To Amy —
Great meeting you
at Winterhawk '98.
Barry Lee Willis

Inscribed
40-
p

T3-BPL-151

America's Music: Bluegrass

by Barry R. Willis

Edited by Dick Weissman
Foreword by Dr. Dan Crary

From Valerie '30

Pine Valley Music

Pine Valley Music, Franktown, Colorado

America's Music: Bluegrass

By Barry R. Willis

Published by:

 **Pine Valley Music**

Pine Valley Music
P.O. Box 701
Franktown, Colorado 80116 U.S.A.
americasmusicbluegrass@compuserve.com

All rights reserved. No part of this book may be reproduced or transmitted in any form or by any means, electronic or mechanical, including photocopying, recording by any information storage and retrieval system without written permission from the author, except for the inclusion of brief quotations in a review.

Copyright 1989 by Barry R. Willis. © renewed with present book title 1992.
First Printing October 1997
Second Printing January 1998
Printed in the United States of America

Library of Congress Data
Willis, Barry R.
America's Music: Bluegrass / by Barry R. Willis
Music: 640 p.
Includes index and appendices
1. Bluegrass music.
2. Bluegrass music History.
3. Bluegrass musicians United States Biography.
4. Bluegrass music United States.

Editors: I. Weissman, Dick   II. Menius, Art   III. Peterson, Jamie L.   IV. Cherry, Bob   V. Dow, Mike
Layout: Tim Speck, Graphic Images design (grafix@worldnet.att.net)

Library of Congress Catalog Card Number 96-092242
ISBN 0-9652407-0-3: Softcover
ISBN 0-9652407-1-1: Hardcover

Table of Contents

About This Book

As you read this book, you may become overwhelmed with all the facts, dates and information which abound. What I tried to do in this book is to paint the picture of what bluegrass is by including a good cross-section of its performers and its events in an order of approximately when they appeared on the bluegrass scene. If you feel that other facts, dates and information should have been included in this book, I'm sorry but I simply ran out of room. Dick Weissman and I had to cut material mercilessly in order to keep the book to a reasonable size.

This book has a theme. As you peruse through the pages and topics at random—or read them one after the other—you may be able to pick it out. The book shows several things about the music I find interesting. And these are things which I think you may like to know, as well, in order to more fully experience and understand bluegrass music.

The book tries to show how tough the musicians had it in the old days. As you read about these people, put yourself in their places and what they had to put up with in order to ply their skills and make a living. You'll find this theme throughout the book.

You'll also find where the music comes from and how the music has changed through the years by virtue of various events and through the musicians' own interpretations of bluegrass music. This last theme is especially prevalent in the "Branches" chapter.

The reader will also become aware how, as the years passed, events occurred to change the direction of America and, as a result, this music. Take note of the events such as:

·   The decline of the Georgia Old-Time Fiddle Contests
·   The beginnings of the Grand Ole Opry
·   The technical improvements in the recording industry and the subsequent demise of the large string bands which were prevalent in the 1920s
·   Bill Monroe taking the Opry by storm in 1939
·   How World War Two helped spread country music to the world
·   How the music changed in 1946 with Earl Scruggs in the Monroe band
·   How the **Flatt and Scruggs** band solidified the popularity of bluegrass

·   How Hank Williams and honky-tonk music, along with Chet Atkins, changed how country music was performed and, as a result, helped to cause a split between country music and bluegrass music
·   The advent of Elvis Presley which resulted in the "bluegrass depression"
·   How Bill Keith changed the complexion of bluegrass when he perfected his melodic style of banjo picking
·   How bluegrass festivals actually saved the music from extinction
·   How musicians began to play bluegrass music with the influences of their own life experiences
·   How women gained footholds in the music— little-by-little
·   Where we are today and where we are going

So look for these things as you read this book. Feel free to read what interests you in any order you choose. I think you'll find the story of bluegrass is all here.

Before we continue, an explanation must be made here about the word "Dobro". The word has been used for many years to identify a certain type of instrument which is also known as a "resonator" guitar or "resophonic" guitar. These guitars were marketed primarily under the National, DOBRO®, Regal brands and many others as time went on. "Dobro" is now an official trademark owned by the Gibson Guitar Company since they bought O.M.I. (Original Music Instrument Company) in 1993. Now that Gibson owns the rights to the name "Dobro," the instrument referred to, if it is indeed the authentic DOBRO®, is correctly identified as either Dobro® or DOBRO®, according to O.M.I.. But whether a player actually used the DOBRO® brand guitar or not, it is loosely referred to here as a resonator guitar of one brand or the other, when it is unclear if the instrument referred to is a Dobro® or not. It could also be identified correctly as "resophonic", but that term, too, is officially trademarked and therefore avoided in this book. I hope this explanation meets with the satisfaction of the people who have spent so much time in developing the Dobro® reputation and with the Gibson Guitar Company which now owns the name.

ACKNOWLEDGMENTS
and Thanks

There are many people who were essential in the research of this book. Without the back issues of *Bluegrass Unlimited*, I probably would not have attempted the project. Thanks goes to Jim Seafeldt of Portland, Oregon, for lending me all his back issues. While I'm at it, I'd like to thank all the contributors to this magazine which I consider a bible of this music. I have learned a lot from its pages.

What I felt was of value in the understanding of bluegrass music is enclosed within these pages. Obviously, I couldn't include everything. That's where a good editor comes in. Dick Weissman helped me organize and pare down all my material to a readable form without omitting what I wanted to say. And thank you, Dan Crary, for writing the Foreword and for your support of this project through the years, to Pete Wernick for your support, and to Dick Pierle and Mitch Jayne for your contributions. Art Menius, your patience and dedication with this work was beyond reproach. Your genius in bluegrass, your editing, and your input was invaluable in helping this project reach successful fruition. And Bob Cherry, your journalism skills and your enthusiasm and support helped a lot, and thanks to my wife Jan for her help in areas of expertise.

I spoke to many, many people involved in this industry known as "bluegrass". They took the time to speak to me and communicate what they feel is important about bluegrass and old-time country music and what I should know about themselves and this wonderful music. Thank you very much. I have listed most of these folks in alphabetical order:

Eddie and Martha Adcock, Janis Adkins, Red Allen, Bob Applebaum, Bobby Atkins, Mike Auldridge, James Bailey, Kenny Baker, Butch Baldassari, Larry Barnwell, Byron Berline, Bill Bolick, Harley Bray, Ed Brown, Bill Bryson, Jim Buchanan, Mike Bub, Larry Bulaich, Wayne E. Busbice, Greg Cahill, Walter Carter, Bob Cherry, Millie Clements, Vassar Clements, Bill Clifton, Charlie Cline, Steve Cooley, Wilma Lee Cooper, Dudley Connell, Sue Coulter, Dan Crary, J.D. Crowe, Greg Deering, Vernon Derrick, Douglas Dillard, Greg Deering, Hazel Dickens, John Dopyera, Jerry Douglas, Mike Dow, Glen Duncan, Stuart Duncan, Jim Eanes, Tony Ellis, Bill Emerson, John Emerson, Chuck Erikson, Bela Fleck, Nick Forster, Bill Foster, Billy Joe Foster, Dave Freeman, Alice Gerrard, Josh Graves, Tom Gray, Richard Greene, David Grier, David Grisman, George Gruhn, Dick Hall, Carlton Haney, Nick Haney, Bill Harrell, Merle Harrison, John Hartford, Murphy Henry, John Hickman, Bobby Hicks, Len Holsclaw, Doug Hutchens, Carl Jackson, Ken Irwin, Chris Jones, Si Kahn, Bill Keith, Pete Kuykendall, Doyle Lawson, Charmaine Lanham, Lance LeRoy, Library of Congress Archives, Del McCoury, John McEuen, Don McHan, Kate McHaney, Vernon McIntyre Jr., Curtis McPeake, Jesse McReynolds, Jim McReynolds, Wade Mainer, Jimmy Martin, Art Menius, Walt Michael, Allen Mills, Dan Mills, Jerry Mills, Barry Mitterhoff, Bill Monroe, Leon Morris, Lynn Morris, Zeke Morris, Paul Mullins, Alan Munde, Bill

Napier, Tom Nechville, Tim O'Brien, Mark O'Connor, Carl Pagter, Jamie L. Peterson, Barry Poss, Ronnie Reno, Neil Rosenberg, Bobby Osborne, Ray and Ina Patterson, Missy Raines, Tony Rice, Slim Richey, Butch Robins, Jim Rooney, Peter Rowan, Charles Sawtelle, Carl Sauceman, Mark Schatz, Earl Scruggs, Curly Sechler, Pappy Sherrill, George Shuffler, Dallas Smith, Larry Sparks, Art Stamper, Ralph Stanley, Jody Stecher, Larry Stephenson, Carl Story, Don Stover, Eddie Stubbs, Tater Tate, Traci Todd, Ivan Tribe, Tony Trischka, Grant Turner, Rick Turner, Butch Waller, Charlie Waller, Doc Watson, Dean Webb, Eric Weissberg, Peter Wernick, Roland White and Tony Williamson. I've probably forgotten somebody. If so, I apologize.

There were some individuals, whose biographical data appears in this book, that I could not reach. As a result, unfortunately, their biographical data could not be verified as I was able to do with the vast majority of protagonists in this book. In putting their sections together, I had to rely on all other available sources available to me. In any case, I did my best to verify the facts.

For many years (and some feel this condition still exists), folk music was an umbrella term which encompassed singer-songwriters, blues, bluegrass, Cajun, zydeco, old-time, Celtic, and world music. While folk music was important to bluegrass at one time (and I certainly don't want to denigrate folk music), bluegrass has come into its own as a completely different and distinctive style. It seems that most of the pioneers of bluegrass I spoke to no longer wanted bluegrass to be a part of folk music. So I changed the title to avoid the "folk" connotation which the term implies. I changed the title of this book from "Folk Music in Overdrive—A Chronological History of Bluegrass Music" (Shucks! I even got Alan Lomax to allow me to use the term, "folk music with overdrive", which he coined in 1959) to a term which more accurately shows what bluegrass music is today.

These past eleven years have been enjoyable—learning what bluegrass is. I pick the banjo a little, but I really had no idea before I started this project what makes bluegrass unique, so powerful, and so effective as a communicative art form. Many of the people listed above have taught me patiently; I have included their words herein. They also taught me how to present this music to the public and how to conduct the business of bluegrass. Their teachings are here.

Also in their descriptions, they gave me a sense of the reverence they feel for this music. I sensed—although they didn't say so—that they had pride that this music known as "bluegrass" was "created" in America. I feel that it's time America recognizes and takes pride in some of its accomplishments, one of which is this music. Americans can also take pride that they "created" rock and roll, jazz, Dixieland (or traditional) jazz, country, old-timey string music, big band, barbershop quartet, western swing, as well as country and western and other styles of music. But, of course, that's another story...

FOREWORD
by Dr. Dan Crary

When Barry first asked me to write a Foreword to this book, it was a few years ago. I sorta' stalled around, and in the meantime the project has grown to about three times the original size. And that's what you want it to do, because this is *the* book about how it really is in bluegrass music today. It will be the most talked-about book ever written on bluegrass, by far.

Barry Willis has tried to tell the whole story, warts and all, and he has done it with a fanatical sense of detail, and an attempt at an evenhandedness with the darker, more controversial material. I say "attempt" because not everyone will agree with all the conclusions this book reaches. But the data it is based on represents the most exhaustive compilation of information about the history and personalities of bluegrass music ever attempted, and certainly ever achieved.

The "skinny" is here, my friends. But the overall effect is to show Bluegrass as a very human enterprise which has moments of greatness and a few not so great, yet maintains its position as one of the great traditional arts of the world.

The road really is rough and rocky in this book, the heroes are noble and human, and the foibles are juicy. But the music has inspired a richly diverse story of the people that play it. Read this book, and you'll love the music more.

Dan

FOREWORD II
An Important Word from Dick Pierle

Barry Willis has a passion for bluegrass. Not just the music but the entire lot of what makes up bluegrass as a whole. I also have a passion for bluegrass. The difference between Barry's passion and mine is that he wrote this book about it. And what a book it is!

My passion for bluegrass started about thirty years ago when I was one of the lucky ones in attendance at that Labor Day horse farm event near Fincastle, Virginia, in 1965, that some refer to as the first bluegrass festival. Since that time I guess I can say that I have had my fair share of bluegrass experiences. When Barry asked me to take a look at his book before it went to the printer, I was delighted to add this task as one more bluegrass experience. What I discovered was extremely "impactual."

The research and interviews in this book are extensive and somehow never give the author a real opportunity to call it quits. I am sure that if he was allowed the space, this book could easily have been five times larger with no end in sight. But he had to stop somewhere and he told me that he was satisfied with what had been assembled. So am I.

Those who read this book in order to find out more about what makes up bluegrass as a whole are going to be pleased and feel more informed, whether they are new to the music or are knowledgeable veterans. Those who read this book who have been around bluegrass as long as, or longer than, I have may have the opportunity to say, "That's not the way I saw or heard it." This brings me to the point I wish to make about this book:

Bluegrass as a whole is a wonderful world of emotionally-charged experiences. People, being what they are, sometimes, if not most often, see or hear things differently from the way others may recall the same event. The author has done as much as is reasonably possible to bring forth the facts that make this book a rewarding bluegrass experience. The book will be enjoyed by anyone that has a passion for bluegrass. *America's Music: Bluegrass* will certainly give everyone in the world of bluegrass something to talk about.

Dick Pierle

Preface

There's something special about this music. You can read about bluegrass, I can tell you about it, or the pioneers who developed it can tell you about it and what it means to them. But, like many things, bluegrass music really must be experienced in order to be appreciated. Notice that I didn't say you had to actually *play* the music to appreciate it.

Nowadays, we can watch great bluegrass groups who have all the skill and precision of their forefathers. The enjoyment we can get from a particularly good performance can leave us high and in love with the music. It's great to be able to do that. Additionally, by knowing a little background of the group, you can really enhance the flavor of the experience. Then the music will work its way into your soul.

You're becoming a real dedicated fan now that you've seen and heard the music and have read a little about it. But there's another step—an easy one—that I advocate to further enjoy the "bluegrass experience." And that step is only now coming of age. We now have access to reproductions of videos from the Grand Ole Opry and other venues, and digitally cleaned-up versions of the early music that the bluegrass pioneers did for their daily bread. We can listen carefully to the old songs without actually having to have the 78 or the LP in our hands. Fine record companies have been extraordinarily careful about reproducing these recordings in compact disc (CD) form. We can listen to the nuances of the way the pioneers did it without having to try to re-create the music from either instruction books and tapes or from a formal class in bluegrass music. While those methods are helpful in developing technical skills and even in providing a certain amount of bluegrass "soul," by thoroughly studying these reproductions, we can really put things into perspective.

Now we can see why the **Stonemans** were so popular. We can see Donna dancing around with her electrified F-5 mandolin strapped high above her waist, picking a great melodic tune and showing the exuberance that leaves the audience loving it. We can now see the great **J.D. Crowe and the New South** at its peak in 1975 with Tony Rice, Bobby Slone, Jerry Douglas and Ricky Skaggs, watch **Bill Monroe and The Bluegrass Boys** on the Opry when Roland White and Vic Jordan were with him, and watch **Muleskinner**, a short-lived band from the early 1970s with David Grisman, Clarence White, Tony Rice, Richard Greene and Bill Keith.

Libraries are beginning to handle these products more and more. And they can be purchased from the various mail order outfits which include the bluegrass genre. So, after you've read about the artists, seen them play, experienced the music and seen the videos, you'll really be on your way to getting some "bluegrass soul." And, all the while, remember: **there's something special about this music**.

About the Author and Editor

Barry R. Willis

I became interested in bluegrass music after listening to country music stations back in the sixties. The music on the radio was okay, but I'd always tune into the station right at the end of the hour before the news when they'd play an upbeat instrumental. Country and western, as you know, has very few of its own instrumentals, so what I listened for were the bluegrass instrumentals. They were uplifting and exciting. I really didn't know what they were at the time, but I knew I liked them.

I moved around with my family and didn't come across bluegrass again until after the military and in college in 1973. I bought a Conquerer banjo (it was very pretty) and asked Jack Flippin (near Sherman, Texas) to show me a few things. I bought the Scruggs banjo book, learned a few tunes, bought the "Foggy Mountain Banjo" LP, and was on my way to being hooked.

My other passion is flying. I've been an airplane pilot since 1965, professionally since 1974. After stints of flight instruction, charter, Alaskan bush flying, scheduled night freight and commuter airlines, I finally got on with United Airlines as a pilot, where I am a captain today.

I started Folk Music Unlimited in 1982 to promote folk and bluegrass groups in Oregon for a while. I had a syndicated radio show, "Barry's Bluegrass Show," on two stations and actually made money at it. This ended in 1985.

In late 1985, I read *The Big Book of Bluegrass*. It filled me with questions about bluegrass and how I could apply what I learned about bluegrass to my radio show, should I ever decide to start another (I never did). A book or pamphlet which started out to be just a deejay helper evolved into what you have in your hands—talk about overkill; I just found it impossible to quit in my search for the truth and in an effort to be as complete as possible. Bluegrass radio show host Wayne Rice later published a booklet just like the one that got me going in the first place. I don't know how he was able to be so brief. I couldn't do it. I guess one of the reasons it grew to such length is because I let the artists add to it and change it however they wanted, with the presumption that this was *their* story—not mine. I wanted to merely act as a vehicle for them to bring their story to you.

The final stages of the production of this book began in 1994 when I solicited the help of Dick Weissman to help me put all these two hundred or so biographies into some sort of cohesive and interesting format. We worked for some time and came up with its existing form and with the decision that I should self-publish; I did.

Dick Weissman

Dick Weissman is the author of six published books about music and the music business. *The Folk Music Sourcebook*, co-authored with Larry Sandberg, won the ASCAP Music Critics Award. His other books include: *The Music Business: Career Opportunities & Self Defense* (Crown, revised ed. 1990) a best seller on the Random House back list and in print for sixteen years. *Audio In Advertising* (co-author Ron Lockhart), *Music Making In America, Survival; Making A Living in Your Local Music Market,* and *Creating Melodies*. He has also written over thirty-five published instructional manuals for banjo, guitar, and on songwriting. He is an Assistant Professor of Music, teaching in the Music Management program at the University of Colorado at Denver.

Dick has a long career as a studio musician, record producer, songwriter, composer and performer. In the sixties, he recorded for Capitol Records in the folk-pop group, The **Journeymen**. His 1993 album, "New Traditions," is an exploration of the banjo in a variety of unusual contexts. Dick writes: "I've always had a great deal of interest in all kinds of American Music. Barry Willis' project was an enormous challenge because he had so much material. This book could have easily have been two or three times as long as the work you are holding in your hands. My job was to retain the most interesting aspects of the book while eliminating unnecessary repetition. We haven't shied away from controversy, but occasionally we edited out the statements that seemed particularly unfair or out of date. Because I am not really a bluegrass musician, I feel that I had less investment in specific points of view or attitudes than people totally immersed in the music might possess."

Chapter 1

The Roots of Bluegrass - Table of Contents

The Roots of Bluegrass

Dr. Dan Crary once said that "bluegrass music is a way of being in touch with your roots."[1] By understanding where bluegrass music came from, we can build a foundation for understanding why it evolved into what it is today. This chapter is a discussion of this music's origins.

The art form of bluegrass music is enjoyed all over the world. It is played in a traditional form, a progressive form, and styles in between. When some people speak of "bluegrass," they actually include all of these categories of bluegrass. But when the old-timers—the pioneers of this music (many of whom are included in this book)—speak of bluegrass, they unfailingly refer to the first bluegrass groups such as **Bill Monroe and the Blue Grass Boys**, the **Stanley Brothers and the Clinch Mountain Boys**, **Flatt and Scruggs and the Foggy Mountain Boys** and very few others. These are the groups which set the original and traditional standards for the genre.

Later groups would never say that they invented bluegrass but would probably say that they followed in the footsteps of the three groups mentioned above. To take this reasoning back in history even further however, we might eliminate **Flatt and Scruggs** from the list because three of the original **Foggy Mountain Boys** were direct descendants of Bill Monroe's group of 1945 to 1948. Taking the same reasoning with the **Stanley Brothers**, this group didn't play bluegrass until Ralph and Carter Stanley added a former **Blue Grass Boy** fiddler to the band and Ralph Stanley added Earl Scruggs's three-finger style to the band's repertoire— a style he learned from Scruggs when Scruggs was with Monroe. So in a very real sense, it's got to start somewhere and many people start with Bill Monroe as *the* person who introduced bluegrass to the world through the very influential and powerful radio station WSM in Nashville.

This chapter often refers to bluegrass music as how Bill Monroe did it as early as 1939 (This does *not* mean that this chapter says that Bill Monroe invented bluegrass). We start at 1939 not because of the style of music being played by Bill Monroe at that time, but

because it was then that Monroe took his music to the stage of the Grand Ole Opry. Before this subject as described is finished, one must go back to even earlier groups who say they played bluegrass even before Bill Monroe organized his **Blue Grass Boys** in 1939. The **Morris Brothers**, for instance, say that they had already been playing bluegrass (with the same instrument combination that solidified the genre) earlier than when Scruggs joined the **Blue Grass Boys** in 1945. They had the three-finger banjo, guitar, fiddle, mandolin and bass.

This book presents the stories of each one of those mentioned above as well as many others involved in the "creation" of bluegrass music. The reader can make his/her own conclusions as to just where this music originated.

Appalachian Music— The Scots-Irish, the Scots, and the Irish influence

According to many sources, one of the reasons that bluegrass sounds like it does is because of its roots from the British Isles.

During the early 1700s, thousands of Scots-Irish immigrants left their homes to settle in the "Land of Promise" called America. Many were brought over as indentured servants to large landowners. After the completion of their period of indenture, many settled in the relatively-lightly populated hills and mountains of the South. The Scots-Irish were a distinct group, as shown hereafter.

"There were Irish Catholics among these eighteenth-century immigrants, and there were Scots, including some Gaelic-speaking highlanders," wrote author Peter Van Der Aherne, "but by far the most important group was the rather confusingly named 'Scotch-Irish.'[2] Among immigrant groups, they occupy a place in the history of American music exceeded in importance only by the Africans. They were originally Scottish Presbyterians who settled in

Top L to R: Ollen Benfield, Homer Sherrill.
Bottom L to R: Lute Isenhower, Arthur Sherrill.

[1] From a 1994 seminar at IBMA, "Knowing the Bluegrass Mind."

[2] A Scotsman once told me that that "scotch" is the whiskey they produced in their country. And he told me that he wants to be known as a "Scotsman" or as "Scottish." So I think that Van Der Aherne's use of 'Scotch-Irish' is incorrect, but accepted in general use.

northeast Ireland in the seventeenth century. Beginning around 1710, they moved on again to North America, partly because of difficulties with the ruling Anglican hierarchy, and partly because, as one observer put it, they could 'neither get victuals nor work.' The Scotch-Irish seem to have been a tough, truculent, fractious people not unlike some of their present-day Ulster descendants, and those who settled in New England soon showed an inability to get on with the established colonists, who, though fellow-puritans, were not Presbyterian but Congregationalist. They then migrated yet again, gravitating towards the frontier regions of the southern states. The tide of immigration lasted until 1740 and then resumed from 1760 'til the Revolution of 1775. During the latter period, they were joined by Scots from Scotland, some of Gaelic-speaking.

"The Scotch-Irish left a musical legacy with clear links with Scottish Lowlands" continued Van Der Aherne. "Sometimes it is impossible to tell by the printed notes which area a tune comes from. 'Here's to Health to All True Lovers' happens to be Scottish, but it could just as easily have come from the Appalachians. 'The Maid Freed from the Gallows' is a typically Scottish tune which happens to have been collected in North Carolina. Quite often a particular American tune can be traced to a Scottish original. A tune from a Scottish manuscript of about 1620 was collected in the Appalachians in a not very different form three centuries later. Well-known American tunes of Scottish origin include 'Rye Whiskey,' 'When Johnny Comes Marching Home,' 'Amazing Grace' (an obvious relative of "Loch Lomond"), 'Run Nigger Run,' 'Shady Grove' and 'The Ox-Driving Song.'

"The Scotch-Irish, as well as being in the right place at the right time in the right numbers, brought the right sort of music with them. Scottish music at that time was among the most archaic in Europe. It was the music of a people on the fringes of urban civilization, and this helps explain why it took the fancy of Americans living in similar conditions.

"And finally, the Scotch-Irish style had the important characteristic of closely resembling African music in many respects."[3]

During the first two centuries of their existence in this country, because of the relative isolation from the culture and music of the rest of the world, the people of

Appalachia developed their own culture and their own music. The music which emerged from all that isolation and, after all that time, had changed from what it was when they moved to the mountains—as one would expect it to do—but the instruments were basically the same with the addition of a few instruments the settlers developed such as the Appalachian dulcimer. The main instrument, just as it was back in the Isles, was the fiddle. The banjo arrived on this scene quite a bit later, probably when minstrelsy was active with the instrument in the 1800s. And the Irish step dancing came out as clogging.

An additional immigration of Irish farmers occurred about 1845 when the plant disease known as the "potato blight" wiped out virtually the entire crop in Ireland. Without money to buy food, even when it was available, men, women and children in the tens of thousands died from starvation and disease; for hundreds of thousands more, the only recourse was emigration. Many of them came to America. Those who couldn't find work in the cities moved to areas they could farm or work in the coal mines. Still others helped build America's railroad and canal systems.

"On the other hand," wrote Van Der Aherne, "we should not think of the Scottish strain as isolated from other British folk music. A look through anthologies of American folk tunes shows English, Irish, and even Welsh tunes alongside Scottish, all blended and adapted into a distinctively American style. The influence of the Catholic Irish is well known, and even possibly exaggerated in the popular mind. The colonists usually called the Scotch-Irish simply 'Irish,' much to their disgust, and it has always been some Irish Catholic settlers, the heyday of predominantly Catholic Irish immigration was the mid-nineteenth century; between 1815 and 1860 two million arrived in the United States, almost half the total of five million immigrants. They were a purely Irish strain, unlike the basically Scottish Scotch-Irish and, though of mainly peasant stock, they preferred the cities to the back country.[4]

"By the time the Irish arrived in force, American music had already acquired a distinctly Celtic tinge, mainly from the Scotch-Irish, making it easy for the Irish and American folk traditions to merge. The Irish country folk brought their rustic tastes to the cities of the United States and helped to blur the distinction

> "The Scots-Irish, as well as being in the right place at the right time in the right numbers, brought the right sort of music with them." —Peter Van Der Aherne

[3] Peter Van Der Aherne, *Origins of the Popular Style, The Antecedents of Twentieth-Century Popular Music* (Oxford: Clarendon Press, 1989), pp. 46-49.

[4] Van Der Aherne continued: "They also had a special relationship with the blacks with whom they shared the bottom of the social heap. The two groups were constantly being compared, with regard to laziness, dirtiness, lying, pilfering, stupidity, and so on—all the vices ascribed to subject peoples since the beginning of time. They often worked together as laborers. In 1839, when Fanny Kemble was writing her diary, gangs of black slaves and Irish were working on the same canal nearby. They were kept carefully apart for fear, as she put it, of tumult, and 'risings, and broken heads, and bloody bones, and all the natural results of Irish intercommunion with their fellow creatures.' Indeed, so much is the importance of this apartheid insisted on that the reader begins to wonder whether it was working all that well..."

between the popular music of the cities and the countryside—and between black and white music. A.L. Lloyd suggested that the influx of potato famine Irish into the English cities may have influenced urban English folk-song, turning it in a more 'folky' direction with the revival of the old modes and the pentatonic scale. Whatever the truth of this, it seems likely that such a process was at work in American cities at the same time."

The music in the Appalachian Mountains evolved, and by the 1930s and '40s was of two types. One was the pure, indigenous style being played on back porches or at barn dances and other local get-togethers and it was sometimes influenced by traditional songs brought from England. According to author Tony Scherman, "The Appalachian songs packed a punch, had a 'primordial intensity' that the mellow, sweeter British versions often lacked. Mountain tunes were also freer, more spacious, rising or falling jaggedly in their spare five- or six-note modes. These people improvised. They 'worried,' or slurred, notes. Repeating a song, they might see fit to change the melody, often with a skill [Cecil] Sharp (English folklorist who moved to America and is known to prefer American-style ballads) found amazing. English singers, despite a more modern seven-note scale, seemed timid, hidebound. There were differences in manner, too—unlike English singers who were sometimes stiff and self-conscious, most hill folk tended to be loose and easy."[5]

The other style of music prevalent in the Asheville, North Carolina, area was the commercially successful, including that which was perpetuated by **Mainer's Mountaineers**, the **Blue Sky Boys**, Carl Story, Red Rector and many others who appeared on WWNC's Farm Hour.

The contribution of the African-Americans to bluegrass[6]

Probably the greatest contribution of the blacks toward bluegrass is the West African invention of the banjo, according to author Randall Armstrong. After the Civil War, the banjo was nurtured by the southern white musicians in the mountain ranges of the eastern United States. "Black banjo players," he wrote, "though not involved in the creation or development of modern three-finger picking, were important in the development of the older styles from which this method was derived. An interesting example is found in the playing of Dock Boggs[7], the renowned white banjoist of the 1930s. Although noted for its unorthodox tunings and counter-melodies, Boggs' style incorporates the use of the thumb for the third, fourth, and fifth strings, the

index finger for the second string, and the middle finger for the first string. Standard bluegrass banjo style, of course, utilizes the same fingering. The black influence to this three-fingered style is evident from Boggs' claim that he derived his technique from 'colored men who picked the banjo.'

"Blacks," continued Armstrong, "also helped develop finger-style guitar playing. The name of black musician Leslie Riddles is especially important here, for he was the main influence for Maybelle Carter's guitar style. Blacks were the sole innovators of 'bottle-neck' guitar playing. This style was the precursor of many resonator guitar styles. Another form of music highly influenced by blacks is jazz.

"Though blacks have written many songs, they were most noted for their gospel song contributions. Bluegrass songs of this type were 'On the Rock Where Moses Stood,' 'Let the Church Roll On,' 'God Gave Noah the Rainbow Sign,' 'Hear Jerusalem Moan,' 'Were You There' and 'I Didn't Hear Nobody Pray.' Black work songs, originating mainly on railroad crews and chain gangs, are represented in bluegrass music as 'Take This Hammer,' 'Nine Pound Hammer' and 'Saro Jane.' Black ballads now used in bluegrass music are 'Reuben,' "John Hardy,' 'Railroad Bill' and 'John Henry.'

"Even a slight study of the music of bluegrass will reveal the presence of blues in bluegrass. Bill Monroe's musical upbringing drew heavily from the runs and phrasings of the black guitarist Arnold Schultz. The musical form of the blues, with all of its vocal and instrumental characteristics, has probably been one of the primary influences in bluegrass music." This style of music is characterized by repetition of stanzas and is represented in the songs "Six White Horses" (by Clyde Moody), "Doin' My Time" (by Jimmie Skinner) and "Mule Skinner Blues" (blue yodel #8 by Jimmie Rodgers as arranged by Bill Monroe), wrote Armstrong.

A 1991 interview with Rick Turner of Gibson USA gave more light on the blues in bluegrass music. "My feeling is that Bill Monroe got a strong influence from blues players from the South in the early '30s and used the blues scales in the context of country music. And that has a lot to do with the high, lonesome sound... A basic chord progression would be like a I, IV, V. But the use of a lot of sevenths would give you a much 'bluesier' sound... The use of additional sixths would cause the music to get jazzier. Also, the use of the flat third will really give you a lot of that bluesy scale... In 1965, at the Newport Folk Festival at a party, black entertainer Lightning Hopkins was sitting in the corner of one of these Newport mansions playing. Bill Monroe walked in with Peter Rowan, and Bill literally grabbed Pete by the scruff of the neck and sat him down in front of Hopkins and said, 'Now listen to this! You gotta listen

[5] *Smithsonian Magazine*, April, 1985, p. 52.

[6] Randall Armstrong, "Blacks and Bluegrass: A Study in Musical Integration." *Bluegrass Unlimited*, November, 1977.

[7] Boggs was known to have played the banjo with a knife.

to this!'" This was Monroe's attempt to tell Rowan where a lot of that bluesy sound in Monroe's music came from.

Gospel music

In 1922, James D. Vaughan "founded a singing school in Lawrenceburg (Tennessee) and soon branched out into the publication of songbooks, records and magazines. From the early 1920s to the 1960s, Vaughan was a major force in the development of gospel music throughout the country. He hired quartets to go out and sing his songs to publicize them, and helped promote a whole new type of singing in the South. His singing schools gave generations of Southerners their first taste of the 'rudiments' of music, and many a country singer started out singing gospel songs from one of his 105 songbooks."[8] Each songbook usually contained about one hundred songs.

First public use
of the term "hillbilly"

The name "hillbilly," which categorized the mountain music which was being recorded for Ralph Peer and Okeh Records (New York), was so named when, after a 1925 session, the group was asked what style of music they played. "Shucks, we're nothing but a bunch of hillbillies from North Carolina and Virginia," said one of them. "Call us anything you want." When the six tunes were released, the group's title showed "The Hill Billies." They saw this and had second thoughts about the name. "Where we came from, if you called somebody a hillbilly, you were looking for a fight," said Tony Alderman, the last living member of the band. Pop Stoneman, after hearing the group's name, laughed so

hard that tears came into his eyes. "Well boys," he is reported to have said, "you have come up with a good one. Nobody will beat it." The name became applicable to all the country music of the day.

Vernon Dalhart—
an early country star

In 1924, Vernon Dalhart, a cowpuncher from Texas, recorded "The Wreck of the Old '97" on the Victor label. The record sold about six million copies in fifty versions by various artists through the years. The success of this record convinced Okeh and Victor Records that there was a commercial market for early country music. Because of this record, and the recordings of Ernest Stoneman, Fiddlin' John Carson and a few others during the '20s, the stage was set for an explosion in the popularity of country music.

Dalhart was born Marion Try Slaughter in northeastern Texas in 1883. His stage name came from two cities in Texas. A 1991 editorial by Dick Spottswood in May's *Bluegrass Unlimited* summarized the recording career of Vernon Dalhart, "Historians generally agree that the term 'country music' applies to the product created by an industry, beginning with Fiddlin' John Carson's first efforts in 1923 and culminating with the Nashville sound and its aftermath. From the first, there has been controversy about tradition versus progress, starting with a light opera tenor named Vernon Dalhart, whose 1924 Victor coupling of 'The Prisoner's Song'/ 'Wreck of the Old 97' seems to be one of the few records of its era to have actually sold a million copies. Traditionalists then and now have dismissed Dalhart as an anemic singer whose style mocked that of genuine traditional performers; to others, he was the performer who sparked the industry in the first place. Be that as it

Courtesy Library of Congress

Article from "Talking Machine World", April 1925.

This drawing of the Hill Billies, from the cover of the Okeh record, was probably drawn to enhance the magazine's desire to add respectability to the group. The group, from Galax, VA, normally dressed in overalls, scarves and hats— typical of the informal groups of the day. Other photos of the group included different instrumentation which included Tony Alderman on fiddle (deceased 1983), Charlie Bowman on fiddle, Joe Hopkins on guitar and Al Hopkins on Clawhammer banjo.

This 1925 recording in New York City included six songs with Alderman (fiddle), John Rector (banjo), Joe Hopkins (guitar) and Al Hopkins (piano). Al Hopkins was probably the first person to turn the piano into a country music instrument.

8 Charles K. Wolfe, *Tennessee Strings*, (Knoxville: The University of Tennessee Press, 1977) p. 52.

Americas Music I Bluegrass

may, he was *the* dominant country music figure of his time and recorded for virtually every label in the business from 1923 to 1928. Nevertheless, sales of his records went quickly into decline with the advent of the real thing by folks like the Carters, Charlie Poole, Dave Macon, the **Carolina Tar Heels** and Jimmie Rodgers in 1926 to 1928; by 1929, Dalhart's records were only being offered for sale on bargain tables in chain stores—never again was he a significant commercial force.

"It's been more than a half century since Monroe first sang 'Mule Skinner Blues' at the Opry," continued Spottswood, "radically altering Jimmie Rodgers' song, itself an alteration of an older, black work song. Since then, Monroe's music has endured and prospered by precisely that kind of re-invention of traditional music themes and values. Bluegrass works because it combines the best of new and old, making the most of contemporary resources in order to validate the past. The balance between tradition and innovation is constantly shifting but always there, and bluegrass will always be exciting as long as its practitioners discover new ingredients and new ways to combine the old ones."[9]

Gid Tanner and the Skillet Lickers

Gid Tanner and the Skillet Lickers

Members of "Laughing" Gid Tanner's **Skillet Lickers**, the first super-popular band in country music, in 1924 included Gid Tanner (fiddle, born in Dacula, Georgia), and George Riley Puckett (banjo, guitar, blind almost from birth). The band's extreme popularity came in 1926 with the addition of Clayton "Pappy" McMichen (fiddle), Bert Layne (fiddle) and Fate Norris (banjo). Later, Lowe Stokes joined on fiddle, changing the dance-band style of the band toward fancy, harmony fiddling. Riley Puckett's rather pop voice of the period was smooth and influenced by the tradition of the minstrel shows as well as black singers. His guitar style, especially his well-conceived concept of bass runs, made him a great asset as a sideman and he recorded widely as a solo artist.

Like many large string bands of the day, the band was strongly influenced by black music. The sound of this band was "blacker" than the sound emanating from

other Appalachian groups. The group recorded 88 sides, 82 of which were released. McMichen continued this style of music (which by 1945 included Dixieland) with his **Georgia Wildcats** until he retired in 1955. Gid Tanner quit performing in 1931 and returned to chicken farming.[10]

Uncle Dave Macon

Uncle Dave Macon— the Opry's first featured star

Macon's first public performance was probably in 1921 at the age of fifty-one. Uncle Dave's nickname was the "Dixie Dewdrop" or "King of the Hillbillies." His first performance earned him seventeen dollars; it wasn't until Fiddlin' Sid Harkreader joined his act could he make a living at music. They soon recorded in New York City. On July 8, 1923, Uncle Dave Macon made his first recordings with fiddler and guitarist Harkreader: "Keep My Skillet Good and Greasy." A year later, he was booked throughout the country on the Loew Theater Circuit; he suddenly found that he was a star.

Macon was able to sense the rather impersonal environment of the Victrola and its recordings. He insisted that each of his recordings be a live, mini-performance in order to entertain the audience; his record sales proved that this method was correct. Yet, most of Uncle Dave's income came from personal appearances. He became even more successful when he teamed up with Sam McGee, a major influence on folk guitar stylings.

When Macon joined the Grand Ole Opry in 1926, he was its first featured star and, according to author Bill C. Malone, brought a wide variety of complex frailing and picking styles which modern banjoists might well envy. And Ralph Rinzler said that, with the exception of the **Carter Family**, Uncle Dave preserved more valuable American folklore through his recordings than any other folk or country entertainer.

David Harrison Macon was born October 7, 1870, in Smart Station, Tennessee. He passed on March 22, 1952. He was elected into the Country Music Hall of Fame in 1966.

---

[9] Dick Spottswood, "Guest Editorial," *Bluegrass Unlimited*, May, 1991, pp. 14, 15.

[10] The band broke up in 1931 when Stokes lost a hand in a barroom fight.

Sam and Kirk McGee

Arthur Smith and his Dixieliners. L to R: Sam McGee, Arthur Smith, Kirk McGee.

Sam and Kirk McGee "from Sunny Tennessee"

This veteran brother duo was in show business in the early 1920s and they were charter members of the WSM Barn Dance which was founded in 1925 by George D. Hay and WSM. Sam McGee, born May 1, 1894, near Franklin, Tennessee, was probably the first person to play an electric instrument on the Opry. Hay was appalled and told him not to do that again. Sam was evidently too "uptown" for Hay's idea of what Opry music should be.

"Flat-top Pickin' Sam McGee" created the style of playing melody and rhythm on the guitar at the same time. "The solo works of Sam McGee were little recorded in his heydays of the 1920s and 1930s" wrote Charles Wolfe. "Nevertheless, the few recordings he did make have been carefully studied by several generations of guitarists. Complex, solo, hot guitar music has been relatively commonplace in black folk tradition, but it was McGee who first thoroughly realized it in terms of hillbilly music and made it available to his country music successors like Merle Travis and Chet Atkins."[11] Author Wolfe described McGee's style as a "unique 'flat-top' style wherein he played both rhythm and melody simultaneously; his 1926 recording of an original piece called 'Buck Dancer's Choice' was very popular and helped establish him as a major influence on folk guitar stylings. He was, in fact, probably the first rural white guitarist really to exploit the guitar as a solo instrument. Before his appearance on the scene, the guitar had been used mainly as an accompaniment to vocal or fiddle music. Even Maybelle Carter's famous lead runs were quite simple compared to what Sam was doing." He recorded "Sam McGee, Grand Dad of the Country Guitar Pickers" on Arhoolie at age seventy-six.

In the early thirties, Sam and his brother Kirk (born 1899) joined Fiddlin' Arthur Smith in forming the **Dixieliners**, an Opry act which toured extensively. The brothers played together for eight years, performing on tour in tent shows with Bill Monroe, Roy Acuff and other Opry stars.

Sam McGee died August 21, 1975, at the age of 82; Kirk, 83, died October 24, 1983.

Clayton McMichen and his Georgia Wildcats

Country music's recognition of Clayton McMichen began when he arrived in Atlanta in 1921 and started winning fiddle contests, competing against "Laughing" Gid Tanner and "Fiddlin'" John Carson. In 1925, he began recording tunes which were jazz-oriented and used fiddle, clarinet and guitar.

In 1926, McMichen joined **Gid Tanner and the Skillet Lickers** on lead fiddle, comedian and as emcee. He was one of the few full-time musicians of the time— even Gid Tanner raised chickens. He was a popular member of the **Skillet Lickers** "whose sound was at least a generation earlier than the kind of semi-pop country that (Jimmie) Rodgers was trying to develop."[12]

Mac was influential in convincing record companies that fiddle music would sell. When he recorded dozens of sweet ballads, he used the pseudonym "Bob Nichols."[13] When McMichen and Jimmie Rodgers toured together in 1929, they were billed equally.

After 1929, Mac won the National Fiddle Championship eighteen of the next twenty-five years. One technique he used to win at fiddle contests included a five-minute version of "Fisher's Hornpipe" where he would play the song in five keys: F, B-flat, G, D, and back to F. He won sixteen National Championships with "Bile Them Cabbage Down." Some of the songs which Bill Monroe later played in his band were note-for-note the way McMichen played them, e.g. "Fire on the Mountain."

Mac wrote "Georgiana Moon," a standard at most fiddle contests. He professionally promoted fiddle contests such as a contest between himself and the hottest fiddlers of the day: Gid Tanner, Leslie Keith, Fiddlin' Arthur Smith and Chubby Wise. He and the others were big names in hillbilly fiddle music and virtually assured that enough people would be in the audience to make the event financially successful.

He quit the **Skillet Lickers** in 1931, forming his own **Georgia Wildcats**[14]. But times were tough and almost no one could afford to buy records. Even Merle Travis recorded with Mac. They recorded on Decca,

---

[11] Charles Wolfe, from an article in *Bluegrass Unlimited*. November ,1971, p. 69.

[12] Charles Wolfe, "Clayton McMichen: Reluctant Hillbilly," *Bluegrass Unlimited*, May, 1076, p. 56.

[13] Pseudonyms were a common practice—Hank Williams was "Luke the Drifter;" Bill Monroe was "Bill Smith;" Sonny Osborne recorded as "Hank Hill and Stanley Alpine."

[14] Who were Slim Bryant (guitar) and Carl Cotner.

Americas Music | Bluegrass

using twin fiddling, guitar and fiddle solos, tenor banjo solos, and harmony scat-jazz singing with crooner Kenny Newton on vocals.

McMichen wanted to leave the string band sound behind and pursue a more modern sound which integrated jazz, pop music, and swing. Mac's music, though similar to that of **Bob Wills and the Texas Playboys** and **Milton Brown and His Musical Brownies**, was not as popular. He was jealous that western swing was not his. Mac stuck with hillbilly music because it was his living, but resented it. And, compared with his **Georgia Wildcats**, he believed that the **Skillet Lickers** "stunk."

Birch Monroe remembered Mac, "One night Slim (Georgia Slim Rutland), I don't know if he knowed it or not, but anyway he played one of Clayton's tunes ahead of Clayton. Well, them old **Georgia Wildcats,** you know, they're full of temper and first note he made on it, why, Clayton was mad already. That was Clayton McMichen. So after Slim and the **Ridgerunners** played it, why, Clayton come on. And he said, 'Now some people play this tune one way and some another.' He said, 'This is the right way to play it.' And he just eat it up, you know. He could beat Slim a hundred ways on that tune because it was probably his tune in the first place. But he was mad as a hornet."[15]

McMichen's **Georgia Wildcats** played the WLS road show at the same time the **Monroe Brothers** were beginning their four- or five-month stint on the show[16]

Beginning in 1945, for the next ten years he played Dixieland jazz and played on WAVE, Louisville. About that time, Mac taught George Barnes how to play fiddle tunes on the guitar. Barnes was a pioneer in playing electric guitar in country swing music. Barnes later joined the **Prairie Ramblers**, the same group which backed up Patsy Montana on WLS in 1934.

Some of Mac's old songs were re-released but he was not allowed to record his Dixieland band. Frustrated, he retired from the music in 1955 to run a tavern.

During the early 1960s, the "folk boom" made a hero of Mac for his time with the **Skillet Lickers**, but history seemed to forget his music was much more. He was stereotyped as a funky, colorful, old-time fiddler. In 1961, he accepted an invitation by Birch Monroe at the Bean Blossom, Indiana, country music show which Birch managed, to play for an appreciative audience. Mac also played at the Newport Folk Festival in 1964. A serious car accident in 1964 thwarted a planned comeback. However, he managed an occasional appearance, such as in 1966 at Bean Blossom when he performed with Neil V. Rosenberg. In 1968, he won first prize at the Kentucky State Championships. Clayton McMichen died in 1970.

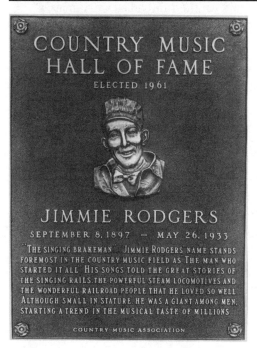

Jimmie Rodgers— the Father of Country Music

Jimmie Rodgers is a name as familiar as Hank Williams in the world of old-time country music, a foundation upon which both the new country music and bluegrass music are built today. His work and performances inspired many artists: Ernest Tubb and Gene Autry are probably the most famous.

The success of Jimmie Rodgers cannot be measured by the amount of money he made during his lifetime. He never learned how to read music and only played simple chords on the guitar. But when he appeared on the scene, there was simply no one else like him, and he contrasted to the immense popularity of the large string bands of the day...bands such as **Gid Tanner and the Skillet Lickers**, Pop Stoneman's **Dixie Mountaineers, Charlie Poole and the North Carolina Ramblers, Earl Johnson and His Dixie Clodhoppers**, the **Fruit Jar Drinkers** and the **Possum Hunters**. These bands became increasingly extinct as bands such as that of Bill Monroe pioneered instrument virtuosity and close-harmony singing. While there may be some discussion as to what the origins of bluegrass music are, there can be no doubt as to the effect that the songwriting of Jimmie Rodgers has had on the music. And, there is no doubt as to who is the "Father of Country Music." Here is a biography of this man.

Jimmie Rodgers was born September 8, 1897, in Meridian, Mississippi. His father worked as a railroad section foreman and spent little time at home. His mother died of tuberculosis when he was four. After

---

[15] Neil V. Rosenberg, "A Front Porch Visit with Birch Monroe," *Bluegrass Unlimited*, September, 1982, p. 59.

[16] Also on the WLS road show were the Cumberland Ridge Runners, the Maple City Four, the Arkansas Wood Choppers, Karl and Harty, and the Prairie Ramblers which Patsy Montana soon joined.

being passed between relatives, Jimmie quit school at age fourteen to work on the railroad as a flag man, a water carrier, and a brake man where he associated with blacks and their music: the blues. Here he learned guitar and banjo songs from black gandy dancers[17].

In 1925, Rodgers acquired tuberculosis, forcing him to quit the railroad and to seek less vigorous work, leading him to pursue music full-time. A lung hemorrhage when he was twenty-seven was almost fatal. He performed as a black-face minstrel in a medicine show, playing waltzes and sentimental numbers on banjo and guitar. In early 1927, Rodgers moved his family, wife Carrie and daughter Anita, to Asheville, North Carolina, to work as a city detective. He formed a hillbilly "ork" (a string band orchestra) called **Jimmie Rodgers Entertainers** and began playing on WWNC, Asheville.

He created the blue yodel as a combination of white music and black music with his own touch of creativity. The yodels were an expression of what the South was going through collectively: that is, the hard times of the 1920s. He became known as "The Blue Yodeler." There were thirteen blue yodels, the last of which was sung between rest breaks on a cot in the studio the day before he died. He wrote very few of the songs he sang. Many of his early songs were written by the sister of his wife, Elsie McWilliams.

Rodgers was "discovered" in 1927 when he answered an ad in the paper placed by Ralph Peer of the Victor Talking Machine Company in Bristol, Tennessee. Peer felt that this recording session would be a good business move for his company—he didn't really care for the music one way or the other and simply wanted to record the local artists, knowing that there was a lot of talent in the area and perhaps a corresponding market demand for such recordings. Rodgers recorded "Sleep, Baby, Sleep" and "The Soldier's Sweetheart." He was paid $20.

Even at the height of his popularity, he billed himself as the **Jimmie Rodgers Entertainers**. He was with this band when the **Entertainers** auditioned for Peer without him[18], and he won a recording contract with Victor after Rogers' devoted wife convinced him to try for a solo contract with Peer. He won it as a solo artist.

On August 4th, 1927, Jimmie Rodgers and the **Carter Family** recorded in Bristol, Tennessee.[19] According to many historians, the "Bristol Sessions" became *the* big launch of country music as we know it now or knew it then. After the Peer recording session for Victor Records, the **Carter Family** went home and

planted the corn, not really believing anything would come from the session. Rodgers then labeled himself as a "vocal artist" and headed straight for New York to make the best of his good fortune. He left even before he was notified by Peer that the recordings he just made would be released. He then came back to RCA and, in November, recorded blue yodel #1 ("T for Texas"). Rodgers quickly became Victor's best-selling artist.[20]

For the next five years, he usually performed as a solo act at tent shows. In 1929, he recorded "Any Old Time" on Peer, one of the first labels to record country music. That same year, Rodgers became the first hillbilly star to record with black musicians. He and a group of black musicians recorded "Frankie and Johnny." In November, he appeared in the nine-minute Columbia film short called "The Singing Brakeman." He never toured above the Mason-Dixon Line.

In 1930, Jimmie Rodgers recorded blue yodel #9 ("Standin' on the Corner") with Louis "Satchmo" Armstrong (trumpet) and Mrs. Satchmo (Lillian, piano). Also that year, he recorded blue yodel #8 ("Mule Skinner Blues") in Hollywood. He recorded "My Good Gal's Gone Blues" with the **Louisville Jug Band** in 1931.

Rodgers built his family a lavish home near Kerrville, Texas, but high medical bills to treat his tuberculosis (also known as "consumption" because of the way it wastes the body) and expensive living later forced him to sell and move to San Antonio. He played twice a week on KMAC until late 1932 when ill health forced him to spend most of the next year on his deathbed.

On May 26, 1933, he recorded the last blue yodel (number 13) "Women Make a Fool Out of Me" on his deathbed. He also recorded several songs including "Old Love Letters (Bring Memories of You)" just before he died of tuberculosis: the same disease which killed his mother. At the studio, he had to rest several hours between each of the twelve recordings. He was propped up on a cot to reach the microphone. He was optimistic, never complaining or whimpering at his ill fate. No one ever heard him mention his illness although he was bedridden, with constant medical attention at his side. He died at age 36, hemorrhaging in the Taft Hotel, New York City.

One month after Rodgers' death, country music's first picture disc was released. It was a ten-inch, 78 r.p.m. laminated RCA record with his picture on it. The song was "Cowhand's Last Ride." In 1961, Jimmie

---

[17] Gandy refers to the Gandy Company of Chicago which made tools for railroad workers. Gandy dancers were known as those persons who used the tools, and who danced.

[18] According to Dr. Charles Wolfe, they were then known as the Tenneva Ramblers because they worked out of Bristol which was on the border of Tennessee and Virginia. They were all there for the audition but argued about the billing on the record. The Ramblers hired a banjo player and recorded without him.

[19] Rodgers and the Carters didn't meet at this session; they first met in Louisville in June 1931.

[20] When one listens to an album of Jimmie Rodgers music, it may tend to be monotonous. It may even become tedious. But when one considers that the songs were all released as singles, and sometimes a year apart, perhaps this can enable one to concentrate on each song, rather than the LP.

Rodgers became the first person inducted into the Country Music Hall of Fame.

30,000 fans dedicated the unveiling of his monument in Meridian, Mississippi, where the Jimmie Rodgers Memorial Museum is located near his first home. In 1978, a U.S. postage stamp was dedicated to him. He and his wife are buried near the Museum.

G.B. Grayson & Henry Whitter

G.B. Grayson and Henry Whitter

George Banman (G.B.) Grayson was born November 11, 1887, in Ashe County, North Carolina. He was nearly blind because of severe eye damage as a baby and grew up "busking" his music on the street, one of the few occupations available to a person with this handicap. By the time World War I rolled around, he was married (he eventually had six children) and settled on the Tennessee-Virginia line. He began performing with his fiddle and singing with nearby musicians such as Tom Ashley and Doc Walsh.

Grayson was a good singer, and when he began recording with Henry Whitter, he took on the vocal duties of the duo. His singing was noticed by various record labels and he soon became recognized as one of the finest old-time singers to ever record.

Henry Whitter was born about twenty years after Grayson, in Fries, Virginia. He was the area's first country musician to record when he went to New York in 1923. He continued to record by himself and with others until he met Grayson in the summer of 1927. They recorded just forty sides together, from October 1927 to October 1929.

Some of the duo's recordings were good enough to make it into the Sears catalogs. But their Victor recording of "Train 45" in late 1927 actually sold 50,000 copies and stayed in print through 1934. Their next-best sellers were stifled by the Depression but still managed to sell relatively well; "Barnyard Serenade" sold nearly 9,000, "The Red and Green Signal Light" sold 6,000, "Little Maggie" sold 5,600, "Tom Dooley" sold 4,000 (released May 2, 1930) and "Going Down the Lee

Highway" (Lee Highway Blues) sold 1,385 copies only because it was released during the height of the Depression. Those 1,385 copies probably went to fiddlers who were trying to learn the tune, according to Dr. Charles Wolfe who wrote the liner notes of the 1984 Old Homestead LPs which were a collection of Grayson and Whitter's songs.

Their recording career together included many tunes which became bluegrass standards: the tunes mentioned above, "Handsome Molly," "Banks of the Ohio" (which they called "I'll Never Be Yours"), "Rose Conley" and "Nobody's Darling."

According to Wolfe, "In 1930, the pair began traveling around to take advantage of their fame; they even made a guest appearance on the Grand Ole Opry, and things were looking up. Then tragedy struck. On August 13, 1930, Grayson was back home and set out hitchhiking to his brother's home. He was hanging onto the running board of a car when it was hit by a log truck near Damascus, Virginia; he was thrown off and killed. Henry Whitter never really got over the shock of the death of his friend and partner. He eventually died of diabetes in 1942."[21] The team of Grayson and Whitter won an Award of Merit from the IBMA in 1996.

Wade Mainer

Wade and J.E. Mainer— a link between the string bands and bluegrass

Wade Mainer is one of the greatest living old-time musicians and one of the few remaining legendary figures of country music and recordings. He is one of the bridges connecting old country and hillbilly music with the bluegrass music of today. Wade is not known as a bluegrass musician, but his banjo-playing style, songs, and music are very deeply entwined in today's bluegrass music.

Followers of bluegrass music, whether they know it or not, are followers of Mainer music. Wade's two-finger style of banjo playing sounds very much like the three-finger style which came to popularity within six years of

[21] From the liner notes of "Ralph Stanley, Short Life of Trouble—Songs of Grayson and Whitter," Rebel Records CD 1735.

the time Wade invented the style. Most banjoists now prefer the three-finger style which seems to be more capable of doing hard-driving bluegrass. There is probably no truth to the idea, as some have suggested, that two-finger style is a precursor to the three-finger style; that style generally originated from a different area of North Carolina and from different musicians such as Snuffy Jenkins. Wade did learn the three-finger style a bit however, and acknowledges that the three-finger banjo style had more *drive* than his two-finger style did. As of 1997, Wade was still using this style—one of the few people to do so.

Joseph Emmett Mainer was born July 20, 1898. Wade Mainer was born April 21, 1907. The brothers were born in Weaverville, near Asheville, Buncombe County, North Carolina. J.E. took up the fiddle, learning from brother-in-law Roscoe Banks, and also played a little frailing banjo. His first fiddle was a miniature, obtained as a prize when he and Wade sold the most of a popular salve during a sales contest. He became pretty good on that little instrument, and in the early 1930s, went downtown to buy a full-sized fiddle which cost $9. In 1910, J.E. left home to work in the cotton mills of Knoxville, Tennessee, at age twelve. Wade was three.

Wade recalled, "I was workin' in the sawmill around about eleven or twelve years old and I guess I stayed with it for two or three years 'cause my dad didn't have much to do back there on the farm. And he give me about fifty cents a week to go a picture show or something.[22]

"Really, what started it all," told Wade, "was when I worked with my brother-in-law, Roscoe Banks, at the sawmill when I was ten or twelve years old. I was just a young fella growin' up on the farm down in Weaverville, North Carolina, and we lived on Rim's Creek. So my brother-in-law had a sawmill and I would go stay with him and he played the fiddle. On Saturday evenings they'd shut down the mill and go get cleaned up good and get ready for a square dance that night. Somebody was always wantin' some music to play for square dances back there in the mountains. So [Roscoe] had a brother by the name of Will Banks that played the banjo but he played the frailin' type. It wasn't very good time with the fiddle, you know. And I'd go set in with them at the square dances. When they'd lay the banjo down to get up and take a break, I'd go over and pick up the banjo and start hammerin' down on it. I learned to frail a banjo first!

"And then, after awhile, I began to think I might just try it with my fingers and see what happens then. I got

to meddlin' with it—pickin' it out note-for-note with my fingers. I kept on and got pretty good with it and got to learn to use my fingers to keep the time with it. It wasn't very long—I guess it wasn't over a couple of months learnin' the two-finger style—and I was workin' at the sawmill with him and after I got to where I could play the two-finger style. I kept better time [than] with the fiddle and all, so my brother-in-law just kept me to play the banjo when he played the fiddle."[23]

By 1922, J.E. had moved to his permanent home in Concord, North Carolina, and married. He later began working as a musician. Wade was working at the Weaverville sawmill near Asheville. Will Banks played banjo with Roscoe at many square dances—the main source of entertainment in the mountains. "I guess, when I was about eighteen to twenty years old (about 1927), I left and started for Concord, North Carolina" said Wade. "I had an old banjo and I had it with me and I stopped off in Marion and got me a job workin' at a yarn mill in Marion, North Carolina, and stayin' in a boardin' house. I'd get the old banjo out in the evenin' and the boarders at the boardin' house, they resented me playin' the banjo—I was makin' so much noise they couldn't stand me. I worked there quite awhile then moved on down to Concord and that's where I began to join up with my brother J.E.." This is where the brothers decided to make music professionally—J.E. on the fiddle and Wade on the banjo. The brothers won fiddle contests and began playing at corn shuckings and other social events. Wade told this writer, "We got so good at fiddlers' conventions taking prizes they finally wouldn't let us enter for prizes."[24] They became influenced by **Gid Tanner and the Skillet Lickers**, the **Carter Family**, Jimmie Rodgers, and **Charlie Poole and the North Carolina Ramblers**. In the latter part of 1933 or early 1934, J.E. and Wade called themselves the **Mainer Mountaineers String Band**.

Wade wrote that in the beginning "There were many times I wished [then] we'd never started playing music. For working in the cotton mill in the day, and J.E. at night would keep me up half the night or longer playing music. I'd get irritated, especially when he'd tell me to get up; he had a new tune he wanted to learn."[25]

 "We were the first to have the bluegrass style—with the drive— *'til it kindly got a little bit, I'll say uptown, faster and higher pitched." —Wade Mainer*

---

22 This may not sound like a lot of money, but in those days fifty cents could buy a week's groceries for a small family. The fact that kids got any spending money was kind of unusual. As Wade's career continued into the Great Depression of the mid-1930s, an admission charge to his concerts of fifteen and twenty-five cents was a lot of money to people in rural America who could barely feed themselves. It's no wonder that Wade quit being a full-time musician in the early 1950s to try to find a "normal" job which would provide some sort of security for him and his family.

23 From a November 1993 telephone interview.

24 From a note to this writer May 12, 1995.

25 Quotation from correspondence to me, following a live interview at IBMA in 1992 and several follow-up telephone conversations.

"We were the first to have the bluegrass style—with the *drive*—'til it kindly got a little bit, I'll say uptown, faster and higher pitched. And when it got into that, it kind of left the **Mainer Mountaineers...**" he told this writer in a 1992 interview. "I didn't do too much lead on the banjo because we had the fiddle for a lead. Well, the fiddle finally faded out when Bill Monroe... Well, Bill wasn't the first one to play the mandolin 'cause the **Tobacco Tags** had the mandolin when we were working for Crazy Water Crystals back in '35 and '36. We had already established the mandolin, but when the mandolin (of Bill Monroe) came in, the mandolin took over the lead for the fiddle. But the mandolin style of Monroe was different," said Wade. "Monroe's style was pitched high, sung high, played high and they sung with a *drive*. We had that same *drive* when we recorded with Clyde Moody. There were two or three [tunes] that we had the fiddle and you can hear the banjo with the *drive* in it."[26]

Ralph Stanley was a banjoist who initially used the clawhammer style then picked up the two-finger style from Wade. Wade recalled that the Carters "was workin' around the Bristol area when Carter and Ralph [Stanley] was just boys. So Ralph and Carter stayed around us a whole lot and learned a lot of our music. You can go back to some of the old recordings and find that they recorded a lot of songs that we already recorded. Ralph was just a little ol' boy, him and Carter both, when I was workin' professional."[27] Still, "There might have been two-finger banjo players before I ever was recognized as a two-finger-style banjo player—I don't know, I never heard of them and never heard anybody say there was anybody else. They always said I was the first they ever heard.[28] A fellow named Mack Crow picked up my two-finger style and later played the three-finger style and I think he became rather famous."[29]

In a 1991 telephone interview, Wade spoke about the difference between his music and the songs known as "bluegrass", "This bluegrass music they play now—most old songs—that's what they started with until they got to the point they were able to write about songs which was of a different content than the songs we wrote about—you know, the love songs that maybe I dreamed up, like I done that 'Maple on the Hill'" (1935) in which Wade pictured himself courting his lover

Sons of the Mountaineers in New York during the 1940's.

sitting on the front porch on a swing...or maybe out behind the house where the big maple tree was.

The Mainer brothers hired the Lay brothers, Lester and Howard Lay, in 1934, and they became **J.E. Mainer's Mountaineers**, working Saturdays on WSOC, Gastonia, North Carolina, on the Wayside Program. Then the group went to WWL for about four months in New Orleans, Louisiana. After the band returned to Concord, the Lay brothers left the **Mountaineers** to stay and work at the cotton mills. Soon Wade and J.E. were doing two shows daily at WBT, Charlotte, North Carolina, in addition to the WBT Barn Dance.

They hired Daddy John Love (guitar, yodeler in the style of Jimmie Rodgers, blues singer) and Zeke Morris (guitar)[30]. The popularity of **J.E. Mainer's Mountaineers** was enhanced with the addition of these two.

Wade told how Zeke was hired into the **Mountaineers**. The band needed a replacement for the Lay brothers. The band was based in Concord at the time when Wade went to Old Fort, North Carolina, to find a guitar player he knew about: George Morris. Wade found George playing in a band at a picnic. Wade joined in on banjo, then asked George if he wanted to join his brother's band. George said yes. Wade then went back to verify his choice with J.E. and they confirmed their decision to hire George. But when Wade returned to Old Fort to find him, George couldn't be found but Claude "Zeke" Morris was there.[31] Zeke told Wade that he could play guitar. Wade and J.E. gave him a try. He fit into the new band "like a glove."

---

[26] From a November 1993 telephone interview.

[27] Ibid.

[28] In a separate note to this writer in 1995, Mr. Mainer related that "There may have been other musicians who have tried to copy my two-finger style banjo picking. It is different from any one I've heard. I have never heard anyone play the fiddle like J.E. Mainer; his fiddling and our music was different from anyone in that era of time."

[29] The two-finger style was actually fairly well established in North Georgia and Southwest North Carolina by the early twentieth century.

[30] This was Zeke Morris' first job as a musician. When he and his brothers, George and Wiley, later formed the Morris Brothers, they sounded similar to the Mountaineers.

[31] Wade, in a 1994 communication said, "I think [it was] in late 1934 or '35 when Zeke joined the band. And George Morris, Zeke's brother, never played in the band when I was in the band when I was with J.E.. He joined J.E. later."

In a 1991 phone interview with Wade, he said that "Zeke was more on the guitar like Riley Puckett was with Gid Tanner [and the **Skillet Lickers**]. To tell you the truth, Barry, I think he was a little better and smoother than the guitar players now. [That's] because the guitar players today, they give it that hard-drive music and they tune way high and they really get on them instruments and really ride 'em—if you know what I mean." This is not necessarily bad, Wade explained. "It's just a different style. It's a harder-drive music that caught on as bluegrass."

They played the music of the day: hillbilly music. In an interview with this writer in October 1990 at the IBMA Trade Show, Wade Mainer told that Bill Monroe very well *could* be the "Father of Bluegrass Music" but said that both groups (the **Mountaineers** and the **Monroe Brothers**) were playing pretty close to the same kind of music during that period. Bill Monroe was still with his brother Charlie at the time and they used guitar and mandolin. The Mainers used banjo, fiddle and guitar.

When asked if the Mainers' style was similar to other bands Wade remarked in 1990, "Yes and no. I don't believe our style was quite like the rest of them...we didn't hear nobody else playing our style of music. We had our own style and sound. I don't think we was all that good (he laughed). But I'll tell you one thing, our songs and records sure went over big with the good people." Wade recalled the old days when they had to travel in a T Model Ford. Because the crowds were so great, they often had to play two shows to accommodate the audience which came on horseback, or by car, or walked up to six miles to hear them. He remembered that they were wonderful people to play music for.

About that time, the group gained Crazy Water Crystals as a sponsor and played on WBT, Charlotte, North Carolina, on the Crazy Barn Dance. The group changed its name to **J.E. Mainer and the Crazy Mountaineers**. Other groups sponsored by the company were the **Dixon Brothers**, **Tobacco Tags**, Fisher Hendley's **Aristocratic Pigs**, Dick Hartman and his **Tennessee Cut-Ups**[32], and the **Johnson County Ramblers**.

Their personal appearances on WBT were sponsored by Crazy Water Crystals; the sponsor kept all the money and gave them only a small stipend. But the group did gain exposure and bookings from the shows—

that's where they made their money. Band members made twelve to fifteen dollars per week—actually a good wage; the band leader, of course, made more than the sidemen (who were generally hired by the leader to fulfill the leader's idea of what his music should be). Wade quit the sponsor several times in an attempt to get a better cut of the profits. When the band finally split from their relationship with Crazy Water Crystals, they returned their name to **J.E. Mainer's Mountaineers**. As useful as the Crystals sponsorship was at one time, the band no longer tolerated the situation of getting only a portion of the gate receipts. Now on their own, they were able to keep the entire gate.

The music business has always had a high turnover in band members; the country bands of this era were no exception. There was no trend to it. Most likely, a musician had to quit because of several reasons including: he was too young to understand how hard the job was; he had to return home to the farm; he couldn't leave his day job; or there wasn't enough money in it. A musician who stuck with it simply loved the music enough to put up with all the hardships that went with the job.[33]

On August 6, 1935, **J.E. Mainer's Mountaineers** began recording in Atlanta, Georgia. This led to a recording contract with Bluebird, RCA Victor's sublabel (a subsidiary of RCA) which handled this type of music. They recorded "Maple On The Hill,"[34] a duet sung by

The Smiling Rangers after Wade Mainer left in 1938. L to R: Homer Sherrill, Zeke Morris, Wiley Morris, Joel Martin.

[32] According to Wade, this was the name of the band.

[33] On the other hand, however, there are many who were not trained for anything else. Or, there were those who chose it as a profession because it was easiest thing they could think of to do for their rest of their working career.

[34] There was another "Maple on the Hill" written about 1895 by a black man named Gussie Davis. Wade's unique version of the song was very popular (it was on top of the charts for two years), and became popular again when later recorded by the Stanley Brothers and the Country Pardners.

Wade explained how he came to write his own "Maple on the Hill": "I never heard of that old song [that Davis wrote]. I heard somebody a-singin' it, a-hummin' it, and I picked it up and kindly got a vision of where I might be at [if I were in that song]. It might be in a porch swing or under a maple tree with my sweetheart or whatever. I changed it maybe a half a dozen times until I got it like I wanted it. I copyrighted that, and 'Take Me in a Lifeboat,' in nineteen and thirty-five. It's right there in the Library of Congress. Barry, I'm not trying to go back and dig up the song and start a whole lot of ruckus over it, I just wish somebody would tell me that was one of Wade Mainer's biggest hits of all times. I'd just like to have a little credit on it, is all. 'Cause I put together my own way and my own arrangement. It stayed on the charts for a couple of years there and every time we were on the WBT Barn Dance we had to sometimes do it twice on a Saturday night."

Little Smiling Rangers, c. 1938. L to R: Wade Mainer, Robert "Bucky" Banks, Morris Banks, Chubby Overcash.

Wade Mainer and Zeke Morris. Wade felt that his arrangement was different enough from the original to copyright it. He also arranged and copyrighted "Take Me in Your Lifeboat." Band members then were still Wade and J.E. Mainer, Zeke Morris and Daddy John Love. The June 1936 Bluebird session of **J.E. Mainer's Mountaineers**[35] helped the group's popularity to grow.

That October, J.E. and Wade Mainer split. J.E. kept the **J.E. Mainer's Mountaineers** name with musicians Snuffy Jenkins (banjo), George Morris (guitar) and Leonard "Handsome" Stokes (mandolin). Just after the split, Wade and Zeke Morris joined with Homer "Pappy" Sherrill on another Bluebird recording. This band was unofficially called the **North Carolina Buddies** and lasted only a very short time. Then Wade founded the **Smiling Rangers** which consisted of Wade, Sherrill, Zeke Morris, Homer Sherrill's brother Arthur, and Wiley Morris at WPTF, Raleigh, North Carolina. Pappy Sherrill stayed on fiddle from 1937 to 1938 when Wade quit his **Smiling Rangers** band to form **Wade Mainer and the Little Smiling Rangers**.[36]

On April 15, 1937, **J.E. Mainer and His Mountaineers** were first heard on WIS (a part of the NBC network at the time) in Columbia, South Carolina. Though the station was then an infant of seven years, it was still rated the 38th most popular station in the U.S.. The **Mountaineers'** daily show aired Monday through Friday. The band was the station's largest puller of mail;

they received 8,305 pieces of mail during the six months from October 1937 to March 1938 without benefit of contests or free offers. They were sponsored on WIS by the Chattanooga Medicine Company. There at WIS was announcer Byron Parker.

Wade's new **Little Smiling Rangers** was formed with nephews Morris Banks (mandolin) and Robert "Bucky" Banks (guitar) with Chubby Overcash[37] (guitar). Steve Ledford[38] (fiddle), who was in the band for several years, influenced their music to sound very much like bluegrass. Ledford fiddled in the style of the old string bands. He lived near Bakerville, North Carolina. It is said that a band's sound comes from how the musicians were raised. Certainly, Ledford's roots helped the **Sons of the Mountaineers** keep the music down to earth—in the old style. Wade's two-finger banjo style also helped perpetuate this sound. They knew that Bill Monroe's music was going over big in Nashville, yet they never had any intention of sounding like Bill Monroe. They only wanted to play, enjoy their music, and make a decent living.

The last band formed by Wade, about 1938 or 1939, was the **Sons of the Mountaineers** with Steve Ledford (fiddle), Clyde Moody (guitar) and Jay Hugh Hall (guitar). They recorded on Bluebird into the '40s: songs such as Wade's "Ramshackled Shack,"[39] "Wild Bill Jones" and "Companions Draw Nigh." Wade, in 1990, was still drawing royalties for "Shack." Wade remembered he and the band members heard the song on the jukebox one night. They wrote down the words to the song and performed it on the air the next morning. In November 1937, Wade married Julia and they eventually worked up a duo act.

In late 1938, J.E. left his **Mountaineers**[40]. Byron "The Old Hired Hand" Parker of Wisconsin took over the group. Parker added Homer Sherrill on fiddle and called it **Byron Parker's Mountaineers**. When Parker later took the band to WIS, it became the **Byron Parker and the WIS Hillbillies** with members Byron Parker, Snuffy Jenkins, Homer Sherrill and Leonard Stokes.[41] Because they were sponsored by Black Draught, they became **Black Draught Hillbillies and**

---

[35] Members included J.E. (fiddle) and Wade (banjo) Mainer, Zeke Morris (guitar, mandolin), Harold Christy (guitar), Beachem Blackweller (guitar) and Junior Misenheimer (banjo). Another band member that spring was the Hillbilly Kid (Boyd Carpenter) (guitar, harmonica) who also worked with J.E. and Wade when they were with Crazy Water Crystals.

[36] Homer Sherrill kept the Smiling Rangers going for a short while then joined Byron Parker and His Mountaineers at WIS, Columbia, South Carolina. There Sherrill met Snuffy Jenkins with whom he would eventually partner and form the basis of the Hired Hands (a band which was to last even after Snuffy's death in 1990). The fact that the Mountaineers and the Hired Hands had all the instrumental ingredients of a modern bluegrass band didn't necessarily make them a bluegrass band as we now know bluegrass. Snuffy was indeed playing his banjo in the three-finger style, but that was a rather primitive version of modern bluegrass and didn't have the *drive* that later banjo players put into their music to make it bluegrass. Don Reno, just learning the banjo at this time, listened intently to Snuffy Jenkins while he played banjo with J.E. Mainer's Mountaineers and learned from him. Zeke joined Charlie Monroe's Kentucky Pardners, which was the band that Charlie formed after he and Bill Monroe split.

[37] Overcash later joined J.E.'s band.

[38] Recording on Rounder Records in 1973 was the Ledford String Band. Their album featured Steve Ledford (fiddle, who recorded with his own Carolina Ramblers and Wade Mainer, among others), Wayne Ledford (guitar) and James Gardner (guitar).

[39] "Ramshackled Shack" made a big hit like "Maple on the Hill" and "Take Me the Life Boat." Probably written by Bill Cox, it is also known as "Sparking Blue Eyes."

[40] Earlier in 1938, J.E. Mainer's Mountaineers were Curly Shelton (guitar), J.E. (fiddle) and Jack Shelton (guitar).

[41] The reader may recall that Jenkins and Stokes were in J.E.'s band at the Mainer brother split and that Sherrill and Jenkins met there at WIS.

Homer Sherrill as well as **Byron Parker's Mountaineers.** Snuffy's brother, Verl "The Old Sheep Herder" Jenkins, was actually the first fiddler but was physically unable to travel so Byron convinced Sherrill to join the band. He was, according to Wade Mainer, "one of the best emcees you ever seen in your life. He could sell a barrel of rotten apples on the radio if he wanted to. He was that good!" He picked up the nickname "The Old Hired Hand" at about age twenty-five from the Crazy Water Crystals Company by virtue of his experience which, by that time, was considerable. Parker had worked with the **Monroe Brothers** and managed their band for a few years.[42] Members of the **Mountaineers** now included Jenkins, Henson Stokes, Leonard Stokes and George Morris. Leonard and George, as a duo, were known as **Handsome and Sambo.**

Wade Mainer's Sons of the Mountaineers, 1938.

Wade Mainer's **Sons of the Mountaineers** at WPTF in Raleigh was Jay Hugh Hall, Clyde Moody, Wade (banjo) and Steve Ledford. Moody and Hall were also known for their band, the **Happy-Go-Lucky Boys**, a name that they had used as a duo since 1933 on WSPA, Spartanburg, South Carolina. They again used this name while they were members of Wade's band when RCA Victor asked Wade's **Sons of the Mountaineers** to record for them. Wade had a disagreement with the label at the time and refused to do it with his **Sons of the Mountaineers.** The other members of his band wanted to do the recording but Wade was insulted that the band members would go behind his back and record under the **Sons of the Mountaineers** name. The other three members of the band, Ledford, Hall and Moody, went ahead with the recording using the name of Wade's band. When Wade found out about it, he threatened to sue so they changed their name to **Happy-Go-Lucky Boys.**

In 1939, Wade formed a new **Sons of the Mountaineers** which included Howard Dixon (Hawaiian guitar), Walter "Tiny" Dodson (fiddle, comedy) and the Shelton Brothers (Jack and Curly who had recently left J.E.'s band). J.E. played fiddle with them occasionally on WNOX's Mid-Day Merry-Go-Round.

About the time that World War II broke out for the United States, in 1941, Wade and his band were at WNOX, performing under contract on the Mid-Day Merry-Go-Round. George D. Hay invited Wade's band to perform on the Grand Ole Opry and take the place of Pee Wee King's band on the Saturday night slot. Lowell Blanchard, Wade's manager at WNOX told him that was a great opportunity for Wade and that he shouldn't miss it. But when the time came for Wade to leave, Blanchard couldn't let him go. That would break his contract with the station and Blanchard had no one to replace Wade's **Sons of the Mountaineers** on the station. Wade missed an opportunity of great potential, he said.

At WROL in Knoxville, Wade's band was sponsored by the Cas Walker chain of supermarkets (there were at least four stores at the time). Wade described Walker as "a nice guy. He was just a country boy. He was a shrewd trader, though." Walker told the bands he sponsored, "If you put things over and get people listening, I'll put you on." There at WROL, Wade and his band supplemented their income with concerts at schoolhouses. At the top of their popularity, *Life* magazine followed him around for a week, taking pictures and preparing an essay on him and his band. Nothing ever came from those activities, though; the War had broken out and gave the magazine something more critical to cover.

In 1941, Wade Mainer, with Tiny Dodson and Jack Shelton, played for President and Mrs. Franklin D. Roosevelt at the White House. The Librarian at the Library of Congress who organized the event asked for "folk music." Although this was not the first hillbilly band to play for a President, Wade recalled in 1990 that he may have been the first banjo player who did. He also remembered that Lily May Ledford, of the **Coon Creek Girls**, played for the President at some time.

Wade, still in Knoxville, quit music for a short while in September 1941 and turned his **Sons of the Mountaineers** over to J.E. who changed the name back to **J.E. Mainer's Mountaineers.** Members of the band then became J.E. Mainer, Curly Shelton, Jack Shelton and Julian "Greasy" Medlin. In 1961, J.E.'s family band, the **Mainers**, featured the Scruggs-style banjo of Glenn Mainer (J.E.'s son). They recorded for Atlantic, Arhoolie, and eventually did sixteen albums for Rural Rhythm. J.E. stayed with the music awhile longer, spending some time in St. Louis with the **Carter Family**, until he died in 1971.

42 According to Wade, "[Parker] took sick when he was with that band and they never did take him back. I think he was the one who started them on the road to success."

By 1945, Wade was back with his **Sons of the Mountaineers** who performed on the BBC for broadcast to the U.S. troops in Europe. This was a job which was obtained by a vote count of the soldiers away from home; the men wanted to hear *his* band more than all the others. The recording session was in New York.

Wade and his band recorded several tunes on King Records in January 1952: "No Place to Lay Your Head" and "Now I Lay Me Down to Sleep." In June, King released "Standing Outside"/"I'm Not Looking Backward." King released Wade Mainer's "Little Birdie"/ "The Girl I Left in Sunny Tennessee" in August. In 1953, Wade and Julia moved to Michigan to work for the Lord. His daytime job was with General Motors. Wade dropped out of the music mainstream for twenty years until he retired from GM.

In 1971, J.E. died just before an appearance at the Culpeper Bluegrass Festival. His music career spanned fifty years and he recorded over 500 songs. He died of an apparent heart attack at his home in Concord, North Carolina.

In the early seventies, Wade's son, Frank Mainer, was at a Tex Ritter concert and introduced himself to Ritter. Ritter recognized the Mainer name and asked if he knew Wade Mainer. Frank said he was his son and that Wade was living in Flint, Michigan, working for General Motors. The word got out about Wade's existence and, before long, he began to receive fan mail again. He retired from General Motors in 1972 and continued to play his music on tour, proving that it was still in demand. Wade then recorded on the IRMA label (one record) and on Old Homestead. He would mostly perform gospel music, having become "born again" in 1953.

Wade won the Carter Stanley Memorial Trophy (the White Dove) at McClure, Virginia, for his contributions to old-time music in May of 1979. In January 1982, at the age of 75, Wade took his first plane ride when he was hired to perform for the F.D.R. Centennial Celebration in Washington, D.C.. The event was designed to be a partial re-creation of the 1941 performance for President and Mrs. Roosevelt and was arranged on both

WWNC, 1938. Wade Mainer (l) with Howard "Panhandle Pete" Nash and Steve Ledford. Pete is playing the harmonica with his nose. He was a one-man-show who played 17 instruments at one time.

dates (1941 and 1982) by noted folklorist Alan Lomax. Wade received the Snuffy Jenkins Award in 1983. In 1983, Wade, Julia, and their son Leon Spain (now deceased) took their music to the Netherlands. In 1985, he received a clock plaque from Detroit Area Friends to recognize his fifty years in music. Wade and Julia were sponsored by the International Folk Music Festival to tour Florence, Italy, in 1986.

The North Carolina Arts Council honored its hillbilly radio pioneers in 1985 with "The Charlotte Country Music Story" featuring performances by Wade Mainer, Bill Monroe, Snuffy Jenkins, Pappy Sherrill, the **Morris Brothers** and the **WBT Briarhoppers**. In 1987, Wade was one of thirteen recipients of a National Heritage Fellowship Award in honor of being an Appalachian five-string banjo picker and singer. This award is worth $5000 to the winners and is quite prestigious because the recipients are nominated by their peers. In 1988, at Zimmerman, Minnesota's Minnesota Bluegrass and Old-Time Music Festival, a plaque was presented to Wade by Mr. Harry Teifs. It signified that on that day, fifty years earlier, Wade recorded "Maple on the Hill" in Atlanta.

In October 1990, Wade Mainer received a Award of Merit at the International Bluegrass Music Association Awards Ceremony at Owensboro, Kentucky. The award noted his significant contributions to the roots of bluegrass music. Upon acceptance of the award, Wade, a trim and healthy eighty-three years old, thanked the group and said, "It's about time! It's about time you started recognizing what we did in the old days." After the trade show, Wade and Julia were driving out of town when some "force" called them back to the event. When they came back into town, he was asked to perform that weekend at the IBMA Fanfest, there on the shores of the Ohio River. He thinks it was Divine intervention.

Wade and Julia Mainer, 1994. Wade was 87 years old.

Other awards of recognition Wade received through the years include Wade Mainer Day, a proclamation from the Mayor of Flint, Michigan, an award from the *Congressional Record*, a Michigan Country Convention Award, and a congratulatory letter from President Reagan. In September 1994, Wade received a plaque for his contributions to the preservation of traditional North Carolina music by the Charlotte Folk Music Society.

Wade plays music by ear, can't read music, and has no formal knowledge about the study of music. The duo of Wade and Julia continued to perform and record together on June Appal Records; the most recent album was issued in 1992 on Old Homestead.

Zeke, George and Wiley Morris

The Morris Brothers— Zeke, George and Wiley

The **Morris Brothers** could very well be *the* first bluegrass band. They had all the ingredients for it in the early 1940s: they had the five basic bluegrass instruments and, according to many, they had the rhythm. With the presumption that Wiley Morris' rhythm was passed on to Clyde Moody, who then passed it on to Lester Flatt, who then influenced Bill Monroe perhaps they were, indeed, the very first.

Often, when an interview is conducted some sixty years after the event, the facts get scrambled. Some of the events included here are actually *that* old. But the interview with Mr. Zeke Morris indicated that he was very lucid and remembered much of the early days during the thirties.

Claude "Zeke" Morris was born May 9, 1916. Wiley Morris was born February 1, 1919. The oldest brother was George. All the brothers were born and raised in Old Fort, North Carolina, McDowell Country, near Asheville.

The story begins when J.E. Mainer was looking for a guitarist-singer for his **J.E. Mainer's Mountaineers** with his younger brother, Wade, who played two-finger style banjo with the group. J.E. and Wade hired Zeke Morris as their guitar player in 1933. Wade had actually arrived at the Morris household looking for the older brother, George, whom they had heard about but was not at home that day. So Wade and J.E. hired Zeke.

Wade and Zeke decided to leave J.E.'s band in the fall of 1935 and partner up in a duo, **Wade and Zeke**, and later on in the **Smiling Rangers, Wade and Zeke**. Zeke remembered, "And then Wade and me come out with that 'Maple on the Hill,' you know. And that really put me and him on top, you know. And we pulled out and left J.E.. It was Wade and me for a long time. Of course, we had Steve Ledford to play with us, and we

had Homer Sherrill to play with us some. But Wade and me, we played together a long time. But Wade and me, we had a unique thing. It was old-timey and stuff, but it was good—the people thought so anyway. But my brother (Wiley) and me, we did our thing and I come out and I wrote that 'Salty Dog Blues' (1935), you know, and that's been my biggest hit of all that we've done, you know. And I still make money off that. 'Cause I was smart, you know—I was an old country boy, but I was smart. I had all the stuff copyrighted and published so I draw royalties every six months through Southern Music Publishing Company. I been pretty big into it.

"And in 1937," continued Zeke, "is when Wade and me dissolved partnership because I wanted my brother into it, you know. And I took Wiley and got him started into it, and then he and I skyrocketed then, you know, 'cause our voices were so close together, you know, in harmony. 'Cause two brothers' voices blend together better than strangers, you know."[43]

"It was a terrible time to try to make a livin', right in the middle of the Depression. But we survived, you know. But we were popular—there's no doubt about that. Wade and me were the most popular duet of all times back in those days. That was due to 'Maple on the

---

"It was a terrible time to try to make a livin', right in the middle of the Depression. But we survived, you know. But we were popular—there's no doubt about that." —Zeke Morris

---

Hill,' you know, and 'Two Little Rosebuds' and songs like that. That's what put us over: 'Maple on the Hill.'"

Having a sponsor was necessary for a band to have a sustaining salary. "Well, it more or less helped the sponsor, really," said Zeke. "We made our money off of our show dates, you know. [The sponsor] just paid for the time on the radio, more or less, so we could advertise our show dates. And I have, in the early days, went into radio stations and bought my own time so I could work my show dates. I'd go in and buy time, you know. 'Cause it was pretty cheap in those days. But after later on down the line, then you *could* get some pretty good sponsors. But a lot of times I have bought my own times."

Zeke and Wiley became the **Morris Brothers** again as a brothers act in Asheville on a daily radio afternoon show at WWNC, sponsored by JFG Coffee (which still exists today). All the Morris brothers played the guitar, so Zeke took up the fiddle at this time to help their sound. Later, they played a daily morning show at

[43] All quotations by Zeke Morris are from a telephone interview with Zeke while he was at his auto body shop in Black Mountain, North Carolina, just over the hill from Old Fort, NC, on November 26 and 27, 1993, unless otherwise noted.

WPTF, Raleigh, North Carolina, and were immediately followed by the **Monroe Brothers**, Bill and Charlie, with whom they became close friends. They were not rivals because their music was so different, said Zeke.

On January 26, 1938, the **Morris Brothers**, Zeke and Wiley (with guest fiddler Homer Sherrill) recorded for RCA Victor for the first time. During this recording session in Rock Hill, South Carolina, the three brothers recorded "Let Me Be Your Salty Dog."[44] It became the **Morris Brothers'** most famous tune. Zeke said that the idea for the song came to him after winning at the slot machines at a bar near Canton, North Carolina, called the Salty Dog. Wiley said that the origin for the name came from when they were kids growing up together in Old Fort. When one would see a girl he liked, he'd say, "I'd like to be her salty dog!" Also, there used to be a drink in Michigan called the Salty Dog.[45] The song later gained great popularity in the bluegrass world. They made much more money from royalties than from the sales of their recordings.[46]

Zeke had started out his career on the guitar. After teaching Wiley how to play, he switched to mandolin.[47] They added the three-finger banjo and the fiddle to the band and they really had a bluegrass sound, said Zeke. He reflected on Wiley and their original music, "Wiley could really play that guitar. You see, I've always could play a mandolin ever since I started out playin'. I could play any of them, you know. But when Wiley and me were playin', once in awhile I would get the fiddle and play a breakdown. But most of the time it was mandolin altogether. And I've got a style that nobody else has got." The sound of this period is captured on Rounder's 1972 recording and release of "Wiley, Zeke and Homer."

"But, now listen," continued Zeke, "I know you've talked to quite a few people. A lot of them will give you the wrong information. But believe me, what I've told you is straight from the horse's mouth. I know all about this stuff and I've always had a excellent memory— [what I've told you] is what Wade and me did together. But Wade and me wasn't together all that much—about three years or something like that? See, Wiley and me have spent pretty much a lifetime

together. And ever since that, I got him on to playin' and singin'. You should have heard him when I first got him. Lord, I worked with him, mercy sakes...to get his timin' right, you know. But after he caught on, I mean he went to town then. And I worked with him right; I had patience with him. 'Cause you can disgust a young person and turn 'em against that. But I'd work with him and showed him. And the first thing you know, there wasn't any better. He come right out from the woods and in no time he was a-goin'. He was a terrific singer. That guy had a mellow voice and I mean he could sing, too. He didn't sing through his nose at all."

It is interesting that the country music which was prevalent in the '30s was mostly that of the big string bands like the **Skillet Lickers** and the **Georgia Wildcats**, for instance, and that Zeke and George didn't use them as mentors. Laughing, Zeke also recalled "The **Fruit Jar Drinkers**, old Uncle Dave Macon. That wasn't music as far as I was concerned. Like I told you, I started playin' when I was eight or nine years old. And you know, I just hit it right off. I could tune my instrument before I could play it. I had a good ear for music. I guess I was gifted from my mother, you know, and it wasn't any problem for me to learn and to learn different instruments. At one time, I could play the fire out of a guitar. But after Wiley and me were doin' our duets and all, just once in awhile I'd take the guitar when we was goin' to do a trio or a quartet number like a gospel song or something. I'd play the guitar then, 'cause I'd play with my fingers, you know; it's a different sound from Wiley with a straight pick. I used a thumb pick and only occasionally used an index finger pick back before we got amplifiers. But after we got amplifiers I just used my natural fingers. But it didn't really make any difference in my playin'. I just wouldn't play as loud. And playin' my mandolin, I don't play it loud at all. I get right up in the microphone with it so I can get over the strings, you know.

"But I developed my own style when I first started learnin', so I never did care about coppin' after somebody else. I never did believe in that. I just did my own thing. Now, a lot of people started to copy Wiley and me, but they've never been able to get it done. There was some boys up in West Virginia, calls their

1936 Martin D-28 guitar. Over the years the Martin D-28 guitar has proven itself to be the most popular model for bluegrass music. The pre-World War II models with Herringbone trim are especially prized by collectors as well as musicians. Photo courtesy George Gruhn Guitars.

[44] Also known as "Salty Dog Blues."

[45] In an interview with Wade Mainer in 1990, Wade spoke about Wiley's idea about the origin of the song. "That song was created by the old, old Shelton Brothers. Now, Wiley may be getting ahead of hisself. That song was done just like I done 'Maple on the Hill' [by the modification of an existing song]. They (the Morris Brothers) changed it and made the different arrangements and all. But that's the way that song was created. I remember that song many, many years before Wiley and I got together." Finally, according to Walter V. Saunders' "Notes and Queries" in *Bluegrass Unlimited*, May, 1990, "Salty Dog Blues" was revised considerably by the Morris Brothers from the 1925 tune by Papa Charlie Jackson.

[46] Earlier in this interview, Zeke mentioned that he was smart, and the reason why is because he copyrighted his songs. Many other artists of the day, and later, hadn't learned that lesson yet.

[47] Zeke's mandolin, the one which he used throughout his career, is the only A-1 Gibson in existence today, he says. Patented in 1898 and sold on the market 1906; he has been offered $15,000 for it. He will leave it to his large family. He also will leave his large collection of 78s to his family.

self the **Morris Brothers**. They tried to copy after us but they just cain't do it, you know. They don't have the voices; they can't do it like Wiley and me did. People who know all about our music are all the time writin' me and sendin' me information. But nobody in the whole wide world can do it like the Morris brothers. 'Cause when we would perform at these places, it was just like down in Charlotte in 1985. Anyway, I have my own style and I've stayed with it ever since I was a kid. Naturally, I got better in my playin'."

The **Morris Brothers** had as its nucleus Zeke and younger brother Wiley. They soon added fiddler Homer "Pappy" Sherrill as a three-piece band in Danville, Virginia. In April 1938, Joel Martin joined the **Morris Brothers** at WBTM, Danville, Virginia, on the Farm Bulletin Program and by early 1939 on the Western North Carolina Farm Hour at WWNC.

Their first banjo player, Joel Martin was one of the pioneers in the bluegrass style of banjo playing as were Snuffy Jenkins, Hoke Jenkins, Mack Crow and few others. Wiley and Zeke now had the basic combination of instruments (banjo, fiddle, guitar, mandolin) which later used in bluegrass. Martin "was a terrific banjo player!" said Zeke. "He played the three-finger style. So he's the one, really, who set the stage for the three-finger banjo pickin'." According to Zeke, Martin was largely self-taught, having no connection or exposure with Charlie Poole, Snuffy Jenkins or others. "He didn't know nothin' about Snuffy. He was from way up in the hills of Virginia—back up towards Martinsville. His whole family was musicians. Wiley and me and Homer, we left Raleigh and went to Danville, Virginia, and we mopped up there and that's where we got a-hold of Joel. He joined us on the five-string banjo. We really had a band, too! Just us three. And Buddy, he couldn't sing, you know. But he could really play a five-string banjo."

Martin played "nothin' like Charlie Poole," Zeke explained. "In other words, it was on the same style that Hoke Jenkins—Snuffy was Hoke's uncle—and Hoke played with Wiley and me for several years, you know. In fact, he was a better banjo player than Snuffy! Old Hoke was a real five-string banjo player. But Joel Martin; you couldn't beat him. That guy was terrific! He's another one who couldn't sing a lick (Zeke laughed). Well, Snuffy couldn't sing either." Martin stayed with the **Morris Brothers** about two years; he was replaced on the five-string banjo by Hoke Jenkins, followed by Don Reno, then Earl Scruggs.

"Wiley and me started the Western North Carolina Farm Hour on WWNC," continued Zeke, "and stayed there until '41 when the War come on. Of course, we went back and played several times after that, you know. But we stayed there from '39 through '41. And we played the whole territory for WWNC 'cause we had two programs. We was on at 5:30 in the mornin' and then we'd come on at 12:05 'til one durin' the day. And we were really popular back in those days, too." It was at WWNC that brother George joined them for two years.[48]

Members of the **Morris Brothers** in late 1939 were Zeke (mandolin), George (guitar) and Wiley (guitar) Morris with Hoke Jenkins (banjo) and Tiny Dodson (fiddle). They were very popular with "Get on Board Little Children" and "Walking in Jerusalem Just Like John." The brothers' harmonies were impeccable. They featured comedy skits of black-faced George, Wiley, Zeke and Hoke. Back in those days there was no racial problem with this kind of entertainment.

Wade Mainer's Sons of the Mountaineers, c. 1938. L to R: J.E. Mainer, Wade Mainer, Clyde Moody (in black-face and dress) Jay Hugh Hall, Steve Ledford. Black-face comedy was common as a form of entertainment in country acts of the day.

In 1941, the band was on WSPA in Spartanburg, North Carolina, with young Don Reno on banjo (Hoke had left for the military). As with many a musician's career, W.W.II interrupted the professional musical career of the **Morris Brothers** and a shortage of gasoline and tires made travel difficult. Zeke recalled that "Don Reno came in after Hoke Jenkins who was with us on the Farm Hour. But I got Don Reno, I believe it was in '41[49] 'cause I went to Spartanburg and started a

---

48 The next time the Morris Brothers returned to WWNC was "in the '70s," told Zeke. "They saw the film that Earl (Scruggs) and Wiley and me made, you know, at Oklahoma State University. We had over 12,000 people. Wiley and me were feature attraction there on Friday night and we had over 12,000 people there watch us. And Earl called there from Nashville, Tennessee. Him, his outfit, and Bill Monroe and his outfit was gonna be at another place there on Saturday night and Earl wanted Wiley and me to stay over so he could do 'Salty Dog Blues' with us on his program. So we did. And after that, Wiley and me left, comin' on back home. But Wiley and me could really sing together."

49 Other sources say it was September 1941 when Reno joined the band.

program there and I got Don and taken him with me and a couple of his relatives. They was one boy named Howard Thompson that... He went with us and we stayed down there. And then Wiley joined me down there a little bit later after he got out of the service. See, they drafted Wiley into the service but he didn't have to stay; he got a medical discharge. So he joined me in Spartanburg. I didn't have to go into the service. I worked in a shipyard in Newport News, Virginia, for a while on a defense job. But I didn't stay there long and then I come on back.

"Don stayed a good, long while—a year or maybe a little more. Anyway, while I was a-playin' on Spartanburg, WSPA, Grady Wilkins[50] from up in Shelby, he brought Earl Scruggs down. We was a-playin' Gaffney, South Carolina, that night and he brought Earl Scruggs down there just right out of high school. We liked Earl's playin' so I gave Earl a job. That was the first professional playin' Earl ever did. And I paid him twenty-five dollars a week. He stayed with us a pretty good while. Then, somewhere along the line, he got a chance to go with Bill Monroe."[51]

In November of 1945, although the Morris brothers hadn't played together since early in the previous year, they re-formed and recorded for RCA Victor in Charlotte, North Carolina. The songs included two Wiley Morris originals, "Tragic Romance" and "Grave on a Green Hillside," and Zeke's "Somebody Loves You Darling." In those days, when Zeke wrote a song and put music to it, they often recorded it after only one practice run-through. Wiley read the words right off their scribblings on the paper.

The brothers performed together from 1937 up through '85. "That's the last concert we did: in '85." They never called it "bluegrass". It was still "country" music—a more derogatory term was "hillbilly" music. The Morris brothers feel that they played bluegrass music before the name became known, that the bluegrass sound was there in their band. They had banjo players such as Earl Scruggs, Don Reno, and Hoke Jenkins, and fiddle players such as Benny Sims and Tiny Dodson.

Zeke feels that bluegrass music as we know it today became popular only because of its exposure on the Grand Ole Opry—in this particular case, through **Bill Monroe and the Blue Grass Boys**. He is adamant that bluegrass was already in existence before Monroe—he and Wiley had been doing it for years already. He knew the **Monroe Brothers** well because he worked with them in North Carolina, but was neither impressed nor influenced; Zeke and George Morris had already been professional musicians for several years before they met Bill and Charlie Monroe.

Zeke elaborated on the music which he played, "But really and truthfully, there ain't no such a thing as bluegrass music; it's just something they come up with. It ain't a thing in the world but country music. They've added a little stuff here and there. 'Cause if you could hear our records—the **Morris Brothers**—you could see where it come from right there. I've got all kinds of records—78s down in my basement—of Wiley and me. Then I've got a reproduction album that RCA Victor done of Wiley and me. Now, Boy, that's terrific in full stereo. You see, those old 78s wasn't in stereo. They can really make you sound terrific nowadays. You can take the sorriest entertainer and they can make him sound terrific! All of my recordings with RCA Victor was done on wax. Now, this album, the master, was done on tape. The engineer that done that come down here from Washington, D.C., and we did it in the band room on account of the acoustics at Owen High School. And that guy knew how to bring it in and cut you down and level your music out. That's the reason that album sounds so good—such good harmony on it—he knew how to record it.

"We really had somethin' back in those days. If we could have waited and come along now, it would have been somethin' to see and watch."
—*Zeke Morris*

"It's not just me a-sayin' it. The whole country—'cause I've had feedback from it—that we were the best. There just wasn't a duet nowhere in the whole world that was like us. Old Joe Clark come all the way from England to see Wiley and me. And he said that we were the world's best! He said, 'Nobody can sing like you fellers.' I've had numbers of people visitin' me from Ireland, Japan. And I'd talk to 'em on the recorder.

"We really had somethin' back in those days. If we could have waited and come along now, it would have been somethin' to see and watch. See, back when we was doin' our recordin', you couldn't play 'em on the radio. They wasn't licensed for broadcast—home use only! Now, the first thing they do when they make one is they send it to all these disc jockeys and they play 'em over and over and over every day. I guess that's what sells for 'em. That's the reason I said we come along forty or fifty years too soon (he laughs). But we didn't have any control over that."

---

[50] This may have been "Wilkie."

[51] On the liner notes of "Wiley, Zeke and Homer" which was recorded in 1972 by Rounder, Zeke mentioned that Earl Scruggs was with the Morris Brothers "until he got his notice to report for induction into the Army." This is the only time I have heard mention that Scruggs went into the service.
    Unfortunately, the Morris Brothers did not record during the time either Reno or Scruggs were in their band. As a result, the Morris Brothers' place in bluegrass history may be lost or incompletely appreciated.

Although the brothers continued to sing and play together through the years, 1972 was their first opportunity to record in many years. It was for Rounder Records where we read on the liner notes, "The Morris brothers have a quiet, gentle appeal and a firm mastery of everything they sing."

Wiley Morris died of pneumonia September 22, 1990. Zeke lives in Black Mountain, North Carolina. He quit performing when Wiley died. And on the topic of what he thinks of the new music that followed in the footsteps of the **Morris Brothers**, "Well, some of it is okay. And they're callin' it 'country' that definitely is not country. You take Garth Brooks, for instance. He's a terrific singer—he's bound to be to make the money that he has. I couldn't call him a country singer. Now Clint Black, you can call him a country singer. He's got the voice for it! Now, Conway Twitty was a country singer. You can listen to his voice and tell. But Garth Brooks and Kenny Rogers do not have the country sound."

Zeke doesn't like how bluegrass has changed through the years. "They're ruinin' it! They're just cuttin' it up. I think that they're just messin' the true country music up. Look what's sprung off from it. And they're callin' everything 'country' anymore; and it's *not* country."

"That's the reason, when Wiley and me walked out on that stage and hit our instruments, no matter how many groups were there it just sounded like a new world had opened up it was so much different, you know. And our voices—we had strong voices but we didn't sing all that loud—we didn't need to. The type of music that Wiley and me did was the true *country*. It changed when they started addin' all this electrical stuff to it like the recordin's they do now. 'Cause you listen to the guys in person and they sound terrible! But the way they record 'em now, it makes 'em sound terrific. They've got all that extra added into it and it makes 'em better than what they are.

"This bluegrass music is the offspring of the music Wiley and me did many years ago. You can listen to the sound and to the bluegrass—they call it now—and you can see where it come from."

"This bluegrass music is the offspring of the music Wiley and me did many years ago. You can listen to the sound and to the bluegrass— they call it now—and you can see where it come from." —Zeke Morris

The Carter Family of Virginia

The **Carter Family** is important in any history of this music because they bridged the gap from the way bands played music before them to the way bluegrass is now arranged. Before this, there was considerable participation by each member of a band in a song, but not much sophistication or thought went into its presentation.

Banjoist Alan Munde described the band in this manner, "I'm not an historian or anything—I'm just a curious observer and I haven't listened to all the music of that era—but it seems to me that the **Carter Family** were important in the sense that they set the model for how a band structured itself. For instance, how a band used the guitar kickoff, and then a verse, and then the harmony joining in on the chorus, and then there is a guitar break. Just the form of the music they played is a model of those that came afterwards. Because a lot of the early string bands—they just played sort of [haphazard] and when somebody was compelled to sing some words—while they were singing, the instruments were just played away. And the **Carter Family**, partly because they were small and were not a string band, were organized. Jimmie Rodgers and the **Carter Family**, I think, were very strong models for all of country music."[52]

Renowned country music historian and author Dr. Charles Wolfe wrote of their importance in country music, "In the past, picking styles had been adapted to voices, leading to all manner of odd tunings and instrumental techniques. But A.P. Carter incorporated this group's vocals into the instrumental sound, which often involved simplifying both melody and rhythm. Others were doing the same thing around the same time, but few got results like A.P. did. The **Carter Family** songs were reduced to three chords played in steady 4-4 time, and this simplification was undoubtedly another key to their success. Keeping the music simple meant keeping

52 1992 interview in Loveland, Colorado.

it down to earth, and it's hard to get much earthier than the **Carter Family**."[53]

Alvin Pleasant Carter, patriarch of the **Carter Family**, was born at Maces Spring, in Poor Valley, southwestern Virginia, near the Clinch Mountains in 1891. "A.P. got his early training in church quartet music about the turn of the century," wrote Wolfe. "It was all-day singings and singing schools that eventually paved the way for gospel music, modern day country music's religious counterpart. In fact, religious music was commercialized and adapted to modern mass media as fast or faster than traditional secular music..."[54]

In 1898, Sara Dougherty was born in Wise County, Virginia. She and A.P. were married in 1915. She played Autoharp and guitar. Maybelle Addington was born in Nickelsville, Virginia, May 10, 1909. Maybelle married Ezra "Eck" Carter, A.P.'s brother, in 1926. She was sixteen; he was twenty-seven. She already played guitar and joined A.P. and Sara Carter as a guitar soloist in the trio they called the **Carter Family**. They soon recorded for Victor, songs including "Bury Me Under the Weeping Willow" and "The Poor Orphan Child." In May of 1928, the **Carter Family** recorded "Keep on the Sunny Side," "Will You Miss Me When I'm Gone" and "Wildwood Flower" on Victor Records. They recorded on Victor until 1935 when they switched to the American Record Company and Decca.

In 1926, Maybelle bought a Gibson L-5 guitar for a hefty $125. She played melody or harmony notes on the bass strings of the guitar while chording the bottom strings for rhythm. Charles Wolfe wrote that "she played the melodic line in front of an Autoharp rhythm back-up, has indirectly influenced almost every country guitar picker, her solo on 'Wildwood Flower' is one of the most imitated in country music history."[55] She used a thumb pick and two steel finger picks, thereby creating a style which some use today. A major influence on Maybelle's guitar style came from A.P.'s partner, black guitarist Leslie Riddles of nearby Kingsport, Tennessee. He and A.P. would take long trips to find new songs. When they found one they liked, A.P. would write down the words (or change them at will), and Riddles would learn the melody on the guitar in order to teach Maybelle. As a group, the **Carter Family** did little touring and changed their style negligibly in spite of the influence of the evolving Nashville sound.

The music of the day was known as "hillbilly" to describe its origins and style. Most often, the music would be supplemented with vaudeville-like comedy which was part of the total entertainment package brought to the people by the bands of that time. An outlandish costume for the main comedian was popular. The practice was carried on for several decades after this period.

On August 4th of 1927, Jimmie Rodgers and the **Carter Family** began recording in Bristol, Tennessee. Author Nolan Porterfield wrote, "Music historians and others fond of dates and places have a special weakness for 'Bristol, August 1927.' As a sort of shorthand notation, it has come to signal the Big Bang of country music evolution, the genesis of every shape and species of Pickin'-and-Singin' down through the years."[56] Though both the Carters and Jimmie Rodgers were at the studios at Bristol at that time to record for Ralph Peer (who was then with Victor Records), they didn't meet until their next Peer session in Louisville in June 1931.

At the peak of their career in 1938, the **Carter Family**'s music was broadcast live on 500,000 watt XERF, Del Rio, Texas, on the border of Mexico and Texas. With coverage all over the U.S., they could simply stay at one place and sell their records by mail. There were two shows daily. The group played there until 1942 even though they stopped recording in 1941.

June Carter (Cash) remembered the original band, "When I listen to some of those old things now, I'm really proud that we came out of Poor Valley and sounded like we did—especially the amazing sounds that Mother, Uncle A.P. and Aunt Sara made. I mean it was just two instruments and three voices, but it sounded like an orchestra. If it needed an oboe, Uncle A.P. was the oboe. Then he would lay out and come in later like a violin section. It was amazing. My uncle, A.P. Carter, when he'd walk into a room, everybody would know A.P. had walked in. He had a charisma that changed everyone. To hear the original **Carter Family** is something I will never forget as long as I live."[57]

The **Carter Family** was elected into the Country Music Hall of Fame in 1970. A.P. Carter died November 7, 1960. Maybelle Carter died October 2, 1978.

The music of the day was known as "hillbilly" to describe its origins and style. Most often, the music would be supplemented with vaudeville-like comedy...

[53] Charles K. Wolfe, *Tennessee Strings* (Knoxville: The University of Tennessee Press, 1977), p. 63.

[54] Ibid., 14.

[55] Ibid., p. 44.

[56] Nolan Porterfield, *Country, the Music and the Musicians* (New York: Abbeville Press, 1988), p. 17.

[57] *Life* magazine—"The Roots of Country Music" September 1, 1994, p. 70.

The Delmore Brothers

The best duet harmonies seem to come from the same families, with the similar voices that siblings seem to have. Such duets included the **Delmore Brothers**, the **Callahan Brothers**, the **Monroe Brothers**, the **Shelton Brothers** and the Bolick brothers (**Blue Sky Boys**).

One of the first duet acts, the **Delmore Brothers**, retained their popularity longer than any of the others who began back in the formative days of country music. Their style was innovative and their new songs were often good enough to "cross-over" to the pop charts—"Beautiful Brown Eyes" and "More Pretty Girls Than One" were two of these songs. Alton did most of the songwriting for the duet, including "Brown's Ferry Blues," "Til the Roses Bloom Again," "Blue Railroad Train," "Gonna Lay Down My Old Guitar," "Back to Birmingham" and "Nashville Blues." They pioneered the style called "Hillbilly Boogie" after World War II.

Their style was important in country music history because it linked the blues, ragtime and shape-note (gospel) singing which were prevalent in the South during the 19th century, with the newer styles of the '30s and '40s which were more complex, polished and commercial. The radio media was important here because professional performers couldn't earn a living playing their music without having a weekly radio show. The shows gave them a salary, a place to advertise their items for sale, and the ability to tell listeners about their upcoming performances.

In addition to bringing sophistication to hillbilly music, the Delmores served in several other ways to provide significant influence on future groups—specifically brother duets:

- they developed a harmony style for Jimmie Rodgers' blue yodels.
- their intricate and delicate harmonies, now made possible by better microphones, became the forerunner for other close-harmony groups such as the **Monroe Brothers**, the **Blue Sky Boys**, the **Callahan Brothers**, the **Girls of the Golden West** and generations of others to follow.
- their songs were more sophisticated than those of the string bands before them. They crafted songs which could be sung delicately and with the feeling that the new, sensitive microphones allowed.
- Alton Delmore was a formidable flattop style guitarist. He taught Rabon how to play the tenor guitar. They were the first group to take an instrumental break on it. They were considerably better instrumentalists than many of their contemporaries and their twin-guitars gave them a sound like no others.

When Rabon (pron. Ray'-bawn) was ten (he was born December 3, 1916), he sang duets with eighteen year-old brother Alton (born December 25, 1908) in the close-harmony style for which they later became famous. Rabon played a little fiddle; Alton, the guitar. They won many talent contests. One early performance was related by Alton, "It came time for Rabon and me to play, and some of the fine bands had already been on the stage and made a big hit with the crowd... The only thing was, we could not play as loud as the others had played... We picked out two of our best ones, I think the first one was 'That's Why I'm Jealous of You.'

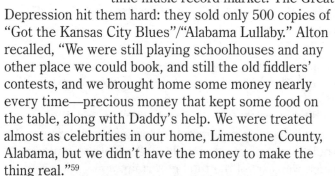

We sang it a lot in those days and it was a good duet song. When we first began to sing, the crowd was kind of noisy. But we hadn't got through the song before there was a quietness everywhere. You could have almost heard a pin drop. Then we knew we had a good chance at the prize even though there were only two of us. When we finished, there was a deafening roar of applause. If the crowd had not quieted down, there probably would never been an act called the **Delmore Brothers**."[58] This success gave them the confidence to pursue their music professionally.

The professional brother act of Alton and Rabon Delmore then began in 1926 when Alton (18) published a shape-note gospel songbook called *Bright Melodies*. After an audition with Columbia Records in 1931, they cut one record then returned home to Elkmont in northern Alabama. They were feeling even more confident about their possibilities of earning a living from the music because Columbia was *the*

The Ramsey

dominant record company in the old-time music record market. The Great Depression hit them hard: they sold only 500 copies of "Got the Kansas City Blues"/"Alabama Lullaby." Alton recalled, "We were still playing schoolhouses and any other place we could book, and still the old fiddlers' contests, and we brought home some money nearly every time—precious money that kept some food on the table, along with Daddy's help. We were treated almost as celebrities in our home, Limestone County, Alabama, but we didn't have the money to make the thing real."[59]

By 1933, the **Delmore Brothers** had twenty-five original tunes. Finally, with five dollars between them, they were given an audition for the Opry by its manager, Harry Stone. Stone asked them to perform one

[58] Charles Wolfe, "The Delmore Brothers on the Opry," *Bluegrass Unlimited*, October, 1989, p. 18.

[59] Ibid., p. 18. The "thing" he was referring to was the realization that he and his brother could earn a living from this music. This would be a big step for them; very few who played music professionally were doing well.

song; they chose "Silver Haired Daddy of Mine." They were hired and replaced the **Pickard Family**[60] on a regular thirty-minute slot. The Delmore's first appearance on the Opry was April 29th, 1933, following the "Harmonica Wizard," DeFord Bailey. There on the weekly show, the **Delmore Brothers** often provided accompaniment for stars Uncle Dave Macon and Fiddlin' Arthur Smith.

In December, the **Delmore Brothers** began recording for Victor's Bluebird label in Chicago. Two of the songs were "Brown's Ferry Blues"/"Gonna Lay Down My Old Guitar." This gave them the popularity needed to convince the Opry to let them go on tour, which was necessary to supplement the meager wages paid by WSM. But even though they got almost as much mail as Uncle Dave Macon, they were not allowed to tour until the success of these recordings proved their worth.

By 1935, Uncle Dave Macon had noticed that the Delmores were getting almost as much fan mail as he did so he asked them to tour with him in a proven circuit of profitable school houses and small-town meeting halls. Macon had used these venues for many years and knew they would work. Alton wrote, "If he (Uncle Dave) wanted to play a week in a certain part of the country, all he had to do was write someone a letter and they would book him and he always made money."[61] These earnings were in addition to bookings arranged by WSM's Artist Service Bureau for its Opry stars which took fifteen percent of the money from the gigs it set up for them. This began a conflict with WSM. A disagreement of the Bureau over the separate tours of Macon with the Delmores caused Harry Stone and Judge Hay to split up the trio. Stone also felt that there was no need to pair up two of the biggest Opry acts together.

In 1937, Stone then paired the Delmores with Fiddlin' Arthur Smith who had just finished four years with Sam and Kirk McGee as the **Dixieliners**. This trio also worked well, but when Smith gained prominence for himself with his recordings on Bluebird, WSM split this group up as well. After the separation, the Delmores were paired with other acts which featured a more primitive, informal fun, and hard-drinking style of music which was still popular. But the Delmores sought to professionalize the music and present it to a more sophisticated audience. Their complaints were noted by Judge Hay and Stone but given little heed. Hay's direction for the Opry was to "Keep it down to earth, Boys." He dressed his acts in overalls and baggy pants to perpetuate the "hay seed" and "hillbilly" image which he felt helped bring the music to the average

country person better. Those who wanted to professionalize the music were treated as outcasts. This conflict caused much friction between the two parties.

By 1937, the **Delmore Brothers** were at their peak of popularity on the Opry. They recorded some eighty sides for RCA's Bluebird label and for Montgomery Ward's mail-order label. They sold 100,000 copies of "Brown's Ferry Blues"—incredible figures for the middle of the Depression—three times that of other top sellers. In 1938, Roy Acuff was hired onto the Opry to take the place of Fiddlin' Arthur Smith. The Opry's manager, David Stone, put Acuff and the Delmores together and soon Acuff and his band became popular enough to tour on their own. The Delmores were then teamed with Pee Wee King's **Golden West Cowboys**.

The **Delmore Brothers** quit the Opry in September of 1938, mostly because of Alton's unwillingness to conform to the Opry as it placed changing demands upon them. And he disliked the iron-firm grip of control the Opry had on its performers; it placed an overbearing friction on the brothers. Alton and Rabon then moved to Raleigh, North Carolina, where they accepted a regular-paying job at WPTF. They toured wherever they could book until they broke up in 1952.

Their style was important in country music history because it linked the blues, ragtime and shape-note (gospel) singing which were prevalent in the South during the 19th century...

In 1944, the **Delmore Brothers** signed with King Records, an independent record label which had just been founded (1943) by Cincinnati record store owner Syd Nathan. To a large extent, their recordings on King were merely re-recordings of the work they had done on Bluebird. They had many hits on King and had good success using electric instruments and the modern sound of "Blues Stay Away from Me." As a result, much of their subsequent work was not released because it was considered too traditional and not up to the caliber of "Blues." They played on Cincinnati's WLW radio as members of the great gospel group, the **Brown's Ferry Four** with Merle Travis and Grandpa Jones.

The **Delmore Brothers** broke up in 1952. Rabon died soon after. Alton continued solo for a while, even recording a hit, but he eventually became bitter and died in 1964. Alton had written more than 1000 songs.

---

[60] Quotation from Charles Wolfe, "The Triumph of the Hills: Country Radio, 1920-50," *Country, the Music and the Musicians* (The Country Music Foundation: Abbeville Press, 1988), p. 69.
   The Pickard Family joined the Opry in 1926 and became its first star singers. Said Dad Pickard, "I am mighty glad of the opportunity to play and sing these old ballads and folk songs. I feel that we are doing something worthwhile, for we are helping to preserve something very sweet and fine, which would otherwise be lost." It is interesting to note, even at this early stage of country music history, that performers were interested in preserving country music, knowing that it would be lost if someone didn't do it.
[61] Wolfe, op. cit., *Bluegrass Unlimited*, p. 19.

Tommy Scott— one of the last purveyors of the "medicine show"

Tommy Scott was one of many musicians willing to pursue any avenue to earn a living in music—especially difficult during the Great Depression. M.F. "Doc" Chamberland hired Scott during this period and taught him the secrets of entertaining the people and selling Herb-O-Lax Tonic. He was given the formula for the elixir after a year, and he started his own show which he called "The Last Real Medicine Show" which included sharp-shooting, bullwhip acts, juggling and magic, sales pitches for his snake-oil liniment, Herb-O-Lax, and lots of live, hillbilly music.[62] Scott soon became "Doc" Tommy Scott.

By 1933, Scott was entertaining on WAIM, Anderson, South Carolina. Later, he performed on WPTF, Raleigh, North Carolina, on WFBC, Greenville, South Carolina, on WBIG, Greensboro, North Carolina, and on WWVA's Jamboree in Wheeling, West Virginia, where he met Charlie Monroe. Monroe and Scott (both on guitars) founded the original **Kentucky Pardners** with Fiddlin' Dale Cole, Tommy Edwards (mandolin) and J.R. "Curly" Seckler (mandolin, tenor banjo) in 1939.

Late in the 1930s, Scott and Seckler formed a business which sold the tonic "Vim-Herb." They performed on WRDW, Augusta, Georgia (later owned by soul music singer James Brown), WAIM, and WSPA, Spartanburg, South Carolina. The duo bought a used circus tent with their last pennies.

Scott remembered, "We set out the first week of April that year and encountered a freak, heavy snow storm that tore our tent to pieces. It wiped us out. Curly went back with Charlie Monroe and I continued with my medicine show."[63] In the 1980s, the show played to 352 different cities and his traveling show included 100 workers, seven show vehicles and eighteen acts which included old-time sharp-shooting, magic acts, country and bluegrass music. Scott recorded with Clyde Moody for Old Homestead Records in 1980.

The Blue Sky Boys, Bill and Earl Bolick.

Homer Sherrill & Snuffy Jenkins

Homer "Pappy" Sherrill and Snuffy Jenkins and the Hired Hands

Going back to the late 1920s, we find thirteen year-old Homer Sherrill playing his fiddle at square dances for fifty cents per night. The fad at the dances was to shuffle and drag your feet through corn meal sprinkled on the floor to enhance the dancers' shuffling effect. Sherrill's professional experience, though, began even earlier when his father promoted his seven year-old son's interest in music in 1922 by buying him a Sears and Roebuck tin fiddle for Christmas that cost $1.98. (As of 1991, he still owned that fiddle.) He took lessons from Dad Williams, Mooresville, North Carolina. "I used to fiddle for my Daddy to help him sell watermelons. By noon, all ours would be sold and we'd leave the other farmers standing out in the hot sun."

About 1934 in Hickory, North Carolina, **Homer Sherrill's East Hickory String Band**[64] played at the Saturday night Barn Dance on WBT, a 50,000 watt station in Charlotte. When the dance became sponsored by the Crazy Water Crystal Company, the band's name was changed to **Crazy Hickory Nuts** and the dance name became the Crazy Water Barn Dance.

The Crazy Water Crystals Company was a significant source of income for hillbilly musicians beginning in 1933. The product had its beginnings in 1877 when sulfate waters were discovered near what is now Mineral Wells, Texas. The company, based in Charlotte, North Carolina, marketed the crystalline residue left after evaporation of the water. The crystals were packaged and sold as a laxative to be mixed with water before usage. "The appellation 'crazy' derived from the name of the original well and was not intended as jocular although the company's insistence that its performers incorporate the

---

[62] People who worked for Tommy Scott's Last Real Medicine Show in America included Stringbean, Clyde Moody, and old-time western stars Kit Carson, Johnny Mac Brown and Colonel Tim McCoy (with more than 200 movies to his credit).

[63] Don Rhodes, "Bluegrass Medicine Man—Tommy Scott," *Bluegrass Unlimited*, January, 1981. A quotation from Mr. Scott.

[64] This band consisted of Lute Isenhour (banjo, from Taylorsville, North Carolina), Homer Sherrill (fiddle), Ollen Benfield (guitar, sometimes spelled Olin) and Arthur Sherrill (mandolin, Homer's brother).

America's Music — Bluegrass

word into their stage names, led to such billings as **Fred Kirby, the Crazy Cavalier** (peculiar for a serious singer of heart songs)..."[65] Other bands during the 1930s who were associated with the sponsor included the **Monroe Brothers, J.E. Mainer's Mountaineers**, the **Blue Sky Boys**, the **Dixon Brothers**, the **Morris Brothers** and the **Tobacco Tags**.

Most of the radio programs were remote broadcasts from school auditoriums in the larger towns of North and South Carolina. Unlike WSM and WLS, WBT had nothing to do with programming the broadcast; it only put it on the air waves, for which it was paid by the Crazy Water Crystal Company which produced the one-hour show. Announcers would introduce the bands and advertise the sponsors.

Many of the entertainers on the Crazy Water Barn Dance consisted of talent from various towns and cities in the Carolinas. It was very common that the artists received no money for their services at the dance, with the exception of mileage expenses and the opportunity to be heard over a 50,000 watt radio station. When Sherrill's group became sponsored by Crazy Water Crystals, they made $10 per person per week—more money than he had ever been paid previously and very good wages for that time. Bill Bolick, in a 1991 interview, told of the station, "At this time, WBT was the only 50,000 watt station in the Carolinas. WSB, in Atlanta, Georgia, was the only 50,000 watt station in Georgia. If an artist could obtain a decent across-the-board spot on either of these stations, he was almost assured of limited success as these stations had possibly ten times as much coverage as smaller stations."

By 1935, Sherrill was working with Bill and Earl Bolick (who later became the **Blue Sky Boys**) in Asheville, North Carolina, where they were sponsored by the JFG Coffee Company. The trio was known as the **Good Coffee Boys—John, Frank and George**. They played for $10 per week per person. The brothers really hadn't played or sung much together until this time, but with Bill singing harmony and Earl singing the melody, the sound gelled and immediately became successful. Bill began playing the mandolin more and more due to fan mail requests. Certainly, the popularity of Bill Monroe's mandolin with the **Monroe Brothers**, who were an unqualified success at this time, was a factor in the taste of the audience and a reason for the requests.

In 1936, Sherrill joined Wade Mainer's band which soon became the **Smiling Rangers**. When Mainer left this band, he formed the **Little Smiling Rangers**. Sherrill kept the **Smiling Rangers** awhile longer in Raleigh, North Carolina.

Soon Sherrill partnered with Bill and Earl Bolick and they became the **Blue Sky Boys**. He was a good breakdown fiddler.[66] In 1938, Homer Sherrill learned "Orange Blossom Special" from its co-composer, Ervin

Rouse; Sherrill is credited for making it one of the all-time popular fiddle tunes in the North Carolina and Columbia, South Carolina, area of the country.

After some time with the **Blue Sky Boys**, in 1938 he went back home to Hickory and stayed until **Byron Parker and His Mountaineers** came to Granite Falls, North Carolina, along with Snuffy Jenkins, George "Sambo" Morris, Leonard "Handsome" Stokes, and Snuffy's brother, Verl, on fiddle. Sherrill joined the band in Columbia, South Carolina, and replaced fiddler Verl "The Old Sheep Herder" Jenkins.

Homer "Pappy" Sherrill in 1994.

At WIS in Columbia, the group's announcer was the self-proclaimed "Old Hired Hand", Byron Parker. Sherrill began earning "big bucks" (five dollars per night) as a full-time member of **Byron Parker and the WIS Hillbillies**, a.k.a. **Byron Parker's Mountaineers**. The group was featured in 1938 on NBC's Saturday Showcase called "Symphony from the Hills." Their comedy act, with George in black-face, was **Handsome and Sambo**. Some famous people who played on the WIS Barn Dance in Columbia at that time (sometimes as guests of **Byron Parker and the WIS Hillbillies**) included Mel Tillis, the original **Carter Family**, Tex Ritter, Red Foley, and Loretta Lynn when she was getting started. Sherrill had earlier played with Fiddlin' John Carson (when Carson was a guest of the **Blue Sky Boys**), and more recently Pee Wee King, Eddy Arnold and Jimmy Davis.

John Morris, of Old Homestead Records, wrote about Byron and J.E. Mainer's band, "It is the same group that recorded on Bluebird Records as **J.E. Mainer's Mountaineers** featuring Leonard 'Handsome'

[65] From the liner notes of "Crazy Water Barn Dance, Snuffy Jenkins and Pappy Sherrill." Notes by Mark Wilson (Rounder 0069)

[66] Actually, breakdown fiddling was what he did best at this stage of his fiddling career and he did very little playing behind the close-harmony voices of Bill and Earl Bolick. Sherrill later became more accomplished and could "do it all" when he was with the Hired Hands.

Stokes and George 'Sambo' Morris on harmony and, for the first time, the exciting three-finger style banjo of Snuffy Jenkins. You might say this is actually when recorded bluegrass music began because even though it was not called 'bluegrass music' then, it had the exact ingredients and pretty much the same sound (a time at which, I might add, Bill and Charlie Monroe were still singing harmony duets only)."[67]

Sherrill then teamed up with Dewitt "Snuffy" Jenkins to begin a duo which continued until 1990 when Jenkins passed away. Jenkins was one of the few people to play the banjo in the three-finger picking style at that time and is known as the first person to play this style on the radio. He had learned from Smith Hammett in Rutherford County, North Carolina. Earl Scruggs was also a student of Hammett. Jenkins was also the first person to play a washboard at Carnegie Hall in New York City. He redesigned the washboard to be a rhythm instrument, playing it with thimbles on his fingertips. He is credited for bridging the gap between old-time and bluegrass music.

Sherrill was known by his first name, Homer, until he and Snuffy established themselves as top-notch entertainers. The name "Pappy" came as soon as he had his first son (July 4, 1940) (named Wayne Irvin Sherrill after the radio station WIS where they played).

These were the days of the "kerosene circuit" where kerosene lamps lit the stage. The roads were muddy, unpaved, and seldom well-marked. Winter snows made it very difficult to make a living in this music. During the summer it was very hot; Pappy recalled the sweat literally dripping off the fiddle at times. In their travels, they wore out cars very fast. Concerts were usually in schools, as southern towns were spread apart and the local school was usually the largest public building which could house a country music performance. There was little advance publicity; word of mouth, hand bills, and radio announcements the day of the concert were often the only advertising for a performance that night. A sign in the local grocery or hardware store helped. Many bands of this era pulled a trailer in which they carried their instruments. The trailer often had the name of the band or the band's sponsor.

In 1948, the band began recording on Bluebird Records with Byron Parker (on vocals only; he didn't play an instrument. He was more an emcee than a singer and he booked the shows). After Parker's health failed him this year, the band soon won a recording contract with Capitol Records, beating out seventy other bands from all the southern states. Sherrill wrote "C.N.W. Railroad Blues," "Cherry Blossom Waltz," "Miller's Reel" and others recorded by **Byron Parker's Mountaineers**.

Byron Parker died at age thirty-seven on October 6th, 1948. The band changed its name to **Snuffy Jenkins and Pappy Sherrill and the Hired Hands** at Snuffy's suggestion.

When Sherrill had stomach ulcer problems in 1958 and had to quit the road awhile, the fiddler for **Snuffy Jenkins and Pappy Sherrill and the Hired Hands** was Roger Miller. This was the same man who later became famous in country music for songs such as "King of the Road" and "Dang Me."

At the 1966 Country Music Jamboree attended by more than 10,000 people, the Country Music Association of South Carolina presented an honorary lifetime membership to Snuffy, Pappy and Greasy Medlin, noting that these three men represented over a century of performing country music. The first Snuffy Jenkins North Carolina Bluegrass Festival was held in Harris, North Carolina (Snuffy's home town), in 1975. Also, the festival park was named in Snuffy's honor. The next year, Pappy Sherrill won first place at the National Fiddlers Championships in Washington, D.C..

In 1982, Snuffy, Pappy, and Greasy appeared with Roy Acuff in the PBS production, "The Last Free Show." Medlin died shortly thereafter.

Dewitt "Snuffy" Jenkins passed away April 30, 1990, in Columbia at age 81 following a recurrence of colon cancer. After Snuffy's death, band members continued as a foursome. **Pappy Sherrill and the Hired Hands** continued to be active in the 1990s and played as much as they wished.

Rose Maddox

America's Music | Bluegrass

[67] John Morris, from the liner notes of "Bluegrass Roots," Old Homestead Records, 1985. The LP was made from Bluebird 78s made about 1940.

The end of the Maddox Brothers and Rose

The story of this band begins in 1937 when they made their radio debut in Modesto, California, on KTRB. That first week, they got 10,000 letters. The studio was five miles out of town but people would still walk to see them perform. Rose Maddox was about eleven. She sang and read commercials on the air. One show in February 1940 was recorded and released on an Arhoolie Records LP. Many of their recordings and transcriptions were aired over the powerful Texas/Mexico border station XERB at Rosarita Beach, Baja California, Mexico.

The group played their raucous kind of American country music up and down the West Coast. Their pay varied between fifty and a thousand dollars. At one time, they owned twenty-five uniform changes. The costumes were elaborately embroidered and profusely decorated with appliquéd flowers, hearts and other designs—a custom-made shirt and pair of pants would cost up to $700.[68] They traveled so much that a new Cadillac—they each owned one—lasted about six months on the road. Between 1949 and 1959, Fred Maddox owned fifteen Cadillacs. They appeared at their gigs, each with their own car, in a convoy.

A 1941 audition for the Opry was unsuccessful because Jack Stapp, an Opry official, didn't consider them "hillbilly" because they were from California. Nevertheless, they appeared on the Opry as a guest in 1949. The Opry brought them in because of the national popularity of their song "Gathering Flowers for the Master's Bouquet." This appearance on the Opry was recorded and later released on Arhoolie Records.

When W.W.II came along, Cal, Fred and Don Maddox were drafted. Cliff had medical problems and didn't qualify for the military. Henry was too young for the draft. They reorganized after the War and continued until they split up. In 1946, the group began their recording career with a 78 on 4-Star Records. In 1952, they received top billing at the Louisiana Hayride where they shared the stage with Hank Williams, Red Sovine, Faron Young, the **Wilburn Brothers**, Jim Reeves, Slim Whitman, Bill Carlisle and the **Browns**.

According to veteran bluegrasser Roland White, the **Maddox Brothers and Rose** were the last word on entertainment. He felt that even though the **Stonemans** were lively and very good at entertaining, the **Maddox Brothers and Rose** band was "Great! The best!" and that the **Stonemans** were trying to imitate this California band. Rose Maddox is Roland's favorite woman singer.

The group was driven apart in 1957 by rock and roll. Rose Maddox recalled, "We could see the change was

Vern Williams and Rose Maddox, 1980.

coming. The big dance halls were going out. The night clubs were not hiring groups. They would pay a single artist as much as they would pay a full group."[69]

Cliff died in 1949, Cal died in 1968, Henry died in 1974, Fred became a night club owner/operator and retired in Delano, California. Rose lives in Ashland, Oregon. She recorded a bluegrass album in 1962 at the invitation of Bill Monroe and Carlton Haney. Her backup band was **Don Reno, Red Smiley and the Tennessee Cut-Ups** with Monroe on mandolin. This led to many appearances at West Coast bluegrass festivals through 1995 and she continued to entertain despite cardiovascular bypass surgery.

Roy Acuff

Roy joined the Grand Ole Opry in 1938. He was its first international star. Roy personifies qualities which lie at the heart of the Opry. A warm, direct human being who treasures the honesty and simplicity of America's folk music, truly he has earned the title of "The King of Country Music."

These sentences, written on the bronze plaque on the Opry house, only begin to tell the story of Roy Acuff, his entertaining prowess, and his importance in the country music publishing business. It is for these reasons, and because a few of the sidemen in some of his bands are well known in bluegrass circles, that he is included in this book which is a history of the country music which became "bluegrass."

Roy Claxton Acuff was born September 13, 1903, near Maynardville, Tennessee, into a musical family. His fiddling father was a Baptist preacher, a lawyer and a judge. Acuff's performance in high school baseball earned him an invitation to join the New York Yankees but an attack of sunstroke in 1920 changed those plans and he knew he had to find an occupation which he could do out of the sun. While recuperating at home, he learned to play the fiddle from the records of the popular old-time bands of the era. After his health returned, he joined George Stevens' touring medicine show.

---

[68] According to a brief conversation with Rose Maddox in 1995, the costumes were sold to Marty Stuart.

[69] Wayne W. Daniel, "The Saga of the Maddox Brothers and Rose—A Country Music Success Story," *Bluegrass Unlimited*, December, 1990, p. 57.

An early Acuff band was the **Tennessee Cracker-jacks**. By 1934, he was on Knoxville's WROL with **Roy Acuff and His Crazy Tennesseans**. An early sideman with Acuff's band was Archie Campbell of "Hee Haw" fame. Acuff and his band began recording in 1936. One of his first recordings was "Great Speckled Bird."

His later bands made extensive use of the resonator guitar, Pete Kirby being one of the first and most notable. Kirby played in a rather simple style compared to what it would become in the early 1950s in the hands of Josh Graves. Acuff's band name was changed by Opry manager Harry Stone to the **Smoky Mountain Boys**[70]. The success of this band led Acuff to ten movie contracts with Republic and Columbia studios.

In February 1938, Acuff and his **Crazy Tennesseans** joined the Opry and were immediately accepted by the fans.[71] He had tried unsuccessfully for years to join the Opry—they weren't accepting any new members. It wasn't until Fiddlin' Arthur Smith was suspended from the Opry for four weeks that Acuff was given a chance as fiddler/singer/entertainer. He auditioned with the gospel song "Great Speckled Bird," forgetting the words the first time, but was invited back and then was successful—the Opry managers understood stage fright.

By 1943, Acuff had stopped fiddling on stage to focus his energies on singing and showmanship. His singing was extremely intense on stage; he often wept during a sad song.

In 1943, Acuff and Fred Rose formed Nashville's first song publishing company. Acuff was a prolific recording artist who knew the importance of keeping new records on the market for his fans to buy. This was an important source of income for the touring musician. Of course, being in the publishing *and* recording businesses gave the royalty checks from each sale an extra boost. Indeed, he was probably one of the wealthiest people in country music. In 1953, Roy Acuff, Fred Rose and Wesley Rose founded Hickory Records. Acuff's own hits on the label sold millions of copies.

Roy Acuff ran for Governor of Tennessee in 1948...unsuccessfully. Dallas Smith (of **Dallas Smith and the Boys from Shiloh**) recalled the event, "I can remember...Roy gettin' up on the stage. And they was wantin' a speech out of him and he says, 'Well, I'm not too good at speeches but I'm gonna show you what I am good at,' and he cut loose on the fiddle."[72]

Acuff's first nickname was "King of the Hillbillies," later modified to "King of Country Music." Roy Acuff passed away November 23, 1992. His funeral was unannounced and attended only by his closest friends.

Byron Parker— the greatest radio announcer who ever lived

Some have given Parker most of the credit for the popularity of the **Monroe Brothers**. This may not be exaggerated because, according to some musicians in this industry who knew them, the two brothers were not a good duo. If this is true, then truly Byron Parker deserves much of the credit for the success of the **Monroe Brothers** duo.

Byron Parker was born September 6, 1911, in Hastings, Iowa. He first performed with the **Gospel Twins**. In 1934, he became an announcer for WAAW, Omaha. After he met Bill and Charlie Monroe there, they moved to South Carolina in 1935 where he became their booking agent for personal appearances, announcer for their radio shows and show dates, and product salesman. The **Monroe Brothers** began playing school houses and worked at WIS and WBT.

"Byron very seldom used scripts," wrote author Pat Ahrens. "His gift was one of perfected ad-libbing. He has been called, by many, the greatest radio announcer ever heard on the air."[73] Someone once said he could have sold struck matches. Wade Mainer said that "he could sell a bushel of rotten apples even if there was only one good one in it." Parker called himself the "Old Hired Hand" for, even though he was young, he had considerable experience in the music business. After every radio show, he signed off the air, "And now, until we meet again either in person or on the air, this is your Old Hired Hand, Byron Parker, saying good-bye, good health, and God bless you every one."

All were saddened by his death in 1948 at age thirty-seven. Perhaps God needed an announcer, was one person's thought. Bill Monroe reminisced that "We liked Byron right off. He had a pleasant disposition—always smiling. He was an asset to our programs and

---

[70] Band members included Pete Kirby (who later became "Bashful Brother Oswald"), Jimmy Riddle (who later appeared on "Hee Haw"), Lonnie "Pap" Wilson and Oral "Odie" Rhodes.

[71] "When I came to the Opry in '38, I'd never seen any of the other performers' shows," he said. He had no real idea of what a show on the Opry should be except to entertain an audience.

[72] From a telephone interview with Dallas Smith of the Boys from Shiloh, February 1993.

[73] Pat Ahrens, "A History of the Musical Careers of Dewitt 'Snuffy' Jenkins, Banjoist and Homer 'Pappy' Sherrill, Fiddler," p. 14.

later on he helped us out by singing bass on our hymns. He had a fine bass voice. He was well-liked by fans. It was a pleasure to have known him."[74]

Pete Seeger

According to *The Folk Music Sourcebook*, "The importance of Pete Seeger cannot be overlooked or overstated. Even today [1976], his audience casts him in the role of cheerleader, but his musical contribution has been great and influential nonetheless. The man's repertory and his acquaintance with a number of musical styles are awe-inspiring. He developed a personal banjo style, with Appalachian roots, and became the first instrumental virtuoso of the urban revival. The contribution to the understanding of traditional banjo technique, and later contribution on six- and twelve-string guitar, paved the way for later generations of revivalist players whose main interest was in style and instrumental technique."[75]

Author Dick Weissman explained that as important as Earl Scruggs was on the banjo, the other main protagonist in the commercial success of the banjo was Pete Seeger. Weissman, as well as Eric Weissberg, initially followed the teachings of Seeger.

Hank Williams

Just a quick note on Hiram "Hank" Williams, probably the most famous country music artist who ever lived. Hank Williams began recording in 1946, songs which were a reflection of the honky-tonk era which was popularized by Ernest Tubb, Hank Thompson and Lefty Frizell. His "Honky Tonkin'" didn't do well, but his 1947 hit, "Lovesick Blues," reached number one on the charts. He became the first country music superstar.

June 11, 1949, was the date of Hank Williams' first appearance on WSM's Grand Ole Opry. Minnie Pearl said that the applause that night was awesome. Every time he sang "Lovesick Blues" he'd bring down the house. She spoke of the time after she agreed that the new singer could open for her in Great Bend, Kansas, "Poor me. I was standin' back there in a dumb-lookin' outfit with a price tag and they were screaming for Hank. When I finally did get on the stage they were still hollerin', 'We want Hank.'"[77] "I never saw anybody have an effect on the Opry crowd the way he did when he was here," said Ott Devine, then an announcer and later a manager of the Opry. "Nobody could touch Hank Williams and the only one who came close was [Red]

The influence of World War II on our music

"Grand Ole Opry star Minnie Pearl once wrote about [how country music was affected by W.W.II], 'I think the War did more to spread and further the popularity of country music than any other influence. World War II and the subsequent wars caused the military personnel to carry the love of country music literally all over the world. This was at a time when country music really needed to gain a foothold...'[76] The way this was done is really quite simple. The War's participants included many country music lovers who would, say, bring out their guitars and sing and play a few tunes for his soldier buddies. Eventually, many of them who had never heard of the music became fans and subsequently took it home with them after the War.

"The Opry was growing by leaps and bounds during the War years," continued Pearl. "We were being joined by new artists practically every month or two as the interest in country music grew. The crowds were large in spite of rationing gas. We all performed at war bond rallies, outside on truck beds, and inside on truck beds, and inside, wherever!"

One of the most important things Ray and Ina Patterson pointed out to this writer is the tremendous influence of World War II on country music throughout the world. The War was effective in taking many country musicians into many countries heretofore unfamiliar with our music. They would carry their guitar, or whatever instrument, and show the world about country music as it was played in America. This was a *definite* influence on the rest of the world and helped create venues for touring Americans later on.

[74] Letter from Mr. Bill Monroe; Nashville, Tennessee, (December 10, 1969). This quotation came from "A History of the Musical Careers of Dewitt 'Snuffy' Jenkins, Banjoist and Homer 'Pappy' Sherrill, Fiddler," by Pat J. Ahrens. A 1970 publication.

[75] Larry Sandberg and Dick Weissman, *The Folk Music Sourcebook* (New York: Alfred A. Knopf, 1976), p. 100.

[76] Don Rhodes, "Bands on the Run—The Johnson Mountain Boys," *Bluegrass Unlimited* December, 1981.

[77] Article by David Zimmerman in *USA Today*, late 1992.

Foley."[78] According to Hank Williams Jr.'s manager, Merle Kilgore, the "only two people I ever saw who laid everybody out was Elvis and Hank Senior."[79] By 1950, his popularity was unsurpassed and he was clearly the leader of commercial country music. At one time, he was earning more than $100,000 a month. 1950 brought the release of "Long Gone Lonesome Blues."

The promoters pushed him until his health began failing; he worked anyway. His wife, Audrey, pushed him and they had marital problems. He began to drink more, which created performing and attendance problems.

Soon, Hank and Audrey reconciled, remarried, gave birth to Hank Jr., and experienced a very productive period. But this didn't last long either. Even though they loved each other, they couldn't live together. They parted ways again. In May 1952, they divorced. He gave up his son and half of future royalties.

Williams' 1951 recording of "Cold, Cold Heart" became a #1 pop hit. Williams pined for his faithless wife, Miss Audrey, drank excessively, took drugs[80], drank some more, fell down and cracked his skull, and drank some more. Certainly, his addiction to morphine as a result of the pain from his back operation in 1952 didn't help him kick his drug problem either. He experienced even more highs and lows. Doctors told him that his back problems were caused by malnutrition during his poor youth when all he had to eat for a week at a time was peanuts. It is now accepted that Hank suffered from spina bifida.

He would drink for four or five days straight. He wouldn't eat. His friends put him into detox, which worked well, and he wished that he could stay sober. His reputation for missing concerts hurt his fame. He was dismissed from the Opry August 1952. He was told that if he was able to "clean up his act" for one year, they would consider hiring him back.

On October 19, 1952, Williams married nineteen-year-old Billie Jean Jones Eshliman of Bossier City, Louisiana. He made the event quite a spectacle by charging from $1 to $2.80 to the estimated 28,000 in attendance; he needed the money. They had two "shows" and made $30,000 from each one.

After his departure from the Opry, his life there at KWKH, Shreveport, Louisiana, continued downhill. He became thinner and looked pathetic. He continued taking drugs, painkillers. Ten weeks later, en route to a concert in Canton, Ohio, on New Years Day 1953, Williams died in the back seat of his Cadillac from an excess of drink and drugs. He was twenty-nine.

"When Hank was ready to leave," recalled Billie Jean, his bride, "he came and sat down on the edge of the bed. He just looked at me, not saying a word.

'What're you lookin' at, Hank?' I asked him. 'I just wanted to look at you one more time,' he said. I stood in front of the mirror, my back to him, and he came over and kissed me on the cheek. Then he said good-bye and left."[81] His song, "I'll Never Get Out of This World Alive," was on the charts.

Ray & Ina Patterson

Ray and Ina Patterson speak of the new music and the old

R ay and Ina have been singing a style of music very similar to the **Blue Sky Boys** and a few other close-harmony duets since the 1940s. "We consider the music we done as 'mountain folk music,'" said Ina. "It's not exactly college folk or modern folk. It's a homespun version of string band [music]. String bands, you see them more for country dances or get-togethers. The duet or family-type harmony that we do is more or less homespun. It stayed within family and close friends. It takes somebody that's been together awhile to do the close harmony. You can't just go out and find somebody that does harmony and immediately get the sound you want even though it's possible to sing together—and it's pleasant. But if you've been singing together awhile, it's just like a band." For Ray and Ina, it took several years of practice before they were ready to go on tour.

"I would say that the style of string band and the folk music that we done is what started [bluegrass music]," said Ina. You see, Bill and Charlie Monroe started out as a duet. They didn't have the close har-mony. They featured more of the high harmony that Bill Monroe is noted for. But still they were a brother duet. That's were they started and now, of course, he is now known as the 'Father of Bluegrass Music.'

"Bill Monroe presented bluegrass music to the world over WSM," continued Ina, "but I believe there was other performers or pickers that helped to establish

---

[78] Jack Hurst, *Nashville's Grand Ole Opry* (New York: Harry N. Abrams, Inc., 1975), p. 177.

[79] Zimmerman, op. cit.

[80] Choral hydrate

[81] Quotation from Nick Tosches' "Honky-Tonkin': Ernest Tubb, Hank Williams, and the Bartender Muse" chapter in *Country, The Music and the Musicians* (New York: Abbeville Press, 1988), p. 250.

the bluegrass sound. The fact that Bill Monroe was on the Opry made a big difference. But if it hadn't been for the others, bluegrass music wouldn't have evolved as fast or as quick as it did. I don't know anything that evolved that only one person caused it to evolve. Anything that evolves must have several outside influences to make it what it is. Now, I'll admit that Bill Monroe had a very big influence. In fact, he may have been the sole, one person that had the strongest influence. But there were other people around him that had a little of the input in order for him to be that influence. I think that bluegrass began before 1945 (even before Lester Flatt and Earl Scruggs were in his band)."[82]

On the liner notes on the Patterson's second County album, Ray and Ina described the change in music, "Some folk music authorities have stated that 1952 was the year of the great change in country and folk music. This may have been the year when everyone became aware of the change, but we feel commercialization began as early as 1945. It was right after the War that we first noticed that radio stations were selecting their records with a certain sound, and pushing aside the basic country type. The only way you could hear the old-time sound was to request it and as time went on, they no longer played requests, and folk, cowboy ballads and mountain music were almost taken off the air entirely. All that was left was the new, modern sound of country music. The sound was described as an 'upgrading' of country music, switching from fiddles to violins to make the music easier to listen to and add appeal to another type of audience. But somehow in the process, they seem to add a false quality and lose the real meaning that is connected to basic country music."

"One of the main gripes we have," said Ina, "is that they are making a conglomerate for sale. You can't identify any music in it. It's a little of this, a little of that, a little of something else, and they put it all together trying to suit everybody with one type of music—and that's our main gripe. I like to keep things separate so you can tell what you're listening to. You can also find out what the roots are and what brought it up to this point. If you have a conglomerate of music it's just a mixture of everything. The biggest thing that I can say that is a drawback to the music, or any artistic adventure, is commercialism. Now anytime you make something strictly for sale, you weaken the product. You've got to make the product what it is and make the market for it. If you can keep it that way you can keep it true, and clear, and clean of all outside influences."

During the late 1940s and early 1950s, there seemed to be a conspiracy at some radio stations against bluegrass and folk music. Ray Patterson told the story which occurred during this time, "We was doing a live radio program on KGFL in Roswell back about 1948

or '49 or '50—back about that time. The program director said, 'I'll give you all a daily program but I don't want you to even suggest that anyone should send in requests. If we allow any kind of requests to come into the station we'll be hearing from the whole kerosene lamp section up here on North Hill.'" Ray laughed, then added, "People would be playing their wind up phonographs." Ina added, "This showed that a few people would say things like that which, in other words, would mean that they looked down on a certain kind of people or a certain kind of music. Then, they would turn right around and hire us for a job because we was different and the other groups was a dime a dozen. They wanted something to break up the form a little bit. We could get jobs when some of the others couldn't. And it would make them mad at us because they didn't think that our kind of music should be hired above them. It wasn't because we was better than them; it was just that our style was rare."

"Now that's why we had the folk boom. Music had gone so far out you couldn't hear a banjo or a standard guitar which was recognizable. If it was a standard guitar, it was played in the bar chord pattern which sounded like a rhythm beat and all. But it didn't have the open string rhythm they are noted for. The mandolin almost went out completely. The Dobro®...you hardly ever heard of. You heard an electric steel, but the Dobro®, no way. Fiddle, you'd still hear it; they never went out. But it was in a little different style. They was doing a different style with the bow. You still heard some of the Texas swing style fiddling." The folk boom of the early 1960s brought back the early music of the string bands and the early country bands "but they done it so well that they improved on it, said Ina. "They done it better than the old timers did but they didn't lose any of the flavor of the music. They didn't polish it to the point to where it sounded artificial."

Ray spoke of touring in the 1950s, "We got along with a lot of the Nashville guys we would be working with—in the big shows there would be twenty-five or thirty entertainers. But we were the only ones who would stick to this basic kind of music because it was basically off limits [for them] to do that. Some of these Nashville-type boys who would play in all the honky-tonks, they'd have their cigarettes all going and that smoke would rise up. When they'd see us come in the door they'd jump into an old **Carter Family** style position and they'd imitate 'Wildwood Flower' or something when they saw us come in the door (Ray laughed). Those was two things which would mix about like oil and water."

Ina spoke of the hard times, "During the early '50s when many of Nashville's stars were having trouble getting good attendance, they would often use only one band and have as many as six stars in one show. Even

Ray and Ina Patterson, c. 1994

then the crowds were often small. One of the reasons for this was that the record companies were overproducing albums. One store had Eddy Arnold albums on sale for fifty cents with a sign 'There's nothing wrong with these albums. They are just molding in the jackets.'

"It used to be that when you were hired by a radio station you advertised whatever they wanted. You might advertise dCon® rat poison one day and insurance the next day. The announcers did that. You didn't have to do any of the commercials. The station paid you a salary for the programs. You could advertise show dates, or your songbooks. That was a side benefit. Then whenever radio stations got away from doing that, they would only take you if you were sponsored or they'd give you a sustaining program and try to sell you—but they wouldn't hire you. Then, the first thing you know, they started going to the top 40/top 50 format and all live entertainment pretty much went out.

"When we played live, the stations usually had two studios: one small and one large. When you did the early morning show we'd use the small one and not many people would come by to see you play. Ray and I did that. But if your show was, say about six or seven a.m., they used the big auditorium so maybe 100 people could attend in that big studio. You'd be surprised how many people would attend the show."

As of 1997, Ray and Ina Patterson live in Colorado Springs, Colorado.

The Crazy Water Crystals of Mineral, Texas

The Crazy Water's souvenir booklet (see photo page 79) boasted thirty-one different bands and one-man acts. Others listed here are Fred Russell's Hillbillies, The Crazy Tobacco Tags, James B. Grady's Huckelberry Pickers, Hilo Hawaiians, Leroy Smith's Moonlight Serenaders, and others which the company sponsored during the 1940s and 1950s.

The photo on page three is from "Souvenir of the Crazy Barn Dance and the Crazy Bands" published by The Crazy Water Crystals Company of the Carolinas and Georgia. The caption for this photo of Homer Sherrill's band (1935) reads:

"Homer Sherrill's Crazy Hickory Nuts are 'adopted children' in the great 'Crazy Water Crystals Family.' They hail from Hickory, the Furniture City, at the gateway to the mountains. Homer Sherrill and the boys have been broadcasting with us on our Barn Dance programs from their very beginning. Just recently, Homer Sherrill's Crazy Hickory Nuts, formerly called the East Hickory String Band, have been employed by the Crazy Water Crystals Company of the Carolinas and Georgia and are at present broadcasting daily from radio station WWNC, Asheville, at 12:00 noon. You will have the privilege of hearing this popular band on most of our Barn Dance programs, and in various personal appearances throughout the Carolinas."

Photo and book courtesy of Homer Sherrill. Reprinted by permission.

J.E. Mainer's Mountaineers with Byron Parker and Snuffy Jenkins on WIS about 1938. This band was also known as Byron Parker and the WIS Hillbillies. Photo courtesy Pappy Sherrill.

"*The Jenkins String Band of Harris, NC, 'The Farmer Musicians,' comprise one of the finest string bands in the country playing the old-time mountain tunes like very few can, and in that 'peppy' style that is peculiarly their own. Thousands of listeners are always delighted when the Jenkins String Band is announced on the Crazy Barn Dance program. The group is composed of C.V. Jenkins, DeWitt Jenkins, Dennis Jenkins and Howard Cole. If you want to hear the genuine, old-time music at its best, don't miss the Jenkins String Band.*"

The J.E. Mainer's Crazy Mountaineers photo below is also from "Souvenir of the Crazy Barn Dance and the Crazy Bands," published about 1935. The caption for this photo reads:

Here is a photo (above) of the Jenkins String Band in 1934 on WBT, sponsored by Crazy Water Crystals Company on the Crazy Barn Dance. This was probably the first time that this 3-finger style of banjo was heard on the air. (*Authors note: This was Snuffy's first professional appearance in a band.*) Caption for this photo from "Souvenir of the Crazy Band Dance and the Crazy Bands":

"*J.E. Mainer's Crazy Mountaineers have put more Crazy Water Crystals programs on the air than any other group, with the possible exception of Dick Hartman's Tennessee Ramblers. These boys receive many hundreds of letters each week from their friends and admirers throughout radioland. This band is composed of J.E. Mainer, Wade Mainer and John Love, all of whom hail from Concord, NC, and also Dorsey M. Dixon and Howard Dixon who came to us from Rockingham, NC. J.E. Mainer's Crazy Mountaineers have been heard by thousands over WWNC, Asheville, and during the past six months over WBT, Charlotte, as well as hundreds of personal appearances throughout the two Carolinas.*"

Photo and booklet courtesy of Pappy Sherrill.

Chapter 2

Understanding Bluegrass Music - Table of Contents

Understanding Bluegrass Music

Definitions of Bluegrass, Rhythm, Theory, and Songwriting

Introduction

> *"If a man listening will let it, bluegrass will transmit right into your heart. If you love music and you listen close, it will come right on into you. If that fiddle's cutting good and they're playing pretty harmonies, it will make cold chills run over me, and I've heard it many times. If you really love bluegrass music, it will dig in a long ways. If you take time to listen close to the words and the melody, it will do something for you."* —Bill Monroe[1]

This chapter is a multi-faceted method of defining bluegrass music, explaining various aspects of its character and substance, and descriptions of how this music has developed into something special. It also includes various aspects of a few of the techniques in bluegrass—things which matter in a musical sense.

There are four different sub-topics/categories in this chapter: 1) introduction, 2) definitions, 3) a "how to" guide of important features in the music, most of which are peculiar to bluegrass, and 4) miscellany which includes topics such as songwriting, videos and other things. As usual, all the subjects written into this chapter come from the words of this music's protagonists.

Glen Duncan, Larry Cordle[2] **and Lonesome Standard Time** was a contemporary bluegrass band in the Nashville area which carried on the traditional bluegrass style with a modern flare for some years in the early 1990s. The following interview in *Bluegrass Unlimited* gives us an idea of the state-of-mind many bluegrass enthusiasts share.

Glen Duncan related that "Recently, a Nashville interviewer asked me, 'Why didn't you and Larry (Cordle) go country instead of bluegrass?' My first thought was, 'Well, we *are* bluegrass; it's a music and a way of life, too.' I was a bit surprised that he asked.

"I'm sure there are a few bluegrass bands who maybe record with the idea of 'If we get big enough, we can go country.' They really don't know what 'go country' means. We know, and we don't want any part of it. I've played coliseum shows and all that stuff and that's a wonderful thing if it's what you want to do. But that's not what we set out to do. The reason we became a bluegrass band and not a country band is because we have never—let me stress *never*—done this with the idea of getting somebody in country music interested in us.

"It's never entered our minds to soften up our music," Duncan emphasized. "Cut back on banjo here and there, change this a little bit to make it more palatable to people who aren't hard-core fans. I've never agreed with that. We believe in bluegrass music with a fiddle, five-string banjo and a mandolin, a guitar and a bass. We also believe in keeping the banjo right up there with it. We keep our sound close to tradition because there's power there.

"Real bluegrass is timeless; I enjoy 'Uncle Pen' as much today as when I was six years old. It's a pure thing and it has depth and you could always get more out of it. But if it was some sort of hybrid, I don't think I'd feel the same way about it," he laughed. "In fact, I don't think I'd want to play it the first time, let alone repeatedly."[3]

What is bluegrass, anyway?

A recent dictionary definition of bluegrass, as interpreted by the Second Edition of Webster's New World Edition of the American Language, listed bluegrass as a noun: "1. any of a large genus (Poa) of temperate and Arctic forage grasses, as Kentucky bluegrass 2. (ff) (often B—) Southern string-band folk music."

---

[1] James Rooney, *Bossmen: Bill Monroe and Muddy Waters.*, Da Capo Press. Quoted from *Bluegrass Unlimited*, June, 1983.

[2] Songwriter Cordle wrote many songs made popular by other artists and has been an integral part in helping to expose bluegrass music to non-bluegrass audiences. He wrote or co-wrote "Two Highways" (recorded by Alison Krauss), "Lonesome Standard Time" (Kathy Mattea, co-written with Jim Rushing), "Highway 40 Blues" (Ricky Skaggs), "The Fields of Home" (Ricky Skaggs) and "Kentucky Thunder" (Skaggs). The band received a Grammy nomination in 1993 for the "Glen Duncan, Larry Cordle and Lonesome Standard Time" album (Sugar Hill).

[3] Brett F. Devan, "The Real Thing—Glenn Duncan, Larry Cordle and Lonesome Standard Time," *Bluegrass Now*, July and August, 1994, pp. 7, 8.

"How come nobody plays bluegrass with a squeeze box anymore?"

According to a contributor to *Bluegrass Unlimited*, "Bluegrass is the music played from the time [Bill Monroe] broke up with Charlie in 1938 until 1945 when he hired Earl Scruggs. During this period, Bill invented and perfected his music while rehearsing his **Blue Grass Boys** in garages all the way from Raleigh to Mobile. Sure, he had high singing and fast picking, but what gave the music so much character was the odd time he played it in."

"There are a good many examples of this in Bill Monroe's Victor and early Columbia recordings. This distinctive aspect of bluegrass disappeared when Earl Scruggs entered the band. The banjo roll straightened all that stuff right out of the music. So you see, the 'Will You Be Loving Another Man' (Columbia 1946) did not mark the beginning of bluegrass as some folks say, but the end of it!

"Bluegrass died in 1945. By the time the 'folkies' got to using the word 'bluegrass' in the '60s, it had already changed into something else. If you want real bluegrass you'll have to go back and listen to Bill with Clyde Moody, Pete Pyle, Stringbean and Tex Willis. That's real bluegrass. And you talk about your women in bluegrass? How about Sally Ann (Forrester) and her squeeze box? Now that squeeze box trips my trigger every time. How come nobody plays bluegrass with a squeeze box anymore?"[4]

Bill Bolick on bluegrass origins

Bolick, veteran of a very popular country band beginning in the 1930s (**Blue Sky Boys**), spoke of bluegrass music and other people he feels are important in bluegrass music, "To me, if it doesn't have the Monroe mandolin and Scruggs banjo, it isn't bluegrass. This is the fast-moving type of country music that Charlie and Bill innovated, and most of it I enjoy very much. I have only the highest respect for Charlie and Bill and the unique style they developed. I will also extend this compliment to Earl Scruggs, although his style of banjo picking isn't truly original. He is the one, however, that made it famous. For the clones and imitators of the above three, I hold very little respect. Though many of them have attained high honors in the bluegrass world and have become financially rich, I feel they have added very little to country music."[5]

Bluegrass defined by its instruments

"All instruments in a bluegrass band are non-amplified," P.A. Richardson wrote in 1965. "Now, certainly you can play in the bluegrass idiom or bluegrass style with amplified instruments, but you cease to be a bluegrass band when the amplifier is used. Country music means a million different things today, and the field is getting so broad that rock and roll and jazz are a regular part of it along with a heap of other rot. So, you can have (and call it) a country band with all sorts of instruments, but it won't be a bluegrass band—not in the least."[6] The author of the passage then listed the required instruments in a bluegrass band: five-string banjo, guitar, resonator guitar, acoustic bass, mandolin and fiddle.

The May 1982 issue of *Bluegrass Unlimited* magazine included the SPBGMA (Society for the Preservation of Bluegrass Music in America) definition of bluegrass music: "We would say it is a non-electric version of country music maintained with certain instruments played a certain way. We would say it is the Monroe style of music which he played back in the '40s continued on."[7]

In John Roehmer's 1980 review of an album[8] which used drums on it, he explained, "As a general proposition, drums don't belong in bluegrass. Not because Bill and Ralph never used them, but because they oversimplify the music and force its subtle rhythms into a monotonous chunking. However, I'm not a terminal curmudgeon; drumming sometimes adds to the music and somebody, somewhere, someday may actually devise a boogie-grass sound that works."

Allen Shelton defines bluegrass

Veteran bluegrass banjoist Shelton gave his definition of bluegrass music, "Today, when you say bluegrass music...it all goes back to Bill Monroe and Flatt and Scruggs when they were with him. There was Howdy Forrester, Chubby Wise, Cedric Rainwater playing bass...and lots of others. I saw these people perform when I was a child. In fact, we walked about five or six miles to get to their shows. You talk about inspiration! They were really laying it down...and that's the sound that stuck in my mind of what bluegrass was.

"I know Bill Monroe has credit for bluegrass music...but actually, the sound as we know it today—and I'll probably get clobbered for this—was when Flatt

---

[4] Lyndo Criscoe, of Blank Ankele, North Carolina, "Letters," *Bluegrass Unlimited*, June, 1990.

[5] Telephone interview.

[6] P.A. Richardson, back cover of *Sing Out* magazine, November, 1965.

[7] Chuck Stearman [President], "Chuck Stearman of SPBGMA, The Promoter's Promoter," *Bluegrass Unlimited*, May, 1982, p. 74. Stearman played mandolin with the Midwest Gospel Singers while they did a radio show on KLCO, Leavenworth, Kansas, and other bands through the years. He has promoted his own festivals extensively and is careful not to allow any electric instruments on stage.

[8] "Operation Boogie Grass" by the Russell Brothers was reviewed in the October 1980 issue of *Bluegrass Unlimited*, p. 27.

and Scruggs were with him. That's when it all came together as we know it."[9]

Bill Monroe on his music

Monroe philosophized about how people should play his music. "I have followed instrumental numbers for so long that I know how they should go. I know if it is getting out of line. I know the minute if you leave the melody and go on someone else's tune. That's studying it and listening to tones and knowing what tone should follow another. Now I know that tunes like 'Roanoke' or 'Turkey in the Straw' don't need changing. They've got everything in them they need. Now if you could come up and play the same melody in another position, why, I'm 100 percent for it. So if you've heard a fiddler all your life—maybe you've danced after him—he still hasn't put enough time on it to really learn how it should be played—maybe he was playing for a square dance and making money and that's all he was interested in. He wasn't interested to learn the number and play it the right way. And that's when a man should learn to follow the melody, is when he's a young boy. He should take time to learn which way it should go, and go that way. If it's 'Fire on the Mountain' or any number like that that's got the notes the way the man wrote it and if it sounds good to you and you think he did a good job with it, you should put every note in it that he did if you can. You shouldn't leave anything out. Many banjo players will cut through and hide behind their licks and not take time to learn which way the melody goes and what notes should follow the other."[10]

Monroe didn't see much reason to change bluegrass from the way he had done it all during his career. "I'd like to keep bluegrass down to earth and put the good sound in it the way it should be played. Bluegrass has got a great feeling in it. A lot of it comes from gospel singing—Methodist, Baptist, Holiness. 'Course it's got a lot of old southern blues and Scotland, the way they used to play music back there in that country—that's

This is the magazine which includes Ralph Rinzler's "Bill Monroe— The Daddy of Blugrass Music". It was written to counter an earlier article in this magazine about Earl Scruggs.

where some of my ancestors came from, you know, Scotland—and old-time, the way they played fiddlin', you know."[11]

In an interview for *Bluegrass Canada Magazine*, he spoke about bluegrass music today, "A lot of them play it in their style, the way they feel about it. But you can still tell it's bluegrass music and that makes me feel good and that they want to play bluegrass music." To the question, "Are you happy to see bands taking your style and making it their own?", Monroe replied, "It won't be theirs. It will belong to Bill Monroe—the music."[12] In this interview, he said that he had written nearly 100 gospel songs, 100-150 instrumentals, and 200-300 others.

When interviewed in his later years, Monroe didn't talk much about bluegrass or its future. Paraphrased, he defined bluegrass as using the basic five instruments, said that it is here to stay, and that young people all over the world will continue to play it. The type of song (pop, rock, folk, etc.), according to Monroe, was not important as long as it fit the above parameters of style and instruments. He acknowledged that he started the art form of bluegrass music. He never named any up-and-coming performers as promising leaders in bluegrass. "You know, there's a lot of them, but I don't get to talk with them and spend too much time with them. And so I really don't know what to say on that."[13]

While it's okay to have new singers in the music, he didn't think the basic character of bluegrass music should change. "A good gospel song or any number like that or 'Uncle Pen'—numbers like that—should be taken care of right and played with the right timin' to it and don't try to put stuff in it that don't belong in it."

When asked about the changes in bluegrass music, he replied, "Well, a lot of them are still playing the old-time way, you know. And a lot of them's puttin' extry notes in and some different sounds. And if that's the way they want to do it...everybody's got his own way, what he thinks he should do in music, so I just wish them all the best. But I do think that if you keep bluegrass down pure and sing it right and play it right, you'll make much more out of it than if you put a lot of notes in there that don't belong in the number. But everyone's got his own way of thinking about music and

[9] R.J. Kelly, "Allen Shelton—Working the Bluegrass Trail," *Bluegrass Unlimited*, May, 1989.

[10] Rooney, op. cit., p. 96.

[11] 1984 interview in Portland, Oregon.

[12] Martin Chapman, "Interview: Bill Monroe," *Bluegrass Canada Magazine*, September/October, 1991, p. 7.

[13] Amy Worthington Hauslohner, "Bill Monroe—The Legend Continues," *Bluegrass Unlimited*, September, 1991, p. 23.

the way he wants to hear it, and the notes he wants to put in it. So you've got to go along with them anyway they want to do it."

In response to a final question at this interview, he mentioned his favorite song was "Blue Moon of Kentucky."

Bluegrass gospel music according to Bill Monroe

In a 1984 interview, Mr. Monroe spoke about gospel bluegrass music and how he has helped bring people to the Lord through his music, "Yes, I have. And I'm proud of that. I've helped a lot like that. And I know that the Lord knows that I have helped down through the years. And he knows I am stronger in it now than I have ever been in my life. And I want to keep on singing the gospel. And I want to help out all the way as long as I am in music. Because you'll never beat gospel singing.

"And a radio that shuns the gospel, you know that's not right! They should always have gospel on...at least on a *Sunday*! But a lot of them have gone so much country that they got to play the top forty and that's all that matters. They don't care what kind of a song it is, what kind of words are in the song. But they should get down to earth, and go back and do something wonderful for some people who sing the gospel all over the world."

About rock musicians doing gospel music, "They is just puttin' on a show. There is no Christian there, I don't think, in a lot of it. It ain't sung right. They are puttin' stuff in there that don't belong in it. It ain't right! It's no good! They ought to sing gospel in the old-time way with the piano and the organ behind them and they don't need drums or all those horns behind them. And they don't need to be hollerin' and screamin'. They just need to do it nature."

Pappy Sherrill's views of bluegrass and country music

In a conversation with Pappy Sherrill in 1991, he named several groups which he classified as "country". Those groups included **Mac and Bob**, the **Delmore Brothers**, the **Blue Sky Boys**, the **Louvin Brothers**, the **Monroe Brothers** (Charlie and Bill) and himself when he worked with Wade Mainer and Zeke Morris. "Now if you get on down to it—into bluegrass—you're getting into harmony singing which is real high and fast. And your fiddlin' and your band music is real fast with banjo, mandolin and the fiddle and the tempo is about four times faster than it used to be—then it's bluegrass." He further elaborated, "Bluegrass has that high, harmony singing and the type of song had something to

do with it. In bluegrass, you don't run into too many love songs; it's usually a train number or a crook number or something like that."

Mr. Sherrill added that bluegrass often adds a capo in order to get the "high harmony" effect. "Back in them days, I don't remember anyone using a capo. If you could get G, C, or D, you had it made—that was country."

Curly Seckler— "To me, the Morris brothers, Wiley and Zeke, were some of the greats."

Curly Seckler played with Charlie Monroe in the early '40s and remembered the **Morris Brothers** band on the same radio station. He recalled that the **Morris Brothers** band played in a style similar to bluegrass today, "but it wasn't as fast as Lester and Earl and us did. We had our music *too* fast, I think. But I didn't have a whole lot to do with it. It was just like a train except when you come to a curve it would throw you out in the woods. It's *too* fast!"

Seckler recalled the Morris brothers, vividly remembering that "Them boys could solid-sing—Wiley and Zeke! To me, they were some of the greats. Of course, I had heard them before I saw them down there [at Spartanburg]."[14]

Vassar Clements— "Bluegrass really goes a long way into anything."

As of 1990, Vassar Clements had played on more than 4,000 recordings—from the Blue Grass Boys to the Boston Pops to the Grateful Dead. On the topic of how music has changed, Vassar commented, "I think society has changed more than music. Music doesn't change that much. The only thing that music does is: the electronics get better, your records sound better, you add different instruments to your band—and maybe that makes it sound different. But in your heart, you haven't changed, I don't think. You're still the same person you were... I'm still the same person I was in 1949 when I first went to the Grand Ole Opry with Bill Monroe..."

Clements spoke about bluegrass music, "You know, bluegrass really goes a long way into anything. Depending on what rhythm you get into and what changes you're playing, you're going to touch on a lot of styles through playing bluegrass: jazz, country, blues and even rock. Somehow, in bluegrass, you really seem to cover all the bases. I think that's really where all the different stuff is rooted..."[15]

[14] Telephone interview, 1991.

[15] Jeffry S. Solochek, "A Master Fiddler—Vassar Clements," *Bluegrass Unlimited*, December, 1990, p. 67.

In a 1992 telephone interview with this writer, Vassar elaborated on that statement, "Bluegrass people, I think, want to define it just as an outcast thing over here to one side and it doesn't mean anything but bluegrass. You can make anything in the world you want to out of bluegrass. It can be souped-up soul music, or it can be jazz if you put the right chords with it, or it can be blues—slow it down. The colored people, a lot of them say that it's just souped-up soul music. You can make just about anything out of bluegrass. And it's hard to play if it's played right. It's a lot of up-tempo stuff and [you have] to think real quick, thinking what would be the neatest thing to put into the next place that's coming up."

Vassar is the type of musician who finds it nearly impossible to play a song twice the same way. He feels that he is a victim of having to learn music "the long way around and having to learn by yourself. And then you just kinda died in that wool—it's hard for you to break it."

Sonny Osborne on what constitutes a bluegrass song

On the back cover of "Encore," the 1980 CMH record by **Heights of Grass**, Sonny Osborne not only said that he liked the group but told a little about himself. "I'm a believer in (if not the originator of) the theory that bluegrass music can be woven into and around every kind of music in existence..." This follows Bill Monroe's statement to this writer which declared that any song can be bluegrass as long as bluegrass instruments are used and the song uses a certain structure and timing peculiar to bluegrass.

Rual Yarbrough— "You can take any song and sing it bluegrass style if you want to."

Bill Monroe seemed to have had something special that attracted Yarbrough's attention. "He definitely had something different. It's a combination, probably, of the instruments that he fitted together, even though he used an organ, an electric guitar, and maybe an accordion. See, after he left Charlie they did several things. Charlie continued to do some other things and used the electric guitar in his group. Bill even tried. I heard him make a comment one time. He said they were trying to put an electric pickup on the mandolin and he said he had tried that back many years ago and it don't work.

"But I think his distinct sound came from his high voice [together] with good harmony. And a lot of people think there is such things as bluegrass songs. But you can take any song and sing it bluegrass style if you want to. You put the bluegrass instruments to it and it could pretty well be used in any of it, you know. Of course, bluegrass, for years, has kept a cleaner type of [words]—they never had any profanity in any of their singin' until fairly recently when a couple people has put some things in it. Bluegrass has always been thought of as a clean, family-type music."

Yarbrough then spoke of timing in the various bands. "**Flatt and Scruggs**' timing was a little different to Monroe's. They've got this thing—I don't know how much you know about music but I don't know anything—I learned that there was three different phases of music. There's one right on the beat, and there's one just behind the beat, and there's one just ahead of the beat. And all those timings got a little different feel to 'em. They're all in time if you're all playin' together. I thought for years and didn't really know what was going on."[16]

"It's hard to play bluegrass if you play it like it's supposed to be played... aggressively, gutsy, and knowing how to put the soul into it"
—*Hazel Dickens*

Yarbrough spent two years with Monroe's band (1969-1970). "Monroe pushed the beat," he said. "It was a different feel. It felt like it was speedin' all the time. Kenny (Baker) would come in there with the fiddle and it felt like it was runnin' away. I never really felt as comfortable with it as I would have liked to have, you know. There are musicians who feel it a little behind the beat—they'll drag you down. There are some that'll keep you right on it. And there are some that'll speed you up if you'll let 'em. By the time you get through an instrumental, you'll just be a lot faster than when you started.

"Me and Jake Landers always thought we had the **Flatt and Scruggs** beat which, I guess, is what you call 'on-the-beat.' Landers plays good, solid rhythm and is known as one of the best rhythm men in this part of the country. So he always played what I always felt was **Flatt and Scruggs**' timing, which I thought was real good. Scruggs has been described as the 'metronome banjo player' and plays on time so well. And Landers does, too.

[16] Phone interview, April 20, 1992, from his home in Florence, Alabama. Clements is featured in the Bluegrass Fiddle chapter.

"I've got some tapes of Earl and Bill in 1948 on the Grand Ole Opry and Earl was so dominant in the group at that time that the announcer, when he would come back, he would say, 'Now back to Bill and Earl.' He included him in the name [of the band], you know. Boy! He was just burnin' that banjo up."

In 1978, Yarbrough spoke of bluegrass, "I think bluegrass is just like country...you know, country took a big rise a few years ago. Now, of course, country is here to stay, but it had its low time. Bluegrass has done the same thing. 1962 was the beginning of Bill Monroe making a comeback. He was real strong back in the earlier days and he had some low times."[17]

Alan Munde—
"There is no such thing as a song that is 'bluegrass'."

During a 1991 interview, Munde spoke of the bluegrass style, "I think it is defined by the instruments and the way they are played...there is no such thing as a song that is bluegrass, I don't think. It's the style [that identifies it]. But I think that the banjo is the marker, for me. Of course, this is coming from a banjo player, too. To me, when Alison Krauss does a song that she does without a banjo, it's just acoustic music. It's not bluegrass. And when Tony Rice plays 'Big Mon' on his guitar without a banjo, it's just not bluegrass."

Munde once had a conversation with Buddy Spicher and Bobby Hicks about bluegrass music; they all agreed that bluegrass was not easy to play. Those two fiddle players had played all kinds of music and they knew just how difficult it is, Munde related. A testament to that thought is represented in the Nashville studio with musicians like Mark O'Connor, Stuart Duncan, Glenn Duncan, Jerry Douglas and Robert Bowlin who all learned their skill of music in bluegrass, and that skill was transferable to other types of music, explained Mr. Munde. Session music requires a good background in music. And bluegrass provides that background.

Ginger Boatwright on "the blues"

Ginger Boatwright spoke of bluegrass being influenced by the blues, "Leadbelly is one of the greatest singers of all time and most bluegrassers don't even know it. He did 'Don't Let Your Deal Go Down,' 'Midnight Special,' 'Take This Hammer and Carry It to the Captain,' 'Rock Island Line' and so many others. Bluegrass has blues roots. I love hearing those dirty Delta blues, I love it when they start singing those double line verses."

About the bluegrass style, "It's so different. It's based on the offbeat. It is the difference between listening to the **Osborne Brothers** sing 'Rocky Top' and listening to Lynn Anderson sing it."[18]

Kenny Baker (L) and Blake Williams. Photo courtesy Jan Willis.

Jerry Douglas—
"We're pretty close to what it started out to be."

According to resonator guitarist Jerry Douglas, there are five different sounds of bluegrass music. There's (1) the brother-duet sound of a full band as defined by the **Stanley Brothers**, (2) the Bill Monroe sound, (3) the **Flatt and Scruggs** sound, (4) the newer versions such as Boone Creek, and (5) the Doyle Lawson kind of power, driving bluegrass. "You hear a lot of those kinds of bands now (referring to #5). Then there is the **New Grass Revival** kind of clones. These aren't that far removed, you know. It hasn't changed that much. I think it's all encompassed within those five or six bands. We're pretty close to what it started out to be. I think that the Stanley sound is the most primitive, even though they started after Bill Monroe, because of where they came from."[19]

[17] Patricia Glenn, "Rual Yarbrough," *Bluegrass Unlimited*, October, 1978. Yarbrough is featured in the Bluegrass Banjo chapter.

[18] Alana White, "Ginger Boatwright," *Bluegrass Unlimited*, September, 1988, p. 31

[19] Telephone interview, 1992.

How do you make Bluegrass?

Don Reno—
"You've got to keep the lead man free because he can't lead and keep time."

And about the timing of bluegrass, multi-instrumentalist Reno said, "Well, you've got to stay kind of on top of it. You don't push, and you don't drag. It's something you feel. You've got to keep the lead man free because he can't lead and keep time. You've got to find the whatever time he starts it at. And if he starts it in the wrong time and I'm playing rhythm with him, that's his bad luck because I'll keep the time he started. I won't push him, and I won't drag him."[20]

Bill Harrell—
"If the audience can't hum the tune, they lose interest."

Harrell spoke about writing instrumental tunes, "I don't write many instrumentals because they are so hard to do and they are so easily forgotten. I don't care how intricate they are; if the audience can't hum the tune as it's being played, even on songs such as 'Orange Blossom Special' or 'Foggy Mountain Breakdown,' well, they lose interest. I don't care how much you write on it, if the audience is not involved, if that melody doesn't strike the crowd so they can simulate it and say they remember it went 'ta-ta-tat,' I say it will never be a great instrumental no matter how well it is played.

"A lot of instrumentals are wonderfully played by some of the modern-day musicians, but I honestly can't tell you what they've played right away because their music is so intricate. I find it's hard to get involved with some of the newer sounds in bluegrass today. I like their music and I keep some of it on the bus to listen to, but I don't understand some of it."[21]

Hazel Dickens—
"Bluegrass has a lot of soul in it."

In a 1979 interview by Ron Thomason, Dickens said, "I am an emotional singer...maybe I'm a masochist. I never get quite satisfied [in concert]...[I don't] try to project something that isn't real."

Asked about the differences in the types of music she plays, "It's hard to play bluegrass if you play it like it's supposed to be played...aggressively, gutsy, and knowing how to put the soul into it. A lot of people play it, and they play and they sing right through it. They think because they are playing fast and singing fast that's bluegrass. But it isn't. Bluegrass has a lot of soul in it. You have to be able to do all those things and keep good time."

In an interview at Owensboro, Kentucky, Dickens spoke of herself and Dudley Connell, with whom she occasionally performs and records, "I been singin' all my life but I really rarely run into people that can hold their own. I don't mean to say that in a braggin' way or anything like that, but there's people that sing and hold back, you know. And then there's people who sing that old, mountain stuff where you just rare back and just let it go—'beltin',' as some people call it. He's the only one I ever run into that understands exactly what I'm aimin' for. I don't have a trained ear. I couldn't read a note of music if you put it in front of me. And I sing, generally, just what I feel, you know—whatever that emotion is. And the next time I sing it, I may not remember how I did it before. A lot of times I don't know what I'm going to sing until it comes out. You see, I can't hear those notes before I sing them. I think that if I were to try to sing music by the book, I'd lose that spontaneity which works best for me.

"And Dudley understands that. And he understands that kind of singing. And I don't know where he learned it either, you know. 'Cause I used to sit in the audience, you know, and listen to him sing. And it seems like every time he was going to approach something, he never knew what he was going to do. You never knew if he was going to do it different than he did the last time, if he was going to put more emotion into it, or what. And that really appealed to me, you know, because when you're singing like that and they can go the same way you're going... He's gotten to the point where he can almost anticipate what I'm going to do. He has an amazing voice!

"When you're singin' up there in front of all these people...it's not a total reality. You can't see. If you're in your living room, you have a lot more control. But on stage, you're just trying to sing on pitch and sing on time and trying to remember all your verses and breaks—because you have to—it's a professional job. But to do all that and then punch it like you want to—get all that emotion in there like you really want to—you know, it's not easy. But it is so much fun..."

20 From an interview with Don Reno by Tony Trischka. Tony Trischka and Peter Wernick, *Masters of the 5-String Banjo, In Their Own Words and Music* (New York: Oak Publications, 1988), p. 85.

21 Carol Ross Jeffry, "Still Alive and Kickin'—An Interview with Bill Harrell," *Bluegrass Unlimited*, December, 1991, pp. 21, 22.

John Starling—
practice makes "together"

John Starling spoke about singing, "Before I started singing with John Duffey, I used to phrase a certain way—and I still do when I'm singing by myself. But when you start singing in a trio (and I'm sure John has changed a couple of things that he used to do with Charlie [Waller] just because it blended better)—but when we first started singing together, we didn't blend very well, because we were 'fighting' each other—we wanted to phrase things differently. After awhile, after you've done a song for awhile, you subconsciously learn to phrase differently. That's what makes trios begin to sound 'together.'"[22]

Don and David Parmley—
"Some groups just don't have either the knowledge or the perseverance to get it right."

Banjoist and band leader Don Parmley spoke of the skill of bluegrass singing, "It takes more than just having the voices to sing each part in a trio, or in knowing how to sing the parts for that matter. You have to also have the ability to know when it *isn't* quite right. Some groups just don't have either the knowledge or the perseverance to get it right." Son David added, "We used to get together in the kitchen or somewhere and record ourselves. Then we'd play it back and listen for mistakes and we were never satisfied until it sounded exactly the way it should."[23]

Jim Eanes—
"If you got no timing, you ain't got nothin'!"

Mr. Eanes was a man with fifty years of experience in bluegrass and country music. He said that *the* main difference in the two types of music—bluegrass and country—is its individual timing. "Everything is the timing. You can be the best in the world, but if you got no timing you ain't got nothin'! Timin' in bluegrass is on top of the music. If you'll notice, bluegrass music has to be played 'on top.' But in country music you can get behind the note or in front of the note or anything and make it work. George Jones proved that! He put a lot of feelin' into his music. And you can do the same with bluegrass. You can put feelin' in bluegrass, but you have to sing on top of the music.

"There's a big difference in playin' bluegrass and a difference in playin' country. In my day, there were a lot of singers that couldn't sing country. And today, there are a lot of country singers that can't sing bluegrass. I'm a very fortunate fellow 'cause I learnt to sing in my early days by singin' what I feel. And if it come out bluegrass—okay. But primarily it was hillbilly music."[24]

George Shuffler—
The music "come from where those Kentucky folks like to dance."

Mr. Shuffler is one of the great bluegrass pioneers who has played with the creators of the music, knows their styles, and knows how to perform it. Describing it is much more difficult than playing it even though he says that "It's one of the hardest music[s] in the world to play."

A July 1993 telephone interview with Mr. Shuffler found him able to describe it in terms that can possibly bring the subtle nuances of this music to the surface so that we can all understand what it is—and what it isn't. He explained that "Bluegrass music—the music part—is played with a *drive*. Like southern gospel and country, sometimes they'll sing with a delayed action—the voices will. But the music's right on the beat. And bluegrass is almost to the breaking point to push it forward. It plays right up on the edge of breaking over into another tempo.

"If you'll listen to any of [Bill] Monroe's old interviews, he says he plays his music with a *drive*, he says. That's what it means. You'll not catch him a-laggin' and you'll not lag either. I've played bass with Monroe several times back in the lean years when he come out of Nashville with two or three and there would be three

George Shuffler

22 Pat Mahoney, "The Seldom Scene As Heard," *Bluegrass Unlimited*, June, 1974, p. 16.

23 Brett F. Devan, "The Bluegrass Cardinals, Synonym for Vocal Harmony," *Bluegrass Unlimited*, May, 1986, p. 9.

24 Telephone interview, January, 1993.

of us—Carter, Ralph and myself. Altogether, we'd just have one good band, you know. They'd book us together for maybe a week or something. You'd never catch him laggin' and if somebody was a-draggin' a little bit, he could look around to me and I would know how he felt. He believed in playin' that stuff right up full speed, you know—not a break in time on it, but just drivin'."

Now we have to define "drive," probably *the* most important element in this music according to Shuffler and Monroe. "If you can define drive, that's all you need to say about it. You just don't lag it, you don't drag it, you don't play with no delayed action. You play 'on the beat' every time, but it's a rush beat." Even slow songs can be played with drive, he said. "If you listen to Travis Tritt talkin' about puttin' drive into your country, that's exactly what he was referrin' to. Don't drag it, don't lag it. Keep it pushed right up there full steam ahead."

Mr. Shuffler's not talking about *speed* of the beat. He elaborated, "You don't speed it. You don't rush it. But you get right up to the breakin' point. The next lick would rush it if you ain't careful. But you play it with the drive—you just push it right up there to the breakin' point.

"That come from where those Kentucky folks like to dance. You can't dance to music that'll drag you. It's like one of these old wind-up 78 Victrolas that you wind up to play the record. When they start windin' down, why, it'll start draggin'. You got to keep a good beat up there—especially if you are buck dancin'. They'll dance just as fast as Ralph could clawhammer. Now, the old-time mountain music—like the **Mainers**—they play their's with a drag almost. If you don't believe it, listen to the old-time stuff. Theirs don't have that drive in it like old man Bill's did! 'Cause he was standin' right behind you with that mandolin and he would chunk that rhythm right up your shirt tail. He plays it with the drive and when he talks about drive that's exactly what he means."

The drive of the **Stanley Brothers** and **Ralph Stanley and the Clinch Mountain Boys** comes from Ralph's banjo, said Shuffler. "Me and Carter kept the music right up there good and full—full speed ahead, you know. But we didn't rush it. We just played it right up there—even on the hoe-downs. And you don't let it slow down. Don't let your mind leave you while you are playin'. Set your foot to pattin' and don't let it slow down. Keep it to drivin'. That's the closest I can define bluegrass—the timin'."

Asked to compare the Stanleys' music to Monroe's music, Shuffler paused to collect his thoughts and continued, "I'd say that Monroe's music and singin' was a little shriller than theirs. The Stanleys' was more melodious—their harmonies in their singin' was—and they played according to their singin'. They didn't try to bust everybody's ears with the instruments and they

kept the instruments under the voices. But it was a little softer, I always thought. I could be wrong, but that would be my interpretation of it. It was just a little softer tone to it, it seemed like, for some reason. Maybe that was just me a-hearin' that, but that's what I heard. And I've been accused of havin' a pretty good ear for what's goin on...you learn to listen to it and if someone in my own group is laggin' or if one of the voices is the least bit sour, why, I can detect it just in a heartbeat and tell which one it is."

In another analogy, he said lazy rhythms just don't work in this music. "You don't play a lazy rhythm in bluegrass music. And that's about as close as I can find words for it." Examples of lazy rhythm would be the pop songs of the day such as those of Bing Crosby, or "Up a Lazy River"-type songs. "That's just an old, lazy beat—something that you would relate to settin' on the side of the river with a can of worms and a fishin' pole; just relaxin' on a hot, lazy day where you don't feel like doin' nothin' but settin' in the shade or fishin' or eatin' watermelon."

But this drive can also appear in slow bluegrass tunes if they're done right. In the first portion of Monroe's "Blue Moon of Kentucky" we find slow music, but it's just half time from the faster speed later in the song. Shuffler explained, "Still, the first beat of it, he don't lag that! It's a different time, but he still pushes that. He don't let that lag either. But he gets a tempo set on that mandolin...and old man Bill, himself, will tell you timin' is ninety percent of it and if you ain't got time you might as well push it under the bed and get back between the plow handles.

"Most of those old bluegrassers, they got so much respect for old man Bill—he set the pace all over this country for bluegrass, and everybody knows to play in that drive. They just don't push it around. I've never heard a banjo player that would drag time. But when they go to draggin' that time, you're killed in bluegrass. You ain't got a prayer or a leg to stand on! And I'd rather have my feet in the fire than to have somebody in the group that's draggin' or laggin' time."

When it works, it's good. "When it don't, it's the sorriest music in the world if it ain't played right! When it works, there ain't nothin' like it! It's sweet as honey. But when it ain't a-workin' it just kills me. Used to, when we'd play, we'd have a grand finale or something. And if there would be a bass player or rhythm guitar player who's standin' next to me who's draggin' a little bit, wantin' to hold back a little bit, I get out of breath and it just wears me out. I can't stand it! I want to kick his—pardon my expression—but I want to kick his hind end right good—wake him up.

"Bluegrass music, if it's played right, I say, is one of the hardest music in the world to play. Now I know that some of these young whipper-doos that's comin' on, they're trying to put every chord they know into every instrumental, you know. But the old-time, original stuff—just three chord stuff like 'Pike County Breakdown' and 'Sally Goodin' and 'Old Joe Clark' and 'Cindy' and all them old-timers—there's just no place for laggin' in it! You just got to drive it to play it! But it's hard to play—to keep everybody awake and alert. I think that's one of the reasons it's so hard to play: you can't get five or six people together and just really drive it and charge that thing with gusto and keep it rollin'. The old Country Gentlemen and the Seldom Scene now, they play with good drive. And the Osbornes are awful good about that. I've played bass with them some, and they'll call on you. Any time you're gonna be playin' with a group you've not been playin' with, you're gonna be cautious."

On the subject of bluegrass singing and harmonies, Mr. Shuffler referred to his old boss in describing the subject, "Ralph Stanley said that George Shuffler is one fellow you can't lose on baritone. We sang so much together I knew where he was goin'. If he'd go high, I'd go low. And you've got to study the man you're singin' with because there's no music to it. It's just like a fiddle tune—you've got to slur and roll your notes. If you've got a good tenor and baritone with a lead, why, you gonna double up and there will be two of you on the same part if you're not careful. You've got to learn your man and stay with him. Jim McReynolds is the easiest man I ever sung with 'cause he sings his straight. But Ralph Stanley's the hardest man a fellow ever tried to sing with in his life—the way he rolls his notes. And I sang with him so long… When Ralph would roll, I would roll with him. You can't put that to music. If it came out in boxes and squares it wouldn't be bluegrass. It's got to be a three- or four-part harmony or it wouldn't be bluegrass."

Asked if bluegrass harmony has any different rules than other types of three- or four-part harmony singing, Shuffler mentioned another music whose harmony structure involves three and four parts: barbershop quartets. Barbershop quartet singing goes back to shape-note singing, some of which Shuffler can do. Barbershop singing uses the same theory of harmony as bluegrass, but barbershop doesn't do a lot of rolls and slurs which are common in bluegrass. He explained that "bluegrass is the only music you can do that in. Others just don't work with it. You take just regular, drawn-out country songs; you don't hear none of that pretty slurs and turns in 'em. And gospel, unless it's a black gospel, you can hear plenty there. But they are singing double half the time—right on top of each other. And two or three of them soundin' the same note ain't no harmony. There might as well be one man up there if you're gonna sing on top of somebody else."

George's **Shuffler Family Band** has in it members who know his every move in a song. "We can stand there and sing a song we've never rehearsed and I'd look at one of them young'uns and raise my eyebrows and they know I'm goin' up. They can read my facial expressions. We're family and we know each other— we've sung together twenty years and it makes a big difference. It's not like you and me pickin' up a lead singer and tryin' to sing a trio; we'd have to do a little woodshed."[25]

The Osborne Brothers, Red Allen and the "high lead" trio, and their use of electric instruments

Neil Rosenberg described one of the major forces which helped shape bluegrass music of the late '50s, "One of the recordings which the Osbornes made with Red Allen was 'Once More' (1957). This was their first performance using the 'high lead' trio. Instead of the conventional country and bluegrass trio arrangement— harmony parts sung above ('tenor') and below ('baritone') the melody—this new approach placed the melody highest in the trio, with the baritone below it, and the tenor part sung an octave lower, below the baritone. The sound resembled that of the pedal steel guitar in two ways. First, on this instrument the melody is often voiced highest, with the harmony parts on lower strings; and second, pedal steel chord changes and melodic shifts are often made by moving a single note within a chord. Such movement occurs in the Osborne's vocal trio. As they developed this style, they became adept at the shifting of parts within the trio. Some of their later arrangements involve harmonies in which the lead is taken by different voices at various points in the song, producing a series of constantly shifting chord inversions.

"In the Osborne's high lead trio, the roles and images of the singers in the group were significantly altered. In modern country the lead singer is, in effect, the center of attention for the audience: the star. When Bill Monroe, who had never sung lead, started his own band in 1938, he had to deal with this fact. He solved the problems it presented by singing lead on the verses and tenor on the choruses. In this way, he preserved the reputation he had earned as a tenor singer and developed a new reputation as a lead singer. Bobby Osborne, too, switched parts this way sometimes, especially with the **Lonesome Pine Fiddlers**. With the high lead harmony, though, he solved the same problem Monroe had solved earlier, but in a different way—by singing lead throughout the song and at the same time singing the highest part. Moreover, Sonny's baritone part was

[25] That's George's expression to indicate that we might have to fight to settle who was going to do what to get the sound right. He recognizes that other groups have to go through these stages and feels fortunate that he works only with veterans of many years. It is a comfort in this business to know that the person with whom you are going to sing knows the music and knows how to follow you.

now the middle voice in the trio and next most prominent. This shifting of musical roles freed the Osbornes from dependence upon the reputation of any single guitarist/lead singer, since the guitarist was now singing the lowest and generally least discernible part. From this time on, changes in band personnel became more manageable and, in terms of the band's overall sound, less significant."[26]

Charlie Cline—
"Music is what extends your feelin's."

Multi-instrumentalist Charlie Cline told this writer that a performer should not copy anyone else's style; that would be counterfeit, and one should play what he feels. Cline is a first-generation bluegrasser who has his own style and plays what he feels. "Music is what extends your feelin's. Each individual has his own identity. And you have to like it. And this is what I'd like to tell the young people of today: it's not going to be all roses; there's goin' to be some thorns. If you love it you'll be willing to endure any obstacle or challenge until you get it."[27]

Mr. Cline advocated that everyone have his own style so that the listeners can tell who is playing without looking up. "Curly and me play more alike, I guess, than anybody. But we're completely different 'cause he plays with Ralph [Stanley] and Ralph's got a mountain sound, and I got a Monroe sound because that's the kind I started playing in the early fifties."

Charlie played with a lot of groups through the years. With each of these, "You have to blend in with the people you're working with. Jimmy Martin didn't want the blues stuff, he wanted more of the progressive style. It's a different style than, say, the bluesy stuff required by Bill Monroe. Chubby Wise was probably the first fiddler of that style. The same thing applies to the way people blend their voices. If the tones are not going together, they're going to have to work it out to where the tones blend together. You have to change. If you know how to change and blend voices, then you get good harmony. And in the wording, some people say the same word in different ways. Some of them may have to talk southern and some may have to learn to talk northern. It's just whoever you're playing with."

Continuing the interview, the Alabama resident spoke about the blues in bluegrass, "The **Lonesome Pine Fiddlers**, I guess, was the first to ever put blues in the music. We put out a number, 'Honky Tonk Blues,'

Charlie Cline

and the chorus is blues. That's when we started trying to put in with bluegrass. The rest is just plain pickin' but we tried to get something different. It's sort of like the high, lonesome sound. Back home we call 'blues' songs 'lonesome' songs. We put a 'boogie blues' beat to it. Jimmy Martin's got a kind of country beat with a bluegrass sound. You know, when you have a band, you've got to have a distinctive sound so you'll know that's Charlie Cline or that's Jimmy Martin. You don't have to read the label to know a song by Ralph; everybody knows who it is by the way his voice sounds."

Charlie spoke about the differences between modern country and western and the country music of the 1950s, "It's no more like it is now. George Strait is gettin' a little bit of that back. You take, like, Ernest Tubb, **Johnny and Jack**, Webb Pierce—they were the Grand Ole Opry! Back in the old days, folks like the **Fruit Jar Drinkers** (and Uncle Dave Macon, Fiddlin' Sid Harkreader, etc.) were always playing music. You go into their dressing room and they were playing. They'd play for three or four hours straight while they were there. It reminds me of bluegrass festivals. I think that's why people like the festivals—because the music is just like it used to be in the old days. We used to have jamborees—we had them in parks, at airports. It was a festival. We had Charlie Monroe, Mac Wiseman, Martha Carson and all of them."

Bill Emerson—
"The problem with bluegrass is that there is too much unprofessional bluegrass."

Banjoist Bill Emerson believes that electric instruments can be used to enhance the sound of bluegrass, just as a piano or drums might in certain circumstances. A gospel tune, for example, can sound good with a piano. But he doesn't like to see it used just for economic reasons. In whatever case it's used, this non-bluegrass instrument must blend with the acoustic instruments in bluegrass music.

"The problem with bluegrass is that there is too much unprofessional bluegrass. It's a type of music that anybody can play anywhere. You don't have to have an amplifier or an AC power outlet. That's the beauty of it—playing it just like it was played a hundred years ago... Program directors, recording executives and promoters should be careful about who they're putting out there to represent the bluegrass idiom. To help it

---

[26] From album cover notes by Neil V. Rosenberg, "Rounder Records Special Series 04."

[27] Interview, 1989, Kissimmee, Florida.

grow we have to concentrate on the best music we have. The dedicated people at IBMA are doing a lot for it. We all need to support that organization. There seems to be a stigma attached to bluegrass—like the Hatfields and McCoys or 'Deliverance.' If that was dispelled, a lot of people would come out of the closet."

And, "The fact that I'm playing an American music that has historical roots in this country means a lot to me personally."[28]

Paul Mullins— "Timin' is eighty percent."

Paul "Moon" Mullins, a fiddler of renown, spoke about the sophistication of bluegrass music, "The term has been kicked around and knocked around in so many ways that some of it is deplorable. But as far as the music is concerned—the real heartfelt music, the way it was designed and supposed to be played—it has as much sophistication as any orchestra that ever played anywhere.

"In our music, timin' is eighty percent. You can even play bad notes, and if you are still on time it will be noticed by very few people. When you play really good notes and you're really on time—really in synch with what's going on—then that's what this whole music is about. That's the reason I rehearsed my band with starts and stops so much. We worked on this until everybody got sick of them. But that's really the way it's supposed to be. Every start has got a new lick in it, and every stop is the same way because every tune is different. It's got to be done that way to have the feeling and have the time and have it all come out even.

"You talk about bluegrass timing. It's got to be on top of the beat just a little bit to the point where you don't rush. Especially if you're going to play an instrumental. It's got to be pushed all the time. That's where the real drive in this music is. Even on some of the slow songs we play, it's got to be right up on top of the beat [to be right]. Especially, the bass player and the guitar player has to be up there."

He explained what he meant with being "on top of the beat." "It's just a tad ahead of the real timin', but not to the point to where it's noticeable that it's rushed." He added that a lot of amateur bands have guitar players and bass players play the same phrases or series of notes when the song is coming to its end, or starting. They are two different instruments altogether. "Good guitar players and good bass players—like the boys in my band—I see them together all the time talking about this right here [in my band] because that's the way it's supposed to be."[29] Mullins explained that this is peculiar to bluegrass and that it came from Bill Monroe.

Eddie Adcock— "The best way to create is to be totally relaxed."

This portion of the 1990 Eddie Adcock interview enabled him to share more about his playing. "Something that I did all my life— I still do this 'til this day, although I don't play it on stage— I hear a lick on an instrument that I like, I'll play that lick *exact* at home in my basement...because there is a neat thing that takes place in the mind—just like some of the finer art in the world—when you hit upon that note exactly the way the guy intended to hit it the first time. Then you can get the idea and the feeling and the emotion that caused him to do it. They're not your emotions; you're working out of his brain even though he may be dead and gone. It does something for you that nothing can do. It's like when you stand and stare at a Van Gogh picture long enough when it starts moving and comes alive. It's the same thing in music. And if you hang in there and try to duplicate it in every way, then you can experience what he experienced when he did even though it may have been fifty years ago. You can feel him go through that."

As a musician—and he said this is the way all musicians should feel—he knows that there is no "best" musician out there; it's only a matter of who's buying it. "I love B.B. King," he explained. "He only knows four licks but I love to listen to B.B. King. Now do you say that Eddie Adcock is better than B.B. King because I know more technique on the guitar than what he knows? Hell no! You just can't say that technique makes you the best. And what about Earl Scruggs? The truth is he's everything that Eddie Adcock is and more. But in truth, it don't have a thing to do with music and art—and we're supposed to be artists... If what you play isn't understood by the audience, what is it? It doesn't have a purpose, it don't need to be here. Just to play a bunch of technique is what we're referring to here. It's just there! Music should have a purpose.

"The point is, no one *can* be better than anyone else. This will remove that competitive edge. The best way to create is to be totally relaxed; that's when all the heavy thoughts come in. You may be great but you may be in one little groove and you can't get out of that groove. And you can never be greater than you are right then and there merely because you aren't willing to change a thing about what you are doing. And if you remove that element of competition, then you have the art left. It's not me trying to outdo you, it's me trying to do the best I can do. This philosophy needs to be spread around. It will help the music considerably."[30]

28 Joe Ross, "Bill Emerson, Banjo Player Extraordinaire," *Bluegrass Unlimited*, March, 1992, p. 27.

29 1991 interview at his home in Middletown, OH.

30 1990 interview at Owensboro, KY.

J.D. Crowe—
"Pickers forget what they're trying to do as a group unit."

In a 1991 interview, J.D. Crowe, as a man with considerable credentials and experience, attempted to define bluegrass "time", "Everybody has their own terminology over timing. Of course, everybody says there's different types of timing, which is true maybe. But to me there's only one kind of timing, and that's being together as a group. I just revert back to the old **Flatt and Scruggs** things. I listen to that, and what made them so solid—they were together! They played as a group and not as individually. That's one of the problems today. Pickers probably are more advanced as far as knowledge-wise—in the mind—but they forget what they're trying to do as a group unit. You know, you've got to work as a unit. The way I would do it myself, you work your breakdowns, your licks, your rolls, and things like that. Then I would see if they would work in certain types of songs. It all is structured around a group sound."[31]

He also explained how timing can be learned without drive and tone, "The drive is the feeling you have. Everybody has their own feel, they way they interpret their music, you know, when they pick up an instrument—the way they hold their hands. The tone comes from that and also from the way you think that you hear it at a particular time."[32]

Crowe then explained he backs up a lead guitar with the banjo by playing rhythm and vamps. This isn't the time for the banjo to be out front, he emphasized. Occasionally, he throws in a note or two, but not enough to kill the guitar—especially an acoustic, which is easy to do with the additional volume of the banjo.

Crowe told this writer that Jimmy Martin's timing (and sound) when compared to other bands such as that

J. D. Crowe and The Kentucky Mountain Boys, c. 1971.

of Bill Monroe "is a little different. To the average person, it's not. But to a picker that's really studied it and knows, there is a difference. Monroe's timing is, what I call, choppy. Jimmy's timing is a little different and is a fuller sound. He likes everything going at the same time, more or less. Jimmy played a different rhythm with his band than when he did when he was with Bill."

When he was a young man in Martin's band, Crowe was very determined and anxious to learn under the patient tutelage of Jimmy Martin. The most memorable thing that Martin taught Crowe was to "'Keep it solid. Don't leave any holes.' And he would point out that's the way Earl and Lester and them worked. 'Now you listen to these records! You hear that banjo at all times. It may not be as loud at times, but you still hear it. That's what you have to do.' I can hear it, but yet it takes that pointing out to really get it in your mind and to remember it—somebody pointing it out to you a lot."[33]

Tony Rice—
"The real important part is to play right, perfectly in time, to play with soul, to hit all the notes really clear and clean."

Tony Rice spent four years as lead guitarist/lead singer in **J.D. Crowe and the New South**. Crowe was a master bluegrass technician and young Rice learned a lot. Rice said of Crowe, "It's the *important* musical knowledge that he has. The real important part is to play right, perfectly in time, to play with soul, to hit all the notes really clear and clean. J.D. has a great influence on my right hand: on my whole theory of attacking a string; how to attack it and when not to attack it; how to get the most tone and volume [out] of an instrument. I guess I'd say I learned to use the instrument efficiently from J.D. Crowe." Rice watched Crowe carefully. "It used to amaze me that you could hit a string that hard without any rattle and get such pure tone. It really takes practice to do that—just to get a clean, smooth sound—something that's not jumbled up with the notes all run together.

"Many people think too much in terms of metronomic time—of playing like a metronome from the beginning to the end of the tune. But you can attack a note *before* the metronome would strike, or you can attack it after. The *feel* of music comes from that. It's not whether or not you're playing with the metronome; it's where you're attacking the notes."[34]

[31] Tony Trischka and Pete Wernick, *Masters of the 5-String Banjo* (New York: Oak Publications, 1988), p. 156.

[32] Ibid., p. 156.

[33] Tony Trischka and Pete Wernick, *Masters of the 5-String Banjo* (New York: Oak Publications, 1988), p. 154.

[34] Jack Tottle, "Tony Rice—East Meets West," *Bluegrass Unlimited*, October, 1977, p. 13.

Del McCoury—
"You gotta be precise."

McCoury, a veteran of over thirty years in bluegrass and an award-winning musician, spoke about the music, "What I can really feel is the old-time structure of a band. When all of the instruments are blending good together and everybody is right on top of the beat, you can feel it vibrating through you. I think if I lost that feel, then it wouldn't mean the same. But as long as I can feel that, and the harmonies are good, and that punch is in it, I'll be okay. That's what excites me in the music."[35]

In a 1991 interview at IBMA in Owensboro, Del elaborated on this by saying, "If you get a whole bunch of musicians together and sometimes one can't stay right on top, he'll get a little bit behind. Boy, does that mess up a band! You can't get solid as long as that is happening. That guy has got to be right on top. And that goes for a country band, Benny Goodman, or whoever; timing is such an important thing. A lot of musicians today don't think about that. It's one of the most important things in music if you're gonna play. You gotta be precise, you know. You can't look out there in the audience and have something distract you. I've had bass players do that. And I know when they saw something that distracts them because the timing went elsewhere. Boy that burns me up! I can't take that. When that timing goes [from me], I'm ready to quit music."

Timing is not something that he learned. "I think it's something you are born with, you know. I've known professional musicians I've played with who have played longer than I have played that I couldn't play a note with because they couldn't play in time. They couldn't play on top of the beat...Jimmy [Martin] is a good teacher. I'm not. I figure if a guy can play in time—fine. If he can't play in time, I don't have time to fool with him. I mean, I'm no teacher. I don't have the patience to teach people. I wish I did. And I don't think Jimmy has the patience he once had at teachin' people, because he was a good teacher. He could teach guys what it was he was doin' in this music. He sure knows timing."

When McCoury played with Monroe, especially on "Rawhide," Monroe would often play syncopated rhythms and go off on a tangent which would worry McCoury. He wasn't sure where Monroe was going, but he would keep his own rhythm on the guitar and Monroe would return exactly on time—much to his relief. "He is *some* musician! He really is."

Del McCoury and His Dixie Pals, c. 1967.

Raymond Fairchild—
"Bluegrass musicians are the laziest people on earth."

"A lot of people tell me to pick one with drive," banjoist Fairchild said in 1982. "They think you have to be playing fast to have drive. But the 'Tennessee Waltz' has drive if the timing's right. Time is drive. Drive is time. You can drive a waltz just the same as when you're burning one up, if everybody's there. Listen to Bill Monroe's 'Kentucky Waltz' or Jimmy Martin's 'Widow Maker' and you'll hear drive.

"I never did try to get hired by any of the professional bands. I knew if I did try to play with any of those groups I'd have to change my style. I never did want to change what I started. When you go to pick with a man like Bill Monroe, you've got to pick the Monroe sound. I could have changed, but I didn't want to leave my work behind. I knew some day I'd put it out my way. You can't do that working as a sideman for somebody else. You know, I've played for years with these fellers and they wanted to do all Bill Monroe, or all Jimmy Martin, or all somebody else. You can't get nothin' going doing that. You can play your head off playing like somebody else, but that ain't going to do you no good. Them fellers are great, they're the ones who made it, but you can't get on stage in front of them at a festival and do their stuff.

"That's what's a-matter with bluegrass. They claim they love it but they don't love it enough to sit down and learn some new songs or new chords. Bluegrass musicians are the laziest people on earth. They want to play something they can use one chord, or something somebody else already has out. You've got to take the old stuff and make it your own way."[36]

[35] Eugenia Snyder, "Del McCoury, Low-Key But Powerful," *Bluegrass Unlimited*, May, 1982.

[36] Wayne Erbsen, "Raymond Fairchild—Making His Own Way," *Bluegrass Unlimited*, March, 1982, p. 17.

Peter Wernick—
"If everybody in the band is playing with the same feeling and timing, I think it's very relaxing as well as energizing."

In a 1985 interview with Peter Wernick, he spoke of the music **Hot Rize** played. In view of the tremendous popularity of his band at the time, perhaps this gives insight into the musical tastes of the general public. "Most of our songs have a simple structure," he said. "We don't hardly have any complicated arrangements in our entire repertoire. I think that gives us much more ability to get to the guts of the music. I'm personally as happy playing a one or two chord song as any. Some of our songs— 'Shady Grove,' 'Sally Ann,' 'John Henry'— are some of the most down-to-earth songs you will ever find. It is not that they haven't been done, but if we chose our own individual way of playing that song, maybe with an interesting new twist or better tone, it is harder to play than a song with a lot of complexities. When you let one or two chords ring and ring, it pushes you to the limits within a confined musical area.

"I think that is one of the reasons bluegrass has been around for so long. The good players over the years have been able to make innovations within the traditional musical boundaries."[37]

In the summer of 1988, at Grass Valley, California's Midsummer Bluegrass Festival, Wernick talked about *timing* at a banjo workshop. "It's great to have something to give you the basic beat. If you can really depend on that, it kind of frees you up—makes you more relaxed. And if everybody in the band is playing with the same feeling and timing, I think it's very relaxing as well as energizing. It makes everybody play better. Whereas if one person is noticeably dragging or rushing, or if there are uncalled-for surges in the music, then it kind of gets people off guard. Whether it's absolutely perfect or not I don't think is the big question because I think there is a lot of enjoyable music that we all listen to on records which, if we carefully, carefully analyzed, you'd see problems like [in] 'Sally Goodin' by **Flatt and Scruggs**. It's a great version of 'Sally Goodin.' It noticeably speeds up at a certain point in the song but that doesn't keep it from being a great cut of music—doesn't ruin it. But what you really need is that feeling like you can really depend on that beat to be there where you want it. I think that's what people are really after."

Ben Eldridge, banjoist with the **Seldom Scene**, agreed, "It really makes a difference. That's what I call

the 'groove.' The band gets a groove. What happens with us (Seldom Scene) is the [music] just kind of plays itself. You don't have to think about it. It's amazing. But when that's not happening, boy! It's hard work."

Tony Trischka—
"This new banjo music is beginning to achieve critical mass."

Tony Trischka's music roots are deep. He spoke of what the bluegrass beat is, "Now here's an interesting point that I just realized. I was jamming with John Masters, who plays banjo for Larry Sparks, one night [probably 1982]—just the two of us—and I was playing the way I usually play rhythmically, and he was playing the way he usually played. And we played for about fifteen minutes and there was some good music being made, but I didn't think we were totally synched in rhythmically. And then I realized, playing with Larry Sparks, he's probably pushing the beat, and so I started pushing the beat a little bit myself, and instantly I synched in with him. And this is something Sonny Osborne describes in his interview—it was like a weight was lifted from my right hand. And it became totally effortless. And I felt at that point that I was playing 'bluegrass time,' and that was two banjos. And I think that you don't need another instrument to be playing ahead of the beat. It's just like there's this imaginary beat going on, a metronome in people's heads, and they're just a little touch ahead of that in a very even way, not just rushing forward out of control."

To obtain this good bluegrass time, "I guess you've got to play with somebody who has it, because I had no idea about what bluegrass time was. I remember playing down at the Berryville (Virginia) festival in 1967 or 1968, and I was jamming with some guys from the South. And I didn't think about it at the time, but I came back to Syracuse and I was playing bluegrass time. There was a different feel in my right hand that I never had before. Then it faded because the guys I was playing with didn't have it and I didn't either. But for that brief moment I was playing bluegrass time. And since then, here and there I've really noticed it, particularly jamming with John Masters. So I think you really do have to play with people that have it, and that's, I guess, to the greatest extent the southern bands where the music came out of."[38]

He reflected on this thing he does with the banjo in relation to the whole of bluegrass music, "I feel that this whole style of music that you're playing, that I'm playing, that Bela Fleck, Bill Millett, Pete Schwimmer and Dave Griffiths are playing, that Butch Robins has

37 Vanna Heflin, "Hot Rize," *Bluegrass Unlimited*, April, 1984, pp. 9, 10.
38 Trischka and Wernick, op. cit., pp. 344, 345.

played, this new banjo music is beginning to take hold to a certain extent. There are enough people out there. It's beginning to achieve critical mass, you might say. It's becoming a style in itself almost. It's a much freer conception of the instrument, not limiting it to Scruggs' style or Reno or melodic style in the traditional bluegrass sense of those styles, but just a person expressing his own music through his instrument—which is what people have done on other instruments. Whereas in bluegrass, for years, it's been people copying. Everyone would copy Earl Scruggs, or everyone would copy Don Reno, or everyone would copy Bill Keith. Don't forget that those three men had to take a leap ahead, a leap forward in their thinking to come up with a totally original style, a new approach, and that was their own music being expressed; then everyone would copy that style.

"But now I see a trend towards people expressing their own music on the banjo rather than copying Scruggs, Reno or Keith. They're getting their technical thing together by learning the traditional styles and then taking it out farther into other realms. I see it with a lot of different people, much more than in the past. It's heartening. If everyone could just be a little open-minded about it, it would help."[39]

> *"In playing country, you're a lot more controlled. In bluegrass, you've got more chances to improvise..."* —Mike Hartgrove

Mike Hartgrove— "I'd rather hear somebody pull out good tone than to play a whole lot of licks."

With experience in both bluegrass and country bands, fiddler Hartgrove compared the two. "In playing country, you're a lot more controlled. In bluegrass, you've got more chances to improvise. I love bluegrass but I never had a chance to play it much 'til I came with the **Cardinals.** I much prefer playing acoustic and I'd always rather hear somebody pull out good tone than to play a whole lot of licks. It's what I strive for, to get the best tone I can, whether it's four or five notes or twenty."[40]

Keith Little on Vern and Ray and "vanilla" bluegrass

Multi-instrumentalist Keith Little spent much of his formative career in the foothills of California during weekends with his buddy, Delbert Williams (son of Vern Williams who used to play a traditional form of bluegrass with fiddler-partner Ray Park in **Vern and Ray**). Little spoke of Vern Williams and Ray Park, "Whereas Ray helped me get on the track of what to play, Vern showed me that the bottom line in music is emotion. I'd always wondered why I liked the Stanley records, and Vern helped me form the opinion that *feeling* is the bottom line. I'm glad I got to see that. I think there's a lot of people that like the music but they don't know why. What I really search for is music that's got the real feeling in it, and lots of over-produced pop music doesn't have it—it's too 'vanilla.' There's nothing that makes your guts rumble around."

The trio in music— more difficult than the quintet

The traditional bluegrass band, of course, has five band members. Its music is often highly structured and leaves only a limited amount of creativity and expression within its confines. Occasionally you'll find a trio. One trio which lasted as an entity for eleven years was **Berline, Crary and Hickman** on fiddle, guitar and banjo, respectively. Crary was later able to appreciate how easy it became with his five-piece **California** than when his **B-C-H** was only a trio. He was able to relax and enjoy the solos of the other lead instruments.

Another trio, which recorded in 1993, was Jerry Douglas (resonator guitar), Russ Barenberg (guitar) and Edgar Meyer (bass). The liner notes of their "Skip, Hop and Wobble" describe just how difficult, and rewarding, a three-piece band can be, "We found that an ensemble of three instrumental voices offers unique opportunities and challenges. First, you get to play a lot, and everything you play is of critical importance. The trio challenges and sharpens your skills by giving you responsibility. You are one-third of the total effort, so your playing is often exposed, if not featured. You will be

[39] Interview for *Banjo Newsletter,* November, 1978.

[40] Brett F. Devan, "Bluegrass Cardinals, Synonym for Vocal Harmony," *Bluegrass Unlimited,* May, 1986, p. 9. Hartgrove left the Bluegrass Cardinals in October 1979 to join country star Moe Bandy for three years. He rejoined in June 1982 for awhile. In 1995, he was with IIIrd Tyme Out.

sorely missed if you get lazy, and you will stick out like a sore thumb if you get sloppy. The relatively spare environment encourages playing that is rhythmically sturdy and 'texturally' interesting, yet it still provides the support and interactive stimulation that help draw out and energize your ideas.

"Though demanding, a trio is extremely flexible and responsive. It is a highly conductive medium in which musical energy is easily transmitted. One player can quickly elicit response from the others, effortlessly taking the lead in imparting dynamic direction. With this degree of responsiveness, rhythm can be handled with delicacy and control. Each player has immediate access to the group's interpretation of time and phrasing. No one person dominates; each is able to influence the others. A trio inspires good listening.

"We are all tone addicts, and with only three instruments there is room in the sound to hear the full range of tone and the full shape of the notes on each instrument. As a player this is intoxicating, but it is also satisfying because the subtleties of your playing stand a better chance of coming through to the audience. And since you can hear more completely what comes out of your own instrument, you are able to play more expressively and with greater finesse.

"Another plus is the degree to which you can absorb and process the music while you are playing. The amount of musical information is such that each player can digest it completely. This makes for music that is in some ways more alive than large-ensemble music. The spontaneous communication among the players can be richly detailed, and the resultant interplay of sounds is active and intimate."

Bela Fleck on jazz and bluegrass— "I do think that they should learn the basics as well as Earl did if they can."

"If a guy hasn't learned tone and timing, that's a basic of music. So if they want to be a jazz banjo player and that's all they want to be, I don't really see why they should learn Earl Scruggs. But I do think that they should learn the basics as well as Earl did if they can— whatever kind of music they're trying to play. Earl's a good example of somebody who knew his basics and applied them to what he did really, really well."[41]

Tim O'Brien— "A lot of players will add stuff to the style."

"A lot of players will add stuff to the style as opposed to creating within the style," said Tim O'Brien who was a bluegrass star with **Hot Rize** at the time of the interview. "There are certain roles that each instrument has within the context of a bluegrass band and you can use those roles in your own way, as opposed to making a new kind of role."[42]

Tim O'Brien

[41] Trischka and Wernick, op. cit., p. 156.
[42] Don Stiernberg, "Interview—Tim O'Brien, *Mandolin World News*, June, 1984, p. 8.

The songwriting

There's something about this music which is wholesome and all-American. There's really nothing more American than bluegrass music. The subjects which bluegrass songwriters tend to prefer are those close to home: relationships, family and hillsides. When Flatt and Scruggs sang songs like "Cabin on the Hill," the audience could visualize themselves on that old farm the song addresses. Modern bluegrass songwriters today usually try to keep within these guidelines. However, today's listeners may not have ever been near an old cabin on a hill, so the imagined image may not be as important to them as to an earlier generation of listeners.

As a result of the existence of a new audience and different media available for songs (cassettes, compact discs, videos, etc.), much of the newer writing has changed to subjects with which people are more familiar: reality topics such as divorce, job stress, split families and other subjects somewhat foreign to the rural audiences of early country and bluegrass music. Country singer Reba McEntire has had tremendous success with her videos of songs that relate to the average person.

According to banjoist Bela Fleck, "There are two ways we can look at bluegrass: One way is to think of it as a 'museum piece,' which implies that it is an isolated bit of history that cannot be changed. The song 'Cabin on the Hill' is an example; it is a good time period it was written in. And heard in that context, it is meaningful. But how many young people growing up away from rural Appalachia can truly relate to the imagery? I like to think of bluegrass music as being alive and growing and meaningful for today, but the heart of bluegrass lies in the honesty of the music. Bluegrass itself was considered a progressive, wild thing at the start. Bill Monroe in the 1940s was unique: a new guy with a new sound. The good bluegrass musicians have been the ones who have taken the music form and added to it the electricity that comes from playing with like-minded musicians. Earl Scruggs, Sam Bush and Jerry Douglas are some good examples of individuals who have added a lot to the music, along with bands like the

Osborne Brothers, the **Country Gentlemen**, **New Grass Revival** and the **Seldom Scene**. In my mind, **New Grass Revival** was definitely bluegrass—progressive, contemporary bluegrass... 'Cabin on the Hill,' while being historically and sentimentally important, is not the future."[43]

Dr. Ralph Stanley. Photo courtesy Dr. Ralph Stanley

The brilliant songwriting of Felice and Boudleaux Bryant[44]

In mid-February of 1982, the Tennessee State Legislature voted to make "Rocky Top" the State Song. Boudleaux Bryant and wife, Felice, wrote the song in ten minutes. Boudleaux explained how it happened, "This was in 1967. Chet Atkins asked us to write some material for an album with appeal to the senior citizens

...to say that Alison Krauss' success is as a result of the popularity of her videos would be an error.

[43] Bela Fleck, quotations from *Inside Bluegrass*, newsletter of the Minnesota Bluegrass and Old Time Music Association, October, 1994.

[44] Boudleaux Bryant was born February 13, 1920, in Shellman, GA. After high school he trained as a classical violinist. At 18, he hired as a country dance fiddler for WSB, Atlanta, with Uncle Net and the Texas Wranglers, and later, Hank Penny's Radio Cowboys. About 1940, he met Felice Scaduto; they soon married.

America's Music | Bluegrass

called 'Golden Years.' The artist was to be Archie Campbell who was doing a show in Gatlinburg [Tennessee] at the time. We went over to Gatlinburg so we would be near him while we did the writing. Well, we spent several weeks writing songs about 'sitting in rocking chairs' and children are all married and gone'—that sort of thing. Finally, Felice got so depressed she said, 'Let's do something different. Let's do something bright, up tempo.' I wanted to hurry up and finish the job we were doing but Felice was insistent, and at last I said, 'Okay, okay,' and started singing 'Rocky Top.' Ten minutes later we had the song down on paper and were ready to get back on the material for Archie Campbell."[45] The first cut of the Osborne Brothers record sold 150,000 copies, and later won BMI's high performance award for the most-performed song.

The Bryants also wrote "Georgia Piney Woods," "Tennessee Hound Dog," "Muddy Bottom" and "I Can Hear Kentucky Calling." Their songs have made stars of performers such as Little Jimmy Dickens, the **Osborne Brothers**, the **Everly Brothers**, Carl Smith, Eddy Arnold, Webb Pierce, Sonny James, Bob Luman and Jim Reeves. Other well-known compositions of the Bryants were Buddy Holly's "Raining in My Heart," and the **Everly Brothers**' "Bye, Bye Love," "Problems," "Bird Dog," "Love of My Life," "A Brand New Heartache," "Wake Up Little Susie," "Like Strangers," "All I Have to Do is Dream" and "Poor Jenny." As of 1991, over 200 million copies of their songs had been sold.

Charlie Cline, bluegrass songwriter— "It's time again for new material."

Cline and his wife Lee have written 300 to 400 songs together. Charlie explained that "What I'm trying to do now is get new, original material in bluegrass. You see, a lot of people have sung these old songs—and they're good—but they are gettin' to where they wore 'em out. It's time again for new material."[46]

Jake Landers, bluegrass songwriter

Jacob Landers, a prolific songwriter, supplied many songs for Lester Flatt, **Bobby Smith and the Boys from Shiloh, Country Gentlemen, Osborne Brothers,**

Bluegrass Cardinals and Bill Monroe. During an early 1960s stint with Bill Monroe[47], he co-wrote "Beyond the Gate." During other phases of his career he wrote "The Secret of the Waterfall" (1971, a big hit for the **Country Gentlemen**)," "I Want to Be a Bluegrass Picker," "Put a Light in the Windows" and fifty others. In the early 1990s, his "Walk Softly on My Heart" was recorded by the country and western band **Kentucky Headhunters** and, as a result, sold nearly a million copies. Writing songs which get picked up by artists who can get the tune massive exposure is really the only way to make money in the tough world of writing bluegrass songs.

Don Reno and the "Nashville sound"

In 1967, **Don Reno, Bill Harrell and the Tennessee Cut-Ups** recorded on television shows such as "Top O' the Morning" on WDJB in Roanoke. To conform to the television station's country sound they hired a steel guitar player and a drummer. Reno hated the sound which "changed my band around to where nobody could recognize it."[48] The music Reno was complaining about was largely classified as "the Nashville sound" which often requires the sophisticated recording techniques such as overdubbing the various music sections: full rhythm sections, horn and string sections, vocals and others.

Pat Enright's opinion of Nashville songwriting

"The Nashville music scene is not geared to bluegrass music," said Pat Enright of the **Nashville Bluegrass Band**. "Songwriters want to write hits and there's obviously a formula for that. When a songwriter gives us or **Hot Rize** or **New Grass Revival** a song, it's usually one they think is the typical bluegrass song. Writers would do well to submit songs to acoustic or bluegrass groups without making them stereotyped. Bill Monroe is a good example of a songwriter who never restricted himself to hackneyed themes and wrote some very personal, sometimes disturbing, songs. That was simply the way he was expressing himself."[49]

[45] Wayne W. Daniel, "Rocky Top," *Bluegrass Unlimited*, April, 1982, p. 21.

[46] 1991 interview.

[47] In 1963, occasional members of the Blue Grass Boys were Raul Yarbrough (banjo) and Jake Landers (guitar, for six months), Kenny Baker and Bessie Lee Maudlin. Landers had already written "I Want to be a Bluegrass Picker," "Luther Smith's Mail Order Bride" and "Put a Light in the Window" (which was co-written by Herschel Sizemore).

[48] Bill Vernon, "Don Reno, Red Smiley, Bill Harrell and the Tennessee Cut-Ups," *Bluegrass Unlimited*, August, 1971, p. 10.

[49] Alana J. White, "Pat Enright," *Bluegrass Unlimited*, December, 1987, p. 60.

Joe Ross on songwriting

Joe Ross, a prolific contributor to *Bluegrass Unlimited*, researched the task of successful songwriting by interviewing many of the best known writers in the 1980s such as Dudley Connell, Randall Hylton, Phil Rosenthal, Billy Henson, Sonny Ludlam, Don McHan and Paul Craft. His conclusions were, "Almost anyone can write songs but very few can write hit songs; songwriting requires a certain degree of creativity and therefore you must find a certain amount of inspiration and motivation within yourself to be successful: Songwriting is work, and only with a good deal of practice at it will you become comfortable doing it. Songwriting is a craft; it can be learned: If you view it as a form of communication, you can learn about the styles, ways, and methods to say exactly what you feel within your soul."[50]

Ralph Stanley— "Singing is the weak spot in bluegrass."

A 1986 interview with Mr. Stanley brought out his opinions of singing in bluegrass, "Singing is the weak spot in bluegrass. Now, I feature singing more than I do instruments. I've always liked it better. If I sing a song, I think people want to hear the song. 'Course, it's good to have some music to take a break, but the song is what they're interested in. The instruments are there to bolster up the singing."

About the development of modern bluegrass, Ralph said, "I think it might get a little crowded. I think it might be harder to make a living at it than the traditional. There's not too much of what I play or what Monroe plays, so that makes a better market for the traditional. There are so many groups that are good among the—what do you call it—'progressive,' but you can't tell who it is unless you are looking at them. Now if you hear Bill Monroe or Ralph Stanley, you can hear who it is right now. What I've always liked to play to is the public. We draw more people like that. I think a lot of bluegrass shows are not promoted. The records are not promoted. You got to put that stuff out there and make people think they're getting a bargain. Then they'll grab it."[51]

The changing music of Earl Scruggs

An August 1978 *Pickin'* interview asked Earl Scruggs how music changes. Earl then spoke with careful, measured words here, according to Don Kissil, the interviewer. "Yeah! You're going to get criticized by some hard-core people—the type that wants to stop the clock. That's a selfish point of view. I think changing is makin' progress. I thought it back in 1960, but I never knew how much progress [actually] did change...

"I got the point firmly across that I wasn't playin' bluegrass anymore. I just admitted it and lots of people for a long time, they didn't want to hear that or believe that. So I finally said to them, that's just your problem. I've got to live with myself. I've been playin' the same thing for twenty-some years. I got bogged down and if you get depressed doing somethin', why...

"In other words, about 95-98 percent of the exuberance a musician is going to project on the stage depends on how happy he is with what he's working with. I got pretty bogged down playing the same thing I did in 1945 and '48, along in there. And now with this change, why, it's almost like I felt when I was twenty-one when I hit the stage. I have too much respect for music to see myself go down and just wither away. So doin' this change is puttin' some spirit back inside of us. So if somebody just don't accept me now...well! I don't try to displease anybody, but if they don't accept me the way I am that's just their problem. I just got to play something that I'm excited about—to do what I'm capable of doin'. And I really never knew what the banjo's capable of doing until I got to playin' with the boys. There's a great inner feel—a real change!"[52]

The origin of "four potatoes"

Mandolinist Bob Applebaum told the story of the origin of the word "potato" when used a tempo-setting phrase to kick off a song. "This comes from Steve Arkin who was sitting around the house one day with Peter Wernick and they were trying to come up with some word for when you need a few 'somethings' up front. What do you say? Well, it was his idea to come up with a phrase. And in that conversation he and Peter Wernick came up with the word to describe the rolls which come up front. Potatoes! There it is! Two New York banjo players did this!"[53]

[50] Joe Ross, "The Sharps and Flats of Bluegrass Songwriting," *Bluegrass Unlimited*, July, 1988.

[51] Barry Brower, "Ralph Stanley—Keeping It Right, Down and Simple," *Bluegrass Unlimited*, February, 1987, p. 13.

[52] On another topic, Earl spoke of his sons and that he "didn't encourage them to pick at all." While he didn't discourage them, he waited to see if they had an interest in playing music before backing them "because if you don't have the interest in this, you'd better get out of the business." Their interest in music seemed to happen all by itself.

[53] Interview with Bob Applebaum in a 1992 interview at IBMA.

Dan Crary—
"The total of this music is more than the sum of the parts."

Dr. Crary spoke about his love of music, "Music is not fun, in the sense of fun, to me. I don't mean that it's the opposite of fun. It's more something I *have* to do. It's something that's happening inside." It has been "happening inside" ever since he first heard a **Stanley Brothers** record in 1951, went "completely bananas," and became what he thinks was probably the only kid in the whole state of Kansas to know that bluegrass was not something you grow out in the fields. He continued, "I like the tonality of bluegrass—the pure chord forms and the harmony. The clichés that happen in bluegrass are my clichés. Something magic happened when they got these five or six instruments together. The total is more than the sum of the parts."[54]

Michael O'Roark—
"You have to understand bluegrass... and that takes years."

At age nineteen, Michael O'Roark founded **Mike O'Roark and the Freebornmen** with his younger brother, Mitch. Author Nancy Cardwell wrote, "Mike recalls that it was a little unusual to grow up during the '60s and really love country music. 'My peers when I was sixteen years old were into the **Beatles** and if you said, "I like Johnny Cash," they'd look at you kind of weird. It was a well-kept secret for a long time.'"[55]

O'Roark spoke about the popularity of bluegrass music, "Sometimes, the singing turns people off. I love it, but to the uneducated ear it takes some getting used to. It's like wine, or the first drink of beer you get. You have to understand bluegrass and be educated in it before you can really know what they're feeling, what they're trying to present, and that takes years. But if you want a record on the radio, the programmers won't do it. You've got to have the soft 'grass first before you can work them into the hard 'grass."

Cardwell continued, "Mike's only complaint is with the hard-core purist who 'considers anyone who doesn't play traditional bluegrass part of a Communist conspiracy to undermine bluegrass music, ruin it, and change it. These same people have never tried to sell it.' Mike points out, 'They're sitting back there with their nine-to-five jobs and they put their records on the stereo and say, "Boy, I really like that." Well, I do, too, but try to sell it to a club owner whose disco has just gone broke and who wants to try country rock because he heard of Waylon Jennings.

'The people that are always condemning country rock with a banjo in it just don't have to make a living at it. I'd love to sit up there on stage with my old D-28 and play straight bluegrass because I love it. But you can't do it if you can't get paid at it and I don't want to go back to reading gas meters.'"

"The people that are always condemning country rock with a banjo in it just don't have to make a living at it." —Michael O'Roark

---

Don Reno—
"You've got to keep yourself in tiptop condition."

Reno said bluegrass music "is not the easiest to play by a long ways. I think that straight country style is easier to learn. There is a different timing and feel to bluegrass. I've had people come up to me and ask, 'Where do you put this run in at?' and I just tell them I put it where I feel it."[56]

He spoke about the rigors of a traveling musician, "You change climates, you change temperatures at least every week. You've got to keep yourself in tiptop condition. If you don't, something will give way. You lose sleep—I have gone three whole days and nights without sleep. Back in the old days you often had to grab what sleep you could in an automobile."

Author Bill Malone—
"There are places in *Country Music, USA* where I was wrong."

Country Music, USA was published at the University of Texas (1968) for the American Folklore Society and was written by Bill C. Malone. It included a chapter on bluegrass, careful not to include it as mainstream country music.

"An early pioneer in the field of country music history, Bill is now considered to be one of the foremost experts on the subject," wrote Fred Burton. "There were no scholarly treatises on the subject twenty-four years ago when Bill started and, over the many years of research and study, his views have changed about some of the material presented in his book. 'I think I know

[54] Mary Jane Bolle, "Deacon Dan Crary—A Man of His Own Cloth," *Bluegrass Unlimited*, May, 1974, p. 23.

[55] Nancy Cardwell, "Mike O'Roark: A Bluegrass Musician in Transition," *Bluegrass Unlimited*, January, 1982, p. 15.

[56] Don Reno, from an interview by Bill Vernon, "The Don Reno Story, Part Five: Don Reno Today," *Muleskinner News*, February, 1974, p. 8.

much more about the subject now (1984) than I did when I started writing my original doctoral dissertation back in 1960. There are places in the book where I was wrong. There are factual mistakes in the book that I'm correcting now. There are points of view which I no longer hold. I think I'm much smarter about the subject now than I was back then.'"[57] One point he no longer feels is important is his earlier emphasis on country music as a part of folk music. "The music is valuable whether it's folk or not. The fact remains that the music is a popular expression which reflects the lives of people and is so meaningful to people."

Malone is also the author of *Southern Music, American Music* (University of Kentucky Press, 1979) and co-edited *Stars of Country Music* with Judy McCullough, editor of the University of Illinois Press. Malone had his own bluegrass band in Texas and Louisiana, **Hill Country Ramblers**, from 1972 to 1978. In 1982, he was nominated for a Grammy Award in the Historical Recordings category for his LP "Smithsonian Collection of Classic Country Music" (Smithsonian Recordings).

Bobby Hicks— "Bluegrass is hard."

"People don't realize it, but bluegrass is hard," said fiddler Hicks. "There's nothing to hide behind; there's no drums."[58]

Garry Thurmond— "Bluegrass has come of age."

Garry Thurmond, a founding member of the **Warrior River Boys** (1965), spoke of today's music and its pickers, "You hear a lot of great pickers today but you don't hear many real singers of traditional songs. Some young performers just simply aren't willing to pay the price necessary for digging back and learning the real traditions. They may learn five or six songs that are old and still popular, but they fail to really dig back down to the roots.

"Young people have a great opportunity today in bluegrass because more and more people are realizing that bluegrass is really getting back to the basics of our heritage. Bluegrass fans now range from northern college professors to southern farmers to New York businessmen. Bluegrass has come of age but we can't forget the early struggles of the Stanleys and the Monroes who made it through those bleak years."[59]

A deejay's opinion of bluegrass— "Honesty is the thing about bluegrass that distinguishes it."

Radio deejay Ed McDonald once said, "I think, with the kind of music we're doing, we have a relationship of one to one that I've never been able to achieve in any other kind of radio. The people respond to the personalities and they respond to the music. It is honest. I guess honesty is the thing about bluegrass that distinguishes it and makes it a cut above a lot of other kinds of music. It's just honest, genuine, with a human quality, and I don't feel like I'm getting a product off some record company's assembly line."[60]

Earl Scruggs— "You have to have a lot of concentration; you have to think of the whole sound."

In the "Workshop" section of the November 1982 issue of *Frets*, we find Earl Scruggs talking about the standards he uses to evaluate his own lead and backup playing, "When I'm doing backup behind a singer, I try to blend in a softness that helps the singer and blends with everything. I try to use the low parts when the voice is going high, and I try to use the high parts when the voice is low. I try to support, or complement, the singer and not fight against the voice. I often hear recordings where everyone is picking at the same time while the singer is singing. For my music, I try to lay back and support the singer. I concentrate on the total sound and not so much on my own picking, although I have to take stock of what I'm doing, too; it's sort of a combination. As to whether I'm doing it well or not—to evaluate my playing—I don't really know how to answer that. If something goes wrong (and it has many times), I just know it and try to help as much as I can or go in a different direction. I will make a change in the middle of a piece to help it if I feel it is not going right. Sometimes it works and sometimes it doesn't.

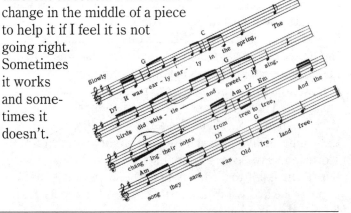

57 Fred Burton, "Bill C. Malone, Texas Hillbilly—Country Music Historian," *Bluegrass Unlimited*, July, 1984, 24.

58 Thomas Goldsmith, "Bill Monroe in the Studio—Recording the Grammy Winner," *Bluegrass Unlimited*, April, 1989, p. 46.

59 Suzy Lowry Geno, "Garry Thurmond and the Warrior River Boys," *Bluegrass Unlimited*, January, 1985.

60 Ed McDonald, WNKU-FM, Highland Heights, Kentucky. *Bluegrass Unlimited*, 1988.

"You have to have a lot of concentration; you have to think of the whole sound. You can't just pay attention to your own sound, thinking that everything will just come together by itself. It won't. If my picking doesn't work, or if its taking away from the singer, I'll just drop back and play rhythm. Or, if somebody else is putting in pretty backup, I'll just go to rhythm. I've always been a firm believer in not letting two or three musicians back the singer at the same time. One is plenty in my ear. More than that really gets busy. I try to direct my attention to the guys on stage and to do it directly, rather than through the monitor. Some can't pick that way. I prefer to hear the natural sound than I do when I hear through the monitors or through the headphones. So, I request that my monitors be set [volume-wise] as low as possible. However, this approach does depend on the stage. If it's an outdoor stage with the wind blowing, I just might need more monitors. Of course, there's the last evaluation when I hear the playback of a recording, but that's really different. The only thing I can do about it then is to re-record it or try to mix it better. I think the evaluation must be continuous, as you are playing."

Bill Lowe—
"If we don't save this music, who will?"

Musician and writer Bill Lowe told of an important part of the music: the musicians. "Young musicians should do more research on this wonderful music. It deserves more than most give it. They should play the music right and good and put their hearts in it. All the ingredients are there... I've ridden for miles and miles and I've talked and talked about this music and how wonderful it is and how, if we do not take care of it, it's going to be like the old antiques and things that people are looking through garages and houses and barns today trying to find. If we don't save this music, who will?" Lowe was distressed about the fact that even in Kentucky, "people know nothing about the **Skillet Lickers**, **J.E. Mainer's Mountaineers**, the **Callahan Brothers** or Uncle Dave Macon. The music is gone—it's all gone from right where it came from."

Chapter 3

Technology and the Recording Industry - Table of Contents

Technology and the Recording Industry

T hings change; we all know that. This chapter discusses how and why bluegrass music got to where it is as a result of the increasing influence of the "electronic age".

Victor Records and the electrical recording process

In 1923, "Victor invented an electrical recording process; in addition to making much cleaner recordings, the electrical method meant fewer pieces of bulky equipment. It was possible to record 'in the field' as opposed to studios."[1] In the next decade, the Library of Congress took advantage of this breakthrough and sent people around the country to preserve examples of vanishing folk music; Atlanta was the city they visited most often. Performers were usually paid a flat fee, usually $25 to $50 per song. There were no royalties. Whether they would record again depended upon sales.

Cliff Carlisle, famous Opry star with his National guitar/resonator guitar, spoke about Ralph Peer and the recording process, "They (Ralph Peer and his field recording engineers) used to carry these portable sets around and go in just anywhere they could find a vacant building, see? And they'd just take a whole big bunch of burlap and hang it up all around, and then they'd have a partition built in it, and they'd put their recording equipment in back, and they'd just go in there, Boy, and start recording. They'd try to locate a central location, see, and they'd call people in from three or four hundred miles away, recording artists. That's the way Victor used to do it."[2]

Eck Robertson and Fiddlin' John Carson— the first country music recordings

In June of 1922, fiddler   marched uninvited into Victor's New York studios and recorded "Sallie Goodin'" and "Arkansaw Traveler." The 78 rpm record was released April 1923 and is acknowledged as the first commercial country record. It sold well and proved that fiddle music (the predominant type of country music at that time) could be a profitable commercial venture.

Fiddlin' John Carson and Okeh Records recognized the popularity of Robertson's record and made an effort to commercialize the popularity of the fiddle; Carson was soon hired to play on WSB radio, Atlanta. Carson's fiddling on WSB in 1923 became what some people acknowledge as the first documented performance by a solo country artist on the radio. With subsequent performances on the station, he became well accepted by the audiences of WSB. It is said that Carson once won a prize for singing 118 different songs in one session.[3]

There is some controversy as to what the "first" country record is. Robertson's tune was the *first* and paved the way for the success of Carson and all country artists who followed. Although Robertson's Victor recording beat Fiddlin' John Carson's Okeh record by several months, Carson was recruited for the express purpose of profit. On June 14, 1923, Carson, from Georgia, recorded on Okeh Records in Atlanta. The songs were "The Little Old Log Cabin in the Lane" and "The Old Hen Cackled and the Rooster's Going to Crow."[4] The first song is known as the first "commercially-released country music record" by some historians. The Eck Robertson recording of a year earlier was much more informal nature than the actual recruitment of a fiddle player to record a song as they did with Carson.

Okeh pressed 500 copies and sold out within a month—much to the surprise of Ralph Peer, then with Okeh Records, who then signed him exclusively.[5] Carson recorded many other tunes in later years for the Okeh and RCA labels in Atlanta; he was probably the first to sell his own records at his performances, thereby establishing a now-well-known tradition.

Carson eventually recorded some 200 songs, mostly in Atlanta; this helped to make Atlanta *the* hot spot for the recording business. Indeed, **Bill Monroe and the**

[1] Charles K. Wolfe, *Tennessee Strings*, (Knoxville: The University of Tennessee Press, 1977), pp. 42, 43.

[2] Nolan Porterfield, *Country, the Music and the Musicians* (New York: Abbeville Press, Inc., 1988), p. 43.

[3] Carson played a fiddle which dated back to the 1700s and was brought to this country in a flour sack from Ireland by Carson's ancestors. Rosa Lee Carson Johnson, better known as "Moonshine Kate," donated her father's fiddle to the Country Music Foundation.

[4] Rounder released the recordings in 1976 with the title "The Old Hen Cackled and the Rooster's Going to Crow." The album is considered by many as a "must" in record collecting.

[5] Band members for the recording session were John Carson (fiddle), Rosa Lee Carson "Moonshine Kate" (guitar, banjo), Earl Johnson (fiddle), T.M. "Bully" Brewer (guitar), Marion "Peanut" Brown (guitar), Land Norris (banjo) and Bill White (banjo).

Blue Grass Boys made all of their RCA Victor recordings in Atlanta. Soon Columbia Records waxed many of Atlanta's other local artists such as Riley Puckett, Gid Tanner, Clayton McMichen and the Darby and Tarleton duo. Ralph Peer left Okeh, joined Columbia, and then Victor.

Earliest country music duet

The earliest documented country duet act is Reuben Puckett and Richard Brooks, who first recorded on January 29th of 1923.

The Bristol Sessions

In July of 1927, Jimmie Rodgers and the **Carter Family** recorded in Bristol, Tennessee. They were just two of nineteen groups who recorded during the two-week recording session of seventy-six tunes.[6] Maybelle Carter was eighteen when she showed up with her guitar for the A.P. and Sara session. It was clear then that the group was destined for much, much more. Ralph Peer described their arrival into the studios of the third Virginia group which Peer initially identified as "Mr. and Mrs. Carter from Maces Springs", "They wander in. He's dressed in overalls and the women are country women from way back there. They look like hillbillies. But as soon as I heard Sara's voice, that was it. I knew it was going to be wonderful."[7]

Jimmie Rodgers recorded solo that day and featured his yodeling. Ralph Peer recalled in a classic understatement, "I thought his yodel alone might spell success."

The Bristol recording sessions were the project of Ralph Peer, who set out from the nation's major recording city of New York to preserve (for a profit) the artists of the day. According to historian/author Charles Wolfe, the arrival in Bristol of Ralph Peer of the RCA Victor company to record local musicians began "the true dawn of country music." Two months later, the records were on sale in the Bristol region. The musicians' friends immediately bought up their records and validated their mountain music. Little did they know they were welcoming a new era in American music: country (or hillbilly) music.

Peer had already worked for Okeh Records and Columbia. Now with Victor, he advertised for additional artists. But he had to convince his new employer that it would be profitable. Victor probably felt that this inferior music would somehow taint the hard-won reputation it had with its opera celebrities. This attitude existed in spite of the major hit for Victor by Vernon

Dalhart, "The Prisoner's Song"/"The Wreck of the Old 97," which sold six million copies in fifty versions. Peer received no money from RCA but they allowed him to own the publishing rights of any song that he recorded.

The choice of Tennessee as a recording site was not indiscriminate. According to Charles Wolfe, "The popular image of the southern mountains as a prime source of folk songs was formed (and still holds today) and this image was to have much to do with the later commercial development of this folk music. Tennessee especially benefited from this image when radio and phonograph records came along; recording sessions were held in Tennessee because the northern recording executives thought old songs could best be found in the mountains, and the founder of the Grand Ole Opry chose Tennessee because he felt the hill country would be most authentic there. And the music, to be sure, was indeed present in the mountains."[8]

The success of these recordings led to the formation of the Peer-Southern publishing company, one of the largest in the world today.

The importance of microphone technology

In 1923, 104 million records were sold. In 1932, during the Depression, only six million were sold. As of 1927, the increasing convenience of having radio entertainment only the flick of a switch away made the sales of records (75 cents each) and phonographs somewhat perilous. And the quality of the reception by radio was often superior to that sound which a phonograph was capable of giving. This phonograph quality improved overnight, but not enough to compensate for the variety of free entertainment offered on the radio. And complicating the situation was the feeling that the record companies didn't want their records played on the radio; they felt that people wouldn't buy their records if they could hear them on the radio for free.

The next few years, including those through the Depression, were very hard on record companies. About the only company that was left after the Depression was Victor. This was mainly because RCA (Radio Corporation of America) had purchased Victor in 1927 and provided enough capital to keep the company alive. Columbia Records, which owned the Columbia Broadcasting System (CBS), was sold in 1927, and had ironically re-joined CBS in 1938 as a subsidiary itself. The Decca Company of England opened up Decca Records in America in 1934 with their main artists being Bing Crosby and Guy Lombardo. These records cost thirty-five cents each.

---

[6] Others who recorded then included Ernest V. Stoneman and His Dixie Mountaineers, Henry Whitter, the West Virginia Coon Hunters, the Bull Mountain Moonshiners, the Blue Ridge Corn Shuckers, the Tennessee Mountaineers and several others.

[7] From liner notes by Charles Wolfe on the double LP album "The Bristol Sessions," by Country Music Foundation (CMF) Records, 1987.

[8] Charles K. Wolfe, *Tennessee Strings*, (Knoxville: The University of Tennessee Press, 1977), p. 6.

The early 1930s brought significant changes to country music—changes which were enabled by the technological improvements to the microphone. This new technical achievement allowed the creation of such period stars as Bing Crosby, the **Mills Brothers** and Frank Sinatra. Country music close-harmony duet singing, such as was that of the Delmore brothers, also found its beginnings as soon as the microphone was developed enough to pick up the softer voices, delicate harmonies and lyrics.

While certain styles of music were naturals to this electronic advancement, others who became popular during the '20s found that their styles didn't fit well into this new radio medium. Up until that time, popular stars such as the **Skillet Lickers** and the **Carter Family** had to nearly yell to be able to record on the recording devices of the day. The music which used electrified instruments (western swing, jazz, etc.) also took advantage of the technology revolution and went their own way.

The recording capital of Charlotte, North Carolina

By the 1930s, Charlotte, North Carolina, was a major recording center for country, blues and gospel. RCA established a permanent studio in Charlotte's most exclusive hotel. Though primitive by today's standards, it was a step up from the portable and temporary warehouse studios of earlier years. The last recordings made by the **Monroe Brothers** were made here in 1937. But Charlotte's recording activity was almost gone after World War II.

"Bluebird was an RCA subsidiary, and after several trips in 1934 and 1935 to the Southwest (i.e. Bristol,

Technician leaning over cylinder-recording machine. In foreground is a 16-inch transcription machine. Photo courtesy Library of Congress.

TN) the company stumbled on a new mother lode during a 1936 stop in Charlotte."[9] In Charlotte, they found **J.E. Mainer's Mountaineers**, the **Blue Sky Boys**, the **Monroe Brothers**, the **Dixon Brothers**, the **Tobacco Tags** and the famed gospel-singing **Golden Gate Jubilee Quartet**. Bluebird returned to Charlotte several times. Although Victor's recordings in Bristol of Jimmie Rodgers and the **Carter Family** were very important, the company only made trips there in 1927 and 1931.

Recording on "wax" in 1938

Wiley Morris, of the **Morris Brothers**, described the process of recording back in those days. He said, "They had two rooms rented for the recording. They used one of them as a studio, and in the other they had the machinery to do the recording. They had one big machine in there which turned a bunch of stuff and there was a big cake of wax with a needle sticking in it. It cut the grooves right then. They let you hear the first song you recorded and that was it. You didn't get to hear no more 'til it came out as a record. I guess the reason was that when you recorded, you put the sound in that cake of wax. And when they played it back, it took the sound back out. Later on, they changed all that. So if you made a mistake, it was a mistake, 'cause they couldn't let you do it over. That cost them money. If you really messed up, I guess they'd let you do it over but they didn't like that.

"I remember they had one mike which was right between me and Zeke. I stood in the middle of the room. We stood side by side and both sang into the same side of that mike. It was a big mike. They had a red light down at the bottom to tell you when to play.

Barrels and boxes full of cylinder recordings. Cylinders were mainly used to record speeches, not music. Photo courtesy Library of Congress.

[9] Richard K. Spottswood, "Country Music and the Phonograph," *Bluegrass Unlimited*, February, 1987, p. 20.

They also had speakers so you could talk back and forth. They told us not to play longer than three minutes. I never will forget that big cake of wax. When that needle was cutting the groove, it sounded like grinding an ax on a grindstone."[10]

The use of one microphone was the norm during the '30s, '40s and '50s

Wilma Lee Cooper recalled that "Back in the old days of show business we only had one microphone, and you learned to use that mike in and out. You worked it. As you came to a low note you leaned a little closer so the note would be stronger, and when you came to a note you were hitting hard, you would lean back a little. The whole band had to learn to work the microphone in and out. When one person finished, he would move back and the next person would move in to the mike to pick his part."[11]

Flatt and Scruggs and the Foggy Mountain Boys also used only one microphone for the entire band. The band exhibited exquisite timing and shuffling when a band member was to take a break. The transition from instrumental break to vocals was just as challenging. Some have said that the hard part about learning to be a new member of that band was learning the intricate choreography associated with each song. More recent bands who have used one mic include **Doyle Lawson and Quicksilver**, **Hot Rize**, and **Lonesome Standard Time**.

George Shuffler in 1949— "I was dangerous"!

Hoke's **Smoky Mountaineers** included the McReynolds brothers and George Shuffler. "We didn't make a lot of money," said Mr. Shuffler. "But we had a good time. Back in the mountains, we occasionally worked a concert without electricity, but most of the places had electricity. We carried a little PA set with two little box speakers and a little amp settin' down at the bottom. And we had microphones and stands; one guy could set it up in two minutes. We plugged it in and we give it a minute to warm up and we was ready to go.

"We only carried one microphone. That was *it* back then. You run over somebody if they didn't get out of the way when it come time for your break. They was in trouble; they would end up out in the front seats if they didn't get back out of the way. You come in from behind and then bow out to the right. I'd just get right in there and I'd put the guitar[12] up under my chin, you know, and

put it right up to that little ol' microphone and let it go. And they knew to get out of the way when it was time for me to take my break. It was showmanship—it looked awful good. But a new man, Lord-a-mercy, he could get this legs kicked and everything else until he learned to get out of the way. 'Cause I was gonna come in there or bust! I was dangerous! I guarantee that I was gonna get my part."

In spite of all the fancy amplification gear he now uses in his own family band, "I miss it. I really do. We got enough sound equipment for our little gospel group to start a radio station. And we don't need all that junk. These younger boys that's in the group, you know, they're out to keep up on this. We sing with a lot of other groups that's got all this high tech stuff and they think we got to be right in with them, you know. Of course, you don't have to move around as much, but I'm so old now that I couldn't get around like I did then no-how."[13]

Juke boxes and the recording industry

Following the repeal of Prohibition in 1933, juke boxes were reintroduced especially in places/joints too small to afford live entertainment. Juke boxes had been introduced in the early 1890s to introduce Thomas Edison's new invention: the phonograph record. They cost the customer five cents per play and featured the records of Decca, Bluebird and Vocalion. For many years, jukeboxes were more significant in determining popularity and generating royalties for recordings than radio.

The transcriptions and border radio

In the late 1940s, many touring hillbilly groups recorded a series of radio transcriptions which gave the bands the freedom they needed to make a better living. Radio program transcriptions were large, wax records on which artists recorded not only their previously-recorded 78s, but also entire fifteen-minute shows as well. Their purpose was to allow radio stations to play an artist's music when they weren't there in person. The successor to this idea was audio tape and later, video tape. The sixteen-inch platters were carried by the artists in the days before high fidelity.

The transcriptions were nothing but a large-diameter record turning at 33 1/3 rpm and played by a 78 rpm needle. At these speeds, the outer grooves had such speed that they allowed the closest thing to high fidelity. This provided the "punch" that was later

10 Wayne Erbsen, "Wiley and Zeke—The Morris Brothers," *Bluegrass Unlimited*, August, 1980.

11 Wayne W. Daniel, "Wilma Lee Cooper, America's Most Authentic Mountain Singer," *Bluegrass Unlimited*, February, 1982, p. 16.

12 He still has that old Gibson he used in those days. "You can hold it up and see daylight though it just about anywhere."

13 George Shuffler during a telephone interview, March 1993.

provided by the 45 rpm record and the improved technology which came with it. As the needle neared the center of the transcriptions, some fidelity was lost because of the lost speed. Nevertheless, many radio stations used them. These were not for public consumption because the public had no phonographs capable of playing them back.

According to collector and veteran performer Ray Patterson, "Even the 33 1/3, 16-inch transcriptions was recorded with a 78 rpm needle. So you had to play them back with a 78 needle even though they was 33 1/3. But they sounded very good! Way back when they was makin' transcriptions that way, they just didn't have a bunch of record companies and people in the business who supplied stations with all kinds of material, see. Well, they was transcriptions companies back in the late '30s and early '40s that just went across the country makin' transcriptions of different kinds of western music—they called it 'cowboy'—they was even brave enough to call it 'hillbilly' music. They transferred these recordings from 78s over to the big 16-inch transcriptions and they would sell them to radio stations. Then as they got more record companies and things got more commercial, radio stations was supplied with an awful lot of records comin' from all directions. In fact, they got so many that they didn't play all of them."

Wolfman Jack, 1973.

Mr. Patterson recalled that recording one of these things was a "one-shot deal"; it was expensive, and once an artist began recording on it there was no going back to try it again except to begin the whole expensive process again. When they began recording, the artists had to have their throats cleared and they had to be ready to go for fifteen minutes.

Bill Bolick, of the **Blue Sky Boys**, refused to have the recording device in the same room where he was performing because it made him nervous and unable to play with the comfort and freedom which produces the best live performances. "So," Patterson continued, "a lot of the stuff they made on the transcriptions wasn't really some of their best material or their best balance on the mike, see. It was just a standard radio broadcast. They recorded quite a few of them. And when they had to go out of town somewhere and be gone doin' their personal appearance shows, they would play these big 16-inch transcriptions. Of course, it had commercials in

there and everything that it needed, and it sounded like they was right there in the studio."

A major use of transcriptions was at the XE radio stations just south of the United States/Mexico border in Texas. They also played 78 rpm records of various hillbilly stars on the stations. One of the first of the border stations was begun by Doctor Brinkley who started XERA in 1931 to tell the world of his surgical/medical skills. Considered a "quack" by many, he nevertheless kept it going for ten years and became a multi-millionaire as a result.

In the 1980s, two albums were released on County (551 and 552) which "convey for the first time on commercial recordings the same music that excited listeners heard as they faithfully tuned in the daily broadcast [at WCYB]. The transcriptions—originally made to substitute for like performances when the band was away on a show date—reveal that there were some real differences between the performers' broadcast music and their early recordings. Not only did they perform a good deal of material that was never released commercially, but the looseness, informality, and good fun that endeared these bluegrass pioneers to their fans comes through on the transcriptions in a way that records rarely, if ever, capture."[14]

U.S. regulations didn't allow radio stations to have more than 50,000 watts of power so the actual antenna for these stations, where the radio license was bought, transmitted up to 500,000 watts from Mexico on the AM band. They were even known to put out a million watts of power at times. The stations reached all parts of the United States after dark, even reaching Canada, and other parts of the world occasionally. The output of XERF's antenna was focused to the north and severely interfered with normal U.S. stations throughout the continent.

Doc Brinkley and other XE station owners often hired many live, hillbilly groups to play daily at the station to help advertise on the station. Brinkley, a pioneer in the use of radio transcriptions, often had the groups record their music on these transcriptions. The groups would record them in San Antonio (and other places) and send them to all the XE stations across the border. Brinkley hired acts such as the **Carter Family**[15], Jimmie Rodgers, the **Maddox Brothers and Rose**, Patsy Montana, Cowboy Slim Rhinehart, the **Callahan**

[17] Jack Tottle, "WCYB—Bristol's Farm and Fun Time," *Bluegrass Unlimited*, October, 1987, p. 25.

[15] In addition to these live performances, in the case of the Carter Family, they would get paid by sponsor Consolidated Chemical Company to record the transcriptions in San Antonio and send them to the stations.

Brothers, the **Delmore Brothers**, Lefty Frizell, Ernest Tubb and Hank Williams. Some of the entertainers who worked at WWL in New Orleans recorded the transcriptions and sent them to the XE stations.

One of the popular entertainers on XERA was the **Picard Family**. They played hillbilly music and advertised anything which would sell: "How many of you have gray hair?" asked Obed "Dad" Pickard. "Well, you just listen to this announcement please. Don't let gray hair cheat you out of your job and cause you a lot of worry. No, sirree, that isn't necessary anymore. Not when it's so easy to get rid of gray-hair worries and handicaps. And here is all you have to do. Get a bottle of Kolorbak from your nearest drug or department store." The product was guaranteed "or your money back."[16] According to *Border Radio*, "The Chicago-based drug manufacturer received as many as 20,000 responses a week to the **Pickard Family** broadcasts, a marketing gold mine for manufacturer and performer alike. 'All my dad's old friends from the Grand Ole Opry on WSM in Nashville and WLW in Cincinnati wanted to know if there were any openings down there,' remembered Ruth Pickard. 'Those other stations weren't paying much money in those days. My dad was making a thousand dollars a week, which was a lot of money in those days, back when the Depression was on. The rest of us got about a hundred a week.'"

Crazy Water Crystals was a laxative which was advertised for anyone suffering from a condition "that was caused or being made worse by a sluggish system." The company's popular, hillbilly Crazy Gang Show was first broadcast from a Dallas studio but later moved to the lobby of the Crazy Hotel in Mineral Wells, Texas, where hotel guests who patronized the Crazy Water Bar would enjoy the show. Cowboy entertainer Jim Turner, who was on the border stations during the mid-forties, said, "When I got to my first border station, I learned very fast that they didn't hire you to sing. They hired you to sell, sell, sell; I was a pitch man. A pitch man's success depended entirely upon his ability to pull mail. The greatest announcers in the country would come to the border, and they wouldn't last overnight. The best radio pitch men came off the carnival or the vaudeville halls."[17]

Brinkley's station was forced to cease operation in 1941 due to Mexican and American governmental interference. Some of the stations would begin anew after the War. The XERB and XERF stations continued with Wolfman Jack playing rock and roll, beginning in 1960. Eventually, the stations ended up playing mostly the sermons of preachers. For the most part, the XE stations were gone by 1986.

Also during this period came the disc jockey who would play records on the radio. "The disc jockey," wrote Bill Crawford and Gene Fowler, "became a dominant force on the airways after WW2 partly because of a court ruling that allowed radio stations in the United States to play purchased phonograph records over the air, a move that had been fought by performers' organizations since the beginning of radio. The postwar years also saw the first glimmerings of television, which threatened to dominate the broadcasting media. Radio operators across the country scrambled for ways to trim costs and the impending video invasion, and the platter-spinning disc jockey was the obvious solution."

According to Dick Hall, "The days of disc recordings and 78s all ended when the wire recorders came in. They were on a spool; they were wire. And I remember the station had one when I left in, like, '48. It was a pain in the butt because they would all get wound up wrong; it was a magnetic-type recording. After the War, the magnetic tape recordings came to the United States, which Germany invented. That's what deleted the transcriptions and such because it was easier to put on a reel of tape. You didn't have those big ol' 16-inch discs to ship around the country." Some transcriptions were made as late as the '50s, but reel-to-reel tape was its undoing.

Mike Seeger recorded in the field with a "portable" tape recorder[18]

Mike Seeger. Photo by John Ullman, courtesy Library of Congress.

Beginning in late 1952, folklorist Mike Seeger went out into the field—into peoples' homes and where they performed—to record their talent. Until this time, this had been nearly impossible because of the bulkiness of recording onto a disc. Now that tape recorders (reel-to-reel) were invented, it enabled him to move around as never before.

His first recordings with his American-made recorder

[16] Gene Fowler and Bill Crawford, *Border Radio* (Austin: Texas Monthly Press, 1987), p. 173.

[17] Ibid., p. 183.

[18] Interview with Mike Seeger, half-brother of renown folk musician Pete Seeger, at IBMA, September, 1992. Seeger is not only an accomplished folk musician, but an author, a record producer and folklorist. He first heard Flatt and Scruggs in 1952.

were of the black guitarist Elizabeth Cotten, and a square dance musician. "But I really didn't get started until '65, '66 when I went into the (Bill Monroe's) Bluegrass Music Park when I recorded Bill Monroe, Lester Flatt and Earl Scruggs, and the Stanley brothers. I didn't interview any of them. I set up a tape recorder on stage and let them do whatever they did. I didn't have much money at the time so I was rather cheap with the tape. I didn't turn it on always when they were talking—which was sad. They had a lot to say...especially Carter Stanley. He was a good talker. He and Mac Wiseman were really good at talking on stage. Even Bill Monroe once in awhile would have something to say. Charlie Monroe had a great laugh (Seeger laughed). Those were the things I remember the most.

"This was not in a festival situation; there were no festivals then," Seeger explained. "They were just country music parks where the local band would have a forty-minute set and they would talk and sing and joke and play music. And then they would sometimes have two bluegrass bands, each doing sets starting at one o'clock in the afternoon. They'd do a set, have a break, do a set, have a break, until ten or eleven at night on Sundays. Families and people would come out from that area of northern Maryland, southern Pennsylvania. Most of the people actually were from Virginia.

"When you think of somebody having the vision to do something like that, it often doesn't start as a vision. Just like Bill Clifton's first bluegrass festival; Bill did have more of a vision than most of the people there. But as far as starting a festival movement, I don't know if that concept was there. Musicians, definitely, were conscious of it being a special event—having so many bluegrass musicians on the same program. That was a big move then in '61. The vision of bluegrass being a world, a community of musicians...I mean, that was an interesting idea of having bluegrass being commercial."

Continuing in this 1992 interview at IBMA, Mr. Seeger said that he wasn't at Carlton Haney's first 1965

bluegrass festival because he had to work that weekend; he only heard about it. But he was able to attend the 1966 event and described it, "It was a *great* event! The feeling was *really* high during it."

The tape recording industry, EPs and LPs

This 45 rpm recording by Flatt and Scruggs was found in a jukebox. The songs were originally recorded in 1961.

The year 1945 brought the introduction of tape recording into the United States from Germany where it had been used since the 1930s. The invention helped allow record companies to exist and prosper in areas which were not known as being centers of the record business— such as the country music industry establishing a hub in Nashville by 1950.[19] The first publishing house in Nashville to pursue this new industry was formed by Roy Acuff and ex-Tin Pan Alley tunesmith Fred Rose in 1943. Rose was already a successful songwriter for some of Acuff's songs. Even though they specialized in country musicians such as Hank Williams, Rose was often able to get pop artists of the day such as Mitch Miller, Tony Bennett, Rosemary Clooney and Jo Stafford to record the tunes of his country artists.

"Hank Williams' songs weren't the first to cross from country to pop," said Dick Spottswood, "but there were enough of them to point to country songs as an important new source for national hits in the waning days of Tin Pan Alley."[20]

The introduction of tape recording also allowed longer songs. And editing. The previous practice of recording directly to disc did not allow editing. Now, the longer songs could be "waxed" on EPs (Extended Play 45 rpm) and LPs (Long Play 33 1/3 rpm). The 33 1/3 record speed had been used since 1926 when Victor used it in the production of sound tracks for movies. Movie film was not to have its own sound tracks attached to it until 1931.

The 33 1/3s were abandoned in 1935 due to poor quality and cost, but not until some important classical

[19] All major labels had an office there. They focused their activities around the star system which WSM's Grand Ole Opry had created.

[20] Richard K. Spottswood, "Country Music and the Phonograph," *Bluegrass Unlimited*, February, 1987, p. 21.

and jazz artists had been recorded (but not country). Program transcriptions continued to use 33 1/3 until 1948 when Columbia reintroduced the product with more quality in a more portable and affordable form—the 33 1/3 rpm seven-inch disc (they did not last long on the market due to poor sales). Even Bill Monroe and the **Stanley Brothers** recorded on these smaller 33 1/3s.

Another significant event about 1945 was when Victor re-invented records with the introduction of 45s (EPs) which had a large hole in the center, and sold phonographs which could play them. Mac Wiseman recorded a 45 which had four songs on it for Dot, a feature which became a standard in the industry in the 1950s. Dot also released its first 12-inch 33 1/3 rpm LP of Tommy Jackson's fiddle recordings, "Popular Square Dance Music" in 1957.

Mail order 45s were only 55 cents each, postpaid from Wayside Music Co., Detroit. From Cincinnati, the Jimmie Skinner Music Company sold 78s at 98 cents each and 45s for 89 cents.

About 1956, country music left the 10-inch 78 rpm format for their music in favor of the 7-inch 45 rpm extended-play (EP) and 7-inch 45 rpm singles. But there seemed to be considerable interest in the LP album format. A few country records were issued as LPs by August 1956, especially on the Folkways and Riverside labels.

The first bluegrass LPs in the U.S.

In 1956, a Mac Wiseman LP was released in England. In January 1957, Folkways released the first LP (#2314) which featured bluegrass music. It was called "American Banjo, Tunes and Songs in Scruggs Style"[21] and had thirty-one tunes by fifteen different artists including Junie Scruggs, Snuffy Jenkins (and his band, the **Hired Hands**), Larry Richardson (**Lonesome Pine**

This EP 45 rpm record had 3 songs on each side. Notice that the label takes advantage of tremendous popularity of the 5-string banjo by the words "Bluegrass Recordings By All Star Artists featuring 5-string Banjo."

Fiddlers), Eric Weissberg and several others. It was produced by Pete Kuykendall and Mike Seeger and gives a good anthology of the modern banjo style. According to Rounder Records' Ken Irwin, this album predated all other LPs of this music, including King Records' **Reno and Smiley** release by several months.

The LP format, a popular medium for other types of music for a while now, was just coming into its own in bluegrass music and it's not surprising that both "American Banjo" and **Flatt and Scruggs**'s "Foggy Mountain Jamboree" featured the five-string banjo because, with Scruggs at the "point", people were hungry for anything with the banjo associated with it. Producers Mike Seeger, Don Pierce and Syd Nathan absolutely knew it was time for such products. It's good that bluegrass music did not remain strictly as singles—as many in that industry would have had it.

The LP "revolution" was now complete but the LP was still not be available to less influential bluegrass bands. The large record companies, in their presumed knowledge that they knew what was best for their artists and all consumers, still forced the smaller groups to put out only singles, most of which were now 45 rpm EPs. But the smaller (independent) labels were more flexible, and moved faster than the big ones. Don Pierce of Mercury put out several LPs in early 1958 by Jimmie Skinner, Carl Story, **Flatt and Scruggs**, and the **Stanley Brothers**.

There were more new bluegrass and bluegrass-related LPs out in February 1958 than ever before. They came from Mercury-Starday (three, in Nashville under Don Pierce), King (two, in Cincinnati), Judson (two, a subsidiary of New York's Riverside label) and Elektra (one, which featured Roger Sprung and his **Shanty Mountain Boys**[22]. Before 1959 was over, King Records had put out **Reno and Smiley**'s "Sacred Songs"; their "Instrumentals" soon followed.

---

[21] This record was re-released in 1990 by Smithsonian Folkways which included 43 re-mastered tunes by 15 five-string banjo players from original tapes and included sixteen previously-unissued tracks. The re-release was called "American Banjo Three Finger and Scruggs Style." Neither the original nor the new version included the banjo playing of Earl Scruggs.

[22] Who were Sprung (banjo), Mike Cohen (guitar) and Lionel Kilberg (bass).

Also of significance was "Banjos, Banjos, and More Banjos" which featured Eric Weissberg and Dick Weissman on one of the first double-banjo duets with bluegrass and frailing banjos. Released originally on the Riverside subsidiary Judson in 1958, the album included the non-bluegrass banjo styles by Billy Faier and Weissman, and the bluegrass style by Weissberg.

Seeger continued promoting bluegrass in 1959 by producing "Mountain Music, Bluegrass Style." He included a twelve-page brochure which was, according to Neil Rosenberg, was "a veritable ethnology of blue-grass music," starting with the history of the original Monroe band. Yet, as historical as the intent might have been, the music was not of Scruggs or Monroe or Stanley, but of the lesser-known group, **Earl Taylor and the Stoney Mountain Boys**, along with the consider-able, individual talents of "B" Lilly, Don Stover, Eric Weissberg, Bob Yellin and Tex Logan.

In October 1959, Columbia released the record known as "the second long-playing album of bluegrass music", "Foggy Mountain Jamboree" (CL-1019), by **Flatt and Scruggs and the Foggy Mountain Boys**. The tunes were compiled from sessions between 1951 to 1957.

The recording industry was moving to still another new format—the stereo LP album—by 1958. That February, RCA Victor introduced stereo versions of all their new albums. Many record companies followed, including Atlantic Records in November 1960. This seven-album set "Southern Folk Heritage Series" was recorded in the field by Alan Lomax. The record was not purely bluegrass but did give a healthy example of it with thirteen cuts. This breakthrough LP reflected the popularity of bluegrass at the beginnings of the folk boom.

The emergence of rhythm and blues

In 1954, one of the new developments in the music industry which was bound to affect bluegrass music was a surge among teenagers in their interest in rhythm and blues music. This led to rockabilly music and the era of Elvis Presley. Record companies picked up on this trend almost immediately and began putting out records which fit this new genre.

The country and pop cross-overs in the '50s and '60s

In a 1991 interview, Paul "Moon" Mullins described what was happening in the record industry during the '50s and '60s, "The people in Nashville were trying to

record 'cross-overs.' By that, I mean a country record that would play on the pop charts and sell to the people who like pop music as well as country; that's what they were striving for. That's when, as I see it, how the industry went to hell. [They were] trying to straddle the fence and play to both audiences and not calling themselves 'country' but calling themselves something else. I agree that some of that music was good, but why didn't they call it 'cosmopolitan'? Why did they have to call it 'country' when it wasn't country at all. Columbia Records spent how many thousands of dollars to make Ray Price a pop singer? You know, he was first called 'the Cherokee Cowboy' when I first started playing his records. They put a whole stringed orchestra behind him and it changed it. And I refused to play that stuff on the air when there was *good* country to play."

The "Nashville sound" and Chet Atkins

Technology was influencing how recordings were being made during the early 1950s. Taped studio ses-sions allowed more consistent recordings. Over-dub-bing and taping made it easier to record a song over if mistakes were made during the take.

According to author Charles Wolfe, "Although the major record companies were sending more and more of their executives to work with the growing Nashville recording scene, two native Tennesseans were really responsible for what was soon to be called 'the Nash-ville sound'. These men were Owen Bradley and Chet Atkins. They, more than anyone else, helped create the special qualities that made a Nashville recording differ-ent from others and made a Nashville recording session a unique blend of creativity and technology."[23]

Producers like Atkins and Bradley brought a sophis-tication to country music; their Nashville sound brought the music out of the hills and brought it "uptown". The idea was to make it more palatable to pop music listen-ers. Instead of fiddles, records had a chorus of violins. The banjo, the steel guitar and other hillbilly sounds were replaced with smooth, polished arrangements with smooth voices such as Eddy Arnold, Jim Reeves and Patsy Cline. Atkins claims only to have simplified the music, but what he helped do is turn Nashville into a billion dollar industry and recording center.[24]

Atkins was a fiddler and guitarist since the early 1940s. After a time with the **Carter Family** and WNOX, he became a studio musician where he helped Hank Williams on a few songs—arranging and playing. Even-tually, he became the most-recorded solo artist in history. He moved to Nashville in 1950 and by 1957 he was in charge of Victor's operation in Nashville and produced records for major country singers. He pro-

---

[23] Charles K. Wolfe, *Tennessee Strings*, (Knoxville: The University of Tennessee Press, 1977), p. 96.

[24] The Nashville sound was a rival to the Bakersfield Sound in the 1960s. There was a refreshing difference in the West Coast music and it was probably brighter and maybe happier than what Nashville was putting out for public consumption. The Nashville sound, according to Harlan Howard, had a lot of "bottom" to it—a lot of bass. Bakersfield country artists such as Buck Owens and Merle Haggard, who had migrated from the Texas/Oklahoma area, took a lot of the bass out and added some "high end" to play better on the AM car radios of the day.

moted over-dubbing, the removal of the heretofore obligatory steel guitar and fiddle, the introduction of horns and strings, and the use of the piano as a lead instrument. He was responsible for Charlie Pride's acceptance into the country music scene. He tried to take into consideration the tremendous popularity of Elvis and rock music and didn't ignore it as so many others tried to do. But even in all this "progress", he found traditional music slipping away from popularity. In 1976, Atkins told *Rolling Stone*, "I've said that I hope country music doesn't completely lose its identity—and I apologized for anything I did in taking it too far up-town, which I sometimes did because we were just trying to sell records." Owen Bradley's piano playing and arrangements are prevalent on the next generation of country music.

Mac Wiseman on an independent record label revolution

In an interview for an article in *Bluegrass Unlimited* in 1987, Mac Wiseman spoke about the music, "Traditional and bluegrass music have been the victims of a kind of musical segregation, as insidious as racial segregation used to be in the deep South. Big record company executives believe in charts, reports from radio stations that never play bluegrass, economic surveys that show low sales in rural localities. They don't know how many records are sold at festivals. They don't know how many people attend festivals and concerts. It's frustrating.

"We need an independent label revolution like we had in the fifties. In those days, King Records and Sun Records—little companies—were recording rock 'n' roll, country and traditional music and getting it racked in record stores. Today's independents would have to make deals with larger companies to distribute and sell their records. There's a lot of talented groups and singers and the more bluegrass music is recorded and made available the more it'll be heard. It's a way to make executives of big record companies aware of the music's potential. Record executives aren't opposed to bluegrass, they're concerned with sales figures. They don't understand how great bluegrass' appeal is or could be."[25]

Wiseman is an advocate of bluegrass videos but insists they must be produced in a professional manner. The 1960s "Hootenanny" television show gave the audience a false impression of our music, he feels. It "evoked a pseudo-side of bluegrass that confused the audience. Bluegrass musicians are serious musicians and shouldn't be presented in a manner that demeans their artistry."[26]

The recording industry is slanted against bluegrass music

Record producer Dave Samuelson wrote in an article about the making of a record, "The costs of recording in Nashville are often prohibitively expensive and the results of bluegrass sessions frequently turn out to be far from ideal. The Nashville establishment has never been receptive to bluegrass, and the attitudes of the major record labels and many studios reflect this. At present, only one bluegrass musician—Bill Monroe—is signed to a major label, and his records in the past decade sometimes have been marred by poor production and careless engineering. Other bluegrass acts working under the Nashville sound system often found their means of music tampered with. Under pressure by their record labels to produce 'hit' material, such major talent as **Jim and Jesse**, Mac Wiseman and Lester Flatt produced some of their most uninspired recordings.

"One of the primary reasons bluegrass recordings from Nashville sound so shabby is that their engineers have been conditioned to use assembly-line techniques. Some of them may balk at the rigid disciplines imposed by recording bluegrass, audibly grumbling about instrument leakage into the vocal mikes, vocal leakage into the instrumental mikes, and the boring repetition of take after take. An experience like this can affect your mood and the quality of the music you record.

"In all fairness, there definitely are a few studios in Nashville that are sympathetic to bluegrass..."[27]

The folk era was in full swing in 1960 when this album was made. The Blue Ridge Mountain Boys were Jake Landers, Rual Yarbrough and Herschel Sizemore with guests for this LP.

25 J. Wesley Clark and J. Michael Hosford, "Mac Wiseman: Once More with Feeling," *Bluegrass Unlimited*, August, 1987, p. 16.
26 Ibid., p. 18.
27 Dave Samuelson, "Making a Record, Part 2," *Bluegrass Unlimited*, January, 1982, p. 16.

Martha Hearon Adcock on sound systems

Martha Hearon joined **II Generation** in April 1973 as sound person. She was a folk musician with a musical background of classical and folk and was an instrument repairperson at Nashville's Old Time Pickin' Parlor when she met Eddie Adcock. She spoke about her future husband, "In their exploration into what some have called 'bluegrass-rock,' the electronic and audio needs made a lasting impression on Eddie. He is most adamant about the requirement of a good sound system for their show. It goes back to the old days of bad systems when somebody would say, 'Turn it up, we can't hear you!' You would turn it up and it would distort and then they would say, 'Turn it down, it's too loud.' Actually it wasn't too loud—it was distorting and the only thing they knew to change was the volume." Adcock says that "a good sound system will help keep a band together so they don't have to worry about anything but just playing their best."[28]

Dean Webb's mandolin playing

Dean Webb, in an interview in for *Mandolin World News*, 1980, described himself as a "light" player now "because I've been electric for some time now. My theory on playing fast at the volume I want is to just bear down on the volume pedal and play faster. If you're playing acoustically and trying to be heard, it takes quite a bit of energy and you start knocking off strings. With the electric thing, breaking strings just isn't a problem. I play acoustically in the studio and I like the warmth an acoustic instrument has."

Videos

Videos—the dramatic acting out of a song's lyrics—are an important method of getting people to buy an artist's records. Nashville's Country Music Television (CMT) and The Nashville Network (TNN) are now dominant in the video field. Now the audience can not only hear a song played, they can see it played in a setting which displays the artists ideas of what the song is all about. The visual image is an important method of getting a recording sold because the modern buyer can relate to it more easily.

Today's methods of exposing music and performers to the public are considerably different from the early days of recording and television. In the old days, a record would get sold only if the purchaser either heard the group live on the radio or saw the group at one of its concerts. It took a long time for a group or a performer to become popular with the public.

Bluegrass singer Alison Krauss has made tremendous strides in bluegrass music by getting her videos in front of the viewing public. Her music has crossed over country and bluegrass boundaries because of its sincerity and ability to project the songwriting to the audience. Her work has transcended the confines of artists such as Ralph Stanley or Bill Monroe in this new video age, and now sells records to audiences who have never even heard of bluegrass before seeing it on the television.

But to say that Alison Krauss' success is as a result of the popularity of her videos would be an error. She is known as a young lady who cares very much about bluegrass, and she is talented enough to have the ability to choose any music field she wants. She has, indeed, had those opportunities and turned them down because she loves bluegrass. As Ron Block put it, "Alison's success has come about mostly through having and continually developing a remarkable voice, playing fervently tasteful fiddle, searching out timelessly believable songs, arranging them with extensive imagination, and founding it all upon an honest love for music and an equally honest disregard for easy popularity."[29]

Compact discs

Compact discs were just becoming accepted in bluegrass music in 1986 after much of the rest of the music industry had already stocked music store shelves with their CD products. The first releases by Sugar Hill were "Down South" by Doc and Merle Watson, and the "Old and In the Way" album (a re-release). Rounder released the classic "J.D. Crowe and the New South" album, Tony Rice's "Cold on the Shoulder," Ricky Skaggs' "Family and Friends," and a one-hour compilation from the **Bluegrass Album Band.** By the beginning of 1990 decade, CDs were, by far, the favorite medium for all kinds of music.

The digital recording technique provided an accuracy in recording never before achieved. Inferior, old, recording projects could come out clean by deleting the "digit" which applied to "noise," tape hiss or scratches. Many recording companies spent a huge amount of energy in "re-creating" valuable, original music which had, up until that time, been undesirable because of the quality of the master recording.

Soon, a compact disc was able to hold so much data that it became "interactive"—responding to the actions of the user. Personal computers became capable of not only displaying data on a screen, they could play music at the same time as video clips of the band playing it were viewed on the screen simultaneously.

28 Pete Kuykendall, "II Generation," *Bluegrass Unlimited*, March, 1975, p. 15.

29 Musician in Transition," *Bluegrass Unlimited*, January, 1982, p. 15.

Radio and Television - Table of Contents

Radio and Television

The protagonists of this chapter tell how they got into this business and how hard it was to keep the job. They explain the importance of the media toward making a living in their art form. The reader will see how the music changed as a result of the changing policies and technologies of radio and television. The feelings expressed in their words are not just words from people who lived a long time ago; they describe *how* they were raised. In order to understand bluegrass music today, we should understand something about how these people lived and played their music. But first, let's introduce their medium.

The beginnings of the radio industry

The first commercial radio station, 8MK, was licensed August 20, 1920. (It is now WWJ, Detroit.) The program "Tonight's Dinner" was the first. Local election returns were broadcast August 31st. KDKA of Pittsburgh, licensed October 27, 1920, offered a semi-weekly broadcast from November 2, 1920, to December 1, 1920.

The first baseball game was broadcast, play-by-play, on August 5, 1921.

Advertising on a commercial radio broadcast was sponsored for the first time by the Queensboro Realty Corporation, Jackson Heights, New York City, on August 28, 1922, over station WEAF, the experimental station of the American Telephone and Telegraph Company. The commercial rate was $100 for ten minutes. H. M. Blackwell spoke for ten minutes about Hawthorne Court, a dwelling in Jackson Heights.

In the early '20s, "Radio was becoming an important entertainment factor. With the record industry centered in New York City, that city's tastes were inevitably those foisted off on records to the country as a whole."[1]

As of 1922, the record business was booming but it was aimed at the more affluent types who would buy recordings of light opera, parlor songs and dance orchestras. Before long, country music would have several artists out on wax, but the record industry felt seriously threatened by the increased number of radio stations; after all, who would *buy* a record when they could just turn on a radio and listen for free? Indeed, RCA record sales fell by over half between 1921 and 1925.

The radio industry was also in a technological change because crystal sets, to which only one person can listen to a broadcast station at a time, were being replaced by radios with batteries and speakers which could be heard by all those in a room. In 1919, there were no more than 5000 receiving sets in America; by 1924, there were over two and a half million. As of 1923, there were 1400 licensed radio stations in the United States. One-third of all money spent on household furniture that year went for a radio receiver: $350 million.

RCA's radio station, WWJZ in New York City, offered 340 soprano solos, 98 baritone solos, seven football games, bedtime stories, six baseball games, boxing matches, harmonica solos, organ concerts, plays and lectures. Listeners loved their new form of entertainment. But material was being used faster than it was being produced.

The '30s and '40s were the Golden Age of Radio. Wherever you turned on the dial was some form of entertainment, comedy, news, drama and suspense. By the early 1940s, some of the stations left their live performance format and hired disc jockeys to spin records with a formula which provided each station with a personality definable to its listeners. Radio became a specialized medium which met listeners' specific desires/habits in an informal, intimate way. And it became a medium which focused on meeting local needs and the needs of a mobile audience.

A radio advertising contract for FM (frequency modulation) broadcasts was signed December 9, 1940, by the Longines Watch Company and provided for the broadcasting of Longines time signals by W2XOR, New York, for twenty-six weeks beginning January 1, 1941. On April 1, 1941, the experimental license was replaced by a commercial license W71NY. This station was operated from 8:30 a.m. to 11:30 p.m. on a frequency of 47,100 kilocycles. FM radio soon gained popularity; public radio flourished on FM and found audiences which weren't there previously.

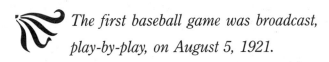

The first baseball game was broadcast, play-by-play, on August 5, 1921.

[1] Richard K. Spottswood, "Country Music and the Phonograph," *Bluegrass Unlimited*, February, 1987, p. 19.

WSB

WSB was one of the first influential radio stations to play hillbilly music. WSB radio went on the air in Atlanta, Georgia, March 15, 1922. By June, WSB put out 500 watts (and 1000 watts in 1925) and was very influential in thirty states when it put out 50,000 watts of power. Prime time was 10:45 p.m.. Broadcasts of this station were heard by an estimated two million people.

Okeh Records, founded about 1920 in New York City, was involved in setting up a studio in remote locations to record local popular talent which radio was already exploiting. In June 1923, Okeh went to Atlanta, with Ralph Peer on staff, where WSB had been operating for over a year. A local retailer convinced Peer to record locally-famous Fiddlin' John Carson. To everyone's surprise, they sold well. Soon Okeh, back at its base in New York City, was to record Ernest V. Stoneman and Henry Whitter. Columbia Records then sent its mobile unit to Atlanta and established a yearly tradition of visiting there to record the local hillbillies.

In 1926, WSB held the first fiddling contest ever to be broadcast over the air with the audience as judges. The contest was decided by letters, telegrams and postcards from listeners in twenty states. The winner of the $50 first prize was won by J.C. Price of Clanton of Alabama. He competed against twenty-two others. Fourth place was won by a future champion of the State of Georgia, a woman named Mrs. J.P. (Anita Sorrelles) Wheeler, fiddler with the **Dixie String Band.**

WBAP of Fort Worth, in January 1924, became the first radio station to regularly use a barn dance (i.e., country music variety show) format. But WSB (Atlanta) and WLS (Chicago) were the first to make substantial commitments to the use of country music in their programming. Author Charles Wolfe wrote, "One witness has said that announcer Lambdin Kay, who ran [WSB], used 'anybody who could sing, whistle, play a musical instrument, or even breathe heavily.' Fortunately, the hills around Atlanta were filled with talented folk musicians, and soon the station became a hotbed of all sorts of musical activity including record making."[2] WSB soon became a powerful 50,000 watt station and helped Atlanta become a center for the country music industry. Also helping Atlanta's popularity were the fiddle contests which centered there for many of those early years.

WSB began its WSB Barn Dance in 1940. Its musicians not only played on the radio weekly but toured regularly to promote the show and try to make a living. Bands present were Martha Carson and her son with her husband James (Carson) Roberts, Bill "Too Old to Cut the Mustard" Carlisle, Mac Wiseman, and Boudleaux Bryant, half of the famed husband and wife songwriting team.

WLS

On April 12, 1923, WLS began broadcasting at the WLS studios in Chicago. On April 19th, the National Barn Dance was aired from Chicago's now-defunct Sherman Hotel. George D. Hay was the announcer. A year and a half later he would be hired by WSM in Nashville to found its own barn dance which he later renamed the Grand Ole Opry. In 1932, the broadcasts were moved to the 8th Street Theater; in 1957, they returned to the WLS studios.

Though the WLS barn dance was unappealing to WLS executives, hundreds of telegrams, letters, post cards and telephone calls came in from rural people.

Most of the stars were vaudeville performers. The first real star was Bradley Kincaid, a Kentucky college student. He made only $15 per week until he learned how to be more commercial in his performances. This wage was in spite of his tremendous popularity with his version of "Barbara Allen." Kincaid recalled that "Sears, Roebuck was operating the station as a way to promote their sales and as a goodwill gesture—they didn't charge anything for the radio time. Up until this point "there was no such thing as a commercial anywhere in radio that I know of."[3] "One thing Sears always prided itself on was responding to every request that came in. When I started singing these old ballads that had been brought over from the old country, people started writing in, wanting copies of the songs. Well, they were songs that hadn't been published—at least not in this country and not in hundreds of years."[4] Kincaid soon announced the sale of his songs in a book for fifty cents each. He sold all 30,000 copies before they came off the presses. Now that WLS executives saw money coming in, his salary went to $100 per week.

Kincaid continued, "Sears, fearing it might be charged with conflict of interest for owning the principal medium on which it advertised, sold WLS to *Prairie Farmer* magazine" on October 1, 1928. WLS also began the booking of its performers into paid venues throughout the community.

The National Barn Dance in Chicago was at its peak of popularity in 1930; they had to deny admission to 10,000 people into one special performance. A year and a half later, WLS began charging admission to its theater which held 200. During the 1930s, the Barn Dance troupers (those who toured in the summertime to play fairs and shows) made $15 per day—excellent wages for the Depression. Soprano George Gobel was eleven in 1931 when he got his start there. By the time the Tom Mix Straight Shooters Show appeared on the scene later that decade, Gobel was making $150 per week.

---

[2] Charles Wolfe, *Country; The Music and the Musicians*, (New York: Abbeville Press, Inc., 1988), p. 59.

[3] Ibid., p. 58.

[4] Jack Hurst, "Barn Dance Days—Chicago's National Barn Dance," *Bluegrass Unlimited*, April, 1986, pp. 57, 58. The article in this magazine was a reprint from a 1984 article in *The Chicago Tribune*.

The barn dance phenomenon

WWVA's Jamboree, Wheeling, West Virginia, became reality in 1933 and could be heard in eighteen states and six Canadian provinces. Other barn dance shows during the 1930s included:
- Renfro Valley Barn Dance (WHAS, Louisville, Kentucky)
- Hill Billy Champions (KMOX, St. Louis, Missouri)
- Sunset Valley Barn Dance (KSTP, Minneapolis)
- Saddle Mountain Round-Up (KVOO, Tulsa)
- Hoosier Hop (WOWO, Ft. Wayne, Indiana)
- Sleepy Hollow Ranch (WFIL, Philadelphia)
- Boone County Jamboree (WLW, Cincinnati)
- Crazy Water Crystals Barn Dance (WBT, Charlotte, North Carolina)
- WHN Barn Dance (WHN, New York)
- Iowa Barn Dance Frolic (WHO, Des Moines)
- WSB Barn Dance (WSB, Atlanta)
- National Barn Dance (WLS, Chicago)
- Grand Ole Opry (WSM, Nashville)

Even though some of these live radio programs were aired on national networks, none of them were any real competition to WLS and WSM. During the next two decades more barn dances came into being:

Painting of George D. Hay hanging in the Ryman Auditorium.

- Old Dominion Barn Dance (WRVA, Richmond, Virginia)
- Big D Jamboree (KRLD, Dallas)
- Farm and Fun Time (WCYB, Bristol, Tennessee)
- Louisiana Hayride (KWKH, Shreveport)
- Mid-Day Merry-Go-Round (WNOX, Knoxville)
- Town Hall Party (Los Angeles)

The Grand Ole Opry, George D. Hay, and the beginnings of WSM

George D. Hay was born in Attica, Indiana, in 1885. The victim of a broken home, after age ten he took many odd jobs to support himself but he read widely, became educated, and was scholarly in his demeanor.

By 1920, he was a reporter for the *Commercial Appeal* in Memphis. Eventually, he got a by-lined column "Howdy Judge" (named after his nickname "Judge" for "George" probably). In 1923, the *Commercial Appeal* bought radio station WMC and Hay became its Radio Editor with a nightly, one-hour broadcast where he told what he had seen during the day on his police beat. One year he covered 137 murders. He began calling himself "The Solemn Old Judge".

In 1923, Hay moved to Chicago's new radio station, WLS. In what was probably the first "talk-a-thon," he raised $215,000 for the Red Cross to help victims of a Midwest storm. His notoriety brought him to the forefront of recognition and he was voted America's most outstanding announcer. At WLS, he helped develop the WLS National Barn Dance for the princely sum of $75 per week.

By 1925, he was offered a job as Manager at WSM in Nashville for $250 to $300 on the basis of his experiences at WMC and WLS. Hay was glad to leave the big city and get back to the South. His new job at WSM included programming at the new station which featured a Saturday night folk music program called the WSM Barn Dance. Hay started work, and the WSM Barn Dance, about three weeks after the station came on the air.

WSM was begun October 5, 1925, when Edwin Craig, a vice president for the National Life and Accident Insurance Company, convinced his company to start a 1000 watt radio station (with call sign WSM which represented the words "We Shield Millions") and to advertise their insurance services on it. Herbert Hoover signed the license. The five-year-old insurance company had recently changed its name from National Sick and Accident Association. The only other radio stations on the air in Nashville at this time were WDAA (a Baptist church station) and WDAD (owned by Dad's Hardware Store). At the time, the WSM transmitter was called "the world's largest radio tower". Studios were set up in the main office building in downtown Nashville.

On November 28th, 1925, at WSM, Judge Hay hired Uncle Jimmy Thompson "the man with a thousand fiddle tunes" to play his favorite fiddle tunes as the first person to perform on the WSM Barn Dance.[5] Veteran fiddler Thompson, about eighty years old at the time, became a professional, touring musician at age sixty-eight; he died in 1931.

The Barn Dance evolved into the Grand Ole Opry on December 10, 1927, at 8 p.m. when the show was renamed by George D. Hay. Here's how it happened. After a time of orchestra music being played over the air, Hay had DeFord Bailey play "Pan American Blues." Then he went back to the microphone and announced, "For the past hour, we have been listening to music taken largely from Grand Opera[6]. But from now on, we will present the Grand Ole Opry."[7]

Renaming the Barn Dance to the Grand Ole Opry was impromptu. DeFord Bailey's tune was an example of American music and Hay's aim was to popularize the music which he saw people enjoying at a country picnic in the Ozarks some years before. Though not played much on record or radio, he knew it had great appeal. No matter what the folk content of the Grand Ole Opry today, Hay insisted that folk music was to be heavily emphasized on the show he created. His cry was "Keep it down to earth, boys." Hay wrote that the Opry was "as fundamental as sunshine and rain, snow and wind and the light the moon peeping through the trees. Some folks like it, and some dislike it very much. But it'll be there long after you and I have passed out of the picture or the next one." Hay closed every show with, "That's all for now, friends, Because the tall pines pine and the pawpaws pause, And the bumble bees bumble around, the grasshoppers hop, And the evesdroppers drop, While gently the old cow slips away."

DeFord Bailey, "the Harmonica Wizard", was a slight man with a hunchback. He was not only the first person to play on the Opry, he was also the first black musician to play on the Opry. He was doing well at the neighboring WDAD when Humphrey Bate, of the **Castalian Springs String Band**, recommended that Bailey get a chance on Hay's program. As a result, he was allowed to play without an audition.

Bailey "was unquestionably one of the most musically innovative performers that ever appeared on the program," wrote Robert K. Oermann. "He was a crippled black man who played a syntheses of white hillbilly music and blues/jazz. His repertoire ranged from railroad songs to fiddle melodies to lazy blues. He could mesmerize an audience with harmonica and nothing more."[8] "Bailey once called Uncle Dave Macon 'the best white banjo player I ever heard.'" The two men were the Opry's first real stars.

The Opry show quickly gained great popularity and soon had to move to larger quarters. Country music lovers trucked in to watch the radio show. But the wealthy people in the city of Nashville (known as the "Athens of the South") were afraid that this music was inferior and would only adversely affect the city's prestige. Hay was able to assuage any ill feelings between his bosses, the city, and his country musicians by opening up lines of communication. Daughter Margaret Hay Daugherty wrote, "This argument to the directors of WSM was that his country cousins were authentic representatives of whatever America was all about; it had its origins in the early settlers and it was a part of the blood stream of America. It was not going to disappear. If it were not given voice today, it would be tomorrow. It was *of* the people and *for* the people and he wanted it to be heard in every hamlet that had a radio. And it was."[9]

As the show became more popular, the term "hillbilly"—earlier a term of degradation—came to connote a zesty, fun-loving, checkered-shirt life style; the "corn crib music" designation was being lost toward a feeling which projected more prestige. What had appeared to the owners earlier as a social heresy was becoming a financial bonanza beyond their wildest expectations.

The power of the station was upped in 1927 to 5,000 watts. In 1933, power would be 50,000 watts on a clear-channel frequency and almost dominated the airwaves.

"Early Opry shows also featured the hammered dulcimer. This lovely instrument was played by Kitty Cora Cline, but after she left the program its intricate,

[5] The exact history of the WSM Barn Dance and the Opry gets blurred very easily if allowed. Judge Hay broadcast Uncle Jimmy Thompson first, said Hay in his autobiography. The show was renamed two years later to the Grand Ole Opry. Some insist that the Opry had existed since that first show with Thompson playing fiddle; still others (and this book) assert that it wasn't officially the Opry until it actually received the name. It may have been the same show as was the Barn Dance in 1925, but the actual name didn't come until December 10, 1927.

"Fiddlin' Sid Harkreader wanted the record set straight about who was actually the *first* to play on the Opry: 'It has been reported in the newspapers that I claim to be the first fiddler who ever played the Grand Ole Opry. That is not true," he said dryly. "Uncle Jimmy Thompson was. What I said was—and you take this down—I said that I was the first fiddler to play on WSM. That was shortly before Judge Hay started the Opry, on November 28, 1925."

Minnie Pearl, who has tried to research the actual origins, noted: "If everybody who claimed to have been on the first show actually had been, there wouldn't have been room enough left in the studio to do anything else,"—Jack Hurst *Nashville's Grand Ole Opry*, 1975, p. 80.

[6] This reference to the Grand Opera was a reference to the Music Appreciation Hour of Dr. Walter Damrosh. The show was educational in nature and highlighted one orchestra instrument during the hour, and a different instrument each week.

[7] Jack Hurst, *Nashville's Grand Ole Opry* (New York: Harry N. Abrams, Inc., 1975) p. 92.

According to Grant Turner, long-time announcer on the Opry, Hay actually announced the new name as "Grand Ole Opera." Turner said that Hay was an educated man and would never slur words in that manner. But the old-timers around the station disliked the term "opera" which sounded somewhat elitist to them. They eventually were able to change it to "Grand Ole Opry." For more details on the origin of the Grand Ole Opry, there are many good books which quote directly from Judge Hay's personal account of the formative days of the show.

[8] Robert K. Oermann, *Frets* magazine, December, 1982, p. 22.

[9] Margaret Hay Daugherty, "George D. Hay: The Solemn Ole Judge—Pioneer P-R Man," *Bluegrass Unlimited*, July, 1982, pp. 31, 32.

delicate, bell-like tones were not heard on the Grand Ole Opry for some fifty years. Grandpa Jones' daughter Alissa brought the hammered dulcimer back in the 1980s."[10]

Another popular act at the Opry was "Obed 'Dad' Pickard, known as the 'one-man orchestra,' [who] supposedly could play any instrument in the orchestra except the clarinet; and on late-1920s Opry shows he performed with fiddle, mandolin, guitar, Jew's harp and banjo. If recorded evidence is any guide, however, Pickard was more of a novelty act than he was a musical prodigy. On the other hand, his **Pickard Family**, as vocal popularizers of authentic folk songs, had few peers."[11]

In 1928, regular pay for Opry musicians became a reality. It amounted to a dollar a minute. Up until this time, musicians were given $5 each Saturday night they performed; this was fine for most artists for they had day jobs. For the full-time musician the new wage helped, but they did the show mostly for the exposure and to advertise their upcoming concerts where a "good" living could be made.

Harry Stone replaced Judge Hay as Station Manager of WSM in 1930. Hay continued as announcer and a few other duties. This was fine with Hay and his family; the pressure of the Station Manager's job caused him to worry, which led to ill health. Hay retired in the late 1940s, partly because of a long-term nervous disorder. Even though he did such a nice job during the early years at getting the Barn Dance started at WSM, he was never the type of person who could handle pressure; the job made him ill. At age sixty-five, he was retired on $165 per month. According to Grant Turner, who joined the Opry as its announcer in 1944, "It seemed like he created something that almost destroyed him. And his family thought that the only way to get him out of this was to completely remove him from the scene and take him to Virginia Beach where it was placid and he could have his friends there and he could look back on his Opry years and not be bothered by a lot of obligation because of his fame. The thing just worried him to death; it got to him... Judge was not a business man and

Painting of Grant Turner hanging in the Ryman Auditorium.

he liked to work in his office in a more or less calm and placid way like working at the radio station. Once a week he would go down to the Ryman theater to emcee the show. But he couldn't hold out as *the* emcee very long. Even when I came there [he was showing that he was having problems]. He had none of the lasting qualities that Roy Acuff or Bill Monroe have...

"A lot of people were after the Judge to get involved in the more or less commercial aspect of the business. This was something he did not want to do. He did not want to have the show raided by people with big ideas of how *they* could make money out of the Opry. It worried him to death. They would follow [us] on the street and say, 'Judge, wait a minute! I'd like to speak with you.' He'd say, 'I don't have time.' And I'd say [to him] that [this] man seems to be sort of insistent that he wants to talk with you.' He told me, 'He just has some scheme on how to make money out of the Opry.'"[12]

It was Harry Stone who soon founded the Artists' Services Bureau to help promote tours and live performance bookings for Opry acts. Stone also hired a music librarian to oversee the increasingly complex world of copyrights, performance rights and publishing royalties. The librarian instituted the policy that enabled outside sponsors to buy time on the Opry. The shows then changed from a rather chaotic string of people playing music to the slick, smooth-running show that we know today. Though Stone may be accused of destroying the folk fabric of the Opry, he must also be recognized as making it possible for country music artists to make a living at their work. The Opry started its tent show tours (used in the summer) about 1931. Bill Monroe started his own tent shows in 1943.

The commercialization of the Opry was now under way. The first tour went out without the Opry icon attached to it; it was simply billed as "Uncle Dave Macon and His Moonshiners." WSM took fifteen percent of the gate; the tour manager took twenty. The artists were abused, expected to tour over terrible road conditions during the week and to be back in Nashville

[10] Robert K. Oermann, *Frets*, December, 1982, p. 23.

[11] Ibid., p. 23.

[12] 1991 telephone interview.

for the Opry on Saturday night. The two acts which dominated this circuit during the 1930s were the **Delmore Brothers** and the **Dixieliners**.

The **Dixieliners** came to the Opry about 1930 when Sam and Kirk McGee joined Fiddlin' Arthur Smith. The McGee brothers, from Franklin, Tennessee, had earlier performed with Uncle Dave. It was Sam who gained the name "Flat-top Pickin' Sam" after he developed a style of guitar picking that played the rhythm and melody simultaneously. He exhibited this on his 1926 recording of "Buck Dancer's Choice." He was probably the first white guitarist to use the guitar as a lead instrument. Even Maybelle Carter's famous lead runs were quite simple compared to what Sam did.

Arthur Smith used the long-bow technique on the fiddle and helped to popularize it on tunes such as "Red Apple Rag," "Mocking Bird," "Pig in a Pen" and "More Pretty Girls Than One." Unfortunately, the band never recorded in its prime. Too bad, for the instrumental prowess of Sam and Arthur made them one of the most influential string bands in country music history. They broke up in 1938 when Smith began doing western movies in Hollywood.

Alton and Rabon, the **Delmore Brothers**, joined the Opry in 1932. They sang in the smooth style learned in the gospel singing schools of northern Alabama and southern Tennessee. They were creative, often shifted harmonies, and displayed tricky timing and blues in their music.

The duo suffered from the abuse of the system. They struggled for respectability amid the relative contentment of the other Opry musicians. They finally left the Opry in 1938 and went on to have a long career on radio and records.

The Opry cast in 1933 included Blythe Poteet, Alton Delmore, Rabon Delmore, Herman Crook, Lewis Crook, Dee Simmons, Nap Bastian, DeFord Bailey, David Stone, Oscar Stone, Oscar Albright, Dr. Humphrey Bate, Buster Bate, Sam McGee, Kirk McGee, Arthur Smith, Robert Lunn, Bill Etter, Staley Walton, Judge Hay, Walter Ligget, Dorris Macon, Uncle Dave Macon, Paul Warmack, Roy Hardison, Burt Hutcherson, Claude Lampley, Howard Ragsdale, Tommy Lefew, George Wilkerson, Charlie Arrington, Tom Andrews, Gale Binkley and Amos Binkley.

By 1942, the cast of the Grand Ole Opry were George D. Hay, **Jamup and Honey** (black-face comedy), Pee Wee King, Minnie Pearl, Uncle Dave Macon, DeFord Bailey, Rachael Veach, Vito Pellettire, Sam McGee, Kirk McGee, Eddy Arnold, Redd Stewart, Bill Monroe, Art Wooten, Clyde Moody, Bill (Cousin Wilbur)

Wesbrooks, Howard Forrester, Stringbean, Roy Acuff, David Cobb and Zeke Clements.[13]

When Roy Acuff joined the Opry in 1938 with his **Crazy Tennesseans**, Harry Stone changed the name to a less hayseed-sounding **Smoky Mountain Boys**. This further showed how Stone was trying to get away from what he felt were demeaning band names: he was trying to professionalize the music.[14]

National exposure for the Opry came the next year when NBC programmed a half-hour of the show on their stations. Even more exposure came in 1939 when Hollywood released "The Grand Ole Opry," a film which featured as stars Roy Acuff, Judge Hay and Uncle Dave Macon. According to historian/author Charles Wolfe, "The fact that such a film could be made indicates the degree of acceptability that country music had, not only across Tennessee but across the nation. Indeed, country music was now ready for its final thrust into the mainstream of American pop music."[15]

Since the early 1930s, the Opry has been structured to feature sponsors in half-hour segments. This format is basically the same used today at Opryland USA. On one particular night about 1960, beginning at 7:30 p.m., Pet Milk was the first sponsor to feature entertainment for the audience. After the announcer read the advertisement, the rest of the half-hour went something like this:

dancers	fiddle theme
George Hamilton IV	"Before This Day Ends"
Bill Monroe	"Linda Lou"
Jerry Byrd	"China Nights"
Dottie West	"I Can Start Running"
George Hamilton IV	"Three Steps to the Phone"

and other acts during the half-hour.

This fast-moving entertainment show then included half-hour segments by Martha White, Faultless Starch, Jefferson Salt, Stephens, Standard Oil, National Life, Roses, De Con, Coca-Cola and finally Mohawk. Other acts that night by various sponsors included the **Glaser Brothers**, Cousin Jody, Del Wood, Porter Wagoner, **Jim and Jesse**, Grandpa Jones, Jimmy Newman, Mark Stewart, **Sam and Kirk McGee**, **Fruit Jar Drinkers**, **Red Cravens and the Bray Brothers** and Johnny Forbes. The show closed down with Bill Monroe doing "Sally Joe" and then the fiddle tune "Blue Grass Breakdown."

Chet Atkins joined the Opry in 1946. He got his start in country music on WNOX in 1944, playing for $3 a night. He remembered that "WNOX was a pretty wild place in the '40s. There were girls everywhere because

13 Although Monroe's entire band was in the photo from which these names came, it is unlikely that his sidemen were actually members of the Opry. Technically, they were in the cast but were probably not members. The Opry's "star" system usually only included the star or, in this case, Bill Monroe.

14 According to Roy Acuff on the 1993 video "Bill Monroe—Father of Bluegrass Music," the manager of the Opry at that time, George D. Hay, named most of the groups himself. Many of them arrived at the Opry without names, he said. It is even said that Hay renamed Bill Monroe's group to the "Blue Grass Boys" when he brought his band there.

15 Charles K. Wolfe, *Tennessee Strings*, (Knoxville: The University of Tennessee Press, 1977), p. 74.

all the men were all gone. I had very bad asthma so I was 4-F. There was a one-armed banjo player; name was Emory Martin. He had a stub of an arm and he would fret the banjo with that; he played well. And then we had Ray Mears. He was an armless musician who played steel guitar with his feet. **Johnnie** [Wright] **and Jack** [Anglin] were there, too. And, of course, Johnnie's wife, Kitty Wells. I played some show dates with them. We traveled by car with a PA system in the front seat and Johnnie had an aluminum bass fiddle we tied on top. One day, he finally took that bass, shot it full of holes, threw it in the river and collected the insurance."

When Chet arrived at the Opry, "Oh, it was really great. They had these wonderful characters like the singing newsman, Jim Day: 'Oh, hello, everybody. Here's the singin' news with a little music to chase away the blues.' And they had those old string bands, the **Gully Jumpers**, the **Fruit Jar Drinkers**. They were all farmers from around there. The music was kind of primitive to me; my dad had always put country music down so I thought a person had to sing with a trained voice like Red Foley. But I got to watching Roy Acuff. He'd sing 'Great Speckled Bird' and cry. People loved it. They'd just throw babies in the air. And Ernest Tubb, he had a truck driver's voice—real low. On stage, he'd look straight ahead like he was having an out-of-body experience or something. And I got to realizing that simplicity had its values. Anyway, I was playing a solo each week on NBC, but they took it off, so I quit the Opry."[16]

The birth of NBC

The National Broadcasting System was "born" in 1926. It was the first radio network. Its creator, David Sarnoff, later became President of RCA. In June of 1927, NBC linked fifty stations in twenty-four states as thirty million people listened to the homecoming of Charles A. Lindbergh returning to New York from his record-breaking flight to Paris.

The Blue Sky Boys

Some early groups, such as the **Blue Sky Boys**, can just as easily fit into the Roots chapter of this book. Indeed, they are there as well. But this group is a perfect example of how the early pioneer groups de-

pended upon radio exposure for a living. As you absorb this biography, you'll be able to pick out this theme as a representative example of individuals and groups who used radio in the early days of hillbilly/country music.

Bill and Earl Bolick, from West Hickory, North Carolina, were two important men in the history of bluegrass music because of their delicate harmonies and Bill's intricate and complex mandolin style. Their music was played before and after Bill and Charlie Monroe split. The **Monroe Brothers**, the **Delmore**

Earl Homer Bill
CRAZY
Blue Ridge Hillbillies

COMPLIMENTS OF CRAZY WATER CRYSTALS CO.
BROADCASTING DAILY

GET CRAZY WATER CRYSTALS FROM YOUR DRUGGIST
CRAZY WATER CRYSTALS CO.
TELL YOUR NEIGHBORS TO TUNE IN ON THESE PROGRAMS
CHARLOTTE AND ATLANTA

made in Atlanta Ga

Brothers and the **Blue Sky Boys** were three of the better-known groups which used the close-harmony duet style of singing; this would later be an important element of bluegrass music.

A major influence to Bill Bolick on the radio was Chubby Parker who sang and played banjo on the WLS Barn Dance until about 1927.[17]

Bill (born October 29, 1917) and Earl (born November 16, 1919) Bolick were raised into a non-musical family. The Bolick family had one of the first radios— battery-powered, of course—in the entire West Hickory

[16] *Life* magazine's "The Roots of Country Music," 1994, pp. 62, 71.
  By 1948, Chet Atkins was back at WNOX, recording for Steve Sholes and RCA Victor. When Mother Maybelle and the Carter Sisters came to town in 1948, he began touring with them.
  As a producer in charge of RCA's Nashville studio in the mid-'50s, "People have given me credit all the time for inventing the Nashville sound, and I don't know about that. Owen Bradley had a lot to do with it and all those musicians like Anita Kerr Singers and the Jordanaires. So I don't like to take the credit."
  As for the music today: "The music has gotten pretty bad, I think. It's all for that damn line dancing they do. Once in awhile there's a good song—and once in awhile, a great song. It's just that there's a conformist attitude. And it's not just the producers, it's the damn radio stations—their play lists have gotten smaller. It's the program directors, its the fans, it's everybody. And it's a damn shame. Back in the old days, we didn't just follow the trends. We tried something different every record. Boy, it was a lot of fun."—p. 71.

[17] Parker "was the reason I persuaded my father to purchase me the banjo. A different Parker, Samuel 'Curly' Parker, worked with us as a fiddler and sang in some of the trios. He and I are the same age. He joined us in 1940 and played with us until the summer of 1949 with the exception of the time we spent in the service."—Bill Bolick, 1996.

area. Because there were so few radio stations in existence, they had no problem picking up distant stations. They listened to 50,000 watt WLS in Chicago during the mid-twenties before the Opry appeared on WSM. In his teens in 1933, Bill Bolick preferred to listen to WLS' Barn Dance in Chicago over WSM and the Opry. He considered WLS as the only station which had any kind of country music in the early days and "it had better entertainers at that time." The station's country show was on Saturday nights. The other type of music on the station was mostly classical and it later added "Fibber McGee and Molly" and "Amos and Andy." Bill convinced his father to buy him a Sears and Roebuck $5 banjo about this time.

The **Delmore Brothers** were becoming popular on the Opry in the early 1930s. Until the **Delmore Brothers** and Fiddlin' Arthur Smith started on the show, Bill really didn't feel there was any group listening to on the Opry. Bill Bolick told this writer, "I felt the Delmores and Fiddlin' Arthur Smith were a great boost to the Opry. However, I don't recall hearing them until sometime in the early thirties." He didn't care for Gid Tanner's fiddle playing, feeling that the talent of Riley Puckett carried the band. Bolick remembered that Puckett did some of his fabulous bass runs with his index finger. And, "I especially liked 'Fiddlin' Arthur Smith'—he was quite unique. A lot of the old-timers had their own style; that's what I think I admired most about them. They initiated or originated their own style and they actually copied from no one. They could sing the same songs and yet not sound like the person they learned them from, which is something that to me is very rare today—especially in the bluegrass field. About all you hear is Scruggs-type banjo. I know there are various variations—and the same as Bill Monroe's mandolin and the same as their singing—but basically it is more or less the same. And to me, when you hear one, you hear it all and I soon tire of stuff like that. But you take people like [Bradley] Kincaid, for instance—distinctly had his own style. There was Riley Puckett—no one has ever sounded quite like Riley. And I don't think that anyone has ever quite come up to the Delmores. I also liked Charlie and Bill Monroe when they worked together; I thought that they were very unique."[18]

Bill never liked the name "hillbilly"; he felt it denigrated the music and felt that the term referred to

more of a low-class, ignorant type of individual: a character who made moonshine, wore patches on his britches, had little schooling and lived in a shack. This image was offensive to Bill, for his birthplace at Hickory, North Carolina, was actually in the "hills" near where the term originated.

"I never refer to old-time music as 'bluegrass' even though some of it is," wrote Mr. Bolick. "The entire time Earl and I were actively engaged in the entertainment business, I never heard any type of country music referred to by that name. It has all come about since we quit entertaining. Too, I never heard the name 'Dobro®' mentioned. I still call it the 'Hawaiian guitar.' I have no objection to the name 'bluegrass' if one wants to classify it that way. I have always classified it as string music, old-time music and country music.

"To me, if it doesn't have the Monroe mandolin and [the] Scruggs banjo, it isn't bluegrass. This is the fast-moving type of country music that Charlie and Bill innovated, and most of it I enjoy very much. I have only the highest respect for Charlie and Bill and the unique style they developed. I will also extend this compliment to Earl Scruggs, although his style of banjo picking isn't truly original. He is the one, however, that made it famous. For the clones and imitators of the above three, I hold very little respect. Though many of them have attained high honors in the bluegrass world and have become financially rich, I feel they have added very little to country music."[19]

Bill Bolick began playing professional music with Homer Sherrill's **Crazy Hickory Nuts** in 1935 on a daily fifteen-minute program on WWNC (Wonderful Western North Carolina) in Asheville, North Carolina. Every Saturday night, they played on the Crazy Water Crystal Barn Dance which was broadcast on WBT in Charlotte, North Carolina. Their pay was three cents for each mile traveled between Charlotte and Asheville. Bolick remembered, "Asheville was a very difficult station from which to work personal appearances. It was in the midst of the mountains. The western part of North Carolina had very few towns of any size and practically no industry. The winter months were usually rough and with a lot of snow; most of the roads were impassable. Although WWNC had excellent coverage for a 1,000 watt facility, most people outside a 25-30 mile radius of Asheville listened to powerful WBT and you, more or less, had to build up your listening audi-

"Most principals felt our type of music was not dignified enough to be presented in their schools. Also, during the Depression days, many felt that you would be taking too much money out of the community. I heard that excuse frequently."
—Bill Bolick

18 This quotation was written by Bill Bolick for the 1976 album "Presenting the Blue Sky Boys" for the JEMF reissue of Capitol ST 2483.
19 From a 1991 letter to me.

America's Music | Bluegrass

ence one at a time. Unless you were on a powerful station or were tremendously popular, it was difficult to obtain bookings.

"Most principals felt our type of music was not dignified enough to be presented in their schools. Also, during the Depression days, many felt that you would be taking too much money out of the community. I heard that excuse frequently." Bill Bolick, in 1976, wrote that "most radio stations— especially, believe it or not, in the South where this music was more popular— were very much opposed to our type of music and it was pretty hard to get a spot on the air. It was almost impossible to get a sponsor through the radio station itself. I suppose it was what they considered a necessary evil; they knew that it was popular with most of their listeners and yet they frowned upon it very much and, I think, really tried to hold the country musician down as much as they possibly could. I think that most of them felt that this type of music was strictly beneath their dignity. In fact, that not only went for the radio stations, but also for a lot of the schools that we played."[20] As a result, it didn't work out financially. Arthur Sherrill left for a day job, leaving Homer Sherrill (fiddle), Bill Bolick (guitar) and Lute Isenhour (banjo) in the **Crazy Hickory Nuts**.

Bolick and Isenhour quit the **Crazy Hickory Nuts** in 1935. Sherrill stayed, with the promise from WWNC that replacements would be hired. But the station failed to follow through on that promise; Crazy Water Crystals soon took their program off the air. Homer Sherrill soon returned to the station again with another group which included banjoist Mack Crowe. Sherrill and Crowe played there on WWNC for free, and for the privilege of advertising their personal appearances over the air. This was not too successful but Sherrill stayed with the program until it went off the air.

In the early fall of 1935, WWNC invited Bolick and Sherrill back to the station with a new sponsor, the JFG Coffee Company of Knoxville, Tennessee.[21] They added Bill's younger brother, Earl Bolick, to fill out the trio. They were named **The Good Coffee Boys—John, Frank and George**. The Bolick brothers really hadn't played or sung much together until this time, but with Bill singing harmony and Earl singing the melody, the sound gelled and immediately became successful. The station paid them $10 per week per person (very good wages for that time, especially for the Depression) and the station, in turn, was paid by the sponsor.

The **Good Coffee Boys** was an unqualified success at WWNC. Within days of their return to the station, they were drawing in more fan mail than the **Crazy Hickory Nuts** ever had. Within weeks, they were getting 40-100 pieces of fan mail daily, but lack of a reliable automobile severely limited their personal appearances.

In March of 1936, the trio of Earl, Bill and Homer was enticed to go to Atlanta to play on the small 1000 watt station, WGST, which was owned by the Georgia School of Technology. They were offered double their salary and the use of a car until they paid for it. The car (a 1934 Ford) became useful to be able to play functions other than at the station. This further increased their income, for personal appearances were the main source of money earned by most entertainers in those days. Their personal appearances were mainly at schoolhouses.

The offer to play on WGST came from Crazy Water Crystals. They were guaranteed $20 per person per week by Crazy Water Crystals for their radio performances.[22] They put out a songbook using the band name **Crazy Blue Ridge Hillbillies**.[23] With their personal appearances three or four days a week, they were each making nearly $100 per week even though they were bucking the 50,000 watt Crossroads Follies Program of WSB. They became immensely popular. There at WGST they became the **Crazy Blue Ridge Hillbillies— Homer, Bill and Earl**. Their daily fifteen-minute show, six days per week, brought in fifteen cents from kids five through twelve, and twenty-five cents from adults. WGST had never before seen the amount of fan mail that the **Hillbillies** brought in.

On June 16th, 1936, the name **Blue Sky Boys** came about when Bill and Earl Bolick[24] auditioned in Charlotte recorded for Bluebird, a subsidiary of RCA Victor which handled this type of music. Although the man they auditioned for, Eli Oberstein (A & R man for RCA), had heard that the brothers sounded like the **Monroe Brothers**, he had to admit there was almost no similarity in the sound of the two bands. They chose the song "The Sunny Side of Life" for their audition. Oberstein liked it and suggested that the brothers take a stage name of some sort. He said that there were just too many acts using the name "Brothers" in them. In a discussion of what their new name should be, Oberstein, Bill, and Earl took the "Blue" from the Blue Ridge Mountains, and the "Sky" from the fact that the

---

20 From Bill Bolick's comments for the 1976 album, "Presenting the Blue Sky Boys" for the JEMF reissue of Capitol ST 2483.

21 Bill Bolick played guitar, Homer Sherrill, the fiddle, and fifteen year-old Earl Bolick joined on guitar.

22 They replaced the Monroe Brothers and the Monroe's announcer and occasional bass singer, Byron Parker.

23 Bill Bolick: "We were given the name Crazy Blue Ridge Hillbillies by J.W. Fincher, president of the company in the two Carolinas and Georgia. As you know, I'm not one to embrace the word 'hillbilly', but with the advantages offered us, I felt I could live with it."

24 Homer Sherrill was not with the band at this time; he was still at WGST. Bill Bolick: "Because of some changes Mr. Fincher wanted Earl and I to make, we returned to our parents' home in Hickory, NC, about June 1, 1936. Arrangements had already been made for us to record June 16 in Charlotte, NC. Homer stayed in Atlanta and Fincher hired two fellows, Shorty and Mack, to take our place. This group took the name of the Blue Ridge Hillbillies and recorded several selections for RCA on the Bluebird label."

land around Asheville was known as the "land of the sky", and they adopted the name **Blue Sky Boys**.

Back at WGST in Atlanta in early 1937, Bill and Earl Bolick re-joined Homer Sherrill as the **Blue Sky Boys**. Bill and Earl had recorded three or four songs as the **Blue Sky Boys** since they left WGST last June. Sherrill never recorded with the **Blue Sky Boys**. As a matter of fact, all of their recordings prior to World War II were recorded by only the duo of Bill and Earl Bolick.

L to R: Earl Bolick, Curly Parker and Bill Bolick at radio station WNAO, Raleigh, NC.

Byron Parker, "The Old Hired Hand," left the **Monroe Brothers**[25] about this time. He then went to Atlanta to convince the **Blue Sky Boys** to work for him. He told them that he would be the band's manager and emcee and give them a salary plus a percentage of the personal appearance receipts; he certainly had done a good job in helping make the **Monroe Brothers** famous. "Without a doubt, at that time, the Monroes were the biggest name in country in the two Carolinas," said Bill Bolick. "Probably the Delmores and other WSM artists were better known throughout the rest of the South." Bolick remembered that Parker always introduced the **Monroe Brothers** in the same manner: "You're listening to the boys that can't be beat and can't be tied." With that sincere, folksy voice, "People ate it up."

Parker only wanted the Bolick Brothers, not Sherrill. But in a pact made earlier between and Bill, Earl and Homer, they agreed not to split up the band. Certainly the offer was tempting because of the money that Parker could make for them. His promotion skills were well-proven. His charisma and salesmanship would certainly, Parker thought, be appreciated by any band. Bill Bolick, in a 1991 telephone interview, told that Parker's words were very close to "I'll make you

famous—like I did the **Monroe Brothers**. You don't need anybody else."

Later in 1937, Homer Sherrill left to join the **Morris Brothers** at WPTF in Raleigh, North Carolina. Because the Bolick brothers had wrecked their car about this time and had no means of transportation to continue entertaining, they quit music for a while—not knowing whether they would ever entertain again. Bolick continued, "We left WGST in December 1939 and moved to radio station WPTF the last several days of the month. We worked over that station until May 1941. We then moved to WFBC, Greenville, South Carolina. While at WFBC, we drew more fan mail than we had anytime previously. We drew 250 to 500 cards and letters daily. We were at WFBC approximately two months when I received a draft notice. At that time, the draft was only for one year. Earl signed up for his year at that time to enable us to get out at the same time and start back entertaining. Unfortunately, it was four years and seven months before we had that opportunity."

After their return from the War in March of 1946, the Bolick brothers realized that their kind of music was being put on the "back burner". They worked at various stations which had previously given them a past history of success—stations such as WGST (for two years) then WNAO (a new station in Raleigh for a year), then WCYB in Bristol, Virginia/Tennessee, in March of 1949, followed by WROM in Rome, Georgia, then KWKH in Shreveport, Louisiana. They then returned to WNAO where they worked until they retired in February 1951. They didn't sing again until the summer of 1963.

Starday's Don Pierce wrote to Bill in 1961 to discuss issuing some of the **Blue Sky Boys**' post-War transcriptions. Their first release was "The Blue Sky Boys: a Treasury of Rare Song Gems from the Past" (SLP-205), re-recorded from transcriptions recorded for the Willys-Overland Company back in 1946-47. After this was issued, the Bolicks agreed to record again. In August 1963, Bill and Earl Bolick returned to music to record for Starday. They rehearsed for three days. Their second Starday album was "Together Again: the Blue Sky Boys" (SLP-257). The Nashville session was in August 1963. Bill Bolick remembered that "It was almost like starting all over. I hadn't sung any harmony and had done very little singing myself. And if I did, it was with a guitar" (Bill normally played the mandolin in the **Blue Sky Boys**). Starday's Don "Pierce wanted us to use a bluegrass-type banjo." The Bolicks flatly rejected this idea because they felt that it would detract from the **Blue Sky Boys** sound. "We did agree to adding a fiddle and bass, as nearly all our post-War recordings were made this way. They also wanted us to use additional instruments on our other album. We were at no

25 Byron Parker told Bill Bolick that he left the Monroe Brothers because Charlie's wife was to take over the management of the band.

America's Music — Bluegrass

time pressured to use any of these extra instruments, as has been stated by some writers. We simply agreed to do it because we were convinced that our sales would be greatly increased if we did use them. You must remember we had had no contact at all with the musical world in more than twelve years. We finally agreed to do the religious album 'Precious Moments' the way we wanted to do it, and the 'Together Again' album using the so-called 'Nashville sound'." The album, "Precious Moments with the Blue Sky Boys" (SLP-269) was recorded at the same session as "Together Again."

The **Blue Sky Boys**, now back into the music part-time, toured occasionally at colleges and on the bluegrass circuit. In 1975, they recorded an album for Rounder then quit music altogether. Bill retired to Hickory, North Carolina, Earl to Suwanee, Georgia.

The Cas Walker chain of grocery stores—a boon to country music and bluegrass

About 1937, Cas Walker began sponsoring country music shows in Knoxville on WNOX and WROL. He liked bluegrass "and explained his rationale for using it on his shows. 'If you have what I call "jumping up and down music"—bluegrass—and something that a child can jump up and down to, you make the children jump up and down and listen to you. And when you please someone's child, you please the papa and mama...every child knows Cas Walker, and that's not bad, when everyone is going to be eating at one time or another.'"[26]

The Grand Ole Opry overtakes the National Barn Dance in popularity

In 1937, WLS and the National Barn Dance suffered a tremendous loss when John Lair took many of the groups he managed for the station and soon founded the Renfro Valley Barn Dance. WLS then changed its format to a more "sophisticated" character. Also, the local musicians union began to require a sixteen-piece orchestra on the show just to get it on the network. It soon had a hundred cast members. The overhead became such that they had to stick to a more profitable type of music: "popular" music (Mills Brothers, Bing Crosby, Frank Sinatra, etc.)

Before 1940s were over, Autry-clone Rex Allen became a star on the National Barn Dance. So did **Homer and Jethro**[27], who had just left John Lair's Renfro Valley Barn Dance to guest on the National Barn

Dance. After three weeks, they became popular and became regular members of the cast. This was quite a boon for the duo for they no longer had to tour constantly to make a living. Plus, they were getting national exposure on NBC.

Though the National Barn Dance continued its existence, by 1946 the Grand Ole Opry had overtaken the Dance in popularity. Jethro Burns described the situation about the Barn Dance at the station in 1949, "Your Gene Autrys and Rex Allens were gone and they didn't seem to realize that every time a big star left, he took some portion of that audience with him. They never tried to stop it. I thought they were going to really perk it up and start bringing in fine new acts. Instead, they let their best acts go, I think, and what they replaced them with was pseudo-country, made up principally of Chicago people who weren't country and weren't pop; they weren't even what you would call 'old-time.'"[28] Management allowed the departure of Patsy Montana's group, the long-time Barn Dance act **Mac and Bob**, and Doc Hopkins who was a former member of John Lair's **Cumberland Ridge Runners**. Management's intent was to treat everybody the same, as members of the family, and not allow any one act to become a star.

The demise of the National Barn Dance continued through the years. In 1957, the 8th Street Theater was closed. Lulu Belle and Scotty retired to their native North Carolina mountains. Homer Haynes and Jethro Burns left to continue their career. In 1960, the Barn Dance moved from WLS to WGN in Chicago. It was put on television at WGN, but the draw of authentic country acts was gone. *Prairie Farmer* magazine then sold the show to ABC. Suddenly the show was playing rock and roll. It was gone. The National Barn Dance died on WGN-TV in 1971.

The beginnings of WCYB and its Farm and Fun Time

On December 13, 1946, radio station WCYB began broadcasting from Bristol, Tennessee, and was heard clearly over the mountain areas of five states with its big 10,000 watts (which later became 50,000 watts). Their Farm and Fun Time Show was the place that **Flatt and Scruggs and the Foggy Mountain Boys** headed for after Lester Flatt and Earl Scruggs formed their own band. It soon became one of *the* important places for a bluegrass artist to play and gain fame.

Among the first to play at the station was the brand new **Stanley Brothers and the Clinch Mountain Boys** band. They played without pay for an hour at noon, on and off for the next twelve years. Other acts on the

26 Wolfe, op. cit., *Tennessee Strings*, p. 88.

27 Homer Haynes died in 1971. Jethro Burns died in 1989.

28 Jack Hurst, "Barn Dance Days—Chicago's National Barn Dance," *Bluegrass Unlimited*, April, 1986.

station during this period were Charlie Monroe's **Kentucky Pardners**, Mac Wiseman, **Curly King and the Tennessee Hilltoppers**, and the **Blue Sky Boys** (in 1949). Later on, the station was to host the **Sauceman Brothers**, Carl Story, the **Shelton Brothers**, Bonnie Lou and Buster Moore, **Ralph Mayo and the Southern Mountain Boys**, **Jim and Jesse** and even A.P. Carter. Several of the groups used electric instruments.

The beginnings of country music on the air in Ohio

On September 1, 1947, Paul F. Braden began broadcasting on WPFB, Middletown, Ohio. He was careful to program his favorite music: hillbilly. Braden hired Ranny Daly to help run the station. He hired entertainers Old Joe Clark and Little Eller and Smoky Ward from the Renfro Valley Barn Dance. They held a jamboree in a large tent on station grounds. A move to inside a barn in 1949 caused it to be a barn dance. By 1954, the station was in full swing, with many touring musicians passing through to play the venue. These artists included **Jim and Jesse**, Frank Wakefield, Hylo Brown, Jimmy Martin, the **Osborne Brothers**, and Red Allen.

This was the station where Paul "Moon" Mullins became famous in his twenty-seven year career playing a variety of bluegrass and country music. Although Mullins made a good living at the station as emcee, he was so popular that he probably made Braden rich. At one point, he had 88% of the country radio market. It was stations like this which seemed to make geographic "hot spots" for the music. Fans of country and bluegrass music seemed to gravitate toward the area simply because of such airwave activity. Because many of its listeners had moved from eastern Kentucky where they

were known as "Briars" or "Briarhoppers", the station became synonymous with "We Play For Briars."

Mullins described his techniques of having a successful radio show, "I did my radio program in the same manner [in which] I prepared myself to go on the stage—to entertain the people that were listening. I did my radio [show] for thirty years in the same manner. I prepared myself so I knew I was gonna make people pay attention to what I was doing. I brought my own records to the radio station[29] and started playing my music— good, bluegrass music: Bill Monroe, **Jim and Jesse**, **Reno and Smiley**, Mac Wiseman. I started playing the **Country Gentlemen**'s records, too. And I had a real hard time with the sales people at the radio station. They refused to sell radio commercials on my radio program because it was 'corn'—because it was so 'country'. They said, 'If you'll change your music then we'll go out there and sell it for you.' I said, 'Man, I'm on a salary. I don't care whether you sell it or not. That's your downfall, not mine.' They refused to sell it and so the station manager who hired me (Paul Braden) called me in one day and says, 'There's something on the air that you're doing that your sales people don't like.' I said, 'I know what it is, too.' But I said, 'You know, I left a real good job. I can go back for the same money I left and I don't have to stay here.' He asked me for a suggestion. I said, 'You keep payin' me what you're payin' me and give me ten percent of what I sell and I'll go sell it myself.' That's when I learned that you could really make a good livin' in this business. So I started selling like I did in Kentucky."

The history of the Ryman Auditorium and the opening of Opryland USA

March 16, 1974, was the date of the last Grand Ole Opry concert to be held at the Ryman Auditorium. The new owners of the Opry moved the Grand Ole Opry show to the new Opry house which cost $16 million to build and has 4,400 seats and air conditioning. The closing of the venerable old Ryman was sad for many because they knew that the "hillbilly dust" (or atmosphere) of the Grand Ole Opry would change forever with the new, modern facility. According to George Gruhn, whose instrument store is on the same block as the Ryman, "There was more great country music played there than any other place on the planet. I may not go so far as to call it a musical instrument, but there's something soulful that lingers there...some of it seeps into the bricks."[30]

A pleading letter[31] from Bill Knowlton, a deejay at WCNY, Syracuse, New York, was addressed to Irving Waugh, the President of WSM and the Controller of the

A painting of the Ryman Auditorium which hangs within its halls.

[29] Later on, after telling record companies what he was doing, they began sending him 45s and LPs.

[30] John McMillin interview for an article in the May 29, 1994, *The Denver Post.*

Grand Ole Opry at the time. Knowlton was concerned about the direction of the Opry away from the type of music Judge Hay had insisted upon in his tenure as General Manager. Knowlton was insistent that Hay's kind of music return to the Opry before it was too late. Hay would not have tolerated drums, tuxedos or a posh Broadway band. Knowlton exhibited sorrow and despair in his letter, and sarcastically congratulated Waugh on his plush, expensive new office. He was sad. But little did anyone know at the time that the Ryman would be preserved, rebuilt, and opened again to country and bluegrass music in 1994.

"The Ryman Auditorium was built in 1891 by riverboat captain Tom Ryman who came to a religious tent meeting to heckle the preacher, only to stay and be converted. He built the structure for the Reverend Sam Jones. The Confederate Veterans reunion was scheduled in 1897 and a balcony was added for the meeting. It then could seat more than 3,000 people."[32]

The WSM Barn Dance was first broadcast from WSM's Studio B in 1925. Two years later, the name of the Dance was changed to the Grand Ole Opry. Before long, crowds clogged the studios and they knew they had to move to a different building or build Studio C, an acoustically-designed auditorium which was to hold up to 500. They built it, but that, too, became full so they searched for an appropriate home. They stayed at the rented Hillsboro Theater awhile, followed by two years at a huge tabernacle across the Cumberland River in East Nashville. In July 1939, the show moved to the newly-constructed War Memorial Auditorium until its capacity was exceeded, in spite of their idea of slowing down attendance by adding an entrance fee of 25 cents. The weekly crowds exceeded 3000 so they moved to the Ryman June 5, 1943, out of necessity—it could hold more than 3,000. Initially rented by WSM for $100 a week, the Opry used the Ryman as its home until 1974. The Ryman Auditorium was the largest facility of its type in Nashville; it became the natural place for a large event such as the Opry.

Opry member Wilma Lee Cooper remembered the nearly intolerable playing conditions at the old Ryman Auditorium, "You could stand on the stage and see daylight coming through the cracks. It got so hot all you could do was one song, but it was home. We lost that in the new building; we lost the closeness to the people."

One man described its interior, "Although I was accustomed to austerity, I was not prepared for the drab-ness of the Ryman. The walls and ceiling were dark and dingy. No light or bright colors were revealed by the bare light bulbs hanging from the ceiling. The seats were battered church benches, the kind made purposely uncomfortable to prevent worshippers from going to sleep during a dull sermon. The individual

The Ryman Auditorium, 1994.

seating spaces were identified by numbers stenciled on the backs of the benches and separated by painted stripes. These seats were approached over an unpainted wooden floor that yielded and creaked under one's feet.

"Sometimes on Saturday night," continued the man, "I would stand in line in front of the building with the farmers in their overalls to see the Grand Ole Opry. I would hope that none of my college friends would happen by and see me there. The Opry was not uniformly liked by the citizens of Nashville. The city called itself 'The Athens of the South.' It took pride in its culture, its universities and colleges, and its way of combining Old South gentility with relatively liberal social attitudes. Country music did not fit this self-image."[33]

Roy Acuff was all for the new facility in 1974 and wanted to tear the Ryman down. While this may sound somewhat heretical from a man who made his best music at the Ryman, according to Grant Turner, "He was afraid that the building would fall in because they loaded, at one point, 3300 people in there and they were all stomping and yelling. And you take that many people, especially in that balcony—if the building had ever caved in... And I think they now allow up to a thousand people in there now (for a tour). And they let them sing 'You Are My Sunshine' so they can say they have sung on the Grand Ole Opry. They have tour buses lined up and they allow 48 people in there at a time. All day long this happens."

Mr. Turner reminisced in 1991 about the different feeling of the new Opry location, "When we've been out here a few years and we can refer to this place as the Old Opry House, then it will take on a character of its own. It's beginning to take on that character now. It

[31] From a December issue of *Muleskinner News*. Year of the magazine is probably 1974.

[32] *Official Opry Picture-History Book*, 1992 Opryland USA Inc., Vol 8, Edition 1, p. 166.

[33] Ralph Grimble, "The Grand Ole Opry—50 Years Ago," *Bluegrass Unlimited*, October, 1990, p.38.

Bluegrass Night, 1994. L to R: Alison Krauss, Bill Monroe, Ricky Skaggs.

took all those years—since 1974—to get it up to the point that it has a character of its own."

If the old Opry location had a distinctive character, many of today's performers and promoters see it only as a business and ignore the charm and mystique acquired over the many years when the Opry was at the Ryman. "None of us can understand why they promote the people who care the least about the Opry," said Turner emotionally. "You see, we have people that love the Opry and will do anything for it. But these other people come in and skim the cream, you know. They get all the publicity. They appear there one time a year and that's about what it amounts to. I don't think they do that much for the Opry although they do help our image among younger people who listen to country music on the modern disc jockey shows. There is always big money behind every one of them. A poor man never gets a chance. And that's not how the old Opry used to work." Grant Turner died October 19, 1991, of a heart aneurysm, two weeks before this writer was to meet and interview him in person at his home in Nashville.

Veteran Curly Seckler also felt that the Grand Ole Opry was changing for the worse. And when the old groups (which he claimed were most responsible for the sound of the Opry) are gone, the Opry will never be the same...and lose its popularity. In 1992, Seckler reflected on this, "It'll never be the same. I heard 'em over there yesterday afternoon. They said there was empty seats in there Friday and they didn't know whether they could fill it—and Garth Brooks was gonna be there! You know, [it] used to [be that] people would call and ask me and want me to get tickets for 'em and I would say you'd have to get 'em five or six months in advance. Well, that's a thing of the past anymore over there. They just don't get the people they used to.

"That thing over in Missouri is the one that's took over—Branson. If they didn't have this 'Nashville Now' thing here, they might as well close the doors over here, in my opinion. They tried to get a bunch of live shows started around here in some of these theaters and hotels but they should have done it years ago before all that was built over yonder in Missouri. Mel Tillis recently said that he would have liked to have been a part of the Grand Ole Opry at one time but he never was asked. Now he says he has a new life going there in Missouri. Now if I was twenty years younger I would leave here and go over there, too. But I've done had my days."

The deleterious use of a staff band at the Opry

In a 1982 article in *Frets*, Wilma Lee Cooper was asked about the use of the staff band at the Grand Ole Opry. "I don't use the staff band of the Grand Ole Opry," she said. "I've seen many country music jamboree shows go under with staff bands because everybody had the same sound when they used the same band. Chicago's WLS went under, and another station in Cincinnati did the same when it went with a staff band. You get away from that original sound [when you use a house band]. That staff out there couldn't cut Monroe's stuff the way he wants it. If Roy [Acuff] had to go without his Dobro® guitar, and his sound...they just don't have it. We lose our individual sounds."

Acuff reminisced, "When we first came to the Opry, we brought our sound. There was no backup band like the one they've got now. If there was anybody that came on, they'd play back of my band. And performers would play in front of my band, too. But then they all sound alike."

And about the "new" Opry, Acuff said, "These people that they're bringing in here destroy us on stage at the Opry. They really do, and I resent it! And I talked to the bosses about it but there ain't nothing they'll do about it." Some of those who go out there, said Acuff, "are so loud they make the audience deaf and you have to back up yourself to stay on stage. They are just out there, to me, just for what little they get out of it: the money."[34]

A
m
e
r
i
c
a
s

M
u
s
i
c
I

B
l
u
e
g
r
a
s
s

34 George Gruhn, "Opry Veterans Looking Back, Looking Ahead," *Frets*, December, 1982, p. 34.

Flatt and Scruggs and Martha White Flour Mills

In June 1953, Martha White Mills became the sponsor for **Flatt and Scruggs** on WSM's daily, early-morning radio broadcast where they performed for the next eleven months. The sponsorship with Martha White continued on both radio and television until the group broke up in 1969. The acquisition of the regional flour company as a sponsor was quite a coup for the band. Their earlier success had led to the contract with the Mill, but this additional exposure on WSM helped their popularity enough to eventually enable the band to take over the Mill's sponsored spot on the Opry which until that time was occupied by a western swing band.

Flatt and Scruggs and the Foggy Mountain Boys was at the top of its form and popularity when Lester and Earl accepted Martha White Mills as their sponsor. The band had been playing on all the popular radio stations of the day including WCYB (10,000 watts), Bristol, Virginia, on Farm and Fun Time, WSM in Nashville, WPAQ (10,000 watts) in Mount Airy, North Carolina, WPTF in Raleigh, and WRVA (50,000 watts) in Richmond, Virginia. (The only significant station on which they had not played was WWVA, Wheeling, West Virginia.) They left WNOX to accept this job on WSM. It was said by the president of the Mill, Cohen Williams, that **Flatt and Scruggs** changed the company into a multi-million dollar business.

In the early 1950s, **Flatt and Scruggs** began video-taping its Martha White shows for later viewing. There are no old tapes or films of these television shows. Earl Scruggs said, "When we were taping programs like the Martha White television shows, they [the studio] would erase the tapes for each next show. You know, you can do that with television video tape just the same as you can a home tape recorder. As far as I know, there's not a-one of them that's available to see today. As I think of it, it is a shame; it's a thing they overlooked, I guess. You know, at the time, those tapes were very expensive so they felt they had to reuse them over and over."[35] (This is the same fate which befell shows video-taped for the Jim Walters Corporation by the **Stanley Brothers**.) Probably the best way for us fans to see these groups in their heyday is to watch either the reruns of "Beverly Hillbillies," the 1964 production of a package show hosted by Ralph Emery, "Country Music on Broadway," viewing of put-together videos in the International Bluegrass Music Museum, or in the documentary "The Nashville Story" from the mid-sixties. These are available commercially.

In a 1978 interview for *Pickin'* magazine, Scruggs spoke a little about the status of the record industry and getting airplay. "It's got to be on a major label anyway because there's too many records comin' through to be programmed to start with. They can't even program all over the major labels much less... It is [very competitive]. More records come out every day than there are minutes in the day. I'm not saying that what they program is the right stuff, but nothin' we can do about that. I sure hate to see a group spend their hard-earned money on these gyp joints in Nashville that surely will relieve you of your money awfully quick. The union was trying to get that stopped but I don't know how far along they got. It'd be a blessing to see these guys put out."

The Old Dominion Barn Dance and the New Dominion Barn Dance

The Old Dominion Barn Dance, managed by "Sunshine" Sue Workman, ceased to exist on October 19, 1957. When Carlton Haney took over as the show's manager, it became the New Dominion Barn Dance. Both shows were broadcast on 50,000 watt WRVA of Richmond, Virginia.

The original show began about 1947 with artists such as Chet Atkins, Grandpa Jones, the **Carter Family**, Merle Travis and Joe and Rose Maphis. In April of 1955, Haney re-formed **Reno and Smiley** and, as their manager, got them an audition with Sue. She gave them a regular spot at $150 per week. They stayed there until Sue decided to close it in 1957 due to poor attendance. WRVA sold it to Haney for $1 and he took over its management. The new, live show was held every Saturday night from 8:00 to 10:30; WRVA broadcast a portion of the show from 9:05 to 9:30. Every third

Bill Monroe at "Bluegrass Night", 1994, the re-opening of the Ryman Auditorium for bluegrass music since closing in 1974. Tater Tate (background) on bass.

35 Quotation by Earl Scruggs in his *Frets* column, March 1982.

Radio and Television

week, the show was broadcast over the CBS network. The show featured artists such as **Reno and Smiley and the Tennessee Cut-Ups** with little Ronnie Reno, Grandpa and Ramona Jones, Scott Stoneman and the **Blue Grass Champs**, Clyde Moody, and others.

In the 1960s, the Virginia Life Insurance company sold the old, decrepit building, closed it down, and the dangerous building was torn down. Haney moved the New Dominion Barn Dance to the smaller Belleview Theater (a movie theater). After the festivals got going, Haney needed the time to devote to the festivals so he closed it down.

Tom Gray on radio programming

Tom Gray spoke of radio programming in the mid-'60s[36], "Shortly after the phenomenon of the bluegrass festival began, the first radio programs that played purely bluegrass [appeared]. I remember when I first heard them; I wondered how somebody could get away with that. There had never been any radio programs of just bluegrass. It had always been sandwiched-in with country or, if you were lucky, in with folk music. But miraculously it did catch on to a certain audience in the non-commercial radio stations if they could find enough people who would pledge dollars to the station if they kept playing bluegrass."

Bluegrass in the movies

In July 1975, United Artists released the film "Five Easy Pieces" which starred Byron Berline, Benny Thomasson, Rual Yarbrough and Johnny Montgomery along with lesser known actors Scatman Corothers, Fanny Flagg, Sally Field, Jeff Bridges and Arnold Swartzenegger (who held the "Mr. World" body-building title at the time).

Speaking of films, Paramount Pictures' "Nashville" was released about the same time. Even though Vassar Clements, Randy Woods' Pickin' Parlor and Nashville's **Misty Mountain Boys** were in the film, it was not really concerning bluegrass music. It was a story about people in the multi-faceted, hydra-headed and multi-million dollar business known as the country music industry.

Part of the preparation for actor Robert Duvall's role as a country singer in the 1982 movie "Tender Mercies" was to observe and spend some time with Charlie Waller and Bill Monroe.

1993 brought the release of "High Lonesome," a full-length film about the history of bluegrass and was centered around Bill Monroe. "Gather at the River," a

1994 film on bluegrass music, was narrated by Peter Rowan and covered a large part of the genre.

Curtis McPeake on radio programming

About the programming of bluegrass music on the radio, Mr. McPeake said, "Program directors will not program it because they're playing top ten play lists. Bluegrass needs to be recognized for what it is, given a place in country music, and a few accolades should be handed down. I don't know how they'd handle that in country music circles. It would be hard to bring in a bunch of bluegrass boys that have been living off this music for thirty or forty years and start recognizing them. But if the large radio stations would start regularly programming bluegrass music and recognize it as being a pure American music, they would introduce it to a lot of people. It has to be classified as top-grade American music, because that's what it is."[37]

Limited airplay for bluegrass

About the lack of airplay of bluegrass records on radio stations, one of the conclusions reached at October 1976 Disc Jockey Convention was that with the many small and independent labels doing such a fine job in producing and marketing this music, perhaps bluegrass and old-time music doesn't need the distribution and production power which major labels can provide.

A letter in *BU*[38] expressed a concern about the lack of popularization of this music due to limited/restricted airplay. The author wrote, "We, as country/bluegrass music lovers, have set back, accepted whatever the semi-country radio stations who will not program bluegrass decided we would hear on the air, and we didn't raise a peep. What they are playing is not country, not rock, it's a crock." The argument he presented was that the lack of popularity of bluegrass was due to lack of airplay but this could change if we want. "Bluegrass music and fans only have limits if we set them ourselves. We don't have to force bluegrass, just give it the exposure. We don't have to apologize."

Bill Harrell on radio programming and the IBMA

An interview for *Banjo Newsletter*[39] brought out some of Bill Harrell's frustrations (and anger) at the state of the recording industry which doesn't allow much bluegrass to be played on the radio. "I know a

[36] From a 1989 interview with Tom Gray at his home.

[37] Joe Ross, "An Interview with Curtis McPeake," *Bluegrass Unlimited*, July, 1992, p. 49.

[38] Berk Bryant of Radcliff, Kentucky. A contribution to "Letters" in January 1991 *Bluegrass Unlimited*.

[39] Ted Miller, *Banjo Newsletter*, December 1987 to January 1988.

young lady in Virginia right out of Washington that can sing country music with any of the big stars that has good songs and records but she can't get airplay. It's very much the same with bluegrass artists—stations don't play them like they should. And there is a definite country flavor in bluegrass today. I never was ashamed of the old 'hillbilly' music, mountain music, country music. That's the only American kind of music there is; the rest of it was invented somewhere else. So what it all boils down to is there is a small handful of people controlling a lot of airplay.

"In the meantime now, we bluegrass entertainers have gotten together and formed the International Bluegrass Music Association with an elected board of officers and we're going to have a way to stimulate stations and try to entice them into playing our records... We'll have a Disc Jockey Convention just like there is in Nashville and I think that with the right kind of lobbying, the right kind of people behind it all, there is no reason why it (bluegrass) shouldn't be considered by any station that plays country music.

"The most stupid thing I ever heard in my life was a sponsor that said that people who like bluegrass wouldn't buy his product. Today, the audience that is bluegrass is composed of everything from truck drivers, farmers, doctors, lawyers, dentists, school teachers and any walk of life that you can find. I find that young people are delving more into the music and playing it. So the market's there, and they drink as many Pepsi-Colas as somebody that likes rock-and-roll.

"We had a bluegrass show on a local Austin radio station a couple of years ago. One of their DJs that knew bluegrass talked them into putting on a show in an open time slot from 6 a.m. to 8 a.m. on Sunday morning. In the two years that it ran, it became one of their most popular shows. They had more letters, calls and response to that show than most others. They even got a national sponsor. Unicopy told their ad people that they wanted to run a spot on that Sunday morning show.

The ad people thought they were crazy, that nobody listened to the radio on Sunday morning at 6 a.m.. So, they didn't want to put it in and mix it with country because, o-o-o-h, it would destroy it. Like, don't put this garbage in my can because it's a little dirtier than yours. That's the way they feel about it."

Harrell admitted that "What we're doing there is cramming it too hard down their throat. I think what should be done is to mix it in with country music. You segregate yourself when you take an hour show. And when they're broadcasting twenty-four hours a day, you'd like to have the possibility of having something played other than just that one hour. I have never, never been afraid to take two or three good bluegrass groups that know how to sing and put them in a package show with the best in country. I can assure you of one thing: they will more than hold their own in that particular package of entertainers. What it all boils down to is that there's a handful of very important people in Nashville, Tennessee, in the record business and that work for the magazines that control what's published.

"Ricky Skaggs [was able to adapt bluegrass music to this system]. All those songs Ricky came out with at first, gosh, we were singing them and had them recorded when he was a little kid. He just used different instrumentation. One thing I'll say for him, he's country, not pop. I'm very proud of him. I think his dedication to Ralph Stanley and Bill Monroe is wonderful. Don Reno and I sang and recorded 'I Wouldn't Change You If I Could' when Ricky Skaggs was a little baby and had a lot of airplay on it. He took a Carter Stanley song and changed the instrumentation. I took an **Ink Spots** song, 'I Get the Blues When It Rains,' just to prove a point and it's on my Rebel album, 'I Can Hear Virginia Calling Me.' We speeded that thing up about ten speeds and used banjo and fiddle and made the prettiest little bluegrass tune you ever saw out of it. Of course, the **Ink Spots** would probably roll over and faint if they heard it."

This songbook, published in 1952 by Ginsberg Music Co. of Roswell, NM, was undoubtedly on sale when the Blue Grass Boys performed at the Opry.

The presentation of bluegrass on the radio

Orin Friesen, award winning host of Bluegrass Country on KFDI, Wichita, Kansas, offered these words of advice for someone starting a local bluegrass radio show: "Strive to be professional in radio. The show should sound just as professional as everything else on the station. You should have commitment, patience and persistence. Do your homework. Keep up with the music and the music business. Continually try to improve yourself and your show. Prepare your show. Don't just throw something on the air. Do what you can to fit your program into the station's regular format. Try to keep the regular listeners. Don't drive them away."[40]

With bluegrass shows now present in all regions of the U.S., Mike Flynn wrote of the audience of his own The Folk Sampler on American Public Radio. "Everybody listens," he said. "There are doctors, lawyers, miners, truck drivers, home makers, the young and the old. What these people all seem to have in common is an interest in something that is down to earth. They write in to say that they enjoy slowing down a little and forgetting about their fast-paced life. They are wonderful people."[41]

Speaking of radio shows, Nick Forster's E-Town became available to public radio stations in the early 1990s and other stations after 1996. An issues-oriented, live, music radio program with an emphasis on the environment, it is recorded in Boulder, Colorado, and features artists such as John McEuen, Peter Rowan, Jerry Douglas and Norman and Nancy Blake.

[40]Joe Ross, "The Radio: Bringing Bluegrass to the Country," *Bluegrass Unlimited*, December, 1988, p. 74.

[41] Ibid., p. 73.

Chapter 5

Comics and Entertaining in Early Country and Bluegrass Music - Table of Contents

Comics and Entertaining

In Early Country and Bluegrass Music

luegrass and early country music used to have comedians in the act, hired just to do comedy. It was an expected part of the show—part of what they called "entertainment"—and it supplemented the music. When the venues changed from the neighborhood school house and park to big, electronically-amplified halls, and television became *the* place most people got their entertainment, the comedian quietly disappeared from the shows. While they were once considered essential for the presentation of a country show, it seems that groups were now able to get by solely on the merits of their musicianship. They would tell jokes or otherwise try to keep the show moving, but it wasn't the same; and it would never be again. The "Toby," or comedian, was gone.

In later years, comedy was brought back: Mitch Jayne, Mike Snider and Ron Thomason as story tellers, and **Red Knuckles and the Trailblazers** (who appeared with **Hot Rize** 1980 to 1990) are a few which come to mind. This was a welcome addition to our music; it was an attempt to really put on a show for the folks and it was very well received by audiences all over the world. Mitch was kind enough to contribute his/our feelings, writing from his soul with an Ozark wit as only he can. Thank you, Mitch.

A look at entertainment in bluegrass music— by Mitch Jayne[1]

*Playing bluegrass music for the fun of it was not just a **Dillard** idea. We came from a part of the country music where music is fun anyway or why on earth would you want to play it? Taking up a banjo or a fiddle is an act of good humor back home, done out of hospitality and warmth of spirit and making a living calls for more serious tools, like axes.*

*That's why, when the **Dillards** left to go out into the big world outside the Ozark Mountains, we loaded up our sense of humor first. After all, we were bringing to strangers the music of home and we wanted to polish it good to show the folks. And you have to remember that everyone we had seen and heard, either playing music on the stage at the Grand Ole Opry or doing the touring shows that got to our little towns, were entertainment people. All the pickers we'd ever seen were performers first, artists second; the whole idea being, apparently, to carry you boldly into a stage setting that defined their music.*

Mitch Jayne

*And it worked. Bill Monroe and his band wore boots in the early days, and dressed like Kentucky squires. Lester and Earl were funny people, joking with their comedian-bass players like Hylo Brown, and making dry comments to each other. **Reno and Smiley** did entire skits of music, taking on clown uniforms and changing their personalities at the same time. As banjo player with the **Hired Hands**, Snuffy Jenkins was a comedian who epitomized the wry, funny little man of country-store humor, and all the stage performers we saw were flavored with the Grand Ole Opry charm of rural comedy. The bass players seemed to be chosen for their ability to caper around that ungainly instrument. They took out their teeth, wore clown clothes, or played a character part. Some, like Lee Mace of the Ozark Opry, rode the bass around stage like an outrageous bronco, acting the fool.*

The Ryman Auditorium in those old days was a performance palace, bringing the glitter and fun of country to the world. Uncle Dave Macon was a showman of the old school who conjured up medicine show magic. Dave Akeman, with his 'Stringbeans' stage name and his soulful painted-on eyebrows, was the essence of the gawky clown, sorry for everything that confused him. Minnie Pearl and Rod Brasfield were actors who make you believe that places like "Grinder's Switch," Tennessee, could actually exist somewhere, and Grandpa Jones brought those mythical places to life with his specs and mustache and flamboyant banjo

[1] Author's note: Mitch Jayne and I met in 1991 at the Grass Valley, California, festival where the Dillards were on tour. Mitch is a fascinating person to speak with, for he has knowledge about the many facets of this music and well-developed opinions on what it takes to be an entertainer in this music. It soon became clear to me that his views and feelings on this subject were identical to mine and would fit into this book. He is well known for his literary humor which has the ability to entertain as well as educate. He is a frequent contributor to bluegrass media such as *Bluegrass Unlimited* and *Bluegrass Now*.

frailing. All of these people made you believe, for a while, what they wanted you to believe: that there is a musical world where everyone who wants to, plays something and the rest of us can join in the fun of it.

So, of course, the **Dillards** *went out to have fun. We didn't know any better—and a matter of fact, still don't. It wasn't supposed to be just fun for ourselves. It was our intention to make it fun for an audience who, if they didn't like us, were unlikely to appreciate what we did. We were going to California, of all places, and for all we knew our mountain music would be as strange to them as jazz to a bunch of Eskimos. All we knew was that bluegrass sells itself if the salesmen are engaging and friendly and willing to share their love of it with strangers.*

Back home it was sort of a family thing: a kid would hear his uncle play a fiddle tune and think "Hot damn! That sure sounds like a neat thing to do." We were pretty sure California people didn't have uncles who pulled a fiddle out of an old pillow case and struck off a tune. We started out, in other words, with the basic assumption that anyone who listened to bluegrass would want to be part of it, some way, and add it into their lives and we would stand in for the missing uncles.

Now what we found when we actually got to California (after a stop in Oklahoma to earn travel money) was a lot of people who were wide open for anything. Folk music had been wildly welcomed in that land of immigrants from the Midwest and every city had a scattering of coffee houses and showrooms all geared to the current idea of folk music, and priced for young people. Clubs like the Golden Bear, the Ash Grove, the Ice House in Pasadena, the Mecca near Disneyland, had every variety of folk you could name: flamenco guitar, bagpipes, Irish music, English folk singers, black protest singers, mountain dulcimer pickers, Schottische dancers, balladeers of all kinds. What they didn't have much of was bluegrass because nobody had gotten around to that yet as a merchandise-able folk item. They thought it was hillbilly and too pedestrian to classify as folk art.

We set in to fix that. We already played the basic American folk music; all we had to do was prove to them that we were folks.

The fact that we were almost immediately successful didn't come as a surprise to us because we honestly expected to be successful. How in the world could anyone not like bluegrass music with its crackling banjo, its joyful overdrive feel, its down-to-earth happy-to-be-here high old sound of four guys cooking up music? We sold the music with the good-natured confidence of backyard hucksters, pleased to be anywhere people had come to be entertained. We loved to hear them laugh because laughter opens doors, and the audience decided to have a good time.

On stage, we tried the old and trusted premise that if you play yourself you'll never fall out of character. I told stories about the Ozarks, mostly lies, but I included us in all the stories because they had us to look at. Rodney played the fool, Dean acted the part of the straight arrow dedicated mandolin picker beset by the foolishness around him. Douglas just towered over us grinning and exuded good nature. We looked like a bunch of rangy hillbillies in town to have a good time. The audience decided to have a good time, too. I'd see the look on the faces of the first row kids. It said, "Well, look at that! I could do that." Or even better, "Hot damn, that sounds like a neat thing to do!" And so off we went, being surrogate fiddling uncles to all these California kids, and it worked for us just fine.

In the natural course of things, bluegrass pickers have a tendency to discover each other and congregate like starlings, admiring licks and harmonies someone else has tried. Bluegrass is an inventive music, after all.

The first time I ever heard a bluegrass band of California origin play, I got uneasy in my bones because the people were missing and the music, good as it was, couldn't find them. Everyone stood tall and unsmiling and took breaks as predictable as sections of a chain link fence. They showed clever time, adept harmonies, and the combined determination of men baling hay before a storm. I realized that they were up tight and playing for strangers—but that's what everybody up one stage does, and it never had occurred to me that this might demand a personality freeze. Where was all the enormous joy that comes from showing off and getting away with it, that "Hey, how about this?" familiarity that makes bluegrass a second language for people who don't even have a first one? Where did the fun go? To use a hound-man's terms, it was like watching somebody set the dogs on a rabbit and then following the dogs when, of course, the purpose of a hound is to bring the rabbit around to you. They had forgotten the purpose of the music which is to bring the people around, and they were playing for each other!

Though the idea of people paying to watch musicians stroke each other was a new wrinkle in my horn, I was to find that it was more the state of the art in those California clubs where we played. Bluegrass was played only for people who already liked it. Fun music presented as Bach, to half-full houses.

Now all this was years ago—over thirty if I haven't lost count—and if this were a simple history of bluegrass and its early problems told by an old codger of the times, my work would be done and I could lay down some place. But that's not the case. Bluegrass music is still at the emergence state we all talked about in the '50s when everybody thought it was ripe to become a dynamic force in country music. Still fenced off by radio stations into early morning/late night corrals, still in a back corner of the Grand Ole Opry, still a separate cultural event that doesn't qualify for a country music award, bluegrass still keeps trying to happen on its own.

And part of that is its own fault. Those old boys who stood up proudly and played for themselves built their own fences. They got clique-ish with this music that belonged to everybody and became purists. Worse, they became imitators of imitators and there is no surer way to kill creativity than that. The experts had given bluegrass an attitude problem.

What bluegrass musicians can do about that today is be conscious of what it is that they do on a stage and remember that our audiences aren't jazz audiences. They are usually family people, anxious to know what the pickers are all about. Some of the most entertaining things I have heard happen on stage weren't comedy routines but simply people talking about who they were and how they got together.

Bluegrass is story music, and it's wonderful if you have a story teller like [Ron Thomason of the] **Dry Branch Fire Squad**. But I have watched a Missouri group called **Radio Flyer** simply captivate a group of people by letting each member tell a little about himself. Audiences can't wait to find out what makes a group tick. They study faces and look for clues, wanting to be part of it. A funny story (and we all have them) adds intimacy to the sharing of our music, makes an extended family out of willing strangers. There is no music less pretentious than bluegrass, which admits out front that it's hand-made. Its most famous practitioners are people who look at it as an honorable living—not an ego trip—and they want their work loved, not dissected. These people don't put on performances; they put on shows!

My advice to a beginning bluegrass band, in the event that they'd ask it, would boil down to three truisms gathered over a long, rewarding bunch of years:
• If it's not exciting, they won't like it.
• If it's not heartwarming, they won't like you.
• If it isn't the fun it looked like, they won't remember bluegrass or you anyway, so why don't you just do something else?

And finally, something we should all remember: bluegrass is not kept alive by people who play music. It's kept alive by the people who like, buy, and support music. These people give it all they've got. Go thou, and do likewise.

The legend of Toby

Toby was the generic comedian through history. When Toby was a member of a bluegrass band (often a musician), the choreography "faintly resembled ballet or perhaps modern dance with musicians ducking in and out and executing near pirouettes in order to reach one microphone. During that time, one member of the band

Cousin Jody - worked with Roy Acuff from 1933 to 1938.

often wore baggy pants, a silly hat, and had blacked-out teeth."[2] The skits were situational, somewhat slapstick, and racially inclined. But in those days, this kind of humor seemed to be socially acceptable.

The best known Toby clown for fifty years was Snuffy Jenkins. Don Reno was the Toby "Chicken Hot Rod" in his comedy spot in his band. And there were Gid Tanner (fiddle), Sam McGee (guitar, banjo), and James Clell "Cousin Jody" Summey who played Hawaiian guitar with one of Roy Acuff's early bands, steel guitar on television, and on the Opry during the '50s. Charlie Monroe's band included the comedy of banjoist Tom (Clarence) Ashley in the black-face guise of "Rastus Jones from Georgia." Ashley later became a partner to Doc Watson during the folk boom.

Toby often played bass. Examples include Cousin Wilbur, Uncle Josh, Old Dad, Humphammer, Cousin Winesap, Kentucky Slim, Uncle Snort, Greasy Medlin, Chicken Hot Rod and Cousin Mort. But these stars came along after the 1930s; the bass wasn't really a popular country music instrument until then. Some other comedians through the years played a variety of instruments. Examples include Uncle Dave Macon (banjo), Stringbean (banjo), Grandpa Jones (banjo) and Gid Tanner (fiddle).

When bluegrass became popular within the cities, Toby seemed to disappear from bands. One of the reasons for this could be because the music shifted venues from concerts at schools and community gathering locations to bars where the audience became less family oriented. And, of course, when audiences became more sophisticated about racial slurs, that aspect of it became obsolete.

Comedy acts yesterday and today

Comedians, as a team or as a solo act—whether they played instruments or not—were always prevalent on the stage of the Grand Ole Opry and other barn

2 Joe Wilson, "Sidelines in American History—When Bluegrass Bands Needed Lighting Rod Salesmen, Part 1," *Bluegrass Unlimited*, October, 1982, p. 40.

dances and live radio shows such as Chicago's WLS National Barn Dance. One of them was **Homer and Jethro** who were Henry Haynes and Kenneth Burns. This team spent most of their time at WLS. **Lum and Abner** were at the National Barn Dance. **Crazy Elmer and Cousin Emmy** were on the Jamboree show at WWVA. "Uncle Junie," "Little Clifford," "Aunt Idy" and Benjamin Francis Ford (a.k.a. Whitey "the Duke of Paducah" Ford) were at the Renfro Valley Barn Dance.

Sarie and Sallie were Mrs. Edna Wilson and Mrs. Margaret Waters of Chattanooga, Tennessee. They were the first full-time comediennes on the Opry. On the Opry at various times with Roy Acuff's band were "Cousin Rachel" (Rachel Veach) and "Bashful Brother Oswald" (Beecher R. "Pete" Kirby) who played the resonator guitar. "Cousin Jody" was James Clell Summey. Lonnie "Pap" Wilson was there. **Lasses and Honey** were actually Lasses White and Lee Davis Wild. Country singer Ferlin Husky played the part of "Simon Crum." "The Mouth of the South" was Jerry Clower and was still active into the 1990s.

Also on the Opry was **Lonzo and Oscar**, led by Rollin Sullivan ("Lonzo"). The "Oscars" have been Lloyd George, Johnny Sullivan and Dave Hooten. By the mid-1940s, the comedy team of Rollin Sullivan and Lloyd George was becoming popular in an act within the band of country singer Eddy Arnold. Sullivan already had the nickname "Oscar" but George didn't have one. Lloyd George remembered, "One night just before the War was over, Eddy checked us all into a hotel. For some time, he'd been looking for a name to go with Oscar but nothing came to mind. As we checked into this hotel a big guy came down the stairs into the front lobby with a huge armful of dirty linen—just covered with it—and this desk clerk yells, 'Lonzo! I've told you a hundred times not to come down the front way with those dirty linens!' Eddy slapped them hands together and said, 'That's it! Your name is Lonzo!'"[3]

Lonzo and Oscar recorded "I Am My Own Grandpa" on RCA. It was written by Moe Jaffe and Dwight Latham from the anecdotes of Mark Twain where Twain proved it was possible for a man to become his own grandpa by a certain succession of events beginning with the premise that if a man married a widow with a grown-up daughter and his father married the daughter, et cetera, et cetera, he would eventually become his own grandfather. The recording was their only gold record. Their popularity led them to resign

Lonzo and Oscar

from Eddy Arnold's band, start their own act, and join the cast of the Grand Ole Opry.

Sara "Minnie Pearl" Cannon and Rodney Leon "Rod" Brasfield frequently teamed up together on the Opry. She was influenced strongly by Elviry Weaver of the **Weaver Brothers and Elviry**. Regulars on the Opry included Louis M. "Grandpa" Jones, Sheb "Ben Colder" Wooley, Don Bowman (who wrote "Make Me a Star" for Chet Atkins) and Speck Rhodes (who, as of 1982, toured with Porter Wagoner).

About 1972, Wendell Watterson and Jimmy Atkins began their comedy team of the **Mayor and Buford**. Watterson was the mayor and the originator of the group. He actually *was* the mayor of Morrow, Georgia. Atkins, the nephew of Chet Atkins, was Buford (named after the north Georgia town). They began playing festivals about 1976.

Yet, as visible as these comedians were on the Opry, bluegrass music groups which were not on the Opry had very few of them. Snuffy Jenkins was classic with some of his routines in the **Hired Hands** band and the **WIS Hillbillies** with Pappy Sherrill. Early country/bluegrass bands such as Wade Mainer's **Sons of the Mountaineers** often included comedy skits, too. Others to be included in these ranks were **Reno and Smiley** act with characters "Chicken Hot Rod," "Pansy Hot Rod," "Mutt High Pockets" and Jeff Doolytater." An all-bluegrass comedy band called **Chicken Hot Rod** operated out of Charlotte, North Carolina, during the 1970s. Later bluegrass bands included the comedy of Little Roy Lewis and, most recently, **Red Knuckles and the Trailblazers**, the **Mike Snider Trio**, and Ron Thomasson of the **Dry Branch Fire Squad**.

Finally, Minnie Pearl, in 1991, said that back in those days there was no differentiation between male or female comedians—they were all called "comics."

Paul Mullins on comedians in early bluegrass acts

Paul Mullins, in a 1991 interview, spoke of the importance of comedians in early bluegrass bands, "The reason for the comedians in the bands [was because] they had to pacify the variety of audience that they would draw when they would come to a small town such as Frenchburg, Kentucky, where I'm from. Lester Flatt and Earl Scruggs had just moved to Nashville when I first saw them in 1962. If they hadn't had a comedian,

America's Music — Bluegrass

[3] Quotation by Lloyd George from *Bluegrass Unlimited*, April, 1980.

they wouldn't have had but twenty-five or thirty people really entertained by their music; they spent probably 55 or 60 percent of their time on their comedy to entertain the people that didn't know about—or didn't care about—the banjo playing and the fiddle playing and gospel singing.

"Probably one of the best comedians in the business was Chick Stripling. He worked with Bill Monroe and Ernest Tubb, and been on the Opry. (Stripling appears on the **Stanley Brothers** video with Pete Seeger and Cousin Emmy). Chick was probably the best there ever was as far as entertaining the audience. He was *more* entertaining to the people on stage. I'm talking about Carter and Ralph and myself and Curley Lambert because he really kept us *up* on stage. After he would tell the audience what he wanted them to hear, then he would turn to us—we only had one microphone then—he would turn to us and tell us what he wanted us to hear about what he had told the audience, which was twice as funny. He really kept us *up* with this.

"The same thing with Charles 'Little Darling' Elza, the one that did the pork chop dance. He was with the Stanleys for a long time when I was with them—maybe five or six months. That reminds me of a story. He always had a certain place he had to sit in the automobile—and that was behind the driver. Ralph and Carter had a new Buick we traveled in. There were six men in that car. The man that rode the 'death seat'—the death seat was the one in the middle up in front—it was really uncomfortable and we would try to rotate and get to where everybody could get a better seat all the time. But 'Little Darling' wouldn't move. He had his certain place he would set on (he was well over six feet tall and weighed 275 pounds). We played a live TV show in Fort Myers on Wednesday and we was leaving there for Orlando for a TV show. Anyhow, we stopped at a drive-in barbecue place to eat. After we ate, we all piled back into the car. He took his regular spot in the car, lit up his cigar, and went to sleep. Well, we all decided to put a surprise on him. What we did was all of us hollar and scream at the same time and then cram on the brakes. And he lost his cigar and he never did know where it went."

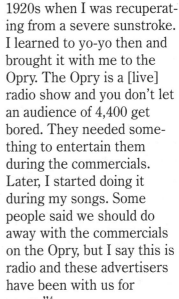

Jimmy Dean Show, 1963. L to R: Jethro Burns, Homer (Henry Haynes), Molly Bee and Jimmy Dean.

Roy Acuff—
"A man should feel that the audience specifically came to see him."

One of Acuff's trademarks was the yo-yo. "The yo-yo is an American toy and it came into being in the early 1920s when I was recuperating from a severe sunstroke. I learned to yo-yo then and brought it with me to the Opry. The Opry is a [live] radio show and you don't let an audience of 4,400 get bored. They needed something to entertain them during the commercials. Later, I started doing it during my songs. Some people said we should do away with the commercials on the Opry, but I say this is radio and these advertisers have been with us for years."[4]

Acuff's idea of performing was to entertain the audience. "There is no use to go out there if you can't entertain them... I have seen about all the Opry stars come here, except for Uncle Dave [Macon] who was already here when I joined. If Uncle Dave was performing today (1977) and speaking in his words he would say, 'Roy, Boy, the old man can still bring them in, can't he?' A man should feel that way—to go out on the stage and feel like that audience specifically came to see him. That way you will go out and do the best you can. You can't go creeping around on stage like an old man. You've got to show the audience there's life in you. If I get to the point I can't do that, it's time for me to quit the stage."[5]

Bill Foster—
"If you aren't enjoying your music, then you're just performing and not entertaining."

Dr. Bill Foster, head of the popular **Foster Family String Band** which won SPBGMA's (Society for the Preservation of Blue Grass Music in America) Old-time Band of the Year several times in a row, spoke about entertaining an audience from lessons learned from his grandfather. He said that his grandfather "felt that you should be the very best musician you can be... But he also felt that only musicians can appreciate great ability

4 Don Rhodes, "Roy Acuff, the Real Speckled Bird," *Bluegrass Unlimited*, May, 1979, p. 19.
5 Ibid., p. 19.

in a musician, and musicians don't buy the tickets and pay the bills. His point, as I see it now after forty years, was that great ability on your instrument makes you a good musician, but not necessarily an entertainer. You've got to have fun with your music, with your show, and you've got to try to make the audience have fun with it, too. Your enjoyment and your love for the music have to be contagious, and folks have to leave a concert feeling that they've gotten something besides hot picking out of it... I have seen many bands try to fake enjoyment, and I don't believe it can be done. The audience knows if you're enjoying your music; if you aren't, then, by Grandpa's standards, you're just per-forming—you're not entertaining."[6]

Entertainers in the old days really had to work at their stage shows and skits. Foster continued, "All those early string bands had a black-faced comedian, you know, Hambone and Rastus. And they would do what is almost a hick version of vaudeville. Whereas a band will come out now and in a forty-five-minute set will do, say, twelve three-minute songs and a little bit of patter in between. Those guys [string bands] might not do but six or seven songs, and then right in the middle they'd have a ten or twelve-minute comedy routine. Some of those are on early records and they are all racially oriented, of course—most of them, anyhow. Some of Charlie Poole's stuff they did with black-faced comedians." Poole, often inebriated, would engage in all sorts of on-stage antics: walking on his hands, dancing on chairs, etc..

Earl Scruggs—
"Today, the comedy's gone."

According to Earl Scruggs, the reception of his new **Earl Scruggs Revue** group was "much better received today than when we (**Flatt and Scruggs**) were playin' country in little ol' schools in the old days. The format of the show has changed. In other words, for twenty-some years, we'd go out and play three, four tunes, turning it over to a comedian who'd do ten to eighteen minutes of comedy. We'd go out and do two or three sacred numbers and another tune or two, stop and sell songbooks, pies and cakes for who ever's sponsorin' the show. Then we'd go back and do another routine and then the emcee would start endin' the show—signin' off the

Earl Scruggs

show—and people would start leavin' the school tryin' to get out before the rush.

"Today, the comedy's gone. If there's any witty lines, they have to fit in with what you're operatin' with; they have to fit in with the song or music. It's more of a musical program now than it was in the old days. The band would probably get called back two or three times for encores.

"In other words, I'd prefer to leave before giving them too much. I think also that the people between fifteen and thirty years old now, in a lot of ways—I can't say that they know more about music than they did fifteen years ago, but they seem to study it closer than they did back then—they seemed to take it for granted in the old days. They'd sit there and wait for you to entertain them and then didn't respond to what you were doing. They might have known more about it then, I'm not arguin' the point, but they didn't respond to what we were doin' and didn't seem to notice the art that we were puttin' into the instrument that we're doing today."[7]

Greasy Medlin, a black-face comedian with Snuffy Jenkins and Pappy Sherrill and the Hired Hands

In 1941, Julian Leonard "Greasy" Medlin joined **Byron Parker and the WIS Hillbillies** which included Snuffy Jenkins and Homer "Pappy" Sherrill. Greasy was hired as guitar player and black-face comedian.

Medlin was born September 18, 1910, in Dentsville, South Carolina. He got his first guitar at age eight, and at age thirteen he joined **Dr. H.E. Foxworth's Travel-ing Medicine Show**. "We sold anything to cure anything you had...anything for dandruff to fallen arches, we had it...sold tonics, oils, soaps, candies, corn medicine..." The act must have been pretty good. Medlin recalled that the Doc was "pretty smart back then...he had people fooled...he knew when to move."[8] The troupe traveled extensively, often in Washington, Virginia, Ohio, New York, Georgia and Kentucky.

Sherrill, in a 1991 phone conversation, spoke about Greasy, "He was a real comedian. He and Snuffy to-gether would really lay 'em down... Now, when I say comedy, they all are not really comedians [today]. I tell you, I've seen some where they don't hold a candle, in any way, shape or form to what we did in the years when we were doing road shows. They come out of Nashville—that's Music City. They're comedians and making money at it but, to me, I couldn't get a good belly laugh out of some of 'em. It's not like I used to hear when they really did comedy."

[6] Interview at his home in Florence, Alabama, 1989.

[7] If my memory serves me correctly, this quotation is from one of Doug Hutchens' "Bluegrass Today" radio shows. If I've misquoted, I apologize.

[8] Quotations from Julian Leonard Medlin in the liner notes of Rounder Records' fifth album (#0005) "Snuffy Jenkins and Pappy Sherrill, 33 years of Pickin' and Pluckin'." The album contained songs recorded in 1971.

Through the years, the **Hired Hands** became famous for its comedy sketches where Snuffy played the clown. Snuffy, the banjoist, wore the bright colors, the baggy pants, the rag hanging out of the back pocket and the rest. He did an excellent of keeping the rube comedian alive from its heyday in vaudeville. Some of their comedy acts included "Hookeyville School," "Snuffy Cures a Snakebite" and "Dead or Alive" with Snuffy playing the part of an undertaker. From then on, it didn't matter which instrument the comedian played—*that* part of the vaudeville tradition had changed.

Sherrill spoke about black-face comedy, which was very prevalent those days. "They used a black-faced man in the medicine shows originally. They didn't think anything about it; they used burnt cork to darken the face and did kind of a colored-man act. The people back then didn't think anything of it. You never heard no racial slurs or carrying on at all back in them days. You never had any problem with that. A person would even say 'nigra' and you never heard nothing about it. We had to stop when they started segregating the schools, [so] Greasy started putting clown makeup on instead. This was about the early 1970s."

On stage, Greasy's appearance was "'store-boughten' hair, his made-up smile, his rope guitar strap on his ancient Gibson, and hear him say, 'You ain't ever heared "Wildwood Flur" 'till you hears Snuffy "wash" it!'...and Snuffy, sittin' there in his baggy britches and stretched suspenders, those infamous shoes (size 12), with his thimbles keepin' perfect time on a one-legged washboard with its upside-down frying pan, a cow bell, and a horn with a chunk broken out...you know he's gonna honk it, but it's funny every time anyway...and the whole while, old Pappy never misses a note...you'll hear Pappy's rendition of 'The Mocking Bird'...and Snuffy's 'John Henry'...and Greasy's 'Bumble Bee'...and much, much more..."[9]

Surrounded by instruments all his life, Medlin played mandolin, guitar, banjo and bass fiddle. During his career, he also played with Hank Williams and with Eddy Arnold. Medlin stayed with the **Hired Hands**, on and off, for many years. He also worked with **Fisher Hendley's Aristocratic Pigs** from 1944 to 1945 as comedian, guitarist and bassist, but spent most of his career with Snuffy and Pappy. Medlin stars, during one of his last performances, in the 1982 University of North Carolina Center for Public Television documentary, "The Last Free Show," with Jenkins, Acuff, Sherrill and others. He retired in Columbia to run a trailer park. He passed away while still a member of **Snuffy Jenkins and Pappy Sherrill and the Hired Hands** group July 15, 1982.

Jim McReynolds on entertaining in 1949—"It's hard to stay up there for two hours and never make people laugh."

Jim McReynolds spoke about the humor in the early shows of Hoke Jenkins' **Smoky Mountaineers** when Jim and Jesse were members. They performed "a lot of comedy. I think that was a big selling point if you had a good, fast-moving show. It's hard to stay up there for two hours, singing one song after another, and never make people laugh. I think that's one thing that's missing in a lot of shows today. There's some good bands out there but you don't see too many people getting into showmanship. To really entertain an audience, you make 'em feel sad one minute and then the next one you get into, you get 'em hollerin' and laughin' with you and that sort of rounds out the show.

Jim McReynolds

"Hoke was doing comedy. I guess he got a lot of it from Snuffy; he was a good showman." Snuffy probably gave advice like, "You got to make out like you're having a good time, whether you are or not."[10]

Bill Harrell— "...make someone laugh, cry or sing..."

Harrell loves to entertain. But his secret of longevity is to present a song to each member of the audience as if they are in his living room. His motto is "If you can make someone laugh, cry or sing, you've made them part of the show."[11]

Ricky Skaggs— "If you're dead, then the audience is dead."

Skaggs spoke about showmanship, "I've always tried to look my best to look clean and decent. But all the musicians got to participate. You can't have some guy on Dobro® who's down all the time—who don't never smile or cut up and have a good time. Can't have a guitar player that's standing there, playing rhythm and looking up a thousand miles away in the sky somewhere

9 Quotation from Pat Ahrens, "A History of the Musical Careers of Dewitt "Snuffy Jenkins, Banjoist and Homer "Pappy" Sherrill, Fiddler," (West Columbia, South Carolina: Wentworth Corporation, 1970)

10 Julie Knight, "Hoke Jenkins, Pioneer Banjo Man," *Bluegrass Unlimited*, September, 1985, p. 29.

11 Ted Miller, "Bill Harrell; An Interview," *Bluegrass Newsletter*, December 1986 - January 1987, p. 6.

thinking about how he'd like to be out fishing or squirrel hunting or something like that. You can't have a banjo player standing there dead-headed and won't look and smile at the crowd or look up and wink at the girls. If a crowd sees that you're having a good time on stage, then they have a good time. If you're dead, then they're dead."[12]

Bill Lowe of the Stanley Brothers— "Music that don't come out and get a hold of you ain't no damn good."

In 1955, Mercury released the **Stanley Brothers'** two quartet numbers: "I Hear My Savior Calling" and "Just a Little Talk with Jesus." Recording with the band at that time included members Curley Lambert (mandolin), Art Stamper (fiddle) and Joe Meadows[13] (fiddle). Bill Lowe sang bass, Meadows sang baritone.

Lowe was often the third part of the Stanley sound, the same part George Shuffler did for many years. He was born May 8, 1930, in Hatfield, Kentucky, where he grew up listening to Bill Monroe and the **Carter Family**. Like many pioneer musicians of the day, he moved around to various radio stations and in and out of various bluegrass-type bands. He spoke about attitudes about the business of music, "I do all I can to get all there is in a song out of it. Music that don't make you either cry, feel good or want to jump up and clog—if it don't reach you right off, come out and get a hold of you—it ain't no damned good. It's like canned food; it don't have no flavor.

"There's more to playing an instrument than just noting it or just playing a chord. The emphasis you put on it has got to come out of your head and down through your fingers and out onto those strings—the expression has got to come off those strings right. If it don't, then it sounds mechanical."[14]

The Mike Snider Trio with Glenn Duncan (R) and Bobby Clark.

An emcee should entertain

Dave Stever wrote an article called "Emcee Work" for the December 1982 issue of *Bluegrass Unlimited*. He said, "Communication with audiences has become more and more important with bluegrass groups today, as opposed to groups playing twenty-five years ago. One reason is the tremendous competition between groups bidding for jobs at festivals and the like. The bands have had to concentrate more on their whole presentations—music, as well as the time when there is an absence of music—on stage."

Mike Snider— an entertainer first, a banjoist second

Mike Snider was nominated as one of the Top Five Comedians in the United States. This banjoist was then overwhelmed with invitations including one to be a regular on the television show "Hee Haw." Now, "I'm as busy as a cat in a sawdust pile."

Born and raised on a farm in Gleason, Tennessee, Snider got his first taste of country music when his father brought home a **Flatt and Scruggs** album. After being thoroughly captivated by the music, he got a banjo when he was sixteen and pursued show business with an overwhelming desire to entertain. He practiced incessantly: before the school bus came, and in the afternoons before feeding the hogs. Soon he entered banjo contests and won many of them including the Tennessee State Bluegrass Banjo Contest (age 21) and the National Bluegrass Banjo Championship (age 23). But his banjo playing, as good as it was, served mainly as a prop for his act which emphasized comedy.

Soon afterwards, through the efforts of fellow Gleason resident Gordon Stoker and others, Snider was invited to play on the Grand Ole Opry...to be introduced by Roy Acuff. The Opry then did something that has never been done before or since: it invited the entire town of Gleason to watch him perform. Those 2000 tickets were gone in forty-eight hours. Snider received four standing ovations during his first Opry performance and received the Key to the City from the Mayor of Nashville. Acuff described it this way, "Never in my forty-five years of performing on the Opry have I witnessed an event such as this. This is very unusual for the Opry. I've never seen a young man so celebrated, and I'm glad he's here."[15] Snider was inducted into the Opry family on June 2, 1990. He has made over a hundred appearances on The Nashville Network's

---

12 Jack Tottle, "Ricky Skaggs: Clinch Mountain to Boone Creek," *Bluegrass Unlimited*, January, 1977, pp. 15, 16.

13 Ralph Meadows was nick-named "Joe" because of the other "Ralph" in the band.

14 Eugenia Snider, "Bill Lowe: Fruit From the Real Vine," *Bluegrass Unlimited*, March, 1985, pp. 13, 14.

15 I lost the source of this quote.

(TNN) "Nashville Now" show. He became a regular member of the "Hee Haw" television show in 1987.

James Bailey—
"People pay their money to be entertained."

"Being a professional musician is being an entertainer. People pay their money and come to a show to be entertained. These people are most important to the performer. A lot of times, you may play to entertain yourself or to entertain other musicians. This may limit your ability to communicate with your audience."

James Bailey said of Roy Clark, "Technically, you know, there are better banjo players and so forth. But Roy Clark has made it by communicating; he makes people feel good just watching him."[16]

Paul Mullins—
"Each time you face an audience, you've got to have something just a little bit different."

On the topic of performing at his best, fiddler Mullins said that the best performance usually came the second day on a tour. "You need to be worn down just a little bit and get over last night. It'll knock the edge off of you. You're a little bit edgy if you haven't played four or five days. You have a tendency to jump at it; you're not real smooth. By the time the second night rolls around, all that apprehension is gone. You do a better show then. Everybody is more cohesive right then.

"Each time you face an audience, you've got to have something just a little bit different. For example, when we play the Moose Lodge in Elizabeth, Pennsylvania (we've played it two times now) the first time we was there (with his **Paul Mullins and Traditional Grass**) we broke the ice for the people. They had just heard some of our music that one of the local disc jockeys played on the air; they didn't know what they was gonna hear at all. They didn't know they was gonna hear real, heart-felt, traditional music. We went back again this last

September (1991) and they knew what to expect and what they was gonna hear. It's so much easier to work for the crowd then." Their band name, **Traditional Grass**, tells people what kind of music they play and what to expect. That helps break the ice as well. When they went back to the same venue the following March, they found that the place was full of traditional bluegrass fans.

He continued, "There is a real cohesiveness between the audience and the stage when people really understand what you're doing. Each member of the band will pick out at least one person in the audience and make eye contact with and play to. When my wife is in the audience I pick her out (he laughed). When my daughter (Chris) is in the audience I pick her out and by her expressions I can tell how we are doing up there. You can't always tell by listening to the monitors. She really knows what is and what ain't. She's only eighteen years old and she really grew up with the people who like hard rock and all that kind of stuff, but she really knows about the big names [of bluegrass music]. I didn't say she couldn't listen to rock and roll—I just said I don't want to hear it. She really loves bluegrass."[17]

Mike Snider

[16] From a 1992 telephone interview.
[17] 1992 interview at his home in Middletown, Ohio.

Chapter 6

America's Music — Bluegrass

Bill Monroe and the Blue Grass Boys
His biography and what others say about him - Table of Contents

Bill Monroe and the Blue Grass Boys

His biography and what others say about him.

erhaps *the* most important person in the history of bluegrass music is Bill Monroe. With that as the introductory sentence to a very important subject, let's see why.

Pete Kuykendall—
"Monroe is still creating" in his eighties.

Bill Monroe, according to IBMA Hall of Honor entrant Pete Kuykendall in a 1989 interview, was still creating and playing his own music at a very advanced age. Mr. Kuykendall explained that "There are people like Segovia and Casals who could play at an advanced age, but were usually not performing their own music, and the ones who created the music stopped creating their music. Monroe is still creating. It is definitely a phenomenon. That's one reason why I give him a lot more credit than I give to, for example, the Flatt and Scruggs connection with

Bill Monroe, 1990.

the band. It's not saying that they didn't create, but they didn't continue to create like Monroe has."[1]

Jake Landers—
"You have to give the guy credit as being an innovator."

In 1962, Jake Landers (guitar) and Rual Yarbrough (banjo) worked for Bill Monroe on a fill-in basis. Also in the band were Monroe, Kenny Baker and Bessie Lee Mauldin. When Landers played rhythm guitar for Monroe he had to adapt to Monroe's rhythm. Landers said, "Monroe's timing is a little bit different than what a lot of people play. He plays a little bit ahead of the beat—the way I feel it—and it takes a little while to get adjusted to that. And there are others whose timing feels like they are playing behind the beat... I wouldn't consider that as *the* correct beat for bluegrass. I'm sure

Bill feels that way, but it's just one of quite a few 'cause there are different interpretations of music with regards to what field you are talking about...jazz or whatever, that interpret it different. So therefore their timing might be a little bit different or their feel for it may be a little bit different."

Nevertheless, Landers considers Monroe as the "Father of Bluegrass Music". As such, it may be assumed Bill Monroe invented it, so what he does is "correct" bluegrass. Others who follow may change it to the way they feel. Their feel, or interpretation, may be "correct" by today's standards, but not absolutely "correct" because it is not *exactly* how Monroe did it. "I'll tell you something else," added Landers. "A lot of people just look at Bill for his music. But the guy is really a talented individual as far as writing is concerned and putting together melodies that endured down through the years. I have a lot of admiration and respect for him. He didn't have a lot of things to go by that a lot of musicians have today. He didn't have all these other things to listen to. So you have to give the guy credit as being an innovator at that point in time."[2]

Doyle Lawson—
"I wish people could understand what he's doing because it's so unreal."

Doyle Lawson is a Monroe disciple and loves what Monroe created and played. He feels that "The new people that are coming along now haven't really taken time to listen to what Bill plays. Bill doesn't play as many notes, but there's a difference in the way he projects. What he does with one note might take me two or three to do.

"I wish people could understand what he's doing because it's so unreal. It's just a little riff that he'll do and suddenly you'll say, 'Wait a minute!' And you back

---

[1] From a March 1989 telephone interview.

[2] 1991 interview.

up the record and listen to it again. And he's just done a smashup riff that you've got to listen to. It's the way he delivers."[3]

Bill Box—
"Bill Monroe looks at a lot of different angles whenever he hires a musician."

In an interview with Bill Wilhelm in 1978, Bill Box, who played guitar with Monroe about 1971, spoke of Bill Monroe, "Bill hires a man not only for his music, he's got to have a fellow that won't hit the bottle on him and will work along with him. You don't always play music when you work for Bill Monroe. You might play music today, and if he needs you out at his place you might build a fence the next day. Bill, he's a workin' man. He's got a farm, you know, and he expects a country boy to know how to handle all that stuff. He knew that I had worked horses and all that. And he has cattle. He looks at a lot of different angles whenever he hires a musician."

Bill Keith—
"Bill's music had a lot of effect on me."

Bill Keith described some of his experience with Monroe in 1963, "When I joined Bill it was pretty intense. I got there on Thursday, officially tried out on Friday night, joined the union Saturday, and played on the Opry Saturday night. And then we recorded right away, which I regretted because the music improved greatly as the band stayed together... Musically, the band was successful. Economically, it was a tough time for Bill and bluegrass music. I think Bill liked what I was doing—in fact I'm sure he did. He wouldn't have asked me to join the band if he hadn't liked it. He hadn't recorded in some time, but in two weeks after I joined the band we practiced up and went to the studio and did six instrumentals and one vocal and then we started whipping up some attention on the Opry and I think some work started to come in. So things were perkin' up. Seems to me—and I'm not trying to imply in any way that I was largely responsible for that but—it was great to be a part of that scene when things were picking back up because there was a low ebb there. This was before the Bean Blossom Festival started and essentially there was not much work and not much money around.

Bill Monroe at the Bell Cove Inn, 1994.

"Bill's music had a lot of effect on me. Strangely enough, I hadn't heard a lot of his music before I went to work for him. I'd listened a lot to banjo things—Scruggs and Reno—and his earlier things, but I didn't know any words. So everything he did had a big effect on me. I remember picking up dynamic ideas he would use where he would play the first lines of a break in one style and then change styles in the last line. I remarked on that. I remembered the variations he would go through, playing one song week in and week out. A lot of things would happen and I would notice them. So hearing his playing had quite an effect on me. One thing—it made me use the style that I had put together less and less in standard bluegrass material and limit it to instrumentals and fiddle tunes and breaks. When I went there, I had mastered most of the rolls. I had my vocabulary; I just improved my technique—phrasing, timing. Earl, on the other hand, when he first was with Bill, used mostly a forward roll but he added considerably to his vocabulary while he was with Bill and really defined his style. I improved a lot with Bill. You couldn't help it. You wanted to. It felt great. It was always getting better. It was a tonic."[4]

"He created his music from the elements of blues, old-timey and old-time music, and the influence of several black musicians from Kentucky," continued Rooney. "All those ideas were swimming around Monroe's head and came out as what we know as bluegrass music."

In a 1992 telephone interview, Keith spoke more of Monroe's contribution to bluegrass, "I think what he added, in addition to being a great mandolin player, was his vocals and the songs that he's written and that bluesy sound, and it was the introduction of the long bow and double stops and bluesy notes with the fiddle. And that's what began to separate bluegrass. That, to me, is what made it remarkable and able to stand out from old-time music and from what his brother Charlie was doing... I feel also that he had an idea for what every instrument had to do to make a band a cooperative effort where everybody fills the gap but there wasn't so much overlap—instead of everybody playing at once. He had a vision and he was able to get what he needed from the many musicians who had worked with him over the years, and in spite of the change in personnel, to build toward that conception which he had in his mind of what music could be or should be. To me, I think that's where he deserves the most respect. Sure, he's a fine mandolin player and a fine singer and he has great rhythm—and those are technical aspects—but the creative aspects,

3 Jack Tottle, "Doyle Lawson and Quicksilver," *Bluegrass Unlimited*, November, 1980, p. 16.

4 James Rooney, *Bossmen: Bill Monroe and Muddy Waters* (New York: Da Capo Press, 1971), p. 82.

to me, is a more global, more encompassing thing than just playing 'Rawhide' and singing the higher notes than you expect."

Kenny Baker—
"He doesn't mind when someone outshines him on the stage."

In an interview[5] with Roger Siminoff, Baker talked about how to be a new person in Monroe's band, "Well, just play the music, keep your mouth shut—truly, that's the basics. He's more lenient now than he used to be. When you're traveling, he hates cutoff jeans and tennis shoes, stuff like that. He doesn't mind when someone outshines him on the stage. He puts this group together, and if one man gets a real good hand it's his own good fortune; there's no jealousy. Maybe at one time there may have been some of that, but not now. Not at all. It makes Bill feel good to see a man sell his (Monroe's) music.

"Gettin' back to my work with Bill," said Baker, "I give Bill credit; he worked with a lot of different people and he had banjo players comin' and goin', guitar players. Bill was always conscientious about being sure that those boys all had money to eat on when we went on these trips. I'll tell you something else. Out of all the time that I worked for Bill Monroe—we'd be out on the road and if that bus was in transit we might sleep on the bus—but if we hit a town playing and that bus was not on the road moving, he always checked us into a real comfortable motel. That's one thing I respect Bill for because he was concerned enough about his boys that he wanted them to be comfortable... But sometimes there was a newcomer in the band and they were maybe a little backward. Anyway, they hesitated to ask for a little advance in money and things and Bill asked me several times to be sure some new guy had money in his pocket to eat on. That's a side of Bill that a lot of people probably wouldn't even think about."[6]

Richard Greene—
"Everything was very black and white."

Looking back on the experience as a Blue Grass Boy, Greene spoke candidly about his ex-boss, Monroe "was a very good teacher and insisted on the rhythm being even (his own, he admits was inconsistent). For the first three months, I wasn't even allowed to play any notes except for my solos. I had to play rhythm the whole time and that's very good for teaching rhythm. In fact, that's where I developed that percussive rhythmic stuff (which is similar to Scotty Stoneman's bouncing bow technique). It's related to the 'Orange Blossom Special' sound where you scrape the bow on the string."[7] Greene was paid $27.50 per show.

When they toured, "I remember when Monroe used to get rooms for us. He'd get one for the band and another for him. The one for the band usually had only two beds and there were four of us. So, we had to become accustomed to sleeping two in a bed." Nevertheless, "I was very fortunate to work for Bill because of the way we focused on his music. It was always easy to get the 'truth' about what we were involved in, which was his way of playing music. If he liked it, it was right. If he didn't, it was wrong. Everything was very black and white... Since that time, I've learned that that approach to music was unique. It was like being a bluegrass major in music school—very unlike these days when you're constantly trying different directions and are never able to say 'Enough!' Even today, I still long for that convenient source of the 'truth' we had in those days. It was never again like that for me."

Greene added that Monroe was not involved in the commercialism of his music. "He couldn't care less about it. It was never an issue. The only issue was to present his music 'correctly' the way he wanted it."[8]

"He was a strict taskmaster, but liked me and he was very supportive. We never had any of the problems that he is so famous for. Just the way I held my hands on the instrument gave me a little different look—a classical look. That added points, especially since I used that technique only to perfect his music. He would do a phrase on the mandolin and I would play the same phrase on the fiddle doubling what ever notes he doubled. He appreciated the way I was able to capture his meaning. He would indicate when he liked something, and that would be a great feeling of accomplishment on the part of his sidemen."[9]

Greene explained the importance of his ex-boss, "Bill Monroe is like the Charlie Parker in bluegrass. Bebop certainly lived during Charlie Parker *and* after. But when he was gone, the originator was gone, the *force* behind bebop was gone. Since the forties on, there have been all kinds of bluegrass bands—not exactly as Monroe plays it—they lived then they will live on. He was the inventor, the originator. It was almost exactly the same as Parker in terms of their relationship to the music they invented. Another one would be Duke Ellington when you talk about once-in-a-lifetime, gigantic figures. Hank Williams."

---

[5] Quotation from an article about Bill Keith in *Bluegrass Unlimited* magazine. Author and date of source unavailable at this time.

[6] Brett F. Devan, "Kenny Baker—One of the Masters," *Bluegrass Unlimited*, February, 1991, p. 24.

[7] Richard J. Brooks, "An Interview with Richard S. Greene, Virtuoso Violinist," *Bluegrass Unlimited*, November, 1984, p. 20.

[8] Ibid., p. 21

[9] Ibid., p. 19.

Vassar Clements—
"If you're really interested in what Bill's doing, he'll take all kinds of time with you."

Clements learned a lot from Monroe. "I would just watch him play. I'd sit down for hours with him while we were in-between shows. I'd sit backstage and try to get note-for-note on the fiddle what he was doing on the mandolin. He'd show me how all the old tunes went, and he was real patient with me. If you're really interested in what Bill's doing, he'll take all kinds of time with you. At least, he did with me. And I learned so much right there, I'll never forget any of it. And I'm constantly using what I learned from him now."[10]

Vic Jordan—
"When it's your turn to play, then let them have it."

Vic Jordan took the place of Lamar Grier on banjo July 27, 1967. He stayed until March of 1969. From Monroe he learned "a lot of the things that really mattered: what to look for in the tone of the instrument. That is, how to get a particular tone for a particular song, and how to play *time*. Monroe had a lot of influence on my timing. He taught me that there's a difference between speed and quickness. Quickness has to do with the individual note; speed is one note after the other. Quickness is touch. Like Monroe said once, 'Everyone thinks I'm fast, but I'm not. I'm quick.'"

Monroe would give helpful hints in effective playing but he never would say, "Don't play that, play this." Jordan continued about Monroe, "He's a stickler for melody. When it's instrumental time, he wants to hear tone, time and melody. No razzmatazz. Now, when he's singing he wants good, solid drive and good fill behind him—pretty good stuff, but don't get flaky back there. When it's your turn to play, then let them have it."[11]

Dick Spottswood—
"Bluegrass has been a major American musical achievement..."

Author Dick Spottswood wrote philosophically about Monroe's band when Scruggs joined. Spottswood said that while Stringbean's banjo never quite fit into Monroe's **Blue Grass Boys**, "Earl Scruggs, on the other hand, not only fit in, he threatened to run away with the show. Surely there were uncomfortable moments as audiences wildly cheered the young man,

whose revolutionary approach to an instrument which had all but been discarded, sounded as dramatic as Monroe himself had ten years earlier. Whether he wanted to or not, Earl Scruggs routinely upstaged his boss for most of the time they worked together—and it's to Bill Monroe's credit that he didn't mind. The argument continues as to whether there was bluegrass before Earl Scruggs; I feel that there was, since the sounds of the mandolin, fiddle, rhythm instruments and vocal duets, trios and quartets were already in place before the war. But there's no question that the banjo was the last foundation block of the bluegrass sound in its classic form. Even the Dobro®, for all its contributions, has never become as essential to the fabric as the first five instruments. This is due surely in part to Monroe's refusal to have one in his band.

"It's remarkable enough that Bill Monroe has survived to begin his 81st year on this planet, given the amount of intensity of his work, the endless miles of highway and endless amounts of bad food consumed over those miles. But that he survives as the world's very best performer on his chosen instrument, as a singer with at least most of his voice (and all of his gifted ear) intact and as a hard-working, professional bandleader whose music continues to instruct and inspire, is truly phenomenal. Pianists like Vladimir Horowitz, Artur Rubinstein and Eubie Blake survived into their eighties and beyond, but these were seated solo performers who worked when they chose rather than under the demanding and less rewarding conditions imposed even on a veteran musician of Monroe's status.

"It would be hard to find another musical figure to whom Bill Monroe's multi-faceted achievements could be compared. Bob Wills comes close. Like Bill, he created a new music synthesizing and expanding on earlier styles, creating a successful formula whose effects have lasted for generations and thereby creating new traditions out of old ones. The comparison fails only when you consider the two as actual musicians. Wills was a congenial old-style Texas fiddler who collected a broad array of talented musicians and allowed them to develop on their own. He created an eclectic mixture of the blues, hoe-downs, country songs, pop songs, western songs, big and small band jazz, though he contributed as a fiddler only to the more traditional pieces he could comfortably play, leaving the hot licks to the likes of Joe Holley, Jesse Ashlock and Johnny Gimble. Monroe, on the other hand, developed a unified set of music principles, teaching each sideman exactly what was necessary to make his music work and drawing his material from a limited range of country songs and composing hundreds—even to this day—to fit the bluegrass aesthetic. Even though Bill's descendants have departed from his model in numerous ways,

10 Rick Gartner and George Gruhn, "Vassar Clements, the Superbow Instinct," *Frets*, July, 1984, p. 15.
11 David Robinson, "Vic Jordan," *Pickin'*, August, 1974, p.6.

it's safe to say that all of them are aware of the model itself and the musical integrity for which it so firmly stands.

"Bluegrass has been a major American musical achievement, not only in its development but in its persistence and world-wide spread. Bill Monroe, who at one time saw those who emulated his music as claim jumpers and competitors, has long since accepted Ralph Rinzler's early '60s designation of him as the 'father' of a discrete musical style. If imitation is the sincerest form of flattery, Bill's thousands of flatterers pay tribute to him each time they pick up an instrument. I think it's safe (or soon will be) to number him among this century's greatest music figures like Igor Stravinsky, Hank Williams and Duke Ellington."

Paul Mullins— ## "It came from the heart and it was good."

In a 1991 interview with this writer, Mr. Mullins spoke about Bill Monroe during the mid-sixties, "He had something good and he *knew* that he had something good. It came from the heart and it was good. But think of how many people made fun of him for singing high and loud and clear and having the show that he had. A lot of people really made fun of him. They called it 'corn' before the word 'bluegrass' really took hold. No wonder Monroe had a hard look in his eye towards all those who came to him with their hand out. I can really understand that. Hell, he had his heart and soul in it. He still does! You know that people make remarks about Monroe being a hard man. Hell! He's not!

Monroe's got a heart of gold. He's a genuine, decent fellow. In the thirty years that I've known him, he's mellowed a lot. Hell, to survive—think what he's done and not changed—you think you don't have to be hard? You'd better be!"

When asked if Bill Monroe invented bluegrass music, he replied, "Monroe set the pattern and Monroe had some things to do with how it was played—the fiddle player especially. He showed Chubby Wise what he wanted him to play. He played the notes on the mandolin for Chubby to play on the fiddle. Chubby told me this himself. That's where the blues is—right there! I don't know if Monroe had anything to do with Scruggs' playing at all.

"When you talk about bluegrass, you got to talk about the blues. Monroe knows about the blues. I'm sure that he had a big influence on Scruggs. I know he did on the fiddle player."[12]

Butch Robins— ## "Bluegrass *is* Bill Monroe."[13]

"I've always been drawn to the energy of Monroe's music, real ultra-high energy, acoustic music," said Butch Robins who was a personal friend of Bill Monroe. It hits you on the quarters, it hits you anywhere Bill Monroe can hear to play rhythm to it, and he can play just about anywhere you can think of to play—and it will be right! The syncopations and everything he does come in extremely funny places and he'll have to do one ten or fifteen times before you can hear it. Some of them are so subtle that when you start getting into it you think you're hearing things.

"Bluegrass *is* Bill Monroe. It started there and it stops there. It's his rhythm chop on the mandolin and it's the power of his voice, the range of his voice, the range of the lead lines he plays on the mandolin. There are a lot of people who have added to it, but that's all they've done. They weren't *it* when they got there and they weren't *it* when they left. They added lead lines, solo breaks, but the thing that made it bluegrass—nobody added. Monroe brought that and he'll take it home with him. He plays with power. He gives every tune a different face, a different color, a different mood that's extremely hard to do, especially in these little two and a half or three-minute energy blasts—and they are intense little blasts. It's the most exciting rhythm I've ever played to by far. I used to try to define it as 'white country people's blues music' but it's more than that. It touches people in rock—from Elvis Presley recording 'Blue Moon of Kentucky' all the way to the **Eagles** who have turned around and used the banjo as a lead instrument out front—and it came courtesy of Bill Monroe. If it hadn't been for him, there would have been no such thing as someone playing a banjo. He was a vehicle for Earl Scruggs. Where else in 1945 could Earl Scruggs have gotten the mass audience he got with Bill Monroe.

"It's a cross of the folkies and the jazz and the blues people 'cause it's down-to-earth music—or at least it's always been billed that way—so the folkies get into it. The blues people get into it because it's real high-

Butch Robins on banjo in 1995 at Carlton Honey's festival with Randall Collins on fiddle and Curtis Blackwell on mandolin.

[12] From a 1991 interview at his home in Middletown, Ohio.

[13] Butch Robins spent four years as banjoist with the Blue Grass Boys beginning in 1977. This is one of the longer tenures for a banjo player with Monroe.

energy, country blues music. Jazz people get into it because it has real complex lines. The melody lines themselves are complex pieces of music in bluegrass, or what I define as bluegrass' Monroe's music."[14]

Robins continued speaking about the legendary Monroe, "He's got such a magnificent dancing rhythm about him. He'll take you all the way to the depth of the blues if you want to go, but there's still a sparkle about it. I think he has to control himself because he lays lead lines down that play more rhythm than what I play behind him. I try to structure my playing around the fact that, when he's playing, whether it's backup or lead, that I should be playing rhythm chunks behind him and not playing rolls that interfere with the staccato effect he might have on the mandolin.

"That man is the ultimate test of being a bluegrass musician. The only way I could ever stand on my feet and say I was a musician is to see the day I could play for Bill Monroe.[15]

In a 1995[16] conversation with Mr. Robins, he recalled there was a significant difference in the performance technique between **Flatt and Scruggs** and Bill Monroe. **Flatt and Scruggs** more or less had certain songs during their act which they always played; they varied very little and it was easy for them to prepare for a performance because it was just a matter of rehearsing their songs. Of course, this polished music and its consistency was one of the reasons why they were so very popular. Monroe's act was much more impromptu and spontaneous than the **Flatt and Scruggs** act. He would rehearse his band very little and often create as he went along. And through the years we can see his mood swings in his music. From the love/torment (lost parents or lost emotionally) songs of the early 1950s to the more violent tunes such as "Stoney Lonesome" in the late 1950s to the more recent "tone poems" such as "Jerusalem Ridge, "The Last Days on Earth" and "Southern Flavor" which show a man comfortable with himself and confident he was deserving of the title "Father of Bluegrass Music" bestowed upon him in 1963 by Ralph Rinzler in *Sing Out!* magazine.

Curly Seckler—
"Bill beat Charlie to the Opry by two or three weeks."

Curly Seckler remembered Bill Monroe's **Blue Grass Boys** in 1944, "Monroe had a accordion and a electric guitar when Lester went to work with him. And when Earl came in there they turned his sound all the

way around. [Monroe] had never played nothing like he calls bluegrass music until Lester and Earl went to work with him. Now that's a true fact! And I never heard of bluegrass music, except what the **Morris Brothers** played, until Lester and Earl went to work with Bill. And Bill had never played no bluegrass music 'til then that I know of.

"Now, he's entitled to that name ("Father of Bluegrass Music")—period! I'm glad he's got it because he deserves it. Because he was out there just a year or two before I went. But I would tell him today if he was over here (at my home) that Charlie lacked two weeks of beatin' him to the Opry. Now, we (**Charlie Monroe and the Kentucky Pardners**) was in Wheeling, West Virginia, when Charlie asked us if we would like to go to the Opry. I told him it was fine with me—wherever he goes. I was working for him. And he said we was scheduled to go in there for an audition in two weeks. Turned around and we was [listening to the Opry] one night and it said 'Bill Monroe and the Blue Grass Boys.' [Charlie] got up and left [the room]. So Bill beat him in there two or three weeks."[17]

Don Stover—
"Bill Monroe was the finest man I ever worked for."

Don Stover worked for Bill Monroe for six months in 1956. Stover said of Monroe, "...the finest man I ever worked for. Sometimes he'd call over to my hotel room and say, 'Let's go,' and we'd figure we were going out to do a show. In the end, we'd be over on his farm plowing with a mule or loading hay bales or chasing fox."[18]

About the reason for leaving Monroe, he told this writer, "There's things that people don't know and there's things that you can say that can hurt other people, and I don't want to do that. And a lot of people who are a star like Bill Monroe don't want to tell you that I been a-working for two years and I can't make a salary. You know what I'm saying? Bill Monroe stayed by his guns and he run through 879 banjo players and 1600 fiddle players and guitar players and he still hung in there. They'd go to work for him awhile and they couldn't get even a week's salary to pay their hotel bill and eat off of because everybody knows the business.

"Lester and Earl already had a Martha White sponsor. They had everything in both hands right there. They had it! But Monroe didn't have nothin'. He ran through all those musicians, but he still stuck right in there and today he's known as the 'Father of Bluegrass

14 Barry Silver, "Butch Robins," *Bluegrass Unlimited*, May, 1979, pp. 50, 51.

15 Ibid., p. 53.

16 From a July 1995 interview at Carlton Haney's festival in Berryville, Virginia. This festival was put on as the thirtieth anniversary of Haney's first festival in 1965. Mr. Robins had been out of the music for some time at this point and was making an intense effort to return.

17 Phone interview with Curly Seckler, June 1992.

18 Jack Tottle, "Big Banjo from Boston: The Don Stover Story," *Bluegrass Unlimited*, March, 1973, p. 8.

Music'... As far as I'm concerned, Bill and Charlie Monroe started bluegrass music. They just did not have a banjo! But if there had been a man, back in those days, who could play banjo just like Earl Scruggs, I believe that Bill and Charlie would-a had him in their band. That's my belief right there!"

Tater Tate—
"This music wouldn't be the same without that mandolin chop."

Mr. Tate[19] spoke about how Bill Monroe deals with a new member in the band, "It's not as bad as probably a lot of people make it sound. If somebody come in, he'll listen for a while—a few weeks or something or other like that—if they's a little something that don't sound just right to him, he'll probably eventually say something to him about it. It's usually something simple that he's not hearin' right and it can be worked out right there most of the time. That's just Monroe. That's just what he wants. Now, down through the years, I've heard a lot of people say how rough he is to work with, you know. I don't know where they got that at unless they brought it on theirselves. From what I've seen of him, he's been a gentleman to me."

Tate spoke of Monroe's music, "In the years past, I believe he used to do more just rhythm chop than he does now. A lot of times now, when a lead instrument like a fiddle would take a break, a lot of times he would be playin' along with it. This music wouldn't be the same without that mandolin chop."[20]

Bobby Atkins—
"Flatt and Scruggs played the best bluegrass music that has ever been played."

"Now, I'm not takin' nothin' away from Bill Monroe or nobody," said banjoist and band leader Atkins, "but in my book, Flatt and Scruggs played the best bluegrass music that has ever been played. As pretty as Flatt and Scruggs sounded with Monroe, Curly Seckler sounded better with them than Monroe did because he matched their voices better. Lester was more like myself—he was more of a country singer than Bill. The phrasing is a little different. He put more feelin' there. Now Bill could sing it, but the thing of it is that Bill couldn't find anyone to sing it with feeling with him after Lester left him. That's his problem, it's not Bill!"[21]

Atkins spoke of what it was like to work for Monroe, "Bill, at that time, wouldn't give you his phone number. I had to reach Bill through Bertha, Bill's sister, who was in the hospital. If I wanted to get in touch with Bill I had to call the hospital and talk to either Charlie or Birch Monroe and leave a message for him to get back to me. I had such a hard time paying bills that I had to tell the motel owner that we were due to go out tomorrow and that I would pay him then. [This was hard on me] and so when we went out the next time, I said this was *it* for me. Our tour ended up in Bluefield, West Virginia, and that's where I left Bill. He set and talked to me for an hour or two, saying that we were just getting to where we could pick and sing together good. He said we got an album to do. When we get back to Nashville I'll pay you $350. I had a wife and three young'uns at home. I said, 'Bill, I can't be out there and be throwed out of the motel. I can't go back like that. I can get by in Greensboro—I got people there—but I can't get by in Nashville. And he said, 'Bobby, your wife's people will look after her until you get back.' I said, 'Well, Bill, that is not their place. That is *my* place.' He tried to convince me to stay but I just told him to pay me what he owed me and I'll be on my way. He didn't pay me what he owed me. He paid me just like he did Vassar. He give me just enough bus fare to get back home. And I went back home and started working for Sears and Roebuck through the Christmas rush. I still kept my music up in spite of the hard times. Carlton Haney called me and asked me to fill in [with Monroe's band] until he could get a band together. All he had was (Tommy or Benny) Jarrell, (Frank) Wakefield and (Red) Allen .

"This is the way I look at it," explained Atkins. "I don't think Bill owes me a dime because I learned enough with Bill Monroe that I figure we are straight. As far as I'm concerned, Bill Monroe is one of the finest singers and musicians that ever lived—in any field! In my book, his timing is perfect. He is the easiest man in the world to sing and play with because of that timing. And I love him. I don't hold no grudges; I may not have known it at the time, but I sure realized it pretty quick afterwards. It's like Carlton Haney says, 'If you've ever played with Bill Monroe, your timing is right.' I thought I had played bluegrass music until I played with Bill Monroe. Then I seen the difference. I learned timing, phrasing, and how to perfect my country singing. Now I know the difference and I'm grateful."

[19] Clarence "Tater" Tate played for many of the great bluegrass bands through the years: bands such as the Bailey Brothers and the Happy Valley Boys (1950), the Sauceman Brothers and the Greene Valley Boys (1950), the Blue Grass Boys (1956), Carl Story's Rambling Mountaineers, Hylo Browns's Timberliners and Red Smiley and the Bluegrass Cut-Ups.

[20] Another fine chop mandolin player, Tate explained in this 1991 telephone interview, "was Curly Seckler when he worked with Flatt and Scruggs."

[21] From a 1992 interview in Owensboro, Kentucky.

Tony Ellis—
"When Lester Flatt and Earl Scruggs came along, it became very apparent what the right sound was."

In a 1991 phone interview with Ellis, who worked as Bill Monroe's banjoist February 1960 to June 1962, he spoke about Bill Monroe as the "Father of Bluegrass Music". He said that Monroe knew what he wanted as bluegrass music "in late 1939 or 1940. I think he was still trying to come up with a firm consensus as to what bluegrass music was to be. But at that point I think he had almost reached a decision as to what kind of music his band would end up being...he was groping around. Of course, when Lester Flatt and Earl Scruggs came along it became very apparent what the right sound was. I think that clearly defined bluegrass music forever... Lester and Earl, more or less, were two of the supports under bluegrass music: the banjo of Earl and the guitar playing and singing of Lester; the harmony they did was so good.

"But Bill's mandolin was really the essence of bluegrass music because of the blues that were involved in it and the excitement and the electricity that came from that mandolin. And that transferred over to the fiddle. You'll hear a lot of fiddle notes being played very much like some of the mandolin notes that Monroe played...and I've never heard anyone else, except for someone who was copying Bill closely, play the notes the way he did. So I feel very clear in my mind that he fully developed that mandolin style, and [that] his mandolin style is the real backbone of bluegrass.

"And, of course, the blues in the singing that he did...especially the blues and the inflection in the singing. was so different than other country music forms... Monroe told me he worked in the fields with black people and that's where he learned harmonies and that's where he learned to feel blues the way that he transposed into music as he was playing it when I was playing with him.

"Other than George Wynn in Richmond, Virginia,[22] I don't know anyone in the world that can play rhythm mandolin like Bill Monroe. When he's excited and really wants to play, he can really build a fire under a band." And this was just with the mandolin keeping rhythm.

"He (Monroe) was pretty demanding. He wanted things *his* way. That was appropriate and I didn't mind at all because it was his music—he *is* the father of that kind of music—and he knows what he wants. He's not there to make a name for himself or for somebody else. He's already made his name. He's done it based on the music he developed and he knows how he wants it done." Ellis then said that Monroe "was *very* patient.

But he would coach you along and tell you that he doesn't have a lot of time to teach you."

They toured a lot. This wasn't hard on Monroe because he didn't do any of the driving. Ellis did 90 percent of the driving when he was there.

Working with Monroe was easy for Tony Ellis, though it may not have been for some others. "Bill was very demanding in some respects. He wanted you to, more or less, 'keep your skirts clean' as the old saying goes. He didn't want his musicians drinking or running around or staying out all night or misbehaving. I went to work for him to learn to play his music, so I did what he wanted me to do and I worked hard and was very respectful to him and so he was very respectful to me in return."

Mr. Ellis was able to study "Monroe music" and explain a part of it. "There's an attitude in your playing that is definitely 'Monroe music' and is different from other groups. It's a different approach; it's a different feel for the note. You might be playing a song that goes from G to C. The guitar could go to C but the fiddle might make a G chord. It's what people today call a polychord. It's an overlay where two different chords are overlaid. And they blend in kind a unique way. That's part of the Monroe style. That happens a lot in his music. It's interesting, and a very *feeling* thing when it happens. You really can feel the intensity of the song or the tune. It's different than just playing straight notes or chords. So when Bill's gone, that will probably drift away rather quickly. I've played with a lot of other mandolin players, and they are great players, but there's something extra there with Monroe."

A 1992 interview with Tony Ellis at IBMA brought out more interesting things about working with Monroe. "When I went to work for Bill I had played the banjo for a couple of different bluegrass bands and had learned some basic things. Don Reno had taught me a world of things. But working with Bill—his timing is so wonderful, the rhythms that he played on the mandolin and his hearing, the subtle things he did in his music that he had you learn and do—all these things seem to come together to form an essence called 'Monroe music.' Bluegrass music, today, covers a real broad spectrum and a lot of different styles and the feelings and colors. But 'Monroe music' was really down to earth and came from country roots and really has the heart and the soul of country people and mountain people and a lot of blues... Bill had grown up playing with black blues players and black singers and worked in the fields with black people and learned harmonies and timing from them. To actually learn what he did there was a strong part of how he developed mandolin notes. He played a lot of blues on the mandolin which were actually harmony notes that he heard black people singing.

22 In 1991, George Wynn had a band in Richmond, Virginia, called the Bluegrass Partners.

"So bluegrass music, while it has a lot of the Scottish and Irish fiddle-type structure, it also has blues in it and some country music and a lot of gospel in it, too. So there is a broad blend of traditional styles of music and singing that he put together in bluegrass music." Mr. Ellis also added that "There is also an Irish influence in bluegrass music because his Uncle Pen was Scots-Irish. His mother was part Cheyenne Indian."

While Bill, Charlie, Birch and the other Monroe children were raised in similar conditions, Bill came out a little differently. Ellis explained, "Bill told me, when I worked for him, that when he was a youngster he couldn't see very well; he had eyesight problems. So he was kind of backwards. He didn't want to get involved in things the other family members did because he felt a little reluctant because of his eyesight. So that may have been the key to his creativity. It made him think and made him feel stronger and with a different perspective."

Frank Buchanan—
"There's something about Monroe's music that drives you."

In 1960, Buchanan[23] joined the **Blue Grass Boys** as lead singer and guitarist in Nashville. Other members of the band at the time, he recalled, were Tony Ellis (banjo), Red Stanley (fiddle) and Bessie Lee Mauldin (bass).

"There's an attitude in your playing that is definitely 'Monroe music' and is different from other groups." —Tony Ellis

Buchanan found Monroe's timing to be different than most bands, and difficult to learn. In a 1992 interview at IBMA, he elaborated, "I thought my timin' was way off when I went to work with him. He taught me that bluegrass timin' stays right up on the top note all the time. The timin' don't go down in that note; it stays up on the top all the time. You're driving, pushin' the beat. That's the best I can describe it. If you get lazy and slack down, he'll [get up right beside you] and drivin' that mandolin will drive you back to the top. He can tell just the minute you are droppin' down. And that's what you call *drive*. And a lot of people gets drive and speed confused. A lot of these banjo pickers—and everybody—think when you're burnin' somethin' up that that's drive. That's not it. When you're playin' the 'Tennessee Waltz' you got to have *drive*. It's hard to describe."

Even though Mr. Buchanan had considerable experience with other bands, he admitted, "We still wasn't drivin' it like Bill Monroe does." What Buchanan was doing before he joined Monroe "wasn't exactly wrong, but it wasn't exactly right either. There's somethin' about Bill Monroe that drives you. He'll make you want to play."

Don Reno—
"He knew whether or not you could make it."

"As far as being a good bandmaster, I think he's one of the best I ever worked with" Don Reno said of Bill Monroe. He would never lose his temper. If you wasn't playing a tune the way he wanted you to play it, he'd keep playing it until you got it, and he'd look at you with kind-of-a-half grin on his face, you know, when you got it right. He made you get it for yourself. He knew whether or not you could make it. And he'd set up a bank on each side of you and drive you right down the middle."[24]

23 Born in Spruce Pine, North Carolina, on March 25, 1934, Frank Buchanan began playing music at age fifteen. He and his brother soon won the first "Arthur Smith Talent Hunt" when the act came to town. By 1956, he had joined Bobby Atkins and Joe Stone on WRVA's Old Dominion Barn Dance for a year. Quotation are from a 1992 interview at IBMA.

24 Rooney, *Bossmen*, op. cit., pp. 54, 55.

The story of Bill Monroe and the Blue Grass Boys—

With Charlie and Birch Monroe. A biography.

William Smith Monroe is often known as the one critical element in the creation of bluegrass music. It is not an accident that he is referred to as the "Father of Bluegrass Music". This is his story.

Dear reader, as you read this biography on Bill Monroe, you'll find a bewildering number of facts, dates and people. The presentation of these in a coherent form is very difficult; it may be difficult to follow, especially since Monroe's musicians often came and went often and at irregular times. For instance, the fact that Monroe sometimes had different musicians for touring than he did when he recorded doesn't help to simplify this story. So, reader, approach this chapter with an understanding that a further explanation of a particular event is often found in the individual biographies (when included in this book) of the protagonists involved.

Bill Monroe was born in Rosine, Kentucky[25], September 13, 1911. Monroe's father was James B. "Buck" Monroe (October 28, 1857 - January 14, 1928) who was named after the fifteenth president, James Buchanan Monroe; there is genealogical evidence that they are related. His mother was Malissa A. Monroe (July 12, 1870 - October 31, 1921). Bill was the last of eight children. Malissa was forty-one when Bill was born.[26] They all helped run the family farm. His mother died when he was ten. She was an old-time fiddler and singer who also played the accordion.

By the time Bill was growing into puberty, many of the other Monroe children had grown up and moved away and Bill was alone. "I started to work when I was eleven and there wasn't a lot of playtime for me...and the evenin' would be lonesome, you know. Well, that's in my music."[27] Bill quit school before completing the sixth grade.

"People used to come to this house," he continued, "and since I was cross-eyed, strangers would laugh at me, and I couldn't see well enough to play ball. After awhile when I saw strangers coming down that road, I would go and hide in the barn." From these feelings of mistrust, anger, and isolation came a fierce determination to create something of his own and hold onto it in spite of some tense working relationships through the years.

An early musical influence was a black fiddler and guitarist, Arnold Schultz. Bill took up the guitar and would back Schultz at dances. Schultz was a local blues and old-time man whom Bill considered "a powerful guitar player". Monroe explained that "There's things in my music, you know, that come from Arnold Schultz: runs that I use in a lot of my music. I don't say that I make them the same way that he could make them 'cause he was powerful with it. In following a fiddle piece or a breakdown, he used a pick and he could just run from one chord to another the prettiest you've ever heard. There's no guitar picker today that could do that. I tried to keep in mind a little of it—what I could salvage to use in my music. Then he could play blues and I wanted some blues in my music too, you see."[28]

Bill switched to mandolin when he began performing with his brothers, Birch and Charlie. His mandolin only had four strings in order to temper the loud volume of the hard-playing young man. The influence of his Uncle Pendleton Vandiver (1869 - 1932) made the fiddle

---

[25] The town's former name was Pigeon Roost and was renamed in honor of Jennie Taylor McHenry (1832 to 1914), a poet who wrote under the pen-name "Rosine." Rosine is considered by some to be the birthplace of bluegrass music because Bill Monroe was born there.

[26] The children were, in chronological order: Harry (9/8/1890 to 8/20/1954), Speed (11/30/1884 to 1/14/1967), John (5/17/1896 to 2/1/1962), Maude (11/17/1898 to 12/26/1961), Birch (5/16/1901 to 5/15/1982), Charlie (7/4/1903 to 9/27/1975), Bertha and Bill. Bertha lives in Rosine as of 1996.

Butch Robins, who worked for Bill Monroe from 1977 to 1981, studied not only the music, but the man and his early life. Monroe often told Robins of his early life; Robins shared many of these thoughts here. Reader, keep in mind that this is how Monroe represented it to Butch, sixty years later.

The Monroe family was fairly affluent by the western Kentucky standards of the day compared with some of the other protagonists of this music who often lived hand-to-mouth. By the time Bill was born, the Monroe family owned three sawmills. The family worked hard, reaping the bountiful lumber of the area. It would be a few years before the lumber industry would dwindle and the coal mining industry would become dominant in the area. It was here, working for his father, that Bill learned his work ethic. He worked hard and became strong, *very* strong. Robins recalled that even playing catch with Bill was quite an experience. Butch caught four baseballs thrown by Monroe, each one was thrown harder than the last. The next one would undoubtedly be harder still (and hurt his hand) so Butch chose to dodge the incoming missile. The ball hit the wall behind him, bounced off the wall, and hit him in the back of the head, knocking him out. "That was the only time I've been knocked out in my life," he said.

Bill was born cross-eyed and with poor vision. He and his brothers attended a shape-note school of music but Bill couldn't see what they were showing on the blackboard. His brothers had to come home, write the symbols used in the music, and show them to Bill up close. It would be some years before his cross-eyed handicap would be corrected.

The early days in the life of Bill Monroe were sometimes violent for, according to a story he told Robins, he was beaten by brother Speed, who had beer on his breath at the time he was abusing the youngest Monroe brother. Perhaps the beatings and his lack of self confidence due to his poor eyesight led to the sometimes violent temper outbursts experienced by those around the man. And perhaps, too, it was a reason for his creativity for which he was also famous. Although this book is not really intended as a psychological treatise of Mr. Monroe, perhaps now we may see why his music was so important to him.

[27] John W. Rumble, "The Music Of Bill Monroe, 1936 to 1994," p. 14.

[28] James Rooney, *Bossmen: Bill Monroe and Muddy Waters*, 1971, pp. 23, 24.

A m e r i c a s   M u s i c | B l u e g r a s s

Uncle Pendleton Vandiver (R) and Clarence Wilson (L)

the instrument of Bill's choice, but since the eldest brother, Birch, had already claimed it, Bill settled on playing a yet-to-be-chosen instrument: the mandolin. As the youngest of eight children, at age eight, he didn't have much choice.

Even his sister, Bertha, played the guitar. Bill later said that if he had his choice he never would have fooled with the mandolin if it hadn't been for the music he played with his brothers. He wanted to play the guitar, too—the way Arnold Schultz played it. This band with his brothers steered him away from his desire to play and sing the blues with a guitar; he was stuck with the mandolin, and the die was cast.

With his brothers in 1927, Bill played the mandolin, Birch played bass and old-time fiddle, Charlie, the guitar. They were known as the **Monroe Brothers**. Birch learned to play the fiddle from Uncle Pen. The elder Monroe brother, Harry, played fiddle (and the two brothers after that, too). Birch played his fiddle in Rosine at local gatherings. "There'd always be dinner on the ground, you know," said Birch. "People'd take big baskets of food, go there and sing all day. Start Sunday morning, sing way in the afternoon. At Rosine they'd go to the Baptist church; a lot of them communities had churches."[29] Birch, Bill, and Charlie didn't play much together around Rosine; Bill was too young. But when Birch and Charlie left for Michigan, Bill and Uncle Pen played together awhile.

When Birch and Charlie moved up north to work in the Indiana and Chicago area in 1928, Bill was about sixteen, and left alone; he moved in with his Uncle Pen. Bill remembered, "I'll never forget the old days. They was wonderful! Back in the early days when all my brothers had left, I would drive four horses and would haul telephone poles or cross ties or coal, you see. And when I was sixteen, I was makin' into a stout man already. But I knew how to work." Mr. Monroe had a definite work ethic; he professed it all his life. He was strong and able to lift anything he could get his hands around; he weighed up to 265 pounds in his prime.

His Uncle Pen "was the first fiddler I ever heard play. He didn't try to teach me. He would just play so I could listen to him. And I would hear him play at old-time square dances. And he was a wonderful fiddler. He kept good timing to his music and played that old sound from years and years ago. And I really loved it."[30] The way that Monroe learned from Vandiver, just listening and doing, turns out to be the same way Monroe would "teach" people in his own band which would come later.

He learned several tunes from Uncle Pen such as "Jenny Lynn," "Boston Boy," "Wedding Tune" and "The Old Gray Mare Came Tearing Out of the Wilderness." Bill Monroe wrote of his Uncle Pen on the back cover of the 1972 MCA album, "Bill Monroe's Uncle Pen": "He was one of Kentucky's finest old-time fiddlers. And he had the best shuffle with the bow I'd ever seen, and kept the best time. That's one reason people asked him to play for the dances around Rosine (pop. 350)... His later years in life he was a crippled man, he'd been thrown by a mule, therefore he had to use crutches the rest of his life... My last years in Kentucky were spent with

Uncle Pendleton on fiddle, Clarence Wilson on banjo. Women unknown.

him. He done the cooking for the two of us. We had fat back, sorghum molasses, and hot cakes for breakfast followed by black-eyed peas with fat back and corn bread and sorghum for dinner and supper." Uncle Pendleton Vandiver died June 22, 1932.[31]

By the time Bill Monroe was seventeen, the foundation had been laid for bluegrass to be created: the blues were there, the country music was there, the fiddle was there, the church harmonies and religious influence were there. Bill was soon to create his own music, but it was not to evolve into its full form until he went out on his own and formed his own band, the **Blue Grass Boys**.

Birch and Charlie left home in 1928 to search for work. Bill joined them a year later. Birch recalled, "We first went to Detroit, worked in Briggs Body Plant 'til the bottom fell out in '29. We'd only been up there, I believe, six months or so when the bottom fell out. When that Depression hit, we went back to East Chicago where we found work in oil."[32]

[29] Neil V. Rosenberg, "A Front Porch Visit with Birch Monroe," *Bluegrass Unlimited*, September, 1982, p. 59.

[30] Interview in Portland, Oregon. October 31, 1984.

[31] Another source says 1930.

[32] Rosenberg, op. cit., p. 59.

Bill joined them in 1929 and obtained a job at Sinclair Oil in East Chicago, Indiana, loading 150-pound barrels—up to 2,000 per day—for nearly five years. The **Monroe Brothers** again became a trio and became popular playing at square dances and local functions. They played on WAE in Hammond, Indiana, for several years.

During the tough times of the Great Depression, only the lucky were able to keep a job. Because he was the only brother working, he supported his kin. Bill recalled that, in those days, "I worked every day for five years and all I got out of it was I spent forty dollars for a mandolin and I got a couple of suits of clothes. I've often wondered if I was doing the right thing. I guess I was. It wouldn't be right not to support your people."[33] Bill was on the company baseball team where he excelled.

In the Chicago area, Bill, Birch and Charlie took leave of their job at the refinery for four or five months and played a little on WAE in Hammond, Indiana. They also had a gig at Gary's WJKS[34] where they played weekly and were able to advertise their square dance dates they would do on the side.

In 1932, the **Monroe Brothers** (now with Larry Moore as a member) began playing for the newly-created touring entertainment unit for WLS[35], Chicago. WLS' National Barn Dance show was one of the first (and most popular) of the Saturday-night radio jamborees. They did square dances and were hired to play for dancers. Charlie was the group's leader, doing the emcee work and providing the entertainment aspect of the show. They traveled in their Packard for WLS until 1934; each performance was a sellout at twenty cents admission. In small towns, half the entire population would turn out. WLS paid them $22.50 per week per man. At that wage they could afford a steak for thirty-five cents and a good room for seventy-five.

It was during this period that the fiddle playing of Clayton McMichen served as the style that Bill wanted his mandolin playing to resemble. Even at this early stage of Bill's career playing the mandolin, he was incredibly fast and skillful. Veteran WLS entertainer Karl Davis (of **Karl and Harty**) recalled, "He took this mandolin and I've never heard anybody play as fast in my life, and I went across the stage and got (WLS cast members) Red Foley and Linda Parker and Harty and I said, 'Come over here and listen to this man play this mandolin.'"[36]

Bill, Charlie and Birch played at the Chicago World's Fair in 1933. Now that they were sponsored by Texas Crystals (a cathartic product similar to the better

known Crazy Water Crystals) on KFNF, Shenandoah, Iowa, and a few months later at WAAW, Omaha, Nebraska (in 1935), Bill was able to quit his job in the oil business in 1934 to become a full-time musician with Charlie. Birch stayed at the refinery until he was laid off, and then he was hired at Cities Service Refinery where he stayed for the next nine years. Birch liked the music okay, but didn't want to leave the security and stability of a day job for the uncertainty of being a full-time musician during the middle of the Great Depression. Birch joined Bill's band about 1945.

Byron Parker, "The Old Hired Hand," joined the **Monroe Brothers**, Charlie and Bill, at WAAW as bass singer and as their announcer. Bill was now married. Daughter Melissa was born in 1936. She later recorded with him in the early '50s for Columbia and appeared on many road shows. Son James William was born in 1941. He started his musical career with his father in 1964 as bass player.

After moving from Omaha, they moved to Columbia, South Carolina, followed by Charlotte, North Carolina, where, in 1936, the **Monroe Brothers**, Bill, Charlie and Byron, moved to WBT's Crazy Barn Dance, sponsored by Crazy Water Crystals (which also sponsored the **Blue Sky Boys**, Fisher Hendley and his **Aristocratic Pigs** and **J.E. Mainer's Mountaineers**).

Author James Rooney wrote that "Bill's tenor was way up there and it had that 'lonesome' quality along with some blues feeling that made it immediately identifi-

Uncle Pen's gravestone. It reads: Pendleton Vandiver 1869-1932. "Uncle Pen" immortalized in song by his nephew Bill Monroe Father of Blue Grass music and member of the Country Music Hall of Fame. Late in the evening about sundown, high on the hill above the town, Uncle Pen played the fiddle Lord how it would ring, you could hear it talk you could hear it sing

able. They had speed too, and Bill's mandolin was more dynamic and melodic than anyone else's playing at the time. He was creating a style on the instrument that also distinguished the **Monroe Brothers** from their competitors. Soon Victor Records (on their country music sub-label, Bluebird Records) got word that the

[33] Rooney, op. cit., p. 26.

[34] WJKS stands for Where Joy Kills Sorrow.

[35] The radios station WLS was owned by Sears, Roebuck and Company and the call letters stood for World Largest Store. It was 50,000 watt station—the maximum the law allowed—and was "clear channel" which means that no other station could use its frequency, permitting it to broadcast its signal in all directions.

[36] Charles K. Wolfe, "What Ever Happened to Karl and Harty?" p. 29. This quote was found in Rosenberg's *Bluegrass—A History* (p. 30) who referred to Wolfe as the original source of the quotation.

America's Music — Bluegrass

Monroe Brothers was in the Carolinas, had a following, and signed them up."[37] Their performances on WFBC (Greenville, South Carolina), WBT (Charlotte, North Carolina), and WPTF (Raleigh, North Carolina) brought them much fame in the Carolinas.

On February 17th, 1936, the **Monroe Brothers** recorded for Bluebird Records. The ten songs recorded that day included "What Would You Give In Exchange" and "This World Is Not My Home." Their royalties were approximately a cent and a half per copy sold. Still, it got their sound out there and they were soon packing them in. "And it didn't take much advertising," said Mr. Monroe. "People listened strictly to your program and you didn't have to put up much paper for your advertising. We worked on a percentage with the schools. I believe they got thirty or thirty-five percent. And then after that was over with, why, we busted it down the middle. We would generally stay in a place a year-and-a-half and then we would move on to another town, you know; I think we moved from Greenville to Raleigh, North Carolina, and stayed there a year-and-a-half."[38]

Ricky Skaggs, in the 1993 video "Bill Monroe— Father of Bluegrass Music," mentioned that much of the music which followed was influenced by the Monroes. He pointed out that the **Blue Sky Boys** followed the music of the **Monroe Brothers**, as did the **Louvin Brothers**, and then the **Everly Brothers** who then influenced the **Beatles**. The musical aspect which runs through all these groups is the same style of harmony which the **Monroe Brothers** had. The Monroes were one of the first bands to try to meld their voices in the close-harmony style. Before them (and a few other close-harmony duos), the non-harmony sound of the big string bands was prominent but not a large factor in the **Monroe Brothers'** music.

During the next two years, the **Monroe Brothers** recorded sixty sides including "I'll Roll In My Sweet Baby's Arms," "New River Train" (written by Charlie Monroe), "Darling Corey" and many **Carter Family** tunes. Half their repertoire was gospel. As a comedy duo, Bill switched instruments to the fiddle and Charlie to the banjo. It didn't go over well so they ceased it.

In April 1937, Parker left the **Monroe Brothers** to eventually form **Byron Parker's Mountaineers** with Snuffy Jenkins and Pappy Sherrill. Parker quit as the Monroes' manager shortly after Charlie became married when, evidently, Charlie wanted his wife to manage

the **Monroe Brothers**. Bill went along with it, reluctantly, for a while. In retrospect, it is often recognized that Byron's managerial competence is one of the main reasons the **Monroe Brothers** was popular; he could sell anything—even the band itself (whether or not they were any good).

Bill and Charlie fought like siblings often do—often physically—and had a philosophical difference as to what the **Monroe Brothers** sound should be. This became evident in the way each man formed his own band and played his own music. Bill and Charlie split[39] early in 1938 in Raleigh, North Carolina. Charlie basically stayed with the old country music formula; Bill became innovative and progressive with his band. They were completely different. Charlie Monroe formed the **Monroe Boys**[40] and Bill formed the **Kentuckians** in Little Rock, Arkansas.

Discontented with the sound of the **Kentuckians**, after three months Bill moved to Atlanta to start another band. He advertised for a guitar man and lead singer in the paper. One of the men who answered the ad was Cleo Davis, a man whose only singing had been behind a plow pulled by the family mule. Davis sounded remarkably like Charlie Monroe when he and Bill Monroe sang together during the audition.

Bill remembered that it "took me about a month to get a new band together. I think I rehearsed every day for a month. To start with, I was getting a singer and a guitar man. That's what I wanted to carry—you know, have some good singing. So that was the first thing that I done. I hired Cleo Davis. And then I got a fiddle player. Art Wooten was his name. And after that, the next man I hired, he played a jug, you know, sounded like a bass. His name was John Miller, from Asheville.[41] And he could play spoons and bones, you know, and could play good comedy—played blackface comedian. We was there in Asheville, North Carolina, three months after I got the **Blue Grass Boys** together. I tried to work over in Little Rock, Arkansas, but it played out there so I came to Asheville (WWNC). Then I moved to Greenville and the jug player stayed with us a short time and then I got a bass man, Amos Garen. And we worked there, I guess, and went to Nashville and tried for the Grand Ole Opry and made it there."[42] He called his band the **Blue Grass Boys**, named after his home state of Kentucky which is known as the "Bluegrass State".

---

[37] Rooney, op. cit., p. 29.

[38] Rooney, op. cit., p. 31.

[39] Despite all the lurid rumors about the breakup, Charlie's wife as manager seemed to be the key issue.

[40] Members were Bill Calhoun (guitar, mandolin) and Lefty Frizell (mandolin, not the famous country star).

[41] Other sources say that this black-face comedian was Tommy Millard which is verified by Millard in his biography in the Pioneers chapter of this book.

[42] Rooney, op. cit., p. 32.
 A further research of the exact sequence of events reveal that the duo of Monroe and Davis got a job at WWNC in Asheville as Bill Monroe and Cleo Davis. Soon Bill hired Tommy Millard (comedy, rhythm, percussion), calling the band Bill Monroe and His Blue Grass Boys. Millard left shortly and was replaced by Amos Garen on bass. When the bass was added, it freed Bill from having to keep rhythm all the time, allowing some picking. They also played on Greenville, South Carolina's WFBC. Soon they were ready to try for WSM and the Grand Ole Opry.

Monroe told how he got hired onto the Opry, "When me and my brother broke up, I decided that I wanted to be on the Grand Ole Opry. Well, he'd done gone up there, Charlie had, and they wouldn't take him on there. And I went up there in 1939 and the Solemn Old Judge and Harry Stone and David Stone were going out to get some coffee and they said they'd be right back and they'd listen to me. They come back and I run over two or three numbers for 'em. And they said I could get started on the Grand Ole Opry that Saturday night or, if I wanted, to go ahead and look for another job. I said, 'No.' I wanted to be right here. They said, 'Well, if you do start here you'll have to fire yourself.'" As of 1996, he still performed there regularly.

In an interview in 1984, Bill Monroe described what he had in mind when he created bluegrass music, "Well, I had some sounds in my mind that I wanted to come out with and see how it would work out: old-time sounds and tones from years and years ago like they would have played a hundred years ago, or a hundred and fifty. And with the different ideas, I was going into the music, you know, like some blues and a little bit of swing and a hard drive. I was going to be sure that I put that in with the mandolin so I could give the banjo a chance, a better chance. And the new style of fiddle playing. And it's a high, lonesome sound in bluegrass music. A lot of holiness, Baptists and Methodists singing in bluegrass music. And the old Scots bagpipe sound in it. So it's just a wonderful music and I'm glad that it belongs to the USA."

He spoke more about that *high, lonesome sound*, "Well, Barry, back when I was real young, I was checking my voice and sounds to see how high I was going to sing and everything. I had sung tenor, you know, a long, long time. And later on, why, I knew I was going to do some solo singing but I was still going to take care of the tenor. And I had to learn and know how to handle my voice and take care of my throat because I was going to sing against a mini-lead singer. And, of course, some of them could really sing high. And so that's one thing I had to work out when I was young. But I got that under control and it worked out fine. It's a wonderful part to carry in bluegrass music—the tenor part—to be sure that that's taken care of right. Bluegrass has a wonderful feeling in it and if you sing something like 'My Rose of Old Kentucky' you can still hear a lot of gospel in it, too. So it's all mixed in there and it's wonderful."

In a different interview, Monroe recalled, "When I started on the Grand Ole Opry, I had rehearsed and we was ready. Our music was in good shape. We had a good fiddler with us—for bluegrass in them days—Fiddlin' Art Wooten. And my singing was high and clear, you know, and I was in good shape, and we was ready to go on the Grand Ole Opry. Really, the only competition we had there was Roy Acuff, and they was two different styles altogether.

"Charlie and I had a country beat, I suppose. But the beat in my music—bluegrass music—started when I ran across 'Muleskinner Blues' and started playing that. We don't do it the way Jimmie Rodgers sung it. It's speeded up and we moved it up to fit the fiddle and we have that straight time with it: driving time. And then we went on and that same kind of time would work with 'John Henry' and we put it on that. And when we started here on the Grand Ole Opry, 'Muleskinner Blues' and 'John Henry' were the numbers we tried out with. And it was something different for them and they really wanted it. It's a wonderful 'time,' and the reason a lot of people like bluegrass is because of the timing of it.

"And then we pitched the music up where it would do a number some good," said Monroe. "If you play in B-natural and sing there and your fiddle is right up there playing where you're at and the banjo, well, it just makes it a different music from where it would be played if it was just drug along in G, C, and D."[43]

At about the same time as Bill Monroe began playing on the Saturday evening country variety show Grand Ole Opry on October 28, 1939, which aired on 50,000 watt WSM[44] in Nashville, Charlie Monroe found WHAS, a 50,000 watt station in Louisville, Kentucky, for his **Kentucky Pardners**.

Larry Sandberg analyzed this music in *The Folk Music Sourcebook*: "Monroe's early recordings with his brother, Charlie, and then with the **Blue Grass Boys** beginning in the late '30s, reveal a personal approach to the old-time style characterized by strikingly gutsy high lead vocals, even higher tenor harmony sometimes going into the falsetto range, and a brilliantly original mandolin style clearly influenced by black music. With the **Blue Grass Boys**, Monroe developed a trio vocal harmony sound (high lead with baritone and higher tenor harmonies) that remains one of the most characteristic aspects of the original bluegrass sound. When gospel songs are sung, and occasionally elsewhere in the repertoire, it is conventional to add a bass part, recalling the four-part harmony of church singing.

"The band's use of a string bass also contributed to the emerging bluegrass sound. Old-time string band music, which was originally played for dancing in the two-step tradition, usually kept 2/4 time. The string bass made it easier for the new music to keep a more flowing 4/4 or cut-time beat. In a useful, though

43 Rooney, op. cit., p. 33, 34.

44 As a side note, WSM radio, because it was owned by the National Life and Accident Insurance Company, stood for "We Shield Millions." Incidentally, WSM's call sign is the same as the name, William Smith Monroe. The Opry had a half-hour segment on NBC radio nationally, much like the TNN show today.

superficial and somewhat dangerous analogy, one might say that the difference between old-time and bluegrass time keeping roughly parallels the difference between Dixieland and swing band timekeeping."[45]

The band's fast-paced style amazed all who heard it. Monroe played in heretofore unfamiliar keys (which matched his voice) and thus demanded more musical competence than had ever been required before in country music. The keys of B-flat or B-natural or E, said Monroe, gave fiddle players "a fit and they wouldn't hardly tackle it and they'd swear that they wanted to play straight stuff and they figured that that's where I should sing. And that's where bluegrass really advanced music."[46]

The band started quartet singing in bluegrass with his creation of the Blue Grass Quartet. Monroe often sang high lead; there was a tenor singer pitched below him. Tommy Magness sang baritone and Cleo Davis sang bass. The vocal harmonies are what stand out in tapes of the 1940 and 1941 Opry shows.

Monroe dressed his band in suits and shunned cowboy costumes which were popular on the Opry stage; this further removed him from the hillbilly image which he despised. Except for the person Monroe hired to be the comedian, they wore white shirts, ties, jodhpurs, riding boots and narrow-brimmed Stetson hats. Though they journeyed through the roughest towns, they were never bothered. "I suppose they thought we were the law,"[47] commented Monroe.

On September 6, 1940, Cleo Davis left the **Blue Grass Boys** and was replaced by veteran guitarist and singer Clyde Moody of Cherokee, North Carolina. Another member of the **Blue Grass Boys** was Tommy Magness (fiddle) who popularized "Orange Blossom Special." The bass player was Willie Egbert "Cousin Wilbur" Wesbrooks, a comedian who dressed the part of the hillbilly with overalls, rag hanging from the back pocket, and with slovenly manner to match. A comedian was an essential part of the entertainment package offered by country bands in those days.

On October 7th, the band recorded for Victor's Bluebird label. While recording on Bluebird, Monroe played guitar on the pre-World War II version of "Mule Skinner Blues." This was the first tune recorded by Monroe and his **Blue Grass Boys** and was the last time the **Blue Grass Boys** recorded a song with Monroe on guitar.[48]

When Clyde Moody left the **Blue Grass Boys** after a year and a half, he re-formed the **Happy-Go-Lucky Boys**[49]. Moody was to return later to the **Blue Grass Boys**.

Monroe replaced Moody with Pete Pyle[50], from Mississippi, already a Bluebird/Victor recording artist. By 1941, Pyle was performing regularly with **Bill Monroe and the Blue Grass Boys** on the Grand Ole Opry. However, because he was still recording on RCA's country music sub-label, Bluebird, RCA would not let him record on a second session with Monroe. He missed out on recordings such as "Live and Let Live" and "Were You There." The second **Blue Grass Boys** recording session for Bluebird was October 2, 1941, in Atlanta with Art Wooten (again, who replaced Magness) and Wesbrooks. Monroe sang occasional lead with the band but relied on others to carry the bulk of the lead singing. The only duet recorded that day included Monroe and Wesbrooks on "In the Pines." In 1942, Pete Pyle went into the U.S. Army. Replacing Pyle as a **Blue Grass Boy** was Clyde Moody who returned to the band for three more years.

In 1942, Bill Monroe bought his famous Gibson F-5 mandolin in a Florida barbershop for $150. The instrument was number 73987 and was signed and dated by Lloyd Loar, July 9, 1923.[51]

Later on that year, members of the **Blue Grass Boys** were Monroe (mandolin), Jay Hugh Hall (guitar), Clyde Moody (guitar), Cousin Wilbur (bass, comedy) and Howdy Forrester (fiddle) who replaced Wooten[52]. Forrester had already pioneered twin-fiddling on WSM with Georgia Slim Rutland. Dave "Stringbean" Akeman was hired as comedian and banjoist. Monroe now had two comedians.

In October 1942, Carl Story joined Monroe's band, replacing Forrester when Forrester joined the Navy. Story remained with Monroe until October 1943 when Chubby Wise replaced him in the fall of 1943.[53] Jim

---

[45] Larry Sandberg and Dick Weissman, *The Folk Music Sourcebook*, Alfred A. Knopf, Inc., 1976) pp. 68, 69.

[46] Rooney, op. cit., p. 34.

[47] Ibid.

[48] For more on this topic, see chapter on Controversies and the chapter on Carlton Haney.

[49] By 1955, Moody had his own Carolina Wood Choppers.

[50] Pete Pyle (April 18, 1920 to March 11, 1995) was born in Burnsville, Mississippi. In 1940, he had a solo spot on the Opry and retained that act after he was hired by Monroe. After leaving Monroe, he worked as a lead singer with Pee Wee King before quitting to start his own Mississippi Valley Boys. He later worked with Jamup and Honey and Ernest Tubb and re-joined Monroe in the mid-'50s. Later, he worked as leader of the house band at Monroe's Brown County Jamboree in Bean Blossom. He is best known as composer of "True Life Blues," "Highway of Sorrow," "Don't Put Off Until Tomorrow" and "Happy on My Way."

[51] Bought in Tampa, Mr. Monroe couldn't recall if it was $150 or $125.

[52] Wooten passed away October 6, 1986, at age 80 in Sparta, NC. He suffered from emphysema and a heart condition. The North Carolina Folklore Society honored him in 1985 with their Brown Hudson Award for his contribution to the state's cultural heritage.

[53] Floyd Ethridge also worked for Monroe during this period but his sequence in the succession of fiddlers in unclear. So are his dates of employment. According to Don Reno in his biography, "the day Bill Monroe offered me a job in 1943, Clyde Moody and Floyd Ethridge and Chubby Wise had just gone to work for Bill and were trying to learn the breaks from Floyd."

Shumate later replaced Wise and played fiddle with the band until Forrester came back from the Navy after the war (October 1945) and claimed his job with Monroe. Forrester didn't stay long and Wise came back.

In approximately 1943, Monroe's band began a six- to eight-year episode of touring with its tent shows. They frequently worked with other Opry acts such as DeFord Bailey, Uncle Dave Macon, and Sam and Kirk McGee. They would put up a tent after obtaining a permit and then go into town to promote the show. The groups brought everything they needed to produce a show. They would sell the tickets, perform that night with maybe two or three complete sets, clean up, tear down the tent afterwards, travel to a new location, and do the same thing all over the next day. The shows were a lot of work, but in order to make money at being a musician they found this was a lot cheaper than renting a building in town and trying to make ends meet in that manner. Originally, Bill had seven trucks and twenty-eight men handling the music, the tent, bleachers, chairs, electric lights and power, and a cook house. Sixty-five dollars covered all the overhead at the site. He put ten people in his stretched Chevrolet bus called "Blue Grass Breakdown." The others in the tent show traveled in the trucks.[54]

Being one of the stars of the Grand Ole Opry, he usually filled the tents to capacity. His band, and others who traveled with it, challenged the local baseball team to a game of hardball. Calling them the **Blue Grass Club**, they took on all comers. This was not only a good diversion from work, it was good business, attracting additional people to the concerts. Bill played shortstop and Clyde Moody pitched. The concept gained considerable popularity and its serious competitiveness caused Monroe to hire professional baseball players. Monroe actually had two teams: one for the road and one near his base of operations. Monroe provided a strong leadership role with his baseball teams just the same as he showed in his music. Monroe made his musicians tote their share of the baseball activities just the same as when they played his music on stage. It is often acknowledged that Stringbean was hired for his strong pitching arm, and that Monroe found later he could play also an instrument.

On February 13, 1945, Bill Monroe and his band recorded on Columbia Records with Chubby Wise (fiddle, who was back with the band after Howdy left), Sally Ann Forrester (accordion), Stringbean (banjo), Bill Wesbrooks (comedy, bass), Curley Bradshaw (guitar) and Tex Willis (guitar, not a member of the **Willis Brothers** who were the well known country swing group). They recorded "Footprints in the Snow," "Rocky Road Blues" and "Kentucky Waltz."

Monroe and his band worked through the war years but did not record, probably because the war effort used most of the materials which made up a 78 record and because of a musicians strike. Howard Watts, using the stage name "Cedric Rainwater", joined Bill Monroe after Cousin Wilbur left in 1944 and did comedy routines with Stringbean.[55] Lester Flatt joined the **Blue Grass Boys** in early 1945 about two to three weeks before fiddler Jim Shumate joined up.

When Flatt joined (from Charlie Monroe's band), he brought better bottom end rhythm and drive to the band. It is sometimes speculated that Flatt got his guitar rhythm from Clyde Moody when Flatt worked with Moody's **Happy-Go-Lucky Boys** earlier in the decade. Tracing this rhythm back a little further, we find that Moody may have picked it up from Bill Monroe when Moody joined the **Blue Grass Boys** in 1940, or even from Wiley or Zeke Morris who were playing their form of country/bluegrass music in the late 1930s, then passed it along to Flatt.

Birch Monroe joined the band on bass in 1945, probably in Bill's touring band, when regular members were Bill, Earl, Lester and Chubby. Birch said about Lester Flatt, "Awful hard to sing with Lester 'cause you can't sing with somebody's that's flat and be yourself. Lester couldn't keep from being flat. And he would have, if you tried to sing with him today, I'd bet a dollar he'd drop you a little flat. Bill knowed that I wasn't my best; he realized what was happening. Then in the meantime Jimmy Martin come to Bill. I helped Bill record two or three records with Jimmy Martin and it's easy to sing with Jimmy 'cause he don't go flat."[56] During Birch's time with Monroe, he wrote "The Beautiful Red Rose Waltz" and "Cabin of Love" (which Bill and Carter Stanley recorded as a duet in 1951).

At Christmas time of 1945, Earl Scruggs joined the **Blue Grass Boys**; Stringbean had recently left, soon to form a comedy act with Lew Childre. Scruggs had earlier played with the **Morris Brothers** and, more recently, with the **Allied Kentuckians** which was led by Lost John Miller. Scruggs' audition with Monroe consisted of "Sally Goodin'" and "Dear Old Dixie." When Scruggs joined, other band members were Wilene "Sally Ann" Forrester (Howdy's wife, accordion), Jim Andrews (tenor banjo, comedy), Jim Shumate (fiddle), Lester Flatt (guitar) and Andy "Bijou" Boyette (comedy).

Historian Dr. Bill Foster conducted the last interview of Lester Flatt before Flatt died. Foster shared some of the context of this interview, "As I recall, the most interesting part of the interview was the part where I asked Lester about his first meeting with Earl Scruggs. He said that Bill Monroe told him one evening

---

[54] Another group which toured with tent shows was Smoky Graves and the Blue Star Boys. Eddie Adcock describes this 1954 experience in the Banjo chapter of this book.

[55] Also with the Blue Grass Boys were Chubby Wise (fiddle) and Clyde Moody (guitar).

[56] Rosenberg, op. cit., p. 61.

at the Opry that there was a young banjo player backstage who wanted to play for them after their part of the show. Apparently, the band had tried several banjo players who were clawhammer or double-thumb pickers and did not like the results; it was not the sound Bill wanted. Flatt told me that when Bill told him there was another banjoist waiting to audition, he said something like, 'Bill, we don't need a banjo picker; they all sound like David.' He went on to say that, after their portion of the show, they gathered in one of the dressing rooms to give Earl a chance to pick with them. Lester told me, 'I hadn't ever heard anything like it!' He (and Bill, as well) was impressed with Scruggs' style and ability, which was like nothing he had ever heard before."

Bill Monroe spoke about Scruggs in a 1984 interview, "He was just a young boy when I started bluegrass music. He was just learnin'. He didn't know anything about playing banjo, you might say. He was learnin' from a man by the name of Snuffy Jenkins. He was the first five-string banjo player that's played that style of banjo and Earl was a young boy learning from him. And when Earl went to work with me—I believe he was nineteen—he was just still learning to play, you know. I wanted the sound of the banjo in my music. Stringbeans was the first banjo player and he was a great comedian and I needed people like that. But I wanted the sound of the banjo, you know, in my music just like I wanted the sound of the mandolin and the fiddle. I had to have that. And, of course, a good bluegrass style of playing the guitar meant a lot, too. And the bass, too. It helps keep the time and it keeps that low note."

The development of Monroe's music was now pretty much complete. The sound was good. It was novel. The band was tight. And people appreciated it. Bill spoke about his music compared to the other music which was featured on the Opry, "If I had got up there and sang everything solos with a little fiddle music behind me or a guitar like Ernest Tubb does, it would have got awful old. But with everybody where they could play their parts good and carrying a quartet or a trio or duet and letting the guitar man sing some solos, it made it good. There's more to it than just one man singing."

They traveled from concert to concert in the "Blue Grass Breakdown" stretched limousine with touring members Birch Monroe (who did the booking, bass singing and bass playing), Chubby Wise, Bill, Lester Flatt and Earl Scruggs. They toured constantly with their tent show.

Between September 1946 and October 1947, Monroe's band recorded four sessions for Columbia

with Monroe, Flatt, Scruggs, Wise and Howard "Cedric Rainwater" Watts. They recorded "Kentucky Waltz," a tune written by Monroe, on Columbia. It was his most popular tune since "Mule Skinner Blues" was released in 1940. In September, Monroe and Flatt co-wrote "Will You Be Loving Another Man?" and "Why Did You Wander?" Monroe's music had evolved into a different sound from only a few years before. People were noticing, and paying attention.

Earl Scruggs made his first recordings with Bill Monroe on September 16, 1946. Birch Monroe recorded in Bill Monroe's quartet that month on "Shining Path." Another tune was "Heavy Traffic Ahead." Performing on radio shows during that time, one of their most popular songs was "Molly and Tenbrooks."[57]

In January 1948, Flatt and Scruggs left Bill Monroe. When they quit, Cedric Rainwater went with them. Shortly thereafter, they formed their own band in direct competition with Monroe. One of the reasons, it is rumored, for the departure was the unlikelihood of making "the big bucks" unless they were the owners of their own band. Other reasons, such as Scruggs' need to go home to take care of his mother, are explored within the biographies of Earl Scruggs and Lester Flatt in the Pioneers chapter of this book. About that same time, Chubby Wise, the "Suwanee River Fiddle Player", left Monroe's band to join Clyde Moody on WARL, Arlington, Virginia. Benny Martin took Wise's place.

As much as it hurt Monroe that he lost most of his band in just a couple of months, he found that hiring competent replacements was easy. His band was *hot*! Good musicians and good lead singers were out there ready to take the job. Such singers were Jim Eanes, then Mac Wiseman and then Jimmy Martin. The fiddlers were many and competent. Also playing with the band were Jackie Phelps[58] (guitar) and Joel Price (bass). Don Reno came back from the Army and became Monroe's banjo player in 1948. In 1949, Rudy Lyle followed Don Reno as Monroe's banjo picker, recording with Monroe from 1949 through 1954.

In 1949, Bill Monroe began writing autobiographical songs (from personal experiences and feelings) such as "My Little Georgia Rose" (recorded for Decca February 3, 1950), "Letter From My Darling," (recorded January 20, 1951), "Memories of Mother and Dad" (recorded July 18, 1952), "On the Old Kentucky Shore" (recorded January 20, 1951) and "On and On" (recorded January 25, 1954). He labeled them as "true songs". He wrote "Uncle Pen" (recorded in 1950) as a happy tribute to a dear relative. "On and On" was a heart-felt song from personal feelings. And, of course, his sacred songs were written from his deep commitment to the Lord. The

57 This song's origin "goes back to the famous match race between [race horses] Ten Broeck and Mollie McCarthy (won by Ten Broeck) which took place in Louisville, Kentucky, July 4, 1878. This same Ten Broeck had run in the first Kentucky Derby (1875) and finished fifth. Monroe recorded it in October 1947. This was the first song which Scruggs "kicked off".

58 Claude Jackson "Jackie" Phelps was one of the few thumb-style guitarists to play with Bill Monroe; he also worked with Roy Acuff. Along with Jimmy Riddle, he was a long-time personality on "Hee Haw." He passed away April 22, 1990.

songs show his depressed personality during this period. Author John Morthland wrote that "Virtually all of them (the above listed songs) are taken at funereal tempos and they make for a despairing body of work, brooding and preoccupied with death. Steeped as they are in archaic language, they fit right in with the tragic mountain ballads that were part of his original repertoire. Even 'Sugar Coated Love' (recorded July 6, 1951), the closest thing to an upbeat song here, isn't really upbeat; in it he merely concedes to having experienced pleasure at some point in the past. But his music remains as awesome as his misery. In this era, only Hank Williams could match him for turning private desolation into art."[59]

In February 1950, Bill Monroe began recording with Decca, leaving Columbia because his competitors, the **Stanley Brothers**, had just signed onto Columbia and Monroe wanted no part of a label who would have anything to do with a label which would record his competitors. Mac Wiseman played guitar and sang lead with the **Blue Grass Boys** for a year[60] until he started his own group and began recording on Dot Records in Gallatin, Tennessee. Soon after that, Jimmy Martin talked Monroe into hiring him in place of Wiseman. In an audition, Martin proved that his voice blended with Monroe's better than Wiseman's did. Martin stayed on and off for several years, continuing to record with Monroe even after he left to start his own band in July of 1951.

Bill Monroe's 1950 booklet of his music was called "Bill Monroe's Blue Grass Country Songs." This was the first use, in print, of the name "blue grass" to describe his music.

In March of 1951, Bill Monroe recorded some songs at Decca using studio musicians—not his **Blue Grass Boys**. Musicians included himself, Thomas Grady Martin (guitar), Tommy Jackson (fiddle), Jimmy Selph (guitar), Owen Bradley (piano, organ), Farris Coursey (drums) and Ernie Newton (bass). The sound was totally different from the sound that Monroe wanted to call his own, and Monroe finally convinced the producers that his sound could only exist if he, himself, was able to instruct the musicians on how to play his songs. Later, Ralph Stanley would have a similar arrangement with Rebel records—they would record whatever he

would want in order to achieve a specific music: the "Stanley sound".

In 1951, Bill Monroe bought the Brown County Jamboree, a country music park at Bean Blossom, Indiana. The Jamboree was established in the mid-'30s. Instead of the normal tent, a barn was built as a concert hall in 1941. Monroe's music personnel connections and skills enabled the Jamboree to grow much faster than before he purchased it. Birch ran the Jamboree except for 1963 when Neil Rosenberg managed it. An annual bluegrass festival was established there in 1967.

About July 1951, Monroe went to the town of Bluefield, Virginia, and hired away banjoist Larry Richardson and fiddler Charlie Cline from the **Lonesome Pine Fiddlers**. Cline stayed with Monroe on and off until 1955. Also about 1951, the **Blue Grass Boys** was the team of Rudy Lyle, Jimmy Martin, Vassar Clements (fiddle) and Joel Price (bass). Early in 1951, Monroe recorded several songs in Nashville: "Letter from My Darling," "On the Old Kentucky Shore" and "Poison Love" which were duets by Monroe and Jimmy Martin. "Rawhide" was a new instrumental which featured Rudy Lyle (banjo), Red Taylor (fiddle), Martin, Monroe and Price. In June 1951, Monroe's manager became Frankie Moore.

Paul Cohen (R), Decca records, is only kidding when he strums a chord or two for Bill.

While the **Blue Grass Boys** band was on tour in Bluefield, West Virginia, about July 1951, Jimmy Martin left Monroe.[61] Carter Stanley quit his position as bandleader of the **Stanley Brothers** and joined Bill Monroe's **Blue Grass Boys** until September. It was a turning point in Monroe's career because up to this point he resented, and felt threatened by, other bands playing a similar sound. Monroe and Stanley worked well together and put this resentment behind them. They recorded two sessions for Decca, on July 1 and July 6, which included songs "Rotation Blues"/"Lonesome Truck Driver Blues." Stanley didn't sing on the first session (he only played rhythm guitar) but did sing lead and played rhythm guitar on the July 6 session on "Sugar Coated Love," Cabin of Love," "You're Drifting Away" and "Get Down on Your Knees and Pray." Other musicians were Rudy Lyle, Gordon Terry and Howard Watts (Ernie Newton played bass on the July 1 session). Ralph Stanley joined them occasionally on banjo.

[59] John Morthland, *The Best of Country Music* (New York: Doubleday and Company, 1984), p. 156.

[60] Some sources acknowledge October 22nd, 1949, as *the* date they recorded together.

[61] Bob Osborne remembered that Monroe's band also included Red Taylor, Rudy Lyle and Joel Price when they did a show at the State Theater one night. It was there in Bluefield that Martin would soon team up with Bob Osborne in the Lonesome Pine Fiddlers. This duo soon left to form their own Jimmy Martin, Bob Osborne and the Sunny Mountain Boys.

These were very lean years in the music business. Some people put the blame on the commercialization of music which was occurring in Nashville with well known country bands. In order to draw a decent crowd, they had to tour together. One such tour included Roy Acuff, Little Jimmy Dickens, **Johnny and Jack**, Kitty Wells and Robert Lunn, a dancer. The Bolick brothers (the **Blue Sky Boys**), who had been in the country music business since the mid-1930s, dropped out of music completely in 1951. Their music careers simply were not providing the income they had enjoyed for so many years so they chose to abandon music. The tastes of the people who bought records and attended concerts was changing.

Elvis Presley came along in 1954 and made a tremendous impact on country and bluegrass music. Former IBMA head Art Menius wrote, "Rock and roll robbed country music of its youth market. Trying to reclaim that youth market has ruined country ever since." Country and bluegrass musicians, in spite of whatever feelings they might have had about the man, his music, or the loss of the venues they once had, felt that anyone capable of making a living in that climate just had to be good. Ralph Rinzler explained it this way, "The reason Bill was in the dumps in the fifties was the takeover of rock and roll at the time of Elvis Presley, and it threatened all of country music for a while. Another factor was that **Flatt and Scruggs** had cornered the market on what was left." Louise Scruggs was a fine manager for her husband's band and helped keep it successful. Monroe had no organization. He cared nothing about the business of music—only about playing music. He was a creator, not a business man. According to author James Rooney, "The one thing he was extremely aware of was that he had fashioned his music. His music didn't just happen and it wasn't intuitive. He consciously did it. The way a painter takes his brush and dips his brush into different colors on that palette, he can tell you exactly where he gets every sound in his music."[62]

Benjamin Franklin "Tex" Logan met Monroe in October 1951. Logan was playing his last show with **Wilma Lee and Stoney Cooper** where he and Buck Graves had been working. They went backstage to meet Bill Monroe and to introduce his "Christmas Times' A-Coming" to him. Monroe immediately wanted to record it and invited Logan to record it. But Logan wasn't able to make the recording session so Monroe used Gordon Terry, his regular fiddle player, to record it.

In June of 1952, Jimmy Martin returned to Monroe's band with fourteen year-old banjoist Sonny Osborne. Osborne was still in school and had to return to school at the end of the summer.

Monroe's "Pike Country Breakdown"/"A Mighty Pretty Waltz" was recorded for Decca[63] on July 26th and released in August. "Monroe composed 'Pike County Breakdown' a number of years ago but he had never recorded it. Mercury released a recording of it by **Flatt and Scruggs** in May—so Monroe found himself again (as with 'Kentucky Waltz' last year) recording a 'cover' of his own composition."[64]

Jim Smoak joined the **Blue Grass Boys** in October 1952 as banjoist, taking Sonny Osborne's place. Smoak (18) was just out of high school. Other band members of the **Blue Grass Boys** were Jimmy Martin and Charlie Cline. This band split when Monroe and Bessie Lee Mauldin had a near-fatal auto accident near White House, Tennessee, in January 1953. (Cline had left the band only a week before the accident.) Although Martin kept the band together for a while, they could do no road shows without Monroe and they were limited to their scheduled appearances on the Opry. It is well known that Monroe hated alcohol and was very intolerant of those who used it. Certainly, one good reason for this hatred came as a result of this event where his car was hit by another car whose driver was drinking. When Monroe's health recovered, he reorganized his band with Smoak,[65] Jack Youngblood (fiddle) and Edd Mayfield (guitar).[66]

According to Butch Robins, one of the features which Monroe seemed to find in his best friends was that of a work ethic similar to his own. Edd Mayfield, Byron Berline and Bill Holden were three of those who weren't afraid of the hard work at Bill's farm. These men were physically strong at the time and became true friends to Monroe. When times were slow musically, Bill would "invite" his band members to work the chores at his farm which was near Nashville. They would work for room and board during slow times of the music.

---

[62] Rooney, op. cit., p. 70.

[63] With musicians Monroe, Jimmy Martin, Charlie Cline, Osborne, Ernie Newton and Owen Bradley, piano on "Waltz."

[64] Neil V. Rosenberg, "Thirty Years Ago This Month," *Bluegrass Unlimited*, June, 1981.

[65] Soon after Monroe's accident, Smoak left to join the band of Little Jimmy Dickens. Smoak has the distinction of being the first and only banjo player Dickens ever carried with his band (1953). In late 1953, Smoak's tenure with that band ended when the Musician's Union pay scale went up and forced Dickens to lay off two of his seven-piece band.

[66] Edd Mayfield (born 1926) was an important singer amongst all of Monroe's lead singers. Mayfield, of Dimmitt, Texas, was not only an authentic cowboy, he and his brothers were extremely popular around west Texas before he joined Monroe. He could, according to Bobby Hicks, "chord a guitar all day long and not get tired." And banjoist Joe Drumright said of Edd, "You couldn't get him out of time, and he played some of the best backing notes you ever heard in your life. Edd was way ahead of his time. There wasn't anyone even close to him back then." These quotes come from Alan Munde and Joe Carr's *Prairie Nights to Neon Lights*. Mayfield went on to record "Panhandle Country," "Christmas Time's A-Coming," "Close By," "My Little Georgia Rose," "Put My Little Shoes Away" and "The First Whippoorwill" among others. He was in Monroe's band various times during the 1950s. He died of leukemia July of 1958.

This photo is on display at the Country Music Hall of Fame. L to R: Bessie Mauldin, Billy Baker, Bill Monroe, Bobby Atkins and Bobby Smith. Courtesy Bobby Atkins.

Carlton Haney, of North Carolina, in 1954, became Bill Monroe's manager and catcher on the baseball team. Haney also began to learn how to play the acoustic bass for the band, but didn't really like it.

On June 26, 1954, Bill Monroe began recording with three fiddles to add to his show-business appeal. The three men who played fiddle in Monroe's band at the time convinced Monroe to try a triple-fiddle sound with his band; Monroe wasn't interested in changing his "sound". Charlie Cline said, "It wasn't Bill trying to change it as much we was tryin' to get him to change it. He wanted to stay with the single fiddle. And Red kept tellin' Bill that it would be something different if he had three fiddles. And when he heard the three fiddles he said, 'Yeah, that's it!' And it really took off. Edd Mayfield was on that and Gordon Terry and Red Taylor...and the first number we did was 'Blue Moon of Kentucky.'[67] There was no banjo on 'Blue Moon of Kentucky' because I was the banjo player and I had to play fiddle. We didn't have no dubbin' in back 'ere. You just played like you did on the show. If you made a mistake you just did it over. There was no albums, there was just 45s." They also recorded "Georgia Rose."[68] The songs that session were "Close By" and "Put My Little Shoes Away."

Bill Monroe changed his music style as a result of these three fiddles. "It was bluegrass through the fifties... When we got with him, he changed his style to the *high, lonesome sound*. It was bluegrass, but it wasn't the *high, lonesome sound* until we started putting the three fiddles in there..." said Cline.

Pete Pyle re-joined the **Blue Grass Boys** for two months. Both men found that Pyle's style, which was fine in Monroe's 1941 music, was incompatible with Monroe's present music. It had changed significantly since the old days—just thirteen years before. Bill arranged a job for him at the Brown County Jamboree he had just bought.

Kenny Baker met Bill Monroe in 1955 and was offered full-time employment anytime he wanted. At that time, Bobby Hicks was Monroe's fiddler. Baker didn't accept employment until 1957.

In June 1956, members of the **Blue Grass Boys** were Bobby Hicks (fiddle), Joe "Spark Plug" Stuart (banjo, comedy), Yates Green (guitar) and Chick Stripling (comedy, buck dancing).

Bill Monroe hired Cajun fiddler Doug Kershaw in 1957 in a further attempt to reach another generation of fans. This was somewhat in the direction of rock and roll, and young people liked it. His tenure with the **Blue Grass Boys** was short though, lasting for only one recording session. Also that year, Monroe's band consisted of Ralph "Joe" Meadows (fiddle), Stuart (banjo) and Mauldin (bass). Eddie Adcock worked with Monroe twice that year in addition to his regular **Buzz Busby and the Bayou Boys** in the Washington, D.C., area. In March, with Don Stover on banjo, Monroe and his band toured in a package show with Ray Price, Ferlin Huskey, Jean Shepard and Hawkshaw Hawkins. In Cincinnati they played to 4500 people.

In 1958, Monroe's Gibson F-5 mandolin was in the shop.[69] He sent it back to the Gibson factory to rework the fingerboard and also wanted some work on the neck. Receiving it after what seemed to be a long time with very little done on it, he was so angry that he took his pocket knife and cut out the mother-of-pearl Gibson insignia. And because they finished it without his permission[70] and some of its original tone had been lost, he angrily scraped the finish off with a pen knife[71]. The mandolin stayed in that condition for several years. Gibson repeatedly offered to repair it but Monroe was too angry. Besides, he loved the sound of his Lloyd Loar and didn't want refinishing to possibly alter it. When Billy Grammer of the Opry talked him into allowing

---

[67] 1990 interview in Owensboro, Kentucky.

[68] "Blue Moon of Kentucky" was recorded September 4, 1954; "Georgia Rose" was recorded earlier on June 26th. Both recording sessions used triple fiddles. The June session used the banjo of Jim Smoak. This according to the *Bill Monroe Discography*, by Neil Rosenberg and Charles Wolfe, a 1989 Bear Family Publication to accompany a four-CD set. But Charlie Cline definitely told this writer that "Blue Moon of Kentucky" was the first Monroe tune to use triple fiddles.

[69] He borrowed the F-4 of Connie Gately (Backwoods Boys Band) for Decca recording session #32 (December 1, 1958). On the next recording session (January 30, 1959), Monroe borrowed the F-12 of Bill Thomas (Cumberland Mountain Boys).

[70] The article "Monroe's F-5 Gets a Facelift" (*Frets*, January, 1981, p. 36) tells a different story. It reads:
"The story really begins in 1951. Monroe, who had bought the mandolin for $150...at a Miami, Florida, barbershop (in 1942) (see 'The Master's Mandolin,' *Frets*, May, 1979) decided to send the instrument back to the factory to have a broken neck repaired. 'I had four or five more things I wanted done to it,' he recalled. 'It needed frets and tuning keys and I wanted to have it refinished because it had gotten pretty scratched up. Gibson kept it four months, and when they sent it back all they'd done was put the neck back on. That's all! I got kind of aggravated.'" For more on this story, see the Instrument Companies and chapter of this book.

[71] This according to Carlton Haney, who saw him doing it. Other sources say it was a piece of glass.

America's Music | Bluegrass

Gibson to finally do the work properly, it was sent to Gibson in Kalamazoo, Michigan, in its own airplane seat. They re-installed the Gibson insignia but left the finish alone. After the repair was completed, with a thank-you note from the repair people who worked on it, Monroe remarked, "Listen to how it rings and keeps on ringing. I've been offered $40,000 for this mandolin but I don't think I would sell it for 450,000. It's meant so much to me and what I wanted to do that I wouldn't put a price on it. Everything is 100 percent. They've done a good job and we've made up and forgiven each other...which I guess is the way it should be."[72]

Touring with Monroe in June of 1959 were Charlie Smith (fiddle), Jack Cooke (guitar) and Buddy Pennington (banjo). They did a series of shows with **Jim and Jesse** which included Bobby Thompson and Vassar Clements who doubled on bass with the **Blue Grass Boys**. While Charlie Smith was Monroe's occasional fiddler with the group, the November 25th recording session for Decca in Nashville included fiddlers Benny Martin and Dale Potter, banjoist Joe Drumright, guitarist Jack Cooke, and bassist Bessie Lee. This release was a "faked" live event; hand clapping was added after the recordings.

Bobby Smith joined the **Blue Grass Boys** in Nashville in November 1960 (as a fill-in guitarist) whose members included Bill Monroe (mandolin), Charlie Smith[73] (fiddle), Tony Ellis (banjo) and Mauldin (bass).[74]

On May 21, 1961, Bill Monroe opened his music park in Bean Blossom, Brown County, Indiana. On October 22nd, the **Blue Grass Boys** played there with Bobby Smith and Jimmy Maynard (guitars) and Vassar Clements (fiddle). Local musicians Birch Monroe and Neil Rosenberg filled out the band. Bill played mandolin on the 1962 "Rose Maddox Sings Bluegrass" album. Other musicians were Donna Stoneman (mandolin), Don Reno, Red Smiley and Mac Magaha. This album was probably Monroe's idea (Carlton Haney also claims credit for the idea) and gave Rose her first exposure to bluegrass music. Monroe played mandolin on the first session, Stoneman the second.

Ralph Rinzler[75] became Bill Monroe's manager in January 1963. He was to be a very important person in the life of the band and in the history of bluegrass music. Monroe's forte was musicianship and he tended to be somewhat lax in the promotion department.

Lamar Grier telling his "story" with Carlton Haney in 1995.

Rinzler changed the band's booking policies and expanded the venues Monroe was to play in the future...places such as folk festivals, colleges and tours to the north and west of the United States. The February/March 1963 issue of *Sing Out!* included the article "Bill Monroe—'The Daddy of Blue Grass Music'" written by Rinzler. The title remained with Monroe for the rest of his life. The article was written because Earl Scruggs had just received tremendous accolades in *Sing Out!* only months before[76] for being "the undisputed master of bluegrass music". Rinzler wanted the world to know that Monroe was its "father" and all others in bluegrass were merely disciples.

In March, because the **Blue Grass Boys** now had two banjo players, Del McCoury and Bill Keith (whom Monroe called by Bill Keith's middle name, Brad, to avoid having two "Bills" in the band), Rinzler moved McCoury to guitar and lead singer. Monroe capitalized on the musicianship of this band which included Keith (banjo), McCoury (guitar) and fiddler Kenny Baker.[77] This very popular group of individuals helped keep his band, and bluegrass, alive in spite of the decidedly folk and rock and roll era.

Monroe spoke of his new banjo player, "Brad Keith, he understands music. He's a good listener and he's a good man to listen to. He's done a lot of good for music and especially for bluegrass. At a time when I needed a boost, I think that Brad gave it to me. I think it came in

[72] Laura Eipper, "Bill Monroe's Mandolin Gets an Apologetic Facelift," *Bluegrass Unlimited*, November, 1980, p. 29.

[73] Smith has played on the Opry once a year with Monroe until recently.

[74] During the entire period that Bobby Smith was with the group, other members with the BOYS were Vassar Clements (fiddle), Joe Drumright (banjo) and Bobby Atkins (banjo).

[75] Ralph Rinzler died July 2, 1994. A distinguished career in this music ended that day, but his life will continue to live on within bluegrass because of his accomplishments as musician, musicologist and historian. He discovered Doc Watson in 1960. Rinzler worked as mandolinist and vocalist for the New York-based Greenbriar Boys and recorded with them and other folk artists such as Joan Baez and Peggy Seeger. In 1967, he took a position as at the Smithsonian Institution where he worked tirelessly for nearly thirty years, promoting the music and crafts of America's indigenous folk artists. Rinzler created the Smithsonian's annual Festival of American Folklife and the Center for Folklife Programs and Cultural Studies. In 1987, he helped the Smithsonian acquire the huge catalog and archives of Folkways Records. His most recent Smithsonian/Folkways productions include a compilation of live performances by Bill Monroe and Doc Watson, and the original Folkways recordings of Doc with Clarence Ashley.

[76] April/May 1962, "Earl Scruggs—and the Sound of Bluegrass" by Pete Welding.

[77] Billy Sage was also a fiddler during this time; Mauldin played bass.

when I needed it. Before he came along, no banjo player could play those old fiddle tunes right. You have to play like Brad could play or you would be faking your way through a number. It's learned a lot of banjo players what to do and how to do it to where they can come along and fill that bill today."[78] Ex-Bill Monroe manager Rinzler wrote that "Having Bill Keith come with [Monroe] reinforced his musical vitality. Keith would hear one of Monroe's phrases and he could pick up and instantly he would echo it back on the banjo and that would excite Monroe because it was an acknowledgment of the subtlety of his creativity right there on the stage."[79]

Monroe was not only relating to a northerner, but a college-educated man as well. It gave Monroe an idea of how universally accepted his music was—how important it was. He began to accept the role given to him by Rinzler—that of being the "Father of Bluegrass Music". He began to enjoy it and became more mellow. Thereafter, when musicians left his band, he wasn't as offended as he was when Lester and Earl left. Monroe began to recognize that they were merely leaving to expand upon what he taught them. He began to understand—and it put him at ease.

In a 1984 interview, Mr. Monroe was asked about how musicians use the **Blue Grass Boys** as a training ground to get experience and credentials. He said he didn't regret that at all. "Not a bit in the world! Bluegrass is like a school of music, and that's the way I have kept it ever since I have been on the Grand Ole Opry and I started it. And people would work for me—most of them would stay for nearly three years—and then they would have learned enough about it and then they go out on their own. I was for them one hundred percent."[80]

Also in 1963, **Bill Monroe and the Blue Grass Boys** played at the Newport Folk Festival and New York Folk Festival for the first time. It was at the Newport (Rhode Island) festival that Bill Keith played "Sailor's Hornpipe" and "Devil's Dream" before a stunned crowd. This was the world's first exposure to a large dose of melodic banjo playing.

Keith stayed eight months, eventually tiring of Nashville and touring. McCoury stayed one and a half years, quitting to go to California with Billy Baker to join the **Golden State Boys**. Occasional members of the **Blue Grass Boys** during that period were Rual Yarbrough (banjo) and Jake Landers (guitar). Other "outsiders" (or those not from the South) to contribute to Monroe's band included Peter Rowan, Richard Greene, Steve Arkin, Gene Lowinger and Byron Berline. Arkin could play the best backup banjo Monroe

had ever heard. Monroe recognized Greene as a potential great bandleader.

Neil V. Rosenberg took Birch Monroe's place as manager of the Brown County Jamboree shows for the 1963 season. Birch continued to run the dances and took over the managerialship again the next year. Rosenberg continued to play at the Jamboree in the house band called the **Stoney Lonesome Boys** as banjoist until he left the scene entirely in 1968.

Gene Lowinger was the fiddler about 1964 for a year or so and is known as Monroe's first Yankee fiddler. In 1964, Monroe's band recorded four times with various musicians including Joe Stuart, Joe Drumright, Benny Williams, Del McCoury, Jimmy Maynard and Norman Keith "Buddy" Spicher. Don Lineberger, a left-handed banjo player, worked with Monroe just before the first bluegrass festival in 1965. By 1966, members of the **Blue Grass Boys** were Peter Rowan (guitar), Richard Greene (fiddle), Lamar Grier (banjo) and James Monroe (bass, Bill's son). Rowan is acknowledged as being the first Yankee lead singer who sang with the **Boys**. Douglas B. Green filled-in on guitar with Monroe in 1967 (April 30th to the end of the summer during a West Coast tour), and the bass in 1969 (March through July). Green would later gain considerable fame with his **Riders in the Sky** western trio as "Ranger Doug". By the fall of 1967, members were Roland White (guitar), Vic Jordan (banjo), Byron Berline (fiddle) and James Monroe (bass). By winter, Vassar Clements and Benny Williams were on fiddle. A year later, the only change in personnel was the fiddler who was now Kenny Baker (for the third time) who stayed with Monroe, on and off, until 1984.

Bill Monroe held his bluegrass festival at Bean Blossom, Indiana, in June of 1967. Roland White was a member of the band about that time. According to Alan Munde in a 1991 interview, "I didn't know him at the time, but Roland would help build the stage or put in the sewer line or a drain or whatever was needed to be done. He said that Birch was so unbelievably tight that before he would send out to buy nails, he would require that the old ones be straightened out first. Another time, during the festival they had one row of concession stands where they had run out of ice that Birch was in charge of. So here you have one concession stand and maybe a thousand people or two thousand. You've got one concession stand and he goes out and buys a pound of coffee and two bags of ice. He would run back and forth all day long rather than [store supplies]. And Roland, just to illustrate the point, said he would drive to California putting in two dollars worth of gas all along the way."

[78] Rooney, op. cit., p. 83.

[79] Ibid., p. 87.

[80] 1984 interview with this writer, Portland, Oregon.

Roland White left the **Blue Grass Boys** in 1969 to work with Lester Flatt's **Nashville Grass**. Taking his place was James Monroe who moved from bass to guitar. Doug Green joined on bass March to September. James stayed until 1972 when he left to form his own **Midnight Ramblers.**

In 1970, Monroe's sidemen were Kenny Baker, Rual Yarbrough (banjo), James Monroe (guitar) and Doug Hutchens (bass). Soon Earl Snead replaced Rual Yarbrough on banjo who left to spend more time at his music business in Muscle Shoals, Alabama. Joe Stuart replaced Hutchens on bass. They were occasionally joined by Tex Logan on fiddle and Dan Jones on guitar. Also that year, Bill Monroe was elected to the Country Music Hall of Fame.

Burial headstone of Charlie Monroe, Rosine, KY.

Bill Box, of Muskogee, Oklahoma, replaced Bob Fowler as lead singer/guitarist with the **Blue Grass Boys.**[81] Greg Kennedy replaced Guy Stevens on bass.

Also about that time, Bill Monroe gave his Uncle Pendleton Vandiver a special monument on his grave. And recently, Bill Monroe was presented with the old Vandiver home site (3 1/2 acres) where Bill lived a year. The gift was from his son, James, on Bill's 60th birthday.

Bill and James Monroe established a booking agency for their bands and others in 1972. Bill was active in helping festivals, in addition to his own at Bean Blossom, get started. He would lend not only his name but also financial support. One such location was with the Colorado Bluegrass Music Society where he volunteered to help put on their first festival in 1973. Monroe brought the talent listed with his agency at no up-front cost to the Society. This festival included the **Blue Grass Boys**, Lester Flatt, the **McLain Family Band**, Hylo Brown, **Country Gazette**, **Bluegrass Alliance**, Dudley Murphy and Hubert Davis. After a few years,

the festival became self-sustaining and Mr. Monroe was no longer a part. He held five bluegrass festivals in 1980:

1) Beaver Dam/Rosine Bluegrass Festival, Rosine, Kentucky.
2) Bill Monroe's 16th Annual Bluegrass Festival, Bean Blossom, Indiana.
3) Second Annual Tarheel Bluegrass Festival, Kings Mountain, North Carolina.
4) Bill Monroe's Sixth Annual Autumn Festival, Bean Blossom.
5) Bill Monroe's West Tennessee Bluegrass Festival, Waynesboro, Tennessee.

In 1973, Bill Monroe invited Lester Flatt to the Bean Blossom festival. The reunion was their first appearance together since 1948 when they parted ways. The event was a significant emotional move to patch up old wounds. On the other hand, Monroe had no intention of easing his policy of being anti-electric instruments. He would still not allow bands with electrified instruments such as the **Earl Scruggs Revue**, **New Grass Revival** and the **Osborne Brothers** to play his festival. But in spite of Bill Monroe's dislike of musicians who grew their hair long, he hired the **Bluegrass Alliance** to play at his Arizona Bluegrass Festival in Payson, Arizona.[82]

March 11th now marks "Bill Monroe Day" in Boston as declared by the city's mayor. The date coincided with Monroe's concert there, put on by the Boston Area Friends of Bluegrass and Old-Time Country Music. In November 1973, Bill Monroe was the Grand Marshall of the Thanksgiving parade during the Grand Strand Honor Roll at Myrtle Beach, South Carolina. He was then inducted into the Honor Roll as a tribute for outstanding personages who have participated in a major Myrtle Beach Grand Strand activity. On September 13, 1975, "Bill Monroe Day" was proclaimed by the mayor of Metropolitan Dade County, Stephen P. Clark. The award was inspired by the Southern Florida Bluegrass Association.

In 1974, the **Blue Grass Boys** members were Kenny Baker on fiddle, Dwight Dillman, the banjo, Ralph Lewis, the guitar, and Randy Davis, the bass. By late 1974, regular members of the **Blue Grass Boys** had become Bob Black (banjo), Ralph Lewis (guitar), Kenny Baker and Randy Davis. Monroe toured Japan with the **Lilly Brothers** in December.

May 9, 1975, was the opening of Bluegrass Musicland Park. Owned and operated by Bill and James Monroe, the park was located in Beaver Dam, Kentucky, near the sight of the log cabin where Bill's Uncle Pendleton Vandiver grew up. The duo planed to hold bluegrass and gospel shows there twice a month and include a museum.

---

81 In August of 1974, Bill Box left to re-form his Bill Box and the Dixie Drifters, then on to Jim and Jesse in 1986.

82 It was a Dick Tyner production which also featured Ralph Stanley and Lester Flatt.

Charlie Monroe died of cancer on September 27, 1975. He was buried in the Rosine cemetery in the Monroe family plot. Now, each annual Rosine Arts and Crafts and Bluegrass Festival pays tribute to Charlie.

In May of 1976, the MCA label released Bill Monroe's "The Weary Traveler."[83] Later that year, Bill Holden joined the **Blue Grass Boys** as guitarist/lead singer who had just left the **Country Gentlemen**. When Kenny Baker severely cut his left hand with a hunting knife in September 1977, James Bryan was hired to take his place on fiddle. Butch Robins was on banjo. Wayne Lewis had recently left **Lillimae and the Dixie Gospel-Aires** to become guitarist and lead singer with Monroe. By 1979, the bass player for Bill Monroe's band was Mark Hembree.

Bill Monroe was presented an honorary degree in bluegrass music late in 1977 by South Plains College of Levelland, Texas. October 28th, 1979, marked Bill Monroe's 40th anniversary as a member of the Grand Ole Opry. An inscribed silver bowl was presented to him by Bud Wendell, the president of WSM.

James Monroe opened Monroe Manor, a club/restaurant in Nashville, in September 1980. It featured the big names in bluegrass music. It eventually became vacant and burned down. About 1984, Bill and James opened up the Bill Monroe Museum Bluegrass Hall of Fame in Nashville. It was not profitable, and about 1986 it was relocated to Music Village USA, Hendersonville, Tennessee, a few miles east of Nashville.

Blue Grass Boys belt buckle. A gift from Bluegrass Unlimited magazine to all the ex-Blue Grass Boys. This particular one belongs to Doug Hutchens.

By November of 1981, members of the **Blue Grass Boys** included Butch Robins (banjo), Kenny Baker (fiddle), Wayne Lewis (guitar) and Mark Hembree (bass). They recorded the "Master of Bluegrass" album on MCA. Also on the album were Norman Blake, Jesse McReynolds and Larry Sledge (mandolin). By December, Blake Williams was the banjoist with the **Blue Grass Boys**; he stayed over a decade with Monroe's band.

Birch Monroe died of a heart attack in Owensboro, Kentucky, on the eve of his 81st birthday, on May 15, 1982. On his gravestone in Rosine is written: "Fiddler, Friend of all. A wonderful brother, a wonderful uncle."

On July 3, 1982, Bill Monroe was a recipient of the First Annual National Heritage Fellowship Award. The award was sponsored by the National Endowment for the Arts. Monroe's award read, "A song maker, a man-

dolinist, and Father of Bluegrass. Once described as 'Folk Music in Overdrive,' this brilliant musical style takes the familiar American country string ensemble of fiddle, banjo, guitar and mandolin into a new dimension. Bill Monroe is one of the few living American musicians who can justly claim to have created an entirely new musical style."[84]

In January 1983, Bill Monroe suffered an auto accident and had to stop work until May. When he began touring again, band members included Monroe, Kenny Baker (fiddle), Blake Williams (banjo), Wayne Lewis (guitar) and Mark Hembree (bass).

Monroe was named Chairman for the recently-formed Nashville Bluegrass Music Association International—an organization created to promote concerts. In February 1983, Bill Monroe was selected to be Grand Marshall at the 1983 Kentucky Derby festivities. This was fitting because he is a native Kentuckian and strove to promote his state at every opportunity. September 13th is now Bill Monroe Day according to the mayor of Nashville. The Day was proclaimed at Monroe's 72nd birthday at Mason's Restaurant, Goodlettsville, Tennessee.

Dale Morris took Kenny Baker's place in February 1985. By October, Glen Duncan was Monroe's fiddler.

On November 13th, 1985, Monroe's home was broken into by a vandal while he was on tour. Nothing was stolen, but most of his valuable vintage instruments, pictures and mementos were broken. His ever-familiar Lloyd Loar Gibson F-5 mandolin was nearly destroyed by a fireplace poke. Evidently, the vandal had selected those items which meant the most to Monroe. Certainly, his mandolin is irreplaceable. Monroe turned to the Gibson factory. They put their best repairman on the job and worked on it for several months. The job was especially difficult because some pieces of the instrument were merely splinters. The worry was that, even though the parts could be put back in the proper order, the unique sound of the instrument would be lost due to the increased presence of glue.

The restoration was completed on February 26, 1986; there was no charge to Monroe. The work was done by Gibson's Charlie Derrington. The pressure on him was great, for he had the whole bluegrass world waiting for Monroe to strum it and see if it was okay. Monroe was pleased, saying that "Gibson never did a better job than for this mandolin...it still sounds tight. It needs to be played, broken in again."[85] There was a

83 Musicians on the LP were Kenny Baker and Joe Stuart (fiddles), Bob Black (banjo), Ralph Lewis and James Monroe (guitars) and Stephen Davis (bass).

84 From General Store, *Bluegrass Unlimited*, August, 1982.

85 Charmaine Lanham, "Bill Monroe's Mandolin Is Restored," *Bluegrass Unlimited*, April, 1986, pp. 40, 41.

second, less valuable mandolin destroyed by the vandal. This, too, was Derrington's job to repair. It took three months to fix the first one. Derrington could pursue the repair of the second one at a slower pace, for the pressure on Gibson and Derrington was off.

Wayne Lewis left the **Blue Grass Boys** in 1986, after almost eleven years with the Monroe band.[86] Tom Ewing took his place with the **Blue Grass Boys** and remained there into the mid-1990s. In March of 1987, Billy Joe Foster, from Oklahoma, was fiddler with Bill Monroe. He and Tater Tate, who mostly played bass, occasionally did twin-fiddle tunes together. Mark Hembree joined the **Blue Grass Boys** as bass player again in August 1988. He was replaced in March of 1989 by Wayne Jerrods. The new guitarist was Scotty Baugus. In May of 1989, members were Tom Ewing (again), Tate, Blake Williams and Billy Rose (bass).

Bill Monroe was named "Honorary Member of the Sonneck Society". It is a society named in honor of the first chief of the Music Division of the Library of Congress, Oscar Sonneck. That year, Monroe won a Grammy for his "Southern Flavor" LP. The title tune is an instrumental. Monroe wrote tunes spontaneously, and sometimes often. "I write for the music and for the sound," Monroe said during sessions for this recording. "I write all the time when I'm on the road. I can write an instrumental in just a minute."[87]

In June 1989, "Bill Monroe was exonerated of all charges stemming from an incident at his farm on May 3. Ms. Wanda Huff of Birmingham, Alabama, filed assault and battery charges after Mr. Monroe allegedly 'hit her with a Bible, knocked her down and kicked her.' No state charges were filed and the District Attorney asked that all charges be dismissed in Sumner County General Court on May 10."[88] Evidently, Ms. Huff insisted that Mr. Monroe swear on the bible that he was not seeing other women. Supposedly, she made harassing phone calls, came to his house, destroyed property and caused a major disturbance. The charges were dismissed and she was ordered to stay away from him.

Bill Monroe celebrated fifty years on the Opry at a TNN television special on October 28th, 1989. MCA Records simultaneously released an LP of live Opry performances, "Bill Monroe Live."

By the fall of 1990, the **Blue Grass Boys** were Monroe, Williams (banjo), Ewing (guitar), Tate (bass, fiddle) and Jimmy Campbell (fiddle, bass). Later that year, Blake Williams left the banjo spot in Monroe's band and joined the **Mike Snider Trio** as bassist.

Bill Monroe underwent a double coronary artery bypass surgery on August 9, 1991. He recovered and continued to perform whenever he could. His eightieth birthday came up the next September 13th. Monroe had a 280-acre farm where he lived and which he worked a little; it's sixteen miles from Nashville. He used to raise cattle, horses and chickens there. It was bought by associates of the Grand Ole Opry in 1995 for a reported $300,000. Monroe was allowed to live on the property as long as he wanted.

On June 14, 1994, **Bill Monroe and the Blue Grass Boys** returned to the newly-opened Ryman Auditorium. **Alison Krauss and Union Station,** which opened for Monroe, was the first bluegrass group to play at the venerable Nashville landmark. The Ryman had been restored to a like-new condition inside and was infinitely more hospitable because of the air conditioning. The pews were the same, but they had been refinished to eliminate graffiti carved into the wood over the years. The old hall, which the Grand Ole Opry had used from 1943 to 1974, was again alive with music. With its upgraded stage lights, sound system, insulation, air conditioning and other amenities, it was Nashville's attempt to counteract all the damage that Branson, Missouri, had done to the city by "stealing" Nashville's artists away from it—but that's another story. Members of the **Blue Grass Boys** that night were Monroe, Dana Cupp (banjo), Tater Tate (bass), Tom Ewing (guitar) and Robert Bowlin (fiddle).

William Smith Monroe passed on September 9, 1996, a few days before his 85th birthday. Ricky Skaggs, who had visited him a few days before, set Bill at ease about his concerns on the demise of bluegrass. He told Bill, 'Don't worry about bluegrass music; it will never die. I will keep playing it." And so will the rest of the world, Ricky.

"Monroe influenced everyone from Elvis Presley to the Grateful Dead. And while bluegrass may sound a bit antique six decades after its invention, it has lost none of it ferocity—until now. For the unmatched performer of this music was always Monroe himself, a brilliant composer, an intrepid instrumentalist and a wonderful singer. No one who saw him in his prime could forget the sound of that near-psychotic falsetto soaring over the sound of a mandolin played so fast that one critic said Monroe was not playing his instrument so much as piloting it. Pyrotechnics, however, were only part of the point. 'It's played from my heart to your heart,' Monroe declared. Even near the end, when the famously fierce voice had thinned to transparency and the fingers were no longer so fleet, Monroe never lost his ability to touch your heart, or make the hair rise on the back of your neck."[89]

---

86 After a summer with Jimmy Martin, He formed his Wayne Lewis Band. He was already owner of a talent agency in Hendersonville, Tennessee.

87 Thomas Goldsmith, "Bill Monroe in the Studio—Recording the Grammy Winner," *Bluegrass Unlimited*, April, 1989, p. 46.

88 *Bluegrass Unlimited*, June, 1989, p. 13.

89 Malcolm Jones Jr., "The Passing of a Patriarch," *Newsweek*, September 23, 1996, p. 75.

My Life In Bluegrass—
An Interview
With Bill Monroe

By Alice Foster

From the program book at the 1969 Newport Folk Festival. Reprinted with permission (3/14/96).

(Written and edited by Alice Foster with thanks to Ralph Rinzler and Hazel Dickens for their help. Taken from three taped interviews with Bill Monroe at Sunset Park, PA., September 29, 1968; Nashville, TN., May 16, 169; Lancaster, PA., May 24, 1969.)

"There's so many people that's played bluegrass music that don't know where the ideas come from, but when you're a kid, you can remember things and the things I can remember, I've fitted them in down through the years to advance bluegrass music, and never just make it into one thing one year and let that be the end of it. I've tried to add something to it every year.

Bill Monroe from his Grammy-winning LP/CD "Southern Flavor," 1989.

"The first music I heard was Uncle Pen and Uncle Birch and a man by the name of Clarence Wilson, and they played numbers like 'Soldier's Joy.' Each town maybe had a little band eight or ten miles from us by the name of Foster String Band—that was back in the twenties, and I remember a band that had a fiddle, a Hawaiian guitar, mandolin—they might have had a banjo. They played breakdowns, dance music and a few waltzes and a little Hawaiian music. Maybe there would be one man who would know a solo, and there was one fellow singing 'Greenback Dollar.'

"There's a long ridge back home called Jerusalem Ridge, and I remember we had to cross that and go on down about a mile to where we come to this real old house called the Lizer place, and this man, Clea Baze that played the fiddle, he lived there. We'd walk back there with a coal oil lantern, and we got there that night and there was a good many in the room listening to them play and they sat in the middle of the room and I thought that was awful pretty music...numbers like 'Turkey in the Straw' and that kind of stuff. They'd play 'Cacklin' Hen' and he could really play that. It was something to go [to] knowing you was going to hear some music that night.

When Bill was twelve or thirteen, he became friendly with Arnold Schultz a local, black musician.

"The first time I think I ever seen Arnold Schultz...this square dance was at Rosine, Kentucky, and Arnold and two more colored fellows come up there and played for the dance. They had a guitar, banjo and fiddle. Arnold played the guitar but he could play the fiddle—numbers like 'Sally Goodin'. People loved Arnold so well all through Kentucky there; if he was playing a guitar, they'd go gang up around him 'til he would get tired and then maybe he'd go catch a train. He lived down at a little mining town—I believe it was called McHenry—or on down further. I used to listen to him talk and he would tell about contests that he had been in and how tough they was and how they'd play these two blues numbers and tie it up. And they had to do another number and I remember him saying that he played a waltz number and he won this contest. And just things like that I have never forgot. He thought it was wonderful that he could win out like that and I admired him [so] much that I never forgot a lot of the things he would say. There's things in my music, you know, that come from Arnold Schultz—runs that I use in a lot of my music. I don't say that I make them the same way that he could make them 'cause he was powerful with it. In following a fiddle piece or a breakdown, he used a pick and he could just run from one chord to another the prettiest you've ever heard. There's no guitar picker today that could do that. I tried to keep in mind a little of it—what I could salvage to use in my music. Then he could play blues and I wanted some blues in my music too, you see.

"Me and him played for a dance there one night and he played the fiddle and we started at sundown and the next morning at daylight we was still playing music—all night long. And, of course, that automatically made you be dancing on Sunday, but that is really the truth—I could say that I have played for a dance all night long. I played guitar with him. I just could second fair—probably any guitar man in the country could've beaten me, but anyhow I played guitar for him. I believe it was the next day about 10:00 there was a passing train come down through and stopped at Rosine, and I believe he caught that train and went back home and that was about the last time I ever saw him. I believe if there's ever an old gentleman that passed away and is resting in peace, it was Arnold Schultz—I believe that.

"People like Clayton McMichen was my favorite fiddler. If you listen to a man like that, you know if he is setting the notes in right. And if you learn to set your notes in a mandolin like that, you know that they're in there right. It's kind of like a lot of other things—putting a motor together—if you know how to put it together, well, it's got to be right. And if you've got an ear for music, for old-time music, you can might near tell. Hearing people like Clayton play years ago, there couldn't be any more notes put in—if you did you'd hurt the number. Learning how far to go with it and when to stop helps a musician.

"I've always been a great lover of Cliff Carlisle's style of singing and, of course, I like Jimmie Rodgers' singing but I think I liked Cliff Carlisle's better. Bradley Kincaid was one of my favorites, and Doc Hopkins.

"The first man that I ever heard play mandolin, I believe his name was Hubert Stringfield. He used to farm on our place and I can remember him playing ball there at Rosine. He could play a mandolin; he could tremble one and play different numbers and I thought it was really nice. Later on, there was two blind fellows by the name of Mac and Bob [who] played on WLS in Chicago and they played a slow mandolin and guitar but they could really play it pretty. They played numbers like 'What Does the Deep Sea Say,' and 'Where Is My Sailor Boy' and 'Midnight on the Story Deep.' And Karl and Harty, they had a mandolin and guitar, and the Prairie Ramblers. They all had a little different style of their own. When they was on the radio and making money, I was trying to learn a mandolin. I had that in my mind, to never play like nobody, and that helped to change the style and with the different ideas and the different people that I have heard... I wanted a style that I could call my own."

Bill first started playing mandolin in Kentucky with Birch and Charlie Monroe, his older brothers. "We didn't play bluegrass music. We want to keep that straightened out with the Smithsonian and Newport."

"There was so few guitars in the country and there was maybe just one good guitar and we had to borrow it, and Birch, he thought he wanted to be the fiddler, you know, and you didn't need two guitars and a fiddle, so about all that was left was the mandolin. Of course, there wasn't no banjos hardly in the country, so I just followed down to taking a mandolin. There was no use to argue, you know. They was the oldest and biggest and so I went on with the mandolin. But it's not heavy to carry around and a mandolin will take a lot of rough treatment, too. Really now, I'm glad that I taken the mandolin because the competition hasn't been bad. I reckon I picked the right instrument.

"To start with, I had a little potato bug mandolin and then I got one from Montgomery Ward—it was a pretty good little mandolin—it cost nine dollars. And then the neck come off of it and I finally got me a Gibson mandolin—it cost forty dollars and I was really advancing then. And that was the first good mandolin I had.

"I was playing rhythm when all three of us was together. I was chording and helping keep time. Then when the guitar and mandolin got together you needed a lead instrument so we didn't have one and I done it with the mandolin. So I started trying to learn what I could, you know, in the way of taking a break between verses and choruses. Seemed like it might have went kind of the way I thought singing should go. And old-time fiddle music, too, had a little influence on me.

"After we (Charlie and Bill) broke up, I knew I was going to have to come up with some kind of a group. I figured on four men, and I didn't know what it would really be like. I knew what I thought that I might have wanted to sound like. Bluegrass, I don't think, would ever have happened—I think it had to have a leader and somebody to keep it in line, you know, to learn the other people. The people that plays music today, they had to have something to go by or they would have been playing like Roy Acuff or Ernest Tubb or something like that that was really popular too, you know.

"When I started trying to originate the music or get it the way I wanted it, I was going to be sure there was a lonesome sound to it because I do know that the country people love the lonesome sound of music. A lot of them was raised up that could sing maybe some blues or so, and they sung it the way it made them feel good.

"It's bound to have come from my background. I told you about writing the banjo number about 'Crossing the Cumberland' the way that I thought it would have been back in the pioneer days, and I told you about writing the old fiddle number called 'Land of Lincoln.' And that's the way that I believe that it would have sounded many years ago. Take Abraham Lincoln when he was a young man and say there was a fiddler there seventy, seventy-five years older than he was. You know that it was bound to have been a long ways back and they was bound to have been some of the oldest tones and ideas in the world that old man would be playing. In this 'Land of Lincoln,' I put every old tone I could think of and made it go that way that I thought Abraham Lincoln might have heard it—a tune like that when he was a boy from some old-time fiddler...

"I wanted to advance old-time music, and it leads back to where people who played and sung in a low key couldn't do much to advance it. Gid Tanner and Uncle Dave Macon and people like that. If they sung, it would still be just as old-timey as the fiddle. I knew there was going to have to be a change made and I had in mind what I wanted to do. But I had to get the men and I had to pick the tunes to develop that style to where it would work on any number. And by training my voice, I changed mine and made it easy to where I could sing, and the musicians played where I sung. Now that has been the step of bluegrass that would've never been done if I hadn't made them play where I wanted them to play. When I started here in Nashville, nobody played in B flat or B natural, so that has been one thing which has give bluegrass such a brilliant tone and it's put the music up where the singin's at. If you played in a low G and sung in a high G, you still hadn't got it right. Now the fiddler—take Kenny Baker—he would play in the high C with me because he knows that's where I'm at— he wouldn't play in a low C because it would be easier. I wanted the music and everything pitched the same, and that's why it's give bluegrass that kind of a tone—if you sing high, the music is up there with you. By changing it, it give country a new sound and it made a music that was wonderful for the people to listen to. Bluegrass music is hard to explain—what it really is, 'cause it's got so many things that it has to have in it that it's hard to pin it down to one thing. The 'high, lonesome sound of bluegrass' has come as close as nearly anything, and it's got a good, solid, driving time to it. Now bluegrass music, it's got more jazz in it than a lot of people gives it credit for—it's been flowered up and it's been worked on and advanced, and a little bit of maybe swing music in it...and a hard drive to it and a good, high pitch and a touch of blues in it. And it's like if you was going to try and make a real good pie, to put everything in it that you could really put in it that you could help that pie along, and that's what I have tried to do for bluegrass.

Home of the Monroe family plot.

"I knew that it would be a mandolin and a fiddle, guitar and bass. It leads back years ago to when I first could remember them playing, you know—Uncle Pen and Uncle Birch and Clarence Wilson. He played the banjo. So then I was on this tent show in nineteen and forty-one and I thought I might need two comedians, you know. I had one, the bass man. So Stringbean had wrote to me for a job and he was a comedian and played the banjo. And with the touch of the banjo, it run to giving us more of the old-time, years-ago flavor. So then that put five in the group and that's what I've kept ever since.

"Then, forming the bluegrass band, the guitar plays a good many runs. Well, we needed rhythm so I really went to work playing rhythm on the mandolin when I wouldn't be taking a break. And that gives the banjo a chance to take his break. And when he's not taking his break, it gives him a chance to play fill-in. And it gives the guitar more opportunities to play runs, you see. That helps bluegrass music. And that's something that was brought along from the start of bluegrass—to learn new runs for the guitar—runs that I have heard, you know, years ago. And making the fiddler play what I thought sounded good, and what I thought was right. And it must've been right because the country people have stayed with bluegrass. They have stayed with it. They have believed in it. They think it's right.

"Back in the early days, you could drive up to a theater and the people would already be there on a morning ready to get them a ticket and see the show. A lot of them was in small towns in the eastern part of Kentucky and West Virginia...coal mining country. Then I have played as high as three theaters in a night and I've played a white theater and go to a colored theater and play. And that's something that I'm proud of. I don't believe anybody else on the Grand Ole Opry could say that they've done that.

Bill Monroe and young Matthew Spray (c.1982) talk while listening to Matthew's tape of Uncle Pen. Photo courtesy Erma Spray.

"There's been different people with their ideas and their way of playing that's helped bluegrass music. For my kind of playing, each year we've added a little something in bluegrass and it makes it more interesting. It's exciting, you know, what this man's going to play that the other man don't play. Just like mandolin, fiddle and the banjo. You know, a lot of people thinks you work against each other. And in one sense of the word, you probably do because if the fiddler's playing a number and then the banjo comes in and he sells his chorus good, the fiddler knows that he's up against it—he's going to have to get to work. And the mandolin, he follows to his part as good as the banjo or better. And it's just vice-versa. If I'm playing and the banjo and fiddle comes in, of course, they get their chances. And that's the way it's kind of been.

"It's not altogether just notes. And to run through a number that suits me that I get any enjoyment out of, I listen for the tones and try to make them satisfy me and please me. And people that understands music like that, they please them too.

"A lot of people claim that I started a monster. They call it that—bluegrass music; that I have got to stick with it, there ain't no way out of it—there's no way to change. If you changed, the people would know you didn't believe in what you was doing. I've said it—that I could originate at least two other kinds of music, but I couldn't hardly do it because people would say, 'Well, you never believed in your music to start with. You just got it started and forgot it. It wasn't good to you and you didn't care about it.' So I guess it's bluegrass all the way.

"I know the years is going to make everything come to an end, you see, and there's times when I dread to think about it because I love to play so well...if I live to be ninety I might still be playing.

"Bluegrass will never die—there will always be bluegrass music. But I just wonder how it's going to be played. But to stay on the side of the country people, you know, you're going to have to keep it down to earth and play it good. And I just hope my son Jim will do it or, if he don't, I hope there'll be some good, high lead singer who's got a lot of will power and enough backbone that he will understand it and study it and will carry it on."

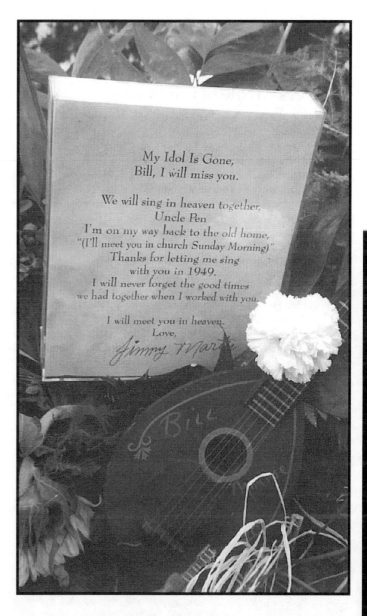

Jimmy Martin's graveside wreath to Bill Monroe. It reads: "My Idol Is Gone, Bill, I will miss you. We will sing in heaven together, Uncle Pen, I'm on my way back to the old home, "(I'll meet you in church Sunday Morning)" Thanks for letting me sing with you in 1949. I will never forget the good times we had together when I worked with you. I will meet you in heaven. Love, Jimmy Martin

Pioneers - Table of Contents

Pioneers

This chapter deals with many of the important figures in early country and bluegrass music. The protagonists appear in a somewhat chronological order of how they appeared on the professional music scene.

The Stonemans and the Blue Grass Champs

Ernest V. "Pop" Stoneman was the father of a large family of musicians who made their own mark in bluegrass music. Author Ivan M. Tribe wrote, "Twice this venerable patriarch of country music, "Pop" Stoneman, had made his way to the top. The Great Depression curtailed the first mark. But surrounded by offspring and through thirty years of poverty, hard labor, and a dazzling quintet of super-picker children, he did it again."[1] He recorded with his spouse Hattie, who is acknowledged by the Library of Congress to be the first woman of importance in country music.

Ernest was born at Monarat, Carroll County, Virginia, May 25, 1893. He played the mouth harp and Jew's harp from an early age and soon learned to pick the banjo and the Autoharp. By the time he went to New York to make recordings for Ralph Peer and Okeh Records and Edison Records in the mid-twenties, he learned to play guitar.

He married Hattie Frosh in 1919 and, over the next ten to fifteen years, taught her to play fiddle. They eventually worked up about 100 songs for recording on many labels. He and Hattie had fifteen children (the first was born in 1920 and the last 1940), thirteen of whom lived to maturity. Pop never told his children to play an instrument, but if they seemed interested he would make them one.

Stoneman and his various bands recorded on labels such as Okeh (his first recording session on September 4, 1924, in New York City), Edison, Gennett, Paramount, Pathe, Vocalion and Victor. He recorded on 78s

the tunes "John Hardy," "The Sinking of the Titanic," "The Hallelujah Side" and "Lonesome Road Blues." His **Ernest V. Stoneman and His Dixie Mountaineers** played a version of string band music that was popular in the Galax, Virginia, area at that time. In 1928, his group included the ukulele, two fiddles, two banjos and a guitar. Pop began recording for Ralph S. Peer, the same music scout who discovered Jimmie Rodgers and the **Carter Family** in 1927. His first recording, "The Sinking of the Titanic," sold over a million copies. His final recording session was in 1934.

Shortly after Scott Stoneman was born (August 4, 1932), the Stoneman family was evicted from their home in Galax so they relocated to Alexandria, Virginia, in the Washington, D.C., area where they endured ten years of dire poverty. The Great Depression hit the Stoneman family hard. Patsy Stoneman (born May 27, 1925) passed out from hunger while in school. Ernest sometimes went three days without food. During this ten-year period, Donna, Jimmy, Veronica and Van were born.

The onset of World War II in 1941 brought regular employment for Ernest at carpentry, and better income. They were now able to replace the canvas on their cottage with a roof. In 1947, he obtained regular, good-paying employment in a gun factory in Virginia as a carpenter.

Veronica, who was also known as "Roni", grew up in D.C. when the area was a center for touring bluegrass bands. "I never knew until I was in the third grade at school that there was another world besides the world of music. I thought everyone in the whole world played an instrument and sang. I thought making music went along with breathing and walking." It was hard for her to relate to the Dick and Jane school books because neither one carried an instrument.

In the years after W.W.II, the family had several combinations of family members performing under band

Ernest V. Stoneman and the Dixie Mountaineers, c. 1928. L to R: Ives Edwards, George Stoneman, Uncle Eck Dunford, Ernest Stoneman, Hattie Stoneman, Bolen Frost.

---

[1] Ivan M. Tribe, "The Return of Donna Stoneman," *Bluegrass Unlimited*, June, 1983, p. 23.

names such as **Pop Stoneman and His Pebbles**, the **Stoneman Brothers**, and the **Blue Grass Champs**. In the early fifties, the Stoneman family, were Patsy, Roni, Van, Calvin Scott "Scotty" (fiddle), Hattie (fiddle), Ernest (guitar), Grace (guitar), John, Bill (banjo), Donna (mandolin), Jim (guitar) and Jack Stoneman (bass). Donna, who claims only a seventh grade education, became a full-time performer at age sixteen in 1949. Two years later, she got her Gibson F-5 mandolin. The bass that Jack used was built like a banjo; it had a stretched head over a frame whose diameter was about two feet. Its neck was fretless.

Scotty formed the **Blue Grass Champs** in 1955 with Donna (mandolin), himself (fiddle), Jimmy (bass), Porter Church (banjo), Veronica Stoneman (Cox) (banjo) and Jimmy Case (guitar). This was the first band to include the term "bluegrass" in it other than Monroe's band. The band was especially lively and had tremendous audience appeal. Donna was very good on the mandolin and danced around to the delight of the public while Scotty—well, there is only *one* Scotty Stoneman. He was considered as "the best" by many who saw him pour his heart and soul into his tunes.

Ernest, now known as "Pop", won $20,000 in 1956 on the NBC network quiz show, "The Big Surprise." Hosted by Mike Wallace, Pop won by exhibiting his knowledge of travel and geography.

The Washington area was beginning to "emerge as the major center of creative bluegrass in the country, and bands like **Buzz Busby and the Bayou Boys**, **Bill Harrell and the Virginians**, the **Country Gentlemen**, and the **Blue Grass Champs** flourished with club work, radio, and local television."[2]

The **Champs** won on the CBS network television show competition, "Arthur Godfrey's Talent Scouts" (which is one of the first times that a full bluegrass band appeared on a prime-time network program). Their arrangement of "Salty Dog Blues" won them each $680, recalled Porter Church who was banjoist with the group. This win, and the twenty-six weeks of appearances at Constitution Hall in 1947, were feats which brought them enough notoriety to appear at regular Connie B. Gay television productions such as "Gay Time" (for sixty-two weeks), Town and Country Time and on WARL radio, Arlington, Virginia. In 1957, the **Stonemans** went to the studios to record for Folkways. Donna didn't record here because she was thoroughly involved with the **Blue Grass Champs**.

The **Blue Grass Champs** (a name that was derived from the group's success in band and instrument contests in the area) entered many competitions and gained considerable notoriety. The **Champs** members evolved to Scott, Donna, Van, Jimmy, Roni and Pop Stoneman, along with Porter Church (banjo) and Lew Houston (who went by the stage name "Lew Childre"

The Stonemans, c. 1970. Standing L to R: Van, Jim. Sitting L to R: Donna, Patsy. Floor: Roni.

after the veteran country radio star who worked with Stringbean in the 1940s). About that time, Scotty won his first national fiddle championship at age sixteen. That summer, the **Champs** recorded "Haunted House"/ "Heartaches Keep on Coming" on the Bakersfield label. This was Donna's first recording.

In 1958, the **Champs** began to include more contemporary songs in their repertoire used on their regular appearances on WTTG television in Washington. Yet, their musical style remained basically traditional.

After two failed marriages, Patsy came back to the Washington, D.C., area about 1961, and formed a band with Bill and Wayne Yates, Red Allen, Bill Emerson, Roy Self and Ed Ferris. This band played some bluegrass, but not exclusively. In 1963, they were only able to earn about $10 per night plus $3 each in tips per person. When they found the venues where the **Blue Grass Champs** had been a success, the pay jumped to $27 and $25 respectively.

Pop retired from his gun factory job in 1962 and the group headed for Nashville which had become the center of the country music industry. They were very well received on the Grand Ole Opry, "however, instead of just doing a brief encore, the **Stonemans** did the whole song over and somewhat without realizing it, took up about eleven minutes of another artist's time which alienated [the manager] from further appreciation of this highly dynamic group. Donna later commented that the entire incident drove them back to the Washington area like a whipped pup."[3]

2 Ivan M. Tribe, "The Return of Donna Stoneman," *Bluegrass Unlimited*, June, 1983, p. 19.
3 Ibid., p. 20.

In January of 1964, the **Stonemans** moved to California where they played at Disneyland, the Monterey Folk Festival, The Ash Grove and The Troubadour clubs in Los Angeles, and at Fillmore West in San Francisco. They recorded an album for World Pacific in Beaumont, Texas. The album included canned applause—the kind they would receive during their stage performances—for their showmanship. They appeared on the "Steve Allen Show" and a Meredith Wilson special. Two years later, the **Stonemans** moved back to Nashville after signing with MGM Records. Their first record was "Those Singin' Swinging' Stomping' Sensational Stonemans." They also recorded a syndicated television show sponsored by Gingham Girl flour for three and a half years.

The Country Music Association awarded them Vocal Group of the Year in 1967. Other than the **Osborne Brothers** in 1971, this was the only time a bluegrass-oriented group ever received the honor.

Ernest V. Stoneman died at age 75 on June 14, 1968. He is known to have recorded under eighteen different names and eight labels. Patsy then took over Pop's place with the **Stonemans** in Texas and remained with the band along with Roni, Van, Donna and Jim.

In 1971, Roni, frustrated by a lack of success, decided to go on her own. She found adequate employment on television (she played the banjo on "Hee Haw" and became well known as Ida Lee, the ironing and bitchy wife on the popular hillbilly show). Celebrity Management, the new promoter for the **Stonemans**, dubbed Roni Stoneman "Fastest Woman in the West." Donna left late the next year.

Scotty Stoneman (40) died due to complications from emphysema and drinking shaving lotion on March 6, 1973. Known for his superlative fiddling, he was practically the only member of the **Stonemans** who didn't electrify his instrument. Since his death, the group never used a fiddle again; "It's hard to replace something when you've had the best,"[4] said Patsy. Hattie died in 1976.

In 1980, members of the **Stonemans** were Van (guitar), Patsy (mandolin) and Jim Stoneman (bass), Johnny Bellar (resonator guitar) and Eddie Mueller (banjo). They recorded on ACE's Country Music Heritage label.[5] Many of the former members of the **Stonemans** left for a ministry of religious work. Patsy told of the group's extreme conservatism, "The **Stonemans** have always been known as party poopers because we don't join the crowd and party all night. So when we get somebody with us, the next thing you know they're calmed down, too. I think we scare the devil out of them,' she laughed."[6]

CMH Records released "The First Family of Country Music" by the **Stonemans**[7] in 1982. The double album was a re-uniting of the group which had played together through the years. The **Stonemans** were presented the first Distinguished Service Award For Lifetime Achievement in Traditional American Music by the Shenandoah College and Conservatory of Music in 1985.

Tommy Millard

Tommy Millard was hired by Bill Monroe in 1939 to be one of the founding members of **Bill Monroe and the Blue Grass Boys**. He worked with Monroe in Greeneville, North Carolina, until Monroe got the audition for his band on the Opry in October 1939. But because Millard's wife was expecting her first child, he felt he should move back home to Asheville and not continue on the road. After the baby was born, the family moved to Winston-Salem, North Carolina, where he played with fiddlers Tommy Hunter and the **Morris Brothers**.

One of his most important contributions to country music of the day was his transition from the racially-degrading black-faced comic to the more acceptable role of the rube comic who wore a freckled face, tattered, baggy pants, oversized shoes and slouch hat. Much of his material came from minstrel shows which often included a large bag containing countless props and instruments. The minstrel shows which flourished from the 1840s were losing popularity in the later part of the century. This type of comedy was picked up by vaudeville and later by medicine shows and country music comedy, which for many years was represented in television's "Hee Haw." In a very real sense, Tommy Millard was responsible for trying to save this tradition of comedy from oblivion.

In 1930, Millard (19) joined his first medicine show, **Lee and Big Chief Tonic**, where he learned the skill of black-face comedy. After some time with this group, he joined **Mitzie Shelton and Her All-Girl Band** which had fifteen women and three men. (Also on the medicine show circuit at the time was Roy Acuff.) Millard even performed on the Opry, telling jokes and doing monologues. But the wages paid at the Opry caused him to get back into traveling medicine shows with Indian Chief Kadat. Author Wayne Erbsen related that "They performed mainly in the small towns and in coal mining areas where they were often paid in script or 'dugalo' as they called it. Their basic method was simple: they came into town, set up a canvas-covered platform to act

[4] Randall Armstrong, "The Stonemans." *Bluegrass Unlimited*, June, 1980, p. 72.

[5] ACE stands for Association of Country Entertainers.

[6] Armstrong, op. cit., p. 72.

[7] Musicians included Eddie (electric guitar, fiddle), Grace (vocals), Patsy (autoharp, guitar, maracas, tambourine, Jew's harp), Jack (guitar), Dean (mandolin), Gene (guitar), Donna (mandolin), Jim (bass), Van (guitar, clawhammer banjo), Van Jr. (guitar), and Randy Stoneman (electric bass), Johnny Bellar (Dobro), Eddie Mueller (banjo) and Donna Kay (vocals, Grace's daughter). Van Stoneman died June 3, 1995.

as a stage, and the five or six performers and musicians would entice the crowds to get close enough to hear the 'pitch' delivered by Chief Kadat or Tommy. They would sell shampoo, soap and snake oil to the crowd."[8] A typical pitch went something like this, "Now Ladies and Gentlemen, I'd like to call your attention to a product here tonight. It's Big Chief Tonic. It's good for stomach troubles, it's good for indigestion, and we highly recommend it for the elderly adults and the young. It will bring out your vim, vigor and vitality. When you and your wife are sleeping in different rooms, after you take this medicine you'll find yourself going up the steps to meet your wife and you'll find her coming down the steps to meet you."[9] They didn't stress it being a cure for anything. It was a good laxative though, the ingredients of which were only known to the Chief.

Millard had a band in the mid-'40s, the **Blue Ridge Hillbillies**[10], which had a regular show on the Mid-Day Merry-Go-Round in Knoxville where he did the comedy in his group. It was here that he changed from blackface to country rube. The change occurred when a black preacher complained about racial overtones of a regular act on the Merry-Go-Round. But according to Millard, "I've had colored people come around and talk to me, shake hands and they had no hard feelings or anything like that."[11]

After playing out in Knoxville, he moved the act to Asheville where he met Bill Monroe who had just separated from his brother Charlie. Bill had just formed a band with Cleo Davis (guitar) and Art Wooten (fiddle). Millard was then hired to emcee and do comedy. Davis, the very first **Blue Grass Boy**, often had trouble controlling his straight-man role with Millard's hilarious skits; Monroe then had to fill that role. It was here that Monroe dubbed Millard with the name "Snowball". Shortly after that, the audition for the Opry came in Nashville so Millard left.

The end of W.W.II brought significant changes in the professions of many musicians. "At the same time the boys were returning from the service," explained Millard, "a lot of little radio stations began to pop up all over the area we were broadcasting in...in such places as Waynesville, Black Mountain and Marshall. Everybody and his brother grabbed a guitar and a fiddle and whatever and started playing on those little stations. They also started playing personal appearances around over the country. I got wind of a lot of them that put on rotten shows, or even dirty shows, and along that time I decided to get out of it. I left the Farm Hour (WWNC,

Asheville) and also left WLOS where I was also working at the time.

"Shortly after that, I gave my heart to the Lord and knew I had to quit show business. The very night I was saved, I was supposed to do a show in Haw Creek, North Carolina, with Carl Story. I went to the stage door and motioned for Carl to come to me. I told Carl I was sorry and that I didn't mean to stand him up, but explained that I was saved and couldn't make this appearance with him. He said, 'Yes, you can,' and dragged me out on the stage and told the people, 'Friends, this is Tommy Millard, comedian, musician, and said he couldn't make this appearance tonight because he gave his life to the Lord. It's not that he thinks there's anything wrong with it, it's just that his life has changed, and he's going into a different profession.' Do you know what the crowd done? They stood up and applauded. I thought they was never gonna stop. When they finally stopped I thanked them but I just couldn't talk much. I did manage to say that if I don't see them in this world again, I'd see them up yonder. They stood up again, and just kept applauding as I went out the back door. And that was the last time I was ever on the stage. After that, I went into the ministry and have been a preacher all these years."[12]

Bill "Cousin Wilbur" Wesbrooks—one of Bill Monroe's early comedians

Willie Egbert Wesbrooks became famous for "The Coupon Song," his comedy showpiece about how he saved up enough coupons to get a wife and was now saving to get a divorce. He was a good singer and yodeler as was demonstrated on the song. His 1970 autobiography was titled "Everybody's Cousin." Wesbrooks talked about the song for which he was famous and recorded with Monroe's band, "I always had to do the coupon song. I'd ask Judge Hay, 'Why can't I ever sing something else beside the coupon song?' He always said, 'No, you're going to make the name of the coupon song and it's going to build the name of Cousin Wilbur'... He made me stay with the coupon song and I did it every Saturday night on the network for a year. He knew what he was talking about. But I got so tired of it—singing it every day, Saturday night, and then on the road. I had to do it on every show on the road. It got a little tiresome."[13]

Wesbrooks, from Gibson County, Tennessee, began his musical career in 1930. Country singer Eddy

[8] Wayne Erbsen, "Tommy Millard—Blackface Comedian, Blue Grass Boy," *Bluegrass Unlimited*, May, 1986, p. 22.

[9] Ibid., p. 22.

[10] This band, at various times, included Carl Sauceman with Jimmy Lunsford and Curly Shelton, Wade and J.E. Mainer, Jack Shelton, Shorty Barton and Red Smiley.

[11] Erbsen, op. cit., p. 24.

[12] Ibid.., p. 24. As of the date of this article by Erbsen, Millard was 75 years old.

[13] From "Notes and Queries," a regular feature by Walter V. Saunders in *Bluegrass Unlimited* magazine. This dissertation on Wesbrooks was in the November 1991 issue.

Arnold's first job was with Wesbrooks' band from 1935 until the band broke up in 1938. Wesbrooks then worked for **Uncle Henry and His Kentucky Mountaineers.** In his next career move, Wesbrooks went to the Opry and asked Judge Hay if anyone needed a musician. Hay told him about Bill Monroe's new band, and a week later he was Monroe's bass player/comedian. He stayed until 1944 and recorded on all of Monroe's Bluebird recordings.

In 1947, after marrying Blondie Leatherman, they performed together as the **Cousin Wilbur and Blondie Brooks Show.** Then he worked a couple years on the Louisiana Hayride and other shows. He and Blondie continued performing for many years after that. Mr. Wesbrooks died in August 1984.

Clyde Moody

Clyde Leonard Moody, was born September 19, 1915, in Cherokee, North Carolina, into a musical family. This pioneer was fully involved in music in 1930 and made almost his entire living from it during the Great Depression—a difficult feat. Moody became country music's "Waltz King" after the release of "Shenandoah Waltz" just after World War II.

His first group was the **Happy-Go-Lucky Boys** with Jay Hugh Hall about 1933 at Spartanburg, South Carolina, on WSPA where they became good enough to acquire a sponsor, Front Liquor Stores, and to be able to afford a car.

In the late 1930s, he joined Wade Mainer (banjo) with Jay Hugh Hall (guitar) and Steve Ledford (fiddle) to form the **Sons of the Mountaineers** at WPTF, Raleigh, North Carolina. The next year, they got a big hit with "Sparkling Blue Eyes." Also during that time, Moody developed the thumb and finger guitar style used later by artists including Bob Osborne, Lester

Flatt and Charlie Moore. And Hall developed an ability to yodel in harmony. They did radio work on WIS, WWNC and WPTF. Just before the band broke up, they recorded for Bluebird in February 1940.

On September 6, 1940, Clyde Moody became a **Blue Grass Boy**[14] in Bluefield, West Virginia, replacing Cleo Davis. The next month, they recorded their first Bluebird session in Atlanta; tunes which included "Cryin' Holy Unto the Lord" and Moody singing lead on his own "Six White Horses." This was Moody's only session with Monroe though he stayed about five years with him.[15]

In those years, Monroe's group traveled about 3000 miles per week and did as many as three shows daily. In addition to the performances, Moody pitched on the **Blue Grass Club** baseball team. He quit Monroe the first time in 1942 to play in his **Happy-Go-Lucky Boys** for a year; he was replaced by Pete Pyle. Moody quit Monroe the final time in 1945, this time to try to make it as a solo artist on the Opry where he hired on as a featured soloist with Roy Acuff's troupe. He recorded in February on Columbia with four songs. He soon formed **Clyde Moody and His Carolina Wood Choppers** and became known as the "Carolina Woodchopper". A few months after that, he signed on with the Bullet label and recorded four songs. These songs, which included a piano and trumpet, were more of a swing nature than earlier efforts.

In 1947, Clyde Moody began recording on Syd Nathan's King Records with Chubby Wise and Tommy Jackson (fiddles) and King's **Sacred Quartet**, which included **Johnny and Jack** and Ray Atkins. He recorded his own "Shenandoah Waltz," co-written with Chubby Wise, and the song became a million seller in 1952. Over the next four years, he recorded over sixty sides. Because of the popularity of Moody's "Cherokee Waltz," "Carolina Waltz" and "West Virginia Waltz," he became known as the "Hillbilly Waltz King". During this period, he performed with crooner Eddy Arnold and Red Foley. Moody also wrote "Next Sunday Is My Birthday" and "I Know What It Means to Be Lonesome."

Moody left the Opry for Washington, D.C., in 1949. In 1950, he joined Connie B. Gay's "Gay Time," a television show in Washington, D.C., with fiddler Chubby Wise. He also performed on WDBJ (Roanoke) and WDVA's Virginia Barn Dance[16] (Danville). He left King Records (after four years) to sign with Decca and did five releases over the next five years, after which he left WBMT, Danville, Virginia, to play on the Louisiana Hayride, Shreveport, Louisiana.

[14] Other musicians were Bill Monroe (mandolin), Tommy Magness (fiddle), Mack McGar (fiddle, mandolin), and Willie Egbert "Cousin Wilbur" Wesbrooks (bass).

[15] Moody re-formed his Happy-Go-Lucky Boys each time he left Monroe. Jay Hugh Hall, an original Happy-Go-Lucky Boy from about 1933, helped reform Moody's band when he left Monroe the first time with Lester Flatt on tenor vocals and mandolin at WBBB in Burlington.

[16] Also on the show were fiddler Bobby Hicks and banjoist Hubert Davis who were members of Flint Hill Playboys. Jim Eanes was there too, and Eanes also kept his own Shenandoah Valley Boys band active.

Disappointed with the financial rewards of country music, Moody quit music in 1957 to earn a living selling mobile homes until 1962 when he returned to music, began recording on Don Pierce's Starday Records, and hosted and performed on the "Carolina in the Morning" television show in Raleigh. Later in the '60s, he recorded for Wango in Baltimore and another session for the Little Darlin' label. Art Menius told this writer, "In 1984, Moody told me, 'If you want to be forgotten, Son, go into local TV.'"

In 1972, still semi-retired from music in Nashville, Clyde Moody recorded on John W. Morris' Old Homestead label. Moody and Doug Green recorded together. He performed occasionally at festivals, on the Opry, and on Lester Flatt's early morning radio show on WSM. In 1975, Moody worked in Tommy Scott's medicine show from August of that year until May 1981 when his health failed and forced him to retire. The duo recorded three LPs. He returned to performing occasionally 1983 to 1985. In his later years, Moody grew embittered with how Nashville treated the pioneers and helped form The Reunion of Professional Entertainers (R.O.P.E.).

Clyde Moody died April 7, 1989, in Nashville after a long illness.

Carl Story

Carl Story and the Rambling Mountaineers

Carl Story, "The Father of Bluegrass Gospel Music", was born May 29, 1916, in Lenoir, Caldwell County, North Carolina. This pioneer was a nearly seventy-year veteran of country music. His father was a local fiddler and passed down his passion for music to young Carl. His mother was also a musician and taught him chords on the guitar. He learned the fiddle at age nine, soon playing the guitar and clawhammer banjo. His first guitar came in the mail after selling twelve jars of Cloverine Salve, then mailing the proceeds along with an extra two dollars.

At age fourteen, Story met nine-year-old Johnny Whisnant (banjo)[17] who is known as one of the earliest banjo players to successfully use the Carolina-style of three-finger picking, later made popular by Earl Scruggs.

He began fiddling professionally in 1932, and in 1934 won a talent contest on Lynchburg, Virginia's WLVA. This awarded him $10 and led to a weekly radio show at the station where he stayed several months, sponsored by a local furniture store. He did this several months. Then he returned home, joining Whisnant and J.E. Clark (vocals) in **J.E. Clark and the Lonesome Mountaineers** on weekends. In October, Story and Whisnant left Clark to form their own smaller band where the idea was to make more money than they had been making with J.E. Clark's band. Story became the leader after they drew straws; he named the band the **Rambling Mountaineers**. They all had day jobs at the same furniture manufacturing company (Lenoir Furniture) where they made ten cents an hour and worked thirteen hours a day.

In 1935, Story and his **Rambling Mountaineers** began appearing at WHKY, Hickory, North Carolina, where they played for free but could announce their upcoming concerts every Saturday. They stayed part-time at WHKY for four years. After one particular concert in Taylorsville where they made the equivalent of seven week's factory wages, they decided to pursue music full-time. Now that they could see the potential of earning "good" money in the music business, the **Rambling Mountaineers** got a booking agent, Hal Houpe, who booked them on a tour in Washington, D.C.. Upon their arrival at the city they only had twenty-five cents among them. They bought all the bologna that a quarter could buy, hoping this would tide them over until the tour was to begin. That evening they played a concert, got paid, and were able to get a decent meal afterwards.

The group obtained a radio spot on WSPA, Spartanburg, South Carolina, in 1938 for a year, with a sponsorship by the Vim Herb Company (La Follette, Tennessee) which manufactured Scalf's Indian River Medicine (this sponsorship lasted several years on several stations). Then they returned to WHKY, soon relocating to WWNC, Asheville, North Carolina, where they were still sponsored by Scalf's Indian River Medicine. About that time, the group recorded for Okeh Records[18], one of the subsidiaries of Columbia, but the songs were never released. These eight recordings were among the first by any groups to feature fiddle and

---

[17] Johnny Whisnant later became the banjo player with Story's Rambling Mountaineers (1934).

[18] Another subsidiary of Columbia was the budget label, American Record Corporation (ARC). Story considered Okeh a step above ARC and a step below Columbia.

Carl Story and the Rambling Mountaineers, c. 1956. L to R: Lloyd Bell, Claude Boone, Bobby Thompson, Carl Story.

the three-finger style banjo;[19] they could be the first bluegrass recordings ever made. Unfortunately, the masters were lost. But in 1973, Puritan Records did release impromptu recordings of the group from 1939.

The oncoming of W.W.II forced the breakup of the group as Ed McMahan and then Whisnant left. Hoke Jenkins took Whisnant's place on banjo until he was drafted. Story still stayed home, hiring Ray Atkins (resonator guitar, age 16) of Erwin, Tennessee. Bonnie Lou and Buster Moore worked briefly for the band. In 1942, Claude Boone, formerly with Cliff Carlisle's band, joined. That summer, Story and his band had a radio show at WWNC. The War made it difficult to keep a band together.

When Bill Monroe called Story and offered employment to play fiddle with the **Blue Grass Boys** late in 1942, Story knew that it might take awhile to get up to the speed at which Monroe played. But both Monroe and Story were confident that he could do it so he left his **Rambling Mountaineers** in the hotel where they were staying and headed for Nashville. He took Howdy Forrester's place who left to join the Navy. Other band members were Clyde Moody on guitar, Stringbean played banjo, Sally Ann Forrester pumped the accordion and Cousin Wilbur Wesbrooks, the bass. Story stayed a year until he was drafted into the U.S. Navy in October 1943. Monroe paid Story a salary plus ten percent of the sales of pictures, candy, and souvenirs which he hawked wherever they went. Monroe also paid all the motel bills. When Story gave notice to Monroe, Monroe hired

Chubby Wise. So, for the next three weeks Story and Wise played twin fiddles until Story left.[20]

Story was discharged from the Navy in October of 1945, and reorganized his **Rambling Mountaineers**[21] in December at WWNC with the same sponsor as before. Story and his band soon moved to WNOX's Mid-Day Merry-Go-Round in Knoxville where, for the next five years, he firmly established himself in the world of this music. Doing comedy with Boone and Charles "Kentucky Slim, the Little Darling" Elza,[22] they played live packed houses, often having to do an additional show to accommodate the audience. These live performances were six days per week. And at Lowell Blanchard's Tennessee Barn Dance in Knoxville, they made weekly appearances which paid members $60 per week; band leaders, such as Story, got double that.

In 1946, the **Rambling Mountaineers'** "Tennessee Border" on the Mercury label was #1 for eighteen consecutive weeks. Story and his band also began recording gospel tunes about this time. The first was "My Lord Keeps a Record." As their reputation for the band's affinity toward gospel music spread, the band, along with several other bands noted for their gospel tunes, drew a crowd of 9,000 in Birmingham at the Civic Auditorium. They were featured to sing this one song at the all-night gospel singing. It took them 45 minutes to complete their appearance, having taken nine encores.

As of this period, the music was still hillbilly. The group had no banjo, so didn't qualify as what we now know as bluegrass. Yet, "They are nonetheless a good, traditionally-oriented, country music band of the period which featured lead guitar or mandolin,"[23] later adding an electric steel.[24]

After a short time at WWNC, the **Rambling Mountaineers** went to WCYB's Farm and Fun Time for a short while, soon getting a better offer at Charlotte's WAYS (in 1951) where they stayed for two years with three fifteen-minute shows. They were now able to receive a salary in addition to being able to plug their show dates.

Story was always energetic and creative when it came to trying to make money in his profession. One of the earliest examples was taking some of the proceeds from candy and souvenir sales with Monroe's band a decade before. Now at WAYS, they received 27,000 pieces of mail in a particular three-week period when Story and his sponsor had a riddle for the listeners to

---

[19] Musicians were Story (fiddle), Dudley "Uncle Dud" Watson (guitar), Ed McMahan (guitar, bass) and Johnny Whisnant (banjo).

[20] This story is a little different from the way Chubby Wise remembered it. Wise recalled that he took Forrester's place.

[21] Other band members were Hoke Jenkins (banjo), Jack (guitar) and Curley (mandolin) Shelton and Claude Boone (bass). Soon Jenkins and the Sheltons left Story to form Jenkins' Smoky Mountaineers at WWNC.

[22] Another version of the band included Boone (guitar), Red Rector (mandolin) and Ray Atkins (resonator guitar).

[23] Ivan M. Tribe, "Carl Story: Bluegrass Pioneer," *Bluegrass Unlimited*, January, 1975, p. 10.

[24] Members were now Story (guitar), Boone (guitar), Hack and Clyde Johnson. When Story, Boone, and the Johnsons sang together, they called themselves the Melody Four.

  After a move to Asheville in 1950, band members of the Rambling Mountaineers were Carl Story (guitar), Red Rector (mandolin), Claude Boone (guitar, bass), Cotton Gaylon (electric guitar, pedal steel), Kentucky Slim (bass), and occasionally Fred Smith (guitar) and Ray Atkins (resonator guitar, electric steel). Rector stayed with Story until 1955.

answer. Only one answer in the 27,000 was correct—and the couple won a new television set. The riddle was:

> My shape causes no one to sigh
> My spirits most always are high.
> Should I fall once that's enough
> You'll certainly find that I'm tough
> What am I?

Mr. Story was looking directly at a pine burr when he made up the riddle.

At nearby Mineral Springs, North Carolina, Story helped get a Saturday night barn dance started there. They called it the Tar Heel Barn Dance; it later became known as the Mineral Springs Music Barn. Carl stayed with it for two years. It exists today in its same format with a new barn which seats 1,000 less than the first building.

There at WAYS, the regular deejay was a blind man who was sick one day and couldn't spin his 78s and the 45s. Story gave it a try and this was the beginning of his career as a world renown disc jockey. He stayed with WAYS until he left for the Tennessee Barn Dance on WNOX, Knoxville. There they went on the CBS network every Saturday night.

In April 1952, Story moved the band to Decatur, Georgia, to replace **Johnny and Jack**'s show on WEAS. **Johnny and Jack**, along with Clyde Moody, moved to the KWKH Louisiana Hayride in Shreveport. In addition to performing at festivals with Bill Monroe, Story still held down his regular job as deejay and singer on WAYS. In August, Mercury released Story's "My Lord's Gonna Lead Me Out"/"Are You Afraid to Die?"[25] They recorded a new Hank Williams composition "Are You Walking and Talking with the Lord?" It is said that Williams personally brought the new song to the studios for Story to record. The next week, Williams was "suspended" from the Opry.

Story signed with Columbia in June of 1953, staying three years. He recorded "Love and Wealth"/"Lonesome Hearted Blues." Later that year, the **Rambling Mountaineers** returned to WNOX for a four-year stay. Ray Atkins stayed in Charlotte, working for the Arthur "Guitar Boogie" Smith show. Red Rector left. Story picked up the **Brewster Brothers**. Recording again for Mercury with Carl Story on guitar, **Carl Story and the Rambling Mountaineers** included Tater Tate (fiddle), the **Brewster Brothers** (William "Willie" on mandolin and Franklin "Bud" on banjo) and Claude Boone (bass). With the addition of Bud Brewster on banjo (and was

the best lead singer Story ever had, according to Story)[26] Story now had, what he considered, a full, bluegrass sound. Story believes Tate to be the best fiddler he ever had in any of his bands. He could play any style and backup anything.

In January 1956, Carl Story and his group left the Mid-Day Merry-Go-Round at WNOX to work for the Cas Walker[27] Show on Knoxville's WIVK radio and WBIR-TV. According to Bud Brewster, "the pace was truly frantic with the day beginning with a 5:30 a.m. radio show, followed by another at 6:15, a 7:00 a.m. television program, then back to the radio for thirty minutes. After a one and a half hour break, there was an equally-long show at noon, a 4:30 radio spot, and another night-time television broadcast on another channel. This was all done live, and doesn't even take into account personal appearances."[28] Story's Columbia contract ended that year and they were soon back with Mercury again.

The **Rambling Mountaineers** played many radio stations and on Cas Walker's television show. At WLOS, Asheville, North Carolina, he stayed three years. They were switched from Mercury to Starday. For a while, the two labels were combined until Don Pierce separated the two and took Starday with him. Story stayed with Starday eighteen years and recorded sixty-two albums with them. They sold 475,000 copies of one EP (extended play 45 r.p.m. record) in three months.

On the February 25, 1956, recording session for Mercury-Starday, the band recorded with a full, bluegrass sound, following Don Pierce's strategy which was to increase sales. He put out a couple of tunes where the other side of the cuts was a gospel tune. The session included "Mocking Banjo," "Banjo on the Mountain," "Got a Lot to Tell My Jesus" and "Light at the River." Musicians included Story (guitar), Bud Brewster (banjo), Willie G. Brewster (mandolin), Tater Tate (fiddle) and Claude Boone (bass).

Banjoist Bobby Thompson joined them in 1956 at WLOS. At a Mercury recording session on August 3rd, Thompson showed off his banjo on "Banjolina," "Fire on the Banjo," Savior's Love" and "Family Reunion." He hadn't begun recording his melodic banjo playing yet.

In 1958, Story revived Arthur Smith's "Feuding Banjos" tune, calling it "Mocking Banjos." With Bud Brewster back on banjo, the Brewster brothers did tradeoffs on banjo and mandolin.

Story reduced his touring schedule in 1960 and became a deejay on WFLW, Monticello, Kentucky, playing occasionally with pickup bands, with Clyde and Marie Denny, and with **Bonnie Lou and Buster Moore**.

25 The Nashville session this month included Rector (mandolin), Boone (guitar) and Atkins (resonator guitar).

26 As of 1992, Bud Brewster could still belt out a song like he used to. He owned a big music store in Knoxville, Pick 'N Grin, on Kingston Pike.

27 Mr. Story told this writer that Cas Walker had a chain of twenty-six grocery stores. They were the biggest supermarkets in East Tennessee and some in Kentucky. They still exist. Story says that Walker, who started years ago with $600, "doesn't know what he's worth" indicating that he's still doing real well. Walker was Mayor twice, on the City Council several times...all with a fourth grade education.

28 Kathy Kaplan, "The Pinnacle Boys," *Bluegrass Unlimited*, October, 1976, p. 14. The article actually was written about Bud Brewster and his part in the Pinnacle Boys but spoke of his earlier years with Carl Story's Rambling Mountaineers.

He worked the following labels: Acme, Starday, Spar, Scripture, Sims, Songs of Faith, GRS and Rimrock. They still traveled occasionally. He did more deejay work at WEAS, and then at WCKI, Greer, South Carolina [where he lived until he died]. Claude Boone and the Brewster brothers remained in Knoxville. Story's "The Lord Keeps a Record" on Starday was the last one which he and Boone and the Brewsters did together.

Mr. Story was proclaimed the "Father of Bluegrass Gospel" in 1974 by the governor of Oklahoma.

In 1977, **Carl Story and the Rambling Mountaineers** had a six-days-per-week, live show at WEAB in Greer, South Carolina, and was the host band. In September 1978, he was named a Tennessee Colonel by the Governor of Tennessee (Ray Blanton), after Story's performance at the Smoky Mountain Festival. In 1985, Carl Story signed a year-long contract to broadcast bluegrass gospel for an hour per day on ZGBC, Dominican Republic, West Indies. As of 1991, he had recorded more than 2000 songs and 55 albums. Carl Story died March 31, 1995.

Lester Flatt

Lester Flatt— one of the reasons bluegrass music is successful today

There are few guitarist/lead singers who are better known in bluegrass music than Lester Raymond Flatt—probably none. His long career with Earl Scruggs and earlier with Bill Monroe made him a legend. And his strong rhythm guitar playing helped make bluegrass music the identifiable entity that it is.

Lester Flatt was born near Sparta, Tennessee, June 19, 1914. He was one of nine children. Young Lester was taught by his father to play the drop-thumb frailing banjo but could never master it so he quit to divert his energies elsewhere. By age seven, he was playing guitar and singing in the church choir. He became well-known near his home for his singing at schools and church programs before he was ten. Later in life, when asked about his musical style, he said that the music he played was simply the same type of music that his family had taught him. As a member of the **Blue Grass Quartet**, singing Monroe's gospel tunes was just an extension of what he'd been doing all along. As a teenager, Lester left to work as a rayon weaver at the Sparta Silk Mill, Sparta, North Carolina.

In 1934, Lester and wife Gladys bought a home in Sparta for $350 down and $5 per month payments. When the mill shut down that fall, the Flatts moved to McMinnville, Tennessee. Before the year was out, however, they were both employed in Johnson City by a silk mill there. The next year found them with the mill in the different location near Roanoke, Virginia. The Flatts did a little local entertaining together as a duo, and there in Roanoke, Lester joined Charlie Scott's **Harmonizers**, playing on WDBJ. Flatt's bout with rheumatoid arthritis forced him to quit the mill and to pursue music on a more regular basis.

Lester and Gladys Flatt moved to Burlington, North Carolina, in the fall of 1940, where Gladys worked for the huge Burlington Industries, and Lester joined veteran entertainer Clyde Moody on WBBB where he sang tenor to Moody and played mandolin with Moody's band.[29] Also, it was during this period when Flatt worked at the mill that he worked with **Jim Hall and the Crazy Mountaineers**.

In 1943, Flatt played with Charlie Monroe's **Kentucky Pardners** in Winston-Salem, North Carolina. Flatt played mandolin with this band only because Charlie played the guitar; he wasn't accomplished on the mandolin but got a pay raise from Charlie to do it. He had to sing tenor to Charlie (just like Charlie's brother, Bill, had done in the **Monroe Brothers** duets). Even though Flatt's voice was capable of this type of work, he didn't like it, and upon leaving Charlie Monroe he vowed never to do it again. There at WSJS (Winston-Salem) they were recorded on a thirty-minute 16-inch disc—a transcription (this was before tape recording). The master disc was then duplicated and shipped to other radio stations allowing the artist to appear at two or more places at once. They played on the Noon-Day Jamboree which was broadcast over seven radio stations and brought tremendous appearance demand. This led to Charlie's purchase of a huge tent which could seat 2,000 people. They would fill it twice almost every night. The band had seven people plus a tent crew.

[29] The name for this band, and Flatt's participation in it, is a little obscure. Indeed, Flatt's biography, written by Jake Lambert, doesn't even mention the group's name. This could have been an oversight on Flatt's part because it was rather insignificant in the entire scheme of things. The band was called either the Happy-Go-Lucky Boys or possibly the Carolina Playboys. Moody had used the name Happy-Go-Lucky Boys since 1933 (in a duo with Jay Hugh Hall), and when Moody left Bill Monroe in early 1941 he may have re-established his band using either name.

It was here, probably, that Flatt noticed Moody playing guitar with a thumbpick and a pick on his index finger. He took the style for his own and it was refined by the time he was with Charlie Monroe in the early '40s.

Although he usually played mandolin with the band, it was here that most of Flatt's guitar playing became refined. As did Clyde Moody, Cleo Davis, Charlie Monroe and occasionally Zeke Morris, Flatt adopted that style which included a thumb pick and a steel pick on the index finger. Flatt played guitar bass runs and melodies with his thumbpick on the low strings while brushing the high strings with his first finger to add rhythm.

After quitting the **Kentucky Pardners**, Bill Monroe offered Flatt a job as rhythm guitarist and lead singer with the **Blue Grass Boys**, which he accepted.[30] Stringbean met him at the bus station in Nashville and ushered him around until performance time. They all played on the Opry that night with no rehearsal. This was March 1945 according to some sources.

Flatt's voice fit well with the **Blue Grass Boys** and Monroe, quick to recognize good talent in his band, began listing Flatt's name on the labels. Out of the next nineteen singles which featured vocals, only three did not feature Flatt singing lead.

At Christmas of 1945, Earl Scruggs joined the **Blue Grass Boys**. According to Jake Lambert's biography on Lester Flatt, "With the addition of Scruggs, Monroe's band became one of the hottest groups working the Opry. Bill purchased a stretched automobile and they were on the road almost seven days a week. When they finished a Friday night show they would head for Nashville and the Opry. Most of the time they would leave as soon as the Opry was over and travel the rest of the night to do a Sunday matinee—maybe four hundred miles away. Flatt said that there were many times Gladys would bring his clothes to the Opry and he would never go home. For both Lester and Earl, the road seemed to be endless. The personnel of the **Blue Grass Boys** in 1946 and '47 were Monroe, Flatt, Scruggs, Chubby Wise and Howard Watts. This band would go down in bluegrass history as being probably the best ever assembled."

Lance LeRoy, bluegrass enthusiast, band manager and well-respected Lester Flatt biographer, gave his opinion of bluegrass at its best, "Looking back on it all, I think it would require someone with extreme tunnel vision to dispute the viewpoint that bluegrass music was first introduced to the world there around Christmas of 1945 when Earl first appeared on the Grand Ole Opry with Bill and the **Blue Grass Boys**. I don't buy this 'bluegrass as we know it today' cop-out. I regard it as being the first time bluegrass music was introduced to the world...PERIOD! It took Earl's three-finger roll on the five-string banjo to supply the music's single most distinguishing characteristic. The four other parts were already here; he added the fifth one that is abso-

lutely essential if you are going to have bluegrass music. The sound of the banjo played with a three-finger roll has always symbolized 'bluegrass' to both fans and the general public as well. I doubt that any other of the instruments even come close.

"Now I'm certainly not suggesting that Earl created bluegrass music," continued LeRoy, "but then again neither did any other one individual. Bill Monroe was the band leader and, as a Grand Ole Opry member, provided the forum. Whether through fate, blind luck or whatever, he assembled what I think is the first and the best group ever to play bluegrass. Nobody has been able to improve on it since. For all this, he richly deserves to be called the 'Father of Bluegrass Music'. It's one of those honorary titles that befits the role he played in that band. Bill Monroe has been symbolic of bluegrass music throughout the world for a long, long time. In reality, though, bluegrass had a number of fathers."

They worked hard and made good money. The road was difficult and Earl was concerned about his mother back home. "I was fully determined to get out of music," said Scruggs. "My cup was 'runneth over' with the aggravations of road life. I was going home. I think the reason Lester put off leaving was because he didn't think I'd leave. When I left, that's when he gave his notice."

Earl quit the **Blue Grass Boys** in early 1948, followed within two weeks by Lester and Cedric. "When I got home, Lester called and said, 'I don't think we'd be happy going back into the mills. Let's think about it.' He said we could stay close around home if I wanted, so I could look after my mother."[31] Lester invested $3300 of his life savings into a car and a sound system and they were on their way.

The original Drifting Cowboys. Back L to R: Cedric Rainwater, Sammy Pruet, Don Helms. Front L to R: Jerry Rivers, Hillus Butram.

[30] Other members of the band were Wilene "Sally Ann" Forrester who played accordion, Dave "Stringbean" Akeman on the drop-thumb (frailing) and the two-finger picking banjo styles, Chubby Wise played fiddle, and Andy Boyette played bass but occasionally featured some tunes on the electric guitar. Jim Shumate joined two to three weeks after Flatt.

[31] Marty Godbey, "The Artistry and Accomplishments of Earl Scruggs," *Bluegrass Unlimited*, August, 1996, p. 59.

Scruggs recalled, "We went to Danville, Virginia. Lester, Cedric Rainwater and myself. Jim Eanes was there. There were just the four of us and we were only there two or three weeks. We called Jim Shumate, wanting a fiddle player; he wanted us to come to Hickory (North Carolina) to work on a radio station there. He was working in a furniture store in Hickory and didn't want to leave. We were there just a matter of weeks." (Eanes didn't make the trip.)

"Mac Wiseman called, wanting a job, and we told him we weren't doing anything. He said he wasn't, either, 'Just sitting in the Shenandoah Valley, going crazy,' he said. He came to Hickory to work with us and told us about WCYB. We contacted the radio station and moved to Bristol within a few days. That's where we started making a living." They got there "about the last of April, the first of May 1948." Also there were the **Stanley Brothers** and Curley King with his band. It was here they were billed as **Lester Flatt, Earl Scruggs, and the Foggy Mountain Boys**.

Lance LeRoy elaborated on the next stage of bluegrass music: the era of **Flatt and Scruggs and the Foggy Mountain Boys**, "In their twenty-one years together, Flatt and Scruggs had more impact on the music, in my opinion, than anything that's gone on before or since." LeRoy, who knew Lester Flatt as well as anyone, continued to describe the situation, "They went their separate ways in early spring of 1948, neither one apparently with any immediate plan to continue playing music professionally."

Some of the songs Flatt wrote through the years were "My Cabin in Caroline," "Come Back Darling," "I'll Never Shed Another Tear," "Down the Road," "Head Over Heels in Love with You," "Why Did You Wander," "We'll Meet Again, Sweetheart," "I'm Gonna Sleep with One Eye Open," "Bouquet in Heaven," "God Loves His Children, "Get in Line, Brother," "I'm Going to Make Heaven My Home," "I'm Working on a Road to Gloryland," "Be Ready for Tomorrow May Never Come," "Little Girl [of Mine] in Tennessee," "Don't Get Above Your Raisin'," "Cabin on the Hill" and "The Old Home Town." He co-wrote "No Mother or Dad" with Curly Seckler.

The remainder of the history of **Flatt and Scruggs and the Foggy Mountain Boys** is discussed in the Earl Scruggs portion of this chapter. Lester and Earl split in 1969. Earl joined his sons in the **Earl Scruggs Revue** while Lester formed the **Lester Flatt and the Nashville Grass** with Lance LeRoy as manager.

LeRoy spoke of how the departure of Earl Scruggs as Flatt's partner presented Flatt with a serious dilemma: whether to continue in music or not. "But without Earl and his 'security blanket' at that crucial

point and without the strength of Earl, who was such an enormous presence, I honestly believe that Flatt would have retired with a gold watch from the (textile) mill in Covington, Virginia, where he had worked, or the one in Sparta, Tennessee, where he had worked at one time, too." LeRoy explained that Lester cared little about the business end of the band—even in personnel problems with his band members. He left those problems to Earl and Louise Scruggs (manager), and later to LeRoy when LeRoy became Flatt's manager. Without Earl and Louise's business sense, Flatt probably would not have ventured into a band of his own. But Flatt could rely on LeRoy to handle those things in 1969. "I've always felt that Earl's role in the total picture of Flatt and Scruggs' career was underplayed and certainly Louise never got more than a fraction of the credit she should have," told LeRoy. "She handled their business just exactly the way it should have been done for more than fifteen years."

Now in Flatt's **Nashville Grass** were Flatt (guitar), Roland White (mandolin), Vic Jordan (banjo, he left Bill Monroe's band to join the **Grass**), Paul Warren (fiddle), Josh Graves (Dobro®) and Jake Tullock (bass).

By 1972, the banjo player for Flatt's **Nashville Grass** was Haskell McCormick. Josh Graves quit the **Nashville Grass** and joined the **Earl Scruggs Revue** for a couple of years. Marty Stuart[32] joined Flatt's band as guitarist Labor Day weekend. He was twelve. He moved in with Flatt's family, toured, and continued his schooling by correspondence.

In a 1980 interview, Marty Stuart described his time with Lester and Gladys and the band, "As I look back on it today, I realize that I have been one of the most richly blessed people in the world, being able to get my start with such a past master as Lester Flatt. I mean, going over the whole realm of music from every respect, to me, Lester Flatt was the greatest. He started me out in a very dignified way and there is no way that I could have ever repaid him... When I go on stage to do my show, I'll always go back to how Lester would have done it. He was always point 'A' in my life and when I think I have got above that, I'll always go back to Flatt. Just like going back to your alma mater."[33]

In 1979, while Lester Flatt was recovering from a visit to the hospital, Flatt asked Curly Seckler to take over the band while he recuperated. LeRoy recalled that "Lester's whole manner changed a lot in those last couple of years and by then he'd totally lost interest in what the band sounded like and so forth, and it showed. But his mind and his perception never wavered. I talked with him in his hospital room on the Sunday before he died, the following Friday, about a contracted festival appearance that was a month away. A big tear rolled down his cheek and he turned his head away quickly

32 Stuart was five when he began learning to play the guitar, and twelve when he started on the mandolin. At age thirteen, he went to a festival with Roland White and played a tune on stage. Then Lester Flatt asked him to join the group as guitarist. Roland White was the mandolinist with the group at the time and when Roland left to join his brother, Clarence, in March of 1973, Flatt switched Stuart to mandolin.

33 Lambert and Sechler, op. cit., p. 151.

and said in a barely audible whisper, 'I don't think I'll ever play another one.' After all the years and all the good times, that was awfully hard on me emotionally, and it shocked me into finally realizing that this is it."[34]

Earl visited Flatt in the hospital before he died. That meant a lot to Lester. LeRoy described Earl's visit, "Earl gave Lester his flowers while he was living. Any fellow **Flatt and Scruggs** fan will know immediately what I have reference to." In the instance Earl visited Lester when he could barely talk above a whisper, Earl stayed with him for more than an hour. When LeRoy tells of the visit to all who ask, he considers it "One of my most memorable moments throughout it all."[35] Earl described the visit to Lester's bedside, "I went to see Lester—I don't know how many days it was before he passed away, but he was really in bad shape. He was in the Baptist Hospital here in Nashville. He could hardly talk loud enough for me to tell what he was sayin'. He wanted to know if we could play some reunion dates together. And my answer immediately was, 'Lester, number one, I want you to get well. Number two, yes we'll play dates together when you get well. But my biggest concern now is for you to get more strength and get to feelin' better; then we'll talk about doin' reunions. So that was kind of the way it was left."[36] Lester Flatt never recovered—he died after an extensive period of sickness.[37]

Lester Flatt died on May 11th, 1979. The **Nashville Grass** became a partnership with all members as equal partners. Soon Seckler and Charlie Nixon became the leaders of the group until Nixon's health failed about 1981. Then the band became **Curly Seckler and the Nashville Grass**[38].

L to R: Lester Flatt, Curly Seckler, Earl Scruggs, mid-1950's. Photo courtesy Curly Seckler.

Curly Seckler and the Nashville Grass

Fifty plus years in the music business has given Curly Seckler solid roots in country music. His contributions to bluegrass are legendary. As a veteran of not only the bands contributing to the roots of bluegrass but of probably the hottest bluegrass band history has ever known, he has done it all.

John Ray "Curly" Sechler was born December 25, 1919, in Rowan County, near China Grove, North Carolina. He took "Seckler" as his permanent stage name after "Sechler" was consistently and incorrectly pronounced "Setsh-ler".

At ten, his mother bought him a guitar and showed him a few chords.[39] In 1935, Curly and his three brothers formed the **Yodeling Rangers** which played local functions before performing on WSTP, Salisbury, North Carolina. Curly played the tenor banjo which, because it is tuned similar as the fiddle and mandolin, was a natural to fit into a country band. The boys were too poor to afford cases for their instruments so their mother sewed each of them a cover with a zipper. Russell Furniture Company sponsored their radio program on WSTP. Because their only compensation was furniture, the brothers soon brought home enough to fill their two-story farm house. This band was not recorded until 1991 in a reunion—for their children. It may be released someday, said Seckler.

---

[34] Traci Todd, "Lance LeRoy, Part 2 of 2," *Bluegrass Unlimited*, February, 1993, p. 47.

[35] Ibid., p. 47.

[36] Doug Hutchens interview for his radio show, "Bluegrass Today."

[37] Members of the Nashville Grass at that time were Curly Seckler (mandolin), Billy Smith (guitar), Tater Tate (fiddle), Blake Williams (banjo), Charlie Nixon (Dobro), Marty Stuart (mandolin) and Pete Corum (bass).

[38] In 1987, Larry Perkins joined the Nashville Grass on banjo. Willis Spears became a partner to Seckler's Nashville Grass and the band became Curly Seckler, Willis Spears and the Nashville Grass. Band members were Seckler, Spears, Kenny Ingram, Marty Stuart, Johnny Warren (fiddle, Paul Warren's son), Perkins (banjo, guitar) and Pete Goble (bass). Seckler described Spears as sounding very much like Lester Flatt and of fine character.

[39] In 1995 he clarified that his first instrument was a Silvertone five-string banjo which he frailed, followed by a mandolin and then a guitar.

Charlie Monroe heard Seckler singing tenor on WSTP and recognized that Curly's style would fit well with his lead. In 1939 (just after Charlie and Bill Monroe had split), and after several months of offers from Monroe to join his band, Seckler (19) finally accepted his offer to be a full-time, touring musician at $20 per week on the tenor banjo. Seckler really didn't want to leave his brothers in the **Yodeling Rangers** or his home, but the offer was too good. They went immediately to WWVA's Jamboree, Wheeling, West Virginia, and called the new band **Charlie Monroe and His Kentucky Pardners**. The band was "more like bluegrass today,"[40] said Mr. Seckler.

In 1941, Seckler and "Ramblin'" Tommy Scott left the **Kentucky Pardners** in Louisville and moved to Anderson, South Carolina.[41] Seckler (now on his new $42 F-2 Gibson mandolin[42]) and Scott then went to Spartanburg, South Carolina, for the same sponsor as in Anderson (Herb Product Company). Wiley and Zeke Morris were there on the station with Don Reno who was thirteen at the time. One of the things Seckler will never forget is what Reno said to him when they first met. Seckler told this writer, "We drove into town there. Of course, back then I had a Packard. And Tommy had one of these Cadillac deals. And we drove up and Don told me many times, 'Good Lord have mercy! They must be multi-millionaires!' Them cars, you know, you could buy 'em for a dollar a dozen back then."[43]

Seckler then joined Leonard Stokes, calling themselves the **Melody Boys**, in Knoxville, Tennessee, playing for Cas Walker's supermarket chain on WROL. "Walker sure was a good man to work for."[44] "We first went to work for Cas Walker there in '42. Lowell Blanchard found out about the mail we was drawing up there—he couldn't get it in the boxes—and Lowell offered us more money so we left Cas and went to work for Lowell on WNOX (on the daily Mid-Day Merry-Go-Round)." Seckler and Stokes then went to Columbus, Ohio, where Seckler worked two years for the main Post Office in Columbus. There was very little gas to travel on in those days—with most of it going toward the War effort—so there was a slight respite from the music.

After the War, Seckler joined **Danny Bailey and the Happy Valley Boys** on WSM's Grand Ole Opry in Nashville (Danny's brother, Charlie, was in the service at the time). Bailey was the youngest member of the Opry at this time. In 1947, Seckler and Mac Wiseman worked together on WCYB as the **Country Boys** with E.P. Williams, Paul Prince, and Curly's brother, Duard (whose stage name was "Lucky").

Seckler then joined Hoke Jenkins' **Smoky Mountaineers** on WGAC in Augusta, Georgia, with Jim and Jesse McReynolds and Wiley Morris (guitar). According to Nelson Sears' book on Jim and Jesse, "About the time Jim and Jesse were singing with Roy Sykes (and the **Blue Ridge Mountain Boys**), Curly had been contacted by Hoke Jenkins who wanted him to go to Augusta, Georgia, to join Hoke and the **Smoky Mountaineers**. Curly told Hoke that he would come if he could bring Jim and Jesse along with him."[45] Hoke accepted and their trios included the McReynolds boys with Seckler. They did numbers like "Six Months Ain't Long" and "Mother's Not Dead She's Only Sleeping." Seckler had worked a lot with Charlie Monroe and his influence was heard on those trios. Seckler recalled that "Jim was doing most of the lead back then except when him and Jesse would do a duet. I was singin' so high that most of the time Jim did a lot of the lead notes on some of the songs. Of course, Jesse was the lead singer, but once in a while we'd switch it around. Actually, their first record deal was on Capitol Records with Nelson King and we come to Nashville here at the hotel and recorded. I'd wrote a number called 'Purple Heart' and we recorded it and I sung the lead on it. Jess' sung the baritone and Jim the tenor. We'd just switch it around."[46]

Seckler was working with the **Smoky Mountaineers** on WGAC when Lester Flatt called March 17, 1949, and asked him to join him and Earl Scruggs in a band they had formed; Seckler couldn't get there fast enough. Jim and Jesse were happy for him and wished him well. This new band that Seckler joined called

Curly Seckler, c. 1944. Photo courtesy Curly Seckler.

[40] This according to Curly Seckler in a note to this writer. He added that he first recordings were made with Charlie Monroe's band in 1946, long after he had left the band.

[41] Shortly after their departure, a young mandolinist/tenor singer named Lester Flatt joined the Pardners and stayed until he joined the Blue Grass Boys in 1945.

[42] He was glad to switch later to the F-5 which had the longer neck. The F-2 "would cramp your hands to death!" he said.

[43] Phone interview, June 1992.

[44] This according to Mr. Seckler in a note to this writer.

[45] Nelson Sears, *Jim and Jesse. Appalachia to the Grand Ole Opry*, (1976) p. 42. A self-published book.

[46] Phone interview, 1992.

Curly Seckler (L) and Lester Flatt. Photo courtesy Curly Seckler.

themselves **Flatt and Scruggs and the Foggy Mountain Boys.** They packed them in! Other band members when he joined were Lester Flatt (guitar), Earl Scruggs (banjo), Art Wooten (fiddle) and Cedric Rainwater (bass). Curly played mandolin. "Well, I held it. Lester, he always said, 'You can't play the mandolin too good, but I like the way you hold it.' [He laughed] I did play some though. He was just jokin'." Curly's nickname (by Lester) was "The Old Trapper from China Grove, North Carolina". Sometimes they would play drive-in theaters where people drove up in their cars; they stood on a stage and piped the music into each car by speaker. Through the years, they toured with acts such as Cowboy Copas, Lefty Frizell, Ray Price and Kitty Wells. Seckler wrote "No Mother or Dad" in 1949.

In November of 1950, Seckler left the **Foggy Mountain Boys** to join Carl and J.P. Sauceman's **Sauceman Brothers and the Greene Valley Boys** in Bristol, Virginia.[47] Seckler told of the rather rapid transition of events in early 1951, "Carter and Ralph [Stanley] was there at the same time. Every now and then Carter would call me about goin' to work with him and Ralph. I said no. He just kept on and finally he upped his salary quite a bit. I went and talked to Carl and J.P. about it. They said if I wanted to do that, go ahead and do it. So I said okay. We had just got up and running and the guy up in Lexington[48] that Lester and us had worked for up there and got that Kentucky Barn Dance going, he called me and said to me, 'Curly, I don't care who you are with down there but I want the band that you are with. If you will, bring them up here to Lexington to do this Kentucky Barn Dance and work for that 'bacca company we had up there in Versailles.' I told him that I didn't know if the Stanleys wanted to go up there or not. But if they didn't, I would bring the **Sauceman Brothers.** He said, 'I want the band you're with—I don't care who they are.' I asked Carter and Ralph and they said yes so I took them to Lexington. We played that program every day and then we'd do that Kentucky Barn Dance."[49] Seckler's time with the **Stanley Brothers** lasted only four months—after a personal problem with Carter. The Stanleys left the station soon after. Carter would soon join Bill Monroe

during the summer until Carter and Ralph re-formed in October at WCYB.

Seckler stayed there at WVLK and brought in Jim, Jesse and Hoke in March of 1952 to work on the same radio show he had earlier with the Stanleys. This time, Jenkins was a part of Jim and Jesse's **Virginia Boys** instead of before, when the brothers were a part of Hoke's band. There Seckler wrote and recorded "Purple Heart" on Capitol. He still receives royalties for that song today. **Jim and Jesse** got a recording contract on Capitol and recorded with Sonny Loden on fiddle[50]. In June of 1952, they recorded in the Tulane Hotel in Nashville—songs such as "Are You Missing Me," "Just Wondering Why" and six others.

Still in the same time frame, Curly Seckler returned to **Flatt and Scruggs** as mandolinist (after Everett Lilly left for Boston) at WPTF, Raleigh, North Carolina, just in time to reap the benefits of the Martha White Flour television sponsorship in 1953. They moved from Knoxville to Nashville. Seckler stayed until 1962. He recorded more than eighty songs with **Flatt and Scruggs** on the Mercury and Columbia labels and was an integral part in the band's music.

They were definitely the hottest bluegrass band around. Indeed, "There were only about ten groups back then doing anything," explained Seckler," and we were the only ones making money. We hit it just right with that TV! Man, when that come in, the mailman didn't bring the mail in a sack, he brought it in a truck. I don't care where we went, we didn't worry about doin' a show. We was wonderin' sometimes if we was gonna have to do the third one. I mean they had crowds. And we worked a lot of the little schools—that was before the big stuff came in. We'd go into those little ol' school-houses and pack 'em in—two shows about every night."

Seckler described why the band was so successful, "It was just different than anything else on the airway, the radio. That was all there was to it! It was just different! Bill [Monroe] couldn't touch it 'cause he didn't have a band. Of course, Earl come in with that banjer and that was so much different. Good gracious! Just like a Martha White biscuit from anything else—it was good! And the people just eat that up, Boy! He put them banjos in every part of the country. That helped, but it took it us *all* to do it. Lester Flatt, if he was alive today would tell you it took all of us to do it. One thing that helped more than anything was we stuck together. That was the whole thing. I could tell you whether Lester Flatt was gonna take a long breath or a short one. We had it down pat."

The band had quite a choreography going when they only had one microphone on stage. Seckler described it,

[47] Bristol is a city where half of it is in Virginia and the other half in Tennessee. This book considers them interchangeable for the purposes of simplicity. Everett Lilly took his place on mandolin.

[48] This was probably Don Horton at WVLK.

[49] Phone interview, 1992.

[50] Loden later became country music giant Sonny James.

"To start, we only had to use that one mike. Then they put one on the bass, I think it was, and we just went in and out, in and out. And now everybody's got a microphone. I've got nothin' wrong with that. But Flatt, before he died he said, 'All them cords is good for is someone to fall down and break their neck.' He never did go modern much. He was something else. He never would go with that little ole tape capo on his guitar until the day he died. You couldn't give him nothin' else."

Josh Graves joined **Flatt and Scruggs** on Dobro® in 1955. "I was glad to see Josh come in with his Dobro®," said Seckler, "but that took me off the mandolin breaks that I could have done. That put me on chops, you know. But I still could do the ones that I had wrote before Josh come in. But now I never was a big mandolin picker like Monroe or nothin' like that."

Seckler left **Flatt and Scruggs** in the fall of 1962 planning to retire, but kept his hand in until the group split in 1969. He ran his own trucking business for twelve years. Still, he yearned to get back into the music business on a more full-time basis. During the early seventies, when bluegrass festivals were becoming popular, he worked mainly as a solo. Occasionally, Flatt would bring him up to play and sing with the **Nashville Grass**.

"It was just different than anything else on the airway, the radio. That was all there was to it! It was just different!" —Curly Seckler

---

In March of 1973, Flatt hired Seckler to take the place of Roland White with **Lester Flatt and the Nashville Grass**.[51] Seckler played guitar; Marty Stuart moved to mandolin. The next few years brought failing health to Flatt so he had to rely more and more upon Seckler to the keep the band going. "Many times we would arrive at a show date and Lester would tell me to go on with the show and not mention he was on the bus. But if he was able, he would come on stage and do a number."[52] "And it got to where he would come on the stage and not do a number and kindly introduce all of us boys and talk a little bit and then he'd leave. He got in such health he couldn't carry a tune."[53]

Flatt asked Seckler to take over the band if he should pass on. Hesitant, Seckler was assured of the group's profitability by Flatt's words of advice, "Curly, if you keep the music down to earth as we always have, it won't take long before they will accept you without me."[54] After Seckler took over the **Nashville Grass**, it lost $20,000 the first two years. But the group stuck with the formula that made Flatt successful and soon Seckler was making good money—more than he made as a sideman; it allowed a modest, comfortable retirement in Nashville where he lives as of 1996. He was baptized in 1978, just in time to convince Lester, one of his best friends, to become a born-again Christian before he died on May 11th of 1979. Seckler took over the reins of Flatt's **Nashville Grass** whose members then became Blake Williams (banjo), Tater Tate (fiddle), Charlie Nixon (resonator guitar), Marty Stuart (mandolin), Billy Smith and himself (guitars).

By the spring of 1981, Willis Spears was the new lead singer with **Curly Seckler and the Nashville Grass**.[55] On January 1, 1987, Seckler asked Spears to be a full partner in the group. They changed the band name to **Curly Seckler, Willis Spears and the Nashville Grass**. Seckler felt confident that Spears could carry on the band if anything should happen to him.

When asked why he didn't go for the big money but preferred the smaller venues, he admitted that he didn't really need the money anymore, he liked being on the road playing his music and, "I enjoy the smaller places now because it gives us a chance to be around our kind of people."[56]

Little Jody Rainwater— comedian, bass player, deejay. He's done it all.

Charles E. Johnson, later known as "Little Jody Rainwater," was born in Surrey County, North Carolina, into a musical family in 1920. He began playing the mandolin with his brother Herman on guitar as **Chuck and Slim, the Johnson Brothers** in 1935. "There was no such thing as getting paid back then," he said. "'Course sometimes they'd pass the hat for us and there'd be mostly pennies and nickels—once in a while, a dime. You know, if we made two or three dollars a day, we felt like we had money."[57] Even when they got a job

[51] This band was originally called "Lester Flatt Show" on their radio station when Flatt and Scruggs split up. A listener contest of name solicitations changed it before Seckler joined. Band members of the band were Flatt (guitar), Seckler (guitar), Haskel McCormick (banjo), Charlie Nixon (resonator guitar), Marty Stuart (mandolin), Paul Warren (fiddle), and Johnny Johnson (bass), with Lance LeRoy as manager.

[52] Ray Thigpen, "Curly Seckler—Willis Spears and the Nashville Grass. A Legacy Lives On," *Bluegrass Unlimited*, February, 1990, p. 21.

[53] Phone interview, 1992.

[54] Thigpen, op. cit., p. 21.

[55] Other members were Seckler (guitar), Kenny Ingram (banjo), Johnny Warren (fiddle) and Bob Rogers (bass). This version of the band was together through 1986.

[56] Marty Stuart, "Lester Flatt Memories," an interview with Curly Seckler, *Bluegrass Unlimited*, May, 1986, p. 81. This interview of Flatt was his last interview before his death.

[57] John A. Hinton, "Jody Rainwater—Bluegrass Reflections," *Bluegrass Unlimited*, January, 1981, p. 36.

playing gospel tunes on the radio, they didn't get paid for it. "We were too dumb to know anything about getting any money out of it," he said.[58]

In April 1945, after a tour in the Marines, Charles Johnson (mandolin) and Woody Hauser (guitar) formed the **Blue Ridge Mountain Boys** in Winston-Salem, North Carolina. The comedy team of **Little Jody and Woody** were together for three years. Soon the **Blue Ridge Mountain Boys** began playing music on WTOB where they began polishing their comedy team performances. As with most comedians of the era, he was dressed in a uniform of some sort and had a stage name. His clothes were baggy pants, suspenders and old shirts; his nickname was "Little Jody" (Johnson's stature is small—about the height of Chubby Wise). About that time, the duo performed during the intermission of a Bill Monroe road tour where he met Lester Flatt; they soon became lifelong friends.

In 1948, Little Jody joined **Smoky Graves and the Blue Star Boys** on WDBJ, Roanoke, as mandolinist/bassist/comedian. He spoke about band comedy, "I'd like to see it get back in the music. Situation comedy is funny, clean and natural. **Reno and Smiley** were masters at it."[59] The **Blue Star Boys** worked enough to make a living. But because they stayed in the Virginias, their fame was only local. That year, Jody was in Roanoke with the **Blue Star Boys**. He recalled, "When Flatt told me, 'We're leaving the **Blue Grass Boys**,' I thought it was the most awful thing I'd ever heard. Flatt, Scruggs, and Cedric, all three were going to leave Monroe. Why, with Chubby Wise, I still say it was the greatest band—the backbone of bluegrass. They asked me then to come with them to handle bookings and advance advertising, but I decided to stay in Roanoke."[60]

By late summer of 1949, in the area of Bristol's WCYB in southwest Virginia, a coal mining strike severely depressed the area. **Flatt and Scruggs and the Foggy Mountain Boys**, which was there at WCYB, decided to leave to seek greener pastures in Lexington, Kentucky. This left a spot open at the station so Smoky Graves, with Charles Johnson on comedy, moved his **Blue Star Boys** to the famous 50,000 watt station and they nearly starved. Then Flatt offered Jody a job again; this time he accepted, as Cedric Rainwater's comedy partner on WVLK's Jamboree and as their booking agent. This radio station is in Versailles, just outside of Lexington.

The duo quickly became a successful comedy act and Little Jody became like Cedric Rainwater's younger brother. Flatt renamed him "Little Jody Rainwater" for promotional purposes. He lost the name "Charles Johnson" except to family and close friends, and by the 1970s, even to them. When Cedric soon left to join Hank Williams' **Drifting Cowboys**, a popular country act in the late 1940s and early '50s, Jody began playing bass with the **Foggy Mountain Boys** and continued his rube comedy, still wearing his comedy costume.

Soon the **Foggy Mountain Boys** moved to WDAE, Tampa, but this too proved unprofitable. They stayed eleven weeks, during which time they recorded their last Mercury session. Band members about this time included Flatt, Scruggs, Curly Seckler (mandolin), Chubby Wise (fiddle) and Little Jody Rainwater (bass). Benny Sims was also a fiddler during this period.

In January 1952, the **Foggy Mountain Boys** moved to WPTF, Raleigh, North Carolina, where the group gained great popularity through their tent shows. The concept, copied from Bill Monroe and the Opry, gave them great flexibility as to venues, packed them in, and became quite profitable. Jody recalled, "I was doing the booking, sleeping in the car about half the time, then doubling back to meet them out at the shows. I was just doing too much, working seven days a week, eighteen hours a day. That's when I decided I had to do something else. I was right at a nervous breakdown." He regretfully quit in May 1952.

Jody joined WSVS in Crewe, Virginia, as deejay June 7, 1952, . This gave him flexibility, steady pay, and good hours. His reputation with **Flatt and Scruggs** helped significantly in the success of the show.

In 1971, Jody Rainwater became a Christian. His music now took on a new meaning. "If people would come and listen to what I have to say, I would enjoy that. If I could just give my testimony, it might help somebody. To have been where I've been in bluegrass music, they might listen to me where they wouldn't someone else."[61]

Bill Keith remembers Don Reno

"Long before I heard any bluegrass groups in the flesh, I had recordings of Don Reno's music—probably as early as the spring of 1958. In the fall of 1957, I bought my first five-string banjo, having been a tenor player before. I bought Pete Seeger's instruction book because it was basically his playing with the **Weavers** that attracted me to the five-string banjo. In that book, Pete suggested getting some records by Earl Scruggs and Don Reno, so I immediately did.

"I was always impressed by the freewheeling, unconventional, and improvised nature of Don's playing. Other players that I was familiar with would have their

---

58 John A. Hinton, "Jody Rainwater—Bluegrass Reflections," *Bluegrass Unlimited*, January, 1981, pp. 36, 37.

59 Ibid., p. 38.

60 Ibid., p. 38.

61 Ibid., p. 40.

Jody's son-in-law, Billy Budd, played bass with Bill Harrell during the late 1980s and early 1990s. Daughter Charlie Rainwater was a bluegrass deejay and festival emcee during the 1970s and 1980s.

breaks more worked out. His music had a flash to it. There was some kind of spark to Don's playing that no other banjo players had....it had more immediacy, as if it were blasting right out of his imagination without too much processing.

"I saw him play on several occasions. The first time was at Watermelon Park in Virginia, in the summer of '59 or '60. Bill Monroe was playing, along with Sonny Osborne, Red Allen, Smitty Irvin, Mac Wiseman and Don and Red, with Ronnie standing on a chair playing mandolin. I have tape recordings of that festival. I used to listen to it a lot and it really got locked in my memory. After hearing that tape so often, it happened more than once that I would be playing along and thinking, 'Gee, I just fell into a nice little lick that I had never played before.' But then the next time I listened to that tape, there would be that same kind of lick, and I would discover it was really Don's. I think his playing was usually a little more memorable because of the flash and spirit that he had.

"One of the reasons I really appreciated Don has to do with Monroe. As you know, Earl Scruggs went to work with Monroe about the time Don went into the service. Earl developed tremendously in those years—particularly noticeable if you listen to the recordings between '44 and '48—and I have always felt it was to a great extent because of Bill's influence, his aesthetics. But once Don got back out of the service and then joined Monroe, he had a problem because Earl had already established a three-finger style and a direction to bluegrass banjo. So even if Don knew that Earl's playing would be very influential on the banjo, he needed to be more than a carbon copy of Earl. He had to establish his own musical identity. And he succeeded immensely.

"Don's approach to the banjo, and the guitar too, was just different from any other player's. He organized notes more like they were sung. You can always sing a single string of notes organized melodically, but try singing a Scruggs-style arrangement or try singing Travis-style. You just can't sing every note. With Don't stuff, his playing is more melodic—that is not a value judgment about other players, it was just Don's way of playing.

"One time about 1964 or '65, I went down to see Don and Red at Sunset Park in Pennsylvania. I arrived before they did and when they came in, it was without Don, who had to stay behind due to a death in the family. I was honored to be asked to play in his place that day.

"At that time, when I was playing with Bill Monroe, there was no interstate from Nashville up to the North-east so we used to take Route 81 and often would stop in Roanoke or in Troutville and visit with Don or Red.

We appeared on a television show they did out of Roanoke.

"I have a lot of memories that include Don and, as has been mentioned in various banjo instruction books, half of the inspiration for what I played in melodic style: 'Devil's Dream,' 'Sailor's Hornpipe,' and all that, I credit to a particular riff that Don played on the bridge of 'Banjo Signal.' There was a little lick in there that I put together with another thing from Don Stover, to play the major scale in the melodic style. Don was very important to me as a musician. There have been a lot of influences, and I hope there still are. He was one of the formative ones."[62]

Don Reno

Don Reno and the Tennessee Cut-Ups

While the biography of Don Reno could easily be included in the Banjo chapter of this book, he and his groups were much more important than that—they were pioneers in the music. Just a cursory knowledge of Don Reno and Red Smiley will show that. Because there is much more research material available on Reno than on Smiley, this section deals with the entire biography of Don Reno as well as the portions of his career when he was with Red Smiley.

A 1991 interview with **Reno and Smiley** historian Eddie Stubbs shared this insight, "They were probably the second group which pioneered bluegrass after **Flatt and Scruggs**. In the era of the '80s and '90s, of all the pioneering groups, they were probably the most overlooked and most under-appreciated. And that has been attributed to a lot of things. Reno was such an individualistic type player, he had great style, but he was also a great guitar player. His guitar playing has never been totally appreciated. I think it's just now getting some credit among the people like Dan Crary and Tony Rice. But it must be remembered that in the era of **Reno and**

62 Alan Munde, "Bill Keith Remembers Don Reno," *Frets*, April, 1985, p. 23.
     An in-depth look at Reno's style can be found in "Remembering Don Reno—An in-depth look at his musical contribution" by Alan Munde, *Frets*, April, 1985, pp. 24-26.

Smiley, they weren't really a bluegrass band. They had the bluegrass instrumentation, but they were a country band. And I think they would have told you that. They worked on country package shows. I think that because they were primarily a country band, that may be one of the reasons why their popularity has not had the longevity that somebody like the **Stanley Brothers**, or Bill Monroe, whose songs have been recorded time and time again.

"If you went back and listened to their live shows," Stubbs continued, "and I have gone back and listened to them—they used to work a boatload of dances—they had a real entertaining show. I saw them once when I was only a very small child. The only thing I remember was Mac Magaha jumping up and down on the stage, jumping all around. But if you listen to their live shows, they did a lot of country music—mainstream country music of the day—I mean, songs like Jim Reeves songs, 'Missing You,' and an old Don Gibson song, 'I Can't Stop Loving You.' They did 'Together Again' which was made popular by Buck Owens. They did more of other people's songs than they did of their own. They were on television in Roanoke five mornings a week for an hour and a half. And Don Reno told me that they could go six weeks without repeating a song on the show."

Reno was always generous with his time. He would help anybody and show anybody anything they wanted to see. Stubbs remembered that at one concert he and the **Johnson Mountain Boys** opened up for Don Reno's group. The **J-M-B** got five encores. Stubbs really felt bad about cutting into Reno's slot. Reno replied, "You're not cuttin' into my time at all. Get out there where you belong. I've had my day. It's your turn now."

Historian Dr. Bill Foster, in 1991, shared some thoughts about Don Reno. "I became convinced that, had he not been such a stellar and innovative musician, he could have been a star as an impressionist or an impersonator. Not only was Don one of the most personable and gregarious men I have ever met, he was one of the best raconteurs. When he told a story, he assumed the characters and the voices of everyone in the story in turn, talking one minute like Uncle Dave,

and the next like Lester Flatt. We sat there, Don and Jerry [Hinton] and I, until just before dawn, and we never picked a note! It was a great evening in my life because it was so enjoyable."

Reno was highly influenced by **J.E. Mainer's Mountaineers**, the **Delmore Brothers**, the **Blue Sky Boys** and Jimmie Rodgers. By this time, the string band music of groups such as **Gid Tanner and the Skillet Lickers** had faded out and was heard only on recordings.

Their band sound was unlike Monroe, **Flatt and Scruggs**, the Stanleys, the **Lonesome Pine Fiddlers**, or anyone in the bluegrass genre. They seemed to be aiming at a different market which included the more modern material and the honky-tonk audience which liked the electric instruments and the more modern Nashville sound. This music was similar to what Smiley had performed as a country artist in Ohio. Then, with the addition of Reno who could play any instrument exceptionally well, the **Tennessee Cut-Ups** did those songs with bluegrass flavor. (By this time, Reno had spent some time with Bill Monroe's band and fully capable of doing solid bluegrass music.) On the slower tunes, Reno introduced a full, chordal style on his banjo which innovated what the banjo could do. Smiley's smooth, mature, lead singing was complemented by Reno's smooth tenor singing. The combination of all this seemed to work; it worked well enough for the records to sell sufficiently to create enough demand for them to reorganize again after disbanding in early 1952.

Don Reno was born in Spartanburg, South Carolina, February 21, 1927, into a family where he was the only one who played music professionally. When he was one year old, Don's father moved the family to a farm near Clyde, North Carolina. He began playing music at age five and had his own guitar at eight. When he was about eight, he heard Snuffy Jenkins for the first time; he then knew that he *had* to be able to play the banjo like that. "So I immediately went in to a show that he was playing, and as soon as I possibly could. And he kind of took me under his wing and told me to put a pick on that third finger and start using it. In about three weeks, I

Price: $7.95

THE MUSICAL HISTORY OF . . .

DON RENO

HIS LIFE . . . HIS SONGS

A Pictorial and Graphic History of the Great American Country and Western Troubadour was able to play any of the stuff that I was playing with three fingers."[63] Although Mr. Jenkins modestly said that he never actually "taught" young Reno anything, Don thought differently about Jenkins. He said, "Snuffy taught me the basic three-finger roll on the five-string banjo when I was just a little boy, and was the first to use three fingers in any kind of style that was different, and the same style is used today on [many banjo tunes]...that's what turned me to banjo." Reno remembered that Snuffy actually sat down and showed him some tunes and "He told me to hit the third, second, and the first strings to start with in G, and then run it up to C and do it, D and do it, back to G and do it." He continued, "Before Snuffy's style, banjo sounded harsh and crude to me. Snuffy and Pappy [Sherrill], whatever I am today, you're the ones that deserve all the credit. This was the combination of a lifetime, the one that is still my inspiration after all these years."

Snuffy had it all together, said Reno. "Snuffy Jenkins is the man that brought it to the front, and he had it just as strong and smooth and going just as good in the early thirties as Earl and I had it going in the late forties, if you want to know the plain truth about the whole situation."[64] Snuffy never told Reno where he learned his style. Reno commented that "I've heard of all these other guys, and heard some of them play, that were supposed to have taught Snuffy. But they didn't have what Snuffy had—he was the authentic third-finger man. The others played with three fingers but they didn't use a predominant roll—it was a messed-up sort of deal—it wasn't clean. Snuffy played 'Sally Goodin' and 'Cumberland Gap' the way Earl and I play it today, and these other guys didn't."[65]

Don Reno's father didn't want him to be a musician. Nevertheless, he and a friend (J.R. Sorrells) decided to make a banjo. They whittled the body out of wood and tanned a mountain cat's hide by soaking it in ashes and water as the banjo head. "After many weeks of work and blisters we came out with a very crude banjo, but at least I could play it. We used screen door wire for strings tuned so low you might play four songs before breaking a string. My brother [Harley] finally gave me a banjo with United States flags drawn all over the head. I sold J.R. Sorrells my half of the banjo we made together for $1.50. I don't know what he did with it but I would give anything to have it now."[66]

Tommy Magness was an excellent fiddler at the time and was performing professionally.[67] He showed Don some of the basics of music and made him back up his breakdown fiddle numbers. Magness was hard on young Reno if he did anything wrong. Magness (Don Reno spells this name "Magnus"), the guitarist and fiddler whom Reno felt had the best timing of anyone in the business, was playing in Reno's brother's band as Don was getting started, and was very influential toward this very important factor of the music. "He kept telling me over and over that if I didn't learn *time* I might as well not even learn to play. He really chewed me real good when I was little, but it was good for me that he did."[68] By the time Don was eight, he could follow Magness very capably. (By the mid-1950s, he was fluent on *all* the bluegrass instruments.)

Reno developed an interest in the guitar before he was ten, put the banjo aside, and followed the **Delmore Brothers** style of picking because he loved it so much. He then formed a duet with Howard Thompson (who was in the first grade) and they would play music at school during every break. He used Ed Russell's guitar in the duo until Russell became good enough to play with them, then Reno went back to the banjo. Joe Medford[69], who was just starting school, joined on fiddle and they added an harmonica player, Lemuel Mackey. Reno was in the third grade when they made their first performance at a high school Halloween party. The foursome played together until December 1938 when the Reno family moved back to South Carolina.

Twelve-year-old Reno did black-face comedy with George Morris with the **Morris Brothers** when he was a member the first time. They played a circuit of school-houses and theaters, hitting them every five or six months. They worked almost every night, traveling in their 1936 Pontiac. They charged between ten cents to a quarter at their concerts and played to between 300 and 1000 people at a time. Most of the audience consisted of rural folks, but when they played in the city even bankers and lawyers showed up—although they were ashamed to admit they liked it.

Reno listened to the **Monroe Brothers** and Byron Parker ("The Old Hired Hand") when he was growing up when that group played on WFBC, Greenville, South Carolina. By the time Don was twelve in January of 1940, he had fully developed his banjo playing to a professional caliber. "I'd learned everything that seemed to be going on banjo just then. I hadn't started what you might call 'innovating' on the banjo, so I took

---

[63] From an interview with Don Reno by Tony Trischka. Tony Trischka and Peter Wernick, *Masters of the 5-String Banjo, In Their Own Words and Music* (New York: Oak Publications, 1988), p. 90.

[64] Bill Vernon, "The Don Reno Story, Part 1: Early Years, "*Muleskinner News*, June 1973, p. 9.

[65] Ibid., p. 10.

[66] Don Reno, "The Musical History of Don Reno. His Life...His Songs" (1975 and 1983), p. 5.

[67] Magness was the fiddler on the original cut of Bill Monroe's "Muleskinner Blues" in the early '40s.

[68] Trischka, and Wernick, op. cit., p. 82.

[69] Joseph Howell "Joe" Medford, April 2, 1932-November 16, 1993. His career spanned many years with Tommy Millard (1948), Mac Wiseman (1951), Charlie Monroe (1951) and Don Gibson (1952-'53).

the guitar because there was more progressive guitar in that era than there was banjo."[70]

By age thirteen, he had a solo radio show on WSPA in Spartanburg where he played harp and guitar together Monday through Friday, 6 a.m. to 7 a.m.. A group of musicians (two guitarists and a mandolinist) heard him on the radio and asked him to join them in Greer, South Carolina. After Reno joined them on banjo, they went to Clyde, North Carolina, and got a fiddler. They named the group the **Tapp Brothers Band** because the brothers were the ones who had the car and the PA set. Their first gig was at WFBC; Reno made $1.50, all in nickels.

Thirteen year-old Don Reno wrote his first song, "Jesus Will Save Your Soul," which he later recorded. One of his main interests at that time was a study of the Bible and had often contemplated being a minister. "I tried to understand as I read, not just read and say, 'Well, well, well,' because the Bible can turn you around if you don't really know how to understand it. You can make it say what you want it to."[71]

About this same time, Earl Scruggs used to listen to Reno on a radio show. Reno was doing then what Scruggs ended up doing later. They had basically the same rolls and the same kind of licks. Reno didn't show Scruggs any technique, though. "Earl was so backward back then," said Reno. "I didn't even know he played banjo for a long time. He and Grady Wilkie used to come over. Finally he did admit to me one day that he played a little banjo (Scruggs was very shy)."[72] By 1942, when Scruggs took Reno's place as banjoist with the **Morris Brothers**, "He had his stuff together. He was a good banjo picker." The only banjo players Reno knew about at that time were himself, Snuffy and Hoke Jenkins and Scruggs.

Back home in April 1940, he got a call to play banjo with his buddy Howard Thompson and Tex Wells as **Tex Wells and His Smoky Mountain Rangers**. Musicians were Reno (banjo), Thompson (guitar), Wells (emcee, and he owned a 1935 Chevy they could travel in), Jay Haney (fiddle) and Walter Haney (guitar). They started a show at WISE, Asheville, South Carolina, which lasted until September.

In September 1940, Zeke Morris took Reno (13), Jay and Walter Haney, and Thompson to WSPA. They convinced George "Sambo" Morris to come out of retirement and now the **Morris Brothers** band was back in business. Soon the Haneys left. Wiley, the youngest Morris brother, soon joined with George, Zeke, Howard Thompson and Don Reno to do their weekday mornings on WSPA. Wiley was considered, by Reno, to be of the music's best rhythm guitarists and "Wiley, Zeke and George had the best trio I've ever heard."

The **Morris Brothers** band was very popular in country music at this time. It is significant to note that the band had all the basic instruments of a modern bluegrass band but that the **Morris Brothers** did not have the impact that the **Blue Grass Boys** did with the same instrumentation beginning in 1946.[73] Don Reno, in a 1973 interview, said that "The **Morris Brothers** actually had one of the first bluegrass groups; Zeke played the mandolin and they had Tiny Dodson on fiddle, George on guitar, Wiley on bass, and Hoke Jenkins was playing five-string with them in the Snuffy style, so they had the basic bluegrass lineup. Hoke played good banjo; he had to go to service, and I took his place. Then, when I left the **Morris Brothers** the second time, Scruggs took my place. That had to be '42 because I remember when Pearl Harbor was bombed, I remember playing Gibson, Georgia, the night before, with the **Morris Brothers**."[74]

Reno quit the **Morris Brothers**[75] to join Arthur "Guitar Boogie" Smith and his recently-formed **Crackerjacks**[76] on WSPA. This band had a hillbilly music style after Smith's **Dixie Land Jazz** band proved monetarily unsuccessful. At that time, Reno bought the Gibson Mastertone (which he would later trade to Earl Scruggs in 1948) from Snuffy Jenkins (who had bought it from Fisher Hendley for $50). Reno learned how to read and write music from Arthur Smith.[77] In the fall of 1943, Reno continued the radio show on WSPA with his own **Carolina Hillbillies**.[78]

According to a story that Reno told folklorist Dr. Bill Foster in the early 1980s, Reno was traveling with Uncle Dave Macon when Reno was about sixteen years

[70] Trischka and Wernick, op. cit., p. 82.

[71] Vernon, op. cit., p. 11.

[72] Trischka and Wernick, op. cit., p. 91.

[73] According to Mrs. Don Reno in 1991, this band was not playing bluegrass music. They were playing "country," or "hillbilly," music. She felt that Bill Monroe started this music called "bluegrass". She felt that the most important event in bluegrass music was the mandolin playing of Bill Monroe.

[74] Ibid., p. 10.

[75] Howard Thompson had quit the Morris Brothers just before Reno; the Morris Brothers hired former Blue Grass Boy Tommy "Snowball" Millard in Thompson's place.

[76] Members of the Crackerjacks were Arthur Smith (mandolin, fiddle, guitar, tenor banjo), and Smith brothers Sonny (guitar) and Ralph (bass).

[77] The group disbanded when Sonny Smith joined the Navy. Arthur Smith went to WBT in Charlotte, North Carolina, to work for the WBT Briarhoppers until he went into the Navy three months later.

[78] With Pee Wee (or Shorty) Boyd (fiddle), Hank Garland (electric guitar), Mary Lou Morris (bass, who worked with Arthur Smith), and Howard Thompson (guitar) until Reno joined the Army. Morris left almost immediately to get married and was replaced by John Palmer (of Union, South Carolina).

At Allen's Tavern, Detroit, Michigan, c. 1954. L to R: Wiley Birchfield, Arthur "Guitar Boogie" Smith, Ray Brown. Photo courtesy Ed Brown.

old. They traveled in Hudson Terraplane automobiles. Evidently, Macon was continually losing his pipe in the car and young Don was always on his knees looking for it. This touring group played the "kerosene circuit", so named because they often played in locations such as schoolhouses which had no electricity. Their cars were loaded up with kerosene lanterns to light the stage for the performers.

Reno noticed that the War had changed the people he used to entertain in the Carolinas. "It seemed as if they were more concentrated to our kind of music while the War was going on, and then when the War was over they were in a happy state and the sad songs didn't mean what they had meant. While the War was going on, North Carolina and South Carolina were two of the best states to play in. But after the War was over, it seemed there was a period when there were other things that the people were more interested in than music."[79]

In another interview, Reno said that the banjo style which he, Snuffy and Scruggs were playing was already being noticed. "It had started making a dent on people around the places where we were playing—the day Bill Monroe offered me a job in 1943, Clyde Moody and Floyd Ethridge and Chubby Wise had just gone to work with Bill and were trying to learn all the breakdowns from Floyd. Sam and Kirk McGee were in the hotel, the Franklin Hotel in Spartanburg, right in front of the radio station. I was working with Arthur then, and after the show these guys took me over to the hotel and were getting a kick out of it. And then Bill came in and they started me all over again with him. He asked me if I wanted a job." Stringbean was not with Monroe yet. In

fact, "He had no banjo at all at this particular time," said Reno who probably had no idea that a banjo in the style of a Reno or a Scruggs could completely revolutionize history—and we're not just talking about *bluegrass* history. Reno spoke of Monroe, "I don't think he really knew at the time, but he liked it (Scruggs' banjo style) better than anything he had heard in a while. He had offered Snuffy Jenkins a job but Snuffy was too well established in Columbia, South Carolina, to take a job and go."[80]

When Bill Monroe came through Spartanburg with a tent show in 1943, along with Sam and Kirk McGee, Floyd Ethridge and Uncle Dave Macon, Monroe tried to hire Reno on banjo. "I told him I was going to join the Army and jack my age up a year. If the Army didn't take me, I would come on to Nashville. The Army took me and sent me to Fort Riley to the horse cavalry. I was offered Special Services (to play as a musician) but I turned it down because I didn't want to take what I call a 'chicken' job. The playing I did was after hours, when the work was done, at Fort Riley, Kansas. Me and Bob Banks would get together."[81] When Reno was stationed in China, he was the company barber and nightly entertainer. His Army outfit was the famous Merrill's Marauders in China, Burma and India.

With Earl Scruggs now in Monroe's band, Reno said that the **Blue Grass Boys** sounded somewhat like the **Morris Brothers**. "I would say the group at that time, Chubby Wise and Earl and Bill's mandolin playing, made the group real unique. Cedric Rainwater played real good bass and Lester played good guitar. [Monroe] had a tight group, the best I ever heard. Bill's music had a little bit more sting to it than the old **Morris Brothers** music. Of course, the singing was high, and back then Bill sang high. He tuned over standard. The music had a real good sock to it. I don't think anyone today realizes what an impact he did have with his music because the Opry officials told him one night that he was turning in more Opry service money (the percentage of the receipts which went to the Opry) than any other artist. He was having overflowing crowds wherever he went. When Bill Monroe was in town, the whole town was out. He worked seven days a week."[82]

In late 1945 or early 1946, Don Reno played rhythm guitar on Arthur Smith's "Guitar Boogie." Reno normally played the lead when the pair played together, but Smith played the lead on this recording which made him famous.[83] And because of this new fame, Smith was more easily differentiated from Arthur Smith, the fiddler ("Fiddlin Arthur Smith"). He became Arthur "Guitar Boogie" Smith.

[79] Vernon, op. cit., p. 11.

[80] Ibid., p. 10.

[81] Reno, op. cit.

[82] Pete Kuykendall, *Bluegrass Unlimited*, July, 1971, p.13

[83] Also on the recording were Cecil Campbell (of the Tennessee Playboys) and Roy Lear.

Ronnie Reno, Don's first son, was born in 1947. He later wrote "Boogie Grass Band" which was recorded by Conway Twitty, and during the early 1990s was the host of a cable network television show. He worked with his father from 1954 (age seven) to 1968 when he went with the **Osborne Brothers**, then with Merle Haggard while Carlton Haney was Haggard's manager. Don's other musician sons are Don Wayne Reno (born 1963) and Dale Reno (born 1961).

When Reno came back from the Army in 1948, he found the tremendous success that Earl was having with Monroe. But he wasn't overly impressed—he preferred to play guitar at the time. Instead of being a clone of Scruggs, he chose to change his style—with the accent on fast chording of the melody and later single-string picking (which he learned from Eddie Adcock in 1953). This was an easy transition; he was an accomplished guitar player and he easily developed these skills for the banjo.

Don Reno and his brother operated a grocery store in Buffalo, near Spartanburg, which they had bought before he left for the service. There in Buffalo, he worked local gigs with John Palmer and the Pruitt brothers as the **Saddle Pals**.[84] When member Pee Wee Gosdin[85] quit music, Reno and Palmer then joined the **Carolina Hillbillies** at WSPA in early March 1948 when Reno heard Monroe's band without Scruggs who had just left. He learned that Monroe would be playing in nearby Taylorsville, North Carolina. "I got to Taylorsville just as they were starting their show. I went backstage, took my banjo out of the case, and walked on stage and started playing. Bill said, 'Boy, I've been trying to find you,' and I said, 'Well, I finally made it.' His group that night was Lester Flatt (guitar), Benny Martin (fiddle), Joel Price (bass fiddle) and Jack(ie) Phelps (electric steel guitar).

"Lester left in three or four weeks.[86] Jim Eanes took his place for a while then left to go form his own group in Danville, Virginia. Jack Phelps played flattop for about eight months after Jim [Eanes] left, and Mac

"The Morris Brothers actually had one of the first bluegrass groups; Zeke played the mandolin and they had Tiny Dodson on fiddle, George on guitar, Wiley on bass, and Hoke Jenkins was playing five-string with them in the Snuffy style, so they had the basic bluegrass lineup." —Don Reno

Wiseman took Phelps' place when he left. Benny Martin left and Floyd Ethridge took his place."[87]

From a different source, Reno noted, "When I heard that Scruggs was leaving, I went to Nashville and Bill was gone to North Carolina. So I doubled back and went to the theater in Taylorsville where he was playing. He had no banjo player with him so I got my banjo out, tuned up, and walked out on the stage and started playing with him. Lester was with him and Bill gave me one of the hardest rows to hoe that night I ever seen. He started playing everything in B-flat or B-natural because I didn't have a capo and he was getting a kick out of it.[88]

"So we went to Mt. Airy, North Carolina, and played some radio shows with him and a stage show. And he took me to a cafe and said, 'I don't know how much you're used to making.' I said that money wasn't the thing. I didn't care what he was paying. He was paying ninety dollars a week and fifteen dollars extra on Sundays."[89]

In mid-1949, Reno (22) left Bill Monroe to form **Don Reno and His Tennessee Cut-Ups** with Benny Martin, Hillis Butram (who only stayed two weeks), then Jimmy Pruitt (fiddle, thirteen years old), Chuck Haney and John Palmer (who was occasionally replaced by Jarvis Haney). They worked WSPA, and in August 1949 opened up WBCU, Union, South Carolina. Neither of the Haneys were related to Carlton Haney, who would be Reno's manager for several years.

By December, they were playing at WDBJ, Roanoke, Virginia, with members Don and nephew Verlon Reno, Bill Haney, Tommy Magness and Al Lancaster. Lancaster left after a month and was replaced by Irvin Sharp on bass until the group left Roanoke. Verlon and Don sang duets. Reno also toured with **Tommy Magness and the Tennessee Buddies** where, on December 27th, 1949, he met Red Smiley. Smiley sang solos and bass in the quartets. This is where "Chicken Hot Rod" was born, a name given to Reno by Magness.

---

84 Other members of the band were Hank Garland (guitar, age 14) and Pee Wee Gosdin. Garland would later become a famous country star on the Opry.

85 Reno said this name is "Gosnell" or "Gonsell."

86 According to both Jim Eanes and Jim Shumate, Lester Flatt and Earl Scruggs had already left Monroe and formed their Foggy Mountain Boys in January. Perhaps this is *after* January and Lester was just filling-in. Eanes didn't start with Monroe until February of 1948 (according to Mr. Eanes). But this is only conjecture—there's no research that says that Flatt ever went back to fill-in with Monroe.

87 Reno, op. cit..

88 Actually, Reno probably never used a capo. "I don't have anything against the capo. If a man wants to use one, well, that's fine. It would take me half a day to get one on, get it adjusted, and then tuned up. And then, after all these years of not using one, if I put one on it would probably throw my neck off so bad I probably wouldn't be able to find anything. (laughs) You know, emceeing and running a band...I had tried to use one years ago a few times, and it seems like I spent more time with the capo and tuning than I did trying to emcee the show or run it."—Trischka and Wernick, p. 90.

89 James Rooney, *Bossmen: Bill Monroe and Muddy Waters*, 1971, p. 51.

It was with the **Tennessee Buddies** group that the duo of Reno and Smiley first recorded together in February of 1951. The group did a radio show on WDBJ, which lasted until Verlon died in a fishing accident in June of 1950.

Don Reno's mother died May 7, 1950. A month later, on June 20th, Verlon drowned in the Cow Pasture River, near Clifton Forge, Virginia, where he and Don had fished a lot. These two events really took their toll on Don but he continued with his music. It must be difficult for the artistic and sensitive personality of a musician to suffer such emotional and personal losses and keep going. He knew that the audience must not be able to perceive the hurt which is within. Somehow, performers must be able to put it behind them; they must put their emotional stress behind them and act like nothing has happened. They remember that they must be entertainers first and musicians second.

After Verlon's death, Don and Red began singing together—thus began an era in bluegrass music. Reno and Smiley stayed together until January 2, 1972 (Smiley's death), except for health problems at the end of 1964, and Smiley's occasional semi-retirements. Still with **Tommy Magness and the Tennessee Buddies**, Remus Bell was later added to replace Verlon. Jack Phelps joined in January 1951.

Reno quit the **Tennessee Buddies** in April 1951. Reno, Smiley and Phelps left Roanoke and joined **Toby Stroud and the Blue Ridge Mountain Boys** on WWVA in Wheeling. Reno and Smiley then left to return to Reno's home in South Carolina in September. They picked up Chuck Haney (mandolin), Jay Haney (bass) and Gopher Addis (fiddle) and formed **Don Reno, Red Smiley and the Tennessee Cut-Ups**.

In Cincinnati, **Don Reno, Red Smiley and the Tennessee Cut-Ups** recorded their first session with King Records on January 18, 1952. King's Syd Nathan was looking for a bluegrass band to round out his complement of country stars which through the years included the **Delmore Brothers**, Grandpa Jones, Clyde Moody, Cowboy Copas and Hawkshaw Hawkins. Author Bob Artis described the record situation this way, "It seemed to be the thing in those days—every major label had at least one bluegrass band on the payroll: Monroe was at Decca; the Stanleys were at Columbia and would soon join Mercury; **Flatt and Scruggs** was at Mercury and would soon join Columbia; the **Lonesome Pine Fiddlers** were at RCA." Nathan's recordings of Jimmy Martin and Bob Osborne in 1951 didn't seem to be sufficient for King, especially since they were together as a band just a couple of months before

Osborne went into the Marines in November 1951. At the King session, Reno featured a finger-picked mandolin in "Let in the Guiding Light." They also recorded "I'm Using My Bible for a Roadmap," "Crazy Finger Blues" and "Maybe You Will Change Your Mind."

The song "I'm Using My Bible for a Road Map" was released in April and did fabulously well. But by the time it was released and achieving great sales, the band had already disbanded because of poor financial conditions. Smiley had gone back to Asheville; Reno had gone back to the grocery store in Buffalo. Reno, John Palmer, Chuck Haney and fiddler Mac Magaha (pron. ma-gay´-hay) worked weekend gigs until June when Arthur Smith offered Reno a good-paying job at WBT (Charlotte) with his **Crackerjacks**, which Reno gladly accepted. Playing banjo and doing comedy, Reno worked with Smith until May 1955. In the meanwhile, Reno and Smiley would continue to record together. Throughout 1952, the Reno and Smiley band was still inactive but King released the other songs recorded in January.

Tommy Faile was with Arthur Smith at that time.[90] The band's comedy act was "Brother Ralph and Chicken Hot Rod" with Ralph Smith (Arthur's brother). Sonny Smith (another brother) played rhythm guitar.

Reno was a good instructor and tried to "show other banjo players just how easy it was. I picked up a fiddle, a guitar, a mandolin, steel, any sound that I heard. I could relate it to a banjo neck. I studied, and I know my neck—the neck on a banjo. You don't know how proud I am to see the new banjo players who have come along and finally come to the conclusion that there is a lot of things that can be done with the banjo, and going ahead and doing it. This is what I tried to start in 1952."[91]

Reno and Smiley recorded their second King session on January 30, 1953. The twelve songs included "Tennessee Breakdown," "He's Coming Back to Earth Again," "Springtime in Dear Old Dixie," "Choking the Strings," "Love Call Waltz" and "I'm the Talk of the Town."[92] On November 8, 1954, **Reno and Smiley** recorded twenty songs for King. Eighteen were written or co-written by Don Reno.[93]

In May of 1955, Don Reno and Arthur "Guitar Boogie" Smith wrote "Feuding Banjos" and recorded it on MGM. It was later to be used in 1972 as the theme for the movie "Deliverance." Reno challenged on the bluegrass banjo and was answered by the tenor banjo of Smith. In the movie, the guitar of Steve Mandell was answered by the banjo of Eric Weissberg. This version was called "Dueling Banjos."

The tremendous success of "I'm Using My Bible For a Roadmap"[94] led to the re-formation of **Reno and**

[90] A smooth singer, he had earlier worked with Snuffy Jenkins and Pappy Sherrill. Reno and Faile started singing together as the Log Cabin Boys.

[91] Trischka and Wernick, op. cit., p. 84.

[92] Since Don and Red were not actively performing together as a band, the musicians included Tommy Faile (bass) and Nelson Benton (drums) who were members of Arthur "Guitar Boogie" Smith's Crackerjacks, along with Red Rector (mandolin) and Jimmy Lunsford (fiddle).

[93] Session musicians included Smiley Hobbs (mandolin), Mack Magaha and Jimmy Lunsford on twin fiddles, and probably John Palmer (bass).

[94] It is often said that King Records was on the verge of bankruptcy when "Roadmap" was released, but that it's fabulous success kept King in business for the next few years.

Smiley and the Tennessee Cut-Ups. People were clamoring to hear and see this group. They re-formed in May 1955 and began working the Old Dominion Barn Dance in Richmond, Virginia, every Saturday night (run by Sun Shine Sue). They taped radio shows every Saturday evening to be played weekdays on 50,000 watt WRVA, and did a live television show every Tuesday on WXEX, Petersburg, Virginia. Other regulars at the Barn Dance were **Flatt and Scruggs** and Mac Wiseman. In July, Benny Williams joined on mandolin. He left in October to work with **Flatt and Scruggs**. Bill Harrell took his place. In November, they hired Carlton Haney to manage them. Haney was recently manager for Bill Monroe and Hack Johnson's **Farm Hands**. On December 24th, they began playing on Connie B. Gay's Town and Country Time in Washington, D.C..[95]

They brought the whole group into the comedy act. Reno was "Chicken Hot Rod". Magaha's mother made Red Smiley a dress and they bought him a wig in New York City when they played the Arthur Godfrey "Talent Scout" television show on CBS on August 15, 1955. They named Smiley "Pansy Hot Rod", Chicken's wife. John Palmer became "Mutt Highpockets" and Magaha was "Jeff Doolytater". The act was called "Chicken and Pansy Hot Rod and the Banty Roosters".

In April of 1956, Reno and Smiley's group returned to Richmond and the Old Dominion Barn Dance. Harrell left because of dwindling band profits and soon formed his **Rocky Mountain Boys**. Reno's son, Ronny, had learned the mandolin by this time and took Harrell's place with the **Tennessee Cut-Ups**.

About that time, **Hack Johnson and the Tennesseans** had a hit record on Colonial Records with Allen Shelton playing "Home Sweet Home" using his Scruggs tuners. King Records' Sydney Nathan wanted his own version and asked Don Reno to do it that night. Reno couldn't find any other musicians to help him on such short notice so he played all of the instruments: fiddle, guitar, banjo, and bass, and sang all the parts, overdubbing like crazy in an all-night session to get the song out.

In 1956, Don Reno wrote "Country Boy Rock And Roll" as a sarcastic parody on rock and roll, for it was taking over their music and they wanted to make fun of it. When Reno recorded the song, it became the first bluegrass recording which featured the flatpicked guitar. **Reno and Smiley** also did parodies on Elvis. With Don Reno's ability to mimic others, it was probably great entertainment on stage.

They worked 342 days in 1956; they put a lot of miles on the cars and drove themselves mercilessly. Smiley's health was failing, especially by November of 1964. But they nevertheless kept a reliable schedule.

About this time, Reno heard Eddie Adcock playing his banjo on the radio. Reno could immediately tell that the instrument needed some work without seeing it or

having met Adcock. But he did make it a point to meet Adcock shortly thereafter and suggested the banjo get a new bridge, new strings and that he play with metal picks instead of plastic. This improved Adcock's playing considerably.

The group worked on Roanoke's WDBJ radio, and on television beginning in December. The "Top O' the Morning" show was the first, weekday, early-morning (6 a.m.) program in the history of television. They commuted back to the Old Dominion Barn Dance until spring of 1957. The television show was so popular that it was lengthened an additional half hour from 6 to 7:30 a.m. The band soon tired of the long commute back to Richmond, quit the Old Dominion Barn Dance, and took over the WDVA Barn Dance in Danville through December 1959. With the addition of "Top O' the Morning," this band now had more television and radio exposure than any group in Nashville. Smiley stayed with the show until about the same time it ended in 1970.

In 1958, the band also had a television show on WSVA, Harrisonburg, Virginia,

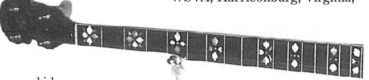

which
lasted seven years. They also played at the Verona Roller Land Skating Rink. The wages earned from these shows were of a subsistence level but kept the band together. Dr. Pepper was their first sponsor, and the soft drink firm continued their support until 1963, using the band to popularize Dr. Pepper and the new Mountain Dew (later distributed by Coca Cola). Dr. Pepper outsold Coca Cola wherever the band played for five years.

Reno and Smiley recorded again for King Records on the 26th and 27th of October 1959. Nathan was known to dislike the sound of the fiddle and mandolin and forced this band, and the **Stanley Brothers**, to record without these instruments. While the Stanleys used Bill Napier and George Shuffler to record leads on guitar (with Ralph on the banjo), Don Reno played lead guitar for his band, Red Smiley played rhythm guitar, John Palmer played bass and Ray Pennington played drums. The songs were "Freight Train Boogie," "East Bound Freight Train," "I'm Blue, I'm Lonesome" and "He Will Set Your Fields on Fire." King later released "Love Please Come Home"/"Under the Double Eagle." "Love Please Come Home" hit the country charts at #29 on the *Billboard* list.

On January first, 1960, Steve Chapman joined them full-time on electric guitar and added a different sound the group—a sound that King Records thought preferable. Don recalled that "Steve played electric guitar with the best taste I ever heard. He made it fit in with

A
m
e
r
i
c
a
s

M
u
s
i
c

|

B
l
u
e
g
r
a
s
s

95 They were still living in Richmond and commuted to this D.C. job. Also on the bill was Jimmy Dean and the Texas Wildcats.

our music and really added a good sound to the **Tennessee Cut-Ups.**" In January, **Reno and Smiley and the Tennessee Cut-Ups** replaced Buddy Starcher's band at WSVA every Saturday night. With all the commuting they were doing, they were barely able to make it back for their show in Roanoke every day.

Don Reno and John Palmer opened an automobile business in Roanoke in 1961. As of 1975, Palmer was still with the business and played with the **Shenandoah Cut-Ups.** While **Reno and Smiley** was on a tour in California in October, **Bill Monroe and the Blue Grass Boys** took their place at their regular television show at WDBJ in Roanoke.

By 1964, regular members of **Reno and Smiley and the Tennessee Cut-Ups** were Magaha (fiddle), Palmer (bass), Ronnie Reno (mandolin), Steve Chapman (guitar) and Sid Campbell (guitar, not a full-time member). Magaha left in October to join Porter Wagoner's band in Nashville.

Don Reno and Red Smiley split in 1964.[96] Smiley formed his own **Bluegrass Cut-Ups.** Carlton Haney stayed in Roanoke for awhile. He was now probably the biggest promoter of country and bluegrass shows that ever was. Don, Betty, Dale and Don Wayne Reno moved to Bedford, Virginia, November 17, 1964. He thought about quitting music, but two weeks later he got Chuck Haney (guitar), Sid Campbell (guitar), Duck Austin (bass), Ray Crisp (fiddle) and Ronnie Reno (mandolin) to regroup as **Don Reno and the Tennessee Cut-Ups.** They recorded "Mr. Five String" on Dot on January 18, 1965, with Jimmy Buchanan on fiddle. The **Cut-Ups** toured the United States until September 1, 1965, when Haney and Crisp left. Don then teamed up with fiddler Benny Martin; together they went to "the big city".

On November 17th, 1965, Reno signed with Pamper Music in Nashville as a writer. "I wanted to get out and do some traveling" said Reno. "I'd get tired of the television studio atmosphere every day. I just wanted to keep on making a living playing music."[97] Reno turned his songs over to Pamper to be published, hoping that his writing skills would be amply rewarded. "This is where your money is," he said. "I'd done what I said I'd do, but they hadn't held up their end so, as Benny Martin would say, I bailed out right fast. In the meantime, I'd gotten around to some new fans that I hadn't had before."[98]

In Nashville, Reno found that the C & W people operated differently than bluegrass people. "I didn't know, when I went to Nashville, that they operated as differently as they did. They hadn't before, but there'd been such a change in Nashville from the time I'd lived there before to the time I went back. I went downtown twice while I was in Nashville that time and said to heck with it, and got out as fast as I could."[99]

September of 1965 brought Carlton Haney's first festival. Reno and Harrell's group was there, as was Red Smiley's group.

During this approximate period, Red Smiley recorded LPs on his own Rimrock and Rural Rhythm labels with his own **Bluegrass Cut-Ups.** He later came back to do some recording with the Reno and Bill Harrell's version of the **Tennessee Cut-Ups** on the Wango label. Smiley later re-joined Reno and they recorded "Together Again" on the Rome label.

About that time, the "bluegrass depression" made things difficult for the musicians of this music. Sid Campbell returned to Ohio to teach school; Duck Austin went back to South Carolina. Reno worked with Betty and Ronnie in Nashville until December 1965 to fulfill some dates. The Reno family moved to Nashville and were there until December 21, 1966.

In the fall of 1965, Don Reno and Benny Martin recorded songs later to be picked up by Hal Smith's Monument label. The songs were "Soldier's Prayer in

[96] Whether the ill health of Smiley was a factor of the split is a point of controversy. Smiley's health was, indeed, failing but, according to Bill Harrell who soon joined Reno's Cut-Ups, Smiley's health was not really a factor in the split. This is verified by the fact that Smiley started his own Bluegrass Cut-Ups in Roanoke which lasted until 1969 when his health truly *did* cause his retirement. The Bluegrass Cut-Ups continued with the Top O' the Morning television show which he and Reno had for so many years.

Carlton Haney explained that Reno was tired of the music business at this time. He was making ends meet but little else. He sought other ways of making a living in the music. He and John Palmer bought about twenty used cars with the intention of fixing them up and profiting from their sales. They hired mechanics and spent money in order to make the business go, but the market wasn't there at that time.

His next step in trying to make more money was to quit his own band and go to Nashville to peddle his songs as a writer. But by 1966, he was back in the performing business full-time.

[97] Ibid., February, 1974.

[98] Vernon, *Muleskinner News*, February, 1974, p. 8.

[99] Don Reno, from an interview by Bill Vernon, "The Don Reno Story, Part Five: Don Reno Today," *Muleskinner News*, February, 1974, p. 8.

Vietnam," "Five By Eight" and "You Can't Make a Heel Toe the Mark." Another band members was Ronnie Reno, with pickup musicians Jackie Phelps, Steve Chapman and Junior Huskey. He and Martin also recorded an album on Alec Campbell's Cabin Creek label with Sid Campbell, Duck Austin and Ronnie Reno. Reno spoke of his split with Benny Martin, "Benny had been used to working by himself. He liked to work too many clubs to suit me...he'd started working the joints [as a C & W musician] where he used electrification, and I didn't go for that too much. So I figured we could do just as well separated as we could together. So, that winter (January 1966) I went to Richmond to WEET and turned all-country."[100]

Reno was in several bands in 1966 until he joined Bill Harrell in the Washington, D.C., area. The band's members included Ronnie Reno (mandolin), George Shuffler (bass) and Buck Ryan (fiddle).

Reno and Harrell partnered December 8, 1966, and they all moved to Riverdale, Maryland, on December 22, 1966, where the Reno family took roots. Reno and Harrell stayed together until 1976. "I'd known Bill (Harrell) since he worked with Red and me in 1955, and I could see that he would make a fine singer and rhythm guitar player. I knew him on down through the years and I knew him to be one of the finest guys I'd ever known. And I figured there couldn't be anybody I could pick that would do a better job taking Red's place with me than Bill, and I was certainly right."

They began recording immediately; Reno and Harrell's **Tennessee Cut-Ups** recorded on the King label in 1968, and recorded three albums for them. They began a weekly television show the next year. The duo were doing quite well financially. Reno wrote most of the material; as of December 1973, he had written 417 songs.

Reno and Harrell recorded on television shows such as "Top O' the Morning" on WDBJ in Roanoke. To conform to the television station's country sound, they hired Don West (steel guitar) and Herby Jones (drums). Reno hated the sound which "changed my band around to where nobody could recognize it."[101] When he played drums and steels in the clubs, "I took them everywhere I went. That's what I was selling on television and I figured that's what I had to sell everywhere else. But it hurt me more than it helped me. My general state of mind was I was either going back to what I'd been playing or I'd quit for good; one of the two. That's why I minced no words when I told them to take the TV show and go with it. That was 1968. We cut four albums for King. I wrote a lot of the material and picked all of it."[102]

In June of 1968, Ronnie went with the **Osborne Brothers.** World Fiddling Championship winner Buck Ryan then took Ronnie's place in the **Cut-Ups.** According to Don, Ryan (who worked with Don until Ryan's death January 7, 1981) is "one of the greatest fiddlers I've ever worked with." In July, they started a television show on WTTG in Washington, D.C.. They hired Jerry McCoury to play bass and put George Shuffler on flattop guitar. Shuffler left January 10, 1969. They hired Del McCoury to replace him. Del stayed about six months then left to form his own **Dixie Pals.** The others with whom they worked were not steady.

Red Smiley retired in 1969. Reno remembered in his biography, "Red's contract had run out at 'Top O' the Morning' TV show in Roanoke and he retired. He went down to his country home and he fished awhile, and when he got tired of that, I knew he wanted to play so I told him he was welcome to work with Bill and me whenever he wanted; I think he worked every date with us from then on, until he died."[103]

Red went back with Don about the spring of 1969, at Warrenton, Virginia. Reno and Harrell were doing well together—about the same as when Reno and Smiley split. Harrcll welcomed Red's return "and let Red have his front seat back again and insisted on doing this. Some people might have thought bad about it, or felt like they were being slid to the back, but Bill was man enough to step back and say, 'Get up there, Smiley, where you belong!' And for this, I will respect Bill Harrell for the rest of my life."[104]

The group's name became **Don Reno, Red Smiley, Bill Harrell and the Tennessee Cut-Ups.** These were the happiest of times for the trio of Reno, Smiley and Harrell. In April 1969, Smiley's old band members continued on by themselves as the **Shenandoah Cut-Ups;** a combination of Jim Eanes' old group (the **Shenandoah Valley Boys)** and the **Bluegrass Cut-Ups** of Red Smiley.

When Red joined Don and Bill, he was taking insulin regularly to maintain his health. They continued working the road jobs heavily. When the audience saw the three of them together, they were able to see how well Don and Bill worked together and it gave them comfort that Bill was an adequate replacement for Red, and that Red and Don had split amicably earlier.

On January 2, 1972, Red Smiley died after a long illness. Don related, "Red's passing away left the **Tennessee Cut-Ups** broken-hearted. We didn't pick our instruments up for six weeks. Red left a vacant place that will never be filled by anyone."[105]

[100] Vernon, Ibid., p. 9. His job at WEET was as manager and DJ.

[101] Ibid., p. 10.

[102] Ibid., p. 10.

[103] Ibid., p. 10.

[104] Ibid., p. 10.

[105] Don Reno, op. cit.

Soon the **Tennessee Cut-Ups**[106], recording in live performances, were Reno, Harrell, Buck Ryan (fiddle), Raymond W. McLain (mandolin) and John Palmer (bass). The recordings were released on Viechi Records.

In November, Doug Tuchman was hired to be the band's manager. Tuchman ran the Blue Grass Club in New York City and edited *Pickin'* magazine. He was their manager until April 1974.

A month later, on December 6th, **Don Reno, Bill Harrell and the Tennessee Cut-Ups** were the first American country music band to perform at the United Nations headquarters in New York City. They also played for the presidential inauguration of Richard Nixon in 1973.

In December 1974, members of the band were Reno (banjo, guitar), Harrell (guitar), Buck Ryan (fiddle) and Ed Ferris (bass). In 1976, Don bought a home in Lynchburg, Virginia, and moved there. In 1977, Harrell was seriously injured in an automobile accident and was replaced by Bonny Beverly on guitar in Reno's band. Harrell came back as soon as he could, performing on crutches, but he would never fully recover from the accident.[107] By the time he did begin performing with Reno again, they lived so far apart that Reno felt it would be best if they dissolved their partnership in April 1977. Reno continued with his own **Tennessee Cut-Ups**[108] and Harrell formed his own **Bill Harrell and the Virginians**, a name he used in 1964 before he joined the **Cut-Ups**. He recorded on the Rebel and Leather labels.

The 1977 Carter Stanley Memorial Award went to Don Reno and Red Smiley on Memorial Day weekend. Reno accepted on behalf of his deceased partner. That July, Reno became a member of *Frets* magazine advisory board.

When Don Reno held a banjo contest in April of 1979, he required more of his contestants than most other organizers. According to the April 1979 issue of *Bluegrass Unlimited* magazine, "He required that each contestant mail him a list of ten tunes. From those ten numbers he returned his selection to the contestant of the three that he would play in competition. None of the banjo-hopefuls would repeat a tune that one of his colleagues had played! The purpose of all this hard work (most places I know of have computers for this kind of scheduling) was two-fold: a) a fairness to the contestant, and b) sheer delight for the audience."

As of 1980, Don Reno had written 457 songs to the best of his knowledge. A prolific songwriter, Reno would sometimes write as many as fifteen songs at one time. They included "Choking the Strings," "Dixie Breakdown," "I'm Using My Bible for a Roadmap" "I

Know You're Married But I Love You Still" (1955, recorded the next year by **Reno and Smiley**).

In 1983, *Reader's Digest* produced a twin-banjo album featuring the banjos of Don Reno and Bobby Thompson.

On October 16, 1984, Don Reno died after an extended illness of sugar diabetes. Evidently, medical tests went awry, poisoning his system. He was unable to recover. He had suffered from chronic bronchitis the last couple of years. He had recorded sixty albums and five hundred songs. He kept a reliable schedule through his illness. Don Reno's wife, Betty, was still working in a textile mill as of 1991. Though Don had made good money through the years, he wasn't able to hold on to it.

Charlie Monroe

Charlie Monroe and the Kentucky Pardners

Much of the early Monroe brothers' biography is in the chapter on Bill Monroe so this biography will skip much of their early time as the **Monroe Brothers**.

Charlie Monroe was born in Rosine, Kentucky, the sixth of eight children, on July 4, 1903. He was two years younger than Birch, but eight years older than Bill. At age eleven, Charlie took up the guitar. Birch played the fiddle and younger sister Bertha, the guitar. Bill was only three.

Around 1936, the **Monroe Brothers**, Charlie and Bill, moved from Omaha to the Carolinas. Beginning in February, and for the next couple of years, they recorded sixty sides on RCA's Bluebird Records. Half their repertoire was gospel. In their duo act, Bill switched instruments to the fiddle and Charlie to the banjo as a comedy skit. It didn't go over well so they ceased it. They played on WIS (Columbia), WBT (Char-

[106] Jerry McCoury left the Cut-Ups March 18, 1972, to join Del McCoury and His Dixie Pals. Ellis Padgett took Jerry's place until he died May 9, 1973. Ed Ferris took Padgett's place and played bass the next several years.

[107] He had to get his hips replaced with metal ones in 1994.

[108] Dale was on mandolin, Don Wayne was on bass fiddle and banjo, Mr. Beverly was on fiddle and guitar, and Steve Wilson was on guitar and Dobro.

lotte), WFBC (Greenville) and WPTF (Raleigh). They switched sponsors from the Texas Crystals Company to Hubert Fincher's Crazy Water Crystals. Charlie Monroe married Elizabeth "Betty" Miller who later became their booking manager. Betty died of cancer in 1966. He remarried in 1969.

"Back in those days, we both were just so hot-headed and mean as snakes,"[109] said Charlie. They sometimes fought physically, as siblings often do, and they knew their partnership had to end. Bill and Charlie split up the **Monroe Brothers** in 1938. Bill went to Little Rock, Arkansas, where he formed the **Kentuckians**. Charlie worked on WNOX, Knoxville, Tennessee, as the **Monroe Boys** with Lefty Frizzell (not the famous country star, mandolin) and was later replaced by Zeke Morris. Bill Calhoun (guitar, mandolin) was also a member. The trio worked on WDBJ for a year, continuing to record for Bluebird.

On July 2, 1939, Charlie Monroe formed **Charlie Monroe and the Kentucky Pardners** in Knoxville. After several months of offers, Curly Seckler finally accepted the job with Charlie Monroe's band as a full-time touring musician on mandolin and tenor banjo. Curly really didn't want to leave his brothers in the **Yodeling Rangers**, or his home, but the offer of $20 a week was too good. He joined the new full-sized band and they went immediately to WWVA, Wheeling, West Virginia, calling themselves the **Kentucky Pardners**, a.k.a. **Kentucky Partners**[110]. The performances featured a wide variety of talent and were *very* entertaining.

Shortly thereafter, Bill Monroe began playing on 50,000 watt WSM on the Opry. Not to be out-done by his brother, Charlie Monroe found WHAS, another 50,000 watt station in Louisville, Kentucky, and played on this station beginning in 1940. They played on the Renfro Valley Barn Dance, and in March began his legendary tent shows in Almo, Georgia. They made excellent money, charging $1 for the 2000 person capacity crowds. When the summer ended, so did the tent shows. They moved to WBIG, Greensboro, North Carolina, staying there for twelve years. During the 1940s, Charlie Monroe manufactured Man-O-Ree, a laxative, and the company acted as their sponsor. He sold the product every chance he got and played on his Noonday Jamboree on WSJS, Winston-Salem, North Carolina.[111]

In 1946, **Charlie Monroe and the Kentucky Pardners** began recording for RCA Victor—44 sides through 1951. On WNOX's Mid-Day Merry-Go-Round they took the place of **Johnny and Jack** who left to join the Opry. They also played regularly on WBOK, Birmingham, Alabama. During the next five years, Monroe recorded extensively with many well-known bluegrass stars such as Ira Louvin, Stringbean, Curly Seckler, and Red Rector (who joined the band in 1947). In 1950, Charlie Monroe's single "Good Morning to You"/"Cold Gray Tomb of Stone" was released on RCA Victor. He was backed by one of the most popular groups in Nashville, Hank Williams' **Drifting Cowboys**.

Charlie Monroe recorded four tunes on his first session with Decca in Nashville on January 20th, 1952.[112] In March of 1957, Charlie retired from music to his farm, supplementing his farm income with his coal mine. He came out of retirement in 1962, and also in 1964, to record on Bob Mooney's Rem label, Lexington, Kentucky.[113]

 "Back in those days, we both were just so hot-headed and mean as snakes."
—*Charlie Monroe*

In 1972, Jimmy Martin asked Charlie to come out of retirement for guest appearances at two festivals. He enjoyed it so much he continued to work with Martin's **Sunny Mountain Boys** for a while. He came fully out of retirement in 1974 and worked with the **Dominion Bluegrass Boys** and with previous members of his **Kentucky Pardners**. Gusto released "Tally Ho!" in 1975. No musicians were listed on the cover. Just before Charlie died, his **Kentucky Pardners** recorded on Pine Tree Records.[114] July 26, 1975, was the first Charlie Monroe Day in Ohio County. A reception was held in his home of Rosine.

On September 27, 1975, Charlie Monroe died in Reidsville, North Carolina. He had suffered from throat cancer for some years and the cancer was probably a cause of his death. He now lies in the family plot near Jerusalem Ridge in Rosine. He was 72.

---

[109] "The Music of Bill Monroe from 1936 to 1994" compact disc album and biographical history of the Monroe brothers and of Bill Monroe's music.

[110] Members were Charlie (guitar), Dale Cole (fiddle), Tommy Edwards (mandolin), "Rambling" Tommy Scott (guitar, who wrote their theme song) and Curly Seckler (tenor banjo, mandolin).

[111] The band also appeared at the Tennessee Barn Dance on WNOX about 1941.

[112] Band members included himself on guitar, Joe Medford (banjo, electric lead guitar), Sonny Miller (fiddle), Rocky Harper (bass) and Ted Mullins (mandolin). The recording session included Bob Foster (steel guitar), Grady Martin (lead electric guitar), Jerry Rivers (fiddle) and Ernie Newton (bass) on "Find 'Em, Fool 'Em and Leave 'Em Alone"/"Those Triflin' Women." By 1953, members of the Kentucky Pardners were Charlie Monroe (guitar), Ted Mullins (mandolin), Buddy Osborne (lap steel guitar), Slim Martin (fiddle), Joe Medford (banjo) and Wilma Martin (bass).

[113] With J.D. Crowe (banjo), Paul "Moon" Mullins (fiddle) and B. Lucas (fiddle).

[114] With musicians Monroe (guitar), Jimmy "Slim" Martin (harmonica, fiddle), Birch Monroe (fiddle), Grady Bullins (guitar), Audene Lineberg (guitar), Roy McMillan (mandolin) and Wilma Martin (bass).

Charlie Cline, Curly Ray Cline, Ezra Cline and the Lonesome Pine Fiddlers

Ezra Cline was born in 1907, in Baisden, West Virginia. Ned was also born in Baisden in 1920 or 1921, "Curly" Ray Cline was born there in 1922, and Charlie Cline was born there June 6, 1931. Ray and Charlie Cline were raised near Baisden by their father who was a good old-time fiddler. At their farm, they raised everything they ate, just like his grandfather of German ancestry who had died in Baisden at 105 years old. The only thing they had to buy was coffee.

Baisden was coal mining country. One day, when Ray and Charlie were loading coal, the whole mountain started to cave in. This was Charlie's impetus to get away from that job and pursue a safer occupation, such as country music, which was actually what he wanted to do in the first place. His early influences were Fiddlin' Arthur Smith, Howdy Forrester and Clayton McMichen. Brother Ned, a multi-instrumentalist, was Charlie's hero. Curly Ray only played fiddle. Curly Ray and Ezra worked in the coal mines of Bluefield, Virginia. Charlie Cline chose to eke out a living in music, and only spent two years in the mines.

The **Lonesome Pine Fiddlers**[115] was formed in 1937 by brothers Ned and Ray Cline, their cousin Ezra Cline, Cecil Surratt, and their friend Gordon Jennings.[116] Ned played the tenor banjo and other instruments very well.[117] Ezra and Curly Ray continued until 1959, at which time they retired. Charlie Cline, a multi-instrumentalist, joined the band in 1945. When Fiddlin' Arthur Smith worked with the band during 1938 and 1939, Curly Ray was influenced by his fiddling style.

In 1939, Cline brothers, Curly Ray (fiddle) and Ned (banjo), with their brother-in-law Ezra, also known as "Cousin Ezra", whose use of the bass fiddle was one of the few in use at the time. They were hired by Gordon Jennings whose group was sponsored by Bi-tone, supposedly a medicinal water additive. Jennings played guitar and sang with the group on WHIS, Bluefield, West Virginia. Often they had to perform other manual, labor-type jobs before they could afford the gas to get to their gigs; Bi-tone didn't pay much. If the group wanted to eat they brought food from home, borrowing electricity to cook.

The **Fiddlers** returned to WHIS full-time in 1945 with Black Draught as a sponsor, among others. The sound was not bluegrass yet. Fourteen year-old Charlie Cline joined the band this year; he played guitar and banjo. Bob "Bobby" Osborne, who later worked with Charlie Cline, remembered, "He played any [instrument] that he picked up, and played it well. I've always admired Charlie Cline for being able to do that right there. He's not the greatest on anything, but he plays anything that he picks up good enough to get by in any group. He can fit in anywhere, singing parts the same way."[118]

After the war, the **Lonesome Pine Fiddlers** joined with another Bluefield, West Virginia, band, **Rex and Eleanor** (Parker) **and the Merrymakers**, to become **Rex and Eleanor and the Lonesome Pine Fiddlers**. This gig is what Charlie Cline considered to be the brothers' first professional job. They played on WHIS five times a day, fifteen minutes at a time; it was exhausting. They arose at 5 a.m. most mornings. They were sponsored by any local company they could find. This was about the same time other bluegrass-type

The Warrior Boys with Charlie Cline, c. 1986

---

[115] The group took its name from a road that was known as "The Trail of the Lonesome Pine" near Williamson, West Virginia, and because their father and grandfather were fiddlers. They played the music of the brother-acts of the day.

[116] Jennings left the group in 1941 and continued in the business later with his own group.

[117] The band split for a short while during W.W.II when Ned joined the service. He was killed in W.W.II at the Normandy invasion.

[118] 1991 interview.

bands were coming to WHIS. Besides WHIS, they also played on WBTH in Williamson, West Virginia; they drove to this performance every afternoon for a year. Charlie and Ezra Cline quit **Rex and Eleanor** in 1949, joining Bobby Osborne and Larry Richardson and Ezra Cline's re-formed **Lonesome Pine Fiddlers**. Curly Ray stayed with Rex and Eleanor Parker and worked the coal mines of Keystone, West Virginia, awhile, playing only weekends.

Back in those days, the number of professional three-finger banjo pickers could almost be counted on one hand. They included Charlie Cline, Larry Richardson, Joe Medford, Earl Scruggs, Snuffy Jenkins, Hoke Jenkins, Don Reno and Johnnie Whisnant. There were few others. With the **Fiddlers**, Charlie Cline recorded two banjo tunes on RCA: "Lonesome Pine Breakdown" and "Five-string Rag."

In November 1949, band members of the **L-P-F** were Ray Morgan (fiddle), Ezra Cline (bass), Larry Richardson (banjo) and Bob Osborne (guitar). These last two musicians significantly increased the popularity of the band by influencing the band to be similar to the sound of the **Blue Grass Boys** which was dominating the country music world. Now that Richardson was with them, they had a bluegrass band. This was not necessarily true at WHIS in 1946. Charlie Cline, in 1990, elaborated on the status of bluegrass—then known as "hillbilly"—music during this period, "People don't believe this or don't understand. To get on a record company back then we had to change our style to bluegrass. It was hot! Anywhere you went on the jukebox, there was the **Stanley Brothers**, **Lonesome Pine Fiddlers**, Bill Monroe, Mac Wiseman. We did twenty-seven numbers for RCA."

In early 1950, the **L-P-F** began a stint at WHIS, Bluefield, West Virginia. In 1951, Osborne and Richardson wrote "Pain in My Heart" which they recorded on the Cozy label. Richardson joined Bill Monroe for a short time, then re-joined the **L-P-F** with Osborne, Charlie and Ezra Cline. Charlie was to work for Monroe on and off for the next five years. He helped Monroe record "On and On," "White House Blues" and "New John Henry Blues." But probably more significant was the event of the first triple fiddling with the **Blue Grass Boys**. The 1954 sessions included Charlie Cline, Merle "Red" Taylor and Gordon Terry on fiddles on "Blue Moon of Kentucky," "Little Georgia Rose" and "Close By."

On June 3, 1951, Richardson left the **L-P-F** and joined the **Sauceman Brothers and the Greene Valley Boys** at WCYB, Bristol, Tennessee. Charlie Cline took his place on banjo and replaced him on the duets with Bob Osborne. They then got a King Records recording contract, which then led to a job at WCYB.

Charlie Cline telling the "story" of bluegrass music with Carlton Haney at Haney's 1995 festival in Watermelon Park, Berryville, VA.

Jimmy Martin soon joined the **L-P-F**. Ezra paid Martin $8 per night plus room and board. They worked together until he formed his own **Sunny Mountain Boys** in August with Charlie Cline and Little Robert van Winkle. Charlie proudly announced to this writer that "I'm one of the first **Sunny Mountain Boys** ever they was. I was the first. Bob and Jimmy got a contract with King and did six numbers. Curly, me, Bob and Little Robert, we did six numbers and went to WCYB on the Farm Hour. We worked schools, theaters, parks and stuff like that there. But when Jimmy and Bob broke up there (October 1951), me and Bob Osborne went with the **Stanley Brothers** in Lexington. This was during the Korean conflict. Bob Osborne worked with Carter and Ralph and me until he had to go into the Marines (November 1951). I stayed with the Stanleys— me, Curly Seckler (who sang tenor to Carter Stanley), George Shuffler and Carter and Ralph went to Lexington, Kentucky, after Bob went into the service. And we went on Versailles, Kentucky, radio every morning at nine o'clock. We played tobacco warehouses, radio shows and I stayed with them—probably less than a year. I was in and out of this band—with the **Fiddlers**, too. Curly [Seckler], he didn't stay with them long after I left. That's when Ralph got to singing tenor with Carter (Pee Wee Lambert had just left in the fall of 1951). Before that, Ralph used to not singin' anything but 'Man of Constant Sorrow' and 'Pretty Polly' and stuff like that. Carter used to try to get Ralph to sing tenor but Ralph never really thought he could do it. I always thought he was pretty good at it, though."

Ezra and Curly Ray Cline had to fill the vacancies of Martin and Osborne and Charlie Cline so they hired Paul Williams (whose real name was actually Paul Humphrey) and Jimmy Williams who were billed together as the **Williams Brothers**. Paul Williams would later join Jimmy Martin's band. The **L-P-F** worked several stations with several personnel changes through the next few years with the band members who included Melvin and Ray Goins, Joe Meadows, James Carson, Udell McPeak and Billy Edwards.

Charlie Cline joined Lee Warren's country band, the **Versatile Westerners**, in 1957. He married Lee in 1958. Both of them then joined the **L-P-F** and she became the first woman with the band. Ezra and Curly Ray semi-retired the band in 1960; Charlie went back with Monroe again. The **L-P-F** continued to perform and record part-time with members Curly Ray, Ezra, Melvin and Ray Goins.

In 1966, Curly Ray Cline left his semi-retirement from music[119] to join the **Stanley Brothers and the Clinch Mountain Boys**. The **Fiddlers** broke up. Curly Ray only did one show with the Stanleys before Carter died. Soon he and Ralph picked up the pieces and founded **Ralph Stanley and the Clinch Mountain Boys**. They were on the road again by December 18th, with members Melvin Goins, Curly Ray Cline, Ralph Stanley and George Shuffler. Larry Sparks was to join soon.

Curly Ray remembered that "Ralph sure had a heavy load to carry. He had a hard time making his mind up whether to go on or not. Ralph had always left all the talking and everything up to Carter and it was like cutting his right arm off, but he finally just picked up and went on and always keeping the old sound, but improving on it as he went along."[120]

Ralph helped Curly Ray finance his first solo record ("Boar Hog" on the Old Homestead label, 1980) by promising to purchase those which didn't sell. The unsold quantity was nil.

After sixteen years of "doing the Lord's work" (Pentecostal), Charlie re-organized **Charlie Cline and the Lonesome Pine Fiddlers** in 1975 with wife Lee Cline, Chuck Carpenter and Derek Sparkman.

Chubby Wise and Charlie Cline rehearse for a performance at Carlton Haney's 1995 festival.

In 1980, Charlie Cline went to work for Jimmy Martin's **Sunny Mountain Boys**, staying until 1986. Where the average duration for a band member in a new band is one and a half years, Charlie is the exception and tended to stay at least five years wherever he would go. His brother, Curly Ray was going on 29 years with Ralph Stanley's band in 1994. He retired in the mid-1990s.

In 1986, Charlie Cline joined the **Warrior River Boys**,[121] a traditional-style bluegrass band. One of Cline's main jobs with the band was to teach them the "high, lonesome sound". They were eager to follow his tutelage, learning to play traditional bluegrass music from a man who, recently having been elected into the Bluegrass Hall of Fame, certainly had the credentials to teach these kids how it was done in the old days. "I wouldn't say I taught 'em," he said. "They just sort of caught on to it." Cline mostly played fiddle. The band, at that time, worked more than any band in bluegrass.

Cline said that in 1992, he was doing better, financially, than he had done in the first forty years of his career. During that time, the band leaders seemed to do the best. This referred to Monroe, Jimmy Martin and Mac Wiseman among others. Now, sidemen (non-bandleaders) in a bluegrass-style band were doing okay. "Back then," he recalled, "bluegrass was played more on the radio than country was,"[122] referring to the more traditional style of country music (hillbilly)—not the country music which artists such as Webb Pierce, Marty Robbins and Hank Williams played. Country and western artists such as these dominated the radio play list and record sales at that time.

Cline re-formed the **Lonesome Pine Fiddlers** in 1992.[123] As of 1996, Charlie and his wife were preachers for the Pentecostal Holiness church in Arley, Alabama.

[119] He was playing part-time with Ezra's Lonesome Pine Fiddlers and also worked part-time in a coal mine.

[120] Janice Brown McDonald, *Bluegrass Unlimited*, September, 1988, p. 25.

[121] Other members of the band were Larry Wallace (banjo), Mitch Scott (guitar), Stan Wilemon (bass) and David Davis (mandolin, nephew of Cleo Davis who was the first Blue Grass Boy). Scott and Davis were partners in the band. Gary Waldrep was on banjo during this period, too.

[122] 1989 interview in Kissimmee, Florida.

[123] Members included himself (fiddle, guitar), Chuck Carpenter (banjo, guitar, fiddle), Bill Sandlin (guitar) and Jarrod Rains (bass).

Jim Eanes and the Shenandoah Valley Boys

This bluegrass and country musician was a veteran of this music from 1939 until his death in 1995. In an environment which sought each musician be a little different than the next, Jim Eanes' smooth, mature voice definitely set him apart from many of the voices that characterize bluegrass music. Eanes told this writer, "When I first started in '39, I was singin' a lot of the big stars' songs, see. And I felt like I had to get my own identity. At that time, it was called 'hillbilly'—there wasn't any 'country' or 'bluegrass' or anything. So I'm still a hillbilly. If you're gonna entertain the fans, you got to do somethin' a little extraordinary and I didn't want to go around copying everybody. That's something that doesn't help you at all."[124] Eanes also entered comedy songs into his repertoire which further separated his identity from the others.

Homer Robert Eanes Jr. was born in Mountain Valley, in the Piedmont[125] section of southern Virginia, December 6, 1923. His father played the five-string banjo in the three-finger style, "but he didn't have the fancy finger work. He tuned it in the old time (C tuning) way.[126] Young Eanes taught himself to play the guitar. His first guitar was a Stella that he bought with the proceeds from selling Cloverine salve. He sang the popular songs of the day: those of the **Shelton Brothers**, Gid Tanner, Bob Wills, Gene Autry and Jimmie Rodgers. In the late '30s, he listened to WPTF, Raleigh, North Carolina, which featured **J.E. Mainer's Mountaineers**, Wade Mainer's **Sons of the Mountaineers** and his **Smiling Rangers**, the **Briarhoppers** and Clyde Moody.

Eanes began his professional career in 1939 as a member of **Roy Hall's Blue Ridge Entertainers.** He used a thumbpick and fingerpick to be able to extract the most volume on the guitar.[127] When Roy Hall was killed March 13, 1941, the band dissolved. Eanes then moved to Galax, Virginia, and then to Knoxville, Tennessee. There in Knoxville, he joined the Tennessee Barn Dance and Mid-Day Merry-Go-Round on WNOX.[128] Eanes and his father then worked as performers at shows and dances with his father's band from 1943 until 1946.

Jim Eanes and Joe Johnson founded **Jim and Joe and the Blue Mountain Boys** that worked on WBOB and also WNOX's Tennessee Barn Dance.[129] During that time, Eanes' group recorded for the National Record Company. Eanes stayed with the **Blue Mountain Boys** until late 1947. He won a talent contest and got to record two sides backed by Pappy Sherrill and Snuffy Jenkins.

In January of 1948, Jim Eanes joined Lester Flatt and Earl Scruggs who had recently left Bill Monroe's band. They played on WDVA, Danville, Virginia. "Lester and Earl called me and wanted me to join forces with them. Lester and Earl and Cedric had all left Bill [Monroe] at that time and formed the **Foggy Mountain Boys.** And he called me and wanted me to be a part of the group and we started working together."[130]

Eanes spoke of Bill Monroe, Lester and Earl, "Earl Scruggs—I think he learned a lot from Snuffy Jenkins, you know bein' down from that area there. He was a young man and he was tryin' to emphasize his type of music. He was just so far ahead of everybody else... 'cause Flatt, he'd worked with Charlie [Monroe] and everything. And workin' with Monroe I think they picked up a lot of pointers. In fact, I think [Bill] Monroe

---

124 From a 7/24/94 telephone interview.

125 This valley also spawned the talents of Jim and Jesse McReynolds, Ralph and Carter Stanley, Don Reno, Red Smiley, Bob and Sonny Osborne, Kenny Baker and Doc Watson.

126 From the album notes written by Jack Tottle for Rounder's "Jim Eanes and the Shenandoah Valley Boys—The Early Days of Bluegrass—Vol. 4."

127 Others who used this configuration were Clyde Moody, Lester Flatt, Carl Story, Charlie Moore, Bob Osborne and Carter Stanley. Hank Anglin, the banjoist of Roy Hall's group, used the three-finger style of banjo picking...he was one of the few—Snuffy Jenkins was just becoming noted for popularizing this style of picking. According to Eanes, Anglin learned the style from Jenkins. Jenkins' style was definitely a big thing in that part of the country—a lot of banjoists were following this style which put rolls together in a fluid form. Of course, Reno and Scruggs became the most well-known of the lot. Even Eanes' father played the three-finger style, but because it was "pre-Jenkins," it was not at all refined. Eanes described his father's style as the three-finger style, but in a low key. What he did was the roll of the three-finger and it enhanced the instrumentals. "A lot of banjo pickers picked up that style from Snuffy," he told this writer.

128 Both of these Saturday-night shows on WNOX were hosted and managed by emcee Lowell Blanchard. The Mid-Day Merry-Go Round was sponsored by Cas Walker and his chain of grocery stores.

129 Also appearing at the Dance were the groups of Carl Story, Archie Campbell, Molly O'Day and Lynn Davis, the Carlisle Brothers (Cliff and Bill) and Charlie Monroe's Kentucky Pardners.

130 Interview, Owensboro, Kentucky, 1991.

had the best group there was durin' that segment. Clyde [Moody] was with him before. And then Flatt came in from Charlie and then they had Earl and Cedric. They just gelled. Monroe—he still wanted his type of music. He still does today! I got to admire the man!"[131]

"Then Bill [Monroe] sent me a telegram. And like every young musician, I had always wanted to sing on the Grand Ole Opry and I had never been there. So I left that group (in February) and went with Bill."[132]

"Monroe," he continued, "was ahead of his time; Monroe had that high stuff. Like me, he wanted to get something different than anybody else, see. And he had his own style of singin' this high stuff—which was eventually called 'bluegrass.' When I went to work with him, I had a hard time because I was tryin' to lead with Monroe singin' in B and B-flat. That was his two favorite keys. That complicated things for me because I had been singin' those ballad-type songs. But I made it. I got through about nine months of it—that was enough!" So he quit after nine months to manage a record shop in Martinsville, Virginia. "I tried [to make my voice fit with Monroe's]. I really tried hard. And I enjoyed it. It was great experience for me. I would say that the best two guys that gave me more experience in this music business was Roy Hall, my first professional job in 1939 and, of course, Bill Monroe, too.

"I was young, you know. I was twenty-five. But hell, you don't know everything. You don't learn everything in this music business—it takes a lifetime! I'm *still* learning. You never quit learning 'cause the music changes so much." Eanes nevertheless tends to stay with the style he knows best. "I'm stayin' pretty close to my type of stuff. I've had people tell me that if I wanted to make a lot of money, I should change my style. Hell, I've worked on this thing all my life and money doesn't mean everything, you know. At least if I record something and I feel it and I play it and they play it on the radio, they know it's me—I ain't copyin' nobody."[133]

In 1951, Eanes formed the **Shenandoah Valley Boys**[134] and the band became popular on WBTM,

Danville, Virginia, and the fifteen-minute radio show was soon extended to fifty-five before a live audience of about 200 people.

Working for Eanes, the musicians made $35/week— good wages in those days. They played on the Shenandoah Barn Dance, eventually playing to as many as 1000 people on a Saturday night. Later, Eanes hired Arnold Terry (bass) and Bill Bledsoe (mandolin). By that time, they had a bluegrass sound, but distinctively smoother than the Stanleys, Monroe or other popular bluegrass acts of the day. This reflected Eanes' affinity for certain country music singers of that time. He understood the commercial country music sound and pursued it within the framework of bluegrass instrumentation.

They recorded for Blue Ridge Records, North Wilkesboro, North Carolina. Arthur Q. Smith was brought into the session to record "Missing In Action," a song he and Eanes had co-written in 1947. The record sold 400,000 copies and enabled Eanes to get a more lucrative contract with Decca in 1951. He actually received four different contract offers. In December, Ernest Tubb recorded his own version of the song on Decca. Through the years, he also wrote "Baby Blue Eyes" (recorded by **Flatt and Scruggs**), "You'd Better Wake Up" (recorded by Mac Wiseman), and "I Wouldn't Change You If I Could" (made famous by **Reno and Smiley**), among others. Later on in 1951, due to the success of "Missing in Action," its sequel, "Return from Missing in Action," was penned and recorded. In September, Decca released "Tomorrow May Be Different"/"Prisoner of War." The "War" song was another follow-up of his successful "Missing In Action" released the previous year. Eanes continued to record in the Nashville style. On November 17th, Eanes and his band recorded "When the One That You Love Is in Love with You," "Gloomy Tomorrow," "Little Brown Hand" and "Kiss Me, Kiss Me." Roy Russell, his regular band member, played fiddle.[135] Eanes' singles usually had country on one side, bluegrass on the other.

---

131 Telephone interview, January 1993.

132 When Eanes went to work with Monroe, other members of the band were Monroe, Don Reno (banjo, he started about a week before Eanes arrived), Benny Martin (fiddle), Joel Price (bass) and Bessie Mauldin (bass). Reno left the band shortly after Eanes left the band and went back to Arthur Smith's Crackerjacks.

133 Telephone interview, January, 1993.

134 The original Shenandoah Valley Boys were Hubert Davis (banjo), Pee Wee Davis (fiddle, mandolin, Hubert's brother), Neely Gilfellen (lead guitar), and was soon joined by Dee Stone (fiddle) and Benny Jarrell (bass, fiddle). Stone and Pee Wee Davis soon left.

135 Other musicians were Nashville regulars Chet Atkins, Jack Shook, and Ernie Newton (one of Bill Monroe's favorite studio bassists).

The next stage of Eanes' career, and in country music in general, came in the mid-50s. According to Pete Kuykendall, "Country music was to suffer greatly from the appearance of Elvis Presley and the rock and roll acts during the mid-'50s." Eanes recalled, "Well, Elvis came along and he put us out of business. I went into radio then."[136] Eanes stayed at WBTM until November of 1953 as an announcer and still actively maintained his band.

In 1955, Jim Eanes began recording with Starday with the first band of his own (he had been using mostly studio musicians).[137] This recording was at the invitation of Don Pierce. All these Starday records were recorded while working at WHEE, Martinsville, Virginia. Eanes' first Starday record was "Your Old Standby"/"Don't Stop Now."

The group stayed with Starday through 1961. It was during these Starday sessions that Eanes developed his own style of bluegrass music. It became noticeable mostly due to the rhythm guitar. As with many individuals who were band leaders looking for a style of their own, the booming rhythm guitar became Eanes' trademark. He lost this trademark in 1964 when Roy Russell died. Russell was not only an important member of Eanes' band, but a good friend. It was 1968 before Eanes was able to even begin playing regularly—with Red Smiley's band. In the late 1980s, Eanes felt that his trademark rhythm guitar was coming back again. He, like many bluegrass pioneers, recognized that success in this music will come only if their band is a little different—somewhat unique—than other existing bands.

Getting that "Jim Eanes sound" was important to Eanes' band's longevity. He explained, "They were Roy Russell, Allen Shelton and Arnold Terry. And we just worked so good together. And we had our own style. I wish I could get back that sock rhythm I had, you know. I'm tryin' for that but I can't find nobody to do it. I guess I'm a little picky but—they try, but they don't have that charisma, I guess. When I first started I had Curly Howard who had worked with Clyde Moody and Don Gibson. And that boy, he's the one that started it actually. I was doin' most of it with my guitar but Arnold Terry was doin' it, too. When Curly Howard left me, I got Arnold doin' most of it and he and I were doin' it together. And I'd do it awhile and he'd do it awhile. I was just like Monroe tryin' to teach me! I was tryin' to teach 'em what I wanted. And although I probably couldn't do it, when I hear something, I know what I want. I'm not the fanciest guitar picker in the world—my handicap or something like that in my left hand—but I do what I want to do what I want to do and I do what I can."[138]

In January 1957, the **Farm Hands** lost their radio station job so they called Eanes, asking for work at WHEE where Eanes was working. Eanes then hired members Allen Shelton (banjo), Roy Russell and Arnold Terry into his own newly re-formed band. Shelton left in 1960 to join **Jim and Jesse**, which soon led him to the Grand Ole Opry when they joined in 1964. Eanes hired Gene Parker in place of Shelton.

Eanes related to this writer that, in 1965, he was going to be hired at the "first bluegrass festival". He recalled the time when "Carlton Haney called me one day and told me, 'I'm going to run a festival.' I said, 'Wha-a-a-t?' He said, 'We're going to hold it at Cantrell's farm in Fincastle. I don't know whether we're going to make any money or not.' He had contacted all the boys who were with me at the time (Arnold Terry and Roy Russell). So we went on up to play. We had a makeshift stage out in the cow pasture. Well, we didn't make any money that first year. So the few people who were there—we asked them if they wanted another festival—they said, 'Yes.' And the next year it was three times that many. So I got paid that year for the year I had played before." Eanes, a solo artist, was backed by **Don Reno and the Tennessee Cut-Ups**.

About the time Eanes was recording a gospel album for Dave Freeman's County Records with Red Smiley's **Bluegrass Cut-Ups** in 1969, Smiley retired. Eanes joined this band at John Palmer's invitation. Smiley's group was playing on the "Top O' the Morning" show on WDBJ-TV in Roanoke, Virginia, at the time. The group combined the names of Smiley's **Bluegrass Cut-Ups** and Eanes' **Shenandoah Valley Boys** and called themselves the **Shenandoah Cut-Ups**.[139] They worked together for about two years around Roanoke, then joined the Wheeling Jamboree where they performed twice a month at WWVA.

In 1971, Eanes left the **Shenandoah Cut-Ups**. The members then hired temporary replacements such as Cliff Waldron, then Udell McPeak, and settled on Wesley Golding. Eanes started working again as a solo and emcee at bluegrass festivals. He re-formed his **Shenandoah Valley Boys** with local musicians.[140] This

---

[136] Pete Kuykendall, "Smilin' Jim Eanes," *Bluegrass Unlimited*, February, 1973, p.10.

[137] Members of this band included Allen Shelton (banjo), Roy Russell (fiddle) and Arnold Terry (guitar, bass).
    Eanes remembered Shelton: "When I hired Allen, he didn't have all that great ability to do it but he learned it real quick. He'd play all night and all day. He'd bunk with me and I'd wake up in the mornin' at three or four o'clock and he'd be sittin' on the edge of the bed playin' his banjo. I'd say 'Go to sleep!'"

[138] Telephone interview, January, 1993. Mr. Eanes has a physical handicap which has slowed down what he might have been able to do if all his digits had been working correctly. In 1936, he had an operation on his left hand to correct the damage of a severe burn to his hand which occurred at age three. This was partially successful but didn't correct the problem of having two unbendable fingers. Perhaps this handicap caused him to concentrate on his singing.

[139] Other members of the Shenandoah Cut-Ups were Tater Tate (fiddle), Herschel Sizemore (mandolin), John Palmer (bass) and Billy Edwards (banjo).

[140] Eanes tried to use John Palmer on bass when he could. He considered Palmer to be the best bassist in the business.

policy of using mostly local musicians continued until 1987 when he started recording with a group on a regular basis. Other than this group, Eanes mainly did solo work where he picked up a band at each festival to back him up. "I can't use my band like I want to—the ones that I record with—because they won't pay it. These promoters they done put the stamp on everything and that's it! I can't blame them for what they do, so I do a lot of solo work. But I've been very fortunate to have a lot of good musicians behind me." In the early 1990s, he recorded regularly with Bobby Atkins whose regular band was the **Countrymen**.

"I started out with the traditional stuff and the mountain music and you combined it all. I don't play country music and I don't play bluegrass—I'm still 'hillbilly.' That's the way I feel about it. I learnt my music by bein' a hillbilly and I haven't changed it. Of course, I can go out and do the bluegrass if they want to call me 'bluegrass,' but primarily, today, I'm doin' what I've been doin' all my life! If I want to sing country songs, I do these tours in Europe where they want country music. I sit down with my guitar on a stool and I sing country music. I sing bluegrass if they want it—anything that comes to mind."[141] Eanes passed away November 21, 1995.

Hylo Brown

Hylo Brown and the Timberliners

Frank "Hylo" Brown Jr. was a significant figure in bluegrass music beginning about 1939 with his own weekly radio show in Logan, West Virginia. Born April 20, 1922, in River, Kentucky, he picked up the name "Hylo" about 1948 because of his wide voice range, both high and low.

In his early years, he worked for Bradley Kincaid, the five-year veteran of the Grand Ole Opry. They recorded on Capitol Records.

In approximately 1950, Brown wrote "The Grand Ole Opry Song" describing the Opry as it existed in the late '40s. It was first recorded by Jimmy Martin on Decca. A few years later, Brown wrote "Lost to a Stranger" and his label at the time, Capitol Records, hired a band for Brown to record it.[142] They also recorded "Lovesick and Sorrow" in 1955.

He founded his own **Buckskin Boys** in 1954 to play on WWVA's Jamboree to capitalize on the fame brought from his own "Lost to a Stranger." Brown also recorded on his own for Capitol during that time.

In 1958, Brown joined the **Flatt and Scruggs** band on their television shows and the Grand Ole Opry. In 1958, sponsored by Martha White Mills, Brown was chosen to form his own band, the **Timberliners**[143], to alternate with **Flatt and Scruggs** on the Martha White television show on WSM. They bought a brand new station wagon and put 70,000 miles on it in just a few months. They still found time to record Capitol's "Hylo Brown" album. Then the technology of videotaping made it possible for **Flatt and Scruggs** to appear on the show while they were on the road.

Hylo Brown and the Timberliners[144] became one of the first bands to play the 1959 Newport Folk Festival and featured Earl Scruggs on banjo (without the **Flatt and Scruggs** band). Vanguard Records recorded their Newport performance. Soon Brown changed the members of his band and added he Melvin Goins who handled the chores of booking, vocals, and comedy as "Hot Rize Charlie." They recorded on Capitol Records.

Hylo Brown's contract with Capitol Records expired in 1961. He then began recording on Starday with artists which included Chubby Wise (fiddle), Curtis McPeake (banjo), Joe Drumright (banjo), Jackie Phelps (guitar), Junior Huskey (bass), Josh Graves (Dobro®), Shot Jackson (Dobro®), Rita Faye (Autoharp), and the **Lonesome Pine Fiddlers**.

During the days when folk music was dominating peoples' tastes, Brown, along with many other bluegrass artists, had a difficult time earning a living. They crossed over to country music occasionally—whatever would bring in a few bucks. Along the bluegrass lines, Brown recorded with the following labels: Rural Rhythm, Vetco, Newland, King's Music City, Rome and K-Ark.

As of 1992, Brown was retired, but still musically active in River, Kentucky.

---

141 Telephone interview, January 1993.

142 Band members were Merle "Red" Taylor, Joe Drumright (banjo), Gordon Terry (mandolin) and Cedric Rainwater (bass).

143 Members of Hylo Brown and the Timberliners were Hylo (guitar), Red Rector (mandolin, who joined in 1958), Tater Tate (fiddle), Jim Smoak (banjo) and Joe "Flapjack" Phillips (bass).

144 Band members were Billy Edwards (banjo), Hylo (guitar), Norman Blake (Dobro, mandolin), Louis Profitt (fiddle) and occasionally Kenny Baker (fiddle) when Baker was not a member of the Blue Grass Boys. Edwards stayed until 1961.

Cleo Davis—
the first Blue Grass Boy, and the
hiring process with Monroe

The life of the early bluegrass pioneers was often from a setting in the Old South as a farmer or from the equally economically-poor areas of states such as Kentucky, Tennessee and West Virginia, where coal mining was the main industry. When a geographical area is so dependent upon one product as described, even a slight downturn in that activity can have the consequences of many of its residents being raised in dire poverty. In these poor families who were trying to eke out a living from the soil or the mines, their playtime activity usually centered around the home in whatever fashion they could entertain themselves. Often these activities were music in the family and music among neighbors. The activities would include weekend summer celebrations for just about any occasion they could think of to get together a community event.

Even though they might live miles apart, neighbors took the time to get together regularly and have an event. These events might be pea shuckings, or corn huskings, or ice cream socials or attendance at a hillbilly band concert when they came to town. Radio play—where they listened to their favorite barn dance show—would only tantalize the residents for when their favorite entertainers would come to town and do a real live concert. Meanwhile, at home on the farm, the lovers of the music would practice their instruments (which were frequently home-made) and they would sing the songs they heard on the radio. One such person is Cleo Davis who was born March 9, 1919, on a farm in the hills of northwest Georgia.

The first concert Davis heard was when Gid Tanner and Riley Puckett came to town in 1929. He then determined to learn the guitar; he made his own. "He searched until he found an oil can to which he attached a sawmill strip for a neck. After punching a hole in the top of the can, he stretched a single strand of screen wire over the top of the can and his one-string 'guitar' was complete."[145]

"I sang and yodeled and strummed that guitar until my sister chased me out of the house," said Davis. "There wasn't a barn, so I had to go out into the woods to play. I kept singing and carrying on 'til I drove all the wild animals back into the river swamp."[146] He soon traded rabbit skins for an harmonica. Then he swapped the harmonica and a pocket knife for an old Stella guitar.

He learned the **Carter Family** guitar style and Jimmie Rodgers tunes. He plowed with the family mule while singing and yodeling his way through many of Rodgers' songs. "It got so that the mule couldn't work

unless I was singing and yodeling. I did notice that the old mule would shake his head when I'd hit a high note. I thought at first he was just flipping off horseflies, but I later realized that he was trying to tell me I was giving him a headache."[147]

In 1938, Davis moved to Atlanta and ended up working as an ice truck driver for $1 per day—more money than he had ever seen before. About Christmas time, Davis' friends in Atlanta insisted he answer an ad in the *Atlanta Journal* for someone who could play guitar and sing old-time songs. Eventually he went, after his friends bought him a guitar at the hock shop for $2.40.

Davis related, "We got to the location in the ad and found it to be a small trailer sitting next to a service station. When we approached the trailer we heard country music coming out of that thing. I was a little hesitant to knock on the door so I waited until the music stopped. Two or three guys came pouring out, and the man inside told them if he'd decided, he'd give them a call. We were then invited in, and I trailed in last. Introductions were passed around but I never did get his name. He said, 'Well, who plays the guitar?' I eventually pulled it out from behind me where I had it hid and said, 'I do, Sir.' He asked, 'Well, what can you play?' 'Oh, maybe a verse or two of "This World is Not My Home" or "What Would You Give in Exchange for Your Soul?" not knowing at that moment who I was talking to.

"My mind then flashed back and I remembered how I had learned those two songs. Several years before, I had picked up the Grand Ole Opry over radio WSM. There I heard people like Arthur Smith and the **Dixieliners**, Clayton McMichen, and the **Delmore Brothers.** I thought the **Delmore Brothers** were out of this world. A little later, some other brother acts came on the scene such as the **Callahan Brothers** and the **Shelton Brothers.** Then I heard two brothers who had exactly what I thought I'd been looking for—the **Monroe Brothers.** I had no idea where they were located and had never seen them, but I had picked up one of their old records of 'This World Is Not My Home' and 'What Would You Give in Exchange for Your Soul?' and that's how I learned those songs. I was awakened out of my thoughts when the man standing before me asked, 'You can sing "What Would You Give in Exchange for Your Soul?"' I said, 'Yes, Sir, I think I can sing that.' So we proceeded to tune up together. But I soon found out that the $2.40 guitar would not tune up to that beautiful mandolin he had. So he tuned down to my guitar and we hit out.

"We had done about a verse and a chorus to 'What Would You Give in Exchange for Your Soul?' when I recognized the voice. I didn't recognize the name, but I recognized the voice. This *had* to be one of the **Monroe**

145 Wayne Erbsen, "Cleo Davis—The Original Blue Grass Boy," *Bluegrass Unlimited*, February, 1982, p. 28.

146 Ibid., p. 28.

147 Ibid., p. 29.

America's Music – Bluegrass

Brothers. I got so scared that I lost my voice and had to quit playing. He asked me what was the matter and I told him I had forgot the song. So we talked for a moment and I tried to calm down. I think he knew what had really happened to me. I had realized that I was standing there singing with Bill Monroe and I was shocked beyond reason. So I finally recovered and he said, 'Let's try "This World Is Not My Home,"' so we tried that. I was beginning to get brave and sang nearly two verses until I got scared to death and lost my voice again. He had to laugh a little about that and kidded me and said, 'You'll get over that.' We did a better job of it the next time.

"His wife, whose name is Carolyn, was sitting at the end of the trailer listening. He said, 'Carolyn, what do you think?' She said that I sounded more like any man she ever heard not to be Charlie Monroe. I seen a grin come over Bill's face and he said, 'Let's try that number again.' I think we did it still a little better that time and he turned around and told Carolyn, 'I think I found what I'm looking for.' I figured he couldn't have been looking for very much to have found it in me. To my amazement, I found out that he was satisfied with our sound and that he and Charlie had split up in Raleigh, North Carolina, some time before and that Bill had formed a group called the **Kentuckians**. He stayed there a few months and either didn't go over too well, or he was unhappy with their sound. So he headed back to Atlanta, Georgia, where he and Charlie had worked a guest spot a few years before.

Bill asked me if I could come back to the trailer the next morning about 8:30. I told him I would, not knowing what was in store for me. So I caught a street car and was right back there the next morning. We drank some coffee, and Bill asked me if I knew any music shops downtown where we could look at some instruments. I told him I did, so we went downtown and looked at the guitars hanging in pawn shop windows. We finally found a big orchestra-type guitar that Bill strummed approvingly. He handed it to me and asked me how I liked it. I'd never played a guitar that cost more than $2.40, so this $37.50 guitar was the most beautiful thing I'd ever seen. I nodded furiously. Bill told the man we'd take it and at that moment, I hit the door hard and fast. This old country boy only had about dollar in my pocket and there was no way I could buy that guitar. Bill paid the man and walked out with that guitar."[148]

Dobro Cyclops model 37 square neck made in 1932. Photo courtesy Gruhn Guitars.

When Davis joined, Bill Monroe taught him how to play the guitar. Monroe knew all the guitar parts his brother, Charlie, used to use when they were the **Monroe Brothers**. Soon, Davis' playing sounded just like Charlie's. Davis believes that Bill Monroe's purpose in hiring him was to keep the "**Monroe Brothers'** sound" together. Perhaps even Bill didn't realize it at the time. But the end result was a harmony and band which Bill and the audiences were used to.

"As the weeks went by, it seemed like Bill and I kept picking up speed until we were playing faster and faster. But we were as good on the slow numbers as we were on the fast ones. I found out quick that you don't make mistakes when playing with Bill, so we practiced never making mistakes. In order to stay up with Bill, I used the old 'Charlie Monroe G' run until it got to a point where I could no longer make it and keep up with Bill Monroe. So I had to find something I could do and keep up with the fast pace that we had set. So with the help of Bill, I modified the old Charlie Monroe G run. I made it into what is now known as the famous 'Lester Flatt G run.' I not only could make it in G, but also in the keys of C, D and even A."[149] Davis didn't use a capo. In fact, he couldn't remember that anyone used capos in those days.

After Christmas of 1938, they auditioned as a duet at WSB, Atlanta, on the Crossroads Follies. But the station only accepted groups, not duos. They went back home.

Soon Davis and Monroe went to Asheville in Bill's new 1939 Hudson Terraplane. They were accepted at WWNC on the Mountain Music Time show, taking the place of the **Delmore Brothers** who had just left for WFBC in Greenville, South Carolina. Davis and Monroe returned home to pick up their belongings to set up their base of operations. "On the way back to Asheville, with Bill's trailer in tow, I had a need to know what Bill was going to call us. I really didn't know his intentions about a band, because Bill doesn't talk much. Bill said, 'Bill Monroe and the Blue Grass Boys.' I questioned Blue Grass Boys, being from the hills of Georgia and not knowing anything about bluegrass. So I asked him about it and he said, 'I'm from

[148] Ibid., pp. 29, 30

[149] Ibid., p. 59. As a side note to what Cleo Davis says here, Wade Mainer, in a conversation with this writer in 1990, told me that the G-run which Davis claims to have invented to keep up with Bill Monroe was being played by Riley Puckett when Wade was a little boy in the '20s. "Riley Puckett was a-playing that G-run and he had several other different runs that he named on that. They picked all that stuff up from him. I know that because J.E. and myself bought a lot of their records with Gid Tanner and the Skillet Lickers and the Georgia Yellow Hammers and all that. We learned a lot of our music and them songs from them boys and all. When we learned it, we put it to our own style of playing. It was something similar to all that which was leaning toward bluegrass. The banjo that I played in the band was leaning up toward bluegrass, you know."

Kentucky, you know, where the bluegrass grows, and it's got a good ring to it. I like that.' He didn't talk a lot, but when he did talk, he made it count."[150]

"We used to get a lot of kidding about that name in the early days. You could hear all sorts of little remarks when we'd play schoolhouses, like 'Bill Monroe and the Glue Brass Boys.' As the years pass by, of course, I'm real proud that I was an original member of the **Blue Grass Boys**."[151]

The announcer often referred to them as **Bill Monroe and Cleo Davis**; their mail often came to the **Monroe Brothers**. Soon Monroe and Davis, together, began auditioning musicians to form a full band. Art Wooten, from Marion, North Carolina, was hired to play fiddle. But he also was a "one man band" which "was like half an organ, with Art sitting with his knees under the thing. He also had a five-string banjo and a guitar built into it. He picked it with one foot and chorded it with the other while at the same time playing the fiddle. He also had a harmonica rack around his neck and played the fiddle and the harmonica at the same time. We used that act on stage with the **Blue Grass Boys** many times."

Tommy "Snowball" Millard, from Canton, North Carolina, joined as black-faced comedian. Davis remembered, "He would always break me up with his act when he'd go out on stage. As a matter of fact, I couldn't even play straight with him while I stood off in the wings and laughed. He didn't sing or play an instrument, though he did have two big tablespoons that he'd play back to back. He would beat those spoons on his knees, between his hands, on his shoulders, under his arms and up and down his legs. He was real good at it."[152]

Monroe's wife, Carolyn, booked many of the gigs they got while advertising on their daily shows. They charged fifteen and twenty-five cents admission and often played to fifty or seventy-five people. "I remember we opened with a fast fiddle tune like 'Fire on the Mountain,' had two or three fast duets like 'Roll in My Sweet Baby's Arms,' maybe an old blues number, a duet yodel, and a skit of ten or fifteen minutes. We had a skit that was mighty popular called 'The Pickpocket Game.' I always came up short on that deal."[153]

Three months after beginning in WWNC, the group followed the trail of the **Delmore Brothers** to WFBC in Greenville when the brothers left. Millard left the **Blue Grass Boys** and was replaced by Amos Garren who played bass. Monroe now felt more comfortable about his music. It was closer to that "sound" he dreamed about. The bass seemed to add a bottom end rhythm to the music which Monroe liked and kept in his band ever since. They practiced in a grease shed behind a filling station. It was there they developed songs like

"Muleskinner Blues" and "Footprints in the Snow." The first quartet was formed.

They worked hard but "We were about to starve to death. Those were bad times and we were not making much money. Sometimes we'd take in $25 to $30 a night in the little shows and we'd play most every night. Bill paid me $15 a week when we were working. When we weren't working, he couldn't pay me anything though he did pay for my haircuts and my laundry. Back in those days, Bill was more like my older brother, though he wasn't much older than me. But he'd been around a lot more than I ever had."

In October of 1939, six months after their arrival in Greenville, they left to audition for the Grand Ole Opry. The guys felt that if Bill Monroe said they were good enough to appear on the Opry, then they were. They auditioned for the Solemn Old Judge, George D. Hay with "Foggy Mountain Top." Then Monroe and Davis did a fast duet with a duet yodel, then "Mule Skinner Blues" and finally "Fire on the Mountain." They got the first spot on Saturday night.

That first appearance on the Opry on October 28th was very memorable. They were the first group to appear on the stage with white shirts and ties. They were probably the first country music quartet to play on the Opry. "When we hit the stage, such performers as Roy Acuff, Pee Wee King, Uncle Dave Macon and Sam and Kirk McGee, who were standing in the wings watching the **Blue Grass Boys** when they pulled the curtain on us, could not believe when we took off so fast and furious. Those people couldn't even *think* as fast as we played, I believe... Those people [the audience] like to played us to death that night. We had done exactly what we started to do."

On September 6th, 1940, Cleo Davis left the **Blue Grass Boys** for Lakeland, Florida, for his own show on WLAK. He was replaced by Clyde Moody. Davis remained in the music through the years in Lakeland, Florida, where he helped found the Florida Opry House which exists today. The **Blue Grass Boys** began its recording career the next month.

"We used to get a lot of kidding about that name in the early days. You could hear all sorts of little remarks when we'd play schoolhouses, like 'Bill Monroe and the Glue Brass Boys.'"
—*Cleo Davis*

150 Wayne Erbsen, "Cleo Davis—The Original Blue Grass Boy, Part Two," *Bluegrass Unlimited*, March 1982, p. 59.
151 Ibid., p. 60.
152 Ibid., p. 61.
153 Ibid., p. 61.

Wilma Lee and Stoney Cooper and the Clinch Mountain Clan

According to author Wayne W. Daniel, "Several factors have contributed to Wilma Lee's acceptance by bluegrass audiences. First of all, there's her voice which has the range, timbre and punch usually associated with the bluegrass sound. The lively, rollicking nature of her stage performances, coupled with an unmistakable aura of sincerity can be described best as old-time, country soul. The instrumentation of the Cooper band, the **Clinch Mountain Clan** (named after the Clinch Mountains near their home), with its fiddle, resonator guitar and Scruggs-style banjo, has long been identifiable as that of a bluegrass band. Finally, there's the matter of repertoire. Many of the songs Wilma Lee has recorded, as well as those she sings on stage, have been drawn from bluegrass sources or have become bluegrass standards due, in part, perhaps, to her own efforts."[154]

The husband and wife team of Wilma Lee and Stoney Cooper grew up near each other in an area of the country in which playing music was a part of their culture. There in West Virginia, they both started playing music due to their family influences and they got together as a duo in 1939 when Stoney, an accomplished fiddler in the style of Fiddlin' Arthur Smith, joined Wilma Lee's family band, the **Leary Family**.

In 1938, the **Leary Family** won a West Virginia contest and soon represented the state of West Virginia at the National Folk Festival organized by Mrs. Eleanor Roosevelt in Washington, D.C.. Wilma Lee was the guitarist. They came back the next year. The recordings became the perfect example of authentic mountain folk music. The group soon began a three-year stint on WSVA, Harrisonburg, West Virginia, where they gained considerable popularity. Beginning in the mid-'40s, said Wilma Lee, "We made our name in the days of the radio—in the days before the success of an artist was measured almost solely in terms of the number of hit records sold."[155]

Wilma Lee and Stoney formed the **Clinch Mountain Clan** during this period with Bill Carver (resonator guitar, mandolin) and Ab Cole (bass, comedy). They considered themselves as just another band which sang the music of their roots. Wilma Lee said, "Well, you know, I never thought we were bluegrass, really. I thought we were just pure old country. True country. We just sung like we growed up." Stoney added, "I never thought we had bluegrass singing voices. Now, Bill [Monroe] seems to think we did! He says Wilma does. He told me, 'You just don't use her right.'"[156] "When we came into Nashville," said Wilma Lee in 1974, "they started classifying music—giving it a name of some kind. And they would say we were bluegrass, but Stoney would say, 'We're not exactly bluegrass. We're just country.' And they would say, 'Yes, you're bluegrass.' Then you don't know what to call yourself."[157]

The **Osborne Brothers** became famous for the high-lead style of harmony. Sonny Osborne once mentioned, "I think Wilma Lee and Stoney and the **Maddox Brothers** had done it."[158]

During the 1947 period while they were at Asheville's WWNC, they recorded for Rich-R-Tone. Soon they were performing daily on 50,000 watt WWVA's Wheeling Jamboree where the band immediately became popular...especially since the audience hadn't heard a resonator guitar before. The group soon became sponsored by Carter's Little Liver Pills (Carter, himself, was an old-time fiddler). Carter hired them to do a series of transcribed radio shows to be broadcast throughout the nation on twenty different 50,000 watt stations. They recorded "Wicked Path of Sin," "Tramp on the Street" and others. "Tramp" sold more than 20,000 copies in Wheeling alone and helped establish Wilma Lee as one of the top female singers on radio anywhere in the States. They stayed on the Jamboree for ten years. Also on WWVA at the time were such personalities as Hawkshaw Hawkins, George Morgan and Toby Stroud.

In 1949, the **Clinch Mountain Clan** began recording on Columbia. This arrangement lasted until 1953 when Columbia dropped the old-timey groups in favor of the more modern country groups such as Lefty Frizell and Carl Smith. The Coopers then switched to the Hickory

---

154 Wayne W. Daniel, "Wilma Lee Cooper, America's Most Authentic Mountain Singer," *Bluegrass Unlimited*, February, 1982, pp. 14, 15.

155 Ibid., pp. 13, 14.

156 Douglas B. Green, *Bluegrass Unlimited*, "Wilma Lee and Stoney Cooper," March, 1974, p. 25.

157 Daniel, op. cit., p. 14.

158 This quotation from a newspaper clipping sent to me by Mrs. Cooper. Origin and date unknown.

label in the mid-'50s and remained there for many years; the **Clinch Mountain Clan** recorded on many labels through their career. Recording on the Hickory label, they had big hits with "Come Walk With Me," "Big Midnight Special" and "There's a Big Wheel." Some of their later recordings were produced with background voices, electric instruments and drums. They departed from the traditionalism they grew up with and once deemed so important.

Wilma Lee and her **Clan** was voted the "Authentic Mountain Singing Group" in 1950 by Harvard's Library of Music. During the early 1950s, their first banjoist (other than Wilma Lee) to be hired was Chuck Henderson of North Carolina, at WWVA. Her own banjo style was what she called the "old flog style" in which she picked out the melody with her index finger. Members of the band soon became Buck Graves, Tex Logan and Johnny Clark (ex-banjo player for Bill Clifton's **Dixie Mountain Boys**). They also played at the Old Dominion Barn Dance on WRVA, Richmond, Virginia.

On February 1, 1957, **Wilma Lee and Stoney Cooper and the Clinch Mountain Clan** joined WSM's Grand Ole Opry and moved to Nashville. In 1974, Wilma Lee was awarded the title "First Lady of Bluegrass" in a television series of "Women in Country Music." In 1976, Stoney was awarded a degree of Doctor of Christian Music by the Victory Institute of Lewiston, Ohio. Their religion showed vividly in their music. Wilma Lee has a Bachelor of Arts in Theology from Davis and Elkins College, Elkins, West Virginia.

Stoney Cooper died on March 22, 1977. The band then went into a transitional state. Like the **Stanley Brothers**, the lead person/emcee for the band was gone. This led to a decision by the remaining partner, Ralph Stanley and Wilma Lee respectively, to choose whether to quit music or continue as the leader of the band. Both Ralph and Wilma Lee chose to go on. Wilma Lee re-formed the **Clinch Mountain Clan** in 1979 and they were back in business on the Opry. She soon recorded the "A Daisy a Day" LP on Leather Records. She continued the use of a resonator guitar in the band.[159]

1981 was Wilma Lee's most active year for jobs; she became more and more musically active after Stoney died. She even took up the banjo again—an instrument she forsook soon after Stoney joined the band. Marty Lanham became her bluegrass banjo player (again. He had worked for Stoney and Wilma Lee in 1976, too). Other musicians who have, through the years, played for the **Clinch Mountain Clan** included Dobro®ist Josh Graves, fiddler Tex Logan, banjoists Johnny Clark and Vic Jordan, guitarist George McCormick and mandolinist James (Carson) Roberts. Also in 1982, Rounder released "Wilma Lee Cooper." Half of the cuts on this album included Stoney's April 1976 session—his last.

She appeared in the movies "Country Music on Broadway" and "W.W. and the Dixie Dance Kings." She received awards from *Music City News*, a citation from the American Legion, is a Louisiana Colonel on the Governor's staff (1961) and is an Honorary Colonel of the State of Alabama as declared by Governor George Wallace. She is a Kentucky Colonel, commissioned by Governor Martha Layne Collins. She and Stoney received a Award of Merit from the International Bluegrass Music Association in 1994, and she was voted into WWVA's "Walkway of the Stars" by the World's Original Jamboree.

Dave Freeman wrote that "She is dedicated to the preservation of the music. A musical novice might call her music antiquated, but the more knowledgeable fans would likely call her genuine. They'd be right. She's a one-of-a-kind original with a voice that encompasses most of the emotions common to us all—victory, defeat, love, heartache, happiness, sadness and desolation—all of these with a dignity uncommon in any business. A legendary performer, Wilma Lee Cooper is the 'Queen of Bluegrass Music.'"[160] She is also known as the "First Lady of Country Music" and as the "First Lady of Bluegrass". As of 1994, she still appeared regularly on the Grand Ole Opry.

Carl and J.P. Sauceman

Carl and J.P. Sauceman— the Sauceman Brothers

The history of country music and bluegrass music is filled with outstanding musicians who can "pick the fire out of that instrument" but never get the recognition they deserve. This lack of recognition is often because of lack of exposure to the public. This applies to the **Sauceman Brothers and the Greene Valley Boys** of Greene County, in eastern Tennessee.

---

159 Gene Wooten was the Dobro or resonator guitar player with the band beginning about 1980 until 1984.

160 Dave Freeman, "Brother Dave's Place. Wilma Lee Cooper: The Preservation of the Music." Origin unknown to this writer.

A m e r i c a s   M u s i c   l   B l u e g r a s s

This writer met Carl Sauceman at a Kissimmee, Florida, bluegrass festival where we spoke briefly and corresponded considerably after that. The main remark I remember that Mr. Sauceman made to me was something to the effect that he and his group were playing the same songs back in their heyday (as early as the mid-1940s) as were being played on that stage in 1989, and he thought the music should have more substance than just rehashing the old songs. To be sure, I'd heard many of the songs before. But to hear him say that was somewhat new to me and enlightening. I had done some preliminary research on the Saucemans and knew the name but little more about him and his group—only that I was in the presence of a living legend. His remark stirred a more thorough research into his music where I found that his group was an early pioneer in the history of bluegrass music. History? Yes. But long-lasting significance? That's another question, for this group was like many we know today who were very good at bluegrass music—even innovative—but who toured very little out of their local area. In the case of the **Sauceman Brothers,** their area was Alabama. Few people in the bluegrass world knew of them, nor were they influenced by them. It seems that the big names in bluegrass that we all recognize are those who were not only full-time in their music, but those who toured extensively in search of new markets. Had the Saucemans toured as much as **Flatt and Scruggs** or **Bill Monroe and the Blue Grass Boys** or **Jim and Jesse and the Virginia Boys,** perhaps history would be written differently. In spite of having to leave out many groups and individuals from this book for brevity—for which I apologize—the Saucemans' group is included because it is one of the earliest true bluegrass groups. Their sidemen were some of the greatest names in country and bluegrass music. They should not be forgotten.

Carl Sauceman, in a 1989 interview, said the reason they never achieved the popularity of the other major bluegrass bands is because, "We were before our time. What we were doing then is what they are doing today. And it just wasn't selling then...Joe Stuart and I were playing at Bill Grant's bluegrass festival in Hugo, Oklahoma in 1986 and Walt Saunders *(of Bluegrass Unlimited)* took us around and introduced us to the **Johnson Mountain Boys.** He wanted us to meet them all. I said, 'Well, I've got to hear these guys. Everybody says they are fabulous.' It's my word to God above, when they sang, I could have closed my eyes and heard us exactly—thirty-five years ago. The *same* sound."

Carl was born in Bright Hope community, Greene County, Tennessee, March 6, 1922. John Paul (J.P.) was born March 7, 1928. Their father, Alvin, was a farmer and gospel singer who sang (often with his family) at revival meetings throughout the area. Carl learned country songs from his mother and from relatives, and listened to the Opry on the radio. He heard the **Monroe Brothers,** Charlie and Bill, for the first time on an old crank-up phonograph. His cousin, Ivan Sauceman, would play the record and young Carl would listen as he passed their house on the way to school.

Much of their entertainment came from playing their own music. Carl recalled, "I was raised on a little farm in east Tennessee. There wasn't any place to play except at ice cream suppers and such." He bought his first guitar for 98 cents at age ten and still owes two cents to his cousin, Everett Gray, he says, for the Sears instrument. Soon, he was winning talent competitions with his cousin, Dulcie Sauceman, who also sang with him at many churches.

Carl recalled that he joined Uncle Dud Watson and a group which was working at WISE,[161] Asheville, North Carolina, in 1940 or '41. The group soon moved to WHKY, Hickory, North Carolina. Though there was little gas and lots of bald tires during these hard, war years, the group managed to exist on money from "show-dates" at North Carolina schoolhouses which had no sound systems or electricity: the "kerosene circuit". In 1942, Sauceman, hoping to improve his financial lot, teamed up with Curly Shelton (another member of the group) to form their own band. They successfully auditioned for Lowell Blanchard's Mid-Day Merry-Go-Round in Knoxville, Tennessee. The band was called The **Carolina Ramblers** (a name selected by Blanchard) and consisted of Carl, Shelton, Rusty Hall, Price Honeycutt and later, Tommy "Snowball" Millard and Tommy Trent, who moved from the Grand Ole Opry to join them. The group stayed there until Sauceman received his draft notice in 1944.

Told that he would be inducted within six weeks of his physical examination, Sauceman returned to his father's home in Greeneville, Tennessee. After some time he "got tired of waiting" and went to WWNC, Asheville, North Carolina. During that time, his brother, J.P.,[162] replaced Shelton as the group's tenor singer. When Carl was finally inducted into the Navy in 1945, J.P. continued with the group on WWNC, playing the Renfro Valley Barn Dance. The group, at that time, consisted of J.P., Red Rector, Red Smiley, Jimmy Lunsford and Fred Smith.

---

[161] At WISE, members were Uncle Dud Watson (guitar, know as the man who made "Kentucky Waltz" famous), Curly Shelton, (mandolin), Carl (guitar), Shorty Baston (fiddle), Price Honeycutt (steel guitar) and Tommy "Snowball" Millard (comedy. Shelton and his brother, Jack, gained notoriety as members of Wade Mainer's Mountaineers.

[162] In 1944, Carl, age 22, got his father's permission to allow his brother, J.P., age 15, to sing professionally with him. Carl and J.P. worked at WWNC'S Farm Hour, in Asheville, North Carolina with Ted and Wanda Henderson with Billy Boy Flower as sponsor. With them were Red Rector (mandolin), Red Smiley (mandolin), Benny Sims (fiddle), Jimmy Lunsford (fiddle), Willie Carver (electric guitar) and Hoke Jenkins (banjo). During this time Curly Shelton worked with Tommy Millard and his Blue Ridge Hillbillies.

In 1946, Carl returned from the Navy to join J.P. and the group at WWNC. Not long afterwards The **Sauceman Brothers,** as they became known, returned to their hometown of Greeneville to begin a two-year stint at a new (as of 1945) radio station, WGRV. The band consisted of Carl, J.P., Benny Sims (fiddle), Thomas Martin (banjo), Claude "Tiny" Day (guitar) and the Saucemans' younger sister, Imogene (guitar, bass).

Carl and J.P. left Greeneville in 1948 and took their **Sauceman Brothers**[163] band to WROL in Knoxville where they worked for sponsor Cas Walker and his chain of supermarkets. While they were known as the **Sauceman Brothers and the Hillbilly Ramblers,** Walker didn't like the name "hillbilly" so he re-named them the **Greene Valley Boys.** They also worked the Dinner Bell Show, a noon-time round-up with Archie Campbell (later of 'Hee Haw' fame).[164]

In 1949, Carl, J.P. and Joe Stuart[165] left Knoxville and moved to Detroit, Michigan, to play clubs. They quickly learned that they didn't like the venue so the **Greene Valley Boys**[166] moved to Bristol, Tennessee, in February 1950. In Bristol, they played on the Farm and Fun Time radio show, replacing **Flatt and Scruggs** there. Charlie Cline was there at WCYB at the time and remembered them in a 1990 interview, "They had a different style. Mostly there was bluegrass quartet. Their style was between country, southern gospel and bluegrass. I remember all that. They had a quartet as good as Lester and Earl had. That's what they were known for in Bristol is the quartet: bluegrass quartet. Their band was the **Greene Valley Boys.**" The Sauceman group stayed at WCYB until early 1952. While there, they signed a recording contract with Capitol Records. Due to a delay in recording sessions, this combination of **Sauceman Brothers** never recorded even though this was, according to Lester Flatt, perhaps their best band and probably their greatest opportunity.

At this time, Carl turned down a chance to go with Bill Monroe and his band. Carl once told Monroe, "That was probably the biggest mistake I ever made." Monroe

Carl Sauceman, 1989 in Kissimmee, Florida

replied, "You done all right. You done all right." And indeed he did. He didn't make the impact on the world that Monroe did, but he certainly did all right. His later-acquired day job in radio station management was probably a correct career choice as opposed to being a full-time musician, he conceded in an interview with this writer. Carl and his band also had the opportunity to join the Grand Ole Opry but Carl was making excellent money in radio and didn't want to uproot his family, including his invalid son, and take the pay cut. "Music had always paid my way, so to speak; it was a living. That was all. I wasn't savin' no money. It's bad to have to say this but I had to leave what I loved so well in order to get myself fixed so I could live without workin' the rest of my life..."

Three major events were to affect the Sauceman brothers in 1952. J.P. went into the Marine Corps, the duo lost their father and Carl formed a new group, moving to WRAG, Carrollton, Alabama, to work for the Roth Hook network. By that time, Joe Stuart had joined the **Bailey Brothers,** Curly Seckler, the **Stanley Brothers,** Larry Richardson, the **Blue Grass Boys,** and Tate had gone into the Army. Don McHan was hired to replace J.P. and sang lead in addition to playing the banjo. Carl commented, "I don't want to discredit anybody, but Don McHan was the only good man I took to Alabama with me. Not only was he a good banjo man, but he could play all the instruments.[167] Although J.P. rejoined the group upon his return from the Marine Corps, the **Sauceman Brothers** name was never revived and the group remained **Carl Sauceman and the Green Valley Boys** through its sixteen-year tenure in Alabama. During that time, the group recorded for major labels, did three live television shows per week in Mississippi in the cities of Meridian, Tupelo and Columbus and did two live radio shows daily. Carl also did disc jockey work, eventually becoming manager and part owner of the station.

Soon the first Capitol release of "Handy Man"/ "Down The Road To Love" came out[168]. On the Republic label they recorded two songs written by Don

---

[163] Members of the band included Ralph Mayo (fiddle), Wiley Birchfield (banjo) and Willie Carver (electric steel).

[164] The Sauceman Brothers had many good sidemen during the years. They included "Tater" Tate (fiddle), Curly Seckler (guitar), Larry Richardson (banjo), Art Stamper (fiddle, 1951) and Don McHan. There was, indeed, a talented band. Others included Carl Butler, Carl Smith, Wiley Birchfield (banjo), Jimmy Lunsford (fiddle), Howard Chamberlain (fiddle) and Benny Sims (fiddle.)

[165] Carl spoke of Joe Stuart: "At one time, Joe Stuart was the greatest mandolin player there was. Something else he'll never get credit for is that finger-style guitar Earl Scruggs used. Joe Stuart is one of the first to start that style. If you don't believe me, listen to the quartet record we made for Rich-R-Tone in 1947." And of Curly Seckler, Carl said: "He can play the finest rhythm you'd ever want in a bluegrass band. He worked with me at Bristol, Tennessee, for about two years and then again in Alabama for one year before going back with Lester and Earl."

[166] Who were Carl, J.P., Larry Richardson, Tate, Seckler and sometimes, Arville Freeman (fiddle).

[167] Dick Spottswood, "Carl Sauceman: The Odyssey of a Bluegrass Pioneer, " *Bluegrass Unlimited,* October, 1973, p. 13.

[168] This was July of 1952 or 1953. The next month band members included Joe Stuart (fiddle), Ben Drinnon (mandolin), Don McHan (banjo) and Bill Wilburn (bass).

McHan: "I'll Be an Angel, Too" and "A White Cross Marks the Grave." While McHan sang lead with the group at first, J.P. began singing lead upon his return from the Corps. Carl recalled that he sang tenor and Monroe Fields would sing high tenor (high baritone). "Monroe would take the electric guitar on Saturday night and if they wanted rock and roll, we could do it. If they wanted Eddy Arnold, Conway Twitty or George Jones, we could do it. Monroe could tone his voice down and sound exactly like George Jones. Ask George himself if you don't believe me. Of course, we did bluegrass, too. But I have to give this band credit—they were versatile." Carl remembered that about 1955 "In Meridian, Mississippi, one record shop was selling two of our records for every one of Elvis Presley's—and that was when Elvis was hot!"

Carl spoke of the old days, "In those days, package shows were becoming popular. There was always somebody calling me to book twin-bills with them: Lester and Earl, Benny Martin, the **Carlisles, Lonzo and Oscar** and others. But we didn't take a back seat to any of them. This was a talented group of musicians. We could turn our back to each other and know exactly what each other was doing. We were busy, too. There were three television shows a week and two live radio shows a day. I did a disc jockey show every day and we'd go to Nashville every three months to tape segments which were aired on WLAC-TV, Nashville. There was a show every night at some school or theater. We did a dance every Saturday night at a local National Guard armory when Fred 'Sparkplug' Richardson would lay down his banjo for a set of drums and he was *fantastic* on the drums. We filled that big armory every Saturday night.

"I was playing bluegrass long before I ever heard the word. In those days, you just called it all 'country' music or 'hillbilly' music. Then the Grand Ole Opry wanted to get away from the word 'hillbilly' in the early '50s. The guys who didn't want to be labeled 'hillbilly' started calling it 'country-western' and they separated from bluegrass and quit calling it 'hillbilly' altogether. When Lester Flatt and Earl Scruggs left Bill Monroe and went off on their own—that's probably when the term 'bluegrass' came about. In all fairness, when Lester and Earl started, we'd been in the business for years, though I'd never thought of myself as a bluegrass entertainer. Our name was the **Hillbilly Ramblers** and Cas Walker made us change it to the **Greene Valley Boys** because he didn't like the word 'hillbilly'. And today (1978) everything is either country-western or bluegrass."[169]

The Saucemans continued to play as a band until December 31, 1962, when Carl quit to stay home and take care of his invalid son whose physical condition was deteriorating, finally dying in 1966. In 1968, Carl

moved, with his family, to Gonzales, Louisiana, where he built and operated radio station WSLG some eighteen years until his retirement.

For a short period in 1975, Carl re-grouped some old members of the **Greene Valley Boys** and played several bluegrass festivals around the country, including the National Folk Festival at Wolf Trap, Virginia, the Kerrville, Texas, festival, the Jazz and Heritage Festival in New Orleans, and Bean Blossom, Indiana.

J.P. Sauceman died of cancer on Thanksgiving Day, 1984. When Joe Stuart, Carl's longtime friend and fellow-trouper died, Carl decided to retire permanently from music. He put his guitar in the case and gave up professional music for good. And while the Saucemans no longer take to the stage, Carl delights that "Carl" still performs regularly in the person of the young man who was named for him: Carl Jackson.

George Shuffler

George Shuffler— a man who has done it all

George Saunders Shuffler was born April 11, 1925, near Valdese in Burke County, North Carolina. He was raised in a musically-inclined family in which all members played an instrument. Young Shuffler began playing his father's guitar at ten years old. His own first guitar cost no more than $6, paid for by his mother's knitting projects.

While growing up, a major musical influence was his church where he learned shape note singing and learned harmony and quartet singing with his little church group. His main idol was Merle Travis to whom he listened on the family's battery-powered radio. He and his family listened to WLW, Cincinnati, where they heard Grandpa Jones, the **Delmore Brothers**, **Curly Fox and Texas Ruby**, Red Foley, the **Coon Creek Girls** and **Lulu Belle and Scotty**. They could also pick up the Grand Ole Opry.

About 1941, young Shuffler's participation in his first band was as the electric guitarist with members Herb Lambert (mandolin), J.D. Walker (fiddle) and Wade

169 Spottswood, op. cit., p. 14.

Turner (guitar). After a few months with this group he, at age sixteen, joined the **Melody Mountain Boys** with John Shuffler (George's younger brother), Merritt "Curly" Williams (steel guitar) and Lester Woodie (fiddle). They played on a station in Lenoir, North Carolina.

The next year, Shuffler and J.D. Walker were hired into the very popular **Charlie and Danny Bailey and the Happy Valley Boys** when their bassist, Junior Huskey, and their steel player, Joe Jones, didn't show up. Though Shuffler had never played bass before, he was able to fill-in adequately. George was paid handsomely at $60 per week so he quit his bakery job and soon left with the band for the Opry, sponsored by Martha White Mills. Shuffler stayed with the Baileys until they quit the Opry (about 1942). He moved back home to Valdese and re-formed his **Melody Mountain Boys.** They worked WKBC, North Wilkesboro, WMNC, Morganton and WIRC, Hickory, North Carolina, among other stations. On one of his occasional visits to WCYB, he and Jesse Fulbright met Carter and Ralph Stanley.

About 1950, Shuffler joined up with **Mustard and Gravy**, which was really the duo of rube comedians Frank Rice and Ernie Stokes. They had an extensive radio network (up to 300 stations) and they often played at movie theaters between movies. The all-day jobs included five thirty-minute concerts per day. Shuffler became married during this time. **Mustard and Gravy** split up and Shuffler went with Jim Bulleit and the Liberty Network in Kentucky.

While Hoke Jenkins and Jim and Jesse McReynolds (as Hoke's **Smoky Mountaineers**) were in Middlesboro, Kentucky, for six weeks into the fall of 1951, Shuffler joined them on guitar and vocals and the band went to WWNC, Asheville, North Carolina, to the Old Original Farm Hour. Shuffler described the sequence of events in Middlesboro and Asheville, "Jim Bulleit came out of Shreveport, Louisiana, up into Spruce Pine, North Carolina, and started the Liberty Network. Well, he hired me and then Hoke (Jenkins), and Hoke called Jim and Jesse. Hoke had worked with Jim and Jesse down in Georgia in Valdosta and all around. They were up in Middletown, Ohio, at the time. They had been out in Iowa and all around out through there—the duet had—and they came back to Middletown. So Hoke called them and they came to Spruce Pine as a duet with Hoke. Then they hired me. I went with them. Then we left there in a little while— that Liberty Network didn't last too long—and we did a daily program out of the Carolina theater in Spruce Pine there for a short while and we played dates throughout Kentucky and where the Liberty Network could reach. And so we got tired of that and it was about to fizzle out, too. So Hoke had been at the Farm Hour years prior to that with Wiley and Zeke Morris and the Mainers and different ones so he called up there and got us a pro-

gram. So we went in there and I don't even know what we called ourselves then. This was at WWNC in Asheville." Shuffler was with them for about a year as a quartet. Working with Hoke Jenkins was a lot of fun for Shuffler. He was pleasant, full of mischief and fun. They worked there until Christmas 1951 when inclement weather prevented performances around the area, then they went home for the holidays.

Carter Stanley called George Shuffler on December 28th, 1951, and asked him to join the band which included Carter, Ralph, Curly Seckler and Charlie Cline. The **Stanley Brothers** was on its way to WVLK, Versailles, Kentucky, to replace **Flatt and Scruggs** which left for Raleigh in September. The Stanleys had just left WCYB. Shuffler joined them on bass at WVLK for "a good, long while" which turned out to be until 1958. Before too long Seckler and Cline left, so the band of Carter, Ralph and George became a trio until they hired a fiddler. Kenny Baker played with them at square dances near Baker's home in Jenkins, Kentucky, while he was still working in the coal mines. Art Stamper joined them on fiddle at WVLK in 1952 and was soon replaced by Art Wooten on fiddle. On April 11th, the Stanleys, with Shuffler and Wooten recorded "A Life of Sorrow" in Nashville. There was a later Rich-R-Tone session in mid-'52 at which Shuffler was not present.

In August 1953, the Stanleys recorded their first Mercury session. Shuffler's bass playing gained significant attention on the four songs which they recorded that day. The "walking" bass fiddle style which Shuffler played with the Stanleys inspired many future bassists. Bill Clifton asked Shuffler to record with him. Tom Gray heard these recordings and patterned his own style after Shuffler's. During that time, Shuffler and his brother, John Shuffler, alternated performances with the Stanleys, with George on 90 percent of them.

Shuffler's cross-picking lead guitar style is strictly his own and difficult to duplicate. He played this style with the Stanleys during the period before Bill Napier, who is also given credit for popularizing cross-picking, and was the first to record on lead guitar with Carter and Ralph. But as Mr. Shuffler explains in the Bluegrass Guitar chapter of this book, the styles were different.

The **Stanley Brothers** moved to Live Oak, Florida, in 1958, with Jim Walter Homes as their sponsor. Shuffler didn't go initially. When he did join them that year, they began to pre-record on tape the television shows to be shown at a later date. They made one tape for each one of the television stations where they earlier had played live. Now, they would simply record one show in Jacksonville on Wednesday and it would be sent out to their stations along the East Coast, the Gulf Coast, and in Tallahassee, a circuit they earlier traversed by car every week.

Their venues dried up during the mid- to late '50s. "Oh Lord-a-mercy! Man, I'll tell you that it was hard to get a date," said George. "We just had to rely on the people that we'd worked for back when we were a-boomin'. They'd book us and advertise us and get us enough people to play to keep up surviving...I know Ralph sold a herd of cattle just to keep the band together. He had thirteen big brood cows and a big bull and calves and he sold every one of them to pay salaries."

That fall of 1958, the Stanleys began recording for King; Shuffler began recording with the group February 1959. The **Stanley Brothers** also recorded for Starday and Blue Ridge labels while based in Florida. Shuffler's part in the recording of the King LP "Hymns of the Cross" is believed to be one of the first works by a major bluegrass group which featured a sideman so prominently since the time when Lester and Earl were Monroe's sidemen.

On July 11, 1960, Shuffler first played lead (cross-picked) guitar with the Stanleys for King Records. He doubled on bass and Curly Lambert was also featured on lead guitar and bass at this session with Vernon Derrick on fiddle.

> "At my age I have to pick about everyday to stay up on it. But I can let up a little bit and pick as good as I ever could. I don't play as fast as I used to." —George Shuffler

Referring to his time with the **Stanley Brothers**, George recalled, "Back when they first started bookin' us in colleges (in the early 1960s) we went from, like, $50 a night back in them little schools, to $1000, 1200 or 1500 a day. And we didn't know whether they was laughin' at us or laughin' with us. But we was payin' bills. And because we were so authentic, we were some of the first that went into the colleges before **Flatt and Scruggs** or Monroe or any of 'em. We played the old-time mountain stuff that they was tryin' to study. And we was doin' 'Rabbit in the Log' and stuff like that and the others were doin' more modern bluegrass, you know. They wanted the old, authentic stuff with a lot of the drop-thumb banjo, you know, and the old style harmony with Carter and Ralph singin' lead and tenor and me singin' bass—and we did that a lot. And you know, we sang so much together that way it sounded like there was an overtone of a baritone in there! It almost sounded like a quartet—our harmony was so close." They played and sang as a trio unless the contract called for a quartet. Then they'd hire a bass player who was "good enough to get by."

The colleges would sometimes film their act, slow it down, and study it. The schools would re-show it, charge admission, and use the films as teaching aids. So by the time the **Stanley Brothers** returned to the venue, the group knew they had to have something different to present to the students. The colleges were the first to turn around the situation for starving bluegrassers. Then the festivals era began and bluegrass became profitable again. Shuffler was with the Stanleys at that time and he appeared at that first bluegrass festival in Fincastle, Virginia, in 1965, with the group.

In spite of Carter Stanley's poor health in late '66, they played a regular schedule. Shuffler told of Carter's continuing ill health, "From the Nashville convention (Fan Club Convention Awards Dinner at Nashville's Noel Hotel) we came over to a little town in Kentucky to do a show. Melvin Goins was with us. Carter played a part of the show but then became ill and had to leave the stage. They wanted to put him in the hospital in Lexington but, instead, he wanted to go back to his mother's in Smith Ridge (Virginia). So we played Frenchburg, Kentucky, on a Saturday night and were returning from this show when we were stopped by a trooper who told us that Carter was hospitalized at Bristol in critical condition."[170] Carter recovered enough to spend Thanksgiving at home, but was soon back in the Bristol hospital. He passed away on the morning of Thursday, December 1, 1966.

Shuffler stayed on with Ralph for several months. He later joined **Don Reno, Bill Harrell and the Tennessee Cut-Ups** (in 1968) with Ronnie Reno, recording a few LPs with them on bass.[171] They were based in the Washington, D.C., area and played WWVA's Jamboree; he stayed two years. Shuffler had admired the base of operations at WDBJ that the **Tennessee Cut-Ups** had. He said that "Don Reno and Red Smiley had the best deal of anybody around, over there in Roanoke, Virginia. They had their sponsors there at that station and they survived. And they'd book us through there, you know. We'd do that television show and we go out [on tour] and have crowds around there."

The Reader's Poll of *Bluegrass Unlimited* named George Shuffler Best Bassist by the seventy-five people who participated in the fledgling magazine's poll in 1967.

Shuffler quit his painting job to re-join Ralph Stanley in 1970. "This time I stayed with him about ten months or a year, but it just didn't work. One thing was that people were asking me to play guitar, but I was actually playing bass. Ralph and I were actually too close, I guess, for me to be a sideman."[172]

---

170 Green, op. cit., p. 36.

171 He replaced Duck Austin.

172 Green, op. cit., p. 37.

In 1972, he began playing guitar and singing with his **Shuffler Family** band which mostly performed gospel music. As of 1991, band members were daughter Jennie and her husband Tony Brittain, daughter Debbie, son Steve (bass) and Jimmy Church (steel guitar).

In a 1993 telephone interview, Mr. Shuffler told this writer of a conversation he and Doc Watson had a little earlier, "At my age I have to pick about everyday to stay up on it. But I can let up a little bit and pick as good as I ever could. I don't play as fast as I used to. Doc Watson and I were talkin', he says, 'George, you play as fast as you used to?' I said, 'No sir. I don't even *think* as fast as I used to!' I've got about three numbers I can still pick at a concert. Outside of that I'm slowed down an awful lot. But I still stay with it."

He recorded a tape with his family band which featured his cross-picking. Shuffler's 1993 guitar cassette featured his cross-picked guitar as well as overdubs on lead guitar and bass. As of 1996, he promoted concerts in Valdese and was a horse trader. The horses and the guitar were the only sources of revenue he produced through the years. His wife's job helped put food on the table when music things got hard during the '50s.

Earl Scruggs

Earl Scruggs and the Foggy Mountain Boys

In all the history of bluegrass music there are only two people, in the opinion of this writer, without whom bluegrass would not exist as it does today: one is Bill Monroe, the other is Earl Scruggs. In all the discussions of who was the most important, John Hartford said it best, "Here's the way I feel about it. Everybody's all worried about who invented the style and it's obvious that three-finger banjo pickers have been around a long time—maybe since 1840. But my feeling about it is that if it wasn't for Earl Scruggs, you wouldn't be worried about who invented it." The same can also be said about Monroe and perhaps others, as well. But few will doubt the importance of Earl Scruggs and his "fancy banjo".

Earl Eugene Scruggs was born in Shelby, North Carolina, in the Flint Hill community January 6, 1924. His family had five children. His father, George, frailed on the banjo. Earl's memories about the first instrument he started playing is unclear, "Actually, I don't remember which instrument I started trying to play first. My father died when I was four so I don't remember his playin', but we had in the house a banjo, a guitar, Autoharp, fiddle, and instruments like that. But my older brother (Junie) picked banjo and my [other] brother who's almost two years older than me (Horace), he played guitar. I believe I started the banjo some. But when I would play with my older brother, he wanted me to play guitar with him because he wanted to play the banjo. So anyway, I started playing guitar back as far as I can remember. My idol at the time—the main person I loved the most—was Momma Maybelle Carter, so that's who I copied."[173] About 1930, Junie Scruggs and Smith Hammett (who played a form of three-finger banjo picking style) sparked Earl's interest in the banjo. By age ten, Scruggs was picking the banjo in the local three-finger style and by his early teens was playing for local dances.

According to Larry Perkins in a 1990 interview at IBMA, the Scruggs brothers, Earl and Horace, developed their timing by starting a song then walking around the house and meeting at the point of origin. They did this on their songs until they consistently were in time with each other after their walk.

Scruggs "credits as one of his most important musical influences was Dennis Butler, an elderly farmer and a 'great old-time fiddle player,' wrote Tony Trischka. "As a teenager, Earl 'played many hours with him and got a lot of basic knowledge.' Rather than giving pointers, Butler would fiddle one tune after another and let Earl experiment and find the best ways to complement his music. Despite references by Bill Monroe and Don Reno suggesting that Scruggs derived much of his style from Snuffy Jenkins, Earl consistently refers to his style as his own. However, he does credit Jenkins among the banjo players who influenced him most. Earl recalls seeing him as early as the fiddlers' convention at which Earl first performed in public, and listening to him on the radio in the late thirties and forties."[174] Other important musical influences were **Roy Acuff and His Smoky Mountain Boys**, the **Carter Family**, and Uncle Dave Macon (with whom Scruggs often traveled after joining the **Blue Grass Boys**). Of Macon, Scruggs said, "He never ceased to drop a bit of enjoyment whenever possible. It was my first experience of seeing a man so well loved by so many."[175]

173 From a live interview on Doug Hutchens' radio show, "Bluegrass Today."
174 Tony Trischka and Pete Wernick, *Masters of the 5-String Banjo* (New York: Oak Publications, 1988), p. 21.
175 Trischka and Wernick, op. cit., p.21.

Don Reno described Scruggs' early banjo playing as similar to that of Snuffy Jenkins. "In 1934 and '35, Snuffy could play 'Cumberland Gap' or 'Sally Goodin.' You couldn't tell... If I had a recording of him then and then you put a recording of Scruggs on it you couldn't tell the difference. Me and Scruggs were little boys, you know, then."

Up until Scruggs was a young man, he was on his family's farm. Then, in 1939,[176] he began playing with the **Morris Brothers** (Zeke on mandolin and Wiley and George on guitars) featuring what was known then as "country" music or "hillbilly" music. Don Reno had just left the band as banjoist to soon join Arthur Smith and his **Crackerjacks**. Earl played with these men for a few months, then quit so that he could take care of his widowed mother at his home in Shelby. He worked for the Lily Mills textile mill near his home until the draft restriction of World War II was lifted. And his mother encouraged him to pursue music as a career.

Returning to music in 1945, Scruggs joined the touring band of **Lost John Miller and the Allied Kentuckians** on WNOX in Knoxville, Tennessee, for about three months. They also had a weekly show on WSM in Nashville, one of many such lesser-known programs on WSM which was not the Opry. About that time, Jim Shumate first heard Earl play. Shumate remembered Scruggs well, and when Bill Monroe needed a banjo player to replace Stringbean, he asked Shumate if he had any ideas. He did. Shumate found Earl with Lost John and asked if he wanted to play with the **Blue Grass Boys** which had legendary status even then.

It was well recognized within the **Blue Grass Boys** when Stringbean was the comedian and banjo player that his banjo style was not appropriate for keeping the kind of rhythm which Lester Flatt and Monroe required. In recordings when Stringbean was a member of the band, his banjo is almost inaudible. Flatt and Monroe had interviewed several banjo players after String gave his notice.[177] When it was rumored that another banjo player might audition for the **Blue Grass Boys**, Flatt didn't want another banjo player because "they all sound like Akeman."[178]

Flatt spoke about the exit of Stringbean and the arrival of Earl Scruggs, "Well, I wouldn't want to say exactly how long [Stringbean was gone] but it was several months, and I know as good as we all loved String—and I love that kind of banjo picking because I was raised on it. My daddy played that style and I tried to learn it and I couldn't; that's how come I quit fooling with a banjo—Bill told me one night after String had gone that he was trying out a new boy on the banjo. I hated to hear that because I was really enjoying the work that we was doing with a banjo. Poor old String—it just didn't fit. He would really drag you [down] on that thumb string on those tunes like we're doing today."[179]

When Scruggs auditioned for Flatt and Monroe, Flatt was "thrilled. It was so different! I had never heard that kind of banjo picking. We had been limited, but Earl made all the difference in the world."[180]

Flatt told about Uncle Dave Macon's comments of Scruggs at the audition, "Well, when he got his banjo out to do a little auditioning for Bill, everybody was ganged around listening just like myself because it was entertaining. And Uncle Dave was standing over there with that gold tooth a-shining, and he listened for a while and he said, 'Aaahh. Sound's pretty good in a band.'—there was two or three playing with him you know. He said, 'I'll bet he can't sing worth a damn.'"[181]

Scruggs told about the audition for Monroe, "I worked in Knoxville for Lost John Miller. I was in a group that tried out for the show there. We didn't make it, but Lost John asked about the banjo player in the group, and I started working with him. Then he came to Nashville to start a Saturday morning program. We still lived in Knoxville and worked there and we would come over to Nashville to do the Saturday show. I was friends with Jimmy Shumate who worked with Bill then. The band included Lester Flatt, Birch Monroe, Jim Andrews on tenor banjo and comedy, Shumate and Bill. Each Saturday, Jimmy would want me to quit Lost John and go with Bill. Then, towards the end of 1945, Lost John disbanded and I told Shumate that I was out of a job and would probably go back home so he set it up for Bill to listen to me. Bill came over to the Tulane Hotel and listened to a couple of tunes. He didn't show much reaction, but he asked me to come down to the Opry and jam some. He showed interest, but I think he wasn't sure exactly of the limits of it or how well it

---

[176] This date is contradicted by both Don Reno and Zeke Morris. But because Mr. Scruggs told it to Peter Wernick in 1995, it is included here as *the* date.

[177] String left the Blue Grass Boys in September 1945 and was not replaced until Scruggs came on board except for the tenor banjo of Jim Andrews.

[178] This quotation from an interview with Lester Flatt by an individual who prefers to not be identified.

[179] Marty Stuart with interview by Curly Seckler, "Lester Flatt Memories," *Bluegrass Unlimited*, May, 1986, p. 82.

[180] Ibid., p. 83.

[181] Stuart, op. cit., p. 83.
    Banjoist Bill Keith remembered that Earl Scruggs once told him about an incident during the time that Scruggs and Flatt worked tent shows with Uncle Dave. Keith was told that Uncle Dave always called Earl "Ernest." Scruggs also told him that things in the promotion of their Bill Monroe and the Blue Grass Boys group didn't always go well. He explained that one evening, after twenty hours on the road to get to a small town venue, they found that the posters announcing their arrival (and their invitation to play against their baseball team) had not been posted properly and that they played neither music nor baseball that day. The group just watched a movie and drove back home.
    Mr. Keith also told that Lester and Earl played at WCYB at the same time as the Stanley Brothers. The Stanleys would listen through the wall to Flatt and Scruggs rehearsing their set and find out what songs they were going to play. The Stanleys would then go up first and play those songs and watch Flatt and Scruggs scramble to change the songs they planned to play during their set.

would fit his music, but he asked me if I could go to work on Monday and I said yes."[182] In December of 1945, Scruggs became a **Blue Grass Boy**. Also in the group were Cedric Rainwater (Howard Watts) on bass, Chubby Wise on fiddle, Bill Monroe on mandolin, and Lester Flatt on guitar.

"Back then," Scruggs continued, "the term 'sideman' wasn't used as it is today. It was a leader and his group, and you all worked together. It was hard work but we had a lot of fun. I loved Bill like a brother and he was always good to me. He took great interest in the work he was doing, and I felt appreciated. He was high on my list as a musician, and he had a solid beat that could support anything you wanted to pick. He would spend a lot of time just tightening up the group. Some rehearsals we wouldn't sing a song. We would just concentrate on the sound of the band.

"We were working all the time. Sometimes we wouldn't see a bed from one end of the week 'til the other. In theaters, we would do four or five or six shows a day from eleven in the morning until eleven at night. Sometimes we would do what was called 'bicycling'. We would play a show in a theater, then while the movie was on, go play in another and come back to the first one while the movie was on in the second.

Lester Flatt and Earl Scruggs meeting the cast of "The Beverly Hillbillies" —popular CBS television show in the 1960's

"It was a must then to make it back to the Opry on Saturday night. Sometimes, if we were over on the East Coast somewhere, it was all we could do to make it back. But the Opry meant so much to the people then in the towns...

"It was hard traveling then on bad roads in a stretched-out car with no place to lie down. Sometimes you'd feel so bad and fall asleep and then wake up and someone would maybe tell a story and we'd laugh and feel good again. But Bill would never let the music go down no matter how tired we were. If a man would slack off, he would move over and get that mandolin close up on him and get him back up there. He would shove you and you would shove him and you would really get on it.

"We played in rain, we played in snow, we played where the power would go off and we would have to play by lantern light with no sound. We had two bad wrecks, but nobody got hurt. The way we had to drive to make dates, it's a wonder we weren't killed. But we made it, and it toughened you up to encounter and overcome these difficulties. It seemed to make Bill

stronger and it brought out the deep feeling and love he had for what he was doing."[183]

Scruggs made his first recording with Bill Monroe, "Heavy Traffic Ahead," on September 16, 1946. Also on the recording were Monroe, Wise, Flatt and Watts. Birch Monroe recorded in Bill Monroe's quartet that month on "Shining Path."

In early 1948, Earl Scruggs quit the **Blue Grass Boys** to move back to North Carolina. Two weeks later, Flatt also resigned. It is said by some that the two men had intentions of getting together again to form a band. Some say that they planned the move with Howard Watts. But Flatt remembered, "Well, I feel like actually maybe Bill might have always had the feeling that we had planned it, but actually we hadn't. Earl, he had to take care of his mother. She was living over in Shelby and he didn't like the idea of staying away from home all the time with nobody there with her. To make a long story short, it was a rough life. I had made it up in my mind to quit but I hadn't said anything about it. Earl was going to go home just to get off the road. We had it rough back then. It wasn't anything to ride two or three days in a car. We didn't have buses like we do now, and we never had our shoes off."

Flatt continued, "Earl had a textile job before he came to Nashville so I think he was just planning to get back and take care of his mother and work at the mill. After Earl turned his notice in to Bill—you know, he was giving his two weeks notice—we got to talking and I told him I was going to quit, too. We decided we might go to Knoxville and work as a team or go to work with Carl Story or some group that might need us. I turned my notice in then, and before my notice was up, fellows like Cedric Rainwater [Howard Watts] said, 'Let me join in with you and we'll form a band.' So that was how it all happened."[184]

The men knew that there was a lot of money to be made in this business with their own band—they had handled the bundles of cash at every concert they played with Monroe—so they decided to go ahead with it. They formed their own band. Flatt, Scruggs, and Cedric Rainwater became **Lester Flatt, Earl Scruggs and the Foggy Mountain Boys**. They came up with the band name from a popular **Carter Family** song, "Foggy Mountain Top," and began using the song as a theme song for awhile.

This new band first played on WDVA, Danville, Virginia, as a trio in January 1948. Their time as a trio

[182] James Rooney, *Bossmen: Bill Monroe and Muddy Waters*, 1971, p. 42.

[183] James Rooney, *Bossmen: Bill Monroe and Muddy Waters*, 1971, pp. 43-45.

[184] Pete Kuykendall, "Lester Flatt and the Nashville Grass," *Bluegrass Unlimited*, January, 1971.

lasted only a few days when they hired Jim Eanes, who was already at the station, to play guitar and sing lead with them at the station. Eanes was with them there at WDVA for two or three weeks.

Eanes related, "Lester and Earl called me and wanted me to join forces with them. Lester and Earl and Cedric had all left Bill [Monroe] at that time and formed the **Foggy Mountain Boys**. And he called me and wanted me to be a part of the group and we started working together. Then Bill sent me a telegram. And like every young musician, I had always wanted to sing on the Grand Ole Opry and I had never been there. So I left that group and went with Bill." Eanes then found that his voice was too low to fit the keys in which Monroe like to sing (B and B flat) so he quit after nine months to manage a record shop in Martinsville, Virginia.

In March, after the **Foggy Mountain Boys** left WDVA, Danville, Virginia, the threesome picked up fiddler Jim Shumate and began playing at WHKY, Hickory, North Carolina, near Shumate's home. They then hired Mac Wiseman and were able to get a job at the very powerful WCYB in Bristol in the last of April, the first of May. There at WCYB, the station allowed them to advertise their songbooks for four weeks; they sold 10,000 books through the mail. They stayed eighteen months; Wiseman stayed until Christmas 1948.

Flatt spoke about this new band he and Scruggs had formed, "We had a good outfit. It wasn't too long until we got a chance at some network stuff. At the time, our type of music was more or less limited to the South. And the people up in the New England states and some of the northern states started talking about the 'new' sound of **Flatt and Scruggs**—and we'd been playing it for years."[185]

On April 18, 1948, Earl Scruggs married Louise Certain. They had met in Nashville in 1946. Her experience as a bookkeeper enabled her to fit right into the position of Business Manager and Booking Manager for the group in 1956. While many people give her credit for some of the band's success, others recognize that Earl was excellent in his management skills and passed on to Louise much of his knowledge about the successful management of his band. Both of them actively, and successfully, managed the band and kept them working through the years.

Earl, in an interview with Doug Hutchens, described the early days of his new band, "We had been married—maybe two or three months and we wasn't makin' anything. We worked a little while in Hickory, North Carolina, and my wife was stayin' with my mother in Shelby. So we moved up to Bristol and I think

about the second week we played Hindman, Kentucky. And it doesn't sound like a lot of money, but we did close to $400 up there. We were on a five-way split. Of course, I had been used to workin' for Bill Monroe for $60 a week so my split really looked good. I think I took my part in one-dollar bills. Anyway, I called Louise down in Shelby and said, 'Come up! I've struck it rich!' She came up and I showed her that bundle of money— and most of it was ones but it looked as big as a limousine Cadillac as far as I was concerned. That was how we got started off and from then on it seem like everything else fell into place. Bristol really had a lot of listeners."

During the fall of 1948, **Lester Flatt, Earl Scruggs and the Foggy Mountain Boys** began a three-year recording stint with Mercury Records.[186] Scruggs elaborated that "Mercury was a very small company. I think we were about their third artist. Murray Nash, who produced all the records for Mercury, would make the arrangements for a studio someplace and we'd record at some radio station."[187] It began with "My

Lester Flatt and Earl Scruggs, c. 1951

Cabin in Caroline," "I'm Going to Make Heaven My Home," "We'll Meet Again Sweetheart" and "God Loves His Children." Musicians in the band and on the recording were Flatt, Scruggs, Wiseman, Shumate and Watts. Flatt's terrific rhythm, using a thumbpick, was solid. Scruggs developed a lead guitar style, using the three-finger style, which was innovative and an entirely new sound. It was very effective on "Jimmie Brown, the Newsboy."

"Flatt and Scruggs seem to have tried to innovate than merely to copy," wrote author Jack Hurst. "They gradually made changes in Monroe's formula, and Flatt acknowledges now that they consciously tried to present 'a little different sound from Bill.' In the mid-fifties, they dropped the mandolin altogether and replaced it with a Dobro® guitar played by Buck (Uncle Josh) Graves, whom they hired from Wilma Lee and

[185] Stuart, op. cit., p. 83.

[186] They couldn't record on Bill Monroe's label, Columbia, because Monroe was on that label and applied pressure that another band like his (the name "bluegrass" was not used yet to identify the musical genre) would not to be hired there; they had to find another label.

[187] Marty Godbey, op. cit., p. 59.

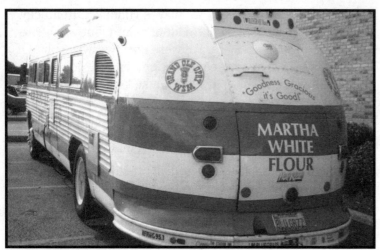

Replica of 1956 Flxible bus used by Flatt and Scruggs and the Foggy Mountain Boys for many years. Bus restored by Don Clark.

Granada banjo for my Gibson RB-3, so the swap was made."[190]

In southwest Virginia, in the area of Bristol's WCYB, a coal miner's strike severely depressed the area. In March 1949, **Flatt and Scruggs and the Foggy Mountain Boys**, which was there at WCYB, decided to leave to seek greener pastures at WROL in Knoxville. They played on WROL's Noon-Day Dinner Bell Show which was hosted by Archie Campbell. Mac Wiseman left shortly after the move to WROL to work at the WSB Barn Dance in Atlanta.

When Lester Flatt called Curly Seckler and asked him to join him and Earl Scruggs in a band, Curly couldn't get there fast enough. He was working with Jim and Jesse McReynolds (and Hoke Jenkins as the **Smoky Mountaineers**) in Augusta, Georgia, at the time. He joined **Flatt and Scruggs** on March 17th, 1949. Curly's nickname (by Lester) was "The Old Trapper from China Grove, North Carolina." This new group packed them in! Their success was unqualified and their popularity was tremendous.

That spring of 1949, **Flatt and Scruggs** recorded their second Mercury session with Flatt, Scruggs, Seckler, Wooten and Watts. The songs included "Down the Road" and "Why Don't You Tell Me So?" On December 11th, they recorded with Flatt, Scruggs, Seckler, Sims and Watts. The songs were "I'll Never Shed Another Tear," "No Mother or Dad," "Is It Too Late Now?" and "Foggy Mountain Breakdown."

Howard Watts (Cedric Rainwater) left the band in late 1949 to join the band of Hank Williams. Charles Johnson joined on bass and soon became known as "Little Jody Rainwater." By the summer of 1950, the group was based at WCYB again after a short time at WVLK in Versailles, Kentucky.

In late summer, the **Foggy Mountain Boys** moved to WDAE, Tampa. But this, too, proved unprofitable. They stayed eleven weeks, during which time they recorded their last Mercury session during a threat of a hurricane (October 20, 1950) there in Tampa. Songs included "Doin' My Time," "Pike Country Breakdown," "Cora is Gone," "Preachin', Prayin', Singing." On the next day, they recorded their own version of the **Lonesome Pine Fiddlers**' "Pain in My Heart." They also recorded "Roll in My Sweet Baby's Arms," "Back to the Cross" and "Farewell Blues." At the following session at that time, they recorded "Old Salty Dog Blues," "Will

Stoney Cooper's **Clinch Mountain Clan**. Flatt also pitched his voice much lower than Monroe's high sound, even though Flatt himself had always sung tenor until he joined Monroe's band."[188]

Toward the end of 1948, Jim Shumate quit and was replaced temporarily by Art Wooten. Wooten recorded on the April-May 1949 recording session with Curly Seckler on mandolin. That fall, Wooten was replaced by Benny Sims on the fiddle. Sims recorded more than two dozen tunes in seven recording sessions with this group beginning with the December 11, 1949, session to the November 21, 1950, session, and helped define the **Flatt and Scruggs** sound. Tunes recorded during that time with Sims on fiddle included "Foggy Mountain Breakdown," "Old Salty Dog Blues," "Farewell Blues," "Head Over Heels in Love," "Will the Roses Bloom (Where She Lies Sleeping)," "Take Me in a Lifeboat," "Doin' My Time" and "Roll in My Sweet Baby's Arms." "When Benny was with the **Foggy Mountain Boys**," said Earl, "everyone always got along great." Sims recalled that "With all five of us and the instruments packed in the car, there was no room left for suitcases. So we just put our clothes into paper grocery sacks and stuffed them wherever we could find room."[189]

"While we were at WCYB," said Earl, "Bill Monroe was in the area and we invited him to make an appearance on our radio program to promote his nearby show dates. Don Reno was with him at the time and approached me on the idea of trading his 1933/34 Gibson

---

[188] Jack Hurst, *Nashville's Grand Ole Opry* (New York: Harry N. Abrams, Inc., Publishers, 1975), p. 245.

   Actually, Mr. Hurst is in error about dropping the mandolin "altogether." The band continued to use the mandolin in the band but with the conscious effort to use it for mostly rhythm.

[189] Jack Tottle, "Benny Sims, East Tennessee Bluegrass Pioneer," *Bluegrass Unlimited*, February, 1996, p. 31.

   Sims (1924 to December 23, 1995) earlier worked with the Morris Brothers, the Shelton Brothers (which at that time included Carl Smith), Jim and Jesse and the Virginia Boys, and the Stanley Brothers. Then he played three years on Knoxville's Mid-Day Merry-Go-Round and then the local television stars Bonnie Lou and Buster Moore. He left music in the 1960s for a full-time job in Johnson City, Tennessee, as an insurance agent, staying active with his music by teaching fiddle occasionally.

   The next Flatt and Scruggs session (May 9, 1951) featured Chubby Wise, followed by Howdy Forrester (October 24, 1951 session), Benny Martin (November 9, 1952, through August 30, 1953, sessions), followed by Paul Warren whose first session was May 19, 1954.

   Sims' last recording was on Curly Seckler's 1995 project on Nashville's Vine Street label which also included Mac Wiseman, Ralph Stanley, Jim and Jesse McReynolds, Jimmy Martin, Grant Turner, Benny Martin, Doyle Lawson and Marty Stuart.

[190] Godbey, op. cit., p. 59.

the Roses Bloom (Where She Lies Sleeping)," "Take Me in a Lifeboat" and "I'll Just Pretend."

On November 21st, 1950, they made their first Columbia[191] recording session with members Flatt, Scruggs, Sims, Seckler and Jody Rainwater. Songs included "The Old Home Town," "Come Back Darling," "I'll Stay Around," "We Can't Be Sweethearts Any More" and "I'm Waiting to Hear You Call Me Darling." About that time, Benny Sims left and was replaced by Chubby Wise on fiddle.

Seckler left **Flatt and Scruggs** in November to join the **Sauceman Brothers**. Everett Lilly became the mandolin player for the band from November 1950 until fall 1952. He was not, as many people have said, restricted to mainly rhythm in order to sound dissimilar to the **Blue Grass Boys**. (Seckler did very little lead playing, but then Seckler never claimed to be a great mandolin player. Seckler likes the story that Flatt used to tell of Seckler's prowess on the mandolin as, "Well, you hold it real good.") But Scruggs did insist on a style which ended up a little different that Monroe's. While his mandolin players were not restricted to strictly rhythm, it may have seemed that way. Scruggs explained, "That's a matter of interpretation. We never asked Everett to stick to rhythm at all 'cause Everett was a good mandolin picker. Now, that's exactly how it was. But if Everett interpreted that was what he was supposed to do, he never indicated that. I'll tell you where that probably came in. What I always insisted on the band doin' is, if you was backin' up somethin' for us to play rhythm and just one person was backin' up. In other words, not everybody would be playin' at the same time while the guy is up there singin' his heart out, tryin' to sing a song, and everybody tryin' to play every lick they can play is like a lot of people tryin' to talk at the same time. You can't get a point across. So I did require, if I was backin' up, for the fiddle and mando- lin to lay off. Then when I drop off, give it to the fiddle player and then the mandolin, and the banjo player'd drop off. And then when the mandolin was doin' it, the fiddle and banjo'd drop off. See, that cleaned it up a whole lot. That was just one require- ment that was probably different than a lot of bands that was goin' around then and still goin' around today. I'm not speakin' of anybody in particular, but sometimes you can hear them all playin' at the same time in the

background of a lot of records. Anyway, that's the only reason Everett was put on rhythm."[192]

In March 1951, the group moved from Florida back to Lexington where, that fall, they had programs on WVLK in nearby Versailles, and WKLX with members Flatt, Scruggs, Everett Lilly (mandolin) and Chubby Wise (fiddle). In June 1951, Scruggs played lead guitar on "Jimmy Brown, the Newsboy" when they recorded the single on Columbia. It was here in Lexington that J.D. Crowe first saw the group. "Their music was so different, so powerful...I never saw or heard anything like that—like it was going to explode. The speed, and even the slow things, had such a timing factor."[193]

Flatt and Scruggs worked the month of July on WOAY, Oak Hill, West Virginia. In September, the band moved to Roanoke, Virginia, playing on WDBJ.

Howdy Forrester, a regular member of Roy Acuff's band, recorded with the band on October 24th; Chubby Wise had recently left. Art Wooten had joined but was not at the recording session that date. The best known tune from that session was "Earl's Breakdown" where Scruggs manually re-tuned his second banjo string to get an effect which he and his brother Horace experi- mented with as kids. The success of this tune led to the development of his D-tuners and later the Scruggs- Keith tuners. Scruggs also came up with the idea of using hooks, initially made from hairpins, to capo the fifth string.

In January 1952, **Flatt and Scruggs** traded their spot on WDBJ in Roanoke with the **Bailey Brothers** at 50,000 watt WPTF in Raleigh, North Carolina, where they spent eight months. Everett Lilly quit in Septem- ber to joined Don Stover, his brother "B" Lilly, and Tex Logan in their **Confederate Mountaineers**. Seckler re- joined on mandolin. Benny Martin joined on fiddle.[194]

Flatt and Scruggs at Oberlin College, c. 1962. Photo courtesy of Mark Schoenberg.

[191] Bill Monroe had left Columbia and begun recording on Decca in November of 1949. He didn't want to be on the label which had two bluegrass bands—the Stanley Brothers started recording on Columbia earlier in 1949. Flatt and Scruggs was now free to join Columbia since Monroe was gone.

[192] July 1996 telephone interview.

[193] Godbey, op. cit., p. 60.

[194] About this time, Benny Martin invented the 8-string fiddle. It is mostly a novelty and he used it for only about fifteen tunes; it is very difficult to play. Martin made one for John Hartford, a man whom Martin considers "the greatest one-man show I ever saw."

Flatt and Scruggs left Raleigh that October for WNOX in Knoxville where they spent several months. That November, the group recorded their ninth session for Columbia in Nashville which featured Flatt, Scruggs, Seckler, Martin and Jody Rainwater. Three songs of the session were played by Flatt and Scruggs while they were with Monroe: "Dear Old Dixie," "Why Did You Wander" (written by Monroe and Flatt and recorded by them in 1946 but never released) and "If I Should Wander Back Tonight." Other songs were "Flint Hill Special," "Thinking About You," "Dim Lights, Thick Smoke," "Reunion in Heaven" and "Pray for the Boys" (timely because of the Korean conflict). "Flint Hill Special" featured Scruggs' D-tuners on both middle strings. It was in Knoxville that the Martha White Mills salespeople told Cohen Williams that he needed the band to sell their flour.

In June 1953, Martha White Mills became the sponsor for **Flatt and Scruggs** on WSM's daily, early-morning radio broadcast where they performed until September 1954.[195] They then moved to Crewe, Virginia, for a weekday radio performance. They continued their WSM Martha White shows by recording them on tape. "We were the first in country music to have a syndicated TV program," said Earl. With the Pet Milk Company as a co-sponsor with Martha White, they were seen on more than forty television stations. During these appearances on WSM, they were simultaneously appearing in Nashville, Chattanooga and Jackson, Tennessee, and at Huntington, West Virginia.

When television came along, they "didn't have video tape then," recalled Curly Seckler. "So we had to travel to [all our live shows]. We rode 2500 miles each week doing six television shows. Plus, we would play a personal appearance at night somewhere in the radius

Earl Scruggs and Lester Flatt, c. 1963

of the television station." Two years later, "videotape came along and we danced a little jig because then we could tape them here in Nashville and send them out to the stations."[196] Additionally, in the early stages of their touring, they included stops in Atlanta, and at Florence, South Carolina. Occasionally they made a trip to Detroit with stops along the way. On occasions, they gave four complete performances in one day.

The band recorded on August 29th and 30th of 1953, but this time it was with a different sound. They added a second rhythm guitar played on the same offbeat as Seckler's mandolin. They hired a studio musician for this and also hired a studio bass player for the session.

In September of 1954, they joined the cast of the Old Dominion Barn Dance, of Richmond, Virginia, in order to appear on the New York Broadway show, "Hayride," at the 48th Street Theater for two weeks.[197] Here, in one of their first tours outside of the South, they found how popular the banjo had become by seeing the number of young folk musicians trying to imitate Scruggs' style. The popularity of Scruggs-style banjo playing had increased to unprecedented proportions and the term "five-string banjo" became a drawing card to concerts and record buyers. Bluegrass (the term was gaining recognition as a musical form) banjo instrumentals were becoming more and more prominent in the music. When Pete Seeger included a section in his folk banjo book about Scruggs' playing method, the group became well accepted in the folk circles. This was very important, for the advent of the Elvis phenomenon would soon make it hard for bluegrass bands to thrive.

The New York show director wanted the group to wear make-up—the traditional reddened cheeks and penciled eyebrows. Flatt refused. "We didn't come here to perform a miracle—just to put on a little hillbilly show," he told the director. "We'll go on tonight like we are and if the folks don't like it we'll go home tomorrow."[198] Their tremendous reception kept them for the contracted time.

The group moved from Nashville to Crewe, Virginia, in May of 1954 to do live shows at WSVS while still recording their WSM shows on tape and making regular Saturday night appearances at Richmond, Virginia's Old Dominion Barn Dance. Paul Warren joined **Flatt and Scruggs** as fiddler in 1954, replacing Benny Martin, until 1977. Warren's fiddle style fell right in with the needs of the band, featuring the fiddle and banjo during instrumentals. The introduction of Buck Graves' Dobro® in 1955 took away some of the fiddle's lime-

[195] The sponsorship arrangement with Martha White Mills continued on both radio and television until they broke up in 1969. The Martha White Company actively sponsored Alison Krauss and Union Station in 1996 just as Flatt and Scruggs had helped them remain a successful company through the years. And, just as Flatt and Scruggs and the Foggy Mountain Boys was the most popular band in bluegrass in the early 1950s, Union Station would also benefit from this symbiotic business arrangement.

[196] Stuart, op. cit., p. 87.

[197] The entire cast of the Old Dominion Barn Dance went up there to do their show before the New York audience.

[198] Ben A. Green, "Flatt and Scruggs—Friendship music hits hearts from New York to Tennessee rural school," *Bluegrass Unlimited*, September, 19xx?. This article was written by Green and included in the September 1956 issue of the *Nashville Banner*.

light and the band had its own, distinctive sound. And Curly Seckler's mandolin breaks almost ceased to exist.

They moved to Nashville January 1955. Jody Rainwater left the band and went into radio broadcasting when **Flatt and Scruggs** left Crewe for Nashville.

By early this year, **Flatt and Scruggs'** series of thirty-minute television shows on WSM-TV was aired in six different cities, sponsored by Martha White Flour Mills. Band members included Flatt, Scruggs, Paul Warren (fiddle), Charles "Little Darlin'" Elza (bass, comedy) and Seckler (mandolin).

Until this time, WSM didn't allow Lester Flatt and Earl Scruggs to become members of the Grand Ole Opry. It is often said that the station felt they owed a certain loyalty to Bill Monroe, and that this new band was an imitation of the original. Finally, there was so much mail that public demand (and Martha White Mills) insisted they appear on the Opry. They took over the Mill's sponsored spot on the Opry which, until then, was occupied by a western swing band. They joined the Opry in January 1955.

The band's entry onto the Opry was actually as a direct result of Martha White's Cohen Williams. He dumped a large sack of fan mail on the floor of General Manager Jack DeWitt[199] and threatened that either he put **Flatt and Scruggs** on the Opry or he was going to pull his company's advertising from the station. But there is more to this story, much more. It is included in the Controversies chapter of this book. "The reason we wasn't on the Opry was because of Bill Monroe," said Scruggs. "That simply was how it was. The reason we got on the Grand Ole Opry was because of Cohen Williams. Because we was the only ones that he thought could have sold his flour for him. We did well (financially), and so did they."

It turned out that the groups *were* different enough. Mr. Scruggs told this writer, "We came here to Nashville with our own style. We didn't have to change our style to be ourselves. I started pickin' when I was about four or five years old and came up with the style I came up with for the rest of my life when I was about ten or eleven. I never really could remember when I came up with the three-finger style. But I never felt that I should quit what I had done all my life after I left Monroe, and let him go ahead and do it, and me try to learn a new style."[200]

Earl Scruggs with his "Earl Scruggs Revue," winter 1977-78

Initially, **Flatt and Scruggs** was treated with cold shoulders by the other entertainers, but only a few weeks went by and they were treated well and welcomed. Grant Turner, announcer of the Opry since 1944, told this story in a 1991 phone interview: "There's quite a story there. Jack Stapp was the Program Director and they had quite a problem there, and Jack realized it because he found out that Bill Monroe was going to be *very* unfriendly to them bringing in this group to be on Martha White's show. So he (Stapp) told Flatt and Scruggs, he said, 'When you come here to do this Martha White show, come in just a few minutes before it's time to go on. And as soon as you get through with your show, leave. Well, you could imagine. Lester, especially, was a very sensitive person and this made him—you're talking about a man who is building up a good career in country music and you're talking to him like he is a second class citizen—it absolutely made Lester very uptight. In fact, he may have told them that he would rather go back to where he was because he didn't come here to be treated that way. It's a wonder that they worked it out."

Several months after Lester and Earl joined the Opry, Josh Graves was hired as bass player and comedian. He had already worked with Esco Hankins, **Wilma Lee and Stoney Cooper**, Toby Stroud, and Mac Wiseman's **Country Boys**. Tom Gray, in a 1989 interview with this writer, felt that the prime years of **Flatt and Scruggs** were already over. "I think the Dobro® rescued them when they were losing some of their spark. The Dobro® gave them a new spark to continue

---

[199] At the time of the meetings, which were held with Cohen Williams and the Opry managers, Josh Graves was not with them yet. Therefore, as Scruggs put it, he was not a factor of the band being hired onto the Opry. When Graves came with the Foggy Mountain Boys, he was hired to play bass. He began playing Dobro with them a month later. Graves feels confident that he was not a factor in the group's admittance into the Opry. He said that it was strictly the pressure from Martha White Flour which exhibited not only proof that his sponsored Flatt and Scruggs group was getting more fan mail than any of the existing Opry members, but he forced this issue by threatening to pull out his substantial sponsorship at the Opry.

And, according to Jim McReynolds as told by former Opry announcer Grant Turner, Bill Monroe had done everything in his power to keep them off the show. Monroe had actually circulated a petition among the Opry members in support that Flatt and Scruggs should not be allowed entry. It was signed by several of the members who, after the band was admitted, apologized to Flatt and Scruggs later for signing it. Evidently, they had been pressured by Monroe to sign it. (See "Strife at the Opry Caused by Bill Monroe" in the Invention of Bluegrass and Controversies chapter.)

Further, McReynolds mentioned that the bitterness in the Monroe-Flatt and Scruggs feud, which is legend, began about this time. Monroe had played occasionally with them down at WCYB shortly after Flatt and Scruggs had left the Blue Grass Boys and had somewhat of a working relationship with them until they challenged his popularity on the Opry. (See Carlton Haney chapter for more on this topic.)

[200] 1996 telephone conversation.

creativity." With Graves playing the "hound dog" guitar (so named by Graves), it became so popular that they put him on Dobro® full-time. "A few people criticized us for doing it," said Seckler, "but now they would criticize us if we left it off."[201] Scruggs emphasized that "Josh *was* an asset to the group. We had a lot of air time and played the same style over and over so much until we thought that an addition wouldn't hurt."

Graves remembered, "When Earl called me, he wanted to know if I would come down for a two-week try-out as a bass player. Well, that was like asking if I wanted a million dollars. I arrived in Nashville and began my try-out on May 14, 1955. The first personal appearance we did after I arrived was Silver Point School in Wilson County, Tennessee. I had my Dobro®, so I asked Flatt if he wanted me to take my old guitar along and he said we could carry it; 'We might even let you do a tune.' So on the show that night I played 'Steel Guitar Chimes' and the audience really seemed to like it. However, neither Flatt nor Scruggs said anything one way or the other. I was in my third week and one day they called and asked me to meet them in the lobby of the hotel. Well, I thought, 'Here I go back to Momma and the kids.' They were still in Richmond. We had purchased a house trailer and I didn't want to go through the moving process until I knew I had the job with Flatt and Scruggs. I was living at the Tulane Hotel and I went down and paced the lobby until they got there. When they arrived, Earl wanted to know which instrument I had rather play: the bass or the Dobro®. Well, after I breathed a sigh of relief, I told them I had rather play the Dobro®, but the main thing I wanted was a job. I never will forget what Flatt said to Earl: 'Well, it looks like we are gonna have to hire us a bass player.' Man, I was tickled to death. I asked them if it was all right for me to move my family to Nashville and Earl said, 'Well, that depends on whether you want 'em down here or not.' I moved them the next week and we parked our trailer at the Dickerson Road Trailer Park."

Graves continued, "Flatt and Scruggs hired Joe Stuart to play bass and put me on Dobro® and comedy. They had seen Jake (Tullock) and me do a comedy routine when we were with Esco Hankins and we had a pretty fair act together. So, with all due respect to Joe Stuart, they wanted me to call Jake and see if he would work for them, doing comedy with me and also playing bass. I called him in Knoxville and he caught the next bus for Nashville. We dug out our old comedy outfits and started our routine all over again. I believe Flatt and Scruggs started us out at about eighty dollars a week."[202]

Flatt and Scruggs now was one of the few bands around that used the Dobro®/resonator guitar. According to Lester Flatt, Brother Oswald was playing "an electric type Dobro® or steel, and he (Roy Acuff) had Shot Jackson playing steel. And I'll tell you something else: a fiddle was so dead you couldn't give a fiddle away. Nobody seemed interested in a fiddle. I was more or less raised on a fiddle and a banjo, and I would keep throwing a fiddle tune in on every show. Now, today it's a different story. A fiddle is one of the hottest instruments going around a festival or in the colleges."[203]

Scruggs recently said, "People will tell you that Elvis killed country music. But we did more business during that time than we ever had. Some acts can go on TV and go over; and some just die. It just so happened that people were hungrier for [our] music than they ever were before... Just about every band here [in Nashville] disbanded during that time. They had one band that played behind the stars, and they survived awhile doing package shows."[204]

On October 2nd, 1955, Earl, Louise, and children Gary and Randy Lynn were in a serious auto accident. The children were fine but Earl suffered dislocated hips and a fractured pelvis, among other injuries. Louise was seriously hurt and received 200 stitches on her face. Both Earl and Louise were in Nashville's Saint Thomas Hospital for about two months. They received 10,000 get-well items. Injuries sustained would continue to bother him through the years.

Earl described the event, "One Sunday afternoon, pretty late in the day, my brother called me and didn't want to excite me too much, afraid I might drive too fast. Anyway, he said something was wrong with our mother. What had happened is she had had a stroke. Back in those days, the only way you could get from here (Nashville) to Charlotte—and Charlotte's about forty miles east of Shelby—you would have to catch a plane out of Atlanta. I believe you'd have to go Atlanta and change and go to Columbia, South Carolina, and change and go to Charlotte. That would take all day.

> "It was a must then to make it back to the Opry on Saturday night. Sometimes, if we were over on the East Coast somewhere, it was all we could do to make it back. But the Opry meant so much to the people then in the towns..."
> —Earl Scruggs

[201] Stuart, op. cit., p. 85.

[202] Jake Lambert, *The Good Times Outweigh the Bad,* a biography of Lester Flatt.

[203] Stuart, op. cit., p. 85.

[204] Godbey, op. cit., p. 61.

And, of course, this being late Sunday afternoon we decided we'd just drive over 'cause we could be over there by early breakfast the next morning by taking our time. So we started drivin' and we had gotten about fifteen miles east of Knoxville—I guess at the time that was during the two-lane highway days along 70 Highway—and we was on the straightest road between here and Shelby about three o'clock (my watch was broken at five minutes before three in the morning) there was a car came out of a side road [with a] boozed-up man and woman in it. That's where it happened. Luckily for us—we had two boys at the time Gary and Randy, they were two and six—one was on the pallet on the floor and one was layin' in the back seat. This was before seat belts. And Buddy, when I hit that car—and everybody said I was drivin' about 55—when I hit that car the seat stripped on the carriage. Louise knocked a hole in the windshield; she messed up her face real bad for several years and had a lot of plastic surgery done. But it dislocated my hips and broke us up real bad. But we was young enough until after three months I had to have a metal hip put in and later have another metal hip put in. But everything came out real well, mainly because our two boys were not injured that much. And after enough years went by, we got to where we could get along all right even though we still have pain with it." Scruggs started flying his own plane to some of his concerts in 1957. This enabled him to be home with his family more often and is easier, physically, than traveling endless hours on the band's bus. Flatt hired Curtis McPeake and Donnie Bryant in Scruggs' place.[205] After this, McPeake replaced Scruggs many times until 1969 when **Flatt and Scruggs** disbanded.

In 1955 and 1956, **Flatt and Scruggs and the Foggy Mountain Boys** won the readers' poll of *Country and Western Jamboree* magazine as Best Country Music Instrumental Group (with less than six band members). The band was the only Opry unit continuously sponsored on radio, television, and personal appearances by one firm: Cohen T. Williams' Martha White Flour. **Flatt and Scruggs** was among the entertainers who recorded transcriptions for the U.S. Armed Forces syndicated show, "Country Style USA." The series aired on over 2,500 stations. In the band were Flatt, Scruggs, Seckler, Paul Warren, Josh Graves, Jake Tullock [206] and Charles

"The Little Darling" Elza (comedy, bass, also known as "Kentucky Slim"). Occasional comedy—no longer black-faced—included skits with Kentucky Slim and Jake Tullock. Slim weighed 275 pounds. Their television shows gave Slim an opportunity to show off his "pork chop" step which was difficult for such a large man.

In October 1957, Columbia released their first LP, "Foggy Mountain Jamboree." Soon Curly Seckler was playing on a part-time basis and the band hired Curly Lambert (guitar, tenor vocals). He recorded on the January 23, 1959, session which included "Crying My Heart Over You" as well as the April 5, 1959, session (on tenor vocals only) which included "Cabin on the Hill." Everett Lilly played mandolin with the band again for eight months beginning in 1958. That same month, a second Martha White unit was formed featuring Hylo Brown and his newly-formed **Timberliners**.

After Scruggs' July 1959 appearance at the first Newport Folk Festival, he was described by the *New York Times* as the "Paganini of the five-string banjo". He appeared there as a guest of Hylo Brown's band, not his regular **Foggy Mountain Boys**. This appearance was probably the impetus which catapulted **Flatt and Scruggs** to stardom during the great folk boom in the early '60s and perhaps helped all bluegrass bands to be accepted into the folk "fold" where the venues were. The Elvis phenomenon had taken the wind out of bluegrass' sails and bluegrass bands had few places to play until the festivals got into gear.

The next year, they played at the Newport Folk Festival and appeared on their first live network television show, "The Revlon Revue: Folk Sound, USA," on the CBS network. Experiencing other kinds of folk music on this program whetted Scruggs' appetite to delve into a style of music which was more commercially appealing to young and urban audiences. Columbia Records pushed this, too. Flatt resisted. In April 1960, **Flatt and Scruggs** recorded with drums for the first time. They continued this practice occasionally. They did their first college and university folk music concerts in 1961. Columbia soon released "Folk Songs of Our Land" which catered to this folk market.

On December 8, 1962, **Flatt and Scruggs** appeared at Carnegie Hall; an album of the concert soon followed. Late that year, "The Ballad of Jed Clampett" theme

---

205 McPeake later went with Lester Flatt and the Nashville Grass. Also, through the years, McPeake kept Scruggs' banjo tightened the way Scruggs liked it and repaired it when necessary. McPeake later worked a couple of years with Bill Monroe. As of 1994, McPeake owned McPeake's Unique Instruments, a mail-order instrument business in Mt. Juliet, Tennessee.

Author Chris Lewis tells how it happened: Pedersen was recording in Nashville with Vern and Ray (Vern Williams and Ray Park). "A big break came when Herb filled-in on a Saturday bluegrass television show featuring Carl Tipton and the Midstate Playboys. One of the viewers was Earl Scruggs. He was so impressed with Herb, he called the musicians' union to get his name and number. When Herb got the call from Scruggs, he didn't believe it. 'I thought it was a big joke.' Herb recalls. 'I thought it was one of my buddies... I said, "Who the hell is this?"'

Earl Scruggs repeated his name and Herb began to recognize the voice. He quickly accepted an invitation to Earl's house. When he got there, Earl picked up the guitar, leaving the banjo to Herb. Earl explained that he was going into the hospital for a hip replacement and wanted Herb fo fill-in for him for a while.

"'I went deaf.' Herb says. 'I couldn't hear anything after he said that. I was 23 and I thought this was insane, that it happened to me.' Herb played a few weekends with Lester then returned temporarily to Los Angeles to play with Vern and Ray at the Ash Grove in 1968. During that trip, Dean Webb approached Herb about taking Doug Dillard's place on banjo with the Dillards. After an audition over the phone, he got the job and moved his family back to California, recording with the Dillards in 1968 and 1969." —Chris Lewis, "The Laurel Canyon Ramblers," *Bluegrass Now*, April 1997, p. 7.

206 Ronnie Williams played bass during this period.

song for the "Beverly Hillbillies" television show (recorded September 24, 1962, and released October 12th) reached #1 on the country music charts. It was the only bluegrass recording to ever do this; it was nominated for a Grammy Award. The show ran on CBS-TV until 1971 and appeared in more than 70 countries. **Flatt and Scruggs** played the theme and made personal appearances on the show until 1968. In these appearances they acted as old friends of the Clampett family from their mountain home. The theme song on the television show was sung by veteran studio musician Jerry Scoggins; the Columbia recording used Lester Flatt as lead singer. Don Parmley, later replaced by Steve Stephenson, was the main studio banjoist for the show until it went off the air in 1973. They wrote "Pearl, Pearl, Pearl" and played it on the show. The record reached #8 on the charts in 1963 and was on the charts for eleven weeks. The show vastly increased the purse of Lester and Earl but didn't help eliminate the "hillbilly" image that they, and many other bluegrass artists, tried so hard through the years to eliminate. In 1965, "Green Acres" began its reign on CBS-TV. **Flatt and Scruggs** recorded the song on an LP of that period. The band also recorded the theme for the "Petticoat Junction" television series.

The band's exposure on television literally changed the lives of kids who would become third-generation bluegrassers. People like Sammy Shelor, Bela Fleck, Craig Smith and hundreds of others loved it so well that they tried to follow in the footsteps of bluegrass' pioneers. Pete Wernick recalled that "Earl was the first person I heard [play the banjo]; later I heard a lot of others, but I keep coming back to Earl because he's the best, not just the first. He dramatically changed my life." J.D. Crowe admitted, "Had I not seen Earl Scruggs, I doubt very much if I'd be playing the banjo." Shelor, upon acceptance of the 1995 International Bluegrass Music Association Bluegrass Banjo Player of the Year Award, said, "If it wasn't for Earl, none of us would be here."

Curly Seckler left for the final time in 1962. Also gone now was the sound of the mandolin as a rhythm instrument, though they would hire an occasional mandolinist; Everett Lilly returned in 1966 for another year with them.

Songs recorded during this period were of a different ilk than earlier recordings of the late 1940s, '50s and early '60s. Their style leaned toward that of the "Nashville sound" and they copied already-popular songs as exemplified in the "Nashville Airplane" and "Changin' Times" albums. They added the harmonica of Charlie McCoy (in late 1963) and other studio musicians. This was a solid link to old-time country fans but failed to please bluegrass fans. They added drums. Gary Scruggs

was included in these recordings in 1967. Later, Randy Scruggs recorded with the group.

At a time when **Flatt and Scruggs** was producing inconsistent music/albums, possibly to the extent they were losing their traditional following in 1966, they recorded with Doc Watson on "Strictly Instrumental" on Columbia. The record, however, came out as more Watson than **Flatt and Scruggs**.

Actor Warren Beatty called Earl Scruggs and asked him to write a tune for his new movie, "Bonnie and Clyde." Scruggs provided "Foggy Mountain Breakdown," originally recorded about 1950 for Mercury. Also heard in the film are Doug Dillard, Glen Campbell and Tommy Tedesco. The tune won a Grammy and earned a "Million-Air" award from B.M.I. for having been broadcast over a million times in the United States.

In 1968, Peer International Corporation published Scruggs' *Earl Scruggs and the Five String Banjo*. By late 1973, the instruction book had sold over one million copies. At that time, Scruggs received a gold book award from Peer-Southern. It was 1968 that the band became the first American bluegrass band to tour Asia.

The period between 1967 and 1969 brought the success of the band's recordings such as "Bonnie and Clyde," but Columbia, after offering Flatt and Scruggs a substantial sum to record, pushed them to alter their sound by using more studio musicians and update their lyrics by introducing material by Bob Dylan. Flatt couldn't relate to this and it made him extremely uncomfortable. Scruggs brought two of his sons in to record with them and was a source of some tension. And the road continued to take energy from the two men, putting them in occasional ill health. After their last 1968 album, "The Story Of Bonnie and Clyde," Lester Flatt and Earl Scruggs finally reached an impasse in styles so they split up. The last time Lester and Earl played on stage together was in February of 1969.

Lester and Earl recorded their final session six months after they broke up (August 21 and 22, 1969). Columbia offered them a tidy sum to come back for one more album. Musicians were Flatt, Scruggs, Randy Scruggs (lead guitar, 12-string guitar), Josh Graves, Paul Warren, Johnny Johnson (guitar) and others.

Soon Flatt and Scruggs were pursuing their own music; Lester Flatt formed the **Nashville Grass** and Earl Scruggs formed the **Earl Scruggs Revue** with his sons, Gary (bass, harmonica) and Randy (electric and acoustic guitars) and Jody Maphis (drums). The **Revue** played a music which some (but not the members of the **Revue**) have categorized as "folk-rock". They performed at urban clubs, colleges, and some festivals until the early 1980s. They pursued the tunes of artists such as Bob Dylan and Joan Baez. Lester Flatt continued in the traditional bluegrass sound by hiring ex-**Blue Grass Boys** Vic Jordan (banjo) and Roland White (mandolin) as well as Josh Graves, Jake Tullock (bass) and Paul Warren (fiddle). Martha White Mills continued to sponsor them. Flatt left Columbia Records to record on RCA Victor. **Lester Flatt and the Nashville Grass** became the first country band to sign with RCA since the **Country Pardners** in the '50s. Flatt was very opposed to non-bluegrass music and associated those long-haired musicians with rock music and marijuana-smoking. In 1971, Flatt and his **Nashville Grass** recorded "I Can't Tell the Boys from the Girls," probably as an affirmation of their beliefs.

Scruggs was known to be a good boss of the **Earl Scruggs Revue**. At a time when some band leaders would hire one bus driver to do all the driving (which may have been fifteen hours a day), Scruggs hired two drivers and would restrict their shift to six hours each. The performance contracts which he approved for the **Revue** included lounges for before and after the concert and catered food for the band members.

In 1973, Scruggs wrote the bluegrass score for "Where the Lillies Bloom," a movie about four children and their life in the Blue Ridge Mountains after the death of their widowed father.

Scruggs had a plane accident in October of 1975 in which he was the pilot. Surgery was required on his wrist and ankle and required several months of recuperation.

Lester Flatt and Earl Scruggs were finally entered into the Country Music Hall of Fame in 1985—an award long overdue. Scruggs was on hand to accept the award in this, the most moving event of the Country Music Association Awards. Scruggs recalled, "I didn't have a speech prepared that night. I didn't have one prepared and I just went up and smiled and bowed and walked off. From the way I'm rattlin' off now it doesn't sound like it, but put me out on a stage to make a speech [and] I just go speechless."[207]

Bill Monroe, Lester Flatt and Earl Scruggs became members of IBMA's Hall of Honor in 1991. It is significant that Flatt and Scruggs were given the award the same year—and therefore the same stature—as the man who is often called "the Father of Bluegrass Music". As of 1996, Mr. and Mrs. Scruggs live in Madison, Tennessee, and he performs occasionally.

Red Smiley— the smooth-singing partner of Don Reno

Red Smiley was the other half of one of the important pioneer bluegrass groups, **Reno and Smiley and the Tennessee Cut-Ups**. His partner, Don Reno, is covered extensively in his own section in this Pioneer chapter.

Arthur Lee "Red" Smiley Jr. was born around or in Asheville, North Carolina, May 17, 1924. He was raised there in an educated family whose father was a friend of promoter and performer Bascom Lamar Lunsford. Red was impressed by the early duet singing of groups such as the **Delmore Brothers** and the **Blue Sky Boys**. When he was about seven, he became interested in playing music professionally after hearing two hoboes play in Bushville, North Carolina (a city now at the bottom of a TVA-created lake). Smiley was already attempting to play the guitar at the time and, shortly thereafter, he started flatpicking the guitar in the style of the **Delmore Brothers**. By age thirteen, he was playing on WROL in Knoxville.

In 1942, Smiley was drafted into the Army where he was critically wounded in Sicily from a bomb explosion which ripped through his chest. He spent more than two years in Army hospitals and finally lost his left lung. But this didn't seem to bother him emotionally or physically; he sang for his fellow patients in Walter Reed Hospital while he recuperated.

Smiley worked on WJHL, Johnson City, Tennessee, in 1944 with Zeke Morris, Red Rector, Howard Johnson and Fred Smith. Smiley had to beg the mothers of teenagers Red Rector and Fred Smith to allow their sons to travel with him. The group played music in the styles of men such as Bill Monroe, Ernest Tubb and Hank Thompson. Also about this time, Smiley played guitar with the **Blue Ridge Hillbillies** on WWNC's

Farm Hour in Asheville, North Carolina, whose members were Rector (mandolin), Curly Shelton (mandolin), Carl and J.P. Sauceman and the leader, Tommy "Snowball" Millard (comedy, bass).

By 1949, Smiley was in Ohio and headed a band as a straight country singer. Soon Tommy Magness offered him a job, which he accepted, in **Tommy Magness and the Tennessee Buddies** at WDBJ, Roanoke, where he met Don Reno. They played an unrehearsed, hour-long show on December 27th, 1949, with Magness, Reno, Smiley and Al Lancaster.

After the death of Verlon Reno in 1950, Don and Red began singing together. Reno stayed with Smiley until January 2, 1972 (Smiley's death), except for health problems at the end of 1964 and Smiley's occasional semi-retirements. It was with the **Tennessee Buddies**[208] group that the duo of Reno and Smiley first recorded together in February 1951.

Don Reno, Red Smiley and Jackie Phelps left the **Tennessee Buddies** at Roanoke in April 1951 to join Toby Stroud's **Blue Mountain Boys** at 50,000 watt WWVA. Dobro®ist Josh Graves was there with **Wilma Lee and Stoney Cooper** at the time. Stroud played a combination of country and bluegrass, sometimes carrying two complete sets of musicians on his tours.

In September, Reno and Smiley re-formed Reno's old band, the **Tennessee Cut-Ups**, in Buffalo, North Carolina, and called it **Don Reno, Red Smiley and the Tennessee Cut-Ups**. They got Chuck Haney (mandolin), Jay Haney (bass) and Gopher Addis (fiddle) for this new band.

A continuing biography of **Don Reno, Red Smiley and the Tennessee Cut-Ups** is found in the biography of Don Reno in this chapter. We now pick up Red Smiley's story after he had his own **Bluegrass Cut-Ups** in Roanoke in 1964.

After Reno and Smiley split in 1964, Red continued the "Top O' the Morning" show with his **Bluegrass Cut-Ups** on WDBJ-TV. David Deese was one of Smiley's first banjoists in his new band. In May of 1969, WDBJ-TV canceled its "Top O' the Morning" show. Smiley, in declining health for many years, decided to retire; his diabetes was giving him significant health problems. He left the group; Tater Tate (guitar) and John Palmer (bass) took it over. They got Billy Edwards (banjo) and Herschel Sizemore (mandolin). Jim Eanes was called by these four to sing lead and play rhythm guitar in the spring of 1969. Tate switched to fiddle. They needed another name for their band so they

combined Eanes' own band name (**Shenandoah Valley Boys**) with Smiley's old band (**Bluegrass Cut-Ups**) and came up with the **Shenandoah Cut-Ups**. They recorded on the Rimrock and Rural Rhythm labels.[209]

But retirement didn't suit Smiley very well so he asked Don Reno and Bill Harrell (with whom Reno had now partnered) if he could join them when his health permitted. They, of course, said yes and, according to Mr. Reno in his autobiography, "The last two years and five months that Red worked with me and Bill Harrell were the happiest years we spent together. Bill Harrell, Buck Ryan and Jerry McCoury were delighted to have Red with us. They really bent over backwards to help me take care of Red's health." They continued to record for Rome Records. Their last recording was waxed May 18 and 19, 1971; it was prophetically entitled "Letter Edged in Black." Red Smiley died January 2, 1972.

The Bailey Brothers

The Bailey Brothers and the Happy Valley Boys

This band, headed by Charlie and Danny Bailey, was a country/bluegrass music act during the mid-1940s and beyond. They worked on many of the radio stations which were part of the bluegrass act circuit and hired many of the well-known bluegrass artists who made it big in bluegrass. For instance, musicians working for them on the "Cas Walker Show" in Knoxville included Benny Birchfield, Jake Tullock, Hoke Jenkins, Johnny Whisnant, Clarence "Tater" Tate, Joe Stuart, Don McHan, Dolly Parton (1954) and Bobby and Sonny Osborne (1955).

---

208 Remus Bell was later added to replace Verlon. Jackie Phelps joined in January 1951.

209 This foursome of Tate, Palmer, Edwards and Sizemore was the basis of the group for the next several years. Eanes stayed with them for three years until 1971. When Eanes left, his replacement was Wesley Golding.

Tate is a veteran bluegrass musician who, for most of his career was that of a sideman. The exception was his partnership with John Palmer as described above and his own band in the military in 1954. He is a Virginian whose first professional job was when he was sixteen years old on WNOX's Mid-Day Merry-Go-Round. By that time, he was a qualified multi-instrumentalist. Throughout his career he played guitar, clawhammer banjo, mandolin, bass and fiddle. His tremendous talent and versatility enabled him to fit easily into bands such as the Bailey Brothers and the Happy Valley Boys (1950), Carl Sauceman and the Greene Valley Boys (1950 AND 1963), Bill Monroe and the Blue Grass Boys (1956, 1984 to present), Carl Story and the Rambling Mountaineers (1956, 1959, 1963), Bonnie Lou and Buster Moore (1958), Hylo Brown and the Timberliners (1959), Lester Flatt and the Nashville Grass (1977 TO 1979), Curly Seckler and the Nashville Grass (1979 to 1980) and Wilma Lee Cooper on the Opry (1980).

When Danny's health failed in 1953, Charlie Bailey and Tater Tate struck out on their own to form their own **Happy Valley Boys**, a name which the brothers had used since 1951. In 1954, **Charlie Bailey and the Happy Valley Boys** played on the "Cas Walker Show" on WROL, Knoxville, sponsored by Cas Walker's chain of grocery stores. Shortly after Tate left the band in mid-1954, Charlie Bailey moved the band to WWVA where he hired Bobby and Sonny Osborne. After four months, the Osborne brothers left the band. Charlie Bailey hired Ralph "Chubby" Collier (fiddle), Jimmy Elrod (banjo) and Ray Myers, the armless musician. Charlie Bailey remembered about Myers that "He was tourin' with us then. He was a great attraction...a great entertainer. He wasn't the greatest musician but it's good to see a guy handicapped like that make it. We played in Canada and we'd built him up quite strong...we turned people away after seven shows. It was about three o'clock in the morning when we got finished at the theater. He was the kind of guy you didn't mind paying money to...'cause he would put that many in the auditorium for you, just to see him perform."[210]

Charlie and Danny Bailey continued to play bluegrass through the years and recorded in 1980 on Rounder's "Just As the Sun Went Down."

The Lilly Brothers— Everett and "B"

The northeastern United States has its share of traditional bluegrass thanks to brothers Everett and Mitchell Burt Lilly (known as "B"[211]). Their eighteen years at the Hillbilly Ranch in the Boston area served as a major bluegrass influence for men who would later be influential in bluegrass on their own: Joe Val, Bill Keith and many others. Their gig in Boston was really the only game in the area.

"B" Lilly was born in Clear Creek, West Virginia, on December 15, 1921. Everett is the better known of the two because of his time with the early **Flatt and Scruggs** band. Charles Everett Lilly was also born in Clear Creek July 1, 1924. The Lilly brothers came from a large family and "The Lilly Reunions" of the family brought more than 75,000 members back to their home in Beckley, at Flat Top Mountain, in the '30s and '40s. This multi-day event often got people such as the President of the United States to speak at their homecoming. And they always had music there, requiring a manager to coordinate the activity.

In 1933, twelve-year-old "B" Lilly played guitar. He and nine year-old Everett sang together locally. Their musical influences were Homer and Walter Callahan (the **Callahan Brothers**, a close-harmony duo) in 1934, followed by the **Monroe Brothers**, the **Blue Sky Boys**, the **Delmore Brothers**, the **Sheltons**, and **Mainer's Mountaineers**. They preferred the lively style of Bill and Charlie Monroe best. Nevertheless, the brothers didn't lean toward one particular group.

Though they may have resembled one of the above groups, Everett pointed out, "The Lilly brothers were not a copy of nobody. We don't have to copy after nobody. We got our own stuff. If you play country music, you're going to sound like somebody else who plays country. On an instrument, you don't use foreign notes, you use American notes. And so does Bill Monroe and so did the **Callahan Brothers**, the **Blue Sky Boys**, the **Carter Family** and all of them. I don't necessarily care for people who relate to me as a copy of somebody else. I'm still playing music (as of 1996) and I'm not copying nobody.

"As far as that bluegrass thing you are talking about, there ain't no such a thing as bluegrass music. It's 'American folk mountain country music.' It's not city music—it's not dignified, high class city music. It's American folk mountain country music. American people play it. It come from the folk mountains all over the place—and not just in Kentucky and not just in West Virginia—all over. You do know that name "bluegrass" is a feud name between Lester and Earl and Bill Monroe, don't you?" he asked this writer.

"I'll tell you exactly how it is!" he continued. "When the **Monroe Brothers** separated, Charlie and Bill, they had a lot of records out but they didn't play together too long. At first, Charlie Monroe hired Lester Flatt to work with him. A lot of people don't realize this. Lester worked with Charlie Monroe and Charlie Monroe took a good name for hisself, **Charlie Monroe and the Kentucky Pardners**. Bill Monroe didn't have a good Kentucky name left so he thought of the Blue Grass State of Kentucky. This name is about where he is from: the state of Kentucky. The grass that grows upon the land is what he named his band after. It had nothin' to do with no type of music. Later, Lester leaves Charlie Monroe and he goes to work with Bill Monroe. Now let me tell you, the **Monroe Brothers** never once called it 'bluegrass' music. Neither did Charlie and Lester Flatt when Lester worked with him. Bill Monroe didn't call it bluegrass music even when he went on the stage. Lester Flatt done the emceein' for Bill Monroe and

[210]Quotation by Charlie Bailey on March 21, 1970, from an interview by Gary Henderson and Walter V. Saunders, "The Bailey Brothers (conclusion)," *Bluegrass Unlimited*, February, 1971, p. 6.

Myers played the electric lap steel. He would sit on a chair, hold a pick between the toes of one foot, and bar the strings with the steel bar which he held between the toes of his other foot. He did very little lead picking, if any. He wasn't a bluegrass musician but he did play in two bluegrass bands: the Bailey Brothers and the Happy Valley Boys and the band of Hack and Clyde Johnson which was probably called the Johnson Brothers at that time.

Myers was truly a sideshow act and billed that way. People would come down just to see how someone without arms could play an instrument. Back in those days, bands would try anything to draw a crowd and "using" Myers was definitely one of the things which helped the band succeed.

[211] Some spell this "Bea"—but incorrectly. Everett explained that "Bea" is a girl's name and that his brother's name should be spelled "B."

when they come out on the stage to open up the show they'd say 'Friends and neighbors, we have a little clean, country, sober show here we hope you will enjoy.'

"Then after that, me and brother 'B' was a-workin' with Lynn and Molly O'Day in WNOX in Knoxville, Tennessee (in the mid-'40s). A man named Lost John and his **Allied Kentuckians** performed a song called 'Rainbow at Midnight.' He also had a early morning program on WNOX and Earl Scruggs was a-pickin' the banjo for him. That's the first time I ever seen Earl Scruggs or heard tell of him.[212] Lost John went to WSM hopin', like everybody else, that he'd get on the Grand Ole Opry. So he took Earl Scruggs and went down there and Bill Monroe hired Earl Scruggs from Lost John. Now he had Lester and he had Earl and they still called it that country stuff. Me and 'B' played double-header shows a lot of times with Bill Monroe when Lester and Earl was with him.

"Okay! Lester and Earl left Bill Monroe and formed their own band. Well, Lester and Bill and Earl wasn't a-speakin' after that because Bill, I guess, was mad at 'em for leavin'. Then people would ask—even when I joined Lester and Earl somewhere back then—people would ask us to do an old Bill Monroe tune, knowin' that Lester and Bill sang together like me and Lester [did]. Lester didn't like to hear them approach him that way. Well, the public gets wise to the way they're askin' somebody somethin' they don't like. So they began to call later, 'Do us an old bluegrass tune' and that is how that name [came about]. It's a feud name between Lester and Earl and Bill Monroe. Nothing else.

"And I'll show you another thing that you keep this in mind. Me and Bill Monroe can go out an play a mandolin all we want to and bark up a tree. And they'll call us 'country.' But the minute you hit a five-string banjo you're automatically called 'bluegrass.' Now I carry a five-string in my band. I'll carry the name 'bluegrass' around but I'll still know exactly where it come from and how it come from."

Earl Scruggs, in a 1996 telephone interview, elaborated on "the feud". "When we was workin' at WCYB, Bill would come through and we'd put him on the program to plug his dates. We were friends. There really was no feud—it was just *he* that got upset."

Mr. Lilly covered a lot of events and time in that last conversation. Now back to 1939. The Lilly brothers began radio performances on the Old Farm Hour on WCHS, Charleston, South Carolina. Early the next year, on WJLS, a brand new station near their home in Beckley, West Virginia, they were known as the **Lonesome Holler Boys**, though not losing their original identity. They were sponsored by the Lilly Land Company which, at one time, called the band **Everett Lilly**

and the Lilly Mountaineers. At WJLS, they worked closely with Lynn Davis and soon-to-be-a-country-music-legend Molly O'Day. The Lilly brothers joined Davis and O'Day again in Knoxville (WNOX) on the Mid-Day Merry-Go-Round and the Tennessee Barn Dance. They were unrecorded. Davis and O'Day's group was sponsored by Dr. Pepper, the soft drink. The **Lilly Brothers** came and went from one station to another, including three different stints at WJLS.

In early 1948, the **Lilly Brothers** band worked on WWVA, Wheeling, West Virginia, where **Red Belcher and the Kentucky Ridgerunners**[213] also appeared regularly on the Wheeling Jamboree. They recorded on the Page label of Pennsylvania. Tex Logan worked for both the **Ridgerunners** and for the **Lilly Brothers**. The **Lilly Brothers** quit the Jamboree in late 1950 and went to WMMN, Paramount, West Virginia. Like other bands associated with the radio stations which featured a barn dance, the **Lilly Brothers** had to go on tour with other acts at the dance. There didn't seem to be enough money in these tours because they had to split the revenue so many ways so they quit WMMN after a month and Everett joined **Flatt and Scruggs** in November of 1950. "B" Lilly moved back home and worked at Beckley.

Flatt and Scruggs had just left WCYB and then went to WVLK, Versailles, Kentucky, where they appeared on the Kentucky Mountain Barn Dance every Saturday night. From WVLK, the group went to WDAE, Tampa, Florida. But this, too, proved unprofitable. They stayed eleven weeks during which time they recorded their last Mercury session. Then Everett joined them in Tampa after Curly Seckler left in November. They also worked at WDBJ, Roanoke, Virginia.

The next year, Everett recorded on Columbia with Flatt and Scruggs's band including Chubby Wise (fiddle) and Jody Rainwater (bass). This May 1951 session included "Jimmie Brown, the Newsboy," Flatt's "I'm Working on a Road" and four others.

At the next recording session in October 1951, Wise had left and "Big Howdy" Forrester played fiddle. Lester Flatt and Everett co-wrote "Over the Hills to the Poorhouse." After a short time in Roanoke, they swapped positions with the Bailey brothers who had a regular gig at WPTF in Raleigh, North Carolina. They spent eight months at WPTF.

In the fall of 1952, Everett quit **Flatt and Scruggs** in Raleigh to join Tex Logan (fiddle) and "B" in Boston. Everett quit Lester and Earl, but only after Logan promised a year of bookings to the brothers up in the Boston area. He re-joined **Flatt and Scruggs** in 1958, and again in 1966. Each time he left, he returned to his brother because he felt bad about leaving his kin; they

---

[212] In this May 1992 telephone interview with Everett Lilly he told this writer, "As far as I'm concerned, Earl Scruggs had more to do with [the creation of bluegrass music as we know it today] than even Bill did hisself—or at least the people think so. Every time they see a banjo they holler 'Bluegrass!'" All quotes from Mr. Lilly in this biography came from the 1992 interview.

[213] This very popular act had as its members Red Belcher (clawhammer banjo and salesman for the band's sponsor), Tex Logan (fiddle) and Smilie "Crazy Elmer" Sutter (bass).

needed each other and wanted to help each other out. When Everett left this time, Curly Seckler took his place. Everett then told Logan about Don Stover who was working in a coal mine in Stovepipe, West Virginia, and they hired Stover. Pete Lane, who was in an earlier group with Logan, was also in the band they now called **Tex Logan, the Lilly Brothers and the Confederate Mountaineers** (or just the Confederate Mountaineers). They played in the Boston area on WCOP and at the Hillbilly Ranch every day for the next eighteen years.

The Boston area was a great area for a bluegrass band trying to make a living. Everett described it this way, "The people loved us up there. It was unbelievable. When we first went there, to us everybody we talked to was a foreigner 'cause we couldn't hardly understand 'em. And they couldn't [understand] us. But as far as our music was concerned, they seemed to understand it. A lot of that place we didn't really understand."

When Tex Logan left the Lilly brothers' band in 1956, subsequent fiddlers were Herb Hooven, Dave Miller, Scotty Stoneman (at different times. "It was hard to keep him straight.") and Chubby Anthony. They renamed the band the **Lilly Brothers and the Confederate Mountaineers** after Logan left. Don Stover was in and out of the band occasionally and was replaced on the banjo by Joe Val, Bob French or Billy Pack.[214]

Everett quit the **Confederate Mountaineers** in 1958 and returned to **Flatt and Scruggs** on the Grand Ole Opry and television shows. He missed his brother though, and after eight months returned to Boston. Nevertheless, he really enjoyed working with Lester and Earl. "They was good to me and I thought I was good to them. My leavin' them wasn't their fault and when you look at it from my angle it wasn't my fault either. I probably made a mistake [leaving them]."

Back in Boston in 1960, Chubby Anthony joined the **Lilly Brothers and Don Stover.** The next year, the band recorded on Folkways (produced by Mike Seeger, 1962) and Prestige International[215] labels.

In 1966, Everett Lilly returned to **Flatt and Scruggs**—the third time—for a one-year stint. He left again to re-join his brother. In 1970, the **Lilly Brothers and Don Stover** recorded a single 45 on Dave Freeman's County label: "Tragic Romance"/"John Henry." Everett's son, Jiles, died in a traffic accident. The Lillys then moved away from the big city and back home to the country in Beckley, West Virginia.

"I'll tell what drove me out of Boston; I might as well tell you exactly. In nineteen and seventy I had a son (Jiles Burt Lilly). He was lackin' two months of being seventeen year old and he played music with me some and he was really good and he played the Hillbilly Ranch a lot with me. We'd even pay him to play with me when my brother 'B' would be off. He went to work with us one night and he told us that he was goin' to a theater to a show and he wouldn't even have to cross the street. I said I'm kindly hoarse I'd appreciate it if you'd come back pretty early and sing with the show 'cause I really need a little help. Well, he called a girl and went over to her house. And on the way back—the expressway that goes over the top of Boston and when you come off of it they is two blind pillars holds the bridge up—and they's a red light there. When he come off of there, and the girl was with him, he had a green light to go. And as he aimed to come through the green light this fire truck run a red light, run through the car they was in, killed him instantly and the fire truck turned over in the middle of the road and hit another car. So that is exactly what drove us out of Boston. Me and my wife couldn't take it no longer so we left Boston and come to West Virginia where we buried him there. If it hadn't been for that we'd probably still be there."

"And I'll tell you another thing. Before me and 'B' went to Japan, Japanese come through Boston. Now, it was with a show called 'Holiday in Japan.' These two Japanese come to the Hillbilly Ranch every night. They asked us, 'What kind of music do you call this?' We said, 'Well, we play "American folk mountain country music", but we said the new name is "bluegrass."' Well, when these Japanese went back to Japan, they asked us if we would come to their country. We told them that we were afraid their people wouldn't understand. One of the brothers taught it in a Japanese college over there so we said yes we would come. But I've had a lot of snow jobs in my life so I didn't figure we'd ever go to Japan. However, he asked to cut a tape of us and we cut it. And he carried it to Japan and they put it out on a record and called it 'Live from the Hillbilly Ranch, Boston.' I didn't even know they'd done that for some time. Then they did contact us and we gave them a price and we went to Japan and did a tour for them (1973)."[216]

By 1975, Everett and "B" had their own **Everett Lilly and Clear Creek Crossing** which included Everett (mandolin, fiddle, guitar) and Mitchell "B" Lilly (guitar), Everett Alan Lilly (bass, Everett's son, who played very occasionally with the band) and occasionally Don Stover (banjo). That winter, Everett Lilly was teaching a class on bluegrass music at Southern Appala-

---

214 Everett Lilly on Billy Pack: "He knows more than any banjo picker I've ever seen. He can note that banjo all over just like a typewriter. And he can pick like Scruggs if you want him to. But you know, the more anybody knows, the worse time you have with 'em. They know so much they don't want to hold nothin' back. That's the trouble with fiddlers, too. Sometimes they know too much in the wrong direction and they try to play over your head and I say, 'Hey buddy, play what fits us and not what you want to hear."

215 Musicians were Everett, Stover, "B," Everett Alan Lilly or Ross Whittier on bass. In 1964, members of the Lilly Brothers and Don Stover were Everett (mandolin), "B" (guitar), Don Stover (banjo), Herb Hooven (fiddle) and Fritz Richmond (bass).

216 This tour used Jerry and Robert Tanaka, Everett and "B" Lilly. According to Art Menius, this label also cut three live albums of the group called, "Holiday in Japan" (parts one, two and three) on TOWA, a Japanese label, in 1974 and 1975.

chian Circuit-Antioch College. He made his home in Beckley, West Virginia, for the next two years.

Everett Lilly and Clear Creek Crossing was Everett's band as of 1992, touring in the East Coast. "B" lives in Melrose, Massachusetts, near Boston. Everett knows he could continue in music with pickup bands for certain events—as many acts do—but he feels that the music which is so important to him is better presented by a group who are not merely involved in a jam session. He had his three sons in the band now: Mark Lilly (pedal steel, guitar, fiddle), Charles Lilly (rhythm and lead guitar, saxophone) and Daniel Lilly (banjo). He also has a drummer and a lead guitar picker. "It's not the kind of music I want to play, but I'll tell you it's the only thing they push on the radio and if you can't do it, you can't get booked. But I don't play with them all the time. When they go on the stage, I go up there on the end and I do about three or four numbers on every set and I do in my style: American folk mountain country style. And for two or three numbers they eat it up—so that's good."

Mac Wiseman

Mac Wiseman and the Country Boys

T his veteran bluegrasser is one of the most significant figures in this music because of his tremendous success as a recording artist and as an executive in the recording industry. He is known as the "voice with the heart".

Malcolm B. "Mac" Wiseman was born in Crimora, Virginia, near Waynesboro, May 23, 1925. He was raised during the Depression on a farm where the community was poor, but still his father had the only wind-up phonograph and the first battery-powered radio in the community. They listened to the WLS Barn Dance and WSM's Opry. Mac was the only musician in the family. At age eleven or twelve, Mac got his first guitar, as Sears, Roebuck, which came in the mail in a cardboard box. He had it for a year before a traveling minister tuned it for him. At age fourteen, young Wiseman sang

on WSVA, Harrisonburg, Virginia, for a Future Farmers of America program. After training at the Shenandoah Conservatory of Music, Dayton, Virginia, and with a scholarship from the National Foundation for Polio, he became a DJ at WSVA. Wiseman's first band was formed for a radio program over WFMD, Frederick, Maryland, in 1945.

Mac's first experience in the professional music world was in Buddy Starcher's band as an announcer. Soon he was asked to sing a few songs and was on his way to becoming a singer. The next year, Wiseman was a member of Molly O'Day and Lynn Davis' **Cumberland Mountain Folks** for nine months. He was their guitar player for some time until they recorded. He recorded "Tramp on the Street"/"Six More Miles" on bass on Thanksgiving weekend. She was one of the most influential people on his singing style; Wiseman considers her "the female Hank Williams of all time". He played bass during the Columbia record sessions and appeared regularly on the Opry at that time.

In the spring of 1947, Wiseman left O'Day's group in WNOX and went to WCYB, Bristol, Tennessee, which had recently begun operations. He played a 6 a.m. solo show where he played for free, but got a percentage of what he could sell. His sponsors included insurance companies, Christmas ornaments, baby chicks, and strawberry plants. The second show, the mid-day Farm and Fun Time, included his **Country Boys** whose members included himself (guitar), Curly Seckler (mandolin), Tex Isley (electric guitar) and Paul Prince (fiddle). The group became popular right away. He was soon busy playing school houses every evening and many afternoons. He had no records out yet.

That fall, Earl Scruggs approached Wiseman about his plan to quit Bill Monroe and start his own band with Chubby Wise and with Wiseman. (As far as Wiseman knew at the time, Lester Flatt had not indicated he might also leave Monroe.) There were no firm plans made at this meeting.

Wiseman soon tired of all the traveling on unpaved mountain roads choked with ice, snow, and/or mud in order to give concert at remote mining camps so he disbanded his **Country Boys** and moved north into Virginia. A few months later, after Scruggs and Flatt had formed their own **Foggy Mountain Boys**, they called Wiseman to replace Jim Eanes. Wiseman started work in the spring of 1948 on guitar, performing first in Hickory, North Carolina, and soon, with the connections he made at his earlier time at WCYB in Bristol, to WCYB's Farm and Fun Time program. They were soon regulars with two hours daily. Wiseman also did the booking for the band which was now booked solid three months ahead. Band members were Flatt, Scruggs, Wiseman, Jim Shumate and Cedric Rainwater. In the fall, their first recordings were "My Cabin in Caroline,"

"We'll Meet Again Sweetheart," "I'm Going to Make Heaven My Home" and "God Loves His Children."

About Christmas time 1948, Wiseman left **Flatt and Scruggs** to join 50,000 watt WSB, Atlanta, on the WSB Barndance. From about that time until the mid-1950s, he toured and recorded extensively with his own **Country Boys** and with others. He had in his band many greats musicians with whom he recorded some very well known bluegrass songs. In 1949, on the WSB Barndance, he and his **Country Boys** toured with comedian/singer Bill Carlisle.

The show at WSB lasted until May so he joined Monroe's **Blue Grass Boys** on the Opry. With Monroe, he recorded "Can't You Hear Me Calling" and "Traveling This Lonesome Road." Wiseman spoke about an appearance on the Opry, "It was the pinnacle then, you almost had to perform there to hang out your shingle as a singer and musician. Today (1987) you can be a country music superstar without being a member of the Opry. It's still the mother church but it doesn't have the influence it once had. Bluegrass fans would rather spend the weekend at a festival, listening to a double-dose of bluegrass, than go to Opryland and hear a few tunes."[217] Jimmy Martin took his place as lead singer/guitarist with Monroe in the Christmas of 1949.

Mac Wiseman, 1995.

Wiseman and his band left WCYB for the third and final time in April of 1951—this time to join KWKH's Louisiana Hayride in Shreveport, Louisiana. On May 23rd, Wiseman began recording for Dot Records at the studios of KWKH, eventually recording his greatest hits including "Jimmy Brown, the Newsboy," "'Tis Sweet to Be Remembered," "Love Letters in the Sand," "Are You Coming Back to Me?" "I'll Be All Smiles Tonight" and "(I'd Rather Live) By the Side of the Road."

In April of 1952, Wiseman took his band to WDBJ, Roanoke, replacing the **Bailey Brothers** which had just left for WWVA. By September, Wiseman was at WNOX. In 1953, Wiseman moved to Richmond, Virginia, after he was offered a key spot as an entertainer, and the manager of the Saturday night radio show, Old Dominion Barn Dance, until 1954, and played gigs throughout North Carolina, Maryland and Virginia. In 1955, Wiseman toured with country favorites Jim Reeves and Hank Locklin.[218] Mac's version of "Wabash Cannonball" was a best-seller near his home in Richmond, Virginia.

When Dot Records, the company for which Mac Wiseman was recording, moved to California in 1956

after being purchased by Hollywood's ABC-Paramount, he became the Director of Artists and Repertoire (A & R) for all their country music performers and ran the company's Country Music Department. Before his move to California, members of his **Country Boys** were Allen Shelton (banjo), Don Bryant, Eddie Adcock and Buck "Uncle Josh" Graves. He disbanded this group before the move. Wiseman's first action with Dot was to negotiate with Carlton Haney, manager of **Don Reno, Red Smiley and the Tennessee Cut-Ups**, to have that band sign a recording contract with Dot. This caused them to leave King Records where they had been since 1952.

In 1958, Mac Wiseman helped found the Country Music Association and became its first secretary. The next year, Wiseman moved from California to Nashville and became popular at folk shows for the duration of the folk music revival period (late '50s to early '60s). In about 1963, he left Dot Records to join Capitol Records. Also about that time, briefly, he had his own Wise Records. In 1966, he managed WWVA's Jamboree show until 1970. In 1969, he left Capitol Records to join Lester Flatt in three epic recordings on RCA Records. The records were "Lester 'N' Mac," "On the Southbound" and "Over the Hills to the Poorhouse." In 1971, Wiseman became a regular on the Renfro Valley Barn Dance, Renfro Valley, Kentucky. The Barn Dance's new owner was Hal Smith.

During that decade, he recorded the non-bluegrass "Me and Bobby McGee," written by Kris Kristoferson. "There was a time when I felt switch-hitting would hurt me with bluegrass fans, but bluegrass fans are loyal and my fans are particularly loyal."[219] He feels that his diversity may help bring new fans to bluegrass.

On October 5, 1973, Wiseman appeared on television's "Dean Martin Show." October 21 was proclaimed as Mac Wiseman Day by the city of Waynesboro, Virginia, to honor its native son. July 3, 1977, was proclaimed Mac Wiseman Day by the Governor of Virginia. Wiseman was recently inducted into the Virginia Folk Music Hall of Fame.

Wiseman left RCA in 1974, looking for another label which promoted bluegrass music. He later ended up on CMH, owned by Arthur "Guitar Boogie" Smith and Christian Martin Haerle, which began operation in Los Angeles in 1976.

When a person gets busy trying to earn a living in this business, it's often difficult to sift through all the

217 J. Wesley Clark and J. Michael Hosford, "Mac Wiseman: Once More with Feeling," *Bluegrass Unlimited*, August, 1987, p. 18.

218 His real name was Lawrence Hankins Locklin.

219 Clark and Hosford, op. cit., p. 16.

tunes sent to him/her to sing and record. Here's the story of one of Mac Wiseman's most famous: "I was playing a show down in Alabama, just playing a series of dates, and I was on my way to Nashville to record and a young guy came right up after the show and said he had a song he wanted me to hear. I always made a practice of having 'em send it to me on tape. I was on my way to the box office to check up on stuff and lots of times you don't have time to listen as carefully as you should. That's the reason for using that method, I never listened to 'em when I was busy or wasn't concentrating. I asked him to send it to me on a tape and he said, 'Well, I don't have any way to put it on a tape.' So, he was such a sincere young man I took time and went back in one of the school rooms there and he started singing this song, 'Remembering,' and it just knocked me out."[220]

In 1986, Wiseman was a Board member of Nashville's Reunion of Professional Entertainers (R.O.P.E.), the purpose of which was to build a retirement home for its members who are in the industry of entertainment. He served two years on the Board of the International Bluegrass Music Association. He continues to perform as a solo into the 1990s.

The Stanley Brothers

L to R: Bill Lowe, Ralph, Bobby Sumner, Carter, c. 1947.

The Stanley Brothers and the Clinch Mountain Boys

One of bluegrass music's first groups was that of Carter and Ralph Stanley. They began playing their version of bluegrass music not too long after Bill Monroe did and, like Mr. Monroe, Ralph

Stanley still performed and recording regularly into the 1990s.

Carter Stanley was born in McClure, Virginia, on Big Spraddle Creek August 27, 1925. Ralph Stanley was born near McClure, in Stratton, Virginia, February 25, 1927. Carter and Ralph were full brothers; the other children in the family were from other parts of the family. Only children Carter and Ralph played music, but the older relatives did play the banjo and fiddle. Their banjo style was clawhammer, also known as frailing or drop thumb. Nevertheless, Ralph remembered that there were "Not too many musicians right around that part of the country where I was raised."[221] His father owned and operated a sawmill in Dickenson County, southwestern Virginia. Back in those days, there were a lot of trees; they have since been logged. Ralph worked in the sawmill only a few days when he was about sixteen.

The brothers' mother played music. She bought Ralph his first banjo and taught them the rudiments of music. The young brothers were influenced by the **Carter Family, J.E. Mainer's Mountaineers, Monroe Brothers** and the Saturday night radio show, Grand Ole Opry, and they knew early that they wanted to play music for a living.

When Ralph was nine, the family moved to near McClure, Virginia, where the present Carter Stanley Memorial Bluegrass Festival is held annually.[222] They kept cows and horses and raised tobacco on their farm. The kids walked nearly three miles to catch the school bus. The boys' parents also influenced them toward church—the whole family sang in church. Carter and Ralph and the other kids sang a little in church, but mostly their parents did that. They had no instruments in church so they had to guess at the key. If they guessed too high they quit and started all over again. During that time, the local dances were a focal point of the Virginia hills culture. The music usually consisted of nothing more than a banjo frailer and occasionally a fiddler. And when they got a rhythm guitar, they had a "big band sound". They played in neighbors' homes and between acts of the school plays.

The family got a radio about 1936 on which they listened to programs from Knoxville, Tennessee, and Bluefield, West Virginia. Others would come to the Stanley farm to listen to the radio. As they listened to the stars of the Opry, "We would just think in our mind how we would like to be people like that, you know."[223] Ralph would play along with the radio until someone

[220] Quotation from the album cover of "Mac Wiseman, Early Dot Recordings, Volume Two." There is no indication on this album who the author is...of any songs on the LP. This album was released in 1988 on Rebel.

[221] *It's the Hardest Music in the World to Play: The Ralph Stanley Story in His Own Words,* self published in Evanston, Illinois, by John Wright, 1987, p. 2. Author Wright later came out with Ralph Stanley's "autobiography" called *Traveling the High Way Home* (University of Illinois Press) in which all quotations from above pamphlet are contained.

[222] When Ralph described this, he was referring to the area near McClure, Virginia. In 1985, the new location for the 15th Annual Ralph Stanley Memorial Bluegrass Festival was in Roxana, Kentucky, where it existed for four years with Ralph's name on it. When it moved back to McClure in 1989, the festival name returned to Carter's.

[223] John Wright, op. cit., p. 2.

other than Carter came into the room; he was too shy to play music in public.

In 1939, Ralph began playing the banjo two-finger and frailing styles (he picked up the two-finger style from Wade Mainer). Carter had recently acquired a guitar. Still in high school in 1943 and with considerable stage fright, the brothers made their radio debut on the Barrel of Fun show at WJHL, Johnson City/Elizabethton, Tennessee. The show had been active for the last decade.

Ralph was in the Army infantry in Germany from May 16, 1945, until he was discharged in October 1946. While Ralph was still in the Army, and Carter was fresh from being discharged, in March of 1946 Carter (guitar) joined Pee Wee Lambert (mandolin), Roy Sykes (fiddle), Ray "Pickles" Lambert (comedy, bass, no relation to Pee Wee), Gaines Blevins (steel guitar), J.D. Richards (guitar) and Jack Belcher (electric Spanish guitar) and formed **Roy Sykes and the Blue Ridge Mountain Boys** to play daily on WNVA, Norton, Virginia, which is twenty miles from the Stanley home. It was a country music band, sponsored by Piggly Wiggly stores for an early morning fifteen-minute show. Pee Wee Lambert was to be a regular fixture with the Stanley duo for the next four years, playing mandolin in the Monroe style.

When Ralph was discharged from the military, he was interested in veterinary medicine. Instead, he joined his brother in the **Blue Ridge Mountain Boys** on WNVA for about three weeks on banjo. This was Ralph's first professional music job. It was at this time that Ralph began to play the three-finger banjo style. He had heard Hoke Jenkins and Snuffy Jenkins play it, and Earl Scruggs! Earl was his biggest influence toward this style. Ralph said, "Earl did take the three-finger and really do something with it. I think he improved it so much, you know, than what Jenkins or any of them had. I really liked his way of playing. And still do better than anybody I've ever heard."[224] Ralph learned the three-finger style by ear and it came out differently than most others; he described it as "simpler".

In December of 1946, Ralph and Carter left Sykes to form their own **Stanley Brothers and the Clinch Mountain Boys** with fiddler Bobby Sumner and mandolinist Pee Wee Lambert. They played about three weeks at WNVA sponsored by the Piggly Wiggly Company. The band was lucky enough to find a brand new station, 50,000 watt WCYB, Bristol, Tennessee, which needed performers for their Farm and Fun Time program. They began about December 26th playing without pay for an hour at noon, on and off for the next twelve years. Their first concert performance was packed at both shows. "We couldn't hardly find a building around big enough to hold the people," said Ralph. "That was about a week after we started at Bristol." And that's the way it was from then on. The mail to the station was heavy and they became very busy with shows six nights per week

and more. Most of the concerts were at schools where they took 60 to 70 percent of the gate. They also played a live show between movies when they booked at a theater.

The "good old days" lasted for some time. The **Stanley Brothers** recorded their first 78s at stations which included WOPI in Bristol, a station which had recorded top performers for years. The recordings were released on Rich-R-Tone (of nearby Johnson City) and soon led to a more lucrative contract with Columbia.

Very late in 1946, because Bobby Sumner was an "unreliable employee," they found Leslie Keith and made him their permanent fiddler. He stayed two years. It was basically bluegrass even though Ralph didn't play three-finger style publicly yet. Ralph Mayo filled-in often on many recordings with them. Successive fiddlers after Leslie Keith were Lester Woodie, Art Stamper, Art Wooten, Joe Meadows and Chubby Anthony. Ralph remembered, "Now Leslie Keith, he was a old-timer and he knew how to make money. And he had a tune called the 'Black Mountain Blues' that was real popular. He'd put out the notes to that and a picture of himself. I believe you paid ten cents or a quarter or something, but he really sold it. That gave *us* the idea to put out a songbook. We couldn't mail them out fast enough. We got to carry the orders home in a box or a basket or something."[225] They were actually making a pretty good living with their little songbook selling at fifty cents each. They sold 20,000 copies.

By early in 1947, the **Stanley Brothers** was booking 90 days in advance. Though their first gig on tour paid $2.35, they were soon popular enough to play to full houses, making up to $400 each night. The bass fiddle rode on the top of the Chevrolet their father had bought for them. They played six to seven nights per week, traveling all the year round, many miles daily. The brothers called Farm and Fun Time home for the next several years, occasionally doing work at other stations and in other areas. Through the 1950s, they recorded on King, Mercury and Starday. "We left Bristol a couple of times," said Ralph, "but we never did stay maybe over two months. We went to Raleigh, North Carolina, once, but we didn't stay in Raleigh too long. I believe we went back to Bristol from Raleigh and, let's see, I imagine the next place we went to from Bristol was Huntington, West Virginia... It was about the time the television station started there and that was among the first TV stations to ever start and we did television there about six months and then we went to the Louisiana Hayride in Shreveport, Louisiana. Well, we didn't like that much and anyhow, why, we got a call there from Lexington, Kentucky. They had a Saturday night jamboree in Lexington and they offered us a good thing. We wanted to get back close to home so we left Shreveport after three or four weeks and we went to Lexing-

224 Ibid., p. 3.
225 Ibid., p. 6.

ton and stayed a few months, I don't know just how many. And we moved from Lexington to Oak Hill, West Virginia, WOAY, and played several months there and then we moved from there to Pikeville. And we went to Versailles, Kentucky. But we didn't stay long. We'd always come back to Bristol. And we played maybe a year or so until other groups started coming in, like Mac Wiseman, Charlie Monroe, and **Flatt and Scruggs** was there awhile in '48. We were on there off and on for twelve years. Left there in '58."[226]

The trio of Pee Wee Lambert, Ralph and Carter Stanley initiated a type of harmony heretofore unused as it featured the high voice of Lambert as high baritone. Due to the influence of Lambert's mandolin style, the group was evolving away from mountain string music, which they had been playing until this point, to an approximation of Bill Monroe's music. Lambert patterned his vocals and picking after Bill Monroe. During this period of time, it was highly advantageous for a new band to sound like the most successful band of its time: the **Blue Grass Boys**. Of course, the music was not known as "bluegrass" then.

In September 1947, the group signed with Jim Hobart Stanton's[227] Rich-R-Tone, agreeing to play only for royalties, and recorded "Little Maggie," "Little Glass of Wine," "Mother No Longer Awaits Me at Home" and "The Girl Behind the Bar." As of 1974, "Little Glass of Wine" had sold 100,000 copies. The group used the studios of WOPI in Bristol and also recorded at Pikeville, Kentucky, at the studios of WLSI radio. Many of these recordings were later available on the Melodeon label; the later Columbia recordings were again released on Rounder Records. Record sales were tremendous. Recording band members were Carter, Ralph, Pee Wee Lambert and Leslie Keith. "And at that time we didn't know A from B. We didn't know about things like that. And he didn't pay us anything, just promised us some royalty on the record. We were glad just to get some records out."[228] They also recorded "Molly And Tenbrooks," which was actually a Monroe song. But even though Monroe played it regularly at his concerts, it wasn't recorded by Monroe until a year after the Stanleys did. The **Clinch Mountain Boys** continued recording for Rich-R-Tone until 1949 when they signed with the major label Columbia Records.

After six months at WCYB, there was a waiting line for sponsors. They had to extend the program to almost two hours. "We were sponsored by a store over in Honaker, Virginia, called Honaker Harness and Saddlery and the 'Glass of Wine' was released. They got us to come one day, one Saturday, and play at their store and

they bought a thousand of this record. And I know they sold that thousand that day. People came out of the mountains, different places. They advertised us on the radio, you see. They sponsored part of our shows on the radio and they got us to come down and play, and advertised that they would have that record for sale. And they ordered a thousand copies of it and run out before the day was over."

In the summer of 1948, the **Stanley Brothers** lost fiddler Leslie Keith to the **Curley King Band**. Keith was then replaced by Art Wooten (with Jim Shumate helping out temporarily until they hired Wooten). With Art Wooten (a former **Blue Grass Boy**) as fiddler who had considerable speed and, because of the presence of Pee Wee Lambert on mandolin and tenor vocals, the band had some of the elements of the **Blue Grass Boys** sound.

Monroe felt highly threatened by the presence of similar bands. (Many years later he was to feel honored by these clones of his band when the "world" gave him recognition that he was the kindly patriarch of bluegrass music.) Ralph continued, "Way back then, Bill didn't want us doing his songs, but he was misinformed a lot and I guess we were, too. About us doing his songs and everything. I mean, he felt like we was trying to ride on his coat tails, I think. Bill was about the only artist in the field at that time, you see, and when someone else come along to getting a little of the attention, that might've hurt a little bit. But after we learned Bill, and met Bill, and he met us, I don't think we got a better friend. I think it was all just rumors and things that caused all of the ill feelings to start with."[229]

Despite similarities to Bill Monroe's music, the brothers began developing their own sound. "Actually, we weren't too happy with the sound. Pee Wee Lambert played the mandolin and sung some like Bill, and we listened to Bill a lot and we were doing a lot of his songs. We were looking for more of a style of our own. But we had a good trio with Pee Wee. Now, as far as I know—I may be wrong but I don't think so—we were the first to put out a high trio in that style. Like 'Lonesome River.' That was good material we had on Columbia, but I think some of our best recordings were some of the Mercurys (1953 to 1958)."[230] When they finally got their "Stanley sound", it was distinctively different than the "Bill Monroe sound".

As the "Stanley sound" became less like that of Monroe, the brothers de-emphasized the role of the hot, lead mandolin, even though Lambert could play that style. The Stanleys were increasingly insistent that people should come to hear their group to hear some

226 John Wright, op. cit., p. 7.

227 Some people refer to Mr. Stanton as Hobe or Hobart; some called him Jim. He went by either name since his full name was James Hobart Stanton.

228 John Wright, op. cit., p. 7.

229 Ibid., p. 8.

230 Barry Brower, "Ralph Stanley—Keeping It Right, Down and Simple," *Bluegrass Unlimited*, February, 1987, p. 13.
According to Art Menius, the Stanleys recorded with a version of the high lead trio before the Osborne brothers did.

Stanley Brothers songs rather than Bill Monroe songs. Of course, nobody called it "bluegrass" yet. In later attempts at finding their own sound, the brothers tried the twin fiddles of Howdy Forrester and Benny Martin (1957) and of Ralph Mayo and Chubby Anthony (1956). This twin fiddle idea was Carter's; he liked to experiment with their music as long as it was kept right and simple. Such songs were "Daybreak in Dixie," "Who Will Call You Sweetheart" and "Cry from the Cross."

Now based out of WPTF, Raleigh, North Carolina, the **Stanley Brothers** began recording for Columbia on March 1, 1949. Columbia especially wanted four songs to be recorded by their newly-signed artists: "Little Glass of Wine," "Little Maggie," "Pretty Polly" and "The White Dove." Bill Monroe was recording on Columbia at the time. He didn't like his "competition" on the same label so he switched labels to Decca. **Flatt and Scruggs** was now free to record on Columbia as well. Ralph explained, "Well, yeah. Bill didn't want Columbia to sign the **Stanley Brothers**. He thought it was too much on his kind of music. I was told by Art Satherly[231] (of Columbia) that Bill said if they signed the **Stanley Brothers** he would probably leave. And so they signed us and he did go to Decca. As for Lester and Earl, I think they always had their aim set on Columbia, but at the time (1948 to 1949, while Monroe was still with the label) maybe they couldn't get on, so they took Mercury and waited until they could get on Columbia (1950)."

The Stanleys were doing well. Before long, they left WPTF and spent time at WCYB, WSAZ-TV (Huntington, West Virginia, where they were the first group to play music on the station) and KWKH (Shreveport, Louisiana) in September of 1950. With the band during this period were George Shuffler (bass), Pee Wee Lambert (who also worked at the Stanley family sawmill and farmed) and fiddler Lester Woodie.[232] Shuffler left the band in 1950.

The **Stanley Brothers and the Clinch Mountain Boys**, as with many bands, became mostly inactive during the winters. This is not to be misinterpreted as having disbanded. The only time that this band actually disbanded was in 1951 when Carter joined Bill Monroe for a few months. During that time, Ralph was relatively inactive in music. He was still thinking about pursuing veterinary medicine. Early in 1951, when Carter and Ralph and Pee Wee Lambert went briefly to Detroit, Ralph wasn't sure if he wanted to continue in the music so he stayed in Detroit and worked for Ford Motor Company for eleven weeks and Carter a few weeks longer. Then in June or July, Carter moved to Nashville to be Bill Monroe's guitar player and lead vocalist, taking the place of Jimmy Martin. Ralph joined Carter and Bill Monroe for a week on banjo as a replacement for Rudy Lyle who had just left the band. The **Blue Grass Boys**, with Carter on lead vocals, recorded "You're Drifting Away," "Sugar Coated Love" and "Get Down On Your Knees And Pray." Carter and Ralph declined the possible co-billing of **Bill Monroe and the Stanley Brothers**. The event of Carter's joining Monroe became a turning point in Monroe's career because up to this point he resented, and felt threatened by, other bands playing a similar sound. Carter and Bill worked well together and put this resentment behind them. But Monroe was still angry at Flatt and Scruggs for reasons which are explained elsewhere in this book. Then on August 17, 1951, Ralph had a serious car accident with Pee Wee Lambert[233] driving. Carter stayed with Monroe until September. Lambert left the band, and the band became "free" to more fully develop the "Stanley sound".

In October, after Carter had left Monroe and while Ralph was still recovering from his injuries, he and Ralph re-formed the **Stanley Brothers** at WCYB. The **Stanley Brothers** soon moved to WVLK in Versailles, Kentucky, with Carter and Ralph, Charlie Cline, Curly Seckler (guitar, mandolin) and Bob Osborne (mandolin, for only three weeks until he joined the Marines), recording for Mercury.

Carter did most of the lead singing; Ralph sang occasional solos. "Anything I wanted to sing lead on, I did," said Ralph. "It just come natural that Carter was the lead singer. He had more songs to sing than I did. I had a few that I sung, but I guess he was a little bit more on the ball than I was and he'd reach out there an' get 'em."[234]

George Shuffler joined on bass December 28, 1951. They paid him a regular salary whether he'd play or not. "We couldn't afford to do a full band that way, but we could just about take George and just about serve as a

---

231 Art Satherly was probably the person responsible for beginning to record music other than the popular music of the '20s. After recording Negro music, called "race music" or "black blues", and finding that the black people loved to hear themselves in their own dialects, Satherly found that then next logical step would be to record the yet-to-be-named "hillbilly" music. This would have worked just as well except that radio was just coming into its own and hired live performers while discouraging records of any type. The radio stations put all the hillbilly music they wanted to hear on the air and took the place of the records which people listened to just a couple of years earlier (before 1920). Satherly was also the first person to record Gene Autry.

232 Lester Woodie was the fiddler for the Melody Mountain Boys before he was hired by the Stanleys. He had worked in the bakery at Valdese where Shuffler had worked, and Woodie played radio shows with the Melody Mountain Boys. Shuffler recalled: 'The Stanleys heard Lester with us on our radio programs. When they got without a fiddle player, Ralph and Pee Wee Lambert came to Valdese and hired him. I bought Lester the first fiddle he ever owned, for $25, and he paid me back out of show-date money.'

233 Pee Wee Lambert sold his mandolin and retired from music in 1960. He was lured out of retirement in spring of 1964 by guitarist Landon Rowe and banjoist John Hickman. Ray Willis played bass. They played the local bars and on WDLR, Delaware/Marysville, Ohio. Lambert died of a heart attack on the way to work June 25, 1965.

234 Brower, op. cit., pp. 14, 15.

full band, you know."[235] Their fiddler became Art Stamper in 1952 while they were at WVLK.

That summer of 1952, the **Stanley Brothers** left WVLK, Versailles, Kentucky, to play a few dates at WVOW, Logan, West Virginia. A subsequent move to Pikeville, Kentucky, at WLSI, was, as George Shuffler put it, "Hat, button overcoat and moved down there and left Versailles." Then they played some time at WOAY. Jimmy Williams[236] joined the **Brothers** as mandolinist. Other band members included Stamper (fiddle), and Shuffler (bass, who intermittently returned home to build his house. John Shuffler played bass in his brother's place). Carter and Ralph both loved being home and tried to be home as much as possible. The radio stations at which they worked were usually set up to allow them to get home often. George was the same way.[237] They recorded again that year for Rich-R-Tone. Later in the year, Williams re-joined Mac Wiseman's **Country Boys** and was replaced in the **Stanley Brothers** in October 1955 by Curley Lambert.

In April 1952, the **Stanley Brothers**[238] recorded some songs for Columbia. This was their first recording session for the duo since November 1950. Songs included "The Wandering Boy," "Sweetest Love," "Let's Part the Best of Friends" and "A Life of Sorrow." This session was also the last for the Stanleys on Columbia. In October, the **Stanley Brothers** was in North Wilkesboro, North Carolina, for a few gigs on WKBC.

In July of 1953, Mercury signed the **Stanley Brothers** and soon recorded the single "Memories of Mother" and "Could You Love Me One More Time." The trio was Carter, Ralph and George. They stayed with Mercury five to six years. Their Mercury version of "Orange Blossom Special" was their first to use bluegrass banjo. Joe Meadows was the fiddler. Yet, as successful as their instrumentals were, the heart of their sound was the vocals of Carter and Ralph. Ralph described their vocals as "simpler, old-fashioned, more down-to-earth, just mountain sound."[239] Yet, in spite of all these efforts to change from Bill Monroe's music, Ralph really respected the man and his music. "As for Bill Monroe," said Ralph, "there's lots of copies. But there's none that get that feeling that Bill Monroe's got."[240]

The **Stanley Brothers** won the top award of Country Instrumental Group at Nashville's Disc Jockey Convention in 1955. This was significant because this bluegrass group was considered to be the same category as the top commercial C & W bands. The separa-tion between C & W and bluegrass had not been made here yet.

By 1958, the music market had changed, mostly due to Elvis and rock and roll music—the effect which is sometimes called "the Bluegrass Depression". The Stanleys felt obliged to leave WCYB, a station which had provided a good source of income since 1946, for the last time. They moved to WNER, Live Oak, Florida, where they started the Suwannee River Jamboree. They worked the area for the next five years and got on the television circuit with the Jim Walter Corporation, shell home builders, as their sponsor. They were so busy with all their work, they really had all they could do. Curley Lambert left in 1958 to join **Flatt and Scruggs**.

Author Barry Brower described this distinctive period in the history of the band, "By the late 1950s, the Stanley name had become firmly established within the bluegrass community. Unfortunately, it was much less well known in other musical circles and outside of the South. Not surprisingly, the realignment of the record industry as a result of the sudden popularity of rock and roll was to have a profound impact on the group. While the conventional country music scene in Nashville accommodated changing public tastes by watering down their music for mass consumption, many bluegrass groups, the **Stanley Brothers** among them, chose to remain honest to the musical form. As a result, a wedge was driven between the two country music camps. Nashville moguls began to view bluegrass as a music of the connoisseur and traditionalist with limited commercial appeal. Many record companies began to review the commercial potential of their artists. It is perhaps the reason Mercury chose to assign the **Stanley Brothers** (in 1958) to their subsidiary Starday label in spite of the group's artistically productive efforts for the parent company. The Mercury sessions were to be the last major label recordings of the **Stanley Brothers**, but their popularity in the South and among a growing number of urban folk revivalists was strong and there were numerous specialty labels willing to capitalize on it."[241] They joined Sydney Nathan's King label in the fall of 1958.

When King Records forced the use of a lead instrument onto the **Stanley Brothers** in the late '50s, Bill Napier, who normally played mandolin with Carter and Ralph, occasionally flatpicked the guitar with the band, thus being the first to bring the lead guitar sound to the band. Napier recorded with the lead guitar and contin-

235 Wright, op. cit., p. 11.

236 He had just left Mac Wiseman's band as mandolinist at WOAY. He often switched between the two bands.

237 Cam Powers filled-in occasionally on fiddle. Powers was an old-time fiddler who was probably 80 years old at the time. Shuffler: "He could play that old-style fiddle; his old arm was as limp as a dish rag."

238 The fiddlers during that time were Art Wooten and Art Stamper.

239 Brower, op. cit., p. 14.

240 Ibid., p. 14.

241 Ibid., p. 15.

ued with the band on mandolin while George Shuffler continued in this tradition as well. It wasn't long before Carter and Ralph realized that this was the sound that would make the **Stanley Brothers** different from other bluegrass bands, for no other bluegrass band relied on the guitar as a lead instrument—yet.

George Shuffler, in a 1994 telephone interview, clarified this issue of using the guitar as a lead instrument. First of all, Mr. Shuffler never traveled with them during the period that Napier picked lead guitar. He did record with them on that first King session by playing bass. "That's the only guitar work he (Napier) ever done with the Stanleys on record. Syd, he wanted to get into the guitar thing on account of the **Delmore Brothers**. I don't know if Don Reno had recorded any guitar; he was *some* kind of a flattop guitar player hisself! He was the first one *after* the **Delmore Brothers**, that is. Anyhow, they were the first and they sold a lot of records for Syd and so he talked Reno and them (**Reno and Smiley**) into doin' some guitar work on some of their stuff. And then it came along that they wanted the

Carter and Ralph Stanley, c. 1951

Stanleys to go from mandolin and fiddle to guitar. And so Bill Napier, he did the first album and they used a lot of guitar on it. Then Bill left and went with Charlie Moore (in 1961) and they called me back in. Curley Lambert played a little guitar during that time right after Napier. He recorded maybe four sides with them, maybe. Then I came in and took over guitar and I worked with the rest of it then. They told me if I wanted to come back on guitar, they'd love to have me on guitar. Curley Lambert recommended me as the best guitar player they could ever find. I appreciated that and told him I did.

"Syd had Napier playin' the guitar kind of like the Delmores did; you know, kind of like a mandolin. And whenever I went back with them that time, there was mostly just the three of us—just Carter, Ralph and myself. So I was on guitar and I saw that single-string stuff just didn't fit 'em. It didn't fill-in like at the end of a line where they would dwell...there's nothing there to fill—just a little single-string—so I started doublin' up on the strings and started to cross-pick the thing and I saw that it filled real good. And that's how it came about. It fit them better than anything that I'd ever heard them do up to that point—that is for backup for 'em. They didn't think much of it at first, but now Ralph carries a guitar player with him all the time, you know."

Ralph described his music in the same way that Bill Monroe described his style: "high and lonesome". But there is a difference. In an interview with this writer, Ralph described the "Stanley sound" as simpler than that of Bill Monroe: "A more simple sound, a mountain sound, more down to earth and old-timey... It's the sound that brother Carter and me created, and it's the only sound we know."[242] His sidemen are allowed very few excursions into their own style. This is so the "Stanley sound" can be maintained through all the personnel changes. Consistency is important. There have been changes in bluegrass music through the years; the most significant change has been toward a more progressive type of bluegrass. But Ralph said, "Actually, it's the same music as we started out with, but it's just been improved."

King released their "Finger Poppin' Time." Hank Ballard's version, also on King, hit the charts the previous month on the Rhythm and Blues category of the charts and proved successful so Syd Nathan decided to have the brothers do it. The flip side was "Daybreak in Dixie."

Napier left in 1961 to join Charlie Moore's **Dixie Partners**. He was still active in music into the 1990s. Shuffler joined the brothers again in Florida.

In 1965, sixteen-year-old Larry Sparks filled-in with the **Stanley Brothers** when they needed a lead guitarist and tenor singer. He never did go full-time with the band. On September 20, 1965, the last recording session of Ralph and Carter together was at King Studios in Cincinnati.

At the peak of their success in 1966, Carter had more and more health problems—reportedly associated with his drinking. On December 1, he died of ill health. Ralph's evaluation of Carter's death was that it was due to cancer of the liver. Carter's death, though not sudden because of declining health in the past six weeks, was unexpected by Ralph. The night before he died Carter and Ralph spoke of buying a bus in which to travel. Carter always wanted a bus.

A letter to the editor of *Bluegrass Unlimited* (July 1976) was from Carter's daughter, Doris Stanley Avery of Live Oak, Florida. She wrote about her father:

Bluegrass, Stanley-style, was born in the hills when Carter Stanley was born. He had a feeling for music, and we will never see his like again. Your article [in the June 1976 issue of Bluegrass Unlimited *by Bob Cantwell] calls him "lonesome". His "lonesomeness" came from within, from a feeling for, and a caring for, music and for people. He often spoke of this friend, or that one—people, his friends, his fans, people such as yourself—they were very important to him. Music was his first love—his life—and he*

242 From an interview in Portland, Oregon in May 1985.

gave it the best he had to give at all times. Sick or well, sad or happy, for Carter Stanley the show went on. I am so proud when I hear someone singing or playing a song which he wrote. He seems so close—at festivals, the mark he left on music is so great you can hear it at every corner.

I remember him too as a humanitarian, and he taught me lessons in human relations I could not have learned from anyone but a man such as he was. She ended the letter, ...*a beautiful part of [Stanley-style music] ended with him, too. But, because of publications such as yours, he lives on—his music, his dreams, the things he stood for, live on...*

George Shuffler was still with the band when Carter died. "I think that Ralph would be the first to admit it just wasn't the same without Carter. We were always the prank pullers—the jokesters. Ralph and I tried, but it wasn't the same. We three were like brothers. I never worked *for* the Stanleys. I worked with them."[243]

Ralph spoke of the new situation without Carter, "It was hard because Carter had always done the emcee work and he was the front man, and done a lot of songwriting. It was hard to do, but it was either do, or don't. So many people would call me and I got letters telling me that they was really behind me and not let 'em down. It was actually my only choice—the only thing I could do. It was just like taking on something new."[244] It took awhile for Ralph to get over his brother's death and accustom his thinking that *he* would be the leader of his new band...if he were to form one. So, about three weeks after Carter's death, Ralph was back in business. Ralph's formation of the new **Clinch Mountain Boys** kept the basic sound that he and Carter had originated. "I'm real proud that I was able to carry on but there's a lot of difference from when Carter was around. Now I have everything to see to...[and] I realize what a burden he had on his shoulders that I didn't have."[245]

By December 18, 1966, Ralph had hired Curly Ray Cline (fiddle), Melvin Goins (guitar) and George Shuffler (bass, guitar) and were on the road doing committed gigs. Goins (from the **Lonesome Pine**

Ralph Stanley in 1995 at Carlton Haney's festival in Watermelon Park.

Fiddlers) was "Big Wilbur" on bass and comedy. By February 1967, Larry Sparks (guitar, lead singer) was a part of Ralph's new **Ralph Stanley and the Clinch Mountain Boys**. Ralph spoke about hiring Sparks. While he had played guitar with the earlier group a few times, "I didn't know he could sing. But when Carter died, why, he played up that way somewhere and Larry called me and said, 'I'd like to audition as a singer for you.'"

That summer, King Records assured Ralph that his new band would continue to be recorded in the tradition of the **Stanley Brothers.**

In 1970, Stanley quit King Records and soon began recording for Rebel; his first LP was "Cry From the Cross." Rebel gave him the unrestricted freedom he needed to fulfill his idea of how his band was to sound: the "Stanley sound". On the session were Roy Lee Centers (guitar, who replaced Larry Sparks), Curly Ray Cline (fiddle), Stanley (banjo), Ricky Skaggs (mandolin, fiddle), Keith Whitley (lead guitar), Jack Cooke (bass, hands), Ed Ferris (bass) and Cliff Waldron (hands). Ralph spoke of Roy Lee Centers, "I really don't know whether he tried to sound like Carter or not. But he did sound a lot like him and, I don't know, it just seemed like it fell in place that he'd do a song just exactly like Carter."[246] Ricky Skaggs and Keith Whitley were in the band when Centers was shot to death in an unprovoked murder (May 2, 1974). Whitley took over the lead singer/guitar spot.

Skaggs and Whitley were two kids who simply idolized the old sound of the **Stanley Brothers**. Ralph reminisced, "We were playing a little club in Louisa, Kentucky, and we were late getting there. The man that ran the place knew Ricky and Keith. We got there and they was on-stage, filling-in for us. And they sounded *identical*, I thought, to the way Carter and me sounded when we first started. And they knew more of our old songs than I did! They wanted to get started in music, so I took 'em on the road with me. I didn't pay 'em much—I paid them all I could—but I had a full group. I wanted to get them exposed and to show people that there was more people who could do that kind of singing."[247] They recorded on Jalyn on January 9, 1971.

Ron Thomason, who worked with Ralph's **Clinch Mountain Boys** in the late '60s, in his *Bluegrass Unlimited* article about Ralph Stanley, spoke of how the **Clinch Mountain Boys** saw themselves, "They liked to work together and get the job done. What could be a tremendous burden of hard traveling performances is enjoyable because each member knows he's with friends. We once talked about the possibility of having the ugliest band on the road. We decided that while this

243 Ron Gould, "The Shuffler Family: Foothills Gospel," *Bluegrass Unlimited*, November, 1977, p. 33.

244 Barry Brower, "Ralph Stanley—Keeping It Right, Down and Simple," *Bluegrass Unlimited*, February, 1987, p. 13.

245 Wright, op. cit., p. 18.

246 Ibid., p. 13.

247 Quotation taken from the Ralph Stanley discography by John Wright.

may be true, there are certainly some close-running seconds. The **Clinch Mountain Boys** take pride in the old-time music they play, too."[248]

Ralph's band toured a lot. Ralph mentioned that "Japan is one of the finest places I've ever played. They're crazy about it in Japan. Europe, they like it over there too, but not like it is in Japan."

In May 1971, Ralph organized the First Annual Carter Stanley Memorial Bluegrass Festival on his land in McClure, Virginia. The Carter Stanley Memorial Award presented at the festival to honor those who support bluegrass went to Bud Wendell of the Grand Ole Opry. The three previous years of the award (begun in 1968) went to Ralph Stanley, Bill Monroe and Snuffy Jenkins. Curly Ray Cline was the 1976 winner of the Award. Cline had just completed ten years' service with Ralph Stanley as fiddler for the **Clinch Mountain Boys**. That year, Ralph Stanley was made 32nd degree Shriner. (There are only 33 and the top level goes only to presidents and such.) On December 11, 1971, Kentucky's governor, Wendell Ford, honored Ralph Stanley and Curly Ray Cline by making them honorary "Kentucky Colonels."

🎵 *"A more simple sound, a mountain sound, more down to earth and old-timey... It's the sound that brother Carter and me created, and it's the only sound we know."* —Ralph Stanley

---

Also in 1971, Ralph recorded an *a cappella* tune with his gospel quartet. His was the first bluegrass band to do so, and its popularity increased rapidly after the event. As of 1971, Ralph Stanley had written 40 to 50 songs.

Ralph lost his 1975 attempt to become Clerk of the Circuit Court of Dickenson County, Virginia. That summer, he was named Honorary Captain of the Belle of Louisville, a boat in Jefferson County, Kentucky. That year, the Ralph and Carter Stanley Scholarship was established by Lincoln Memorial University. It is an award to a student from Dickenson County, Virginia, recognizing traditional mountain musicians. Part of the funds for the scholarship was to be from tape sales by Ralph's band. At the 1976 annual Carter Stanley Memorial Festival, Ralph was awarded an honorary Doctor of Arts degree from Lincoln Memorial University, a small liberal arts college near Cumberland Gap, Tennessee.

Beginning about 1988, Ralph Stanley was hard at work promoting his Stanleytone banjos for sale at the festivals he attended. The Stanleytone is a copy of his Gibson 1927 Granada.

Ralph once had an opportunity to join the Opry. "I turned the Grand Ole Opry down. I don't remember what year it was. I was either offered a regular spot or a open spot any time I wanted to go through and guest—I took that—because, you know, if you get on the Opry you're supposed to play the Opry every other Saturday night. That's when you make your living. Back when Carter and me first started, we would have liked to have had the Grand Ole Opry. But when I was offered it, I didn't figure I needed it. I was doing all the playing I wanted to and getting all the bookings I wanted. After his passing, I just didn't want to get tied down."

He told this writer that he would like to be remembered as "a fella that give the best of my life to bluegrass music; done my best to do it the right way. Respect it. Never lower the name down. What I mean by that is always going on the stage right, neat, nice clothes—instead of jeans and shorts and things that I've seen a few do. And a music that I respect and love."

Ralph has three children and has a farm which has horses and squirrel dogs. He loves to hunt and fish. As of 1996, he lived in Coeburn, Virginia. Ralph Stanley was the first member of Bill Monroe's Hall of Fame and he and his brother became members of the International Bluegrass Music Association's Hall of Honor in 1992.

Curley Lambert— from western films to bluegrass

The legendary Curley Lambert had over three decades of bluegrass experience. Starting his career in 1946, he continued his music until his death in 1982.

Richard Edward (Curley) Lambert was born in Brodnax, Virginia, into a musical family June 13, 1930, where he soon learned the mandolin, guitar and bass. At age sixteen, he left home to pursue a professional career with Al "Fuzzy" St. John, who appeared in western films as a comical sidekick. This lasted intermittently for a few years until, in 1949, he took up music as a vocation in Durham, North Carolina. He played electric mandolin in a country band for a year then returned to acoustic (guitar, bass) with Bill and Mary Reid's **Melody Mountaineers** in 1950. With this group, Lambert played three times weekly on live television in Lynchburg, Virginia. He played on three of their recordings: two for Columbia and one for Starday. In late 1950, Lambert began his U.S. Army stint and formed his own **Blue Ridge Mountain Boys** which had an emphasis on the music of **Johnny and Jack** (not exactly bluegrass).

Back from the Army about 1953, Lambert re-joined the **Melody Mountaineers**. He also played mandolin with Bill Clifton's **Dixie Mountain Boys**, recording extensively with the band on Starday, Mercury and Blue Ridge, singing tenor and baritone until 1958. He recorded on "Living the Right Life Now" and "Little White Washed Chimney."

In October 1955, Lambert replaced Jimmy Williams on WCYB, Bristol, with the **Stanley Brothers**[249] on mandolin, remaining about ten years. The decade included recordings on Mercury, Starday, and with Syd Nathan's King labels. He supplemented his weekly $50 **Stanley Brothers** income with frequent appearances in the area.

Lambert left the **Stanley Brothers** in 1958 to replace Curly Seckler with **Flatt and Scruggs**. This was a particularly popular time for the band which recorded "Crying My Heart Out Over You" and "Ground Speed." His voice and style didn't seem to fit the needs of the band so he after a short term. He then worked as an attendant in a Richmond, Virginia, mental institution until he joined the **Stanley Brothers and the Clinch Mountain Boys** again, this time in Live Oak, Florida, where they were on television. Lambert left the **Stanley Brothers** again in 1963, to join **Charlie Moore, Bill Napier and the Dixie Partners** on WJHG-TV, Panama City, Florida. He stayed three months, then joined the recently re-formed **Masters Family** for eight months, after which he returned again (for the fourth time) to the **Clinch Mountain Boys**. Soon he became musically inactive except for occasional work with Ralph after Carter's death. In 1967, Lambert quit the music business, selling his instruments, until 1971, when he joined **Chief Powhatan** (Floyd Atkins) **and His Bluegrass Braves** for a couple of years. Also that year, he was with **Raymond Lumpkin and the Bluegrass Ramblers** and the **Foggy Mountain Five** near Richmond, Virginia.

In 1973, Lambert re-joined Charlie Moore in his **Dixie Partners**[250] for about two years. They appeared on the WWVA Jamboree, and they recorded on the Old Homestead label. The next year found him as the bass player with **Bob Goff and the Bluegrass Buddies**. In March 1975, Lambert joined the **Goins Brothers**, staying with that band several years. Then he re-joined Charlie Moore in Richmond for awhile. In August 1980, Lambert re-joined Powhatan's band on mandolin. He was with this band until he passed away on October 22, 1982, in Richmond, Virginia.

Jim and Jesse McReynolds

Jim and Jesse McReynolds and the Virginia Boys

The McReynolds brothers are still playing bluegrass today—after fifty years in the business. Retirement isn't something they talk about much; they just seem to want to play and sing and entertain. And they do it just as well today as they did when they first formed their first band in 1947. Even though the McReynolds family grew up near the Stanley brothers, Jim and Jesse didn't fall into the pattern set by Bill Monroe as did Carter and Ralph. They continued a more traditional vein which featured the mandolin/guitar combinations of the **Blue Sky Boys**, the **Monroe Brothers** and many other similar duets of the 1930s and '40s. Their early music was very much in the style of these groups...until they got a banjo in their band in 1949. In the chronology of brother duets, a well known group which came onto the music scene just before Jim and Jesse was the **Louvin Brothers**, Ira and Charlie.

James Monroe McReynolds was born in the Carfax community, near Coeburn, Wise County, Virginia, February 13, 1927. Jesse Lester McReynolds was born there on July 9, 1929. Carfax was not much more than a coal-loading stop on the railroad as it passed through the area. Years ago, the railroad workers, desiring more train cars to pass through the area declared, "We need more cars—and that's a fact!" thus the name of the community was born.

Their parents taught them a love of gospel music. Their father, who was a fiddler, often invited relatives and neighbors to play with him at home for Saturday night dances. Their brother-in-law, Oakley Greear, encouraged them toward music because he was a fiddler

[249] Other band members at the time were Carter and Ralph Stanley and Ralph Mayo (fiddle). Later he worked with Art Stamper, Bill Napier, George Shuffler and Chubby Anthony.

[250] Other band members included banjoist Butch Robins, Johnny Dacus, Terry Baucom and Ben Green.

and owned the radio to which the family and neighbors listened on Saturday nights in the late 1930s. In 1941, Jim and Jesse won Best Duet at an amateur contest in St. Paul, Virginia. This was a good start on a musical career, but World War II interrupted any such plans even though they were both too young to volunteer. Instead, they stayed around Carfax and worked in the coal business. At age fourteen, Jesse actively began learning to play his dad's fiddle. He learned some from Greear, who owned the mandolin that Jesse would soon pick up and start playing. Jim joined the Army in 1945.

With Jim out of the Army in 1947, the brothers now began their pursuit of a full-time career in the music business. In their early performing years, they at first called themselves the **McReynolds Brothers, Jim and Jesse, and the Cumberland Mountain Boys.** Some concert attendees, though, actually expected to see the outlaw Jesse James so they searched for another name. They began playing daily on 250 watt WNVA, Norton, Virginia. "In the pattern of many other country acts, they used the radio station as a base of operations and from it publicized their nearly nightly shows in the broadcasting area, mostly in the eastern Kentucky coal mining towns."[251]

They played at WJHL, Johnson City, Tennessee, and WFHG, Bristol, Tennessee. The band did not have a banjo, this absence was conspicuously different than the sound we know today as bluegrass. By 1948 at WCHS, Charleston, West Virginia, Marion Sumner played fiddle, Jay Hughes, the bass. Jim brought back with him from the Army a new Gibson A-50 f-hole mandolin. He tried to play it—and Jesse the guitar—but neither had much success so they traded instruments.

In 1949, Jim and Jesse traveled to Augusta, Georgia, to play on a mid-day radio show on WGAC for a year. This band was Hoke Jenkins' **Smoky Mountaineers.** Musicians were Jenkins (banjo, nephew of Snuffy Jenkins), Curly Seckler (multi-instrumentalist), Jim (guitar) and Jesse (mandolin). Jesse began developing cross-picking here as an effort to duplicate on the mandolin that he heard on the banjo of Hoke Jenkins who used a form of three-finger picking style which mainly used backward rolls. Jesse's mandolin virtuosity was significant in their popularity with bluegrass audiences. On March 17, Seckler was asked to join Lester Flatt and Earl Scruggs and play mandolin with the **Foggy Mountain Boys**; he left immediately.

In 1950, after a short stay at KXEL, Waterloo, Iowa, and then WMT, Cedar Rapids, Iowa, the McReynolds brothers moved to Wichita, Kansas, to work on KFBI. They played no bluegrass on this station which featured **Sons of the Pioneers** and other western music.

The next year, Jim and Jesse moved to WPFB, Middletown, Ohio, where they worked for Smoky Ward

as a featured duet on Ward's television and radio variety show using the name, **McReynolds Brothers.** Jim and Jesse also performed on the show as the **Virginia Trio** with Larry Roll (lead vocals, rhythm guitar) and Dave Woolum (bass) on the show. Roll was a solo singer and the brothers were duet singers. They sang mostly gospel tunes. It was with this band that they made their first recording for Gateway Records and featured Jesse's cross-picking. With Gateway they recorded eight songs, issued ten years later as "Sacred Songs of the Virginia Trio" by Ultra-Sonic Records (c. 1961).

By 1952, the brothers were working hard at making a living in the music and were now in a position to hire Hoke Jenkins, who had given them one of their first jobs in the music. Jim recalled, "We were looking for a banjo picker and we got Hoke to come work with us. He was with us in '52 when we did our first recording on Capitol Records. We had a good relationship with Hoke. He was a lot of fun to be around. Back in those days it was hard to make it in this business. There wasn't too many big deals or a lot of money floating around but we had a lot of fun. One thing about the early days of this business, you had to believe in it and enjoy it because sometimes all the payoff there was the enjoyment you got out of it." Hoke's wife, Rose, recalled, "Some weeks they would make money and some weeks they wouldn't make any money. But we did just as well with six of us home and with one salary as I do now. It's just a difference in the time and the economy."[252]

Still in 1952, Jim and Jesse signed a recording contract with Capitol Records. The band name was changed from the **McReynolds Brothers and the Cumberland Mountain Boys** to the shorter **Jim and Jesse and the Virginia Boys** by Capitol's (Ken Nelson) request in October when the recordings were released. On March 16, they recorded "Air Mail Special" on Capitol. Musicians on a June 13th recording session for Capitol Records were Sonny James (fiddle)[253], Hoke Jenkins (banjo), Curly Seckler (guitar), Bob Moore (bass) and Jim and Jesse. The session featured bluegrass songs such as "I Will Always Be Waiting for You" and Ira and Charlie Louvin's "Are You Missing Me?" Jesse featured his by-now-fully-developed innovative split-string mandolin playing on "Just Wondering Why." After some time at WWNC in Asheville, the group moved to the Kentucky Barn Dance at Versailles, Kentucky, on WVLK in 1953.

Soon they had their own fifteen-minute segment at WCYB's Farm and Fun Time in Bristol, Jesse was drafted December 2, 1952. On March 16, 1953, **Jim and Jesse** recorded just before Jesse left for a tour of service in Korea. They recorded "My Little Honeysuckle Rose," "A Memory of You" and "Too Many Tears."

251 From the liner notes by Scott Hambly in the CMH LP "The Jim and Jesse Story."

252 Julie Knight, "Hoke Jenkins—Pioneer Banjo Man," *Bluegrass Unlimited*, September, 1985, p. 29.

253 Sonny James was the same one who later made it big as a Nashville singing star with "Young Love, First Love." His real name was Sonny Loden.

In Korea, Jesse met and teamed up musically with Charlie Louvin. **Jim and Jesse** later recorded an album of tribute to the **Louvin Brothers** (CBS Records) which included much of the music written by the Charlie and Ira Louvin, including "When I Stop Dreaming" and "Are You Missing Me?" Jesse mentioned that the music he and Charlie Louvin played in Korea was all country music, also known as "hillbilly" music. Jim added that when bluegrass [hillbilly] music was separated from the "Nashville sound", that's when things really changed. Jesse recalled that "We tried to expand as we went along. We tried to do enough variety that we could be accepted on a country show, or on a radio show where they might have played Bill Anderson, or any other Nashville act." Jim added, "In those days, the only people that were really making any money with bluegrass music was **Flatt and Scruggs**. And they were doing it with television in the '60s."[254]

Jesse was discharged in 1954 and the brothers band moved to Danville, Virginia, in 1955 to play on the Saturday night WDVA Barn Dance as well as on early morning and mid-day shows as a re-formed **Jim and Jesse and the Virginia Boys**. They had to start all over again to regain the momentum they had lost as a group. They continued to record for Capitol until January 24, 1954. But soon, lack of income drove them to other stations such as WBBB, Burlington, North Carolina, and Knoxville's Tennessee Barndance and Mid-Day Merry-Go-Round on WNOX in mid-1955.

That summer of 1955, **Jim and Jesse** played on the prestigious 50,000 watt WWVA's World's Original Jamboree but in November, to get away from a harsh winter, they moved to Live Oak, Florida, on Halloween and helped form the Suwanee River Jamboree on 250 watt WNER where they played live and featured bluegrass. Band members included Don McHan (banjo), Joe Meadows (fiddle), Dave Sutherland (bass) and Chick Stripling (comedy). Their geographic exposure was very little so Jesse supplemented his income as a disc jockey on the station. They stayed at WNER for several years, enjoying a somewhat stable base of operations and had a syndicated radio show throughout the South. Syndication was used by bands to attempt to hang onto their audiences—and careers.

Jim and Jesse and the Virginia Boys began its first, weekly, thirty-minute television show on WCTV in Tallahassee in 1956. Sponsored by Ford Tractor Com-

Jim and Jesse with Bobby Thompson (banjo) and Vassar Clements (fiddle), 1956.

pany, members included Meadows, Bobby Thompson (banjo), Don McHan (bass) and Stripling. McHan, who was actually a multi-instrumentalist who played all the bluegrass instruments, moved to bass when Bobby Thompson came in on banjo. Ford also sponsored them in Savannah on WSAV-TV and on WALB-TV, Albany, Georgia. Joe Meadows left in 1956 and was replaced by Vassar Clements in 1957 who stayed until 1961. Meadows returned to **Jim and Jesse** later.

The group acquired a job playing in Pensacola, Florida, on WEAR-TV and WTVY, Dothan, Alabama, about 1957. These jobs were sponsored by John Dodson's Marina and Crestview Mobile Homes Companies in Florida. Sponsorships for a touring band were nearly essential to its continuing longevity and they were glad to have them wherever they could find them.

After three years with Capitol, Jim and Jesse had signed a recording contract with Starday. Songs included "Border Ride" and "Let Me Whisper." The brothers had an arrangement where Starday would only distribute the records; they would have to be recorded, mixed, and produced elsewhere. It was a commercial success, but this arrangement with Starday was similar to several years ago with Ultra-Sonic and Gateway: beyond their control and without royalties.

In January 1959, **Jim and Jesse** left Florida and moved to Valdosta, Georgia. The **Stanley Brothers** replaced them in Live Oak. Soon Martha White Flour Mills began a sponsorship of **Jim and Jesse** on their tours, some television shows, and occasional guest spots on the Opry beginning in 1961. The sponsorship by Martha White helped their popularity immensely and helped get them on the Opry as permanent members (1964).

Jesse explained how they got the Martha White sponsorship, "In Valdosta, we was working television shows for Ford Tractor and a construction company. This was before they had videotape and all the shows had to be done live. **Flatt and Scruggs** did Tennessee and West Virginia, and they (Martha White Mills) had another group doing Chattanooga, Atlanta and northern Georgia and in that area. So they moved further south into Valdosta in north Florida. And when they come down there, they had to have another group to cover that area and it happened that we were in that area at the time. And the people at the TV station, when they came down to buy their TV time, they were inquiring

[254] Robert K. Oermann, "Jim and Jesse: Testing the Boundaries of Bluegrass Music—With a Little Help from Charlie Louvin," *Bluegrass Unlimited*, September, 1982, p. 21.

about a band. And the manager of the television station was a friend of ours—we had worked for him before—and he recommended us. That was in Albany, Georgia. We were the only ones available in the area at that time. Talk about being in the right place at the right time!"[255] Also this year, they were featured at WGOV's Lowndes (pron. Lowns) County Jamboree in Valdosta.

About 1960, the band began videotaping their shows for play at a later time. This reduced their 1500 miles per week driving commitment to stations such as WSFA-TV, Montgomery, Alabama, and WJTV, Jackson, Mississippi. Also reducing their mileage was a move to Prattville, Alabama (close to Montgomery), from Valdosta. Here, band members included Allen Shelton (banjo), Jimmy Buchanan (fiddle) and Don McHan (bass).

Don Law offered them a recording contract with Columbia on December first, 1960. The December 7th recording session songs included "Flame of Love" and "Gosh, I Miss You All the Time." This band[256] was popular and added to **Jim and Jesse**'s fame. This configuration of the **Virginia Boys** really put the band on the map. On the strength of their Columbia recordings and with the prestige of being sponsored by Martha White Flour, they made their first guest appearance on the Grand Ole Opry on January 28, 1961. On May 5, 1961, they recorded the very commercial and somewhat successful "Diesel Train" for Columbia with Shelton, Clements and McHan.

In 1962, Columbia Records assigned **Jim and Jesse**[257] to the new Epic label, a Columbia subsidiary designed to cater to country and bluegrass audiences. They produced six albums with Epic through 1966. Their first LP was "Bluegrass Special," produced by Don Law and Frank Jones. The duo's music was not restrained by the confines of traditional bluegrass. Regarding their many years of stretching bluegrass boundaries, Jim said, 'When we first moved to Nashville, bluegrass wasn't doing that well. We had to get something on the record charts before we could get any work. And the only way we could get on the record charts was to get booked country. So that's where we went. In Europe, bluegrass and country are not so segregated as here... In Germany, England and France

Jim and Jesse and the Virginia Boys, 1995.

we were on a tour with Johnny Cash and Tammy Wynette and Marty Robbins. When we played Paris we went on right in the middle of all the acts and we got more encores than anyone else on the show—including Cash.'"[258] Martha White Mills and Pet Milk sponsored many of these package shows in which a bluegrass band would tour with country music stars who were also having a lot of trouble making ends meet. The tours were helpful in keeping many bands alive, but it was obvious that country and hillbilly music was not as popular as rock and roll or "the British invasion" which occurred about this time.

The June 22, 1962, session included "Sweet Little Miss Blue Eyes," "She Left Me Standing on the Mountain" and "I Wish You Knew" with musicians McHan (guitar), Shelton (banjo), Buchanan (fiddle), Douglas Kirkham (drums) and David Sutherland (bass). They also recorded their own composition, "Stoney Creek."

By the summer of 1963, the full force of the "folk boom" had hit and was beneficial to groups of this genre. Jim and Jesse played at the 1963 Newport Folk Festival. Bill Monroe's band was there at the festival with banjoist Bill Keith. Doc Watson was there, and others. On June 22nd, they recorded their first sacred album, "The Old Country Church," as a representative example of an important tradition in the McReynolds performances. Shortly thereafter, they recorded "Y'all Come."

Jim and Jesse then recorded "Bluegrass Classics" on Epic. Released on October 1, 1963, it was along the same vein as "Bluegrass Special." Both Epic LPs did well and kept them in the music full-time—something a lot of musicians couldn't/wouldn't do.

On March 2, 1964, they recorded "Cotton Mill Man" and "It's a Long, Long Way to the Top of the World." On fiddle now was Jim Brock, taking the place of Jim Buchanan who had just left to join Arthur Smith. "Cotton Mill Man" reached #43 on the *Billboard* Country Charts in 1964, and was their best seller until "Diesel on My Tail" came out in 1967 and reached even higher. These hits were of significant importance to the group and helped put them "on the map". Allen Shelton considers "Cotton Mill Man" as the first musical highlight of his early career as

[255] Telephone interview, March 24, 1993.

[256] Their fiddler was Vassar Clements; the banjo player, Allen Shelton; their electric bass player, Don McHan; and their comedian, Dave Sutherland, who called himself "Joe Binglehead."

[257] Band members were Allen Shelton (banjo), Don McHan (guitar), Jim Buchanan (fiddle, age 21), Dave Sutherland (bass), Jim and Jesse.

[258] Oermann, op. cit., p. 24.

a **Virginia Boy**. On the April 20th session for Columbia/Epic, they recorded with saxophone player Boots Randolph; the songs were all gospel. Other sessions in 1964 were March 2 and December 30.

Jim and Jesse McReynolds became regular members of the Grand Ole Opry on March the second, 1964, at the invitation of Opry Manager Ott Devine. Their first performance as members was March 7th. Thus, they became the first bluegrass band to join the Opry since **Flatt and Scruggs** in 1955. A dream come true, Jesse remarked, "If it wasn't for Martha White, I guess we wouldn't be here today." Jim agreed, "It's still the greatest country music show there is. It's something special to be a part of."[259] The group took over Martha White's fifteen-minute early morning show on WSM which **Flatt and Scruggs** had held since 1953. Perhaps because of the Opry influence, **Jim and Jesse** began using electric guitars and steel guitars; becoming more a part of the Nashville sound. They played more recent material which also contributed to the change.

The brothers bought a farm near Gallatin, Tennessee, moving there in 1965. Today, the Double J Ranch is their home.

Jim and Jesse and the Virginia Boys recorded the "Berry Pickin' in the Country" album on Epic in 1965; it was a collection of Chuck Berry tunes which went over very well, crossing over the border from bluegrass to country and rock; it became a financial success. Songs included "Memphis," Maybelline" and eight more tunes written and recorded by Berry.

By 1967, the popularity of this hillbilly/country kind of music was waning and the effect on **Jim and Jesse** was accentuated when Martha White discontinued their sponsorship. Also, 1966 was the last time they appeared at the Newport Folk Festival. They had to change their approach to music to survive. Jim and Jesse again strayed from bluegrass when they went country and western in their recording of the single "Diesel On My Tail," recorded in late 1968 on Epic. The song made it onto *Billboard* magazine's #18. This song was the most successful since the time when they changed over to electric and steel guitars. An album of the same name soon followed and it remained a best-selling album for eighteen weeks. The group had suddenly found a new popularity and were voted Most Promising Vocal Duo for 1967 by *Record World*. This seems rather ironic for a duo which had been in the business since the late 1940s.

In June 1967, the brothers launched a syndicated television show entitled "Country Music Carousel." This led to a similar, but more sophisticated, "The Jim and Jesse Show." This was their most ambitious syndication plan so far; they independently produced the show in a series of taped television shows. In the late

1960s, Jim and Jesse recorded their "Salute to the Louvin Brothers" (Epic label, August 1969. The Louvins broke up in 1963; Ira died in 1965.) and Charlie and Ira Louvin gained increased fame due to this exposure. Also during this time, they recorded the albums "Sing Unto Him a New Song," "The All-Time Great Country Instrumentals" and "We Like Trains." Following the success of "Diesel on My Tail," the 1969 recording of "We Like Trains" transcended bluegrass and ventured heavily into the realm of pop country with all the instruments to match. Into the early '70s, they recorded "Freight Train" and "Mandolin Workshop" (Hilltop, 1972).

Carl Jackson (14) joined the group in the spring of 1968. He was allowed by his parents to tour with **Jim and Jesse and the Virginia Boys** (this was the only group his parents trusted with their son). This job proved to be the launching of a very successful musical career. By the time he was twenty-one, Jackson had recorded for Capitol, succeeded John Hartford on "The Glen Campbell Goodtime Hour" and become a respected session man, songwriter and producer in Nashville.

Having left Epic in 1971, Jim and Jesse McReynolds began their own record label, Old Dominion Records, in the spring of 1973. Now that they were producing their own records, they were able to keep busy enough to hire musicians full-time. Additionally, in November they signed with the Opryland label. Keith McReynolds, Jesse's son, joined on electric bass. Jim Brock was the fiddler. It was on this label that they recorded John Prine's "Paradise." A ecological protest song about strip coal mining, it is a reminder of where the duo were born and raised.

By 1974, the festivals were in full swing and gave an enlivened shot into the lives of bluegrass bands. As a result, **Jim and Jesse** was back to playing mostly bluegrass.

The brothers brought back many former members of the **Virginia Boys** in spring of 1980 for their newest CMH Records double album, "The Jim and Jesse Story."[260] Band musicians were Carl Jackson, Jim Buchanan, Don McHan, Lloyd Green, Bobby Thompson (who also produced the album) and Allen Shelton.

Jim and Jesse McReynolds were admitted into the Virginia Country Music Foundation Hall of Fame in 1981.

During the late 1980s, concert attendees may have noticed that Keith McReynolds was not walking onto the stage with his electric bass strapped to him. He had his bass on a waist-high stand on the stage, waiting for his performance. He didn't know it at the time, but he had multiple sclerosis. All he knew is that the weight of the bass was increasingly heavy to carry on and off the

259 Michael R. Drudge, "Jim and Jesse, 25 Years on the Grand Ole Opry," *Bluegrass Unlimited*, May, 1989, p. 61.

260 The LP has great biographical liner notes. This type of double LP is what CMH specialized in. When they signed an artist, many of the tunes they planned to record would be the ones which the band already made famous, but CMH always insisted that they be recorded again on their own state-of-the-art equipment.

Americas Music — Bluegrass

stage. But he soon became so weak that performing became difficult so he had to quit. Keith continued to tour with his father as a member of the audience. Benefits were held for Keith in 1992 and 1995. By 1996, the disease had rendered him virtually helpless.

By 1990, **Jim and Jesse**'s new banjo player was Raymond W. McLain. Early in the year, the electric bass player was Mike Drudge; the fiddler was Jimmy Campbell. Blaine Sprouse took Campbell's place on fiddle in the fall. Drudge explained how, as a newcomer, he got his job with this very popular band. The secret, he found, was persistence. He worked for five years just to get to ride with them on the bus. He explained that after he got to know them and they felt comfortable with him, he told Jim that he played bass, sang baritone, and knew every song they ever did. This was his first full-time, professional music job. Drudge soon founded his own booking agency, Class Act Entertainment. During McLain's recent years with the **McLain Family Band**, they toured about 140 days per year; now that he was with the McReynolds', he toured 250 days per year.

Jesse still practices daily in his pursuit "to be the best mandolin player in the world and that's something I'll be working at all my life. That's my goal though I don't think nobody would live long enough to really achieve that. I learn something every time I pick up the instrument, really...something that I hadn't done before or something that I hadn't noticed I had done it before."

Jim and Jesse McReynolds were inducted into the IBMA Hall Of Honor in 1993. In 1995, the touring group included Jim, Jesse, Jimmy Campbell (fiddle), Raymond McLain (banjo) and Ray Kirkland (electric bass).

Charlie Waller

Charlie Waller and the Country Gentlemen

After nearly fifty years in bluegrass music—and nearly forty of that in one group—Charlie Waller has indeed become a legend in this music. He and his music have changed with the times and, as a result, his group has been able to not only been able to maintain its presence but also thrive.

Charles Otis Waller was born in Jointerville, Texas, on the Texas-Louisiana border on January 19, 1935. When he was very young, the family moved to the Shreveport, Louisiana, area where he lived until he was age six, at which time the family moved to Washington, D.C.. His first guitar was a $15 Stella and his first good guitar was a $35 Gibson bought from a friend. A strong influence to Waller's country music was Hank Snow and other hillbilly music. And he was heavily influenced by Mac Wiseman, Don Reno, **Flatt and Scruggs**, and Bill Monroe (when he was singing with someone else, not singing solo).

Waller got his first professional job in Washington, D.C., in 1948; he was thirteen years and sang with Richard Decker (13) and Jack Jackson who taught him a lot on the guitar. To augment his income from his club work, he parked cars where rising-star Roy Clark frequented. It was always a thrill for Waller to be with Clark, picking together until a car would come to be parked. Here he met fiddler Scott Stoneman, who helped him develop as a musician.

Beginning in the early 1950s, Waller played clubs in the Baltimore and D.C. area with Earl Taylor and Sam Hutchins. He was with **Earl Taylor and the Stoney Mountain Boys** until the time he began working with Buzz Busby and his **Bayou Boys** in Washington, a full-time job in 1955. A full-time salary was something that Waller hadn't experienced before this. Busby and this band were important figures in the area, helping to make it a center for bluegrass during this period. The band was a hot item because of Busby's television show. Then the band received an offer to appear regularly on the popular stage show, Louisiana Hayride, on KWKH, Shreveport, Louisiana. Band members were Busby (mandolin), Waller (guitar), Don Stover (banjo), John Hall (fiddle) and Lee Cole (bass).

In early 1957, the **Bayou Boys** moved to D.C. for a series of gigs. After a local concert, the band had a bad auto accident. People in the wreck were Busby, Eddie Adcock, bassist Vance Truell, and friend Sonny Presley. Waller was not in the band at this time. Busby was seriously hurt, as was Truell. Immediate replacements had to be found to fulfill the band's obligations so Busby asked Bill Emerson to take over the band. Emerson hired twenty-three-year-old John Duffey to play mandolin (who was playing with **Lucky Chatman and the Ozark Mountain Boys** at the time) and formed the replacement band with Larry Leahy (bass) and Charlie Waller (guitar). Soon Tom Morgan became the bass player. On July 4, 1957, they decided to go on without Busby's presence and changed the band name to **Country Gentlemen**; they played their first gig at the Crossroads Tavern. They shared in the material. Emerson recalled that "John wanted to do those pretty trio numbers and Charlie had his Hank Snow style. I had the straight-ahead bluegrass where I could really work on the banjo. Whatever we came up with we'd try, and if it worked we'd leave it in. If it didn't, we'd try something else. There was plenty of material available. John even got a song from Carter Stanley. It was our first record (recorded October 1957) called 'Going to the Races.'"[261] "Heavenward Bound" was on the flip side. This was a song Duffey wrote earlier and played with Lucky Chatman. Recorded at the studios of WARL, John Hall was added on fiddle. Hall played fiddle with them for a year.

Alleged personality conflicts with Duffey and Emerson caused Emerson to leave. They went through several banjo players including Peter V. Kuykendall (using the stage name Pete Roberts)[262] who was already well known for his folklore work with Mike Seeger on several projects and was recently with **Benny and Vallie Cain and the Country Clan.** Porter Church worked with the **Gents** on banjo for a couple of weeks then Eddie Adcock took over the banjo spot that winter. Kuykendall is credited for helping Eddie Adcock learn how to sing the baritone vocal part which proved to be essential for the trio. Kuykendall was with the group until June 1959, playing fiddle, banjo and bass until he left to pursue full-time activities with the Library of Congress. Busby got out of the hospital two months after the accident and re-formed his **Bayou Boys.** Jim Cox took Morgan's place on bass with the **Gents** and was then replaced by Tom Gray in 1960. Heavily influenced by George Shuffler of the **Stanley Brothers,** Gray's walking-style of bass playing fit right in when the trio was singing and no one else was playing their lead instruments as backup. Gray stayed four years,

On May 13, 1961, the **Country Gentlemen** appeared at a university (Oberlin College, Ohio) concert for the first time. Band members were Waller, Adcock, Duffey and Gray. Their appearance here helped to form today's policy of almost universal acceptance of folk bands at college campuses and this was two years before Bill Monroe's **Blue Grass Boys** started touring out of the South. After the **Gents** paved the way at colleges, Ralph Rinzler took over the **Blue Grass Boys,** followed the lead of the **Gents,** and put Monroe's band on the map by booking the band in a much larger variety of venues and areas of the country. In September of 1963, the **Country Gentlemen** played at Carnegie Hall. Ed Ferris had taken the place of Tom Gray on bass in mid-'64. Other band members were the same from 1959 until early 1969.

Jimmy Gaudreau, who later became integral to the **Country Gentlemen**'s sound, spoke of the band's sound, "You knew instantly, when you put on a **Country Gentlemen** record, that it was a different type of bluegrass. They were forerunners and innovators of that type of sound. It all had a lot to do with the personality of the group. Adcock's banjo struck you as completely different, not only in the way he played, but the tone he got out of the banjo was unlike anything else you ever heard. That particular band was made up of four individual stylists that happened to work well together."[263]

Duffey was the first one to realize that their band was just copying other bands of the day such as **Osborne Brothers and Red Allen.** He spent many hours in the Library of Congress looking for songs which would make the **Gentlemen**'s sound distinctive. They were very successful with songs such as "Copper Kettle," "Long Black Veil" and "Handsome Molly." Adcock was given free reign to follow his own style. Duffey's rendition of "The World is Waiting for the Sunrise" "came from the realization that you cannot play like somebody else and expect to create anything that's your own."

In 1966, the **Country Gentlemen** got it's first hit with "Bringing Mary Home" on Dick Freeland's new Rebel label.[264] It reached #43 on the *Billboard* magazine music charts. Actually Bill Clifton had recorded and released the song just before the **Gents'** version but it was barely noticed. A survey by WAMU in 1981 showed that the D.C. area considered the **Gents'** version was the top among all bluegrass songs. Also in 1966, according to an article by Bill Vernon, "The Sound That Changed the Color of Bluegrass," in a 1976 issue of *Muleskinner News,* the **Gents'** had an opportunity to appear on the "Tonight Show." But when the talent

Classic Country Gentlemen, 1963. L to R: Eddie Adcock, John Duffey, Tom Gray, Charlie Waller.

261 Joe Ross, "Bill Emerson, Banjo Player Extraordinaire," *Bluegrass Unlimited,* March, 1992, p. 22.

262 As Mr. Kuykendall explained, determining just who was a band member was (and still is) difficult because of the rapid turnover in many bands and because someone might be unable to play at a certain time with the band and they would get a substitute. While that substitute may be *in* the band, he may not actually qualify to be a regular member of the band. This applies to all bands included in this book.

263 Marty Godbey, *Bluegrass Unlimited,* December, 1980.

264 They had been recording on the Folkways label.

buyer, Skitch Henderson, asked for a kickback, Duffey suggested that he have sex with himself (or words similar). According to Mr. Vernon in a 1996 conversation, probably the only pure bluegrass act to appear on the show was **Flatt and Scruggs**, and even then, all they did was play a tune—they weren't invited to the couch with Johnny Carson.

With successive performances and recordings, the **Gentlemen**'s style became categorized as "progressive", thereby setting the stage for other musicians and bands inclined toward this style of bluegrass. Some have said that the progressive nature of their music was a forerunner to what is now known as "newgrass", but at the time, Waller and company didn't consider themselves progressive. They were just doing the music with which they felt comfortable. Even though they were doing "far out" tunes such as "Exodus" and "Greensleeves," they would still do "Katy Dear" and "Jesse James"-type songs. They were merely entertaining people, making a lot of people sit up and listen.

In 1969, John Duffey left the **Country Gentlemen**, needing a break from touring and the music business in general. He semi-retired from music to his instrument building and repair business. Rhode Island Yankee Jimmy Gaudreau (age 22) replaced him. Ed McGlothlin then replaced Ed Ferris on bass, followed by Bill Yates on December 3, 1969. Yates stayed until November 1988.

Adcock left the **Country Gentlemen** after eleven years in early 1970, and was replaced by Bill Emerson on banjo who stayed three years. In 1971, Adcock started his own **II Generation**, a newgrass-style band. Gaudreau left the **Gents** to join Adcock and was replaced by Doyle Lawson on August 30, 1971. One week after Doyle Lawson joined the band, Len Holsclaw, longtime friend of the **Country Gentlemen**, became manager of the group.[265] Band members for the **Gents** were Waller, Lawson, Emerson and Yates.

The **Country Gentlemen** began recording on Vanguard Records in 1973; with Rebel they had dreams of excellent promotion which never occurred. The band played regularly in the Washington, D.C., area. Jerry Douglas was the session resonator guitarist during the summer of 1973, joining as a member in July of 1974 for one and a half years (and again for ten months beginning in 1978). Ricky Skaggs was the fiddler with the group, bringing the sound of the fiddle to their recordings for the first time in fifteen years (Carl Nelson had earlier recorded "Orange Blossom Fiddle" with the group).

Bill Emerson left the band June 1, 1973, to join the Navy. A very successful concert with the **U.S. Navy Band** that year almost caused the recruitment of all the **Gentlemen** into the Navy. Waller and Bill Yates were too old (the age limit was 35), but Emerson did join and he soon formed the Navy's **Country Current** and

The Country Gentlemen, 1971. L to R: Jimmy Gaudreau, Bill Emerson, Bill Yates, Charlie Waller.

eventually the **U.S. Navy Bluegrass Band** which continued after he retired in 1993. Doyle Lawson was about to join but changed his mind at the last moment, feeling that he had just reached a point in music where he felt good about his music and his career, and to leave this very successful group now would be a disservice to his past efforts and to his fans. Another event which may have precipitated Emerson's departure was a shooting after a concert. The band had finished a show at the Red Fox Inn in Bethesda, Maryland, and were walking to their cars. Suddenly, a car sped by and a shot rang out. Emerson grabbed his arm in pain where the bullet had pierced it. He recovered fully. The band kept up a reliable schedule in spite of this tragic event. Coincidentally about this time, they started dropping their regular gigs at the Shamrock, finding that there was very little money in it.

Mike Lilly took Emerson's place on banjo, staying a couple of months. When Lilly left in November 1973, James Bailey took his place until August 1974. After Bailey left, Doyle Lawson took his place on banjo, followed a few weeks later by Bill Holden who stayed until Bailey came back in September 1976 (he stayed until February 1979). Holden then joined the **Blue Grass Boys**. Ricky Skaggs left that October and went back to Kentucky to work for J.D. Crowe where he stayed many years.

In 1973, *Muleskinner News* named the **Gentlemen** Band of the Year for the second year in a row; Charlie Waller was Best Blue Grass Singer, Bill Emerson won Best Banjo Player, Bill Yates won Best Bass Player....Ricky Skaggs was named Most Promising Fiddler for the second year in a row. Other awards for the band this year were for best song and album.

Members of the **Country Gentlemen** in 1979 were Waller (guitar), Rick Allred (mandolin), Kent Dowell (banjo) and Bill Yates (bass). Allred and Dowell recently came from the **Bluegrass Blend**. Early in 1981, the top three songs voted by the listeners of WAMU, Washington, D.C., were by the **Country Gentlemen**: "Legend of the Rebel Soldier," " Bringing Mary Home" and "Fox on

265 He had just been asked to be bass player for the newly-forming Seldom Scene but declined because of possible conflict of interest with the GENTS. Instead, John Duffey, John Starling, Mike Auldridge and Ben Eldridge hauled Tom Gray out of musical retirement to do the job for the Scene.

the Run." In the fall of 1981, members of the band were Waller (guitar), Jimmy Gaudreau (mandolin),[266] Dick Smith (banjo) and Yates (bass).

Norman Wright joined the **Gents** as mandolinist in 1986. A former member of the **Bluegrass Cardinals**, he wrote many of the **Gentlemen**'s songs. By 1988, members of the **Country Gentlemen** were Waller, Keith Little (banjo, who joined in 1987), Wright and Yates. Charlie Waller won SPBGMA's Bluegrass Guitar of the Year (Rhythm) from 1984 through 1988. Then he was retired from the competition.

Kevin Church joined the **Gents** on banjo in early 1989.[267] Members of the band were Charlie Waller (guitar), Norman Wright (mandolin, multi-instrumentalist), Church (banjo, lead guitar, buck dancing) and Jimmy Bowen (bass, multi-instrumentalist). **Charlie Waller and the Country Gentlemen** is still active in the 1990s and won several awards in 1996 at SPBGMA. The "classic" Country Gentlemen became members of IBMA's Hall of Honor in 1996. They are John Duffey, Eddie Adcock, Charlie Waller and Tom Gray.

Hubert Davis and the Season Travelers

Another one of the unsung bluegrass pioneers was Hubert Davis who was later known for owning and running the Bluegrass Inn venue in Nashville. Hubert Davis was born in Shelby, North Carolina, in 1932, eight years after Earl Scruggs was born there. His father played banjo, the first of which he made from a tin pan and a stick of wood. Hubert spoke about the banjo his father made for him, "It didn't have no frets and he made a little round mark where the notes was at. He didn't have a drill, he'd heat an iron rod and burn the holes for the keys. He whittled the keys out of wood."[268] This was in the days before Earl Scruggs became popular in their home town of Shelby.

Davis watched Scruggs there in Shelby as he grew up. When Scruggs became a popular banjo player, he left town. Davis remembered that when Scruggs was about seventeen, he was just as good as when he went to work with Bill Monroe four years later. Occasionally, Scruggs would come home from touring with Monroe. During those times, Scruggs gave Davis tips on how to play better three-finger style banjo. Soon, at age fifteen, Davis chose music as a career, left Shelby, and began recording with Don Gibson and Pee Wee Davis (Hubert's brother) and Pee Wee Peeler on RCA in Charlotte, North Carolina.

"When Earl Scruggs was with Bill Monroe," said Davis, "my goal was to learn to pick the banjo, and when Earl quit, to come here (Nashville) and take his job. I was sent word I could have done that—but it wasn't that I didn't want it; I was just young and scared, I guess. Lloyd McGraw came up and played the first Saturday night after Earl left, but he didn't stay with it...and that's when Don Reno came in."[269]

In 1948, after a brief stay in Gastonia playing bluegrass music with the **Murphy Brothers**, Davis joined Jim Eanes' **Shenandoah Valley Boys**. They soon got a contract with the Blue Ridge label and with Decca. Davis left the group for a brief period; Allen Shelton took his place until he returned. By that time, Bobby Hicks was on fiddle. They recorded "Home Sweet Home"[270] and "Cotton Picker's Stomp."

Davis recorded four sides with Bill Monroe in 1954, even though he never joined Monroe's touring band. Hubert and his brother, Pee Wee Davis, played together in various bands through these years until 1962 when Hubert moved back to Shelby, working at a mill for a year. Then Hubert and Pee Wee Davis organized the **Bluegrass Ramblers** in Asheville.

Hubert moved to Nashville about 1972. About that time, he formed the **Season Travelers**. This group played regularly at Davis' Bluegrass Inn.

Through the years, Davis recorded with Don Gibson on RCA Records, Jim Eanes on Blue Ridge, Rich-R-Tone and Decca Records, Bill Monroe on Decca, his **Bluegrass Ramblers** on Trepur Records, the **Davis Brothers and the Bluegrass Ramblers** on Spires Records, **Hubert Davis and the Seasons Travelers** on Music City and Stoneway Records. Hubert Davis died May 4, 1992. His group disappeared. Soon, the Bluegrass Inn was out of business.

Red Allen and the Allen brothers. L to R: Neal, Harley, Ronnie, Red, and Greg Allen.

---

266 Again. He returned when Spectrum split up.

267 Church's father, Porter Church is a former banjo player for the Gentlemen.

268 Bruce Nemerov, "Hubert Davis—Down Home Banjo Picker," *Bluegrass Unlimited*, January, 1977, p. 18.

269 Ibid., p. 20.

270 When Shelton left the band, he joined Hack Johnson's Farm Hands where, in 1955, he recorded "Home Sweet Home" using Scruggs tuners.

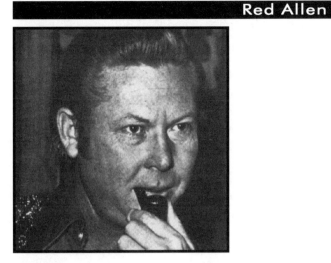

Red Allen and the Kentuckians

Red Allen is known for helping "invent" the high-lead trio style of singing with Bobby and Sonny Osborne, and for his soulful singing. Red Allen's **Kentuckians** served as a breeding ground for many known well bluegrass musicians today. He never cared to make it big in the bluegrass music business; he just wanted to work near home and raise a family. As a result, Red Allen's fame nowadays seems to come when linked to other stars such as David Grisman, Frank Wakefield, Bill Keith or the **Osborne Brothers**. His four sons later had their own **Allen Brothers** band.

Harley "Red" Allen was born in Hazard, in eastern Kentucky, February 12, 1930, and raised in nearby Pigeon Roost. Those raised in that area of the country are known as "Briarhoppers". He was exposed to music by his family. About 1949, Allen began playing bluegrass music professionally in the Ohio area.[271] In 1952, Allen changed the band name to **Red Allen and the Kentuckians**. By using his name in the band name, he was able to capitalize on his popularity in the Dayton area with his earlier band.

Allen joined the Osborne brothers in late 1956. He remembered that "They had no sound other than the regular bluegrass pickin' when they come with me. Their sound was the same as everybody else. They hadn't reached that high lead [that they became famous for]. They wouldn't have reached that...high lead if it weren't for me. They sounded like Bill Monroe and Flatt and Scruggs and everybody else had. [The way that sound developed was] we was comin' back from Wheelin' one night and we had this song called 'Once More.' We'd already cut one session [in Wheeling]. We'd do two shows at the Jamboree and we'd do two shows after the Jamboree. We was comin' back and a fella named Ray Anderson was comin' back with us. Ray had his family in his car and we was comin' back and we got to Zanesville, Ohio. We'd been rehearsing this song, 'Once More,' and I didn't like the way I was singin' lead on it and we didn't like the way the timin' was on it. And so Bobby was drivin' and I was in the back seat layin' down and Sonny was on the passenger side and Bobby started singin' 'Once More' and he got a little high. I was sung out. I was tired and I didn't feel like gettin' the lead to it there and Sonny hit the baritone to it and I hit low tenor. Now that's exactly how it was born. We sung it through and Sonny said, 'What in the hell was that we was singin'?' I said, 'Hell I don't know but it was prettier than what we've been singin'.' They honked at Ray Anderson, pulled him over, and sang 'Once More' for him and he said that 'was the prettiest stuff I've ever heard in my life.' Nobody had ever done that before. The way we got it—I lucked on it because I was so tired I didn't want to reach up and strain and sing the lead so I just went to something else."[272]

Allen and the Osbornes stayed together as the **Osborne Brothers and Red Allen** for thirty months—until April of 1958. Then Allen went home and played locally in Dayton until 1960.

Red Allen's sons' band, **Red Allen and the Allen Brothers**, was formed in 1970 with Greg, Harley, Ronnie and Neal Allen. Ronnie played drums in the band until they hired a drummer; he then switched to bass. The band appeared as "long-hairs" with blue jeans and flannel shirts—an appearance which occasionally kept them from being hired at some events. They were later accepted on WWVA's Jamboree after audiences heard their music and ignored their appearance.

When asked about his feeling about modern bluegrass compared to what it was when he was playing, Red Allen replied, "I don't pay much attention to it. Everybody sounds good to me—what I hear."

Red Allen died April 3, 1993, of lung cancer complications.

[271] Members of Red Allen and the Blue Mountain Boys were Allen (guitar), Dorsey Harvey (mandolin), Noah Crase (banjo) and Johnny McKee (fiddle).

[272] This quotation and others, except as otherwise noted, were from a 1991 telephone conversation with Mr. Allen at his home in Dayton.

Curly Seckler told this amusing anecdote about Red Allen. "I've known Red Allen since he was a kid. The closest I ever got to gettin' locked up in jail was over Red Allen. I was working with Jim and Jesse in '51. We was working at WVLK just out of Lexington. Lester and us went in there, you know. And I left Lester and them, I went to work with Jim and Jesse up there. But I went to the Stanley Brothers first. But that's a long story. I went into Bristol and then took the Stanleys up there and that fell through. But anyway, Red was up there and doing shows. We didn't know that he wasn't keeping his kids up—supporting them. We got the word when we went to Richmond, Virginia, which was on April Fool night. He didn't go. I guess he got word that they was goin' to pick him up. And so when our show with me and Hoke Jenkins and Jim and Jesse was over, two private guys come up to me and said, 'We've got a warrant for your arrest.' Of course, Hoke Jenkins was always pulling a joke, you know. And I thought it was April Fool. I ain't done nothin'. This is a joke. They said, 'Well, you're Red Allen ain't you?' I said, 'No, I ain't Red Allen. Red ain't with us tonight.' They said, 'Well, we've got orders to pick up the blonde-headed, curly-headed guy that played the guitar.' At that time, I was playing guitar with Jim and Jesse. Danged if they didn't take me to jail! They didn't even want to see my driver's license or nothin'. They just said they had orders to pick me up. They didn't lock me up, but it was about a hour before them dudes turned me loose. And ole Red, he found it out, and he called me and said 'Dad'—he always called me Dad—'I hear you got problem!' I told him that if he was down there I'd break his neck. That really happened." — From a 1992 phone interview with Mr. Seckler.

Jimmy Martin and the Sunny Mountain Boys

Banjoist Raymond Fairchild spoke of Jimmy Martin, "The Greatest! He's my all-time favorite entertainer. When Jimmy Martin steps to the mike, his timing, it's there! Jimmy Martin is one who'll never be equaled."[273]

Bluegrass probably wouldn't be what it is today without Jimmy Martin. When he left Bill Monroe's band in the early 1950s to form his own, he took Monroe's bluegrass rhythm with him and passed it on to all who became members of his band. His hard-driving style of bluegrass became well known in the bluegrass world, especially at the hands of banjoist J.D. Crowe.

Jimmy Martin's legacy in bluegrass is multi-faceted and includes his wonderful, crowd-pleasing music presented in a showman style which few bluegrassers can reach. It includes his own rhythms of bluegrass which is close, but not identical, to that of his mentor Bill Monroe. It includes a history of missed concerts due to excessive drinking. His behavior off-stage kept him from becoming a member of the Grand Ole Opry where he had performed several times and achieved tremendous crowd acceptance. And his social relationships with most of the big names of bluegrass, with which he has worked at one time or another, virtually disappeared. He seemed to offend almost everyone at one time or another to the point that they wouldn't speak to him. But his legacy also includes his tremendous music, for which he lives. He loves bluegrass, knows it well, and has turned many a promising blue-

grass musician into a great one. Just ask J.D. Crowe, Alan Munde, Bill Emerson and Paul Williams. This is his story.

James H. "Jimmy" Martin was born in Sneedville, Tennessee, August 10, 1927. As he was growing up and developing his musical skills, he sang in quartets around the family farm. He sang in church a lot, and he played as many as two funerals a day with his little group. Later on, he played mandolin daily with a guitar-player friend on a radio station in Morristown, Tennessee. They did this for no pay, hoping for exposure. Their day jobs were as painters. He especially liked the sounds of Bill Monroe and learned all of Monroe's songs while Flatt and Scruggs were with Monroe. Jimmy Martin's first guitar was a "Gene Autry," purchased for $10.

Martin (22) saw **Bill Monroe and the Blue Grass Boys** for the first time at the Grand Ole Opry in the summer of 1949. He auditioned for Bill on the spot. At that time, Mac Wiseman was singing lead. Martin felt that Wiseman's voice didn't blend with Monroe's and convinced Monroe to hire him after singing a song. Their voices blended so well that Monroe was able to eliminate the need for the trio singer, which was costly to a band and inconvenient when musicians were coming and going so frequently into Monroe's band.

Martin remembered meeting the legend—his idol—Bill Monroe, "I was kind of scared and nervous but I just wanted to see him and meet him. I really didn't know what I was going to do but I did want to sing with him. I got down there and got me a room at the Sam Davis Hotel where I could see the Opry, then get back to the hotel without getting lost. I went down and got me a ticket for the first show up in the balcony. I thought Bill would be a little man; I'd never seen him before. But then I saw a man walk across with a mandolin, and he was a pretty good sized fellow. He was wearing a red shirt and white pants and a white hat. And I said I betcha that's Bill Monroe right there. Chubby Wise and Rudy Lyle was there with him. They sang 'Brakeman's Blues.' Then I decided, after Bill went off, to go find the back door where the entertainers came out. It was back in an alley and I asked some people, is this where the Opry stars come out, and they said yes. So I stayed there. Directly, Bill came out. He didn't have his white hat on but he had on his red shirt and white pants. I was still a little nervous. But I went up to him and told him who I was and that I listened to him on the radio at home.

"I told him I played with a group up in Morristown and that I was playing mandolin, but that I wasn't as good as him. And I told him I also played guitar—his style—and could sing lead and some tenor, but not as good as him. And that I could sing bass and baritone in

273 Janice Brown McDonald, "Raymond Fairchild," *Bluegrass Unlimited*, May, 1989, p. 26.
This writer agrees. Whenever a person asks me whom to listen as a good example of what bluegrass is, I always recommend they listen to any of Jimmy Martin's records, but especially those with Crowe and Williams. His music always shows bluegrass at its best.

the quartets and knew all his songs. He said, 'How about coming back here and singing one with me?' I said, 'I'd like to.' So he took me in the back. You know how nervous I must be—getting to sing with my idol. He told Mac Wiseman to let me have his guitar, the same one Lester Flatt played with, and that made me thrilled. He asked me what songs I would like to sing. He just had a new one out called 'The Old Crossroads' and said he hadn't sang that since Lester left. So we sang that. Then he asked me to sing a solo, so I sang 'Poor Ellen Smith.' Then he asked me how good I was at following fiddle tunes, so they played 'Orange Blossom Special.' Then he looked at Chubby Wise and said, 'Chubby, how do you like that boy's guitar playing?' I never will forget this. Chubby looked at Bill and said, 'Oh Lordy, son, he's flat got it, ain't he?'"[274] He was hired; Wiseman left the band Christmas 1949. Monroe liked Martin's style of singing. He put in just the right amount of lonesome whine into his voice, and Monroe would match it with his tenor.

Martin played and recorded with Monroe for Decca, on and off, from early 1950 until early 1954 on tunes such as "New Mule Skinner Blues," "Uncle Pen," "I'm On My Way Back to the Old Home," "Little Georgia Rose," "Wicked Path of Sin," "Walking in Jerusalem Just Like John" and "On and On." Band members who recorded with Monroe and Martin during this period included Rudy Lyle (banjo), Vassar Clements (fiddle), Joel Price (bass), Red Taylor (fiddle), Charlie Cline (fiddle), Sonny Osborne (banjo) and numerous studio musicians.

In July of 1951, Martin left Monroe,[275] planning to form a band with banjoist Larry Richardson in Bluefield, West Virginia. Richardson didn't show up (he was hired by the **Sauceman Brothers and the Greene Valley Boys**[276]) so Martin teamed up with Bob Osborne (who was playing guitar at the time) in the **Lonesome Pine Fiddlers (L-P-F)**. Their voices seemed to blend well. Osborne took up the mandolin to complement Martin's guitar. The duo was hired by **Ezra Cline and the Lonesome Pine Fiddlers** and included Charlie Cline in this band in which Ezra paid $8 per night plus room. The **Fiddlers** immediately got a recording contract with King Records in Cincinnati. This led to a job on WCYB, Bristol, Tennessee, which was then known as *the* place for bluegrass bands to work.

In August, Osborne and Martin left the **L-P-F** to form their own **Jimmy Martin, Bob Osborne and the Sunny Mountain Boys** at WCYB with members Bob Osborne, Jimmy Martin, Curly Ray Cline, Charlie Cline

and thirty-nine inch-tall Robert van Winkle. Their first recordings were on August 27th on King Records: "She's Just a Cute Thing," "Blue Eyed Darling," "You'll Never Be the Same" and "My Lonely Heart."[277] The monetary rewards at WCYB were too little to keep them together so they split in October. Martin went to Knoxville to work for Cas Walker and Osborne stayed in Bristol and used the name **Bob Osborne and the Sunny Mountain Boys** for about a month.[278]

In April 1952, Martin left Knoxville, joining **Smoky Ward and the Barrelhead Gang** on WPFB, Middletown, Ohio. They had a daytime show six days a week and a Saturday night barn dance. At the dance, thirteen-year-old Sonny Osborne frequently came to hear him. Martin taught him a few things on the banjo. By that summer, Sonny Osborne was playing banjo on the Saturday night shows on WPFB.

Martin spoke of how he took young Osborne under his wing and got him the job with Monroe, "Sonny was helping me—I was working there in Middletown, Ohio, on a radio station on a Saturday night barn dance. Sonny was working on Saturday night—he lived over there in Dayton—and he was learning to pick the banjer and I'd go home with him and teach him all I knew about the banjer, you know, and bluegrass music. Then Bill Monroe called me and wanted me to come to Nashville. He couldn't find nobody that could play a guitar well enough and sing well enough to record a album and he asked me would I come down there and record a album with him. So I heard that Bill didn't have too good a

Jimmy Martin (R) at age 12 with his brother at home.

274 Rhonda Strickland, "Jimmy Martin—King of Bluegrass Tells It Like It Is," *Bluegrass Unlimited*, July, 1986, p. 16.

275 Carter Stanley took Martin's place with the Blue Grass Boys for the summer, followed by Edd Mayfield on a more permanent basis.

276 Larry Richardson (banjo) left the L-P-F in June 1951 to join the Sauceman Brothers at WCYB. Charlie Cline took Richardson's place in the Lonesome Pine Fiddlers on banjo.

277 Martin and Osborne were accompanied by Charlie Cline (banjo, fiddle), Curly Ray Cline (fiddle) and Ralph Guenther (bass).

278 In October 1951, Bobby Osborne joined the Stanley Brothers (for a month at WVLK, Versailles, Kentucky) when Carter Stanley returned from his summer with Monroe's band. Then Bob joined the Marines in November 1951.

banjo player.[279] And by that time, Sonny wasn't too good, but he was good enough to cut a record with Bill anyway. So I got Sonny in the union there. And they wouldn't let him into the union (Sonny was too young) unless I would sign for him. So I signed for him and he went with me to Nashville and I introduced Sonny to him and he let Sonny record the session."[280]

Then, after the session, "I remember that Paul Cohen, who was the head man (Artists & Repertoire)—the big chief—of Decca Records. I remember in the lobby of the Tulane Hotel where the recording studios was then. Everybody used it—Columbia people and everybody. Down in the lobby, this Paul Cohen said, 'Bill, I'm going to tell you something. If you'll keep this Martin boy with you, you'll sell a *lot* of records, 'cause you and him sound good together.' Bill said, 'Well, I'm going to try to.' And so, then Bill asked me to come back to work with him awhile. And I told him I would if he would let Sonny work all summer with him. And Sonny was young and Bill didn't want to work him, and he said, 'I will let him work if you'll be responsible for him.' So I was just like, you say, a dad to Sonny. He roomed with me and would go to eat with me and everything. We was together just about like father and son. Sonny really appreciated it and I enjoyed doing it for Sonny 'cause I thought that after Bob [Osborne] got out [of the Marines] that we would try to go back together as **Jimmy Martin and the Osborne Brothers** if I could get Sonny good enough on the banjer and learn him to sing baritone. So we did just that. We finally got back together after he got out.

"But Bill promised me that if I would go back with him, that all the single records that he put out would say a duet with Bill Monroe and Jimmy Martin. Then I stayed with him and the first record that come out was 'In the Pines.' So I went down to the record shop to see if my name was on it. So my name wasn't on it. So that night I asked Bill, I said, 'Bill, I thought you promised me that you would put my name on there as a duet by Bill Monroe and Jimmy Martin.' And he said, 'Well, ain't it on there?' I said, 'Bill, you know you didn't tell them to put it on there 'cause it ain't on there.' And it was things like that was the reason I put in my notice again and left Bill Monroe.[281]

"And another reason I left Bill Monroe the second time was that at the time [of] the Decca album, Paul Cohen said he would record me anytime I wanted to record. So then RCA Victor offered me a contract. Then, also Columbia Records. And so I went up to Bill Monroe and said, 'Bill, would you care if I recorded a album for RCA Victor or Columbia records? It won't be on the same label as you.' Bill didn't want me to record and I said, way in the back of my mind, 'If you're going to be against me that much I'm just going to leave.' But I didn't tell him why I was leaving. He asked my why I was leaving and I told him, 'Well, Bill, if you don't know I ain't a-gonna tell you. So I just left. But Bill Monroe told me then, and held my hand for about five minutes or ten and said, 'Anytime you want your job back or if you're anywhere broke and need the money, just call me and I'll pay you plane fare and get you back with me.' I said, 'Bill, I hope you can find somebody who can take my place and make you a good guitar player and lead singer.' He said, 'Jimmy, there'll *never* be nobody who can take your place.'" Martin stayed with Monroe a year and a half that time. In April 1952, two weeks after giving notice to Monroe, there was no replacement singer/guitarist. Martin left anyway to record with Smoky Ward's band on WPFB in Middletown, Ohio.

There at WPFB, Martin formed a band with J.D. Crowe and Bill Price. He spent a lot of time with them to bring them up to his recording standards. He had to teach Crowe to sing baritone and Price to perform and sing. "That's when I hired the Osborne brothers," said Martin. "I just couldn't get a harmony enough (with Crowe and Price). J.D. couldn't learn to sing baritone and I had a mandolin player by the name of Bill Price, and he couldn't keep rhythm, so I couldn't record. So I said that the best thing I could do is team up with the Osborne brothers 'cause we *can* sing together. When I let J.D. go, he hugged my neck and started crying. I said, 'J.D., if something ever happens that me and the boys can't get along, you keep learnin' the banjo what I've showed you and I'll come back and pick you up." He hired Crowe the second time in 1956.

About the Osborne brothers, Martin remembered, "Bob and Sonny had a real good ear for music and singing and both had good voices. One thing, you didn't have to show them the same note over and over again—you'd show them one time and they'd have it. And when you'd get on stage with them, our trios came out on the mike just like we rehearsed them."[282] He explained how they got together in August 1954, "They [Bob and Sonny Osborne] was in Knoxville and formed their own band but they come to Dayton, Ohio, where I was working. I had J.D. Crowe and a bunch of boys with me which couldn't sing good[283]. I was offered a RCA Victor contract and I had to have some good singers with me.

---

279 Martin told me later that he believes that Monroe didn't even have a banjo player at that time.

280 They recorded "In the Pines," "Footprints in the Snow" and "Memories of Mother and Dad," among others.

281 Neil Rosenberg, in *Bluegrass: A History*, may have touched on the reason Martin's name didn't appear on the label. He wrote: "After 1948, Monroe would take precautions to prevent the kind of publicity that Flatt and Scruggs had received being given to his band members. Never again, for example, would his lead singer's name be identified on his record labels."—p. 86.

282 Leon Smith, "Talking with the Stars: Two Interviews from a 'Bluegrass Hornbook,'" p. 9.. Note: *Bluegrass Hornbook* was a summer radio program on National Public Radio.

283 They were J.D. Crowe and Bill Price.

Bob and Sonny come up there and talked to me and said they'd get along with me if we'd go together as **Jimmy Martin and the Osborne Brothers.** So we went together like that. They wasn't making too much in Knoxville. They just quit.

"So when we went together, the first thing we done [is] we rehearsed real good and got our singing and music and then we went up to Detroit[284] to a big Saturday night show, which is a big city. And the first time we went up there we encored about three or four times and the guy hired us right then in Detroit. And then we went down and made some records: '20/20 Vision' and 'Save It, Save It' for the RCA Victor people. Then, in just a few weeks, they come up on the charts as #5, the best-selling record for the RCA Victor people in country music. I think 'I Don't Hurt Any More' was number one."

Jimmy Martin and the Osborne Brothers signed with Steve Sholes of the RCA label for four songs, one of which was "20/20 Vision" (recorded by Gene Autry earlier in the year). It became a #1 hit in the Detroit area. The November 1954 recording session also included "Chalk Up Another One," "I Pulled a Boo-Boo," and the very successful "Save It, Save It." The band, consisting of Martin, the Osborne brothers, Red Taylor (fiddle) and Cedric Rainwater (bass), played every Saturday night on the Big Barn Frolic in Detroit, which was similar to the Grand Ole Opry. It was broadcast live on CKLW radio. The group was paid $225 per Saturday. They were offered regular employment on the Wheeling (West Virginia) Jamboree for $10 per night and turned down the offer. **Jimmy Martin and the Osborne Brothers** was on its way.

"I remember when that record ("20/20 Vision") come out," continued Martin. "There was WEXL—the biggest country music station in Detroit—was on from about one o'clock 'til about five every evening. Then me and Bob took our record out there. We was interviewed on that show. The disc jockey said, 'What kind of music do you play?' We said, it kindly like Bill Monroe and Lester Flatt and them. And the guy says, 'Well, we never get no requests for that kind of records.' So I said,

Jimmy Martin and the Osborne brothers, c. 1955. Photo courtesy Ed Brown.

'Well, can I ask you one thing, sir?' He said, 'Yes.' I said, 'Would you just play both sides of this record and if you don't get no calls, no cards or letters, then we'll just give it to you and you can take it home for a souvenir or just break it and throw it in the garbage can.' Well, he played it right then and we stopped every phone line, I think he had five comin' in. And for hours it was stopped, asking him to play it again. So it wasn't but a few weeks that it was the number one record on his show, and the number one jukebox record and the most-selling record of all record stores in Detroit. And that's when Webb Pierce had out 'He's in the Jail House Now.' But we was overriding it very much there."

Also in 1954, Columbia Records' Troy Martin asked them to move to Nashville and work on WSM for Martha White. The Osbornes were for it, but Martin knew how difficult making a living in Nashville was; his experience with Monroe had taught him that. They stayed in Detroit until they broke up on August 5, 1955.

Unable to get along with Sonny Osborne, Martin split to form **Jimmy Martin and the Sunny Mountain Boys.**[285] The Osbornes left for WWVA. J.D. Crowe joined Jimmy Martin's **Sunny Mountain Boys** again in July 1956 when the band was in Detroit replacing Sam Hutchins on banjo. The band became Martin, Earl Taylor and Crowe. These men, along with Gordon Terry (fiddle) and Cedric Rainwater (bass) recorded the "Grand Ole Opry Song" and "Before the Sun Goes Down." Earl Taylor would leave in 1957 to partner with Hutchins in the **Stoney Mountain Boys.**[286]

Martin hired Paul Williams on mandolin when Taylor left. Williams normally played guitar, but because of his fine tenor voice, Martin taught him how to play the mandolin so they would not have two guitars for the trio. He played a round-hole F-4 Gibson mandolin. He thought it gave a brassy sound, distinctive enough to enable listeners to know that it was *his* sound. Williams was one of Martin's favorite singers. "The greatest band I ever sang with and ever had," he said, "was when Paul Williams and J.D. Crowe joined me."[287]

---

284 They were almost immediately hired as regulars in the Saturday night barn dance at WJR in Detroit. They became very popular.

285 Band members included Earl Taylor (mandolin), Sam Hutchins (banjo), Junior Huskey (bass) and Don McHan (banjo). The Osbornes left on Aug. 5, they were replaced Aug. 7.

286 Also joining the band in Detroit (for a very short time) was Frank Wakefield on mandolin. Billy Gill played bass with the band, too.

287 Paul Williams' name was actually Paul McCoy Humphrey. He was partner to Jimmy Williams when the two were just beginning their career. They were known as the Williams Brothers. According to Jimmy Williams, "Humphrey was too hard to spell or say so Williams just stuck." Paul Williams later went on to gain fame with the Lonesome Pine Fiddlers, a partnership with Red Ellis, and with Charlie Moore and Bill Napier.

When he hired Crowe again, "I was his daddy just like I was Sonny's for five years. He eat out of my refrigerator and slept in the same house. I always would rent a house big enough for him and Paul Williams. They knew how to play and sing like I like it. I don't know if it's my way of doing things, but those were the biggest-selling records that I've ever done. We were making more money than me and the Osbornes ever did. But me and the Osborne brothers—I want to make it awful plainly—we had an awful tight band. If we had stayed together as long as me and J.D. and all of us, I believe we would have been the top band in bluegrass."

Martin's singing style forced a change in Crowe's music style—toward more bluesy licks, straighter playing, and more hard-driving. He taught Crowe that timing is 75 percent of playing bluegrass. The first recording that the **Sunny Mountain Boys** did after Crowe became banjoist was "Dog Bite Your Hide" and "I'm the Boss of This Here House." The band soon became Martin, Crowe (banjo), Johnny Dacus (fiddle) and Paul Williams (mandolin). This was Martin's favorite group and brought the most success—especially significant because the band was competing with Elvis' popularity. While other bluegrass bands were having significant problems finding venues for their music, Elvis didn't affect the success of Martin's band at all. While others told him that he would have to get an electric guitar to compete, Martin said, "I think we was on the Louisiana Hayride as guests two times and I think we took two and three encores with the banjo, mandolin and guitar, and they hired me a bass player. And it's been doing that ever since. Elvis didn't hurt me whatsoever. I would have liked to open up his show for him and showed him how bluegrass could win over at his show."

This band, considered by many as one of the best versions of the **Sunny Mountain Boys**, was soon offered a good salary and a regular spot at Shreveport's Louisiana Hayride on KWKH. Elvis Presley, at a D.J.'s convention in Nashville, walked up to Jimmy Martin and told him that he was an admirer of Jimmy Martin and that he owned all of Martin's records. Elvis had been employed earlier by the Louisiana Hayride, making only $18 per week and sleeping in his car. He recommended that Martin not go to work down there unless he wanted to go broke; a year later, Martin joined anyway. He paid J.D. Crowe and Paul Williams $25 apiece for a Saturday night; Martin made $50. Upon his arrival at the Hayride, KWKH told him to drop the banjo and mandolin and get an electric guitar; it would go over better. Martin did not, and they got three encores. Their exposure on the CBS radio network (weekly nationwide) helped their popularity and exposed many new listeners to hillbilly music. They stayed on KWKH about two years and toured Texas during that period. The band of Martin, Crowe, and Williams recorded

"Ocean of Diamonds," "Saphronie," "Rock Hearts" and "It Ain't Like Home."

Crowe and Williams "both stayed with me for five years until Williams got messed up with a woman," continued Martin. "My half-sister married Paul Williams and got him to quit and talked church-going to him and told him that he couldn't both play bluegrass music and live for the Lord. That's the plain facts and I do want it put into the write-up." Martin pointed to my recorder. He also insisted that even though he didn't get along with his half-sister and step father, he loves Paul Williams and he knows that Paul Williams loves him.

Jimmy Martin and the Sunny Mountain Boys, early 1960's. L to R: Unknown bass player, Mike Miller, Chris Wheeler, Jimmy Martin, Vernon Derrick, Ray Patterson. Photo courtesy Ray and Ina Patterson.

A higher salary offer from WWVA in May of 1960 caused a move to Wheeling where booking agents all over the eastern seaboard were anxious to have him appear at their venue. The group was on top of the world. They recorded "My Walking Shoes," "Widow Maker" and "Sunny Side of the Mountain."

The acknowledged steps for success for a country band in those days was five-fold, and Martin did them all. They were: WWVA Jamboree, Wheeling, West Virginia; WRVA's Old Dominion Barn Dance, Richmond, Virginia; WCYB's Farm and Fun Time Hour, Bristol, Tennessee; KRLD's Texas Jamboree, Dallas, Texas; and finally, the pinnacle of success, WSM's Grand Ole Opry, Nashville, Tennessee. Although he made guest appearances on the Opry and met with the audience's approval, Martin's group never actually joined the cast there at WSM.

Their appearance on the Opry went over big. Martin recalled that "Stringbean said, 'My boy, you tore the house down, you sounded great! But you shouldn't of done that. It may be awhile before you are on again.' And it was. It wasn't long after, we found out WSM had pulled my records and wouldn't play them. At that time, 'Widow Maker' was on the country music charts in *Record World*, *Cash Box*, and *Billboard* magazines." Mr. Martin explained why his records were pulled from the shelves, "All I can say is somebody in Nashville didn't like me and didn't want me working and playing show dates out of Nashville. But I remembered how Lester Flatt and Earl Scruggs played the early morning Martha White show on WSM for a long time before they ever did guest appearances on the Opry. And they were very popular all over the world at that time. So it didn't hurt my feeling too bad. Someone must have thought that, by pulling my records and not getting them played on WSM and not letting me do guest appearances on the Opry, that I'd just leave Nashville. But I fooled them. I'm still here."[288]

When Bud Wendell became the manager of the Opry, Martin began making Opry guest appearances again. Even though Martin and the manager talked about him being a member of the Opry, he was never officially asked. Just before Opryland opened up in 1974, Wendell promised to make Jimmy Martin a member of the Grand Ole Opry. "But I was told that Bill Monroe asked them to not make me a member. And he [Monroe] did keep Lester Flatt and Earl Scruggs off that for about twenty years[289]. But their sponsors, Martha White, told them (the Opry) to put them on or they would quit being a sponsor. You see, they were quitting Martha White and [would] go back to Knoxville if they couldn't get them on the Opry. Then they tried to hire me and the Osborne brothers to come down there and take over Martha White.[290] Bob and Sonny wanted me to do it, but it was so tough when I worked with Bill Monroe that if Lester Flatt and Earl Scruggs couldn't make it down there with Martha White, I'm not gonna go down there and try it.

"I remember one time, you see Bill Monroe and Earl Scruggs and Lester Flatt wasn't speakin'. [This was] because they was popular. Now, had they not have been popular Bill Monroe would have spoke to 'em. You know what I mean? But he's kind of a man that can't stand for somebody to walk up and brag on another outfit. He wants them to brag on Bill all the way. I'm not that kind of nature. There's other people besides me that can play bluegrass music and play it good."

In 1960, J.D. Crowe left the **Sunny Mountain Boys** to work in a car parts store and was replaced by Shorty Edgar, then Paul Craft. Crowe's departure left only Paul Williams with the band. Martin wanted to hire the Bray brothers (Harley (banjo), Nate (mandolin) and Francis (bass)) but the brothers wanted to stay with Red Cravens; they felt they were just starting to put things together and that they would soon "make it" as a full-time bluegrass band. (In actuality, they soon disbanded and now are only legends in the annals of bluegrass.)

Bill Emerson joined after Paul Craft got the mumps.[291] Emerson spent a total of five years with Martin—through 1965. He was Martin's banjo player at Carlton Haney's first bluegrass festival in 1965. Martin found banjoist Emerson after listening to one of Emerson's records. Martin "recalls thinking that if anyone could replace Crowe it would be Emerson. Martin hired Emerson and remembers being very impressed with the man as well as his musicianship. After playing with Martin only a week, Emerson asked Martin which songs they would be doing Saturday night at the Jamboree, wanting to study them and get them down perfectly so he wouldn't make himself or Martin sound bad. Martin gave Emerson all his records and he learned all of the songs by Saturday night. It is exactly that quality which Martin says he has always looked for in his band members and has had much trouble finding in the years since that last classic band. He still speaks highly of Bill Emerson, says he was a pro, and that they got along excellently together, never having an argument or a cross word."[292] They[293] recorded "Tennessee, I Hear You Calling Me," "The Last Song," "Stormy Waters," "Theme Time" and "This World Is Not My Home."

In 1962, they[294] took a break from KWKH and went to Las Vegas, Nevada. This was the first bluegrass band to play Las Vegas, working six nights per week, six shows per night at the Golden Nugget. They were very popular, but as Martin recalled, "for the money they wanted to pay us, I wouldn't go back. We were playing as many shows as Hank Thompson and we had them standing plumb in the streets. And they liked it. But I found out what they were paying Hank Thompson. I told them I wasn't coming back for near nothing. I don't think bluegrass should be treated that way."[295] They then moved back to Wheeling. After two years on the

288 Rhonda Strickland, op. cit., p. 20.

289 Actually, Flatt and Scruggs became sponsored onto the Grand Ole Opry as members by Martha White in 1955. So it was more like seven years from the time that Lester and Earl left Monroe's Blue Grass Boys until the time they actually joined the Opry. I'm not sure what Jimmy Martin was referring to by his reference to twenty years. Additionally, I'm told by one of the involved parties, who asked not to be identified because it just wouldn't help to know who said it, that Jimmy Martin was not asked to become a member of the Opry because of his somewhat offensive manner. It certainly wasn't because he wasn't well-accepted by the audience. It almost goes without saying that he and his band were very popular wherever they would go. But Martin's rather abrasive nature was not hidden from the Opry managers. Therefore, no invitation to join the Opry came.

290 This was the Mill's early morning show on WSM which Flatt and Scruggs had been at for the previous eleven months. Even Flatt and Scruggs was not a regular member of the Opry yet.

291 Bill Emerson, in a 1995 conversation, elaborated that he filled-in for a show or two while Craft was ill with the mumps. Two months later, Emerson took Craft's place on banjo when Craft left the band.

292 Strickland, op. cit., p. 19.

293 This band now included Martin, Emerson, Williams, Lois Johnson (bass, snare drums, piano) and Kirk Hansard (drums).

294 The band added Zeb Collins as bassist and comedian. Johnson moved to guitar.

295 Strickland, op. cit., p. 20.

Jamboree, Martin moved to his present home at Hermitage Hills (near Nashville). Soon Paul Williams married Martin's sister and retired from the business.[296]

From this time began a period of hiring many other musicians into the **Sunny Mountain Boys**. Through the years, a list of the members of Jimmy Martin's band resembles a *Who's Who* in bluegrass music. Here are a few of the better known musicians: Tom Adams, Hylo Brown, Vassar Clements, Vernon Derrick, Billy Edwards, Bill Emerson, Dave Evans, Josh Graves, Doug Green, Vic Jordan, Doyle Lawson, Don McHan, Vernon McIntyre, Alan Munde, Herschel Sizemore, Garland Shuping, Blaine Sprouse, Tater Tate, Marshall Wilborn, Benny Williams, Rual Yarbrough and Bill Yates.

Bill Emerson left as Martin's banjo player August of 1966, and was replaced by Vic Jordan[297] until July of 1967. Chris Warner played banjo with the group during this period then banjoist Alan Munde joined Jimmy Martin's band in 1969 staying until 1971.[298]

"I hired Al Munde because I needed a banjo player bad. And he didn't know my style. And he still can't sing baritone. But I let him work with me two years trying to let him sing baritone and trying to teach him. But he never did learn it. But I learned him how to play on the banjer. He'd just put in anything he wanted to, you see, whether it fit or it didn't…" Where Munde played a tune the way *he* felt like it, Martin tried to teach him how to play the song exactly as it was done on the record. "He finally learned that and soaked it into his head pretty good. In other words, if I sing 'Sunny Side of the Mountain' today, you can't go up on the neck today, and I sing it tomorrow and [you] don't go up on the neck. You're just changin' it all the time on me. So I told him if he was going to change it like that, then I'm gonna have to change my words to the song and rewrite it. That's one thing that's hurtin' bluegrass today is the pickers just a-pickin' it every way and not gettin' it down pat where it sounds good. Each guy is just trying to out-pick the

other. And band-wise, that hurts it. You gotta have harmony in your band with instruments as well as harmony in your singin'. Every man's gotta know what the other'n is gonna hit. And today they pick anything they want to and say they can't pick the same thing twice.

"You got to study it if you're going to make money. A lot of these bluegrass people today don't study. They just get 'em a little band, get 'em a bus, and they think that's it. A lot of people, some of the **Blue Grass Boys** even, ask me how I got to where I am today. I say, 'Buddy, it would take a long time to tell ya and you wouldn't go through what I went through to get to where I got. Money don't come easy."

About 1972, Martin lured Charlie Monroe out of retirement to play a couple of festivals. He liked it so well that he stayed on awhile longer with Martin. In 1973, the readers of Carlton Haney's *Muleskinner News* voted Martin Entertainer of the Year. In 1980, Jimmy Martin called a square dance in the movie "Coal Miner's Daughter."[299] He was awarded the Carter Stanley Memorial Award for his contribution to bluegrass that year. Gusto Records released Martin's "Will the Circle Be Unbroken."[300]

Audie Blaylock was twenty when Martin hired him to play mandolin; this was his first professional job. With Martin, he learned timing, music in general, proper volume and tone quality in his tenor voice, and got a college education in bluegrass music. It was tough, at first, working for Martin. "He pretty much just tells you what you are doing wrong," said Blaylock. "And that's where—well, musicians have fragile egos; it's hard to take. That's where they get the idea that he's hard to work for. Because he is going to be on you all the time until you get it… It was constant pressure [for me]. But then I realized it was sink or swim. One day something clicks. You play a certain thing and you say to yourself, 'Hey, that's what he was trying to tell

[296] Paul Williams left the Sunny Mountain Boys in 1963. Except for a couple of reunion tours in 1987 and 1988, he kept in the music with the gospel group Northside Trio in Morristown, Tennessee.

[297] Jordan had just spent a year and a half with Wilma Lee and Stoney Cooper. Band members then became Martin, Jordan, Vernon Derrick or Vassar Clements (fiddle) and Bill Yates (bass). By 1968, members of the Sunny Mountain Boys were Herschel Sizemore (mandolin), Chris Warner (banjo), Bill Yates (bass) and himself.

[298] By 1971, the Sunny Mountain Boys were Ronnie Privette (mandolin), Munde (banjo), Jimmy and Ray Martin (bass, Jimmy's son, born 1955). In October, Munde left to join Byron Berline and the Flying Burrito Brothers. Privette left the Sunny Mountain Boys to join the Bluegrass Alliance. From 1971 to 1973, musicians with Martin's band included Darrell Sanson (mandolin), Sheridan Sanson (bass, brother of Darrell), Tim Spradlin (banjo), Martin's two sons; Jimmy Jr. (drums) and Ray (electric bass) Martin, Gloria Belle (guitar), Privette (mandolin) and Kenny Ingram (banjo). Gloria Belle Flickinger began working a few shows with Martin in the summer of 1968. Johnny Dacus (fiddle) re-joined the Sunny Mountain Boys in late 1973. He was also with the band in 1957 with Crowe and Paul Williams.
      MCA Coral released Jimmy Martin's "Moonshine Hollow" in 1971. Musicians on the recording were Paul Williams, Lois Johnson, Kirk Hansard and Bill Emerson; it had been recorded earlier with different band which included Kenny Ingram (banjo), Ronnie Privette (mandolin), Ray Martin (electric bass) and Jimmy Martin Jr. (drums).
      The period of 1974 to 1980 included musicians Marc Pruett (banjo), soon followed by Tommy Hunter, Steve Sutton and Freddy Harris (mandolin), Blaine Sprouse (fiddle), Gloria Belle (guitar), Dwight Dillman (banjo) and Ray Martin (bass). Sprouse left in the summer of 1975 to join the Lost Kentuckians. Then joined Jimmy's only daughter, Lisa Sarah Martin (vocals), with Steve Sutton (banjo), Freddy Harris, Kenny Ingram (banjo), Vernon Derrick (fiddle), Dave Radcliff and brothers Terry (bass) and Billy (guitar) Smith. Derrick later went with Hank Williams Jr. for eight years.

[299] Members of his Sunny Mountain Boys at that time were Charlie Cushman (banjo), Vernon Derrick (fiddle, mandolin) and J.T. Gray (bass).

[300] Musicians on the album included Kenneth Ingram (banjo), Doyle Lawson (mandolin), Vernon Derrick (vocals), Lisa Martin (vocals), Robert "Bill" Yates (bass) and Don Coburn (drums).

me all along.'"[301] In a 1991 interview, Martin spoke of Blaylock and the difficulty of playing Martin's style of bluegrass, "He was just average. Even after six years he never did get the Jimmy Martin rhythm. A lot of guys who have worked with me the last few years just meet me at the show dates and I don't have time to show 'em and teach 'em and that was my regret with Audie. He didn't stay around me long enough to really get the rhythm. Two of the best rhythm mandolin players that I've ever had as a Sunny Mountain Boy is Paul Williams and my son, Ray Martin.

"You see, Bob and Sonny, we used to rehearse when they first come with me in Detroit for about three to five hours every Tuesday and every Thursday, and I taught 'em everything that I knew that I thought could help 'em. And I believe, if you will listen to their shows and their timing, then you'll have to agree that they have the Jimmy Martin timing. And I'm sure, if they would tell the truth, then they would have to say they learned it from Jimmy Martin. And I'm not thinking I'm the greatest in harmony singing, but I know every part and I have taught people and helped 'em. A lot of 'em, when they are interviewed I've noticed, they don't want to give me no credit. You take Sonny Osborne. Before he will give Jimmy Martin any credit he will give it to Bill Monroe—and Bill Monroe never showed Sonny Osborne nothin'. But he always brags about working with Bill Monroe. I guess all this corruption and problems we're having now came after we all got popular. Of course, I don't think I'm any more popular than them. And I damn sure don't feel they are any more popular than Jimmy Martin. That's the reason; the bitterness is on account of the popularity. Now, if I wasn't popular they would be the first to shake my hand. And I love 'em all just like a brother. I just wish it wasn't that way."

Martin is known as a tough taskmaster. "I'm no tougher than Lester Flatt and Earl Scruggs or Bill Monroe or any tougher than George Jones. Just like a ball club. If you ain't got a good leader, they'll never win in the World Series. And the toughest leader—and the one that gets the hardest on them—that's the one that'll win the World Series. Then they hug the leader's neck, 'We won it didn't we!' As far as changin', I've not changed the way of combin' my hair. I've not changed the way of dressing. And I've not changed my way of singing. And I've not changed my way of explaining bluegrass music. I want my band to play as good as J.D. Crowe and Paul Williams back in '58. And don't change it in nineteen and ninety-one 'cause they'll still like it that way 'cause it's good and it's together."

Jimmy Martin, c. 1992.

Even though Monroe was seventy-nine years old at the time of this 1991 interview with Jimmy Martin, "I still believe that if Bill didn't have some lazy boys just like I have [had] in past time—you got them lazy pickers that pick lazy; they want to sleep all the time—if Bill had somebody... I would say, today, let me play the guitar, J.D. Crowe the banjer or Earl Scruggs the banjer, and Chubby Wise the fiddle, and had a good bass player like my son or like Terry Smith who is with the Osbornes and go on that Opry and cut "Mollie and Tenbrooks" you would hear Bill Monroe sound like a new man because they are draggin' him. They are trying to play chromatic stuff behind him and I know he don't want it. But they still play it. And it don't fit his voice. Then if you take a weak banjer player or a weak bass player behind Bill Monroe, well, his voice is so strong that even though he is hittin' the notes, it's gonna sound bad. 'Cause his voice is too strong for them weak players. When I played with Bill Monroe, I tried to play that guitar just as loud as he played the mandolin. Scruggs did it fine. The rest of these guys stand there half asleep and don't come up with him. That's what hurts me.

"The people today don't love it. They just want to make money and have fun. I tell them, 'Boys, it's a job. If you don't work at it and bring it from your heart and put your soul in it and give it all you got and talk about it and love it, you ain't gonna make it.' I'm payin' $170 a day for a man. The good ones like J.D. Crowe, Paul Williams, Chris Warner, them kind of guys, I've offered a salary for them to stay with me. They just got tired of traveling and had to quit."

Charlie Cline[302] enjoyed working for Martin, saying that Martin is honest and reliable. "The only ones who say it's hard to get along with Jimmy Martin are the

---

[301] By May of 1983, members of the Sunny Mountain Boys were Billy Gill (mandolin), Dana Cupp Jr. (multi-instrumentalist), Charlie Cline (fiddle), Martin (guitar), Mel Mattish (bass) and Lisa Martin (vocals) and probably Tom Adams (banjo). Adams was Martin's banjoist from 1983 to August 1985. Other formations of the band at this time were Audie Blaylock (mandolin), James Bailey (banjo), Charlie Cline (fiddle) and Kenny Lewis (electric bass). Through the years which followed there were numerous bass players.
Strickland, op. cit., p. 22.

[302] Cline first began working with Martin when Martin joined Ezra Cline and the Lonesome Pine Fiddlers when Martin was in Knoxville back in 1951. Then Martin and Cline went with Monroe for three years until Cline joined the military (1953). When Ezra Cline retired [about 1959], Curly Ray Cline went back with the L-P-F, and in late 1966, with Ralph Stanley's Clinch Mountain Boys. Charlie Cline joined Martin's band in 1980 for a more secure paycheck than he was getting when he was running his own band with his wife, Charlie Cline and the Lonesome Pine Fiddlers.

ones who have grown up learning to play just anything and not really working out bluegrass the way it should be played," said Cline. "And Jimmy just tells them the way it is. And he wants his songs played the way he recorded them...Jimmy's completely different. He has a different style from Bill Monroe and the **Lonesome Pine Fiddlers** and Don Reno or anybody; they've got to learn his style... We've had a lot of people off and on. Everybody thinks that music is just a happy-go-lucky thing. Most people don't understand it's a job. If you're working at a job, you got to do a *good* job. I find in bluegrass today, people don't take it to heart like they used to... [This is because] times are a lot easier than they were back then. It's easier to make money now. They all talk about how money is not worth much today but look at how much more money people are making. Sidemen are making more today than what whole bands were making back then."

Cline continued, "But the young people have sort of grown away from the traditional bluegrass; they've modernized it. People are taking banjo lessons and mandolin and fiddle lessons and Pappa and Mamma are paying for these. Back then you had to dig it out for yourself. I had to sweat it out for myself. Nobody showed me nothing. I had to learn it myself. But when you get it handed to you on a silver platter...when people have to dig out and learn it themselves, they're going to think a lot more of it."[303]

"I like to do a good-worded song, bluegrass-style," said Martin. "I want to do what the *song* has in it. When the Osborne brothers and I were together, we went down to cut a session. We got there and Troy Martin played a Gene Autry song, '20/20 Vision.' Sonny and Bob said we couldn't do that song because of the way Gene Autry was singing it. The way he sang, it didn't fit bluegrass. But me and Sonny and Bob got together in a room and worked it up, and the more we worked it, the better they liked it. But at first they thought we couldn't do it... And the same thing happened with 'I Pulled a Boo-Boo' and 'That's How I Can Count on You.'"[304]

With new band members in the 1990s[305], "I'm having a good time," said Martin. "I enjoy my band greater than anything I've had in the past fifteen years. It seems like all of them are interested in Jimmy Martin's music and singing. Chris Warner, my banjo player, is back with me for the second time and he's been back three or four years now. Audie Blaylock has been with me seven summers. When guys stay with you that long, you get to where they know you and what you are doing and it makes it so much easier on stage than it is to have a new guy who doesn't even know the breaks. It makes me so much more happy."[306] That summer, members of Martin's band were himself (guitar), Ray Martin (mandolin), Charlie Cline (fiddle, finger-picked guitar), David Nance (resonator guitar) and two others.

In Iowa, Bob Everhart gave Jimmy Martin a plaque which made him the Ambassador of Bluegrass Music of the United States. Jimmy Martin still tours the bluegrass circuit as of 1996. He is known as the "King of Bluegrass Music". He was inducted into the IBMA Hall of Honor in 1995.

Don McHan

Don McHan has a long history as a sideman in bluegrass, beginning about the time Jimmy Martin formed his own band in 1952. They were both working for Cas Walker's chain of grocery stores in Knoxville, for WROL and WIBK at the time. He worked with Wade Mainer's **Sons of the Mountaineers** (1951), followed by **Carl Sauceman and the Greene Valley Boys** (1952), the **Bailey Brothers** (1952), **Jim and Jesse and the Virginia Boys** (beginning in 1956 and occasionally through 1987) and set up his own recording studio in 1962. McHan began an extensive involvement with the Southern Baptists in about 1973 and had his religious radio program on several radio stations by 1982.

McHan was one of the first three-finger banjoists. He recalled there were others in the area at the time including Scruggs, Snuffy Jenkins, Hoke Jenkins, Johnny Whisnant, Hoyt Herbert from North Carolina, and Wiley Birchfield from Bryson City, North Carolina, who worked with Carl Sauceman, the Louvin brothers and Mac Wiseman. Mr. McHan sent the following biography:

I was born July 11, 1933, and raised just outside the Smoky Mountains National Park of western North Carolina, and although I've traveled at least half way around the world, I still live in the Carolina mountains (Bryson City, North Carolina) today. My mother once told me that I literally cut my teeth on a Gene Autry guitar she put in my crib. I do know I started learning the guitar chords at age four. My dad bought me a nice mandolin when I was ten. After that, I started buying my own instruments.

[303] Strickland, op. cit., p. 23.

[304] Ibid., p. 24. In 1985, members of the Sunny Mountain Boys were Martin, Tom Adams (banjo), Audie Blaylock (mandolin) and Charlie Cline (fiddle). The next year, band members included Chris Warner (banjo), Cline (fiddle) and Blaylock. Marshall Wilborn was bassist for a few weeks in 1986; then he received a full-time offer from the Johnson Mountain Boys which he couldn't refuse.

[305] By 1990, members were Audie Blaylock (mandolin), Vernon Derrick (fiddle), David "Little Sweets" Nance (resonator guitar), Lynwood Lunsford (banjo), Ray Martin (electric bass) and Bert "Sasquatch" Hoffman (drums).
    In early 1991, the Sunny Mountain Boys included Chris Warner (banjo) and Blaylock (mandolin).

[306] Martin Chapman, "Interview: Jimmy Martin," *Bluegrass Canada Magazine*, July/August 1991, p. 8.

I know you've heard poverty stories about country artists. Mine is that I bought a fiddle for $4 and paid for it a quarter at a time; there was no bow with it. We had an old dilapidated couch with a plywood bottom. I tore strips from this which had resin on the edges. This served as a bow until I could get one. I went on to learn some of my favorite fiddle tunes like "Orange Blossom Special," "Listen to the Mockingbird" and "Black Mountain Rag." Then I heard the ringing five-string banjo in the modern-day type of pickin'. This was Hoke Jenkins who was working with Carl Story out of Knoxville, Tennessee. Snuffy and Earl Scruggs were both from my home state in the foothills of the mountains. I knew Hoke was getting this sound with three fingers and with picks; I had a thumbpick but no fingerpicks and no way to get any. I bent some of my mother's old-fashioned metal hairpins to fit my fingers. And that's how I learned to play the banjo.

Now on to writing and demo-ing. I wrote my first song when I was fourteen. I had my first major label-cut of a song when I was nineteen. To date, I have written or co-written over 3000 songs; I have over 300 cuts of songs on record. The best seller so far has been "The Pill" by Loretta Lynn. I co-wrote one song with Harlan Howard which was recorded by Waylon Jennings. I've recorded some songs myself that have shown up within the top thirty stateside and overseas. I'll mention only one or two: "If This Rose Could Talk" and "Modern Day Roman Soldier."

Now to demo-ing. I'm not sure that I was the first country music demo artist, but I was one of the first. I can trace it back to the spring of 1965 when I advertised as Laurel Music Studios in Songwriter's Review out of New York. I was the first with a few things that I may not get credit for: the Nashville number system that musicians use, for instance. I was using numbers over lyrics for melody by 1960. I did this because I wrote a lot on the riverbank (fishing) without having a tape recorder, and I used numbers for melody notes over the words so that I could keep the melody in tack until I got back to the studio. I sent two or three lyric sheets into Nashville and the numbers were still over the lyrics. Someone picked up on it and, of course, they have now developed it to an advanced stage for session musicians; I think guitarist Grady Martin was the first to use a high-gauge third string. Anyway, I put high-gauge strings all the way up and used it on a few independent sessions in the late sixties. I called it a "Chimeatar". Now we've heard it on so many sessions the last number of years.

There's probably no way to completely protect a songwriter's ideas. Very few people take a songwriter's words and melody outright. The danger lies in someone re-writing your ideas. I remember I sent a song to Nashville entitled "It Would Be Heaven If It Wasn't Sin." You heard it as the hit, "Heaven's Just a Sin Away." Nothing I could do...title, words and melody were different. So anyone can do a "twist off" of a songwriter's idea and re-write it...and most times legitimately, I guess. So when you have a great idea, write it as strongly as you can for one thing, then protect it as best you can. At least a dozen of my ideas have been exploited through the years.

In closing, let me say that I love songwriters and have tried to help them. Two percent of them may be crabby and difficult, but 98 percent of them are "the salt of the earth".

The Osborne Brothers

Bobby and Sonny Osborne are pioneers in bluegrass who have not only had a career of over forty years in bluegrass, they have contributed to its style and popularity. They worked with some of the biggest names in bluegrass and kept their own style for most of those years.

The brothers were born into a musical family. Bob (a.k.a. Bobby) was born in the coal mining town of Hyden, Kentucky, in southeastern Kentucky's Leslie County, on December 7, 1931. Seven years later, Sonny (born Roland) Osborne was also born in Hyden (October 29, 1938). Bobby learned music and the guitar from his father who also ran a grocery store and taught school. In 1942, the Osborne family moved to near Radford, Virginia, and three years later moved to Dayton, Ohio, where the musical career for the Osborne brothers began. Their father had a good education and the family was able to survive the Depression relatively easily. He worked thirty years for National Cash Register in Dayton until he retired. Their grandfather had a grocery store, a sawmill and a blacksmith shop; when he died, the boys took over his enterprises. The younger Osbornes helped their father farm the land just outside of Dayton. Though the elder Osbornes were educated, both Sonny and Bobby were both lured away by the music before they finished high school. When Bobby heard the sound of the banjo, it was all over; they have been in music ever since then.

Bobby began listening to the Grand Ole Opry about the time the family arrived in Radford. Just after World War II, Bobby got a new Martin D-28 guitar for Christmas. His father showed him three basic chords—"That's all. Nobody from that day to this has ever shown me anything. I learned it on my own."[307] By age sixteen, he felt confident enough to play in front of people.

It was 1946 when Bobby heard Earl Scruggs on the Opry and became Bobby's main influence toward bluegrass. He explained it this way in a 1991 interview with this writer, "In my years of learning to play, the Grand Ole Opry played the biggest part of even hearing country music to start with. Mom and Dad had a battery radio and then a electric radio in the late '40s.[308] Of course, we always listened to the Grand Ole Opry on Saturday night—there was nothing else to do. But Ernest Tubb was the first guy I got to listen to.[309] That was back in about '46 or '47. He was the first guy I ever got to see on the stage. I saw him in Memorial Hall,

Dayton, Ohio, around 1946. I said then that's what I'd like to do. I already had a guitar, trying to play exactly like him at that time and sing. He just inspired me to want to do that. I kept following him right on down until I was about sixteen when my voice kinda changed. I [used to sing] his songs low and the keys he was [in] and went to where it is now. I still sing his songs but I have to do it in a higher key. So I got this little ol' job playin' the guitar at this WPFB radio station down there [in Middletown, Ohio][310]. That must have been in about 1948.

"But let me back up to even before that. I was listening to the Opry one Saturday night and heard Earl Scruggs play 'Cumberland Gap.' That one—I couldn't figure out. I didn't know nothing about Bill Monroe or mandolin or nothing. I just heard that banjo play 'Cumberland Gap' and I could not figure out what in the world was taking place right there. So then I kept tuning to the Opry and it took me three weeks or a month to ever hear that again. Finally, I heard them play that again and I found out that it was Bill Monroe's **Blue Grass Boys**. And they came to Memorial Hall down there in Dayton, Ohio, and I got to see that. I got to watch Flatt and Scruggs and Chubby Wise and Bill Monroe and Cedric Rainwater together one time on the stage in Ohio. And after that then, that turned me to bluegrass.

"My voice was already high enough—I didn't know what harmonies were—that the tenor singer was supposed to do this or whatever. All I knew is that it was good music. So I got to try to learn how to sing Bill Monroe songs. I bought me a songbook and got to learn those songs, but I still did Ernest Tubb songs and I still played the guitar, too. And when I saw Lester Flatt—I played with a straight pick—when I saw Flatt play with a thumb pick and a finger pick I threw the straight pick away and got me a thumb pick. I wanted to be like him. So I played the guitar like that for a long time. The style of guitar that Lester Flatt played was like Bill's brother, Charlie. Back in those days of Merle Travis, there was no straight picking. It's like Riley Puckett, too. Everybody seemed to do it."

Bobby and Sonny received their first exposure as entertainers there on WPFB. Sonny explained what they played, "There was no such thing at this time as bluegrass. If you played the guitar or banjo and sung that type of thing, it was hillbilly music...and at times you were embarrassed to admit that this was the kind of

Larry Richardson

224

---

307 Carol Sue Jeffrey, "Back to the Basics—Bobby Osborne," *Bluegrass Unlimited*, February, 1991, p. 38.

308 Back in those days, many homes didn't have electricity, and the battery-powered radio was often their only connection with the outside world. In many cases however, the lack of electricity wasn't because of lack of wealth in the household; it was simply because the electric lines hadn't reached their part of town yet. The battery-powered radios were probably more plentiful during those years.

309 Tubb played electric guitar with Chuck Swain and Larry Richardson (banjo).

310 In June of 1947, Bobby formed the Miami Valley Playboys in Dayton with McKinley Dixon (guitar) to play on WPFB. This was Osborne's first professional job. He played electric guitar, Junior Collett, the guitar, and Dick Potter, the electric mandolin. In June of 1949, Bob began singing "Ruby" live on WPFB. The station manager got so many requests for it that he asked Bob to not sing it again. Osborne had learned the song from a record by Cousin Emmy on the jukebox in a bar. He began singing it here at WPFB.

music you listened to and tried to play."[311] In Dayton, they played at Charlie's Nite Club where they worked four nights per week and made $43.50 each for the week's work. It wasn't much money, but it didn't seem to matter then. "But then, we were all very young and very green, and man, did we ever want to pick—it was life itself,"[312] Sonny exclaimed.

On July 21st, 1949, Bobby Osborne and his friend, banjoist Larry Richardson, first played together there on WPFB. Osborne quit school as a sophomore and left home to play music. The next month found Richardson and Bobby jobless and unsuccessfully auditioning for a job on eight radio stations until they were hired at WBRW, Welch, West Virginia. They formed the **Silver Saddle Boys** with Eddie King (fiddle) and Buck Duncan (tenor guitar), playing until October 12th. Bob recalled that "everybody back in those days was tryin' to do the same thing that I did. They were tryin' to find some group they could play with and love this music and make a name for himself and get started in it somewhere."

The duo joined with Rex and Eleanor Parker on October 23rd, playing square dances for $30 per person per week on WHIS, Bluefield, West Virginia. While Bob was in Bluefield, younger brother Sonny was trying to learn how to play the banjo and came into contact with Larry Richardson. Sonny used to watch his brother and Richardson practicing. It looked easy so he bought a Kay banjo for $100. It *was* easy for him. The first tune he learned was the **Stanley Brothers'** recording of "We'll Be Sweethearts in Heaven." Bob soon taught his brother the forwards-backwards roll the way Earl Scruggs performed it and Sonny's banjo picking really fell into place after that—especially after Sonny began practicing eight hours per day.

After three weeks with the Parkers, Bob Osborne and Richardson joined the **Lonesome Pine Fiddlers (L-P-F)** with Ezra Cline (bass), Ray Morgan (fiddle), Richardson (banjo) and Osborne (guitar, he hadn't started playing the mandolin yet). They recorded Bob and Larry's "Pain in My Heart" the next March on the Cozy label (soon reissued on 78 by RCA Victor). Bob stayed with the group for nearly two years. After a short break from the **Lonesome Pine Fiddlers**, Bobby and Larry re-joined the group on January 4, 1951.

On June 3rd, 1951, Larry Richardson (banjo) left to join the **Sauceman Brothers** at WCYB. Charlie Cline took Richardson's place on banjo with the **Lonesome Pine Fiddlers**.[313] Charlie and Bob did all the singing then, instead of Bob and Larry. The **Fiddlers** immediately got a recording contract with King Records in Cincinnati.

Soon, Jimmy Martin came onto the **L-P-F** scene. Bob Osborne explained, "Jimmy Martin came up there (about July) with Monroe and the **Blue Grass Boys** (with Rudy Lyle, Red Taylor and Joel Price) and they came up to the station that day. Jim was getting ready to leave Bill Monroe and he wanted to know if he could come up there. Larry went to Bristol to work with the **Sauceman Brothers** and we never worked together after that. We never re-joined the **L-P-F**. It became Jimmy Martin and myself who were doing the singing when he worked with the **L-P-F**. So Jim had some contacts in Nashville and everywhere, by being with Bill Monroe, of course." They worked there in Bristol just a short while.

"When Jim came up there and started workin' (with the **L-P-F**), I had never had my hands on a mandolin. All I knew about it is Jethro (Burns) played one and Monroe played one.[314] He told me he couldn't play a mandolin—although he could play it fairly well—and he was determined to play the guitar so I went out and bought me a little ol' cheap mandolin (a Gibson A-50 model) and went to work learnin' that. He and I got to singin' together. That's how Jimmy Martin and me got together the first time and when we got to singin' together.

"Then from there, in about August, is when he and I got Charlie Cline and Curly Ray Cline and Little Robert van Winkle and we went to Bristol and got on that Farm and Fun Time down there. This was when the **Sunny Mountain Boys** was formed for the first time." The name of the group, **Jimmy Martin, Bob Osborne and the Sunny Mountain Boys** came from the fact that they used the **Carter Family** song, "Keep on the Sunny Side of Life," as their theme song and agreed to use that for the band name. This was a mutual agreement and did not come from just one of the duo.[315]

In July, while at home in Dayton, Bob Osborne recorded with Sonny (13, he had been playing the banjo four months), Louise Osborne and Jimmy Martin on the Kitty label. The group was called **Lou Osborne and the Osborne Family**. This was the first recording of Bobby on mandolin, Sonny's first recorded performance (though he had already been performing locally), and of Bobby, Sonny and Jimmy Martin together.

311 From album cover notes of "The Osborne Brothers' Bluegrass Collection" by Sonny Osborne, April 27, 1978. CMH-9011.

312 Ibid.

313 This band was called the Lonesome Pine Fiddlers. The band did not have a name change until years after Bob Osborne had left and the band became Ezra Cline and the Lonesome Pine Fiddlers.

314 Bob also told this writer that since Bill Monroe was a mandolin player and a tenor singer, Bob figured that since he was a tenor singer, he should play a mandolin just like Bill.

315 Bob Osborne feels that he did more for the name 'Sunny Mountain Boys," in getting it started, than Jimmy Martin did in those early years. But now that Martin has exclusive use of the name, "He's satisfied with it—I sure as hell am!" said Bob.

The reader may sense a little animosity here but it's really not. Bob considers his time with Jimmy Martin about the same as with the L-P-F, the Parkers and others he played with in the old days. These experiences were building blocks to where he and his brother would end up eventually—an important factor in the history of bluegrass as a duo. What he and Sonny accomplished together is, by far, the most important thing to him.

Bob and Jimmy recorded "She's Just a Cute Thing," "Blue Eyed Darling," "You'll Never Be The Same" and "Lonely Heart" for King Records on August 27th. Other musicians included Curly Ray Cline (fiddle), Charlie Cline (banjo, fiddle) and Ralph Guenther (bass). "Then Jim and I parted company there," said Bob. "All of us parted company there—Curly Ray and Charlie, too. And I kept the name **Bob Osborne and the Sunny Mountain Boys** on WCYB in Bristol for a short time—without Jimmy Martin. Jimmy went to Knoxville"[316] and later re-joined Bill Monroe with Sonny Osborne (summer of 1952). Osborne carried on with the band until he joined the **Stanley Brothers**.

Carter and Ralph Stanley had re-grouped in October 1951 and were returning to WCYB together. Bob, in a 1993 telephone interview, explained that "Carter Stanley, at that time, had been playing with Bill Monroe.[317] Ralph had gotten into an accident of some sort and he was out of commission so they were completely out of commission right at the time.

Larry Richardson and Happy Smith.

Well, Ralph got into the car wreck (on August 17th) and it laid him up. And Carter went to work singing with Bill Monroe until Ralph got back to where he could travel again. Then they went back together. They had left WCYB a long time before that and they came back to there. And Pee Wee Lambert, their previous mandolinist, never did come back to work with them any more. So when they started back together again there at WCYB, I let my group go and I just went with them. They (the group I left behind) were myself, Curly Ray Cline and Charlie Cline and Little Robert."[318] Bob stayed there with the Stanleys about three weeks until he went into the Marine Corps." Bob joined the Ma-

rines in November. His replacement in the **Stanley Brothers** was Curly Seckler who came from Carl Sauceman's band at WCYB. That winter, Sonny occasionally played with Red Allen at WPFB.

By the spring of 1952, Sonny Osborne was thirteen years old and was playing banjo on the Saturday night shows at WPFB in Middletown, Ohio. The story of Sonny's being hired by Monroe goes like this: Jimmy Martin began working in the Middletown area after Knoxville (where he went after he split with Bob Osborne). One Sunday in July of 1952, Martin took Sonny with him and they drove over to the country music park that Bill Monroe had just purchased in Bean Blossom, Indiana. Monroe only had one member— fiddler Charlie Cline—so Martin worked with him that day and soon both Martin and Sonny joined Monroe's band. The new Monroe band then left directly for Nashville. L.E. White joined on fiddle. Martin had to sign Sonny's union card because Sonny was too young to play when hired by Monroe. They recorded on Decca in Nashville at the Tulane Hotel. Songs included "Footprints in the Snow," "In the Pines" and "Pike County Breakdown." He became the youngest person ever to record with the **Blue Grass Boys**.[319] At the end of summer Sonny quit to return to school in Dayton.

Sonny told of his rather rapid rise to the **Blue Grass Boys**, "I'll tell you, this is the truth. I had no business being there—I'd been playing seven months or something like that and I had no more business being there than a kid working with the band, you know...'cause I didn't know my *time*. I didn't know any *time*; I didn't know any good licks, so it's evident on those things I cut with him. I didn't know how to be a trouper and I didn't carry on and do nothing, you know."[320]

While Bob Osborne was in the Marines but home on leave in October of 1952, Sonny and Bob recorded for Gateway using the band name **Sonny Osborne and His Sunny Mountain Boys**.[321] The tunes included "Raw Hide," "Cumberland Gap," "Train 45" and "White House Blues." They recorded "covers" of best sellers by **Flatt and Scruggs**, Monroe and others; subsequent sessions always included new songs. This Gateway session of twelve songs was later released on several

---

[316] Quotation from a 1991 interview in Grass Valley, California.

[317] The actual chronology was that Carter joined the Blue Grass Boys as guitarist and lead singer during the summer of 1951 until September. After Ralph was pretty much recovered from his August 17, 1951, auto accident, Carter and Ralph re-formed the Stanley Brothers in October and hired Bob Osborne, Curly Seckler and Charlie Cline.

[318] Little Robert van Winkle wrote "Close By" in the 1950s.

[319] On these recording were Monroe, Martin, Osborne, Charlie Cline (fiddle) and Ernie Newton (bass). Sonny recorded with Monroe on the sessions of July 18 and July 26, 1952.

[320] From an interview on March 18, 1967, with Neil V. Rosenberg, "The Osborne Brothers," *Bluegrass Unlimited*, September, 1971, p. 9.

[321] This was actually before Jimmy Martin began using this name. Recall that Martin and Bob Osborne had used the name Jimmy Martin, Bob Osborne and the Sunny Mountain Boys a few months previous and Bob kept the name when Jimmy left. It was a good name so Sonny just picked it up again for these recording sessions. Musicians were Sonny (banjo), Carlos Brock (guitar, who was later a Blue Grass Boy), Enos Johnson (mandolin), Billy Thomas (fiddle) and Smokey Ward (bass). It is doubtful that Bob was at that first Gateway session.
    Another Gateway session was in December 1952 with the same personnel (except Bob Osborne). A February 1954 Gateway session included Sonny, Enos Johnson (guitar), Bob Osborne (mandolin), L.E. White (fiddle) and Les Bodine (bass). Songs included "Gun Powder" and "Blue Waves."
    A March 1956 session for Gateway included Red Allen (guitar), Sonny, Bobby (mandolin, fiddle), Art Stamper (fiddle) and Les Bodine (bass). Tunes included "Hand Me Down My Walking Cane," "Jesse James," "Swanee River," "Silver Rainbow," "Banjo Boy Chimes," "Wildwood Flower" and "Auld Lange Syne."

other labels. The records were promoted heavily by the Jimmie Skinner Music Center/Record Company by mail order and are still available from Vetco Records. Altogether, at least fifty titles were cut for Gateway between 1952 and 1956. The majority of the tunes were released during the '60s on many different labels. Sometimes, Sonny released the songs under the name **Hank Hill and the Tennessee All-Stars, Stanley Alpine and the Sweet Mountain Boys** or **Stanley Alpine and the Tennessee Bluegrass All-Stars.**

In May 1953, Sonny recorded "A Brother in Korea" on Gateway—a story about his brother Bobby who was serving overseas. Sonny also recorded "Sunny Mountain Chimes." This was a very, very popular record (it sold more than 60,000 copies) and was used as the theme for the radio station, WCKY. This is before Jimmy Martin adopted the "Sunny Mountain" name for his group. Bob Osborne recalled that the name of Sonny's group when he recorded with Sonny may have been **Sonny Osborne and the Sunny Mountain Boys.** Sonny worked for Monroe again that summer, planning to join his brother when he got out of the Army.

Bobby Osborne got out of the Marines on November 10th, 1953, and joined his brother in Dayton for a couple of dates. Then they went to work for Cas Walker in Knoxville (WROL) with L.E.

The Osborne Brothers. L to R: Bob Osborne, Dale Sledd, Sonny Osborne, Ronnie Reno, c. 1971.

White (fiddle) and Enos Johnson (guitar). The band name was the **Osborne Brothers and the Sunny Mountain Boys.** They stayed there, struggling to make a living, until June 1954. Then they went back to Dayton, Ohio, and joined Jimmy Martin. Then the band became **Jimmy Martin and the Osborne Brothers.** They worked at WPFB awhile.

In July of 1954, Bobby, Sonny and Jimmy moved to Detroit for a year to play on WJR radio and live television working for Casey Clark's CKLW-TV (Windsor, Ontario, across the Detroit River from Detroit) and soon to Wheeling, West Virginia, at WWVA in 1955. Sonny remembered that it cost them more to commute to WWVA for the shows they were doing down there than they got paid. He also remembered that "We spent a lot of time singing to ourselves in a car—going somewhere—where most of the time not many cared very much if we got there or not. Not many fans, I mean. I guess we wanted to pick this music a lot more then. I don't believe I could do that all over again."[322]

When White left the next year, he was replaced by Ray Crisp in April 1954 until Joe Stuart took his place. Cas Walker's supermarket chain sponsored the band on WROL, Knoxville. On November 16th, **Jimmy Martin and the Osborne Brothers** recorded six songs for RCA Victor in Nashville. The six songs were "Save It! Save It!" "Chalk Up Another One," "20-20 Vision," "I Pulled a Boo-Boo," "She Didn't Know the Difference But I Did" and "That's How I Can Count on You." Also in the session were Red Taylor (fiddle) and Cedric Rainwater (bass). Also in November, Bobby Osborne bought his famous prewar Gibson F-5 mandolin from Charlie Bailey for $350.

In mid-1955, the brothers moved from Detroit to WWVA, Wheeling, West Virginia, for four months with **Charlie Bailey and the Happy Valley Boys.** Jimmy Martin stayed in Detroit, hired Sam "Porky" Hutchins and Earl Taylor, and called the band **Jimmy Martin and the Sunny Mountain Boys.**

About that time, Bobby tired of the music business and moved back to Dayton where both Bob and Sonny quit music. Bob drove a bread truck for White's Bakery for a couple months. He was married by this time. "Lost twenty-eight pounds and quit" (he laughed). Bob and Sonny then drove cabs. Bobby recalled that it was "The best job I ever had in my life! You was your own boss. If you want to get out there and make you some money, you could. If you wanted to set on your butt, just be nothin', you could do that, you know." During the time Bob was driving the bread truck, Sonny and Bob began playing music again on the weekends at the Royal Crest Restaurant. They had great crowds, good acceptance, and soon they were back to performing full-time. "I quit [music] twice, and the last time I got into it I said I ain't gonna quit anymore. It's something I want to do and I'm gonna go broke—or whatever—tryin'. I never quit anymore after that."

They recorded for Gateway Records in 1956, and for MGM in 1957. The MGM contract came about mainly because of a demo tape, hand-carried by Tommy Sutton to Wesley Rose (Artists and Repertoire man for MGM Records) of Acuff-Rose. The tape included "Ruby" on it, a song Bobby Osborne had been singing since 1949. This was the first record on which twin three-finger

322 Sonny Osborne, album cover notes, CMH-9011.

style banjos were heard. Bobby played the second banjo. While with MGM, they recorded "Rocky Top," "Roll On, Muddy River" and "Ruby." The sixteen songs recorded at this session came out on Rounder Records' Special Series 01, "The Osborne Brothers." Art Stamper was the fiddler with the band from January 1956 to October 1956.[323]

About October of 1956, the **Osborne Brothers** joined the cast of WWVA's The World's Original Jamboree in Wheeling and moved there. Red Allen replaced Enos Johnson in late 1956, and stayed until spring of 1958. Charlie Bailey was also in this band at WWVA. They stayed at WWVA seven years. This band was called the **Osborne Brothers and Red Allen** and consisted of Bob, Sonny and Red Allen. Bob and Red quit their jobs at National Cash Register after the success of "Ruby" and when they became regular cast members of WWVA's Jamboree.

Their MGM recordings were being blasted all over the airwaves via the powerful WWVA. Soon the recordings of the **Osborne Brothers and Red Allen** were in every household—MGM did an excellent job of distributing their records. Johnny Dacus played fiddle after Stamper left, Ricky Russell, the resonator guitar, Red Allen, guitar, and Ray Anderson, bass. This band configuration never recorded.

In 1957, the **Osborne Brothers** began using drums on their recordings, beginning their reputation as innovators in this music. Their 1957 recording of "Once

Bobby Osborne (L) with Terry Eldredge, 1993.

More" showed the band's emphasis on vocal work. Sonny sang baritone, Red Allen, low tenor, and Bobby, high lead. The song was their first which used this "high lead" trio concept of harmony and paved the way for many of their songs to come. The genius of the high lead is that the lead singer became less important and thus replaceable.

"Rocky Top" was recorded by the **Osborne Brothers** in 1967 and featured (for the first time since 1960) a pedal steel guitar. Most of their subsequent recordings have included this instrument. The importance of "Rocky Top," written by Boudleaux Bryant,[324] cannot be underestimated in the progression of their career. It sold 84,000 copies in three weeks—a feat unheard of in bluegrass music. Sonny said, "It opened a door that would not have been opened, and that has not been opened for, any other bluegrass group except maybe **Flatt and Scruggs**. It opened the door that has allowed us to go into the part of the business that no one in our whole side of the business—bluegrass—has been, before or since."[325]

Paul Craft associated himself with the **Osborne Brothers** as a songwriter in 1958.[326] In April, Red Allen left the **Osborne Brothers and Red Allen** after thirty months with them. They became the **Osborne Brothers** and no longer did another artist receive co-billing with the pair. Their singing signature was cast in stone, and other singers merely filled-in their trio. Johnny Dacus, their fiddler, took Allen's place in the trio but left before the recording session of February 1959 when Ira Louvin filled-in. That summer, guitarist Ray Anderson filled-in the trio.[327]

By the fall of 1959, the **Osborne Brothers'** new band members were Benny Birchfield (bass, banjo) and Jimmy Brown Jr. (guitar). Brown left and Birchfield began singing with the trio, played the guitar, and stayed longer in that position than any others up until late 1964 when he left when the band joined the Opry. Sonny considers Birchfield to be the greatest harmony singer in the business—next to himself, of course.[328] This trio last recorded together in 1962 or 1963.

The **Osborne Brothers** played in what was probably the country's first bluegrass band concert at a college in February of 1960. It was at Antioch College,

---

323 While Stamper was a band member he recorded "Ruby," "Who Done It," "Teardrops in My Eyes" and "My Aching Heart."

324 Boudleaux and his wife, Felice, also wrote "Georgia Piney Woods," "Tennessee Hound Dog" and "Muddy Bottom."

325 Glenna H. Fisher, "The Osborne Brothers," *Bluegrass Unlimited*, July, 1984 p. 17.

326 This 1937-born Arkansas banjoist/songwriter got interested in bluegrass music in 1951 after he heard Earl Scruggs play the banjo. Though he did play banjo with various bluegrass groups such as Jimmy Martin and the Sunny Mountain Boys in 1961, his fame came as a songwriter.
    With the Osborne Brothers in 1958, Craft's songs included "Blue Heartache" and "Midnight Flyer." These two songs, when recorded, included the harmonica of Charlie McCoy—an indication of this phase of the band's music. He also wrote "Stand Beside Me" for the Osbornes in addition to "Fastest Grass Alive," "We're Holding On (To What Used To Be)" and "Bent, Broken and Blue."
    Craft's other songwriting contributions include: for the Lewis Family, "Will He Call Out My Name," "Won't It Be a Happy Time," "Come Walk With Me," "Sailing, Sailing," "I'm Working My Way" and "Gonna Go Walking"; for Joan Baez, "Till Teardrops Kiss the Morning Dew"; for the Seldom Scene, "Bottom of the Glass," "Raised by the Railroad Line" and "Keep Me From Blowing Away"; for Bobby Bare, "Drop Kick Me Jesus (Through the Goal Posts of Life)"; and for Ray Stevens, "Honky Tonk Waltz."

327 He had recorded on the Mountaineer label a year or so earlier with Sonny and Bob assisting him. Anderson did not record on the MGM label.

328 Sonny laughed when he said this. And in a separate interview, Bobby laughed when he told me that was Sonny's opinion of his singing—not Bob's. A 1991 interview.

Yellow Springs, Ohio, not far from Dayton. In October, they recorded with electric lead guitar and pedal steel guitar; they were well accepted. The **Brothers** used non-bluegrass instruments because they fit well into the songs and filled-in while Sonny and Bobby stopped playing their instruments to concentrate on the trio vocals. Adding further to the experimentation to try to get more audience, they used Doug Kershaw on electric guitar in a recording session in February 1962.

The **Osborne Brothers** left WWVA in 1963 and moved to Nashville. That year, the group signed with Decca Records. Their first recordings were released in the fall. Also in 1963, Sonny wrote *Mel Bay's New Bluegrass Banjo*, the first book on Scruggs-style banjo picking.

Working there in Nashville about 1963 brought another significant change to the music of the **Osborne Brothers**: They began using drums and integrating "the Nashville sound" into their music. In a 1991 interview with this writer, Bob Osborne described the use of electric instruments with the band which he said was not really new for them, "If you go back there [to the MGM recordings] we had an electric steel guitar. That was before we were at the Opry or anything; we just didn't have drums on it. Country, if you'll recall the rock and roll era, just about took country out. Just about wiped it out until the late fifties when country started coming back. By the time we got into the early sixties, you had the Webb Pierces and the Carl Smiths and the Faron Youngs who were dominating the industry with electric instruments and using the new sound equipment which was being brought to Nashville and making the guitar sound so wild. We just jumped in and got our share of it. That's all. It paid off and really worked out good in that period of time. We gained a lot by doing that. We were programmed [on radio stations] in the country market as well as the bluegrass market. The folks that were buying the country market material... Well, all we did was, instead of just having solos, we added harmony to it. But Sonny and me never laid that mandolin and banjo down there and we got a lot of airplay and we were considered as both bluegrass and country. And we got a lot of airplay that folks in blue-grass never did get and haven't got until this day. So I think we did an *awful lot* to further bluegrass music.

"Monroe has been here twenty years longer than us, you know. But for a period of time, I think we took bluegrass places where it will never be taken any-more—I'm talking about the White House, we played there, and Lake Tahoe at Harrah's Club with Merle Haggard. That was another good thing. Of course, he was number one at the time and through him we took bluegrass to people who wouldn't walk five steps to

Sonny Osborne, 1993.

hear a hundred hours of it. And people blame us for going with the Nashville sound—but what is it now? It's still the Nashville sound. It never hurt us any and we gained a lot of new fans. We lost some of our old ones, but for every one that we lost we added a whole bunch to it."

On August 8, 1964, Bob and Sonny Osborne joined the Grand Ole Opry. That December, Benny Birchfield left the band; he was replaced by Gordon Cash, who was then replaced by Dale Sledd in the fall of 1965.

Sonny was always innovative. In 1965, he was the first to use the five-string resonator guitar when they recorded "Making Plans." The next year, Sonny used his top-tension Vega banjo in the recording of "Up This Hill and Down." Its special tuning and distinctive bassy sound and the addition of a piano made this their most successful record up to this date. They also added an electric bass that year, first used on "The Kind of Woman I Got." They soon hired electric bassist Ronnie Blackwell into the band. Benny Birchfield re-joined on guitar in September. In 1970, Sonny recorded a song on his new, experimental 6-string banjo. The 6th string was lower than all the others and tuned to G, .025 gauge. He used it extensively until 1975.

The **Osborne Brothers** recorded on Decca and later MCA.

The **Brothers** used amplified mandolin, guitar and banjo in 1969, trying to fight the effect of playing with large, package shows where their acoustic instruments could hardly be heard by an audience that had sat through sets by other groups which used electric instruments with batteries of giant speakers. Their hit, "Tennessee Hound Dog," was the first song to come out this way. In 1971, "Georgia Piney Woods" came out the same way but was augmented with an overdubbed string section.

In 1971, the **Osborne Brothers** were voted Best Vocal Group by the Country Music Association at the Opry-sponsored "Early Bird Blue Grass Special," a concert at the annual DJ convention in Nashville. That year, Ronnie Reno played guitar for the **Brothers**. He moved from bass when they hired Ray Kirkland to fulfill the bass duties with the band. Reno also did twin-mandolin numbers with Bobby. Reno left to join Merle Haggard's **Strangers**, then Dale Sledd returned to take his place. Dennis Digby joined on bass. Robby Osborne, Bobby's son, was added to play drums. When Digby left, Robby took over on bass. In spite of all these changes, Sonny and Bobby were able to keep the sound tight and consistent.

The **Osborne Brothers** played for President Richard Nixon on March 17, 1973. They were on the bill there with the **Merle Haggard Show**. This was the first bluegrass band to ever play inside the White House. Sonny said, "The place is awesome—it really is. We got to tour the whole thing—just wander around for a whole night."[329] Also that year, Bobby Osborne and Dale Sledd were involved in an auto accident in September in Morristown, Tennessee. Bobby's hand was injured and Sledd suffered multiple injuries which caused him to be in intensive care at the hospital. Robby Osborne filled-in for guitarist Sledd.

When MCA released "Fastest Grass Alive," musicians included Sonny, Bobby, Sledd, Robby Osborne and Dennis Digby, along with several studio musicians. It was on this album cover that Bobby first wore a hat—a black one. From this point on he would almost always perform with one. Bob also felt strongly that it was his job to dress as neatly as possible on stage. He began wearing a tuxedo on stage, feeling that the audience wants to see a performer take pride in his or her appearance.

The **Osborne Brothers**, having used electric instruments for several years, switched back to acoustic in 1974. Also, the drums were eliminated. In October 1977, Dale Sledd (who wrote "Sledd Riding") returned to the use of an amplified guitar on their shows. Sledd left the group in December.

The **Osborne Brothers** were selected as the Bluegrass Band of the Year for 1978 by *Music City News* (Nashville)...for the eighth year in a row! Sonny and Bobby Osborne played a thirty-minute part in Marty Robbins' movie, "The Drifter." Jimmy D. Brock joined the band February 24th.

Sonny likes working with his brother, Bobby. "I know my role and he knows his. And I never have to ask him anything and he never has to ask me anything. On stage, I can look at him and I know what he's going to do, and he does me the same way. He realizes what I am musically, and I realize what he is musically. I respect that he respects that, too. I enjoy hearing him sing and he enjoys hearing me play. It's good." He is most proud of "the origination of the harmony which hadn't been done before. That was in 1957 or 1958. It completely changed bluegrass harmony around. It opened another door for people to go through."[330]

Abbreviating subsequent band members with the group, the list includes Jimmy D. Brock, Buddy Spicher, Don Collins, Blaine Sprouse, Paul Brewster, Shawn Camp, Glen Duncan, Tommy White, Steve Thomas, Terry Smith, Raymond Huffmaster, Gene Wooten and Terry Eldredge.

Terry Eldredge joined the group about 1988, taking the place of Jimmy Brock (electric bass). Eldridge brought the acoustic bass to the band. The group was just trying out the acoustic bass after having used electric for many years. As Sonny said in 1991, "We'll never go back to electric; the acoustic bass fits our music." When Terry Smith arrived to play bass with the group, Eldridge moved to guitar, enabling him to sing more. It seemed easier to sing while strumming a guitar than plucking a bass.

The Osborne brothers, Bob and Sonny, were voted into IBMA's Hall of Honor in 1994. They continued performing into the late 1990s.

Author with Bob Osborne at Grass Valley (the Capitol of Bluegrass in California) in 1992.

329 Ibid., p. 16.
330 Ibid.

The Goins Brothers

Some pioneers of this music seem to avoid the limelight of notoriety, they just keep on playing good bluegrass music and earning a living. The brothers Goins of near Bramwell, Mercer County, in the coal-mining area of West Virginia is a good example of this type of band.

Melvin Goins was born December 30, 1933; Ray was born January 3, 1936. They were raised in a large musical family. They didn't have electricity in the early 1940s and their father didn't own a car. Growing up in Bluefield, West Virginia, the brothers listened on their battery-powered radio to **Rex and Eleanor Parker and the Lonesome Pine Fiddlers** on WHIS, and to Bill Monroe on the Opry. After 1947, they more enjoyed WCYB's Farm and Fun Time (noon to 2 p.m.) where they heard the **Stanley Brothers**, **Flatt and Scruggs**, Mac Wiseman, Charlie Monroe and **Curly King and the Tennessee Hilltoppers**. When Ray and Melvin were small and working in the family corn field, they'd tell their father that they would be willing to miss dinner if he would let them listen to WCYB. They were now officially fans of bluegrass music.

During the late '40s and early '50s, there were bluegrass shows on Sunday at Glenwood Park, West Virginia, and Doran Airport in Richland, Virginia, which featured the biggest names in bluegrass at the time. The two boys saved their nickels all week to be able to attend the concerts. Physically getting to the concerts was tough. They had to walk about four miles through the mountains to the main road where they caught a bus or street car. It cost twenty cents to ride it to Franklin, West Virginia. They didn't have enough money to buy anything to eat when they got there, but worked around that with the sack of ginger cakes and jar of Kool-Aid their mother sent with them. They used to get there

early to get a ringside seat. They could hardly wait for **Bill Monroe and the Blue Grass Boys** to arrive on stage, with the riding pants with leggings, the Stetson hats and broad ties.

The brothers soon began playing their own music. Melvin got his first banjo by trading a guitar, four chickens and a rooster. Their first performances were in 1950 on Gordon Jennings' radio show at WKOY in Bluefield.[331] In the early 1950s, Ray and Melvin were with the **Lonesome Pine Fiddlers** at WLSI, Pikeville, Kentucky, with Ezra and Curly Ray Cline for several years. They made $12.50 per person each week. Their main source of income came from their "candy shows". These were appearances—usually local in nature—where "It was a free show...we would do into these little communities and play these little ball parks, fields, close to grocery stores—any place where we could find a big place in the road where we could assemble a lot of people for a free show. We had what they call a 'candy show' and we done free entertainment and sold candy...for a quarter a box and gave away gifts and prizes [in the candy box]." The crowds were often as large as a thousand people. The concerts would return to the same location as long as the crowds remained. They made about the same amount of money as if they had charged admission. They used a sound system for the first time during these concerts. Rather crude by today's standards, it did help project the music to the audience.

They continued working for the **Fiddlers** and their own **Goins Brothers** band for some years. Melvin and Ray then joined the **Blue Grass Boys**[332]. They re-joined the **Fiddlers** in 1960. The foursome of Curly Ray and Ezra Cline and Ray and Melvin Goins began recording again, doing four albums for Starday, one of which featured Hylo Brown. They stayed in this configuration until 1964 when they played at WCYB-TV in Bristol, Tennessee.

The band members all had day jobs, playing with the **Lonesome Pine Fiddlers** on a part-time basis. Melvin re-formed his **Goins Brothers** band without Ray. In 1966, Melvin joined the **Stanley Brothers and the Clinch Mountain Boys** full-time, playing guitar, bass, and doing comedy as "Big Wilbur". After Carter Stanley's death in December, he remained in Ralph's band for two and a half years.

In May of 1969, Melvin re-formed his **Goins Brothers** band again with Ray who had been operating a country store near Elkhorn City, Kentucky. The two brothers would operate as a full-time touring band from this time on. Their first bluegrass festival was at Bean Blossom in June. The **Goins Brothers** started their own festival near Beckley, West Virginia, in 1971. The brothers won the 1981 Carter Stanley Memorial Award.

---

331 Jennings was a founding member of the Lonesome Pine Fiddlers in 1937.

332 While the brothers were with Bill Monroe's band during the late 1950s, band members were Bill Monroe, Merle "Red" Taylor (fiddle), Melvin (guitar) and Ray (banjo) Goins and Billy Edwards (bass).

The Goins brothers are still active as a band into the 1990s. They recorded for Rebel, on their own label, and in the 1990s on the Hay Holler labels. Melvin Goins received Promoter of the Year award several time from SPBGMA. In 1994, Ray experienced serious health problems and missed the 1995 festival season.

Bill Clifton

Bill Clifton is a pioneer in bluegrass music whose excellent education and upbringing were not deterrent enough to sway him from the call of making music. In his recording and band projects, he hired some of the biggest names in the music while he operated his own band and gained everlasting status in bluegrass music.

William Marburg, later known as Bill Clifton, was born April 5, 1931, on a farm in Baltimore County, Maryland, away from the source of the music. Although his parents didn't provide a significant influence toward music, at approximately eight years old he was introduced to hillbilly music through farm hands who *did* know the music and who *did* listen to it on the radio.[333] He was influenced by the **Carter Family**, the **Morris Brothers**, early artists on the WWVA Jamboree and WSM's Grand Ole Opry, as well as local radio artists.

He recalled that during the times he was learning to play music, "Most of us never committed our songs to memory. We always used sheets off the music stand. We did this until we had to get out and do it live [from memory]. Then our repertoire became considerably smaller." He noted that Buddy Starcher was one of those who never committed any song to memory—even his own tunes.

Before he was twenty, Clifton was playing country music on several radio stations and shows in Virginia and Maryland; the Hayloft Jamboree in Charlottesville, Virginia, was the first—in 1949. He formed his own **Dixie Mountain Boys**[334] in 1952. They played WWVA's Jamboree in Wheeling, West Virginia, until November 1953. This early band recorded for Stinson Records but the tunes were never released. His Blue Ridge record-

ings from this era were released in 1954/1955. And later on in the mid-'70s, the Bear Family Records album "Bill Clifton and Paul Clayton" brought to light, for the first time, most of the 1952 recordings made for Stinson. Neither Clifton nor Clayton were blessed with a brother so they worked as the **Clifton Brothers**.

In the military from 1954 to mid-'56, Clifton recorded with many artists and frequently used the band name **Dixie Mountain Boys**. In an interview with this writer, Clifton said, "I didn't really keep a band on the road. I accepted dates, and when I did them everybody was paid as a member of the band. But they weren't full-time with me. They did other things, too." Later, he recorded for Starday Records using the well-respected artists of the day, such as John Duffey, Charlie Waller, George Shuffler, Mike Seeger, Ralph Stanley, Tommy Jackson and others.

In 1961, Clifton booked country and bluegrass bands weekly into a summer-long series of concerts at Oak Leaf Park in Luray, Virginia. These were held every Sunday from May through September. Many students of bluegrass say that the July 4th "Bluegrass Day," which re-united Bill Monroe with former **Blue Grass Boys** on stage for the first time, was the first bluegrass festival. But it was only a one-day affair and didn't have the flavor of Carlton Haney's multi-day festivals which began in 1965. Bill invited all the bluegrass artists he could afford; it was low budget and used only 8 x 10-inch flyers. Clifton remembered that none of the groups there had spoken to one another for many years except Bill Monroe with Carter and Ralph Stanley. Monroe, said Clifton, particularly avoided Flatt and Scruggs. Clifton wanted to help get them all together by inviting them to the same event but when Flatt and Scruggs found that the Stanleys were planning to attend, they declined the invitation. Clifton recalled that Carlton Haney wanted too much for **Reno and Smiley** which he was managing at the time; he wanted as much as

Bill Clifton (R) introduces Bill Monroe at the 1963 Rhode Island Festival.

333 Peter Kuykendall's liner notes of Bill Clifton's "Blue Ridge Mountain Blues" cited Clifton as a "city-billy." Clifton denies that the word applies to him because the term usually refers to a more urban individual who was raised in, and played music in the big city which, according to Clifton, he did not.
334 With himself (guitar), Johnny Clark (banjo) and Winnie Sisk (fiddle, who was soon replaced by Bill Wiltshire).

Monroe wanted. Clifton couldn't afford them. That July 4th, they got 2250 paid attendees at $1 each; children were admitted free.

Clifton received an advanced college degree (MBA, University of Virginia) and worked as a stock broker until he found that he could make a living playing music. This realization came to him in Britain so he pursued music for the next fifteen years there, with occasional breaks for recording events with County Records in America. The list of people on his records would fill a *Who's Who* in bluegrass music with each formation of his **Dixie Mountain Boys**.

He came back to the U.S. for three weeks in 1972, at Pete Kuykendall's request, to perform in festivals at Indian Springs, Maryland, Bean Blossom, Indiana, and McClure, Virginia. Clifton returned to the U.S. for the final time in 1978, and settled in Mendota, Virginia,[335] where he lives today. Returning to the bluegrass circuit after all those years in England placed him in the position of having to submit tapes to festival promoters as if he were an unknown; he couldn't pick up where he left off. His previous profession as a stock broker proved too difficult to re-enter and still be flexible enough to play his music so his day job became a loader of trucks. Together with Red Rector and Don Stover, he formed the **First Generation** and they began performing at festivals and concerts in the U.S. and in Europe.

Eventually, he was able to re-establish his reputation on the bluegrass circuit with musicians such as Don Stover (banjo), Red Rector (mandolin) and Art Stamper (fiddle). In 1991, he recorded with Stover and others as **Pick of the Crop**. He recorded over twenty of his own records through the years. He is one of the founder directors of the Newport Folk Festival and is included in the Smithsonian Collection of Classic Country Music.

In a 1976 British publication, John Atkins wrote, "Regretably, like far too many of his contemporaries, Bill's reward from the media has been virtually non-existent, and many lesser talents and considerably lesser human beings have received far greater accolades. In terms of the people who make and intimately know the music, Bill has unconditional respect, and I suspect that at the end of the day this means more to him than the shallow plaudits."

As of 1996, he continued to pursue his music and frequently contributed his talents to IBMA. He ran his own Elf Records label and Mendota Music publishing company.

Bill Harrell and the Virginians

This veteran of over forty years in bluegrass music is one of the pioneers who has paid his dues. Most of his career was as leader of his own **Virginians**, but many know him as an ex-partner of the legendary Don Reno. An enduring musician and a tireless promoter of bluegrass music, he has earned the respect of those who know and understand this music.

George William Harrell was born in Attoway, Virginia, September 14, 1934. The Harrell family later moved to Maryland where they lived in one room with his father's sister. The menu was very limited on his father's meager salary. They had no car; there was a two-mile walk to the streetcar. Young Bill helped pay the bills by hauling bottles off in a home-made wagon of two-by-fours and lawn mower wheels. Eventually his father was able to buy a home in Riverdale, Maryland—a "fixer-upper" shack. "It looked like a chicken house."[336] It took a year to fix it up.

"I was interested in bluegrass as a kid; learned to play guitar and sing by the 'trial and error' method of finding chords in a chord book and singing the song. When the tune didn't fit the song, then I found the chord. That's how I learned to play and sing." Harrell recalled, "I got the mandolin when I was in college. My mother bought it for me[337] in order to play with the **Rainbow Mountain Boys** which was formed in college with myself (mandolin), Dave Swan (banjo), Pete Ross and Mo Lebowitz and played weekly on WDON, Wheaton, Maryland." About 1953, Harrell played mandolin with Smitty Irvin's band with Jack Gibson (guitar), Smitty Irvin (banjo) and Stoney Edwards (bass).

In 1955, Reno and Smiley hired Bill Harrell as a mandolin player. Harrell recalled that "Ronnie Reno was

[335] He chose Mendota, according to Tom Gray, because he has always been a fan of the Carter Family and he wanted to be near the Carter fold and be a part of that music.

[336] Carol Ross Jeffry, "Still Alive and Kickin'—An Interview with Bill Harrell," *Bluegrass Unlimited*, December, 1991, p. 21.

[337] The Martin mandolin cost $100; his mother paid $7 per month for it.

a little boy; he was learnin' to play and too little to play. About that time, **Reno and Smiley and the Tennessee Cut-Ups** were members of the Old Dominion Barn Dance in Richmond, Virginia, and I went there on Saturdays and played that." Harrell told the famous duo, "I want to play mandolin with you. If I do anything wrong just tell me or knock me off the stage—but just let me try it."[338]

The group sounded good—good enough for Connie B. Gay to offer them a job on his television show, "Town and Country Time," hosted by Jimmy Dean. They had Reno (banjo), Smiley (guitar), Mac Magaha (fiddle) and John Palmer (bass). Harrell filled-in as an extra and was paid as a sideman. On Christmas Eve of 1955, he got his union card so that he could play the television show (he had been playing without a card on the Old Dominion Barn Dance at Richmond). "I was able to play on the TV show and Don didn't tell me anything until the last moment and he asked me, 'Have you got your union card?' I said no. That's how I wound up playing mandolin with them for twenty-six weeks on Jimmy Dean's 'Town and Country Time.'"[339] The group left the Barn Dance soon after this television gig began.

Harrell was drafted in 1956. Knowing that he would soon join the military, he formed **Bill Harrell, Smiley Hobbs and the Rocky Mountain Boys**[340]. They played daily on WARL in Arlington, Virginia. They recorded "Reno Bound" and "Rocky Mountain Ramble." When banjoist Donnie Bryant was drafted, Eddie Adcock took his place on banjo with the band in the Washington, D.C., area. The band of Harrell, Adcock, Smiley Hobbs and Carl Nelson broke up in 1957 when Bill Harrell joined the military.

Harrell spent fifteen months in the Army hospital due to an auto accident[341] and was medically discharged in 1959. He and Buzz Busby worked the Leonardtown, Maryland, area. Harrell recorded with Starday in 1959 and 1960 songs such as "Eating Out of Your Hand," "One Track Mind," "Tragic Highway," "I'll Never See Her Anymore" and "Love Is a Stranger."

"In 1961, Smitty (Irvin), Stoney Edwards, Buck Ryan and myself got a band together and we ended up playing "The Jimmy Dean Show" on ABC network once every six weeks through 1963. I got a record contract with United Artists in 1961 and recorded 'The Wonderful World of Bluegrass Music.' I had Smiley Hobbs on mandolin and twelve-string guitar, Buck Ryan on fiddle,

Smitty Irvin on banjo, Stoney Edwards on bass fiddle, and I played a guitar. It was released in 1962." The band was advertised as the **Virginians** on the show.

"In 1966, I began my partnership with Don Reno. It was **Don Reno, Bill Harrell and the Tennessee Cut-Ups**. At that time, Reno and Red Smiley had separated. They just wanted to go their separate ways—for what reasons I don't know and don't even care to say.[342] Don Reno and I became partners and later on we would occasionally bring Red Smiley back into the band and then we had a three[-way] partnership for a while before Red Smiley died. Red had diabetes real bad and he got the flu which made him very, very sick. He couldn't hold anything down on his stomach so he couldn't take the massive doses of insulin without eating—sort of a chain reaction. That's the way I have it set in my mind that Red Smiley died."[343]

Harrell had a driving accident early in 1977 in which he went to sleep in a car, hit a telephone pole, broke both legs and left him with a bad back. "Don and I were working together and, at that time, we had Ed Ferris (bass), Buck Ryan (fiddle), myself on guitar and Don Reno on banjo. A fellow named Bonny Beverly took my place playing guitar and siging while I was recovering from these broken legs. And when I went back to start playin' some of the shows I still had casts on, and crutches. Shortly thereafter, I think Don wanted to keep Bonny Beverly in addition to me, and I didn't think we needed another guitar player—we had a fiddle player— so I said, no, I didn't want to do that. Shortly after that, Don called up and said he wanted to separate the partnership. There was no ill feelings about it or anything. We just settled up our partnership business and I went along with it."[344]

Bill Harrell and the Virginians, 1995.

[338] "Don Reno, Red Smiley, Bill Harrell and the Tennessee Cutups," *Bluegrass Unlimited*, August, 1971, p. 9.

[339] From a telephone interview, July 18, 1993.

[340] Members were Paul Champion (banjo), Carl Nelson (fiddle), Smiley Hobbs (mandolin) and himself (guitar). Champion, of Orlando, FL, died February 14, 1986, in Gainesville. During his 30-year musical career, he performed with Charlie Waller, Buzz Busby and Bill Harrell, among others. He authored a book on five-string banjo playing and applied his musical talent while working with young people in a drug-rehabilitation program.

[341] In this accident, he was being driven to the train station to begin his military leave. The car was run off the road. Bill lay in the field most of the night. The first time he walked without a cane or crutches was when he got married August 12, 1959, to Ellen Anne Morgan. She passed away December 14, 1982. They had three children. Mitch Harrell, born August 6, 1963, is the only one who continued in his father's profession. He records for Pine Castle Records.

[342] The separation was not because of Red Smiley's failing health. His health problems would come into the picture later; it was not a factor here.

[343] 1992 telephone interview.

On April 16, 1977, Don Reno and Bill Harrell split up. Harrell re-formed **Bill Harrell and the Virginians**. "So then I got Ferris for the group which lasted a long time. I had Darrell Sanders on banjo, Carl Nelson on fiddle, and Ed Ferris[345] on bass fiddle. Larry Stephenson came into the group around 1978 and stayed for five years and later joined the **Bluegrass Cardinals**."

When Larry Stephenson went with the **Cardinals**, Harrell hired Eddie King on mandolin, followed by Paul Adkins for four years. When Adkins left, he formed his own **Borderline Band**. Harrell proudly told this writer that "Larry Stephenson and Adkins both have their own groups and I'm very proud of those two young men who I feel as though, and they will tell you this, too, that I put them there where they could be seen. I didn't do much more than feature them on our shows and expose them to thousands of people." Bill Harrell lives in Davidson, Maryland. Members of Harrell's **Virginians** in 1994 were Mitch Harrell (guitar), Carl Nelson (fiddle), Michael O'Farrell (bass) and Bobby Lundy (banjo).

Red Cravens and the Bray Bros.

Photo courtesy Harley Bray.

Red Cravens and the Bray Brothers of Illinois

In the mid-'50s in Illinois, a bluegrass band was formed with Robert "Red" Cravens (guitar), and brothers Harley Bray (banjo), Nate Bray (mandolin) and Francis Leon Bray (bass). They were still relatively unknown even at the time when the band folded in

1963. Even a recording contract on Liberty and a booking contract with the Jim Denny Artist Bureau of Nashville, Tennessee, didn't assure the success of this fine band. Now, looking back, we have a chance to listen to their recordings and yearn to have heard the band in person. Though they are one of many fine bluegrass bands in America during the Elvis and folk eras, they were simply unable to overcome the tremendous odds that were stacked against them.

The Bray brothers were born in Champaign, Illinois, and were raised in a family which loved both classical violin and old-time country fiddle playing. Harley initially learned a pre-Scruggs three-finger banjo style from his father in 1947. It was an index finger pivot-type roll, not the roll style that Earl Scruggs made famous. Harley later patterned his picking style after '50s-style Scruggs.

In 1951, Red Cravens played banjo on a radio station in nearby Urbana, Illinois. He had a large collection of bluegrass records and exposed his neighbors, the Brays, to bluegrass; they began jamming together. Francis first played cello, then bought a half-size bass. Nate took up the mandolin. Harley and Nate were obsessed with the music and played five or six hours a day. Harley sometimes went through three sets of strings a week. Nate worked hard and fast at developing his skills on the mandolin.

There was something special about Nate's mandolin playing. One of his disciples who played with the **Bluegrass Cardinals** for many years, Randy Graham, said, "His playing was just so neat. He'd take an ordinary run or phrase and maybe sharp one note or make some slight change in sequence or timing that would make all the difference in the world."[346]

They formed **Red Cravens and the Bray Brothers** in 1954 and became part of the cast of the Hillbilly Jamboree at WBLN, Bloomington, Illinois, the following year. Harley described the Jamboree, "The Bloomington show in 1955 was a very good stage experience. No one played there who became famous, but the guy in charge aspired to be on the Grand Ole Opry and operated it as such. Everyone kind of milled around on the back of a large stage and visited, waiting their turn to perform. Acts consisted of mostly local country music acts. We were the only bluegrass band in the area."[347]

Also in 1955, they traveled to Nashville. Harley recalled, "We expected to find lots of bluegrass records as well as some bands playing in the area. We had trouble finding either, the only records being those of Monroe and **Flatt and Scruggs**." Nevertheless, they pressed on in their relentless pursuit of playing traditional-sounding bluegrass music.

344 1992 telephone interview.

345 Ferris and Harrell spent nearly eighteen years together. He quit Harrell's band several years before he died June 24, 1993.

346 Frank Godbey, "Who in the World Are the Bluegrass Cardinals? *Bluegrass Unlimited*, May, 1976, p. 14.

347 From notes to me January 1992.

In the summer of 1960, Harley, Nate, Francis and Red took an apartment in Urbana, Illinois. They played a weekly show on WHOW, Clinton, Illinois, occasionally joined by John Hartford. The shows were taped, but most of these recordings were lost because there were only two tapes which were used over and over again. What was salvageable was collected in 1972 by Rounder Records and released as "419 W. Main"[348] and "Prairie Bluegrass" (1976). On the cover of Rounder's "419 W. Main," Cravens told readers:

I had this Crown tape recorder that was a good recorder. Said we'll do it like a radio program. We put the boom out and everybody got around except that in bluegrass you should have the mike up close to the banjo and to instruments when they take a break. Otherwise, you won't be able to tell one instrument from another when they're taking a break. So that's where you used different mikes and the engineer comes in usually. But what we do is use the little wooden box method. Now, from the stage shows, I was in the habit of picking up and getting right in the mike if I had a little break or a special little run to do. Nate had his mandolin right up around his neck. No problem there. He'd sing into the mike and the mandolin was almost on the same plane so the only problem then was the banjo and that's why Harley was the one to use the little wooden stool. He wouldn't be taking a break. We'd be singing and we'd have to learn not to trip over it. It was sitting right there in front of the mike. We'd be singing and we'd be all in there smelling each other what they'd had for supper that night real close, singing a little trio harmony. Then we'd back off. Had to operate in the studio during the tape just like we did on stage. We'd back off and Harley would come in with the banjo and take a break. Sometimes we'd play in tandem like the **Cream** *with certain bluegrass runs, and other times I'd run around him. We just kinda play off*

Red Cravens and the Bray Brothers. L to R: Nate Bray, Red Cravens, Harley Bray, Bill Sherman, Francis Bray, Jimmy Raines. Photo courtesy Harley Bray.

together. But there were a few accidents with this stool thing. I woulda had another mike but we couldn't afford it. Sometimes we'd fall off and we'd have to stop. We finally got where we didn't bang our instruments into another. That happens at first, you know. You're miking everybody else's instrument so close and you gotta come in right now. You got a half a beat to get in there and, if you miss it, why, I used to go over and shut the tape off and then we'd all have a big argument (laughs). You remember and we'd get it on again and by God and the next time we'd get right in there. Somebody coulda got their teeth knocked out but they never did.

A reviewer of "Prairie Bluegrass" in a 1987 *Bluegrass Unlimited* loved the record. He wrote, "Nate's intense, forceful mandolin seemed to be the source of their awesome drive, although a similar case could be made for Harley's dynamic banjo. At any rate, they maintained an energy level that would blow away many of today's bands. Red's guitar and Francis Bray's bass provided the solid rhythmic showcase in which Harley and Nate could really strut their stuff." The album was produced by John Hartford.

After a successful appearance at the Grand Ole Opry on July 17, 1961, and due to their radio exposure, college concerts, and a performance at the Opry, **Red Cravens and the Bray Brothers** signed with Liberty Records and traveled to California to do the recording. Liberty renamed them the **Bluegrass Gentlemen**. The **Kingston Trio** had just broken up and the folk boom was in full force all over America. Until the bluegrass festival scene appeared in the mid-1960s, the folk boom was what seemed to keep bluegrass bands alive by providing folk festivals at which they could perform.

Harley wrote, "We recorded an album in Hollywood, California, for Liberty called 'The Bluegrass Gentlemen.' I can't say how commercially successful the record was except we didn't receive a large amount of money for it—but received some. Many people have called or written saying they had bought the record and

348 Named after their apartment in Urbana.

liked it. We met John Hartford through the record. He heard it and looked us up. He then sat in on some recordings we did in 1962. The Liberty record was re-released during the 1970s in Japan. I have never seen one, but Red Cravens was given one by a friend who was traveling through Japan. In the 1970s, I heard that the Liberty record was selling for $50 as a collector's item.

"The Liberty record had several songs that are not bluegrass material: 'Lover,' 'Malaguena,' 'Shanghaied,' 'Tobacco Road,' etc.. We put these on [the recording] in hopes of expanding the audience for bluegrass music. Other more traditional tunes were 'Little Glass of Wine,' 'Poor Little Ellen,' 'Little Maggie,' etc.. This was one of the earliest recordings—to my knowledge—that consisted of non-traditional material played with blue-grass instrumentation. We were one of the few, un-known bluegrass bands of that time to record on a major label."[349]

By the summer of 1963, the folk boom had begun to fade. Their recordings for Liberty didn't work out well financially and there was an economic recession throughout the nation. Financially, the group wasn't doing well so they left California, returning to Illinois and WHOW. Back at WHOW, they struggled to make a living on the Corn Belt Country Style program. From this program, Rounder Records assembled some of the recordings for their album released in 1976, "Prairie Bluegrass." The band was never recorded except for the WHOW tapes and Liberty Records. They went on tour with **Wilma Lee and Stoney Cooper**, Jimmy Dean, Roy Acuff and others. This also was not lucrative so they all got day jobs. That summer, Cravens was laid off from his day job and left the Midwest for California[350]. Eventually even Harley and Nate gave up as a full-time band. Red and Harley then began work for Bell Telephone. Nate was a very fast typist and began as book-keeper for a music company in Champaign, Illinois. Francis became a nurseryman who lays out landscapes.

Nate Bray became sick with Hodgkin's disease in 1966; he died in 1970 at the age of thirty-three. Harley resurfaced in the mid-1980s in Seattle, Washington, as banjoist with **Friends of Sally Johnson** which later evolved into **Williams and Bray** with members Harley (banjo), his wife Shera (guitar) and another locally prominent musical couple, fiddler Vivian and mandolin-ist Phil Williams. Their CD, "Winter Moon," appeared in 1993 on Voyager Records to critical praise.

Bill Foster— folklorist, banjoist, academician, hillbilly.

Dr. Bill Foster has a long history of recording and playing old-time bluegrass music—music in the favor of traditions which go even further back than the early Opry. His **Foster Family String Band** of Florence/Muscle Shoals, Alabama, is well-schooled in this tradition.

In a 1989 interview in Kissimmee, Florida, Foster spoke about modern bands which don't have the heritage that he and his family have, "Sometimes I get a little bit put out by some of the younger groups that buy records... Sometimes I get the feeling that they just bought the records and learned the songs and don't really understand anything they're singing about. I think that some of the best musicians, even the younger ones, are the ones who have at least grown up in the part of the country and have known old folks who have really lived the music. I don't hold it against them, though; I'm not saying that I resent them. I'm just saying that the feeling for the music may be a bit stronger with us." In spite of these feelings, one of the family's favorite bands is **New Grass Revival**. The **Foster Family** likes to play old ballads, traditional songs, novelty songs and gospel.

"I'm also interested in the heavy, heavy black influence that has come into [early bluegrass music]. I've seen stickers on instrument cases which read 'Bluegrass Music is White People's Music.' Monroe and Hank Williams and practically all of those old masters and formers of bluegrass music, at some time in their life, played with some black musician such as Schultz with Monroe, and Rufus (Rufe) Payne, also known as "Tee Tot," with whom Hank Williams supposedly worked.

---

[349] Telephone interview, 1992.

[350] He lives there as of 1992.

"My interest in the mutual give-and-take between traditional white and black folk music has been increased as I have had the opportunity to talk and play with such stellar performers as Wilson Pickett, the **Commodores** and other black musicians, and have experienced the ease with which we can play together because of the common background. W.C. Handy, who was born in Florence (Alabama) and who worked in a lumber yard at McFarland Bottoms, mentions in his biography that he learned much of his music from a white fiddler and that some of his most famous blues tunes drew heavily from fiddle tunes which he adapted, and to which he gave his own unique mark."

In 1975, Dr. Foster (he was an English professor at the University of Northern Alabama as of 1994) was hired by the state of Alabama to do a television show called "Bluegrass Roots" which would focus on southern folk music as it evolved down one of its many paths—to become bluegrass. The one-hour show soon became a series of ten shows and was aired during the fall and winter of 1976 on the Alabama Public Television Network. It was well received, selected as Best Series of the Program Year, and was subsequently shown by public television networks in several other states for the next ten years. He wrote and produced other projects of a similar nature through the years.

His family band was a consistent winner of SPBGMA's Old-Time String Band of the Year award. They cut eight LPs through 1989, and toured forty weekends during the year until the late 1980s when they began to cut down on their appearances.

Pete Kuykendall

Pete Kuykendall

Peter Kuykendall has near-legendary status within the bluegrass community because of his co-founding, editing, contributing and managing activities with the magazine which has proved to be *the* information source for bluegrass enthusiasts: *Bluegrass Unlimited.* But his time as a bluegrass musician with some prominent bluegrass bands should not be forgotten either.

Peter V. Kuykendall (born January 15, 1938) won the National Banjo Championship in 1956 and played in a local bluegrass band. About that time, "Pete Roberts" became Kuykendall's stage name when he became a disc jockey, thinking that Roberts would be easier to use than Kuykendall. Just out of high school, he became a deejay on a Fairfax, Virginia, radio station while attending college. Kuykendall is probably the first bluegrass discographer with a compilation which soon appeared in *Disc Collector*, which was *the* source of this type of material at that time.

In early 1958, Kuykendall performed as banjoist Pete Roberts with the **Country Gentlemen** when Bill Emerson left. Kuykendall's replacement with the band

Pete Kuykendall, 1989.

was Porter Church for a short time followed by Eddie Adcock in the winter of 1958.[351] He left the **Gents** to pursue recording activities with the Library of Congress. In early 1962, Kuykendall joined Red Allen and Frank Wakefield as a member of the **Kentuckians** for a year.

The idea for *Bluegrass Unlimited* came about in 1966 when a local D.C. couple, Diane and Vince Sims, missed a **Stanley Brothers** concert; the event wasn't publicized. Diane Sims suggested to local deejay Gary Henderson that they put together a newsletter to notify people of such concerts. Sims had a mimeograph machine in her basement and was willing to do most of the legwork. Soon Kuykendall was in the project along with Dick Freeland and Dick Spottswood. The first issues were put together at Sims' house, stapled together in one corner. It continued this way until late 1967 when the newsletter became too much for her to handle. Kuykendall then recruited some others for another year. Sims then left the project. Alice Gerrard (of **Hazel and Alice**) took over for six months. Sally Gray, Tom Gray's wife, handled it for another six months.

With the threat of another bluegrass publication, *Muleskinner News,* Kuykendall decided to go full-time with *Bluegrass Unlimited.* 1975 circulation of *BU* was 9200; 1988 circulation was about 12,000, 1996 circulation was 25,000. He was awarded an Award of Merit by the International Bluegrass Music Association in 1988; he was elected to the IBMA's Hall of Honor in 1996.

351 An accomplished musician and singer, Eddie Adcock credits Kuykendall with much help on singing baritone. Adcock's baritone singing seemed to make pull the Gents' sound together and, along with his distinctive banjo playing, it seemed to be *the* necessary ingredient for the band's phenomenal success.

John Duffey—
a mandolin player who would rather be known as a singer. A biography of the "Father of Modern Bluegrass".

Now known as the "Father of Modern Blue-grass"[352], John Duffey was born in Washington, D.C., March 4, 1934. His father sang in the Metropolitan Opera for twenty-five years; as a result, Duffey listened to a lot of opera. But he was more impressed by the music of the Grand Ole Opry: Bill Monroe, Lester Flatt and Earl Scruggs in the late '40s.

At seventeen years old in high school, John Duffey started playing the guitar. He had tried the banjo earlier but decided to concentrate on the guitar after he couldn't get the hang of the banjo. He then pursued the mandolin—because no one else he knew had one. "At that time in the early 1950s," he said, "the only person that really seemed to know some [mandolin] licks was Monroe. That was it!"[353] Soon he was with David Swan and the **Rainbow Mountain Boys** and **Lucky Chatman and the Ozark Mountain Boys.**

Let's now set the stage for the beginning of the **Country Gentlemen.** In June of 1957, members of **Buzz Busby and the Bayou Boys** included Busby (mandolin), Eddie Adcock (guitar), Bill Emerson (banjo)

and Vance Truell (bass). A serious auto accident oc-curred and Busby, Adcock and Truell needed time to recuperate. It became necessary to find replacement musicians to fulfill the band's concert obligations in Washington, D.C.. The task fell to Bill Emerson who then hired twenty-three year-old John Duffey to play mandolin, Charlie Waller, the guitar, and Larry Leahy, bass. Waller had played a few dates with the **Bayou Boys** recently and knew the songs.

It became a matter of question as to when Busby would return to music after the healing of his injuries so the band members decided to go out on their own; they changed the name and began their careers as the **Country Gentlemen** on July 4th at the Admiral Grill in Bailey's Crossroads, Virginia. At the formation of this group was John Duffey (mandolin), Charlie Waller (guitar), Bill Emerson (banjo) and Larry Leahy (bass). Emerson was replaced on banjo by Pete Kuykendall in early 1958, who then was replaced by Porter Church, followed by Eddie Adcock in late 1958. Tom Morgan replaced Leahy on bass.

During that time, Duffey used fingerpicks with his mandolin on certain cuts.[354] They developed a large following in the Washington, D.C., area. Duffey wrote many of the songs which the group played. He also played resonator guitar in the three-finger roll style on his own single, "Travelin' Dobro Blues," as well as many of the songs done during this period by the Gentlemen.[355] He would also over-dub the resonator guitar on some recordings. Duffey spent twelve years with the group. He quit his full-time surgical supply job (driving a truck) to play full-time with the **Country Gentlemen** in 1958. Within two years, they were playing full-time at the Shamrock in Georgetown, Washington, D.C..[356]

In 1961, Duffey changed his mandolin style to a more progressive, jazzy style. The **Country Gentlemen's** version of the song, "The World Is Waiting for the Sunrise," changed the course of blue-grass history because of its progressive nature. As he became more mature with the music, "It didn't take me long to realize, when I went out and tried to make a few bucks, you're not going to get anywhere trying to play someone else's style."[357] "I was trying to play more like jazz rather than straight down-stroke bluegrass. I just

352 This is a title given him by the *National Observer* magazine.

353 Dix Bruce, "John Duffey Interview," *Mandolin World News*, Vol VI, #II, Summer, 1981, p. 10.

354 Duffey also did a song with Bill Clifton using his fingerpicks in a 'Travis style' method of guitar picking on his mandolin. He didn't recall the name of the song at this interview, but admitted that it didn't seem to catch on. "It never interested anyone but me so I said, 'The hell with it. It must not be that good.'"

355 Another song with his resonator guitar is "Comin' Back But I Don't Know When."

356 The Shamrock, in Georgetown, Washington, D.C., was an important venue for bluegrass bands during the '60s. Artists who would frequent the place included Country Gentlemen, Bob Goff and his Bluegrass Buddies, Bill Harrell, Little Jimmy Dickens, the Osborne Brothers and Ricky Skaggs. The Shamrock is one of the reasons the area became known as the "Bluegrass Capital of America." Richard "Mickey" Woodward and Roger Woodward were the owner/managers of the bar.

357 Bruce, op. cit., p. 12.

wanted to incorporate this style into bluegrass because that's the style that I like."[358]

Duffey likes to entertain. "There's one thing that every human being will always enjoy, and that's a laugh. You cannot go wrong with that. I think people want to appreciate music, but mostly they want to be entertained."[359] And along those lines, "I think of myself as a singer. I honestly do. I don't consider myself a picker. I'm a singer."[360]

The **Country Gentlemen** got its first hit with "Bringing Mary Home"[361] on Dick Freeland's new Rebel label[362] in 1965. With successive performances and recordings, the **Gentlemen**'s style became increasingly categorized as "progressive" thereby setting the stage for other musicians and bands inclined to develop along these lines.

On March 4, 1969, Duffey left the **Country Gentlemen**[363], needing a break from music and touring and the music business in general. He also suffered much frustration with only the promise of royalties but no monetary reward by various recording companies. "It was like savin' up to go on tour. The other guys Eddie and Charlie, wanted to go most anywhere for fifty bucks and I told them than we'd never get a decent price if you keep on doing that! I don't want to save up to go on tour! I should get *paid* to go on tour. In addition to that, there were the hassles of the business, and I was getting pretty successful with my instrument-repair business.[364] Hell, I could stay home and not put up with all that sh— and get by."

In the early 1970s, the *National Observer* named John Duffey the "Father of Modern Bluegrass". While the term "father" usually indicates that someone invented something, it is doubtful that Duffey actually put a concerted effort into creating modern bluegrass. But John did help define this music by being there in the beginning of the movement which led to modern bluegrass. And beginning in 1971, he helped form the **Seldom Scene** which continued in this progressive nature. About the time that bluegrass musicians were multiplying in numbers due to the advent of bluegrass

festivals, musicians with talent were pushing its limits and showing their influences of rock and roll. Their new art form was now played with beards and long hair and sometimes being called "newgrass". Carlton Haney responded to its tremendous popularity by holding festivals for just this kind of music. Mr. Duffey feels that his bands, in spite of this progressive nature, have *added* to bluegrass music—and not taken anything away it. Asked if the **Seldom Scene** was an extension of the **Country Gentlemen** he replied, "I don't really think so. I think we're just our own separate selves. Every once in awhile we might do an old song we used to do, but we just do it. I guess there was a lot of music created in the early **Country Gentlemen** era that lots of people nowadays pick up on. But as far as being an extension of it, I don't think you could say that."

In 1971, the **Seldom Scene** was formed with John Duffey (mandolin), Ben Eldridge (banjo), Mike Auldridge (resonator guitar), John Starling (guitar) and Tom Gray (bass). They were individuals who wanted to play professionally (with the avowed purpose of playing for fun) but also held down day jobs in their D.C. area. They began performing regularly at the Red Fox Inn, Bethesda, Maryland, in January of the next year, staying until 1977. It was there at the Red Fox Inn that Duffey invented the saying, "You don't sit on our stage and we won't play on your table."

In 1973, the **Seldom Scene** provided the sound track for the NBC network television program, "The Past Dries Up," which dealt with the history of the C & O Canal.

The *Muleskinner News* magazine Readers' Poll voted the **Seldom Scene** as Best Bluegrass Band in 1974, 1975 and 1976. But as Mr. Duffey explained, "We've never considered ourselves a traditional bluegrass band."[365] "We've always considered ourselves an acoustic band, and it was a good thing. That's what really set us apart."[366]

In 1977, the **Seldom Scene** began playing regularly at the Birchmere (known now as "the house that John Duffey built") in Arlington, Virginia. The Birchmere

358 Live interview, January 23, 1993. I finally got an interview with John after several years of trying. John, at this stage of his career was thinking more of figuring out how to retire than being interested in giving interviews to anyone who may ask. But he was very cordial to me and I was thrilled to be with this legend of our music. I arranged an interview at his convenience—while he was "on duty" during a tour. The interview took place after a concert in Boulder, Colorado's Boulder Theater where we flew out together in the back of a United Air Lines Boeing 757 where I conducted this interview. The Seldom Scene, with Duffey, Auldridge, Eldridge, John Starling and T. Michael Coleman, were on their way to San Francisco's Bay Area for some gigs. He and I exchanged airline jokes and had a good time. He also explained that the reason he didn't used to fly at all was because of several aviation accidents about the time he was getting started in the business and even earlier. He still doesn't like it, but goes ahead and submits to the wishes of the other band members who would like to do a tour such as this.

359 Bruce, op. cit., pp. 12, 13.

360 Ibid., p. 13.

361 The song, written by Duffey, Joe Kingston and Chaw Mank, probably came from North Carolina folklore. Rod Serling's television show "Twilight Zone" later included an episode which was similar to the song.

362 Freeland sold Rebel Records to Dave Freeman in the late 1970s.

363 They still had that gig at the Shamrock.

364 Live interview, 1993. He didn't own a shop. He was given space in a basement for a shop at Arlington Music. He was the first person to do Martin Guitar warranty work outside the Martin factory.

365 Quote from Duffey in an interview by Art Menius.

366 Pat Mahoney, "The Seldom Scene As Heard," *Bluegrass Unlimited*, June, 1974, p. 16.

moved to its present location in Alexandria about 1981. "The [Birchmere] was like a place ought to be. We didn't change to the Birchmere because of the condition of the place or anything like that. He was also offering more money. So what we did for a while was play every other week at the Red Fox and every other week at the Birchmere. Right after John Starling left and Phil (Rosenthal) came with us, Phil had only played one night with us at the Red Fox and then we went on and played regular Thursday nights at the Birchmere."[367]

In September of 1977, John Starling left the **Seldom Scene** to pursue private medical practice. Duffey says he left to pursue "ear, nose and wallet." Phil Rosenthal took Starling's place as lead singer and guitar player.[368] Phil Rosenthal left the **Seldom Scene**[369] in June of 1986 and was replaced by Lou Reid[370]. With the **Scene**, Reid fiddled, sang, and was the lead guitarist. The **Seldom Scene**'s "Blue Ridge" LP won the award for Best Bluegrass Album from the National Association of Independent Record Distributors (NAIRD) in 1986.

Tom Gray left the **Seldom Scene** in October 1987. The band was in a stage of transition then, and Gray wasn't interested in the change of style or in playing electric bass. T. Michael Coleman joined on fretless electric bass. Lou Reid left the band in 1992. John Starling filled-in until Moondi Klein joined as their full-time lead singer. These transitions in the band membership "was the beginning of my headaches" said Duffey in a 1996 telephone interview.

The **Scene**'s fifteenth and twentieth anniversary albums (Sugar Hill) were both nominated for a Grammy. At the end of 1995, Klein, Auldridge, and Coleman left to go full-time with **Chesapeake**; Dudley Connell joined the **Seldom Scene** on rhythm guitar and as lead singer. Fred Travers joined on resonator guitar and Ronnie Simpkins joined on acoustic and electric bass on New Year's Eve of 1996. This new version of the band, according to John Starling, is the best ever. Duffey told why. "Well, the first thing about it is that Dudley is the first *real* rhythm guitar player we ever had. And now we all play in time. To have that guitar on stage like that is 'something else.' And he's a great lead singer, too.

"The sound difference in the band is interesting; it seems that when we sing the trios, it doesn't sound any different. Of course, Dudley's lead voice is different. Fred is also singing some lead. I guess the biggest thing you would notice in our sound is the guitar. With the combination of Dudley and Ronnie, our timing is really good; it seems that nothing ever goes wrong now. Knock on wood."

Bluegrass and the world lost John Duffey on December 10th, 1996. John was an act unto himself. He had such a presence on-stage you just *had* to watch him. He commanded the attention of the audience. This writer had trouble focusing on the other members of the **Scene**. John Starling conceded that Duffey was "sometimes difficult to deal with from a professional standpoint, but he was also true to himself and he never changed. John was one of a kind."

MidSummer Bluegrass Festival, Grass Valley, CA, 1988. L to R: Ben Eldridge, T. Michael Coleman, John Duffey, Lou Reid, Mike Auldridge.

Jake Landers— the Master Sergeant of bluegrass

Jacob "Jake" Landers was born in Lawrence County, Alabama, August 14, 1938. He was raised in a musical family, listened to, and was influenced by, Eddy Arnold, Little Jimmy Dickens and others on the Opry in the late '40s and early '50s. By age ten, he played guitar. During high school in the '50s, he sang modern country and western songs of the era (Faron Young). He jammed occasionally with Rual Yarbrough after Rual moved there in 1956. He became interested in bluegrass after a stint in the Army when he began playing with banjoist Melvin Hallmark.

After a tour of active duty in the military, he joined Herschel Sizemore, Rual Yarbrough, Billy Sizemore and Bob Dooley (fiddle) as the **Tennessee River Boys** in late 1957. Landers played guitar, piano and banjo. By early in 1958, they had a television show on WOWL. The base core of the group remained Sizemore,

367 Live interview, 1993.

368 Rosenthal wrote "Brother John," "Walk with Him Again" and "Take Him In."

369 He left to his home to run his American Melody Records.

370 Reid had extensive bluegrass experience in bands such as Doyle Lawson's Quicksilver (1981), with Ricky Skaggs (1985) before that, with Jimmy Haley and the Bluegrass Buddies, and with Southbound.

Yarbrough and Landers and from 1959 to 1962, the trio toured northern Alabama. Initially, they used the name **Country Gentlemen**. When they heard that the name **Country Gentlemen** already existed, they changed their name to the **Dixie Gentlemen**.[371] They recorded for Dot[372], for Time Records[373] of New York as the **Blue Ridge Mountain Boys**, and for United Artists[374]. Vassar Clements was with the group during this period until he joined Bill Monroe in 1961. In 1962, Landers and Yarbrough worked for Bill Monroe on a fill-in basis. Also in the band were Monroe, Kenny Baker, and Bessie Lee Mauldin.

The **Dixie Gentlemen** split in 1969. They partnered up again in 1971 and changed their band name to **Rual Yarbrough and the Dixiemen**[375] after Yarbrough came back from the **Blue Grass Boys** and returned home to Alabama to set up his luthiery shop. The **Dixiemen** recorded "The Greatest Day of My Life," a gospel album for Old Homestead.

By 1973, Jake Landers' day job was in the newspaper business in Muscle Shoals, Alabama. He went to work full-time for the Army Reserve that year.[376] By 1976, Landers had cut back his playing considerably but did manage to record "Jake Landers: Singer, Writer" on Old Homestead.[377] All the tunes on the album were written by Landers.

Al Lester spoke of Landers, "He can play any key or chord...any kind of song—even reels and square dances. I always hire Jake when I tour as a single. There aren't many guitar players who can play bluegrass and country equally well, but he's one of them. He plays good harmony and he's a good arranger."[378] In a 1992 telephone interview with this writer, Landers was flattered by this statement, adding that the key to this versatility is a love of many diverse kinds of music—not just bluegrass.

By 1979, Landers had his own **Landers Family Band**[379]. They worked together four years, during which time they recorded two LPs for Old Homestead.

The **Jake Landers Band** was founded in 1991 with himself, Larry McWilliams (fiddle) and James Killen (bass). That November 9th was a reunion for the **Dixie Gentlemen with Vassar Clements**. It was the first time in twenty-plus years that they had been on stage together. They recorded the album "Take Me Back to Dixie."

Del McCoury

Del McCoury— the rightful heir to the "high, lonesome sound"

Del McCoury is a significant contributor to the second generation of bluegrass musicians and vocalists. When he got his job with **Bill Monroe and the Blue Grass Boys** he was virtually unknown. Then, like a lot of bluegrassers who like to play in the traditional vein, he learned what he had to know about bluegrass from Mr. Monroe and went out on his own to start his own band. Though his was a good band through the years, it wasn't until the late 1980s when he and his band began to gain significant recognition for songwriting, excitement and singing. This new recognition may be partially a result of the existence of the International Bluegrass Music Association members who were recently able to vote for their favorites in the field of bluegrass: Del and his band consistently came out on top in several of the voting categories. The awards which the band accrued became multiple, and all of a sudden Del McCoury had come onto his own—after only thirty-plus years in the business. *The Southern Bluegrass News* included a record review of McCoury's "Don't Stop the Music" which said, "No one can argue that Del McCoury is not the rightful heir to the 'high, lonesome' throne of bluegrass music. No other performer that I can think of so seizes the genre and shakes the fruit from the tree quite like him... With the emphasis these days (1991) seeming more and more bent on breaking the bluegrass 'mold,' Del proves that he could have recorded 'Don't Stop the Music' thirty years ago with just as much validity."[380]

371 The Dixie Gentlemen band members were Jake Landers (guitar, banjo, piano), Al Lester (fiddle), Raul Yarbrough (banjo), Bill Smith (bass) and Herschel Sizemore (mandolin).

372 "Greatest Bluegrass Hits" with Tommy Jackson on fiddle.

373 "Hootenanny Bluegrass" and "Bluegrass Back Home."

374 "The Country Style of the Dixie Gentlemen" produced by Tommy Jackson with Vassar on fiddle.

375 Members in February 1971 included Landers (guitar), William Smith (bass), James Bryan (fiddle) and Yarbrough (banjo).

376 Another version of the band in 1975 included Red Rector (mandolin), Joe Stuart (guitar), Johnny Montgomery, then James Whitten (bass).

377 With himself (guitar), Yarbrough (banjo), Al Lester (fiddle), Buddy Whitten (Dobro, brother of James Whitten) and Joe Stuart (mandolin).

378 Patricia Glenn, "The Master Sergeant of Music—Jake Landers," *Bluegrass Unlimited*, June, 1982, p. 44.

379 With Jake (guitar), daughters Wanda (electric bass) and Phyllis (tambourine), Larry McWilliams (fiddle) and Melvin Hallmark (banjo).

380 From a record review of "Don't Stop the Music" (Rounder Records), *Southern Bluegrass News*, March/April 1991.

Delano Floyd McCoury was born in Bakersville, North Carolina, February 1, 1939. When he was two, his family moved to York, Pennsylvania, where he grew up influenced by his older brother, G.C. (Grover Cleveland Jr.), who taught him to play guitar at age nine and forced him to stay up after his bedtime to listen to the Grand Ole Opry. About 1950, G.C. introduced Del to the music of **Flatt and Scruggs** on a 78 of "Roll in My Sweet Baby's Arms" and "I'll Just Pretend" on the family wind-up victrola. McCoury also listened to the banjo music of Don Reno, Allen Shelton and Ralph Stanley.

The "high, lonesome" sound of bluegrass music had a certain "hook" for young McCoury. All the rest of the music he heard seemed mundane. "A lot of my kinfolk played mountain music all through the years. I heard something different when I was growing up that I thought was a lot better than old-timey stuff. The stuff I heard was modern, Man—this Bill Monroe and **Flatt and Scruggs** stuff. There was more excitement in that music. Country music was so draggy and this had some zip to it."

Del soon (1953) began to play banjo after hearing Earl Scruggs on the records. It wasn't called bluegrass then; it was just called "music", he said. He liked lead instruments and "Once I heard that banjo I thought that was the only thing I wanted to do is play

The Del McCoury Band, 1990.

that. Then I found out later that when I was playing in a band I had to sing. I was forced to sing in every band I ever played in. And a lot of times I didn't want to sing, but I *had* to sing. And so, then when I went to work for Monroe, I went for the banjo job, see, 'cause I'd been playing it about ten years by that time, and again he was wanting to make me sing. So I took that job. And he told me that if you play guitar and sing lead, you're going to like that better. Of course, I auditioned singing with him. He must have liked the way I sing. We had two tenors in the band then. I'd usually sing tenor before that. But you know, from that time on I never did really want to play an instrument. I got to an age where I didn't want to do it no more. Then when I got my own band, it was much easier to get musicians than singers so I said, well, I'll just sing and play the guitar."[381]

McCoury continues the Monroe tradition by assuring that his music has a lot of the blues in it. "The blues have a lot in them for a singer," he said. "There's more

melody that you can get out of a slow, bluesy tune. You can turn it and twist it and this and that. I like to see what I can get out of it."[382]

Del's first professional job (just out of high school at age 18) in 1957 was with the **Stevens Brothers**[383] on the radio in Chambersburg, Pennsylvania. He played banjo and was lead singer. The duo of McCoury and Keith Daniels remained with the band for a year until they founded **Keith Daniels and the Blue Ridge Ramblers**[384]. They played often throughout Maryland, Virginia, Delaware, Pennsylvania, and at the New Dominion Barn Dance in Richmond, Virginia, and in early 1962 recorded on the Empire label.

Shortly thereafter, McCoury went into the military, getting a medical discharge in June 1962. Then Del (guitar) and his younger brother Jerry (bass) joined Melvin Howell in Baltimore with the **Franklin County Boys**. The brothers' next move was to join Jack Cooke's new **Virginia Playboys**[385] with Del as banjoist. He and Cooke filled-in for a short tour in the Northeast with the **Blue Grass Boys** which included Monroe, Kenny Baker and Bessie Lee Mauldin.

Del was soon invited to join Monroe for a full-time job. He and Bill Keith auditioned for the banjo job at the same time early in 1963. McCoury recalled, "I started to work for him in February [1963]. And the way it worked out—we found out later that there was a hotel in Nashville called the Clarkston Hotel; it was right beside the National Life and Accident [Insurance] building. That's where they did the Friday night Opry, in that building; when Bill told me to come down there he told me to come to the Clarkston Hotel, he told Bill Keith the same thing. I waited about a month before I came down. I must have played with him like in December or January [for the audition]. And by the time I got there we both had a room at this hotel and he came in town and auditioned us both the same day. Of course, I went down to the hotel, carrying [my banjo], and Bill Keith did, too. We didn't know each other.

"He took us both up into the National Life building and we auditioned for him. He had his own guitar, Bill did, and he said, 'Now, I want you to play the guitar and sing.' I thought, 'Man, what is this? But I did. I played guitar and sung. So he hired Bill Keith (on banjo) then.

381 From a 1991 interview at IBMA's trade show, Owensboro, Kentucky.

382 Robert Gordon from his "Picks" article sent to me by The Keith Case Company who was his agent in December 1993.

383 With Keith Daniels (fiddle, mandolin), Curly Stevens (guitar) and Kenny Stevens (mandolin). McCoury had taken the place of Paul Chaney who was with the band until then.

384 Members of this new band were Daniels (fiddle, mandolin), McCoury (banjo), Frank Campbell (guitar), Lloyd Herring (guitar), Sterl Sauble (Dobro) and Wes "Jellybean" Paine (bass).

385 Kimble Blair played fiddle, Cooke, the bass. Cooke had just quit Bill Monroe's Blue Grass Boys to start his own band.

And he told me about all this. I guess he wasn't sure I was gonna want to do this. He said, 'The only thing I know to tell you is that I will try you out for two weeks and if you want to keep doing it I'll get you in the union. So that's the way we did it. He got me in the union there in Nashville.

"I sang with him before this, you know, when Jack Cooke and myself helped him out on a few dates. And I played banjo and sung a part—it could have been baritone. I sung all parts back then, you know. At that time—this was at the New York University—he told me, 'If you come to Nashville I'll give you a job.' He needed people. Jack wouldn't go. He'd done did his tour with Monroe. He also had his own band, **Jack Cooke and the Virginia Playboys**, and I played in that band. Well, the job excited me but I liked that job with Cooke 'cause I could play the banjo, see. So about a month later—I thought about this for a month—I went down there. In the mean time, he heard Bill Keith. He probably liked Bill Keith's playing. And Bill [Keith] was ready to go with Bill [Monroe]... You know, he told me that he '...needed a lead singer the worst in the world. I can't find one. Can you sing lead?' I said no 'cause I didn't know if I could sing with him. 'Cause I had always sung parts. I'd sung tenor and baritone. But my problem was I knew I'd have to learn a lot of songs, verses and things. I did it. At the time, I didn't like it. But now I'm glad I did it."

McCoury didn't really know the impact that being in this band would have on his career. "I was going in there doing two things I wasn't sure I could even do. You know, I wasn't rehearsed at this stuff when I went with him. Now, I was rehearsed at pickin'; I could have picked anything he played. I knew that. I knew I could pick with Monroe. But now play rhythm and sing lead—I didn't know that. So he put me in a tough situation there, you know. I had to learn it pretty fast. And I thought, this can't sound good. It's unrehearsed. But he was easy to sing with. You had to sing pretty hard; I found that out. He was really powerful in those days. I had to really put out because he was so powerful."

McCoury found that he was in a band led by a strict taskmaster, yet each lead singer was required to sing each song the way the singer heard it. "I found out he sings to his lead singers," said McCoury. "If his lead singers sing *this* way, he'll sing that way. If the lead singer changes, he'll change. He's a tenor singer at heart and he sings to his lead man no matter what the guy sounds like. And I think he likes variety in lead singers. I really do. I really thought he was actually an easy man to work for. I really did. I was kind of backward and bashful then and I didn't talk much. And Bill Monroe was the type of guy if he don't feel like talking—and you sense this—then you get along good with him, see. But if you force yourself on him you could become an enemy of his pretty quick. He's temperamental and kind of moody. And he's got a lot of talent. But I got along good with him. And he never actually would say now do this or do that. That's the reason I think he sung to the lead singer. As long as you sung good timing, and good strong rhythm, and you sing strong, he never said anything to you." They recorded, in January of 1964, "Roll On Buddy" and "One of God's Sheep."

When Kenny Baker quit Monroe's band, McCoury recommended his friend and Kenny Baker's cousin, Billy Baker, to Monroe and Billy was subsequently hired. Then "I happened to mention this California thing (a temporary job with the **Golden State Boys**) to Billy and he really wanted to go to California. I was single and everything and I didn't really want to quit Bill, but one thing led to another and we did. We both quit and moved to California," feeling that it would be easy for Monroe to replace him. That was in January of 1964. McCoury and Baker left Monroe to join the **Golden State Boys**[386] with McCoury on banjo. "We played a tour out there. They really wanted me to take a job with [this band]. I didn't take it serious, you know." A better-paying situation presented itself when McCoury and Baker founded their own **Shady Valley Boys**[387] near Norwalk, California. McCoury moved to guitar when he was twenty-five.

He didn't like it in California. In July, due to low monetary returns, the group moved back to McCoury's home in York County, Pennsylvania, where he was in Billy Baker's **Shady Valley Boys** with Bill Keith, Jerry McCoury and Kenny Haddock.[388] McCoury also joined his father's logging business at home. The band separated in 1966 when buddies McCoury and Baker parted ways.

Del founded **Del McCoury and the Dixie Pals** in the summer of 1967. Original members were himself (guitar), Jerry McCoury (bass), Larry Smith (banjo), Bobby Diamond (fiddle) and Dick Laird (mandolin).[389]

---

[386] Band members were Hal Poindexter (guitar, uncle of Tony Rice), Eric White (bass, brother of Clarence and Roland White) and Skip Conover (Dobro). Don Parmley was with the band earlier but was playing with Vern and Rex Gosdin when McCoury arrived on the scene.

[387] Members included Steve Stephenson (banjo) and Mel Durham (bass). The band evolved to Don Eldreth on banjo, Clifford Bare on bass, and then Jerry McCoury on bass.

[388] In addition to working with Chris Warner (banjo) and Vernon "Boatwhistle" McIntyre (bass).

[389] Through the years, the band's mandolinists were Dick Laird (1967-1969), Dick Staber (1969-1974, 1977-1978), Don Eldreth (1974-1981), Ronnie McCoury and Herschel Sizemore (1978-1980).
The banjoists were Larry Smith (1967-1969), Don Eldreth (1969-1970), John Farmer (1970-1971), Bill Runkle (1971-1977), Walter Hensley (1977-1978) and Dick Smith (1978-1981, until Smith joined the Country Gentlemen). The fiddlers were Bobby Diamond (1967-1970), Billy Baker (1970-1971, 1973-1974), Bill Sage (1971-1973), Bill Poffinberger (1974-1977), Sonny Miller (1977-1981, died November 24, 1981, in an automobile accident). The bass players were Jerry McCoury (1967-1969, 1972-1973, 1978-at least 1982), Dewey Renfro (1969-1972, 1973-1978) and Danny Renfro (1978-1979).

Their base was New Freedom, Pennsylvania. On December ninth and tenth, 1967, they recorded for Arhoolie.[390] They then recorded for Rounder, did an album for Grassound, and later recorded for Revonah. An LP on Leather Records was latter reissued by Rebel, and they recorded several more for Rebel.

The band recorded extensively through the years and changed band members regularly. In December 1979, the **Dixie Pals** recorded "Strictly Bluegrass Live"[391] in Mito, Ibaragi, Japan. It was released on Trio Records. Soon, Sizemore left and was replaced by Ronnie McCoury, Del's fourteen-year-old son.

In 1987, Lance LeRoy became the band's agent for about two years. The **Johnson Mountain Boys** had just split up so LeRoy's Lancer Agency had an opening. That year, with son Robbie McCoury on banjo and son Ronnie on mandolin (since 1981), they became the **Del McCoury Band**. Ronnie won IBMA's Mandolinist of the Year three times as of 1996.

Del McCoury was named Top Male Vocalist in 1990, 1991 and 1992 by IBMA, and in 1991 the McCoury name was among the IBMA finalists in almost every category the election process had. They shared top honor for Recorded Event of the Year for their "Families of Tradition" album. Their recordings for the Rounder label have become best sellers. They continue to perform and record into the late-1990s.

Bobby and Dallas Smith

Bobby Smith, Dallas Smith and the Boys from Shiloh

Bobby and Dallas Smith are members of the Bluegrass Hall of Fame. In their thirty-year career, they recorded about thirty albums and tapes as of 1993. We lost Bobby Smith June 24, 1992. Dallas wrote the following so that we might remember his brother and the dedication he had to this music,

Bobby Smith was loved very much. He played bluegrass music for thirty years. Bobby touched and brought happiness into a lot of people's lives with his music. He had terminal cancer and passed away June 24, 1992. Bobby's last request was to perform for his fans in Bean Blossom, Indiana. He attended the festival but was very sick and unable to perform. Bobby and his music will be missed very much.

Alcohol was a big problem with many bands which toured in the old days; it was very prevalent with the **Boys from Shiloh**, too. Dallas, though he doesn't have any scientific information to prove one way or the other, feels that Bobby's problem with alcohol may have been a large factor in his early demise. He spoke about this serious problem, "It wasn't something that ran in the family. It was just something that happened, and I'm almost sure that it was from drinking. Now Bobby drinked a lot. Of course, I, back years ago, did too. But I quit drinking about three years before he did. He quit the last ten years of his life because he wanted to live a Christian life and that's what Bobby did fer the last ten years of his life. We were both raised up in moonshine country. It was good stuff—better than what you could get from a store. I know I drank some that ran a good 190 proof! And they had some that wasn't. The good stuff ran higher proof. The stills was mostly back on the ridge and in the hollers; they had plenty of it."[392]

Toward the end of Bobby's career, he handed the reins to his brother who had played in the **Boys from Shiloh** from the beginning. Dallas told him, "Bobby, I'm not used to all that emcee work; you've always done that. I don't know whether I can or not. He said, 'Well you've done it all along. You just didn't know it. You can do it.'" Dallas continued with the group, recording and performing, carrying on the tradition as **Dallas Smith and the Boys from Shiloh** per the advice of Bobby Smith and Bill Monroe.

Bobby (born January 23, 1937) and Dallas (born June 13, 1934) Smith were born and raised in Overton County, near Cookeville, east middle Tennessee, into a musical family. Dallas remembered, "My daddy played the old thumb banjo (frailing) and my mother played the guitar and then, of course, my aunts and uncles all played guitar or somethin'. The (Lester) Flatts lived across the hill from us and we were all kinfolk. They lived over in the next holler from us and Lester would come over on Saturday night and they'd have a square dance at somebody's house every Saturday night and ever so often they'd come to our house and they'd set all the furniture from the living room out in the yard along with the two-dollar linoleum and they'd have a square dance in the living room there. I know Lester came over an awful lot and he'd pick and sing along with

390 With McCoury (guitar), Bill Emerson (banjo), Wayne Yates (mandolin), Billy Baker (fiddle), Tommy Neal and Dewey Renfro (bass).
391 Members were Del McCoury (guitar), Dick Smith (banjo), Sonny Miller (fiddle), Herschel Sizemore (mandolin) and Jerry McCoury (bass). This was the only recording with Sizemore in the band as a member.
392 Quotations from a February 1993 telephone interview.

my aunts and uncles and my mother. Lester used to straight-pick back then. I do remember that. He didn't always use a thumb pick. Some time after that is when he used a thumb pick.

"We finally moved off into town in probably the early '40s. Lester came down to board with us and he got him a job at one of the mills—I don't know whether it was the ax handle mill or the [wagon wheel] spoke mill. Of course, back then times were real hard. I remember one morning he came to the breakfast table and he looked at the coffee and the coffee was weak that morning, evidently. He looked at it and he says, 'Humm,' he says. 'Looks like the coffee and the water had a lawsuit and the coffee come clear.' Of course, my daddy was pretty high tempered and he just reached over and picked up a pan of biscuits and throwed 'em at him. And then Lester got mad and my dad was mad and so Lester packed his suitcase and moved somewhere into Virginia. I guess that's where he probably started his musical career.

"We used to go over to Sparta in the '50s when him (Lester) and Gladys lived over there. They lived about half block from where his brother lived.[393] This was after he went to work with Bill (Monroe). But it was just a little framed house he lived in over there."

Bobby and Dallas played together as the **Smith Brothers** for a while. The brothers listened to Lester Flatt on the Opry every Saturday night. "Bobby and I used to follow any of the bands that came to town," Dallas recalled. "We'd always tried to get in the shows. I remember one time—this was back when Bill and Lester was playin' the Bangham schoolhouse. That was right out of Cookeville about seven or eight miles— Lester had got me and Bobby in free. We had walked about six mile I guess to where they were playin'. We had to walk over there. We were real young at the time and I remember Earl Scruggs tunin' Lester's guitar while they were playin'. Earl was just pickin' along on his banjo and I remember him just reachin' over and tunin' a string on that guitar. And I thought, 'Boy, he's got an ear!'"

Back in 1948, Roy Acuff ran for Governor of Tennessee...unsuccessfully. Dallas remembered the event. "I can remember all the way back to when Roy Acuff ran for Governor 'cause Bill [Monroe] was supposed to be there along with his ball team, the Blue Grass Boys. Back then, the colored people and white people had separate fairgrounds. And Acuff held his speech over there—I guess because of the ballpark over there. Bill didn't show but the ball team did. I forget what they said was wrong with Bill that time, but anyway, he didn't show up. Of course, I was real disappointed at that. And then I remember Roy gettin' up on the stage. And they was wantin' a speech out of him and he says, 'Well, I'm not too good at speeches, but I'm

gonna show you what I am good at,' and he cut loose on the fiddle."

Bobby quit school early, at the eleventh grade in 1952, but finished it much later. Except for a tour in the Army which began at the time when Dallas got out of the Navy, Bobby's full-time work was always as a musician. He married and went up to Dayton to join his older brother, Dallas, where they played music in the area with Don Swaford in a trio. After working in Dayton, Ohio, during the summer months with Bobby, Dallas (now 18) joined the Navy.

Bobby and Sonny Osborne and Red Allen were there in the Dayton area about the same time that the **Smith Brothers** was there in the '50s. Dallas said, "I remember Bobby and Sonny both were drivin' a cab up there in Dayton. And they were playin' over in Wheelin' on the weekends. But it seemed like there was a lot more goin' on in Nashville than in Dayton so we moved to Nashville. Nashville was more open then for young artists who come into Nashville at that time than it is now. It was easier to make it then than it is now (1993). I've learned a lot more about it since Bobby died than I ever learned in my life—I had to. Bobby wasn't never one for askin' people questions. But I don't care; if I don't know, I'll ask."

The **Smith Brothers**, Bobby and Dallas, along with Don Swaford (whose stage name was Don Ford) who played electric guitar mandolin and bass, went to Nashville to seek their fortune. "We picked up Marion Sumner to play fiddle with us and Lord, we run all over Kentucky and Cincinnati and Dayton and we played all the little places. Lester was now at Madison, Tennessee, and had a nice place up there and he was gonna set us up with a talent agent out of California. He was stayin' at the Sam Davis Hotel and Lester called down and set up an appointment for us to go on down there. We went over and sang him some songs there in the room and he said he liked it and he wanted us to do some songs on tape [for him to take home to California]. He was leavin' town that Friday. Of course, in Nashville we was lost. We didn't know where to do this at [so we never followed up on the tape]. So

393 Lester's brother, Leonard, lost three fingers in the mill at Sparta where he worked. This ended his music playing with his brother in the 1940s.

we ended up leavin' town just like we came in."

They stayed together until Bobby went back to Nashville in November 1960 where he got the idea that perhaps he could get hired by Bill Monroe. He first went to Nashville with Johnny Montgomery. Bobby practiced Monroe's tunes for the next six months. There at the Ryman Auditorium, they were able to obtain employment as sidemen when an extra musician was needed for a performance. In 1961, Bobby Smith joined the **Blue Grass Boys**[394] as a fill-in guitarist.

Bobby played a smooth rhythm guitar. This was a bit different than other recent guitarists with Monroe who played harder. According to Bobby, Monroe had a different timing. "But now Bobby, before he ever took the job with Monroe, he worked awfully hard to develop that timing. Bobby had one of the fastest double licks on a guitar that I've heard down through the years in all the bluegrass bands. He had the fastest hand I ever seen. He hit a down lick *and* an up lick when he hit it. One boy in Nashville now that has a similar lick is Charlie Cushman. It's hard to learn Monroe's timing, but he didn't leave Monroe because he couldn't exactly get his timing the way Monroe wanted it. He left because there wasn't enough money there; at least you can get by on it now. But back then you didn't make much money at all—if you made any at all." According to Bobby, you had to really love it to play it.

When Bobby joined the **Blue Grass Boys**, Dallas went to New Jersey and formed a country music group (the **Cherokee Boys**). Dallas told this writer, "Of course, back then it was all called 'country' music. We did some bluegrass songs and also did a lot of the country songs. I worked a lot of the clubs along the coast of New Jersey. When Bobby quit the **Blue Grass Boys** in early 1962, he formed the **Boys from Shiloh**."[395] They recorded "The Boys From Shiloh" on the Sims label. He called Dallas a few years later to join the band. Except for a short time with the **Greenbriar Boys**, Bobby stayed with the band until he died.

The next year, the **Boys from Shiloh** had a television show in Bowling Green, Kentucky. By 1964[396] they had a television show in Nashville which lasted a year. The group wore Confederate uniforms on stage—part of the challenge to be different from the next band. Dallas, in a 1992 interview at IBMA, described it this way, "A lot of the people up north didn't know what the Confederate uniforms was. They thought we were some kind of busboys or something. So we finally got away from that." The costumes were just for the purpose of putting on a show; there was no significance in the fact that the uniforms were Confederate except, perhaps, that a Civil War battle took place at Shiloh.

In 1967, the group, with Ken, the youngest Smith brother on bass, began a two-year stint with the WWVA Wheeling Jamboree. They recorded two albums for Rural Rhythm. They toured extensively in the east and were very popular. But they only traveled in the east. A trip to the western or central states wasn't worth it, they decided. That would have put more miles on the body and car, cost more to get there, and often wouldn't pay as well.

The band played a part in "Payday" in 1971, a movie which was the story of a musician which starred Rip Torn. In the movie, Dallas sang tenor with Torn and played electric bass, Bobby played steel guitar and the whole band had parts in the movie. It took three weeks to complete their part in the movie.

The group played regularly at Earl Snead's Bluegrass Inn at Nashville, later owned by Hubert Davis. They also played quite a bit at Tut Taylor's Pickin' Parlor when Randy Wood was building instruments there.

In 1976, Bobby Smith partnered with Josh Graves for two years. They recorded an instrumental album for Vetco and two albums for CMH. "We had been workin' an awful lot just before Bobby and Josh joined up," continued Dallas. "And I got to drinkin' real bad. And I had to take some time off. So I did and I moved back to Cookeville and I was off for a year or two when Bobby and Josh joined forces. And one day they were comin' through Cookeville. Bobby called me and I was all bleary-eyed and I then recognized that I've got to get off this alcohol. About a week or two later I straightened up enough and moved back to Nashville. Bobby and Josh had split then and I went back to work."

The 1993 band, with Dallas Smith at the helm, now had as its members Earl Snead (banjo), Tim Graves (Dobro®), Dallas Smith (guitar), Harold Jones (fiddle) and Joe Pointer (bass).

Dr. Neil V. Rosenberg— author, scholar, folklorist, musician, enthusiast.

Another section on Dr. Rosenberg is included in the Regional Bluegrass chapter of this book which describes the history of bluegrass music in the San Francisco Bay Area. This section continues his biography.

---

[394] Members included Bill Monroe (mandolin), Charlie Smith (fiddle), Tony Ellis (banjo) and Bessie Lee Mauldin (bass). During the time that Bobby Smith was with the group, other members to join the BOYS were Vassar Clements (fiddle), Joe Drumright (banjo) and Bobby Atkins (banjo). Ellis recommended Bobby Smith for the job.

[395] Bobby left the Blue Grass Boys (at the same time as Vassar Clements left) to organize the Boys from Shiloh with himself (lead and rhythm guitar), Big Al Holderfield (banjo), Charlie Nixon (resonator guitar), Earl White (fiddle) and Johnny Montgomery (bass).

[396] In 1964, the Boys from Shiloh recorded "Dear Heart" which did well on the national charts. Musicians were Bobby Smith (guitar), Rual Yarbrough (banjo) and Herschel Sizemore (mandolin). Others of that era included Al Holderfield, Johnny Montgomery (bass), Charlie Nixon (resonator guitar), Bruce Weathers and Richard Hoffman (fiddle), Tom McKinney, Frasier Moss and Marty Lanham (banjo).

Married and beginning graduate studies in folklore and ethnomusicology at Indiana University in 1961, Rosenberg began meeting and playing music with old-time country and bluegrass musicians in southern Indiana and Ohio, a hot-bed of bluegrass activity.

Rosenberg wrote, "I began my involvement in the Indiana music scene at the most public and high-profile of the country music performance venues, the Brown County Jamboree in Bean Blossom. Every Sunday afternoon and evening from early spring to late fall, country music shows were held in the 'barn' on this private park site located on the main road from Indianapolis to the county seat, Nashville, Indiana. Scenic Brown County is a popular tourist destination, but in 1961, the Brown County Jamboree was not one of the county's tourist attractions. A seedy, rundown place, the Jamboree was an embarrassment to those members of the local chamber of commerce who knew about it. Its owner, Grand Ole Opry star Bill Monroe, had a loyal following, but he and the Jamboree had fallen on hard times. Shows were poorly attended. In the late 1950s, it was discovered by the Bloomington High School folk-music revival scene. A couple whom I'd met through this scene took me to Bean Blossom to see Monroe."

In June of 1961, Rosenberg and friends went to see Bill Monroe at Bean Blossom, Indiana, just twenty miles from his university in Bloomington. There were no more than forty people in the audience that day. Bill Monroe soon arrived with his band which was Shorty Sheehan (fiddle), Bobby Smith (guitar), Tony Ellis (banjo) and Bessie Lee Mauldin (bass). Rosenberg got a chance to play a tune for Monroe, "Bury Me Beneath the Willow," and Neil never forgot Monroe's encouraging, "That boy's gonna make a fine banjo player." Rosenberg became a frequent addition to the Bean Blossom house band with Shorty and Juanita Sheehan.

On October 22, 1961, Rosenberg played his first full show with Bill Monroe on-stage at Bean Blossom. Rosenberg remembered that "I was very nervous. I kept asking what key the next song was going to be in. I think Bobby Smith gave me the wrong key intentionally one time. (This, he found, was a sort of on-the-job hazing.) I didn't have any time to decide what banjo tune to play and I blew a lot of breaks. I didn't even know 'Georgia Rose,' which Bill said was a good number for the banjo. I remember apologizing to him after the show. He said, 'That's all right—you done the best you could.'" Rosenberg also recalled that Monroe stood right next to him on stage with his mandolin right in his ear. Neil figured that this was Monroe's way to teach him the timing which he required. Vassar was the fiddler at the time, Birch played bass, Jimmy Maynard and Bobby Smith played guitars.

Rosenberg was still at Indiana University in 1962 when Mayne Smith joined him and began attendance in the folklore program. They played in the **Pigeon Hill Boys.** Back in Berkeley, California, in 1963, Neil and Mayne played the final **Redwood County Ramblers** gig. In 1963, 1964 and 1965, Rosenberg won the banjo contest at Bean Blossom. During that time, he played banjo with **Bill Monroe and the Blue Grass Boys** several times and in 1963 managed Monroe's Brown County Jamboree at Bean Blossom. Monroe's booking agent/manager at the time was Ralph Rinzler and wanted Rosenberg to run it because he could do it more efficiently than Birch Monroe was doing. Bill was furious at first, but soon recognized that Neil was doing a good job.

Rosenberg began as the banjoist with the house band at Bean Blossom's **Brown County Boys**[397] at that same time. They changed their name in 1965 to **Stoney Lonesome Boys** and did occasional gigs in the area.

Rosenberg finished grad school in 1968 and had more time to develop his own style of music—which didn't include much bluegrass. After a 1968 move to Memorial University of Newfoundland in the Department of Folklore, he became an archivist and professor of folklore, continuing into the 1990s to teach on both the graduate and undergraduate levels on such topics as folksong, ethnomusicology, oral history and Canadian folklore. He received a Ph.D. in folklore in 1970.

In 1974, Rosenberg published *Bill Monroe and His Blue Grass Boys: An Illustrated Discography* (Country Music Foundation, Nashville, 1974). His *Bluegrass: A History* (University of Illinois Press, 1985) is generally acknowledged to be a definitive work on the music known as bluegrass. As of 1991, he had published over fifty essays in books and numerous articles in scholarly journals. His regular contributions to *Bluegrass Unlimited*'s "Thirty Years Ago Today" has brought him great renown. From 1984 to 1991 he was a deejay on "Bluegrass Country" at CKIX-FM in St. John's Newfoundland, Canada, where he lives and teaches. Neil Rosenberg received a Award of Merit from IBMA in 1986. In 1991, Rosenberg was voted Bluegrass Feature Writer of the Year for the third year in a row by SPBGMA. His band, **Crooked Stovepipe**, released a commercial cassette tape in 1993 and a CD in 1995.

The John Edwards Memorial Collection and Foundation (JEMF)

Australian John Edwards was twenty-eight when he was killed in a car wreck on Christmas Eve of 1960. He died on the way to the airport, planning to leave Australia to come to the United States to be closer to the music which he loved: early American country music. He was to be affiliated with the Folklore Department at the University of California at Los Angeles.

[397] Other members were Roger Smith (fiddle), Vern McQueen, Osby Smith and Jim Bessire.

He knew as much about early country music as almost anyone at the time. He had a collection that included two thousand 78s of early country music, many songbooks, picture folios and other memorabilia, and much correspondence from important figures in the music. There were also field tapes, interviews of famous early stars, LPs and 45s. The total collection included 14,000 items though the 78s are the most well-known.

He bequeathed all of his records to American collectors. His will stipulated that the entire collection remain intact and be moved to the United States. Although he was Australian, due to the efforts of several dedicated enthusiasts, his wish was granted—but not easily. Because of the size of this extensive collection of folk and country music, the John Edwards Memorial Foundation (JEMF) was founded to house it.

The John Edwards Memorial Collection spent twenty-one years at UCLA's Folklore and Mythology Center but the Board of Directors of JEMF felt that UCLA was not providing enough funding or institutional support, and that the collection was not being fully utilized. Its subsequent relocation to the University of North Carolina at Chapel Hill was intended to return the collection to the South where the music began. It was also evident that the University had a history of support for this type of thing and that the collection would be cared for and adequately utilized. The UNCCH purchased the JEMF in February 1983. Folklorist Archie Green facilitated the move; it was incorporated into the Southern Folklife Collection. It can now be accessed by interested parties for research in this field.

Bluegrass Banjo - Table of Contents

Bluegrass Banjo

Of all the instruments used in a bluegrass band, none seems to identify the genre more than the banjo. When a person hears a five-string banjo, most people think of bluegrass. And when one thinks of bluegrass, those thoughts are generally linked with the banjo.

Jerry Douglas related that it is easy to identify the bluegrass genre. He said in a 1992 telephone interview, "But for bluegrass music in general, people think of banjos, mandolins, high singing. Everybody has a different definition but I feel that a real bluegrass band does have a banjo and is important in its role in the band." Asked if a song could be bluegrass without a banjo, he said, "I think it's still bluegrass music. Just because you take one instrument away from it doesn't mean it's not bluegrass. The banjo is an important instrument in bluegrass music, though. It's really hard to classify exactly what bluegrass is."[1]

This chapter covers this topic, some of the history of the banjo, and some of bluegrass' significant banjo players who are not discussed in the Pioneers chapter, the Roots chapter, or the Branches chapter of this book. For instance, Earl Scruggs is a pioneer in bluegrass music, not just a banjo player, so his biography is in the Pioneers chapter. Those who appear in this chapter are placed in an approximate chronological order in which they appeared on the scene as a professional bluegrass banjo player.

The history of the banjo

Chuck Ogsbury, of Ome Banjos[2], was kind enough to contribute this historical data on the banjo. The words were borrowed from his catalog.

Combining both the thump of the skin drum with the twang of the hunting bow, the banjo is one of the oldest of all stringed instruments. Its rhythmic, percussive melodies were first brought to America by African blacks during the early 1700s.

In the early 1800s, the banjo was adopted by a handful of white musicians such as Joel Sweeney[3] and Dan Emmit. These early players altered its construction somewhat and began to spread the banjo and its music throughout America in traveling minstrel shows during the 1830s and '40s.

The following decades changed the banjo in even more ways. The neck was shortened and frets were added to improve playability. Innovative tone rings provided both greater volume and the improved tone necessary for large concert halls. The minstrel's enthusiastic "stroke-style" of playing gave way to the gentle classic finger-style. Elaborate ornamentation transformed many instruments into stunning works of artistry and design. By the end of the 19th century, the traditional five-string banjo had reached a peak in its development. Thanks to virtuoso players like Alfred Farland and Fred Van Eps, it had become one of the most popular musical instruments in Victorian America.

The early decades of the 20th century took the banjo from the parlors of Victorian America into the dance halls and concert theaters of the great cities. Electricity was lighting the streets and "jazz" was electrifying the nation! Banjos began to need greatly increased volume and resonance to be heard over the other instruments in the jazz bands, and a new, high-spirited playing style started to develop that was very different from that of the traditional five-string. Steel strings quickly replaced gut, the fifth string was eliminated, the scale length and tuning were changed, and the instrument was played with a flatpick instead of with the fingers—giving birth to the modern tenor and plectrum jazz banjos. This lively period brought fantastic innovations in tonal systems and resonators, as well as numerous other technical advances and artistic embellishments. It was truly the Golden Age of the jazz banjo.

Closed-back, or "standard" side wall resonator banjos were first made in the mid-1870s, as five-string instruments by Henry C. Dobson of New York. This design did not reach wide popularity, however, until William L. Lange offered it on his Paramount banjos in 1921. Tenor and plectrum players, such as Michael Pingatore and Harry Reser, soon discovered its improved volume and resonant characteristics and this style quickly became one of the most popular banjos ever offered.

---

[1] 1992 telephone interview.

[2] Ome is based in Boulder, Colorado. A short description of the history of Ome/Ode/Baldwin banjos is in the Instrument Companies and Makers chapter of this book.

[3] Sweeney is often the man given credit for adding the fifth string to the instrument. The famed banjo made by Joel Walker Sweeney in 1840 is in the Los Angeles County Museum.

When urban musical tastes changed during the 1920s and '30s, the five-string banjo returned again to the rural folk tradition. The remnants of the classical style were transformed into the old-time finger style of players like Charlie Poole and Snuffy Jenkins [Poole and Jenkins picked quite differently—author] and eventually became bluegrass. The old minstrel "stroke" playing evolved into the well-known frailing style of players such as Uncle Dave Macon, Pete Seeger, and the more subtle clawhammer playing of Wade Ward and Fred Cockerham.

Top-tension banjos were first made and patented by George Teed of New York City. Around 1886, he added a deep-walled resonator. Later, classical player and composer Joseph Cammeryer of Brooklyn modified the design and took it to England where it became popular as the English "zither" banjo. Plectrum artist Eddie Peabody is credited with bringing the design back to America where it was further refined by the Vega Company of Boston and became one of the most unique jazz banjos of the late 1920s and '30s.

The Great Depression brought the Roaring Twenties to a crashing end. Changing musical tastes and new recording techniques soon brought the same fate to the popular use of the jazz banjo. The bright, enthusiastic sound of the banjo did not begin to re-emerge until after World War II with both a revival of Dixieland jazz and also in a spirited new form of music called "bluegrass". Bill Monroe, Earl Scruggs, and other bluegrass musicians borrowed heavily from both traditional and jazz playing styles to create their hard-driving tunes. Even the type of banjo adopted for this music was an unusual mix of styles—a rare five-string version of an instrument designed primarily for four-string jazz.

"A great deal of ink has been spilled in the banjo world over the controversy of the fifth string," wrote Karen Linn. "Through the years, most banjoists have credited Joel Walker Sweeney with the invention of the fifth string. Presumably this happened sometime during the late 1820s. The new string generally was assumed

Earl Scruggs about 1963 using his tuners at Oberlin College. Photo courtesy Mark Schoenberg.

to be the short thumb string. Evidence suggests that if Sweeney did 'invent' the fifth string, it was probably the bass string, not the thumb string. Perhaps the most convincing evidence of this is the painting, 'The Old Plantation' (painted sometime between 1777 and 1800), in which an African-American banjoist plays a gourd banjo that clearly has a tuning peg placed halfway up the neck."[4] The work of Dr. Cecelia Conway and others establishes that the "fifth string" as we call it today was not the fifth string added. The short drone string goes back to Africa. The round head, however, only dates to the mid-19th century, according to Conway.

Thomas Jefferson, in 1782, wrote in his "Notes on Virginia" that "the banjar is the chief instrument of the American Negro."

And another point of discussion might be when an instrument with an animal skin stretched across it becomes a banjo. A Japanese instrument has that same feature, and *it* is not a banjo (either samisen or the jaymisen, which are very similar). And whether the banjo is a uniquely American instrument is, according to George Gruhn, highly debatable, for some researchers note that the banjo's first appearance in the gourd and string form goes back to 1678 in Martinique in the Caribbean where it is noted that the *banza* was played by blacks.

Following the further evolution of the banjo in America, research shows that the tenor banjo, because of its similar tuning to the mandolin and increased volume, overtook the mandolin in popularity around 1920. Accordingly, the mandolin orchestras died out and the banjo orchestras began appearing in the 1930s. The tenor banjo was invented in 1907 and rose to popularity, according to many sources, with its association with the tango dance craze which arrived in America from Argentina in 1910. Originally called the "tango banjo", it became a part of "Dixieland" music which had begun during the tango craze decade. The makers of the five-string banjo picked up on the tenor banjo (and the "plectrum" banjo—so named because the plectrum is another name for the flatpick) craze and converted their production to these instruments. It was during the 1910s and 1920s that most of the resonator and tone ring designs so common today were created.

4 Karen Linn, *That Half-Barbaric Twang—The Banjo in American Popular Culture* (Illinois: The University of Illinois Press, 1991), p. 2.

The Gibson company (today the Gibson Guitar Corporation) entered the tenor banjo market in 1918 and "wasted no time in using a combination of aggressive marketing, innovation, and quality production to gain a competitive position."[5] Soon Lloyd Loar, the man behind Gibson's Master Series mandolins and guitars, enabled the banjo to join the Series and it soon became the "Mastertone." Most of the five-string Mastertones from this period are converted tenor banjos. Resonators were introduced to their banjos in 1925. Gibson's five-string or RB (regular banjo) was introduced in 1924 in the -3 and -4 styles. The archtop came along at this time and the flathead came along in the early 1930s.

The first banjo was patented in 1859

Patent number 25,872 was a five-string banjo and was registered to Mr. S.F. Van Hagan in 1859. Though many people may think that the five-string came after the four-string, that is incorrect because no plectrum or tenor banjos were manufactured until well after 1900.

Picking styles

The earliest bluegrass banjo style, and the one which thrust bluegrass music into the limelight, is the three-finger style made popular by Earl Scruggs. It featured the melody note of a tune surrounded by a continuous stream of fill-in notes. Usually the melody is plucked by the thumb. The Thumb, the Index finger, and the Middle fingers move in a variety of patterns including forward motion (TIM) or backward motion (MIT) as well as combinations such as TITM.

According to "Doctor Banjo", Peter Wernick, the melodic style can be defined as every note picked having a melodic value. The technique of melodic banjo picking is that the player must always switch fingers and strings for each consecutive note played. This allows the right hand to move more freely and quickly through melodic passages and allows each string to ring a little longer (to sustain). Bobby Thompson and Bill Keith are usually given credit for "inventing" this style and its application to bluegrass music.

Don Reno and Eddie Adcock played and popularized the single-string style. This style imitates the flat pick, often using consecutive notes on a single string to play the melody. The player uses a higher or lower string if the melody requires it. The right hand picks this string alternatively with the thumb and first finger. This style

obviously prohibits the sustain achieved by the melodic style. It's rather difficult to do well and, as a result, not as popular as the Scruggs or melodic styles. A good example of this single-string style can be found on the Don Reno recording of "Follow the Leader." Greg Cahill, leader of **Special Consensus**, uses this style in many of his instrumentals as does Don Wayne Reno, Don's son.

Bill Keith described his music as "melodic" rather than "chromatic". "In all fairness," he said, "most of the tunes that I was into used more notes of a major scale. The word 'chromatic' refers to, shall we say, non-scalar notes. If you are in the key of C, which is the white keys on the piano, then the black keys are the chromatic tones in the C scale. The word 'chromatic' started to apply when things got into a bluesy and a more angular way of playing that was not my original approach. Bobby Thompson was the first that I was ever aware of [who did that]. Ask Doug Dillard. He told me once that somebody brought a tape across the country of a jam session or something that I was playing in and he heard this and out came 'Banjo in the Hollow' which had sort of a melodic little thing in the front of it."[6]

Bobby Thompson, Courtney Johnson and Jack Hicks who introduced a style called chromatic which uses the chromatic scales in addition to the major notes called for in the melody. This enhances the song, adds flair and sophistication to the song. The use of flatted 3rds, 5ths, and 7ths gives it a more "modernesque" sound.

One man's history of melodic banjo picking—well before Bobby Thompson and Bill Keith

1972 was the year of the release of "Magnum Banjos" by Brown, Sullivan and Company. The group never became well known, but the twin banjo LP did among bluegrass banjoists. It featured the twin banjos of Ed Brown and Fred Sullivan.

Ed Brown, in an interview at IBMA in 1992, described early melodic banjo playing. He began by speaking of Billy Faier.[7] "I first heard of Billy Faier in 1966. I got holt of a banjo player I had known for several years at the time in the Chattanooga area. His name was Bob Johnson. Bob had an album of Billy Faier's which was released in 1957 and he called it "The Art of the Five String Banjo." And on that recording, he was playing with three fingers on his five-string banjo and

---

[5] George Gruhn and Walter Carter, *Acoustic Guitars and Other Fretted Instruments* (San Francisco: GPI Books, 1993) p. 124.
In a conversation with Mr. Gruhn in 1996, he noted that Gibson was actually a minor player in the manufacture of desirable tenor banjos. The more popular brands include Vega, Bacon and the current banjos like Ome. "Bluegrass players are wild about Gibson Mastertones but that doesn't mean that anybody else is. It happens that the bluegrass banjo is 90% of the market these days. Old-timey players, in general, don't care for Gibson."

[6] From a 1992 telephone interview.

[7] Billy Faier played a long-necked, open-backed banjo in style dissimilar to bluegrass styles. He mostly played folk tunes in a classical style, sometimes accompanied by a guitarist. His prime was the late 1950s. His two LPs on the Riverside label, according to Larry Sandberg in his *Folk Music Sourcebook*, featured "a triumphantly unique concept of the instrument, based on tasteful adaptations of traditional and original elements." He recorded three LPs, his last in 1973 for Takoma Records.

he had a guitar player (Frank Hamilton) with him. And he played 'Sailor's Hornpipe' basically the way bluegrassers do it today except that we've souped it up and speeded it up and put a few more notes in it. But it had a lot of melodic-type banjo playing. Of course, he got a lot of pull-offs and push-offs and a lot of ornamentation, but he also played 'Mrs. McCloud's Reel.' Later on, we put that on the second (and last) 'Magnum Banjos' album.

"I also have a recording released in about 1926 on the Sears and Roebuck Record label by Fred Van Eps, another famous banjo player. And he was playing with two or three fingers, whatever he was using, the 'Sailor's Hornpipe' about like we do it today. It was a little less notes than a modern bluegrasser would do today but the basics were still there. He played some other fiddle tunes on there, too. One of them was a fiddle tune that Tommy Jackson called 'Lead Out.' A little 'Arkansas Traveler' on there.

"So what I'm tryin' to say, I guess, is that melodic banjo pickin' has been around for a long time... And then there was a lot of melodic-type banjo playin' in other aspects of music that's been around even longer than that. Back in the 1800s they had it. They had written music for it. Classical banjo playing [which was used back then] is kind of a ragtime-type stuff—but they do it with three fingers and bring out the melody a lot more prominent than the standard Scruggs style would."

Charlie Poole

Charlie Poole— an early form of three-finger playing

Charlie Poole was born in Alamance County, North Carolina. With his **North Carolina Ramblers**, he pioneered the technique of singing to a full string band which served as a bridge between the era of string bands and the era of vocal

stars. He recorded 110 sides with his **Ramblers** under many labels including the song "Don't Let Your Deal Go Down." This song, along with "Let Those Brown Eyes Smile at Me" and White House Blues" were later re-done by **Flatt and Scruggs** on Columbia. Poole was a very popular string band performer of the twenties, and one of the few who were professional musicians with no other means of support.

By 1923, Poole had a form of three-finger banjo playing, just as concert banjoists of late 1800s had their own. Some history buffs may recall that Charlie Poole's version of "Flop Eared Mule" for Puritan Records (3002) showed an inclination toward a three-finger style earlier than 1923. He died before he fully developed the style. (Snuffy Jenkins, whom we will discuss later, had never heard of Poole or followed his style. Jenkins' style was patterned after individuals near his North Carolina home.)

Poole died of a heart attack at age 39 in 1931 while celebrating[8] a contract to go to Hollywood to play in a short feature, like Jimmie Rodgers did with his "Waiting for a Train."

Mack Crowe and Clay Everhart: Two very early three-finger banjo players

"Uncle" Mack Crowe (January 5, 1897, to November 8, 1966) billed himself as the "Banjo King of the Carolinas". He played in the 1920s in a touring, vaudeville string band which played the Loews Theater circuit. The **Blue Ridge Ramblers** had ten members in it and the pictures of the band which exist today can lead us to assume that their instruments were probably furnished by the Gibson company.

Crowe usually won top banjo honors wherever he competed. His acrobatic antics were celebrated and well-remembered. He never used a strap, relying on muscular strength to hold up and manipulate his Mastertone. According to one man's remembrances, "My father told me that Mack would have as many as ten vests made up out of very thin material, and during his showpiece ("John Henry") where he twirled the banjo, he would take off one vest at a time, then at the end he'd remove the last one and never stopped his banjo picking during all of this."[9] These show antics probably overshadowed his three-finger style, little of which is known today. He was recorded, but few recordings survive.

Another early three-finger banjoist whose music came along at the same time as Snuffy Jenkins's early playing was Clay Everhart (June 9, 1890, to December 31, 1963) from Lexington, North Carolina. Everhart reportedly learned to play his three-finger style from a man named Cooper. Apparently Everhart and brothers

[8] He drank himself to death at the party.

[9] Clarence H. Greene, "Mack Crowe and Clay Everhart—Early Carolina Banjo Pickers," *Bluegrass Unlimited*, March, 1986, p. 64.

Tom and Dewey Cooper played as a trio, using guitar, fiddle and banjo respectively, as the **North Carolina Cooper Boys** and recorded for Okeh Records in late September 1927, and again in October 1931, for Columbia.

Johnny Whisnant told of a 1935 banjo competition where "I won second place in a banjo contest against Tell Reed and old man Clay Everhart...Hess Starr...and Hubert Lowe, he was a banjo player back in that day, too...and he was good. They all played like Snuffy Jenkins, you know, or similar to that. Even though this Lowe fellow was a better banjo player than Mr. Everhart, he didn't have that sound; he didn't have what I wanted. When I seen Mr. Everhart play with them three-fingers, I had to know that..." Whisnant then hired Everhart to teach him that music. Clay Everhart played an original flathead Gibson Granada 5-string.

Lute Isenhour

According to **Blue Sky Boy** Bill Bolick, Isenhour was one of the best five-string banjo players of the day (1935). "Isenhour picked a three-finger style similar to the bluegrass style. However, he didn't slur the strings or try to syncopate the melody." It was very similar to the playing of Snuffy Jenkins. Bolick and Isenhour played music together as young lads growing up, occasionally performing near their homes.

Snuffy Jenkins

Photo courtesy Pappy Sherrill.

Snuffy Jenkins— *the* pioneer bluegrass banjoist?

Don Reno knew Jenkins well and remembered, "There was other fellas that played with three-fingers before Snuffy, but he was the first one who ever put it together. It's like seeing a river winding and you don't know where it's going and then finally you see it straightened out going into the ocean. That's the best way I can explain it. When I heard Snuffy, I could see that he unwound something and straightened it out to the point where it did have a flowing melody to it and not a bunch of jerks and stops and this, that, and the other thing. He had perfected, as far as I'm concerned, a three-finger roll."[10]

Dewitt "Snuffy" Jenkins was born in Rutherford County, Harris, North Carolina, on October 27, 1908, into a musical family. The family band included Dewitt on banjo and guitar with his brother, Verl, on fiddle. Verl played for dances and fiddlers' conventions in the 1920s. Dewitt played in the popular melody-led two-finger banjo style.

In 1913, Dewitt Jenkins (5) got his start in the entertainment world doing a clog dance for a sawmill company show and, as he put it, "Folks thought I was wormy, I danced so fast. So they put me to chewing tobacco, and I haven't got rid of the worms yet!" His first instrument was the fiddle but because he was too small to use the bow, he picked it like a mandolin. Soon, both he and Verl played guitar at local social functions. The young boys each built their own banjos: one from a wagon hub and one from an automobile brake drum. From these primitive instruments Snuffy knew he wanted the real thing; he bought a new Sears and Roebuck in 1927. He was a self-taught musician who played "by ear" and could not read a note of music. When he liked a song that he heard, he would simply remember the tune and adapt it to his banjo playing which was, until about 1927, a two-finger style of picking.

Dewitt and Verl began performing for square dances in 1927 with Dewitt's new Sears banjo. That year, Dewitt met Smith Hammett and Rex Brooks of Cleveland County, North Carolina. He related, "So I heard those fellas playing and that kind of stuck with me a little bit and I picked it up from them."[11] It was with this influence that he switched from the two-finger style to the three-finger style.

Rex Brooks played with his fingernails and a thumbpick. It wasn't loud. Snuffy remembered that Smith Hammett "played with his fingernails 'til his middle finger got so sore from playing for dancing he couldn't stand it and he went to using his index and ring fingers with picks." Hammett never recorded. Brooks and Hammett also directly influenced Earl and Junie Scruggs.

By 1934, Dewitt and Verl had their own **Jenkins String Band** on WBT, Charlotte, North Carolina, where they were sponsored by Crazy Water Crystals Barn Dance. This was probably the first time anyone had ever played this three-finger style banjo style on the air. By that time, Dewitt had established himself as one of the first pickers of the five-string banjo in the three-

10 Trischka, "Snuffy Jenkins," *Bluegrass Unlimited*, October, 1977, p. 20.
11 Ibid.

finger style—not that he was the first, of course, but he was in the right place at the time to receive this recognition.

Also in the Cleveland County area were Don Reno and Earl Scruggs. "I don't claim to have taught Scruggs or Reno either one," said Snuffy, "but I was about the first to go on the air with this type of playing. And any time that they just happened to be around, I was glad to show them anything I could."[12] Snuffy told Tony Trischka, "Don Reno claims that I taught him everything he knows 'cause he was playing in South Carolina, too. In fact, I sold him a banjo—a pre-war gold plated banjo for $90. He traded Earl and now Earl's got it. I noticed that me and Earl got pretty much the same lick on a lot of stuff."[13]

In the fall of 1936, Dewitt joined **J.E. Mainer's Mountaineers** at WSPA, Spartanburg, South Carolina.[14] Jenkins and the band then recorded for Bluebird. This was Snuffy's first time recording. Some historians label these recordings among the first commercial recordings of what would later be called "bluegrass music". For the next ten years, they traveled more than 250,000 miles and entertained more than 600,000 people.

In late 1938, J.E. Mainer left his **J.E. Mainer's Mountaineers**. Byron Parker, known as "The Old Hired Hand", took over the group and called it **Byron Parker's Mountaineers** there at WIS in Columbia. This band soon changed its name to **Byron Parker and the WIS Hillbillies**. Band members were Parker, Snuffy, Verl (fiddle), George Morris (guitar) and Leonard "Handsome" Stokes (guitar). Verl was the first fiddler but was physically unable to travel so Parker convinced Homer "Pappy" Sherrill to join the band in October of 1939. Dewitt and Pappy Sherrill began a merger of friendship and musicianship to create a legacy that lasted until Jenkins' death in 1990. Dewitt played banjo, guitar and the washboard. Earl Scruggs heard Jenkins about this time, when Snuffy and **Byron Parker and the WIS Hillbillies** played near the Jenkins home.

During this period, Dewitt Jenkins was named "Snuffy" because he would frequently rub his nose with the back of his hand and sniff. Instead of "Sniffy", they labeled him "Snuffy". He told that the nose-rubbing came from the times he was doing his comedy routines when "I was playing the role of a woman—dress, pocketbook, and all. I kept wiping my nose with the sleeve of that dress and Byron started calling me 'Snuffy'. The name stuck and today even my wife calls me Snuffy."[15] According to Don Reno, Snuffy "was great on the banjo then. He was playing then as good as Scruggs was playing in '48. He's definitely the man that got his stuff together. I'll tell you that first."[16]

Television was just getting started in 1953, and many radio stations jumped on the bandwagon to start their own television shows using the same artists they had on their radio shows. On November 7th, WIS featured the **Hired Hands** on the first day of the brand new television show they were running. They soon had their own early-morning show, "Carolina in the Morning," which led to a prime time Wednesday night show and a Sunday morning gospel show.

Snuffy talked about his music. "I've never called my music anything other than 'country.' We were playing bluegrass years before it received the name... You hear some of the old stuff today but it's not like we have always done it."

In 1956, Snuffy's banjo playing was included in what we now consider the first bluegrass album, "American Banjo, Tunes and Songs in Scruggs Style" (Folkways 2314).[17]

In 1958, Pappy Sherrill left the music business to go into the grocery business—he had a stomach ulcer and had to quit the road to get away from the pressure. His replacement in **Snuffy Jenkins, Pappy Sherrill and the Hired Hands** on the fiddle was Roger Miller, who was stationed at nearby Fort Jackson, South Carolina.[18]

On August 14th, 1966, the Country Music Association presented Snuffy, Pappy and Greasy Medlin with an honorary lifetime membership and a plaque stating that the three men represented over 100 years of continual country music performing. In 1970, Snuffy won the third annual Carter Stanley Memorial Award for his outstanding contribution to bluegrass music.

On April 30, 1990, Dewitt "Snuffy" Jenkins (81) passed away in Columbia, South Carolina, following a recurrence of colon cancer. He is credited as bridging

---

12 Pat Ahrens, "The Snuffy Jenkins Story," *Bluegrass Unlimited*, November, 1967, pp. 1-2.

13 Trischka, op. cit., p. 21. In 1937, Dewitt Jenkins moved to Columbia and met Fisher Hendley whose band was Fisher Hendley and the Aristocratic Pigs. Hendley was also a banjo player. He sold his old, gold-plated Gibson Granada to Snuffy. In 1943, Snuffy bought a banjo he liked even better from a pawn shop for $40 and used this one for the rest of his career. He sold the Granada to Don Reno in 1940 for $90. In 1948, Reno traded that banjo to Scruggs with a Martin guitar for a 1934 RB-3 (with a -4 neck) Mastertone which Scruggs had. Scruggs used the Granada (#9584-3) throughout the Flatt and Scruggs era.

14 J.E. and his brother Wade Mainer had just split. J.E. kept on with his Mountaineers while Wade teamed up with Zeke Morris and soon formed his own band.

15 Ray Thigpen, "A Legend in His Own Time," *Bluegrass Unlimited*, June, 1987, p. 11.

16 Tony Trischka and Peter Wernick, *Masters of the 5-String Banjo, In Their Own Words and Music*, p. 90.

17 This record was produced by Peter Kuykendall and Mike Seeger. It is sometimes called: "American Banjo, Scruggs Style." It featured Oren Jenkins, Junie Scruggs, Larry Richardson, Eric Weissberg and several others. See Technology and the Recording Industry chapter of this book for more on this topic.

18 The lead guitarist at the time, Lacy Richardson, recalled: "Roger didn't have a car so I would give him a ride to the TV station. All the time he would be doing these funny sounds that he later made famous on his million-selling record 'Dang Me.'" After a few months Miller was transferred from his military post so Pappy came back—to stay.

the gap between old-time and bluegrass music. Don Reno said of Snuffy, "He's one of the finest gentlemen I ever knew, and he really taught me how to play a banjo."[19]

Hoke Jenkins

Nephew of Snuffy Jenkins, Hoke Jenkins was one of the earliest banjoists to successfully apply the three-finger roll to country music. His fame never reached the proportions of his skill, probably because the banjo playing of Earl Scruggs overshadowed all other banjo players during that time, and Hoke's playing didn't have the "drive" to set it apart as a lead instrument.

Hoke Jenkins was born into a musical environment August 4, 1917, in Harris, North Carolina. His father played fiddle, his brother Oren, the banjo. His Uncle Snuffy didn't teach him to play the banjo. It was mainly Hoke's environment that fostered that desire. And it was Hoke that introduced the washboard as a musical instrument to Snuffy, who is often given credit for popularizing it by using it in his comedy act.

By age sixteen, Hoke was fluent on most stringed instruments used in country music. His style of playing the banjo was different than Scruggs and Snuffy because he had sort of a lope in his playing—his three-finger style mostly used a backwards roll; it was not as polished as Scruggs' style. As banjo instructor Pete Wernick put it, when a person's roll is restricted to either the backwards or to the forward roll, the melody has a hard time fitting in. The result is that the melody may be forced into a position which isn't convenient to that particular roll. The music is choppy. Wernick recalled listening to Hoke Jenkins' early work with **Jim and Jesse and the Virginia Boys** and labeled it as being

somewhat primitive and old-timey. But Jenkins had another attribute which kept him ably employed as a country music performer: comedy.

Hoke's first radio performance at age twenty-two in 1939 was with the Franklin brothers and two others on WSPA, Spartanburg, on a Saturday show from one to five p.m.. Fiddlin' Arthur Smith played backup fiddle. Later in 1939, he became the banjoist the **Morris Brothers** with Zeke, Wiley and George Morris in Asheville on WWNC's North Carolina Farm Hour. Hoke stayed two years until he was drafted. Zeke Morris spoke of their music, "We had a good, clean, wholesome stage show along with the music. Hoke was an extremely good banjo player and he was comical with it. He was as good an entertainer as you could find anywhere and he was a good person along with it."[20]

When Hoke was drafted in 1940, Don Reno took his place with the **Morris Brothers**, followed by Earl Scruggs. Hoke served nearly five years in the military and got out in 1945. He then joined Carl Story late that year at WWNC. They soon moved to Knoxville where they performed regularly on the Mid-Day Merry Go-Round on WNOX.[21]

Country music did very well financially after the War. Hoke started his own **Smoky Mountaineers** in 1945.[22] This lasted two years. According to Hoke's wife, Rose Jenkins, "With the radio business, they did well if they stayed two years." It seemed like profitable show dates in one area which were promoted through radio exposure ran out after awhile. "It would get old,"[23] she said.

In 1948, Hoke and Carl Smith moved to WGAC, Augusta, Georgia. The Shelton brothers, who were with the band at the time, stayed behind at WWNC. Smith was soon to become a big star on the Opry. Jenkins' band did well in the Augusta area, mainly due to Hoke's popularity. Various musicians came and went. When the Murphy brothers left his band, he called Curly Seckler about working with the group. Seckler said he would join if he could bring the McReynolds brothers, who were just beginning their music career. The trio of Seckler, Jim, and Jesse were glad to find a job in spite of the low pay. Seckler left to join **Flatt and Scruggs** in Bristol on March 17, 1949. Hoke continued with his **Smoky Mountaineers**; Jim and Jesse soon moved on.

Wiley Morris was with Hoke and his band occasionally. He described their appearances in Augusta, "Back in them days, we was chargin' 35 cents and 60 or 75 cents. But when I first started, it was 15 and 25 cents general admission. We was sponsored by schools and theaters; we wasn't guaranteed nothin'. We furnished

[19] Trischka and Wernick, op. cit..

[20] Julie Knight, "Hoke Jenkins—Pioneer Banjo Man," *Bluegrass Unlimited*, September, 1985, p. 26.

[21] Other performers there at WNOX were Archie Campbell, Molly O'Day, the Carlisle Brothers (Bill and Cliff) and others.

[22] Other members included Carl Smith (guitar), Jack and Curly Shelton, and Skeets Williamson (fiddle) on WWNC's Farm Hour.

[23] Knight, op. cit..

our own advertising and the people who sponsored us put up the advertising. At times, we had good crowds."[24]

Soon their good fortune left them. "It finally got so bad to where they didn't draw a crowd," said Rose Jenkins. "People were going for bigger name groups and Hoke decided to quit awhile." He tried the vending machine business in Charlotte, the stone cutting business, the farming business and worked in a sawmill. But Hoke was a musician—not trained for anything else—and music was where his heart was.

In 1951, Hoke was called by the **Bailey Brothers**, Charlie and Danny, to go to Raleigh and play with their band.[25] Charlie Bailey remembered that "Hoke was one of the few banjo players that can play banjo without using a capo on it...he could play anything."[26] In 1952, Hoke stayed in Raleigh for six months then re-joined Jim and Jesse and Curly Seckler, who were now in their own **Jim and Jesse and the Virginia Boys** and had a Capitol recording contract. The McReynolds brothers were working hard at making a living in the music and were now in a position to hire Jenkins who had given them one of their first jobs in the music. Nevertheless, times were very hard as a full-time musician. Hoke quit after four years, returned to the vending business in Charlotte and kept a band to play at local events.

Through the next twenty-some years, Jenkins pushed himself hard to make ends meet and support his family. He stayed busy and played hard. He had a heart attack in 1965, another two years later, and then a third. He wouldn't slow down; he didn't know how. In 1967, Hoke Jenkins died from his fourth heart attack. The **Smoky Mountaineers** played that evening's concert without him, not knowing whether or not the heart attack he suffered that day would be fatal.

The Hoke Jenkins Memorial Award was presented every year at the Snuffy Jenkins Old-Time and Bluegrass Music Festival in Cliffside, North Carolina, to honor those who have made outstanding contributions to old-time country or early bluegrass music.[27] The festival ceased in 1988.

Hubert Davis on Scruggs and Reno

Davis spoke about the music and banjo playing of the late 1970s. "You can't beat the original with whatever it might be. Don Reno and Earl Scruggs, I guess you could say, was the first and they gonna be there from now 'til I'm ninety years old. I don't care whose style of banjo's gonna come up, boom overnight and be on top maybe for a time—but it won't stay. And Scruggs

is gonna move out from under an' be right back up on top. And it's a-doin' it today."[28]

One of the first banjo instruction books

In 1948, Pete Seeger's *How To Play The 5-string Banjo* was first published. The 100 copies sold out in three years. The second printing of 500 copies in 1954 also sold out in three years. Both these printings were mimeographed. The third edition in 1961 yielded 3000 copies. A record to accompany this book was available on the Folkways label. Some of Seeger's students included Roger Sprung, Eric Weissberg and Billy Faier.

Johnny Whisnant

Johnny Whisnant— one of the early three-finger banjo style specialists

One little-known early banjoist who was one of the first to successfully make the transition from the early, choppy banjo styles to the smoother Scruggs style was Johnny Whisnant. His father was his first influence toward the banjo; by age five, he was playing, though confined to bed. He and Snuffy Jenkins began playing the banjo at about the same time but were in different parts of the country when they learned their styles so their learning processes were completely separate. Whisnant learned the three-finger style from Clay Everhart. He began his professional career with Carl Story in 1934, just before Story started his own Rambling Mountaineers.

[24] Knight, op. cit., p. 27.

[25] Hoke was to take the place of Willis Hogsed who joined the Army.

[26] Knight, op. cit., p. 29.

[27] Recipients have included Snuffy, Pappy Sherrill, the Morris brothers, Wade Mainer, Jim and Jesse McReynolds, Mac Wiseman, Greasy Medlin and Roy "Pop" Lewis.

[28] Bruce Nemerov, "Hubert Davis—Down Home Banjo Picker," *Bluegrass Unlimited*, January, 1977, p. 21.

Johnny Whisnant was born in Lenoir, North Carolina, on December 12, 1921, was drafted into the Army in 1942, and got out in September 1945. A War injury in 1945 caused his picking to suffer so he couldn't be hired into a band again as he had planned to do after the service. His skill and confidence returned in 1947 when he joined Charlie and Darrell Lane on WCRK, Morristown, Tennessee. In 1950, Whisnant moved to WIVK, Knoxville, to play with Willy Brewster and Jake Tullock, followed that year by Clyde and Hack Johnson on the WNOX Mid-Day Merry-Go-Round. Beginning in 1951, and for the next three years, he played in Raleigh with the Bailey Brothers, in Knoxville with Carl Butler, in Roanoke with the Bailey Brothers, back to Knoxville with the Brewster Brothers, and then with Carl Butler again. At one time during this period, he played on WKBC in North Wilkesboro with his live, one-man show called "Cousin Johnnie and His Banjo."

In 1957, Whisnant was in Florida where he formed the **Cherokee Ramblers** and worked as a mechanic by day. Back in Knoxville in 1959, he worked with the Brewsters and Charlie Bailey again. The next year, he moved to Ellicott City, Maryland. There he met, and occasionally recorded with, Al Jones, Benny and Vallie Cain and Buzz Busby. He began teaching banjo about that time, refined his patented tuners, and built banjos. He and his wife moved to Knoxville and retired. Here he died on February 2, 1992.

Stringbean

Dave "Stringbean" Akeman

Born in 1914 in Annville, Kentucky, David Akeman began playing the banjo as a teenager. By 1930, he was with Asa Martin's band on WLAP, Lexington, Kentucky. On the first show, Martin forgot Akeman's name and called him "Stringbeans" which matched his 6'2" slim build.[29] The name stuck. Martin worked with Stringbean and trained him to be a comedian. He was a natural, and continued to do comedy throughout his career.

In late 1939, Stringbean played a short while with Charlie Monroe's **Kentucky Pardners** in Greensboro, North Carolina. He did comedy in some black-faced and non-black-faced routines. He had his own band the next year called **Stringbean and the Kentucky Wonders.**

Very successful in his role as a comedian, he never wanted to turn back to simply being a musician. Stringbean continued playing on WLAP, and with **Cy Rogers and the Lonesome Pine Fiddlers** through 1939 when he was hired by Bill Monroe as a baseball pitcher on the band's very competitive team. A comment by Stringbean's brother elaborated on String's two times he was with Bill Monroe, "As far as I know, Bill didn't even know he played banjo when he hired him. After he found out he could play, he went to playin' a little with Bill's band. Then he left Bill to go with Charlie [Monroe] and then went into the service and then he came back and went with Bill again."[30]

In July 1942, Stringbean joined Bill Monroe's **Blue Grass Boys** on the Grand Ole Opry, playing clawhammer banjo (a Vega Tu-ba-phone banjo), doing comedy and playing baseball. He was Monroe's first banjo picker, and his banjo was used mostly as a rhythm instrument. Stringbean recorded on Columbia Records as one of the **Blue Grass Boys**; the banjo is barely audible. Also in the band were Bill "Cousin Wilbur" Wesbrooks (bass), Howdy Forrester (fiddle), Clyde Moody (guitar) and Monroe. Cousin Wilbur and Stringbean worked a number of comedy skits together. Stringbean's comedy included a skit with black-faced comedian Andy "Bijou" Boyette, from Florida.

Jim Shumate joined the **Blue Grass Boys** in early 1945, two or three weeks after Lester Flatt joined the band. String and Shumate then did a comedy act together. Shumate recalled that "People used to come up to Stringbean after he'd left Monroe and say, 'You know that Earl Scruggs can really pick a banjo.' String would say, 'Yea, but you ought to hear both me and him play at the same time.' He never would let himself down, and he never would say that Earl could pick."[31]

"Uncle Dave was the greatest entertainer I've ever known," said Akeman. "He would play to an audience forty-five minutes and then go back for seven or eight encores. It takes a hoss to do that."[32] Macon took String under his wing and taught him many banjo licks and entertainment techniques. Uncle Dave willed a Gibson banjo, which he used on stage, to String. Gruhn Guitars now has possession of this banjo.

29 His nickname is also correctly, and more often, spelled and pronounced "Stringbean."

30 Charles K. Wolfe, "String," *Bluegrass Unlimited*, June, 1982, p. 48. This quotation by Robert Akeman, Stringbean's brother.

31 Wayne Erbsen, "Jim Shumate—Bluegrass Fiddler Supreme," *Bluegrass Unlimited*, April, 1979, pp. 15, 16.

32 Wolfe, op. cit., p. 49.

That fall, Stringbean left the **Boys** to join fellow entertainer/comedian Lew Childre with whom he worked the next three years.[33] String was replaced in the **Blue Grass Boys** first by Jim Andrews on the tenor banjo and then by Earl Scruggs at Christmas time. String and Lew performed hilarious comedic skits and played old-time music on the Opry and in tent shows. With this group, Stringbean became famous for his "short pants" costume which was copied from Slim Miller who was a fiddler and comedian at the Renfro Valley Barn Dance and no longer active in music.

Stringbean and his wife were murdered November 10, 1973, by an apparent robber at their home. The murderers were later found and prosecuted.

Curtis McPeake

Curtis McPeake— a studio banjoist who played with the greats

Curtis McPeake was born in Scotts Hill, Henderson County, Tennessee. His father played some fiddle and banjo and young McPeake got his first guitar at age nine. Curtis started his career in 1945 on WTJS, Jackson, Tennessee. He played steel and mandolin with the band and they broadcast a fifteen-minute show every Saturday morning. They played live performances at ice cream suppers, pie suppers, theaters, coon dog trials, store openings, etc.. He formed his own **Rocky Valley Boys** in 1948, playing electric steel guitar. In 1953, he switched to banjo. His band began broadcasting weekly on WXDL, Lexington, Tennessee.[34]

He recalled, "I used to go to **Flatt and Scruggs** shows and would sit as close to the front as I could. I'd catch three or four licks and would go home and work on them. The first time I saw Earl he had those covered

tuners on his banjo. Some people thought he had an RB-250, but he actually was playing a Granada with a bow tie fingerboard that the factory had put on. One night after a show, he hunkered down on the edge of the stage and told me how he had those covered to keep them a secret. That's partially true, but he had made such a mess putting them on his banjo he didn't want people to see them."[35] Their shows were as "Hot as a firecracker!" he said.

In early 1956, McPeake joined **Flatt and Scruggs** to substitute for Earl who had been seriously injured in an auto accident the previous October. He played for ten weeks the first time, and several other times later. He remembered that "It was a wild time and we had a ball. Lester was a jewel to work for and he always seemed to think a lot of me. I clowned a lot with him. Earl is more reserved, but he's always friendly. Lester was outgoing. I had more real fun with **Flatt and Scruggs** than any bunch I've ever been with. There was no fussing and no quarreling. There were a lot of crazy antics and it was absolutely a madhouse." He recalled that others who substituted for Earl during this time were Donnie Bryant and Haskell McCormick. During future periods of Scruggs needing a replacement, McPeake was almost the exclusive choice.

McPeake then worked awhile with Bill Monroe's band, recorded eighteen sides with him, and played Carnegie Hall with him. At Carnegie Hall, "I was so nervous that I couldn't even tune my banjo much less play it. We were all just a bundle of nerves because we were afraid we might not be accepted well in New York City, but we did really well. In fact, I encored when I did an instrumental. I was so nervous I couldn't have found the seat of my britches with both hands."

Monroe "would teach you to play his style as he wanted it played. I have a lot of respect for Bill and we're still good friends. His music was a little less free-flowing than when I played with **Flatt and Scruggs**, but I have great respect for his ideas and style."[36]

McPeake left Monroe in early 1962, then joined the staff band at WSM. He did session work during the 1960s, then spent nearly two years with **Wilma Lee and Stoney Cooper**. He left in the summer of 1963 to return to Nashville to re-join WSM's staff band, staying with WSM until 1969 when he joined **Danny Davis and the Nashville Brass** where he stayed until 1987. Nashville was changing the sound of its music in the mid-'50s and '60s. Trumpeter Danny Davis was assistant to RCA's Chet Atkins in the 1960s and wanted to

---

[33] Childre played an Hawaiian-style Martin guitar. He would buck dance, do comedy, yodel and ad lib commercials and was one of the best one-man acts in the business, according to Whitey Ford "The Duke of Paducah," country comedian of the '40s through the '60s. Childre was a member of the WWVA Jamboree in the early 1940s. In 1943, he had a daily show on the nationwide Blue Network. He joined the Opry in 1945. String and Lew went their separate ways in 1948. Childre retired from the Opry in 1959, died in 1961. Old Homestead Records released some of Childre's many transcriptions on "Lew Childre on the Air—1946."

[34] Sponsored by an Arkansas flour mill.

[35] Joe Ross, "An Interview with Curtis McPeake," *Bluegrass Unlimited*, July, 1992, p. 43. Mr. Scruggs verified this story in a 1996 conversation with this writer.

[36] Ibid., pp. 43, 44.

start his own style of music. His concept was to move to Nashville, start his own band which featured brass horns, and have a strong "country" sound. Davis' idea for his music was to have a strong presence of the five-string banjo. Atkins approved of the idea and said "good luck" in his new venture. Davis made a few recordings with studio musicians including Sonny Osborne on "The Nashville Brass Play the Nashville Sound." When Davis decided to go on the road, he needed a banjo player so he hired Curtis McPeake who was an Opry staff musician and studio player at the time. "It wasn't bluegrass and I lost a lot of bluegrass contacts, but the pay was better. I have a lot of respect for bluegrass music. I just don't have much respect for all that goes with it."[37] He elaborated, "You couldn't call me a purist. Bluegrass has not been given room to grow. Country music can change and go with every wind that blows and is still considered country. But not true with some bluegrass purists."[38] After his time with the **Brass**, he formed a bluegrass group known as the **Natchez Express**.

McPeake spoke of the development of his individual style and how others might start out learning the banjo: "Learn to do some of the stuff that Scruggs did. Then start branching out and finally you'll be able to develop some licks on your own. Quit saying, 'This is exactly the way Earl played this on Thursday. And this is the same finger Earl used.' This is fine, but why should I want to play every note and every lick with the same finger he did? He already did that thirty or forty years ago. All these players are doing is recreating what he already created, which means they don't have any creativity of their own. Put that banjo in your hand, put the picks on, and play. Let me clear the air by saying Earl Scruggs is my hero and friend. There are some great pickers past and present but nobody is Scruggs and they never will be either. Be yourself!

"I've never asked him to show me a lick. I don't really like to do that. That would've been an intrusion. I've heard Earl play some of my licks, but not on stage. I have walked by Earl when he and Flatt were rehearsing at the old Ryman and Earl would face me, do one of my licks, and grin. But do you think he'd ever use that on stage? No way! He did his own style. He was the forerunner. He cut the trail by hard rehearsing. Lester would tell me how Earl used to work that reverse roll on his britches all the time—on his leg, you know, just tapping out rolls. He played what was natural for him even though it isn't necessarily easy for everyone else."[39]

"I got out of bluegrass because I wanted to feed my family and put my daughter through college. I still enjoy playing it. I now do straight, traditional bluegrass mixed with a lot of gospel. I'd like to do more bluegrass gospel. I don't do the progressive stuff but I'm all for it. The

purists would like to chase them out, I suppose, but I've got no qualms with guys that are doing their own thing. I might not personally like their style, but more power to them."

Curtis McPeake owns McPeake's Unique Instruments, a mail order business he's had since 1977.

Bobby Atkins

Bobby Atkins and the Countrymen

Bobby Atkins is still playing the banjo professionally—after forty years—and few people know it. He is one of many unsung heroes in this business who put their heart and soul into the music.

Bobby Atkins was born in Shoals, North Carolina, May 22, 1933. He was raised in Gold Hill, near Madison, North Carolina, up to his teens at which time the family moved to Summerfield, North Carolina, close to Greensboro. At five years old, Atkins could already play three chords on the guitar, having been taught these three chords by his mother, Alice Atkins. Soon, young Bobby was accompanying his father, Clinton Atkins, on the instrument while his father played the fiddle, the Autoharp and clawhammer banjo. According to Atkins in a 1991 interview, his father was one of the finest guitar pickers and singers who ever lived. He would play the guitar with every finger on his right hand and didn't use a pick. Bobby said that he'd never seen anybody else play that style. His mother played the banjo, guitar, fiddle, autoharp and keyboard instruments and was a fine singer.

At fourteen or fifteen years old, he heard Don Reno play "Foggy Mountain Breakdown"; the next day, he got some finger picks. The first time he heard Earl Scruggs was on WPTF, Raleigh, North Carolina. Atkins swapped a good watch for his first banjo (though it is not the one

[37] Ibid., p. 45.

[38] Ibid., p. 45. Modified slightly by Mr. McPeake in 1995 for clarity.

[39] Ibid., pp. 47, 48.

he performs with today, he still owns that banjo). He practiced at every opportunity, including at the drive-in between movies. He played exactly like Scruggs until he felt the need to play his own style which included more bluesy notes.

During an interview with Bobby Atkins in 1991, he spoke of the early days. "At the time that I started playing banjo there weren't but seven banjo players that I know of. The only ones I remember were Earl Scruggs, Don Reno, Allen Shelton, Sonny Osborne, Hubert Davis and myself. Now, the Jenkins people, they played banjo, too, but they hadn't perfected the banjo pickin' that we play now. We all learned from the way Scruggs played it. There's no way that a banjo picker can get through a show unless he hits a Scruggs lick or a Reno lick.

"I'm a bluesy banjo player; I play a lot of blues. In fact what bluegrass is, is fast blues. So I don't care what people think—I play it my way. Because the way I see it, if somebody wants Earl Scruggs they're going to buy Earl Scruggs. The same goes for Reno, Monroe or Bobby Atkins. Atkins is different now."

Bobby Atkins joined the **Blue Grass Boys** the first of three times in 1954 (the other times were 1958 and 1961). This time it was for only three days.[40] "I got so homesick that I came back home, for I had not been away from home before. Atkins spent several years in the **Dixie Mountaineers**[41] on WRVA's Old Dominion Barn Dance in Richmond, Virginia, and the New Dominion Barn Dance (which began in 1957). He spoke about the last time with the **Blue Grass Boys**, June 1961, when he took the place of Tony Ellis[42]. "Bill let me do a lot of blues and loved it in our stuff at that time. Bill let me do that, and I'm proud of that." Atkins had a distinctive sound that audiences could recognize when he was playing with Bill Monroe, and a distinctive sound audiences recognize now.

After eight months with Monroe the final time (in 1961), Atkins formed the **Appalachian Music Makers** with members Joe Stone (guitar), Tony Rice[43] (guitar), Frank Poindexter (resonator guitar) and others. They worked WUBC-TV in Greensboro, North Carolina. In 1969, the **Appalachian Music Makers** recorded the

soundtrack for a low budget film, "The Preacherman," and its sequel a year later, "The Preacherman Meets the Widow Woman." They did all the background music and singing. On the second movie, they had bit parts in it and did all the music. Bobby renamed the band **Bobby Atkins and the Countrymen**, and that is the name the band still goes by today.

A 1991 interview with Atkins after his IBMA showcase performance led to a few comments about Scruggs and the beginnings of the bluegrass genre. "Scruggs was not the best lead singer in the world but he sung good with groups. He sung good bass and he sung good baritone. But that rascal's timing on that banjo was perfect; it was just like a machine. And he joined [Monroe's band] and throwed the drive to it, see. He had some blues notes, too. Earl Scruggs, in my book, is one of the finest banjo pickers that ever lived. And he really knew that neck, too. When he backed up a group he was all up and down that neck. That's where bluegrass music began, in my book. And I'm not puttin' down Bill Monroe. He is a fine person and a fine musician. Bill was lookin' for something different. And when he had Lester Flatt and Earl Scruggs with him, he had what he was looking for. He had the blend, he had the drive, he had the blues, he had it all together. He had what he had been looking for years."

Bobby Atkins and the Countrymen. Photo courtesy Bobby Atkins.

Atkins reflected on the importance of keeping the old timers around to keep the music right and of his appearance at IBMA with his **Countrymen** with Vassar Clements, "It's going to take people like myself, like Scruggs and people that's played down through the years with [Bill Monroe] to really keep it going. And you know what hurts me? They don't even recognize

[40] Atkins took Hubert Davis' place on banjo.

[41] With Joe Stone (guitar), Frank Buchanan (mandolin), Art McGee (fiddle) and Kemp Atkins (bass).

[42] Atkins left his partner, Joe Stone, and the Dixie Mountaineers for a temporary 8-month stint with Monroe. Atkins never did not record with Monroe however. Musicians were Monroe, Mauldin, Bobby Smith, Atkins and Billy Baker (fiddle). Baker worked awhile until Vassar Clements joined the band. Though Vassar was fully capable of playing the sophisticated style he is known for, "At that time he didn't. Because Bill wouldn't let him. People asked him, when we were together then, why he wouldn't let Vassar fiddle like Vassar could fiddle. But Bill said he didn't want that. He wanted it to sound like his records. I played like he wanted me to play and Vassar played the way Bill wanted him to play."

[43] Rice stayed with them until he replaced Dan Crary in the Bluegrass Alliance in 1970. On their first movie, Tony Rice was with them.

me. They don't recognize the roots—like here tonight (at IBMA, 1991)... It really hurts a person who half-starved to keep it going. I don't even think my name was mentioned on the microphone [when we were introduced]."

Bobby Atkins is a member of the Bluegrass Hall of Fame. He continues to play and record in 1997.

Eddie Adcock

Eddie Adcock

There are several significant banjo players in bluegrass music who have been on the "cutting edge" of this music. Eddie Adcock is one of these who always "pushed the envelope" of the music and he always seemed to be in bands with individuals who felt the same way. His legendary tenure with the **Country Gentlemen** thrust him into stardom, but with this band his status as one of bluegrass' most accomplished musicians (he also plays the guitar with equal skill) had just begun...

Eddie Adcock was born in Scottsville, Virginia, on June 21, 1938. He had several brothers who played a little music in the family. His first instrument was a guitar at age seven, then he changed to mandolin. The first banjo player he heard was Ralph Stanley—on the radio soon after the War. His first banjo was his brother Bill's heavy cast, metal-body Gretsch tenor banjo. Although Adcock played guitar and mandolin, the banjo was the instrument which was most sought after in bluegrass bands at the time. His first group was the **James River Playboys** in 1953 with his brother Frank.

They played on WCHV and WINA, Charlottesville. He played mandolin in this group and, later, plectrum banjo.

In 1954, in Crewe, Virginia (WSVS), Adcock, age 15 or 16, joined **Smoky Graves and the Blue Star Boys**.[44] His mother had earlier given him a calf to raise, and when he received an offer to play banjo with Smokey Graves he sold the calf and used the money to buy a Gibson RB-100 five-string. Adcock made $45 per week plus percentages of songbook sales. "But," he said, "there were weeks that went by where I didn't make anything."[45]

Adcock told of the tent shows he used to play during the year with Graves. "The tent shows were really nasty. Sometimes we had to set them up in the mud. We often were in a cow pasture, sometimes at a fairgrounds. We would go into a town and get permission to set up a tent. We would advertise on our radio shows. Then we would find a farmer and go up to his house and ask if we could set up a tent there.

"Many times it would be raining or sleeting or snowing, and after taking everything down we wouldn't get away until two or three in the morning. The band raised and lowered the tent every night we had to do it. We did the whole thing. I can't even put up a pup tent now but back then I could get one of the big ones that would hold 150 people up in a pretty short time." He also said, "The [cost] overhead was real low—almost nothing. A few posters and a trailer at the closest theater and the radio program and we could get a crowd of 150 people. Some of the bigger groups were staying in the buildings and only having fifty at the show. We could keep the cost down. It was the only way that the little guys like Smokey, who was very smart at this kind of thing, could survive."[46]

While Adcock was a member of the **Blue Star Boys**, Don Reno showed him how to play a proper three-finger roll. Adcock had used three fingers, but mostly with a single-string style and a cross-picking type roll. Reno also showed Adcock how to set up his banjo properly and to use metal fingerpicks. Up until that time in 1953, Adcock was still using plastic picks on his fingers and a metal one on his thumb, which is backwards to "bluegrass propriety". Adcock, in turn, showed Reno his style of single-string banjo playing.

After a short period in 1956 with Mac Wiseman's **Country Boys**, Adcock joined Bill Harrell's **Rocky Mountain Boys**[47] in Washington, D.C.. The band played music in the bluegrass style, strongly influenced by rock and roll music which was becoming popular. Scott Stoneman labeled Adcock a "rock and roll banjo picker"—a label which fit. They made about $12.50 each

[44] Those members were Adcock (banjo, age 15), Herman Yarbrough (steel guitar), Graves (fiddle, guitar) and Paul Johnson (bass, a.k.a. Little Jody Rainwater's).

[45] From a 1990 interview at Owensboro, Kentucky.

[46] Pete Kuykendall, "II Generation," *Bluegrass Unlimited*, March, 1975, p. 9.

[47] He replaced Donnie Bryant who joined the military. Band members were Harrell (guitar), Carl Nelson (fiddle), Smiley Hobbs (mandolin), Adcock (banjo) and Roy Self (bass). Adcock had earlier replaced Bryant in Mac Wiseman's band.

for their three or four nights per week performances. Adcock's tenure with Harrell's band was fairly short. He also worked with the **Stoneman Family** during the same period.

Harrell said, "Eddie was playing super great! He was a few years younger than me and I sort of had to act as a chaperone to play at some of the clubs—he was like seventeen. Sort of an interesting facet was during that time bluegrass was hard to sell in a lot of places and one of the terrific things I thought Eddie added to the band was that he could play sort of a, if you will, a Merle Travis style banjo like Merle would play on the guitar. He would do a lot of Elvis Presley things and we worked six nights a week in the Washington area in clubs and things before I got drafted."[48]

"When Bill Harrell went into the service (1956), the band broke up. Adcock found work at a TV station in Norfolk, Virginia, as the emcee for a musical program. He also worked for the **Virginia Playboys**, a jam group, and also played guitar in a rock 'n' roll band. Following the 1957 accident with Buzz Busby's **Bayou Boys**[49], Adcock joined **Bill Monroe and the Blue Grass Boys**, with whom he remained until joining the **Country Gentlemen** in late 1958."[50]

In 1957, Bill Monroe called Adcock to join as banjoist on the road. Adcock worked there about six months.[51] Adcock said, "I worked on Bill's farm, too. When you worked with Bill, you worked with Bill at everything. We planted tobacco and all when I was with him. He was out there with us right alongside doing his part, too. I don't regret that at all. It was good training. It's helped me a lot since then. We used to work six to eight hours per day on the farm, and then go play a show that night."[52] They made $14 to $17 per night. This was split between four people. "I made less money with Bill Monroe than anyone I ever worked for in my life."

In another interview, Adcock told this writer, "I was with Bill...at a time when he wasn't drawing flies. That's not to say anything bad about him, because all of bluegrass was rough then. We worked some places that didn't even have floors. Sometimes I went two or three days without food. We worked places with no floors in them. A theater in Kentucky, for example, I remember two old pot-bellied stoves for heat. They'd shovel coal in them for heat and sit right on the plank seats on the dirt...[in Nashville with Monroe] I had a room in the Clarkston Hotel. The biggest part of the time, I had money to buy something. My room looked out on the back alley, so it was a little cooler there. I'd buy a loaf of bread and I'd set it out on the window. I ended up just eating bread. At first, I'd set bologna out there; I'd eat one piece of bread, so I could stretch it—that type of thing. It was a very short while, in fact, until Bill moved me out on the farm, along with Edd Mayfield."[53] People like Marty Robbins and Porter Wagoner generously helped him out with a little food and money. "I quit music and decided I wasn't going to be hungry anymore. I barely had scraped enough money to take the bus home." He got a bill-paying day job.

In the winter of 1958/1959, after a two-week period when Porter Church was in the **Country Gentlemen**, Eddie Adcock was asked to join as banjoist; the band had already cut three singles by that time. "The **Country Gentlemen** wanted me to go with them but I didn't care to go back on the road... John and Charlie came over and set from ten o'clock 'til four a.m. one night begging me—trying to persuade me... They needed a banjo player and they needed one bad! They begged and pleaded."[54] He finally agreed to join the band. "When I said 'yes,' I hated myself."[55] Adcock was twenty.

Adcock admits that his being hired into the **Country Gentlemen** wasn't because he was the best banjo player around; it was because he was the only banjo player available. He was not at all interested in working for wages similar to what he made with Monroe. But according to Duffey and Waller, they wanted him because of his unique banjo style. Another reason for Adcock's reluctance to join was that the **Gents** was not original—they were copying other people's materials (albeit doing it well). But when Adcock joined, the band added considerable originality and began creating their reputation as being innovators.[56]

> *"People don't realize it, but...**Ian and Sylvia**, Judy Collins, Joan Baez, people that played second billing to us...[later] did a lot of the material that we pulled from the Library of Congress that was in the public domain."* —Eddie Adcock

[48] I lost the exact source of this quotation, but presume that it came from: Bill Vernon, "Don Reno, Red Smiley, Bill Harrell and the Tennessee Cut-Ups," *Bluegrass Unlimited*, August, 1971.

[49] Discussed fully in John Duffey biography in Pioneers chapter of this book.

[50] Quotations from the album cover, "The Country Gentlemen—25th Anniversary 1957-1982," p. 11.

[51] Edd Mayfield played guitar; Red Taylor had just taken Kenny Baker's place on fiddle.

[52] Kuykendall, op. cit., p. 12.

[53] Bill Vernon, "The Eddie Adcock Story," *Muleskinner News*, Vol. 7, No. 7.

[54] 1990 interview at Owensboro, Kentucky.

[55] Don Rhodes, "Eddie and Martha Adcock—Finding Their Place in Bluegrass Music," *Bluegrass Unlimited*, April, 1982, p. 36.

[56] Interestingly, Duffey didn't talk much on stage. He wouldn't emcee. It was Waller and Adcock who were goof balls on stage for the first few years.

This was the band which really kicked off the musical career of Eddie Adcock. The twelve-year stay with the **Gentlemen** was one of the key ingredients to the group's success. "It's just a magical thing. It's a combination; it's just something that works. I don't question it."[57] John Duffey said of Eddie Adcock, "I consider him quite innovative. He did, and most likely still does, more with his left hand than any player I've seen playin'. Other than that, he was an excellent baritone singer."[58] Charlie Waller told that "It wasn't until we got Eddie that we got that certain kind of magic sound. Duffey and Eddie just worked well together. That was the combination that sold."[59]

After joining the **Country Gentlemen**, Adcock's first recordings were "The Hills and Home" and "New Freedom Bell." On these cuts, Adcock's style strongly resembled the pedal steel of Bud Isaacs. About that time, tuners were becoming popular on the banjo but Adcock didn't use any gadgets to re-tune the string. He didn't own them. He merely did it with his fingers.

"People don't realize it, but...**Ian and Sylvia**, Judy Collins, Joan Baez, people that played second billing to us...[later] did a lot of the material that we pulled from the Library of Congress that was in the public domain. We brought them to the public...like 'I Never Will Marry.' That's one that got real popular in the folk days. Pete Seeger and everyone pulled from our material."[60]

In 1968, "The Sensational Twin Banjos of Eddie Adcock and Don Reno" was recorded. They did it with no rehearsal, face-to-face across a two-sided, stereo Sony microphone. Adcock did mostly the lead, Reno, the tenor harmony.

Adcock left the **Gents** in 1970 (he was replaced by Bill Emerson). He went to California where he began a jazz, jazz-rock, and country-rock band, performing under the name "Clinton Kodack." He explained he's always had trouble doing anything but bluegrass under his real name. He did well financially. This lasted until he returned to the East Coast and formed the **II Generation** the next year with Jimmy Gaudreau (mandolin), Wendy Thatcher (guitar) and Bob White (bass). Soon Martha Hearon[61] joined the group which was playing regularly at Bethesda's Red Fox Inn. She would later marry Eddie and receive considerable recognition from the bluegrass community for her singing.

In 1978, Adcock invented the Gitbo, an instrument which is a combination of electric guitar and electrified banjo. He can select either instrument by flipping a switch, the sound could be like either a guitar or a banjo. It resembles a double-necked electric guitar with a banjo head buried in a lower corner. "It's on seven bluegrass albums, and no one knows which ones they are." At that time, Adcock was also playing a banjo made by Harry Lane. "The Lane banjo is the best acoustic banjo that I have ever played in my life," he said. The group was called **Adcock** and featured Eddie's son, Dennis, on bass.[62]

Eddie told how he gets his peculiar, recognizable banjo sound. Of course, the skill of a musician is a significant influence on the way an instrument sounds, but he described how his banjo setup is different than the way others may set theirs up. "My banjo is a ways deeper. I'm now playing a Stelling. It's like all the others except that it's built a little bit deeper. Your total tone change comes from the distance between the inside back of the resonator and the shell. The other thing that is different about mine is a wider neck. It's good for single-string playing."[63] Some details of set-up are also different. Adcock's Stelling Virginian was presented to him by Geoff Stelling on November 7, 1987. He continued using his Lane banjo occasionally.

In 1984, Eddie and Martha Adcock left bluegrass and went to work for David Allan Coe, with Eddie as Coe's band leader where they made excellent money. They stayed a year, then left to form **Eddie Adcock and Talk of the Town**—a return to bluegrass and newgrass. This band changed its name to the **Eddie Adcock Band** in 1990. The core members of this band, for several years, were Eddie (banjo, lead guitar), Martha (rhythm guitar) and Missy Raines (bass).

In 1990, he formed an alliance to record and perform as the **Masters** who were Adcock (guitar), Jesse McReynolds (mandolin), Kenny Baker (fiddle) and Josh Graves (Dobro®). They performed awhile as a band and received the IBMA award for Instrumental Recording of the Year in 1990. And Eddie's production of, and membership in, the "Classic Country Gents Reunion" helped gain the **Country Gentlemen** the Recorded Event of the Year prize.

Adcock has recorded on more than 100 albums and written around 150 songs and instrumentals including "Another Lonesome Morning," recorded by Emmylou Harris. He was the first five-string banjo player whose records were heard in France and was subsequently named "the Earl Scruggs of France". The **Eddie Adcock Band** actively toured and performed into the 1990s.

---

[57] 1990 interview at Owensboro. He was also referring to the present combination he thinks works—the trio of Eddie Adcock, Martha Hearon Adcock and Missy Raines (who left the Adcock band in 1992).

[58] Brawner Smoot, "Music in Motion," *Unicorn Times*, December, 1978.

[59] Kuykendall, op. cit., p. 12.

[60] Smoot, op. cit., p. 3.

[61] Born October 29, 1949.

[62] And Neil Good on drums.

[63] 1990 interview at Owensboro, Kentucky.

Rual Yarbrough and the Dixiemen

Rual Yarbrough was born in Lawrenceburg, Lawrence County, Tennessee, January 13, 1930. Though not raised in a musical family, the area gave him ample influence from Opry stars such as Bill Monroe and others who would tour through the area. At age twelve, Yarbrough started learning guitar, then mandolin, the fiddle and then bass fiddle.

In 1955, Yarbrough joined **Gene Christian**[64] **and the Hillbilly Pals** in Lawrenceburg as their bass player. But the band needed a banjo player so Yarbrough began learning the instrument at Christian's suggestion; it was awhile before he became proficient with the instrument. In a 1992 telephone interview he described the situation. "I just started off. Of course, back then it was hard to learn—nobody to teach you. I picked what I could and began picking here in Alabama with (Herschel) Sizemore. I was not capable of pickin' in a group but sometimes these things just happen; you just get into it. If the interest is there somebody will, maybe, tolerate you. Nobody had much goin' for them on the outside. I guess [Christian] could see I had the interest and I might could learn it, you know. So we just [eventually worked something out]."

Yarbrough learned the three-finger banjo style the hard way: listening to records and picking up pointers whenever he could. "I liked the three-finger style the first time I heard it. There's no way you can get that sound except with the three fingers. You know, Stringbean was Bill Monroe's first banjo picker; he was a two-finger banjo picker. He was a frailer, too, but his lead pickin' was with two fingers."

Yarbrough moved to the northern Alabama area of Muscle Shoals in 1956. In 1957, near his home, Yarbrough, Herschel Sizemore (mandolin) and Lendon Smith, joined together in a band which was he remembered was called **Tennessee Valley Playboys**. Here Yarbrough began playing banjo publicly.

Soon Yarbrough and Sizemore formed the **Country Gentlemen** with Jake Landers. This was a tough time to start a band but because it was only part-time, it was enjoyable. They worked on WOWL-TV as the **Country Gentlemen** and were sponsored locally. Upon realizing that Charlie Waller's **Country Gentlemen** had already recorded and been on the radio, they changed the band name to **Dixie Gentlemen** and soon recorded[65] on the Florida-based Blue Sky label.

In 1960, the band recorded "Greatest Bluegrass Hits" with Tommy Jackson (fiddle) for the Dot label. In 1962, for United Artists, they recorded "The Country Style of the Dixie Gentlemen." Produced by fiddler Tommy Jackson, the album featured a full rhythm section furnished by UA's studio musicians and included Vassar Clements on fiddle. Then, fitting right in with the folk boom, they recorded "Hootenanny N' Bluegrass" and "Bluegrass Back Home" on the Time label.

Instead of going full-time into their music with the **Dixie Gentlemen** and quitting

This songbook, from the Dixie Gentlemen, came out about 1969. In addition to song lyrics, the booklet has several photos including one of Randy Wood who was working at Rual's Music Service at the time.

---

[64] Christian was a former fiddler for the Blue Grass Boys, leaving them to form this band with Yarbrough.

[65] With members Yarbrough (banjo), Landers (guitar), Al Lester (twin fiddles with Vassar Clements who was full-time with Jim and Jesse) and Wesley Stevens (bass). Lester soon left the group with Vassar filling-in as time permitted.

America's Music | Bluegrass

their day jobs, they kept their part-time arrangement. Landers kept the band together part-time and Yarbrough found jobs with Jimmy Martin (1966, intermittently for a few months), substituted for Earl Scruggs on the "Flatt and Scruggs Show" in Utica, New York (1967) when Scruggs was in the hospital, **Jim and Jesse** occasionally and with **Bobby Smith and the Boys from Shiloh** (1968). Sizemore joined Jim Eanes's **Shenandoah Cut-Ups** in Roanoke, Virginia.

While Yarbrough was working as the banjoist for Bobby Smith's **Boys from Shiloh** in 1968, his day job was as owner of Rual's Music Service in Muscle Shoals, Alabama, a business which included a retail store and instrument repair (by Randy Wood). The group recorded in Wayne Rainey's studio with Tut Taylor in Concord, Arkansas, for James Joiner's Tune Record Company which was based in Florence, Alabama. Yarbrough recorded first his solo LP, "Rual Yarbrough Picks the 5-String," for Tune.

In 1969, Rual Yarbrough joined the **Blue Grass Boys**[66] full-time—his first and only full-time job in the music (he had worked a week with Monroe in 1962) and stayed with this band for the next two years. Yarbrough recorded twenty-one or so songs with Monroe on Decca.

It was tough for Monroe to keep a band in the late fifties and early sixties. Monroe only paid his band members when they worked, and they didn't seem to work often enough for Monroe to be able to pay his band members enough to stay with him as a band. It seemed to Yarbrough that they picked up a new member every time they went out on tour. The next year, he quit Monroe to pursue luthiery and to further his business in Muscle Shoals. There they built Sonny Osborne's six-string banjo neck.

In early 1971, Yarbrough re-joined Jake Landers to re-form the **Dixie Gentlemen** band which would now be called **Rual Yarbrough and the Dixiemen**. They recorded "Rual Yarbrough and the Dixiemen Featuring James Bryan on Fiddle" for Old Homestead in 1973. At Christmas of 1972, Old Homestead Records released "The Dixie Gentlemen Together Once More." This was a reunion of the old group with Sizemore and Clements on the album with Yarbrough, Landers, Bryan and Johnny Montgomery. The next year, Old Homestead released their "California Cotton Fields." Beginning about 1974, Jake Landers was in and out of the **Rual Yarbrough and the Dixiemen** for the next couple of years. Yarbrough, Joe Stuart and Red Rector did some work together and recorded on Old Homestead.

As of 1992, Yarbrough (62) didn't pick much any longer, with the exception of gospel music with James Whitten in church for a needy cause.

Bill Emerson

William Hundley Emerson Jr. was born in Washington, D.C., January 22, 1938. He played guitar first, but when he heard the banjo in country music he began to play that instrument. He traded his electric guitar and amplifier for a Belltone banjo and soon moved up to a Gibson RB-100. John Duffey showed him the basic rolls and chords on the five-string. The country tunes he listened to were those of Wayne Brown who was Mac Wiseman's banjo player on WBMD in Baltimore. Emerson also heard Buzz Busby (and his **Bayou Boys**) on his television show when Don Stover was banjoist. In 1954, Emerson soon got a lot of help from Smitty Irvin, who later played with Jimmy Dean and with Bill Harrell.

The first live bluegrass he heard was John Duffey (mandolin) and Bill Blackburn (banjo, guitar) in a parking lot in Manassas, Virginia. His banjo influences were Scruggs, Reno and Ralph Stanley. Emerson said, "Scruggs was about as close to perfect as you can get and Reno was the most innovative. I wouldn't say that one's better than the other because all three have their strong points."[67]

Emerson's first professional job, in 1955, was with **Uncle Bob and the Blue Ridge Partners** at WINX in Rockville, Maryland, every Saturday morning. This was a group of men with guitars, mandolins, and fiddles but no banjo. They invited him to sit-in and he got paid for it. After later playing with Roy and Curly Irvin and Art Wooten, he joined Buzz Busby's **Bayou Boys**. They played in small Baltimore clubs, on a radio show in Salisbury, Maryland, and he recorded with Busby. This was actually his first real "professional job where I felt pressure to play his music the way he wanted it. Buzz was great. He'd been playing with Scott Stoneman, Don Stover and Charlie Waller and had some excellent

---

[66] Members of the Blue Grass Boys also included Kenny Baker (fiddle), James Monroe (guitar) and Doug Green (bass).

[67] Joe Ross, "Bill Emerson, Banjo Player Extraordinaire," *Bluegrass Unlimited*, March, 1992, p. 21.

records out. He was a professional."[68] Also with Busby's band occasionally was Charlie Waller who was also playing with **Earl Taylor and the Stoney Mountain Boys** at the time.

The **Country Gentlemen** was formed in 1957 when Emerson, "Buzz, Vance Truell and Eddie Adcock were playing in a club at Bailey's Crossroads, Virginia. After the gig one night, they wanted to go to North Beach, Maryland, which was a real 'hopping' place. I went home instead," told Emerson. "They got in the car and hit one of those concrete bridge culverts. They were all pretty badly banged up. It broke the neck clean off Eddie's banjo. He had them bring it into the hospital with him so he could watch it. We still had that job so Buzz said, 'You better get some people in there to hold it for me.' I got Charlie Waller, John Duffey and Larry Leahy on bass... Later we hired Carl Nelson to play fiddle. You could say I brought all of the elements together, and we decided to stay together."[69]

Emerson left the band in early 1958 so he could do something different. He soon did some recording with Bill Harrell: "Eating Out of Your Hand," "One Track Mind" and "I'll Never See You Anymore." He also worked occasionally with Bill Clifton, Mac Wiseman, the **Stonemans** (for 1 1/2 years), and Buzz Busby. He then joined Red Allen and Frank Wakefield when they came to town which was just after Allen had left the **Osborne Brothers**. They did a lot of local clubs and some 45 r.p.m. recordings. Emerson also recorded with Harry and Jeanie West.

In 1959, Emerson won the National Champion Country Music Contest in Warrenton, Virginia, and was awarded the first production Vega Earl Scruggs Model—the same one which Earl had on "The Price Is Right" television show.

In early 1961, Paul Craft was with Jimmy Martin's band but was sick and the group needed a banjo player for a job in Patterson, New Jersey, so they picked up Bill Emerson. Emerson told this writer, "I met him on the Pennsylvania Turnpike and we went to a motel room and ran through the tunes for his show. I already knew most of his stuff because I had been thinking about the possibility of working for him. Afterwards, he said Paul Craft was planning to leave and offered me a job. I accepted and stayed with Jimmy about five years altogether. "It was a lot of fun, and that was my education right there. Just about everything I've used down through the years I learned from Jimmy. He's a master, and right off the bat I could see the value of what I was getting from him."[70]

"Jimmy wanted you to fit with what he was doing. He never said to me, 'I want you to play it like J.D..' But he would say things like, 'Instead of hitting just one string, I want you to reach down and grab a whole handful to make it sound full. Keep the tone of that banjo in there all the time.' He showed me how to keep my banjo pointed at the microphone and how to work in and out. Jimmy didn't play the banjo himself, but he could two-finger it just enough to show you what he wanted. You know, Earl Scruggs said the most important thing to him is how he gets in and out of a break. Jimmy taught me that was very important. Jimmy would say, 'Hit those pick-up notes just like a fiddle would, and keep them separated. You don't want one string loud and the next not loud enough.' He showed me how to put the emphasis, rhythm and dynamics into my playing and singing. He also taught me about show business in general. There wasn't any part of it that Jimmy didn't instruct me on."[71]

"We did the Grand Ole Opry four or five times as a guest. We were regulars on the World's Original WWVA Jamboree out of Wheeling, West Virginia. Shortly after I went with him, we did a week at the Golden Nugget in Las Vegas. We did a USO thing for the troops in Newfoundland. We also played in every country music park and nook and cranny that Jimmy could get us into.

At the IBMA award ceremonies in 1996 when Jimmy Martin was admitted into the Hall of Honor, Bill Emerson described what it was like to tour with Jimmy Martin. "I spent nearly five years with Jimmy Martin on the road and I'd like to tell you a little about the man that I worked for. First, I'll never forget the sound of that Martin guitar in my ear—the power and the thunder of it. And, I'll tell you, I've never heard anything like it since and I'll never forget it. It's indelible. And I'll never forget the packed houses that Jimmy drew and the way he could capture that audience and get 'em right there in the palm of his hand. He'd do it every time.

"The first tour I ever long took with Jimmy was to Las Vegas, Nevada. We played the Golden Nugget and we played it for two weeks, six nights a week and six shows a night. That was tough—forty on and twenty off.

"When we left to go to Las Vegas, this is the way we traveled: Jimmy had a '59 Cadillac. We'd line the instruments in the trunk: a couple of guitars and a banjo and a mandolin and a snare drum and a couple of boxes of records. And then we'd cram the shaving bags in the holes that were left. And then we'd lay the garment bags on top and Paul Williams and I would push as hard as we could to get that trunk lid down. And then we'd put the bass fiddle on top and the cowboy hats would go on the back window ledge. And that's the way we'd go down the road."

[68] Joe Ross, "Bill Emerson, Banjo Player Extraordinaire," *Bluegrass Unlimited*, March, 1992, p. 21.

[69] Ibid., p. 22.

[70] Ibid., p. 23.

[71] Ibid., p. 23.

Continuing with the earlier quotation with author Joe Ross, Emerson further described what it was like to tour with Jimmy Martin. "Instead of stopping at restaurants to eat, we 'jungled.' That's bologna, cheese, bread, mayonnaise, mustard, tomatoes and those little salt and pepper shakers you buy. We'd find a picnic table somewhere by the side of the road and have a great time. You know, we'd play Friday and Saturday nights at the Jamboree, go upstairs to the WWVA studios and broadcast a live show. By the time that was over, it was about 11:30 p.m.. We'd load the car and away we'd go. We wouldn't get back to Wheeling until the next Friday. We traveled all over the country like that all year long. I wouldn't want to do it again, but I wouldn't take a million dollars for the experience. There was no bus, just Jimmy's Cadillac. The bass would go on the top. Sometimes we didn't have a bass player. It was just me, Jimmy and Paul Williams. I'd been with Jimmy about a year before Kirk Hansard and Lois Johnson came along.[72]

"Jimmy deserves more recognition. Look at what he's done for bluegrass. Jimmy's an intense individual and believes in himself. I've been with him on stage and he's had 5000 people in the palm of his hand. He's just that kind of an entertainer. Jimmy knows the business inside and out. He's had some great musicians like J.D. Crowe, Alan Munde and Doyle Lawson come out of his bands. He helped us all."[73] Emerson returned to Virginia in 1962 to live permanently.

In 1964, Emerson returned to Jimmy Martin with Vernon Derrick (fiddle), Bill Torbert (mandolin) and Bill Yates (bass). Earl Taylor played with them for a while during that period. In 1966, Emerson left Martin again. He joined Wayne Yates to form a band and soon he and Wayne Yates and Buzz Busby were working together. When Yates and Busby left, Cliff Waldron came in as mandolin player and then switched to guitar. He and Emerson soon became partners (about 1967) as **Bill Emerson and Cliff Waldron and the Lee Highway Boys.**[74] When Mike Auldridge joined Emerson and

> "*Jimmy deserves more recognition. Look at what he's done for bluegrass. Jimmy's an intense individual and believes in himself. I've been with him on stage and he's had 5000 people in the palm of his hand.*" —Bill Emerson

Waldron's band, Emerson "realized Mike's potential and I did everything in my power to keep him in my band. He was a big selling-factor and he helped take us out of the old-time mode."[75]

Emerson recalled how the band name changed, "We'd been together about six months when Cliff Waldron suggested that [we change the name of the band]. We started out just playing traditional stuff. And the **Lee Highway Boys** was a very traditional-sounding name. So when we started coming up with all this more contemporary material, we decided that we should call ourselves something other than the **Lee Highway Boys** as a band name. So Cliff Waldron made the suggestion that we call ourselves 'the New Shades of Grass.' So it was **Emerson and Waldron and the New Shades of Grass.**"[76]

In early 1970, Emerson went back to the **Country Gentlemen** and joined Charlie Waller, Jimmy Gaudreau and Bill Yates in a four-way split.[77] He tried to bring Mike Auldridge into the **Gents** with him but Auldridge wouldn't go on tour with them.[78] They found a Dobro®ist to go with them when they found Jerry Douglas. And it was Emerson who convinced Ricky Skaggs to quit his day job in Manassas to join the **Gents**.

Gaudreau "left about a year after I went with them,"[79] said Emerson. "Jimmy Gaudreau decided he wanted to do other things. Doyle Lawson was playing guitar with J.D. Crowe and we'd see him at bluegrass festivals. Doyle and I had a lot in common in that he had played banjo and mandolin with Jimmy Martin. He was from the same [musical] school. Doyle was ready to leave J.D. and I offered him that job. The band was at a peak at that time. We toured Japan, signed with Vanguard Records, and were voted Best Band in '72 and '73. Doyle was a catalyst and he and I thought alike musically; we played off each other and the whole thing gelled. We came up with some good material. A lot of people think this was the best **Country Gentlemen** configuration."[80]

---

[72] Joe Ross, "Bill Emerson, Banjo Player Extraordinaire," *Bluegrass Unlimited*, March, 1992, p. 23.

[73] Ibid., p. 23.

[74] Ibid., p. 23.

[75] Ross, op. cit., p. 25.

[76] From a 1995 telephone interview.

[77] Waldron took over New Shades, Ben Eldridge took Emerson's place on banjo, and it became Cliff Waldron and the New Shades of Grass.

[78] Auldridge stayed on with Cliff Waldron's New Shades of Grass. This band was named after an LP which Emerson and Waldron did when they were partners. Dave Auldridge later joined the New Shades band on guitar.

[79] Gaudreau left to form the II Generation with Eddie Adcock et al in October 1971.

[80] Ross, op. cit., pp. 25, 26.

Just after Jerry Douglas began (his first summer) with them in 1973, Emerson left to join the U. S. Navy. The Navy was "a way to not only assure my future and give my family some security, but also a way to give something back to my country and I like the professionalism and esprit de corps at the **Navy Band**. It's a way of life, and I've benefited from it."[81] He concentrated on the management aspect of his band more than the performance part. He played very little banjo for the first ten to twelve years, though he did play his banjo in the Navy's country band, **Country Current**. He later formed a band configuration which played bluegrass at festivals and other events.

Bill Emerson's banjo playing comes mostly from his right hand. "I'm a right-hand type of banjo player. The banjo is a rhythmic thing; I've always felt the right hand is important to the dynamic and timing but you have to do something with your left hand, too." He tries to cater his playing to the guitar player. "I find it's easier for me to adapt to them than it is for them to adapt to me... It's a whole different thing playing with a Charlie Waller than it is with a Tony Rice. They're both great guitar players, but there's two different things going on there. To play with a person, you have to know them musically, know what to expect and how the feel of the rhythm is, what they're trying to accent, where their dynamics are, and support that. Well, you know, the lead guitar in bluegrass is a relatively new thing. Thirty years ago we didn't have the virtuosos on guitar that we do today, but good rhythm is important. People today need to listen to the greats and ask what they're doing that I'm not. The timing and dynamics are everything. Rhythm is the foundation of it all."[82]

On June 10, 1984, Bill Emerson was inducted into the Virginia Country Music Hall of Fame. The award was from the Virginia Folk Music Association. Others in this Hall are Patsy Cline, Roy Clark, the Statler Brothers, Eddie Adcock (1987), Jim Eanes (1988) and Tony Rice (1990). In 1986, Emerson teamed with singer/songwriter Pete Goble to record two albums for the WEBCO label: "Tennessee 1949" and "Dixie in My Eye."

Bill Emerson retired from the United States Navy on June 1st, 1993. As of 1995, he was recording for the Pinecastle Webco Recording Group, performed regularly across the nation, and was represented by Acoustigrass Entertainment of Strasburg, Virginia. He performed with Mark Newton, Emory Lester, and Bob Goff Jr. as the **New Group**.

Tony Ellis

Tony Ellis

Paul Anthony "Tony" Ellis was born in Sylva, North Carolina, July 29, 1939. His early experience in music was mainly old-time as taught by his grandmother. Here he learned frailing, modal tunings and other non-bluegrass playing styles. He would later abandon bluegrass and go back to this music.

During Ellis' formative years as a bluegrass musician, he spent valuable time with Don Reno, learning his style.[83] Reno was very generous with his time and anxious to help. Reno personally recommended Ellis to Bill Monroe for the open banjo job in 1960. But after Ellis went to work with Monroe, he had to un-learn the Don Reno style of banjo playing.

The audition with Bill Monroe was in competition with several other banjoists. Ellis said, "He could see that I was nervous; he gave me a chance to calm down. He went to lunch for about two hours and told Jack Cooke to go over some tunes with me to show me the way he wanted them played. Jack worked with me a long time, with backup, breaks, phrasing. I wouldn't have made it if Jack Cooke hadn't helped me like he did. He'd say, 'Let's do it this way.' He showed me how to lead into tunes...what strings to hit at what point...how to back off to another note, or go forward to another note, roll it in or roll it out. Just everything right down to the finest detail." After a couple of hours with Cooke, Ellis played for Monroe again. "'Now *that's* the way I want it played.' Then Bill added, 'This other fellow plays better than you, but Bessie likes you.'"[84] So Ellis got the job.

81 Ross, op. cit., p. 26.

82 Ross, op. cit., p. 30.

83 Joe Drumright was one of Ellis' favorite banjo players. A very personable and popular person, "He really loved the instrument and loved bluegrass music. When he played, he just sparkled," he told this writer.

84 Bill Workman, "Tony Ellis," *Bluegrass Unlimited*, November, 1986, p. 50. Additionally, Bill and Bessie Lee Mauldin were living together at the time.

Beginning in February 1960, Ellis played banjo, guitar and bass, and sang baritone with **Bill Monroe and the Blue Grass Boys**. He stayed until June 1962.[85] He recorded twenty-five tunes on four Decca albums[86] with Monroe including "Mr. Blue Grass," "Blue Grass Ramble," "Blue Grass Special" and "I'll Meet You in Church Sunday Morning."

When Ellis joined Monroe's band, he had an intense desire to learn bluegrass the way Bill Monroe intended it to be. He worked hard to play bluegrass music properly and considered that Monroe was the ultimate source for this kind of music—this was where he wanted to be. According to Mr. Ellis in a 1990 interview at IBMA, Monroe was a good teacher and very patient but his time restraints were great. Certainly Monroe's task of teaching another new musician how to play his music must have been considerable for a person who hires so many of them. There were 175 people who are acknowledged to have played regularly as **Blue Grass Boys**.

In May of 1962, just one month before he quit Monroe, Ellis toured with Mac Wiseman[87] for two weeks. After leaving Wiseman, Ellis abandoned bluegrass music to pursue the banjo using the tunings he had learned as a child growing up. He became inventive with the instrument and in 1987 Flying Fish released Ellis' solo album "Dixie Banner." A pleasant and interesting yet simple album, it definitely was not bluegrass. It featured members of the **Red Clay Ramblers**, his son, Bill, and clawhammer banjoist/dancer Stephen Wade. He also founded his **Appalachian Travelers** band.

In a phone interview with Ellis in January 1991, he said that he loves bluegrass, preferring the traditional early Monroe or **Flatt and Scruggs**-type music to the newer, more progressive bluegrass as is often played today. Referring to bluegrass as country music, he said, "Country music is a rural music and it was just real straight and simple and expressed human emotions and feelings which were, to me, to be more in touch with reality than the modern forms which [are] more orchestrated and arranged and loaded with a lot of hot licks and flurry." He also indicated that there is a place for the modern styles, as well. The new stuff eliminated boredom.

Tony Ellis retired from his career as a Senior Cost Clerk in 1992 and went back into the music business full-time, in addition to operating a bed and breakfast in Ohio.

J.D. Crowe, the Kentucky Mountain Boys, and the New South

One of the second-generation banjo players who gained fame with the skill and drive of Earl Scruggs or of Don Reno, as the premier banjo player with Jimmy Martin's band and with his own bands, is J.D. Crowe.

James Dee Crowe was born in Lexington, Kentucky, August 27, 1937. In 1950, Crowe began in music by playing the guitar and electric guitar in country music. His original goal was to play electric guitar behind Ernest Tubb, but when he heard **Flatt and Scruggs** his goals changed. At age thirteen, Crowe went to the barn dance every Saturday night to watch Earl Scruggs pick with Lester Flatt and their **Foggy Mountain Boys** when they would rehearse and play for a live radio show on WVLK, near Lexington. He idolized Earl.[88]

When Crowe actually started learning the banjo at age thirteen, there weren't any banjo instructors to give lessons. He bought 78s, slowed them down, and learned a lot of his technique in this manner. "I remember I used to get up in the morning," said Crowe, "and I'd catch the school bus and I would play until the school bus came. Then, when I got in, I would play like two or three hours and I would go do the chores or whatever I had to do, and then I'd eat dinner and then come back and I would play again. And then during the time that I didn't have to go to school, I would play like six or eight hours a day—I mean constantly. I mean keep it in my head."[89]

[85] During this time, Bobby Atkins spent eight months with Monroe as his banjoist.

[86] Curtis McPeake also played banjo on the LPs.

[87] Wiseman's rhythm style, Ellis noticed, was noticeably different. This was mainly due to the fact that Wiseman didn't use a capo and seemed to give a broader spectrum of highs and lows.

[88] Even today, he vividly remembers the power exuded by Scruggs. When he was on the stage, he literally dominated anything else that was going on. Scruggs is, in the eyes of Crowe, one of the main reasons bluegrass exists today.

[89] Trischka and Wernick, op. cit., pp. 155, 156.

[90] Leon Smith, "Talking with the Stars: Two Interviews from 'A Bluegrass Hornbook,'" p. 24. Note: "Bluegrass Hornbook" was a summer radio program on National Public Radio.

At fourteen, Crowe won first prize at a talent contest. This led to a performance on the radio—a show that was heard by Jimmy Martin who was driving through Lexington at the time. Martin sought out the studio, tracked down Crowe, and asked him to join the **Sunny Mountain Boys**. Crowe joined the band during the school's summer break in 1953, along with Bill Price (mandolin).

Jimmy Martin spoke of Crowe, "I always liked the way J.D. picked and I always called him the 'number one Jimmy Martin banjo player' because he stayed with me and got the style down that I liked. It suited my voice. He pitched right with my guitar and he's a banjo player that can pick kindly the way anyone sings, you know.'[90] Martin spent a lot of time teaching Crowe timing, good rhythm, and back-up playing. Crowe "complained that he couldn't play as loud as Jimmy would have liked. Martin would tell him, 'Never say I can't. Say I can, I will, I do believe.'"[91] Crowe followed this advice and became, in the opinion of many, second only to Earl Scruggs in bluegrass banjo playing.

Martin, in a 1972 interview with Doug Green, said that when J.D. Crowe went to work with Martin at age fourteen, he didn't have a style. "But as the public knows and the lovers of bluegrass music tell me," said Martin, "after he worked with me for five years, he had a style! And that style was the way Jimmy Martin wanted him to pick the banjo. Because he said he would always stay with me, I would never have to worry about another banjo player. A man can work on something if he knows he'll be there because today it's very hard to give a musician a lot of your time and after you teach him how to pick and the crowd gets to liking the sound that he picks, then he goes to work for somebody else."[92] Crowe's style became that which Martin required of all his band members and subsequent banjoists with the **Sunny Mountain Boys**. They had to play like Crowe only because that was the style Martin required for his band. Martin's style of bluegrass forced a change in Crowe's banjo playing toward more bluesy licks, straighter playing, and a more hard-driving style. Martin taught Crowe that timing is 75 percent of playing bluegrass.

Martin was very hard on musicians: he would often push them very hard to learn his songs. Martin insisted that prospective musicians know his songs before applying to him for a job. "How in the hell can you work with me and you don't know my songs?" asked Martin. "It's just like going down and asking a man for a plumbing job and him not knowing how to plumb!"[93]

Crowe learned a lot about Jimmy Martin's style of bluegrass—the way Martin insisted that it sound. One such lesson which Martin taught was a feeling for the music he loves. "I feel this style," said Crowe. "I feel what I'm doing, and I want my musicians to get the same feeling. You can't play bluegrass music unless you feel it. If you're going to sing a sad song, sing it just as lonesome as you can. And if you're going to do a toe-tapping tune, then's the time to move around a little bit."[94] And following that thought, Crowe professed, "I believe the musicians today all ought to try harder and the music would be better."[95]

In a 1991 interview, Mr. Crowe spoke of those formative days. "When you're a kid and you're learning, of course everything is great. Nothing's wrong; Man, it's all fun! That's the way it should be—the way it's supposed to be, you know. Once you get into it and really learn all the aspects and how things really work—you only do that by experience, by being in it and around the musicians themselves and doing it a long period of time—then you can tell what the business is like. But when you're young and starting out it's all great."

In 1955, for two and a half months during a summer break from high school, Crowe played with Mac Wiseman in his **Country Boys**. Like many bands of the period, Wiseman went through a lot of musicians. Band members here were Wiseman, Crowe, Benny Williams (bass) and Curtis Lee (fiddle). Crowe hadn't been playing long, only four or five years, and was "very loose" as he described it. It was "a learning stage; a very early learning stage. It was like a lot of them back then. They was hirin' younger people 'cause...well, there weren't very many banjo players around back then. The ones that *were* there, they had other jobs so they were playing for somebody else."[96] Also touring with them was **Reno and Smiley**. Crowe became influenced by Don Reno's banjo playing.

In 1956, J.D. Crowe re-joined **Jimmy Martin and the Sunny Mountain Boys**, replacing Sam Hutchins on banjo. Also in the group were Earl Taylor, Paul Williams (mandolin) and Johnny Dacus (fiddle). Crowe stayed with this band until 1960.

Jimmy Martin signed with Decca in 1956. On December first, the band's second Nashville session included Crowe, Taylor, Martin and studio musicians Gordon Terry and Cedric Rainwater. They recorded "The Grand Ole Opry Song," "I'm the Boss (of This Here House)," "Dog Bite Your Hide" and "I'll Drink No More Wine."

91 I misplaced the source of this quotation. All I can recreate is that it is by author Strickling on page 19.

92 Douglas Green, "As My Granddaddy Always Used to Say," *Bluegrass Unlimited*, September, 1972, p. 7.

93 Ibid., p. 7

94 Ibid., p. 8.

95 Ibid., p. 9.

96 From a September, 1992, interview at IBMA, Owensboro, Kentucky.

In early 1958, **Jimmy Martin and the Sunny Mountain Boys** first appeared as guests on KWKH's Louisiana Hayride, soon joining the cast of the show. Other members of the cast included country artists Johnny Horton and David Houston; guests included Johnny Cash, the **Louvin Brothers**, George Jones and Bob Luman. There was a different guest every Saturday night. They stayed about two years and toured extensively.

In February 1958, they recorded for Decca with Crowe, Williams and Martin: "I Like to Hear 'em Preach It," "Voice of My Savior," "Ocean of Diamonds," "Saphronie," "I'll Never Take No for an Answer" and "Rock Hearts." Their November recordings were "Night," "It's Not Like Home," "She Left Me Again," "Hold Whatcha Got," "Bear Tracks" and "Cripple Creek." Martin, Crowe and Williams hired Chubby Wise (fiddle) and Lightnin' Chance (bass). On these recordings Crowe played bluesy notes which reflected his R & B exposure in those days. As a matter of fact, his activities in this area were so extensive that "If it hadn't of been for Scruggs I might still be playing electric guitar today instead of banjo."[97]

In 1960, they became regulars on the WWVA Jamboree. Early that year, Crowe left the **Sunny Mountain Boys** to work in a car parts store, playing locally in small bands at small venues just to keep his hand in music.[98]

In 1963, J.D. Crowe formed the **Kentucky Mountain Boys**.[99] This was mainly a local band formed with the intention of just having fun and "keeping my chops up." It would still be a few years before he would pursue this music as a business and as a full-time occupation. They played a couple nights per week, playing mostly bluegrass and country music in the only place in town which allowed bluegrass music in Lexington.

In 1968, the **Kentucky Mountain Boys** recorded "Bluegrass Holiday,"[100] so named because they had a regular gig at the Holiday Inn North in Lexington. The album was recorded only to be sold to the Holiday Inn tourists; there was no intent for national distribution. It was a good album but poorly recorded at the brand new LEMCO Studios for the LEMCO (Lexington Music Company) label. It was later released on Rebel, said Crowe. Subsequent records included "Ramblin' Boy" (renamed "Blackjack" on Rebel, 1978) and then "Model Church."

In August of 1971, members of **J.D. Crowe and the Kentucky Mountain Boys**[101] were Crowe (banjo), Doyle Lawson (guitar), Larry Rice (mandolin), Bobby Slone (fiddle) and Jim Hatton (guitar, drums) and were still based in Lexington. About this time, Crowe changed the name of his band from the **Kentucky Mountain Boys** to **J.D. Crowe and the New South**. The new name opened up the horizons for a new sound "which could be anything... We took that name so the music wouldn't be labeled—so we could do any kind of music we wanted. Any time you've got the word 'mountain' in your name you can figure out what it is. I was trying to reach out a little further than strictly bluegrass."[102]

In 1973, they recorded "J.D. Crowe and the New South" which was released in 1975 by Starday/Gusto. Musicians were Crowe (banjo), Tony Rice (guitar), Larry Rice (mandolin), Bobby Slone (bass) with several electric instruments and drums.[103] The sound, revolutionary for the day, is still progressive by today's standards; it showed the heavy influence of the "Nashville sound".

The group has had a difficult time explaining and justifying all those electrified instruments, which alienated many bluegrass fans. Basically, though, the reason for it is "to be different and to get a broader audience."[104] Crowe said, "I love Monroe, Ralph Stanley and Don Reno; I think the world of them. I love their music. But I can't make a living at doing what they do and I shouldn't be condemned for it."

In 1975, as soon as their Starday contract was over they recorded an LP for Rounder, "J.D. Crowe and the New South," with Crowe, Tony Rice, Ricky Skaggs, Jerry Douglas and Bobby Slone (bass). Their Starday album of the same name hadn't even been released yet. This Rounder album is the LP which is often given

---

97 Joe Ross, "The Talented J.D. Crowe," *Bluegrass Unlimited*, November, 1990, p. 20.

98 Crowe was replaced in Martin's band by Shorty Edgar, then Paul Craft, and later Bill Emerson. Crowe's departure left only Paul Williams with the band. Martin wanted to hire the Bray Brothers, Harley (banjo), Nate (mandolin), and Francis (bass), but the brothers felt that they were just starting to put things together with Red Cravens and the Bray Brothers and didn't want to spoil the opportunity. Ironically, this band was gone by 1964.

99 With Bob and Charlie Joslin and many local musicians which later included Doyle Lawson (mandolin) and Bob Morris (guitar). Morris soon left and was replaced by Red Allen.

100 With Crowe (banjo), Doyle Lawson (mandolin), Red Allen (guitar) and Bobby Slone (bass).

101 Also known simply as the Kentucky Mountain Boys, it didn't matter to Crowe on way or the other. "It was just a name" he told this writer. However, after he formed his new band and had a reputation which would sustain a band, he included his name in J.D. Crowe and the New South.
     In October of 1971, Tony Rice left the Bluegrass Alliance to join Crowe's band. His brother, Larry, was already a member as mandolinist, replacing Doyle Lawson who had left to join the Country Gentlemen, and was heavily influenced by the mandolin style of John Duffey. Bobby Slone was still on bass. Slone had joined in the mid-'60s and was previously with the Kentucky Colonels.

102 Ross, op. cit., p. 20.

103 Besides Crowe, Rice and Slone, J.D. used Hal Rugg, Pig Robbins, Ray Eddington, Buddy Harmon, Kenny Malone and Dennis Digby. In a 3/9/93 telephone conversation, Crowe remarked: "They were session pickers and they did a lot of recording with everybody and I just wanted to use them to see what it would do."

104 From a January 23, 1995, phone conversation.

credit as being "one of the most influential bluegrass albums of the decade." Crowe modestly commented on this recognition which the album received, "It probably did help rejuvenate the interest in bluegrass with the younger pickers because everything was kind of dead about that time; there was nothing exciting happening in the way of groups. There was good groups out [there] but they were kind of older and they died down and they were just doin' their regular, same old thing. And we came out with that album with some different material on it with the acoustic drive and everything and I think it really did stir the interest back."[105]

Crowe explained why he now had two albums of the same name released the same year by two different record companies, "That deal was that we recorded that Starday LP before we got the Rounder deal. And what happened is that the Starday people held it up. Earlier they was excited to get us in the studio and they wanted us to record. So we did. And then they held it up! I kept waiting for a release. In other words, I got real frustrated at that bunch. That's the way some record companies operate. But what happened was, see, I signed a contract to do [that] album and couldn't do an album for two years after that, so I was tied up from '73 to '75. So that really ticked me off. I don't know why they never released it after they was the ones that wanted us to go in and do it anyway. And after the two years was up I recorded with Rounder. Then what did Starday do? Nothin' but release that one."[106]

1981 marked the return of Crowe to a more traditional style of bluegrass music when he performed with the **Bluegrass Album Band** with Tony Rice, Doyle Lawson, Bobby Hicks and Todd Phillips. This LP for Rounder was very well accepted and eventually stretched to five LPs and CDs. Its acceptance also gave an indication of the tastes of bluegrass audiences which now seemed to crave the more traditional sounds of bluegrass. The album was a commitment which Tony Rice made to Rounder to produce albums (this was after Rice had split from Grisman in 1979). Skaggs was not available so Rice and Crowe got Doyle Lawson. Jerry Douglas joined on Volume 3 and Vassar Clements took Hicks' place on Volume 5. In 1983, the musicians did a tour as a band, not simply as recording musicians, and made occasional festival appearances through the 1980s.

In 1982, a country and western album came out which exhibited a change in Crowe's style away from bluegrass. "Somewhere Between" (Rounder) featured Crowe (banjo), Bobby Slone (fiddle), Wendy Miller (mandolin), Keith Whitley (guitar) and several electric instruments. Whitley stayed four years with the group.[107]

Crowe has served as an inspiration for banjoists such as Bela Fleck, Greg Cahill, Steve Cooley and Pete Wernick. Crowe explained why he has his **strings** extraordinarily high off the head, "It's not because I wanted it that way, but because I had to have it that way. Years ago, in the '50s, you had one microphone, maybe two if you were lucky. I played so you could hear the banjo no matter where it was. That's why you learned to play hard and you had to have high action to do it. But now I don't play that hard. I've heard it on records and tapes and you lose a little of the tone. So I've let my action down to where it's a little easier to play."[108] Crowe announced his retirement from performing in 1989, but couldn't stay retired and kept up his New South into the 1990s.

Doug (L) and Rodney Dillard, c. 1989.

---

[105] Interview 1992.

[106] Telephone conversation with Mr. Crowe, March 9, 1995. He loves working with Rounder and feels that it is one of the best of the independent labels.
    Larry Rice left in 1974 and Ricky Skaggs filled-in for nearly a year.
    In October of 1975, Skaggs and Douglas left the New South to form Boone Creek. Rice left at the same time to help David Grisman found the David Grisman Quintet. Jimmy Gaudreau joined on mandolin, staying four and a half years. Harley Allen joined the band for a very short time after the Japan tour when they were back at the Sheraton Inn in Lexington. Glenn Lawson joined on mandolin during this same period. Lawson stayed with the band two and a half years. Harley Allen then left to play with his brothers and Lawson moved to guitar. Lawson recorded on the New South's "You Can Share My Blanket" on Rounder. It included musicians Crowe, Lawson (guitar), Gaudreau (mandolin), Slone (fiddle), Charlie McCoy (harmonica) et al.
    In 1978, the New South, having lost Glenn Lawson, consisted of his replacement, Keith Whitley (who had left Ralph Stanley's band), Crowe, Jimmy Gaudreau, Bobby Slone and Mike Gregory. Gene Johnson was with the band about this time for a year. Johnson, as of 1992, worked for Diamond Rio as mandolinist.

[107] Beginning in 1983, Paul Adkins was the lead singer for the New South for two and a half seasons. Also with the band were Bobby Slone (fiddle), Wendy Miller (mandolin) and Randy Hayes (bass). Adkins was replaced by Tony King and they recorded "Straight Ahead" released on Rounder in 1987 with guests Sam Bush, Jerry Douglas and Steve Bryant.

[108] Ross, op. cit., p. 23.

Doug Dillard

The Dillards and Doug Dillard

The story of the **Dillards** band could easily fit into the Pioneers chapter of this book. For simplicity, the story of both banjoist Douglas Dillard and the group he helped found is presented here.

One of the most significant banjo players in bluegrass is Douglas Flint Dillard. He reached fame in the banjo world in the early 1960s with the group he founded with his brother Rodney: the **Dillards**. His innovative banjo tunes and rhythmic drive became standards for many people trying to learn how to play the banjo. The group's influence on the music in southern California cannot be overestimated. Many people began their bluegrass career as a result of listening to this group.

Doug was born March 6, 1937, in Salem, Missouri; Rodney was also born there, on May 18, 1942. Both of the boys were highly influenced toward bluegrass and old-time music by their father, Homer, who played music and was an accomplished clogger. About 1953, Doug got his first banjo and began picking two- and three-finger style in a local Salem band. Upon seeing **Flatt and Scruggs** on the Opry, he knew he wanted to be on the show. Doug and Rodney formed the **Ozark Mountain Boys** in 1956 and soon began television appearances on the Ozark Opry. Doug bought a classic Gibson Bella Voce tenor banjo in an Oklahoma City pawn shop for $295, converted it to a five-string, and still uses it today. The group soon recorded "Mama Don't Allow"/"Highway of Sorrow" on the K-Arc label of St. Louis using the name, the **Dillard Brothers**.

The **Dillards** was formed in 1962 with Doug, Rodney (guitar), Dean Webb[109] (mandolin) and Mitch Jayne (bass). They played together about a month, mainly rehearsing. Their first concert was at Washington University. In the summer of 1962, the **Dillards**

began their move from their home in the Ozarks west to Los Angeles and continued to teach Mitch to play bass in the back seat of the car on the way to California.

Jayne related, "We didn't get to California until November—it was after Thanksgiving—of 1962. You see, we left in the summer and then we stopped and worked in Oklahoma City for a month. I remember that Rodney's Aunt Decky gave us a turkey for Thanksgiving dinner—that's how I remembered that—and we got paid at the Buddeye and they kept us an extra week because we did so well and they gave us a bonus. So we had $500 and a turkey and a one-wheeled trailer hooked to the back of the car. And we forgot about the turkey after we got out there—you know, the shear thrill of Los Angeles and downtown Hollywood and Melrose Avenue and everything. And it got *really* ripe!"

The first thing they did was to set up in the lobby of Hollywood's premier folk club, The Ash Grove, and played until they were noticed. It didn't take long for people to notice their high energy music and entertainment skills. Jayne said, "What I figured made us **Dillards** so successful was that we took it on as a mission to bring bluegrass to the ignorant people who had never been exposed to a class act. Those places we'd play back then didn't know what a banjo was and they'd try to dance to saxophones and pianos and all that outlandish stuff. Douglas would even have to show some man how to dance with his wife by getting his claws in her flanks himself and capering around with her. I think we left a trail of believers all the way to California, judging by the cars that would chase after us sometimes, wanting to go along."

"We hadn't been in town very long before we got that job on 'The Andy Griffith Show,'" said Jayne. "We had the Elektra contract within about two days of the 'Andy Griffith Show' thing. One of Andy's staff people had seen us in *Variety* with a picture and a write-up about us being signed by Elektra. He noticed that and he came down and saw us at The Ash Grove and they thought we were just perfect for this part. So we auditioned for Andy and his staff and Andy liked us and

Rodney Dillard (L) and Steve Cooley of the Dillards.

---

109 Webb, from Lone Jack, Missouri, was highly influenced by Bill Monroe and Red Rector and was working in local bands and was flexible enough to go with the band to California.

all of a sudden we were employed where, just a month before, we hadn't been employed at all. All of a sudden we were on the TV show we had watched at home.

"The show had only been on the air two years by the time we got there and they were trying all kinds of things in the first year and they wanted to get Andy involved in a musical thing. They called Clarence and Roland White and Billy Ray Lathum and Roger Bush and Leroy Mack who were the **Country Boys.** They were mainly background music for some singer who was the person who was going to get a record contract on the show. The writers of the show hadn't written-in the Darling family yet and they were looking for some group to fit in just right and they found us. We were straight out of the Ozarks and were pretty rangy looking."[110]

This is another instance of "being in the right place at the right time." They caught the tail end of the folk boom and exposed many, many people to bluegrass music there in Los Angeles. The television appearances lasted until 1965. They acted the parts of the Darling family, playing the hillbilly image to the hilt.

They began recording for Elektra in 1964; their first album was "Backporch Bluegrass." They met Byron Berline about that time and invited him to be on their next record, the instrumental "Pickin' and Fiddlin' with Byron Berline, Fiddle." Their next Elektra album was "Live—Almost," recorded at The Mecca in Los Angeles.

In 1968, Doug Dillard left the band and struck out on his own. He then toured Europe with the **Byrds.** Doug Dillard, David Jackson, Gene Clark and Bernie

The Dillards as they appeared in the 1990's. L to R: Dean Webb, Mitch Jayne, Rodney Dillard, Steve Cooley. Photo courtesy Mitch Jayne.

Leadon formed the **Dillard and Clark Expedition** and recorded "The Fantastic Expedition of Dillard and Clark" album and "Through the Morning, Through the Night" on the A & M label. In 1970, when Gene Clark left, Doug changed the name of his band to the **Dillard and the Expedition with Byron Berline.** Dillard added ex-**Kentucky Colonels** Billy Ray Lathum (guitar) and Roger Bush (bass). He recorded with the **Monkees** using an electric Rickenbacker banjo, and with Hoyt Axton.

The **Dillards,** now consisting of Rodney Dillard, Dean Webb and Mitch Jayne, hired Herb Pedersen to take Doug's place on banjo. Doug was not to return to the **Dillards** until they did a reunion tour in 1989. However, occasionally they got together to do family things such as the "Homecoming" album.

By 1972, the **Dillards**[111], under the guidance of Rodney Dillard, had changed their acoustic music to electric. Like many musicians, they were trying to find the best way to make a living. They also became rather rock-oriented in their music. The **Dillards** changed back to acoustic in 1989 when they did their reunion tour with Doug, Rodney, Dean and Mitch.

The next year, Doug Dillard began a long period of time doing studio work in Los Angeles in the "Popeye" and "Bonnie and Clyde" movies and on albums. On that second movie, he did all the music during the movie except the theme which was done by **Flatt and Scruggs and the Foggy Mountain Boys** ("Foggy Mountain Breakdown" was originally recorded in 1949). He did studio work until he started his own **Doug Dillard Band** in 1977. He recorded on Glen Campbell's "Gentle on My Mind."

---

[110] Roland White, in a 1996 telephone interview, explained that the Country Boys had already been on two episodes of "The Andy Griffith Show" as a hillbilly band before the show staff decided they wanted to write the Darling family into the script. Roland had already been drafted into the Army so wasn't around the band to be a part of this directly. Actually, by the time that he returned from the Army, the band had changed its name to Kentucky Colonels.

The Dillards were interviewed for the part; they were just right for the Darling family with their coon skin caps and Ozark upbringing. And they instantly hit it off with Griffith who is a southerner from Mt. Airy, NC.. They were also chosen because they were better actors than the Country Boys. Roland and Clarence were just too shy to be as animated as the part called for. Roland also said the Dillards even had the dumb, hillbilly facial expressions which helped make the part famous. Clarence: "We didn't look dumb enough!"

[111] Still in 1972, Jayne retired from the Dillards to write books and articles for various magazines. He became a school teacher. He described a sense of kinship which might occur within a bluegrass band after it breaks up: "I never forgot my friends for a minute, and they didn't forget me. You form some very close bonds from years of playing bluegrass, which I don't think you'd get from a symphony orchestra or acting in the movies. Bluegrass pickers play on hot stages in a newly-cut hay field, or on truck beds, or in the small clubs who cater to our music and travel together across America in vans or busses, talking about things they have in common, sharing the road. In a very satisfying way, bluegrass is as American as the green lady who welcomes people in New York harbor. It's the only thing of its kind, and has an indelible worth. No music that I've ever heard has a pull on me like bluegrass, and I think it's for all the right reasons... Bluegrass is the music that reminds us joyfully what America is all about... It may not be very big, but it glows with a light no one will ever put out." Source: Mitch Jayne, "Bluegrass and the Return to Mayberry," *Bluegrass Unlimited*, November, 1986, pp. 33, 34.

Doug Dillard formed the **Doug Dillard Band** in 1977. Their first record was "Jackrabbit"[112] on Flying Fish. Doug, Rodney and friend Byron Berline appeared on film in Bette Midler's "The Rose" in 1979. In 1980, banjoists Doug Dillard and Bill Knopf collaborated on the instruction book *The Bluegrass Banjo Style of Douglas Flint Dillard* (Alamo Publications).[113]

In 1986, twenty-three years after the **Dillards** first appeared on the "Andy Griffith Show" as the **Darling Family**, they returned for a reunion of the fictitious family. Rodney was now forty-two, Doug and Dean were approaching fifty, Mitch was fifty-seven "and deafer than a cypress stump." These reunion tours continued into the mid-1990s due to the popularity of the Darling family. Rodney, Mitch, Dean and Doug appeared regularly at the events but Griffith would rarely (if ever) appear at this type of event where people came to praise him publicly.

Flying Fish released "Heartbreak Hotel" in 1988. Musicians in the **Doug Dillard Band** were David Grier (guitar), Doug (banjo), Ginger Boatwright (guitar) and Roger Rasnake (electric bass). Guest fiddler/mandolinist was Jonathan Yudkin. Douglas worked with Rodney to help produce it and they received a Grammy nomination for the work.

In 1989, the original **Dillards** conducted a reunion tour after an absence of twenty-four years. About the idea of a reunion tour, Jayne humorously wrote, "They have been after us to get back together and pick a few tunes and they want me to tell some more stories about the home town and people and such. I've a good notion to go, just to get back together with the boys who never did come home, and good luck catching them up! Last I heard, Dean was selling Rolls Royce cars and trucks to country music stars that have made it big in his home town. [Rodney] has the plaster dog and bird bath concession at Lake of the Ozarks and owns an English Tudor double-wide trailer home and a paddle boat shaped like a swan. Douglas Dillard owns a fleet of miniature dunking booths called Dumpa-Dwarfs or something like that, and picks the banjo for weddings."

The songs and comedy routines during the tour were similar to that of years before and they found their audiences not only receptive to their act, they were enthusiastic about seeing this famous foursome again. Many individuals of the audiences recalled their music and antics and music from the **Dillards'** early days at The Ash Grove and were grateful for their re-appearance. Mitch sold his 1989 publication, *An Up To Date Biography of the Original Dillards...and Other Lies (Vol II)*. They recorded a homecoming album which included all the people who had ever been members of the band

through the years. Doug did this reunion tour for a short while then returned to his own **Doug Dillard Band**. The tour was both fun and financially rewarding for the quartet which added close friend Steve Cooley, regular banjoist with Rodney's **Dillards**, to do the guitar flatpicking in the act. Jayne and Rodney said that because the pressure of making a living was off, they were having the time of their lives...enjoying it to the hilt. The tour highlighted the historical importance of the group. Rodney said, "I'm just beginning to realize that we made a difference."

Allen Shelton

Allen Shelton

Jim Eanes spoke of the banjo playing of Allen Shelton, "If I was to consider who was one of the best banjo pickers around, I would seriously have to consider Allen Shelton 'cause I worked with him so much. There was a lot of banjo pickers but I can't place one guy and say he is the best. Reno, he had his style; I liked him. Earl Scruggs had his style. J.D. Crowe's got his style. So you can't say who's the best in the business. But Allen was more of a type of a banjo picker that could play anything. He could play Scruggs, he could play Reno; he could do anything. And he was far ahead of a lot of banjo pickers because he played country stuff on the banjo. On my early recordings, he didn't pick it, he barred it like a Dobro®! He didn't feature the other kinds of styles, like Reno-style, but he could play it. You know, he and Reno played a lot together. Reno was just up the road sixty miles. I used to go up there and fill-in for Reno when they would go out on the road. I'd take my band and do his TV show, see."[114]

[112] Musicians included Douglas Dillard, Ray Park (fiddle, guitar), Bill Bryson (bass), Skip Conover (resonator guitar), Byron Berline (fiddle) and Sam Bush (mandola). It was recorded at the 1979 Telluride Bluegrass and Country Music Festival. Producers were Rodney Dillard and Keith Case.

[113] A new member of the Doug Dillard Band in 1982 was Ginger Boatwright. There were several other band members over time including David Grier on lead guitar. In September, Steve Cooley joined Rodney's Dillards as banjoist and lead guitarist. He had formerly been with Bluegrass Alliance, Katy Laur Band and Gateway. Other members of the Doug Dillard Band were Kathy Chiavola and John Yudkin at various times.

[114] Telephone interview, January, 1993.

Banjoist Shelton spoke of his job as a sideman, "When you're playing behind a guy singing, you want to complement what he is doing. You don't want to sound so far out that people are looking at you instead of listening to the guy sing—that's not what it's about. You're backing him... You're trying to make him sound good. I think a lot of pickers lose that. But to me, that's my job."[115] He spoke from experience—the North Carolinian is one of bluegrass' veteran banjoists who took up the banjo in the late 1940s. Since then he's played with **Jim Eanes and the Shenandoah Valley Boys** (1952, 1957), Mac Wiseman (1953), **Hack Johnson and the Tennesseeans** (1953), **Jim and Jesse and the Virginia Boys** (1960s, 1980s) and recorded several solo LPs.

Allen Shelton was born in Rockingham County, North Carolina, near Reidsville, July 2, 1936, and was the son of a sharecropper whose family raised tobacco, corn, etc.. His father was a multi-instrumentalist who played square and round dances. Fourteen year-old Allen joined his father when the banjo player quit. His father teased him when he was learning the banjo; Allen was "trying to use the rolls real slow." His father told him that "my right hand looked like a big spider crawling."[116] His teachers were his father and Hubert Davis. His formative days of learning to play banjo also included years with close friend Bobby Atkins. Allen's early idols were Bill Monroe and Chet Atkins and he loved the playing of both Earl Scruggs and Don Reno. He'd listen to **Reno and Smiley** on WDBJ in Roanoke then flip the dial to **Flatt and Scruggs** in Raleigh from 1:30 to 2:00 p.m. daily. Shelton said, "Well, I can't really say that nobody ever set down and really showed me back then, but I learned fast. Whoever was playing, whether they were real good or bad, didn't matter. If you stood and listened long enough, there'd be some little lick or something that you liked that you could pick up."[117]

Shelton went to work for Eanes in November 1952 after his audition of "Cumberland Gap." Somewhat of a beginner, Shelton practiced incessantly and became better quickly. Shelton, on the liner notes of "Shelton Special" (Rounder Records 0088), recalled how he got the job with Eanes. "I was listening to [Eanes] every day on the radio. Hubert Davis was playing banjo for him. Hubert got so he was there part of the time and part of the time he wasn't. We went down there one time and I played at Jim's dance—they had a regular Saturday night thing in Danville—and he asked me if I wanted a job. I stayed with him six months and then I got a call from Mac Wiseman which was a much better

job." Wiseman's job was at the Old Dominion Barn Dance in Richmond, Virginia, at the time. Wiseman, he recalled, "didn't carry a bass and he'd play very little rhythm on the guitar. And if a hard-driving style was ever needed, *there* is where you had to put it."

After Shelton left Wiseman's **Country Boys**, he joined Hack Johnson's **Tennesseeans** which played on WPTF, Raleigh, North Carolina. He stayed for two and a half years with the band and did four sides for Colonial Records. Johnson quit music soon after the radio station let him go. Curly Howard then took over the band and they changed their name to the **Farm Hands**.[118] In 1955 at WPTF, Shelton recorded "Home Sweet Home" for Colonial Records using peg tuners. Its immediate success caused King Records to have Don Reno record his own version of the song. The flip side was "You Don't Have to Be from the Country."

Shelton re-joined Jim Eanes' **Shenandoah Valley Boys** for the second time in 1956 at WHEE in Martinsville, West Virginia. Shelton spoke of this time with Jim Eanes, "We were playing three dances a week, at least four hours a night. He sang everything—all the popular country songs of the day. And then you played your square sets. That's a big challenge; you have to learn a lot of backup and a lot of lead...things you don't normally learn in a big band." They recorded on Mercury, Starday and Blue Ridge.

According to Jim Eanes, Shelton "put a handle on his banjo like an electric guitar and tuned it so he could bar it with his finger and we worked up the arrangements using that. He would just push it with his wrist and it would change the tone."[119] This device enabled the banjo to duplicate the sound of the pedal steel.

The material which Shelton and Eanes did was rather commercial and varied to appeal to the rural audience there at WHEE. "When I was working for Jim Eanes out of Martinsville, only fifty miles from Roanoke, [Don] Reno was on Roanoke and he hear could me and I could hear him. I thought it kind of odd, you know, as soon as I worked out 'Under the Double Eagle' and played it two or three times, just a month or two later it came out on a King record with Reno. Of course, it was completely different the way he did it. I don't hold any hard feelings."[120]

Much of his time with **Jim and Jesse and the Virginia Boys** was with Vassar Clements (fiddle), David Sutherland (bass), then Jim Buchanan (fiddle) and Don McHan (guitar). "You could tell just the way it clicked and the way people responded. Of course, when you play that much you get kind of numb to what you're doing. All you can really go by is how people accept it.

115 R.J. Kelly, "Allen Shelton—Working the Bluegrass Trail," *Bluegrass Unlimited*, May, 1989, p. 63.

116 Ibid., p. 57.

117 Pete Wernick interview April 5, 1984, for his book *Masters of the Five-String Banjo* (New York: Oak Publications, 1988), p. 134.

118 Members of the band were Shelton, Roy Russell, Curly Howard (guitar) and Joe Phillips (bass).

119 Pete Kuykendall, "Smilin' Jim Eanes," *Bluegrass Unlimited*, February, 1973, p. 10.

120 Liner notes by Tony Trischka from "Shelton Special."

We did a Columbia (Records) breakfast one morning and we did 'Diesel Train' on it. Man, they wouldn't let us off the stage. We knew then we had to be doing something."

Shelton worked as a pipe fitter from the late 1960s until re-joining **Jim and Jesse** in 1984 for a few years, then gradually disappeared from the music scene and went into the building trades.

Don Stover

Don Stover and the White Oak Mountain Boys

Don Stover is one of the greats of the bluegrass banjo. If one listens to the bluegrass music of the fifties, sixties and seventies, Stover can be heard with many popular groups of the day. His fame is small because he toured very little, preferring to stay somewhat local.

He was born in Ameagle, West Virginia, March 6, 1928, and grew up in the coal mining country around White Oak, West Virginia. There he was influenced by, and began playing the two-finger style playing of, Wade Mainer. Then he began playing clawhammer banjo with other locals.

During the mid-'40s, Stover heard Earl Scruggs (with Monroe on the Opry) and the three-finger picking for the first time on the radio. This style of picking was certainly foreign around White Oak; no one knew how Scruggs did it—or even how many picks he used. Stover tried to duplicate Scruggs' playing but their live performance schedule offered few opportunities to hear enough to be able to discern the necessary elements of the style. The purchase of the single "Foggy Mountain Breakdown" enabled him to copy the style—three years later.

"It was a shock to me the first night I heard the Grand Ole Opry," said Stover. "I heard the banjo and I recognized the banjo but the guy was playing it different from what I played. I couldn't find out how until... There was an old pack peddler—what we called 'pack peddlers'—came through our hometown. He had a big leather bag and he'd sell ladies' shoes and little girls'

dresses. No wheels. No transportation. He just packed all that stuff in there. One of them told me one time he knowed this fella Scrubbs. He put the 'B's in there. He said, 'I seen this guy Scrubbs play that banjo.' And I said, 'Well, how does he play it?' He said, 'He tickles it with his fingers like this' (Stover animated this movement on his right hand). And I saw him do that and I said, 'What do you mean?' Then he said, 'Well, he's got some steel picks on those.' But he's got 'em on backwards. That didn't make no sense to me. I took my mother's best sewing scissors and took a Prince Albert tobacco tin can and I made me some things to wrap around my fingers. (He laughed when he said that he first put the picks on backwards). What a rat race that was! I had a terrible time.

"And I would listen to Earl and Lester and Bill Monroe on the Wall-Rite Program on Saturday nights. And on Sunday I'd set all day and pick my banjo and drive my poor mom just crazy as a dog. She run me out of the house. I'd go sit down under an apple tree somewhere and pick-pick-pick eight hours a day. And she'd come to the back door to shake out a mop or broom and see me sittin' out there in the field and she'd yell out to me, 'Are you still at that stuff? Why don't you give it up! It's driving me crazy.' And me, too! But I just wouldn't give it up. I finally got to where I could play 'Bluegrass Breakdown' and 'Mollie and Tenbrooks.' Earl and Lester disappeared from the Opry when they formed their own band and went down to WCYB in Bristol. That's the only banjo I heard for a long, long time.

"I heard Don Reno the first night he ever went with Bill Monroe. Poor Don was a great banjo player. We all know that. But Don was having to play the same stuff that Earl left with. So therefore he couldn't shine on his own and he couldn't play Earl's stuff like Earl could play it. Later on, he got his own style and things going for him like it should have been done. This change was when he got with Red Smiley. He went back to his way of playin' the banjo—the way he heard it in his head. It's awfully hard for two people to play banjos just exactly alike; they don't hear it and don't think it the same way. It's been written that I pick a lot like Earl Scruggs. I don't know whether it's true or not. I just pick the what I feel in my soul and the way I learned it when I was very young, and the way I feel.

"But I can pick old-time clawhammer and do some old-time mountain songs. That kind of helped me out, too, when bluegrass had some hard times in the fifties, early sixties; my clawhammer kind of bailed me out right there 'cause I could play all those folk shows, you know. I could sit down at the Library of Congress, play at their lunch break. And I played bluegrass circuits and folk shows, too."[121]

In the late 1940s, Stover worked full-time as a coal miner and part-time with the **Coal River Valley Boys** on the local WOAY. During that time, the **Lilly Broth-**

Bluegrass Banjo

ers were playing on WWVA's Jamboree with members "B" (guitar) and Everett (mandolin) Lilly, Red Belcher (banjo) and Tex Logan (fiddle). By August 1952, Stover had left the mines of West Virginia and began music full-time when he joined the Lilly brothers and Tex Logan in Boston.[122] The **Confederate Mountaineers** played regularly on WCOP at the Plaza Club, and then at the famous Hillbilly Ranch where they played for eighteen years, seven nights a week. The bar became a Mecca for touring musicians including Bill Monroe who once played with them in an all-night session. When Stover would occasionally leave the band, he was replaced by Joe Val or Bob French on banjo.

In 1954, Stover recorded on WRC-TV with **Buzz Busby and the Bayou Boys** in Washington, D.C.. The next year, Stover and the **Bayou Boys** moved to KWKH's Louisiana Hayride in Shreveport. Also appearing on the Hayride about that time were country stars Elvis Presley, Johnny Horton and the Browns.

Stover worked with the **Lilly Brothers** until 1956, then joined **Bill Monroe and the Blue Grass Boys** for six months. He recorded on Decca on the songs "Sitting on Top of the World" and "Molly and Tenbrooks" and on Monroe's "Knee Deep in Bluegrass" album. Later in 1956, Stover left Monroe to join the **Lilly Brothers** again. They recorded, on Event Records, records that were later reissued by County Records as "The Lilly Brothers and Don Stover."

With the **Lilly Brothers**, Stover recorded on the Folkways and Prestige labels. He also recorded with the **Brothers** on the album produced in 1958 by Mike Seeger and Alan Lomax, "Mountain Music Bluegrass Style" (Folkways).

In 1966, Stover took time out from the **Lilly Brothers** to play with **Bill Harrell and the Virginians** in Washington, D.C., for a little less than a year. Mr. Stover told this writer that he just had to get away from that seven-days-a-week job they had up at the Hillbilly Ranch up in Boston.

When the Everett and "B" split the band up in September 1969, Stover stayed on in the area to form the **White Oak Mountain Boys**[123] (which lasted until 1976) and recorded on Rounder Records (reissued on compact disc in 1995). Stover likes to do an occasional old-time music tune and used the old clawhammer banjo in his act. But the old-time music has a different timing to it and may make some of his musicians uncomfortable with music other than traditional bluegrass. He explained that this was one of the reasons his musicians

would go back and forth between his band and Joe Val's **New England Bluegrass Boys**.

In 1976, he appeared on the "Johnny Carson Show" and on Doc and Merle Watson's "Good Deal in Nashville" album. In 1978, Stover, Doc and Merle Watson, and Tex Logan played two weeks at the Olympics in Mexico City after which Stover moved back to Massachusetts. In 1979, Stover played with Bill Clifton and Red Rector as the **First Generation**. Continuing to work with Clifton and Rector, they recorded as the **Pick of the Crop** band until Rector passed away in 1990, Stover also worked as a solo act, retired to West Virginia for nearly four years, and finally to Brandywine, Maryland. He played on an occasional album and at an occasional bluegrass festival into the mid-1990s. He died November 11, 1996.

John Hartford

John Hartford is sometimes acknowledged as a great bluegrass musician. But his true roots and love in music is the old-timey styles. Indeed, though he has been in various bands which played bluegrass music, few of them played the traditional style of bluegrass such as that of **Flatt and Scruggs** or Bill Monroe's bands. He told this writer, "I'm not sure I'm qualified to be in your book 'cause I'm just what I am and the tradition that I come out of is old-time fiddling. I love bluegrass a whole lot, and I've played it a lot but I don't know if I'm that, or just what I am. But there is one thing that is definitely sure: that this music, or a lot of the use of this music, originally was dance music, and a whole lot of it now serves as a demonstration of people who want to do their tricks. And I think people get frustrated because they want to dance. I love to dance and I love to move my body. I love it when audiences

---

[122] Everett had just left Flatt and Scruggs (Everett went back to Flatt and Scruggs in 1957). They wore Confederate uniforms. This went over well down South but not so well up North. The idea, though, was show business and not a protest: a different style of dressing—a way of being identified.

Bill Keith started playing the plectrum banjo in the Boston/Cambridge-based Dixieland bands and later took lessons from Don Stover when the Lilly brothers were a part of Tex Logan, the Lilly Brothers and the Confederate Mountaineers. Bill Keith is just one of the future bluegrass banjoists whom Stover influenced. According to Jim Rooney: "In 1959, I met Bill Keith at Amherst College. He was playing a long-neck Pete Seeger-style banjo and was just learning how to play Scruggs-style banjo. I took Bill to hear Don Stover at the Hillbilly Ranch and I think it is fair to say that Don's playing had a profound affect on Bill."—Letter to *Bluegrass Unlimited*, January 1992, p. 8.

[123] Members included himself (banjo), Bob Tidwell (mandolin), Bill Phillips (guitar) and Dave Messer (bass). Through the years, members included Bob Jones, Buzz Busby, Dave Dillon, Al Jones, Fred Bartenstein, Bob Dennoncourt, Carl Rebello, Jack Tottle and Herb Applin.

get up and dance with me. We dance and carry-on and whoop and holler and have a good time. [Incidentally], Bill Monroe started out as a dancer."[124]

Hartford is a genuine person who loves to play and entertain. It is this quality, and because of all the exposure he received on television in the '70s, which makes him an asset for bluegrass music. In 1984, Hartford received the Million-Aires Award for his "Gentle On My Mind" song which was played four million times on the air—more than any country song in BMI history. Even though the song is not at all bluegrass, he gained significant recognition which rubbed off onto bluegrass.

Born in New York City on December 30, 1937, he was raised around St. Louis, Missouri, where he began, at age eleven, playing his father's fiddle when his father wasn't looking. By thirteen, he played the mandolin, and then a Vega Whyte Ladye plectrum banjo which was bought for $2 at a Goodwill store; he modified it to accommodate a fifth string. Local dances exposed him to fiddle music. Stringbean, who was playing on the Grand Ole Opry at the time, exposed him to the frailed banjo. Hartford could pick up the portion of the Opry sponsored by Prince Albert Tobacco which was broadcast over the local NBC affiliate, KSB, in St. Louis. "If you got out on the road, or on a clean night had a wire strung up, you could pick it up straight from Nashville."[125] He listened for Stringbean and Brother Oswald Kirby (who was the resonator guitar player/comedian with Roy Acuff's **Smoky Mountain Boys**). He didn't hear **Flatt and Scruggs** until 1952 when that band came to town. Then, like many who heard Earl Scruggs play the banjo, he was hooked when he saw the show.

Kicking around the music in the Midwest included a founding role with the **Ozark Mountain Trio**, as a disc jockey, and with the **Ozark Mountaineers**. After Glen Campbell recorded Hartford's "Gentle On My Mind" on Capitol in 1967, he gained instant fame (Hartford had recorded the tune first for RCA). That year, Tommy Smothers hired him to write for "The Smothers Brothers Comedy Hour" along with another five-string picker, Steve Martin.

Hartford experimented with various banjo parts in the 1960s and came to the conclusion that it isn't the tone ring which is the most important part of the banjo. Indeed, he played a banjo with a wooden tone ring (a Deering) for years. He likes a banjo to be "nice and dead and have lots of mid-range." Even if a person wants a tinny banjo sound, it's not entirely dependent upon the tone ring. "The tone ring has a lot to do with it. The sound of the tone ring has a lot to do with it. The thickness of the head has a lot to do with it. The bridge has a lot to do with it, and the gauge of the strings has a tremendous amount to do with it. And the pitch of the strings has a lot to do with it. It depends upon your

fingerpicks—whether you're using thin fingerpicks or fat fingerpicks. So, everyone of those is a variable. And your attack, too—whether you're playing on top of the beat or behind it or whatever. That has a lot to do with it. And the distance from the bridge that you play. And also, too, action has a lot to do with it. You can take a banjo that is real dead-sounding and lower the action down where the strings ping on the frets and make it sound tinnier than hell. So, there's a lot of knobs to turn. And there's another trick, too: the tightness of the head makes a difference. And you can actually loosen or tighten the truss rod because what that does is loosens or tightens the pot and lets it breathe."[126] Hartford's 1992 Deering banjo has two additional frets which give him two full octaves and moves the bridge up more to the center of the pot and gives more vibrating space around the bridge on the head.

In 1971, John Hartford founded the **Dobrolic Plectral Society** with Tut Taylor (resonator guitar), Norman Blake (multi-instrumentalist) and Vassar Clements (fiddle). It is often referred to as the **Aereoplane Band** because of the LP of the same name. Hartford's 1976 "Mark Twang" received a Grammy Award for Best Ethnic or Traditional Recording. The next year, he was selected for inclusion into the 14th edition of *Who's Who in America*. During the summer, he occasionally serves as a relief pilot for crews on the General Jackson showboat that runs on the Mississippi River. As of 1996, he lives near Nashville and performs regularly.

Bobby Thompson

Bobby Thompson— banjo innovator and studio musician

Banjoist Vic Jordan wrote "Jordan's Hornpipe" as a direct reflection of Bobby Thompson. "I think Bobby is the finest there is," said Jordan in 1974. "Not everyone can appreciate how good he is. I played bass with **Jim and Jesse**—which was a disaster because

124 Telephone interview, March 18, 1992.

125 Ibid..

126 Ibid..

I'm no bass player but I wanted to get with the group so bad that I'd have done anything. I watched Bobby play and do some fantastic things. But the people just looked at each other like, 'When are we going to hear some breakdowns?' I guess he was just a little too smooth—a little too good for them. Now Bobby's doing nothing but recording studio work and everybody says, 'Boy, I wish we could see Bobby Thompson.' When they had him they didn't appreciate him."[127]

Robert C. Thompson was born in Converse, South Carolina, July 5, 1937. At age fourteen, he began learning to play the banjo. He bought his first banjo during high school for $25. Six months later, having found that he played the rolls backwards, he corrected his technique. A high school talent contest gained him and some friends on a weekend radio show in Spartanburg. Thompson said of Scruggs, "Earl Scruggs was my idol. For his style, he is the best—bar none! Nobody touched Scruggs' authority. Nobody has it like Earl. It's his choice of notes—not how many, but the feeling."[128]

His first professional job was in 1955 after high school with the **Pritchard Brothers** where Brenda Lee was the group's girl singer. Shortly thereafter, he was playing banjo and bass on a television show in Greenville, South Carolina.

In 1956, Thompson joined **Carl Story and the Rambling Mountaineers** for about a year and a half (the group played at WLOS in Asheville for three years). With this band, in August, Bobby Thompson recorded "Banjolina" and "Fire on the Banjo" on Mercury using Scruggs-style banjo playing. While working with Story, Benny Sims, the ex-fiddler from **Flatt and Scruggs** who was then playing with **Bonnie Lou and Buster** with whom the **Rambling Mountaineers** toured often, suggested to Thompson that he play fiddle tunes on the banjo; Sims couldn't understand why some banjo player hadn't done it before. Thompson worked up "Arkansas Traveler" on the banjo. But the style didn't catch on. And when Thompson joined **Jim and Jesse** in late 1957 and played these fiddle tunes, his melodic banjo style just got lost. People wondered what he was doing. They preferred that he stick with the familiar styles of Earl Scruggs and Don Reno. He just played his melodic style off stage. As for his recordings, the first instance of his melodic picking was on "Border Ride" while with **Jim and Jesse** around 1959.

Thompson played banjo with **Jim and Jesse and the Virginia Boys** while they were headquartered in Valdosta, Georgia.[129] He stayed with them for nearly two years. He spoke of Jesse McReynolds, "Jesse is the kind of fellow that is open to anything. We had two different kinds of tunes: what we would play on stage, and the bus tunes. Jesse would get up at daybreak and write a tune every morning. Vassar Clements was the fiddler with the band, and he and I would get up and add our parts. The next day there would be another tune. We never recorded any of these tunes except 'Border Ride.' People at concerts like to hear what they're used to so we just kept that stuff on the bus."[130] In 1960, Bobby Thompson was drafted into the military.[131]

In 1965, still in the Army, Thompson first heard Bill Keith playing "Sailor's Hornpipe" and the applause Keith received. He remembered the lack of audience response when he played in that melodic style in the late 1950s. He thought, "Damn. He's doing what I've been doing," and started playing the banjo again with a new dedication.

After four and a half years in the military, in 1965 he moved to Columbia, South Carolina, then back to Spartanburg for a couple of years, and then to Nashville to join with **Jim and Jesse** for the second time in 1967 with Jim Brock on fiddle. On a particular one-week tour at the Lake of the Ozarks,[132] Missouri, Vic Jordan substituted on bass and joined later as their banjo player in 1972 and in 1988.

Thompson used the melodic style of banjo playing on **Jim and Jesse**'s recording of "Diesel on My Tail." He also used bluesy licks, which he copied from guitarist Jerry Reed, on that album. On this album, he used a five-string Dobro® instead of a banjo. (He used the Dobro® more than the banjo during this period.) Allen Shelton would later pick up on this and play the instrument with the band. The band's April 2, 1968, recording session for Epic included the melodic "Sugarfoot Rag."

Thompson worked with **Jim and Jesse** for one and a half years until 1968 when he tired of the road travel. He began a day job in a machine shop[133] for six months to a year and gradually got into studio session work in Nashville, alternating between guitar and banjo. He preferred to play banjo but found more demand for a guitarist. Bobby Dyson, one of Nashville's leading bass players, told him that if he learned to play rhythm guitar

---

127 David Robinson, "Vic Jordan," *Bluegrass Unlimited*, August, 1974, p. 9.

128 Ted Belue, "The Legacy of Bobby Thompson," *Bluegrass Unlimited*, September, 1990, p. 36.

129 I have read several times that Thompson began with Jim and Jesse by playing bass in Valdosta, Georgia. In a telephone interview with Mr. Thompson on September 18, 1992, he told me he never did play bass with the group.

130 Dick Weissman, "The Nine Lives of a Nashville Cat, Bobby Thompson," *Frets*, February, 1989, p.28.

131 Allen Shelton took his place on banjo that fall.

132 Some have written that Bobby Thompson played bass with Jim and Jesse on this one-week tour. He did not; both Vic Jordan and Thompson say that Vic did. Vic Jordan's tenure as bass player with Jim and Jesse was short; after only a few days with the band he confessed that he really wasn't good enough bassist to continue with the group. He was really a banjo player who wanted to play with the group and thought he could fill-in with his limited knowledge of the bass. But Jim and Jesse's music is more than just three chords. Jordan split from the group amicably.

133 He manufactured the antenna which was used on the lunar landing module on a NASA space shot.

he would hire him for demos.[134] "I was the worst rhythm guitar player in the country and I appreciated Dyson using me, but why he did it I don't know."[135] Thompson became one of Nashville's most requested session musicians.

The guitar was his salvation in the studio. He was able to work much more often and make a living at it. When he became proficient on rhythm guitar, he was able to quit his day job when got to the point where he was working as many as fifteen sessions a week. "About once a month," he told this writer, "we'd cut something so good it would keep your love of music alive. But most of those good tracks were never released. I've got tapes at home that were never released but are better than ninety percent of what you hear on the radio."

Thompson's first session was with Trini Lopez where he played banjo. There he met Grady Martin, Jerry Reed, Frank Jones and Jack Clement who started using him for sessions. He did a number of **Monkees** sessions. One of his first and more prestigious jobs was as the guitarist with the studio band of the new television show, "Hee Haw," which first aired in 1968; twenty-five years later it was still going and one of the staff musicians was Bobby Thompson. Originally, Thompson and the other musicians were called to do six months of taping at one time. By 1974, the "Hee Haw" backup band members were being shown on camera. And being spotlighted for his banjo mastery was Bobby Thompson. This exposed him to a lot of viewers who recognized him as the guy with the beard who never smiled but played awesome banjo.

By 1971, Thompson was working all he wanted. Soon known as an innovative and well-respected musician, it got to the point where he played either guitar or banjo on most of the music coming out of Nashville. In 1974, he recorded the single "Foxfire"/"Devil Dance."[136] His banjo was a Baldwin; he often stuffed a towel in the head to mute it.

Thompson was thoroughly immersed in Nashville's music by 1978. He, along with Larrie Londin, Joe Osborne and Reggie Young started up a production company called Hit Men which produced some new artists and some established artists such as Sonny Curtis, Dobie Grey and Scottish artist Frankie Miller. The music ran the gamut between country, pop and rock.

In 1987, Thompson was diagnosed as having Multiple Sclerosis. He quit playing in October 1988. Because of all that studio session work in Nashville, he receives a regular disability pension check through the Musician's Union. He had a crippling stroke in the early 1990s but recovered sufficiently by September 1992 for a telephone interview with this writer. He walked with a cane. But before his health failed, Bobby was able to teach his son and his step-son the basics of playing the guitar who then became an avid guitar player. Bobby's spare time is devoted to the building of period-correct Kentucky rifles (pre-1840 frontier America).

Thompson loved his job as a professional musician and would like the reader to know that "The music business has been very good to me. I've seen a lot of changes in twenty years in the studio and I'm thankful that everybody used me so much. They're a great bunch of people."

After a few months of a new "improved" "Hee Haw" show in 1993, it was taken off the air; the older shows, with Bobby Thompson, were being re-run. In 1995, even that ceased.

Bill Keith

Bill Keith— innovator and inventor

The contributions to bluegrass music by William Bradford Keith are legendary; they changed bluegrass music. His melodic banjo playing is often called "Keith style" picking. He didn't actually invent the method of re-tuning strings which Earl Scruggs used in songs such as "Flint Hill Special," but he did help invent the D-tuners which make the songs easier to play and have a much cleaner look on the banjo.

Tony Trischka wrote, "Earl Scruggs gave us drive, syncopation, and the smooth, three-finger right hand roll. What he didn't provide for us, though, was a way to play scales or the long, flowing melody lines that grow out of them... With this new style, it became possible

134 Demos, in the Nashville music business, are new songs put to tape in hopes they will be recorded by a popular star, therefore making a good profit for the demo maker and the writer. There isn't a lot of money in demos, but doing a large quantity of them can help a musician make a living.

135 From a personal note to this writer October 1992.

136 "Foxfire" was released on Capricorn and was also released on the "Peaches" LP put out by Capricorn in 1974. The melodic picking featured musicians Thompson (banjo), Steve Schaeffer (bass), Kenny Malone (drums), Shane Keister (keyboards), Jimmy Colvard (electric guitar) and Stu Basore (steel guitar).

for a banjo player to pick fiddle tunes note-for-note as the fiddler would. In addition, an entirely new repertoire of exciting licks and runs grew up; and suddenly, there was something to play besides Scruggs style."[137]

Bill Keith was born in Brockton, Massachusetts, in 1939. Around 1952, he played the plectrum banjo in the Boston/Cambridge-based Dixieland bands. He studied the tenor "Dixieland" style of banjo chord construction and music theory at Exeter Academy and Amherst College.

In 1957, he bought and began playing a $15 long-neck five-string banjo. He used Pete Seeger's instruction book and strove to learn Earl Scruggs' style. He was influenced by Pete Seeger, the **Weavers**, Don Stover, Don Reno and the **Lilly Brothers**. He was already somewhat accomplished on the ukulele, piano, tenor banjo and plectrum banjo. His five-string style was patterned after Pete Seeger's style for the next couple years, then he began concentrating on Scruggs style—still with a long-neck banjo. Keith and Jim Rooney began playing local gigs around the Amherst, Massachusetts, area.[138] He made his first television appearance with this banjo on a local television station near college in 1957. He also played in a local bluegrass band and soon stepped up to a Gibson bluegrass-style banjo. In 1964, he tried the resonator guitar and the steel guitar.

The Lilly Brothers. Everett (L) and B were an influence on Bill Keith.

A significant influence on Keith was Billy Faier who played "Sailor's Hornpipe" using the banjo in a hammering-on style. Nevertheless, "My inspiration was a fiddler. When I heard a fiddler playing 'Devil's Dream,' I said *I* could get those notes to come out in that order on the banjo. I know where those notes are—I just have to play the notes, not rolls. That was the winter of '59 to '60. This was when I first played 'Devil's Dream.' It wasn't recorded until '61." Probably the actual occasion for developing this melodic style of banjo playing was due to weekly visits to Nova Scotia fiddler (living in Massachusetts) June Hall. She would play many fiddle tunes, including "Devil's Dream" for him. That is where he decided that he wanted to play the melodic-style banjo. Keith also began developing "Sailor's Hornpipe" into a medley with "Devil's Dream."

In reference to some authors who had written that Thompson was playing this melodic/chromatic music while he was with **Jim and Jesse** several years before Keith played it with Monroe, Keith replied, "I spoke to Jim and Jesse themselves and they don't really remember Bobby playing fiddle tunes 'cause when I got down to Nashville (1963) there were a lot of people saying that they had never heard that before. And Jim and Jesse were among them."

But "I never met Bobby [Thompson] until after I had worked with Bill Monroe. He had already worked with **Jim and Jesse** and we know that he recorded quite a few things with them including 'Dixie Hoedown,' one of my favorites which has a little bit of what later became his style, I think. Other things like 'Banjolina' were pretty much 'Scruggsy' rolls and not all that melodic. In fact, there are only parts of the 'Dixie Hoedown' that are. The fact is, when I began working with Bill Monroe in the spring of '63, Bobby Thompson was with the Army National Guard in South Carolina and he told me he used to listen to Bill Monroe on the Opry on Saturday nights when I was playing. I was featured on the fiddle tunes with that band on six instrumentals which had a lot of melodic stuff in them. So I feel that I could have had an influence on Bobby. But I don't feel that I influenced him in the direction he took in the bluesy thing and the stuff on 'Area Code 615.'"[139]

During the early 1960s, Bill Keith started transcribing many of Earl Scruggs' songs onto paper. He did this by using tablature. When asked if he invented this technique of teaching and writing, he replied emphatically, "Absolutely not! I learned from Pete Seeger who points out that the lute players of the 18th century used it. He adapted an earlier form of it to the banjo and the first time I saw tablature was in Pete Seeger's book in 1957."

Keith also learned a lot about bluegrass music from Don Stover when the **Lilly Brothers and Don Stover** had a band. The 1961 "lessons" were merely visits to Stover's house—Don wouldn't demonstrate, said Keith. "In '61 and '62, I saw heavy amounts of Don (Stover) at the Hillbilly Ranch where he and the **Lilly Brothers** alternated half-hours with another band. And I spent

137 Tony Trischka, *The Introduction of Melodic Banjo* (Oak Publications)

138 They formed the Connecticut Valley Folklore Society to promote an Odetta concert. Other members were Buffy Sainte-Marie and Taj Majal. In 1952, Keith and Rooney starred in the Connecticut Valley Folklore Society Music Festival. Promoted by Manny Greenhill, who later promoted stars such as Doc Watson and Joan Baez, it also starred Buffy Sainte-Marie and Winnie Winston, Scruggs-style banjoist.

139 "Area Code 615" is covered in the Studio Musicians chapter of this book.

many an evening there nursing a few beers," he told Pete Wernick in a January 1984 interview.

In September of 1961, just before Keith went into the USAF, he (banjo), Jim Rooney (guitar), Joe Val (mandolin), Herb Hooven (fiddle) and Fritz Richmond (bass) recorded "Livin' On The Mountain." It was released in the spring of 1962. (Between the time of the recording session and its release, Eric Weissberg's "New Dimensions in Banjo and Bluegrass" was released, said Keith.[140]) They played as the **Berkshire Mountain Boys** at Club 47, Cambridge, Massachusetts, and featured Keith's melodic-style of banjo playing. One tune on the LP was "Devil's Dream." That same month, he won the banjo contest at the First Annual Philadelphia Folk Festival with "Sailor's Hornpipe" and "Devil's Dream."

In the summer of 1962, Bill Keith started traveling around and went to Washington. In the fall, he joined the **Kentuckians** with Red Allen (guitar), Frank Wakefield (mandolin) and Tom Morgan (bass) in the Washington area and at WWVA in Wheeling, West Virginia; he took Pete Kuykendall's place with the group. His association with Morgan was an apprenticeship in banjo-making there in D.C..

That December, while working with Red and Frank and Morgan in D.C., he saw Earl Scruggs in concert. The concert was at Johns Hopkins University, Baltimore, with Merle Travis opening the show. After the show, Manny Greenhill introduced Keith to Scruggs. Keith showed Scruggs his book of tablature. Peer International had recently published a book of Earl's tunes in music notation. Keith, able to read music, found many errors and explained them to Scruggs who could not read music. Scruggs was impressed so he asked Keith to go to Nashville to work on another book which Scruggs was asked to write for Peer.[141] This was like a call from heaven for Bill Keith: Earl Scruggs asking for his help. Keith had literally spent countless hours transcribing Earl's solos note-for-note and had totally absorbed all of his work. Keith joined Scruggs in Nashville in early 1963, and began working on *Earl Scruggs and the 5-String Banjo*.

The book came out in 1968 from Peer International Corporation. Keith did all the tablature and exercises and did the recording of the album as well. "It was my tape recorder and my roll of tape and my microphone which was set up in his back room and we wrote out the text that he had to say on record. And since he had to play the exercises as they appeared in the book, I had to play them for him because he couldn't read the tablature. This was something he had played, but he couldn't tell what it was [by] lookin' at it. Then I would turn the machine on and he would play it for the instructional record."[142]

Keith explained, "When we were workin' on it he told me I would be gettin' my share and he gave me the shake of his hand and I guess I was a little too green not to insist on having it all down there in writing. After all [he was] my hero and so forth. It was later I saw mention in *Time* magazine that the book had sold a million dollars retail. And I hadn't gotten my first penny—not to mention anything for the record which was retailing for ten bucks apiece. And I knew that you can have those records pressed up for less than a dollar. Here he had zero production expense doin' it in the back room on my machine. I just thought, 'Hey! There's hundreds of thousands of dollars here. Why doesn't he deem that it's time that I should see some of it?' So I asked. I had always been welcome at his house. I seemed to be then until I brought that up. His wife kind of snickered and said, 'You should have had a contract.' I was real bitter about that and it wasn't until several years later that I finally decided I'm not goin' to live with this and resolve it. I went to a friend who was a music lawyer and we went through and...Earl spent a lot more money on his lawyers than what he ended up offering my lawyer...but it was a pittance on what he had implied [that I would get]. And, in the process, I'm permanently on his 'out' list."

Everywhere Keith went at this point—whenever he played this medley of "Devil's Dream" and "Sailor's Hornpipe"—jaws would drop. And once in March of 1963, backstage at the Opry at the old Ryman Auditorium, Bill Monroe and Kenny Baker were back there at the dressing room. Baker came back to where Keith was and said, "If you want a job with Bill Monroe, you've got it." Rual Yarbrough was Monroe's banjoist in the Nashville area but Monroe needed a regular banjoist for touring. Del McCoury, who had played one performance on banjo with Monroe was offered a job at the same time as Keith and both men auditioned for the banjo job the same day. Monroe asked McCoury if he could play guitar, an answer which was in the affirmative, and hired him on guitar and lead singer. Keith was then hired on banjo.[143] Bill Keith was the first Yankee to join the **Blue Grass Boys**. Because Monroe didn't want two "Bill's" in the band, he always called him "Brad" after his middle name, "Bradford."

[140] Eric Weissberg and Marshall Brickman got their first exposure to the melodic style of banjo playing while Bill Keith was performing one night. In a 1993 telephone interview with Weissberg, he seemed to recall that this event was at the apartment of Charlie Rothchild, not a concert performance. The song that Keith picked that night in the melodic style was "Salty Dog." They soon came out with their own album of melodic banjo playing, "New Dimensions in Banjo and Bluegrass" (1963). It was accurately named.

While Eric Weissberg and Marshall Brickman were the first to come out with an instrumental LP featuring melodic picking, Bill Keith is quick to point out that the first time those men had seen that kind of playing was when they saw him in concert.

[141] In the fall of 1964, Scruggs met Burt Brent at Fort Campbell Army Base, Kentucky who helped provide illustrations and photographs for the book.

[142] Phone interview, June 15, 1992.

[143] For more on this topic see Del McCoury biography in the Pioneers chapter of this book.

Keith learned a lot about bluegrass music while with Monroe. Those days with Monroe added to his understanding of how to make music that works—to make it do what you sense it should do—rather than simply following established rules.

Monroe capitalized on the musicianship of this band which included Keith, Del McCoury (banjo and guitar), and fiddlers Vassar Clements or Kenny Baker. This helped Monroe keep his band, and helped keep bluegrass alive in spite of the decidedly folk and **Beatle** era. Keith stayed ten months, until December. Keith left Monroe's band because the place the band appeared, Hootenanny, had blacklisted his youthful banjo idol, Pete Seeger. Keith quit because of a principle.

Late in 1964, Keith joined the **Jim Kweskin Jug Band** in Boston. He used his Gibson five-string banjo (in G tuning) with a flatpick. He bought a steel guitar while with this group. Members included Maria Muldaur and later Richard Greene (fiddle). Keith stayed four years with Kweskin...and away from bluegrass music. The group disbanded in 1968.

Back in the period with Red Allen, Bill Keith and college friend Dan Bump decided to go into business together building a banjo. They eventually settled on re-engineering banjo tuners. They built this business up in the winter of 1963, when most of the work was done by Bump because of Keith's touring schedule with various groups. Bump sent the first D-tuner prototypes to Keith while he was in Nashville working for Monroe. Keith showed the pegs to Scruggs who approved of them. Production of the finished product began on a more serious basis in 1964. Scruggs wanted to lend his name to the product but was under contract to the Vega Company and was not allowed to do both unless he was involved as a shareholder with the new company. They all put up money and they were on their way. In 1968, the Cambridge company began making pewter objects. Eventually Bump lost interest in business and sold the Beacon Banjo Company back to Keith about 1989. Keith expanded it to sell many musical items by mail order.

In 1969, Keith joined **Ian and Sylvia and the Great Speckled Bird**, playing country rock for a year. He commuted between Canada and Boston for this job. He played some banjo, but mostly steel guitar. When this ended about 1970, he moved to Woodstock area where he partnered with Jonathan Edwards, made a few records, and toured. Edwards then decided to retire since he had achieved significant success with his music. Keith then joined the **Blue Velvet Band** with his old pal Jim Rooney (guitar), Richard Greene (fiddle) and Eric Weissberg (guitar, banjo).

Bill Keith helped form **Muleskinner** in 1972, which wasn't much more than a put-together band for a television gig in Hollywood, California. Members were himself, David Grisman (mandolin), Peter Rowan (guitar), Clarence White (lead guitar), Richard Greene (fiddle) and Stuart Schulman (bass). The concert video was released in 1992. The group was formed to lead off a concert for Bill Monroe which was to be televised. **Muleskinner** musicians had been practicing the previous week at their gig at The Ash Grove. As it turned out, Monroe had trouble getting there from his Sacramento gig. He eventually called and told them to go on without him.

About 1975, Keith worked with Judy Collins. In 1977, he toured in Europe with Tony Rice and David Grisman. This was followed by a tour of Japan with the **David Grisman Quintet** with Richard Greene and himself as guests. They toured as two separate groups: one with Greene, Grisman and Todd Phillips, the other with Grisman and Joe Carroll. Shortly after this tour Keith, having spent much of his time between America and Europe, moved back to the U.S..

Bill Keith became an original columnist with *Frets* in 1979. In 1989, he was settled in Woodstock, New York, where he teamed up with Eric Weissberg, Kenny Kosek and Jim Rooney as the **New Blue Velvet Band** and where he lives today. With this band he made his fifth trip to Japan and occasionally toured Europe. They weren't interested in pursuing the festival circuit full-time and were content to enjoy a home life as well as playing their music. Today, Keith also pursues an intense interest in personal computer technology. His 1993 CD was "Beating Around the Bush." In 1995, he was in Richard Greene's the **Grass Is Greener** instrumental band with Greene (fiddle), David Grier (guitar), Tim Emmons (bass, whose place was taken by Gene Libbea that fall), and Kenny Blackwell (mandolin until the summer of 1995 when Butch Baldassari took his place). Tony Trischka took Bill Keith's place in late 1995.

Walter Hensley. An abbreviated biography with Earl Taylor and the Stoney Mountain Boys.

One of the accomplished banjoists of the 1950s was Walter Hensley, known for his years with **Earl Taylor and the Stoney Mountain Boys**.[144]

In 1957, Earl Taylor left the **Sunny Mountain Boys**, re-forming his **Stoney Mountain Boys** in Baltimore with Charlie Waller[145], Sam Hutchins and Vernon "Boatwhistle" McIntyre. Walter Hensley filled-in on weekday gigs. Taylor said of Hensley, "When I met him he still didn't have no National banjo picks—

---

[144] The Stoney Mountain Boys at that time included Taylor and Sam "Porky Hutchins" who had just left Jimmy Martin's band. Other members during this 1957 to 1959 period included Tommy Vaden (fiddle), Fred Keith (guitar) and Curtis Cody (fiddle).

[145] Waller soon became a founding member of the Country Gentlemen (July 4th). Band members then became Taylor (mandolin), Hutchins (guitar), Hensley (banjo), Tommy Vaden (fiddle) and Vernon "Boatwhistle" McIntyre (bass).

he's made his own out of Pet Cream cans. Lord have mercy, Walter Hensley just knowed so much on that neck...it was just impossible to make him miss a note! You could just say to him, 'Play "Ghost Riders in the Sky"' or just anything, and he had it."[146]

The band recorded for Folkways in 1958, "Mountain Music Bluegrass Style" (FA2318, released November 1959). The album became a bible for other bluegrass bands during the soon-to-be-growing urban folk and bluegrass revival. Because of the speed at which the band played, their style of bluegrass became known as "hyper grass". It was probably this speed distinction which attracted folklorist Alan Lomax to begin to promote this band, and in 1959 named the music "folk music with overdrive".

The next milestone accomplished by the group was on April 3, 1959, when Alan Lomax booked the group into Carnegie Hall, becoming the first bluegrass band to play there. The concert at the Hall was promoted as "Folksong USA" and included Jimmy Driftwood, Memphis Slim and Muddy Waters. Musicians at the time were Earl Taylor (mandolin), Hensley (banjo), Hutchins (guitar) and Boatwhistle (bass) with Curtis Cody on fiddle as a guest artist. Alan Lomax recorded the Carnegie concert for United Artists as "Folk Song Festival at Carnegie Hall" (USA 6050). The group also recorded "Folk Songs from the Bluegrass."[147]

Back in Cincinnati in 1961, they played the next three years, six days a week, at the Ken-Mill Restaurant. They recorded one album with Jim McCall as lead singer. This led to an offer to join the Grand Ole Opry but these men preferred to stay around home in Ohio rather than relocate to Nashville. This reluctance to tour as the Opry acts did is one of the reasons the **Stoney Mountain Boys** is not better known.

In 1961, Leon Morris entered the U.S. permanently from Canada; he joined Earl Taylor's **Stoney Mountain Boys** in Detroit. Members were Earl Taylor, Morris, Hensley (banjo), Billy Baker (fiddle) and "Boatwhistle." In Detroit, "It was pretty bad—hard to get any work. So I pawned everything I had—a Gibson RB-150, my record player and everything but my guitar,"[148] said Morris. They moved to Chicago but things weren't any better. Then they went to Kansas City and managed to play several times a week. Morris, Taylor and Hensley went to Baltimore, then Hensley and Morris relocated to Arlington, Virginia, while Taylor and Boatwhistle stayed in Cincinnati. Vernon "Junior" McIntyre, Boatwhistle's son, took Hensley's place on banjo in the new version of the **Stoney Mountain Boys**. The band

broke up later that year. Hensley dropped from the music scene. He re-emerged during the late 1980s as leader of **Walt Hensley and the Dukes of Blue Grass**, playing clubs and festivals in the D.C./Pennsylvania area. Jim McCall and Taylor shared the band as partners occasionally, the last time in 1970 in Cincinnati. Taylor died in 1984.

John Hickman

John Hickman

This venerable banjoist from Columbus, Ohio, has been playing since about 1955 when he heard Earl Scruggs play the banjo on **Flatt and Scruggs** recordings. He traded in his guitar for a banjo and started playing in the two-finger style. Then, exposed to the three-finger style, he learned the backwards roll first, not knowing there was anything else. After a year, Robbie Robinson (who designed the Fender banjo) showed him the forward roll. Hickman recalled, "So it probably took three years to figure out everything everybody was doing with their right hand...but somehow I don't regret taking all that time because it seems like you get everything more solid that way. You gain something. You learn how to play all those tunes in a lot of different ways."[149]

Hickman performed on his banjo (bought in 1957) in a group immediately after high school. His style of banjo playing was strongly influenced toward perfection by Eddie Adcock, Allen Shelton and Earl Scruggs. Veteran banjoist Bob Yellin said of Hickman, "He, more than any other banjo player, has combined the Scruggs style and the Keith or melodic style."[150]

While in the USMC (1962), Hickman played around the West Virginia area with Buzz Busby, and in other areas with Red Allen, Frank Wakefield and the **Ken-**

[146] Tom Ewing, "Earl Taylor: One of the Bluegrass Greats," *Bluegrass Unlimited*, September, 1976, p. 12.

[147] The "folk" term was very popular in those days in order to take advantage of the "folk boom" which was in full swing throughout the nation in 1960. Shortly thereafter, Jim McCall replaced Hutchins.

[148] Fred Geiger, "Leon Morris," *Bluegrass Unlimited*, September, 1982, pp. 35, 36. When the group broke up in late 1961, Morris began driving a Yellow Cab around Alexandria, Virginia, and was a member of the Yates Brothers with Bill and Wayne Yates. Morris quit playing full-time in 1962 until 1969 when he met Buzz Busby. Morris surfaced again in 1995 at Carlton Haney's festival in Berryville, Virginia.

[149] Jack Tottle, "Berline, Crary and Hickman—Part 1," *Bluegrass Unlimited*, September, 1980, p.17.

[150] Mark Greenberg interview, *Frets*, December 1984, p. 28.

tuckians, and with Mike Auldridge and Ben Eldridge. These were the days of the folk boom. In a 1991 interview, he elaborated, "The folk boom did a lot for bluegrass, actually. It sort of brought the banjo, especially, into focus a little more." And "Working with Red Allen was a real treat. He was a real good rhythm guitar player, I thought, and still is." He was the type of band leader which adhered to the more traditional sound but he didn't put restrictions on the styles of individual band members.[151]

In 1964, John Hickman started his own trio with Pee Wee Lambert (mandolin) and Landen Rowe (guitar). Shortly after that, he joined the **Dixie Gentlemen** of Columbus, Ohio, whose members were Sid Campbell (guitar), Ralph "Robbie" Robinson (mandolin) and Charles "Chuck" Cordell (bass).[152] On November 10, 1967 Cordell and Robinson died in a plane crash on the way to Washington D.C. to work with Red Allen (reportedly). They were members of the house band at the Astro Inn in Columbus, Ohio. The band ended. Hickman subsequently joined **Earl Taylor and the Stoney Mountain Boys** with Taylor, Sid Campbell and Boatwhistle McIntyre, playing with them on WWVA as well as with Red Allen's **Kentuckians** with Sid Campbell and Bob White (bass).

It was here that Hickman met Don Reno and they became friends. In an interview with this writer in 1985, Hickman spoke of Reno's banjo style, "I think it seems to be as everyone else does it—you pick up things from different people and interpret it in your own way. I think, in his case, Arthur 'Guitar Boogie' Smith was an influence. Arthur Smith played the plectrum banjo and Don picked up a lot of the single-string things from that and also some of his sliding chordal moves that he did." Hickman occasionally filled-in with Reno and Smiley's **Tennessee Cut-Ups**.[153]

Hickman moved his family to southern California in early 1969, not knowing if there was any bluegrass there or not. After playing a short while with his brother George Hickman and Scott Hambly (mandolin), he met Byron Berline, Alan Munde, Clarence White, Roland White, Doug Dillard and John Hartford. Hickman began recording with these local artists and also appeared on the "Smothers Brothers Television Show."

July of 1973 found John Hickman as the banjo player with **Corn Bred**.[154] They played regularly in Westminster (near Los Angeles), and recorded on the Briar-Takoma label. While Hickman didn't normally

enter banjo contests, he did enter one in Japanese Village when he was with this band, and won the contest. His band won the Best Band contest as well.

In 1975, Byron Berline formed **Sundance** with Hickman (banjo), Dan Crary (guitar), Allen Wald (rhythm guitar) and Jack Skinner (bass). In 1976, brothers John and George Hickman opened up a stringed-instrument repair store in Redondo Beach. John then quit his day job as a lumber buyer for Builder's Emporium; this was his last day job until 1995 when he and Berline opened up a shop together in Oklahoma.

By June of 1977, Hickman was in **Gold Rush** with Alison Brown (resonator guitar, banjo, guitar), Stuart Duncan (mandolin, fiddle) and Larry Bulaich (guitar). Bulaich remembered those days when he, Brown, Duncan, Barry Silver and Dick Tyner had a regular gig at the Magic Mountain theme park near Los Angeles. "When Dick quit, this was the end of **Pain in the Grass** and we renamed myself, Alison, Stuart, and Barry Silver, **Gold Rush**. John Hickman joined us, and that— right there with my friendship with John—was the beginning of my education in bluegrass. I mean, he taught me so much just by example or by just talking about it—its history: where it comes from and how it's survived, and so forth. I've never believed that John Hickman has been as much appreciated as he should be. I thought he knew more about bluegrass in one little finger than the rest of us in our whole body. He is an amazing, amazing person. His playing, his knowledge; he just seems to be on top of everything. John played with us and Alison Brown played Dobro and occasionally would play a banjo duet with John. Stuart played fiddle and mandolin and myself, guitar, and Barry Silver played the upright bass. And the band was getting the job done there at Magic Mountain."[155] He was also playing with Berline's **L.A. Fiddle Band** and with **Cheyenne**, a local band.

Hickman left **Gold Rush** in June of 1978. About that same time, **Berline, Crary and Hickman** was formed with musicians Byron Berline (fiddle, mandolin), Dan Crary (guitar), and John Hickman (banjo). **B-C-H** played for years without a bass. Crary's rhythm guitar was so strong, even when he took a break, that Berline and Hickman's timing never missed a beat.

Hickman spoke about listening to other bands, "There's something I like, I guess, about all of them. I've listened to all of them, but mostly in the past few years it's right back to Flatt and Scruggs. It seems like

---

[151] Another member in the Kentuckians was Frank Wakefield who also had that freedom to play creatively in the band. "That's one of the things that made Frank Wakefield so popular. At that time, nobody was playing what is now considered to be traditional-type mandolin. I think Wakefield was one of the creators of the kind of mandolin playing that is happening today. And that's simply because Red didn't put any restrictions on what he played."

[152] There was another Dixie Gentlemen group headed by Rual Yarbrough, Herschel Sizemore and Jake Landers which began in 1958.

[153] One particular time was when Reno was sick. There he played on the "Top O' the Morning" show on WDBJ in Roanoke. This was a live, two-hour program which aired daily at 6 a.m. and was the first television show of its kind anywhere.

[154] Corn Bred at that time included his brother George Hickman (bass), Darryl Boom (guitar), Jody Cifra (fiddle) and Tom Sauber (mandolin).

[155] From a 1993 interview.

[156] Tottle, op. cit., p. 18.

every time I set down to listen, I drag out the old '50s recordings I have on tape of their live shows and it just fascinates me more every time I hear it. The way Scruggs did it, he just about said it all."[156]

In a 1985 interview, asked how he would like to be remembered after he has departed, he feels that the greatest tribute he could receive would be to have people playing his licks and tunes. He continued in the 1990s in California with co-members Crary, Berline, John Moore and Steve Spurgin. The band has consistently won top honors at IBMA until breaking up in late 1995. Hickman moved to Guthrie, Oklahoma, where he and Berline opened an instrument-repair store and performance venue.

Raymond Fairchild

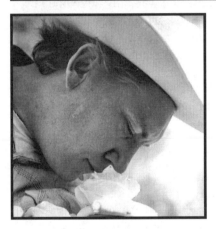

Raymond Fairchild

Doodle, of **Doodle and the Golden River Grass**, said that "Raymond Fairchild is the best banjo player there is, or ever will be, and when they made him they threw away the mold."[157] Some of the truly amazing bluegrass banjo players are those who are largely self-taught; Raymond Fairchild falls into this category.

Born near the Great Smoky Mountains of North Carolina in 1939, he only finished the fourth grade but was completely at home in the woods. His first influence toward music was at his aunt's cabin where they played harmonica and guitar. The banjo was not to be found however; it was considered the instrument of the Devil. He decided to play it anyway—at age twenty. He picked up an instruction book, some picks which he put on backwards at first, and started playing his home-made, fretless banjo. He listened to WCYB's Farm and Fun Time where he heard good examples of bluegrass music.

On a trip out of the mountains into the big city (Asheville), he was highly influenced by hearing Earl Scruggs and Don Reno records on the jukebox. Though impressed by them, he made a deliberate effort to create a different sound; his style became fancier. He worked on his speed, too, and plays as fast as other band members can stay with him.

In the mid-1960s, Fairchild played for tips near the Hillbilly Campground in Maggie Valley. He often played with Frank Buchanan (guitar, mandolin, who earlier recorded with Bill Monroe) and three others. They played from 8 a.m. to midnight, seven days a week. His work as a stonemason supplemented his tip income until he became a full-time musician. He and the **Frosty Mountain Boys** of Georgia recorded on the Rural Rhythm label as well as his own **Maggie Valley Boys**.

Fairchild began guest spots on the Opry in 1972. He spoke of the experience, "When you step in front of those WSM microphones on the Grand Ole Opry, that's the highest you're going in this type of music, Buddy."[158] He is known to be the first banjo player since Earl Scruggs to bring the house down at the Opry.[159] That appearance immediately led to a performance on television's "Hee Haw."

According to Sonny Osborne, "Raymond is creative with his playing. He doesn't play like anybody else. As far as technically, he does everything he needs to and does it correctly. He gets a good tone out of the banjo...and it's not many times that you can see a three-piece band with one lead instrument that can compete with many of these people running around with five- and six-piece bands. But **Raymond Fairchild and the Crowe Brothers** can do that and do it successfully."[160] Fairchild performed on the stage comfortable with his sound because the Crowe brothers gave him the confidence he needed. "If you go out there with a bunch of 'frammers' behind you, it hurts."[161]

At one time, Fairchild used Wilfred Messer on fiddle with his band. Messer died in 1975. He then hired his son, Zane, on lead guitar to fill-out the sound which he feels is all they need in their band. By 1981, they were recording on the Skyline label.

Fairchild was awarded Bluegrass Banjo Player of the Year by SPBGMA 1987 through 1991. He was then retired from the competition. He continued to perform into the 1990s. Beginning in 1994, Fairchild toured less to spend more time as host to the Maggie Valley Opry House which he runs with his wife.

[157] Janice Brown McDonald, "Raymond Fairchild," *Bluegrass Unlimited*, May, 1989, p. 23.

[158] Wayne Erbsen, "Raymond Fairchild—Making His Own Way," *Bluegrass Unlimited*, March, 1982, p. 16.

[159] ...and as being one of the first musicians to perform on the Opry with a loaded .38 revolver. And, according to author Janice Brown McDonald, he and the late Marty Robbins were the only people to receive six standing ovations at the Ryman Auditorium.

[160] McDonald, op. cit., p. 26.

[161] Ibid.

Don Parmley and the Bluegrass Cardinals

Don Parmley is a Kentuckian who loved bluegrass music and the banjo ever since he heard it on the 5:45 a.m. WSM radio show by **Flatt and Scruggs**. He's played this music, and created history, on both coasts of America and knows what it takes to play bluegrass properly and how to succeed in the business.

As early as 1953, Parmley played in a bluegrass band (the **Wayne County Playboys**), and on the radio in 1956. Back home in Monticello, Kentucky, Parmley found several groups with which to play, but **Flatt and Scruggs** was really the only group able to make ends meet in the music. Knowing this and having become married, Parmley sought greener pastures in August by moving to California that year. He supplemented his playing income by driving a Trailways bus. Three years later, son David Parmley was born.

There was actually a substantial amount of bluegrass in southern California at the time: the **Kentucky Colonels** evolved from being the **Country Boys** with Clarence, Roland and Eric White (1963, but were disbanded by 1966); Butch Waller's **Pine Valley Boys** came down from San Francisco to look for work in 1963 but disbanded in late 1964; the **Dillards** arrived from the Ozarks in 1962 and played extensively in Los Angeles for a few years; Byron Berline would soon make his mark (in 1969) after a tour with the **Blue Grass Boys**; and there was the **Golden State Boys**.

Parmley played nearly four years with the **Golden State Boys**[162] with members Hal Poindexter (Tony Rice's uncle), Herb Rice (Tony Rice's father), Leon Poindexter (resonator guitar) and Parmley (banjo). Herb and Leon were partners in the band before Parmley joined. In 1962, Parmley left the **Golden State Boys** with Vern and Rex Gosdin who were then members of

the band. All three left at the same time, picked up Chris Hillman, and formed the **Blue Diamond Boys**. Parmley cut his first banjo album that year.[163]

In 1964, about the time that the **Blue Diamond Boys** broke up, Parmley became the studio banjoist for the "Beverly Hillbillies" television show, replacing Steve Stevenson, until 1973 when the television show left the air. Only the theme the show was played by **Flatt and Scruggs**; the rest of the music was played by studio musicians.[164]

In early 1974, when David (called "Butch" by his father) Parmley was fifteen, he became one of the founding members of the **Bluegrass Cardinals**.[165] David was originally on the bass, but when Bill Bryson took over that spot David moved to guitar. They followed the high-lead vocal trio style which was fully developed by the **Osborne Brothers and Red Allen** in 1957. The "Bluegrass Cardinal sound" comes mainly from the duo of Don and David Parmley. Trios in the group have included others, but that certain sound has remained consistent through the years.

David could really sing high. According to Don, "He could sing anything that Bob Osborne could sing but two or three frets higher. Then when he went through puberty, his voice started changing. Actually, that's why, in a lot of songs we do, I sing baritone part of the time and lead part of the time. 'Cause during that time he was having problems with his voice and I would take over and sing lead on the bridge and let him go to baritone. In a lot of that stuff, we got to doin' it like that back then and we still do."[166]

The group was named by Don's wife. "She got the idea from this little decoration of a cardinal on our refrigerator door," Don related. "It seemed like a good band name and then when she found that the cardinal is the state bird of some of the states where bluegrass is played a lot, then it seemed real logical so we adopted it and had it registered in Washington."[167]

Don Parmley and his Bluegrass Cardinals, c. 1983. L to R (standing): Don Parmley, Mike Hartgrove, John Davis; (kneeling): Larry Stephenson, David Parmley.

162 They worked on channel 13 there in the Los Angeles area for three years and were sponsored by Cal Worthington's auto dealership with a new station wagon in 1962, 1963 and 1964.

163 I believe this is Crescendo Records' (GNP 98) release called "Blue Grass and Folk Blues—5-String Banjo," by Don Parmley with Billy Strange (12-string guitar), LeRoy MacNees (resonator guitar), Chris Hillman (mandolin), Vernon Gosdin (guitar), Equen Gosdin (bass) and Hal Blaine (drums).

164 On the subject of the musicians for the show's theme, evidently Lester Flatt was not chosen to sing the words; this task went to veteran studio singer Jerry Scoggins.
    During this "folk era," the bands that Parmley was in made inroads in translating folk music into the bluegrass style, the John Herald Band was one of those doing it on the East Coast. Parmley was the only member of the Blue Diamond Boys who went on to pursue bluegrass full-time when the group broke up. Hillman became famous in rock music as a member of the Byrds, among others. The Gosdin brothers went into mainstream country music.

165 With Don Parmley (banjo), Steve Stevenson (guitar) and Randy Graham (bass).

166 Interview with Don in February 1993 at the MidWinter Bluegrass Festival, Ft. Collins, CO.

167 Brett F. Devan, interview with Don Parmley, Bluegrass Unlimited, June, 1981.

The **Cardinals'** first album, "The Bluegrass Cardinals," was released on Briar Records (a Decca subsidiary) in 1976. Members of the band[168] quit their day jobs about this time. There in Los Angeles, they were "probably the only regularly-working, straight bluegrass band in the L.A. area...no one east of Death Valley knows anything about us."[169]

In November of 1976, the **Bluegrass Cardinals** moved to Virginia.[170] The move from Los Angeles to the Washington, D.C., area promised to be more financially rewarding. Mr. Parmley moved the band "because there was so much work there. Several bluegrass bands in the area, you know, the **Seldom Scene**, the **Country Gentlemen** and such. There were a lot of them. Ninety-five percent of the festivals were back there some place. So it didn't make no sense to live in California if you were gonna do most of your work on the East Coast or somewhere back in that area."[171] Soon after that, Jack Davis (father of bassist John Davis who was hired this year and spent the next several years with the band) was hired as booking agent. The band reaped the benefits of his considerable work; this established their reputation.

That summer, they recorded their second album, "Welcome to Virginia,"[172] on Rounder. In April 1978, the band signed with CMH (until 1982).[173] In 1981, Sugar Hill re-released the 1964 recordings by the **Hillmen**: "The Hillmen,"[174] with musicians Chris Hillman (mandolin), Don Parmley (banjo), Vern Gosdin (guitar) and Rex Gosdin (bass).

The **Bluegrass Cardinals** was voted Bluegrass Group of the Year for 1982 by Holland's *Country Gazette*. Lance LeRoy became their full-time manager.

Larry Stephenson joined the **Bluegrass Cardinals** in 1983 after spending an enjoyable four and a half years with **Bill Harrell and the Virginians**. "When I first came with the [**Bluegrass Cardinals**] I had a tendency to sort of overpower Don and David in the trios and I had to learn where to soften up and where to rear back and hit it. You've got to learn to sing who you're singing with."[175] Don added, "We worked with him quite a bit on that." Stephenson stayed about five years.

In 1984, the group made a change from acoustic bass to electric. Dale Perry joined in February 1985 on electric bass. He left after about three years, returning

August 1990 after some time with the **Lonesome River Band**. When he came back, he re-introduced the acoustic bass.

In 1988, the **Bluegrass Cardinals** put a 1956 SceniCruiser bus into service. Don and David had spent the last two years repairing it—inside and out—for service as one of the **Cardinals'** tools in the music business. It is completely equipped as their second home and enables a one-day journey of over 1000 miles between gigs. They continued to play a traditional style of bluegrass music through the 1990s. David Parmley left the band in 1993, eventually forming **Continental Divide** with Scott Vestal.

Vic Jordan

Vic Jordan

Victor Howard Jordan was born October 19, 1938, in Washington, D.C.. As a youngster, he moved around the globe because his stepfather was in the military. As a teen, his grandfather gave him an old Bacon Blue Ribbon banjo which no one in his family actually played. In 1957, the Jordan family moved to Norfolk, Virginia, where young Vic was influenced toward bluegrass by Harlan Bumgardner, banjo player with the **Cripple Creek Boys** who played on WCMS, Norfolk, Virginia. He was later influenced by Allen Shelton when Shelton was with Jim Eanes' **Shenandoah Valley Boys**.

Jordan's first professional band was a bluegrass band, the **Delta Ramblers**, while he was in the USAF in

---

[168] Band members were Don (banjo) and David (guitar) Parmley, Randy Graham (mandolin), Dennis Fetchet (fiddle) and Bill Bryson (bass).

[169] Frank Godbey, interview with Don Parmley in early 1976, "Who in the World are the Bluegrass Cardinals?" *Bluegrass Unlimited*, May, 1976, p. 13.
   The Kentucky Colonels had the same identity problem. The Colonels were just about to go "national" when Clarence White was killed. Nevertheless, the point is that it's nearly impossible for a full-time bluegrass band to exist away from the east coast states. There's just too little work out west. Another example is Weary Hearts who eventually gave up their Arizona home and moved to Nashville—where the work is.

[170] Within two months of the move back east, members of the Bluegrass Cardinals were Randy Graham (mandolin), Don Parmley (banjo), David Parmley (guitar), Warren Blair (fiddle) and John Davis (bass).

[171] Interview with Don Parmley, February 1993.

[172] With musicians Don, David, Graham (mandolin), Blair (fiddle) and Davis (bass). Members remained the same until 1982.

[173] Graham left the band in November 1978, returning ten years later. He finally had to quit about 1991 because of throat problems. Mike Hartgrove joined on fiddle in April 1979 only to leave in October, but returned in June 1982.

[174] For more on this topic, see Controversies chapter.

[175] Brett F. Devan, *Bluegrass Unlimited*, May, 1986, p. 10.

Lake Charles, Louisiana, in 1958. (He played drums in some rock groups, too.) The musicians made $5-10 apiece. Jordan's banjo style resembled Don Reno's, having learned from Reno's "Double Banjo Blues" and "Remington Ride." The group's theme song was Reno's "Banjo Signal." He studied Reno's style and was just learning Scruggs' style. "The main thing was availability of records," he remembered. "Reno and Smiley seemed easier to get and I had those when I went to Louisiana, and then I tried doing the Scruggs stuff. I was influenced as much by one as the other back then."[176]

In November of 1964, Jordan joined **Jimmy Martin and the Sunny Mountain Boys** in Nashville for two months. While with this group, Martin insisted his banjo playing sound exactly like J.D. Crowe who had just left. This was to assure the "Jimmy Martin sound". As Jordan explained it, "Whoever was on the record, that's what it was supposed to sound like." This restriction finally bothered him enough to leave in January of 1965. He explained another reason why he quit, "We only worked about four dates in two months. And since Jimmy was not on the Opry, there was nothing else to do when we weren't on the road. And Wilma Lee and Stoney Cooper offered me a job and I started working with them." Jordan stayed with the Coopers a year and a half.

Jordan said, "We didn't have a Dobro® player when I was with Wilma Lee and Stoney; it was electric bass, lead guitar and banjo and Stoney played fiddle and, of course, Wilma Lee played rhythm guitar. And sometimes they included an extra rhythm guitar because they usually carried a front man to sing the third part with them. And then Joe Edwards, who was playing lead guitar at that time, would double on fiddle with Stoney when they would do a waltz or something. But they weren't doing a whole lot of bluegrass when I was with them. It was more country with a tinge of bluegrass. They wanted to get into country full-time and I made the mistake of telling them that I played the drums. And Stoney wanted me to play drums most of the time and banjo just occasionally. And I didn't want to do that; that wasn't what I was about, you know."

He recalled a break from **Wilma Lee and Stoney Cooper and the Clinch Mountain Clan** (when he toured with **Jim and Jesse** June 20 to 25, 1966, with Jim, Jesse, Bobby Thompson (banjo) and Jim Brock (fiddle)). On this particular one-week tour at the Lake of the Ozarks, Missouri, Jordan substituted as a bass player. But after only a few days with the band, he confessed that he really wasn't a good enough bassist to continue with the group. He was a banjo player who wanted to play with the group and thought he could fill-in with his limited knowledge of the bass. "I wanted to get in the band real bad and that was the only thing I could think to get me in the band." But Jim and Jesse's music is more than just three chords as many bluegrass bands use, he explained. He split from the group amicably, and joined later as their banjo player in 1972 and in 1988.

Back to the time he was with Wilma Lee and Stoney, in August of 1966, "I forget who went with Jimmy when I left [to join the Coopers] but he was needing somebody again so I went back with Jimmy for eleven months (when banjoist Bill Emerson left). While with Martin, he recorded with Vernon Derrick or Vassar Clements on fiddle and Bill Yates on bass on February 2, 1967. The songs for Decca were "Uptown Blues," "Union Country" and "Livin' Like a Fool." "After that eleven months is when Jimmy and I had kind of a parting of the ways (July 23, 1967). What I told him is 'Jimmy, it would better for you to find a banjo player who suits you and for me to find another place to play.' So we parted amicably. I hung up the phone about twenty minutes and James Monroe called me and asked me if I was interested in going to work for Bill. I said yes. So I was out of work for about twenty minutes."[177]

Jordan started work for **Bill Monroe and the Blue Grass Boys** on July 27, 1967, with Roland White (guitar) and James Monroe (bass). At various times during his tenure with the band (which lasted until March 1969), fiddlers of the **Blue Grass Boys** included Byron Berline, Benny Williams or Kenny Baker. For Monroe, Jordan recorded "Virginia Darling," "The Gold Rush," "Sally Goodin'," "Walls of Time," "Kentucky Mandolin," "Crossing the Cumberlands," "Train 45 Heading South" and "Is the Blue Moon Still Shining?" On "Walls of Time," Roland White stood on a Coke box to sing up beside Monroe.

The time with Monroe was a creative period for Jordan. "I always had a good relation with Bill," he recalled. "I always worked hard at it! Anybody I ever worked for, I always worked hard at their music. Their music came first—before anything! I committed myself to whatever group I worked for. I did that with Monroe, **Jim and Jesse**, with Jimmy Martin, with Lester, Wilma Lee and Stoney, everything!

"When **Flatt and Scruggs** parted ways, I thought that would be a good move for me so I left Monroe and went with Lester (and the **Nashville Grass**) on March 18, 1969, staying with him until March 22, 1971. Jordan was the first banjo player with Flatt's group. Flatt never told him how to play either. The band consisted of Roland White (mandolin), Paul Warren on fiddle, Josh Graves on Dobro® and Jake Tullock on the old doghouse bass."[178]

---

[176] Quotation from a telephone interview, October, 1992.
[177] Ibid..

Bill Monroe paid you when you worked; Lester Flatt paid a salary. He recorded on the "Flatt Out" album in December 1969 and did occasional studio work as a session musician.

When Flatt wanted to add a second banjo player, the band had four terrific lead instrumentalists. Jordan explained, "We were already splitting practically every instrumental break four ways as it was, and then he wanted to add that. He was just not aware that there had been double banjos used countless times through the years. You know, the Osbornes and so forth. It was not anything new but he thought it was. It was no big deal between Haskell McCormick and I, and it wasn't a problem between Lester and I. But it just got real crowded. I think that Lester was trying to change his sound a bit—toward a more distinctive band sound and away from the **Flatt and Scruggs** format. But it seemed like none of us hardly ever got to play a full break—we always had to split it up. There was Paul (Warren), Josh (Graves), Roland (White) and me. And when we only got to play four bars and we were done, we hardly ever got warmed up."[179]

In an interview with Dick Weissman, Jordan spoke about his former employers, "Well, Jimmy Martin wants you to play just what's on his records. He was very specific, and he didn't want you to play too freely. Working with Bill Monroe was really a good learning process. He emphasized good time and tone. I learned about how to arrange a song from him. I'd say working with him was a good school. He always knew what he wanted. He basically wanted you to play the melody of fiddle tune, like Bill Keith had done. Roland White and Byron Berline were in the band, and we spent a lot of time jamming together.

"Lester Flatt hadn't really followed what was going on with banjo music that much," continued Jordan. "I played 'Little Maggie' for him in the melodic style and it was a revelation to him. After awhile, he started getting out to more of the festivals and he got a better picture of where the music had gone.

"Jim and Jesse were willing to accept melodic style. Jesse was still writing a lot of tunes when I was with him. We'd pick on the bus or in motels and Jesse did his Daffy Duck imitation. We had a good time. I played on some of **Jim and Jesse**'s records. Bobby Thompson was a big help to me."

Jordan is well known for his melodic style of banjo playing; he first heard it when Bobby Thompson played on **Jim and Jesse**'s "Border Ride" record. Then he listened to Eric Weissberg and Marshall Brickman doing double-banjos on "New Dimensions in Banjo and Bluegrass" (Elektra Records, 1963).

On December 21 and 22 of 1972, while still with **Jim and Jesse**, Jordan recorded the "Pickaway" LP for Atteiram as his first solo attempt.[180] Other solo projects are "Christmas Songs of Our Land as Played on the American Banjo" (July 1973, Gusto) and "Nashville Banjo"[181] (April 1978, Sugar Hill) which he recorded when he was a full-time Nashville studio musician. In February 1973, Jordan wrote "Jordan's Hornpipe." He stayed with **Jim and Jesse** until July of 1974, and continued to record with them for the next sixteen years.[182]

With Kenny Baker, he recorded "Portrait of a Bluegrass Fiddler" (September 1968) and "Kenny Baker Plays Bill Monroe" (March 1976). With Jesse McReynolds, he recorded on Jesse's solo LP "Me and My Fiddle." With Red Rector, Jordan recorded on "Ballads and Instrumentals," and with Mike Auldridge he recorded on "Mike Auldridge."

He joined **Jim and Jesse** for the third time October 1988. In August 1990, Jordan and others formed **Old Hickory** and stayed together about a year.[183]

In the 1992 phone interview, Mr. Jordan mentioned that he really likes the banjo playing of Bela Fleck... "And I'll tell you who I'm most impressed with these days is Alison Brown. She's an incredible musician! She's clean, has good tone, good drive—all the things I look for in a banjo player. Plus she's innovative as well."

In the 1990s, he likes being a full-time studio musician on rhythm guitar and banjo. He doesn't have to tour, learn songs, or learn shows. He merely learns his part in a song to be recorded, plays it, and forgets it. He feels it's more enjoyable this way. He also substitutes in various bands occasionally, and does some record producing. He played guitar for Wayne Newton one and a half years in Vegas and in Branson, Missouri. "I stayed in Missouri for a year. But there is just not enough independent work and it doesn't pay well. But I had a good time and made some friends and came back to Nashville in March 1995."

178 Michelle Putnam, "Vic Jordan—Still Pickin' Away," From a July 1996 telephone conversation. *Bluegrass Unlimited*, December, 1991, p. 28.

179 From a July 1996 telephone conversation.

180 Musicians included Jordan (banjo), Norman Blake (guitar), Charlie Collins (guitar), Buck White (mandolin), Butch Robins (bass) and Jody Maphis (drums).

181 Musicians included Jordan (banjo, guitar), Charlie Collins (guitar), Jim Baker (steel guitar), Duke Dumas (bass), Bobby Hicks (fiddle), Jesse McReynolds (mandolin) and several others.

182 LPs include "The Jim and Jesse Show" (May 1973), "Superior Sounds of Bluegrass" (July 1973), "Paradise" (December 1973), "Jim and Jesse Today" (October 1980), "Jim and Jesse and Charlie Louvin" (September 1981) and "25th Anniversary Album" (February and March 1989).

183 Others were Charlie Derrington (mandolin), Jim Hurst (guitar), Kent Blanton (bass) and Gene Wooten (resonator guitar).

Dave Evans

Dave Evans and River Bend

Dave Evans was born in Portsmouth, Ohio, on July 24, 1950, growing up in Columbus into a musical family. At age nine he began and singing picking banjo in the clawhammer style; he soon learned the three-finger style from a neighbor. "When I started playing the banjo I had trouble remembering the tunes, so I got to singing the melodies. When I played 'John Henry,' I sung it right along. So even if I couldn't pick it and get the right licks, at least I could sing it. I always relied on my singing to learn the songs right."[184] After he became a fully-developed entertainer, he was known for his ability to simultaneously pick the banjo competently and sing soulfully.

About 1965, Evans met John Hickman who inspired him toward a professional career. Hickman was in Columbus with the **Dixie Gentlemen** at the time, and gave lessons to Evans at a local music store. Evans was very motivated, learned fast and practiced continuously. On the day after high school graduation in 1968, Evans joined Earl Taylor's **Stoney Mountain Boys** in Yakima, Washington, while the group was on tour there. He quit after seventeen months when he returned home after his mother died. Emotionally troubled, his religious faith kept his thought processes straight. "I know my God too well to go out and get into trouble, 'cause I'd have certain penance to pay when I got home."[185]

He stayed in the Columbus area, working with local bands until Jimmy Martin hired him. But they never actually played together. The story goes that Evans was planning to get married soon, and Martin expressed an opinion of this event that upset him. He related that Martin told him, "'Yeah, if you marry that girl'—you know how he tells the banjo players—'you won't be able to pick the banjo anymore.'" This negative attitude put an end to his employment with Martin after only one day.

Dave Evans' next jobs were with **Larry Sparks and the Lonesome Ramblers** in 1973 for a year, and in 1975 with **Lillimae and the Dixie Gospelaires** on weekends. He also had a day job, but the lure of full-time music was too much; he quit both jobs then joined the **Boys from Indiana**[186] for a year. In this band, he was, for the first time, a lead singer.

He played with Melvin Goins for a short time then founded his own **River Bend** in 1975 with Gerald Evans, Dennis Barrett (guitar) and Art Wydner (bass). By now he was known for his sensitive, yet powerful, lead singing—often being compared to Carter Stanley and Larry Sparks. His new band recorded on Vetco.

In 1990, Evans had an altercation when his son rode a bicycle through a judge's yard and the judge made him angry—so angry he shot up the judge's house. At the trial, he tried to plead his own case but that same judge threw the book at him. Evans was sentenced to fourteen years in jail with no time off or chance for parole. In September 1995, he was released to a half-way house, and then released on probation in January 1996.

Tony Trischka

Tony Trischka, Skyline and the Tony Trischka Band— a step beyond tradition

The story of Tony Trischka could just as easily fit into the Branches chapter of this book because of where he went with the music—some of it was kind of far-out. And though even *he* considers some of it as experimental, we place him in a chapter about the banjo and its players. His interpretations of what banjo music could be makes him a subject of controversy, but that does not denigrate his other contributions to bluegrass music.

184 Herschel Freeman, "Dave Evans—The Voice of Traditional Bluegrass," *Bluegrass Unlimited*, January, 1981, p. 11.

185 Ibid., p. 12.

186 With Paul Mullins, Harley Gabbard, Aubrey and Jerry Holt.

Tony Trischka was born in Syracuse, New York, January 16, 1949. His father played piano. His parents listened to Pete Seeger and the **Weavers**, and Tony was exposed to that. "But my first exposure to the banjo break in 'Charley and the MTA' by the **Kingston Trio** got me excited, and from there I got into Scruggs and Monroe" in 1963. Trischka began playing banjo out of Pete Seeger's instruction book. He already played guitar and soon became accomplished on the pedal steel guitar. His first banjo teacher was Hal Glatzer who taught him the Scruggs-style. "I have a vivid memory of my first lesson there, learning 'Lonesome Road Blues' and 'Reuben James' a la Eric Weissberg from the 'Folk Banjo Styles' record. In the space of one lesson, I was learning Scruggs-style, playing those characteristic licks. It was so exciting going from total ignorance at one moment and an hour later coming out thinking I'd been given the knowledge of the ages, this mystical thing."[187] After a year and a half of lessons, he began learning tunes off records and playing in jam sessions; he began learning to play by ear.

Two main influences on his playing were Don Reno and Bill Keith. Keith was just coming out with his new melodic style. Trischka admired both banjoists but admitted that "Keith has had a very strong influence on many people. Reno less so I think, but I still do a lot of Reno style; it feels punchy to me. It really helps to drive—to play Reno style. It's more percussive because you're damping the note almost every time you hit it, because you're going thumb-index, thumb-index on the same string as opposed to fanning it out over several strings."[188]

In 1965, Trischka attended Carlton Haney's first bluegrass festival in Fincastle, Virginia, where he was able to see the founding fathers of the music. Trischka said, "Bill Monroe had a very profound effect on my music. You might not be able to pick out any particular notes, but just in terms of an amazing depth of feeling. Seeing his band with Peter Rowan, Richard Greene and Lamar Grier in the mid-sixties was just...literally, a transcendent experience. I mean, I was only seventeen or eighteen when I was listening to them, but it's the highest I'd ever been listening to music. Words can't describe how important that was to me."[189]

"Listening" is the best way, he feels, that one can learn this music. He suggests to his students that they listen to "The standards. It's great and wonderfully subtle stuff. Just listen to the Rounder and County reissues of some of that early **Flatt and Scruggs** stuff. Just listen to the greats. Listen to Reno. I'd say listen to a wide variety of the different stylists. In other words, if you just listen to Earl and J.D. Crowe—who are both geniuses, of course—or other people that play like

them, you're limiting yourself. And it's good to listen to everybody and see who you like. Listen to Crowe for sure. Listen to Stanley. Listen to the modern guys.

"One thing is, I find that some people will tend to latch on to the modern players at the expense of Scruggs. And I think that you need the Scruggs to solidify your right hand particularly—just to get the strength and power of bluegrass—then you can play anything else with more integrity and just more firmness. Because Scruggs style is so much of what the banjo is about, you really need that."[190]

About 1969, Trischka became interested in jazz, being tired of the limitations of bluegrass. He felt an inner need to play differently—he heard things "differently because of something inside of me." The next year, he was the banjoist with the **Down City Ramblers** of Syracuse, New York. Trischka told this writer, "The **Down City Ramblers** was my first real band. I don't mention it much because we were almost exclusively a local Syracuse band. But I did learn a lot."

Also about that time, he worked with Danny Weiss in a group called **Country Granola**. In 1971, Trischka was a member of the **Down City Ramblers** as well as **Country Cooking**, a group which featured Peter Wernick, Russ Barenberg, John Miller and Nondi Leonard. In 1971, Rounder released "14 Bluegrass Instrumentals" by **Country Cooking**. These recordings, though common in style by today's standards, caused quite a stir when released. Some people loved them, and others, who liked their bluegrass straight, didn't.

In successive albums, Trischka re-defined the limits of the banjo with the acknowledgment that it is an instrument which has limitations such as lack of sustain and a rather narrow acceptance by bluegrass fans as to how the instrument is to be played. The style that Trischka put on record is not so much a break with tradition as a stretch of it with the addition of his personal techniques, not the least of which is a superb knowledge of the banjo, of bluegrass, and the inspiration of jazz. The album is now considered a landmark in a new direction for the bluegrass genre. Assisting him in this endeavor was mandolinist Andy Statman who can go just as far out. The result is an experiment in chords and rhythm.

"I was listening to the new John Hickman record [today]," said Trischka, "and he has a very identifiable style. It's very well-ordered. He has a certain number of things that he does that are just wonderful—really beautiful. To me, it's a very well-ordered, logical type of sound. Whereas, with me, I find that mine is maybe a little less logical. There are certain things that I will repeat, but there's a lot in my playing that surprises me when I'm playing—things that I've never played before.

187 Interview by Peter Wernick, *Banjo Newsletter*, November, 1978.
188 Ibid.
189 Interview with Lee Kessler for *Banjo Newsletter*, October, 1986.
190 1984 interview by Pete Wernick for *Masters of the 5-String Banjo in Their Own Words and Music* (New York: Oak Publications, 1988), p. 343.

If I'm really inspired when I'm playing, that will happen. Notes will come out that I never knew existed. I know the instrument well enough since I've been playing for fifteen years, so my fingers will just, most of the time, go to the right places. It's really getting tapped into some other source besides myself and I really feel that in all my music—at least in the music I compose— really in everything. It's not me that's coming up, it's the notes that are there that are being channeled through me."[191]

Though a methodical technician, Trischka is heavily involved in emotion when he plays. He just turns off his conscious mind when the moment is right. "When I'm playing very hot and heavy, I get into a very emotional state; I become very unconscious of what I'm doing. I'll listen to tapes of what I've played after a concert and be very surprised at what I've done. That's why I enjoy listening to what I do because it's not like I did it; it's like hearing someone else. It is a very unconscious thing, although obviously there's a lot of practice that goes into doing that. You have to have a certain facility on your instrument and know the neck fairly well to do that."[192]

He likes taking chances in his playing. "That's what I enjoy about it—painting myself into a corner and then seeing how I'm going to get out of it. That's the thing with taking chances; I just need that challenge and I need to challenge myself."[193]

In 1973, Trischka moved to New York City where he joined **Breakfast Special** with Kenny Kosek, Andy Statman, Stacy Phillips and others. 1976 was the first of two consecutive years that Trischka was hired to be the musical leader of the Broadway show, "The Robber Bridegroom." That year, he also appeared on the "Merv Griffin Show."

Not every good banjo player can explain what he/she does. Trischka can do that, and this makes him an excellent teacher. In 1977, Trischka authored *Teach Yourself Bluegrass Banjo*. Already published were his *Melodic Banjo* (1973, Oak Publications), *The Banjo Songbook* (1975, Oak) and *Bill Keith Banjo* (1978, Oak) with Bill Keith.

Barry Mitterhoff, Danny Weiss, Trischka, Larry Cohen and Dede Wyland got together to form **Tony Trischka and Skyline** in 1980. This new band relied more upon vocals than any of his previous bands. By 1982, they were recording for Flying Fish Records.

Trischka authored *Hot Licks for Bluegrass Banjo* in 1983. Two years later, Trischka returned to his bluegrass roots with "Hill Country" on Rounder Records. The following year, he won Banjoist of the Year award in the *Frets* magazine Readers' Poll. He was also a guest columnist for the magazine. He appeared on The Nashville Network's "Fire on the Mountain" television

show in 1984 and 1986. In 1987, Trischka appeared on Ralph Emery's "*Frets* Awards Show" on TNN. *Masters of the 5-String Banjo* was published by Oak Publications in 1988. Co-authored by Trischka and Peter Wernick, it included 400-plus pages of interviews with important bluegrass banjoists. 1988 was the third consecutive year that *Frets* readers voted him the Banjo Player of the Year. He composed and performed a soundtrack for a Scott Paper promotional film. His credits also include numerous liner notes for various albums.

By 1990, his band was the **Tony Trischka Band** which was soon re-named **Big Dogs**. Trischka lives in Fair Lawn, New Jersey, and continues to create music, teach and play bluegrass of all kinds. His new band, called **World Turning**, is an act which tells the history of the banjo through a narrator, spanning African music, American slave music, minstrel music, old-time music, bluegrass and progressive music. In 1995, he appeared on "CBS Sunday Morning" with host Charles Osgood. He took Bill Keith's place in The **Grass Is Greener** in late 1995 or early 1996.

Pete Wernick

Peter Wernick and Hot Rize

Peter "Dr. Banjo" Wernick is a pioneer in banjo and bluegrass instruction along with his contributions in several significant bands. He initiated bluegrass instruction camps where legions of students have benefited from his vast experience in the three-finger banjo technique. And, as President of the International Bluegrass Music Association (IBMA), he serves the bluegrass community as spokesman and behind-the-scenes activist for the well-being of bluegrass music.

Peter Wernick was born in the Bronx, New York, February 25, 1946. His father played harmonica. At

191 Wernick interview, op. cit., 1978.
192 Ibid.
193 1992 telephone conversation.

America's Music — Bluegrass

296

twelve, young Wernick became interested in the banjo after listening to Earl Scruggs play "Shuckin' the Corn" on the "Foggy Mountain Jamboree" album. Wernick now patterns his picking style after Scruggs—by far his favorite banjo player. He learned by trial and error—there was no tablature to follow when he began learning the banjo in November of 1960.

Wernick worked hard at learning this music and, in 1964, while attending undergraduate studies at Columbia University in New York City, joined his first bluegrass band, the **Orange Mountain Boys**.[194] He was a deejay for the college's WKCR. It was there, in March 1966, where he bought his 1931 Gibson RB-1 from Porter Church who was then the banjoist with **Red Allen and the Kentuckians**.

Wernick began graduate studies in Sociology in 1966 and received a PhD. in 1973. His nickname, "Dr. Banjo", has stuck ever since.

In 1969, Wernick worked with Butch Waller and Rich Wilbur in **High Country**[195] in the San Francisco Bay Area. "That was my biggest bluegrass experience up to that date because these guys were actually making a fair part of their living through this music. They already had a respectable following and they were more professional at it than anybody I had ever played with before."[196]

There in California, he also performed with bluegrass traditionalists **Vern and Ray** (Vern Williams and Ray Park[197]). This experience was one which Wernick considers one of the most important in his bluegrass education. "It gave me a deeper understanding of what bluegrass was all about," he said in 1996. "Vern and Ray were both country guys who really knew all about bluegrass and felt it in their bones. When I'd be up there playing with them on stage, I felt like I just *had* to produce and play the kind of music that would fit into what they were doing. I couldn't just go on little flights of fancy because everything going on the stage really had to mean something or it just wouldn't sound right."[198]

In 1970, Wernick moved to Ithaca, New York, to work at Cornell University as a Research Associate. That year, he formed **Country Cooking** with members Russ Barenberg (guitar), John Miller (bass), himself (guitar, banjo), Nondi Leonard (Wernick's future wife[199], vocals) and Tony Trischka (banjo and steel guitar). They recorded two albums on the newly-formed Rounder

Records: "14 Bluegrass Instrumentals" and "Barrel of Fun." By 1974, **Country Cooking** had lost Barenberg and Miller to jazz. A third album on Flying Fish with the group featured Alan Senauke and Howie Tarnower as the **Fiction Brothers**.

Wernick was an accomplished banjo instructor by this time, having taught as many as six students per week during the past ten years. He then put much of his enthusiasm for bluegrass music into writing *Bluegrass Banjo* which was published by Oak Publications of New York in 1974. He explained how the book came about, "It wasn't as difficult as you might think for such a large book because I had already been teaching one-on-one to a lot of people for ten years. When I realized I would be writing a book, I just sat down at the typewriter as though I was teaching one extremely long lesson to one person who needed to have everything spelled out very carefully. And since I had already been doing it, it just fell right out from memory."[200] The book gave him the earnings and courage to quit his job at Cornell to pursue his music career full-time in 1974.[201] As of 1996, the book had sold more than 200,000 copies. He later put out a series of "Music Minus One" play-along tapes (1974), *Bluegrass Songbook* (Oak Publications, 1976), three video tapes (beginning in 1985), and a book on banjo players co-authored by Tony Trischka, *Masters of the 5-String Banjo—In Their Own Words and Music* (New York: Oak Publications, 1988).

In 1975, he, Trischka, Barenberg and Miller recorded an EP (7-inch, 33 1/3 r.p.m.) as the **Extended Play Boys**. He and Nondi moved to Boulder, Colorado, in 1976. **Country Cooking** then disbanded.

Pete Wernick (L) and Ben Eldridge at a 1988 banjo workshop in Grass Valley, CA.

---

194 Band members were Bob Applebaum (mandolin), Hank Miller (guitar), Ed Goff or Chet Stone (bass).

195 Wernick: "I think of Rich as a significant figure in music; he wrote some really good songs." A posthumous CD of his songs was released in the early 1990s.

196 Karen Quick, "Peter Wernick—Dr. Banjo," *Bluegrass Unlimited*, April, 1987, p. 51.

197 Ray Park is from Treat, Arkansas, and learned about bluegrass from an early age through his family. Williams is from a farm in Newton County, Arkansas.

198 Quick, op. cit..

199 Wernick met Nondi Leonard in 1969 on a trip to Colorado.

200 From an interview in Eugene, Oregon, summer 1985.

201 The $6,000 per year he received in 1974 from the book royalties was actually more than he was making at Cornell.

He began playing banjo in Colorado with the **Rambling Drifters** a.k.a. **Drifting Ramblers.** In this group, he worked with guitarist Charles Sawtelle[202] and Denver's Warren Kennison[203]. Sawtelle, the manager of the Denver Folklore Center at the time, also ran their sound system and told jokes. The Center was begun by Harry Tuft in 1962 and was a gathering point for acoustic musicians; Wernick was a banjo teacher at the center. Tim O'Brien taught mandolin and fiddle there, and Nick Forster was an instrument repairman at the store.

Wernick's first solo effort was "Dr. Banjo Steps Out"[204] for Flying Fish Records. He used an electronic phase shifter on the record. Though some may feel uneasy with electronic gadgets in bluegrass music, he used it simply because he thought it sounded good... He said, "When you get electronic gimmickry in there, there is a temptation to use it just as a gimmick—just to get a flashy effect—where I try to only use it where it helps the music communicate somehow better."[205]

In January of 1978, **Hot Rize** was formed with Wernick (banjo), Sawtelle (electric bass), Tim O'Brien[206] (mandolin) and Mike Scap (guitar). Scap left after three months and Sawtelle moved to his main instrument, the guitar; the band asked Nick Forster to play electric bass.[207]

From 1978 to 1990, **Hot Rize** combined the best of traditional bluegrass with original songwriting. **Hot Rize** members, though they came from different areas of the country (New York, Texas, West Virginia), seemed to learn bluegrass in a similar manner. When they combined their talents into a band, their commonalties easily overshadowed any regional differences in the way they liked their bluegrass music. The way they melded their opinions of

Hot Rize, 1989. L to R: Pete Wernick, Nick Forster, Tim O'Brien, Charles Sawtelle.

what bluegrass should be gives us a clear example of just how pervasive this music had become in American society. They learned the lessons of the bluegrass masters well, and the hard-driving quartet also was among the most entertaining of the modern bands. This was also because of a part of the show they performed as their '50s country music alter egos, **Red Knuckles and the Trailblazers.** Their complete personality change on stage was awesome and convincing. The audience almost had to ask if they were, indeed, the same people.

1980 was the year of the first **Red Knuckles and the Trailblazers** performance. By 1981, the act was a regular part of the **Hot Rize** show. In September of that year, **Hot Rize** performed on the Grand Ole Opry for the first time. The first record for the **Trailblazers** was recorded live and released in 1982 by Flying Fish. **Hot Rize** albums to this point were "Hot Rize" (Flying Fish, 1979) and "Radio Boogie" (Flying Fish, 1981).

Wernick began teaching bluegrass music's first instruction week in 1980. It was a banjo class at the summer Haystack Program on the Oregon coast at Cannon Beach. The classes were well attended and well received. Starting in 1985, the Program added several more teachers including the rest of the **Hot Rize** band, teaching the techniques of being a band as well as instrumental skills. Wernick's class was a concept which has since proliferated. The next year, Laurie Lewis and Jerry Douglas taught along with **Hot Rize.** Lewis later directed similar programs elsewhere. The Haystack Program led to Wernick's five-day Banjo Camps which have been held several times a year throughout the nation beginning in 1984.

---

202 Guitarist Charles Sawtelle was born in Austin, Texas, September 20, 1946. In 1971, he played guitar with the Country Blue Boys, Windsor, Colorado. The band changed its name the next year to the Monroe Doctrine Bluegrass Band which played regularly in the Denver area. Sawtelle was partner in a company which provided sound systems for concerts. He also played in the Twenty-String Bluegrass Band with Lynn Morris.

203 As of 1996, Kennison was actively involved in the promotion of traditional bluegrass in Colorado, and as banjoist with his own True Blue.

204 Musicians included Tim O'Brien (fiddle), Andy Statman (mandolin) and Charles Sawtelle (guitar). Also on the album were three members of Country Cooking: Tony Trischka (banjo), Russ Barenberg (guitar) and John Miller (bass, fiddle).

205 From 1985 interview.

206 Tim O'Brien was born March 16, 1954, in Wheeling, West Virginia, and raised there. He learned to play rhythm guitar in Wheeling from Roger Bland, a banjo player who played with Lester Flatt's Nashville Grass. O'Brien was influenced toward the mandolin by Monroe, Grisman and Sam Bush.
    O'Brien arrived in Boulder, Colorado, in 1974 and worked at the Denver Folklore Center, played fiddle with Towne and Country Review, and played guitar with Ophelia Swing Band for three years.

207 On May 16, 1955, Nick Forster was born in Beirut, Lebanon. His family moved to upstate New York when he was two. At age eleven, young Forster was given a guitar and he followed folk music of the Kingston Trio, Ian and Sylvia and Jellyroll Morton. Through high school he was influenced by the Beatles and Doc Watson, and he took up the banjo and mandolin.
    Additionally, a fifth member of the group was Frank Edmonson. He acted as road manager, soundman, and bus driver for the band and is given much of the credit for the proper handling of the Hot Rize sound—very important to a band's relaxation index. Edmonson went on to perform this role for Alison Krauss.

Hot Rize changed from the Flying Fish label to Sugar Hill in 1985 and the label released "Traditional Ties." Other bluegrass bands were changing to Sugar Hill as well. Flying Fish seemed to be staying with diverse types of folk music.

In 1986, Peter Wernick was voted by the Board of Directors of the International Bluegrass Music Association to be the first President of the organization. He remains in this position as of 1996.

On May 1, 1990, **Hot Rize** broke up. Tim O'Brien left to pursue a solo career. Rather than replace him, the band members chose to pursue other projects. **Hot Rize** won Entertainer of the Year award at IBMA September of 1990. Tim O'Brien formed the **O'Boys**[208] in 1990 and works and records with various musicians and with his sister, Mollie O'Brien. He won IBMA's Male Vocalist of the Year in 1993. In 1991, Forster created a syndicated radio show, "E-Town," which he co-produces with his wife and on which he serves as host and plays music in the staff band, the **E-Tones**. E-Town was originally heard on National Public Radio stations and, as of 1996, heard on over one hundred commercial and non-commercial radio stations. Wernick continues his banjo camps, started a performing duo with his wife, Joan (Nondi), and formed the **Live Five,** a bluegrass- and jazz-flavored band in 1992 which records for Sugar Hill. Sawtelle records and performs with various musicians, notably Peter Rowan. He owns and operates the Rancho DeVille recording studio. **Hot Rize** re-grouped for reunion tours in 1992, 1994 and 1996, proving that the success of the band was much more than just a band of fleeting success. It was more than that, and the audiences were glad to have the four men back.

Red Knuckles and the Trailblazers. L to R: Waldo Otto, Wendell Mercantile, Slade, Red Knuckles.

Alan Munde and the Country Gazette

Alan Munde is a veteran banjoist who has done it all: he has performed in a long-lasting band, recorded extensively, written many tunes, taught banjo, taught bluegrass in a university as a faculty member and sold bluegrass paraphernalia in his own mail-order business.

Munde was born in Norman, Oklahoma, November 4, 1946. His brother and sister were the musicians in the family; they played the accordion. In 1960, he became interested in playing the guitar after listening to Pete Seeger's guitar instruction record. Alan's older brother, Mike, had brought that record home when he returned from the Navy about that time. Mike lost interest and Alan gained it. Alan switched to banjo because he liked the sound of it and discovered that Seeger played banjo. He joined his first group about age sixteen: the **East Ridge Ramblers**. He frailed initially, changing to the three-finger style after hearing Earl Scruggs on the "Foggy Mountain Banjo" album. Subsequent influences became Bill Monroe, Bill Keith, and especially Doug Dillard.

Munde explained that "The guy who played the banjo in a way that just really thrilled me and still does to this day, is Doug Dillard. The **Dillards** were real popular and visible, and his banjo playing conveyed this unbridled sense of joy to me. That's the real essence of what I'd like to do...this incredibly joyous music that you couldn't deny." When Munde first saw them in Oklahoma he was seventeen. "I had a banjo and could bang on it. But that was really the first group that I saw that could really do it. And man, I can still see them in my mind. That was *it* for me!"[209]

Bluegrass Banjo

---

[208] It is significant that Nick Forster was Tim's harmony singer and guitarist for the first two years. He was very helpful to the band sound.

[209] Nancy Cardwell, "After Twenty Years—Alan Munde and the Country Gazette," *Bluegrass Unlimited,* October, 1991, p. 21.

Alan Munde with Japanese shamisen. Photo courtesy Jan Willis.

As with many musicians of the day, Munde learned mostly by listening to records; tablature was nearly non-existent. He hung around the Mike Richey Guitar Center and listened to Richey (now known as "Slim", who owns and runs Ridge Runner Records) play music and talk. Because of the variety of music at the store—Slim was primarily a jazz guitarist—Munde got a broad education in music.

Munde met Byron Berline in 1964 while they attended the University of Oklahoma in Norman. Berline had recently cut his instrumental record with the **Dillards**. It was also during this period that Munde met banjoist Eddie Shelton. They played a lot together. Munde, just beginning to play the banjo, learned much from Shelton—especially about melodic picking. Munde and Berline played in the **Oklahoma Bluegrass Gentlemen** at the university with two other members who were not college students.[210] Still in college, Munde joined the **Stone Mountain Boys**.[211]

Courtney Johnson (of the original **New Grass Revival**) introduced Munde to Sam Bush and Wayne Stewart[212] in 1968. The next year, the trio founded **Poor Richard's Almanac** which is often acknowledged as a precursor to newgrass music. Munde did this awhile[213] until he was drafted (April 1969) but he was rejected

from the Army for medical reasons (high blood pressure).

In October of 1969, Munde met Jimmy Martin during a DJ convention in Nashville; he soon auditioned for him in Nashville and went on tour with **Jimmy Martin and the Sunny Mountain Boys** the following Thursday. He considers this as his first professional job even though he had already recorded a record with Harlow Wilcox, a project which did very well.

Doyle Lawson was with the **Sunny Mountain Boys**[214] at the time, and also at the audition. Lawson recommended that Munde could do the job. He felt that Munde could learn, and with his help, progress rapidly to the point where Martin would want him to be. Munde played with the band until October 1971. Of the thirteen songs recorded with Jimmy Martin, two were "Singing All Day and Dinner on the Ground" and "I'd Like to Be Sweet Sixteen Again."

When Munde joined Martin, he was, as he reflected on his music at that time, not an accomplished banjo player. He was at the stage at which he was still learning. He learned by copying other banjo artists—using their breaks and techniques. In the phone interview with this writer in December of 1990, Munde insisted that this was not bad. For him, it was a stage of development; it was not where he intended to end up.

Country Gazette, 1990. L to R: Dawn Watson, Chris Vandertuin, Alan Munde, Steve Gardner.

---

[210] They lived in Oklahoma City and were Walter Hawkins (guitar) and Albert Brown (mandolin). There was no bass player.

[211] According to the liner notes of "Stone Mountain Boys Reunion Album" (1978, Ridge Runner Records), the Stone Mountain Boys organized in 1966 with these original members: Alan Munde (banjo), Mitchell Land (mandolin), Louis 'Bosco' Land (guitar) and Harless 'Tootie' Williams (bass). The band as most people knew it, however, featured Ed Shelton (banjo) and Lonnie Craft (guitar) with Mitchell and Tootie. This was the band seen most often at festivals and shows." Occasionally, beginning in 1965, Munde traveled down to Dallas to play in the band with Mitchell and Tootie, the most constant members.

   Berline also joined them when he could. Berline, in fact, credits the Stone Mountain Boys with his decision to play bluegrass fiddle. Shelton became the permanent banjo player in 1968 when Munde left.

[212] Munde, in 1995, explained it this way: "I met Courtney Johnson at the Mountain View Folk Festival in Mountain View, Arkansas. He went back to Kentucky and he knew Sam Bush and Wayne Stewart and he told Wayne Stewart about this banjo player he heard that was from Norman, Oklahoma. Wayne, the free-spirit that he is, sort of picked up and was going to move to California. He stopped through Norman on his way, spent the night, we picked and had a good time. Instead of going to California, he went back to Kentucky. He kept in touch with me through letters and possibly we talked on the phone. There was a fiddle contest in Independence, Missouri. And at that time, I was sort of going with Lue Berline, Byron's dad, and Byron's brother, Leonard. Lue, Leonard and I went to this contest in Independence and I guess I communicated this to Wayne. So Wayne and Sam also went to this contest in Independence. It was at that place that I met Sam Bush."

[213] He worked there in Kentucky as Poor Richard's Almanac from January 1969 until May of 1969. They did a home recording which was later released as "Poor Richard's Almanac."

[214] Also in the band were Vernon Derrick (fiddle) and Gloria Belle (bass).

Martin taught Munde the basics of professional playing: producing good tone, developing a good sense of timing, and playing clearly. He looked at this bluegrass banjo player as he did with all his job applicants—as a prospective professional musician. Jimmy Martin "had a real presentational approach to playing bluegrass in that whatever you played had to be heard and understood by the audience. He would always say, 'If you play a lick and you can't make it come out and be heard, you might as well not have played it.'"[215] "Jimmy was real obsessed with the music. When he spoke about the music he had a pretty clear view of it. And that view was that he was an entertainer that loved the music, and the music was the larger part of the entertainment. And if the people didn't understand it, then it was less than it could be. What I used to compare it with is when you are telling a joke and get all the way to the punch line and then say, 'Oh, yeah. Did I tell you the guy was Chinese?' Martin wanted it all crystal clear. He wanted you to play ideas which were to the point and [which fit] into where he wanted it to go."

In a 1991 interview, Munde related, "When I was with Jimmy Martin he paid the union scale which was about $35-45 per day that you worked. Actually, I just took what he paid me and didn't say a word. If you worked every day, that wasn't bad. But if you worked only Saturday and Sunday it wasn't good. I believe there was also a per diem for the days that you traveled. But he only paid us on the days that we actually performed. When Byron [Berline] worked for Monroe, he only got paid about $25 per day but he worked a lot more [and it ended up with a lot more pay]. During the first two years I was with Jimmy Martin I just barely made over $2000 total. That's just the standard way in Nashville; you have the artist and then you have the band. The artist makes the money and the band could be just anybody standing up there. This was in country music more so than in bluegrass. Some bands paid a weekly salary... When I went to Nashville I had a banjo and a guitar and I had some clothes and I had $300. When I left Nashville I had the same car, the same clothes, I had to sell the guitar, I

Country Gazette, c. 1978. L to R: Joe Carr, Alan Munde, Roland White, Mike Anderson.

didn't have any money, and I drove home on a car where the nut was welded on because it was the only way it would hold the wheel on. But I could play better! I was twenty-two when I went there and I didn't have anything else to do."

Munde explained that having a new member in his band must have been rather difficult for Martin, too, for Martin's background included the perfection of Bill Monroe's band, and he had been in the business forever. He knew what he wanted his sidemen to play—each note of it—and pushed all of his musicians toward this end. Sometimes he was difficult to play for if the sideman heard a song differently than Martin, who wasn't very forgiving when it came to the sound quality requirements of his band. Martin had learned a lot from Bill Monroe but also learned the elements of other Grand Ole Opry stars such as Eddy Arnold, Little Jimmy Dickens and Ernest Tubb. The elements he learned included the concept of playing in a smooth, slick and an organized single-vision kind of way. He wanted those ideas played on the banjo to be just as smooth and driving, and with a tone that was sparkling, full, and rounded, and with the feel which matched his guitar playing and singing. And that was difficult to do. Munde further challenged that "whoever thought that playing bluegrass was easy hadn't played to the limits which professional bluegrass requires." And being a banjo player under those circumstances, as Munde was, was a real experience from the past realities of the non-professional bands he had been with before.

In October of 1971, Munde quit the **Sunny Mountain Boys**. He moved to the West Coast the next January where Byron Berline (fiddle) and Roger Bush (bass) were organizing **Country Gazette** in Los Angeles. The earliest banjo players with the group were Herb Pedersen and Pat Cloud. Munde joined in January of 1972.[216] "When I worked with Jimmy Martin, I played his material and played it his way. When I went to **Country Gazette** the question became 'What do you want to do?' Up until I joined, I just tried to recreate

215 From a telephone interview with Alan Munde in December 1990.
216 Munde was the first permanent banjo player to join the band.

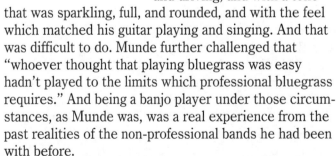

what had happened before. I had never given a great deal of thought to creating new things. Twenty years later, I've developed some understanding of what I have to offer and how to best go about getting it out."[217]

The **Country Gazette** was a band whose members were anxious to pursue music full-time and profitably. Soon Berline found a way to employ the members of the **Gazette** by providing a bluegrass act as a part of the European tour that the folk-rock **Flying Burrito Brothers** had a commitment for in early 1972. Most of the **Flying Burrito Brothers** band had already disbanded so Berline put together a tour for the **Brothers** with **Country Gazette** as the bluegrass element.[218] The first time Munde met these individuals was at the airport in New York, on the way to Europe, on January 2, 1972. Munde admitted that, for a while, he was a lousy electric guitar player. But as time went on, he became more comfortable and became confident enough to turn up the volume of his guitar on stage to an audible level. He called it "earning your volume."[219]

Still in 1972, they worked the summer at Disneyland as **Country Gazette**. Recording that summer, their first United Artists album was "Traitor in Our Midst."[220] This began a period of Munde recording for Hollywood movies through Berline's connections. They included "Can Ellen Be Saved?", "Bounty Man" and Disney's "The Nashville Coyote."

Alan Munde (L) and Joe Carr, 1995.

Country Gazette began another European tour as the **Flying Burrito Brothers Revue** in February 1973—this time as a separate act in addition to performing within the larger band.

That summer, the **Gazette** recorded their second United Artists album: "Don't Give Up Your Day Job" with Berline, Munde, Kenny Wertz and Roger Bush. In July 1973, Wertz left and was replaced by Roland White (guitar). This group recorded "Country Gazette Live" on the Antilles label. Recorded at McCabe's, Santa Monica, the record was released in 1975 by Transatlantic Records LTD of London, England.

In 1975, Berline left to start his own **Sundance**. Dave Ferguson, who formerly played with Texas' **Stone Mountain Boys**, replaced Berline on fiddle with the **Gazette**, then the **Gazette** toured Europe for the third time. **Country Gazette** proved to be the most popular bluegrass group in England and Holland. In Holland, they sold out all eight appearances. Ridge Runner Records released number 0001, "Alan Munde's Banjo Sandwich." This album used Munde, Ferguson (fiddle), Doc Hamilton (guitar), Roland White (mandolin) and Roger Bush (bass). Munde played a Stelling banjo here.

In September of 1976, Kenny Wertz re-joined the **Country Gazette** with Munde, White and Bush. The band decided not to hire another fiddler. Instead, they put Roland White on mandolin—which is where he wanted to be. Wertz and Bush departed this year so Munde and White hired Bill Bryson and Joe Carr occasionally.

The release of "Sam and Alan Together Again for the First Time" (Ridge Runner Records 0007) was so titled because it was the first reunion of Munde and Sam Bush since they'd worked together in **Poor Richard's Almanac**. Bush was then full-time with his own **New Grass Revival**. The bass player on the new album was John Cowan, also of the **Revival**. The album was his best work to that date, said Munde. Mike Anderson joined **Country Gazette** as bassist in 1978; Joe Carr joined as mandolinist.[221]

Munde began as a staff contributor to *Frets* magazine as it began operations in 1979; the magazine lasted ten years.

In the December 1982 issue of *Bluegrass Unlimited*, Herschel Freeman quoted Munde in his article "Country Gazette—At Home on the Range." Munde said that when **Country Gazette** was hired by Oklahoma's Artist-in-the-Schools program, "They wanted the performers to be more than just entertainers going out and doing their thing; they wanted it to be a teaching tool, also. If we were in a history class, we might talk more about where the instruments came from, and how they came to be where they were at the

[217] Cardwell, op. cit., p. 24.

[218] On this tour were Berline (fiddle), Munde (banjo, electric guitar), Kenny Wertz (guitar), Roger Bush (bass), Don Beck (steel), Eric Dalton (drums) and Rick Roberts (electric guitar, who was the sole remaining member of the Brothers). The Country Gazette was Berline, Munde, Wertz and Bush.

[219] Munde still (1991) insists that he continues to be a lousy guitar player. He edited this work and inserted this statement into the draft copy. This give us an idea of his humility and excellent sense of humor. Munde is well known for his casual dress (no matter what the event) and his excellent sense of humor. He was once asked it he would ever sell out to rock 'n' roll. He replied, "I don't know. Nobody has ever offered."

[220] Herb Pedersen guested on guitar, Skip Conover on the resonator guitar, and Chris Smith on guitar.

[221] Anderson came from the Sunset Harmony Boys of Fort Worth, and other bands before joining the Gazette. Eventually, he recorded on the Gazette's recordings including "The Tracker," "Eleanor Rigby" and his own "Highland Dream." He left awhile to study the art of piano tuning, restoring and rebuilding. He set up shop in Weatherford, Texas, and re-joined the group in 1988. His Gazette albums include "All This and Money, Too" (Ridge Runner) and "American and Clean" (Flying Fish).

Joe Carr also joined in 1978 as mandolinist/guitarist and emcee full-time with the band. He eventually recorded on the same albums as Anderson did in addition to "America's Bluegrass Band" (Flying Fish). He later became a faculty member of the Country/Bluegrass Department of South Plains College, Levelland, Texas. Carr "published" tapes on playing bluegrass mandolin.

time of the formation of the music. For an English class, one thing we did was to have a college-level creative writing class write ballads, and then we would take the words back to our motel room and compose melodies to go with them. This showed them how the 'folk process' worked from beginning to end—in capsulized form.

"The elementary school kids were more in awe than anything else. You know, kids are raised to television and all the entertainment is on a screen which you can turn and manipulate. Whereas, to have live musicians in front of them making sounds, singing, and being human brought a reaction. It sort of stirred a lot of things in them. They started remembering, 'Oh, my uncle has a guitar,' or 'My grandfather plays piano a little bit,' and it sort of brought it home to them, I guess."

In 1983, Munde recorded his fourth and fifth banjo albums, "Festival Favorites: Volume I" (1980) and "Festival Favorites: Nashville Sessions" (1982) on the Ridge Runner label (later reissued on Rounder). Gene Wooten (guitar, resonator guitar) joined **Country Gazette** after six years with **Wilma Lee and Stoney Cooper** and session work with Jimmy Martin, *et al*, in 1984.

1985 was the year that Munde owned and ran Alan Munde's Banjo College, in Norman, Oklahoma. It was mainly a mail-order business where he sold banjos and banjo paraphernalia.

Munde began his career as faculty at South Plains College, Levelland, Texas, in September 1986. He told how he got started with his position in the college, "The band did some shows and workshops at the school in 1981, and again in 1983. I returned by myself in 1985 and did a couple of days of private instruction as a guest instructor and a concert. I really enjoyed the educational environment and the opportunity to teach and play bluegrass in the part of the country I come from." By 1990, Alan Munde was an Associate Professor of Music in the Country Music/Bluegrass Program at South Plains College, Levelland, Texas (near Lubbock). Joe Carr, another veteran of **Country Gazette**, was also an Associate Professor of Music there.

Munde loves to play but feels that teaching is very rewarding in its own right. "When you play, you get immediate feedback. In teaching, you watch the growth and gradual evolution of musicians in a more extended context. I can't imagine not performing, but after [being[this closely involved in teaching, I can't imagine myself doing without it either." Just as Eddie Shelton helped Munde to learn effective banjo playing when he was just learning, Munde feels an obligation to help someone else learn—continuing the tradition.

In 1985, Billy Joe Foster[222] replaced Bill Smith on bass with the **Gazette** and also played fiddle. In January 1987, Munde, White and Wooten recorded "Strictly Instrumental" for Flying Fish. Guest artists were Billy Joe Foster (fiddle), David Grier (guitar) and Kathy Chiavola (electric bass).

By 1987, Munde was an experienced musician and music instructor. He was able to note a deficiency in how people learn to play bluegrass music. He explained, "People usually learn a few banjo rolls. Pretty soon they can play 'Foggy Mountain Breakdown' and that's the style they play everything in. It's the same when the whole band comes together. If they just play through stylistic elements on their instruments, there's very little content. They may play well, but they don't play anything; there aren't any musical ideas being brought out. Too many groups select songs that just show off style. That's one place where bluegrass has fallen down. (In 1995, he added that he has noticed that a lot of the newer groups today seem to have overcome this obstacle. "I now hear a lot of very wonderful music and really great songs being played in bluegrass now. Things have gotten a lot better since I made that earlier statement.")

Munde said that through his some thirty years of playing experience, he has "developed a clearer picture of how to go about relating to people through music. Some bluegrass groups believe they must be commercial, and tend to give the audience what they think it wants. The other side of the coin is the performer who just plays and the audience shows up to see what he's doing. The decision I've finally come to is that it's best to find those things in myself and the music that the people like, rather than try to change their outlook or mine. I've learned to find that middle ground where the audience and performer can come together."

In a 1987 interview, he admitted that he likes the West. "I like the frontier—or western—attitude about things. People are more laid back, have a good sense of humor, and are not quite as serious. I think there's a geographic determiner in the lay of the land."[223]

Members of the **Country Gazette** in 1990 were Munde (banjo), Dawn Watson[224] (mandolin), Chris Vandertuin (guitar) and Steve Garner (bass). They recorded "Keep on Pushing" for Flying Fish.

As of 1995, Munde and partner Joe Carr continued to teach at South Plains College, to tour as a duo, and they wrote *Prairie Nights to Neon Lights—the Story of Country Music in West Texas* (University of Texas Tech Press: 1995) which gained critical acclaim.

222 Foster is from a farm near Duncan, Oklahoma. He got started in bluegrass from his father's influence. He saw the Osborne Brothers in 1965, which further solidified his musical direction. His first band was Special Edition as banjoist. That began in 1973 and then he got a call from Alan Munde. With the Gazette, he played all the instruments. He later joined the Blue Grass Boys and Ricky Skaggs' band.

223 George A. Ghetia, "Friday Morning with Alan Munde," *Bluegrass Unlimited*, July, 1987, p. 24.

224 Watson was a student at Munde's Bluegrass Music Program at South Plains College. Then she joined Petticoat Junction before joining the Gazette. In 1989, Dawn Watson became Arizona State Mandolin Champion.

Larry McNeeley—
a Hollywood banjo player

Larry McNeeley was raised in Lafayette, Indiana, into a musical family. His mother sold her beloved piano and borrowed an additional amount to buy Larry a next-to-the-top-of-the-line Vega banjo—her son's obsession.

Early in young McNeeley's musical life, he was influenced by the resonator guitar of Shot Jackson who was with **Johnny and Jack** at the time. He was better (by his own standards) on the banjo, so he quit the resonator guitar. The same thing occurred with the piano. "I never could keep the two hands going in opposite directions, so I just couldn't see it continuing."[225]

In 1965, McNeeley began his professional career with two years as a **Pinnacle Mountain Boys** performer in Tennessee. Charlie Collins (fiddle) was his roommate and the person who introduced him to the melodic stylings of Bill Keith. They worked together, making as little as $3 per gig in their travels; they moved to Nashville in 1967, playing and living on the streets, waiting for someone famous to discover them. Dr. Perry "Doc" Harris, a man with close Nashville ties, became that person. McNeeley got a job working for Shot Jackson and Buddy Emmons; he had earlier been refused employment there... It's who-you-know in Nashville that counts, he found.

The next year, McNeeley (17) joined **Roy Acuff and the Smoky Mountain Boys** full-time in Nashville. But McNeeley was quite independent and tended to do what he wanted. "How am I going to apply that to a roll? That's probably why I've had so many problems with my musical career. I seldom bend for anyone else."[226]

He left the band early in 1969 and later confessed that he has mellowed out since then. He went to work for Roy Acuff Jr., doing country-rock style music.

Beginning in 1969, he did three seasons with "The Glen Campbell Goodtime Hour" after John Hartford left. His first album was "Glen Campbell Presents Larry McNeeley," which he deems as "the most unorganized mess I ever encountered in my life."[227] He left Campbell's show in 1972 to explore studio work in Hollywood, eventually becoming very successful. Carl Jackson took his place on the Glen Campbell show.

Larry McNeeley's banjo can be heard on an episode of "The Waltons" television show, and Walt Disney's film "Apple Dumpling Gang." The **Larry McNeeley Band**[228] was formed in 1978 and they recorded on Flying Fish. In late 1984, McNeeley moved back to Nashville from California. Bill Knopf took over his place on the television show "Dukes of Hazard."

Greg Cahill and
the Special Consensus

Chicago is the birthplace of Greg Cahill, on December 22, 1946. In his late teens, his interest was peaked by the acoustic, string music of the folk boom. At his high school graduation in 1964, Cahill saw a man play **Kingston Trio**-type banjo, and he dabbled in this instrument through college in Winona, Minnesota. Cahill bought Pete Seeger's banjo instruction book. He loved reading the book for its anecdotes but learning to play what Seeger taught didn't satisfy him. There really wasn't anyone to interpret the book to him. He played a little guitar and a little banjo.

225 Jim Hatlo, "Larry McNeeley," *Frets*, November, 1982, p. 25.

226 Ibid., p. 26.

227 Ibid.

228 Musicians were McNeeley (banjo), Geoff Levin (guitar) and Jack Skinner (guitar, formerly of Byron Berline's Sundance). Bassist Johnny Pierce soon replaced Skinner.

229 From a February 1992 interview at Ken Seaman's Mid-Winter Bluegrass Festival in Fort Collins, Colorado.

There in college, he had a folk trio, the **Rye Town Singer**s. The guitar player in the group, Pat Frawley, had **Flatt and Scruggs**' "Foggy Mountain Banjo" album, "and once you hear that it's all over. It's a common story; I just couldn't get enough," he said.[229] Cahill obtained his own copy of the classic LP and casually began learning the banjo. Another favorite album was J.D. Crowe's "Bluegrass Holiday." He loved Scruggs but spent more time learning what Crowe did on the banjo.

After the military, about 1971, Cahill really started playing the banjo. He took a few lessons from Richard Hood, banjoist with the **Greater Chicago Bluegrass Band**, and was on his way toward playing the instrument correctly. Cahill already had the motivation to learn the banjo; Hood's main contribution to his playing was to tell him to which records to listen. He slowed these down to 16 r.p.m.. Cahill explained, "I spent a lot of time listening and playing with records and by 1974 or '75, I decided I would take a year off to play music. I finally decided I had the bug too bad, so I quit my day job and practiced eight hours a day. I couldn't get enough. I couldn't do anything but eat, sleep and drink the banjo. I was listening to old Scruggs and J.D. Crowe records, and I never went back. I just kept doing it, squeaking by on no money and practicing a lot. That's when the band started getting together just playing for fun and for parties. But then we started traveling and performing more."[230] In graduate school, pursuing a Masters in social work, he still managed to practice four hours per day. He graduated in 1973 and worked in the field of social work where he tried to teach kids alternative activities to using drugs. He started giving banjo lessons.

In a 1992 interview with this writer, he explained how he puts tone and drive into his playing, "I got the drive that most people seem to say that I have mostly from Crowe. I'd slow those records down and hear even the rolls. They'd smack you in the face. I'd get right next to the speaker and spend hours there. It was like being in a trance. I'd do it over and over... I was very meticulous about it because I really wanted to learn how to play. Through that year, I was practicing a lot. Even on Christmas morning I got up early and practiced for a couple of hours. I would say that, after six or seven

The Special Consensus Bluegrass Band, 1993. L to R: Marty Marrone, Greg Cahill, Darren Wilcox, Drew Carson.

months after playing every day, I would say that I could do okay with the Scruggs stuff or the Crowe stuff. What I got from that was the drive, boy. I'd break strings a lot so I talked to Crowe about it after a couple festivals. This was before J.D. Crowe's Extra Light Gauge Strings by GHS. He just said you don't have to hit it that hard, you just got to hit it square. So I looked at my fingerpicks and saw that I was hitting them on the edges. So if I just hit it square I wouldn't have to hit it so hard. I bent my picks a little. The main thing I got from him was to hit the strings head on—hit the string with the fat of the pick so I'm going to get the most out of the tone. Then you don't have to play hard at all. So I started using light gauge strings and I wasn't breaking that many strings and was getting all that drive. And I think that's the key to playing with drive—it's just being real true, hitting the string, and just practicing over and over to really just hit the string right square on that pick so that you get the most out of the tone.

"So when I started doing that, I thought I should have my own style. And, boy, I tried to intellectualize it. I made up these licks and all this stuff that I could never pull off, and I just got really frustrated. So I decided that I'd just keep playing and I'd play a little bit of what I like here, and eventually I started making up breaks with maybe a little of the Crowe break, and the second break would be the Scruggs, and the third one maybe would be a melodic thing or a fiddle-type break or a Reno-style. And that's how your style develops. You just begin selecting stuff that you're hearing the way you hear it and all of a sudden you're playing it differently than anybody else because you hear it differently and you have different things you like more than other things."

Mr. Cahill then described the role of backing up in a bluegrass band. "Usually, somebody is backing up. The first thing is, you want to make sure you're not all backing up at the same time. And that's when I chop: when somebody else is backing up. I don't want to get in anybody else's way."

Some banjo players feel that you should never start chopping because that loses the drive of the tune, especially if it's a driving tune or a faster tune. "They say just always do some kind of a roll and keep that

230 David McCarty, "Taking Bluegrass One Year at a Time," *Bluegrass Unlimited*, May, 1993, p. 25.

305

drive going even if you're way in the background. I don't know about that. Listening to Doyle Lawson's band now or the **Cardinals**' band—any of them who get the real clean sound sort of like a southeastern sound—and there's a lot of banjo chopping there to be real clean so that one instrument at a time might back up. You don't want to get in the way of the vocals. So what I'm thinking [is] I want to enhance the vocalist if I'm playing backup. And that means I'm doing it when nobody else is playing backup so that it's not too busy and I'm kind of playing around the melody that the person is singing. So you're really meshing the music with the vocal, which is another instrument in the ensemble. And that's the concept of backup to me. You don't want to play the melody in backup because that's what the singer's doing. All the instruments backup at different times. I think it's what you work out, and the sound that you want with the people you're playing with. You don't want to end up in competition; it should be musical. It's a team effort and a sharing thing.

"And different songs can be backed up differently. I think you just have to get a sense of each song, really. And listen a lot. You listen to all these records with different stylists—how they backup a fast song or a slow song. You start with general categories: a medium song and then a specific song. You listen to four versions of 'The Old Home Place' and see how each person played it and played backup. And then you start hearing differences and you get that sense. And it's all comparison, I think. You'll eventually start picking out what appeals to you, and you start applying it to your own playing and you've got your style."

Greg Cahill formed his **Special Consensus Bluegrass Band** in 1974, and by 1975 it was a band committed toward performing more regularly. Their first album was "The Special Consensus Bluegrass Band" on the local Tin Ear Records in Chicago. Their second LP was "Blue Northern." Their third album was "Freight Train Boogie" LP on Turquoise. In 1980, Cahill recorded his solo banjo album, "Lone Star." His other solo effort was a mandolin/banjo instrumental album, "Blue Skies," in 1992 with Don Stiernberg. In 1989, "Hole in My Heart" was recorded for Turquoise Records. Martin Marrone (guitar) joined in 1990. Don Stiernberg joined on mandolin for the bigger shows. Their "Hey Y'all!" was released in 1991 on Turquoise, followed by "Green Rolling Hills" in 1993. Their "Roads and Rails" came out in 1995 on Shy Town Records with members Cahill, Marrone, Darren Wilcox (bass) and Drew Carson (mandolin).

Greg Cahill continues to perform and record full-time in the 1990s.

Carl Jackson

Photo courtesy Chuck Ogsbury.

Carl Jackson

One of the younger-generation banjo players and songwriters to come along and make an impact in bluegrass music is Carl Jackson. His teen days as banjo player with **Jim and Jesse and the Virginia Boys** gave no hint that he would, in his late thirties, win awards for bluegrass songwriting and have a career of producing bluegrass and country hits.

Jackson was born in Louisville, Mississippi, September 18, 1953. He grew up in a musical family and excels on the banjo, guitar, resonator guitar, mandolin, bass and in writing music. His father was a part-time luthier. As a youngster, Carl, with his father, Lee Jackson, Lee's brother Burgess, and his Uncle Pete had a band: the **Country Partners**. It was the banjo influence of his Uncle Burgess that led him toward the banjo as his primary instrument. He took four or five banjo lessons from Bud Rose. At nine, he played at his first paid performance. His main banjo influences were Bill Keith, Bobby Thompson, Earl Scruggs and Allen Shelton.

In 1964, young Jackson won the Arthur Smith Talent Contest in Mississippi. As the winner, he got a recording contract with Smith's K-Art Records so Smith brought him up to North Carolina to his studio. His first songs were his own banjo tunes: "Five-String Trot" and "Rebel March." Jackson related, "They were on Arthur's label—45s—and I'm sure he probably only pressed up, you know, 500 copies or whatever. But that was the prize for winning. It was great because Arthur played mandolin on the session. Jimmy Buchanan was with him at the time and played fiddle on it. Bud Rose went with me and I played Bud's banjo on it. I was about eleven then.

"I remember that many people, like Charlie Louvin tried to get me on the Opry but they wouldn't let me on because of my age. And I wasn't a member of the Union and all that. But I remember George Morgan took me over and put me on the Ernest Tubb Record Shop, which was a live show immediately following the Grand Ole Opry."

In the spring of 1968, at age fourteen, he joined **Jim and Jesse and the Virginia Boys** at various events including the Opry. The group made weekly Opry appearances, but Jackson was homesick and occasionally left the group on weekends to go home. "I was a kid then and I wanted to go home. I didn't realize what kind of pressure I was puttin' on them to just get somebody else on the spur of the moment. I think Jim was a little perturbed at me for that."[231] Still with the **Virginia Boys** in August of the next year, Jackson recorded on **Jim and Jesse**'s popular "We Like Trains" album. Jackson's solo LP came May 1971; "Bluegrass Festival" was cut on the Prize label.[232]

In 1972, Jackson left the **Virginia Boys** to play guitar with Alabama's **Sullivan Family**. He then broke away and journeyed to Columbus, Ohio, to help form **Country Store** with close friends Jimmy Gaudreau (mandolin), Bill Rawlins (bass), Keith Whitley (guitar) and himself on banjo. The band in its original form would last little more than a week. Glen Campbell's touring band came into town to play the State Fair and, being big fans of his, Carl and Keith went out to see the show. Afterwards, they ran into Campbell's banjoist at the time, Larry McNeeley, who persuaded Carl to come by the next day for a jam session. After picking awhile, McNeeley suddenly told Carl he had been looking for someone to take his place with the touring show[233] and that Carl Jackson was that man. He was introduced to Glen Campbell and hired on the spot as banjoist and fiddler; he stayed twelve years with the Arkansas farm boy. Meanwhile, Jackson recorded several solo albums including "Banjo Player" (Capitol, 1973), "Old Friends" (Capitol, 1977), "Banjo Man—A Tribute to Earl Scruggs" (Sugar Hill, 1981), "Song of the South" (Sugar Hill, 1982) and "Banjo Hits"[234] (Sugar Hill, 1983).

A label change to CBS Records occurred in 1984 where he recorded four singles, all of which were released. They include "She's Gone, Gone, Gone" and "Dixie Train" which went top 40s. He also filled-in for Lou Reid in the **Ricky Skaggs Band**. He left Glen Campbell to strike out on his own. His studio work in Nashville included harmony with Emmylou Harris, Dwight Yoakam, Vince Gill and many others.

In 1990, the International Bluegrass Music Association members voted "Little Mountain Church House" as Best Song of the Year. It was co-written by Jackson and Jim Rushing and was recorded by **Doyle Lawson and Quicksilver**. The song was also recorded by Ricky Skaggs and the **Nitty Gritty Dirt Band**. Since then, he and John Starling won a Grammy for the Best Bluegrass Album, "Spring Training" (February 1992). In 1992, he won the Dove Award for the Best Southern Gospel Song of the Year ("Where Shadows Never Fall," recorded by Glen Campbell). Vince Gill recorded Jackson's "No Future in the Past." It became Jackson's first number one record and was R & R's (*Radio and Records*) Song of the Year in 1993.

Other accomplishments included his membership in **Angel Band** along with Emmylou Harris, Vince Gill and Emory Gordy Jr. when they recorded the bluegrass gospel LP for Warner Brothers, "Angel Band." His songwriting credits included "Letter to Home" (Glen Campbell), "Breaking New Ground" (**Seldom Scene** and **Wild Rose**), "Put Yourself in My Place" (Pam Tillis), "Against the Grain" (Garth Brooks), "Close to the Edge (**Diamond Rio**) and "You Don't Know How Lucky You Are" (Patty Loveless).

In 1994, he entered into a joint publishing venture with Jim Rushing and Larry Cordle near Music Row in Nashville.

Tom Adams— the "right hand man" of the Johnson Mountain Boys

Tom Adams has a long history in music: his entire family participated in bluegrass since the late sixties. He was Banjo Player of the Year at IBMA for 1992 and 1993. His Rounder Records recordings include sessions with the **Johnson Mountain Boys**, **Delia Bell and Bill Grant**, the **Lynn Morris Band** and with the **James King Band**.

Tom spoke about his music, "My dad taught me to play a song so that it can be understood; to try and play the melody and listen to the other people in the band. You can't 'do your own thing' and make it sound right."

Tom was born November 17, 1958, and began in music career playing guitar and mandolin in 1968. In January of the next year, he began playing banjo. Tom and his brother, Dale, were integral members of Pennsylvania-based **Adams Brothers and Dad** (with his father, Tom Sr.) from 1968 to 1979. After his father's death in 1979, he and Dale continued playing music as

231 Katy Bee, "Carl Jackson and Marty Stuart—Mississippi's (Young) Bluegrass Veterans, " *Bluegrass Unlimited*, January, 1987, p. 44.

232 Musicians were Jim and Jesse McReynolds, Jerry Reed (guitar), Jim Brock (fiddle), Jim D. Brock Jr. (bass, Jim Brock's son, and later went on to play bass with the Osbornes) and his father Lethal Jackson (guitar).

233 Larry McNeeley was planning to seek his fortune as a studio banjo player in Hollywood.

234 With musicians Jesse McReynolds (mandolin, twin fiddle), Jim McReynolds (guitar), Jim Brock (fiddle), Lee Jackson (guitar), Jerry Reed (guitar) and Jim Brock Jr. (bass).

the **Adams Brothers** until 1981. In 1980, the **Adams Brothers**[235] recorded "Ahead of the Crowd" on the Baldwin label.

In 1983, he played with Dale and Chris Warner and Warren Blair and other local musicians in **Double Eagle Band** until 1983. Then he joined Jimmy Martin's **Sunny Mountain Boys** as banjoist, staying until August of 1985. The next year, he joined the **Johnson Mountain Boys**. When this group broke up in 1988, he joined the **Lynn Morris Band**. He returned to the **J-M-B** in 1991 until 1995, then returned to Lynn Morris late in 1995 until he quit the band on November 15, 1996, for personal reasons at home.

The Tennessee Banjo Institute, November 1-3, 1990, Cedars of Lebanon. Photo courtesy Bobby Fulcher.

235 With Tom (banjo, guitar) and Dale (bass) Adams, Chris Warner (mandolin) and Jeff Toal (guitar).

NOVEMBER 1-3, 1990   CEDARS OF LEBANON

Chapter 9

Bluegrass Mandolin - Table of Contents

Bluegrass Mandolin

If the banjo is known as the "fifth child" of bluegrass because it was the last one to fit into the mold of the five instruments basic to a bluegrass band, the mandolin may be the first.

The family tree of the mandolin goes back even further than the guitar's to the lute lineage of the 1100s or further. Italy became the center of manufacture for the mandolin in the 1700s with its ribbed, rounded back and flat top. Mozart used one on-stage in one of his operas in 1787.

There are three basic styles of mandolins: the bowlback or "taterbug" style; the carved top and back Gibson "A" and "F" styles; and the flattop, flatback style such as the Martin "A" models and some of the models made by Lyon and Healy and others.

The Gibson company's entry into the mandolin market began with a departure from the earlier bowlback design to Orville Gibson's easier-to-use carved back and top. The "F" style mandolin was invented by Orville Gibson about 1898 and was so named for its Florentine points and scrolls. Walter Carter wrote, "The f-holes that would be touted as one of the many innovations with Gibson's F-5 mandolin in 1922 were, in fact, a 19th century idea by Barrows Music Company of Saginaw, Michigan, in the late 1890s."[1] Others during that period also claim the invention.

By the late 1800s, mandolin clubs and orchestras began their appearance in the United States. By 1910, the bowlback style would be replaced in favor of the newer flatback styles and Gibson carved back models which began its development through instrument makers such as Orville H. Gibson.[2] The Gibson company, which was interested in dominating the mandolin market, was just the company to take advantage of the large market for mandolins for, at that time, they were,

according to George Gruhn and Walter Carter, "the most pervasive force in the American fretted instrument industry in the twentieth century." Martin Guitars and other companies also made mandolins. From the 1890s until 1990, Martin made quite a number of mandolins but the instruments were never a serious competitor in this field to Gibson.

Lloyd Allayre Loar[3], an employee of the Gibson company from 1919 to 1924 who was in charge of testing and approval, went on to help develop Orville's mandolin design. In 1922, the Gibson Company began to build the F-5s. Innovations into the new mandolins included the long neck, the f-style sound holes, the raised fingerboard, parallel tone bars and adjustable neck rods. During the time Lloyd Loar was with the company, according to George Gruhn and Walter Carter, "This much is true: Loar-signed mandolins are considered by most collectors and players to be the finest ever made. The most highly-respected mandolin makers today, from individual luthiers to the Gibson company itself, have modeled their instruments on the Loar F-5. Loar mandolas, mandocellos, and guitars also inspire the highest regard."

Mandolin workshop in Winfield, KS, 1983. L to R: Sam Bush, Roland White, Bobby Clark. Photo courtesy Jan Willis.

Loar contributed much to the design of many of Gibson's instruments during the time he was employed there. While at Gibson, he wore many hats: credit manager, factory production manager, purchasing agent, repair manager and design consultant. But one should not forget that he was only one of amny people in the company who were developing the company's instruments and continuing to keep the company thriving through the years with new products. Walter Carter wrote, "Among his specific contributions were: graduated soundboards (tops) and backboards (backs), longitudinal tone bars, f-holes, longer playable necks, sizing of air chambers, and hand 'tuning' of tone bars

[1] Walter Carter, *Gibson Guitars, 100 years of an American Icon* (Los Angeles: General Publishing Group, 1994), p. 40.

[2] 1856-1918, born in Chateaugay, New York.

[3] Lloyd Loar, 1886-1943, was born in Cropsey, Illinois. He was an accomplished mandolin player and, at the age of twenty, was performing professionally on Gibson mandolins in both concert and solo settings. From June 1, 1922, to December 1, 1924, he signed the labels of as many as 350 Gibson instruments. An estimated 250 were mandolins. He left the company to pursue the development of the electric guitar.

and f-holes. He also developed a new banjo design with the tone chamber supported by ball bearings. Loar's major contribution was 'tuning'— not adjusting the string pitches, but the art of tuning the various structural components of the instrument to specific pitches so that the whole instrument worked as a coupled system (acoustically speaking), producing the best tone possible from the sum of its parts.

"Since an adjustment to one part of the instrument affects the tuning of another part, one can appreciate the hours of trial and error that preceded the development and subsequent finalization of the dimensions of Gibson's Master Model instruments."[4]

According to luthier/musician/historian Tony Williamson, "Loar also influenced the look: elegant but not ostentatious. Profusely ornate instruments did not appeal to Loar—sound *did* matter. This is why people prefer these instruments—because of the sound! This is why Monroe laid down the F-7."

The key to the volume, explained Williamson (Mandolin Central, Siler, North Carolina), was that the F-5 had the bridge right in the middle of the top and was able to take full effect of the vibrating strings. Some mandolins, which had the bridge further back, didn't vibrate the top as much and therefore couldn't produce the same volume as the instrument with the bridge exactly in the center of the vibrating sound board (the top). Williamson also mentioned that most bluegrass players who own the Loar F-5s took out the Virzi Tone Producer which, while it was meant to enhance the tone of the instrument[5], at the same time, the tone enhancement took some of the volume away from the instrument. And because the volume became important in country and bluegrass music, owners often opted to have more volume over the more mellow tone. The Virzi was an extra-cost item on Loar's F-5s built in 1924.

George Gruhn agrees that the bridge in the middle of the top does, indeed, take full effect of the vibrating strings, "But the fact is that that's certainly by no means the whole story. The F-12 and the F-7 pre-War models did not have the bridge in the middle, but they still have a darned good sound. They have f-holes and the parallel bass and treble bars. And that seems to have more of an impact than simply putting the bridge in the middle. In fact, I've seen folks do long necks with

F-4 Gibson mandolin made in 1917. The F-4 was Gibson's most deluxe model until the introduction of the F-5 in 1922. Photo courtesy Gruhn Guitars.

bridge in the middle, but with oval sound hole. It still sounds like an F-4; it doesn't sound like an F-5. Putting the bridge in the middle does *not* produce a Bill Monroe sound. Putting parallel tone bars and f-holes is critically important. It's the bracing and sound holes that are probably more critical than the bridge position."

In a conversation as to whether an "F" model sounds better for bluegrass than an "A" model, George Gruhn has researched the mysteries of an instrument's sound and explained, "It's not the body shape that counts. You can take something like a Gibson 'A' with f-holes like the new A-5 model and try to compare that sound with the new F-5L model, and the A-5L and the F-5L sound essentially the same. And in 1924, Gibson did do a custom A-5, Loar-signed, the long neck, f-sound hole and the parallel braces. And, by golly, it sounds like an F-5. If you compare the sound of the short-neck, oval-hole 'A' or 'F' with an F-5, they are notably different."[6]

The heyday of mandolins and mandolin orchestras was over by 1920 and the tenor banjo was gaining dominance over the mandolin; it was tuned and played similar to the mandolin and was louder—able to compete better with other instruments in a band. There were very few mandolins constructed by any manufacturer after 1924. They certainly did not have the attention given it today. Gruhn continued, "The quality of the construction of mandolins in the late 1920s was still excellent even though Loar had left. But they didn't sell worth a flip because no one wanted one. The quality in the mid-'30s wasn't all that great but it was still pretty good. The quality of the '50s and '60s was worse than pre-War, '70s was pretty poor. Starting in the mid-'80s, it began to improve. The quality of the new ones is pretty decent, but the late '20s mandolins were still a whole lot better than today's new ones. Martin mandolin quality didn't go down at all during the '30s. Lyon and Healy continued to make mandolins into the '30s and their quality was as good as ever. Martin's quantity went down, but the quality didn't."

In the early '70s, Steve Carlson moved to Bozeman, Montana, and opened the Back Porch Pickin' Parlor. He bought Flatiron Mandolins (a company from Boulder, Colorado), sold the Pickin' Parlor, and began making mandolins. About 1988, Carlson sold Flatiron to Gibson and became President of Gibson's Montana Division. The next year, Gibson opened up a 20,000 square foot

[4] Carter, op. cit., p. 84, 84.

[5] According to George Gruhn in a 1996 conversation: "As to whether the Virzi enhances tone or not is debatable. It certainly does not make them mellower; it gives them perhaps a little more 'trebly' sound, less of a bark and perhaps a little more sustain. But tone enhancement is a very subjective thing. It may make them sound less bluegrassy, but it sure as heck doesn't make them sound more mellow."

[6] George Gruhn, 1996 interview.

factory to build Gibson and Flatiron products including most of Gibson's acoustic instruments.[7]

Bill Bolick of the Blue Sky Boys

In 1935, as the **Blue Sky Boys** were becoming more popular at WWNC in Asheville, North Carolina, Bill Bolick began playing the mandolin more and more due to fan mail requests. The sound of Bill Monroe's mandolin with the very popular **Monroe Brothers** was a definite factor in the taste of the audience and triggered considerable fan mail. As the popularity of Monroe on the mandolin grew, so did the requests that Bill Bolick play it in his own group. He eventually dropped the guitar altogether. The Bolick brothers, Bill and Earl, also felt that even though they both began playing guitars with their singing, the mandolin sounded much better with their style of singing than two guitars.

Bolick played the mandolin in a manner which introduced a third harmony part while he and Earl were singing. This style of mandolin playing is much harder to do than concentrating on playing breakdowns or leads on the mandolins like the bluegrass musicians do today, said Bill Bolick in a 1991 interview. It requires a greater degree of concentration.

Bill Monroe nearly killed off the mandolin as a bluegrass instrument

Bill Monroe is often given credit as being the main person to popularize the instrument. According to an article by George Gruhn and Doug Green[8], the popularity of the F-5 can be contributed to the fact, more than any other, that Bill Monroe played one. If he were playing the F-7, which he was playing during the '30s, *that* would be the instrument which is popular today.

Ironically, Monroe may also have been the one who almost sealed the demise of the instrument's popularity. The story goes that after **Flatt and Scruggs** was finally allowed to play on the Grand Ole Opry (1955), Bill Monroe was finally forced to accept the fact that the extremely popular band of

Lester and Earl would be on the same show. Monroe had, for years, been able to keep them off until this time. But now that they were on the Opry, Lester and Earl wanted to sound different than the **Blue Grass Boys** and not use a mandolin as a lead instrument. Their mandolin players were significantly less important in the **F & S** sound than in the **Blue Grass Boys**. It almost seemed that the mandolin players were being restricted from playing altogether. This restriction nearly destroyed the possibility of the mandolin becoming popular since only one person was now allowed to play the mandolin in bluegrass music on country music's greatest venue, the Grand Ole Opry.

The distinctive picking styles of Jesse McReynolds— an innovator in bluegrass mandolin playing

In 1949, Jim and Jesse McReynolds with Hoke Jenkins' **Smoky Mountaineers** traveled to Augusta, Georgia, to play on a mid-day radio show on WGAC, Augusta, Georgia (for a year). Musicians were Hoke Jenkins (banjo, nephew of Snuffy Jenkins), Curly Seckler (multi-instrumentalist), Jim (guitar) and Jesse (mandolin). It was here that McReynolds brothers solidified their harmonies and established their own sound.

Jesse described how he invented cross-picking, "It's what we call the backwards roll—the banjo roll. I didn't really know how the banjo roll went; I'd never seen anybody do it. I'd just heard [it] and was going strictly by sound. At the time, the boy who played banjo with us, Hoke Jenkins, played the banjo that way. He never played the forward roll. He played it backwards and really, I guess, I thought that's the way it was supposed to go. The way I worked it out, that's the only way I could do it to any speed."[9] Jesse's technique emphasizes the upstroke—not picking the third string of the mandolin with a down stroke—the first string with an upstroke, and then an upstroke on the second. The first, or E strings, are the equivalent of

Mandolin workshop in Winfield, KS, 1983. L to R: Barry Mitterhoff, Tim O'Brien, Jethro Burns, Jesse McReynolds. Photo courtesy Jan Willis.

---

[7] In 1994, Gibson manufactured some of its banjos and guitars in Nashville.

[8] *Bluegrass Unlimited*, March, 1973.

[9] Scott Hambly, "Jim and Jesse, Reprising Their 'Epic' Best," *Bluegrass Unlimited*, August, 1986, p. 10.

the fifth string on the five-string banjo which is usually sounded as a "drone" string. Even though Jesse had already learned some of these techniques before he met Hoke, he perfected his cross-picking techniques during this period. His mandolin virtuosity was significant in their popularity with bluegrass audiences.

In 1951, with **Jim and Jesse and the Virginia Boys** recording for Capitol, Jesse featured his by-now-fully-developed, innovative split-string mandolin playing on "Just Wondering Why." He described his split-string playing as fretting one of the two strings of one of the four pairs of strings with a fingernail. So, one of the strings in a pair is fretted while one is left open enabling three-part harmony on the instrument instead of two.

Red Allen on Frank Wakefield, David Grisman and Bill Keith

In 1960, "Me and Frank Wakefield and Tom Morgan and Bill Emerson got together and called the band **Red Allen and the Kentuckians**." Wakefield was "the best mandolin picker in the country," said Red Allen. "Frank is one hell of a musician...he picks a good mandolin. You can't take his talent away from him, you know."

Red Allen's 1963 band was the one which he considered had the best sound, the ideal sound, of any band he ever had in his **Red Allen and the Kentuckians**. Members at the time were himself (guitar), Porter Church (banjo), Craig Winfield (resonator guitar) and Jerry McCoury (bass). Red Allen told this writer that "It was a drivin', clean pickin', hard singin' band."

Over the many years of his band, he "hired people who could pick and gave them a free hand as long as they didn't pick exactly like somebody else. David (Grisman) played jazz when he played with me (late 1965). Like Bill Keith; Bill was playin' that chromatic banjo when he was with me (fall of 1962, just before he joined the **Blue Grass Boys**). I turned Bill loose and let him play what he wanted to. And I sung and picked that guitar hard and sung that fast drivin' stuff—him and Grisman both."[10]

The family tree of the mandolin goes back even further than the guitar's to the lute lineage of the 1100s or further.

Frank Wakefield

Considered one of the greatest mandolin players who ever lived, Franklin Delano Wakefield was born in Emory Gap, Tennessee, June 26, 1934. He and his brother played locally. His sisters also played guitar, but not publicly. Frank was six when he began learning the guitar; his first performance was at age thirteen in a church in Emory Gap. In 1950, Wakefield moved to Dayton, Ohio, where he began playing the mandolin—choosing the instrument just to be different; he was already somewhat proficient on the harmonica and guitar. His first mandolin, a Stradolin (similar in shape to an A-style Gibson), cost two dollars. He listened to the mandolin playing of Bill Monroe and Jesse McReynolds and taught himself how to play by ear.

In 1953, Wakefield recorded his original tunes "New Camptown Races" and "Leave Well Enough Alone" on the Wayside label. In 1957, Wakefield was a member of Detroit's **Chain Mountain Boys**.

Before long, he was working with Red Allen. The story goes that Red Allen saw Wakefield playing mandolin on his front porch in Dayton and asked him to join him in a band. Wakefield explained, "In those days, I lived on Montgomery Street and he was livin' down on West Third Street; he had to pass by my house to get to where another musician lived. It was just by accident. I was settin' on the porch playin' the mandolin and he had a guitar, walkin' down the street—didn't have no car or nothin'—so it happened just exactly that way. We just began to pick together. He didn't actually ask me to join him [in a band]. He got me to go down to the Circle Bar with him. I didn't think I was good enough to play but he got me up there anyway. I thought I was makin' a fool of myself."[11]

[10] From a 1990 telephone interview.

[11] David Grisman told the story that Frank Wakefield met Red Allen through him. "I got them this gig at Carnegie Hall, and while they were at Carnegie Hall, they auditioned for a gig at Gerde's Folk City. The guy who ran Gerde's didn't know them from Adam. Pete Roberts was playing banjo at Carnegie Hall and they got the gig at Gerde's. But I guess they were just making real low money 'cause just Red and Frank came up. They stayed at my mother's house—where I was living—and they hired Bob Yellin to play banjo with them. It was just three-piece for two weeks. That's how he met Frank."

America's Music | Bluegrass

314

Frank Wakefield

"Red showed me a little kickoff. He probably forgot about that. He's about five years older than me and the strange thing is [that] when you're that young and somebody's about twenty-two or three, they seem old to you. You know how that is? They really do! And it seems like you're older than they are when you get up to be a certain age. He was my elder then and he actually showed me a kickoff to a song. And heck, I just experimented around with it and hit the notes right about half the time. But it finally worked with practice."[12]

Red Allen formed a band with Wakefield and Dorsey Harvey. Together, with other local musicians, they called the band **Red Allen, Frank Wakefield and the Kentuckians**. Wakefield stayed with the band, off and on, until Allen passed away in 1992. Wakefield explained, "I played with Jimmy Martin after I left Red. Then I'd get mad with Jimmy and I'd go back to Red. I'd say to Jimmy when we were practicing, 'Now this ain't the way Red does it!' Jimmy would get mad and say, 'Damn! If you don't like it, why don't you go back with Red.' There I'd go. That was in Detroit, around '56 or '57. That kept goin' on 'til about '60. And from about '60 to '66, we played in D.C.. I went to D.C. and started playin' and then Red came down there. He follered me down there and I follered him to Dayton."

Wakefield's day job was an auto glass installer, working both jobs in order to raise his four children. In his own, special way of "backwards" talking he joked, "I have kids older than me now." Between his two jobs, he was able to make a decent living. Red Allen didn't do as well because he didn't care to have a day job.

In 1959, Wakefield and Allen re-formed **Red Allen, Frank Wakefield and the Kentuckians** in the Washington, D.C., area. Other musicians were Bill Emerson (banjo) and Tom Morgan (bass). Occasionally Porter Church (Frank calls him "Porter Synagogue") was their banjoist; Church stayed with the band until Bill Keith joined them in 1962. "We was really amazed at Bill Keith's banjo playing when he first began to pick with us. I think we was probably one of the first bands he ever picked with. We really took a likin' to it. We was super hot. We got to play Carnegie Hall and big shows like that."

In 1960, Wakefield bought a 1923 Lloyd Loar Gibson F-5 for $150. He has been offered a new Cadillac and $10,000 for it.

Ralph Rinzler took David Grisman to see Bill Monroe at a festival at New River Ranch in Rising Sun, Maryland, in August of 1961. Grisman got a new idol in Monroe. Also there was Frank Wakefield, mandolinist for the Baltimore-based **Franklin County Boys**.[13] Wakefield became Grisman's friend, teacher and influence. Grisman "took lessons from me for about five years, and he's copied me for about thirty years. He still

does. He mostly has my right hand. And actually the left one, too. A lot of stuff he picks you can't tell whether it's me or him. And he took some of my songs, like 'Cedar Creek,' at least he told me that he took that tune and a couple more. He said he didn't mean to steal it, he just took half of it and changed it [to] 'Cedar Hill.' He apologizes in some write-ups. I don't mind 'cause that means I'm the father of it."

In 1962, Bill Monroe told Wakefield, "Now you can play my style as good as me...get your own style... And when I got my own style, he wouldn't give me a job at his bluegrass festival; it didn't sound bluegrass enough."

Wakefield, while a member of **Red Allen, Frank Wakefield and the Kentuckians** in 1964, recorded "Red Allen, Frank Wakefield and the Kentuckians" on Folkways. Wakefield was probably the best (or one of the best) bluegrass mandolinists in the world at the time; most who knew him during that time recognized this. Another great mandolinist was Nate Bray whom Bill Monroe recognized as the "second best."

During this period of Wakefield's career, he recorded a number of gospel tunes and was deeply involved with religion. Because so many writers have danced around this subject, he explained it here very carefully so as not to be misunderstood: "Actually, I was writing a lot of instrumentals then. I don't do that much anymore because those times are gone now. I played for too many phony preachers. I decided not to call any tunes 'Jesus tunes.' I played for these preachers who would get people into coffins and take people's money... This one guy, when I was in Chillicothe, Ohio, in about 1951, he got a person to get into a coffin. He announced it and advertised it that way—we was doin' a radio show. We got 10,000 people there in this big tent he had and he painted this person up like a dead person. He put him a coffin. In the middle of July in Chillicothe, Ohio—the southern part of Ohio—it gets awfully hot there. Before he got through with the sermon to explain the situation, the guy had to come up for breath. And what happened was it scared people. They tore the tent down, knocked posts down and over. We was in the back of a semi truck, me and the guitar picker; we got under the truck. Everything was fallin'. He was goin' to explain the situation [but never got the chance]. We played for people like 'at. And then he tried to get us to get in the coffin. We was only about sixteen then. We wouldn't hear of that 'cause we was afraid of it. We played for people like 'at. I got so, for awhile, I got to callin' all those tunes 'Jesus tunes.' I was a real faith believer. And I got so I wasn't that way as I got older and wiser, and I quit foolin' with religion.

"What I found out was that they use religion to control people. That way, you can control the masses if you get them afraid of somethin' or believing in

[12] From a telephone interview November 1992. The other quotations here are from the same source unless otherwise noted.

[13] Members of this band included Frankie Short (guitar), a resonator guitar player, and Lamar Grier (banjo).

Frank Wakefield

somethin'. That way you can control 'em and have them under your hand. I studied about things like this a lot. You see how things really are, then you change your opinion and the way you look at things." At about the same time that he lost religious faith, his creative period on the mandolin seemed to end.

Wakefield considers himself a bluegrass musician, admits he plays further out than Monroe, but still retains the lonesome sound. Wakefield told Grisman that his definition of bluegrass is: "When it don't sound a lot like Bill Monroe, then it's not really bluegrass."

In 1964, Wakefield, in addition to his jobs with Red Allen, auditioned for and was accepted into, the **Greenbriar Boys**. A serious auto accident occurred just before his first gig with them. He actually went through the roof of the convertible and it put him in a coma for a month, semi-conscious for nearly a year. He eventually regained his skills and re-joined the band. But after this recovery, his playing, according to David Grisman, was never the same—it was more abstract, more distant from the traditional bluegrass which he was playing before the accident.

Wakefield even has a hard time describing what he does and how it is different than the mandolin styles of others. Nevertheless, "I hear Tony Rice doin' some of my stuff. He recorded one of my songs, 'New Camptown Races'—a lot of people recorded that tune. I think I wrote that in '53."

Wakefield recorded the "Frank Wakefield" LP on the newly-formed Rounder in 1972. It featured many of his own compositions, including "Waltz in Bluegrass." His backup band for the album was **Country Cooking**.

In 1975, Frank Wakefield and David Nelson were part of the **Good Old Boys**. He later changed the band name to the **Frank Wakefield Band** and began alternating between the two names. A 1975 album by the group,

"Pistol Packin' Mama," featured Don Reno (banjo), David Nelson (guitar) and Chubby Wise (fiddle) and was produced by Jerry Garcia. Re-issued on CD in 1992, it sold in the rock and roll section of record stores because of Garcia's name on it. In 1978, his **Frank Wakefield Band** was based in California's Bay Area.

Frank quit drinking alcohol about 1979. A "friend" got him to try acid once by sneaking it on him. It sent him on a "trip" for twenty-four hours. He was so out of control of his faculties that he never wanted to do that again. "I had every kind of vision there was. I was scared of everybody—almost died!"

As of 1994, Wakefield still played bluegrass and his "Frank Wakefield music" using **Summit** to back him up at gigs. He taught mandolin and was based at his home in Saratoga Springs, New York.

James Bailey on Doyle Lawson

When James Bailey joined the **Country Gentlemen** for the first time at age sixteen, one veteran mandolinist who influenced him tremendously was Doyle Lawson. "Doyle [Lawson] was very generous in spending time with me and showing me exactly how things should be done. He showed me that you have to present yourself in a professional manner so that you can demand respect. Musically speaking, simplicity is a concept for Doyle. In relating to an audience, you have to keep the music down on a level that the general public can understand."[14] "Doyle was a mover and a shaker in that situation as he is in any and every situation he is involved in."[15]

Doyle Lawson and Quicksilver— "Simplicity is the purest form of music."

Sometimes it is difficult for a person to fit into just one chapter of this book; Doyle Lawson is one of these men. He is not only a legend in this music as a sideman and a band leader, he achieved great renown as a mandolinist. Though he didn't invent the style of playing he or his band does, he took it to lengths which helped popularize not only a clean, melodic style of mandolin picking, but also his band's close, four-part harmonies— especially in the gospel genre.

Doyle Lawson was born in Fordtown, Sullivan County, Tennessee, April 20, 1944. At three weeks of age, he and his family moved to nearby Kingsport. At four years old, he was allowed to stay up to listen to the Grand Ole Opry. This was the heyday of the **Blue Grass Boys**, and Lawson was mostly influenced by Bill Monroe's mandolin playing. He knew *that* was what he wanted to do when he grew up.

14 Bill Evans, "James Bailey, Multi-instrumentalist and Bluegrass Entertainer," *Bluegrass Unlimited*, May, 1982, p. 87.
15 From a 1991 interview at IBMA, Owensboro, Kentucky.

Lawson spoke of the mandolin and of Bill Monroe, "Monroe made the mandolin a lead instrument. Now when you heard the **Callahan Brothers** or the **Blue Sky Boys,** they used the mandolin, but it didn't have the authority. At that time, the fiddle and banjo is what people would listen for. But Monroe commanded attention with his pickin'. It was so different that I fell in love with it.

"The first record we had in the house was the **Flatt and Scruggs** 78 r.p.m. recording of 'I'll Never Shed Another Tear.' The flip side was 'I'll Be Going to Heaven Sometime.' I never will forget that. I about wore the grooves off it. I loved the sound of it—the way they projected their feelings, their emotions."[16]

His father sang in quartets about 1950 and exposed his son to this style of music. Once Doyle got into gospel music as a professional, his father began exerting more influence on the boy. Doyle recalled what his father told him. "He said, 'Why don't you sing those songs like the writers wrote 'em?' And I said, 'Well, Dad. I don't read music.' So he said, 'You need to learn how to read shape-note music. So he sat down and taught me the basics of the old shape-note style. That was a big help—I've got to admit. Of course, I'm guilty of straying away now and then to make it suit the way I feel."[17]

In 1955, at age eleven, Lawson, with Bill Monroe as his inspiration, borrowed the mandolin of a fellow church-goer. He wanted to match Monroe's style note-for-note. But finding he was unable to do that, he felt better about it when he learned that he should have his own style—one that was comfortable to him.

Lawson likes to "play real clean. If you can't play it clean, then don't play as much. Play a little less so that people can hear it. The hardest thing, when I was getting started, was getting as much volume on my up strokes as on my downs. If you don't have the same volume on the ups and the downs, you have highs and lows in your playing. You can't be clean that way."[18] He also emphasized that right hand position can be crucial to achieving good timing and even sound. Lawson explained, "I can play more than I play; I've never played at my peak. I never try to stick every note I know into one song. That's not the way it's supposed to be. Simplicity is the purest form of music. It's where

people can feel it and listen to it and enjoy it without trying to figure out what you're doing."[19]

In 1962, when Doyle Lawson was seventeen, he realized that to get a job playing professional bluegrass music he would have to learn instruments besides the mandolin (on which he had concentrated thus far), so he took up the banjo. The reality of the role of the mandolin in bluegrass music in those days seemed to be that only Bill Monroe gave primary status of the mandolin in a bluegrass band. Probably another band with the mandolin as lead might be accepted and successful, but it would be risky because audiences normally identified a bluegrass band with the banjo as the lead instrument.[20]

He left school in 1963 to become the banjo player with Jimmy Martin, taking the place of J.D. Crowe. He sounded very much like Crowe. Martin taught Lawson timing and the wrist technique for playing fast on the mandolin. Lawson learned the drive of bluegrass of Jimmy Martin. "I definitely inherited his drive. I can honestly say that, and that was very intentional. I've always liked that drive. I liked the drive that Monroe had, but Monroe has the drive with the mandolin and far too many times, the band wasn't supportive of him as they needed to be, in my opinion. But I like the drive that Jimmy Martin had and, of course, **Flatt and Scruggs** had the drive. And the Stanleys had theirs in

Doyle Lawson and Quicksilver, 1987. L to R: Doyle Lawson, Ray Deaton, Scott Vestal, Russell Moore.

---

16 Jack Tottle, "Doyle Lawson and Quicksilver," *Bluegrass Unlimited*, November, 1980, p. 16.

17 Doyle, in this conversation with this writer in 1992, spoke about the shape-note style of learning to read music which was taught until the late 1950s by Cecil DeWitt all over the country (and these schools still exist today).

    Doyle described shape-note music in this way: Every note has its own identity. Each of the eight notes has its own shape which is put on lines and spaces just like a conventional musical staff. One note may be a large diamond shape (the "me" note. A "do" is a half-diamond. A "la" is a square block) on the staff and students are taught to identify that shape to a certain note and sound. Once you identify that shape, it's fairly simple to pick out a melody. One can then find himself in a position of being able to read the shape-note music, but not being able to read conventional music which has the notes on the staff with ovals of various types. "What I mainly was interested in was being able to recognize each note and the timing and stuff like that so that I could then take the song and pick it out and say, 'Hey that's a good song. I've never heard it, but I can read it.'" Lawson described this as a forerunner to modern southern gospel music. They called it "Jubilee Gospel" when Doyle was growing up in the '50s and had strong African-American roots.

18 Tottle, op. cit., p. 7.

19 Ibid., p. 22.

20 Bands with mandolinists as a lead instrument, such as Jim and Jesse and the Virginia Boys, did exist, but were rare.

their own way."[21] When Lawson later worked with J.D. Crowe, Bill Emerson and Bill Yates, they all seemed to have come from the same school of drive. From there, he just applied his own ideas to fit within that drive.

In late July of 1963, Lawson quit the **Sunny Mountain Boys** after six months and went to Louisville where he was a free-lance musician at local events and worked with Lonnie Peerce (fiddler) and Ginger Callahan (frailing banjo).

Doyle Lawson joined Crowe's band in 1966, then known as the **Kentucky Mountain Boys**, as guitarist (and later as mandolinist when they soon became full-time in the music). He stayed three years. In 1968, Red Allen, who was on guitar for a year, was with the band when they began playing at the Holiday Inn in Lexington, Kentucky. This new venue was quite a coup! Up until then, the only jobs they could get were in the familiar places such as bars and parties. The group was so pleased that they could play at such a class establishment that they named the "Bluegrass Holiday" album after the motel.[22]

In 1969, Lawson left Crowe's band and joined **Good 'n' Country** as the mandolinist, only to return later that year to the **Kentucky Mountain Boys** as guitarist.[23] They played casual gigs around Lexington. Some of their music was electrified. Lawson explained, "We were experimenting with it when I was on my way out, as a matter of fact. We were looking at it real hard and started incorporating drums and things like that. But it never got past that point until after I left. The idea was to broaden our appeal if we could, because West Coast rock was hot then and John Denver had 'Country Roads' and things like that. There was an acoustic appeal, but it was almost a joint venture between the two—everybody wanted electric, but they wanted to sound acoustic. This can be very easily explained because our acoustic band was sounding small.

"In that period also, I might point out that, Carlton Haney was probably the biggest country music promoter in the world. Along about that time of 1969, '70, '71, he was doing 240 shows a year all over the country. He'd do shows in Philadelphia and then do one in the South. In those days, we worked quite a few of his shows where we had Merle Haggard, George Jones, Jerry Lee Lewis, Loretta Lynn or Lynn Anderson—whoever. Just pick a name. But while Carlton's real love was bluegrass, he made his living from country. In his tours he'd usually include a bluegrass act. He used the **Osborne Brothers** a lot. He used Lester. He used us. But the bottom line is that when we had to follow a big act, we went out there with four pieces. We were all acoustic and they [the audience] were used to all the amplification and the drums and all that. Boy, I'll tell you one thing, you can get lost in a hurry with that. We had to figure out how to compete. We had a shot at these shows, and one of the reasons for doing this or experimenting in that was that reason—so people could hear us."

In late 1971, Lawson left Crowe's band to join the **Country Gentlemen**, replacing Jimmy Gaudreau on mandolin.[24] Now fully versed with his style on the mandolin, Lawson now only had to adapt it to the **Country Gentlemen** style of bluegrass music. He does, however, feel that he introduced East Tennessee music to this band which was considered to be rather "northern". He stayed seven and a half years, recording the "Tennessee Dream"[25] LP on County Records in 1977, and did session work for other musicians.

Lawson left the **Country Gentlemen** to form **Doyle Lawson and Foxfire** April 2, 1979. Original members were Lawson (mandolin), Jimmy Haley (guitar) and Terry Baucom (banjo).[26] Banjoist Baucom spoke about four playing in a band, "In a four-piece group, everybody's got to be tight if the whole thing's gonna

[21] Tim Stafford, "A View From Home—A Discussion with Doyle Lawson," *Bluegrass Unlimited*, October, 1987, p. 44.

[22] The masters for the LP were destroyed later, which means that the album will probably not come out on a re-mixed CD.

[23] By 1970, members of this band were Lawson (guitar), Larry Rice (mandolin), Jim Hatton (guitar), Crowe (banjo) and Bobby Slone (bass).

[24] Band members became Charlie Waller (guitar), Lawson (mandolin), Bill Emerson (banjo) and Bill Yates (bass).

[25] Other band members on his "Dream" album were J.D. Crowe (banjo), Kenny Baker (fiddle), James Bailey (banjo, guitar), Jerry Douglas (resonator guitar), Pete Goble (guitar) and Bobby Slone (bass).

[26] Louis Pyrtle took up a position with the band playing bass, resonator guitar, and fiddle. Pyrtle changed his stage name to Lou Reid. Baucom was the most well-known of these men at this time, having already been with Charlie Moore, and with Ricky Skaggs in Boone Creek.

come off. I think I play a bigger role on the banjo now than I did in **Boone Creek**. Because Flux (Jerry Douglas) was there, I kind of laid back—you know, just kick things off and take a break. Now he ain't there and it makes a big difference."[27] Lawson agreed, "With four people you've got to pump all the time. You don't have time to slack."

The emphasis on Lawson's band was vocals, not instrumentals. Just as the **Stanley Brothers** had their flatpicked guitar, and Bill Monroe's **Blue Grass Boys** had its twin fiddles, Lawson's "gimmick" to stardom was tight harmony vocals. Many times, the gospel tunes would feature the black gospel music he learned as a boy in church.

Foxfire's first gig was at Buddy's Barbecue in Knoxville, Tennessee.[28] Within just a few days, the name of the band was changed to **Doyle Lawson and Quicksilver**. "I'll tell you how I came up with the name 'Quicksilver.' It's important to me [that you tell your readers]. When I chose 'Foxfire' I did my research and went through all the band names and did the best I could—I didn't want to take the name that somebody else was using. Of course, I had heard of, maybe, a band before [using that name], but no one that I could see. So it became **Foxfire**. Well then, shortly after that we started getting feedback. People had found out and people were calling. One lady called and she was in tears about how they's had that name for five years. And I told her, 'Listen, you don't have anything to worry about. We're gonna change.' Because, really, the last thing in the world that I would want is to be mistaken for somebody else, you see—to go in something as who you are.

"And so I was living up in Virginia and I had come home to Kingsport to visit with my parents and I told Mom, 'I need another name.' So we talked it over awhile and she said, 'You know, "Quicksilver" is a good name.' She said there's a definition of 'Quicksilver' that is: unstoppable—a force to be reckoned with. That set my ears to listening real hard and I thought I liked that

and what we were all about—we were a force to be reckoned with. It just fit the scenario. So by the time Lou Reid and I had got back home, it had become **Doyle Lawson and Quicksilver**." That August of 1979, on Sugar Hill, the band recorded "Doyle Lawson and Quicksilver."[29]

In 1981, Sugar Hill Records released "Rock My Soul," a record which had tremendous success especially because of its close, four-part gospel harmonies, some of which were *a cappella*.[30] The album got a gold record for its sales.[31] Doyle explained, "I think that opened the doors as much as anything I've done as far as setting us apart from the next band. The worst fear you have is being locked into a category; you never want someone to say, 'Well, they sound real good but they sound a lot like this guy and this guy.'"[32]

The first Doyle Lawson and Quicksilver Family Style Bluegrass Festival took place near Denton, North Carolina, in July 1981. Also this year, Lawson recorded with Tony Rice, J.D. Crowe, Bobby Hicks and Todd Phillips on Sugar Hill's "Bluegrass Album Band" LP which was dedicated to traditional bluegrass music. The project eventually expanded to five LPs and onto compact disc.

A 1983 issue of the Dutch Magazine *Country Gazette* named **Doyle Lawson and Quicksilver** their top bluegrass band.[33] They recorded on Sugar Hill. By 1983, Randy Graham was on bass when they recorded "Heavenly Treasures" album on Sugar Hill. These men recorded "Once and For Always" in 1985.

By May 11, 1985, Doyle Lawson's **Quicksilver** had three new members: Russell Moore (guitar), Scott (banjo) and Curtis Vestal (electric bass). The new members came from **Southern Connection** of Asheville, North Carolina. Ray Deaton joined **Quicksilver** on bass in late 1986.[34] They recorded "Only God" for Lawson's own SSK Recording (which is the abbreviations for his family members' names. Lawson also owns his own publishing company as well). The reputation of this band became widespread enough for it to not

---

[27] Tottle, op. cit., p. 22.

[28] Buddy's featured bluegrass music and barbecued ribs, a popular combination pursued by Buddy Smothers when he moved from Alabama in 1954. Buddy's closed sometime during the late 1980s.

[29] Musicians were Lawson (mandolin), Baucom (banjo), Haley (guitar), Reid (bass) with guests Jerry Douglas (Dobro) and Bobby Hicks (fiddle).

[30] Band musicians were Lawson (mandolin), Terry Baucom (banjo), Jimmy Haley (guitar), Lou Reid (bass) and guest Bobby Hicks (fiddle).

[31] The award reads: "Presented by Disc Jockey Records to Doyle Lawson in recognition of Disc Jockey's best selling bluegrass gospel recording. 'Rock My Soul,' 'Heavenly Treasures' and 'Beyond the Shadows.'" Miniatures of all three records are framed and on Doyle Lawson's wall but only the "Rock My Soul" LP was actually gold.

[32] Stafford, op. cit., p. 48.

[33] Lou Reid had just left the year before and was replaced on bass by an original Bluegrass Cardinal, Randy Graham. One of the reported reasons Reid left Quicksilver was because they were touring 258 days a year. Reid stayed with Skaggs' group for four years until he started with Seldom Scene. Reid later formed his own Lou Reid, Terry Baucom and Carolina. His place in the Scene was taken by Moondi Klein.

[34] By 1987, Doyle Lawson's Quicksilver band consisted of Lawson, Ray Deaton (bass and bass vocals), Scott Vestal (banjo) and Russell Moore (guitar, lead vocals). These band members remained the same through 1989. That year, they recorded "The News Is Out" on Sugar Hill; their guests were Jerry Douglas (resonator guitar) and Glen Duncan (fiddle, piano).

In September 1990, members of Quicksilver included Russell Moore (guitar), Jim Mills (banjo), Mike Hartgrove (fiddle, who had spent the last ten years with the Bluegrass Cardinals) and Ray Deaton (bass). In September of 1991, Russell Moore and Ray Deaton left Quicksilver to join Mike Hartgrove, Terry Baucom and Alan Bibey to form IIIrd Tyme Out. Members of Lawson's group then changed to Jim Mills (banjo, from North Carolina), John Bowman (guitar) and Shelton Feazell (bass). Lawson's "My Heart Is Yours" CD featured Lawson (mandolin), Russell Moore (guitar), Ray Deaton (electric bass), Jim Mills (banjo), Mike Hartgrove (fiddle), with guest Jerry Douglas (resonator guitar).

have to worry about new material. Distinguished songwriters like Pete Goble, Paul Craft and Carl Jackson regularly send him their best songs. Lawson was named Bluegrass Mandolin Player of the Year for 1986 through 1990 by the Society for the Preservation of Bluegrass Music in America (SPBGMA), then retired from the competition. As of 1996, members of **Quicksilver** were Steve Gulley (guitar), Owen Saunders (fiddle), Dale Perry (bass) and Barry Abernathy (banjo).

Jimmy Gaudreau

Jimmy Gaudreau

One of bluegrass' best known mandolinists is the venerable Jimmy Gaudreau, of Wakefield, Rhode Island. Born July 3, 1946, his interest in bluegrass was stimulated by Scruggs' banjo in "The Ballad of Jed Clampett."

The first several years of Gaudreau's professional career is varied and complicated. Here's an attempt to straighten it out. By age twenty-two, he was with the **Country Gentlemen**, replacing John Duffey. He left after two years to form **II Generation** (pronounced "Second") with Eddie Adcock, Tony Rice and Bill Rawlings. This configuration, however, never became a band; it ended up being himself, Adcock, Wendy Thatcher and Bob White in October 1971. In late 1972, Gaudreau formed **Country Store** with Carl Jackson (banjo), Keith Whitley (guitar) and Bill Rawlings (bass). When Jackson left for "Glen Campbell's Goodtime Hour," they were soon joined by Jimmy Arnold on banjo. When **Country Store** wasn't doing quite as well as Gaudreau thought it should, he left and joined **J.D. Crowe and the New South** in October 1975, staying four and a half years, taking the place of Ricky Skaggs. Soon Gaudreau recorded his "The Jimmy Gaudreau Mandolin Album."

Gaudreau's next move was to form **Spectrum** with stellar musicians Bela Fleck (banjo), Mark Schatz (bass)

and Glenn Lawson (guitar); this group cut three LPs on Rounder. When the band split up in 1981, Fleck joined **New Grass Revival**, Lawson left music again, and Gaudreau went back to the **Country Gentlemen** for awhile. In 1985, he joined the **Tony Rice Unit** with Tony Rice, Wyatt Rice and Mark Schatz. During this period, he cut "Classic J.A.G," a project funded by WEBCO Records.

In a 1994 conversation, Gaudreau said that it was easy to work with Tony Rice and that he lets his musicians go wherever their talents lead them—within the **Unit** framework, of course. And, combined with the tremendous amount of satisfaction gained by playing with Rice, Gaudreau, as of 1994, really had no desire to leave. He said, "Playing with Tony Rice is like playing with the Pied Piper. Once you hear that rhythm guitar and the power of the whole rhythm section, it's hard to leave it knowing that if you do anything else you can't duplicate it. I don't know any guitar players who can play like that!"

About 1994, Gaudreau formed **Chesapeake** with Moondi Klein, Mike Auldridge and T. Michael Coleman as a side venture, but it soon developed into a full-time band.

David Harvey

David Harvey

David Harvey is the son of mandolin great Dorsey Harvey who played with Frank Wakefield and Red Allen in the Dayton area. By age fourteen, young David was playing all the major festivals with Red Allen's **Kentuckians**. He became full-time in music at age seventeen.

He described the area where he grew up playing music, "Dayton, at that time, was very economically depressed, and for someone my age there wasn't a whole lot to do as far as work. A lot of my friends ended up being hoodlums—stealing for a living. So when I had the opportunity to go on the road full-time, I took it."[35] Harvey's significant bands began with the **Fall City Ramblers** and **Red Allen and the Kentuckians** among others back in Dayton. After a move Colorado

35 David McCarty, "David Harvey," *Bluegrass Unlimited*, May, 1990, p. 31.

Americas Music I Bluegrass

Springs, Colorado, in 1978, he spent seven years with Phil Easterbrook in Dave's **Reasonable Band**. Harvey founded the three-piece band in 1978 to fill an ad for "a reasonable band" for parties (jazz and swing). John Ramsey was then hired on banjo and mandolin full-time and the band became half bluegrass and half jazz and swing. John became too busy in 1981 with his music store, Original Folklore Center, so Phil Easterbrook replaced him about 1982.

The Reasonable Band, c. 1980 in Colorado Springs. L to R: Steve Haas, Phil Easterbrook, David Harvey, Doug Fulker.

About 1986, David Harvey joined Larry Sparks' band on mandolin and fiddle. "When I was with Sparks, people would tell me how well I fit in because Larry plays very bluesy and I would play a lot of bluesy stuff to fit in with him. I did learn a lot from him about the right way to play fiddle in a bluegrass band because I was playing a lot of swing fiddle. But it's a totally different thing to play bluegrass fiddle. Larry says he can't play fiddle (but I've heard him play a few notes), but he can tell you exactly how it should sound. And if you listen to him, you'll be playing right."[36]

Sparks also taught him about mandolin playing. "If you lay down the melody first and give them a very defined version of the melody first, then on your second or third break you can improvise around the melody. That's something that playing with Larry Sparks really showed me. Larry can play hot and he can play bluesy and he can play soulful and anything else that he wants to play. But something he always stressed is to play to the people—not above their heads. And you can tell—if you're paying attention—the minute you start losing them if you start playing a bunch of stuff they don't know and can't relate to."[37]

In October 1988, David Harvey left Sparks to play with his wife, Jan, and her sister, Jill Snider, which soon became **Wild and Blue**. They continue to perform and record into the 1990s.

When Ricky Skaggs changed his mandolin picking style

After Ricky Skaggs had been with Ralph Stanley's **Clinch Mountain Boys** for awhile, his playing

changed. It evolved from the Monroe/Seckler style of mandolin playing to his own. Stanley didn't mind. Skaggs remarked, "When you get so comfortable on an instrument, you get to where you want to branch out a little bit. You want to do [it] a little different than you played the last break last night of the day before. You want to keep on trying— keep pushing. If you don't, your music gets stale—or I mean it does to me."[38] But Skaggs also recognizes that others may not be motivated in the same manner. Ralph Stanley, he noted, hasn't changed.

Butch Baldassari— from Arizona to Nashville

There are many musicians who make their living as sidemen in various groups and figure that with a lot of "pots in the fire" they can do what they love and still make ends meet. Jerome "Butch" Baldassari is one such mandolinist who not only has played bluegrass in bands such as **Weary Hearts**, the **Kathy Chiavola Band**, **Lonesome Standard Time**[39] and the **Grass Is Greener**. He is also the leader of the **Nashville Mandolin Ensemble** which is similar to the mandolin orchestras early in this century and he conducts regularly-scheduled mandolin instruction camps (similar to Pete Wernick's banjo camps) where a person endeavoring to improve his/her skills on the mandolin can spend a few days with Butch and other students.

Baldassari was born December 11, 1952, in Scranton, Pennsylvania. In 1972, already with some experience in music on electric guitar, he saw the mandolin played at a folk festival and then pursued to learn the instrument. He played in various bands around Scranton until 1974 when he moved to Nashville where he got a job as an instrument repairman at the Old-Time Pickin' Parlor. In 1977, he moved to Las Vegas, Nevada, where he played in several groups, including his own.

In November 1985, Baldassari joined his first full-time band, **Weary Hearts**, whose band members were Mike Bub (bass), Eric Uglum (guitar) and Ron Block (banjo, guitar). This band came into existence after

36 Ibid., pp. 34, 35.

37 Ibid., p. 36.

38 Jack Tottle, "Ricky Skaggs: Clinch Mountain to Boone Creek," *Bluegrass Unlimited*, January, 1977, p. 11.

39 Lonesome Standard Time was scheduled for breakup September 9, 1995, he then joined Richard Greene's the Grass Is Greener in August 1995.

winning the Best Band contest at Wickenberg, Arizona. By 1994, he had three solo LPs: "Evergreen—Mandolin Music for Christmas," "Old Town" and "A Day in the Country." Baldassari is a frequent contributor to various periodicals, produces records, and records with many artists.

Larry Stephenson

Larry Stephenson— a third-generation bluegrass musician/singer with great roots

Since 1974, Larry Stephenson has been playing bluegrass. This second-generation bluegrass mandolinist has made his mark in the music with his incredibly clear, high voice. As of 1994, he has played a major part, even as a sideman, in some great bluegrass bands. His voice is quite unmistakable and his **Larry Stephenson Band** popular.

Larry Stephenson was born in Harrisonburg, Virginia, in October 24, 1956, and grew up in King George, Virginia. "My daddy, his family and brothers and sisters, all played little dances around the Shenandoah Valley through the years. So when I was about four or five years old, he got me started (with the gift of a mandolin) and I've been hittin' it ever since."[40] With his new mandolin, he was taught three chords and he found that it was easy for him. At age nine, Larry and his father began making performances around Fredricksburg and Richmond area on television, live, and on radio.

In high school, Stephenson had a band called **Larry Stephenson and New Grass** with his father, Ed (guitar). He listened to all the popular bluegrass mandolinists but didn't copy anyone; he idolized the voice of Bobby Osborne but didn't try to copy his style. "I don't try to copy Bobby, because I have learned that you have to eventually move on and do your own thing if you want to accomplish anything in this business."[41]

In high school, where rock music dominated, "I was made fun of and kind of laughed at. But I really wasn't an outcast; I had a lot of friends, but they were all doing other things on weekends when I would be going to bluegrass festivals with my parents. I didn't feel square because I was doing what I really enjoyed. It never made any sense to me to go over to Fredricksburg and ride around McDonalds on a Saturday night when I could be doing something I really enjoyed. I could look at girls at the bluegrass festivals as easily as I could look at them at McDonalds."[42] He graduated high school in 1976; the band ended about that time.

Larry Stephenson joined Cliff Waldron in 1977 for a year. The band was initially **Cliff Waldron and the Gospel Way**, but soon returned to the well-known name, **Cliff Waldron and the New Shades of Grass**.[43] Through 1978, Stephenson worked with **Leon Morris and the Bluegrass Associates** and recorded on Morris' "Places and Friends I Once Knew."

In January 1979, Stephenson joined **Bill Harrell and the Virginians**[44]. He remarked, "It was a great learning experience and Bill not only gave me the opportunity to learn more about the music, but I also learned a lot about music as a business."[45] Stephenson loved working with Harrell, mostly as his tenor singer. "He was a great boss. I wouldn't trade those four and a half years for anything." His 1982 solo album was "Sweet Sunny South" on the Outlet label.

Larry Stephenson left the **Virginians** in June of 1983 to join the **Bluegrass Cardinals** where he stayed five and a half years. "I had a lot of leeway with the **Cardinals**, as I not only played mandolin and sang tenor, we also got more into the 'high-lead' trios," he said. "I also did a lot of emcee work which helped me a lot. I recorded three albums with the **Cardinals**: 'Home is Where the Heart Is,' 'The Shining Path' and 'On Stage in Nashville.'"[46] "I had to really rare back and find out what kind of a singer I was. I really grew as a singer there. My voice got stronger and higher." Don Parmley, leader of the band, joked that he had to hold Stephenson back; his piercing tenor voice was so strong. His time

---

[40] Brett F. Devan, *Bluegrass Unlimited*, "The Bluegrass Cardinals, Synonym for Vocal Harmony," May, 1986, p. 10.

[41] Frank Overstreet, "Larry Stephenson—Born to Play Bluegrass," *Bluegrass Music News*, Fall, 1991, p 13.

[42] Don Rhodes, "Larry Stephenson—Taking Control of the Spotlight," *Bluegrass Unlimited*, September, 1990, pp. 30, 31.

[43] Band members then were Arthur Penn, Billy Wheeler, Steve Wilson and Waldron. With Waldron, Stephenson recorded on Rebel's "God Walks the Dark Hills."

[44] Band members included Carl Nelson, Darryl Sanders, Ed Ferris and Harrell.

[45] Overstreet, op. cit., p. 13.

[46] Ibid., p. 13.

with the **Cardinals** enabled him to find what he was capable of doing in music and gave him a sense of fulfillment that kept him from quitting music; his day job financially enabled him to stay in music as a sideline.

Stephenson founded his own **Larry Stephenson Band** in early 1989 with Rick Allred (banjo), Mark Keller (guitar) and Doug Campbell (electric bass). Stephenson likes having his own band. He said, "It has felt better over the last year or two with my own band than it ever has felt. It makes a difference when you get a great bunch of guys together and you're performing your own style of music and kind of taking control of what is happening with your life. When everybody around you is working hard and playing good, it just feels real good."[47] This band soon recorded "Timber" for WEBCO.

Stephenson likes to record not only the old bluegrass standards but songs from other types of music. He feels, "You have to give them modern, up-to-date songs they can relate to. That's how we'll draw more younger people to this music. It really irritates me to hear some bluegrass singers say they can't find any new material and have to record the same songs over and over again. There is no excuse for that when there are good, obscure album cuts to find and remakes to be made of hits from other musical fields."[48]

In 1991, a two CD set of thirty-nine songs came out which was a continuation of the work that the **Bluegrass Band** did in 1981 and '82. Band members then were Alan O'Bryant, Ed Dye, Blaine Sprouse, Butch Robins and David Sebring. This new compilation, on B Natural 1 Records, used musicians Robins (banjo), Ricky Simpkins (fiddle, mandolin), Larry Stephenson (mandolin), Wyatt Rice (guitar), Wayne Henderson (guitar), Arnie Solomon (mandolin) and Ronnie Simpkins (bass).

As of 1995, he had seven recording projects with WEBCO Records which by that time was a part of Pinecastle/Webco Records. He was inducted into the Virginia Country Music Hall of Fame on June 23, 1996, in Crewe, Virginia.[49]

---

[47] Rhodes, op. cit., p. 29.

[48] Ibid., p. 32.

[49] The Virginia Hall of Fame was formed in 1972 to recognize Virginia-born talent that had achieved national stature and/or had helped to promote and preserve country music. Others in the Hall are Roy Clark, Jim and Jesse McReynolds, Mother Maybelle Carter, the Statler Brothers, the Stanley Brothers, Bill Emerson, Eddie Adcock, Tony Rice, Ray Pillow and Bill Harrell.

Chapter 10

Bluegrass Fiddle

The "Devil's Box" is one of the five basic bluegrass instruments. This chapter features a recent history of American fiddle music and biographical sketches of several important fiddlers as they chronologically appeared on the American fiddle music scene and the bluegrass music scene. A further study of this instrument would reveal that, in certain segments of the world, the fiddle is, by far, the most important instrument in that culture. While this book does not delve into those areas, they include Cape Breton, Ireland, Nova Scotia, parts of Canada and others. The fiddle was certainly the predominant instrument in the Appalachians when the Scots-Irish settled the area beginning about 1710. And it was still the main instrument when the music emerged from the mountains as "old-time" two centuries later.

In 1913, the Georgia Old-Time Fiddlers' Association was founded to begin contests in Atlanta. The larger contests gave the champion the title of "Best in the County". Because of the poor roads and rough country, within a county was all the further a person could travel in a day and the extent of most men's contesting. These contests were the breeding grounds for the fiddlers who played in the string bands of the 1920s, some of which continued their playing beyond that period. The contestants, such as Fiddlin' John Carson and Eck Robertson, were the men who first waxed recordings for the country music genre.

According to author Charles Wolfe, in the period of the nineteenth century, "Fiddlers in the eastern half of [Tennessee] also used a short, or 'jiggy,' bow in their playing; this made their music rather choppy and full of short, highly rhythmic passages. By the 1920s, many old fiddlers were playing the 'long bow,' or 'Texas' style, which depended more on complex fingering and yielded smooth, long passages, and the 'short bow' style was on its way out. But the 'short bow' style often made up in excitement and drive what it lost in technical finesse, and

it certainly fulfilled its purpose. It was dance music, not especially listening music, and like ballad singing, the 'short bow' style is in danger of extinction today."[1]

Wolfe continued, "At the most basic level, the contests were community affairs, often held in rural schoolhouses or meeting halls. A description of such a turn-of-the-century contest held in the Smoky Mountains was published by folklorist Louise Rand Bascom in 1909:

The convention is essentially an affair of the people and is usually held in a stuffy little schoolhouse, lighted by one or two evil-smelling lamps and provided with a rude, temporary stage. On this, the fifteen fiddlers and follerers of banjo pickin' sit, their coats and hats hung conveniently on pegs above their heads, their faces inscrutable. To all appearances they do not care to whom the prize is awarded, for the winner will undoubtedly treat. Also, they are not bothered by the note-taking of zealous judges, as these gentlemen are not appointed until after each contestant has finished his allotted 'three pieces.'

To one unused to the mountain tunes, the business of selecting the best player would not be unlike telling which snail had eaten the rhododendron leaf, for execution and technique differ little with the individual performers, and the tune, no matter what it may be called, always sounds the same. It is composed of practically two bars which are repeated over and over and over again until the fiddler or the banjo picker, as the case may be, stops abruptly from sheer fatigue. The tunes are played at all the dances, whistled and sung by men and boys everywhere. The mountaineer who cannot draw music from the violin, the banjo or the "French harp" is probably non-existent... The women are also endowed with musical talent, but they regard it as the men's prerogative and rarely touch an instrument when their husbands or sons are present.[2]

Photo courtesy John Ramsey.

[1] Charles K. Wolfe, *Tennessee Strings* (Knoxville: The University of Tennessee Press, 1977), p. 15.
[2] Ibid., pp. 19, 20.

In 1917, Fiddlin' John Carson warned would-be contestants in the Georgia Old-Time Fiddlers Contest that the convention would be confined to fiddlers and that there was no need for "fancy violinists" to apply. In explaining this policy, Carson stated, "We have had fancy fiddlers who played a half-hour at a time and never strike a tune. They'd fiddle and fiddle and do all kind of stunts and never get nowhere. The may go all right in the Grand Opery, but they don't belong in a fiddling contest for the championship of Georgia. That's flat! Nothing goes but old-fashioned fiddlin'. Just pure elbow grease and awkwardness and the tune that gets into your feet. I figure that any tune that will let a man keep his feet still ain't worth the playing."

A good description of the difference between the fiddle and a violin was given by contestant/judge Colonel Eb T. Williams: "A fiddle is an old, common instrument, clumsily and roughly finished, with wire strings, the bridge a thick piece of wood set in the wrong place; the sound post sometimes in front, instead of behind the bridge, and not infrequently a mouse hole gnawed in the 'f' holes as big as a goose egg where several generations of mice were born and raised."[3] A violin, of course, was given a significantly different description which described its beauty.

Contestants often played Scottish and Irish reels and breakdowns with an occasional ballad. Such tunes were "Leather Britches," "Soldiers' Joy," "Arkansas Traveler" and "Bile Them Cabbage Down." The contestants went to the Atlanta conventions to study the music. An old saying describes this, "As a pianist goes to Chicago or Boston for a post-graduate course with a famous master, so do the Georgia fiddlers attend the Atlanta conventions." They jammed with one another, not to enjoy it, but to learn new tunes, licks and styles.

Times change. And along with them, technology and people's tastes in music were also changing. "One old-timer lamented the fact that the 'good ole tunes' were passing away. 'These here phonografts and the radio are corruptin' our boys and gals worsen a circus or a stage show.'"[4] The popularity of the fiddle in those years was unequaled.

Fiddlers learning tunes from each other at an early Georgia Old-Time Fiddling Convention (contest). Photo courtesy Library of Congress.

In the mid-1920s, the fiddle contest at Atlanta still existed but it seemed like less and less people showed up for them. Soon the large string bands would dominate the airwaves. The conventions ended in 1935 when fiddlers became scarce and the Georgia Old-Time Fiddlers' Association no longer sponsored the event. The then-famous announcer Professor Smart described it this way, "We used to have just fiddlers and old-fashioned tunes but the phonograph and the radio have changed all that. The folks in the mountains and flat woods want something different now. So we're going to have string bands and hillbilly orchestras and quartets and even a big hog-calling contest with a fat hog for a prize." This last sentence contained considerable sarcasm, regretful that an era in American music had come to an end.

Ralph Rinzler's history of American fiddle music

On the liner notes of "Pickin' and Fiddlin'" (EKL-285, 1964), Ralph Rinzler gave a quick history of American fiddle music:

The main body of American traditional fiddle music consists of dance tunes imported from the British Isles or developed here but showing strong influences of the British models. Of the four most common types of dance tunes which come to us from Britain (including, of course, Ireland and Scotland), the reels and hornpipes have persisted in the Southern and Western U.S. while jigs and strathspeys, still current in the Northeast and in Canada and Nova Scotia, have almost completely disappeared or have been altered to suit the faster, more driving, tempo of the reel, square, and clog dance so popular in the south and west of the United States. The lilt of the jig and strathspey along with their characteristically ornate ornamentation and constant cross-bowing have given way to more frequent double-stopping and syncopations (either delaying or anticipating the beat). Thus a number of jigs and strathspey tunes have survived in southern and western American fiddling in slightly altered form. Hornpipes, while common enough, are more frequently played as showpieces by fiddlers of accomplishment than as tunes for dancing.

3 Wayne W. Daniel, "The Georgia Old-Time Fiddlers' Conventions," *Bluegrass Unlimited*, August, 1982, pp. 43, 44.
4 Ibid., p. 46.

Birch Monroe— a veteran fiddler with an opinion or two

In a 1982 interview with Neil V. Rosenberg for *Bluegrass Unlimited*, Birch Monroe spoke eloquently about "the blues". He insisted that a song doesn't have to be slow to be blues. A good example of fast blues is "Carroll County Blues." He said, "Clayton McMichen and them good fiddlers played it so many times. Clayton was something special as a fiddler. So was Arthur [Smith]. They could play blues. Arthur was the best on blues of any of 'em... They was the best there was. Big Howdy [Forrester] and Chubby [Wise] was real fiddlers but they couldn't write like them fellers. You see, them fellers wrote their own tunes so much. Clayton wrote a lot of his tunes. But Big Howdy and Chubby didn't write that much, I think.

"Vassar [Clements] is real good. If you don't think Vassar's good, let him follow somebody on 'Katy Hill' or something like that. He can really jump and he gets some of the prettiest notes of any of 'em on pieces like that.

"Kenny [Baker] is a good musician—guess he's doing well now with his records. He's playing—he's got a better chance than the others, now. Bill (Monroe) will back him, too. And that's what you need.

"Them fiddlers! I feel sorry for 'em, running around, having to go through all them motions to sell. Jumping around—Curly Ray Cline being right on the floor almost, jump up to the mike, scoot up to the mike and back and hasn't never looked at the audience yet in his life. And to sell, to me, you got to look at the audience. I wouldn't give you a nickel to look around and jump around and you never look at the audience 'cause you're playing for 'em and playing to 'em. But I guess more power to him."

About using electric instruments, "We just used it for dances, a few times. As light as I play, why, electric probably would help me. But most fiddlers, it just makes a big noise. Just a-drives them strings and with that electric, why, it takes something away from their tone. Last time Arthur [Smith] was up here he had his fiddle electrified. And it wasn't the same Arthur Smith. He said he wanted it electrified so he could walk around on stage and not have to stand in one spot. Back when we first knowed him, why, he could get everything out of that fiddle."[5]

Eck Robertson— one of the first "long bow" fiddlers

One way a professional fiddler made a living with his music was on the contest circuit; it paid enough for some to pursue fiddling on a more-than-casual basis. Alexander Campbell "Eck" Robertson (1887-1975) was one of these men. One of his contest tricks used "triple stops" which bowed three strings simultaneously. At one particular event he was being beaten by the famous "Georgia Slim" Rutland who was using a double-shuffle bow stroke to confuse or "wow" the judges. Robertson had to do something even more clever so he placed a match stick under a string, bringing it up off the bridge even with two others. Then he tuned into a discord and played "Sally Goodin'" using all three strings at the same time. Another contest method of achieving the 3- and 4-string harmonies—and more common—was to loosen the bow hair from the bow completely and place the bow underneath the fiddle while the bow scraped across three or four strings simultaneously.

Robertson is also significant in history because he was one of the first to leave the "short bow" style of fiddling for the "long bow" style which was used in Texas. His recordings for RCA on June 30, 1922, for RCA are acknowledged as the first in country music. At this recording session in a duet with Henry Gilliland, a former Justice of the Peace in Altus, Oklahoma, they performed "Arkansas Traveler," "Turkey in the Straw," "Forked Deer," and "Apple Blossom." Eck came back the next day to recorded solo: "Sallie Goodin," "Ragtime Annie," "Done Gone" and "Billy in the Low Ground" among others.

Robertson recorded again in 1929 for Victor and was his last session until 1940 when he recorded one hundred selections for the Sellers Transcription Studio in Dallas, but none of these recordings were found. His last public appearances include the 1965 Newport Folk Festival and the UCLA Folk Festival in California in his late '70s.

Fiddlin' John Carson (far right) and his string band in the mid-1920's. Uncle Am Stuart is next to Carson. Photo courtesy Library of Congress.

5 Rosenberg, "A Front Porch Visit with Birch Monroe," *Bluegrass Unlimited*, September, 1982, p. 62.

Clark Kessinger—
an early fiddler

Clark Kessinger recorded extensively during the 1920s. Author John Burke wrote, "An excellent old-time fiddler from West Virginia, Kessinger was one of the smoothest and most advanced players to have recorded during the twenties. His recordings with his cousin Luches (billed as the **Kessinger Brothers**) were highly influential, and it seems to me they must have contributed to the development of the long-bow-stroke Texas style.

"Clark Kessinger was a fiddler who did an unusual bow lick which he called 'triple bowing' which involved bouncing the bow on the two middle strings in such a way that the wood of the bow drums on the strings just after the hair sounds them. To do this, you have to set the hair tension just right and then, with a very loose wrist and no arm motion, set the bow bouncing erratically on the two middle strings."[6]

Fiddlin' Arthur Smith

Fiddlin' Arthur Smith

Arthur Smith is probably the most-direct descendant for modern day bluegrass fiddlers. Though he wasn't the first to use the "long bow" technique of playing, he was the most influential. There are a few fiddlers today who like to use the "short bow" or hoe-down technique, but they are few. Long bow seems to be the best method to fit a whole lot of notes into a phrase smoothly and with the least effort.

When compared with other fiddlers of his time, like Clark Kessinger, Clayton McMichen, Doc Roberts and others, Smith was often faster, more aggressive and daring. Smith got his speed from his fast fingers. His "long bow" technique enabled him to get two notes to a "short bow" fiddler's one. Bill Monroe liked his style because it had blues in it and he noted the fiddle beautifully. Smith's style is largely created by himself and self-taught. One modern fiddler who admits to emulating Smith's style was Paul Warren, who for many years was known as "America's greatest breakdown fiddler".

Jim Shumate, the well-known fiddler with Bill Monroe and **Flatt and Scruggs**, spoke of Smith, "He was a genius, a flat genius, when it comes to playing the fiddle. He fiddled stuff like nobody else—like nobody you ever heard. Smooth...he didn't fiddle a whole lot of fancy stuff, he was flat, down to earth. Like Earl [Scruggs] on the five-string. Earl don't play a lot of fancy banjo, but what he plays is right—it's *there*! And that's the way the Smith fiddlin' was. He didn't do a lot of fancy, showoff, kick-up-the-dust stuff, but when he fiddled a tune, it was fiddled just like it ought to be."[7] Lester Flatt believed that Arthur Smith was one of the first that played that lonesome stuff on a fiddle. He was among the first to bow two strings in harmony at one time ("double stops").

Fiddlin' Arthur Smith was born in Bold Springs, Humphries County, Tennessee, west of Nashville, April 10, 1898. When the Arthur Smith of "Guitar Boogie" fame came along, the quickest way to differentiate between the two was to add "Fiddlin'" to the first one. (There was also a third: Arthur Q. Smith was a Jim Eanes associate and songwriter.)

Four year-old Arthur Smith followed his father's footsteps in attempting to play the fiddle, propping it up on the floor. He learned from his father and the fiddlers of the area who frowned upon open-string playing and insisted on doing it the hard way.[8] By age fifteen, he was playing fiddle at local dances with his sixteen year-old wife. One of the songs he wrote was adapted from a brass band and called "Indian Creek."

At eighteen, finding that professional fiddling just didn't pay the bills, he began working full-time with the Nashville, Chattanooga, and St. Louis Railroad (the Dixie Line). His first job was that of crosstie cutter, and later as a mechanic for the Line where he met Harry Stone, a fellow Line employee, who later became the emcee at WSM's Grand Ole Opry. Still playing locally at square dances, Smith developed a reputation above all others in the dance band with the instrument which was

[6] John Burke, "Country Fiddling," *Bluegrass Unlimited*, April, 1972, p. 18.

[7] Wayne Erbsen, "Jim Shumate—Bluegrass Fiddler Supreme," *Bluegrass Unlimited*, April, 1979, pp. 15, 16.

[8] Byron Berline, who knew both Eck Robertson and Arthur Smith, explained what "the hard way" and "open tuning" are. "Eck played a lot of open-string stuff. In fact, he recorded 'Sallie Goodin' with the D and G tuned up on the fiddle. He left E and A alone. That's what that means—you don't have to use your little finger at all. You just use the first three fingers and it gives it a more open sound—it gives it that ringing sound. It's the same tuning you use for 'Black Mountain Rag' except when you play in A, you don't tune the E string down to E-sharp; you just leave it where it is. But you tune the D and G up a fret. So, doing it the 'hard way' is where you would not use any open tuning."

the dominant (and loudest) instrument in bands of this type during this period.

In 1925, George D. Hay, manager of WSM's Barn Dance (not yet named the Grand Ole Opry) hired Arthur Smith for a solid half-hour of solo fiddling. Smith played his originals such as "Blackberry Blossom," "Dickson County Blues," "Florida Blues," "Pig In A Pen," "Beautiful Brown Eyes" and "Peacock Rag." He popularized Ervin Rouse's "Orange Blossom Special."

After a few weeks of playing solo on the show, Smith formed a duet with his cousin, Homer Smith (guitar). (They were often mistakenly billed as the **Smith Brothers**.) The duo soon had their own thirty-minute set on the Opry and both retained their full-time jobs on the railroad. Smith continued his railroad job until the mid-'30s.

In 1932, Smith joined Sam (guitar) and Kirk (banjo, guitar) McGee, called themselves **Arthur Smith and the Dixieliners** and quickly became the most popular string band of its day and on the Opry. Sam and Kirk McGee were already famous for their work with Uncle Dave Macon and earlier professional work. The McGee brothers dropped Uncle Dave, whom they considered more of an entertainer than a musician, in favor of the quality instrumental work of Smith. Arthur Smith and the **Dixieliners** could be hired for $25 per performance—one-third the rate of the most popular Opry acts at that time. Their performances/appearances kept them very busy and unable to record together.

The **Dixieliners** was a no-holds-barred, hard-driving, no compromise string band. The audience loved it. Smith was a good lead fiddler and was backed by the McGees. But the act rarely had Smith doing backup fiddle for the McGee's segment of the show. As a fiddler from the era of the big string bands of the 1920s, Smith originally felt that fiddle music should not be used to back up dancers or singers, but strictly as a lead instrument. He later changed his mind and began writing songs with lyrics. The change of attitude may be due to the fiddle losing its place in a band as *the* lead instrument.

For a while, the McGees couldn't get Smith to sing. After they did, they "couldn't get him to stop," laughed Kirk. A typical set at their performances included the piano of Arthur's oldest daughter, with Kirk sharing the emcee work and Sam donning a red wig as the "Toby" or comedian.

According to Charles Wolfe, "The trio promoted their personal [appearances] in all sorts of ways. For a time, they had an agent who distributed handbills and posters announcing upcoming shows. A more innovative way of advertising was to buy 'trailers'— short film clips to be shown after the movie feature at local theaters where they were to appear. These trailers—the group had a dozen different ones which

they posted for nine dollars each—showed still photos of the group, gave the time and the place, and had fiddle music in the background. Ironically, the fiddle music was dubbed off of old records by Clark Kessinger since the **Dixieliners** had not recorded themselves."[9] "Blackberry Blossom" became his signature tune, playing "a showy, repetitive line that he keeps extending just when it sounds like he's run out of gas."[10]

The Opry management then teamed Smith up with the **Delmore Brothers** in 1934 (they had joined the Opry the year before), the tours being arranged by WSM and the Grand Ole Opry. The style of the band featured close-harmony vocals as opposed to the mainly instrumental work when Smith toured with Sam and Kirk McGee (which still continued through the next several years). The Delmores had a recording contract with Victor-Bluebird already. Soon their contacts would help Smith make his first recording in 1935, at age thirty-seven, after over twenty years of professional playing. He recorded with the **Delmore Brothers** on RCA's Bluebird label. The recordings featured his own "Blackberry Rag," "Red Apple Rag" and "Fiddler's Dream." In 1936, he recorded "More Pretty Girls Than One," "Beautiful Brown Eyes" and his own "Pig at Home in a Pen." They continued recording together through 1938. During the thirties, Smith competed in contests, and the fame he received became invaluable in later years.

Because of his strong personality and his status as one of the premier performers on the Opry, Smith was given much leeway—more than most other Opry performers. However, when he failed to appear at one of the contests sponsored by the Opry, he was suspended for four weeks in 1938. He was replaced on the Opry by a young fiddler just who was just getting his start: Roy Acuff.

Meanwhile, and for the next year, Smith played with **Jack Shook and His Missouri Mountaineers** and with Herald Goodman's **Tennessee Valley Boys**.[11] Smith's

Fiddlin' Arthur Smith and his Dixieliners (Sam McGee, left).

[9] Charles Wolfe and Barry Poss, liner notes for County's "Fiddlin' Arthur Smith and the Dixieliners." (County 546 and 547)

[10] John Morthland, *The Best of Country Music* (New York: Doubleday and Company, 1984), p. 74.

reputation helped the success of the band as they toured the southern states. The next year, Smith became the leader of the group, moved to Tulsa, and hired a third fiddler, the famous Georgia Slim Rutland. Goodman's band now had three of the Southeast's best and most popular fiddlers. They never recorded together. During that time, Smith worked with Curly Ray Cline and the **Lonesome Pine Fiddlers** and Cline learned much from Smith.

In 1940, Smith recorded eight sides with **Bill Monroe and the Blue Grass Boys** who were Tommy Magness (fiddle), Clyde Moody (guitar) and Bill Wesbrooks (bass). During that period, Smith quit his **Tennessee Valley Boys**, and for the next six years joined groups such as the **Shelton Brothers** (Louisiana), **Zeke Phillips and His 49ers** (Birmingham, Alabama), the **Bailes Brothers and Little Evy** (Huntington, West Virginia), the **York Brothers** (West Virginia), cowboy singer Rex Griffin (Birmingham), The Saddle Mountain Roundup at KRLD in Dallas, and later back with Herald Goodman's radio show.

Beginning in 1946 and for the next three years, Smith joined cowboy singer Jimmy Wakely in California in a group which featured Smith's fiddling. Smith wrote and recorded "Crazy Blues" on Capitol. He also appeared in western films with Wakely. In one film, Smith was supposed to be filmed on a horse. But when the horse moved, he fell off. Many of the audiences that Smith played to while with Wakely were wealthy patrons at the Last Frontier Hotel in Las Vegas who had never heard a country fiddler. "When he started playing, those people would often get up and dance between tables. They would holler and yell. He really made them go."[12] This time of touring with Wakely, and his appearances in Hollywood's western music, gained Smith tremendous national exposure, for Wakely was nearly popular as Gene Autry at the time.

In 1951, Smith worked as a carpenter and was almost completely out of music. In 1963, Smith recorded his only solo album; it was on the Starday label. His son, Ernest was the guitarist. About that time, Smith was invited by folk revivalist Mike Seeger to go to Nashville to record "the old songs" with Sam and Kirk McGee on a Folkways LP. This was the first time that Smith recorded with the McGees. This event led to the resurrection of the **Dixieliners** and they toured extensively. A second Folkways record was waxed in 1968.

Fiddlin' Arthur Smith died of cancer in Louisville, Kentucky, February 28, 1971.

Chubby Wise— the first bluegrass fiddler

In an interview for the November 1985 issue of *Frets* magazine, guitarist Charles Sawtelle told editor Phil Hood, "I think I learned the most from Chubby Wise. What Chubby does that is so great is he says what needs to be said in a concise and beautiful way. He is real conscious of tone, and conscious of playing as a 'member' of a band, really subtle and not too flashy. Sometimes he follows the melody perfectly and sometimes what he plays follows the phrasing perfectly. It's like Scruggs when he played the banjo with the **Foggy Mountain Boys**—he played every word that Lester Flatt sang, not just the melody or his impression of the melody. Musically, he somehow caught the feel of the exact words."[13]

Fiddlin' Tommy Cordell was quoted, "Chubby makes the fiddle sing like a singer sings. He told me that once you start a break, you should never take the bow off the strings. It should just be like a sea gull flying over the ocean waves. He said that's how smooth you've got to get it." And Rosenberg's *Bluegrass: A History* declared that "Chubby's solos on the early recordings of Bill Monroe and Flatt and Scruggs have never been surpassed... Chubby was a pioneer, essentially feeling his way to create his own style. His immediate successor in the **Blue Grass Boys**, Vassar Clements, had the advantage of being able to learn from Chubby's recordings, and that's how the basics of the style were handed down through successive Blue Grass Boys fiddlers."

Robert Russell Dees was born October 2, 1915. His mother died within two weeks of his birth and he was adopted by a Lake City, Florida, fiddler, Robert Wise and his wife. By age eight, now known as Russell Wise, he was playing the banjo which Mrs. Wise had bought him

[11] With Goodman's band, Smith joined fiddler Howdy Forrester, Joe Forrester (bass), Billy Byrd (guitar) and Virgil Atkins (banjo). Howdy, in later years, joined Roy Acuff's Smoky Mountain Boys.

[12] Charles Wolfe and Barry Poss. op. cit., liner notes.

[13] Phil Hood, "Charles Sawtelle—Physical Guitar," *Frets*, November, 1985, p. 43.

330

while he recovered from injuries incurred when a steel beam fell on his leg. When he heard fiddler Bryan Purcell, the Florida State fiddling champion, "I knew right then that I'd found my instrument," he declared.[14]

During the Depression, young Wise and his uncle played for dances in kerosene-lighted halls and barns around Lake City. His first professional job paid thirty-seven cents. For years thereafter, he barely made enough to pay for strings. He dropped out of school in the seventh grade to work on his uncle's farm and to fiddle evenings and weekends. He learned most of his technique by listening to the radio and records; there was no one around to instruct him. At eighteen, he married Rossie, moved to Jacksonville, Florida, and drove a cab. He continued to fiddle for money on the side.

In 1939, Chubby Wise and his friend, Ervin T. Rouse, went to the train station at 3 a.m. to see the exciting, new, streamlined Orange Blossom Special in Jacksonville owned by Seaboard Airlines. Those were the glory days of trains, and each train had its own name. After viewing the magnificent beauty, it was Rouse's idea to write a tune in honor of the train so the two went to Chubby's apartment at 809 E. Adams St. and wrote "Orange Blossom Special." The melody took forty-five minutes to create while the lyrics took longer, with the help of Ervin's brother, Jack. The tune was published and, in June of 1939, recorded on Bluebird by the **Rouse Brothers**. With the consent of Wise, the song's only author became Ervin Rouse. Wise remembered that he told his partner, "Ervin, I've got to get to work. You can have it if you can do anything with it." The song soon gained popularity with Bill Monroe and Fiddlin' Arthur Smith. Wise never made a dime from it but "that song has been good to me. I play it all the time. It's opened doors for me."

Wise moved to Gainesville, Florida, in 1942 to play with the professional country band, **Jubilee Hillbillies**. It was here, during a broadcast on WRUF, that one of the other band members dubbed him "Chubby". After a futile effort to keep the **Jubilee Hillbillies** together (during the War years, he was ineligible for military service because of the earlier leg injury), Wise joined Bill Monroe as their fiddler. He found the job by tuning in the Opry one rare Saturday night when he wasn't fiddling, and heard **Bill Monroe and the Blue Grass Boys**. Monroe announced that his fiddler (Carl Story) was joining the Navy. So Wise took a train to Nashville to meet Mr. Monroe to ask for a job.

"I walked up to him like a big old rooster and said, 'Bill, my name's Wise from Florida and I want to be your fiddler.'

"He said, 'Play me a breakdown,' and I played him one or two things.

"He said, 'Have you got your clothes with you?'

"I said, 'Yeah.'

"He said, 'Get 'em. We're leaving in two hours.'" Story and Wise played together as Monroe's fiddlers for two weeks until Story joined the Navy in October 1943.[15]

Though Chubby Wise is often given credit as being Bill Monroe's most significant bluegrass player—and he was certainly that during the forties—Wise was nevertheless following in the traditions set by Monroe's earlier fiddlers: Wooten, Forrester, etc. But to say that he was just another in the long succession of Monroe's fiddle players may also be a mistake. He was with Monroe's band when Lester Flatt and Earl Scruggs helped establish Monroe's new "bluegrass" sound. And he was powerful enough to keep up with the tremendous power of Monroe's mandolin, Flatt's rhythm guitar, and Scruggs' fancy banjo which was taking the world by storm.

Now that Wise was with a new band, and with a style different from what he was accustomed, Monroe changed Wise's fiddling style from country and dance rhythms to that required by Monroe for appearances on the Opry. Monroe taught Wise how to play bluegrass fiddle and made sure that he included a lot of blues notes in the music to give it that certain feel which Monroe wanted in his band. Monroe obviously saw potential and began teaching him fiddle tunes and other "Monroe sound" characteristics. Wise remembered, "Many was the night we'd sit up, hour after hour, in some two-dollar motel. He'd play his mandolin and say, 'Now, Chubby, I want it to sound like that.' And I'd try to make that sound with the fiddle. He didn't want a lot of notes but he wanted me to make a lot out of every note I played. It was Bill Monroe who taught me to play the long, blues notes. You don't get that feel in country [music]." Wise was successful in the transition and stayed with Monroe until January 1948.

In 1946, members of the **Blue Grass Boys** were Flatt, Scruggs, Wise, Monroe and Howard "Cedric Rainwater" Watts. Wise felt that this band, though the sound was somewhat revolutionary, was highlighted by the terrific banjo of Earl Scruggs. During this period and until 1949, he also recorded with Hank Williams, Clyde Moody and Red Foley. Wise wrote the music to "Shenandoah Waltz"; Moody wrote the words.

Chubby Wise was more than a great fiddler. Carlton Haney pointed out that Mr. Wise recorded the first several gospel hymns on Monroe's early Columbia sessions. Lester Flatt got the credit for being the guitarist on the sessions of September 17, 1946, and

---

[14] Sam Hodges, "True Bluegrass," *The Orlando Sentinel, Florida*, April 30, 1989. Mr. Hodges interviewed Mr. Wise backstage at that year's Kissimmee Bluegrass Festival. I saw the two sitting in Wise's car together in an interview which lasted at least an hour. I also tried to speak with him there but Chubby, probably tired by this time, referred me to Mr. Hodges for the same information I would undoubtedly ask of him. I asked Hodges to send me a copy of his article. Thanks, Sam.

[15] Other band members of the Blue Grass Boys were Clyde Moody (guitar), Stringbean (banjo) and Cousin Wilbur Wesbrooks (bass, comedy).

Chubby Wise and the Bass Mountain Boys, c. 1987.

October 28, 1947. A conversation with Mr. Wise verified that Wise did indeed play guitar on "Shining Path (CCO 4615) and "Wicked Path of Sin" (CCO 4616) on the September 1946 session; and on the October 1947 session he recorded his guitar playing on "That Home Above" (CCO 4882), "Remember the Cross (CCO 4883), "Little Community Church" (CCO 4884), "Shine Hallelujah Shine" (CCO 4888) and "I'm Travelin' On and On" (CCO 4889).

In the chronology of Bill Monroe's fiddlers, Jim Shumate joined the **Blue Grass Boys** in 1944 (about two weeks after Lester Flatt joined) and stayed until Howdy Forrester came back from the Navy to claim that job (October 1945)—his right, since he was legally entitled to it by the rules of Selective Service. Forrester didn't stay long though (he went to work with Roy Acuff), and Wise was soon back with the **Blue Grass Boys** for consecutive Columbia sessions from February 1945 through October 1949.

In January 1948, Chubby Wise left the **Blue Grass Boys** to work on WARL, Arlington, Virginia, with Clyde Moody in the radio band headed by Connie B. Gay, the **Radio Ranch Men**. This lasted until September of 1949 when he re-joined Monroe. (At that time, the **Blue Grass Boys** included Rudy Lyle, Mac Wiseman and Jack Thompson.) Wise stayed only about six months until Lester Flatt called him and asked him to join him and Earl Scruggs in their **Flatt and Scruggs and the Foggy Mountain Boys.** He stayed with Lester and Earl a short time, playing on WVLK, Versailles, Kentucky, and on Lexington's Kentucky Barn Dance. He recorded "I've Lost You," (written by Flatt and Everett Lilly) and "Jimmy Brown, the Newsboy."

After he quit **Flatt and Scruggs**, he stayed on in Washington, D.C., for a while, freelancing when he could. Though he was making a living with his music, it was nothing spectacular. During this period, he recorded "Mansion on the Hill"/"Honky Tonkin'" with Hank Williams. On posters and marquis where he would appear, his name would be referred to as "and many others." He and Rossie still refer to that era of their lives as the "many others" days. He ate a lot, drank a lot and played beautiful fiddle. At one point, he weighed 275 pounds.

In 1954, Wise moved to Nashville, joining **Hank Snow and the Rainbow Ranch Boys** until March 1970. During this most happy time in his career, he also played fiddle for Hylo Brown, Mac Wiseman, Red Allen, the **Stanley Brothers**, **Hazel and Alice** and Frank Wakefield.

After leaving Nashville in 1970, he went to Houston, Texas. His wife became his booking agent in addition to her job as a nurse. He worked rodeos, nightclubs, or anywhere else he could find a job. One day, Hank Williams Jr. called and asked him to join his band, but Chubby was tired of being a sideman and insisted on pursuing his music as a solo act. He spent seven years in Texas where he mastered Bob Wills' western swing, and he was a regular at Gilley's, the "Urban Cowboy" honky-tonk.

His health worsened, so he and Rossie decided to semi-retire to the Washington, D.C., area where he had fiddled for Clyde Moody. He returned to Florida in 1984, for his health...and it was home. Wise moved into in a nice, comfortable, mobile home trailer in Lake City, Florida, complete with pink flamingoes and a decorative wishing well. He lost 100 pounds after a gall bladder and pancreas illness that, in combination with emphysema, nearly killed him in 1987. Bluegrass musicians held benefits to help with his medical bills.

Still active on the bluegrass circuit in 1994, Wise gave the credit for his fame to two sources: God and Bill Monroe. "Whatever talent I got, God give it to me. And I learned bluegrass from Bill Monroe. I was nothing but a country fiddler before I went to work for Bill. Bluegrass was always my first love. As long as I'm alive and able to put that fiddle to my chin, I'll be cuttin' 'grass."

From a October 26, 1993, telephone conversation with Wise at his home in Florida.

Willis: I had a conversation with Carlton Haney some time ago and he talked about you a lot—about the early days with Bill Monroe, **Flatt and Scruggs** and stuff, and I wanted to find out if what he was saying was completely accurate. He kept on saying, "Well, why don't you call Chubby and find out if it's true?"

Wise: I'm pretty sure that it is because Carlton is really up on the bluegrass. You know, I started with Bill in 1943—which is about fifty years ago. As a matter of fact, one of Carlton's festivals is one of the first festivals I ever played! Berryville, Virginia, in '67. I believe they called it Watermelon Park. And I've been working festivals off and on for Carlton ever since. Of course, he hasn't promoted one in some time. But Carlton was a good bluegrass promoter, and I tell you what...if there's

America's Music | Bluegrass

anything you want to know about bluegrass, that's the man to talk to. Brother, he could tell you.

Willis: Well, he talks a lot about those first recordings with Bill Monroe and where you were also playing the guitar on them. Is that true?

Wise: That was some of Bill Monroe's bluegrass quartet. I played guitar on some of those things. I did play guitar on some of those gospel tunes. I don't remember which ones—I can't help you there but I remember that I did some of them. *(This is discussed more fully earlier in this biography.)*

Willis: And I asked Carlton if you were given credit on those Columbia tunes. Carlton said, "Not unless you ask him." So I'm asking you.

Wise: Yes, I was doing the guitar work there. And Flatt's name was on there. I played the fiddle on all of Bill Monroe's old Columbia 78s. Yessir! Not the bluegrass tunes—some of the gospel tunes I played guitar on, and I can't remember how many there were. But all his old Columbia 78s you hear a fiddle on, that's Chubby fiddlin'. When I quit, Benny Martin went to work for Bill. Howdy [Forrester] never did work for Bill again. I quit in '48. Clyde Moody and I went to the Washington area and went to work for Connie B. Gay, the promoter up there. He had a show called "Gay Time" at Constitution Hall. At that time, he had different artists: he had Pete Castle, you know the blind singer; Hank Penny, Grandpa Jones, Jimmy Dean, Billy Grammer, Roy Clark and a number of them on "Gay Time" in Arlington, Virginia, on WARL. That was back in 1948. Connie B. Gay did all that; as a matter of fact he kind of got country music started in that area. Let's give him credit on that. As you know, he's been dead for some time, but I don't guess they'd ever heard of country music in that area before Connie started it.

Willis: You came from a "swing" background before you joined Bill, didn't you?

Wise: It wasn't exactly swing, it was "country". I was with a group in Gainesville, Florida, called the **Jubilee Hillbillies** and we were on WRUF, a University of Florida radio station, and we had a daily show five days a week, Monday through Friday. And we did personal appearances and we did a lot of concerts and dance work in them days. It was all concerts and dance work. And we did a lot of country. We didn't do any bluegrass but we did some western swing—some of the Bob Wills tunes. And we did a lot of the old pop songs back then. If somebody, at a dance, wanted to hear "Stardust," why, we could play "Stardust" for them. If they wanted to hear "Wabash Cannonball" we could play that for them.

I'm not braggin', but we were versatile because we had to do it all! We had to perform school auditoriums and then turn around and play a dance. I really hadn't played bluegrass until I started with Bill.

Willis: Do you think that he taught you that "something" which we now know as "bluegrass"?

Wise: Yes, he did. He taught me to play bluegrass, Bill did. I'd never played bluegrass until I went to work for him.

Willis: Did it actually exist before Earl Scruggs joined?

Wise: Yea. That was before Earl. When I went to work for Bill, the late Clyde Moody was playin' the flattop and singin' with him. And Stringbean was playin' the five-string with us. And a gentleman named "Cousin Wilbur"—'cause Cousin Wilbur Wesbrooks was a comedian and played bass. And Howdy's wife, Billy. Some people called her "Sally Ann"—Wilene. She played accordion and sang with us. She was one of Bill's right-hand men. Of course, she sold tickets on the show. We was out under a tent when I worked for Bill.

Mr. Wise described the kind of music which Bill Monroe played in the early 1940s and earlier with his brother, Charlie.

Willis: Do you know where Mr. Monroe got the timing in his music we now know as bluegrass? Did he get it from the fields he worked when he was growing up?

Wise: No. Before he really played bluegrass, he and his brother Charlie—as the **Monroe Brothers**—sang a duet but it wasn't strictly bluegrass. It was kind of a mountain flavor but you couldn't call it "bluegrass". He didn't start bluegrass until, I don't think, until he went onto the Grand Ole Opry, really.

Wise died January 6, 1996.

Chubby Wise (L) and Charlie Cline, 1995.

Jim Shumate—
a consummate fiddler

Jim Shumate was born into a musical family October 21, 1921, and began playing the fiddle at twelve or thirteen there on the family farm in Wilkes County in northwest North Carolina. He already played banjo and guitar. After he bought recordings of Fiddlin' Arthur Smith he lay the other instruments aside.

Shumate said, "The fiddle is a very important instrument, and there's all kinds of music in it. If you can get it across to an audience that you're gonna get some of that music out of the fiddle, then they're gonna listen."[16] Shumate's fiddling resembles that of Fiddlin' Arthur Smith because of his long bow technique where the left hand does most of the work.

A technique of strengthening his left hand, which he feels gives him an advantage over some of the fiddlers today, frees "his arm and wrist for the pyrotechnical bluesy music which now characterizes his style." He described it. "I'd put the fiddle between my knees to hold it steady so my left hand would be free to slide up and down the fingerboard. That's something you can always rely on—to slide in and out of notes. If you put your upper finger in position first, then you can always gear in the lower finger in the slide."[17]

In early 1943, Bill Monroe first heard twenty year-old Shumate while he was performing on WHKY, Hickory, North Carolina, with Don Walker's **Blue Ridge Boys**. After fiddler Howdy Forrester left Monroe's band to join the Navy (October 1942), Carl Story took his place, followed by Chubby Wise and Floyd Ethridge. And in early 1945, Jim Shumate joined Monroe and stayed until Forrester came back after the War to claim his job (October 1945).

Shumate joined the **Blue Grass Boys** two or three weeks after Lester Flatt joined the band. "Lester and I was both kind of rookies together when we joined Bill."[18] Also with the **Blue Grass Boys** at that time was Stringbean (Dave Akeman) who played banjo. String and Shumate did a comedy act together.

Shumate soon learned that Monroe like to play in keys which were unfamiliar to most fiddlers. "Oh, my!" declared Mr. Shumate. "That was the first time I'd ever hit B or B flat and I'd never played anything in E 'til I got on the stage of the Opry. The one thing about Monroe, you didn't know what to expect. Sometimes when we was getting ready to play a tune, he'd whisper to me, 'This is going to be in B flat or B natural.' With Monroe, you had to be set and ready for anything. But one thing about him; he'd never let me down. He'd always kick it off with the mandolin, which gave me a chance to feel out the first verse and be ready, 'cause he'd always expect me to come in to kick off the second break. I had to do the second break—always. If there was any doubt in my mind, why, there was a look I'd give him and he'd take it himself, because he knew I wasn't ready. On some of those I'd never played—me being a rookie to start with—why, sometimes he'd have to make two rounds before I'd have it figured out. The one thing about it, you didn't practice with Bill. He'd check you out, I reckon, before he hired you." Shumate recalled that the only time he did rehearse was on "Are You Waiting Just For Me?" a popular Ernest Tubb recording. Monroe and Flatt had worked it up the night before they were to do it on the Opry. The song received acclaim and was imitated by other performers. "...The one thing about it, we set the pattern doing it on the Opry."[19]

Shumate was the first fiddler who introduced the policy of having the fiddle kickoff a tune.[20] Lester Flatt introduced him to that arrangement when Flatt and Monroe were having trouble with the kickoff of a song. Their timing was off. Shumate continued, "Lester said, 'Jim, see if you can kick that thing off with the fiddle.' He'd been hearing me in the background, I was kinda kicking it off a little. So I just kicked it off and when I wound up and turned him in, he hit that thing right on the button. So we kicked it off three more times before we hit the stage. And Man, it was right! From then on, we kicked off everything with the fiddle... If Monroe had something that he wanted to kick off, he did. If Lester

16 Robert Hefner, "Master Bluegrass Fiddler Jim Shumate," *Bluegrass Unlimited*, June, 1984, p. 36.

17 Ibid., p. 37.

18 Telephone interview, January 1993.

19 Erbsen, op. cit., pp. 17, 18.

20 In an interview for *Bluegrass Unlimited* in June of 1984, he elaborated on his earlier statement about the rhythmic shuffle introduction to a fiddle kickoff. "Far be it for me to say that nobody else had ever done the kick-off or anything else before. We just hadn't heard anybody else do it." p. 37.

had one he wanted to sing, Monroe left it usually up to the guys because he was straight with us. Bill was [straight] all the way through. If he thought we could handle one better the way we wanted to do it, why that's the way he let us do it. After all, if we flubbed, he was the one that took the rap."[21]

This period was so busy with music, baseball, booking, and traveling, that Monroe did not record from October 1941 to February 1945. They did, however, record transcriptions.[22]

In the summer of 1945, Monroe hired comedian Lew Childre. Stringbean and Childre worked up some comedy skits and became good buddies. "We hired Lew Childre to work with us on a tent show one season," said Shumate. "He was an actor, a good musician, dancer, this, that and the other. He and Stringbean got to fishin' together and they decided to come up with their own outfit—just the two of them working as a team. So Stringbean quit. Bill told me (when they were working down in Mississippi) that Stringbean was quittin' and asked me if I knew anybody in North Carolina that could play the banjo. I said, "Yeah, I know a fella, but he don't play Stringbean-style.'" Shumate referred to Earl Scruggs who lived in Shelby. Shumate had remembered Scruggs from a few years before. They were backstage in Hickory on Shumate's show (called "The Opry") when Scruggs was playing with Grady Wilkie who played guitar and sang.

When Childre and Stringbean left, it caused the event which would revolutionize Bill Monroe's music: the banjo spot was open so Monroe had to find another. They tried to fit clawhammer players in there (most of the banjo players of that era played similar to String) but their rhythms didn't seem to fit what Monroe was doing. After interviewing several of them, Monroe and Flatt were probably frustrated. Monroe *did* want the sound of the banjo in his band but couldn't find anyone who could play his rhythms—until Earl Scruggs.

Shumate got in touch with Scruggs who was playing in Nashville, touring with Lost John [Miller] and the **Allied Kentuckians**. Miller and his band were playing on a small Nashville station on which, as Shumate puts it, "Anybody could pick on the station if you was pretty good but you couldn't make the Opry, of course. I looked on the schedule—I was livin' at the Tulane Hotel at that time there in Nashville—so they was on the early morning [show], about five o'clock. So I went up the next morning and met Earl and asked if he would be interested in playin' with Bill. He said, 'Yes! I'd be interested.'"[23]

"Earl came down to the hotel room. I called Bill and he came over there and brought his mandolin. We took the mandolin, fiddle and banjo there in my room. That was a good get-together—we had a lot of fun. Earl was as nervous as all get out. Boy, he really laid timber to that banjo. Bill had never heard nothin' like that. I said, 'What do you think?' Bill said, 'Gosh, that's good. I'm gonna hire him.' So he went ahead and hired him... When Earl hit the stage, he really tore that place up."[24]

Scruggs fit right into Monroe's music and enhanced the sound in such a significant manner that the entire sound of what Monroe was doing began to change a bit. The "Monroe sound" didn't *completely* change, but it did evolve more toward what is now known as bluegrass music—and Scruggs seemed to be the catalyst. Too, Flatt's rhythm guitar was ideal for this change. And Wise's fiddle was ready for anything, having been an integral part of Monroe's band for several years now.

Scruggs' appearance on the Opry was without Shumate, however. Shumate had to give up his job when Forrester came back from the War to claim his job in late 1945. "When Howdy joined up, that left Bill with three fiddlers, Howdy, Birch Monroe, and myself. Birch had been singing bass on the gospel songs and fiddling old-time hoe-down numbers." The three fiddlers worked on stage together for a week before Shumate left for his North Carolina furniture business. When Shumate twin-fiddled with Forrester, he admitted he wasn't nearly as proficient as Forrester. Shumate always played lead, Forrester would second it.

"So I come on home—I had my notice in—and John Miller, he was playin' a stint back through Tennessee and back into Carolina. He said, 'If you'll play fiddle for me I'll give you a ride back and pay you good.' So I come to North Carolina that way. And Earl stayed up there as far as I know because the following Saturday night I tuned in he was with Bill on the Opry. He just tore the place up as usual."[25]

Shumate stayed active in music in Hickory when he joined **Dwight Barker and the Melody Boys** on WSJS-TV. He also managed a country music park and had his own bluegrass show on WHKY.

In January 1948, Lester and Earl left Monroe and soon formed their own **Foggy Mountain Boys** with Cedric Rainwater. After a short while as a trio, they added Jim Eanes as lead singer on WDVA in Danville, Virginia, for four to six weeks until Eanes got a call from Bill Monroe. The opportunity to play on the Opry for this ambitious twenty-five year-old musician was overwhelming so he left **Lester Flatt, Earl Scruggs and the Foggy Mountain Boys** for the big time. With

[21] Erbsen, op. cit., p. 18.

[22] Transcriptions were often entire shows which were recorded for airplay as if the band were actually there in the radio studio.

[23] Telephone interview, January, 1993.

[24] Erbsen, op. cit., p. 20.

[25] Telephone interview, January 1993.

Eanes gone, in March, they called Jim Shumate to join them on fiddle.

Shumate remembered, "Lester, Earl, and Cedric Rainwater came over to the house and said they'd pulled out from Bill and were organizing their own show and were going to call it the **'Foggy Mountain Boys.'** They said they were going to use 'Foggy Mountain Top' as the theme song and they needed me to play the fiddle. I debated around awhile because I really didn't want to, but I thought, well, since they went to all this trouble I may as well. So we decided to just split down the board. Lester said they were going to need one more man[26] so they were going to hire Mac Wiseman; I'd never met Mac. So we got set up and did our first program over WHKY in Hickory. I think we worked a week there. We went from there to WCYB in Bristol, Virginia, and there we set the woods on fire. Everywhere we went we turned them away. We played everywhere—at school houses, ball parks, auditoriums, and airports."[27] Wiseman acted as their bookkeeper. And because he could type, he was responsible for answering fan mail as well as the band bookings.

"We had no trouble at all getting work. Goodness gracious! If we did anything, we turned 'em down." They soon signed with Mercury Records. Shumate quit **Flatt and Scruggs and the Foggy Mountain Boys**, about the last of 1948, while they were at WCYB. Benny Sims took his place. Just after Shumate left the **Foggy Mountain Boys**, he played fiddle for about a week with the **Stanley Brothers** when Leslie Keith left; they soon hired Art Wooten on a more permanent basis.[28] After Shumate quit the Opry and the professional circuit limelight in the late 1940s, he kept a slower pace of performing. His 1980 solo album was "Bluegrass Fiddler Supreme."

In 1984, Shumate talked about his business, "Now, Joe Blow can cut a record. Back then, people seemed more particular. The one thing I regret in all my business is that I didn't cut a record with Bill Monroe because to me he was just a prince of a man, and I know I would have thoroughly enjoyed it."[29]

As of 1995, Shumate lived in Hickory, still played occasionally, and recorded for Heritage Records. He retired from working in a local furniture store. An early 1990s recording was chosen for inclusion into the Library of Congress. In June 1995, he received the Folk Heritage Award from the North Carolina Arts Council.

Jim Shumate tells of fiddlers Lester Woody, Leslie Keith, Buck Ryan and fiddling contests

About 1948, Jim Shumate was Lester Woody's fiddle instructor. The Stanley brothers asked Shumate to play fiddle with them. Shumate had to decline but referred Lester Woody of Valdese, North Carolina. "They come to hire me but I didn't want to go back to work right then so they asked me if I knew of any fiddlers anywhere. I said, 'Well, yes. I knew a good one.' Me and Lester played here at Hickory together. We did a lot of twin-fiddling together. He was kind of startin' out. I guess you could say we kind of learned together but he

Buck Ryan

was quite a bit younger than me. So I sent him Lester and he went with 'em and done a real good job, I understand. Yea, Lester turned out to be a real good fiddler."[30]

"That [Leslie] Keith was some fiddler," said Mr. Shumate. "But the worst I ever saw Keith hurt was when I beat him in a fiddler's convention. He'd take that 'Black Mountain Blues' and win every convention in the country. He could do that thing. When a man writes a song, it's his, you know, and he could handle it like nobody else. So we did a show at the National Fiddler's Convention at Richlands, Virginia, in 1948. We had Buck Ryan on the program who was playing fiddle for Jimmie Dean at the time, Leslie Keith, who was doing a show out of Bristol, Chubby Wise and myself. I was fiddling with Lester and Earl. There was a huge crowd—about 9,000 best I can remember.

"They run a fiddler's convention sort of like a beauty contest. They started off and matched to see who was going to go first, and I came out last. I usually like to get in the middle, or pretty close to first. That gives you a chance to pick your tune. I would have picked 'Orange Blossom' if I could have got on first. But Chubby Wise got to play first, so he played 'Orange Blossom.' Keith came up next and he did the 'Black Mountain Blues.' Then Buck Ryan came up and did 'Listen to the Mockingbird.' He really laid the timber to that thing—he could really play it. So I said, 'Cedric

[26] Actually, in a different interview with Mr. Shumate, he said that the foursome debated on whether to hire a woman or a man.

[27] Erbsen, op. cit., p. 21.

[28] This date may be when Mr. Shumate was on a vacation from Flatt and Scruggs. Mr. Shumate couldn't recall, in 1995, which it was.

[29] Hefner, op. cit., p. 37.

[30] Telephone interview with Jim Shumate, January 1993. Woody managed a radio station in Alta Vista, Virginia, well into the 1980s.

(Rainwater), what in the dickens am I going to play?' He said, 'Play the "Lee Highway Blues" and them fellows can't touch you with a ten foot pole.' That made me feel more confident, because those boys were good fiddlers—they were the best. So I played 'Lee Highway' and just laid them boys in the shade. So the first round the judges dropped off Keith. The next round they dropped off Chubby. The next one they dropped off Ryan, and that left me standing there. That made me feel good. I'd taken that thing by a landslide.

"I remember that Mac Wiseman backed up all of us on guitar. That way, they'd have no feudin'. Nobody could say, 'If I just had so and so behind me I could have won.' The only disadvantage I could see to those guys was that Mac was working with us at that time and he knew that 'Lee Highway' up onc side and down the other. Every time I'd turn, he'd be right there. So that was a lick in my favor, too."[31]

Leslie Keith

This pioneer bluegrass fiddler began fiddling about 1928 at age eleven. When he got his own fiddle at age nineteen, he played square dances and concerts. His mentors were Fiddlin' John Carson and Doc Roberts. During the Depression, Keith and his partner hoboed a lot, singing and playing for their supper.

Keith's "Black Mountain Blues" became very popular and was recorded by fiddlers Curly Fox and Tommy Magness under the name, "Black Mountain Rag." Keith used this tune in fiddle contests where he competed frequently and even held his own contest in early 1938 when he and Joe Woods decided to hold a fiddlers' contest near Bluefield, West Virginia. The main attraction was a challenge of competition against Fiddlin' Arthur Smith of the Opry who was easily the biggest contest draw at that time. Smith was paid $100 plus bus fare. The word of the competition got out. Twenty-seven fiddlers competed and 9,400 people paid 25 or 50 cents each for admission. Leslie Keith recalled, "We started the contest about 12:30 and before long everyone was weeded out except me and Smith. The thing was judged by applause meter and the people who heard Smith on the Grand Ole Opry was rooting for him and the people from all over West Virginia was rooting for me. He played 'Listen to the Mockingbird,' 'Bucking Mule' and 'Bonaparte's Retreat' the first time around. I played two tunes—I don't remember what they were—and then I played 'Black Mountain Blues.' After we'd tied three times, the people wanted us to play a fourth tune. And we tied again. Just left it at that."[32]

Leslie Keith's main recognition in bluegrass fiddling came from his two years with the **Stanley Brothers and the Clinch Mountain Boys**, beginning in late 1946, when he took the place of Bobby Sumner. But Keith, now famous for his "Black Mountain Blues (Rag)," had to be talked into accepting the job. Carter promised an equal cut between himself, Ralph, and Pee Wee Lambert. While Carter was on the phone, Carter's father grabbed the phone and said, "I'll tell you, Les. You come and get with these boys and if you don't make as much money as you think you ought to, why, I'll make the difference up out of my own pocket."[33] He joined, making the next day's noon show.[34] Their first gig on tour paid $2.35. Keith slept with his feet out the window every night to be hoarse enough in the morning to sing bass. They always played to a full house, making up to $400 each night. The bass fiddle rode on the top of the Chevrolet their father had bought for them. They played six to seven nights per week, traveling all the year round, many miles daily.

In 1948, Keith lost his position to a faster fiddler, Jim Shumate, recently with Bill Monroe. Also, the Stanley brothers wanted a fiddler who could emulate the bluegrass style of Bill Monroe—which was becoming very popular. Shumate was actually full-time with **Flatt and Scruggs** at the time and filled-in only until the Stanleys could find a more permanent fiddler. They found Art Wooten, who also had the considerable speed of a bluegrass fiddler and was a former **Blue Grass Boys** member.

Keith joined Curley King (guitar) and his **Curley King Band**[35] awhile, then followed this with a brief stint with the **Blue Sky Boys**, and with Slim Whitman on KWKH, Shreveport.

He retired from music in 1957, and later had a heart operation which inhibited his ability to get his fiddling up to speed. He made Tucson, Arizona, his home in the '70s and played in two bands during that time: **Leslie Keith and His Boys** and the **Pima County Blues Chasers**. Leslie C. Keith died of a heart disorder on December 28, 1978. He was 71.

Benny Martin— from truancy to fame

Benny Martin was one of **Flatt and Scruggs'** fiddlers in the early 1950s and helped create the sound we know today as "bluegrass music". He recorded on the group's first session with Curly Seckler and Jody Rainwater on November 9, 1952. He helped solidify the

[31] Erbsen, op. cit., p. 23.

[32] Bob Sayers, "Leslie Keith: Black Mountain Odyssey," *Bluegrass Unlimited*, December, 1976, p. 15.

[33] Ibid..

[34] The Stanley Brothers band had a bluegrass sound even though Ralph didn't play three-finger style yet. And Carter was just learning Lester Flatt's strokes. Their comedian was Cousin Winesap.

[35] With Don Campbell (electric Hawaiian guitar) and Dick Leonard (bass).

Flatt and Scruggs sound during his time with the band when he recorded on "Flint Hill Special," "Why Did You Wander" and others.

Young Martin preferred fiddling to school, so at age fourteen he moved to Nashville to ply his trade on WLAC radio with **Big Jeff and the Radio Playboys.**[36] He met numerous people there who would lead him to jobs with such notables as Hank Williams, Flatt and Scruggs and a contract with Mercury Records (and later CMH).

During the early '50s, his manager was Colonel Tom Parker, who also managed Elvis Presley. Martin recalled, "Tom Parker was my manager when he took on Elvis. I went along with Elvis' early shows. We opened up in Richmond, Virginia, and had [from twenty to thirty-five] dates right down the East Coast. And then 'Heartbreak Hotel' came along. We found that song with Mae Axton there in Jacksonville, Florida, and I brought it to Buddy Killen [at Tree Music], and Elvis got it from there."[37]

Martin opened up for Elvis frequently, but the audience was there to see Elvis. Parker once asked Martin to help keep Elvis' fans from charging the stage, but when he saw the fire in their eyes, he stepped aside and let them go.

In the early 1960s, Martin worked at the Famous club in Washington, D.C.. When the festivals became active, he was hired at many of them. He arrived at the events a little earlier than he was scheduled to play and hired a back-up band from those he met there.

Martin is the inventor of the eight-string fiddle in 1952. Another who owns one of these is John Hartford. Martin plays about fifteen tunes on the very difficult instrument.

After a short period of partnership with Don Reno in 1965, Martin went on to record many LPs with Flying Fish and CMH from 1975 to 1980.

Martin gave an insight on managers and his misfortune, "I've had thirteen personal managers and a whole lot of parasites (Tom Parker was a *good* one, he acknowledged). I guess I've been rolled more than any other person who's fifty-four years old. I've been robbed twelve major times right here in Nashville. I woke up in 1975 with not a fiddle to play on. A person can destroy himself and not even realize he's doing it."[38]

Martin makes occasional public appearances into the 1990s. He lives in the Nashville area.

Paul Warren—
"The World's Greatest
Breakdown Fiddler"[39]

Paul Warren, of Lyles, Tennessee, grew up listening to Fiddlin' Arthur Smith on the Opry during the 1930s. Each time he heard Smith on his neighbor's battery-powered radio, he tried to hum the melody long enough to be able to apply it to his own fiddle when he got home. Warren excelled in the old-time, double-stop breakdowns. Lance LeRoy remembered him, "His noting and bowing were always accurate and incisive, and he was superb at playing with blinding speed if the tune called for it. His greatest characteristics were his ability to retain the piquant and stimulating 'old-time' flavor of a breakdown or country jig, while at the same time applying flawless professionalism and dogmatically insisting on learning what he felt was the most authentic version of the melody line of each tune through every means available to him. It's doubtful if the storied Uncle Jimmy Thompson, the Opry's first fiddler, knew more old fiddle tunes." Neil V. Rosenberg further described Warren's playing. Though "not the hot fiddler that Benny Martin was, he was very good at the old-time tunes which he and Scruggs would sometimes feature with banjo and fiddle alone, and he was a solid and steady musician for providing backup on every kind of country song."[40]

Warren joined **Flatt and Scruggs and the Foggy Mountain Boys** as fiddler on February 16, 1954, replacing Benny Martin.[41] Warren stayed with **Flatt and Scruggs** until its breakup in 1969, recording over 250 songs with them on Columbia. Then he chose to join the more traditional **Lester Flatt and the Nashville Grass.** From the time he joined Flatt in 1954, he had played continuously with him for twenty-five years until Flatt died in 1979. Through the phenomenal touring exposure of **Flatt and Scruggs**, Warren became the most widely-heard fiddler in bluegrass music.

Paul Warren died in Nashville January 12, 1978, at the age of fifty-nine.

---

36 According to Art Menius, Big Jeff and his wife owned Tootsie's Orchid Lounge beside the Ryman. Lots of great players started with Jeff's hillbilly boogie band.

37 Edward Morris, "Benny Martin Profile," *Bluegrass Unlimited*, January, 1984, p. 23. Also, according to Art Menius, Parker managed Hank Snow, but dumped Snow for Elvis.

38 Ibid.

39 This is the title of a 1979 CMH LP "Paul Warren with Lester Flatt and the Nashville Grass—America's Greatest Breakdown Fiddle Player." Warren never recorded his own solo album. This record is a selection from Lance LeRoy's personal collection of those tunes taped by LeRoy at various Nashville Grass recordings from February 1969 to February 1976.

40 Neil V. Rosenberg, liner notes for the Bear Family four disc set, "Flatt and Scruggs 1948-1959."

Tex Logan—
the man who wrote "Christmas Time's A-Coming"

This West Texas fiddler has had a substantial influence on bluegrass music of the northeastern United States. While performing there with the **Lilly Brothers**, Tex became influential to a young, new generation of New England area bluegrass players who would have their own impact in the music. These men included Peter Rowan, Jim Rooney, Joe Val and Bill Keith.

Benjamin "Tex" Logan was born in Coahoma, Texas, in 1927 and started playing fiddle during his last year in high school. He remembered how he suddenly became enamored with the fiddle, "It suddenly hit me one day; I remember it very plainly. Going home from school, suddenly I had a feeling in my arm. The big thing is the bow. You've got to have that rhythm in the bow or know what to do with the bow. I could feel it, and I went in the bedroom, shut myself in there, got my fiddle out. I hadn't played in a long time and kind of played, kept sawing around until I could kind of play 'Arkansas Traveler.' That's how I got going pretty good."[42] Logan was highly influenced by the fiddle playing of Tommy Magness (who played the original "Muleskinner Blues" and "Katy Hill" with Monroe in 1940), and he also liked Curly Fox. From his father's fiddling, Tex's playing became "mountain-style" rather than the western swing and Texas contest-style of fiddling which was so prevalent in the area.

In 1947, after graduation from Texas Tech University in what was probably his first professional job, Logan played fiddle with **Jerry and Sky and the Melody Men**[43], so much so that he requested a reduction in his course studies and resigned as research assistant for Boston's Massachusetts Institute of Technology (M.I.T.). He faced this fiddle versus college dilemma until he eventually received a doctorate degree in engineering. He left **Jerry and Sky** in 1948 and went home to Texas where he played weekends with **Hoyle Nix and His West Texas Cowboys**.

In 1948, he was the fiddler with the **Lilly Brothers** on WWVA, Wheeling, West Virginia. Also at the station was **Red Belcher and the Kentucky Ridgerunners**[44]. Logan fiddled for this band, too. This was probably the first bluegrass music he played (until this time, he had played mostly old-time music and western swing). Soon after this, he switched to **Hawkshaw Hawkins and Big Slim, the Lone Cowboy**.

Logan returned to M.I.T. in 1949 to finish his degree, simultaneously fiddling for the **Lane Brothers** (Pete and Frank, whose real name was Locanto), an old-time country band in Cambridge. Logan. The band helped popularize country music on WCOP in Boston and helped start the Hayloft Jamboree on the station. They performed as many as seven nights a week at clubs like the Hillbilly Ranch.

Logan was awarded a bachelor's (and later a master's) degree in electrical engineering from M.I.T. in

Three famous fiddlers (L to R): Charlie Cline, Tex Logan and Byron Berline. Author is in the background. Berline was telling the story of how he recently (1995) got Bill Monroe and Earl Scruggs together to play "Sally Anne" on his latest CD.

---

[41] He was a seasoned veteran by the time he joined, having been with Johnnie and Jack beginning in 1938 (for thirteen years with the group) and having recorded on RCA Victor, standards such as "Poison Love" and "Ashes of Love" with the non-bluegrass group. That group joined the Grand Ole Opry in 1952.

[42] 1989 interview with Alan Munde and Joe Carr for their *Prairie Nights to Neon Lights* (Lubbock, Texas: Texas Tech University Press, 1995), pp. 104-105.

[43] The resonator guitar player was Ralph Q. Jones who later built resonator guitars. Jerry Howorth and Sky Snow had a popular country music act in the Boston area.

[44] Which consisted of Red Belcher (clawhammer banjo, emcee), Smilie "Crazy Elmer" Sutter (bass) and Logan (fiddle).

1951, and eventually received his PhD. at Columbia University in New York. In October, he joined **Wilma Lee and Stoney Cooper** on WWVA. Josh Graves, who was also a member of the band at the time, introduced Logan to Bill Monroe at a large concert in Baltimore. Logan had written "Christmas Time's A-Coming" two years earlier and offered it there for Monroe to record. Monroe liked it and offered to record it with Logan on fiddle. But a car problem kept him from the recording session. Monroe's regular fiddler, Gordon Terry, recorded it.

Logan described how the song came about, "I was working out of WWVA, Wheeling, West Virginia, in 1948, with Red Belcher and the **Lilly Brothers**. It was the first year of my life I had not been home for Christmas. Riding through the bleak, rolling hills of Ohio, covered with snow and coal dust, making personal appearances, my thoughts returned to home and Christmas. It was then, in the back seat of Red Belcher's Hudson, that I composed the lyrics to 'Christmas Time's A-Comin'.' The **Lilly Brothers** and I did the song a number of times on WWVA but I expressly wrote it for Bill Monroe. The thought of him hitting the high tenor on that song gave me chill bumps."[45]

In the fall of 1952, Logan was in a band with Don Stover on banjo and the Lilly brothers, Everett and "B." Everett had just left **Flatt and Scruggs** to re-join his brother in their own group in Boston. They called themselves the **Confederate Mountaineers** and, dressed in Confederate uniforms, they were the first Boston-based bluegrass band. They played on WCOP and at the Hillbilly Ranch. Logan left Boston in 1956 to work at Bell Labs in New Jersey. He and the Lillys continued to play festivals and occasional shows for many years. He played on Mike Seeger's important "Mountain Music Bluegrass Style" LP which is acknowledged as being the first of its kind in bluegrass music.

In 1978, Tex formed a band with Pete Rowan called the **Green Grass Gringos** featuring Lamar Grier on banjo and Barry Mitterhoff on mandolin. The **Gringos** broke up in 1983. Tex then organized the **Northeast Seaborn Band** with Danny Weiss (guitar), Barry Mitterhoff (mandolin), John Carlini (guitar) and Larry Cohen (bass). After this band, Tex then joined forces with Jimmy Arnold for about two years. In 1994, he retired from Bell Labs to his home in Madison, New Jersey.

Bobby Hicks— from Bill Monroe to Ricky Skaggs

Bobby Hicks is one of bluegrass' fiddling legends. Born July 21, 1933, in Newton, North Carolina, he was the only one in his family who chose to pursue music as a career. He became interested in this music from listening to the Grand Ole Opry on Saturday nights; he began playing fiddle at age eight. As early as 1948, he was making a name for himself when he recorded with Jim Eanes and Hubert Davis. While he was experimenting with the fiddle, "I used to take my fiddle apart. I took the strings off of it, dropped the bridge and everything. I put it all back together and tuned it exactly to "A"—without a pitch pipe or anything, because my ear was so used to hearing that key. I guess you'd call that perfect pitch; I can't do it now, but I used to. I think I lost the knack from using a tuner. You use a tuner for so long you get so you depend on it."[46]

In the early fifties, he recorded on Jim Reeves's "Am I Losing You?" which became his first #1 hit. He helped form the **Flint Hill Playboys**, but his next move was to gain him tremendous fame within the bluegrass world: he joined **Bill Monroe and the Blue Grass Boys** in 1954. Here he recorded the well-known instrumental standards "Cheyenne," "Big Mon," "Monroe's Hornpipe" (these three were recorded solo), "Scotland" and "Panhandle Country" (these two were recorded with Kenny Baker), "Roanoke" and "Wheel Hoss" (with Charlie Cline), "Stoney Lonesome" (with Charlie Smith) and "Tall Timber" (with Gordon Terry and Vassar Clements). Hicks recalled that Monroe "spent a lot of time teaching me how to play, and I really give all the credit of what I know to Bill. I learned the correct way to play bluegrass music from him. I learned a lot about my own instrument from him and how to put the music together instrumentally to make everything fit where it sounded and felt right. I learned when and when not to play and how to work around the vocals. He didn't tell me when or where to play but he'd give me some idea of what he wanted me to play in some places or how he wanted it to sound. He would try to get a sound with his mandolin that he wanted to hear from the fiddle. He didn't lay anything down note-for-note; he would leave that up to me. He would play the song, and if there was one specific place he wanted a certain sound, like if he wanted a long bow here or something else there, he would tell me. I just learned by listening to him play."[47] Hicks and Tater Tate played

[45] John Holder, "Christmas Time's A-Comin'," *Bluegrass Unlimited*, December, 1982, p. 60.

[46] From a September 1995 interview at IBMA.

[47] Traci Todd, "Bobby Hicks—an Interview," *Acoustic Musician*, September, 1995, p. 23.

twin-fiddles with Monroe's band just before Hicks left the band in the summer of 1956 when he was drafted. Kenny Baker took his place with the band.

Back from the military in 1958, and again with Monroe, times were hard for bluegrass music. He was happy with Monroe but just wasn't making enough money so he joined Porter Wagoner in the spring of 1960. But the pay wasn't much better there than with Bill Monroe, so in 1962, Hicks left to join the touring band of country singer Judy Lynn, taking the place of Buddy Spicher. He was featured often on the fiddle tunes in the band's repertoire. It was at this time (1963) that he began using a low "C" fifth string to his fiddle, bringing a new dimension to his fiddling, enabling it to sound like a viola. This idea was that of fiddler Johnny Gimble of **Bob Wills and the Texas Playboys.** When Hicks brought it back to bluegrass music, he became *the* person who popularized it in bluegrass. Hicks arranged many of Lynn's songs and stayed with Judy Lynn's country band until he tired of touring and moved to Reno, Nevada, where he formed his own band in 1971. Hicks chose Reno because he knew the area, the hotels and the people there from touring there earlier with Judy Lynn. He and his new **Bobby Hicks Band** played regularly at the Hee Haw Nevada Club and the Bit and Spur Club.[48] This lasted until 1975 when he quit his Reno band and moved to Greensboro, North Carolina, where he cared for his ailing mother.

When he got back into the bluegrass festival scene in 1977, he soon discovered that he had become a legend. He began teaching fiddle, guitar, banjo and mandolin to as many as sixty students at a time. He began doing festivals on weekends, became the top billing of the groups with whom he played, and recorded on many albums during this period.

1978 marked the first time Hicks recorded solo project.[49] In 1981, he joined up with the **Ricky Skaggs Band.** On stage, Skaggs and Hicks continuously changed instruments to show their tremendous versatility. Playing with Skaggs was a fun job (and still is, as of 1996) and he recorded with other artists during this period. He recorded on the "Bluegrass Album" (released in 1981, volume one and two) and on Doyle Lawson's **Quicksilver** albums. In April of 1982, Ricky Skaggs' hit single "Crying My Heart Out Over You" featured Bobby Hicks on fiddle and reached number one on the *Billboard* charts, and that year, Skaggs was inducted into the Grand Ole Opry. Their early 1990s recording of "Wheel Hoss" won a Grammy. Hicks, in 1996, appeared as a featured guest on CNN's "Prime Time Country" television show. He continued studio recording and occasional public appearances.

"Working in the country music field," said Hicks, "has always paid better than when I was in bluegrass." Hicks continues to be an important sideman in Skaggs' **Kentucky Thunder** band, but he will always be remembered for his contributions to bluegrass music of the 1950s.

Vassar Clements

Vassar Clements—
the jazz bluegrass fiddler

One of the more incredible fiddlers in bluegrass music is Vassar Clements. His five Grammy nominations and 2,000 recording performances are just part of his fifty years in music. When fiddlers reach a certain point of excellence in the command of their instrument, fans begin to prefer one musician over the other because of their style. (Certainly, the style of Kenny Baker is different than that of Clements, for example, and a fan may prefer one style over the other.) Technically, Vassar may not be any better than other fine fiddlers, but Vassar's style of bluegrass music has cemented his sound in the annals of its history. It's not old-time, nor is his style a clone of any fine fiddling you can hear in bluegrass. It is basically jazz. Its creativeness and improvisational characteristics are unique and therefore deserve careful attention.

Vassar Clements was born April 25, 1928, in Kinard, Florida. At age six, he got a guitar. But when he soon began playing the fiddle, he found it more challenging and decided to stay with it. His mother allowed him to stay up late and listen on their battery-operated radio to Chubby Wise on the Opry with the **Blue Grass Boys.** Wise became Vassar's first major influence on the fiddle and he feels Wise was the smoothest player, could get the most out of bluegrass music, and was the "all-time greatest bluegrass fiddler". In a 1992 phone interview,

---

[48] Bobby had played a few shows at Harrah's while he was touring with Judy Lynn but he did not play there after he left Judy and formed the Bobby Hicks Band.

[49] His "Texas Crapshooter" LP on County Records had one side bluegrass and the other swing music. The bluegrass side included himself (five-string fiddle), Sam Bush (mandolin), Alan Munde (banjo), Roland White (guitar) and Roy Huskey Jr. (bass). The swing side included Buddy Emmons, Buck White (piano), Bucky Barrett (electric lead guitar), Bruce Nemerov (acoustic rhythm guitar), Joe Allen (electric bass) and Karl Himmel (drums). County released it on compact disc in 1993 (CO-CD-27061)

Vassar related that Chubby "had the prettiest tone I ever heard."

Clements' major exposure to music in Florida was big-band swing music. This music was his most significant influence toward his style for which he later became known. "I had to teach myself," he told this writer. "I didn't really have anybody to show me. I didn't know how to hold the bow or how to tune. To start with, I just tried to get the bow to where it wouldn't squeak. It was maybe a year before I could get it to one end and change without noticing it. I really felt real good about that and then it dawned on me that I had to move my fingers and get something that made sense. So the tunes that I would hear and get in my head [were learned strictly by ear—and very slowly]."

Vassar's experience with Bill Monroe began when he was a teen. Millie Clements, who handles Vassar's business matters and is Vassar's historian, said, "Vassar played the Opry with Monroe when he was fourteen. Monroe is just like family to Vassar; he's just like a daddy. And he always has been. You see, Chubby Wise and Vassar's stepfather were good friends. And Bill used to come out to his mother's house and play. And Vassar played guitar then. I don't imagine he was very good at that age, but that was his first instrument and he was playin'. So, one time, they let him sit in with them down there when they were pickin' there at the house. And after that, every time they'd come to town, Vassar'd get out there and watch 'em from the outside. He couldn't go into the beer joints 'cause he was too little to go in. He'd stand outside and look inside."

In 1949, at twenty-one, Clements learned that Bill Monroe was looking for a fiddle player, so he took the bus to audition for Monroe, unannounced. Clements told that "by the time I got to the Opry in Nashville all I had was my return ticket and enough change to buy a box of crackers or something. I had probably one or two changes of clothes and I didn't even have my fiddle. I had bought an old fiddle for about $3.50 and it was stolen from me at the bus station when I left it behind the counter for a while. I caught the bus anyway. You know when you are younger you don't think about it that much. So as it turned out when I got here, Monroe had one and I used his.

Vassar Clements

"So I waited out back of the Opry for Monroe. And after he finished playing, I went up to him and told him that I could play the fiddle. Shoot, I was still in school at the time! Anyway, he said he'd give me a tryout. And when he named off the tunes, they were the ones I'd learned by listening to Chubby—just lucky, I guess. So he ended up hiring me."[50] "He asked me if I had any money. I said no. He asked me if I had a place to stay. I said no. And so he gave me $20 and told me to go to the hotel with these other guys. And that's the way that started."[51] So Clements began playing fiddle with the **Blue Grass Boys**[52], his first real job just out of high school. Vassar was in and out of this band until 1967.

Vassar's first recording with Monroe was in 1949. A subsequent tune, "Brown County Breakdown," was actually written by Vassar. Monroe, as the leader of the band, simply took the tune and put his name on it. Vassar also wrote the music to "Uncle Pen." In 1957, Clements joined **Jim and Jesse** in Live Oak, Florida (taking the place of Joe Meadows).[53] Gordon Terry replaced Vassar in Monroe's band.

During the period from 1959 to October of 1962, Clements worked occasionally with Rual Yarbrough and Jake Landers and the **Dixie Gentlemen** in the tri-cities of Muscle Shoals, Florence, and Tuscumbia, Alabama. He recorded on "The Country Style of the Dixie Gentlemen" on the United Artists label. During the period between 1962 until 1967, Clements worked mostly out of music with a potato chip franchise in Tallahassee, Florida. In 1962, Vassar and Millie began dating and Millie hired him as a bass player for a band (rock and roll) which Millie was managing. They married soon after.

He joined Faron Young's band in 1967. His time with this country singer allowed him to develop his own style which became more improvisational than specifically bluegrass or jazz. He left in February 1971.

At this period in the history of bluegrass and country music, very few groups used a fiddle—it was not at all popular. Millie Clements continued, "They just wouldn't use the fiddle unless it was something on the Opry which was some hard-core, traditional sawing, old-timey stuff. A good example would be the way Roy Acuff played the fiddle. That was the kind of fiddlin' which was goin' on." The groups of Ray Price and Faron

[50] Rick Gartner and George Gruhn, "Vassar Clements, the Superbow Instinct," *Frets*, July, 1984, p. 15.

[51] Phone interview, 1992.

[52] Also with the band when Clements joined were Rudy Lyle (banjo), Mac Wiseman (guitar) and Jack Thompson (bass). Jimmy Martin was traveling with the band but hadn't yet started playing with the band.

[53] Jim Buchanan took his place when he left Jim and Jesse in 1961.

[54] With Martin (guitar), Vic Jordan (banjo), Bill Yates (bass) and Gloria Belle (bass).

Young used the fiddle, but few others. Vassar took up the tenor banjo and played Dixieland jazz in a place which resembled a pizza parlor: the Dixie Landing Club. He played bass there too, as well as occasional fiddle, from May to October of 1969. There in Nashville, he did what pickup session work he could. In Nashville, about the same time, Vassar worked a dozen or so gigs with Jimmy Martin's **Sunny Mountain Boys**.[54]

From February through October of 1971, Clements further stretched his style while playing in John Hartford's **Dobrolic Plectral Society** with Norman Blake and Tut Taylor. With Monroe, he did studio sessions for bluegrass music; with Faron Young, his sessions were country music; with Hartford, the doors opened to all kinds of music. Hartford was very popular at the time because of his "Gentle on My Mind" record.

When he left the **Society**, Clements joined Earl Scruggs and helped form his **Earl Scruggs Revue**. He also played with Dickie Best. Then he did the "Will the Circle Be Unbroken" LP (1971) where Vassar was hired by **Nitty Gritty Dirt Band** and John and Bill McEuen after a recommendation from Earl Scruggs. "Vassar had been doing *some* session work," continued Millie, "but when somebody tells you to mark off a period of *days* for a session, it kind of blows your mind! It ended up taking about two and a half weeks. Anyway, it wound up [that] Vassar did every session except for four. And that was when Merle Travis cut some and he had to go back on the road with Earl." The "Old and in the Way" LP followed on October 8, 1973. Vassar left the **Revue** in this year.

In 1973, Vassar and Millie formed the **Vassar Clements Band**[55] which began recording on Mercury. It included many electrified instruments and drums to accentuate his desire to have more rhythm—which he felt was missing from standard bluegrass instrumentation. With his new band, he avoided being restricted by the confines of what Nashville thought his sound should be. His band played jazz-rock with country roots, in addition to bluegrass. Because he had drums, he had to have electrified instruments to be heard. "With these people [which] I got together, it just gelled and worked out right. So no matter what kind of instrumentation we had didn't mean, really, I was leaving any form of music. I was just adding a lot more to it. And as far as losing the bluegrass audience—they never let me know that [I had lost them]. A lot of them came to see me and ask me what am I doing and what kind of music is that. They said, 'That's not bluegrass.' I said, 'What tune do you want to hear?' If they said, 'Little Maggie,' I'd play it. And I just said, 'This is just the way we play it now.' And I figure if I lost any, I gained 'em back—if not by the music, [it was] bein' nice to 'em and explain what I

was doin'. I was doin' the same things Ricky [Skaggs] was doin' in the eighties. My ambition was to do all kinds of things. You don't want to just learn one thing and quit learnin'. I still ain't quit learnin'."[56]

The first tour of the **Vassar Clements Band**, in 1974, was set up by Keith Case of Casino Artists at the time. Case soon started Stone County and later moved to Nashville and formed Keith Case and Associates.

Clements doesn't read music, allowing what he feels and hears to dominate his style. Banjoist Alan Munde spoke of Vassar, "It's real interesting and exciting just to watch him. It's hard to know where he's going. You just have to keep your eye on where you are; where you're supposed to be. If you go with him, you might never find your way back!"[57] He's the type of player who improvises at almost all times, who cannot play the same tune twice the same way. As of 1997, Vassar and Millie Clements live in Hermitage, Tennessee.

Paul Mullins

Paul "Moon" Mullins and Traditional Grass

There are some figures in this music who were at the right place at the right time to influence not only the music, but also potential musicians and bluegrass lovers. Paul Mullins was tremendously influential on both counts because of his varied experience as a fiddler through the years, and for his time in the broadcast media. People who heard him in either setting were exposed to a true pioneer at work. This is his story.

Paul Mullins was born in Frenchburg, Menifee County, in eastern Kentucky. The folks who come from that area of the country are known as "Briarhoppers".

---

[55] Members were Vassar, Bob Hoban (piano), Doug Jernigan (steel), Clay Caire (drums) and Mr. McBride (bass).

[56] Telephone interview, May, 1992. Vassar's reference to Ricky Skaggs meant that Vassar's new music was similar to what made Skaggs famous: with the same instrumentation, it was up-tempo, and doing bluegrass music with non-bluegrass instrumentation.

[57] George A. Gretia, "Friday Morning with Alan Munde," *Bluegrass Unlimited*, July, 1987, p. 25.

This was the poorest area of the state where the only industries were squirrel hunting, making whiskey, raising tobacco and making molasses. He began playing guitar in his early teens.

In 1955, Mullins (18) joined the Army. During his stint in the Communications branch in Alaska, he learned how to play the fiddle, mandolin, and improved on the guitar. His inspiration to play fiddle was through Bob Bolden and Bill Moore, two very good fiddlers who provided Mullins the proper role model for a young person interested in pursuing the instrument. Shortly after leaving the Army in 1958, Mullins played in a little band near Monticello, Kentucky. Carter Stanley saw him perform, offered him a job, and Mullins soon began as fiddler for the **Stanley Brothers**.

In January 1959, Mullins and the **Stanley Brothers** moved to Live Oak, Florida. He remembered that "As good as Carter and Ralph were, and have only fifteen people show up, kills you—it broke my heart."[58] Mullins said, "Carter was a master at keeping the audience interested in what you are doing on stage. He had people sittin' in the palm of his hand from the very outset. It was a pure honor to stand beside them, but often there would be so few people in the audience that I'd feel ashamed; I felt empathy with them. I had to do something about it...and I did."[59,60]

Mullins left the **Stanley Brothers** (1959) for a period. When he returned to the group after a few months, they were on live television. "Well, this absolutely destroyed me—to face a live TV camera—because I didn't have enough confidence in what I was doin'. Plus, at the time, Carter and Ralph was changin' their music. They had added the guitar as one of the lead instruments which they didn't have before. They had used the mandolin, the banjo and the fiddle. They added Bill Napier. He played guitar awhile and then Curley Lambert played guitar awhile. Both of them were mandolin players, you know. What changed their music was Syd Nathan, the owner and president of King Records. He wanted the guitars. [His reason was that] he didn't want fiddles on his record. That's another story in itself. They were lowering the keys that they were playing their tunes in. When I learned their tunes, it was off their records. And when they changed the

keys, that changed the whole complexion of the tune—especially to the fiddler.

"Anyway, we had to play live TV. I lost my confidence and I couldn't play good enough to suit me." Mr. Mullins was so nervous that he sometimes would vomit before he went on the air on television. "Me and Carter talked about it. I told him that I would find some way to learn, to break myself of being shy in front of the microphone. I left [the group] in the December of 1959." In 1991, he reflected on this fear of the microphone and he feels that his problem was lack of confidence. In his efforts to fight his fear of performing on live television he had to convince himself that no matter how bad you are, somebody will like you. He did this, but it took awhile.

Mullins decided to pursue a challenge for a shy person: go on radio with his own show. He figured that this would help him solve his problem of lost self-confidence. A month after he left the **Stanley Brothers**, he became a disc jockey on WGOH, a new station in Grayson, Kentucky. It was there that he discovered that

The Nu-Grass Pickers, a group Paul Mullins played in the early 1960's. L to R: Noah Crase, Paul Mullins, Don Edwards, Sid Campbell.

the timing necessary to read a commercial on the air took a certain talent that he didn't have. So he took the commercials and did them *his* way, which was more informal and folksy. Later on he was able to read a commercial on the air, but it took a long time to learn this skill.

In August 1960, Carter called him and asked if he was over his sickness yet. He was, so he went back to the **Stanley Brothers** on live television in Florida. There he made about $65 per week. He then recognized that his job at WGOH paid better than that so he quit

[58] Carter was once approached by Chubby Anthony for a job. He was down on his luck and needed a job to feed his family. Mullins switched to bass and Anthony joined as fiddler.

[59] Glenna and Bernie Fisher, "WPFB—Where the Bluegrass Tradition Lives On," *Bluegrass Unlimited*, February, 1985, pp. 30, 31. During the 1960s, he obtained employment in the radio business where he played a format of country music sprinkled with bluegrass. He really got rolling at WPFB in 1964.

[60] On tour with the Stanley Brothers and the Clinch Mountain Boys in Sevierville, Tennessee, he saw eleven year-old Dolly Parton on the front row. She was a girl from a poor upbringing "who really knew what it was like to sweep the front yard" (poor southerners swept their yards with brush brooms. One wanted a clean-swept yard without a blade of grass.) in the same way many other poor people were raised in that part of the country during that time. Mullins and many other famous bluegrass musicians are from the poor areas of Kentucky, Tennessee, West Virginia, etc., and could relate what it is like to grow up dirt-poor.

Many of the quotations in this biography are from his home in Middletown, Ohio, in 1991.

the Stanleys for the last time.[61] He got a job on the radio station in Mt. Sterling, Kentucky, in January 1961. He stayed there until April when he was offered a better-paying job on WTCR[62] in Ashland, Kentucky. He stayed with this station through the fall of 1963. Here he learned how to find his own sponsors and how to sell products on the radio. He also played as fiddler with the **Bluegrass Playboys**[63]. During this period where hootenannies were big in the "folk boom", he toured awhile with the **Bluegrass Playboys** knowing that he could get his radio job in Grayson any time he wanted. The band played at Carnegie Hall and at the McCormick Place (in Chicago). That summer of 1963, Mullins emceed a weekly television show in Huntington, West Virginia. He then returned to the 5,000 watt Grayson radio station for $150 per week.

In the fall of 1964, Paul Mullins joined the **Log Cabin Boys**[64] as mandolinist and fiddler, on WGOH. It disbanded in October when Mullins moved to Middletown, Ohio, to work for WPFB on October 20th. WPFB had less power (1000 watts), but a larger audience than the Grayson station. Its range encompassed Dayton, Cincinnati and the whole Miami Valley between the two cities. The Ohio area was a hotbed of activity for bluegrass at this time; nearly every night there was some bluegrass activity/concert going on.[65]

Mullins became one of the few people in this business who could make a living as a deejay playing bluegrass on the radio. He mixed one bluegrass record with two more conventional country records. This aspect of Mullins' career is the second way he influenced bluegrass as described in the opening paragraph. Many people heard the broadcasts of country and bluegrass music and were influenced toward bluegrass for the next twenty-five years. The broadcasts actually helped make the region a hot spot for bluegrass. His programming was carefully planned to present country entertainment which included bluegrass music; it was entertainment first, and listeners got a dose of bluegrass music without differentiating country from bluegrass. Lack of categorization of the music was not only an important factor in the station's success, it led to

comments from people who said that if it weren't for him and his radio show, they wouldn't be playing bluegrass music today.

Mullins continued, "In 1967, I started doing commercials for Lake Jewelry, the biggest record store I was ever in. They weren't big when I started doing radio commercials in 1964, but as my radio program caught on, they kept increasing their record selection. In the meantime, I had added a part to my program called 'Hymns from the Hills.'[66] Steve Lake, of Lake Jewelry, started putting on concerts at Chatauqua Park. This was the first bluegrass festival in the area. I promoted it on my radio show and 8,000 people showed up. Monroe saw that I had an audience and said come to Bean Blossom. Well, I promoted that and took 3,000 to 4,000 people with me. Me and Grant Turner were the emcees at that first Bill Monroe Bean Blossom Festival.

"In the meantime, Monroe had offered me a job. I had a band with Noah Crase (banjo) and myself and a couple more musicians.[67] That band was called the **Valley Ramblers**. We would double with Jimmy Martin, with Monroe, just about everybody. Bill didn't want to pay near as much money as I was makin', but I really wanted to go play the fiddle. I can play Monroe's music. And Monroe liked my style. He liked my attack with the bow. He called it a 'southern bow.'[68] I didn't know anything about [categorization of styles like Monroe did]. He was really powerful right then. We had a jam session with Noah Crase and, I think, Roland White was playing the guitar at that time. We played 'Roanoke' and 'Wheel Hoss.' We played it 'all the way to the fence.' I *really* wanted to go with him but I knew what it would be like. I knew what the 'death seat' was. And I've been to Nashville several times and to this day (1991) the first thing I would do when I got to Nashville is move." Mullins was also offered a job by Bob and Sonny Osborne but he had to refuse for the same reasons. He was determined to make a good living on the air. As he looks back on this today, this was probably a good decision. As the success of his radio shows on WPFB continued, he eventually got to the point where, on the

[61] He was replaced by Vernon Derrick.

[62] WTCR stood for Town and Country Radio and was owned by Connie B. Gay.

[63] With Elmer Burchett (banjo), Walter Adams (guitar), Thurman Endicott (mandolin) and June Thompson (bass). Occasionally, his friend from the Army, Tom T. Hall, played bass with the group.

[64] Other members were Sid Campbell (guitar), Ross Branham (banjo), Danny Milhon (Dobro) and June Thompson (bass).

[65] Also in the area was Jimmie Skinner. He had his Jimmie Skinner Music Center in Cincinnati. Mullins spoke of Skinner: "Jimmie Skinner couldn't keep time—he didn't know meter. He was a great songwriter and a good performer in his own right, but still his timing would never fit what we play at all. He didn't understand the bluegrass timing. I played the fiddle with him on stage. It took a bass player and a lead musician like Rusty York to really understand what he was going to play next. You had to play with him a long time to understand it. When I played with him on a record, if I were to have kept perfect, bluegrass time, I would have been way off. "

[66] This was thirty minutes of old-time and bluegrass gospel music daily. This program stayed on until Mullins left in 1989. Then his son, Joe Mullins, continued the program on a different station.

[67] The Valley Ramblers also included David Cox (mandolin), Don Warmouth (guitar) and Bobby Gilbert (bass).

[68] Mullins uses a "short bow" technique on the fiddle which was prominent in the fiddle world before Eck Robertson and others began winning contests with a *long bow* style. Mullins' short bow technique gets a lot of drive from the rapid action of the bow moving back and forth on the strings. The fancy "Texas fiddling" is more easily applied to the long bow while hoe-down music is a natural for short bow. Mullins is one of the few who use short bow today. Curly Ray Cline and Charlie Cline also use it.

morning shift, he did 25 to 30 thirty-second commercials in one hour.

In September 1974, the **Boys from Indiana** was formed by Mullins and Noah Crase and the Holt brothers, Aubrey and Jerry, along with their uncle, Harley Gabbard (resonator guitar). They recorded "Atlanta is Burning" for King Bluegrass Records. Artists in the recording were Aubrey and Harley Holt, Mullins and Crase. The **Boys from Indiana** won the *Muleskinner News* reader's poll as Most Promising New Band in 1975. Dave Evans was on banjo and, for the first time in his career, a lead singer.

In 1981, Mullins left WPFB for two years. But the popular demand of his audience brought him back. He formed **Paul Mullins and Traditional Grass** in 1983, with himself (fiddle), son Joe Mullins (banjo, guitar) and Mark Rader (guitar).[69] With a change of station management and format in 1989, Paul Mullins quit WPFB after twenty-seven years at the station. He retired (Joe eventually took over the band), but that allowed him to go full-time with **Traditional Grass**. The group gained critical acclaim and toured nationally, even playing the 1995 University of Chicago Folk Festival. The band went on hiatus in September 1995 after banjoist Joe Mullins bought a radio station.

The status of fiddling in the 1950s

A review by Richard K. Spottswood of Roy Russell's album, "Fiddlin' Time," in the November 1978 issue of *Bluegrass Unlimited* told of fiddling in bluegrass music:

The estate of country fiddling fell to something of a low mark in the 1950s. After the Hank Williams/honky-tonk era, Nashville producers began to find the sound of the fiddle more and more out of line with the new images and styles they were developing. It remained as a mainstay in bluegrass, but there were no fiddlers who blazed new and exotic trails the way Bill Monroe and Earl Scruggs had done with their instruments. Good fiddlers abounded during the early days of bluegrass—Chubby Wise, Art Wooten, Howdy Forrester, Vassar Clements and Merle "Red" Taylor are names that would only begin the list. Still, only Scotty Stoneman and Benny Martin extended the fiddle's role beyond simple solos and backups. Their drive and inventive powers were truly extraordinary, but it wasn't until the 1960s that others began to take their work seriously, and their contributions have never been adequately explored in print. The rest were lucky to get abbreviated spots to play short, sped-up versions of old breakdown tunes (waltzes, polkas, and other less hectic dance tunes were passé by then) during radio programs or personal appearances. Even then the fiddle tunes were regarded as little more than "specialties" designed to complement the rest of the proceedings. The bluegrass records of the period bear me out. The many banjo instrumentals (and, of course, the Monroe mandolin tunes) all allow the fiddle one or two breaks, but almost never was it allowed to become the focal point.

Tommy Jackson—studio fiddler extraordinaire

On December 9, 1979, renowned fiddler Tommy Jackson died at age 53. For over twenty years, he was Nashville's premier studio fiddler. He probably played on more records than any other fiddler in history—on recordings which ranged from **Bob Wills and the Texas Playboys** to acid rock to Hank Williams to Bill Monroe to Tammy Wynette. Jackson's fiddle albums on Dot were very popular at square dances during the '50s.

He didn't consider himself a bluegrass fiddler. "I've always played enough of it to get by," he said, "because with that stuff you have to play it pretty much all the time just to stay up with it. I've always concentrated on having a variety of things to do. When you're making a living at it, you don't know 'til you get into the studio what you're going to be asked to play."[70]

After his death, his son Mychael, an aspiring rock musician, spoke about his father, "If I could sum up anything he ever tried to stress to me about music, it was to be an artist. He was definitely an artist; he felt that he was confined to this hoe-down style, but that was his bread and butter. He tried to get the record companies to take (record) something besides hoe-downs, but they wouldn't. And in a sense, he understood why. He was practical; as much as he loved jazz, he knew he couldn't get too far above people's heads or it wouldn't sell. He was pretty well frustrated with the music business by the time he died. He felt he had been forgotten. Even in the Nashville papers, he used to say, he got more publicity on the sports pages for his fishing catch off Center Hill Lake than he did for his music. It was really sad toward the end; he wouldn't even talk about the music business and I couldn't even get him to pick up his fiddle and jam around the house."[71]

And in a comment by Charles Wolfe, "It was, ironically, a trap Tommy himself had helped build twenty years before when he forged his square dance style and developed the back-up style for the studios. It was an economic trap, and he grew increasingly bitter and more alienated from the music scene—especially the newer musicians and producers. The drinking got worse and worse."[72]

[69] In 1991, members of Paul Mullins and Traditional Grass were Paul and Joe Mullins, Rader, Glen Inman and Gerald Evans. This band was selected to play at the Smithsonian...above others.

[70] Charles Wolfe, "Tommy Jackson—Nashville Fiddler," *Bluegrass Unlimited*, September, 1980, p. 43.

[71] Ibid., p. 47.

[72] Ibid.

Kenny Baker—
"The best bluegrass fiddler alive today"

The man known for some years as the "best bluegrass fiddler alive today" was born June 26, 1926, in Burdine, near the coal-mining town of Jenkins in eastern Kentucky on the Virginia state line. His early idols were Tommy Dorsey and Glenn Miller—the popular music of the day. His father was an old-time fiddler, as were many of his relatives. They played so much that Kenny had no intention of becoming a fiddler; young Baker chose to take up the guitar instead. The Baker family later moved to Wise County, Virginia, into the Dotson Creek community. It was twenty miles from the home of Carter and Ralph Stanley and twenty-two miles from Jim and Jesse McReynolds.

Although Baker regularly receives accolades as being the best bluegrass fiddler, he nevertheless feels that Chubby Wise wrote the book on bluegrass fiddling. Baker spoke of Wise, when Wise, Lester Flatt and Earl Scruggs were members of the **Blue Grass Boys**, "When Chubby Wise came in, he heard those numbers a lot different than the rest of the **Boys** and Chubby started playing a lot of stuff that I play today. He started the style."

Kenny Baker fell in love with fiddle music when he heard the music of **Bob Wills and the Texas Playboys** during the '40s and '50s and a recording of Stephane Grappelli. He was also heavily influenced by the country-style fiddling of Bobby and Marion Sumner, and the Stanley's band.

Howard "Big Howdy" Forrester is Baker's favorite fiddler. "Howdy was the greatest fiddler that ever walked across the stage," he said. "Really and truly, the way he done hoe-downs—anything he played—it was done so masterfully," said Mr. Baker. "He knew exactly what he wanted to do and he knew how he wanted it to sound. As far as I'm concerned, any time Howdy laid a number down, you'd pretty well have to say it was done *right*.[73] Now I'll tell you, Clayton McMichen[74], back in the days of [Fiddlin'] Arthur Smith and all those people...from what I heard of him (McMichen), he was so versatile. He could play a good hoe-down and he also played good songs. I think Clayton was far ahead of people that was playin' back in the late thirties, early forties.

"I'll tell you another man I think was the instigator of a lot of people's playin'—whether they realized it or not—was Curly Fox. Curly played practically the first double stops (two strings in harmony) ever I took notice of. He had a lot of influence on a lot of people's playin' now. They classified Curly as a show fiddler, but I'm speaking a little more technically. Curly was kind of underrated in the fiddle world. The prettiest backup I ever heard was Curly playing after Texas Ruby's (his wife and partner) singing. Really what carried me away with Curly's work was the way he backed up songs. And back in those days I never heard no man's fiddle like Curly's did."[75]

Baker also likes Mack McGarr who was, he felt, fifty years ahead of his day. On the Opry, McGarr played in keys not normally used by the other fiddlers at the time—keys such as E, B and B flat. "That's where the word 'modernization' in music came from right there," said Baker.

Up until 1945, Baker was normally a guitarist. But one day while he was in the Navy in Okinawa, he played the fiddle for the first time publicly at a Red Cross-sponsored square dance. There he played the only two songs he knew: "Rubber Dolly" and "Ragtime Annie." He alternated between the tunes for over three hours and "From that night on I never had a guitar in my hands again."[76] He was then reassigned to USO duty, playing the guitar and fiddle.

After the military, he worked the coal mines at home in eastern Kentucky and played music at night. He had no intention of becoming a professional musician. Coal mining, according to Baker, is a good living and a respectable job. He played several years of swing fiddle with country music artist Don Gibson in Knox-

[73] Howdy Forrester and Kenny Baker recorded "Red Apple Rag" (County 784, 1983).

[74] In a 1991 interview, Baker spoke about fiddler Clayton McMichen who played in Gid Tanner and the Skillet Lickers through the 1920s and later with his Georgia Wildcats. He said that during the 1930s, McMichen was the best fiddler around because he was so versatile. He could play any of the music style of the day. However, just because he chose not to specialize in country music, he was not the most influential in the music we know now as bluegrass.

[75] Brett F. Devan, "Kenny Baker—One of the Masters," *Bluegrass Unlimited*, February, 1991, p. 23.

[76] This is not entirely true. He played lead guitar on the radio later on and did two albums for the Puritan label with Josh Graves in which Baker played lead guitar and didn't play the fiddle at all. Kenny told me that this quotation is true, but you have to read between the lines. The fiddle is still his main instrument.

ville "until I heard 'Roanoke' and 'Wheel Horse.' The first time I ever heard 'Roanoke,' I thought it was the prettiest piece of music I'd ever heard. I'll bet you I put three dollars worth of damn nickels in that jukebox in Knoxville."[77]

He met Bill Monroe when Monroe and his band were based at WCYB's Farm and Fun Time and on a tour into Baker's area. Bobby Hicks and Gordon Terry played fiddle for Monroe at that time, and Baker liked the way Hicks played "Roanoke" and "Cheyenne."[78] "I was there with Don (Gibson) and I first met Bill there," said Baker. "At one point, [Bill] asked me if I was satisfied where I was playing. I'd do an instrumental tune every day on the show and I noticed Bill would be settin' right out in the audience when I would be doin' my number. I don't know whether he made a point to be there just for that or what."[79] Monroe must have seen something in Baker's fiddling he liked; he was offered a job with the **Blue Grass Boys** any time he wanted to join.

Baker went with Monroe part-time in the autumn of 1957 until 1959. He quit professional music during the period of 1959 to 1961, for music didn't seem to pay the bills very well. In actuality, he had to work as a coal miner so that he could afford to play music professionally. Back with Monroe the third time in 1964 (he was with Monroe again in 1961), he replaced Benny Williams. When Baker finally decided to join Monroe full-time in 1968[80], he really wanted to play. Monroe had to let Williams go. Baker left coal mining behind, now able to afford to do this because his family was grown. He stayed until October 12, 1984. All told, he stayed with Monroe twenty-four years. Now that he was with Monroe full-time, "I had to change my way of fiddling all around and really get after it..."

"When I joined Bill, this fella Joe Stuart set me down and showed me how to play bluegrass fiddle. Up until then I was doing mostly swing music—what I call 'jump music.' But Stuart was playing bluegrass licks all right, but he was putting too many meters in the line. In other words, he was trying to put too much in the line than I thought had to be there. I worked there maybe a month

Author (center) with Josh Graves (L) and Kenny Baker, 1992.

and I told Bill that I couldn't cut it. So Bill told me, 'Why don't you play what you feel.' So when he gave me a full reign to go I had no problems." Monroe told Baker, "Now, don't you listen to what somebody else is playing; you play what you feel and what you hear. That's why I want you."[81]

In a 1991 interview, he spoke about the change of fiddle styles when he left Gibson for Monroe, "It wasn't that tough. You just had to know what people were expectin' out of you. I did make a big change, though...I've always played what I've felt regardless of what kind of music [I would] play. I'm not a—what you call—a great blues player. Josh [Graves] is. Not me. I can play a fast blues—that gut-bucket stuff.

"A lot of people can play country fiddle but a lot of the best country fiddlers can't play good bluegrass—the technique is different. It's what you hear and what you're used to. They want to play the breakdown licks just like they do a song or something like that and you just don't do it. They play too mechanically. Mechanical fiddlers apply themselves to learn that number one way and they'll never change, not one phrase, not one note, nothing about it. Every time they play it—whether they feel up to playing it or whether they don't—it's exactly the same. They work out their patterns and they set their notes in there and that's exactly what they play ten years from today.

"On any number that Bill does, I don't have to worry about playing some licks that somebody else recorded because nobody hears like me and I play what I hear. I wouldn't say I'd take some number and any note I'd make on it would be necessarily right, but I would stand behind it enough to say, well, that's the way I hear it.

"There's a lot of mechanical music being played today, and bluegrass is definitely not mechanical. It's strictly a heartfelt music; it's got ta be. You got ta like it to play it because, money-wise, there's no living to be made for no sideman out of it. Some people love to live in the country just so they can exist from day to day. That's just like a bluegrass sideman. If he loves his music he can stay with it; if he don't, there you go."[82]

[77] Devan, op. cit., p. 20.

[78] Baker and Hicks later recorded the "Darkness on the Delta" LP (County 782, 1980)

[79] Devan, op. cit., p. 20.

[80] Mr. Baker recalls the date was March 14, 1967. However, Byron Berline recalls that the date must be exactly one year later, due to his recollection of when he joined the military and had to leave the Blue Grass Boys. For convenience, we'll just go with the 1968 date.

[81] Liner notes from the LP "Kenny Baker—Portrait of a Fiddler," County Records, 1968.

[82] James Rooney, *Bossmen: Bill Monroe and Muddy Waters*, 1971, pp. 68, 69. Later re-printed by Da Capo Press.

In 1958, Kenny Baker recorded on his first album, Monroe's "Knee Deep in Blue Grass." Baker played fiddle on Bill Monroe's second album, "I Saw The Light."

In Jim Rooney's book on *Bill Monroe and Muddy Waters, Bossmen*, Baker talked about some tunes that Monroe had kept from other fiddlers, "After I got to playing his stuff a little bit, he told me about these old numbers of his Uncle Pen's. He said he was saving them back for the right fiddler, the man he thought could play them and do them right. That's what he told me the first time I worked for him. They've got that old sound and that *drive* is in there. I've listened to fiddle music all my life and some of those numbers I've never heard before. Had he been a fiddler, Boy, he would have been something else."[83]

Kenny Baker (L) and Josh Graves "Partners in Bluegrass" at the 1989 Rocky Mountain Bluegrass Festival. Warren Kennison on banjo.

Baker continued, "There's no more music in the world that you can play like bluegrass music; particularly the fiddle. I've always found that you can play more from what you feel than any set pattern that most music is. In bluegrass, you've got the melody to go by but you play more or less what you feel. With someone like Don Gibson or any other modern country singer you knew exactly what lines you were going to play and all. That's the difference. In bluegrass you're more on your own. The tempos differ in bluegrass. A lot of times the same number will be played in different tempos, depending on how you feel when you go into it, I suppose. Bill will kick off some numbers, you know. One day he'll have a pretty good pace on it, the next day he'll have it a little bit slower. He never does the same number twice alike. There's always some change in that number every time he does it. I've always said that bluegrass music is nothing but a hillbilly version of jazz. He'll let a man work a long time and see if he does have possibilities and the ability to adopt his way of playing. It was five or six months before he ever undertook to show me an old number."

In 1968, Kenny Baker recorded his first solo album on County Records, "Portrait Of A Bluegrass Fiddler."[84] Also during that year, Baker recorded the album "High Country" with fiddler Joe Greene for County. Other County Records LPs he recorded through the years include "A Baker's Dozen Country Fiddle Tunes," "Kenny Baker Country," "Dry and Dusty," "Grassy

Fiddle Blues (1974)," "Kenny Baker Plays Bill Monroe" (1976), "Frost on the Pumpkin," "Red Apple Rag" (1983) and "Farmyard Swing."

A surprise for many Kenny Baker fans is how well he plays the guitar. Just after Abe Samuelson bought Puritan Records, he and Josh Graves recorded "Bucktime" for Puritan. Graves recalled, "Baker called me and wanted to hire me to do this album. I said hell yea. I didn't tell him I was quittin' [the **Nashville Grass**]. And when he come down, he was playin' guitar and it baffled me, you know. But we went to Chicago and cut our first album in 1973. And we did another one in 1974. So it's out on the Rebel label. He scared me to death. I thought, 'Why in the world does a fiddler want me on his session? But as it turned out, it was the best album we ever cut—or will cut." The LPs were well received and became known as "The Puritan Sessions."

In September of 1977, Baker incurred severe lacerations in his left palm when a hunting knife slipped in his hand. The doctors predicted a full recovery. He never fully recovered from this injury and was difficult, painful even, to play guitar like he used to. Even the fiddle became difficult at times. James Bryan filled-in with the **Blue Grass Boys** awhile.

Baker quit Monroe the last time in 1984, and still says, in 1995, that "Bill Monroe was the greatest musician who ever walked across the stage." Baker then joined up with banjoist Bob Black, Alan (guitar) and Aleta (bass, guitar) Murphy in a band for the summer.

He then partnered up with Josh Graves. A 1991 interview with Mr. Baker revealed, "I'll tell you what. We have not sat down and worked one number out yet." What they do on stage is worked out right there on the stage. They love the informal nature of their new "group" and so do the fans. They initially wanted to try this partnership for five years but they enjoyed it so much that they couldn't see any reason not to continue beyond that point and into 1996.

In the summer of 1990, Baker and Graves joined Jesse McReynolds and Eddie Adcock to produce a jazzy, eclectic CD for CMH Records, "The Masters." The idea for the project was probably that of CMH producers Billy Troy (Josh's son) or the late Martin Haerle.

---

[83] Ibid., p. 94.

[84] Musicians were Del McCoury (guitar), Vic Jordan (banjo), Roland White (probably mandolin) and Doug Green (bass).

"Whose ever idea it was to put us in these white suits was kind of a bad lick on their part. And you can print that, too," said Baker.[85]

As of 1996, Baker raised cattle near Nashville. This required that Graves limit the bookings so he could keep up with his cattle. During his career, he wrote 120 to 140 instrumentals; "Freida" was the most popular and continues to pay him royalties.

Mike Hartgrove tells of the origin of the five-string fiddle

Mike Hartgrove[86] spoke about the use of the five-string fiddle, "The five-string concept, adding a low 'C' viola string, has been around for a lot longer than most people realize. I think Bobby Hicks was the man who really brought the five-string fiddle into bluegrass, but the western swing fiddlers have used them as far back probably as the late fifties. J.R. Chadwell was one of the early pioneers and I believe he predated (Johnny) Gimble and Red Hayes in using one. The five-string fiddle is directly related to the saxophone that some of the western swing fiddles used a lot, like Bob Wills. If you'll listen to some of the arrangements used by the swing players like Gimble and (the late) Joe Holley, their phrasing is a lot like the horn players. The fiddlers needed a lower range to play these sax lines so they went to the fifth string."[87]

Art Stamper

Art Stamper— the "Lost Fiddler"

During a 1960s recording session with the Stanleys, Carter Stanley instructed Stamper to make his fiddling

on the record sound like Benny Martin, and another like Gordon Terry. Stamper responded, "Now, Chase (Carter's nickname), if you want Benny Martin or Gordon Terry to cut the album, why didn't you just hire them to cut this album and leave me home? Carter patted me on the back and that's all that was said. I've got a lot of respect for both of them as fiddlers, but I can't be them and me, too! There's only one Kenny Baker and there's only one Benny Martin and there's only one Art Stamper or Marion Sumner."[88]

Art Stamper was born in Knott County, Kentucky, November 1, 1933. He was influenced by Marion and Bobby Sumner, two early bluegrass fiddlers with the Stanleys. His family was musically-inclined, so at nine he began playing fiddle. By thirteen, he was playing dances and pie suppers. About 1950, Stamper left his home to start playing out-of-state gigs. He joined with "Texas Bill," then with **Buster Pack and the Lonesome Pine Boys**, and then with the **Sauceman Brothers** at WCYB.

About 1952, he joined the **Stanley Brothers** at WVLK, Versailles, Kentucky with George Shuffler, Pee Wee Lambert, Carter and Ralph. They recorded on Rich-R-Tone: "Little Birdie," "Are You Waiting Just For Me?," "The Little Girl and the Dreadful Snake" and "The Little Glass of Wine."[89] He worked on and off with this band until September 1953 when he went into the military. Out of the military in 1955, Stamper re-joined the **Stanley Brothers**, staying until January 1956.

In January 1956, Art Stamper and Red Allen joined the **Osborne Brothers** and then began recording on MGM in 1957. They recorded "Ruby," "Who Done It," "Teardrops in My Eyes" and "My Aching Heart"— twelve tunes in total. Stamper stayed ten months, then quit full-time music to pursue cosmetology (hair dressing) at a school in Louisville.[90] He recorded thirty-eight songs with Carter and Ralph through the years. Taking a break from his business in 1978, Stamper played fiddle full-time with the **Goins Brothers**. About 1982, County Records released "The Lost Fiddler." The title came from his absence from music for so long.

Stamper took violin lessons for three years beginning in late 1979. His teacher "said I'd have been a good violinist if she could have kept me off 'Sally Goodin' and some of those old hoe-downs. I'd practice half an hour, and I'm telling you, I'd get so bored playing those scales! I'd have to play some *old* tunes when I got through just to get my mood out—it was like being thirsty for water and trying to substitute something else."[91]

[85] Devan, op. cit., p. 24.

[86] Mike Hartgrove joined the Bluegrass Cardinals on fiddle in April 1979.

[87] Brett F. Devan, "The Bluegrass Cardinals—Synonym for Vocal Harmony, *Bluegrass Unlimited*, May, 1986, p. 12.

[88] Marty Godbey, "The Lost Fiddler—Art Stamper," *Bluegrass Unlimited*, November, 1982, p. 26.

[89] This was their third recording of this last tune. The first time was with Leslie Keith as fiddler, and later with Bobby Sumner.

[90] Later he opened up his own shop and called it A Way of Art. This was his day-job for many years until he sold out and began playing music again.

[91] Godbey, op. cit., p. 26.

America's Music — Bluegrass

About fiddling, Stamper said, "I've been working on my touch for three years and I'm still working on it. There's no way that you can ever master an instrument no matter what it is. I believe in self-inventory; I think you need that. That's why I never criticize anyone's fiddling. I say, 'They're doing the best they can on their level.'"[92]

He quit his hair dressing business in 1983. Through the years, he had won several awards for creativity and had cut the hair of Mark Schatz, Bela Fleck and other noted players. Again active in bluegrass at age fifty-eight in 1991, Stamper helps out when needed on tours such as with Larry Sparks and with the **Goins Brothers**. Stamper played very briefly with Bill Monroe in the mid-'80s, then spent the early 1990s with Ralph Stanley. He loves to play, but dislikes travel; this keeps his appearances somewhat scarce. As of 1996, he lived on his farm in Shepherdsville, Kentucky.

Jim Buchanan

James Buchanan is a sideman with extraordinary credentials which include **Jim and Jesse**, the **Greenbriar Boys**, the **David Grisman Quintet** and **Mel Tillis and the Statesiders**.

He was born in North Carolina, January 1, 1941, into a musical family. His fiddle idol was Benny Martin and was highly influenced by Arthur "Guitar Boogie" Smith, Mel Tillis, Jascha Heifitz and the **Doobie Brothers**. "My ambition," Buchanan told this writer, "is to create and play music in a fashion that people will feel as well as hear. My goal is to achieve a level of communication with mankind so as to meet them where they are!"[93]

At age eleven, Buchanan played professionally with **Joe Franklin and the Mimosa Boys** from Morganton, North Carolina; he toured with them until 1959. This group did the "Ed Sullivan Show" in 1957 and also worked on WCYB-TV in Bristol, Virginia, as their staff band. After high school he pursued theology in a seminary. He began attendance at a bible college in 1975, and two years later was ordained into the Gospel ministry. In 1970, he began a twelve-year stint with Mel Tillis in Nashville, doing television, movies, radio and stage, off and on for nearly twenty years until April 1989.

In 1960, Buchanan worked for Arthur "Guitar Boogie" Smith in Charlotte, North Carolina, for a year on WBT. He helped Arthur Smith record his "Guitar Boogie" at WBTV in Charlotte on January 9th.

Then in Prattville, Alabama, at age twenty, he joined **Jim and Jesse and the Virginia Boys** on May 15, 1961, for three years; he took the place of Vassar Clements with the band. According to Allen Shelton, who was the band's banjo player at the time, Buchanan improved

three-fold during those years. The group performed on radio, television and concerts. In March of 1964, he left **Jim and Jesse** and joined Arthur Smith's band again until early 1965 when he joined the **Greenbriar Boys** in New York City for a year. In April of 1966, Buchanan returned to Jim and Jesse whose band had recently joined the Grand Ole Opry. He left the McReynolds brothers again in early 1969. He also played with the **Pete Drake Band** during this period, followed by a year with **Tompall and the Glaser Brothers** in Nashville and did movies, television, radio and the Opry.

Through the years, Buchanan recorded with Hank Snow, Alabama, Ringo Starr and dozens of other big names in Nashville. He appeared on many of the popular television shows which originated in Nashville. He also sold real estate around Nashville, a job which he could schedule work around his music commitments.

From 1984 to 1987, Jim Buchanan was a member of the **David Grisman Quintet**. Filling the shoes of Grisman's earlier fiddler, Darol Anger, proved difficult because Anger and Grisman had played so long together and knew "Dawg music" very well. But he was able to learn all the songs in the way Grisman had created them and he also added his own influences from bluegrass music. Buchanan's bluegrass timing gave a dimension to Grisman's music which gave it a connection to bluegrass—and less influence from jazz—than had been there before he arrived (or has been since).

1984 was a busy year for him. He recorded and helped arrange the "Here Today" LP, touring awhile with this band. He also played with Dan Fogelberg, Stephane Grappelli, and toured extensively in Europe. He stayed with Grisman until 1987 when he joined **Mel Tillis and the Statesiders** again. He also had a full-time job as General Manager of Innovative Sound Studio in Winston-Salem, North Carolina.

Buchanan replaced Blaine Sprouse with **Jim and Jesse** awhile in 1991. In 1992, he signed a contract with C.E.D. Records as an artist and producer. As of 1996, he lived in the Nashville area.

Triple fiddles was actually introduced into country music before Bill Monroe

In a 1992 conversation with banjoist Ed Brown, he remembered that triple fiddles were actually used long before Monroe's 1954 band which included fiddlers Charlie Cline, Red Taylor and Gordon Terry. Cline claims that triple fiddles were first used here but Ed Brown recalled that Gid Tanner's late 1920s band used them. "A lot of his recordings had three fiddles on it. Some of it they would do in unison but some of it they would do with harmony. 'Rock the Pallet' was one of

92 Ibid., p. 26.
93 1992 interview at IBMA, Owensboro, Kentucky.

them; 'Ride the Old Buck to Water' was another. They done a lot of that stuff. It was Lowe Stokes and Gid Tanner and Clayton McMichen. And Bert Layne was another one who played with them. Stokes and McMichen and Layne were the better fiddlers—Gid was not a real good fiddler. He apparently was an entrepreneur—a businessman." While the above is true, the arrangements by these early fiddlers were unrelated to what Monroe did.

There can be *no* doubt that Monroe's triple-fiddle venture enhanced his 'high, lonesome' sound and helped the band's popularity.[94]

Gene Lowinger—
reminiscing with a 1960s
Blue Grass Boy[95]

Lowinger was born in Newark in 1942. He jammed at Greenwich Village Park in New York City with Roger Sprung, Eric Weissberg and others. In 1963, he bought a $15 fiddle, played with the **Bluegrass Ramblers**, the **Down State Rebels**, and in 1964 with the **New York Ramblers** when they won the Band trophy at Union Grove, North Carolina, with members David Grisman, Jody Stecher (guitar), Winnie Winston (banjo) and Fred Weisz (bass). He played Carnegie Hall, Town Hall and Gerde's Folk City. "Being students, we city boys studied every record assiduously, learned every song note-for-note, and could recite chapter and verse of each artists' discography. We copied, imitated and eventually, in the hands of artists such as David Grisman, developed our own sounds. But we never lost or reverential awe for the masters... It was no passing fancy for us. It was a quasi-religion."[96]

Gene Lowinger fiddled for Bill Monroe from May 1965 to February 1966.[97] The hiring process for Lowinger into Monroe's band is interesting and probably typical of the many different musicians Monroe hired through the years. Monroe told Lowinger to show up at the Ryman and bring his fiddle and he'd put him on the Grand Ole Opry, and to wear a shirt and tie so people would respect him. That next night, they rehearsed "Bill Cheatham" and one other. Ten minutes later, the **Blue Grass Boys** were called to play. Monroe told the audience, "I got a surprise for you folks—a young new fiddler from New York. If you like him, I'll hire him. What are you going to play, son?"

Lowinger was already scared to simply play with Bill Monroe on the Opry, but now he was shocked to learn he hadn't been hired yet. He played the tar out of "Bill Cheatham" and the crowd went wild. Bill asked the crowd if they wanted to hear another and, of course, they give their emphatic encouragement. He played another one. Monroe came up behind him with that legendary mandolin chop of his and pushed the timing of the twenty-three year-old kid. The audience was awed into silence. Monroe leaned over and whispered, "You're hired."[98] And another Monroe disciple was born. Lowinger: "It was not only the music, it was the man and his discipline. This work taught me an important lesson and that is every important thing I've done in life needed a mentor. Monroe was that mentor, and I learned."[99]

While he was with Monroe, he wrote *Bluegrass Fiddle* and sent it off the *Sing Out!* magazine to be published. It was misplaced or lost until Oak Publishing found the manuscript in 1972 and published it. His first royalty check was $10,000.

Sidemen with Monroe barely made survivable wages. When Lowinger began with Monroe in Nashville, he had $200. When he left he had $200. Lowinger met a member of the Nashville Symphony Orchestra who convinced him that he was wasting his time with that bluegrass kind of music and that he could actually earn a good living with classical music. In L.A.'s Ash Grove folk club, Lowinger gave Monroe two weeks notice. He left under good terms and was replaced by Richard Greene.

Even before he quit Monroe, Lowinger had applied to three schools which could teach him how to play symphony music. Each required that he play a particular Mozart piece as an entry audition. He took a few lessons to prepare for the test. Even though he understood the rudiments of reading music, he was unschooled enough to not be recommended for the test. But he finally talked his way into an audition. He recorded the audition piece and played it endlessly—he memorized it. At the audition, he amazed them by performing it flawlessly without reading the music. They were definitely impressed. But when they presented him with another piece to be read and played there, he couldn't do it. And they wouldn't allow him to show his talents on a country tune. Eventually, Lowinger was admitted into the Mannes College of Music in New York City. He studied three years, got a diploma, and in another two or three years had his masters degree in music from the Manhattan School of Music.

---

94 Incidentally, Bob Wills also used three fiddles on many of his recordings of Texas swing.

95 Most of this biography came from Don Kissel's "Triumph of the Will" article in the April 1992 issue of *Bluegrass Unlimited*.

96 Gene Lowinger, Guest Editorial, "Bluegrass Then and Now." *Bluegrass Unlimited*, February, 1993, p. 31.

97 While Lowinger was a member of the Blue Grass Boys, other members were Pete Rowan, Lamar Grier and James Monroe (bass). Lowinger was only the third Northeast city boy to get a job with Monroe (after Bill Keith and Peter Rowan).

98 Don Kissil, "Triumph of the Will," op. cit., p. 34.

99 Ibid., p. 35.

In 1972, he was fully employed in the symphony music business. One of his free-lance jobs in about 1979 was as violinist in "The Nutcracker." Tragedy struck when a dancer fell off the stage into the orchestra pit and onto his neck. The fall crushed a vertebra in his neck and kept him from playing the violin professionally for the rest of his life. He was thirty-five. But instead of being crippled for life, he was able to come back through self-discipline and perseverance. He became a photographer and a computer programmer; he specialized in the photography of bluegrass artists.

In a Guest Editorial for the February 1993 issue of *Bluegrass Unlimited*, Lowinger, absent from bluegrass for many years, gave a perspective of a person who was able to see the differences in bluegrass between the mid-'60s and 1993. In the editorial, he related that he played again with Monroe when he was called in 1989. Here he played a tune with Monroe at the Lincoln Center, New York City. "My love for the music was rekindled. When I began to listen to bluegrass again I was pleased, but not surprised, to find new dynamics at work which gave rise to the third generation of bluegrass. The emergence of women as performers (although there were a few early on, such as Hazel Dickens and Alice Foster nee Gerrard) in what was a male-dominated style of music has been the most important and profound change in the music's history. Alison Krauss, Laurie Lewis, Kathy Kallick gave us another view of life, another vocal sound and another touch on the strings."[100]

Bluegrass, as it is played today, is now a function of all its different influences which, in the first generation, was simply a product of musicians from south of the Mason-Dixon Line. While the music may continue to progress and adapt to the new ideas from all over the world, Lowinger commented that "the greatest impact on the music and the way it is performed comes out of the recording studio. The technology of the studio has been transported to the stage. This may have had a positive effect on the sound of the music; the look of the performers on stage and the cohesiveness of the band has, to my thinking, suffered. In the years when I was cutting my teeth on the bands at Sunset Park, et al, a big part of the excitement was in watching the performers move in and out of the microphones. Now, a band on stage, strung out in a straight line, with each performer having its own voice microphone and instrument microphone, may have an electronically balanced sound, but they look as thought they're each standing in a bucket of cement. That old-time bobbing and weaving was as much fun to watch as the music was to listen to. The bands sounded like and *looked* like a well-oiled machine. And those moments of confusion, when paths got crossed, always added to the fun for the audience.

Playing in a band like that was a real treat. Having Bill Monroe chomp chords right behind my gave me a rock solid rhythm on which to build the bounce of a tune like 'Bill Cheatham' or the drive of a piece like 'Mule Skinner Blues.'

"There was also something aesthetically pleasing about watching two, three or four singers lean into one microphone to sing cheek to cheek. You knew they had to have worked out the voice balance. There were no sound checks before the performances, it wasn't done electronically."[101]

Richard Greene

Richard Greene— a Yankee bluegrass fiddler

Richard Greene is a classical violinist who switched to playing bluegrass before he was twenty. Greene was born in Los Angeles, November 9, 1942. Greene recalled that learning music "was all my mother's doing; I didn't really want to do it. She wanted my father and the other Greene children to take lessons, and we all did. My father never really wanted to play violin either. At the time, he got a really fine instrument which I now have. None of us wanted to play, but I got good at it. I had a little bit of dexterity and talent."[102] When he was thirteen, "I quit when I was big enough to stand up to her and say 'No.'"

In 1960, Greene played in his first group, the **Coast Mountain Ramblers**, in Berkeley, California. Band members were Greene (fiddle), Ken Frankel (guitar) and Dave Pollack (banjo). Greene's main bluegrass fiddle inspirations were Eck Robertson, Chubby Wise, especially Scott Stoneman, and *all* the other **Blue Grass Boys** fiddlers.

In college, his friends played the repertoire of the **New Lost City Ramblers**. They coaxed him to join, which he did reluctantly, and soon found what playing music with a beat and good rhythm was like. In the

100 Lowinger, op. cit.

101 Ibid.

102 Joe Ross, "From Bluegrass to Classical and Back Again," *Bluegrass Unlimited*, July, 1994, p. 51.

early sixties, Greene played some gigs with Chris Hillman at The Ash Grove in Hollywood, California. When Hillman left suddenly to play bass with the **Byrds**, "I was upset because we lost a very good mandolin player."

He formed the **Dry City Scat Band** in 1961 and played bluegrass and old-time music.[103] After seeing the amazing Scott Stoneman (with the **Stonemans** at the time — within a year Scott would be with the **Kentucky Colonels**) at The Ash Grove in 1963, he decided to play the fiddle full-time. Seeing Scott Stoneman was a revelation for Greene. He told this writer, "Scotty is and will always be my favorite fiddler, number one. And he may be my favorite player of any instrument. He brought an intensity to playing music that I had never seen before, and I have hardly ever seen afterwards— just shear animal, fire and strength."[104] "Stoneman would tighten his wrist around his bow like he would a stick or tire iron. He only played with three fingers on his left hand. I think he had an injury and only played with his three weak fingers. His index finger was always up in the air. And his violin! It had a gap between the top and sides big enough to put a magazine through it. The instrument wasn't even stuck together. The guy was playing without any proper technique on a violin that wasn't even in one piece and achieved the most amazing sound I ever heard!"[105] Besides that, the ideas he came up with on the fiddle were completely revolutionary—not just the licks themselves but the meaning underneath all of it—the intensity. So he inspired me to become a musician. I was not a musician until I saw him—I was a real estate broker—then I changed my life." Greene was about twenty years old at the time.

But there was more to Scotty's life than fiddling. Greene explained, "He would stay at my house in those days and there was no way he could be sober for half a day. He was an extreme alcoholic in the final stages of alcoholism. The final stages lasted several years for him, but it doesn't get any worse than that particular case of alcoholism. I took him to the hospital for de-tox. And, of course, he couldn't hardly perform when he got drunk. I think he finally died a couple of years later. I think they found him outside of a market—he had been drinking after shave lotion because he couldn't get any

booze at that time of the morning. He was in Nashville when he died. He was a tragic character."

Soon after that, Greene began playing with Butch Waller's **Pine Valley Boys**[106] in the San Francisco Bay Area. Then he and David Grisman went east together to find play bluegrass. "I had already had the job with the **Greenbriar Boys** as their bass player. After I had gotten that job, I then met David Grisman for the first time and we became, immediately, very close friends. We became inseparable. He needed to bet back to New York (where he lived) and I needed to get back to Massachusetts to play with the **Greenbriar Boys** so we decided to go together." Greene joined the **Greenbriar Boys** as bassist for $65 per week in 1964. This was just to get a start in the music business on the East Coast. He also recorded his fiddle on Red Allen's "Bluegrass Country" (County 704). "This was the first bluegrass recording session of my life. I was with Red Allen, a real veteran, and I was scared to death! Playing with Red Allen was 'the real thing,' I assure you."

The next year, Grisman convinced him that he really could get a job with Bill Monroe; just go up and ask him—so he did. In 1966, Bill Monroe hired him as his fiddler. Members of the **Blue Grass Boys** then were Peter Rowan (guitar), Richard Greene (fiddle), Lamar Grier (banjo) and James Monroe (bass). Greene took the place of Gene Lowinger, who was Monroe's first Yankee fiddler[107]. In five sessions from October 14, 1966 to January 23, 1967, Greene recorded fourteen tunes with the band. Most of these cuts are on Monroe's 1967 LP "Bluegrass Time."[108]

Greene recalled he was asked to help Monroe tend his farm between gigs. "That was misery. I always managed to escape those duties by playing meek. When it came to farm work, I said I didn't really know how to do that, and I complained about back problems. I'd just get out of it. On the road, the **Blue Grass Boys** did all the driving. Bill never drove, so I just told Bill that I didn't really know how to drive and that took care of that. The other **Blue Grass Boys** had too much pride. They had to be martyrs. We were all extremely dedicated to the music, and that was part of it—to rise to those other challenges. I did move some hay but that wasn't too bad."[109]

> "Monroe's tunes were all highly melodic, as were Ralph Stanley's. If you get their melodies down on a piece of paper, you've got something! There are some very deep melodic truths in what the great bluegrass artists had." —Richard Greene

103 Members were David Lindley, Pete Madlem and Chris Darrow.

104 Interview at IBMA's WorldWest, Palo Alto, California, March 25, 1995.

105 Ross, op. cit., p. 51.

106 With Sandy Rothman (banjo), Waller (mandolin), David Nelson, and occasionally Herb Pedersen (banjo) and David Grisman (mandolin).

107 Rowan is acknowledged as being the first Yankee lead singer who sang with the BOYS.

108 This LP was recorded in the days before over-dubbing in the studio. Usually, you never got a second chance to redo your break if you didn't like it.

109 Ross, op. cit., p. 52.

While with Monroe, Greene played twin-fiddle on the Opry with Buddy Spicher. He recalled that Spicher was brilliant at instantaneously being able to play harmony to his lead. Greene would show him what he was going to do one minute before going on stage, and Spicher learned it then.

"After I left the Monroe band, I *never* again played in a band with as good rhythm. I'm going to make an absolute value judgment and say that something is better than something else. I'm not afraid to. Once you've played in a band with a relatively-youthful Bill Monroe giving you mandolin back-beats, you will never again play in a band with as good a rhythm. That's it! There's all kinds of other bands out there—great bands. The **Flatt and Scruggs** band was a great band but it was different."

Greene left Monroe at a time when they had only one gig per week; and that was on the Opry. His weekly income was about $37. Byron Berline took his place with the **Blue Grass Boys** in March 1967. Greene joined Jim Kweskin's **Jug Band** with Bill Keith (tenor banjo, pedal steel), Geoff and Maria Muldaur and Fritz Richmond. Greene left the **Jug Band** in 1969, then joined **Seatrain**[110], a country-rock band which recorded four albums.

Bluegrass music as a profession has been notoriously difficult to survive in without some sort of a day job. While Richard has always made his living with his violin, most of it was away from bluegrass. But now that the 1990s are here, the climate for a touring bluegrass band seems to have improved enough for Greene to make a distinct shift back to the music he loves so well. What brought him back? "The music brought me back" he exclaimed. "The music and the fact that it looks like one is able to have a business at it instead of a hobby. The Bill Monroe band that I was in dissolved for lack of work. And that was my last view of bluegrass as a business. A few years ago I was touring with a bunch of banjo players for Rounder Records, and I saw how many CDs they were selling on the job and people were actually coming out to see this stuff! A light bulb came on and I thought, 'Maybe I can do this for a living?' I always wanted to; it just never seemed feasible. And the music is just great to play. I hope this bluegrass thing will allow me stay in bluegrass; all I want to do is bluegrass.

"Monroe's tunes were all highly melodic, as were Ralph Stanley's. If you get their melodies down on a piece of paper, you've got something! There are some very deep melodic truths in what the great bluegrass artists had. And some of the newer ones, too. The newgrass thing has not survived, and my **Grass Is Greener** band is not like that in any way. It seems that the more Monroe-like or **Flatt and Scruggs**-like the bluegrass is, the better it's going to go over and also, the better I like it—I mean, let's get some personal taste into this. Those guys are hard to beat; their arrangement ideas, their solos, their vocal harmonies, it's hard to beat that... And the bluegrass audience is my favorite audience to play to—it always has been."

In 1973, Greene helped assemble **Muleskinner** to backup Bill Monroe when he was to come to town. "I contracted the band; it was my job to get it all together for Bill and I assembled Clarence White, Peter Rowan, Bill Keith, David Grisman, Stuart Schulman and myself to be the Bill Monroe band. (they all happened to be around at that time for one reason or the other) but Monroe had car problems and didn't show up. Then came 'air time' and there's a full audience out there (at the KCET studios) so what were we going to do? We had only a couple of days to get this band going.[111] "There are two CDs relative to that concert out now (1995). One of the soundtracks and four extra tunes that didn't get onto the video—the live video program which was approximately a half-hour. The first appearance of this live performance is on this 1995 compact disc. And the other CD is the studio recording that the band made after the video for Warner Brothers.

Soon Greene was a member of the **Great American Music Band**[112]. They played a rather progressive style of music. By 1975, he began playing with **Loggins and Messina** for audiences as large as 85,000. He was paid well and well cared-for. Though this was a great job for a sideman, he chose to leave to produce records. He soon began doing session work and taking violin lessons again. He practiced daily for the next several years. He recorded "Ramblin'" on Rounder after the violin lessons and soon formed his own **Richard Greene Band** in 1980. The band recorded "Blue Rondo" on the Sierra Records label. During that period, he played many gigs with Eddie and Martha Adcock. Eddie played electric guitar and electric banjo; Martha, rhythm guitar.

Bringing us up-to-date with Greene in the 1990s, we find him fronting his own **Greene String Quartet** as well as producing albums and performing on jingles and film sound tracks in Los Angeles. In 1993, he returned to bluegrass with the formation of the **Grass Is Greener**. "The Grass Is Greener"[113] was the band's

---

[110] With Peter Rowan (guitar), Andy Kulberg (bass), Larry Atamanuik (drums) and Lloyd Baskin (keyboards and vocals).

[111] They did a gig at the Ash Grove as a warm-up for the show with Monroe. The band didn't tour after this video gig at KCET. Clarence Whit was killed within a month of this gig.

[112] With David Grisman (mandolin), John Carlini (guitar), Ellen Kearny (guitar) and Joe Carroll (bass). The original version of the band was with himself and Vassar Clements at the Great American Music Hall and called themselves the Great American Fiddle Band.

[113] With Kenny Blackwell (mandolin), David Grier (guitar), Bill Keith (banjo) and Tim Emmons (bass). Chris Thile played on the demo for the Grass Is Greener which Greene submitted to IBMA for the 1993 showcase. Thile appeared with the band at the showcase then left the band. Kenny Blackwell took over the mandolin spot from that time on, until Butch Baldassari replaced Blackwell in the spring of 1995. One cut on the album, "Panhandle Country" commemorates Thile's contribution to the band, which was very significant, said Greene.

1995 Rebel (REB-1714) project. His "The Greene Fiddler," which came out in 1994 on Sierra (SXCD 6005), was a compilation of his earlier work. His 1996 work was "Wolves a-Howling."

The tragic story of the incredible Scotty Stoneman[114]

In a 1992 telephone interview, Everett Lilly described Scotty Stoneman, "I've had a lot of fiddlers with me and I've played with what they call the 'best fiddlers,' like Big Howdy Forrester, Benny Martin, Chubby Wise. They are great fiddlers in what you call the bluegrass field. And Tex Logan worked with us. But I don't know nobody that could carry Scotty Stoneman's case when it come to playin' the fiddle on the stage. And I'm speakin' the truth! I have never seen his match and probably never will. And I don't know why anybody could fiddle like that. I've often wondered was it because he was peeled up, drunked up, or doped up or what. But he had more life than three fiddlers had on the stage. He was a showman. He didn't seem to be anybody very smart. All of his smart went to his music some way. When he did, his fiddle on the stage it had an entirely different sound [than other fiddlers]. I've heard a album he cut. The album is great but it don't give him justice in no way!"[115]

Scotty Stoneman came out to the West Coast in 1965 with the **Stonemans** and asked the **Kentucky Colonels** for a job. Roland White recalled, "They had been out there two or three different times and at this point here was probably their last time out there. They came out for two or three months and had a bunch of gigs they were doing: hootenannies, television and stuff like that. They rented a little apartment and stayed out there for that time. Well, in this instance, they had been there over a year, maybe a year and a half. And they finally just threw him out of the band. You can't have that [drinking]. They just left him! So he was down on Skid Row. And so Ed Pearl heard about it from someone else and they went and found him and brought him to The Ash Grove. He didn't even have a fiddle at that time. He was institutionalized to dry out, but he didn't stay very long. So he wasn't in good condition when we got him but he begged to have somebody to play with and that he would do better, you know. And if he couldn't do it, he would just not be on the stage and embarrass us; he would just say, 'Well, I can't do it,' and that's what happened. As far as we know, they just left California without him. When he came with us, in a way, they were glad that someone else had him. Maybe it

was that he disappeared on them—I don't know the real story because I never questioned those people on Skid Row. He just said his family left him."[116]

They loved his fiddling but recognized that he had a drinking problem. They hired him for as long as he would stay sober. "The deal was that he was to not drink, and whenever he felt like he had to go back to drinking and falling down, he could just leave—and that's the way he did it." Roland continued, "He was terrific! He was a gentleman; he was a great guy! He would never embarrass you anywhere you went, you know. He was just very polite. But he was just a really, really sick man. I really felt bad for him because of his sickness." So Scott Stoneman stayed sober while he was with the **Kentucky Colonels**. "If he started drinking, then it would affect his playing," said Roland. "We saw him perform with his family (the **Stonemans**) in a couple instances where they would hold him up and laugh at it and he couldn't play well."

Roland spoke to Pop Stoneman about how Scott came about drinking so much. Evidently, he was such a great fiddle player as early as age eleven that he was in demand by bands in the Washington, D.C., area whose members where much older. Scott played and toured with them and learned how to drink.

The **Kentucky Colonels** recordings with Scott Stoneman on the fiddle "provide a valuable insight to the skills and eccentricities of this brilliant musician. Though his unrestrained approach to the instrument sometimes led to a questionable choice of notes, it is possible that no other bluegrass fiddler has played with the same ferocity, inventiveness, and perhaps technical mastery Scott Stoneman brought to the instrument."[117] He died in early 1973 due to complication with alcohol, barely forty years old.

Byron Berline with California, c. 1994. L to R: Dan Crary, John Hickman, Byron Berline, Steve Spurgin, John Moore.

[114] Most of this anecdote was told to me in early 1994 by Roland White in a telephone conversation. It wasn't easy for Roland to talk about this because, even thirty years later, the tragic story of one of the world's greatest fiddlers was so close to Roland's own life.

[115] Telephone interview, 1992.

[116] From a March 8, 1994, telephone interview.

[117] Barry Brower, "Remembering the Kentucky Colonels—The Bluegrass Life of Roland White," *Bluegrass Unlimited*, February, 1987 , p. 28.

Byron Berline—
the man who changed
bluegrass fiddling

One of the most significant second-generation fiddle players in bluegrass is Byron Berline. As *the* person who introduced the fancy Texas style of contest fiddling to bluegrass music in 1967, Berline is probably more qualified than anyone to speak of the differences between Texas fiddling and bluegrass fiddling. In a very emphatic manner, Mr. Berline was kind enough to define the differences, "The thing is, about Texas fiddling—now get this straight! I want you to understand this if you can—the Texas fiddler, to do it true Texas style, may swing the notes a lot. It's a jazzy, swingy [form] with a lot of improvisation. I didn't do a lot of that fiddling with Bill Monroe—just the simple fact that he does not like swing in his music. And when I did 'Sally Goodin' it was based on the Texas style, but I didn't swing the notes as much as they would. And we played it at a much faster tempo than the Texas fiddlers. So, indirectly, I did bring it to [Bill Monroe] but I didn't take the true Texas form to bluegrass music." Staying within the parameters which Monroe required, Berline introduced his music which he says "was Texas-flavored. I was the only one who had actually studied the style of that kind of fiddling and played with Monroe."

Berline feels that one of the reasons that Texas fiddling came into existence was the many influences of the area upon old-time fiddle music. These influences include swing, Mexican music, and jazz. The style is flashier and more interesting for the fiddler. The style also included a long bow technique which was different from the style typical of Appalachian fiddling. Berline continued with the 1992 telephone conversation. The style was "developed into what it is today—even like Mark O'Connor has done it and Benny Thomasson was doing it in the '40s and '50s when Benny was a young kid—they developed it through the contests, you see, trying to get farther out with it but staying within the

parameter of the tune. Of course, swing influenced it and the type of rhythm that was used behind the fiddle made that style what it is. Instead of using straight chords on the guitar they might use piano or use chords and slap-rhythm type stuff. They would use jazz chords behind the fiddle. This wasn't done in bluegrass or mountain-type music. [The way I did] 'Sally Goodin' seemed to fit in Monroe's music. Now, when I did the album with the **Dillards**—that was before I played with Monroe—that brought it out probably more so than any other record before then...the 'Pickin' and Fiddlin'' record. It was Texas-style fiddling used with a bluegrass backup."

In a 1991 interview, Alan Munde commented on the importance of Berline in bluegrass music. By hiring Byron, "I think it was that Monroe put some stamp of approval on the Texas fiddle/breakdown playing. Maybe Byron was the first to capture Monroe's attention. And he was young enough and wanted to do it. And he *could* do it—he could play bluegrass and then turn around and play "Sally Goodin'" at a tempo that was more in line with what bluegrass people liked. I don't know if Monroe really liked Texas-style fiddling, but he liked what Byron did. I think it created an opening for people like Mark O'Connor and Sam Bush, although they didn't come into it until later. They were certainly influenced by Byron's influence in the music." Byron was not a pioneer in Texas-style fiddling, but he was *the* performer who brought it to bluegrass music.

In a 1991 interview, Berline spoke about old-time and Texas fiddling, "Here's what I did. I played 'Sally Goodin' the way Eck Robertson did it. I had my own style on it but I learned it more from Eck Robertson who was a Texas fiddler. He's the one, as far as I'm concerned, who developed 'Sally Goodin' into what it is today. He had the first recording of that in 1922 on Victor. I knew Eck. He and I were at the 1964, 1965 Newport Folk Festival together. My dad and I have four cuts on there which will be released on CD soon. I don't know if Eck will be on it."

Byron Berline was born in Caldwell, Kansas, July 6, 1944, and brought up just across the border in northern Oklahoma. At age five, he entered his first fiddle contest and he won his first contest at ten. He learned to play from his old-time fiddle-playing father, Lue, his mother, and other musician relatives who hauled him around to many of the Southwest contests. His main influences were Benny Thomasson, Eck Robertson, and Lue, who was a collector and student of the fiddle and who had competed in fiddle contests since 1920. In 1942, Lue won all of the contests he entered that year in a five-state area. Through the years, most of the fiddles Byron played were originally his father's.

In 1962, at the University of Oklahoma, Norman, Oklahoma, on a football scholarship, Byron began playing fiddle with Bill Caswell in a folk group called **Cleveland County Ramblers** (until 1964). In 1964, Berline met Alan Munde and they soon formed the **Oklahoma Bluegrass Gentlemen**. Munde was recently enrolled in the University of Oklahoma and was just beginning to play the banjo. Berline and Munde jammed with the **Stone Mountain Boys** of Dallas, Texas. This was an important band in Berline's career development toward bluegrass. Berline and Munde went down to see them, and played with the band whenever they could.[118]

On November 23, 1963, Berline met the **Dillards** at the University of Oklahoma. The band really impressed him and it was then that he knew that he wanted to be a bluegrass musician. Berline recalled this most memorable moment, "The night I met the **Dillards**, I didn't know those guys from Adam. They were standing there, ready to go on stage for a show at the University of Oklahoma, and somebody introduced me to them and said, 'You guys ought to get together and play.' They saw my fiddle case and said, 'You play the fiddle, huh?' I told them I did. But I didn't know bluegrass, and I didn't know what *they* sounded like. Doug said, 'Let's get together after we're done. I'd like to hear you play.' And I said, 'Okay.' Well, I went and listened to them and they were just mind-boggling. As soon as they got through, they took off out the door and I went to try to find them. About thirty minutes later, I finally spotted them coming out of the student union there at the college, all packed up and leaving. I said, 'Aw, I'm sorry I missed you guys. I tried to find you.' And Doug said, 'Wait a minute you guys, I want to hear this guy play the fiddle.' So I got my fiddle out, he got his banjo out, and the first song I did with them was 'Hamilton County Breakdown'—the fastest song I knew—the closest thing to bluegrass. Oh man! By the time we got though, they all had their instruments out; Mitch took the cover off his bass, Rodney got his guitar out. And we just stood there for two hours, playing one fiddle tune after another."[119]

They liked Byron and invited him to play on their next album titled "Pickin' and Fiddlin'" (Elektra Records) in July of 1964. This was the first bluegrass album featuring old-time fiddling, and his fancy Texas-style added new dimensions to bluegrass music. This was Byron's first opportunity to play with a three-finger style banjo picker and a full bluegrass band. In addition to his playing with the **Dillards**, Berline and banjo player Ed Shelton played weekly on local television.

In 1964, Byron Berline won the National Old-Time Fiddle Championship at Missoula, Montana. Simultaneously, there was a National Old-Time Fiddle Championship at Weiser, Idaho. The two contests competed against each other for some years; soon the contest in Missoula ceased. Berline went on to win the Championships in Weiser 1965 and 1970. Lue also competed in the Senior Division of the contest and consistently placed in the top.

In 1965, Berline and his father played twin fiddles at the Newport Folk Festival. It was here that Byron met Bill Monroe. The invitation to join the **Blue Grass Boys** when he finished college came here. He began working for Bill Monroe in March of 1967[120]; he succeeded Richard Greene on the fiddle. Seven months later, in September, Berline was drafted into the U.S. Army (Special Services division) as a musician and javelin thrower (which he had pursued in college after quitting football). "I hated to leave [Monroe] 'cause I didn't feel I had learned near enough. And he never would say anything. I'd say, 'Bill, am I doing this right or wrong?' And he'd say, 'Oh, you're doing just fine.' He knew I was going into the Army, and he didn't want to bug me about anything."[121] But Monroe did ask him to put some bluesy notes into the songs; this was easy for him. "I knew what he meant...he just wanted me to have a good time. We got along great 'cause he liked the way I played the old-time fiddle tunes. Of course, I learned 'Virginia Darlin' and we worked up 'Gold Rush' together, and 'Sally Goodin',' of course. He loved to just sit and play old-time tunes, one right after the other. We had a great time together. We had a great relationship together, and we still do."

On August 23rd, 1967, a **Blue Grass Boys** recording session with Berline (fiddle), Monroe, Vic Jordan (banjo), Roland White (guitar) and James Monroe (bass) produced "Gold Rush," "Sally Goodin'" and "Virginia Darlin'."

When Berline left Monroe for the Army in September, he was replaced by Benny Williams.[122] While at Fort Polk, Louisiana, he played in his own **Southern Bluegrass Boys**.[123] In 1969, Berline was released from the Army. He was hoping to re-join the **Blue Grass Boys** but Kenny Baker was the fiddler with Monroe at that time so Berline decided to go to California to record on the "Dillard and Clark" LP with Doug Dillard (in June). "After I went out to California I knew I wasn't going to go back to Nashville so I really didn't even ask him if I

---

[118] Band membership consisted of Ed Shelton (banjo), Tootie Williams (bass), Mitchell Land (mandolin) and Lonnie Craft (guitar).

[119] Roger H. Siminoff, "Byron Berline, A Night to Remember," *Frets*, March, 1982, p. 27.

[120] According to Kenny Baker, *this* was the time that Baker joined the group as their fiddler. But Byron probably relates it more accurately because of the relative time that he joined the military. Baker was probably a year off, joining on March 14, 1968.

[121] From an interview at the Peter Britt Bluegrass Festival, near Medford, Oregon, in 1985.

[122] Horace "Benny" Williams recorded on Monroe's November 9, 1967, Nashville session. Vassar Clements also recorded at the session. Kenny Baker replaced Benny Williams and recorded with Monroe on November 14, 1968.

[123] Members included Travis Stewart (guitar, who played a short time with Bill Monroe), Dennis Lucas (banjo) and Gene Alford (bass).

America's Music | Bluegrass

358

could come back. Up until I got out of the Army I had planned to go back with Monroe."

Following the "Copperfields" LP with the **Dillards**, he moved to California permanently. This move for Berline and his wife, Bette, proved very beneficial for both the fiddler and for the L.A. area which thirsted for a good fiddler. And he was a natural, fitting into the session system even though he didn't read music. His instinctive ability in music enabled him to be gainfully employed in most facets of show business. He also recorded with the **Nitty Gritty Dirt Band** on the "Uncle Charlie and His Dog Teddy" LP (Liberty), which contains the top-40 hit, "Mr. Bojangles."

Berline played music with Doug Dillard and Gene Clark's **Dillard and Clark Expedition** for a short time. Clark left the group in late 1970, so Roger Bush and Billy Ray Lathum joined Dillard and Berline and they formed **Dillard and the Expedition with Byron Berline**. This lasted for two years. He also recorded extensively on records, television, and the movie soundtrack for "Vanishing Point" (Dillard and Berline wrote and played the theme for the movie). When he recorded his fiddle on the **Rolling Stones'** "Honky-Tonk Women," "Mick Jagger thought the sound they were getting was 'too slick.' He therefore insisted that the session be moved outside into the street—microphones, wires and all. There, to the astonishment of passersby—and of a nearby construction crew which was told to hush up during the recording—the cut was completed satisfactorily, traffic, noise, and all."[124]

In June 1970, Berline won his third First Place at the National Old-Time Fiddle Championships. He beat Dick Barrett and Lloyd Wanzer.

Berline called Alan Munde and Roger Bush to join him in **Country Gazette** for a tour with the **Flying Burrito Brothers** in January of 1972. Basically a rock band, the **Flying Burrito Brothers** spread bluegrass by including it in their concerts. Munde joined on banjo and electric guitar. They toured extensively, including Europe.[125]

When the **Flying Burrito Brothers** dissolved in 1972, partners Berline and Bush continued **Country Gazette** with Kenny Wertz and Alan Munde. Herb

" Byron was not a pioneer in Texas-style fiddling, but he was the performer who brought it to bluegrass music.."

—Alan Munde

Pedersen occasionally played banjo. A demonstration tape was cut and hustled around to various Los Angeles-based record companies. Eventually, United Artists signed the band, though there was some resistance at the label. "What do we need a bluegrass group for?" snorted one top executive. "We've already got the **Nitty Gritty Dirt Band**!" They recorded "Don't Give Up Your Day Job" for United Artists (1973) and soon recorded "Country Gazette Live."[126]

In 1975, Berline left **Country Gazette** and formed **Sundance** with John Hickman (banjo), Dan Crary (guitar), Allen Wald (rhythm guitar) and Jack Skinner (bass). The first recording was "Byron Berline and Sundance," a 1976 MCA album.

In the spring of 1978, **Berline, Crary and Hickman** was formed with musicians Berline (fiddle, mandolin), Crary (guitar) and Hickman (banjo). 1981 (June) brought Sugar Hill's "Berline-Crary-Hickman."

Berline began writing a regular column for *Frets* in 1979. Still, he didn't read music. His wife, Bette, was helpful in transcribing his thoughts into musical annotation for the monthly articles.[127]

A new group came into existence about 1980; Sugar Hill released "Byron Berline and the L.A. Fiddle Band."[128] As a band, they occasionally played locally in the Los Angeles area but they mostly got together for fun.

A re-creation of **Sundance** occurred occasionally with Berline, Skip Conover (resonator guitar, lap steel), Rick Cunha (guitar), Steve Spurgin (drums), Don Whaley (electric bass) and Pete Wasner (piano). "It's the most fun group I think I've ever played in," said Berline. "We have four lead singers. They're all great musicians. They all write, and they're absolutely wonderful."[129] He began using the mandolin more. "Learning mandolin helped my fiddling, especially on things like double stops. I can write things on the mandolin sometimes, just sitting around, that I can take right to the fiddle." We won't see Byron's other two bands on the road. With so many people in the band, he'd have to charge more than promoters would want or can pay.

[124] Jack Tottle, "Berline, Crary and Hickman, Part 1," *Bluegrass Unlimited*, September, 1980.

[125] Members of the two bands included Berline, Munde, Bush, Kenny Wertz (banjo and guitar), and Don Beck (guitar, pedal steel). Wertz had played with the Scottsville Squirrel Barkers with bluegrass mandolinist Chris Hillman in San Diego.

[126] "Country Gazette Live" was recorded November 1974 at McCabe's, Santa Monica, CA, and distributed by Transatlantic Records, London, England. The guest resonator guitarist was Skip Conover. Roland White joined the Country Gazette on guitar in 1973 when Wertz left in July.

[127] Bette later played piano on his "Jumping the Strings" album (1990).

[128] With members Berline, Hickman, Dennis Fetchitt (fiddle), Bruce Johnson (fiddle), Roger Reed (guitar), Skip Conover (Dobro) and Dennis Reed (bass).

[129] Roger H. Siminoff, "Byron Berline, A Night to Remember," *Frets*, March, 1982, p. 29.

The *Frets* Readers' Poll of December 1983 awarded Best Country/Bluegrass Fiddler to Byron Berline.

In an interview in 1985, Mr. Berline said that bluegrass music on the West Coast was getting more popular and would continue to do so. And this is in spite of the fact that there aren't many clubs in which to play. As of 1995, he played with Dan Crary, John Hickman, Steve Spurgin and John Moore in **California**—their version of bluegrass from the lower West Coast. The group broke up at the end of 1995. Byron then opened up a music store with John Hickman in Guthrie, Oklahoma. Berline and Hickman continued to tour with the **Mason Williams Band**.

Blaine Sprouse

Blaine Sprouse— a third-generation fiddler who learned from the masters well

This Martinsburg, West Virginian was born October 11, 1956. His father was able to keep Blaine's interest in music up by giving him a good exposure to music through his own playing of clawhammer banjo, guitar, and he even had a radio show in Winchester, Virginia. Blaine began playing guitar at age nine—two years before he was influenced by Kenny Baker's fiddle playing, which caused him to switch instruments. At sixteen, he won the West Virginia State Fiddling Championship. He played with the **Sprouse Brothers** (Douglas (bass) and Rodney (mandolin) Sprouse) around the Waynesboro, Virginia, area and with **Bill Emerson and Cliff Waldron and the Lee Highway Boys** in the late 1960s.

Sprouse turned full-time when he joined the **Sunny Mountain Boys** in the fall of 1973. He toured with them until 1975 when he quit the music to do some cattle ranching in Illinois. This tough job of being a cowboy gave him the perspective needed to pursue music as his career. Besides, he missed being on the road. In April 1976, he was one of the founding members of **Bluegrass Strings**.

In 1977, he filled-in with the **Blue Grass Boys** when their regular fiddler, Kenny Baker, was out after cutting his left hand badly with a hunting knife. This gave Sprouse an opportunity to meet the big names of bluegrass music and was definitely the right place at the right time. That same year, Sprouse moved to Nashville and then joined James Monroe's **Midnight Ramblers**. In 1977, the Midnight Ramblers band had an auto accident which killed their bass player, Tommy Franks. Franks was driving himself and James Monroe to Nashville when the van collided with the back of a semi. Monroe was only bruised and shaken. The other members of the band, Alan O'Bryant (mandolin) and Sprouse, were getting to Nashville by other means. The band fell apart.

Then Sprouse joined Charlie Louvin's country band for two years. He explained how the style of this band was different than in a bluegrass band, "You're not out front as much as you are in a bluegrass band. In a bluegrass band, you're such an integral part of everything that's happening. In a country band, unless you're playing with a band where the fiddle is a featured part of the music, you're just there to play a little riff here, a little thing there, maybe backup one verse in the song."[130]

Sprouse quit Louvin's band in 1979 and joined **Jim and Jesse**. During that period, he recorded his solo LP, "Blaine Sprouse," on Rounder. In 1981, he recorded "Summertime." In 1982, Sprouse was in the **Bluegrass Band** with Butch Robins (banjo), Alan O'Bryant (guitar, mandolin), Eddie Dye (resonator guitar, bones) and David Sebring (bass). This was a band which fulfilled the visions of Sprouse, Robins and O'Bryant. Robins had recorded his solo album "The Fifth Child" just before founding this band and was ready to promote it. The band existed for ten months until bookings, which were mainly on the West Coast, ceased to provide enough revenue for them to continue. Their Voyager Records LP was "Another Saturday Night." Sprouse joined the **Osborne Brothers** after the **Bluegrass Band** folded.

The 1984 "Snakes Alive" LP was recorded by **Dreadful Snakes** with musicians Sprouse, Jerry Douglas, Pat Enright, Bela Fleck, Roland White and Mark Hembree. This group, explained Sprouse, "came about as sort of a jam session turned into a band. We used to jam at the Station Inn (in Nashville) quite a bit. Some tapes were made and Rounder acquired one of them somehow, and they were interested in making a record."[131]

130 Wayne W. Daniel, "Blaine Sprouse—Pick of the Bluegrass Fiddle Crop," *Bluegrass Unlimited*, November, 1982, p. 27.
131 Ibid., p. 29.

In a 1988 interview, Sprouse spoke of other fiddlers. About Vassar, "My perception is that he doesn't really think about what he's going to play until he plays it. The major difference between Kenny Baker and Vassar Clements—this is my opinion—[is that] Kenny Baker [will play] a certain break on [say] 'Mule Skinner Blues' exactly the same way every time, which is really hard for someone like me to do. Yet Vassar might play 'Mule Skinner Blues' fifty times and never play it the same way twice."

About Howdy Forrester, Blaine likes "his ability to write these tunes that are so monstrously hard to execute. He has written some of the technically hardest tunes for a fiddle player to play. They're good tunes."[132]

Sprouse was with (though not a member of) the **Nashville Bluegrass Band** in 1985 when they released "My Native Home" on Rounder. That same year, Rounder released Sprouse's "Brilliancy." Soon, Central

Rear (L to R): Blaine Sprouse, Tim Ellis, Keith McReynolds. Front (L to R): Jesse and Jim McReynolds.

Sun Video Company released "Two Fiddles, No Waiting" which included Sprouse and Baker on fiddles, Fleck (banjo), O'Bryant (guitar), Sam Bush (mandolin) and Terry Smith (bass).

In February 1987, Sprouse quit the **Osborne Brothers** to pursue a four-year degree in business administration at a college in Nashville. Soon after leaving the Osbornes, he toured Europe with Roland White, Billy Smith and Terry Smith as **Blue Ridge Connection**. Soon after this, he joined up with **Jim and Jesse**, staying until 1991 when he returned to law school.

One of Sprouse's main objectives is to play to fit a singer's style—to complement it. It's too easy to overpower a singer, he says. Not one to give out unsolicited advice, if asked, he will tell young musicians, "Have fun with it. Don't get so caught up in trying to play something perfectly that you lose what I think music is basically all about—enjoying yourself while you're doing it. I think you learn more when you're having a good time. This certainly is true for me."[133]

John Hartford speaks of plugging-in the fiddle

John Hartford's fiddle for many years was a five-string with a low "C" on the 5th string which he electrically amplified until 1987. He found a better way to produce a true, fiddle sound instead of the unreal way that most fiddles sound which have electrical pickups. His new plugged-in system sounds as though he is playing into a microphone. The secret is to bypass the system amplifier; going straight into the PA system produces the truest sound possible. He explained in a 1992 interview, "If your instrument sounds real electric and is going through an amp and the amp is being miked, you're not hearing the instrument. What you're really hearing is the cardboard speaker of the amp..." But Hartford became dissatisfied even with this tone and went back to playing directly into a microphone.

---

132 Ibid., p. 29.
133 Ibid., p. 30.

Chapter 11

Bluegrass Guitar - Table of Contents

Bluegrass Guitar

The term *guitarra* appears in Spanish literature of the 1300s, but it probably refers to instruments similar to the lute which was the dominant instrument of the Middle Ages and Renaissance. By the 1500s, the guitar (though not yet in its modern form or tuning) had become an instrument of the common people of Europe.

The guitar, as we know it today in bluegrass music, followed a lineage which we can trace back to Germany and Austria. Simultaneously, the classical and flamenco guitars were being developed in Spain and eventually reached America in that form. As for the modern guitar, this story is best told by telling the story of C.F. Martin and Company as is done in detail in the chapter of Instrument Companies and Makers in this book. While C.F. Martin was not the first guitar maker in America, none was more influential. His work in the 1800s was highly respected and became a basis of the modern bluegrass guitar. Of course, there were other guitar makers. While Orville Gibson can be considered as a 19th century maker, his influence would not be recognized until the 20th century. And Lyon and Healy's Washburn brand claimed to produce 100,000 units in 1897. "By comparison, Martin's annual output in the sixty years since C.F. Martin opened shop averaged 123 guitars. Martin's annual guitar production would not even top 1,000 until 1919."[1]

This chapter deals with biographical sketches of some bluegrass guitarists and some of the guitar's relevant modern history in a somewhat chronological order of their appearance upon the bluegrass scene.

Riley Puckett— none were better in the twenties

When Bill and Earl Bolick and Homer Sherrill began on WGST, Augusta, Georgia, in 1936, guitarist Riley Puckett was there at the station. Bill Bolick was a performing guitarist but admits he couldn't come close to Puckett's skill, considering it better than later stars such as Lester Flatt and Charlie Monroe. Bolick considers Riley as doing the best bass runs he ever heard in an old-time band.

In an interview with this writer, Pappy Sherrill spoke with reverence about Riley Puckett, the blind guitarist with Gid Tanner's **Skillet Lickers**. "I seen Riley Puckett play. He played with his first finger coming up towards his body instead of picking down with a thumbpick like Zeke (Morris) does. And he played an old metal guitar."

Bill Monroe's opinions of the lead guitar in bluegrass music

Bill Monroe, in 1984, told this writer how he felt about have a lead guitar in bluegrass music. "I love it. But there's very few bluegrass guitar players that can take lead on the guitar and play a good lead so you have to let them keep the rhythm... I love a guitar that can take the lead on it, you know, in the old-time style and put a lot of blues in a lot of it. I really love that. But they ain't every guitar player that can play that."[2]

Photo courtesy John Ramsey.

Raymond Fairchild on guitar players and "frammers"

In a 1980 interview for *Bluegrass Unlimited*, Fairchild spoke of rhythm guitar players. "A lot of people will tell you the woods is full of guitar pickers. The woods is full of 'frammers'—not guitar players. You can name rhythm guitar players on your right hand.

---

[1] George Gruhn and Walter Carter, *Acoustic Guitars and Other Fretted Instruments* (San Francisco: GPI Books, 1993), p. 30

[2] Not taking anything away Mr. Monroe's comment, there is possibly another factor why the flatpicked guitar was not widely used in bluegrass. This is the fact that the guitar was simply not loud enough to compete as a lead instrument. There were probably plenty of guitarists capable of flatpicking the guitar in a bluegrass band but they would have been lost because they couldn't have been heard in Monroe's band. For many years, Monroe only had one, two or three microphones for the whole band, and none of them was dedicated so that the guitar could be heard over the louder banjo, fiddle or mandolin. It would be a few years before the guitar was allowed to have its own microphone which would allow it to be heard adequately. But even then, Monroe hired a guitarist to play rhythm only—he already had three other lead instruments in the band. Therefore, Monroe more or less established a tradition early in his career that the guitar should be used strictly for rhythm, with only occasional flourishes to taste.

What I like to hear is straight, solid pickin'. I've been into it for twenty-five years and, with all honesty, I'll have to say I've had *one*—the one I've got now—Wallace Crowe. He's the best rhythm picker I've ever heard in my life. The best bass player, too, Wayne Crowe; he's the best man I've ever heard. It don't take a stage full to play music. You take three men and all of them pushing time and it sounds right."

The lead guitar music of the Stanley Brothers

Recording with Syd Nathan's King Records in 1958, the Stanley brothers were forced to use the guitar as a lead instrument for their recordings. Ralph, in a 1985 interview, told the story of using the guitar as a lead instrument. "We used to use a mandolin back when we first started and used it a long time. We recorded several numbers with a mandolin. But most bluegrass [groups] used the mandolin and we wanted to get away from it and sort of get a different sound with the guitar." In that particular King recording session, Bill Napier played lead guitar and George Shuffler played bass.

Bill Napier— one of the first flatpickers

Back in 1954, Bill Napier went to Detroit from his Virginia home to work in a factory. During this time, he pursued the playing of the mandolin with a serious dedication. He employed the tips learned back home from mandolinist Pee Wee Lambert when the **Stanley Brothers** would come to town. Little did he know that he would not only join the **Stanley Brothers and the Clinch Mountain Boys**, he would become an integral part of the "Stanley sound" when they began recording on Syd Nathan's King Records in 1958.

Napier was born in Wise County, Virginia, December 17, 1935, raised in a family of eleven children. Only Bill and one brother showed an interest in music. In July of 1957, Napier traveled to Bristol,

The Stanley Brothers

Virginia, auditioned for a job with the Stanley brothers and got it. He joined them on mandolin that fall. He played mandolin with them until, as he described it, "In '59, they needed a change in sound. That's when I just laid the mandolin down for awhile and took a lot of my mandolin licks and transformed them over to the guitar." (George Shuffler also had a cross-picking style on the guitar with the Stanleys, but mostly played bass when Napier was on guitar during the late fifties.) Napier wrote and recorded the mandolin tune "Daybreak in Dixie" while he was with the Stanleys.

A telephone interview in May of 1994 brought out Napier's opinion of the origination of the lead guitar in music. "As far as I know, when that style started, the only one prior to me was Don Reno in the **Reno and Smiley** recordings.[3] It's just a three-finger roll with a straight pick." Not only was Napier cross-picking with the Stanleys, "I did flatpicking *and* cross-picking, like on their old recordings in about '59 of 'Old Rattler' and 'Mountain Dew.' Those two numbers were just straight flatpicking. They revived an old one called 'Sweet Thing' and that was cross-picking. I don't know who started calling it 'cross-picking,' but at the time I first started recording it George Shuffler was playing upright bass on the same session."

Mr. Napier remembered how the lead guitar picking with the Stanleys came about, "Well, the Stanleys were with Mercury Records in Nashville when I went with 'em on the mandolin. Then our first session for King Records was strictly the bluegrass instruments: mandolin, guitar, fiddle, banjo and upright bass. Well, Mercury had let them go because of a slump in sales—and their first recordings with King sold very slow, too. So Sydney (Nathan) suggested that they needed a new sound. We even thought about Dobro®—**Flatt and Scruggs** already had that going good and strong. So just by accident, while I was puttin' on a new set of strings on the guitar and usin' some of my mandolin licks to knock the slack out of 'em so it would be in tune for a TV show, that's when the Stanleys decided that's the style that Syd Nathan might like. So we had to go in and pretty well audition for King after we'd already done an

[3] Don Reno's "Country Boy Rock and Roll" was the first acknowledged recording of flatpicked guitar (1956). Others who are given credit for flatpicking the guitar, such as the Delmore brothers and Sam McGee, picked it in a style which we consider a precursor of what we now call "flatpicking."

album. So Sydney accepted and said that's what we've been lookin' for and he had us to stay in town and record twenty-four sides. And that's when the cross-pick and flatpick work started with the Stanleys. At that time, there were only four of us: Ralph and Carter on the banjo and guitar, George Shuffler on the upright bass, and I was on the second guitar with the lead out cross-pickin' and flatpickin'. George knew some guitar, that's for sure. He just never used it when I was with the Stanleys."

Mr. Napier continued, "Then from there, since I started the style, that's one thing I wanted to keep when I joined my partnership with Charlie Moore (1961) because that automatically put our records with our own sound, you know. And because I started it all with King Records, that pretty well helped Charlie Moore and I to help swing a ten-year contract with them. In fact, I never did even touch my mandolin during my entire career with **Charlie Moore and Bill Napier**. And that was an even dozen records for King Records and two or three for Old Homestead.

"There has been some confusion on some write-ups about me and George Shuffler, and I've been knowin' George since the late '50s. George is a tremendous upright bass player, so is his brother, John Shuffler—they actually played the bass just alike. But the only thing that even touched the style of guitar playin' that I do was some stuff that Don Reno did back in the middle to late fifties, along in there. Don did almost a mandolin style of flatpicking on his guitar. He did a terrific job. As far as rolling the straight pick, that's what a cross-pick is: when you roll a straight pick. Now Jesse McReynolds does that on his mandolin. It's the same thing as taking a straight pick and doing a three-finger banjo roll. I can't compare what I do with what George does. What George does, I like. I would say it's more relaxed. Because of my mandolin work, I seem to put a bit more a-drive to mine. My style can be used equally well with a waltz as a breakdown. I guess it's a more active pick—more use of the right hand."

In addition to the fact that King Records pushed them into the guitar as a lead instrument in 1959, Carter Stanley realized that this was what was neces-

sary to make their band's sound immediately identifiable from other bands. It would add a gimmick to the band to increase band recognition, popularity, and record sales. The gimmick which Bill Monroe used was twin and triple fiddles. The lead guitar became an essential ingredient to the **Clinch Mountain Boys'** sound. Napier continued, "It was to set the Stanleys apart from Monroe because, as Bill used to say, they were right down his shirt collar when it come to sound. He had a funny way of saying things, but that's the way he said it. **Flatt and Scruggs** did the same thing with the Dobro®. It did **Flatt and Scruggs** a lot more good than they even imagined."

Napier also enjoyed doing some of the booking and being the band's comedian as "Grandpap[4] Napier" who was a cranky old character with a long gray goatee and a gray wig. Comedians were very popular and common in bluegrass bands during that period; most of the time they wore outlandish costumes for immediate identification. Napier continued this comedy character in the first two years of his partnership with Charlie Moore.[5] His pay averaged $50-75 weekly. "It wasn't bad pay if you got it," said Napier. "That's what most people were promised back in those days but it depended on the business. If it's there, you got it; if it's not, you toughed it out."

Bill Napier left the Stanleys in 1961 to further his career and become better known as a musician. He then partnered with Charlie Moore[6] in **Charlie Moore, Bill Napier and the Dixie Partners**. Moore had been in charge the **Dixie Partners** since 1957 and had recorded for Starday already. They played on television shows in Greenville and Spartanburg, South Carolina. They recorded for American Records of Cincinnati, Ohio. Napier played guitar and banjo after he and Charlie moved to Panama City, Florida, to play on WJHG-TV.

The **Dixie Partners** recorded 108 songs on King; their first King LP was "Folk 'n Hill."[7] Their best known song, which was on the LP, was "Truck Driver's Queen." It was later popularized by Jimmy Martin's **Sunny Mountain Boys** on the Decca label and by the **Willis Brothers** on Starday. Napier said, "I would say that the popularity of 'Truck Driver's Queen' was the

---

[4] This is sometimes found incorrectly as "Grandpop."

[5] When Napier dropped the act, Henry Dockery took it up—the old man-appearance, not the name—and they called him "Uncle Henry." Napier explained that it was slapstick. The Stanley's original comedian, no matter who played him, was called "Cousin Winesap," first played by Ray Lambert in '48, the bass player.

[6] This hard-driving bluegrasser from Piedmont, South Carolina, worked full-time in the bluegrass music business beginning about 1956. He recorded as early as 1952 for Decca while still in high school. His choice to pursue music as a career came easy after weighing what other careers were available to him. He picked the one which was his love—the one which was the easiest for him, too.

By 1957, Moore's Dixie Partners went to work in Greenville, South Carolina's The Carolina Promenade Party, and then the band's own gospel show on WSPA, Spartanburg, South Carolina; their sponsors were a sausage company and a tombstone company. Soon his Dixie Partners became so popular that he quit his full-time deejay day job to play on WSPA-TV. Moore continued to work with "Cousin Wilbur" Wesbrooks and Kent Wiseman on a television show in Asheville, North Carolina. In 1958, the band recorded on Starday and Design Records.

Moore's picking style included a thumb pick and a first finger pick following in the styles of Carl Story, Lester Flatt, Carter Stanley and Clyde Moody. Most other guitarists of the day were adapting to the use of the flatpick.

[7] Musicians included Jimmy Williams (mandolin), Henry Dockery (bass) and Ray Pennington (snare drums). The drums were King's idea for the recording and reluctantly accepted by Napier and Moore. Pennington used brushes on the drum to keep the volume soft.

During the mid-sixties, the Dixie Partners used the talents of Ralph Mayo (bass), Benny Williams (12-string guitar), Jimmy Lunsford (fiddle), Paul Mullins (fiddle), Johnny Dacus (fiddle), Audie Webster (mandolin), Jim McCall (mandolin), Eb Collins (fiddle), Sid Campbell (guitar) and Benny Birchfield (bass).

best thing that ever happened to the career of Moore and Napier."[8] Now that Napier was away from the sideman role as with the Stanleys, he was free to write more freely and play more expressively. Being his own boss was good for him and his career.

They recorded extensively on King records. Moore was a prolific songwriter; among other things, he translated "The Fiddler" and a reworked version of Mac Wiseman's "The Irish Rebel" into "The Legend of the Rebel Soldier."

The group left WSPA-TV to join a television show in Greenville for a year. They then moved to Florida at WJHG-TV for a year. This stay was frustrating because if they were to play any gigs, they would have to drive at least fifty miles to a population center. There at the station, Moore would read the farm news, news headlines and weather forecast—complete with a weather map. He was soon to return to the Spartanburg/Greenville area, never to stray too far after that.

In 1965, Moore and Napier's **Dixie Partners** returned to WSPA-TV. The **Partners**[9] played other engagements, local and distant. These band activities and Moore's disc jockey work, plus their WWVA morning television show, Jamboree, kept them busy.

Napier and Moore split up the **Dixie Partners** in 1968. They separated as friends and still continued playing together. Their last recordings were on Old Homestead in 1978. Moore led the **Dixie Partners** until he passed away in 1979.[10] Napier partnered a year with Larry Taylor (mandolin) in 1980, recording twenty-four sides on Old Homestead. As of the early 1990s, Napier was still well and playing both mandolin and guitar with his wife in a duo act called **Bill and Carla Napier** in a "relaxed bluegrass sound" similar to what he did with Charlie Moore.

George Shuffler and his cross-picked guitar[11]

George Shuffler was with Jim and Jesse's first group after the McReynolds brothers left Hoke Jenkins' **Smoky Mountaineers** in 1951. It was here that Shuffler

George Shuffler

became inclined to play guitar in a style similar to what Jesse was doing on the mandolin. By the time he joined the **Stanley Brothers** (1951), he used his cross-picking guitar style quite a bit. Mr. Shuffler spoke about the introduction of this style into the Stanley band. "Everybody was playing single-string stuff then.[12] There were actually only three styles of guitar playing years ago: the Delmore brothers' single-string, Merle Travis' style, and Maybelle Carter style, and didn't neither one of them fit the Stanleys. Especially in the 1960s, ninety percent of the time it was just Carter, Ralph and me traveling together. If a contract called for four people we'd pick up somebody. Standing behind them, playing single-string stuff, it didn't give me any fill at the end of a line. Carter really didn't like the cross-picking that much at first—not worth a nickel. Carter said, 'Is that

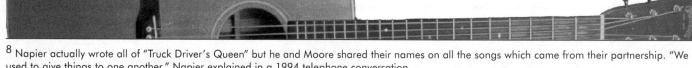

---

[8] Napier actually wrote all of "Truck Driver's Queen" but he and Moore shared their names on all the songs which came from their partnership. "We used to give things to one another," Napier explained in a 1994 telephone conversation.

[9] Band members were Moore, Napier, Johnny Dacus (fiddle), Eb Collins (fiddle, mandolin). They were occasionally joined by fiddlers Chubby Anthony and Paul "Moon" Mullins.

[10] On December 24, 1979, Charles Benjamin Moore died of complications from a hernia treatment in Richmond, Virginia. He was in a coma for the last three weeks. About the time of his death, members of his Charlie Moore and the Dixie Partners were Moore (guitar), Ben Green (banjo), Curley Lambert (mandolin), Lester Woodie (fiddle) and John Davis (bass).

[11] A biography of George Shuffler appears in the Pioneers chapter of this book.

[12] This reference to "single-string" playing is Shuffler's description of flatpicking as we know it today.

[13] Clarence H. Green, "George Shuffler," *Bluegrass Unlimited*, September, 1991, p. 36. I modified this quotation with bits from a March 1993 telephone conversation with Mr. Shuffler.

all you can play?' I said, 'No, but that's all I want to play. 'Cause it fits!' But one of our engineers in Cincinnati at King, Chuck Seitz, did like it and he encouraged it."[13] Shuffler indicated that with Ralph chunking the rhythm during a song, they had to have something with the guitar which would fill-in "and I come up with that and I could just fill-in and keep the music goin' while they stopped to get their breath. So that's how it derived, really. After we got to sellin' records, I could do anything I wanted to. I lost all my fast-pickin' and compromised to do that."

Shuffler's style is difficult for most people to master; it involves picking down strokes on two strings and upstrokes on one. He explained, "Most people do it backwards." By using the open key of D to take advantage of more high strings, "you can start on the lower strings and work your way up. Otherwise, it's hard to come out right with it because you can't keep a consistent roll. My cross-picking is solid, it's two down and one up. That's the only way you can do it and get a consistent roll, you know. It keeps the chord progressions and keeps your right arm a-goin'. 'Cause if you try one down and two up—and that's the way Bill (Napier) played—you get off track that way. You hit a lick and you have to break your stride to stay with the tempo."[14]

In 1960, George Shuffler was with the Stanleys in Florida when they recorded their first King LP. According to Shuffler, "Bill Napier helped us do our first album. Bill called his pickin' 'cross-pickin' but I didn't. Bill called me the other day and we talked for thirty to forty minutes—he's up in Michigan somewhere and we're good friends—but he played one style and I played another because mine was solid rolls and Bill's was more of a hop-skip-jump. It wasn't as consistent [as] with rolls, you know. He played the guitar more like the mandolin; he had the fast wrist. He did the 'Good Old Mountain Dew' album, then I came in there, and Curly Lambert did part of it and I did the rest of [the album]."

Shuffler told an anecdote about his old Gibson guitar, "About the time that Bill Monroe was feudin' with Gibson, everybody who picked a Gibson instrument took paint remover and took the name off the Gibson. We was doin' television, and I wasn't gonna give them no advertisement either so I took the name off. I stripped it plum down, took all the finish off it. We was breakin' into the colleges and people wanted to know what instrument I was playin'—that was before people was so well versed on the instruments. They didn't know what kind of guitar I had, they didn't know the shape of 'em or nothin'. They didn't have no identification to go by so I just let 'em guess and said, 'I don't know.'"

Doc and Merle Watson

Doc and Merle Watson

In the legends of flatpicked guitar music, few stand more prominent in its roots than Doc Watson. He didn't break new ground when he picked a fiddle tune on the guitar; credit for being the first is generally given to Don Reno and the pickers with the **Stanley Brothers**: George Shuffler and Bill Napier. But Doc was different. First, because his playing was so dominant as to demand attention, and second, because he made the guitar *the* lead instrument of the band—not just another lead instrument. He opened the way for a new generation of flatpickers in bluegrass music who are today represented by Dan Crary, Clarence White, Tony Rice, Norman Blake and many others.

However, "You know, Barry, that I don't play bluegrass as such. Acoustic music has been categorized as bluegrass, bluegrass. There is only one bluegrass style and there's other acoustic styles which are traditional, a lot of them are, and I'm involved in that. I began to listen to the radio as I grew up. I heard people like Grady Martin and Hank Garland when they were pickin' in country music playin' fiddle tunes. And I wondered if I could learn to play fiddle tunes with the flatpick. And I began to do some of that. I didn't really work hard at it—you know how a boy is, if he's not absolutely, totally absorbed in music. And I wasn't; I was just a casual player for a long time. I loved it, but not totally absorbed in it like a lot of kids you can't get them away from the guitar or the violin or whatever. In the early '50s, I ran into a fellow, Jack Williams, and I played the electric guitar with a country swing group for a good eight or ten years until the folk revival started and Ralph Rinzler came along. He got me started in the folk revival and people began to hear me flatpick the guitar and play lead on it and the bluegrass players jumped on it. Don Reno preceded me at playin' lead on a flat-top. When I was put on the folk festivals all over the country on the college campuses, the young fellas that loved bluegrass grabbed onto the style. And I guess, maybe, I'm responsible for people in bluegrass playin' lead on the guitar.

"Out of the many albums I have done, I have done one bluegrass album, just to see if I could do bluegrass music and sing some it and play some of it on the guitar. I guess it was successful; it won an award. It was 'Ride the Midnight Train' and was the last our son, Merle, played music on. He played some frailin' banjo on two tunes on it in combination with Bela Fleck's bluegrass banjo. The 'Strictly Instrumental' album with Flatt and Scruggs was done in 1967; Merle had just begun to playin' solid with me along about that time, and he didn't play on that album either. Anyway, the blue-grass album was recorded in '84. I was just a set-in on the 'Flatt and Scruggs with Doc Watson, Strictly Instrumental' (Columbia Records) It was their own album and they wanted me to play some hot guitar on it, or what they called hot guitar, so I set-in and played a bunch of the tunes and enjoyed it awfully well. They released it on CD.

Doc Watson

"I have loved bluegrass and liked a lot of the things that Bill Monroe did," said Doc. "I love the **Nashville Bluegrass Band** (**NBB**). Love that fiddle. I don't play bluegrass as such but once in awhile would do a tune. Sometime, when you get a chance, take a good, hard listen to Jack Lawrence and I and you'll find quite a wide variety of things which are not bluegrass."

"Bluegrass is an offshoot from traditional music and Bill Monroe spawned the idea, but Flatt and Scruggs, I think, helped it to mature when they joined the group. They really helped to make that music come together. Of course, Bill, he was the chief in there and it went the way he wanted it to. But you've got to have good musicians to make a thing come alive. To me, and I think you'll find this if you talk to any real authority on bluegrass—and I don't consider myself one—bluegrass is a combination of four instruments. Of course, you've got to have the bass to set it on, if you'll pardon the expression. The foundation. But you've got to have the banjo, the mandolin, the fiddle and the guitar. And a good bluegrass band will have a guitar player in there that occasionally will play some lead or fill bits. It's not just flatpickin' the guitar. A lot of bluegrass bands use a hot guitar lead a lot. **NBB** don't. They don't need it. That bass player is important and a good player knows when to play and not to play and how to play true notes, especially if you play an acoustic. You've got to tune the thing good first, and then be able, like a fiddler, to be

able to play exactly on the mark because you don't have frets to go by. An accurate hand, let's put it that way, and a good ear. There's your quote: An accurate hand and a good ear makes a good bass player."

Arthel "Doc" Watson was born in Stoney Fork Township[15], North Carolina, in the Blue Ridge Mountains, March 3, 1923. He lives only three miles from where he was born and raised. He was blinded by an eye disease as an infant. Doc told this writer, "I was blind by the time I was a year old. I got an infection at birth, and the capillaries that feed blood to the eye were real weak in my eyes and they couldn't withstand the infection. It destroyed the corneas and later, scar tissue grew into the inner part of the eye and they couldn't do a transplant."

Despite his loss of sight, he seemed to have had no problem learning to play an instrument. Doc said emphatically, "Music is sound! A blind child learns to see with their hands: the shape of things. The neck of the guitar is almost like you were lookin' at it. You find the frets, you find the strings, and you tinker around with it and find out what fret gets what note. I learned by ear; I never took any formal lessons and neither did my son, Merle.

"I started out (on the guitar) with the thumb and finger strum like the **Carter Family** style. That's what I began to first learn on the guitar. And then I heard Jimmie Rodgers play the guitar and I realized he was using a flatpick so I got me one. My youngest brother and I were lookin' at a little book that came with the first guitar that I worked up for my very own. He and I worked one summer pulling a cross-cut saw and I bought me a guitar with my part of the money cuttin' wood for the tannery, and he ordered him some clothes. Anyway, this little book showed you how to hold your flatpick and said it was the way Nick Lucas held his pick. So my brother showed me how to hold my flatpick."

His first remembrance of music was at an early age in church, the unaccompanied singing they did in those days. "My first instrument was the harmonica, as far back as I can remember. I'd get one every once in awhile—they didn't cost much then. My dad showed me a little bit about the harmonica, by sound of course, and talked to me about how to learn it. But my first stringed instrument was a little homemade banjo without frets.[16]

[15] Deep Gap is a post office which split off from Stoney Fork later. It is part of the same community. Doc: "I was born is what is now known as the Deep Gap community but it was originally called Stoney Fork Township."

[16] Both his parents were musicians. His father, General Dixon Watson, built Doc's first when Doc was about eleven. It had a cat-skin head.

He'd pick and I'd listen and I'd figure out what he's a-doin'. He showed me the best he could how to play a few of the old frailing licks on the banjo. And when the guitar came along, it was my first love.

On the album cover of "Pickin' the Blues" he is quoted, "My first introduction to the blues was on the earlier recordings that came with our first wind-up victrola. We called it a 'graphophone.' This was about 1929 or 1930 and, there was, I believe, a record or two in there by John Hurt, and the 'Blue Ridge Mountain Blues' by Riley Puckett. In the next year or two, we got some **Skillet Lickers** records, and then Jimmie Rodgers came along. Even though I was just a young'un, I began to figure out what the blues were. All music to me is universal. There's some things I can't relate to, but there's a lot of things in the universe I can't understand, either. But if a song has something to say, whether it's an old-timey thing or whether it's jazz, I'm liable to latch on to the melody if it fits my notion."

The name "Doc" came from his appearance in a furniture store window in 1941. Doc told the story, "A good old buddy of mine named Paul Grier, when we were both about nineteen, were doing a little radio show from O.P. Lute's Furniture Store in Lenoir, North Carolina, on a station in Hickory, North Carolina, WHKY. We were doing a show by remote control from the showroom window in the furniture store. A little audience would gather there in the store every Saturday morning and, Man, we thought we were big wheels. People would come by and stop and listen, and they had a speaker on the outside and about block the street. We thought we were doing something great. Anyhow, the radio announcer looked at Paul and said, 'Your name is Paul, what's a good, short name for Arthel there?' And he said, 'Well, I don't know...'

Doc Watson (L) and Jack Lawrence, 1996.

And about that time a girl in the audience shouted out, 'Call him Doc!' And it stuck. So that's the way it was...nothing more to it than that."

In 1946, Doc met Rosa Lee Carlton and they soon married. Son Eddy Merle Watson was born February 8, 1949, in Deep Gap. He was named after Eddy Arnold and Merle Travis. Nancy Watson was born in 1951. "Rosa Lee really liked Eddy Arnold, and Travis was my favorite guitar player at the time.

Folk musician Tom Clarence (T.C.) Ashley (1895-1967) is an important figure in old-time music scene even back into the 1920s. At a concert in New York City in September of 1959, Ralph Rinzler and Eugene Earle went to see Ashley perform old-time mountain music with his troupe which included Clint Howard, Fred Price and Doc Watson. While Rinzler and Earle loved what Ashley was doing, they noticed the terrific flat-top picking of Watson. They saw a chance to try to preserve the music of this man and they asked Watson if he would record for Folkways. He agreed. This event was probably *the* event which propelled Watson toward Stardom. Meanwhile, Watson began gaining fame when he played solo at New York City's Gerdes's Folk City. Ralph Rinzler produced "Old-Time Music at Clarence Ashley's" (FA 2355 and FA 2359) with this band of Watson, Ashley, Fred Price and Clint Howard. "And then Fred and Clint and I did a bunch of things on our own after Tom went his own way with Tex Isley. In 1967, there was the three of us at the Seattle Folklore Society. And if you have it on Vanguard, the old-timey concert was made up from those shows."

Rinzler wrote, "Doc was an incredible example of a performer living with, and performing within, both his local community tradition and in the artistic traditions of the regional Southeast. Doc had his community music that he played with Gaither (Doc's father-in-law who played the fiddle)—hymns and ballads, very deep, old, regional music. That was his down-home music. Now, outside of that, he knew a lot of other music he learned off records and radios. He knew a lot of contemporary music from the repertoires of people like Elvis Presley and Chet Atkins, and he could play that equally well. That was his face-to-the-world music. And, at the time, he saw an unbreachable wall between the two of them."[17]

In 1963, Doc Watson, Price, Howard and Ashley played at the Newport Folk Festival. The folk boom was in full force and this quartet was not left out. During this festival, Watson accompanied Bill Monroe's band. Monroe had never heard fiddle tunes played on the guitar so well and so fast as Doc could do.

Merle Watson, Doc's son, by 1964 had learned how to play the guitar and became Doc's rhythm guitarist, road manager and companion, making the touring much more bearable for the blind musician.

"Merle was a very talented young fellow," said Doc. "Let me tell you about it. I was on the road on my first concert tour in 1964 and I had done about half of it and was at The Ash Grove at Easter time working a week or two as an opening act for somebody else—I don't remember who—and Ralph Rinzler calls from my home here in Deep Gap. He said, 'Doc, I've got some good news for you.' And I said, 'Son, lay it on me.' He said, "Merle has started learning the guitar. He's playin'; you wouldn't believe how much he has already learned. And his mama, little ol' Rosa Lee, had taught him his first chords and he just took it and went with it. And Merle didn't learn things from me except listening to melodies. He sat down in the corner, just like I did, and figured out his own way of playin' things." Within a year or so, Merle was playing lead guitar in the finger-picking style. Doc's fame was growing, and they landed their first recording contract with Vanguard.

It was during this period during a West Coast tour that Clarence White noticed the incredible flat-picking of Doc Watson and began finding ways this guitar style could fit into his bluegrass band.

These were good times for the duo but tended to drop off somewhat after 1967, perhaps because Merle had a problem with stress (chronic headaches) which kept him off the road occasionally. Merle wanted to quit the road entirely. Doc related how Merle came to continue playing on a full-time basis with his father, "We had just played the 'Today Show' in New York City and Merle said, 'Dad, I believe I'll quit the music business.' And I said, 'Well, Son, I'll tell you what I'll do. If you'll stay with me—I can't manage this by myself; I'll just have to let this trickle down to about nothing... If you'll stay with me, we'll take the expenses off the top and split the profit.' And he said, 'I believe I'll stay then.'"

In 1965, Doc and Merle were using Martin D-18s. Merle also used a Goya and a Gibson. It was about this time that they switched to J.W. Gallagher's mahogany G-50 guitars. Doc said, "I loved the tone of the guitars. They had somethin' that I loved. I like the neck. Of course, they have been improved along the years. J.W. came by one Easter, he had been to the Union Grove shindig down there, he and his son. They came by and he had four guitars with him. Some of them were much more expensive than the one I picked, and I tried 'em all four. And I went back to the first one and I said, 'J.W., I like this one. He said, 'Doc Watson, it's yours and there's no string attached except for the ones that are on it. You take it and pick it and enjoy it.' I said, 'Well, J.W., I'll give you a letter of recommendation.' He said, 'I don't want a full endorsement; I don't like to tie people down.' That's the way the guy was; he was a good ol' boy and his son, Don, is a good man. I'm playin' a Gallagher cutaway now (1996) and my grandson Richard, Merle's son, has one. I guess that G-50 was really the first guitar meant for flatpickers. I was flatpickin' pretty good by that time and I sure worked on that old guitar and made it sing. I think they thought mostly of fingerpickers before that.

"Here's something I wish you would include in the article: Merle learned, I guess, three times as fast as I did. In a month or two, he was playin' finger-style. I'd say that by the end of June, he could play 'Little Darlin' Pal of Mine' and 'Never on Sunday'—a bunch of things. You wouldn't believe how fast that young'un learned. He didn't tackle 'em to record 'em, but he was pickin' *good*. I asked him, when we went to the Berklee Folk Festival (he went with me to play backup guitar), 'Son, you want to do the lead on "Stagger Lee"?' 'Gosh no! Let me play backup for awhile.' But he could have done it. He had the shyness that his mama had, bless her heart. I don't know if a dad could have had a better son than he was. I'll brag on the boy because I have every right to. There was a lot of slide players that wished they could play as good as Merle can. And Merle was a good flatpicker, too. But that CD on Sugar Hill, 'Remembering Merle,' features Merle on flatpickin' and finger-style and slide and banjo. That'll give you an idea of what a versatile musician he was."

Doc and Merle were sponsored by the U. S. State Department in a cultural exchange with Africa in 1968, touring much of the continent. That tour was "Like boot camp in the Army physically. It was appreciated by the people; they couldn't understand the language in the songs but they *loved* the music. And, believe it or not, in an African country way below the equator called 'Swaziland,' they dearly loved Jim Reeves, the country singer, his music. Somebody told me about that and we did one of his songs on the end of the shows and Boy! They'd scream and hollar. I don't know why they liked his songs. He really pleased those people.

In 1972, Doc was featured on the "Will The Circle Be Unbroken" album. This was another pivotal point in success of his career. The stellar success of this album opened up a whole new audience to this kind of music and secured the Watsons' career in music. He shared a Grammy with the other musicians on the album. "I was about not to do that, and I don't care if you print this in your article, in fact, I wish you would print it. I was about not to do that album because they didn't invite Merle to pick on it. And it really hurt my feelin's bad.

"Bluegrass is an offshoot from traditional music and Bill Monroe spawned the idea, but Flatt and Scruggs, I think, helped it to mature when they joined the group." —Doc Watson

I'll tell you how thoughtful Merle was about things; he had a business head on him. I got off in the corner with Merle and I said, 'They didn't invite you to play on this album and I'm hurt bad and I'm not gonna do it; I'm not going to fool with that.' I just kind of hesitated when John McEuen asked me to. And he said, 'Yea, Dad, well it hurt me, too. But I'll tell you, after I thought about it, if you'll play on it, it'll enlarge our audience.' Our music was kind of at a low ebb at the time. And Buddy, it helped the **Nitty Gritty** as well as us. It got us heard in a lot of audiences and our jobs began to pick up shortly after that record was released. I told Merle one day, I said, 'Son, I'm sure glad you persuaded me to pick on that record because you had some good sense right there.' I was so angry I didn't even stop to thing about it."

The next year, Doc won a Grammy from the National Academy of Recording Arts and Sciences (NARAS) for Best Ethnic/Traditional Recording with his "Then and Now" album on Poppy.[18] The next year, he and Merle won in the same category with their "Two Days in November" album, also on Poppy.

Fretless electric bass player T. Michael Coleman joined Doc and Merle in 1974. Theoretically, Doc was to retire this year, but he stayed on the road and in 1979 they won their third Grammy, this time for Best Country Instrumental Performance with their United Artists album "Live and Pickin'." Watson switched labels to Sugar Hill in 1985 after their very successful "Pickin' the Blues" which came out on Flying Fish in 1985.

Watson built a utility shed at his home—quite a feat for a blind man. He told this writer that if he had been able to see, and handle the education aspect of the field, he would have loved to have been an electrician or a carpenter. He would still have picked the guitar, but the other jobs would have kept him off the road—which he hates, but concedes is necessary to earn a living as a musician.

On October 23, 1985, Merle died of a tractor accident on his family's North Carolina farm. That year, he was voted Best in the Country Guitar Finger-picking category by a *Frets* Readers' Poll. Doc was voted Best in Bluegrass Flatpicking. Jack Lawrence[19] took Merle's place touring and performing full-time (he had done a few dates with Doc earlier).

In 1987, T. Michael Coleman, who had spent the last thirteen years as fretless electric bass player for Doc Watson, joined the **Seldom Scene**.

Watson's favorite albums are Vanguard's "Southbound" (1966), United Artists' "Memories" and "Look Away." And he loves Flying Fish's "Pickin' the Blues." He continued to perform into 1996 with Jack Lawrence. On local jobs, Doc uses his buddy, Charles Welch, and grandson, Richard.

Clarence and Roland White

Clarence and Roland White, the Country Boys, and the Kentucky Colonels

In the 1990s, most bluegrass fans know that Roland White is the mandolin player for the **Nashville Bluegrass Band**. Some may have forgotten, however, that he played guitar with Bill Monroe and mandolin with Lester Flatt and Alan Munde, and that his brother, Clarence, was a pioneer flatpicker, and that their early bands from California were of significant influence in that part of the country. Here is a discussion of Clarence White, Roland White and their very important bands.

According to Charmaine Lanham, "I don't know anybody in bluegrass music who is a guitar player who is not influenced by Doc Watson and Clarence White! Tony Rice was influenced by Clarence White—he followed him around and learned from Clarence White. He plays, what I consider to be, the Clarence White style in the Tony Rice way. David Grier; the first words out of his mouth will be that Clarence was the biggest influence in his life. And, of course, he's got his own style, but you can hear Clarence's influence. And you can also hear it in Marty Stuart's acoustic and electric guitar playing. And 'Clarence White' will be the first words out of his mouth. He plays Clarence's electric guitar and has the biggest collection of Clarence White memorabilia, I think, that exists.

The White brothers (real name LeBlanc. Their father came from Canada and was naturalized into the United States.) were born in Maine. Roland Joseph (born April 23, 1938, in Madawaska), Eric (born July 9, 1943, in Lewiston) and Clarence (June 7, 1944, in Lewiston) were three of five children. Their father was a multi-instrumentalist who collected instruments which the children played, and their mother was a collector of country music records. Clarence was five when he first strummed a guitar. His fingers were so small that he had to have his twelve year-old brother,

[18] Musicians included Merle on lead and slide guitar, Vassar Clements on fiddle, Norman Blake on resonator guitar, plus a rhythm section.

Roland, fret the chords for him. In 1954, the boys' father moved the family from Maine to Burbank, California, where he accepted employment at hydroelectric projects. The three brothers and a sister (Joanne) won a talent contest which led to the boys doing a television show every Saturday night as **Three Little Country Boys**; Joanne no longer played with them.

Clarence was ten when they settled in California. The musical direction of the brothers was provided by older brother Roland. As the group's leader, Roland soon got them jobs on local television, radio and stage shows, conducted the continual practices, and insisted that the band sound develop as far as it could. Clarence, influenced on the guitar by his father and family friend, Joe Maphis, said, "I spent almost every hour with my guitar. It was my whole life—all-acoustic playing at first—until my late teens when I began to get interested in electric guitar."[20] Maphis introduced the boys to all sorts of different guitar styles through his collection of 78 r.p.m. records. Maphis also passed on his hard-driving right hand techniques.

About 1955, Roland and Clarence and Eric heard Bill Monroe play "Pike County Breakdown" and were fascinated at the speed at which he played. When Roland heard **Flatt and Scruggs** play "Dear Old Dixie" on the radio, this fascination led to the purchase of seven (buy six and you get one free) records from the mail-order Jimmie Skinner Record Shop in Cincinnati. He and his brothers soon began playing in this style after they met and began playing with Billy Ray Latham on banjo in 1958, calling themselves the **Country Boys**. LeRoy (MacNees) Mack was on resonator guitar. They practiced two to three hours a night, seven days a week; they soon knew 200 bluegrass songs. Latham sang a high lead like Bob Osborne.

In 1959, the **Country Boys** began playing often at The Ash Grove club in Hollywood. This was their first opportunity to play for people who were there for the sole purpose of listening to music. By 1960, the band was playing almost enough to make a living at it (they were still living at home); they played nearly every week at colleges and folk festivals. The folk boom was in full force on the West Coast. They made two appearances on the "Andy Griffith Show" on television beginning in 1959, and they backed Griffith in his LP recording, "Songs, Themes and Laughs from the Andy Griffith Show," on Capitol.

Eric left the band in 1961 to get married and was replaced by Roger Bush. They made a Midwest tour, then Roland was drafted. Clarence began experimenting with the use of the guitar as a lead instrument. Reno's recording of "Country Boy Rock and Roll" was influential toward this style change as well as Doc Watson's personal appearance at The Ash Grove. The young guitarist, Clarence, was amazed at what Watson could do on Leslie Keith's "Black Mountain Rag." He hadn't heard fiddle tunes played on the guitar like that before. He'd heard Earl Scruggs pick the guitar, and Bill Clifton, Mac Wiseman, Charlie Waller and perhaps Edd Mayfield, but Watson's picking was a revelation of unprecedented proportions. Clarence loved it and began working on how this flatpicking thing would fit into the bluegrass context of their band. He began the complex task of using the guitar in a bluegrass band as not only rhythm, but lead as well. Roland White recalled, "Doc Watson was playing a lot back then but he wasn't bluegrass. He wasn't in a bluegrass band: Actually, his was the first band, other than the Stanleys, to feature some lead guitar playing—but not in that hard-driving flatpicking, bluegrass style."[21] Doc Watson could certainly flatpick with hard *drive*, but he didn't specialize in bluegrass. Clarence White did.

The band recorded "Bluegrass America"[22] when Roland was in the Army in 1962. Though Clarence was mainly a rhythm guitar player at this point, the record-

Roland White with the Nashville Bluegrass band, 1995. L to R: Roland White, Gene Libbea, Pat Enright, Alan O'Bryant, Stuart Duncan.

---

[19] Lawrence, from Mooresville, North Carolina, also worked at the McIntyre Guitar Company in Charlotte, North Carolina, since 1983. Even in 1996, Lawrence continued to tour with Doc as half the duo's act.

[20] John Delgatto, "The Too-Short Career of Clarence White," *Frets*, July, 1986, p. 13.

[21] From an interview near Ashland, Oregon, in 1985 with Roland White who mandolinist with the Country Gazette at that time.

[22] Recording there were Clarence, Mack, Latham, Roger Bush (bass), Joe Maphis and Jody Sanders.

ing also showed his flatpicking and got such a good response that the band's music would never be the same. Bobby Slone joined on fiddle in late 1962 and the band soon became the **Kentucky Colonels**.

Clarence's cameo appearance on Elektra's "New Dimensions in Banjo and Bluegrass" in 1963 was soon followed by the **Kentucky Colonels**' own "Appalachian Swing" for World Pacific Records in 1964. "Swing" sold well and became the first album where future flatpickers could learn their trade. It was later re-issued on compact disc by Rounder Records.

Roland came back from the Army in 1963. The **Kentucky Colonels** toured in the folk circuit in the East and Midwest in 1963 and 1964 and got an earful of bluegrass at the 1964 Newport Folk Festival where they appeared on the program along with the **Osborne Brothers**, the **Greenbriar Boys** and the **Stanley Brothers**. Doc conducted an unforgettable guitar workshop with Clarence, who was not very well known yet. The meetings with Watson changed Clarence's playing emphasis on guitar solos and breaks, and they almost immediately appeared in the **Colonels**' repertoire. Recalled fledgling banjoist Jerry Garcia, "Oh God! He was good. He's the guy who really set up modern bluegrass guitar players—he started them all going."[23]

By 1965, Clarence had expanded his field of influence to guitarists such as Duane Eddy and James Burton who were a part of the folk-rock era. Clarence eagerly pursued this new genre but the rest of the band wanted to play bluegrass. Clarence said, "It wasn't so much that I was getting bored with acoustic bluegrass— I could feel so many new things in the air. I wanted to get in the stream of a new kind of music that combined what you could call a 'folk integrity' with electric rock."[24] He then put away his D-28 and bought a Fender Telecaster, intending to develop his skills sufficiently to make a living as a studio musician. He learned a whole new "touch" on the instrument in addition to chord structures and scales. While he was working with the **Byrds** (1968 to 1973) he was in great demand as a studio musician.

A main factor in the success of Clarence as a lead guitarist was his knowledge of simple rhythm. Roland spoke of this, "He had years of just playing rhythm. He knew that real well. That's where I think people make a mistake. They don't know good rhythm and they get into playing a bunch of hot licks. This is true for mandolin, too. That mandolin chop is real important."[25] When they hired Scott Stoneman (in 1965 for a few months) as

their fiddler, Clarence did little lead playing—content to let the exciting fiddle of Stoneman have the glory.

By the mid-'60s, bluegrass had lost a lot of its popularity throughout the nation. Making a living in this climate of the **Beatles** and the **Rolling Stones** was difficult, so the group began playing with electric instruments and they hired a drummer in 1965. Clarence's session work with the Los Angeles-based folk-rock group, the **Byrds**, in late 1966 or early 1967, led to offers for him to join that band, which had finally become sufficiently profitable for him to actually become a member in 1969 or 1970 for about three years. The **Kentucky Colonels** split up about 1966; Roland free-lanced on electric bass wherever he could.

With the band non-existent, Roland was hired in Los Angeles to play guitar with Bill Monroe in May of 1967, replacing Doug Green. He then moved to Nashville where he lives today. Other members at that time were Byron Berline (fiddle), Lamar Grier (banjo) and James Monroe (bass). He stayed with the **Blue Grass Boys** until mid-February of 1969. Roland and banjoist Vic Jordan left Monroe at the same time (separately) and began working for Lester Flatt's **Nashville Grass**. Flatt was just forming his band after a split with Earl Scruggs.[26] Now that Flatt had his own band, members included Roland (mandolin), Vic Jordan (banjo), Paul Warren (fiddle), Flatt (guitar), Josh Graves (Dobro®) and Jake Tullock (bass).

The **Byrds** broke up in 1973; Clarence joined the short-lived **Muleskinner**. Roland left Flatt's band in March 1973 to re-join Clarence in the **Kentucky Colonels** with banjoists Herb Pedersen, then Alan Munde. They did a quick West Coast tour and a European tour followed by the Indian Spring Bluegrass Festival (the only festival that Clarence played) and then worked as the **New Kentucky Colonels** with Roland, Clarence and others for a short time.

Clarence was killed at the age of twenty-nine on July 14, 1973, in a Palmdale, California, drunken driver mishap just off the Sierra Highway, one of the main boulevards which runs through town, where the venue was located. The driver drifted from the road and into the area where the band was standing. She hit Clarence first. Roland described the event, "What we figured happened was he was next to me and he was pushed into me and knocked me over his car. And then it pushed him back onto her car again and that's what killed him, I'm sure. If we had been in the parking lot, where we should have been, the total incident would

[23] Delgatto, op. cit., p. 13.

[24] Ibid., p. 14.

[25] Barry Brower, "Remembering the Kentucky Colonels—The Bluegrass Life of Roland White", *Bluegrass Unlimited*, February, 1987, p. 28.

[26] "According to Roland, this was a very difficult time for Lester Flatt. His twenty-three year association with Earl Scruggs had come to an unceremonious end when Lester called it quits after a show on the Opry. He had become increasingly dissatisfied with the direction the band was taking. At the urging of Earl, Earl's wife Louise (who helped to manage the group), and their producer, Lester was being asked to perform more and more material—Bob Dylan, other modern songs—that was not suited to him nor to his liking. 'Earl was having some physical problems too, that affected their stage shows,' recalled Roland, 'and Lester Flatt felt, even though they were selling a lot of records, that they shouldn't do any more of that material. Lester was really hurt that Earl had let it go so far that it got to the point where he had to just walk off. His best friend was Earl Scruggs.'"—Brower, Ibid., p. 29.

not have happened." Roland suffered a dislocated shoulder.

Many modern bluegrass guitarists remembered Clarence. Pat Flynn said, "In his acoustic playing, it was always a 'roll' of notes, a lot of beautiful patterns rolling out. And rhythmically it was very urgent. Whenever the banjo handed off the solo to Clarence, he had a lot of power there. It didn't let down... Clarence was always out in front when bluegrass was trying to be assimilated into a more modern setting."[27]

David Grier said, "Clarence was the first guitar player I ever heard when I was growing up. I was too young to remember it, but he would come over to the house and play, and my dad had tapes of that. He would play them and say, 'Did you hear that!' And I would say, 'Yeah, Dad, I heard that.' Listening to Clarence, I developed a different sense of thinking—just the way he would do it, always thinking in a different way. And he was economical. He didn't have to play a whole lot of notes to get things said."

Phil Rosenthal: "To me, Clarence really blazed a trail through a lot of unexplored territory. He had a big influence on my playing—and not just licks necessarily. There's a certain richness and sweetness of tone that he got on a lot of his things. Each note has a fat, full sound to it."

Marty Stuart said, "I was about fourteen when I really started catching on to Clarence. On a Saturday night, I would go to the Opry and would play the Martha White Show. There was a lot of great guitar players down there, but Clarence was the alternative to what-ever was goin' around. It offered me an identity of my own, just to walk into the Opry knowing my hero was someone like him."

Stuart Duncan recalled, "He had that technical ability to let a note ring, where a lot of people would be blocking it with their other finger while they were doing another phrase."[28]

Charles Sawtelle spoke of White's influence on him. "When I first got tapes of Clarence White, I honestly couldn't listen to them; they were so intense. It was such a huge impact for me that I couldn't listen to them all the way through. I could only listen at first to about half a song."

Tony Rice said, "The essentials of guitar, as I play it, come from him. One real, concrete thing I learned from Clarence is the way I hold a pick. All of my left-hand technique I learned directly from Clarence, too—real efficiency of movement. Trying for a smoother sound, not being frantically loud. Concentrating on tone and making a line or phrase smooth... It sounded like he was squeezing the notes out, rather than impulsively firing them off."

Roland White explained, "If we worked up a tune and he was going to take a guitar break, he just did it. And the first time he did it, that's the way it was. Whether he sat down by himself before or not—you know, a lot of times he couldn't have. He started with the melody and then just went in there and picked it. Of course, it got a little better each time we did it, but pretty much what he did the first time he'd almost have his whole break nailed down. It was just in him to do that. He was really amazing. It was no real effort; it seemed easy for him. It affected me a whole lot because I could see, when I got back from the Army, that he had it all together. I thought, 'Gee, well, *I* need to get to work!'

"My mandolin playing is more influenced by him now that it was back then. And one reason is that when I first joined **Country Gazette**, I was the guitar player. So I got to listening to tapes and things and I really zeroed in on that part—being the guitar player of the band—which I hadn't before. And I listened to Clarence's rhythm guitar playing, mostly, and some of the lead things he did. I learned a lot from that. Not so much copying it, but just listening to it, thinking about it, and re-evaluating my guitar playing. It changed my playing; it changed my mandolin playing a whole lot. My playing is a lot simpler now. I didn't set out and say, 'I'm gonna change'; it just happened."

Roland's new job with **Country Gazette** took his mind off his brother's death. He spoke of that job which lasted until 1986, "I really enjoy what I'm doing now. I enjoy working with Alan (Munde). I've learned a lot from him. He's a good musician and a good person. We (the **Kentucky Colonels**) realized way back that we had something of our own—that we weren't really working for anyone else—just basically doing our own thing. Working for Bill and Lester was good, but working for someone else is not the way to do it. If you can have your own little group and do what you want to do, it's a lot easier."[29] You can be more creative when you have your own group, he said. He joined the **Nashville Bluegrass Band** in 1989. With Roland White on mando-lin, they won Grammys for their "Waitin' for the Hard Times to Go" and "Unleashed" Sugar Hill CDs. Roland's solo CD in 1994 was "Trying to Get to You" on Sugar Hill. Roland also played informally with the **New Kentucky Colonels** in 1996.

---

[27] Russ Barenberg, "He Was Somebody Different—Musicians Remember Clarence White," *Frets*, July, 1986, pp. 15, 16. The rest of these quotations about Clarence are from the same article, pages 16, 17, 25 and 58.

[28] Ibid., p. 17.

[29] Brower, op. cit., p. 30.

Norman Blake

There are certain musicians whose instrumental style doesn't necessarily fit into one category of music and as a result is difficult to place into a specific genre. Norman Blake is one of those people. He's basically an old-time music, guitar flatpicker who has played in several significant bluegrass-type bands and therefore picked up a reputation in bluegrass. At the same time, he played his music in bands, some of which he founded, of a folk orientation. He feels comfortable either way but his recent performances have tended to lean mainly toward folk music. Today, his performances with his wife Nancy, on cello, further separates his music from bluegrass. He described his style in this manner, "My guitar playing is innovative in that I play long lines of notes on top of a bass line. It's improvisational—very much like jazz."[30]

Norman Blake was born March 10, 1938, in Chattanooga, Tennessee, and grew up in Sulfur Springs, Tennessee, and Rising Fawn, Georgia. His first influences toward music were Roy Acuff, the **Monroe Brothers** and Merle Travis. He later became influenced by everything he liked. Blake quit high school to play mandolin in a band, and music has been the focus of his life ever since. His guitar flatpicking was among the earliest; occurring about the same time as Clarence White's.

He began his bluegrass career in the mid-'50s in Knoxville at the Tennessee Barn Dance on WNOX. Like many full-time musicians of the day, he moved from station to station to find lucrative employment and good recording contracts. After WDOD and WROM-TV in 1956, he joined the **Lonesome Travelers** and began his recording career. By 1959, he was with **Hylo Brown and the Timberliners**, followed by a band in the military. In 1969, he did session work with artists such as Bob Dylan, Kris Kristofferson, Joan Baez and the **Nitty Gritty Dirt Band** (for which he received a gold record and a Grammy on the legendary "Will the Circle Be Unbroken" LP). He played guitar and resonator guitar while touring with Johnny Cash and for the country star's summer television show. He also toured with June Carter's road group.

In 1971, he formed the **Dobrolic Plectral Society** with himself (guitar, mandolin, Dobro®/resonator guitar, fiddle), John Hartford (banjo, fiddle), Tut Taylor (Dobro®/resonator guitar) and Vassar Clements (fiddle). The band lasted three years. In 1973, Blake's band included Taylor (Dobro®/resonator guitar) and Charlie Collins (guitar).[31] Then, after nine months with **Red, White and Blue (Grass)** with Ginger and Grant Boatwright, he began a solo career.

In 1974, Norman and Nancy Blake began performing together as a touring husband-and-wife team.[32] Nancy loves Norman's type of music: "I've gotten a lot out of country music and I want to give something back to it. I'm doing what I feel might express that by playing Norman's music the best I know how. I wouldn't trade what I know for First Chair in the London Philharmonic."[33]

In 1981, Norman Blake won Best Bluegrass Guitar award in the *Frets* Readers' Poll. His band, recording on Rounder, was **Rising Fawn Ensemble** where he is featured on the mandolin. He was voted Best Multi-Instrumentalist by the *Frets* Readers' Poll in 1986. His music was described by the *San Francisco Examiner*: "What Blake does is important, of course, but the glory of his string sounds, the Tennessee-Georgia twangy drawl of his vocals, and the awesome blend of the Blakes (Norman and Nancy) produces an American music of incomparable purity and integrity."[34]

---

[30] Ken Moffitt, "Norman Blake, "*Bluegrass Unlimited*, November, 1982, p. 11.

[31] This was probably the Rising Fawn String Ensemble.

[32] They had met in 1972 at a performance where they both played. She is a native of Independence, Missouri, where she studied the classical cello at age twelve. After high school, she entered the Nashville Youth Symphony. It was in this city that she became aware of the other kinds of music that Nashville had to offer. She now plays fiddle, mandolin, guitar, bass, and single-row accordion. Her own solo LP, "Grand Junction," won Best Eight LPs for 1986.

[33] Quotation taken from the Blakes' public relations biographical description.

[34] Ibid..

Dan Crary

Another significant guitarist in bluegrass music is the legendary Doctor Dan Crary who, as of 1997, was a professor of speech communication in a major California university. Not only has Crary served as model for future guitar flatpickers, he was the first flatpicker to delve into the newgrass genre of bluegrass music. He is a consummate international representative of bluegrass music and the guitar, a patient guitar instructor, and author of books and songs.

Crary was born September 29, 1939, in Kansas City, Kansas. He got his first guitar at twelve years old in 1952, and became one of only two people he knew who played the instrument. His first guitar was an arch-top, f-hole Gretsch, bought from Ernest Caudill. He took lessons from Caudill for one year and started listening to bluegrass music. "So when I heard somebody fingerpicking on the radio, for all I knew they were doing that with a flatpick. I didn't know what fingerpicking was. So I started imitating fingerpickers with a flatpick, which is a pretty good way to get ready for cross-picking—when you learn what that is. So I've always done that. And jumping around from string to string—I've never been afraid of it, because I thought that's what you did."[35]

In 1957, Dan Crary graduated from high school in Kansas City and moved to Chicago to study Theology at Moody Bible Institute. He soon began a part-time (and occasionally full-time) occupation as a disc jockey which lasted through 1974. He joined a folk band in Lawrence, Kansas, in 1960. In 1965, he moved to San Francisco to attend the Golden Gate Baptist Seminary where he received Bachelor of Divinity. In 1968, he moved to Louisville, Kentucky, to pursue his Ph. D. in Theology at Southern Seminary, staying a year. There in Louisville he formed the **Bluegrass Alliance**[36] and worked at the Red Dog Saloon.

Soon the contest era at bluegrass festivals began. But Crary never entered a contest; by the time the contests were in full swing, he was a professional flatpicker (one of the few) and asked to judge contests at many locations. The **Bluegrass Alliance** was finally allowed to play at bluegrass festivals in 1969. Their first one was at Carlton Haney's Camp Springs, Reidsville, North Carolina. It caused a stir in the bluegrass community because of the "newgrass"[37] nature of the music, Crary's lead-guitar flatpicking (which was new to bluegrass at that time), and possibly because the performance attire was more "casual" than to what the audience was accustomed. Their material included some contemporary songs—this further alienated them from traditional audiences. They did *not* use electric instruments at this time...that came later. "People were surprised that a band would have a lead guitar playing a break in everything..." he said. "I don't want to claim too much here. I hope that, as a band, we influenced the resurgence of interest in guitar as a lead instrument in bluegrass. If that turns out to be true historically, I'll look down from Glory, or up from perdition or whatever, and be glad."[38] That year, the group produced its first album on the American Heritage label, "Bluegrass Alliance."

Crary was still inclined on a teaching career in some field, and in 1970 he went back to his home in Kansas City to pursue a Doctorate in Speech Communication, intending to teach at the collegiate level. Fiddler Lonnie Peerce took over the **Bluegrass Alliance** and soon hired Sam Bush as the group's guitar player. Soon Bush and Peerce recruited Tony Rice into playing with the group at Reidsville. Rice was a follower of the flatpicker Clarence White so the group was able to continue with a lead guitarist in the band.

Crary earned his Ph.D. in Speech Communication from the University of Kansas in 1974. He then began working as a professor of speech communication at California State Fullerton. Soon, Crary met Byron Berline, who was already a veteran of Bill Monroe's **Blue Grass Boys**, the **Flying Burrito Brothers**, **Country Gazette** and was a studio musician. They formed **Sundance**[39] in 1975. The next year, Sundance signed with MCA to produce its first album, "Byron Berline and Sundance."

35 Jack Tottle, "Berline, Crary and Hickman—Conclusion," *Bluegrass Unlimited*, October, 1980, p. 35.

36 Members were Buddy Spurlock (banjo), Wayne Stewart (guitar, mandolin, vocals), Lonnie Peerce (fiddle), Ebo Walker (bass) and later Dan Jones (mandolin).

37 According to Art Menius, the Bluegrass Alliance coined the term "newgrass," the title of their second LP. While with the Alliance, Crary cut his first solo LP, "Bluegrass Guitar," which remained among the top one hundred selling albums for some fifteen years.

38 Tottle, op. cit., p. 35.

39 With Allen Wald (guitar) and Jack Skinner (bass).

In 1977, Crary's "Lady's Fancy"[40] LP was released on Rounder. The musicians of **New Grass Revival** were in the area so he was able to use them on the album. Crary was working full-time during the day so the recording sessions turned out to be all-night experiences.

Berline, Crary and Hickman was formed in 1978 with musicians Byron Berline (fiddle, mandolin), Crary (guitar) and John Hickman (banjo). Crary said, "It's really interesting to work with only two other musicians, especially for the guitar player, because it puts other restraints on the guitar. The guitar has to carry things it doesn't have to otherwise."[41] Crary began touring foreign countries as a solo about this time, and in 1979, began writing a regular column on the guitar for *Frets* magazine.

In 1981, Sugar Hill released "Berline-Crary-Hickman." In 1983, Sugar Hill released Crary's "Guitar." On this new album were Bela Fleck (banjo), Sam Bush (mandolin), Mark O'Connor (fiddle) and T. Michael Coleman (fretless electric bass, who was also working with Doc Watson). In 1984, Sugar Hill released "Night Run" by **Berline, Crary and Hickman**.[42] In 1985, during his tour of Australia, Crary received a plaque to show that he was now a Country Music Ambassador.

In about 1987, Crary and guitar maker Bob Taylor (of Taylor Guitars) collaborated to create a new kind of guitar which was designed to be friendly to microphones, especially with professional players. Together with a new system of bracing and with the best qualities of other fine guitars, the result was the "Dan Crary Signature Model." They tried many combinations of necks, woods, bridge position, and other combinations to come up with the prototype he plays today. "Certainly, it is the most perfect guitar for what I do that I have ever played," said Crary. "And there are lots of other great guitars around. But this one has a different kind of bracing system which is specifically designed to work well over a microphone."

B-C-H hired Texan Steve Spurgin in 1989 to play electric bass and sing lead for the group. They then released "And Now They Are Four" on Sugar Hill. Spurgin soon became well known for his songwriting on subsequent albums. That year, Crary recorded the solo album, "Take a Step Over," on Sugar Hill.

In 1990, they hired John Moore to play mandolin and guitar whose credits included the soundtracks of "Blaze" and "El Diablo" and employment at Disneyland. They renamed the band **California**. The band went on to win numerous awards at IBMA. The band broke up in late 1995.

Crary on flatpicking: "The musicians I know who I have played with for many years are still around because they loved the music so much that they did not quit no matter what, including destitution and poverty and having record contracts canceled and so on. They stayed with it. I'm one of those people. The guitar grabbed hold of me, and at times when I thought maybe it was not very important and didn't give it the due that it deserved, I couldn't let go. So everybody has a destiny. It may not be a Clarence White or Doc, but it's damn sure worth checking out and pursuing. You could find a lot worse things to do with your time."[43]

Larry Sparks

Larry Sparks and the Lonesome Ramblers

The biography of Larry Sparks could fit equally well into this book's chapter on Pioneers except for his age. He is much more than a fine guitarist, he is one of the most soulful singers in the bluegrass business. Here is his story.

This self-taught, second-generation bluegrass musician from Ohio gained prominence in this music when he joined Ralph Stanley's new **Clinch Mountain Boys** in early 1967. Born September 25, 1947, in Lebanon, Ohio (between Cincinnati and Dayton), Sparks began playing the guitar at five years old with his sister Bernice who taught him guitar chords and voice control. He liked the songs of Hank Williams and noticed that the music of Bill Monroe (the first bluegrass music he heard) was different and catchy. He was also influenced by other bluegrass stars such as the **Stanley Brothers**. He recorded his first record at age five, standing on a

---

[40] The tune "Lady's Fancy" was an adaptation from Howdy Forrester's "Say Old Man, Can You Play the Fiddle?"

[41] Tottle, op. cit., p. 35.

[42] The trio used a bass player for the album, Jerry Scheff, who used to play for Elvis Presley. Skip Conover played Dobro.

[43] David McCarty, "Dan Crary on Flatpicking," *Bluegrass Unlimited*, pp. 26, 27.

chair to reach the mike. They played in church during those times, and that upbringing helped his gospel songwriting later on.

He was raised on a farm. Probably the first influences toward bluegrass for Sparks (and many others in the area) was the bluegrass on the radio at WCKY which was out of Cincinnati at the time

Larry Sparks and the Lonesome Ramblers, 1996.

in the late '50s and early '60s. Sparks was also influenced by Tommy Sutton when Sutton had his daily radio show at the same time period on nearby WPFB, Middletown, Ohio. The show was, according to Sparks, an influence on him as well as others in the Dayton/ Cincinnati area. He still remembers that Sutton started every show with **Flatt and Scruggs**' "Flint Hill Special." The bluegrass traditions continued after Sutton when Paul "Moon" Mullins began his very popular country/bluegrass show on WPFB. It was Mullins, former fiddler for the **Stanley Brothers**, who introduced Sparks to the Stanleys.

Sparks became very involved with his music in his early teens. By the time he could see that he could make a living from music and other jobs to gain full independence, he quit school. A lot of his classmates quit, too. He said that quitting school was "cool" at the time.

In early 1965, Larry Sparks (17) played music with the **Stanley Brothers** on a fill-in basis. He stayed with the group, on tour, part-time for two years. He *really* worked at the career of being a musician. He worked for tips, for $5 per night, or for the kitty. $15 per night was big money in the average bar where he worked. While still filling-in with the **Stanley Brothers**, Sparks recorded on the Jalyn label, using his own name.

By February of 1967, Ralph Stanley had reorganized the group that he and Carter had as **Ralph Stanley and the Clinch Mountain Boys** with Larry Sparks singing lead and playing lead guitar. This was quite a responsibility, for filling the shoes of Carter as lead singer was difficult to imagine. This was somewhat of an unlikely succession to power because Sparks had done very little lead singing with the Stanleys; what he had done was mostly harmony. But he had practiced at home and reached a significant level of competence there. In Ralph's new band, Melvin Goins played guitar, Curly Ray Cline played fiddle, George Shuffler, the bass.

As earlier noted, Sparks is renown for his soulful singing. He described it this way, "It's really something you can't explain: how you get a feeling for a song. When I sing with feeling, I kind of picture what the song is about when I sing it. For instance, I took the words to 'Blue Virginia, Blue' and rearranged them so that I could visualize the situation and sing it with feeling really sing it from the heart. You may have a good song, but unless you have a love for the music you don't 'get it.' You get those words and you work with them and you humble yourself to that song if the song is worthy of you humbling yourself to. Each person must feel the song in his own way. It was the same with Hank Williams—he actually lived his songs after he sung 'em."

In the fall of 1969, Larry Sparks parted from the **Clinch Mountain Boys** and formed his own **Larry Sparks and the Lonesome Ramblers**.[44] Sparks' band did some twin banjo/mandolin material in a manner in which was different from other groups yet still in the traditional bluegrass mode. He and Bernice wrote a lot of the songs—which he feels helped the band tremendously. Of course, he also recognized that his fame gained with the **Stanley Brothers** and with Ralph's band was also a key to his success. He felt that the moment where he was sure that he could make a good living in this business was when he released "Bluegrass, Old and New" in 1971. This album was the first album which has what he considered to be the true **Larry Sparks and the Lonesome Ramblers** sound. Up until that point, his music was very much like that of the **Clinch Mountain Boys**.

In 1972, Sparks began recording for Starday, followed by Old Homestead Records, and in 1980, Rebel Records which he feels has an excellent distribution network for bluegrass records. That year, Sparks moved from Nashville to Richmond, Indiana, to record two albums.

From the '70s for the next decade, members of the **Lonesome Ramblers** have included some of the best talent bluegrass had to offer. His sidemen included Mike Lilly (banjo), Art Wydner (bass), Wendy Miller (mandolin), David Cox (mandolin), Joe Meadows (fiddle), Dave Evans (banjo), Tim Maynard (banjo) and Tommy Boyd (banjo, resonator guitar). From 1986 until about 1988, members of the **Lonesome Ramblers** included Sparks

[44] Members were his sister Bernice (rhythm guitar), Joe Isaacs (banjo), David Cox (mandolin) and Lloyd Hensley (bass).

Americas Music | Bluegrass

(guitar), David Harvey (mandolin, fiddle), Barry Crabtree (banjo) and Larry D. Sparks (bass, his son). On September 6th, 1981, in Jackson, Kentucky, Larry Sparks was presented the Kentucky Colonel Award by Governor John Y. Brown Jr..

Sparks described how his 1953 Martin D-28 is so important to him. "It takes years, really, to be close to your instrument. It works that way. I could take my guitar now—I've been off work for two weeks—I haven't even had it out of the case—I could hit the stage Friday night and everything I know I don't have to think about. It's there! With another instrument, it won't have the same feel. This one's been with me so many years. It's sort of like you know what your guitar's gonna do and it knows what you're gonna do. It's difficult to explain. After you've played an instrument so long, it's a part of you."

The music of Larry Sparks is distinctive and, he feels, strictly his own while still staying within the confines of the structure of traditional bluegrass. Contributing to this special sound is his approach and execution to the songs, many of which no other bluegrass artist does. As of 1996, members of his band included Mark Poe (bass), Scott Napier (mandolin) and Jim Britton (banjo).

David Grier (L) and Butch Baldassari at Rocky Grass in 1996 as members of the Grass Is Greener.

David Grier

One of the fine, recent flatpick guitarists who is achieving great fame is David Grier. His 1992, 1993 and 1995 Best Bluegrass Guitar awards from IBMA indicated his prowess on the instrument.

David Grier, son of ex-Blue Grass Boy (1965 to 1967) banjoist Lamar Grier, was born in Washington, D.C., September 23, 1961. He was influenced by Clarence White and James Burton. After playing in the D.C. area for awhile, he placed Second at the National Guitar Flat-Picking Championships at Winfield, Kansas, in 1980. He played electric guitar in a country-rock band for two years then, in 1985, moved to Nashville. After two months, he joined the touring **Doug Dillard Band** with Dillard, Ginger Boatwright and Kathy Chiavola where he recorded on two albums, "What's That?" and "Heartbreak Hotel" (which was nominated for an Emmy).

In 1989, Grier left Dillard to join the **Tony Trischka and the Big Dogs** whose members included Andrea Zonn (fiddle) and Debby Nims (bass). The next year, Grier recorded "Climbing the Walls" on Rounder with Mike Compton (mandolin), Blaine Sprouse (fiddle), Roy Huskey Jr. and Billy Rose (bass). Other recent recording endeavors were with **Country Gazette** on their "Strictly Instrumental" album, with Kenny Baker and Blaine Sprouse on their "Indian Springs" album and with Stuart Duncan on his first solo album, and his own "Freewheeling." His "Lone Soldier" Rounder CD was nominated for IBMA's Instrumental Recording of the Year. He has played on over sixty different recordings and continues into the 1990s.

Bluegrass Bass - Table of Contents

Bluegrass Bass

The bass player's role in bluegrass music is just as important as any of the other band musicians yet, because he/she usually doesn't take flashy breaks which astound the audience, he doesn't seem to get the recognition that an instrument of this importance deserves. A former bass player for the **Seldom Scene**, T. Michael Coleman, performed his own composition about this unsung hero. His song highlights the bass in the act and brings focus to the instrument. He introduces the song to the audience by asking how many bass players there are in the audience. After the expected minimal response is noted, he then answers his question by asking, "Who cares?" Though humorous, it does seem to illustrate the plight of the relative standing of the bass in bluegrass.

Bass playing to modern players such as Mark Schatz and Missy Raines (in separate 1995 interviews) interpret their role as bass player in a bluegrass band as being "totally interactive where everyone listens to everyone else and each becomes an integrate part of a whole interwoven rhythmic fabric. No one leads; all support. The focus is on whoever is in the forefront—vocalist or soloist. *They* lead the charge and the band is in full support and carrying them along at the same time," said Schatz. "Each player attacks the beat with confidence and strives to create *drive* through total rhythmic blend with the other musicians. The bass provides the pulse—the lower end thump that supports and drives the whole band along."

Schatz, a professional bass player since the mid-seventies, mentioned that being in the "groove" with a band is "like flavor—there are many things that taste good, but each is different and with its own ingredients." He described the difference in playing the bass with both old-time music and bluegrass: "Each form has its own feel."

George Shuffler— the bass is difficult to play in bluegrass music

George Shuffler has achieved several acknowledgments of his capability by the voters of *Bluegrass Unlimited*. Back when he was playing with Don Reno and Bill Harrell, he was voted the Best Bass player in bluegrass music several times.

Shuffler's first exposure to the walking-style of bass playing was Cedric Rainwater in the early 1940s version of the **Blue Grass Boys**, he told this writer in 1993.

Author (L) with George Shuffler

From this playing, Shuffler figured out that "There's a note on that bass for your left hand for every time you pull a string. Every time you hit a note with the right hand, your left hand should be in a different position if you are playin' a 4/4, waltz time, drivin', walkin'-type bass. I showed Tom [Gray] that and he learned a lot off the old Stanley records."

Tom Gray

Tom Gray

Tom Gray has been playing the instrument since becoming influenced by Josh Graves when Graves played occasional bass and Dobro® with Mac Wiseman's **Country Boys** in the early '50s, and by George Shuffler when he played his "walking" style of bass with the **Stanley Brothers**. And because Tom Gray played bass with one of the most influential bands

The Country Gentlemen, 1962. L to R: Eddie Adcock, John Duffey, Tom Gray, Charlie Waller. Photo courtesy Tom Gray.

of the 1960s (**Country Gentlemen**), he became one of the most influential bluegrass bass players of all time. He was voted into IBMA's Hall of Honor in 1996 as one of the four "Classic Country Gentlemen" who are Gray, Eddie Adcock, John Duffey and Charlie Waller. Admittance into the Hall had previously been for individuals in the music. This was the first time the honor was extended to a band.

Gray was born February 1, 1941, in Chicago, Illinois. His family moved to Washington, D.C., in 1948. Shortly thereafter, he began playing accordion and piano. In 1959, Gray made his first recording, playing the guitar, with Jerry Stuart, Smiley Hobbs, and Pete Roberts (Kuykendall) on the classic "Mountain Music Bluegrass Style." He recorded "Nobody's Business" with the **Country Gentlemen** before he became a member of the band. He filled-in often with the band.

1960 began his long career as bassist when he took the place of Jim Cox as bass player with the **Country Gentlemen**. The band also included John Duffey (mandolin), Charlie Waller (guitar) and Eddie Adcock (banjo). Gray had already accepted a job with Bill Harrell but was reluctantly released from this commitment. He played with the **Gents** on a part-time basis until 1963 when he quit his job as a cartographer (map maker) with *National Geographic Magazine* after the band signed with Mercury. His absence from the magazine, however, proved to be only temporary; he returned within two years seeking the job security that a young bluegrass band in 1964 couldn't offer. Besides, the **Gentlemen**'s spontaneity was being replaced with set lists. The music became less enjoyable for him. Now on a part-time basis, Gray played bass with **Bill Emerson and Cliff Waldron and the Lee Highway Boys**, the **Bluegrass Association**, and **Benny and Vallie Cain and the Country Clan** of Falls Church, Virginia. He played in and out of these groups during the 1960s until he joined the **New Sunshine Jazz Band** in 1969 based in Washington.

In 1971, Gray began playing bass as a founding member of the **Seldom Scene**. Other members were

John Duffey (mandolin), John Starling (guitar), Ben Eldridge (banjo), Mike Auldridge (resonator guitar), and for the first two months, Dave Auldridge (guitar, vocals). Gray recorded fourteen albums with **Scene**, sixty-two with others.

Tom Gray was the recipient of *Frets'* 1980 Best Country/Bluegrass Bass award in their Readers' Poll. He also won in 1981 and 1985. In 1983, he was awarded Best Bass Player by SPBGMA (Society for the Preservation of Blue Grass Music in America). A similar award was given to him in the 1970s by *Muleskinner News*.

In June of 1986, Phil Rosenthal quit the **Scene** as guitarist/lead singer and was replaced by Lou Reid. Though it didn't happen right away, many of the **Scene** members felt that with Reid's help they could take their band sound toward a sound which would appeal to a larger audience. Gray was asked to use an electric bass and to record with drums. When asked if he was being intimidated into playing the electric bass with the **Scene**, he said, "Yes. But it only came from two people within the band and two other people in the business who were close to us. But all the fans loved it the way it was. I didn't want to disappoint them... We had had several discussions on the necessity of changing our style. But once I was gone, perhaps it sent a message that the **Scene** was preparing to change its style. And I think a few people didn't care for that idea. And perhaps the message got to the guys in the band that they shouldn't antagonize their existing fans. So a lot of the style changes that had been discussed had not totally taken place.

"I got to feeling that I was the one who was holding back everybody else. We had tried to record an album with this updated sound. (He used both upright and electric bass.) But there was this desire to appeal to this wider market and I was asked to play electric on the whole thing. I said, 'My heart's not in it, but I'll try it.' And we rehearsed that way and we went into the studio and started recording. It was a disaster! Each time we would try to lay down a track, there would be something which was not mechanical enough. We'd have to leave out some frills that John was doing on the mandolin that didn't fit. I have to leave out some things I was doing on the bass. The drummer, although he was playing basically without frills in a very steady country beat, had to continually simplify his pattern. We kept trying to make these rhythm tracks upon which a vocal track would later be added. And each time we would do it, it would become simpler and simpler. But still it wasn't the kind of rhythm track that was wanted. "I reached the point where I decided if I get one more word of unwanted advice, I'm going to blow up. Sure enough it happened. I blew up and packed up the Fender bass and left the studio. Ever since then I have no desire to see an electric bass, let alone play one.

"Back to the story of me and the **Seldom Scene**, I began to feel like I was an obstacle to progress. I thought that I could either fight for the way I want it to be, or I could go ahead and change and try it and see if it becomes more commercial, or I could just leave and let them try it with someone who wants to do that. I figured if it was never tried, then the band would never know whether or not it was to succeed. If I had stayed it couldn't have happened. If I would have stayed, I would have blown up—I couldn't have stood it." This was in September 1987. On October 3, 1987, Tom Gray left the **Seldom Scene** after sixteen years with the band. "When I hear them, I hear in my head the way I think it should be. But that's not the sound that is in the air. So it is frustrating for me to listen to them."[1]

He then joined **Paul Adkins and the Borderline Band** on January 16, 1988. Gray noticed that the audience for this band was noticeably older than the audience of the **Scene**. He made a lot less money with this new band compared to when he was with the **Scene** but he insisted that it was still a lot better than it was thirty years ago when the only venues for most second-generation bands (such as the **Country Gentlemen**) were bars. The festival situation can help any young band getting started.

When the **Borderline Band** began touring extensively, Gray didn't want to quit his day job to follow them so he quit that one and was picked up by Gary Ferguson and his band in September 1990.

The most rewarding night of Gray's career was the November 10, 1986, concert which was to be recorded as "15th Anniversary Celebration" by the **Seldom Scene** and friends on Sugar Hill (released in 1988). That concert was arranged by John Starling.

Mark Schatz

Schatz was born April 23, 1955, into a musical family in Philadelphia, settling in Boston in the mid-sixties. He played classical cello at age ten. His first performance was in 1971, as electric bassist in a high

The Tony Rice Unit, 1988. L to R: Rickie Simpkins, Jimmy Gaudreau, Mark Schatz, Tony Rice, Wyatt Rice.

school rock band. Soon he played jazz. He was given a mandolin, learned the guitar, and studied music at Berklee College of Music (Boston) for a year beginning in 1975. Schatz played mandolin and old-timey banjo on the streets of Boston and Cambridge, Massachusetts, and played bass in **Mandala**, an international folk ensemble. Here he learned to clog, which added to his showmanship on stage. "This gave me the 'bug' to pursue music full-time," he told this writer in 1995 at the RockyGrass festival, Lyons, Colorado. Schatz met banjoist Bela Fleck on vacation from Haverford in the summer of 1977.

His college degree in music came in 1978 from Haverford College, which is just outside Philadelphia. He joined Jack Tottle's **Tasty Licks** in January of 1979 on bass and made his first recording, "Anchored to the Shore," with that band. This was followed by Bela Fleck's "Crossing the Tracks." "Bela and I played on the street in the summer of '79. Then we moved to Lexington, Kentucky, in the fall of '79 to form **Spectrum** with Glenn Lawson and Jimmy Gaudreau which lasted until 1981," he told this writer.

Subsequent moves in his music career included the period of January of 1982 until 1985 where he relocated to Nashville and played country music on electric bass. He re-entered the acoustic world in 1985 when he joined the **Tony Rice Unit**. In 1990, he performed with **Tim O'Brien and the O'Boys** and played on all of Tim's recordings. Mark's performance experience with the percussive dance ensemble **Footworks** (formerly the **Fiddle Puppet Dancers**) encouraged him to pursue his own solo recording in 1995, "Brand New Old-Time Way," on Rounder which features his clawhammer banjo playing. It straddles the old-time and bluegrass worlds, he said, and helped him win Bass Player of the Year at IBMA in 1995.

---

[1]All quotations with Mr. Gray came from a 1989 interview at his home in Kensington, Maryland.

Acoustic and electric basses in the Bluegrass Cardinals

In 1984, the **Bluegrass Cardinals** made a change from acoustic bass to electric. Don Parmley explained why, "Oh, everybody in the band likes the electric bass. I was probably the last one to admit it. You can hear 'em good when you're on stage and they're more accurate; generally they're on pitch better, depending on who's playing it. You always get somebody here or there who wants to know why you're not using the upright bass anymore but to the biggest majority of 'em it doesn't make any difference."[2]

The Bluegrass Cardinals, c. 1985. L to R: Larry Stephenson, Mike Hartgrove, David Parmley, Dale Perry, Don Parmley.

Dale Perry joined in February 1985 on electric bass. He left about three years later, returning August 1990 after some time with the **Lonesome River Band**. When he came back, he re-introduced the acoustic bass to the **Cardinals**. Dale (who in the mid-1990s was in Doyle Lawson's **Quicksilver**) remarked, "For traditional bluegrass, upright bass is ten-to-one better than electric. There's no way you can make an electric bass sound like an upright bass no matter what you do to it."[3] Don Parmley doesn't care one way or the other.

Acoustic and electric basses in the Osborne Brothers

Terry Eldridge joined the **Osborne Brothers** about 1988, taking the place of Jimmy Brock who played the electric bass. Eldridge brought the acoustic bass to the band. The group was just trying out the acoustic bass after having used electric for many years. As Sonny said in 1991, "We'll never go back to electric. The acoustic bass fits our music."

Eldridge described the difference in basses, "To me it's just a more true sound. It's just like the difference between an electric and a non-electrified fiddle; the tone is there." He feels that you can accentuate the notes better with an upright bass. It not only fits the **Osborne Brothers** band, but also bluegrass music. When Terry Smith arrived to play bass with the group, Eldridge moved to guitar so that he could sing more. It seemed easier to sing while strumming a guitar than plucking a bass.

Nick Forster

Forster had never played the bass before he joined **Hot Rize** in 1978. In the beginning of his bass career, he was bored for a year. But as time went on he found that "It's more interesting now—I guess because I know how to play the bass better now. I understand the role of the bass in the bluegrass context—at least in this band's style—you know, supporting each solo differently. I play a little different for a guitar solo than I would a mandolin solo."[4]

Nick Forster

[2]Brett F. Devan, "The Bluegrass Cardinals, Synonym for Vocal Harmony," *Bluegrass Unlimited*, May, 1986, p. 11.

[3]Brett F. Devan, "The Bluegrass Cardinals, The Traditional Sound of the Creative Original Vocal Trio," *Bluegrass Unlimited*, November, 1991, p. 19.

[4] From a 1985 interview in Eugene, Oregon, with this writer.

Chapter 13

The Dobro and Resonator Guitar - Table of Contents

The Dobro® and the Resonator Guitar

If the banjo is the "fifth child" in bluegrass music, the sixth is undoubtedly the DOBRO®—or resonator guitar. While the instrument came into existence in the late 1920s, it wasn't until Josh Graves played it with **Flatt and Scruggs** in 1955 that it came into its own as a bluegrass instrument. And because it has since played such an important part in bluegrass music, this chapter will discuss its beginnings as a truly American instrument and discuss some important people who played the instrument.

The first well-known player of the instrument in country music was Beecher "Pete" Kirby (or "Brother Oswald") who worked with Roy Acuff's **Smoky Mountain Boys**. Cliff Carlisle was also popular on the instrument during the '20s and '30s. Other groups (and their resonator guitarist) which used the instrument were Molly O'Day's **Cumberland Mountain Folks** (Carl Butler), Gene Autry's group, Toby Stroud's **Blue Mountain Boys** about 1953 (Buck Graves), Wilma Lee Cooper's **Clinch Mountain Clan** (Stoney Cooper in the early '40s, and later Bill Carver and Buck Graves), Carl Story's **Rambling Mountaineers** (Ray Atkins, 1950 to 1953), Mac O'Dell's **Bob and Mac** (George "Speedy" Krise), **Johnny and Jack** (Ray Atkins until "Poison Love," after which Shot Jackson took over), **Flatt and Scruggs** (Buck Graves), Cliff Waldron's **New Shades of Grass**, the **Seldom Scene** (Mike Auldridge, Fred Travers), Buck White's **Down Home Folks** (Jerry Douglas) and many more through more recent history. Shot Jackson manufactured his own version of the instrument, the "Sho-Bro"—a combination steel guitar-type instrument.

The most significant event in the popularization of the DOBRO® or resonator guitar was when Buck Graves began playing the instrument with the bluegrass band called **Flatt and Scruggs and the Foggy Mountain Boys** in 1955. Graves picked it with the three-finger style that Earl Scruggs taught him. And Pete Kirby was one of the first to take the instrument from the realm of Hawaiian music to country music as a lead instrument. Some may recall that Robert "Tut" Taylor, a renown collector of rare instruments, played the instrument with a flatpick. The flatpick was well suited for country and blues, but didn't catch on in bluegrass like the hard-driving three-finger style of Graves.

Cliff Carlisle

Cliff Carlisle— one of the first in country music

One of the first people to play the DOBRO® was Cliff Raymond Carlisle of Spencer County, Kentucky, who was born in 1904. Carlisle was the man who refined the style of using a sliding bar on steel guitars. He played his metal-bodied National DOBRO® in a style which was as much Hawaiian as it was blues. His steel guitar (also known as "Hawaiian" at the dawn of the Jazz Age) playing was popular during the '20s and '30s. His style was the forerunner of the electric steel and pedal steel sounds of modern western swing. Hawaiian groups originally popularized the style when they toured the U.S. before World War I. Carlisle later made the instrument more popular by making the style a little jazzier, which paved the way for further development of music on the DOBRO®/resonator guitar during the '30s.

During the height of the Depression, radio stations paid only $5-10 per week for singers. Through the years, Carlisle played on WLS (Chicago), WLV and WBT (Charlotte, North Carolina), WWNC (Asheville, North Carolina), WAIR (Winston-Salem, North Carolina, in 1938), WCHS (Charleston, West Virginia), WMMN (Fairmont, West Virginia) and WIS (Columbia, South Carolina). These were the same stations which were part of the bluegrass music circuit and gives an idea of the similar roots of all types of country music, including bluegrass music which was just another form of country music during its formative years.

In 1934, Carlisle recorded his own composition, "The Girl in the Blue Velvet Band," on the American Record Company, a New York label. He recorded it with his brother, Bill Carlisle, when they were known as the **Carlisles**.[1] Cliff recorded with Jimmie Rodgers in 1931.

During the brothers' stay at WNOX in Knoxville at the Mid-Day Merry-Go-Round, they were able to remain a long time and enjoy some fame, too. Bill Carlisle recalled, "I did the comedy on our show, with a character called 'Hotshot Elmer.' We'd work as the **Carlisle Brothers** and then, while Cliff was handling the show, I'd go backstage and change into my rube clothes. That was Hotshot Elmer, and I'd be barefooted. During the act me and my brother had a mock fight and we'd get a chair between us and I could stand flat-footed and jump over the chair. And jump back. I just started doing that and people would laugh about it. So it come natural to me when I'm singing sometimes just to jump, you know. Of course, I'm not getting as high as I used to"—a comedian's studied pause—"but I'm staying up there longer."[2] Cliff Carlisle died in 1983. Bill continued regular appearances on the Grand Ole Opry into the 1990s.

Speedy Krise

George "Speedy" Krise was born in Hinton, West Virginia, May 7, 1922. He was nicknamed "Speedy" because of his slow mannerisms and a hesitation in his speech. Krise's resonator guitar style was of the old school which sticks closely to the melody, varying occasionally with portions of the Hawaiian style.

He played his resonator guitar and electrified Hawaiian guitar in 1941 at WJLS radio, Beckley, West Virginia, with artists such as Little Jimmy Dickens, the **Lilly Brothers**, Walter Bailes, and Skeets and Dixie Lee (Molly O'Day) Williamson. The sponsor on the show was Dr. Pepper.

Krise's own **Blue Ribbon Boys**[3] broke up when he went into the service.

Dobro Cyclops model 37 square neck made in 1932. Photo courtesy Gruhn Guitars.

After Krise returned from the military in 1946, he joined and recorded with Molly O'Day and Lynn Davis and their **Cumberland Mountain Folks** on WNOX. The next year, he recorded with Archie (of "Hee Haw" fame) Campbell's band on the Mercury label. They, with Red Kirk, called themselves the **Old-Timers**. That same year, Speedy formed the **New River Gang** which included "Southpaw" Thacker (guitar). After that, Speedy and Fred Smith formed a duet, the **Arkansas Travelers**, singing and doing comedy on NBC-TV's Knoxville affiliate. Krise then joined Jack Shelton's **Green County Boys** whose members included Fred Smith and Benny Sims. They recorded on Mercury.

Krise began writing songs in 1950, soon recording many of his own on Capitol[4], and again for Capitol in 1951.[5] In 1954, he moved to West Virginia to play with the **Dixie Drifters**[6] on television and radio. He moved to Akron, Ohio, after that and retired from active music, still making an occasional appearance with his sons.

Tut Taylor—
a pioneer in Nashville music

Robert "Tut" Taylor is more than a musician who played the resonator guitar just prior to the time that Josh Graves made his mark with the DOBRO®. He is more than an instrument trader and he is more than an instrument maker. He's all of that. But the man from Georgia also an innovator in the music business.

Taylor was one of the first to commercialize and specialize in vintage acoustic instruments for bluegrass pickers. He trained many today-well-known luthiers and, in 1970 opened up GTR[7] with George Gruhn and Randy Wood in Nashville which later became Gruhn Guitars.

Awareness of his importance in the bluegrass world was brought to the attention of the public by writer Bobby Wolfe when he wrote Taylor's biography for *Bluegrass Unlimited* in 1988. Wolfe points out that "During the old deejay convention days, back in Nashville during the '60s, Tut used to block a whole floor of rooms in

---

[1] Bill Monroe recorded the tune on Columbia with Mac Wiseman in the next decade.

Carlisle also partnered with yodeler/musician Wilbur Ball. When Carlisle met Ball, probably in the early 1930s, Ball was the one who yodeled. Ball taught Carlisle how to yodel, who then became so good at it that Ball never did it again. The duo often played with Jimmie Rodgers who was then playing a very good ukulele. Ball remembered that Rodgers never sang a song the same way twice, making it difficult for others who recorded with him. Cliff and Wilbur spent many years together as partners.

[2] Chet Hagan, *The Grand Ole Opry* (New York: Henry Holt and Company, Inc., 1989), p. 156.

[3] Members were Krise, Ed "Rattlesnake" Hogan (bass), Roy and Carl Barbour (mandolin and guitar).

[4] With Carl Butler, Tater Tate (fiddle), Hoke Jenkins (banjo) and Jake Tullock (bass).

[5] With Carl Butler, Jake Tullock (bass), Art Wooten (fiddle) and Smokey White (guitar).

[6] With Billy Jean and Red Lydick.

[7] GTR stood for the partners of the store: George Gruhn, Tut Taylor and Randy Wood.

a downtown Nashville hotel, call people all over the country, and ask if they were coming this year. He was the spark plug that made a lot of these things happen at the deejay conventions when it was in town. You had all the lobbies of the hotel taken up with the [displays of the] publishing companies, instrument makers, and there were hospitality suites all over the place. And there was the underworld of country music taking place: bluegrass music, day and night, pickin' in the halls. Tut Taylor is one of the people who made these things happen and people didn't know it."[8]

Taylor was born in Baldwin County, Georgia, November 20, 1923, into a family where most members played an instrument. The family moved to nearby Milledgeville when a Works Progress Administration dam covered his birthplace with water. His father's pay, working for the W.P.A. during the Depression, was $7.50 every two weeks. They were so poor they didn't even notice the Depression.

The nickname "Tut" came from his brother, probably because young Robert was a fan of Buck Rogers and comic books. Tut's main early influence toward music was two blind, black men who played music. He tagged along whenever they were in town.

At age ten, Taylor began playing banjo, and then the mandolin. Soon he was playing the lap steel. In 1938 or 1939, he heard the sound of the resonator guitar (Brother Oswald) on the Grand Ole Opry and fell in love with it. He wrote to Roy Acuff asking what the instrument was. After Acuff's wife, Mildred, wrote back and told him what it was, he immediately went out and bought an original DOBRO® at a pawn shop for $27.50. Not knowing how to play the instrument, he learned it by himself, in his own style, with a flatpick. In 1945, Earl Scruggs gave Taylor fingerpicks, which did nothing but hurt his fingers.

Soon Taylor became a collector of instruments, his favorite being the only A-5 Gibson mandolin made by Lloyd Loar when Loar worked for Gibson. At one time, his collection of resonator guitars numbered sixty-seven; then he ran out of room at home. Even with three phones in the house, he had trouble keeping up with all the telephone inquiries about the instruments.

An expert on many instruments, Taylor figures that when Bill Monroe bought his Lloyd Loar mandolin, he probably didn't recognize the label when he bought it. "If he did," Taylor told this writer, "it didn't mean anything. I'd say they were first recognized as good instruments by pickers first, then along in the '50s things like that came together and were recognized."

After a move to Nashville in 1970, Taylor helped found GTR. He sold out to Gruhn in 1973. With a sign-painting business as his day job, he was chosen to paint the huge murals on the walls of Nashville's Old-Time Pickin' Parlor, which he founded with Randy Wood and Grant Boatwright. In 1972, Taylor recorded "Aereo-

Plain" on Warner Brothers. He later partnered up with Norman Blake, beginning to extensively record his unique resonator guitar style on labels such as Warner Brothers, Rounder, Tennessee, and his own King Tut Records. There in Nashville, he picked with the **John Hartford Band** for nearly two years. That band, and Norman Blake's **Dobrolic Plectrolic Society** were the only professional bands he picked with during his career.

In September 1973, Taylor purchased the assets of the Grammar Guitar Company (but not the name). His plans at the time were to move the booming operation of the Tennessee Dulcimer Works into the building at 500 Arlington Ave, Nashville. Bob Givens, from the West Coast, moved to Nashville to join Taylor in business operations. Their plans were to produce Givens' Master Model and also Artist Model mandolins. On the drawing board was a banjo patterned after the 1937 to 1940 top-tension model. About that time, he left the bluegrass scene, and in 1978 left Nashville to his present home near Maryville, Tennessee. He had lost a lot of money in 1976 (as did many people) when many of his Bi-centennial instruments didn't sell. When he received an offer to open a shop at Hee Haw Village, he and his wife did that. In the early 1990s, he became a factor in the Rich and Taylor banjo company, which went now out of business.

Josh Graves

Josh Graves— the man who popularized the DOBRO®/resonator guitar in bluegrass music

T his is *the* man who brought the DOBRO®/ resonator guitar to the forefront of America's music: bluegrass. With his three-finger style of playing, he put a drive into the music of **Flatt and**

Esco Hankins and his Tennesseans in
Knoxville, TN, 1943. Top L to R: Gene
Jackson, Esco Hankins. Bottom L to R:
Henry Horn, Buck Graves. Photo courtesy
Josh Graves.

Scruggs which not only helped popularize the band, but
served as the catalyst for a renewed popularity of the
instrument. Prior to the mid-1940s, none of the resonator guitar's players played bluegrass. Graves has served
as *the* mentor for all subsequent resonator guitar
players.

Josh Graves was born in Tellico Plains, Monroe
County, in East Tennessee, in the foothills of the Smoky
Mountains (in the Alanwick community) on September
27, 1927. Named "Burkett" at birth, his nickname
"Buck" was given to him when a neighbor watched him
get swatted by his mother when he mounted a horse as
a little boy. The neighbor shouted, "Look at Buck
Jones!" and the name "Buck" stuck with him ever
since. The name "Josh" came later.

His family was musically inclined but didn't take it
as seriously as young Burkett. When he was two or
three, the Graves family moved to Maryville, Tennessee, in a wagon. His mother played pump organ, his
father, the mouth harp. Buck influenced his brothers to
music. He originally tried the five-string banjo but found
that his fingers were too short to fret properly.

At the age of nine, Buck was inspired to play the
resonator guitar when he saw Cliff Carlisle in a concert
in Wildwood, Tennessee. He then got a Stella guitar
with a raised nut from a music store which promised
that if he took sixty one-dollar lessons, he got to keep
the guitar. The company moved out of town before the
lessons were complete, so he kept it. His next instruments were an S.S. Stewart guitar, a Stradolin mandolin,
and a metal-body National guitar. He preferred picking
the resonator guitar.

Graves grew up a fan of Jimmie Rodgers; his father
had bought Rodgers' records for him. On some of those
records, Rodgers was backed up by Bill and Cliff
Carlisle of the **Carlisle Brothers**. Graves recalled, "He
didn't play anything fancy, just the old slides, but I liked
what he was playing and he was my idol."[9]

Graves' first significant music job was in 1942 (he
was fourteen) at WROL in Knoxville, Tennessee, with
his first resonator guitar—an all-metal National. This
band was the **Pierce Brothers**, which played every
Saturday night. Since Graves was the only member
without a day job, the other band members helped him
get by financially.

The next year, Graves played with Esco Hankins'
Tennesseans in Knoxville on Cas Walker's program.
This was his first professional job, making $35 per
week. "I didn't own a car until I was thirty-three, but I'd
walk around with a roll [of money] in my pocket."[10] He
worked there until 1947 when he went home. In 1949,
he went back to Hankins for another year, playing
guitar. About that time, he bought his first DOBRO® for
$8, a steel National. He gives names to his guitars; one
is called "Cliff" after Cliff Carlisle, another is "Julie."
Josh told this writer that he talks to Cliff. It's "the most
sensitive I ever played in my life." Today, he plays
"Elbert" and others, considering Cliff and Julie too
valuable to take on the road.

The origin of the name "Uncle Josh", he reminisced
in a 1992 interview, was "In the '30s, there was an old
man from the Carolinas that did monologues and called
himself 'Uncle Josh'. He was rich, and in show business
as a hobby. When I started, bands always had slapstick
comedy. I played an old man with a gray wig and
blacked-out teeth. Another fellow, Wade Cass, did a
woman's part. We called ourselves **Uncle Josh and
Aunt Jeroshia**. It just stuck, I guess. With Esco
Hankins it was 'Josh.' With **Wilma Lee and Stoney
Cooper** it was 'Buck'—Stoney thought that sounded
better. Up in the Northeast it's 'Buck'—they won't have
'Uncle Josh.'" He quit this band in early 1949 because of
the poor pay, and worked at construction for a couple of
years.

In 1949, he played guitar, bass and fiddle. Using a
borrowed fiddle at a contest, he beat well-known old-
time fiddlers Carl Story and Clayton McMichen who
were there competing.

In 1950, Josh Graves joined **Wilma Lee and Stoney
Cooper** on the WWVA Jamboree, Wheeling, West
Virginia. It was with the Coopers that he occasionally
met with Earl Scruggs, who was also on the show.
There Scruggs taught Graves the three-finger roll, and
soon Josh began to develop the style of playing the
DOBRO® with banjo-like, three-finger rolls. He had it

[9] Arlie Metheny, "Kenny Baker and Josh Graves—The Best Years of Their Lives," *Bluegrass Unlimited*, January, 1988, p. 26.

[10] Bobby Wolfe, "Josh Graves—Father of Bluegrass Dobro," *Bluegrass Unlimited*, November, 1990, p. 21. He was single at the time with no significant
financial responsibilities.

pretty well perfected by the time he joined **Flatt and Scruggs** in 1955.[11]

When Stoney Cooper offered him a job playing DOBRO®, he asked Graves if he played in a style like that of Brother Oswald Kirby. The reply was that he didn't copy anybody's style but Earl Scruggs'. Graves offered to audition if Cooper would buy him a $16 bus ticket to Lexington, Kentucky. Up until this time, he made $35 per week. When Cooper offered him $50, Graves was "floored" and eagerly accepted it. "He scared the hell out of me—I'd never seen $50 a week." Cooper later told him that he was pleased that Graves hadn't asked for $100 a week—he would have paid it.[12]

In 1954, Graves joined Toby Stroud's **Blue Mountain Boys** for a short period. That same year, he played bass and DOBRO® with Mac Wiseman's **Country Boys**. About this time, he paid $70 for "Julie." He spoke about his new DOBRO®, "Early on with **Flatt and Scruggs**, we used one mike. With six of us you had to have something to cut it. Nothing is going to cut a banjo, but 'Julie' came as close to it as any I've seen."[13] DOBRO® "Julie" was later stolen at a Loews theater in Syracuse, New York, when he worked with the **Earl Scruggs Revue**. He eventually got it back.

In the spring of 1955, Graves joined **Flatt and Scruggs**, staying until 1969 when the band split up. He joined originally as a bass player, and did one or two numbers per show on the DOBRO® while they tested the audience reaction to the instrument. Whereas other styles of DOBRO®/resonator guitar playing may not have fit into the hard-driving music that **Flatt and Scruggs and the Foggy Mountain Boys** played, Graves' style seemed to fit right in. Before long, he was asked which instrument he would rather play with the band. He jumped at the chance to play his DOBRO®. Jake Tullock then was hired to play bass.

Graves spoke of Earl Scruggs and the music they played together, "He'd go one way and I'd go another. I guess that's what made it so clean. Earl did a lot for me and I appreciated it. He was the greatest. Our tuning and timing had to be right. And he wouldn't let us pat our feet. Poor Paul [Warren], he couldn't play without patting his foot. I've seen Earl walk over and put his foot on Paul's. Paul would start patting the other. Earl just figured you didn't have to do it to play."[14] Graves feels that Scruggs is the best musician alive today.

He was still known as "Buck" and hadn't lost the "Uncle Josh" handle yet, either. His first recordings with **Flatt and Scruggs**, released on Columbia September 3, 4 and 5, 1955, were "Gone Home" and "Bubbling in My Soul." The weekly schedule of appearances with the group consisted of a daily, early morning show for sponsor Martha White Mills, live television appearances and concerts throughout the South, and the Saturday night appearances at the Grand Ole Opry. He didn't get a day off until six months after signing on. During the 1960s, the **Flatt and Scruggs** band "played every major college in the United States and overseas. The money was good," said Graves. When Curly Seckler was in the band, they traveled about 2,000 miles per week.

When Flatt and Scruggs split in 1969, Graves continued with the more traditional sound of **Lester Flatt and the Nashville Grass**. According to Graves, the reason for him choosing one band over the other was not because of a musical preference (certainly the two men's groups were very different) or a personal preference of Flatt over Scruggs. "Hell no! I just wanted to make a living." Graves recruited Roland White, Vic Jordan, Jake Tullock and Paul Warren into Flatt's new band. Graves stayed two years then went with the **Earl Scruggs Revue** for two years. Here he found it necessary to learn new licks to fit into this rock-oriented band. He made good money with them and put out several albums.

During this period, Graves and fiddler Kenny Baker recorded two albums for the Puritan label which were released in 1973. "The next year, Graves partnered with Bobby Smith for a while and recorded for Vetco and CMH. He then broke away from all other bands to perfom on his own."

On October 12, 1984, Josh Graves and Kenny Baker formed a partnership. Graves had grown tired of playing solo and all the driving, "So late in 1984 I was going up into Kentucky to do an album and they needed a fiddler.

Josh Graves with "Cousin Jake" Tullock. Photo courtesy Josh Graves

---

[11] He didn't have an opportunity to use this style with Hankins because of the slow speed of his country music.

[12] Graves sincerely admired Stoney Cooper. Cooper taught him his present attitude on dressing for the audience. Cooper insisted that his stage appearance should make the audience comfortable—that is, he should dress casually. He left his suits in the closet. "Let me tell you something," Graves explained. "If I walk up on that stage, I have a lot of friends settin' out there. If I've got a $500 suit on they think I'm above them. I want to be down to the level where they are."

[13] Wolfe, op. cit., p. 22.

[14] Bobby Wolfe, "Josh Graves—Father of Bluegrass Dobro (conclusion)," *Bluegrass Unlimited*, November, 1990, p. 29.

Sheet music cover. Top: Wilbur Ball. Bottom L to R: Wayne Raney, Cliff Carlisle. Courtesy Ray and Ina Patterson.

I said, 'How about Kenny Baker?' They said, 'Can you get him?' And I said, 'I'll try.' I called Kenny and asked him if he'd left Bill, and he said he had. I asked him if he'd go up to Kentucky to do this album with me, and he said yes. So I said, 'Would you want to do a show on Saturday night after we do the album,' and he said yes... So I booked a Saturday night..."[15]

The partnership has worked out well for both of them. "When Kenny was with Bill Monroe—no disrespect to him—and when I was with Lester Flatt," said Graves, "you had about twenty tunes that you played. And you had to do that every day, and you get tired of doing the same thing. Here's what I like about what we are doing now. We go out, and if we want to stay a month, we'll stay and do what we want to do and play what we want to play...things that we never got a chance to play before. I think it works better that way.

"Kenny and I have talked about this quite a bit, but these three years together have been the happiest time I've had in show business. We'll stop along the roadside at a produce place and get some tomatoes and cucumbers and sit down and eat them—just like the old days when we first started."[16]

Josh Graves gave some advice to DOBRO®/resonator guitar pickers: "The thing they overlook is that you've got to learn that neck. Bright lights bother me and I had to learn to look off. I hate to see a fellow keep his eyes glued to the neck. I see that and wonder if he's afraid he's going to miss it."[17]

He enjoys the status of being the most-copied resonator guitar player in the business. One of his disciples is Jerry Douglas who has, according to Graves, "gone on to fancier stuff, but I'll tell you he's a genius! He can do everything. He can play it straight or whatever he wants to. He's a fine fellow."[18] Indeed, some of the success of Jerry Douglas has been enjoyed by Graves. At the acceptance of a Award of Merit at the International Bluegrass Music Association 1992 awards ceremony, Graves joked, "I knew if he kept playing as well as he does, I'd become famous."

In 1994, Graves sported a new Paul Beard guitar. And after ten years with Kenny Baker, the duo was trying to decide whether or not to retire. Regardless, Graves continued to perform and record. Graves wrote "Come Walk with Me" when he was with the Coopers, and later wrote "Shuckin' the Corn," "Fireball," "The Good Things Outweigh the Bad" and "Roustabout." He lives with his wife, Evelyn, modestly in the same house they bought when they moved to Nashville to join **Flatt and Scruggs** in 1955. He became sponsored by The Gibson Guitar Company in 1995 when Gibson bought DOBRO®.

Mike Auldridge

Mike Auldridge— from tradition to the feel of modern music

One of the premier resonator guitar players in the world is Washington, D.C.-born Mike Auldridge (December 30, 1938). He grew up knowing the big band music of Benny Goodman and Tommy Dorsey. At age fourteen, he began playing the guitar in a style similar to Travis-picking, then the banjo at sixteen, and the resonator guitar at twenty-two. His

[15] Metheny, op. cit., p. 26.

[16] Ibid., p. 27.

[17] Wolfe, op. cit., p. 24.

[18] Wolfe, "(conclusion)," op. cit., p. 31.

interest in the resonator guitar began in the early '50s when he heard his Uncle Ellsworth Cozzens playing resonator guitar at family gatherings. (Cozzens had played resonator guitar and banjo on Jimmie Rodgers' earliest recordings in the late 1920s.) But Auldridge didn't get serious on the instrument until he was in his early twenties.

After moving to Kensington, Maryland, in 1950, Auldridge heard Josh Graves playing DOBRO® with Wilma Lee and Stoney Cooper. Auldridge learned to play the instrument by slowing down **Flatt and Scruggs** records with Graves on them. In 1965, he jammed with Graves and decided then to devote all his musical activities to playing the resonator guitar.

In college, with a major in art and music, he met Ben Eldridge, John Starling and Gary Henderson. This led to a full-time resonator guitar job in 1968 with **Emerson and Waldron.**[19] When Bill Emerson left the band in early 1970 to join the **Country Gentlemen,** Auldridge stayed on with Waldron to soon form **Cliff Waldron and the New Shades of Grass**, based in Bethesda, Maryland.

In 1971, he became one of the founding members of the **Seldom Scene** with John Duffey (mandolin), John Starling (guitar), Ben Eldridge (banjo) and Tom Gray (bass) in a band which promised to just have fun and not take their music to the point of full-time. They managed part-time until their popularity drove them all to quit their day jobs to pursue their music full-time—this was in 1976 for Auldridge.

In 1973, Auldridge began recording his solo albums. These include "DOBRO" (Takoma/Devi Records, 1973), "Blues and Blue Grass" (Takoma, 1974), "Mike Auldridge and 'Old Dog'" (Flying Fish, 1977), "Mike Auldridge and Jeff Newman" (Flying Fish, 1978) and "Eight String Swing" (Sugar Hill, 1982).

In 1975, he began learning to play the pedal steel guitar, practicing ten to fourteen hours each day, which he still does today. He recorded with it on "The New Seldom Scene Album," and on Doyle Lawson's "Heavenly Treasures" and "Once and For Always" albums. Auldridge recalled that, "I really enjoy playing the steel. It sounds kind of corny, but every morning when I wake up, I can't wait to get to it and discover something new on it... I think the steel is gonna become more accepted in bluegrass just as the DOBRO® has been."[20]

Very prolific in the studio as a session resonator guitarist for various artists, as of 1989 he had recorded on approximately 200 albums with various artists in several different fields of music. As of 1995, he remained a stalwart member of the **Seldom Scene** as well

as **Chesapeake** with Moondi Klein (guitar), Jimmy Gaudreau (mandolin) and T. Michael Coleman (electric bass). In January 1996, Klein, Coleman, and Auldridge left the **Scene** to pursue **Chesapeake** full time.

Jerry Douglas

Jerry Douglas— a third-generation dynamo

This third-generation bluegrass resonator guitar player has done more—much more—than pick up the gauntlet of earlier resonator guitar players from whom he learned his instrument. He applied the basic style of Josh Graves with his own upbringing and culture to delve into a type of music quite unimagined by his predecessors. Indeed, the style of music which Douglas plays so frequently now—new acoustic—didn't even exist before his generation.

Author Bobby Wolfe, who writes frequently about resonator guitarists such as Tut Taylor and Jerry Douglas, described how times have changed for musicians born after 1950:

Newgrass, bluegrass-fusion, country-rock, new country, super-picker. All these terms and more have been used to describe or explain the new breed of hot pickers such as Jerry Douglas. They are usually in their late twenties or early thirties. Their parents were born in the '30s or early '40s and were working people of the southeastern United States—that large group of parents responsible for the 'baby boom' of the '50s. These

[19] With Cliff Waldron (guitar), Bill Emerson (banjo), Bill Poffinberger (fiddle), Garland Alderman (mandolin), Ed Ferris (bass), and later Ben Eldridge (banjo) and Dave Auldridge (Mike's brother, guitar). His day job became a commercial artist for the *Star-News* in Washington. He created the artwork for many Seldom Scene albums as well as for the cover of *Bluegrass Unlimited* magazine—its original and present logos. The design for *BU*'s first cover used "Harvey," the banjo of Ben Eldridge obtained from Bill Emerson in September 1966. It was an original gold-plated, flathead TB-6 once bought from a pawn shop by banjo luthier Tom Morgan in the late '50s. The name "Harvey" was given because its original owner was Harvey R. Brasse. The logo for *Bluegrass Unlimited* was changed about 1970 to include a cluster of instruments instead of a single banjo.

[20] Steve Robinson, "Mike Auldridge—Not So Seldom Scene," *Bluegrass Unlimited*, September, 1985, p. 40.

parents were determined that their children were going to have a better childhood than they. The times were prosperous and allowed this to happen or maybe their determination was partly responsible for the prosperous times.

As a result, a new generation of pickers was born into a situation that allowed the time to learn to play, that gave them a better selection of instruments and parental encouragement to 'do their thing.'[21]

Also, by the time these pickers were ready to play, bluegrass festivals were now providing a ready venue at which they could play and pursue their careers in music.

Jerry Douglas was born in Warren, Ohio, May 28, 1956. At five, he played mandolin and got a Silvertone guitar for Christmas about 1962 or '63. Growing up around Warren in the early 1970s, Douglas was heavily exposed to music by his father whose band was called the **West Virginia Travelers**.

Douglas became interested in playing the resonator guitar at a 1966 concert in Middletown, Ohio, where he saw Josh Graves (with **Flatt and Scruggs**) and the resonator guitar player who was with Roy Acuff's band at the time. Jerry liked Josh best. Other early influences were Mike Auldridge, Ry Cooder and Albert Lee. Douglas related, "After the **Flatt and Scruggs**

Crucial Country, early 1980's. L to R: Mark O'Connor, Roy Huskey Jr., Peter Rowan, Jerry Douglas.

show, I asked Dad to raise the nut on the Silvertone, and I'd play it. He did that the next day and then cut a piece out of a tubular hacksaw for my first bar. We just tuned it to open G and I started playing it. We kept our guitars on a cedar chest in the bedroom. We came home one day and found the Silvertone folded up. [It] couldn't stand the sun coming through the window. I was devastated. This was about a year after I'd started playing the Silvertone—DOBRO® style."[22]

There were only two bluegrass bands within a 150 mile radius of his home in Ohio; heavy metal was the predominant music of the area during the late '60s to early '70s. Young Douglas had no one to take resonator guitar lessons from so he learned from records. He learned the three-finger roll from listening to recordings of Josh Graves and watching other musicians play the instruments. In a very real way, Jerry Douglas learned

his instrument in the same manner in which the early bluegrass pioneers learned their music. These pioneers, and Douglas, experimented around until they "invented" their own style of playing bluegrass and other forms of music. After getting an excellent foundation in the basics of bluegrass, he went on to express himself in music forms such as country and western, jazz and new acoustic.

He soon got an "f" hole resonator guitar. His next one was a 1932 "Lady Dobro." He also gave lessons to Ron Messing and Dan Huckabee. He got his third resonator guitar (which is on the cover of "Fluxology") and played it 1974 to 1980. After that he obtained an R.Q. Jones which he used until he got one from Peter Slama, a Czechoslovakian immigrant, about 1990. The Jones "has good volume and a variety of tones... It starts out with a more even tone. It's not as 'twangy' as a DOBRO®." He later began playing a lap steel instrument on stage. In 1992, he used the Jones resonator guitar as well as a Tim Sheerhorn (of Michigan) and the Peter Slama. Each has its own characteristics and gives him more flexibility for performing and recording, depending upon what he wants the sound to be.

Douglas didn't practice much in his formative years, relying on his band sessions with his father's **West Virginia Travelers**[23] to hone his skills as a musician. "Playing with a band makes the difference," he said. "That's where your timing comes from. That's where your dynamics come from. You just adapt to different situations."[24]

The **Country Gentlemen** was his first professional touring band. After having spent a summer with the band in 1973, he joined the group full-time on May 26, 1974, after high school graduation. He stayed one and a half years (he was to join again in 1978 for ten months). Ricky Skaggs was with the group about that time (on fiddle) and spoke about Douglas and the **Gentlemen**, "They had fiddle, banjo, bass and guitar, but no mandolin. That's where Jerry's rhythm got so good from—by playing without a mandolin—because he had to fill that gap. He's got a rhythm lick on the DOBRO® that's just amazing. It's so *there*! It's like a drum, without having

[21] Bobby Wolfe, "The Jerry Douglas Story," *Bluegrass Unlimited*, August, 1991, p. 20.

[22] Ibid., p. 21.

[23] Other members of the West Virginia Travelers were Dave Clark (mandolin), Harry Shafer (banjo), Ray Sponaugle (fiddle) and Bernie Crawford (bass).

[24] From an interview in June 1985 at Jacksonville, Oregon, at the Peter Britt Bluegrass Festival. Other quotations in this biography were from a telephone interview in 1991 unless otherwise noted

one."[25] It was with the **Gentlemen** in 1974 that Skaggs labeled Jerry Douglas with the nickname "Flux". But Jerry said he would just as soon forget about it.

Douglas played resonator guitar on the landmark Rounder Records album, "J.D. Crowe and the New South," when he was a member of that group in Lexington for three months in 1975. Other members were Tony Rice (guitar), Ricky Skaggs (mandolin, fiddle), Bobby Slone (bass) and Crowe (banjo). His presence on such an album served notice to the world that he was about to be the latest in the succession of competent and innovative resonator guitar players which began with Pete "Oswald" Kirby and Cliff Carlisle.

In October of 1975, Skaggs (mandolin, fiddle) and Douglas left Crowe's **New South** to form **Boone Creek**[26] which lasted until 1978. Douglas then returned to the **Country Gentlemen** for eight months and then joined **Buck White and the Down Home Folks** (later known as the **Whites**) in January 1979 and stayed for seven years. "They wanted more of a country band," said Douglas. "Their banjo player had quit so with that it gave me a wide open space to work with. They were great and I could do most anything I wanted."[27]

From that time to the present, he cemented his reputation as the most popular and most-often-used resonator guitar player in bluegrass by appearing on the albums of David Grisman, Tony Rice, Bela Fleck, Emmylou Harris, Jerry Reed, Hank Williams Jr., Glen Campbell, Ray Charles, the **Nitty Gritty Dirt Band**, his own solo albums and, of course, the **Bluegrass Album Band** series of albums beginning in 1981. The *Frets* magazine Readers' Poll voted Jerry Douglas as Best Dobro®. His wins as Best Bluegrass DOBRO® from SPBGMA were 1984 through 1988. After leaving the **Whites** in 1985, Douglas signed with MCA, leaving Rounder Records.

His varied recording and live performances exposed him to working with a drummer where he decided that he liked playing with drums. "After you get used to playing with drums, there is just a 'bottom' that is gone when [you get back to the bluegrass rhythm section]."

He feels that drums free up the mandolin to play more effective melody.

For MCA, he recorded "Under the Wire," "Changing Channels" and "Plant Early." He signed with Sugar Hill in 1991. He had played on over a thousand recordings by this time. As of 1992, Jerry Douglas was one of the most requested studio instrumentalists in Nashville, along with Mark O'Connor. By this time, he'd been in the business for nearly twenty years and was still a young man; he was having trouble getting used to people labeling him as a "veteran". It seemed like only yesterday that he was the "up-and-coming star". "It's fun, but it's not new to people any more. It's like 'Okay, top this.' Now, if you don't play anything surprising which will jump out at people—if you play the same thing they were raving about years ago—[they won't be satisfied]."

When asked for advice for an aspiring musician, he said, "Don't give up. The DOBRO® is a very discouraging instrument when you are first learning how to play. There were a few times when I really wanted to quit because I just thought I had reached the end. I couldn't get beyond a certain point. But there are plateaus that you reach throughout your playing career. I still reach those plateaus where I feel I'm not doing any good with the instrument. But that goes away, so you just have to keep trying. Young players have a lot more to listen to than even five years ago. Just soak up everything you can and listen to everything you can."[28]

His favorite experiences are when he toured Japan with J.D. Crowe, Bobby Slone, Tony Rice and Ricky Skaggs, and in the countries behind the Iron Curtain where western musicians are elevated to the status of heroes. His production of "The Great Dobro Sessions" won Instrumental Recording of the Year, Recorded Event of the Year at IBMA and a Grammy in 1995. He won DOBRO® Player of the Year that year and every year given. As of 1996, he was endorsing Gibson's DOBRO®. He was appointed Vice President of the IBMA in September 1996.

---

[25] January 1973 issue of *Bluegrass Unlimited*.

[26] Jerry Douglas and Ricky Skaggs founded Boone Creek with Terry Baucom (banjo, fiddle) and Wes Golding (guitar). Their albums were "Boone Creek" (Rounder) and "One Way Track" (Sugar Hill).

[27] Wolfe, op. cit., p. 24.

[28] From 1985 interview at the Peter Britt Festival, Jacksonville, Oregon.

Chapter 14

Branches of Bluegrass— Modern Outgrowths, e.g. Newgrass - Table of Contents

Branches of Bluegrass

Modern Outgrowths, e.g. Newgrass

The three generations of bluegrass musicians

As the pioneers of bluegrass get older, their disciples and students carry on their work. These students will then pass it on to others. Based on the presumption that both the masters and the students were of the same approximate age when they began to play bluegrass music professionally, this music culture has evolved to have a sort of hierarchy with the first musicians as masters because they "invented" it.

The first level (or generation) of the hierarchy would include Bill Monroe, Flatt, Scruggs, the Stanleys, Curly Seckler, the Clines, Jim and Jesse McReynolds, and others whose music career began during the thirties and forties. A second generation of bluegrassers might include Cliff Waldron, Eddie Adcock, Mike Auldridge, John Duffey and those whose music began in the mid-fifties with the presumption that they followed the previous work of the first generation. The third generation of bluegrass musicians might include those whose music began to develop about the time of the folk boom of the early 1960s and beyond. As of the 1990s, we are probably in the midst of the fourth generation bluegrass musicians.

The third and fourth generation bluegrass disciples grew up with different social, educational, technological and even governmental influences (wars, depressions, for example) than the first two generations. When a person's main musical influences on the radio are the **Kingston Trio** and the **Beatles**, he/she can't help producing a music which is different than someone such as Bill Monroe who credits a black blues guitarist as a main influence.

Vince Gill, at the 1993 Country Music Awards Show, told the audience that country music had not changed through the years, that it had grown. Bluegrass certainly has done both. Because of the different backgrounds of each person who plays this music and write songs for it, they each play it a little differently. Only Bill Monroe properly plays "Bill Monroe music". Except for others who copy it as closely as they can (and they call it "bluegrass music" in most circumstances), most people who play this music want to develop their own style of bluegrass music and not be accused of playing anyone else's style. Thus, the music has changed. Some might call the "growth" of the music "contemporary" bluegrass.

There is no shame in whatever path a person decides to take—whether a person chooses to be a direct clone of Bill Monroe's mandolin playing, or to play a more abstract style of mandolin playing such as that of Sam Bush or John Duffey. There is merely a difference in how the person chooses to view the music—his music—each according to his own bias. It's no wonder that the music is not the same as it was fifty years ago. Because people change, music will change as well; bluegrass music has changed accordingly. Only now, we have a number of varieties of bluegrass from which to choose. Many super third-generation musicians brought the influences of rock and roll, or folk music, or modern country music or jazz to the forefront of their bluegrass. Some have even gone beyond that. The following is a discussion of a few of these individuals. Perhaps it will give the reader an idea of not only how the music has changed, but why. Women are excluded from this chapter because there is a chapter devoted strictly to women in this book.

Bluegrass in the 1950s

"The 1950s was a singularly important decade in the history of bluegrass," wrote author Jack Tottle. "Many of the performers whose names would become synonymous with bluegrass music during the 1960s and 1970s began their recording careers in the fifties. It was a period of successful experimentation, of new blood, and of growing musical diversity. More top-quality bluegrass material may well have been written and recorded than in any subsequent decade, and these tunes and songs still form the core of the bluegrass repertoire.

"When things were going well, bands worked hard. They would often be playing one or more radio shows daily, and additionally driving to live, evening performances night after night. The pace could be numbingly intense, but it honed voices and reflexes to a keen edge. The results included a host of classic performances, many of which were preserved on record."[1]

Beatniks and the folk music revival

By the late '50s, the folk music revival was gaining resurgence. It included bluegrass music and Appalachian styles of old-time music and was concurrent with the rise of Beatniks during "the beat generation".[2] These styles appeared mostly on college campuses.

---

[1] From album cover notes written by Jack Tottle for Rounder's "Jim Eanes and the Shenandoah Valley Boys—The Early Days of Blue Grass—Volume 4."

Five years later, Hippies appeared on the American scene and embraced traditional music as their own, shunning the more commercial types such as classical or jazz.

At Carnegie Hall in a concert on April 1959 promoted by Alan Lomax ("Folksong '59"), **Earl Taylor and the Stoney Mountain Boys** was the sole bluegrass band represented among the other groups which were predominantly folk. This is a good example of how bluegrass music was being accepted by the folk community. This led to a Capitol Records contract for the group. Lomax seemed to always represent bluegrass bands of lesser renown (with the exception of the smooth, professional **Flatt and Scruggs** band) in his promotions. Examples are Earl Taylor's band, and **Fairchild, Doodle and the Golden River Grass**.

The "folk boom" was just getting started and was to be a dominant music in American society until the **Beatles** and the "British invasion" came in 1963. United Artists Records recorded a concert, released in November as "Folk Song Festival at Carnegie Hall." In March 1962, **Peter, Paul and Mary**'s first LP came out on Warner Brothers; Bob Dylan's first LP came out on Columbia. With the folk boom in full force, bluegrass received considerable recognition from labels such as Elektra, Prestige and Folkways which released bluegrass records and associated them with folk music. Between this action and the exposure of bluegrass acts at folk festivals, bluegrass bands were able to survive a little while longer until the bluegrass festivals became their salvation and enabled many bands to not only exist, but to flourish.

An early, perhaps the first, commercial example of the word "bluegrass" by a non-bluegrass musician was the release of two major label LP's by Walter Forbes. The frailing and two-finger style banjoist, using an open-back banjo, used the word "bluegrass" in the titles of his albums.

One Folkways bluegrass album which was directed at the folk market was "Folk Songs from the Southern Mountains" by the **Lilly Brothers and Don Stover**. This LP included not only songs in the style of the **Blue Sky Boys** and the **Monroe Brothers**, but also bluegrass versions of folk songs such as "Barbara Allen" and "John Hardy." A similar effort was Elektra's "Folk Banjo Styles" by old-time music banjoists Tom Paley and Art Rosenbaum as well as the full-blown bluegrass of Eric Weissberg and Marshall Brickman in their own melodic-style version of "Devil's Dream" which Bill Keith had recently made popular when he joined Bill Monroe's band about this time.

An LP by Ray Charles, "Modern Sounds in Country and Western Music" (ABC-Paramount) included Charles' rhythm and blues version of Monroe's "Blue Moon of Kentucky." In April of 1962, Columbia released **Flatt and Scruggs**' contribution to folk music with "Hear the Whistle Blow (A Hundred Miles)"/"Legend of the Johnson Boys."

Dave Freeman on newgrass music

"I feel a lot of the younger people are forcing it, saying in their minds that they're going to come up with something new because they feel they have to. It's the thing to do: come up with something new and different. Even old-time groups are doing it—bizarre combinations of instruments, the most obscure tune they can find."[3]

Tony Rice

Tony Rice— charting the unknown with the acoustic guitar

While Tony Rice's story can easily fit into this book's chapter on guitar players, Tony Rice is much more. He's not just a flatpicker, he's an innovator of guitar licks that only the most accomplished players can duplicate. He ventured beyond bluegrass into untested areas of acoustic music to find his own music.

Anthony Rice was born in Danville, Virginia, June 8, 1951, and grew up in southern California. Young Tony was first influenced toward bluegrass by the 78 r.p.m. record of "Foggy Mountain Special" by **Flatt and Scruggs**. Rice's father, Herbert Rice, played guitar and

A
m
e
r
i
c
a
s

M
u
s
i
c

|

B
l
u
e
g
r
a
s
s

2 The term was coined by Israel G. Young, founder of the New York Folklore Center.
   When the bluegrass festivals came into being in 1965, bluegrass music had its own venues. Bluegrass no longer had to worry about being booked into folk festivals or changing their instrumentation to conform with rock and roll. Eventually, bluegrass thrived within its own society; more bands came into being and many were able to make a full-time living from their music.

3 Charles Wolfe, "Dave Freeman and County Records," *Bluegrass Unlimited*, October, 1982, p. 54.

mandolin during the early days of bluegrass and was a definite influence in getting the music in front of Tony; Herbert founded California's **Golden State Boys**[4] which is acknowledged as the second bluegrass group in southern California.[5] Tony's uncle, Hal Poindexter, played guitar with this group.

In 1960 at age nine, Tony Rice's first performance was on the Town Hall Party, playing the guitar; he had already tried the mandolin but decided to stay with guitar. He sang "Under Your Spell Again." Also on the show was the **Country Boys**, with Clarence and Roland White. Clarence was yet to make his mark on bluegrass with his dazzling flatpicking, but Rice described his rhythm work as "thoroughly amazing." Tony walked right up to Clarence, his hero, and said, "Hi! How ya doing?' Clarence taught him some lead, and from that point on, White was his mentor. Rice learned much from White[6], including the playing of various fiddle tunes. Doc Watson became a major influence to Rice when Watson began playing regularly in that area.

In the early 1960s, Tony Rice and his brothers Larry and Ronnie, with Andy Evans on banjo, began a bluegrass band, the **Haphazards**, although, they admit, not a very good one. "When we sang, we sounded like rats with real high, squeaky voices. I sang lead, and at various times everybody sang lead in unison since nobody knew anything different."[7] But they became good enough to play at many events.

Rice and his family then moved to Florida (1965) and soon after, North Carolina. About 1970, Tony Rice played some casual dates with **Appalachian Music Makers**[8]. Within a year, they recorded sixteen tracks for release on singles. The Old Homestead label eventually released these on LP after Tony became well known. When the offer came to play the sound tracks of the movie "The Preacherman Meets the Widow Woman" (about 1970), Rice was already with the **Bluegrass Alliance**. He came down from his home in Kentucky to play guitar with them for the sound track. The group also played on the movie's sequel, but Rice was not with them. Tony's day job was as a sheet-metal worker.

By the summer of 1970, Rice was an accomplished guitarist and joined the **Bluegrass Alliance**[9] in Reidsville, North Carolina, in early September of 1970.

"I was just sitting on a park bench at this festival, playing the guitar, and Sam Bush heard me and we started talking. At the time, two original members of the **Bluegrass Alliance** were leaving, One, of course, was Dan (Crary) and the other was the mandolin player, Danny Jones. I took Dan's place and Sam took Danny Jones' place."[10]

This was Rice's first attempt to join the difficult world of full-time, professional music. And making it even more difficult was trying to fill the shoes of guitarist Dan Crary who had just left. During tough financial times, Rice was unable to afford a $12/night sleeping room. He had to move in with Courtney Johnson for a while. When Jack Tottle interviewed Rice just after he joined the **Alliance**, Tottle noted that Rice's playing "was also a bit quiet and the listener was forced to strain in order to hear what he was playing. In short, Tony clearly had plenty of musical ability, but it was early to judge how far he would go with it."[11]

Tony Rice, 1976.

After a year with the **Bluegrass Alliance**, Rice left to join **J.D. Crowe and the New South**[12], a progressive group just outside mainstream bluegrass. Tony's brother, Larry, had been playing mandolin in the band for the past two years. Doyle Lawson, their guitarist, had recently left to join **Country Gentlemen**. He stayed with this band four years.

---

[4] Initial members of the Golden State Boys were Herbert (mandolin), Leon Poindexter (bass) and Walter Poindexter (banjo); two of whom were uncles of Tony. Later, Walter was replaced on the banjo by Don Parmley. Larry Rice was a member of the group about 1962 when Bobby Slone joined on fiddle. Tony was never a member of the group.

[5] The first group was the White brothers' Country Boys which later became the Kentucky Colonels.

[6] The Martin D-28 that Clarence was playing was later to be Tony's. That particular D-28 was not the one Clarence used for solos, though he did play some lead on it. Rice explained: "Actually, Clarence's D-28 wasn't in shape to use for lead at all, the neck was so badly warped." After Rice bought it, he had it repaired

[7] Jack Tottle, "Tony Rice: East Meets West," *Bluegrass Unlimited*, October, 1977, p. 10.

[8] With Frank Poindexter (Dobro), Bobby Atkins (banjo), Kemp Atkins (bass), Marshall Honeycut (snare drums), Shirley Tucker and Rita Williams (vocals).

[9] Also in the band were Lonnie Peerce (fiddle), Buddy Spurlock (banjo, soon to be replaced by Courtney Johnson) and Ebo Walker (bass).

[10] From a February 23, 1995, telephone interview. Tony mentioned that no one was really "in charge"; the Bluegrass Alliance was totally a group effort. In other words, it wasn't Sam's group, it belonged to all of them.

[11] Tottle, op. cit., p. 10.

[12] This also could have been J.D. Crowe and the Kentucky Mountain Boys because the name changed about the same time that Rice arrived.

While with Crowe, Rice and the group recorded for Japan's King Records and they were paid $1000. After it was done, Starday/Gusto asked to release the album in the U.S.. Starday Records released "J.D. Crowe and the New South" (Starday SLP-489)[13] in 1977 and featured Tony and Larry Rice, Crowe and Bobby Slone. It also included a piano, a pedal steel, and drums. It was not the same music as the Rounder album of the same name which was released about the same time.

In November of 1974, Ricky Skaggs joined the **New South**; he replaced Larry Rice. According to Tony, "Skaggs came in under the pretense that we return to the traditional-oriented sound. If we wanted to choose new material, that was okay, just as long as it was in that context. It was an incredible sound, I thought."[14] During the year that Rice was with the band with Skaggs and Jerry Douglas, the band returned to acoustic music and abandoned the electric instruments. The **New South**'s second album, "J.D. Crowe and the New South" (Rounder 0044), then came out. It featured Skaggs (fiddle, mandolin), Douglas (resonator guitar), Crowe, Tony Rice and Bobby Slone. During this period, Rice recorded "Tony Rice—Guitar"[15] and "California Autumn"[16] on Rebel.

Appalachian Music Makers, 1968. L to R: Bobby Atkins, Tony Rice, Shirley Lewis, Frank Poindexter. Photo courtesy Bobby Atkins.

Crowe let his band members practice new tunes on stage at the clubs but this didn't allow sloppiness in the music. Rice agreed, "Especially with J.D. Crowe, it only took about one time to find out what kind of mistakes you'd made. Next time, you didn't make them."

The **New South** worked regularly in the Louisville and Lexington, Kentucky, area and used electric instruments, following the lead of the popular **Osborne Brothers.** Crowe felt that electric instruments were right for the club circuit. Rice recalled, "It was a difficult time for me. It was frustrating to know that here's J.D. Crowe and Bobby Slone and Larry—three guys who can

really play and sing great bluegrass music. And we're plugged in—but we could be doing just as good or better if we weren't. On the other hand, it paid good. You develop a lifestyle out of this that becomes a circle. You go into a bar and hook up your instrument on Monday night and play 'til Saturday night. Then, the next week you do the same thing again. This goes on week after week, year after year. You bring home a steady amount of income, but I couldn't do it again."[17]

Rice feels strongly that the true sound of an instrument cannot be truly reproduced by adding internal pickups and microphones. One must allow the instrument to produce its sound first, project it out the sound hole, and only then it can be effectively amplified by a microphone. He remarked on the group's use of electric instruments, "I felt it was bogus. I didn't mind so much that we were plugging-in and adding drums, but we were still doing the same material. I asked, 'Well, now that we're louder, why are we still selling ourselves as a bluegrass band? Why are we still playing "No Mother or Dad" this way?'"[18]

On the subject of acoustic sound reproduction, Rice is very sensitive about the way a soundman performs his task when his band is performing on stage. He has been known to politely advise the audience that there is a problem with the sound system and that he and his group will take a few minutes to allow the soundman to correct the problem. Hopefully, it would be better when they reappeared on stage. This contrasts to the way some other groups may handle the problem: yelling at the soundman to get it right, or just continuing to play in spite of the handicap of not being able to hear the other band members on stage. The first method makes it unpleasant for the audience, but the second makes it miserable on the musicians. Rice's method may not work effectively either, for he often insists on using very sensitive studio mics outside. They are very difficult for a sound man to handle no

[13] Starday SLP-489, Gusto 0010, and Japanese King 5052 are all the same album recorded in Japan.

[14] Logan Neill, "Tony Rice—A Distinctive Talent," *Bluegrass Unlimited*, August, 1989, p. 19.

[15] Musicians were Rice, Crowe, Larry Rice and Slone.

[16] Musicians included Rice, Tom Gray, Mike Auldridge, Larry Rice, Ben Eldridge, Ricky Skaggs, John Starling, J.D. Crowe and Jerry Douglas.

[17] Tottle, op. cit., pp. 13, 14.

[18] Neill, op. cit., p. 19.

In a 1995 interview, Tony described the "plugging-in" with Crowe's band: "It was very specifically the electric instruments that I didn't like. As a result, it magnifies the six-nights-a-week routine by a hundred fold. It would have been routine enough if it was just straight-ahead bluegrass five nights out of the week. That would get on anybody's nerves after a certain time. And to be doing it electrically, also..."

matter what his experience. One technique of playing acoustic music through microphones, which is recommended by many acoustic musicians, is that once a soundman has done the sound check and established the proper equalization, the soundman should lean back and let the band members mix the sound themselves from that point on by moving back and forth around the microphones. Veteran bluegrassers such as Rice, Ralph Stanley and others who perform this music can be very "picky" and perhaps ultra-sensitive about how they on stage hear themselves and how the audience hears them. But this method works well for them.

"When I bought the D-28 which belonged to Clarence White, I was in Los Angeles. Coincidentally, (David) Grisman was in Los Angeles doing sessions. Grisman and I got together while we were there and it could have been at that time that we mutually decided that we should be playing together in some kind of format. It was then that he dropped a couple of hints that he would like to have me as part of a full-time band. There in Los Angeles in March is where Grisman and I first met and I heard a tape of his music and liked it. We were there to play on Bill Keith's first album, "Something Bluegrass."[19] And then, after the session, Grisman came home with me to Kentucky and he sat in and played a couple nights with the **New South** which was the last configuration of the **New South** that I was in. And then, from there on, we really befriended each other and we started talking on the phone occasionally, just to 'shoot the breeze' more or less. And it was sometime in the summer of that year that we started talking seriously about collaborating on something—be it a group project, or a recording, or whatever. And I think I give notice to the **New South**—it had to have been in August of '75. I know I had given notice and then we played in Japan. I had been with Grisman, staying at his house and playing with him, before I went to Japan." The tour in Japan was himself, Crowe, Skaggs, Douglas and Slone.

After leaving Crowe, Tony became a founding member of the **David Grisman Quintet** in the San Francisco area in October 1975. He remarked, "That stuff was pretty complex for someone who had been a three-chord bluegrass musician all his life. I began studying chord theory and I learned to read charts."[20] Much of Rice's music theory education and guitar playing instruction came from John Carlini who worked with Grisman in the mid-'70s. Fitting into the new style

which Rice pursued, he recorded "Tony Rice"[21] (Rounder, 1976), "Acoustics"[22] (Kaleidoscope, 1979), and "Manzanita"[23] (Rounder, 1978).

Rice left this band when Grisman, in 1979, went to play with violinist Stephane Grappelli whose style was closer to where Grisman wanted to go with his music. He was replaced by Mark O'Connor on guitar. With his reputation as a superior flatpicker firmly in tact, Rice began to pursue some of his own ideas: he formed the **Tony Rice Unit**. His style, once called "spacegrass"— akin to Dawg music and jazz—became his own. Occasionally touching on traditional bluegrass, his music still followed the bluegrass tutelage of Clarence White. The **Tony Rice Unit** recorded "Still Inside"[24] (Rounder, 1981), "Mar West"[25] (Rounder, 1980) and "Backwaters"[26] (Rounder, 1982).

Rice didn't restrict himself to any one style in his music. During the same period when he recorded his "spacegrass" material, in 1980, Sugar Hill released "Skaggs and Rice." The tremendous fame of the two men brought excellent sales. The next year, 1981, "The Bluegrass Album" was released on Rounder. Traditional in scope—a tribute to **Flatt and Scruggs** and Monroe— it brought together Tony Rice (guitar), Bobby Hicks (fiddle), Doyle Lawson (mandolin), J.D. Crowe (banjo) and Todd Phillips (bass). The individuals collectively became known as the **Bluegrass Album Band**. The tunes were released on compact disc in 1988 and 1989. Perhaps because of the success of this venture, David Grisman and Herb Pedersen (banjo, composer of "Old Train," a standard of the **Seldom Scene**) recorded the "Here Today" album along with members Jim Buchanan (fiddle), Vince Gill (guitar) and Emory Gordy Jr. (bass).

Much of Rice's playing during this period was all instrumental and in his "spacegrass" style. Perhaps, though, that term is insufficient to describe what he does. Jimmy Gaudreau, in a 1994 interview, described what Rice was doing musically at that time as "bluegrass rhythms with a lot of space to improvise." Suffice it to say, it is basically his own, it is progressive in nature, and it has little in common with traditional bluegrass.

Returning to bluegrass music occasionally, his **Bluegrass Album Band** project proved he could still play some wonderful bluegrass when he wanted. A 1989 interview brought the following comments: "I'm a bluegrass musician forever in my heart. But I want to explore and unearth some other things along the way.

---

[19] Bill Keith's "Something Auld, Something Newgrass, Something Borrowed, Something Bluegrass" LP (Rounder RB-1) was released in 1976. On the album were Keith, Tony Rice, David Grisman, Jim Rooney, Tom Gray, Vassar Clements, Ken Kosek and Al Jones.

[20] Ibid., p. 19.

[21] Musicians included Larry Rice, Crowe, Todd Phillips, Jerry Douglas, Richard Greene and Darol Anger.

[22] Musicians were Rice, Sam Bush, Richard Greene, Todd Phillips and Mike Marshall.

[23] Musicians were Rice, Jerry Douglas, Todd Phillips, Sam Bush and Ricky Skaggs.

[24] Musicians were Rice, John Reischman, Todd Phillips and Fred Carpenter.

[25] Musicians were Rice, Todd Phillips, Sam Bush, Richard Greene and Mike Marshall.

[26] Musicians were Rice, Todd Phillips, Wyatt Rice, John Reischman, Fred Carpenter and Richard Greene.

When I think that piano, drums and soprano saxophone are appropriate, I add them. I really wanted to get out of restricting myself to one format. But I am very much a guitar player, but the challenge of the music lies elsewhere now."[27] He added that, as much as he loves bluegrass, "The beauty of any music form is that there are a lot of variations to be explored. As soon as you become a die-hard anything, be it jazz or bluegrass or whatever, you are letting someone make a puppet out of you, and you are depriving yourself of a whole world of music."[28]

In 1983 and 1984, Tony Rice won the Best Flatpicking Guitar poll of *Frets* readers. This category included flatpicking, jazz, pop, or progressive. His 1984 Rounder album, "Cold on the Shoulder,"[29] won Best Album. His "Church Street Blues"[30] came out in 1983 on Sugar Hill Records.

As of about 1985, the **Tony Rice Unit** had almost completely left the jazz-oriented instrumental music. Tony returned to doing mostly bluegrass with a mixture of vocal and instrumental tunes; it was bluegrass without banjo. Although he would throw one or two of his "spacegrass" numbers into a show, he realized that jazz was not really where their market was.

Tony Rice is not a tough taskmaster. In a 1994 interview, mandolinist Jimmy Gaudreau described him as being "extremely easy to work with. He loves to give you the space to play what you want to play. As a matter of fact, if the members of the **Unit** weren't like that, they would be gone in a hurry because he doesn't like to hear the same stuff all the time. If you get up there and really 'blow it out' as they say, he loves to see that. That's the kind of players he likes to have in his band." By the summer of 1988, members of the **Tony Rice Unit** were Tony (guitar), Wyatt Rice (guitar), Jimmy Gaudreau (mandolin), Mark Schatz (bass), Jerry Douglas (resonator guitar) and Rickie Simpkins (fiddle).

In the summer of 1988, Rice underwent surgery to correct a deviated septum; an operation which was performed by Dr. John Starling, former lead singer with **Seldom Scene**. This helped his breathing capability, but he has had many vocal cord problems through the years. As Gaudreau explained, Rice is not a sophisticated singer—he doesn't use his diaphragm to project his voice—he uses his lungs and his vocal chords, thereby putting unnecessary stress on the vocal cords. To help alleviate this, he quit singing in August 1994 to rest his vocal cords awhile.

Rice was awarded Best Bluegrass Guitar of the Year by SPBGMA for 1984 through '87 and 1991 through 1994. His "Tony Rice Plays Bluegrass" (1993, Rounder)

won a nomination for a Grammy. "Tone Poems," (1994, Acoustic Disc label) with David Grisman, won critical acclaim. His 1995 project with guitarist John Carlini, "River Suite for Two Guitars," came out on Sugar Hill. Rice's "Crossings" was an instrumental album of gospel music and did quite well for him in the gospel market. And he recorded several projects with his brothers, Larry and Ron. The **Tony Rice Unit** won Instrumental Group of the Year at IBMA in 1995.

Peter Rowan

Peter Rowan— tradition and beyond

It would be improper to tell the story of bluegrass and where it may lead without including Peter Rowan who was a guitarist and lead singer for Bill Monroe in the mid-60s and is still an active performer today. He did a fine job in the band and was one of the early Yankees to play with Monroe. He learned a lot about music from Monroe, then went out on his own to found many bands and a style of singing and music which he can truly call his own. He's played with bluegrass bands, rock bands and new acoustic bands since his days with Monroe and still performs either style with equal dexterity. After banjoist Tony Ellis left Monroe, Ellis had an opportunity to tour with Peter Rowan. He enjoyed this very much, saying that Rowan "...was one of those musicians who could really get you cranked up."

Rowan grew up in Massachusetts during the 1950s when rock and roll influenced all youths of the era and, as a teen, he had his own rock band call the **Cupids**. His influence toward bluegrass was through friends Tex Logan, Bill Keith and Joe Val. He even played as one of the members of the **Charles River Boys**.

[27] Neill, op. cit., pp. 17, 18.

[28] Ibid., p. 20.

[29] Musicians included Vassar Clements, Jerry Douglas, Todd Phillips, Sam Bush, Bobby Hicks, Larry Rice, J.D. Crowe, Kate Wolfe and Bela Fleck.

[30] Musicians were himself and Wyatt Rice on guitars.

[31] Logan B. Neill, "Peter Rowan, Bluegrass Adventurer," *Bluegrass Southern News*, September/October, 1989, 10.

In 1964, Rowan began as lead guitarist and lead singer with **Bill Monroe and the Blue Grass Boys** where he co-wrote "Walls of Time" with Monroe. Rowan said, "I learned from Bill Monroe how important those dynamics are when you sing. It's probably the most important element in the music."[31] He regards his tenure with Monroe as sacred. "When you stand next to Bill Monroe, you quickly learn to become your own man. He'll take you by the hand and show you the way it's done. He lets you make all the mistakes until the feeling of the music takes over and guides you."

When performing his music, Rowan draws from *all* of his experience, not just bluegrass. "What I discovered is that, in the most happy circumstances when the music really flowed naturally, all the elements that went with whatever we were playing sort of breathed on their own. That's why I can look back at **Seatrain** and **Old and in the Way** today and say, 'Hey, we really did that well!' And all of that music continues in some form or another in what I'm doing today." He left Monroe in 1967.

Rowan, then on his own, tried out some of his own musical ideas in the electric-acoustic folk-rock ensemble **Earth Opera** which included David Grisman. Though the band was short-lived, Rowan recognized that rock music was fertile ground from which to earn a living. This led to the formation of **Seatrain** (a rock/jazz/country fusion group) which thrust Rowan into public recognition as a songwriter. It was with this band that he wrote "Panama Red" which became a cult favorite through the **New Riders of the Purple Sage** (**Seatrain**'s members didn't like the song and would not perform it). Richard Greene, who had just left Jim Kweskin's **Jug Band** in 1969, joined **Seatrain** and recorded an album. Greene recalled that there in San Francisco, in an all-electric band, "the bluegrass numbers we did turned out to be the hottest numbers on our live shows. It was bluegrass with drums. That audience never really heard the 'Orange Blossom Special' before and they just loved it." They played to the rock audiences of the early 1970s with attendance of twenty to thirty thousand.

Peter left **Seatrain** in 1972 to spend some time in the Southwest with the Navajo Indians where he wrote "Land of the Navaho" and learned to play "Tex-Mex" music with Flaco Jimenez.

On October 8, 1973, Rowan recorded on the enormously successful "Old and in the Way" album with David Grisman (mandolin), Jerry Garcia (banjo), Vassar Clements (violin) and John Kahn (bass). This Round[32] record eventually sold more copies than any other record in this field with the exception of "Will the Circle Be Unbroken." It was recorded live in San Francisco and released in 1975. Rowan remembered,

"We wanted to do all kinds of stuff. It was a fun group because we had our hearts into playing all the time—playing the music was the most important part of it." Rowan wrote much of the band's material which included "Midnight Moonlight," "Panama Red" and "Land of the Navaho." "That album is the most natural-feeling of all the bluegrass albums I've heard. It was just us playing our music. We recorded a lot of shows and I've listened to some songs that were played totally different ways depending on which night it was. That was one of the neat things about that group."[33]

In 1973, Rowan was a member of the short-lived **Muleskinner** band with Clarence White, David Grisman, Bill Keith, Richard Greene and Stuart Schulman. They produced a record and a video tape of the concert. In 1975, and for the next three years, Rowan was in the **Rowans** with his brothers, Chris (guitar, keyboards) and Lorin (guitar). They recorded on Electra/Assylum records. The brothers continued to perform and record together into the 1990s.

Sugar Hill released Rowan's "Walls of Time" LP in 1982. Musicians included Ricky Skaggs (mandolin, mandola, guitar), Alan O'Bryant (banjo), Sam Bush (fiddle), Jerry Douglas (resonator guitar) and many others. Rowan spoke of this project as "another step further in my view, in my approach to bluegrass music, which is to use traditional Irish roots and to be very free about the sound of the language, the accent, not to inhibit bluegrass into a regional United States kind of bag. You see, bluegrass is a vibrant form and allows for other forms of music to influence it and come into it. But to have it successful, you have to have your roots strong."[34] In another quotation, he said, "I suppose that there is some danger in having your music judged on what phase you happen to be going through, but I sort

Bill Monroe and his Blue Grass Boys, 1966. L to R: Richard Greene, Bill Monroe, Peter Rowan. Photo courtesy Bill Bongiorno.

32 Round was the Grateful Dead's label. CD re-issue was on Sugar Hill.

33 Neill, op. cit., p. 11.

34 Stephanie P. Ledgin, "A Candid Conversation with Peter Rowan," *Bluegrass Unlimited*, April, 1986, p. 14.

of look at it as building on an idea. If you remember, the **Beatles** did that a lot."[35]

In the early '80s in Nashville, Rowan formed **Crucial Country**, an informal group of friends who gathered to play their style of bluegrass. Those friends included Jerry Douglas, Rowan, Sam Bush, Mark O'Connor, Bela Fleck and Roy Huskey Jr.. An artist needs constant reinforcement for his skills to be honed correctly and he feels that "Encouragement is the secret. I received more encouragement from Nashville on a truly musical and personal level than I received from the West Coast in recent years. And now, living in Nashville is kind of like I finally surrendered. I finally went back to where I started from—from being there in the '60s with Bill Monroe. And it's great to hang out with Bill again.

"I've also learned something I don't think I ever had before, which is a respect not only for the vague thing called 'talent' that other people may have, but a respect more for the artistry that people employ and develop to enlarge their talents or project them. Now I listen to it more from a point of view of the art of it and I can respect it as art. I can just see things from a different point of view there, like the amazing amount of work and technology, the amount of, well, musical knowledge, really—call it 'artistry'—that producers and artists do to make those records come out. It's a skill and it is an incredible thing to behold.

"Also, being in Nashville has changed my mind about performance. I don't believe any more that it's just enough to go out there and be inspired. Now, part of the artistry for me is the challenge of how to fulfill, and get the essence of that inspiration into a performance and present it to an audience. And that means understanding the technology, how to interpret the acoustic guitar through electronics to make a larger, more beautiful sound so as to not be a victim of technology, but to control technology."[36] He likes Nashville. He feels that it has some sort of magic there, for "if you stay there long enough, you will eventually surface with a lot more feeling in your music, just because it takes a lot of commitment to stay there, takes a lot of guts, I think."[37]

In 1986, Rowan recorded an album of Bill Monroe songs, "The First Whippoorwill." This was his tribute to solidify his link with the bluegrass community. He doesn't want his fans to forget that an important part of his music is bluegrass-inspired. Rowan said, "Bluegrass

has narrowed itself and certain things needed to be restated and brought up-to-date in the tradition of Bill Monroe. Some of the variations and subtleties in the music, I thought, needed to be restated."[38] "I feel that, contrary to what many people think, most of the fans in bluegrass stand up on their own two feet. The more-adventuresome players stand the risk of being criticized, but never by the fans. Bluegrass fans are the most open-minded fans in the world—completely open-minded. They really are."

Rowan knows that the very competent musicians he often plays and records with have very strong bluegrass roots, but they choose not to be a clone of anyone. He refers to Tony Trischka, Alan O'Bryant, Eddie Adcock, and Bill Keith, among others. "We're not showing off. We're having fun. The reason bluegrass is gonna live is because people can have fun with it. So my vision is to keep the music full of joy and full of the gravity of its tradition, but let it grow a little bit to get some breathing space in there, otherwise, everybody's gonna be a carbon copy of everybody else."[39]

The 1988 Sugar Hill release, "New Moon Rising,"[40] did very well. "I was glad that 'New Moon' got the recognition that it did. That album, and the one that I just finished, are so close to the heart of what I'm trying to say. And I suppose that's what every artist ultimately wants."[41]

Frustrated by the lack of acceptance of his type of music, and bluegrass, on the radio, he pointed out that in country music today, "You're hearing fragments of so many styles of music that weren't there a few years ago. I've always done that with my music—borrowing from here and there and rolling it up into a package." Commenting on music in general, Rowan believes that "Music has been simplified to a degree to where the lowest common denominator is factored in, rather than the richness that's in the music—like selling ice cream cones when they say, 'This is vanilla and we know that a certain number of you like vanilla.' But if any music is good enough, it should be able to stand on its own merit"[42] beyond strict commercial success.

1990 was the release of Rowan's "Dust Bowl Children—Ecology of the Spiritual Landscape." This was Rowan's first solo recorded project which included no supporting musicians, thus avoiding "the inevitable compromises of a group situation where you rely on other people to provide the flavor you are looking for.

[35] Neill, op. cit., p. 11.

[36] Ledgin, op. cit., p. 18.

[37] Ibid., p. 18

[38] Ibid., p. 14.

[39] Ibid., p. 15.

[40] Members of Peter Rowan and the Nashville Bluegrass Band included Rowan (guitar), Alan O'Bryant (banjo), Pat Enright (guitar), Stuart Duncan (fiddle) and Gene Libbea (bass).

[41] Neill, op. cit., p. 11.

[42] Ibid., p. 11.

I've had to face up to a part of me that has long wanted to come forward."[43]

After "Dust Bowl Children," Rowan left Nashville and relocated to near Austin, Texas. "It's really where I feel most at home," he said in a 1995 interview at RockyGrass. "It's very conducive for songwriting. Language and figures of speech are very strong in Texas music. I had to make a move away from the Nashville scene in order to clarify my own vision. In the end, of course, I like a balance between the excitement of Nashville and the solitude I need to create, to reflect, and meditate away from the oligarchy of commercial success."

Rowan recorded "Awake Me in the New World" in 1993. "It's the story of the discovery of the New World through the eyes of innocence based on Columbus' second voyage. This was a departure for me but completed the vision of 'Land of the Navajo' and brought the Spanish-Caribbean side of my music to fruition; I think I have to move beyond history and nostalgia.

"My latest album (1994) is 'A Tree on a Hill' with my brothers Chris and Lorin. It's good to get that 'buzz' of family harmony again. With my brothers, we went back to older country roots of the **Carter Family** and **Stanley Brothers**, did tunes like 'Man of Constant Sorrow,' 'Darlin' Pal of Mine' and 'Fair and Tender Ladies.' This was touching home base! But now I'm off again. Each project creates another... I think it's most important to stay challenged, keep seeking inspiration. If I learned anything from Bill Monroe, it's to keep on creating no matter what! My next projects for Sugar Hill are an album of blue yodels—Jimmie Rodgers style—with Jerry Douglas on resonator guitar and a bluegrass album of new songs with Charles Sawtelle and Richard Greene among others. Somewhere down the line is another 'Dust Bowl Children'-type album. I'm really happiest writing what connects with an audience when I sing. Maybe other singers will pick up on my tunes as well. The songs know...they tell me...I'm just a vehicle. I'm working on that mandolin chop now; it's like a brush-stroke or a Samurai sword slash—it cuts through, and that's bluegrass!"

Rowan was featured in the 1994 video, "Gather at the River," to help tell the story of bluegrass at IBMA.

David Grisman—
"Dawg" music and more

David J. Grisman is one of the more-astounding mandolinists in bluegrass music. Astounding because he not only plays bluegrass music in the traditional way, he also created his own music genre which he calls "Dawg".[44] This musician, who was born March 23, 1945, in Hackensack, New Jersey, was introduced to bluegrass by Ralph Rinzler[45] and steeped in the traditional bluegrass of Red Allen where he developed a feel and understanding for the music one can only achieve by learning from a master such as Allen. Grisman gives Rinzler credit for opening up his artistic side.

Grisman's first musical passion was the music of the early days of rock and roll such as Chuck Berry, Buddy Holly, the **Five Satins**, et al.. But, according to Grisman, this music "got real vapid and lame. Elvis went into the Army and Buddy Holly got killed. Frankie Lyman O.D.'d (over-dosed on drugs)." Grisman soon began playing folk music of the "folk boom" and, with friends Fred Weisz and Jack Scott, would later form their own bluegrass band, **Garrett Mountain Boys**, in the early '60s.

Grisman's first encounter with bluegrass was "a record of **Earl Taylor and the Stoney Mountain Boys** singing 'White House Blues.' I was blown away. I couldn't believe anybody *sounded* like that."[46] He was

[43] Ibid., p. 11.

[44] The name "Dawg" was a nickname given to Grisman by Jerry Garcia during the "Old and in the Way" period.

[45] According to Grisman, Rinzler was a personal friend and mentor of the young lad from Hackensack. Grisman: "We met when Ralph was twelve years old and I was two. My mother, Fanya Grisman, was Ralph's art teacher, and had brought me into class. Years later as a teenager listening to the Kingston Trio, I re-encountered Ralph when he came into my junior high school English class and played the guitar, banjo and mandolin. This was the first mandolin playing I can remember hearing. And did I remember! From that day forward, Ralph was my musical guru. Beyond that, he taught me countless other lessons too numerous and profound to detail in this limited space.

    "Ralph's tireless efforts have not been in vain; he has provided easy access to our own folk culture for future generations. And for that, Ralph, I thank you personally and on behalf of those future generations." Rinzler died July 2, 1994, at age 59. Source: David Grisman, "Remembering Ralph," *The Acoustic News*, Winter 1994/1995,

[46] Jon Sievert, "Red Allen—David Grisman, Bluegrass Reunion," *Bluegrass Unlimited*, May, 1992, p. 24.

sixteen. He jumped into bluegrass mandolin playing with both feet and did some professional playing.

Rinzler, who was the mandolin player with the **Greenbriar Boys**, was fully involved in folk and bluegrass music. He was skillful, knowledgeable, and served as the boys' guru in bluegrass and old-timey music. He taught the boys some tunes in his basement. He had live recordings of Bill Monroe as early as 1956 and from other bluegrass concerts he had attended. It got to the point that Grisman and his friends would crave the music enough to work in Rinzler's garden in order to hear it. Rinzler was not Grisman's teacher, though he did show him some of the basics. It would be several years before proper lessons would enhance his mandolin playing considerably.

On August 9, 1961, Rinzler took Grisman (16) to see Bill Monroe and his band at New River Ranch in Rising Sun, Maryland. Grisman got a new idol in Monroe. Also, it was there that he first saw Frank Wakefield, mandolinist for the local **Franklin County Boys**. On that stage were two of the greatest Monroe-style mandolin players in the world. Wakefield became Grisman's friend, teacher and influence. From this exposure, Grisman presumed that all mandolin players played like that. He took up that style, continuing to listen to and appreciate other kinds of music.

In 1963, Grisman recorded on his first LP, "The Even Dozen Jug Band" (released later as "Jug Band Songs of the Southern Mountains"), as mandolin player with the **Even Dozen Jug Band**[47].

By that time, Grisman had a good handle on what bluegrass music was and he attended concerts and events at every opportunity. One "festival" he wanted to attend was in Union Grove, North Carolina. He informally re-formed his old band (**Garrett Mountain Boys**) into the **New York Ramblers** to play at the event so that they could get paid some of their expenses of getting there. The band subsequently won first place in the Bluegrass Band category at the prestigious contest. The New York band members were Grisman (mandolin), Winnie Winston (banjo), Gene Lowinger (fiddle), Eric Thompson (guitar) and Weisz (bass).

It was at this time that the group met Steve Mandell, who took over the guitar position. Fred Weisz (guitar, bass) took over the banjo. Frank Benedetto joined on bass. With this combination of musicians, at Benedetto's house, they recorded for the first time—an EP. They made four copies of the record, one for each of the musicians. Songs included "Orange Blossom Special" (Weisz on fiddle), "Voice of My Savior," "Blue Ridge Cabin Home," and one other. The record was never released publicly.

In 1963, they played at Carnegie Hall and on the "Hootenanny" television shows. These men were clearly a major part of the second generation of New York bluegrassers/old-timey musicians. The first generation probably consisted of Roger Sprung and his **Progressive Bluegrassers**, Mike Seeger and the **New Lost City Ramblers**, Eric Weissberg, the **Greenbriar Boys**, Steve Mandell and Ralph Rinzler. Grisman's interest in this type of music was now fully developed.

Grisman had a friend, Artie Rose (later of **Harry and Jeanie West** and now one of the partners in Grisman's Acoustic Disc label), who couldn't learn by ear very well. In order to teach him "Katy Hill," Grisman used tablature to show him how to play the song. This soon expanded to others songs. Rinzler saw this and got Oak Publications to back a book on this subject. Grisman spent one and a half years writing and transcribing the book. There was a chapter on Bill Monroe, Frank Wakefield, Bobby Osborne, and others. He got $200 for it but they never published it. Grisman told this writer, "They wanted me to write my own versions of songs. At the time, I didn't feel qualified to do that and I thought that would be the way to learn... So I sort of gave up on this book." But it was through this exercise in studying the music that Grisman learned many solos. A couple of years later, he showed this manuscript to Jack Tottle who wrote his own mandolin instruction book published by Oak in 1975; there was no mention of where he got the idea, according to Grisman.

In April of 1963, Grisman, 18, met Red Allen. Grisman wrote his first composition, "Cedar Hill," the same year.

In 1965, Grisman left New York and moved to the San Francisco area temporarily (permanently in 1970) and then back to New York . Back in New York, Grisman had a personal relationship with Dave Freeman (before he founded County Records). Grisman often went over to Freeman's house to tape much of his enormous record collection. Because he was integrally connected with the folk scene in New York City and helped Red and Wakefield get gigs, they asked him to produce an album and sell it to Folkways. This became "Red Allen and the Kentuckians, Bluegrass Country" (County 704) by **Red Allen and the Kentuckians**. It

> *"Technically, I don't think bluegrass is any harder than the music I'm trying to do. It's mostly a case of keeping your head into bluegrass."*
> —David Grisman

A
m
e
r
i
c
a
s

M
u
s
i
c
|

B
l
u
e
g
r
a
s
s

[47] Led by Jim Kweskin, other band members were Stephane Grossman, Maria Muldaur, John Sebastian, Steve Katz, Fred Weisz, Joshua Rifkin, Peter Siegal, Danny Lauffer and Bob Gurland. Readers may recognize some of these names as well-known folk singers/musicians.

was recorded at Mastertone Studios[48] with Red Allen (guitar), Porter Church (banjo), Wayne Yates (mandolin), Richard Greene (fiddle) and Bill Yates (bass).

Grisman related how this record came about. "[Red] didn't really ask me. He had a tape of one of those times they were playing Gerdes Folk City. He brought up a tape and said he sold this tape to Moe Asch of Folkways. I thought that they had some better material for a Folkways album—like mandolin instrumentals and more folk-oriented material—and I told Red that. I suggested he record some more stuff. Red told me to set it up and he would do it. He wasn't really looking to do it; I sort of suggested it. So I just called up Moses Asch[49] and he gave me a budget—probably $1500 for the session."[50] Grisman asked Red if he needed a fiddle player; Red Allen then hired Grisman's friend, Richard Greene, after an audition with "Sally Goodin'." Allen soon hired Grisman, who was still a student at New York University, to play with the group.

In 1967, Grisman (22) abandoned the bluegrass life, citing lack of financial support, and went to California where he eventually created "Dawg" music. Over the next twenty-five years, he made a living from this music but found an occasional urge to return to bluegrass for a "bluegrass fix".

Grisman was becoming a jazz freak after listening to "Bass Ball" on the Philips label which featured bassist Francois Rabbath and included only bass and drums. Also contributing to this jazz state of mind was Django Reinhardt, John Coltrane's "A Love Supreme," Stephane Grappelli, and "Eric Dolphy at the Five Spot." Nevertheless, he was still a bluegrass lover and purist, preferring the traditional styles of the pioneering groups to the more progressive groups which came along in the late fifties. "I once went up to Eddie Adcock and told him how great the **Country Gentlemen** were when Bill Emerson played banjo with them. I just went up to Eddie Adcock and insulted him." Adcock recognized that Grisman was drunk (for the first time in his life) and was very understanding.

In February 1973, David Grisman helped form **Muleskinner** with Bill Keith (banjo), Peter Rowan (guitar), Clarence White (guitar), Richard Greene (fiddle) and Stuart Schulman (bass) to play at a performance with **Bill Monroe and the Blue Grass Boys**

Red Allen and his Kentuckians

which was a taped television event. The video, "Muleskinner," was recorded on the night in which Bill Monroe was supposed to be there in Hollywood at KCET's television studios but Monroe failed to make it in time for the performance/recording. The recording of the event occurred regardless—with only **Muleskinner**. The group was formed strictly for this event and played only a couple of times before this. An LP of the group, recorded separately with bassist John Kahn and drummer John Guerin, was released about a year after the event. The videotape, presumed to be lost for some time, was released to the public June 1992.

Grisman was also a founding member of **Earth Opera**[51] with Peter Rowan and recorded two records for Electra. He appeared on the enormously successful "Old and in the Way" LP by the band of the same name which featured himself, Jerry Garcia (banjo), Peter Rowan (guitar), Vassar Clements (fiddle) and John Kahn (bass). This band existed from March 1973 to November 1973. The LP came out in 1975 from a live performance at The Boarding House.

The **Great American Music Band** was formed in 1974 to play in San Francisco's Great American Music Hall. Early versions of the band included Jerry Garcia and Taj Majal. It actually started as the **Great American String Band**. Grisman described the events, "We played two nights at the Great American Music Hall and there was a gig which was a co-bill there for Richard Greene and Vassar Clements. Richard hired me for that gig and we put together a band to play our part of it and I think we got Eric Thompson (guitar), Sandy Rothman (banjo) and a bass player named Bing Nathan. But Bing couldn't make it the second night. And Eric Thompson was at a party in Berkeley where Taj Majal was playing bass. We called him up and he came over that night. And Garcia played in that one. And David Nichtern, who wrote 'Midnight on the Oasis' and was in Maria Muldaur's band, he got interested in my tunes and that was his passion—learning this Dawg music. He wanted to be my guitar player and he left Maria Muldaur right when they had that hit record. He came up on stage and played many of my songs like 'Dawg's Rag' and he knew the whole thing."[52] The band existed about a year.

---

[48] It was recorded November 28-December 1, 1965.

[49] Moses Asch, founder of Folkways Records, died of a heart attack at the age of 81 on October 19, 1986, in New York City. Over the last forty years, the label has released over 2,000 albums of folk and other music.

[50] Interview June 10, 1992, at the Denver Zoo, Colorado.

[51] A rock group which he formed in 1967.

[52] Interview, June 10, 1992.

In 1974, Grisman wrote the score for the movie, "Big Bad Mama," and in 1975, for "Capone." In 1976, he composed the score for "Eat My Dust," and in 1978, the score for "King of the Gypsies."[53]

Late in 1975, the **David Grisman Quintet** was formed with Grisman (mandolin), Todd Phillips (2nd mandolin), Bill Amatneek (bass), Tony Rice (guitar) and Darol Anger (fiddle). They played Grisman's Dawg music—a fusion of bluegrass and jazz with acoustic instruments. The idea came about mostly as a result of Grisman jamming with Richard Greene and figuring out that people really would come out to see a strictly instrumental band (both men realized that neither one was a singer). When Greene left to join **Loggins and Messina** that year, Grisman decided to go on with it and see if it would work.

Tony Rice can be given much of the credit for the formation of the **Quintet**. Grisman explained, "It was his idea. I met Tony Rice at this Bill Keith session. I had heard of him but I had never heard him play. I'll never forget it because it was like seven in the morning and Bill Keith went to the airport to pick up Tony at the airport to the house where we were all staying in Washington, D.C.. He woke me up to meet Tony Rice. Well, we played a tune and I remember thinking, 'Wow! Clarence White is back!' I had never heard anyone do what Clarence did until I heard Tony Rice. We just sort of hit if off right away—playing-wise. Then I played a tape I had made while playing at The Boarding House and he flipped out on it. Everybody else was, like, yawning and I was playing this tape of 'Dawgology' and Tony Rice said, 'I've been waiting all my life to play this music.' He made me go back to Lexington, Kentucky (where he lived), and hang out with him for three days and all we would do was wake up and show him these tunes. I showed him how to make a major 7th chord—I mean I didn't know much myself. He was real interested...and he'd start calling me every two weeks [asking] 'When's the gig? When's the gig?' What gig, I asked myself?

"Meanwhile, I had Todd Phillips and Joe Carroll who would show up. I had a band but I didn't have a gig. We just liked to play this music. I had met Todd at a mandolin class in San Francisco [where I was giving lessons]. Todd was making mandolin bridges and he said he would trade me bridges for mandolin lessons. Pretty soon I had new bridges on every mandolin and I didn't need any more. He didn't need any more lessons. I started showing him harmony parts and thought that we could really work on these tunes. One day, Todd came

over to the house with Darol [Anger] and he knew all of Richard Greene's licks from the **Great American Music Band** And so we were rehearsing. What for? And Tony Rice would be calling me up and ask, 'When's the gig?' So finally I said to Tony to come out here and we would rehearse, we can't just do a gig. So he came out and stayed about a week then called me from Japan. He said, 'I just gave J.D. Crowe my notice.' And I didn't have anything going! I mean, on a level of where I could hire somebody. He was playing in the best bluegrass band in the world with Ricky Skaggs and J.D. Crowe and Jerry Douglas! He just went back to Lexington, packed up his stuff and he and his wife just moved into my basement. We rehearsed four months without ever playing a gig."

"The David Grisman Rounder Album" in 1976 featured bluegrass greats Tony Rice, Vassar Clements, Bill Keith, Jerry Douglas, Ricky Skaggs and others.

Mandolin World News[54] was created in the basement of Grisman's house in 1976. "The David Grisman Quintet"[55] LP was released in 1977 on Kaleidoscope. *Billboard* magazine recommended it for both the pop and jazz categories. His Warner Brothers Records project with Stephane Grappelli/David Grisman "Live" was also very important in Grisman's career.[56]

In 1979, Grisman began writing for *Frets* magazine. Also in 1979, his "Hot Dawg" was released on a major label and featured Grappelli, Tony Rice and others. Mark O'Connor joined the **Quintet** for a year after Rice left in 1979 to form his **Tony Rice Unit**. His "David Grisman—Quintet '80" was released on Warner Brothers in 1980 and featured Grisman, Darol Anger, Mike Marshall, Mark O'Connor and Rob Wasserman. Grisman recorded the "Here Today" album with Jim Buchanan (fiddle), Herb Pedersen (banjo) and others in 1982. And Grisman won the Best Mandolin division *Frets* magazine Readers' Poll so many times, beginning in 1983, that he was retired to the Gallery of the Greats.

Grisman's style of "rhythm without drums" has spread. In the late '80s, when he played with the NBC Tonight Show Orchestra, drummer Ed Shaughnessy said that he'd been using Grisman's records in clinics to show his students rhythm without drums. Grisman's earlier recordings used a second mandolin for rhythm, but those players wanted to do more soloing than strictly rhythm so Grisman hired drummer George Marsh. And later, Joe Craven provided an entire rhythm section for the band.

David returned to bluegrass in 1989, letting folks know that he hadn't forgotten his roots. He recorded

---

[53] Appearing in the film were Grisman, Andy Statman, Buell Neidlinger, Matt Glazer, Diz Disley and John Carlini.

[54] Its editor was Don Stiernberg who, in 1992, was the mandolinist with Special Consensus Bluegrass Band. Dix Bruce edited and managed the magazine 1978 to 1984. It folded in 1985. Dix is also the author of several Mel Bay instruction books.

[55] Musicians were Darol Anger (fiddle), Tony Rice, Grisman, Bill Amatneek (bass) and Todd Phillips (second mandolin).

[56] Recorded September 20, 1979, at the Berklee Center for the Performing Arts, Boston (except for one tune), musicians included Grappelli (violin), Mike Marshall (mandolin, guitar), Mark O'Connor (guitar, violin), Rob Wasserman (bass) and Tiny Moore (electric mandolin). Its production coordinator was Craig Miller, who is Grisman's manager of many years.

"Home Is Where the Heart Is" on Rounder. The album featured many past and present bluegrass greats. "Technically, I don't think bluegrass is any harder than the music I'm trying to do. It's mostly a case of keeping your head into bluegrass. I always listen to a lot of it, pure stuff: **Flatt and Scruggs** radio shows from 1953 and '54, the **Nashville Bluegrass Band**, Bill Monroe records, **Stanley Brothers** records. That keeps my head in bluegrass so that when I go into the traditional mode, it's familiar... If you study a style the way that I've studied bluegrass, you don't lose it."[57]

In 1992, "Bluegrass Reunion" featured some of the musicians Grisman worked with through the years. They include Jerry Garcia, Red Allen and Herb Pedersen, among others. The idea of Grisman's "Reunion" LP came from all those individuals doing a concert together at California's Strawberry Music Festival. "They needed another act for their spring festival and asked me to put a band together," said Grisman. "So we had this gig and I said, 'Gee, why don't we make a record since we have to put a bunch of material together and I've got this record company and studio?'" "Reunion" was the fourth release on Grisman's own Acoustic Disc label. Others on this label, which won Grammy nominations, were "Dawg '90" and "Garcia/Grisman."

About Red Allen, Grisman related that "Red gave me my first job in an authentic bluegrass band [and] also gave me my first job as a record producer. Now, I get to hire him and produce a record with him on my own label."[58] Allen died April 1993, shortly after the release of the recording.

The "Bluegrass Reunion" project stayed with the concept of bluegrass of the '50s. Grisman said, "For me, bluegrass was perfected in the 1950s and you can't take it any further than that except on the interpretive level of: it's not Carter Stanley any more, it's Jerry Garcia. I haven't heard anything that's better than the original thing; you just can't get past the original vision. That's a limitation. But once you accept that, you're home free. Consequently, the contemporary bluegrass I like most is the stuff that pays the most homage to that, such as the **Nashville Bluegrass Band**, Doyle Lawson and the group that Tony Rice and J.D. Crowe work with.[59]

"Still, bluegrass seems to be in a healthy state with as many people getting interested as ever. Things have got to change, I know that. But the precepts need to be studied and adhered to for it to succeed. It's like classical or chamber music; if you're going to play it, you have to remain true to that style or else it becomes something different; it's not that style anymore. I don't think there are any new places to take bluegrass from a stylistic standpoint. Other things have been done with

instruments used in bluegrass, such as what I'm doing with my band. But I don't consider what I do to be bluegrass. I'm sure Bill Monroe doesn't either, although some third party might.

"There's never been a proper perspective for bluegrass in the music industry, it just hasn't gained the respect or economic position that it deserves. All those guys were trying to make it in the music business in some form or another. It's just that at their particular place in history, what they knew was folk music learned from a real oral tradition. I guess there must be something about learning a song from your grandmother when you're two years old as opposed to learning it off a record or out of a book. No matter what you do, it'll never be the same. But I think what we've done on this record is close."[60] Grisman continued to tour with his band, playing to sell-out crowds, into the 1990s.

Andy Statman—"What led me out of bluegrass was going through bluegrass."

"When I was fifteen, I'd been playing and listening to bluegrass—I was a fanatic—for several years already. I took some lessons from David Grisman, and his method was basically teach yourself. David also had access to the entire recorded and also live-show catalog of bluegrass, so he let me tape everything he had. I would go home and slow down the tapes and figure out the stuff. And when I couldn't figure out something, I went back to him. In the course of two years, I took about six lessons. I learned basically every mandolin

Andy Statman

57 Dix Bruce, "David Grisman," *Bluegrass Unlimited*, February, 1989, pp. 19, 20.
58 Sievert, op. cit., p. 25.
59 Mr. Grisman was probably referring to the Bluegrass Album Band which recorded on Rounder.
60 Seivert, op. cit., p. 27.

solo by Bill Monroe, Frank Wakefield, Bobby Osborne and others that was recorded between 1939 and 1967. I learned how to play all these styles, plus I started learning what fiddle players were doing. I would spend an hour trying to figure out whether Bill Monroe would do two tremolo strokes on a note or three. I had become musically and technically on top of all the developments of the mandolin up to that point—I've studied everything that had been done and I could do everything that had been done... I was a fanatic.

"What led me out of bluegrass was going through bluegrass. I had come through it around 1966. By that time, I'd realized that the only thing for me to do further would be to get down South and join a bluegrass band. And I realized that, culturally, these groups are just on a whole other trip that I am. Musically, I'd begun developing a style and I was also beginning to find bluegrass very, very limiting, and I started listening to jazz. I needed outside influences to take bluegrass further, either within that style or go somewhere else. I got more and more into jazz and into ethnic music, which led me back to Jewish music." Statman soon fused all of his knowledge, interests and styles into his own... "I'm open to everything," he said.[61]

Poor Richard's Almanac— an early version of newgrass

Alan Munde, Wayne Stewart and Sam Bush recorded a tape in 1969 which became "Poor Richard's Almanac." Often acknowledged as a precursor to newgrass music, the tape of the recording was made in Stewart's grandmother's living room on a home tape machine. They hung her quilts around the room to deaden the sound. The album was released in 1969 on American Heritage. When the band dissolved, Sam Bush went with **Bluegrass Alliance**; Stewart seemed to drop out of music. Munde described **Poor Richard's Almanac** as "kind of the first young band that played in a new instrumental style which is the melodic banjo style of Bill Keith, and Sam did, sort of, the Texas fiddle style of Byron Berline. And maybe we were the first band that picked up on those trends. We played instrumentals but we played them in a much slower tempo; it was more in line with the Texas fiddle-tune style with the bluegrass element throwed in with the banjo in the melodic style and I played fiddle tunes. It was one of the early bands that followed: first Bill Keith on the banjo and then Byron Berline on the fiddle."[62]

This could be classified as "newgrass", depending on what definitions one might use. Munde continued, "If to play newgrass takes a new technique and a new style of playing the instruments, possibly we were among the early players who played in the new styles

that you needed to have those techniques together in order to play newgrass music.

"'Poor Richard's Almanac' was more than just an album," Munde continued. "It was an actual group that performed—not much, but we did some. And Wayne Stewart and Sam, more than I, were very, very interested in what the **Beatles** were doing and what the **Country Gentlemen** were doing. You know, they had done some Bob Dylan stuff and some James Taylor things. And Wayne and Sam, early on, performed those kinds of songs. Now after I left, Courtney Johnson played banjo in **Poor Richard's Almanac** and they did **Beatles** stuff and more things like that. And maybe that incarnation of the group was getting more into those kinds of things, so I guess it could be newgrass but we never recorded it and I don't think Courtney and them ever recorded it as **Poor Richard's Almanac**. Certainly Courtney and Sam went on to become the **New Grass Revival** (after the **Bluegrass Alliance**)."

Sam Bush

Sam Bush and the New Grass Revival

Sam Bush was born in Bowling Green, Kentucky, on April 13, 1952. Before he was a teen, he was motivated toward music by his father. At eleven years old, he bought his first mandolin and two years later got a fiddle. While growing up, he was influenced by Byron Berline, Tommy Jackson and "Texas Shorty" (Jim Chancellor) on the fiddle, and Red Rector and Hank Garland on the mandolin. He was especially impressed by the sounds of the **Greenbriar Boys**. One of Bush's favorite fiddlers is Tex Logan. "When I learned to play, it was in square-dancing style. That may be part of the

[61] Henry Rasof, *The Folk, Country and Bluegrass Musician's Catalogue* (New York: St. Martin's Press, 1982), p. 75.

[62] From a December 14, 1993, telephone interview.

strength, right there, that I've always beat out the rhythm as I play. I think part of the strength lies in the rhythm."[63]

"One thing that made me want to play was watching **Flatt and Scruggs** one time," said Bush. "I used to watch **Flatt and Scruggs** every Saturday afternoon. Lester was up there emcee-ing and all of a sudden this little boy comes up to him and tugs him on the sleeve and Lester says, 'What do you want?' (Little boy answers), 'I wanna pick.' And so Lester pulls a pick out of his pocket and says, 'Well, here.' And this little boy went over and they had about two or three coke boxes so he could reach the mike and he just picked the dickens out of it. It was Ricky Skaggs. And I said, 'I wonder if I could...I bet I could do that!'"[64] According to Art Menius, this was on a regular Martha White television show. It was prearranged and Skaggs was paid; it was his first gig.

Soon Bush took up the fiddle. A year later he began entering contests: first in Weiser, Idaho, then in Texas. The contests were judged completely differently; he won handily in Weiser where the emphasis was on old-time fiddling, but lost badly in Texas where the accent was on Texas fiddling.

Later in his career he said that he prefers playing mandolin over the fiddle. "I feel like I have more command of the mandolin. Playing fiddle's like being on a surfboard that's coming out from under you."[65] Since he plugged in the fiddle electrically, "I enjoy it a lot more. One of the main reasons is because I don't have to play so hard and I don't have to fight the rest of the group to be heard when I'm using a pickup."[66] Before he was out of high school, he had won three Junior National Fiddle Championships. He never entered the adult contest for lack of time.

Recalling a very influential event in his inspiration toward bluegrass music, Bush said, "One of the greatest things I saw—and this may be in 1966—was the reappearance of Kenny Baker. He, Vassar Clements and Bobby Hicks were the legends that none of us had ever seen. Baker had already been with Bill Monroe. Later that night, Del McCoury played and that really blew my mind because [David] Grisman played with him. He had Billy Baker on fiddle and that was one of the hottest sets I've ever heard in bluegrass music."[67]

Carlton Haney, in a 1995 interview, told an anecdote about when he first came into contact with young Bush. "I believe it was in 1966, the second festival. A little

boy out in the field was playin' the fiddle—about nine or ten years old, I thought he was. And I noticed him and he saw that he was doin' good and thought I was gonna get him and bring him up on stage and let him play and show people that the kids are gonna start playin' these instruments in bluegrass. So I asked Bill [Monroe] could I bring him up there would he play with him and he said, 'Sure, I will.' It was just a kid and I let him play and that was it.

"And it was eight or ten years later I met a man at Camp Springs, North Carolina, and I'm tellin' this 'cause somebody led me into it. So he asked, 'Do you remember the kid that played at the second festival?'

"I said yes.

"'Did you get his name?'

"I said no.

"He said, 'It's me! Sam Bush!'"

Getting back to the biography, Bush and Wayne Stewart began listening to the jazz of Barney Kessel, Joe Pass, Stephane Grappelli and Svend Asmussen and they started playing the bluegrass type of music. In the spring of 1969, Bush and Stewart met Alan Munde and soon recorded "Poor Richard's Almanac" on the American Heritage label. This was Bush's first recording. It was released in 1970. In October, Munde was replaced by Courtney Johnson.[68] Soon, Bush (just graduated from high school) and Johnson joined the **Bluegrass Alliance** with Dan Crary and Wayne Stewart. Dan Crary had formed the band in 1968 and really put them on the map with his flashy, lead-guitar picking during the summer of 1969. When Crary left, he formed **Sundance** in 1975 with Byron Berline and others.

In 1970, the American Heritage label produced a second album for the **Bluegrass Alliance**, "Newgrass,"[69] and an album of instrumentals for Dan Crary, "Bluegrass Guitar." A review of "Newgrass" in *Bluegrass Unlimited* by Walter V. Saunders brought these comments, "I must confess to being a traditionalist of the first magnitude, thus it has been difficult for me to accept the new directions recently taken by some of our leading groups. Apparently, they have been cognizant of something I am only now beginning to realize: that if this music is to survive it must have an endless supply of fresh, new material. The **Alliance** are demonstrating one direction this search can take. They are following a path blazed by the **Country Gentlemen**, pioneers of modern bluegrass, yet no one can accuse them of imitation for they have a sound all their own

[63] Robert Hefner, "The Fiddling of Sam Bush," *Bluegrass Unlimited*, February, 1985.

[64] Ronnie Lundy, "The New Grass Revival," *Bluegrass Unlimited*, November, 1978.

[65] Alana J. White, "The Fiddling of Sam Bush," *Bluegrass Unlimited*, September, 1989, p. 23.

[66] Hefner, op. cit., p. 21.

[67] White, op. cit., p. 19.

[68] From Hiseville, Kentucky, Johnson began playing the banjo at age twenty-five. He'd been playing guitar since age seven. Alan Munde was Johnson's greatest influence in his banjo style. Johnson died June 7, 1996.

[69] Two other Bluegrass Alliance LPs were "The Bluegrass Alliance" (Old Homestead 90115) with Lonnie Peerce, Garland Shuping, Darell Samson, Danny Wiley and Martin Townsend and "Love of the Mountains" (1982, Old Homestead 90118)

built around slightly folk-oriented trios and dazzling instrumental virtuosity. The **Alliance** have drawn from a wide variety of sources for the material presented here. Broadway numbers, folk-rock, and delta blues are some of the avenues they explore, ample proof that bluegrass music is where you find it. Dan Crary's endlessly inventive guitar passages are much in evidence throughout the set. A tremendous LP, as good if not better than their first."

Bush played the guitar in the **Alliance** for a few months until "I looked across the field and saw the world's skinniest guy sitting on some guy's case, playing the guy's guitar. It was a D-45, and he sounded just like Clarence White." Bush introduced himself to Tony Rice and invited him to join the **Bluegrass Alliance** with Courtney Johnson, Ebo Walker[70], Lonnie Peerce and himself at the end of 1970. They were based in Louisville, Kentucky.

On September third, 1971, Tony Rice left the band to join **J.D. Crowe and the New South.** Tony's brother, Larry, was already playing mandolin in the band. In November, Curtis Burch[71] (from Brunswick, Georgia) joined the **Alliance** on resonator guitar and guitar to take Rice's place.

At Thanksgiving of 1971, Sam Bush started the **New Grass Revival** with former members of the **Bluegrass Alliance** Burch, Johnson and Walker; they played regularly in the Louisville area. Lonnie Peerce stayed to lead **Bluegrass Alliance**[72], continuing that name and tradition. The **Revival**'s first album came out on Starday that year. This poem by Radio John Topanga Canyon on the album cover of the album explains their social differences with the bluegrass community:

The Arrival of the New Grass Revival
Curtis, Courtney, Ebo and Sam
* The New Grass Revival Bluegrass Band*
They've already gotten nationwide approval
* Which is pretty damn good when you live in Louval*
Tho' other more traditional folks have ask for removal
* Of excess locks of hair*
But the New Grass Revival they don't care, cause their heads and hands are not
* there*
They are somewhere all pickin' fast
* And you bet your ass*
They play that grass

Butch Robins

And do a lot of things to it also not recommended by the Chief But then
* This ain't the first Bluegrass Band That's been on relief You could help relieve this problem*
* Und buy dis oblem*

Soon the **New Grass Revival** was being promoted by Carlton Haney. Bush said, "I have to admire Carlton for always sticking with the young bands during that time... He was the old-time bluegrass promoter who would let us play our weird stuff—he'd just put us on late."[73] Keith Case promoted the **N-G-R** for the next ten years beginning in 1973. They recorded "New Grass Revival" for Starday in 1973. But these events were only partially successful at providing enough money to keep the band together. The rest was provided by the enthusiasm of young Sam Bush.

In 1973, Ebo Walker left the **Revival** and was replaced by bass player Butch Robins (the noted banjo player). The band moved to Nashville to take advantage of Robins' connections with the Starday label, with whom Robins recorded. Robins left the band in late '74 to join Tut Taylor in his instrument repair business, Dulcimer Works, in Nashville. John Cowan replaced Robins.[74] Cowan's background as electric bassist was strong in rock and country/rock but nonexistent in the specialized field of bluegrass. He relied upon the tutelage of Sam Bush to fit his style into what the **Revival** had become.

Cowan's addition to the band was more than significant. Courtney Johnson described the advent of Cowan into the band, "John just lets us play more than we ever did before. John just knows more about his instrument than most people do. He's capable of playing with us and that's turned us all loose."[75] Burch said of Cowan, "John brought a whole new vocal scene into the band. It was weak up until that point but now the band has a good, strong lead singer...and whoever sings with John,

---

[70] Ebo Walker's real name was Harry L. Shelor Jr.. He selected the name because he played the electric bass, an "O" model, in a walking style. The song "Ebo Walker" by the Dillards was just a coincidence.

[71] Burch's early recollections of bluegrass were the Stanley Brothers on a Jacksonville, Florida, television show and Jim and Jesse live at his future high school. Burch's favorite Dobro player was Shot Jackson, "One of the greatest Dobro players there ever was." Lundy, op. cit., p. 12.

[72] Members became Peerce (fiddle), Garland Shuping (banjo), Chuck Nation (mandolin), Dave Cosson (guitar) and Steve Maxwell (bass). Shuping had just left the Bluegrass Gentlemen. Glenn Lawson played bass with the Alliance but soon switched to mandolin for the duration of his six month's stay. Peerce died May 31, 1996.

[73] White, op. cit., p. 21.

[74] Robins and the Revival recorded an LP which has never been released; but it has been widely bootlegged, according to Art Menius.

[75] Lundy, op. cit., p. 13.

you get a good blend. He's inspired the rest of us and I've learned a lot of things from John about singing.[76]

Sam Bush's wife, Kathy, ran their sound system during concerts. Johnson's wife, Hazel, cared for the band instruments, changing broken strings during concerts. Cowan's wife, Liz, set up the equipment, eliminating possible smashed fingers of the performers—not a trivial matter when your living depends on such seemingly small things.

They plugged-in when Cowan joined—to be heard. "We're not talking about a loud rock show," said Bush, "but a country show with microphones set up normally. If you follow a band with all steel guitars and two Fender Telecasters, you'll find the bluegrass band doesn't sound like big, real music. The Osbornes found out real quick that the way to success on these shows was to be as loud as everybody else—not for bluegrass players or fans, but for the average country music audience which did—and still do—far outnumber the kind of show[s] you usually play. And that's what got us doing it, too."[77]

About performing as a warm-up band, Bush related that playing in front of new audience "keeps us tough... One guy can yell out, 'We want Willie,' and wipe out the applause you just got. It's not personal; he's just so enthused about Willie Nelson, he can't wait. But Boy, it's hard not to take it that way when you're up there doing the most important thing you do."[78]

In 1977, Sam Bush and Alan Munde recorded "Sam and Alan—Together Again for the First Time." The

Sam Bush (L) and Roland White at the Winfield Workshop, 1983. Photo courtesy Jan Willis.

New Grass Revival recorded "Too Late to Turn Back Now" for Flying Fish which was recorded live at Telluride Bluegrass Festival in Colorado. The Revival played the event nearly every year.

In 1979, the New Grass Revival began a two-year tour with Leon Russell. The impressive size of the audiences with Russell's draw of the rock crowd brought this remark, "It was a weird experience to go from drawing fifty people in a club to playing in front of 26,000 almost every night. It was amazing—and terrifying, too."[79] Sam Bush supplemented his earnings in the New Grass Revival by being a studio recording artist with players such as Doc Watson, Tony Rice, John Hartford and others.

When they finished touring with Leon Russell in 1981, Courtney Johnson and Curtis Burch left the New Grass Revival to form the Barren Country Revival.[80] By the end of the year, Bush and Cowan re-formed the New Grass Revival with themselves, Bela Fleck (banjo) and Pat Flynn (guitar). Fleck had just left Spectrum.

Now, with four great musicians in the band, the next task was to get a big label to record them. This wasn't easy for they were still considered "bluegrass" by Nashville music executives and therefore not a "player" on country music radio and unsuitable for a chance on one of the big labels. But it wasn't long before they landed contracts with independent labels Sugar Hill and Rounder for the next five years. In 1984, they recorded "On the Boulevard" for Sugar Hill which, the next year, won the Best Acoustic Album award. Bush's 1984 solo LP, "Late as Usual," was on Rounder. He successfully fought off a bout with cancer during this period and was off the road for several months.

In December of 1985, the New Grass Revival signed with huge Capitol Records. This was their chance to hit it big on the country music charts. Interestingly, Capitol put no reins on the group; they were free to chose what to do...only that they were expected to put out singles. New Grass was responsible for the success of their ventures. They recorded three LPs with them and gained several Grammy nominations along the way. Their 1989 recording of "Friday Night in America" was their attempt to make their mark on the world of music. Cowan said, "As far as the band goes, I think we did our job and I think we've made our most successful, accessible record so far. And if this doesn't get any airplay, then I'll throw my hands up because we've got good songs by good songwriters. There's no bullshit songs on there."[81] The recording sold about

[76] Ibid., p. 14.

[77] White, op. cit., p. 22.

[78] White, Ibid., p. 24.

[79] White, Ibid.., p. 21.

[80] In 1987, Courtney Johnson's new band was BJT and featured band members Johnson (banjo, 5-string Dobro), Curtis Burch (Dobro), Ruth Burch (guitar, Curtis' wife), Tom Timberlake (guitar), Lou Ann Timberlake (electric bass, Tom's sister) and Hazel Johnson (mandolin, Courtney's wife.)

[81] Phil Hood, "New Grass Revival," Frets, June, 1989, p. 37.

75,000—better than any of their others. But as Bela Fleck said in 1990, "It still wasn't enough to break into, and be a contender in, the country market. Those were medium sales [for country artists]. It was great for us because we never cracked that kind of numbers before. We hadn't even come close to that. So, obviously, if **New Grass** had stayed together..."

Since then, Sam Bush won the reader's poll of *Frets* magazine as Best Mandolinist three times. His band won Best Band of the Year category, and Album of the Year.

In late 1989, the band decided to break up, effective spring of 1990. Each had projects they wanted to pursue. Bush joined the touring band of Emmylou Harris and also continued his activities of studio recording. John Cowan became the electric bass player for **Chris Daniels and the Kings**. But by June, he was making heavy-metal music. Bela Fleck founded his **Bela Fleck and the Flecktones** to play his version of rock and jazz.

Ricky Skaggs

Ricky Skaggs—
a bluegrass artist who made it big in country and western

Ricky Skaggs made the big leap from the low-paying business of bluegrass to the very profitable world of country/western music. Yet, as bad as those in bluegrass may feel about him deserting it for "the big bucks", his music frequently showed that he took his bluegrass roots with him and he exposes them whenever he can. The result is that Mr.

Skaggs helps spread bluegrass music to audiences who may not have heard it before. Skaggs doesn't claim that his band plays bluegrass music—only bluegrass-influenced music. With his background in traditional bluegrass groups, he certainly knows the difference.

About his use of electric instruments, Skaggs said, "Bill Monroe would never have used them but that is no reason not to use them. I wasn't afraid to go with instruments like that in my band because I can mix them in there with the acoustic music in a way that they're just instruments just like everything else. If you can do it in a way that enhances the music, then I don't think there is anything wrong with it."[82] And "When people complain because my music isn't bluegrass, I understand. But you know, in order for Bill Monroe to come in and do something like he did on 'Wheel Hoss,'[83] he has to have respect for the kind of music that I'm doing right now."

Ricky Skaggs was born July 18, 1954, in Cordell, Lawrence County, eastern Kentucky, five miles from the nearest store. He was schooled through grade three in a one-room schoolhouse which included all eight grades in that single room. When he was five years old, he was taught to play melodies on the mandolin. He'd already been singing in church with his mother holding him in her arms. He played local churches, theaters, schools and radio shows with his family.

The Skaggs family, with Ricky (age six) on mandolin, and his father on guitar, played on WTCR, Ashland, Kentucky. "We did bluegrass and country. Back then bluegrass wasn't really called 'bluegrass.' Bill Monroe was the only guy that played bluegrass. Most people just played kind of mountain-ish country stuff like the Stanleys and **Reno and Smiley**. We did a lot of George Jones songs like 'Window Up Above' and 'Cup of Loneliness' and some Molly O'Day songs, too."[84] At seven, following a recent family move to Nashville, young Skaggs played the mandolin on television when he appeared on **Flatt and Scruggs**'s syndicated television show which was sponsored by Martha White Flour. At about age eight, he began playing guitar; at thirteen, he began learning the fiddle. Skaggs played occasionally with the **Stanley Brothers**. Here, Carter Stanley said to Skaggs, "One of these days Bill Monroe's gonna have to take a back seat to you, Boy."[85]

Soon, teenager Skaggs teamed up with Keith Whitley—about the same age and with similar musical tastes. They loved and played only the songs of the **Stanley Brothers**—all their songs! One night before Ralph Stanley arrived for his gig at a club on the Kentucky/West Virginia border, Skaggs and Whitley were asked to sing and play until Stanley and his **Clinch Mountain Boys** arrived. They sang the only songs they

[82] Jim Hatlo, "Ricky Skaggs—Nashville's Latest Star Paid his Dues in the Trenches of Bluegrass," *Frets*, March, 1985, p. 31.

[83] Monroe overdubbed his mandolin on the record. Skaggs was amused at seeing one of his heroes in a modern studio using headphones.

[84] Jack Tottle, "Ricky Skaggs: Clinch Mountain to Boone Creek," *Bluegrass Unlimited*, January, 1977, p. 8.

[85] Robert K. Oermann, "Ricky Skaggs Remembers the Stanley Brothers," *Bluegrass Unlimited*, May, 1981.

knew: **Stanley Brothers** songs. Ralph then arrived with his band and he walked into the club where he heard the kids doing his songs from the Mercury, Columbia and Rich-R-Tone labels—mistakes and all. Skaggs remembered that Ralph "wasn't really smiling; he was looking off somewhere like he was reminiscing, in a way. It turned out that he was. Afterward, he said, 'Boys, the first time I saw y'all it just brought back so many memories of me and Carter.' That really blew me away."[86] This soon led to a friendship, a couple of festivals, and an offer from Ralph to join him after they finished high school.

In 1969, Skaggs (age fifteen) joined Ralph Stanley's **Clinch Mountain Boys** where he played fiddle and mandolin for two and a half years. Other members were Roy Lee Centers (banjo), Keith Whitley (guitar), Curly Lambert (mandolin) along with Ralph on banjo and probably Curly Ray Cline (fiddle). All of a sudden the boys, Ricky and Keith, found themselves playing blue-grass professionally with one of the biggest names in the business and recorded eight and a half albums with Stanley and the band.

The next year, Skaggs and the Whitley brothers, Keith and Dwight, began playing radio shows on WLKS in West Liberty, Kentucky, taping the weekly shows in Skaggs' parents' garage. Skaggs left the **Clinch Mountain Boys** about 1971. His day job was at the VEPCO (Virginia Electric and Power Company) power plant in Possum Point, Virginia. It was here that banjoist Bill Emerson talked Skaggs into joining Charlie Waller's **Country Gentlemen**[87]. In October of 1972, Skaggs joined as their fiddler. Bill Emerson told of Skaggs' hiring into the **Gentlemen**, "I found Ricky in Manassas (Virginia), working for VEPCO and out of music. I was responsible for him joining the **Country Gentlemen** in the fall of 1972. He recorded two Vanguard albums with them—the second was 'Remembrances and Forecasts.' Ricky stayed with them for about a year after I departed for the **U.S. Navy Band** in June 1973. During that time, I encouraged him to become a solo artist and develop his lead vocal capabilities. He subsequently left the **Gentlemen** and eventually became a band leader with **Boone Creek**. He developed valuable connections when performing with Emmylou Harris—which helped him break into the country music field."[88]

Skaggs left the **Country Gentlemen** in October 1974 to record his first solo album "That's It." In November of 1974, Skaggs joined (or filled-in with) **J.D. Crowe and the New South** in Lexington for a year, replacing Larry Rice on mandolin.[89] The following October (1975), Skaggs and Douglas left the **New**

South to form **Boone Creek** with Terry Baucom (banjo, fiddle), Wes Golding (guitar) and Earl Grigsby (bass). Their albums were "Boone Creek" (Rounder) and "One Way Track" (Sugar Hill).

In addition to performing briefly with the **Seldom Scene**, Skaggs also performed with Emmylou Harris on a European tour. His arrival into Harris' band caused the demise of **Boone Creek** in January 1978. Skaggs joined Emmylou Harris' **Hot Band** when Rodney

The Country Gentlemen, 1974. L to R: Ricky Skaggs, Doyle Lawson, Bill Yates, Charlie Waller.

Crowell left. "I learned a lot working with Emmylou," said Skaggs. "One of the reasons I went with Emmylou was to be able to take my roots of traditional bluegrass and old-time mountain music and try to learn something about drums, piano, pedal steel guitar and electric guitar. I had never worked with these instruments before so it was something new for me."[90]

Even though he switched to country music, Skaggs has always considered Bill Monroe as his mentor. One bluegrass song which made it big on the country (*Billboard*) charts was Skaggs' recording of Monroe's "Uncle Pen."

In 1980, Sugar Hill released "Skaggs and Rice." That same year, Skaggs left Harris to work with **Buck White and the Down Home Folks**. Between these two bands, he gained considerable renown.

The following year, Skaggs left Buck White's **Down Home Folks** and joined up with Bobby Hicks. On stage, Skaggs and Hicks continuously changed instruments to show their tremendous versatility. Playing with Skaggs, Hicks was not held back as he was when he played for

[86] *The Big Book of Bluegrass* (New York: Quill, 1984), p. 156.

[87] Other members of the Country Gentlemen when Skaggs joined were Charlie Waller, Doyle Lawson and Bill Emerson. Dobroist Jerry Douglas was with the Gentlemen when Skaggs recorded "Remembrances and Forecasts," James Bailey was banjoist.

[88] From a personal note circa 1992.

[89] Other members were Tony Rice (guitar), Jerry Douglas (Dobro) and Bobby Slone (bass).

[90] Susan Moore, "Ricky Skaggs—Country Boy at Heart," *Bluegrass Unlimited*, March, 1986.

the country-style band of Judy Lynn. Skaggs also let Hicks record with other artists.[91]

Skaggs was voted Best Multi-Instrumentalist in 1981 and 1982 by the *Frets* Readers' Poll. In April 1982, Skaggs and Hicks' single, "Crying My Heart Over You," made #1 on the charts. Now twenty-eight years old, Skaggs became the youngest person to ever be a member of the Opry on May 13th, 1982. The next year, Skaggs was voted the Top New Male Vocalist by the Academy of Country Music and the Best Male Vocalist by the Country Music Association. In 1981, and for the next two years, Skaggs' band was awarded Bluegrass Act of the Year from *Music City News*. In 1987, he was co-winner of a Grammy for Best Country Instrumental for "Fireball," on an album with J.D. Crowe's **New South**: "Bluegrass: The World's Greatest Show." (Also on this album were **Seldom Scene** and the **Country Gentlemen**.) The Gospel Music Association awarded him the Ralph Stanley Dove Award. August 21st is now Ricky Skaggs Day in his home town of Louisa, Kentucky. In 1984, he was recognized by *Esquire* magazine as "The Best of the New Generation: Men and Women Under Forty Who Are Changing America." In a nutshell, he has "encouraged other artists to put the country back into country music."[92] In 1985, Skaggs was voted Entertainer of the Year over the more "country" groups such as **Alabama** which had won for the last three years. The award was a category of the awards given by the Country Music Association.

John Cowan, with the **New Grass Revival** at the time, spoke about how Skaggs changed his style to comply with country and western music, "When Ricky Skaggs was making bluegrass records, he sang every song in a high tenor. But when he started making country records, he lowered all the keys. And, at first, that really threw me. I thought, 'Well that doesn't sound like Skaggs, he's not up there really humping it.' And then I figured out that, whether it was conscious or not, his voice sounded a little more pleasing in a lot of ways. It may be that he took out the bluegrass part that alienated a lot of people."[93]

"There is definitely a new trend in country music," said Skaggs. "The market for bluegrass isn't as small as many perceive. Bluegrass is a form of country music and it always has been. If we try to make it out like something as different as rock and roll, then we're just fooling ourselves. It started out as a kind of country music and then Bill Monroe heard a hot banjo picker named Earl Scruggs and threw that in there because he wanted to innovate. He wanted to be the one out there

doing something different. What I wanted to do was to get away from playing just totally acoustic bluegrass music so I could try to mix two styles together and do something different. I kind of see myself here in the '80s as doing what Monroe did in the '40s as far as trying to work with something traditional—trying to keep it the same, yet change it and update it. I want to give it a new breath of life."[94]

Beginning about 1990, Skaggs' **Kentucky Thunder** band had eleven #1 hits on the country charts. Nearly half of them were adaptations of bluegrass songs. Before Bill Monroe died, he made Skaggs promise to keep on playing bluegrass music. Skaggs was glad to oblige. He formed a five-piece, touring bluegrass band in 1997.

John McEuen

John McEuen—putting rock music and drums into bluegrass

During the twenty-one years that John McEuen was a member of the **Nitty Gritty Dirt Band**, he studied bluegrass music and tried to inject it into the band whenever it was appropriate—in fact, he was *the* person who kept bluegrass in the band.[95] Keeping bluegrass in the band was, perhaps, one of the main reasons the band became popular at bluegrass festivals. McEuen said, "I was fortunate to be in a band where we allowed each other the freedom of musical expression." He left the **Dirt Band** in 1987 to "find what else was out there." When he left to continue solo performing which he began with the **Dirt Band**, he also began in earnest getting his music out in film scores.

[91] Hicks recorded on the "Bluegrass Album" and Doyle Lawson's Quicksilver albums. Hicks switched between the genres of C & W, swing, and bluegrass to find where the best living could be made. If one was drying up, the other would undoubtedly be profitable.

[92] *Esquire Register Edition*, December, 1984.

[93] John Cowan, "New Grass Revival," by Phil Hood, *Frets*, June, 1989, p. 40.

[94] Ibid., p. 45.

[95] Some examples of his bluegrass influence can be heard on the following Dirt songs: "Buy for Me the Rain" (1967), "Mr. Bojangles" (1970), "Some of Shelley's Blues (1971), "Dream" (1974), "American Dream" (1979), "Long Hard Road" (1982), "Dance Little Jean" (1981).

This led to doing the music scores of "The Man Outside," "Braving Alaska" (National Geographic Society's first Emmy nomination), the ten-hour Warner Brothers mini-series "The Wild West," and working with Tommy Lee Jones and Sissy Spacek in "The Good Old Boys" movie. As both star and director, Jones worked very closely with McEuen to create the desired musical support.

He produced his own solo albums, "String Wizards" and "String Wizards II," for Vanguard Records. He often used percussion and drums in his music, giving bluegrass to the younger generation which seemed to reject all music if it didn't have that heavy drum rhythm in it. The sales of his "String Wizards" CDs (1992, 1993) seems to indicate that his methods of spreading bluegrass were correct.

McEuen tried to describe what he does, "I think the bluegrass I do is not necessarily bluegrass—I use the bluegrass instruments and I try and bring them out to a wider format. I like percussion; I avoid full drum kits with bluegrass music. That's not what I try and achieve and it bothers me as much as many people when the early '60s **Flatt and Scruggs** records started having drum kits on 'em to make that 'Nashville sound.' They didn't blend. It was like having four people singing separately instead of singing in harmony—they didn't blend. Sometimes four people can sing, like the Australian pop group, **Little River Band**, and you can't tell it's four people (he also refers to the harmonies of **New Grass Revival**). It's a lot of parts that blend in so well that it sounds like one person."[96]

McEuen spoke of Bill Monroe, drums, and music, "I think what helped Monroe move along was that he was first with the words and both with the name and the music so you could identify [his music]. You didn't have to say, 'Well, what is that sound'? So it made it easier to market. And he was consistent with his delivery of material—he kept writing music. He didn't just write eight songs and stop. He's still writing in the last many years, you know. He's been prolific both writing and producing.

"It's important for percussion to be added if you want to try and draw some new people in because people who are not aware of it or are not attuned to it can be tricked into listening to it if there's something that helps them lock into the rhythm pattern." Referring to the "Return to Dismal Swamp" song on his first "String Wizards" CD, he continued, "Well, one thing that I felt was necessary for this tune was to have percussion in it. And I like kick drums in the sense that it helps drive it along. I didn't want to depend solely upon strings for percussion. One thing that is missing from bluegrass is everything below 200 cycles where there is a lot of activity available, frequency-wise. Usually, the only thing down there is the occasional bass

note, but you can put things on a record that are, say, 300 cycles and below, and at ten thousand and above, that are not normally a part of bluegrass. And I like the highs and lows and I wanted a kick drum on there and the other thing I wanted to do is try and keep people in tune because the song has three different sections and a lot of fast notes flying around and might sound like a bunch of noise if you tried to absorb it, say, if you tried to take the bass off and it was just the guitar, mandolin, fiddle, banjo. It would probably drive *me* crazy. It would be nice to sit around a pick it that way, but after I put the drums on I played it on my test market which is my living room with my six kids of varying ages. The fifteen year-older, who was into rap music at the time, heard the kick drum. He sat there with a couple of friends and about half way through it they go, 'This is really cool!' And I firmly believe that had I played them a version without the kick drum, around the middle of the song they would have said, 'Are we going to a movie, or what?'"

The 1994 telephone conversation with Mr. McEuen, he then addressed the "Will the Circle Be Unbroken" album which he and the **Dirt Band** did back in 1972. McEuen said, "It sold over a million units and was the highest volume of any record in the bluegrass genre. I want everyone to know the importance of Earl Scruggs in the project; it simply would not have existed without Earl Scruggs. Besides his major artistic contributions, he was the one who introduced my brother and myself to Mother Maybelle and brought in Roy Acuff and Vassar Clements and Junior Huskey and gave us that ability to have that record.

"It's one of those things that I've always felt was overlooked. I've heard the other **Dirt Band** guys and they talk like *they* made that album. My brother put that together! I got Earl and Doc involved first, and my brother took it the rest of the way, came up with a title, did the art work, shot the pictures. To make a long story short, Earl told me about a year ago, 'John, about that "Circle" album. I don't mean that "Volume II," I mean that Volume One. Now I like those other boys in that band but they didn't "get it," did they?' And I said no. They *didn't* get it! He came to see me because I played 'Randy Lynn Rag.'"

"So please, remember that the credit for all this should not go solely to the **Dirt Band**, but principle credit should be given to my brother and Earl and then the other people along with the **Dirt Band**. The main reason we could get the budget and the credibility to make this record was because of 'Mr. Bojangles.' We got along really well and he liked the idea of the album. And I think it helped give him a boost in his career and he knew where it came from. He knew that my brother and I put that thing together—against all odds."

Earl "was attuned to the realities of what made something happen because Louise (his wife) was a manager and he knew what people asked him in interviews. That album got him a lot of exposure. I think that album helped a lot of people. One major accomplishment on that album was getting Vassar Clements recognized, and getting him out of the sideman world. It was the first step, of course. It put the light on him so he could shine; *he* did it eventually. And Doc Watson. It didn't *make* Doc but it sure gave him some credibility and it got him out to a lot of people he wouldn't have reached otherwise.

"We cut that album for $22,000 in six days. We recorded about six hours a day—all two-track. My favorite personal accomplishment on that album was when Bill Keith asked me how I did 'Lonesome Fiddle Blues.' [He laughed]."

As of 1996, McEuen continued to record on Vanguard Records. His latest project was "Acoustic Traveller" which included, as McEuen put it, "unknown stars" to help him on the project. He believes that Vanguard has a lot of potential to become a significant "player" among the independent labels. "Vanguard is working at re-establishing themselves as a new label with new product and new artists which will again put them in the vanguard. People will soon look to them for great things like we did in the '70s."

The first newgrass festival

In 1972, Carlton Haney promoted the first Newgrass Music Festival at the Camp Springs "Blue Grass Park" at Reidsville, North Carolina, which he used for his conventional festivals for many years.

Mark O'Connor, 1979, with his famous white fiddle.

Mark O'Connor— from fiddle contests, through bluegrass, and journeys beyond

In a 1985 interview for *Bluegrass Unlimited*, Sam Bush spoke of Mark O'Connor, "The only thing wrong with his playing is that he never makes a mistake. I just don't think I've ever met anybody that is so gifted and has such a beautiful touch on the fiddle."[97]

Alan Munde spoke of O'Connor, "Though he comes from a traditional background and was with David Grisman's group, he also played with a sort of fusion jazz/rock kind of band. He's interesting to play with, in one sense. Then on the other hand, he plays so well it makes everyone around seem trivial. He's a powerful musician. When he plays he just takes over."[98]

Mark O'Connor's biography could fit into any one of several chapters of this book because of his many styles of music and accomplishments. He is the only person to have won national championships on three different bluegrass instruments: the mandolin, fiddle and guitar. Those who play music with him are nearly overwhelmed at his ability to fit into their music—almost instantaneously. He has such a grasp of all styles of music that the artist merely has to play a song and O'Connor is immediately enhancing it in the same style with a power and precision seldom found in music. O'Connor's career led him to be a premier studio musician, playing on sessions with nearly *all* bluegrass' greats. But because his own music largely took him away from bluegrass as a profession and performer, he is included in this chapter which has to do with where bluegrass music has gone.

[97] Robert Hefner, "The Fiddling of Sam Bush," *Bluegrass Unlimited*, February, 1985, p. 22.
[98] George A. Ghetia, "Friday Morning with Alan Munde," *Bluegrass Unlimited*, July, 1987, p. 25.

O'Connor's background was old-time fiddling and contests and he never really was in a full-fledged, touring bluegrass band. Yet he is widely accepted by the bluegrass audience. He described it this way, "I suppose my roots are traditional American fiddling, and more specifically the Texas style. I played that style all through my teen years and my outlet was mainly fiddle competitions. But occasionally, fiddling and fiddle contests would fall under the larger umbrella category called 'bluegrass' because a lot of fiddling contests took place at bluegrass festivals. So I kind of came in through a side door without really having spent any time, really, doing bluegrass music. I got associated with it because old-time fiddling was not as popular a categorization. It was just easier to call what we did 'bluegrass.' So, I never played in a professional bluegrass band and I never made my living as a bluegrass player. But once in a while I would jam with bluegrass musicians."[99]

When asked if bluegrass was difficult to play, he pensively explained, "I would say that I play bluegrass like I play Irish music—I don't really know how to do it—I just sort of fake my way through it because it wasn't something that I really studied or really took on for my voice in music. It was mainly old-time fiddling. It was almost an accident that I ended up in bluegrass because I wanted to play my fiddle tunes but a lot of people didn't know how to play them the Texas way. So they played the bluegrass way [and] I would end up playing—sort of bluegrass. And a lot of great players are in the bluegrass genre, and I wanted to play with great musicians. Old-time fiddling has always crossed [over to] the bluegrass style, basically because Bill Monroe was a great composer of fiddle tunes. And his fiddle tunes, some were old-timey and some of them took on a bluegrass beat. Old-time fiddling is definitely a part of bluegrass but the bluegrass style was developed to play along with banjos and vocals (the bluegrass style harmony). I never really took that on to try to become an expert at it. Sometimes you end up playing bluegrass because someone hires you to do so. Or you get hired to play country and western, and I can still be an old-time fiddler through this whole thing. As a professional musician, you try to be flexible and try to adapt to the style and keep pace."

Mark O'Connor (center) with award-winning fiddlers Jenny Anne and Luke Bulla, 1990.

O'Connor spoke about fiddling styles, "And my favorite style of fiddling is definitely Texas-style. It's a slower style, which means you have more of a chance to put a lot more notes in there. Bluegrass fiddling is too fast for the feel that you can put into the Texas style."[100]

It is difficult to describe the style of what O'Connor plays today. "I would say that I've got it down to 'American music' now. I'm an American stylist; I play 'American music.' American music includes traditional fiddling from America, blues, jazz, swing, bluegrass and a fusion of these things including modern composition... When I improvise, [my playing] comes out of feeling it through experience. Hopefully, it has gained some structure in the way I feel. When I write, I am always thinking about structure and the different elements that make music pleasant to listen to."

He feels that the best fiddlers in the field of bluegrass today (1991) are Stuart Duncan and Alison Krauss. O'Connor said, "Somebody has to carry it on. And the young people today are responsible for the next generation—just like I'm probably an inspiration to a lot of little Texas-style and contest fiddlers running around. Maybe they should be learning from the old masters, but it's neat when you can model yourself after a player who is in his prime at the time. Like, when I was learning guitar—sure I loved Doc Watson—but Tony Rice and Clarence White were at their prime and that's what inspired me to really get into the intricacies of their style. But if I was, personally, going to learn how to play bluegrass or study the style, since I'm older than Stuart and Alison I would probably look at people who were at their prime when I was very inspired and influenced, especially Byron Berline, Kenny Baker, Benny Martin, Chubby Wise." Vassar inspired O'Connor as well, mainly because of Vassar's playing on the first "Will the Circle Be Unbroken" album.

Mark O'Connor was born in Seattle, Washington, August 4, 1961. At three, he was intrigued by the music of Bach and Beethoven. At six, he began taking classical guitar lessons. As his interests changed, he learned flamenco and folk music. At age ten, O'Connor won his first instrumental competition at the University of Washington—a formal classical/flamenco contest. The next year, he began taking fiddle lessons from Barbara Lamb in the Seattle area.[101] His parents wouldn't buy

[99] From an interview in Grass Valley, California, 1991.

[100] Bonnie Smith, "Mark O'Connor: Winning It All by 14," *Bluegrass Unlimited*, April, 1976, p. 39.

[101] As of 1991, Lamb was the fiddler with a rather progressive-sounding, all-woman, bluegrass-genre band, Ranch Romance.

him a fiddle initially, hoping that he would concentrate his efforts on only one instrument, so Mark tried to make his own out of cardboard. His interest in this instrument was spawned by watching Cajun fiddler Doug Kershaw on the first Johnny Cash Show in 1969. He also started playing the banjo, resonator guitar and steel-string guitar. "His apparent skipping around from one instrument to another was very different from the normal childhood inability to maintain interest long enough to master it. By working on the special qualities of each of the instruments, he was able to give himself a sense of perspective about the one thing they all had in common: the music he wanted to play."[102]

O'Connor soon met Dick Ahrens, a banjoist, and began to play guitar with him regularly. In the summer of 1973, O'Connor finished second at the Weiser, Idaho, Junior-Junior (12 and under) division of the National Old-Time Fiddle Championship. He had been playing the fiddle seven months. There in Weiser, he taped many of the fiddle jam sessions. From these tapes he learned many of the Texas-style licks which were to be included in next summer's Weiser contest.

In August 1973 in Woodenville, Washington, at the first bluegrass festival he had ever attended, he won first place in guitar, second in banjo, and third in fiddle. His prize was a $650 Givens mandolin. In 1974, O'Connor won the Junior Division (18 and under) of the National Old-Time Fiddle Championships; at age twelve, he was the youngest person to win this division. He also won in 1975, 1976 and 1977, becoming the first person to win four times. He also won the Jr-Jr Division, becoming the first person to win both divisions.

Upon his arrival in Nashville in 1974 at the Old Time Pickin' Parlor, the twelve year-older was invited to sit in with Brother Oswald Kirby (resonator guitar, banjo) and Charlie Collins (fiddle, guitar, mandolin). The duo was told by Tut Taylor that the kid was good, but he didn't really say *how* good! The story goes that the kid was invited on stage and "...was asked what he would like to play, and his response was 'Bill Cheatham.' Charlie said, 'Well, at least this boy knows how to pick the songs!' After a couple of licks, Oswald and Charlie about fell off their chairs and everyone in the whole Pickin' Parlor was giving each other glances of disbelief. Someone got on the phone and within twenty minutes many new faces began showing up in the audience, including Vassar Clements and Dr. Perry Harris. Dr. Harris, in charge of the Grand Master's Fiddling Contest at Opryland, immediately invited Mark to be a contestant the following June."[103]

On July 26, 1974, the young man gave his first performance on the Opry as a guest of Roy Acuff. Comments by some indicated a possible belief in reincarnation, for no one could play like that after only one and a half years of practice. A week later, he recorded "Mark O'Connor, 4-time National Junior Fiddle Champ" on the Rounder label with Norman Blake (mandolin) and Charlie Collins (rhythm guitar). Tut Taylor produced this album which came about from his appearance at the Pickin' Parlor.

O'Connor spoke of his Opry appearance at a very young age, "It was all real new to me. I really didn't understand too much about it and I really didn't care at the same time. If I got to play on the Opry or this and that, it really didn't matter to me; I was just having fun with the music."

In December 1974, he acquired his famous white fiddle from idol Benny Thomasson before Thomasson moved back to Texas. On this fiddle he has the signatures of many of his hero fiddlers.

He won Nashville's Grand Master Fiddle Contest on June 15, 1975, winning $1000. Sam Bush (who took third) commented, "Mark absolutely outplayed everybody; no doubt about it. The older guys really didn't expect it at all and it was really interesting to see how they reacted! It will be interesting to see what direction he'll go in music. I'm sure he'll be very effective in whatever he does."[104] He was the youngest to ever win this title. That week, he recorded the "Pickin' in the Wind" album on Rounder.

After a 1979 tour of Japan with Dan Crary, O'Connor (guitar) joined the **David Grisman Quintet** with David Grisman (mandolin), Darol Anger (fiddle), Rob Wasserman (bass) and Mike Marshall (mandolin, guitar). He replaced Tony Rice. In a 1991 interview, he described how he was able to fit in, "It was very complex and you had to do a lot of studying, you know. It would be the same as learning any great musician's music. It requires a lot of adaptability. When you're in a band, it's not just a jam session anymore. It's literally getting down to the finer points of the rhythm and harmony and figure out how to make this person's music sound the best." He recorded his violin and guitar on "Quintet '80," "Mondo Mando" and "Grappelli/Grisman Live."

In February 1981, O'Connor (violin) joined the **Dregs**[105]. They recorded "Industry Standard." That year, he became the first person to win the Open at Weiser National Old-Time Fiddle Championships for three consecutive years, and the same for the Grand Master's Fiddle Championships in Nashville. He was then required to sit out the next year as did every winner.

102 From the liner notes on "Mark O'Connor—4 Time National Junior Fiddle Champion."
103 Bonnie Smith, "Mark O'Connor: Winning It All by 14," *Bluegrass Unlimited*, April, 1976, p. 36.
104 Ibid., p. 37.
105 Members were Steve Morse (guitar), Andy West (bass), Rod Morgenstein (drums) and T. Lavitz (keyboards). They also toured and recorded as the Dixie Dregs.

In 1982, O'Connor appeared on the television show, "Young Artists at the White House,"[106] with Merle Haggard where they performed for President Reagan. He was voted Best Overall Instrumentalist by the *Frets* magazine Readers' Poll. He won the International Mandolin Championship, Kerrville, Texas.

He left the **Dregs** in 1983 to perform with such artists as Doc Watson, John McEuen, Peter Rowan, Chris Hillman and Bela Fleck. He became an exclusive user of Ovation Instruments and endorsed them. The contract required that he give clinics for the instruments as well as providing technical advice for product development.

He then moved to Nashville to try his hand at being a recording session player. In the 1983 and 1984 *Frets* Readers' Poll, O'Connor won Best Multi-instrumentalist and Best Country/Bluegrass Fiddle categories. He then retired from entering competitions. For the next several years, O'Connor was active in recording work in Nashville and signed with Warner Brothers Records. He was voted Best Fiddler by the Academy of Country Music for 1986 through 1994. He is listed in *Esquire* magazine's list of outstanding men and women who are changing America.

Mark O'Connor retired from studio work in October 1990; he felt like he had reached the top. He had recorded on over 450 records in six years and earned $150,000 per year. His plan was to do personal appearances and do his own music.

1991 was the first of four consecutive years that he won the Country Music Association's Musician of the Year award and Vocal Event of the Year (over Chet Atkins) for his "New Nashville Cats" album. The album included fifty-three of his favorite musicians.

"Letters"

The March 1986 issue of *Bluegrass Unlimited* included this letter from Dan Mazer, which gave an insight into modern bluegrass: "The plain fact is that the **Country Gentlemen** and the **Osborne Brothers** were the first to open the form to new ideas: the Osbornes by amplifying themselves to reach the straight country audience, and the **Gentlemen** in two ways: by selecting modern material and, more importantly, by presenting themselves on-stage in a more relaxed manner than the formally-attired groups fronted by Monroe, Martin and the Stanleys. This relaxation led directly to the greater interest of young people in bluegrass, since they looked and sounded much less 'establishment.' They are, in fact, *the* reason that bands now appear on stage in clothes that don't match, and select material from classical to new wave, if it suits them."

Bela Fleck— more than an innovator

Veteran banjoist Vic Jordan described Bela Fleck as one of the more incredible musicians associated with the banjo. In a 1992 telephone interview, Jordan said, "I'm impressed every time I hear him play; he's a banjo player first. He's what I've always wanted to be, in a way. And that is a banjo player first and a particular style of music after that. I like the instrument but I never pushed it to the envelope like he has and succeeded with it. He's done extremely well. I think he got there by his interest in the world of music rather than just a style of music. You see, most of us came up aiming at bluegrass. That's what we wanted. We wanted to play that style of music. And that's what we did. And I think Bela looked at it, 'This is a great instrument for music,' period. And I think he approached it that way. He's kind of like Jesse McReynolds—he's not afraid to step out and try something different and try different tunes and different styles of playing. This is a la Bobby Thompson and, if you stop and think of it, Earl Scruggs. Nobody had ever played like that. He's an innovator. Don Reno, Eddie Adcock, Bill Keith, Bobby Thompson—these people were innovators. The rest of us came along and copped off of that. Bela is one of the innovators. He took it and he just went with what he heard."

Bela (pronounced Bay-la) Fleck was born in New York City on July 10, 1958. At about age fifteen, he heard "Dueling Banjos" and "Beverly Hillbillies." Although he didn't even know what instrument was being played, he was hooked. Fleck auditioned on the guitar for entrance into the New York High School of

---

106 This was actually a series of four PBS specials.

Music and Art, a school which accepts only musically and artistically gifted students, and was accepted. Meanwhile, he continued practicing on the banjo up to seven hours per day, taking lessons from Tony Trischka, Erik Darling and Marc Horowitz. The biggest influence on his banjo style is Trischka, and then Scruggs.

Upon graduation from high school in 1976, Fleck spent the summer in Boston with Gene Schwartz (fiddle) and Mark Schatz (bass) in an eclectic group which featured a lady who sang Broadway-type songs and others. They developed, by playing on the street, the ability to hold a crowd. "Whatever you play," said Fleck, "has to be able to appeal to somebody who might not really know what you're doing."[107]

Fleck's credentials thus far were his experience playing with **Brownstone Hollow** and **Wicker's Creek**. He then chose to work full-time with **Tasty Licks**[108] in the late 1970s. After **Licks** broke up, Fleck re-joined Schwartz and Schatz.

In October of 1979, Bela Fleck and Mark Schatz founded **Spectrum**[109] in Lexington, Kentucky, with Jimmy Gaudreau and Glenn Lawson[110], two former members of J.D. Crowe's band.

In 1980, Rounder released Fleck's first solo album, "Crossing the Tracks." Other musicians on the album included Pat Enright (guitar) and many other well known giants of this music. This record is one of his early solo albums and reflects the influences of Trischka and Peter Wernick on left hand technique, and the instruction toward drive and tighter timing with the right hand as taught by guitarist Pat Enright. "The great thing about Pat," said Fleck, "was that he was the first guy I ever worked with who played traditional music who was really *good*. I had fallen into the trap of going to festivals and hearing bands who weren't hitting it and had said to myself, 'Well, that's not great music.' After meeting Pat, I wanted to understand the old styles of banjo playing for the first time and put quite an effort into trying to master them."[111]

When **Spectrum** disbanded in November 1981, Fleck joined the **New Grass Revival** in Nashville with members Sam Bush, John Cowan and Pat Flynn. The band members insisted that they were doing the music they loved to play so if success, such as a top-twenties record came their way, it would merely be incidental to their desire to play music.

Fleck was voted the Best Country and Bluegrass Banjo Player and Best Dixieland and Jazz Banjo Player by a *Frets* magazine Readers' Poll in 1982, 1983 and 1984.

New Grass Revival broke up in January of 1990. In June, he spoke about his time with the **Revival**, "I was happy about what we did but there was a lot of stuff that I wanted to do that wasn't right for that band. I didn't want to bring things to the band which weren't right for that band, so what I ended up doing instead was doing solo records. When we got off the road, everybody would, like, cool out. That is where I could get it out of my system. I could produce records and write and play jazz, study, and be hired as a session artist—whatever. I was trying to get it out of my system so that I could find a balance where I could feel right."[112]

He formed **Bela Fleck and the Flecktones** with brothers Roy "Future Man" and Victor Wooten and Howard Levy (who later left the band). Fleck said, "I felt that if I didn't do this band, I would always regret it because I found musicians that were like me: they were wide open and didn't care what kind of music it was so long as it was really good and they really wanted to do something special and new. Oddly enough, we were able to have successes that went way past what had happened in **New Grass** and was even much less commercial in a certain way. I always felt that was very strange because I always felt that 'commercial' was simpler. And **New Grass** was trying so hard to find something that would work for the 'country' market which was really a hard thing for us to do because it really wasn't what **New Grass** music was all about. But I was inspired by all the work and success that **New Grass** had and when I started playing this weird stuff I was surprised how quickly I got an audience for 'doing my own thing.' We found a ready-made audience in the jazz market and the college crowd. And maybe, if **New Grass** was together now, we would be reaching some of this audience. But the timing was such as it was."[113] As a result of his move, "I found myself in a position of being written up in *Time* magazine and *Musician* magazine and being on the 'Tonight Show' and things like that—some of the things **New Grass Revival** was unable to do."

[107] Quotation from *The Big Book of Bluegrass* (New York: GPI Publications, 1984), p. 164.

[108] Members were Jack Tottle (mandolin), Robin Kincaid (guitar), Fleck (banjo), Stacy Phillips (Dobro) and Paul Kahn (bass). Their first album was "Tasty Licks" on the Rounder label and included as a guest artist Bobby Hicks (fiddle). Fleck recorded on both of the Tasty Licks albums released on Rounder.

[109] Some Spectrum LPs were "Opening Roll" (Rounder 0136) with Jimmy Gaudreau, Fleck, Glenn Lawson, and Mark Schatz, "Too Hot for Words" (Rounder 0161) with regular members and Jimmy Mattingly on fiddle, and "Live in Japan" (Rounder 0181) recorded October 1981 in Tokyo and Hiroshima with the same personnel as "Too Hot."

[110] Glenn Lawson was born February 20, 1951, in Harrison County, Kentucky. He won the Red Foley Award for his music in 1973 and 1974. He joined the Bluegrass Alliance December 1974. In August of 1975, he began with J.D. Crowe and the New South on mandolin, switching to guitar when Gaudreau came in October 1975. Lawson stayed two and a half years with Crowe's band.

[111] Alan White, "Bela Fleck," *Bluegrass Unlimited*, September, 1986, p. 35.

[112] 1990 interview at Telluride Bluegrass Festival by this writer.

[113] From an interview at IBMA, September 1995.

Dan Crary—
a bluegrass flatpicker who records New Age music

In 1990, Dan Crary recorded "Thunderation" for Sugar Hill, a record intended for airplay on the New Age radio stations. It was not a record of bluegrass-type flatpicking, but had the flavor necessary to be completely different music than he has played on records before.

Dan Crary with daughters Jenny and Julie.

Tom Gray on the breakup of the Seldom Scene and the contemporary music influence on the Scene

Acoustic bassist Gray described how the departure from the **Seldom Scene** occurred, "There were a couple members of the band who strongly wanted to have a more contemporary band; they wanted to update the material. They wanted to find new performing venues. They wanted to get away from the bluegrass circuit. They didn't want to play bluegrass music so much anymore even though everyone did recognize that that was where our bread and butter was coming from. It was good bread and butter as far as the bluegrass business is concerned, but there was a desire to find a larger market. In order to do that we needed to update our sound—update our image—and it would be very advisable if I were to be playing electric bass, so I was told.

"There were several things that happened for several years before I finally left that made me feel frustrated. It really started when we began recording with a drummer. A country drummer is not conducive to playing any kind of bass other than just simple rhythms. It was very hard for me to play with a country drummer. I played jazz with lots of drummers, but it was different there. A jazz drummer will play fills and

flourishes and use it as rhythm and another backup dynamic sort of thing. A country drummer is very little in dynamics but just very predictable pounding like a pile driver. It was as predictable as could be and not much fun to listen to for me.

"But when we went into the studio, trying to be more commercial by having a drummer, all of a sudden I couldn't play the kind of bass I want to play. Some tunes, I would go ahead and play it the way I wanted to play it anyway and often in the mix we would just eliminate the drums because the two of us clashed.

"Although I like electric bass in its element, I don't care for electric bass with standard bluegrass. I think if it's electric, it should be played as electric and it should be able to contribute just as an acoustic bass should be able to contribute what it can—which is what I have been trying to do for many years in a backup function as well as a rhythm function. There are a lot of holes in music which deserve to be filled. Sometimes, if a song is too monotonous, I feel it needs help and I want to play some notes to give it some help where I feel it is appropriate. And there are ways to do that with an acoustic bass which are somewhat between the sounds of a simple bass line and a jazz improvisation. A bluegrass player has to play with much more taste and control than a jazz player. You have to be very sensitive as to what is going on and figure out where to use certain techniques and where not to. Between jazz and bluegrass, you can use a lot of the same things but you just have to focus differently. You would be surprised at the overlap of interest between bluegrass and traditional jazz. They are both improvisational musics that have a lot of tradition behind them."[114]

After the breakup of Hot Rize— the Tim O'Brien ordeal with the record industry

The end of an era came May 1, 1990, when the very popular **Hot Rize** broke up. The members were then free to pursue their own projects. The split occurred when Tim O'Brien, whose songwriting had been reaping great rewards on the country charts mainly through the singing of country and western singer Kathy Mattea, obtained a contract to work on RCA; O'Brien had been anticipating a move from **Hot Rize** for at least two years already. O'Brien and Nick Forster went as a pair. He also intended to work more with his sister, Mollie. Tim also toured with his new **Tim O'Brien Band** which featured much of his own material.

O'Brien then recorded a duet with Kathy Mattea, anticipating a chart-buster which would be the start of O'Brien's C & W career—where the money is. In an unprecedented move by the record companies to which O'Brien and Mattea belonged (RCA and Mercury respectively), both companies were to promote the single.

When interviewed by Fred Langner (of the Oregon Bluegrass Association) in 1990, Langner suggested that O'Brien's career progression was much like that of Ricky Skaggs. O'Brien said, "Well, Ricky is a real master who went into it with a solid idea of what he wanted to do. I'm much more songwriter-oriented and am not solid country. All the guys in **Hot Rize** had listened to, and were fans of, folk music, blues, and rock and roll, and my music shows that influence. One big change is that I'm not writing songs exclusively for a bluegrass band any more—I write just what I feel like writing."

When asked about how the other members felt about his departure, he replied, "We're really close friends and we all feel that we've accomplished a lot of the things we set out to do. I told them several years ago that some record companies had showed interest in me and that if the right deal came along I was going to go for it. It all came about gradually over a long time. We were together almost exactly twelve years plus about three months

Hot Rize. L to R: Pete Wernick, Nick Forster, Tim O'Brien, Charles Sawtelle.

before Nick joined the band. In that time, we had a few disagreements but that was a lot like a marriage...you have to work at it to make it work."

The November 1990 issue of *Westword*, a Denver periodical, included the following in the "Off Beat" column:

Deal, schmeal: Earlier this year, Tim O'Brien thought his career was about to take off. Instead, it's in a holding pattern... At first, the label [RCA] was so enthusiastic that it joined Mercury in a rare co-promotion of an O'Brien duet with Kathy Mattea released this summer. But after getting his best songs on tape at Colorado Sound Studios—and receiving plenty of encouragement from RCA along the way—he was grounded. Last month, following a management switch at RCA's Nashville division, the new bosses decided they didn't like the album and dropped O'Brien from the company roster.

The article by Gil Asakawa continued,

The record's shelved unless O'Brien can convince another label to buy the masters from RCA. Worst of all, he's contractually barred from even re-recording new versions of those songs for five years. For now, O'Brien's living off savings and planning to perform regionally through the winter... "I've been through the wringer but I'm trying to be as optimistic as possible. At this point, I really don't have any choice."

He continued to perform and record with Mollie and with his own band. In March 1991, the matter seemed to be settled. RCA let him out of their previous contract—with restrictions. O'Brien re-recorded the same songs for Sugar Hill Records and had to pay RCA a percentage of the profits if the disc sold well. "I'm over the RCA thing," said O'Brien. "They didn't know what to do with me—they didn't have a clue." It seems that O'Brien didn't fit the mold of current country artists of the day (Garth Brooks, Clint Black) as perceived by RCA, and the recordings were not commercial enough.[115] "As of now, my new record seems to be doing well; there's tentative plans for a video from it. As of the end of '91, Nick Forster has left my group to concentrate on his new radio show, 'E-Town.' I hope to decide on guitar players within the next few weeks (Scott Nygaard filled the spot). Mark Schatz will continue on bass."

O'Brien, in 1996, wrote to this writer how he felt about the debacle in which he was involved. Now with a better understanding of the record industry, he wrote, "My deal could have gone sour from within any record label in Nashville. It is the nature of the record industry in general, and especially at the major label level, that an artist is only as secure as his or her last sales figures. And in the case of a new artist, he/she is only as secure as his/her personal champion at the label. In my case, my A & R representative (Artists & Repertoire is the department that signs and develops acts to record) at RCA lost her job and the whole regime changed soon

---

[115] From a 1991 note to this writer, O'Brien: "...I'm doing my best to keep my feet in the bluegrass world while expanding into the folk and country formats as well. Also have been writing regularly with various Nashville writers, as songwriting brings in about half my income.

"While I've flirted with different formats for my band (from a six-piece that includes drums, electric guitar, piano, Dobro, bass, and me to doing occasional solo and duo gigs), I've come to the conclusion that a trio consisting of myself, a guitar and an acoustic bass is the simplest and most economical way to go. There's plenty of room in the music but it's still enough pieces to 'kick some butt' with a band sound. Jerry Douglas continues to play some with me when his schedule permits. When it does, it gives me and the other two a lift. But he's not easily replaceable so we've learned to do quite well with a trio format when Flux isn't there. It feels great!"

Together with sister Mollie, their "Wichita" earned a nomination for Best Bluegrass Song at IBMA in 1995.

after. Almost the next day, nobody seemed to know my name. This is an old enough story; just change a few names and it could apply to hundreds of people who either never succeeded, or in the case of people like Marty Stuart or Vince Gill, people who eventually found a winning combination for mainstream success at another label.

"I feel lucky to be able to continue what I do, in spite of the experience with RCA. I have had interest in my songs from major label acts and producers, and expect to connect that way again eventually. More importantly, with Sugar Hill, I've been able to develop my bag—my sound—and personal style without the pressure of having to measure up to a Garth Brooks. Now, several years after the RCA fiasco, I feel secure as an artist and feel I have a niche in the marketplace that only I can fill. The new 'Americana' chart in the trade journal *The Gavin Report* (which measures airplay of acts like me) proved for the first time what I suspected all along: that people are listening and appreciating my music (my 'Rock in My Shoe' CD was #1 for five weeks in the summer of 1995).

"As far as my own place in bluegrass, I've continued to do sporadic reunions with **Hot Rize** and some special jam performances with people like Bela Fleck, Jerry Douglas, Sam Bush, and Tony Rice at various festivals. I just have the itch now and again, and I won't ignore it. On my own records, there is, I think, a regular scratching of that itch as well, whether it means an old-time-sounding arrangement or two from within my band, or a guest appearance by a good three-finger banjo player like Pete Wernick or Ron Block. While I wouldn't want to paint myself as a bluegrass artist in the classic sense, I will admit that, both as a business man and as a musician, I'm at home with my bluegrass background, and I embrace it as an essential part of my makeup."

Women in Bluegrass - Table of Contents

Women in Bluegrass

In a chronological order of important women in country music, Cousin Emmy was probably the first, followed in approximate order by Patsy Montana, Molly O'Day, Lulu Belle Cooper, Wilma Lee Cooper, Martha Carson, Rose Maddox, Dottie West, and then a host of others. These were pioneers in country music, not just women's music. This chapter is a brief sketch of several women in bluegrass music. Sara and Maybelle Carter are included in the Roots portion of this book.

F. Paul Haney's article in *Bluegrass Unlimited* brought women's music to light. This article on women in bluegrass/country music tells the reader how the pioneer women singers "took real chances on destroying their life styles and reputations by ascending the stage and following their dreams of musical expression. They found an immense amount of resistance in that male-dominated world of stage and concert, but there were a few daring souls who vanquished fear and went on to fame and fortune. The lucky ones who survived and made it did so mainly by becoming bumpkins or cowgirls or sisters of male performers or just cousins. In short—novelties."[1]

While women did have a hard time breaking into this male dominion, women weren't the only ones to face a society which was not receptive to their potential contributions. The pioneers of this music, whether they were men *or* women, faced numerous obstacles daily. Making a living at this music was a tremendous step for any of them. Women who pursued a career in this music had to have the same drive, determination, and love of the music as the men had. Just as there were very few men who had the qualities necessary to make their career in hillbilly music, there were gender differences in the American society which produced far fewer women who felt the need to pursue this music beyond their doorsteps.

But all things change, and so do American values and the role of women in society; it became acceptable for women to have a career of their own. Women became more and more confident and competent as entertainers. They studied this music—the music of the pioneers and the music of the day's best and most popular entertainers. They became performers on a competent skill level and they were now contributing to the progress of the music in innovative ways. They came out with their own versions of what we now know as bluegrass music.

Most of the early women pioneers were part of an already-existing band. But as time went on and bluegrass music became popular, many women went on to front their own bands. This considerably helped women gain the respect and approval of almost any bluegrass audience.

Women in bluegrass

Betty Fisher, leader of her own **Dixie Bluegrass Band** (which was begun in 1972) spoke of women in bluegrass, "The reason I think there are not many women in bluegrass now is because it is not as glamorous as country music. There's not as much money to be made as in country music. But I think that is changing to a certain extent. A few years ago, there were not many women in country music, but now there are a lot."[2]

The first woman to broadcast on the radio

Probably the first woman to broadcast on the radio and record country music was Roba Stanley from Galax, Virginia, the Georgia State Fiddle Champion in 1920, and who performed on WSB, Atlanta.

A woman beats Fiddlin' John Carson at his own competition

Anita Sorrells Wheeler was the first woman to win the Georgia Old-Time Fiddler's Convention in Atlanta. It was September of 1931 when she beat Fiddlin' John Carson (who was the godfather of the convention and actually tried to keep her out of the contest because she was a woman) and Gid Tanner. She was surprised at Carson's attitude at the time because she always had considerable support from her husband (her playing gave her husband the excuse to go to the dances where she played so he could socialize while she played). She never entered the contest again.

In 1935, Wheeler became the fiddler for the all-woman band, **Oklahoma Cowgirls** (none of the six had ever seen Oklahoma). They toured for a year in Georgia, Alabama, Michigan and Chicago. She survived two husbands and still played as of 1990.

[1] F. Paul Haney, "A Sampling: Women in Bluegrass," *Bluegrass Unlimited*, December, 1989.

[2] Don Rhodes, "Betty Fisher—Born to be Free," *Bluegrass Unlimited*, November, 1976.

Cousin Emmy— and all the rest followed

Cynthia May Carver was born the next to youngest of eight children in 1903 near Glasgow in Barren County, Kentucky. The family's two-room log cabin had "cracks between the walls so big that you could a-throwed a cat between them without touching a hair."[3] While she was growing up in the family's sharecropper home, she was a hard-working farmer's daughter who knew every facet of tobacco growing and harvesting.

The first time she heard a radio was as a young girl when she was in town at a grocery store. Right then she knew she wanted to be a radio entertainer. This enthusiastic exclamation to her parents was rewarded by her mother with a whipping. Nevertheless, she continued to dream and rehearse for her first performance on the radio.

An energetic child, she used her work in her father's field as opportunities to practice entertaining her co-workers. She "would use her singing, dancing, and leg-slapping routines as bribes to get the other children to do her part of the work."[4] As with others from that part of the country, she was uneducated but never perceived her lack of schooling as a handicap. She only joked about it later when she began entertaining.

She inherited music talent from her musical family. She eventually learned to play fifteen different instruments including rubber gloves and her cheeks (by slapping them with her hands). She filled the rubber gloves with air and coaxed a tune by regulating the amount of air escaping from them. She was the first person to win the National Old-Time Fiddlers' Contest, Louisville, Kentucky, in 1936. But as good as she was on the other instruments, the five-string banjo was Cousin Emmy's trademark.

She was bold when it came time to sell herself to a radio station. She would tell a reporter, "Darlin', I'm the sweetest singer of mountain ballads that ever came out of the foothills." To the manager of a radio station she'd say, "I know and can prove that I can outdraw...anybody else. So you go ahead and put me on top of that there pile where I belong." And she copyrighted most of her songs. "I learned that right quick when they began stealing them songs from everybody and making money on us poor old hillbillies, and we didn't make a dime out of it. I thought it's time to do something about it. I learned this right fast after I got out of them sticks."[5]

She began at WHAS, Louisville, Kentucky, about 1935 (for two years). She had a way of endearing herself to the audience by telling them to "Pull your little chairs up to the radio." In 1937, she began at Wheeling, West Virginia, as a member of the famous WWVA Midnight Jamboree which aired every Saturday night from 11 p.m. to 2 a.m.. Of the nearly fifty performers, women comprised about twenty percent of the total. It was there that she taught Grandpa Jones how to play the frailing banjo.

By 1939, she had an entire band which was called **Cousin Emmy and Her Kin Folks**. They had their own program on WSB (Atlanta) every Friday night at 10:30. After stints at WHAS and WNOX, in 1941 she took her act to 50,000 watt KMOX in St. Louis where she appeared twice daily and it was here that she probably reached the acme of her radio career. Sponsored by a cough remedy product and a hair dye product, in 1942 she and her **Kin Folks** recorded transcriptions for coast-to-coast play for a drug company. She and her group were given considerable coverage in the December 6, 1943, issue of *Time* magazine. Cousin Emmy, when describing her part of the show, is quoted, "First I hits it up on my banjo, and I wow 'em. Then I do a number with the guitar and play the French harp and sing, all at the same time. Then somebody hollers, 'Let's see her yodel,' and I obliges. After that, we come to the sweetest part of our program—hymns." In addition to her "wailing and stomping" her "pious and profane hillbillery," she included old folk songs in her repertoire which proved to be quite valuable in the eyes of folklorist Professor R. M. Schmitz.

Back in Louisville at WAVE about 1944, she and her group were described by a member of her band (steel guitarist Mac Atcheson), "When she'd do a show she'd pack the house twice every night, practically, at those little school houses. Ah, she was a showman that wouldn't wait! She played

[3] Wayne W. Daniel, "Cousin Emmy—A Popular Entertainer Country Music History Almost Forgot," *Bluegrass Unlimited*, October, 1985, p. 64.

[4] Ibid., p. 64.

[5] Ibid., p. 66.

banjo and sang 'Ruby' and all those songs like that, then she'd play fiddle—played good fiddle. She'd play old hoe-downs and stuff like that and dance around the stage. She was a real character."[6]

She appeared in the movie, "Swing in the Saddle" (Columbia Pictures, 1944), "The Second Greatest Sex" (Universal Pictures, 1955) and with cowboy Jimmy Wakely in "Under the Western Sky."

In the fall of 1945, she was a regular on the WSB Barn Dance, then she went back to KMOX. In 1947, she recorded for Decca. Her biggest tune was "Ruby" (which Bob Osborne heard her sing and later applied it to his own band). The album of 78s were later reissued as two 45 r.p.m. records on the English Brunswick label under the titles "Kentucky Mountain Ballads, Volume 1 and Volume 2."

In 1961, she was "discovered" by Mike Seeger and the **New Lost City Ramblers** when she was playing at Disneyland's Country and Western Night where she was introduced as the "first hillbilly star to own a Cadillac." The **N-L-C-R** band helped her revive her career with various tours, television programs and festivals. In 1968, an LP of her works came out on the Folkways label, "The New Lost City Ramblers with Cousin Emmy."

Cousin Emmy died April 11, 1980, in Sherman Oaks, California. Her epitaph, if were to be engraved on her tombstone, could be advice she once gave to Tom Paley: "Don't give up. If you set out to do something, do it or bust. Just keep on and you'll get it."[7]

Patsy Montana— "That was the birth of Women's Lib right there as far as I was concerned."

She was not a part of the bluegrass music movement or even a part of the country music which served as the basis for bluegrass. She was just a country girl who found herself in the middle of the western music at Chicago's largest station which played country music, WLS. She is one of the first women to break into a man's world and leave an eternal impact on the world of country and western musics.

Many historians give Patsy Montana credit for paving the way for women in music—women such as Tammy Wynette, Loretta Lynn, Dottie West and others. "Really, I wasn't aware of breaking the ice for anyone but me," Montana told this writer. "There wasn't as many girls around, naturally. There's more girl singers

around now than there ever has been. And I don't think that's bad."

Patsy Montana was born as Rubye Blevins near Jessieville, Arkansas, October 30, 1914[8]. She tells people that she was born anywhere between 1908 and 1925. The specifics are her secret. She has fun with this—"This was how I figure I'm going to have the biggest funeral in the business 'cause everyone is going to come to see how old I am… I'm going to have the last laugh; I'm going to be cremated." Raised in a musical family with ten brothers and no sisters, "That got me ready for a man's world later on."[9] She was the only child who later made her living in music.

At age fourteen, Montana played her first professional singing job. She recalled in a telephone interview, "They were opening a big bridge—that's a big thing in the South, you know. They had the Governor there and all that stuff. And they offered me five dollars to play one song. Well, I couldn't play the guitar so I hired my brother to play the guitar. And I sang one of Jimmy Rodgers' songs—yodeling and ever'thing. We laughed all the way through it. When we got through, he thought he should have three dollars because he played the guitar. Well, I stood my ground right then. That was the birth of Women's Lib as far as I was concerned. I paid him two and a half, I took two and a half." (She chuckled as she told this story.) When she realized that she could sing and get paid for it, she decided to pursue it as long as she could. She continued playing local jobs, never really considering a career in music.

When she started out in the business in the early 1930s, the only woman in professional music she could remember was Kate Smith who was very popular back then. Montana was mostly unfamiliar with country music artists. She had only heard of Bill Monroe, probably because the **Monroe Brothers** had recently played there at WLS when she arrived.

In 1934, Montana was just getting her start in radio in California when her hometown of Hope, Arkansas, called and asked her to submit their watermelon into the contest for the World's Largest Watermelon at the World's Fair in Chicago. This trip, pulling that big watermelon in a trailer, was to be combined with a vacation for her and some of her brothers. Her mother asked her to go by WLS in Chicago and say hello to Hal O'Haloran, her favorite announcer. There at WLS, "I ran right into the **Prairie Ramblers** and they was auditioning for a girl singer. And I never went home." The **Prairie Ramblers** were asked by the station to audition a girl singer "to augment their act, 'cause the girls weren't particularly popular then. They were just sort of, more or less, used to put color on the stage. And in

[6] Ibid., p. 67.

[7] Ibid., p. 68.

[8] This birth date comes not from Mrs. Rose, but from Melvin Shestack's *The Country Music Encyclopedia*, (New York: Thomas Y. Crowell Company, 1974). Another date, from her fan club, has her born in 1912.

[9] Quotation from a 1990 telephone interview.

those days you had to be somebody's sister or aunt because you didn't *dare* travel with four men alone. That just wouldn't look nice to the public. Just like Roy Acuff and his group—well, Rachael was supposed to be Oswald's [Kirby] sister. So that made it okay. But they weren't even kin. So girls weren't very important then. So I can see now that I did come in as an independent person and sort of carve a space, I guess, for women as a girl soloist."

The **Prairie Ramblers** had been at the station for a year already when she began working with them on the National Barn Dance in 1934. All of her first, important records were recorded with this group. They traveled together in one car. There were four large men and, when the weather was inclement, a bass fiddle in the car. They played on any radio stations which would have them. She would even pay a station to let her sing. She made good money back then—$60 per week. That is what the Musician's Union made WLS pay the band members.

Montana added in 1991, "You know the **Prairie Ramblers**—the four guys that I worked with—they actually would be called bluegrass today. In fact, they came to WLS when they were called **Kentucky Ramblers.** When I came along and brought the western mode[10], why, they changed it to **Prairie Ramblers.** They played the exact same instruments that Bill Monroe does now but the name 'bluegrass' didn't come along until Bill Monroe." But she admits that the banjoist had only four strings on his banjo.[11]

Montana had earlier recorded in Hollywood but did not further her career there. It was on WLS that her career really started to take off. The 50,000 watt station was very important to all musicians of the day. While WLS was a full-time career, she also raised a family with two girls. She was the first woman to have a million-seller, "Cowboy's Sweetheart." Many others got their start on this station...acts such as Gene Autry, Red Foley, **Lulu Belle and Scotty**, and **Homer and Jethro**, and the **Monroe Brothers** (who worked the WLS road show, not the radio station).

Patsy and her husband, Paul Rose, moved from Chicago to California in 1952. Not desiring to play night clubs, she quit music. But this didn't last long. She came back in music in various capacities for many years. As of 1991, she still was involved in music. "As long as I can sing on key, and as long as people will pay me, then I'll let 'em," she said.

On April 26, 1981, Patsy Montana was honored by the National Museum of the United States—the Smithsonian Institution—for her lifelong achievements in the performing arts. Also that year, Cattle Records, the German label, released 1000 copies of the monaural "The Cowboy's Sweetheart." The album featured such cowboy songs as "I'm an Old Cowhand," and "I'd Love to Be a Cowgirl (But I'm A-Scared of Cows)." The recording featured Montana with the **Prairie Ramblers.** She remained on the WLS National Barn Dance with the **Ramblers** until 1953, recording over two hundred singles.

> "Well, I think country music is here to stay. I don't imagine that Judge Hay would like how things have turned out now, but you've got to remember that the world is changing."
> —Patsy Montana

In a 1991 interview, she talked about this new music we have today on the Opry and on the radio. "Well, I think country music is here to stay. I don't imagine that Judge Hay would like how things have turned out now, but you've got to remember that the world is changing. Everything is changing. Country music used to use three chords—beyond that you was getting too fancy. And you'd have to sing through your nose. All that is gone now. Country music has 'went to town' you might say. And that's not bad. I think we have pretty good musicians nowadays. This is the best new crop we've had in a long time."

She wrote about 200 published songs. They included "Sweetheart of the Saddle," "Cowboy's Sweetheart" and "Give Me a Home in Montana." She recorded on RCA Victor, then Decca, then Columbia and others. Recently she did an album called "Cowboy's Sweetheart" for the Flying Fish label with Cathy Fink and her group. In April 1991, she recorded, along with **Riders in the Sky** and comedian Baxter Black, a PBS television show called "Texas Connection." She continued to make occasional appearances through 1992 with her daughter, Judy, as a duo until Judy's untimely death that year. Rubye Rose lived in Southern California until her death May 3, 1996.

[10] She dressed in the style of Gene Autry, the famous "singing cowboy" who, according to one source, made $600,000 in 1939 through record sales, radio, films, tours and canny product marketing. According to Ms. Montana, Autry was just getting started at the time she got started and wasn't making that kind of money. She said that when Autry asked WLS for a raise and didn't get it, he quit. That's when Roy Rogers (Len Sly) got his big break—by taking his place. Rogers had been dubbing-in for Autry in some of his movies already—they were built alike. Autry once told Montana, "Everybody tells me that I can't sing, and I can't ride, and I can't act, and I have ten million to prove it." During the mid-eighties Autry put up 34 million dollars for the Gene Autry Museum in California.

[11] This sound was probably not as close to bluegrass as she might remember. She was not well-versed in bluegrass and did admit that she couldn't recall if the banjo player used finger picks or not. Looking at photos of the Prairie Ramblers from that period, the banjo in the picture appears to be a 5-string. This is confirmed by individuals this writer spoke with who performed with her in her later years. In a close analysis of a release of these recordings, I could detect no frailing or fingerpicked banjo in the bluegrass style. In any case, the main instruments used by the four musicians were guitar, fiddle, mandolin, and bass with one of them doubling on banjo.

Lulu Belle and Scotty on the WLS Barn Dance

Promoter John Lair helped seventeen year-old Myrtle Eleanor Cooper (born Christmas Eve 1913) get a job at Chicago's WLS Barn Dance in 1932. Her first audition was a failure because she wasn't accustomed to using a microphone; she nearly blasted everybody out with her volume. A couple of weeks later, after some practice, she got the job. Initially, she worked with Red Foley, an established star, in music and comedy. She could sing and play the guitar. But she became popular when she teamed with "Skyland Scotty" Wiseman[12] to become **Lulu Belle and Scotty,** as named by John Lair, who booked them into the Dance. They sang together from 1933 to 1958.

Lair guided her career at the station; the most important managerial act he performed was to let her act naturally. She was a resourceful, self-confident girl who always had been one to keep on top of the situation. A natural born comic with a sort of sixth sense about putting herself over on stage and on the air, Lulu Belle immediately established a warm rapport with the audience. Even though her daddy got her the job, she was determined to keep it. She dressed in high top shoes that laced very high. Her mom fixed her up with pigtails and a big bow to cover up where the pigtails connected to her hair. This gave her a "girl next door" image to which the audience could relate.

Scotty and Lulu Belle performed their first song on December 13, 1934, the somewhat prophetic "Madame, I've Come to Marry You." The duo was also known as the **Hayloft Sweethearts** and featured down-home music with a lot of novelty tunes and comedy skits.

By 1936, Lulu Belle's popularity had peaked when she was voted Most Popular Woman on Radio by *Radio Guide.*[13]

In those days, one measure of a performer's popularity was the amount of mail received from listeners. This duo measured up respectfully. Also, it is reported that they held many box office records at theaters, parks, county and state fairs. In 1943, *Billboard* magazine listed them along with the **Weaver Brothers and Elviry,** the **Hoosier Hotshots, Sons of the Pioneers**, and Roy Acuff as one of the six best money-getters in the country music business.

Lulu Belle and Scotty were featured on seven films "Shine on Harvest Moon" (Republic, 1938), "Country Fair" (Republic, 1939), "Village Barn Dance" (Republic, 1940), "Swing Your Partner" (Republic, 1942), "National Barn Dance" (Paramount, 1943) and two others.

Some of the most popular material they did in their act was on the NBC Alka Seltzer National Barn Dance. Their most popular tune there was "Does the Spearmint Lose Its Flavor on the Bedpost Overnight?" Others were "I've Got to Quit Kickin' My Dog Around," "When Grandpa Got His Whiskers Caught in the Zipper of His Shirt" and "Which Would You Rather Have on Hand, a Grand Baby or a Baby Grand?" Scotty composed some of these. He also took Bascom Lamar Lunsford's "Mountain Dew" and added more verses to it. But they weren't allowed to sing it on the radio. Lulu Belle explained, "You weren't allowed to sing anything about liquor or cigarettes or divorce or anything that sounded the least bit shady or crude." Scotty bought the rights to "Mountain Dew" from Lunsford for a reported $25 but generously shared half the royalties with him. He also wrote "Have I Told You Lately That I Love You?", a song which sold ten million records through various artists. Scotty was inducted into the National Songwriters Association Hall of Fame in 1971.

Lulu Belle and Scotty remained with the WLS Barn Dance until their retirement in 1958. In the '70s, Lulu Belle served two terms in the North Carolina General Assembly representing three counties. She was the first Democrat to do this since 1922, and the first woman to do so.

Scott Wiseman died of a massive heart attack in 1981 in Gainesville, Florida. Lulu Belle later remarried in Florida. Lulu Belle and Scotty were nominated to the Country Music Hall of Fame for 1979 and 1980.

Evelyn Perry, the Coon Creek Girls, and the Renfro Valley Barn Dance

The **Coon Creek Girls** group was the crown jewel of John Lair's Renfro Valley Barn Dance. They played authentic mountain and hill-country music and it was the first female hillbilly band in the country. The band was formed just for the Barn Dance which was first broadcast October 9, 1937, at Cincinnati's Music Hall. Two years later, Lair moved the Barn Dance to the new barn constructed for the show in east-central Kentucky constructed for the show.

Evelyn Perry was one of the original members of the **Coon Creek Girls**. She was raised in Ohio with a fiddle in her hand. One of her first occasions to play professionally was on the *Prairie Farmer* magazine portion of WLS' amateur hour program in Chicago. But she found that the rules of the Musician's Union did not allow her to play the fiddle but had to sing. She did so reluctantly. This led to a meeting with John Lair who

---

[12] Scott Wiseman was born November 8, 1909, near Ingalls, North Carolina. He learned how to frail on the banjo before he was ten. When he was eleven, he sold a pig for $4.95 and bought a mail order guitar. By the time he was in his teens he was a serious collector or folk songs and a regular performer at square dances. He was the president of his senior class in college and he helped pay his college expenses as an announcer/performer/program director on WMMN, Fairmont, West Virginia. He joined the WLS Barn Dance in 1933, when the very popular Bradley Kincaid left the Dance. He was billed as "Skyline Scotty" because he came from that part of North Carolina which is known as "the land of the Sky."

[13] What made this more impressive is that she was in competition with the world—not just country music. She came in fifth behind Jack Benny, Eddie Cantor, Nelson Eddy and Lanny Ross.

Lily May Ledford. Photo courtesy Eleanor Wilson.

spoke to her about his idea of having an all-woman band perform at a barn dance he was starting up in Cincinnati. Already lined up for the show were Lily May Ledford, the **Girls of the Golden West**, and the **Corn Huskers** (which included Red Foley), and Whitey "The Duke of Paducah" Ford.

When Lair got around to forming this all-woman band, he assigned the ladies stage names which were flowers—he thought it was cute; after all, they were only women and women weren't often viewed with the full respect men could get with the same level of competence as a band. Evelyn Perry became "Daisy" on fiddle, Esther Kohler became "Violet" on mandolin and guitar. Lily May L edford on banjo and fiddle and her sister Rosie Ledford who played guitar were already named after flowers. When he introduced them, he played up the uniqueness of the band being all women and called them the rather pejorative "Coon Creek Girls from Pinch 'Em Tite Holler, Kentucky." John Lair's show traveled extensively in a large bus. The troupe included Red Foley, Aunt Idy, Little Clifford, and the **Coon Creek Girls**.

The **Coon Creek Girls** played the Barn Dance which was broadcast on WLW in Cincinnati, and went on tours for the country music show. They had a weekday show on WCKY at Covington, Kentucky, where, as Perry remembered, "People started coming in and after a few weeks it was so crowded we didn't even have room to play so they had to begin sending out tickets. They didn't cost anything, but the audience had to have a ticket to get in. We'd leave either right after the morning broadcast on WCKY or on Saturday night or Sunday morning after the Barn Dance on WLW. In the

theaters where we played, they'd just run a cheap movie and we'd play again and so on. We had big crowds 'til it got to the point where they'd just cut out the movie altogether and they'd empty the theater and another crowd would come in and we'd sometimes do as many as five shows in one day. Admission was 25 cents and 35 cents. I've got pictures of people lined up for two blocks to get in. We were really popular; I suppose because we were different.

"Those were the days of early, early radio. We played theaters, schoolhouses and I think every fair. I don't remember ever having a day off—Sundays included. Lots of times, of course, the roads were bad and if we had 150 miles to go to the next town we would start out after doing three to five shows and travel all night and a lot of times we wouldn't get to the next date until it was time to go on stage. We would come back in and do the Barn Dance on Saturday nights."[14]

Lair paid the girls $20 each week "regardless of how many shows we did and we knew John was making a lot of money. Out of our salary we paid five nights of hotels, we kept an apartment, we bought food and everything."[15]

When Lair moved the Barn Dance to Renfro Valley, Kentucky, in late 1939, Violet and Daisy left the band. Lily May's sister, Minnie, joined them as "Black Eyed Susan" for a while. Violet and Daisy joined the **Callahan Brothers**, Bill and Joe, and toured Tulsa, Oklahoma, where they met fiddlers Howdy Forrester and "Georgia Slim" Rutland. They also worked dates with Bob Wills' **Texas Playboys**. About a year later, they moved back to WLW's Boon County Jamboree where Violet's sister, Viola, joined on accordion and they played cowboy songs as the **Rangerettes** for another year. Years later, Lily May, who had a distinguished and prolific solo career, recorded a solo album featuring her singing and frailing banjo picking. Pam Perry, Daisy's daughter, played with the **New Coon Creek Girls** awhile.

Molly O'Day with Lynn Davis and the Cumberland Mountain Folks.

[14] Brett F. Devan, "Evelyn "Daisy" Lang Perry—An Original Member of the Coon Creek Girls," *Bluegrass Unlimited*, December, 1989, pp. 35, 36.
[15] Ibid., p. 37.

Molly O'Day

Molly O'Day had a strong influence on traditional country singers such as Wilma Lee Cooper, Jeanie West, Rose Maddox and Rose Lee Maphis. She was called "The greatest woman that ever lived" by Norm Carlson, tape editor of the Stanley Brothers Tape Club. Carl Sauceman, in a 1989 interview, spoke of her, "She was fabulous! She not only was a good singer, she was a *great* show person. Great! She would have an audience eating out of her hand in no time flat. She had that big ribbon in her hair and that big flower-tailed dress. She was fabulous, Man."

O'Day became famous singing the songs written by Hank Williams before Hank sang his own songs... Fred Rose, of Acuff-Rose Publishing Company, recognized that the combination of O'Day's singing and Williams's songs would be a winner. He was right.

This early country musician was born on July 9, 1923, as LaVerne Williamson in McVeigh, Pike County, Kentucky. She was raised in a musical family and listened to the National Barn Dance (WLS) and Grand Ole Opry (WSM). She listened to Lily May Ledford (**Coon Creek Girls**), Patsy Montana (with the **Prairie Ramblers**), Lulu Belle Wiseman, and Millie and Dolly Good (**Girls of the Golden West**). Her first entertaining was at local events with her brothers Skeets (fiddle) and Duke (banjo). In 1939, LaVerne joined Skeets as "Mountain Fern" (when his band played with Johnnie Bailes) in **Fiddlin' Skeets and Smilin' John, the**

Happy Valley Boys on WCHS. They then spent some time at WBTH (in Williamson, West Virginia) and WJLS (Beckley, West Virginia) where "Mountain Fern" became "Dixie Lee." By 1940, her old group had disbanded so she joined Mr. Lynn Davis' **Forty-Niners**. This opening in Davis' group occurred when one of the women lead singers had left the group which was then playing at WHIS, Bluefield, West Virginia. They then joined the Renfro Valley Barn Dance where the **Coon Creek Girls** and the **Holden Brothers** were appearing.

Lynn Davis and LaVerne "Dixie Lee" Williamson married April 5, 1941. That summer, the **Forty-Niners** became sponsored by Dr. Pepper at WJLS. In September, they left the mountains for WAPI, Birmingham, Alabama.

It was during this time that a starving musician and emerging alcoholic offered to sell her one hundred songs for $25. Familiar with his work because she had used several of his songs in her music already, she was tempted. But she felt it unethical to receive so much for only $25 and suggested he keep working on his own to get his songs published. This songwriter was Hank Williams.

In the summer of 1942, the Davises moved their operations to 50,000 watt WHAS, Louisville, on the Early Morning Frolic and on CBS's network show Renfro Valley Barn Dance. Because the War forced many people to stay home as a result of limited gas and tire rubber, the popularity of the radio show grew in the "valley where time stands still". Another WHAS musician at the time, Clayton McMichen, told the duo that there was another Dixie Lee in the area so she changed her name to Molly (similar to WWVA's Milly Wayne) O'Day (an Irish flavor to her choice of Day for a surname—her choices were Day or Knight).

Molly's most popular tune at the time was "The Drunken Driver," a song for which she received 4,000 requests in one day. By that time, she had developed her own singing style and dropped her earlier mimicking of yodels, so popular when she was growing up.

In the spring of 1944, the Davis duo left Kentucky to play again on WLS, this time as the **Cumberland Mountain Folks**[16]. That year, they worked at KRLD, Dallas, during which time they recorded over 100 transcriptions for the Sellers Transcription Company of Fort Worth. In Knoxville on WNOX's Mid-Day Merry-Go-Round in 1945, also on the bill were the **Sauceman Brothers and the Greene Valley Boys**. There they re-formed the **Cumberland Mountain Folks** with Burk Barbour, Everett and "B" Lilly, and Johnny Harper (bass, comedy). On December 6, 1946, Davis and O'Day and the **Cumberland Mountain Folks** recorded their first session for Columbia.[17] Some of O'Day's most

---

[16] With the Lilly Brothers, Everett (mandolin) and B (banjo) Lilly, with Speedy Krise (Dobro) and Fiddlin' Burk Barbour.

[17] Other musicians were Skeets Williamson (fiddle), Speedy Krise (Dobro) and Mac Wiseman (bass). They recorded the popular "Tramp on the Street" as well as songs Hank Williams had sent O'Day through the years: "The Drunken Driver," "Six More Miles" and "When God Comes and Gathers His Jewels." The songs were released July 1947.

and the **Cumberland Mountain Folks** recorded their first session for Columbia.[17] Some of O'Day's most popular songs later made her famous because of their applications to the bluegrass genre. These include "Tramp on the Street," "Matthew 24," "Poor Ellen Smith" and "After the First Fall of Snow."

They then joined WROL, Knoxville, on the Dinner Bell Show (a rival to WNOX's Mid-Day Merry-Go-Round). Other performers on the show were **Flatt and Scruggs**, Archie Campbell, Carl Butler, and Carl Smith.

In the fall of 1952, after an operation for tuberculosis which removed half of a lung, O'Day put all her efforts into the pursuit of the ministry for the Church of God. She and her husband soon ran a gospel music store, the Molly O'Day Music Center. They recorded in 1964 on the Rem label and in 1968 for GRS. In 1974, they were regulars on their own bluegrass gospel radio show daily on WEMM-FM, Huntington, West Virginia.

Martha Carson

One of the prominent figures in women's music was Martha Carson after she split from her husband, James "Roberts" Carson in 1951.[18] Born Irene Amburgey in 1921, she became one of the earliest women to pursue music alone—as a gospel singer.

Irene and her sisters were the **Hoot Owl Hollow Girls** in the late '30s on WSB, followed by a move to WHIS in James Roberts' band. In 1940, Irene Amburgey (by now Irene Roberts) and her sisters joined Lily May Ledford in the **Coon Creek Girls**. James and Irene took the stage names **James and Martha Carson, the Barn Dance Sweethearts** on WSB's Barn Dance in Atlanta. The duo recorded on RCA Victor, the White Church label, and Capitol (by 1949).

The couple divorced and split in 1951 and began separate careers in country music. Martha Carson immediately had a hit with "Satisfied," and was a big success for Acuff-Rose Publishing Company. She then joined the Grand Ole Opry as a gospel singer and used the **Jordanaires** for backup when recording. She was an influence on Elvis' gospel tunes.

Little Roy Lewis spoke of her, "Martha Carson, the gospel singer, was a big influence on our group. She would fill both sides of the stage at Bell Auditorium in Augusta when she came to town. I remember we saw her in a long dress with her guitar having her name on the side. She had beautiful auburn hair and looked like a doll. Her group rode in two green limousines."[19] As of 1991, Martha Carson lived in Nashville.

Lillimae Haney and the Dixie Gospel-Aires

One of the early women in the bluegrass gospel genre was Lillimae Haney. Many of her sidemen had extensive experience in the music and would become better known through their exposure with Haney's group. Sidemen who played with the band included George Smith, Jimmy Dutton, Wayne Lewis, Dave Evans, Junior Stennett, and family members.

Haney was born near Roundhead, Ohio, March 23, 1940. She was named after Lily May Ledford. Her father, from Kentucky, picked guitar in the Maybelle Carter style. Lillimae's father taught her and her sister, Wilma Jean, the guitar and mandolin as children. The sisters were performing in churches by the time she was eight. Soon the trio of the father and the two **Haney Sisters** were traveling to perform. While growing up, Lillimae was influenced by Bill Monroe, **Flatt and Scruggs**, Molly O'Day, Rose Maddox and Wilma Lee Cooper.

When Wilma Jean married, she left the group to Lillimae and her father. Charles Whitaker joined on mandolin and soon married Lillimae. Noah Hollon joined as banjoist...and they had a bluegrass band.

Lillimae quit music for a year and a half when she lost her eldest son in an auto/train accident. Then she re-formed her band as **Southern Gospel Singers** and began recording in 1959.

In the early 1960s, the band changed its name to **Lillimae and the Dixie Gospel-Aires** and eventually to **Ms Lillimae and the Dixie Boys Quartet** in the mid-1980s. They recorded on Cincinnati's Arco label in the 1960s on Jack Casey's Rome Records in 1974, and on the Gloryland label in 1976.

[18] After the breakup from his wife in 1951, James went on to achieve his own notoriety in this music.

[19] Don Rhodes, "On the Hallelujah Turnpike with the Lewis Family," *Bluegrass Unlimited*, June, 1980.

Hazel Dickens— an authentic voice from the hills of West Virginia

You won't hear Dickens on mainstream radio these days. Her voice isn't radio smooth. But then, you don't listen to Dickens' music with your ears. You listen with your soul."[20] Sometimes called the "queen mother of bluegrass", Hazel Dickens is well known for her heartfelt, soulful songwriting and singing. Her approach to making a living in music was different than most other ladies of this music. Ms. Dickens told this writer, "I think I began to be more of an independent-type person instead of trying to fit into the mold. And I did more political songs and wrote a lot more of my own songs. When I say 'political' I mean working class people, not the other kind of political. I guess I concentrated more on the plight of people in the work force and how they reacted to society or how society reacted to them. I guess you might call them socially-oriented songs."[21] "

During the period when women were becoming readily accepted into country and western music, it was different in bluegrass. It is much more difficult for women to be accepted as authentic bluegrass singers. She pointed out that while, as of 1992, there are many women in bluegrass, very few of them made it in the traditional vein of bluegrass.

Hazel Dickens was born in Mercer County, West Virginia, in the heart of the Appalachian Mountains, which was a very poor economic area while she was growing up. Her family moved often among small mountain communities. She was one of eleven children in the musically-oriented family. Dickens recalled, "During the Depression my father had lost about everything. The last children that came along—I was third from the end—really suffered the consequences of all that because there was not a lot to raise us on. He had a truck and hauled timber for the coal mines, and hauled coal for people and did whatever he could do with his truck. Soon mines began closing down."

Music in the neighborhood was commonplace and was a main form of family entertainment. "There always had been music around. My father was a very good singer and sang in the church—he was a Baptist minister. That encouraged us to sing. When my brothers began playing instruments, they were largely self-taught as far as I know. My father used to play old-time banjo but he later got rid of that when he got religion. There was music in church though. In fact, one of my brothers would go down to the Church of God and play."

On the family's radio they could pick up the WWVA Jamboree and WSM's Opry. There were also a lot of local stations which featured local musicians doing country and bluegrass music. "I worked off a lot of the old-time people like the **Carter Family**, the **Monroe Brothers**, the **Stanley Brothers**—people like that. I listened to all those people. I had records by all of them and I would go to see as many of them as I could. But there was not a lot of women who were doing aggressive bluegrass—trying to do it in the style in which it was supposed to be done. The two bluegrass albums I did with Alice (as **Hazel and Alice** 1965 to 1976) was not at all modern. It was very, very traditional. We even took some of the old **Carter Family** songs and re-worked them into bluegrass. And the **Delmore Brothers**. You know, just getting material that other people hadn't wore out."

Dickens began her career in 1955 and soon joined Jack Cooke's band as bassist. Her job at the Continental Can Company tin can factory made the purchase of an acoustic bass possible. She freelanced with her bass for some time. Her swing shift interfered with her music so she soon quit that job to pursue music full-time. But to her, "It was just a fantasy; it didn't last too long." She played in many bands during this period when she was beginning to play professionally. It would be some time before she would be in a band which would gain significant recognition.

She became disillusioned with music when she found she didn't get pay equal to men. But this is only one of the reasons she quit music awhile. She elaborated, "Jobs weren't paying very much at all at that time; it was hard to get jobs. And much later on, I [really] did become disillusioned with music and did stay away from it for awhile because there just weren't many opportunities for women—particularly in bluegrass. Now if you wanted to do top-forties country

20 Keith Lawrence, *Messenger-Inquirer*, July 5, 1996.

21 From a 1992 telephone interview. Unless otherwise noted, all quotes are from this interview.

Women in Bluegrass

435

music you could go to Nashville and, if you were good enough, become the next Loretta Lynn or whoever.

"Kitty Wells was a role model for women," she told this writer. "She was one of the first to have a hit record, 'It Wasn't God Who Made Honky-Tonk Angels.'" This 1952 song was a rebuttal to Hank Thompson's song which came out just before that, "Wild Side of Life." Wells felt offended by the song, which she felt was sexist, and recorded her angry tune which blamed men for the wicked, unfaithful women mentioned in Thompson's song. Little did Kitty Wells (33) know the impact of her song on the music of the day—it thrust her to the forefront of country music and began a long career as the first "queen of country music".

Dickens developed her guitar playing into the Maybelle Carter style, among others. It was actually quite varied, "I had to fit into each band whatever was needed and sometimes I would be singing, like tenor to the male lead singer, and then they would get me up to do a Kitty Wells song...so I had to switch back and forth."

Beginning in 1965, Hazel Dickens and Alice Gerrard worked together as **Hazel and Alice** until 1976. They recorded two LPs for Folkways (which were bluegrass), two for Rounder, and others. About half of the material was inspired by working people. She played her own songs, backed by either a bluegrass band or an old-timey band, for organizations such as the Organization of Women Coal Miners, the United Mine Workers, and the National Organization for Women. On Labor Day in 1980, she played at the White House as a spokeswoman for working people. "The women's movement found us," Dickens said of **Hazel and Alice**. "We didn't go looking for them. We were just doing our music. And they liked seeing two women up there on stage."

"I guess I run the gamut from very old time—like unaccompanied—singing, to old-time music, to bluegrass. And I can sing country-western, too. I can hold my own with the best of them if I want to get into that mood. But it would not be the country-western you hear today, it would be mostly like the fifties."

On her 1973 LP "Come All You Coal Miners" about coal mining, five of the songs were used on the soundtrack of the movie "Harlan County, USA" (released about 1978). The movie people called her for the film after hearing that album. "This may be the first time that a woman from my background was involved in anything like that." It won an Academy Award for Best Documentary. She also did an appearance in the movie

Hazel Dickens (L) and Lynn Morris after receiving IBMA award for "Mama's Hand," 1996.

"Matewan." Because John Sayles was involved in this movie, it got more attention and became better known than her first. She appeared on camera here for the first time. She sings in the beginning of the film (unseen), in the church scene with a hat on, and at the grave site scene. "It got me more recognition, but I don't know if it got me any more work."

She told how could she manage to record such controversial songs including "Black Lung," a tribute to her oldest brother who died of the disease. "I got away with it because I never tried to make it in music. If I had gone to Nashville, I would have had to clean up my act and water down my songs until they were as bland as everything else on the radio. It seems like the more lonesome a song is, the more I like it. My people were that way, too. We moved quite a bit. We were poor and we had to go where the work was. When a coal mine would play out, we'd move on to the next coal camp."[22]

In 1983, Rounder released Hazel's, "By the Sweat of My Brow" LP. Edward Morris, of *Billboard Magazine* wrote the liner notes: "Although she left West Virginia long ago, Hazel Dickens still voices the region's prevailing fears and grieves whether she is pleading for social justice, scolding a selfish lover or recalling the terrible twisting of the soul that occurs when a youngster at last decides to leave home and family. Her songs are textbooks on surviving sadness by accepting inevitability. Still, they are never cynical or self-pitying; and like well-crafted essays, they stand up under the closest inspection."[23] Her "Mama's Hand" won Best Song at IBMA in 1996.

[22] From a 1992 telephone interview. Unless otherwise noted, all quotes are from this interview.

[23] Hazel sent this July 1996 update to the above: "My song, 'Mama's Hand,' has been on the *Bluegrass Unlimited* National Bluegrass Survey Chart for nine months come September. Recorded by Lynn Morris, it has been number one on both the album and song charts for four months. It has been nominated for Song of the Year. My song, 'Pretty Bird,' was used on the sound track of a movie that came out this year called 'The Journey of August King.'

There have been two re-issues on CDs of Hazel and Alice albums on Rounder. 'Hazel and Alice' came out in 1974 and sold 20,000-plus copies. The Judds said that record inspired them to begin singing. The second re-issue was, and is, on Smithsonian/Folkways called 'Hazel Dickens and Alice Gerrard—Pioneering Women of Bluegrass.' It's the first two records we recorded in 1965 and 1967.

The Second Annual Ralph Rinzler Memorial Concert on July 6, 1996, was a 'tribute concert' in my honor as part of the Smithsonian Festival of American Folklife.

Rhonda Vincent and the Sally Mountain Show

She's so young that it's difficult to view her as a pioneer in women's music. But in view of the fact that she's been playing for thirty years already, and because many of today's women stars give her a lot of credit for being a significant influence on them, Rhonda Vincent therefore serves in a pioneer status. She began her musical career at age three, recorded at five, began playing mandolin at seven, and had her first single at nine ("Muleskinner Blues," voted Best Single Recording of 1974 by the Society for the Preservation of Blue Grass Music in America (SPBGMA)).

Rhonda was born in Kirksville, Missouri, July 13, 1962, and is the oldest of the Vincent children. She wrote in her own biography, "I started singing at age three. My mom and dad and I were in the car on the way to someone's house that was having a birthday and they started singing 'Happy Birthday.' And I joined them by singing the third harmony part. They said they couldn't believe it, so they sang it over and over, and each time I would join in and sing harmony."

The Vincent household was a center of musical activity where she grew up in Greentop, Missouri. People came over to socialize and play music nearly every night until ten p.m.. When she got home from school, her father and grandfather were sitting there waiting for her to play music with them. There was never a thought that she was the only woman/girl in the area doing it. It was expected of her and she accepted it.

About 1965, Johnny Vincent, patriarch of the Vincent clan, was in a car accident which crippled him extensively. He claims that his faith in God allowed him to continue with life and music and to start his band soon after. In 1967, the Vincent family had their own television program at KTVO, Ottumwa, Iowa, near their home, and also had a radio show on KIRX, Kirksville, Missouri. That year, the family recorded a gospel album on which she sang two songs (she was five). Their Grandpa Bill performed with them until his death in 1972.

While Rhonda was growing up, Johnny was careful to nurture her interest in the music and not let her get burned out. Once, in 1970 when he sensed she was losing enthusiasm, he took her to see the phenomenal Donna Stoneman of the **Stonemans**. He knew that if she saw her it would inspire Rhonda to play even more. The same thing happened when he tried to get her interested in playing the fiddle—which she was also interested in. Johnny then brought home a double set LP by Benny Martin. She was so inspired that she learned every tune on that record.

Rhonda won the Missouri State Fiddle Contest in 1973. The next year, Rhonda (9) won Best Single from SPBGMA for her recording of "Muleskinner Blues"/ "Satisfied." In 1977, she won the Missouri State Fiddle Championships again. In 1976, she was chosen Miss Kahoka Bluegrass as well as in 1979. (This was at the city's Kahoka Festival of Bluegrass Music in Missouri.) Rhonda graduated from high school in 1980 and began attending Northeast Missouri State University with an accounting and data processing major, still touring with the band.

In 1982, members of their family band now known as the **Sally Mountain Show** were Johnny Vincent (banjo), wife Carolyn Vincent (bass), daughter Rhonda Vincent (mandolin, fiddle, guitar), son Darrin Vincent (guitar, fiddle), and son Brian Vincent (mandolin). The band name stemmed from a mountain near the Vincent family home where early in the 20th century there lived a woman in her nineties who played old-time fiddle and claimed to be the composer of "Sallie Goodin'." The old lady's name was Sally Mosely; local people called the towering hill "Sally Mountain."

Rhonda married Herb Sandker whom she had met playing fiddle in his dance band on December 24, 1983. In 1985, the **Sally Mountain Show** appeared on the "Fire on the Mountain" show. Rhonda appeared on the "You Can Be a Star" show on TNN in April. She moved to Nashville on May first and performed with Jim Ed Brown on the Grand Ole Opry. She toured with Brown's show until November first then returned home. In 1986, Rhonda signed with Rebel. She later gave birth to three daughters, Sally (1986), Tensel (1988) and Brooke (1990). The last child only lived three days due to absence of a left ventricle in her heart.

Rhonda was voted Female Vocalist of the Year by SPBGMA 1984 through 1988, then she was retired from the competition. Other awards from the Society in the past include one for her fiddle playing and one as Most Promising Mandolin Player. On August 25, 1990, the **Sally Mountain Show** appeared on the Grand Ole Opry for the first time.

One of the nicest compliments a musician can receive is to have a successful performer give credit to the one who gave that musician the most influence and to acknowledge it on stage. This is what Alison Krauss did on the stage of IBMA in 1991 as she accepted several awards including Female Vocalist of the Year. Krauss praised Rhonda Vincent for being her main influence. Krauss got her start in performing when she toured with the **Sally Mountain Show** when Rhonda was working with country singer Jim Ed Brown.

Only recently has Rhonda understood that she is somewhat of a pioneer in the business. Since she has become well known, it seems that many more women have joined the ranks of the bluegrass world. If plagiarism is the sincerest form of flattery, Rhonda has been flattered many times by women who sing her songs with the same phrasing as she does. This seems to happen often nowadays.

Rhonda Vincent and the Sally Mountain Show

Ginger Boatwright

As a significant figure in women's bluegrass music, Ginger Boatwright had to suffer the same trials and tribulations as any other bluegrass musician trying to make a living in this music.

Ginger Hammond was ten when her father, Hap Hammond of Pickens City, Alabama, founded the **Magic City Ramblers.** It was through this band that Ginger gained valuable exposure to bluegrass. She attended the Birmingham Southern Conservatory of Music and took up the guitar. She met Grant Boatwright at one of his concerts. They got together to form **Grant and Ginger** and soon married. Dale Whitcomb joined on banjo and they became **Grant, Dale and Ginger** in the local area.

In 1969, the trio was in Chicago with the name **Red, White and Blue** (grass). Their first LP, "Red, White and Blue (grass)—Very Popular"[24] came in 1972 on the General Recording Corporation label of Atlanta. And because the album reached into the top ten in both the country and pop music charts, the work enabled them to be the first bluegrass band to be nominated for a Grammy. In 1969, Ginger was diagnosed with cancer; this was only the beginning of her medical problems through her life including a large, brain blood clot. She was once given only three weeks to live. Always looking forward, "When I see children who are born with spina bifida or some other serious handicap, then I tell myself that I've got no right to complain or wallow in self pity. Hey, I've got it good."[25]

They switched to Mercury in 1977, about which time Ginger and Grant divorced. Ginger soon bought Nashville's Pickin' Parlor and formed the **Bushwackers**[26]. The band ended two years later. She felt burned out due to being on the road for seventeen years already and wanted to quit music.

In 1982, she received an offer to join the **Doug Dillard Band** with Doug Dillard (banjo), David Grier (guitar) and Roger Rasnake (bass). She decided to give music another try and soon recorded on the very popular "What's That" and the Grammy-nominated "Heartbreak Hotel," both on the Flying Fish label.

Boatwright learned her considerable emcee skills when, with **Red, White and Blue** (grass), she didn't have an instrument to tune between songs. She felt uneasy about just standing there with nothing to do so she began talking on the mike and became a real entertainer at the same time.

She spoke of being a woman in bluegrass, "I never saw it as a problem. My answer to people who at first reacted negatively to me was that Bill Monroe had Bessie Mauldin with him for a long time. A lot of the old-timers used women singers—they used whoever was the best and available at the time." By 1995, she had remarried and moved to Alaska.

24 Musicians were Grant Boatwright (guitar), Ginger (tambourine), Norman Blake (mandolin, Dobro, guitar, mando-cello), Dale Whitcomb (banjo) and Dave Sebolt (bass).

25 Lee Grant, "In Tune with Ginger Boatwright," *Bluegrass Unlimited*, December, 1996, p. 42.

26 With Susie Monick (banjo), April Barrows (bass, guitar) and Ingrid Reese (fiddle, guitar).

Laurie Lewis and Grant Street

This West Coast musician has played traditional bluegrass with her fiddle, bass and guitar, but she quickly evolved to her own style which could be categorized as less traditional and more "Laurie Lewis." She was IBMA Female Vocalist of the Year in 1992 and 1994.

Laurie Lewis was born in Long Beach, California, in 1950, into a musical family but spent her early days in Texas and Michigan. At seven, she took piano and later, at twelve, classical violin lessons. But she quit both instruments because of discomfort with written music. Upon her arrival back to California (Berkeley) in 1965, she started playing guitar. After seeing the **Dillards**, she was hooked on bluegrass and even took banjo lessons. She began frequenting Paul's Saloon in San Francisco where the area's bluegrass activity, with **High Country** as the pivotal band, took place.

She considers herself primarily a vocalist even though she has a terrific command of the fiddle and other instruments. "I always used to sing in kindergarten," she said. She "failed miserably" at piano lessons so she began studying the violin. Vocally, she considers Ralph Stanley as one of her mentors in addition to early Billie Holiday, Doc Watson, Benny Martin, Ray Park, Benny Thomasson, Jody Stecher and Kenny Baker.

In 1974, Pat Enright invited her to play bass in **Phantoms of the Opry**[27] and on a tour to Nashville. Members of the band encouraged her participation in fiddle contests and she soon became the California Ladies Champion twice and a Third in the Open Division.

Lewis is a founding member of the **Good Ol' Persons** with Kathy Kallick in 1974 and a former member of Peter Rowan's **Free Mexican Air Force**, **Arkansas Sheiks**, and **Blue Rose**[28] (which was the 1988 idea of frailer Cathy Fink).

Lewis and Greg Townsend founded Marin Violin Shop about 1981. She later sold her half of the shop to Townsend after she found herself unable to both run a shop and tour with her band.

By 1983, Laurie had begun touring the East Coast extensively to expand her financial horizons. Her **Grant Street String Band** (the name of the band came from her address in Berkeley) won Second Place at the Kentucky Fried Chicken Bluegrass Festival in Louisville. The next year, they appeared on Garrison Keilor's "A Prairie Home Companion" radio show. The band[29] dissolved soon after they had recorded "Grant Street String Band" on Bonita Records. The members split up the band to pursue their other interests.

Flying Fish released Laurie's "Restless Rambling Heart"[30] in 1986. To promote her new album, she reformed her band and shortened the name to **Grant Street**.[31] She was now committed to pursuing her music with a full time band. The Chicago label released Lewis' "Love Chooses You" LP in June 1989. The following year, this record was chosen Best Country Album of the Year by the National Association of Independent Record

Laurie Lewis and Grant Street. L to R: Laurie Lewis, Tammy Fassaert, Tom Rozum, Tony Furtado.

---

27 With members Gene Tortora (resonator guitar), Robbie MacDonald (banjo) and Paul Schelasky (fiddle).

28 The Sugar Hill record also featured Cathy Fink (frailed banjo), Marcy Marxer (guitar), Sally Van Meter (resonator guitar) and Molly Mason (bass).

29 The band consisted of herself, Steve Krause (banjo), Tom Beckeny (mandolin), Greg Townsend (guitar) and Beth Weil (bass).

30 Recording band members were Lewis (fiddle, guitar, bass, hardingfele), Tim O'Brien (mandolin, guitar), Greg Townsend (guitar, her partner at a violin shop, Spruce and Maple Music in Berkeley, California), Mark McCornack (banjo), Markie Sanders (electric bass) and others.

31 Grant Street then included as its members Tom Rozum (mandolin), Tony Furtado (banjo), Tammy Fassaert (bass), and later Scott Nygaard (guitar). Rozum was a veteran of Arizona's Summerdog and Flying South as well as San Diego's Rhythm Rascals. Fassaert is a Canadian who plays a German carved-top instrument. Furtado, of Pleasanton, California, won the National Bluegrass Banjo Championship in Winfield, Kansas, in 1987. After spending a short time with the Bay Area's Heartland ("the band that takes time out for supper") he joined Grant Street. Nygaard was a well-known guitarist in Seattle before joining Lewis' band and is a veteran of Hurricane Ridge Runners, the Scott Nygaard Trio, and many others in Seattle.

Dealers and Manufacturers (NAIRD). Also, she was presented a commission as a Kentucky Colonel. The next year, she was introduced onto the Grand Ole Opry by Hank Snow. She has recorded on Bonita, Bay, Spaniel, Flying Fish, Gayleo Music, Deep River, Grass Roots, Police, Redwood and Rounder Records. Her 1995 Rounder CD "True Stories" included Tom Rozum (mandolin), Mike Marshall (guitar), Todd Phillips (bass), Rob Ickes (pronounced Eyeks, resonator guitar), Jim Nunally (guitar), Cary Black (bass), Nina Gerber (guitar), Peter McLaughlin (guitar), Scott Nygaard, David Balakrishnan (violin) and others. She was booked by Under the Hat Productions. Her "Who Will Watch the Home Place" won Song of the Year at the 1994 IBMA awards ceremony.

Lynn Morris

Lynn Morris and the Lynn Morris Band

Nowadays, there are several good bluegrass bands led by a woman including Laurie Lewis and **Grant Street**, Vicki Simmons and the **New Coon Creek Girls**, Andrea Roberts with **Petticoat Junction**, Alison Krauss with **Union Station**, and Lynn Morris with the **Lynn Morris Band** based in Winchester, Virginia.

Lynn Morris was born in San Antonio, Texas, October 8, 1948, and raised in the farming town of Lamesa, Texas. Her family enjoyed music but were not performing musicians. The area of Lamesa did not have a lot of music so her exposure to live music was limited. The radio, the only station in town, provided a significant influence toward this end. She especially liked

Hoyle Nix (who played with Bob Wills' **Texas Playboys**) and the **Chuck Wagon Gang**, a gospel group from Lubbock, Texas, only sixty miles away.

Morris took piano lessons at age six, managing to struggle through that for a year. At age eleven, she received a baritone ukulele. Soon, she began taking guitar lessons from the same person who taught Buddy Holly to play, Clyde Hankins. At age fifteen, she began learning the classical guitar and pursued that throughout high school. It was not common at that time for girls to play guitar so she kept this to herself. She had little exposure to others who played the instrument.

She went to college at Colorado College in Colorado Springs, majoring in art. It was here that she heard her first bluegrass band, the **Twenty String Bluegrass Band**. In that band, two of the musicians were Charles Sawtelle (guitar) and Mary Stribling (bass).

By 1970, she wanted to learn to play banjo. Lynn's first banjo was her sister's beginning banjo. But this three-finger banjo playing interfered with her classical guitar playing. She explained that the hand positions between the two instruments are completely different. "At that point, I was having such a good time with the banjo that I just put down the classical guitar and never picked it up again."

Joe Dareing, in Colorado Springs, was her first banjo instructor. Lessons occurred over approximately a three-month period. About that time, she also learned to finger-pick the guitar in the folk style. She learned how to frail from an instructional national public television show which was taught by Laura Weber. In Denver, she observed Dick Weissman, famed frailer of Boulder, Colorado, who toured for years with the **Journeymen**. An even stronger influence toward frailing for Morris was the late David Ferretta who was proprietor of his own acoustic music store and The Global Village coffeehouse in Denver. She credits Ray and Ina Patterson, then of Woodland Park, Colorado, as a major influence toward her decision to become a professional musician. Morris recorded with them occasionally in their home, using only one large mike—in the traditional style.

Upon graduation from college in 1972, Morris (banjo) and Mary Jo Stribling (bass) founded **City Limits Bluegrass Band** with Patrick Rossiter[32] (guitar, resonator guitar) in Denver. The full-time band lasted six years until Stribling left the band. There were no personnel changes during the band's existence.

In 1974, Lynn Morris won the National Banjo Picking Championship at Winfield, Kansas. The prize was $100—not much by today's standards but gladly accepted. She won at Winfield again in September of 1981. That time, the prize was a banjo. The long interval between wins is attributed to the contest regula-

32 Rossiter came to Denver that year with a new college degree in geology. He is a self-taught musician, plays the banjo, and was a bluegrass programmer with Denver's KCFR. Stribling is a Denver native who earlier played washtub bass for the Twenty String Bluegrass Band. Stribling later formed Denver's Mother Folkers and was still popular in the 1990s. The band recorded "City Limits—Live!" on Biscuit City Records, Denver. It was recorded May 1976 at Denver's Oxford Hotel.

440

Whetstone Run, 1984. L to R: Lee Olsen, Lynn Morris, Mike Gorrell, Marshall Wilborn.

nearly two years. Morris freelanced for two years, working with California's Laurie Lewis occasionally.

Upon the demise of the **Johnson Mountain Boys** in 1988, the **Lynn Morris Band** was founded with members Lynn Morris (guitar), Marshall Wilborn (bass), Tom Adams (banjo) and various mandolin players.

In 1990, Lynn Morris was elected to serve on the IBMA (International Bluegrass Music Association) Board of Directors as a representative of Artists and Composers. She won Female Singer of the year at IBMA in 1996. She also won Best Song for "Mama's Hand" written by Hazel Dickens.

tions which require a champion to wait five years until he/she is eligible to compete again.

Morris then joined a country band on guitar and vocals. With this band she did two USO tours in the Pacific region in 1980. After the completion of the USO tours, her father was seriously injured in a car accident and she moved back home to Texas. There she stayed for a year until Pete Wernick told her of an opening for a banjoist in **Whetstone Run**, a full-time band based in State College, Pennsylvania. She stayed with **Whetstone Run**[33] for four years beginning in the spring of 1982. At the end of the summer, Bill Harris quit and this opened a spot for a bassist. Morris recommended a good friend, Marshall Wilborn.[34]

By the spring of 1986, Morris and Wilborn were married and left **Whetstone Run**. Wilborn auditioned for **Jimmy Martin and the Sunny Mountain Boys**. He played for a few weeks while the couple planned to move to Nashville near Martin's band. Then Wilborn received a full-time offer from the **Johnson Mountain Boys**[35] as bass player. The **J-M-B** was the hottest band in the country at the time, and because **J-M-B** played more often than with Jimmy Martin, the job had the potential of more favorable monetary returns. He accepted the offer, taking the place of Larry Robbins. The couple then moved to their present home in Winchester, Virginia, closer to the **J-M-B**. Wilborn stayed

"Letters"— women in jam sessions

There still seems to be sexual bias in bluegrass festival jam sessions, according to a contributor to *Bluegrass Unlimited* in 1989. Kathy White of Griffin, Georgia, wrote, "I would like to comment on men who think that women can't or should not pick. Being a woman banjo picker, I've run into quite a few of this breed! I've walked up to jam sessions at festivals with my banjo and I could see the expressions on a few faces that say, 'On no, I bet she can't pick nothing in time' or 'Can't wait to show her up with my hot licks.' But they would ask me to sit in with them, expecting a $40 banjo to be pulled from my home-made plywood banjo case. It was pure satisfaction I felt when they saw I can pick my 1930 Gibson banjo! I even had one guy (a banjoist) ask me why I didn't learn to play a 'girl's' instrument like a bass or guitar and leave the 'men's' instruments alone! The men who think women can't play as well as men should listen to groups like the **New Coon Creek Girls** or **Sidesaddle**. They haven't heard Alison Krauss fiddle 'Dusty Miller' yet. Guys who think women can't pick should buy some of their records and listen real carefully."

---

[33] Band members were its leader Lee Olsen (mandolin), Mike Gorrell (guitar), Bill Harris (bass), Tad Marks (fiddle) and Morris (Scruggs-style banjo). Olsen formed Whetstone Run in 1976. A professional musician since then, his influences were the styles of Buck White, Jethro Burns and Bill Monroe. Gorrell had been with Whetstone Run since 1977 and was considered the backbone of the band with his strong rhythm guitar and singing, combined together to give the group its special sound. Born and raised in southeastern Ohio, Gorrell worked as a disc jockey and applied those skills to his emcee duties with the band.

Over the years, Whetstone Run has included a variety of musicians and recorded "Bluegrass" for LEMCO Records (1978), "Dixie Hills" and "Time Sure Flies" for Red Dog Records. Whetstone Run's 1984 LP on Red Dog Records was "No Use Frettin'" with musicians Morris, Olsen, Gorrell, and Marshall Wilborn.

[34] They had met in Austin, Texas. Marshall Wilborn was born March 12, 1952, in Austin. He played banjo for some time but the need for a bass player in that area caused the switch of instruments to bass. In Austin he played with the Alfalfa Brothers. Wilborn is also a talented songwriter; he wrote "Mountain Girl" and "The Black Pony."

[35] Members were Dudley Connell (guitar), Eddie Stubbs (fiddle), Richard Underwood (banjo), David McLaughlin (mandolin) and Wilborn.

Sally Van Meter

Women have come a long way in country music since Cousin Emmy hit the stage about 1935. Women are not just "cute" anymore. They don't take a back seat to men when it comes to experience in bands, awards for their recording projects, or status within the international bluegrass community. Sally Van Meter is a resonator guitar player who has accomplished a lot with her music. Her work was included on Sugar Hill's Grammy winner "The Great Dobro® Sessions" album which was a gathering of the top ten resonator guitar players in the country; her excellent work with the **Good Ol' Persons**; her own **Sally Van Meter/Tammy Fassaert Band**[36]; her solo resonator project "All in Good Time;" and her appointment as Vice President of the International Bluegrass Music Association.

Sally Van Meter was born October 7, 1956, and began playing the guitar about age seven (she's self-taught) and followed these up with the slide guitar, resonator guitar and banjo. She grew up in Stirling City in northern California. She became a member of the **Good Ol' Persons** in 1976 as banjoist and resonator guitarist.

She has a lot of well-formed opinions on what bluegrass is and what it should be. "There's a lot of percussion in bluegrass. And I don't think that's necessarily a bad thing unless it detracts from the music. I think *that's* the line [you can't cross if you want to play bluegrass]. If it detracts from the soul part of the music, then you've lost it. If you're sitting there listening to a great song but all you can focus on is how loud the snare drum sounds, then you've lost it. But if you hear it and feel it as one, whole, integrated music, then I think it's okay."[37]

And "I think you have to be constantly evolving, create and re-create, because everything's forward motion. But I still love traditional, and I'm just as happy doing that as I am doing anything else."

Being a woman in bluegrass can still be a problem. Though Van Meter is confident she was chosen for "The Great Dobro Sessions" album because of her virtuosity, she often receives an attitude from some men that "she plays pretty good for a woman." Van Meter responded, "I met Oswald Kirby who was a wonderful gentleman and a really good player, and he was probably one of the first of an earlier generation who didn't say, 'Well, mighty pretty lady, isn't that great?' I can't tell you how many times I've had that said to me. And it took me years not to be mad about it. I'm from California where we're pretty serious about feminism. It's important to turn it all into a community that works together instead of finding things that separate us. That's what playing music is all about."

"To me, music's a very strong river that runs deep, and I think it's important to show that. Sometimes I like it when people say, 'Wow, I didn't expect this!' I've seen barriers change, which is a really nice thing for me and for other players who are women.

There's another aspect of Van Meter's position as a lover of good acoustic music. She plays CDs of good acoustic musicians for kids when she can, "and they were completely turned on by it," she said. "And now they're admitting that they like something other than **Judas Priest**; they're admitting that they like something with some intense musical duality that you can still hear. It was really neat because they'd come up and ask if I taught folk guitar, or if I knew someone who did. I'm starting to be real encouraged by seeing the kind of interest that's beginning to come up because I used to be that younger generation and now I'm that middle-to-older generation. It went fast! I've been in music for almost twenty years."

"I'm still hoping to see more women instrumentalists out there because there really are very few that have it as their primary focus. Alison Brown is one, I'm one, Alison Krauss is a great fiddler, Laurie Lewis plays fiddle. But when you look at that and you look at the ratio of men to women, it's still pretty slim. It's not surprising though, because fifty years ago women just didn't have dual careers."

She has recorded with artists such as Peter Rowan, Kathy Kallick, Tony Furtado, John Reischman, Laurie Lewis and others, and on labels including Kaleidoscope, Planet Bluegrass, Strictly Country, Flying Fish, Rounder, and Sugar Hill. She resigned her position within the IBMA in mid-1996; fellow resonator guitarist Jerry Douglas took her place.

---

36 Members in 1994 were Van Meter, Fassaert (bass), Jim Nunally (guitar), Avram Siegel (banjo) and John Reischman (mandolin).

37 Julie Koehler, "All in Good Time," *Bluegrass Now*, November/December, 1994, p. 20. All other quotes are from this source unless otherwise notes.

Alison Krauss and Union Station—the youngest ever into the Opry

Things rarely change rapidly in bluegrass history. It takes time—many years—for a person's influence to reach proportions of significance in this music. There are a few exceptions: Earl Scruggs, Bill Keith and Alison Krauss. These individuals seemed to have come up with something so significant that it thrust them into stardom almost immediately. Scruggs had been playing professionally about five years before he became famous, Keith had been playing bluegrass only a couple years, and Krauss had formed her own group only eight years earlier when she became the youngest person to become a member of the Grand Ole Opry on July 3, 1993. (Ricky Skaggs was twenty-eight when he became a member.) Her's was the first bluegrass act to join the Opry since 1964 when the **Osborne Brothers** and **Jim and Jesse** came on board.

Alison Krauss was born in Decatur, Illinois, July 23, 1971, and grew up in Champaign, Illinois, after age three. Krauss said, "My parents put my brother (Viktor) and I in every program you can imagine: swimming, gymnastics, art classes, and sports... They wanted to make sure we had things to keep us interested."[38]

The incident which brought her to the fiddle was a string program at her school. At age five, she took violin lessons on a half-size violin. At six, she began listening to such tunes as Hank Williams' song "Honky-Tonk Blues." At age nine, she attended her first fiddle contest, bought a book of fiddle tunes, and began learning the fiddle just for the fun of it. She came in fourth in the Twelve Years and Under category in her first contest.[39] Though these contests in Illinois were not as competitive as those in Texas, they prepared her for what was to come. Even at this early age she exhibited on uncanny ability to remember tunes, note-for-note, weeks after she heard them only once. She liked rock and roll, disco, and musicals like "Grease" and "Saturday Night Fever."

Her motivation to be a great fiddler came when "This one girl came up to me and said, 'Don't worry, my bowing used to be just as bad as yours.' Immediately I decided, 'Not for long, Honey!'" She began playing at events with Viktor, her mother and her father and discovered she liked to sing. By the time Krauss was a teenager, she held five State fiddle championships.

In 1983, she became highly motivated toward bluegrass by **J.D. Crowe and the New South** when Ricky Skaggs and Tony Rice were members. She also listened intently to Mark O'Connor, **Boone Creek**, and the **New Grass Revival**. She learned to sing harmony by listening to the recordings of Ricky Skaggs.

She soon teamed up with Francis Bray (of the early '60s **Bluegrass Gentlemen** a.k.a. **Red Cravens and the Bray Brothers**) and John Pennell[40] in Pennell's newly-formed **Silver Rail**, when she was twelve, for two years. As Pennell's new fiddler, "I didn't know there was such a thing as improvising... We always worked out the tunes, had no idea people made up their solos as they went...so I had a whole new world right there. They said, 'Play in the spaces.' I said, 'Play *what* in the spaces?'"[41] In 1983 and 1984, she was SPBGMA's Most Promising Fiddler in the Midwest. In 1984, she won the fiddle contest at Winfield, Kansas.

In 1985, Alison (14) and Viktor (bass) Krauss and Jim Hoiles (old-time fiddler) and Bruce "Swamp" Weiss (guitar) produced an album of fiddle tunes. Alison joined **Classified Grass** in Indiana. Pennell started another group, **Union Station**. Krauss replaced Andrea Zonn in this group while Alison was still with **Classified Grass**. Dave Denman and Mike Harman joined **Union Station** about the same time. She was inspired and motivated toward perfection in music with this group. They began doing a few festivals and she soon became the focal point of the band; the band became **Alison Krauss and Union Station**.

---

[38] Charlene A. Blevins, "Alison Krauss and Union Station—It's a Band Thing," *Acoustic Musician*, September, 1995, pp. 9, 10.

[39] Andrea Zonn won second place, and later fiddled with Union Station (before Krauss came in), with Tony Trischka's Big Dogs, Vince Gill, Lyle Lovett and others.

[40] She gives Pennell credit as being one of the most important people who introduced her to the finer points of songwriting—which became her standard later on. While she later was accused of leaving bluegrass music in some of her 1990s material, she told *Newsweek*: "I wasn't into doing something different, but songs as good as 'That Makes One of Us' deserves to be catered to."—Blevins, op. cit., pp. 20, 21.

Finding new material is "my favorite part of my job. There's nothing like finding the right song. If you get a really good song, a lot of times they arrange themselves. It becomes really obvious," she said.

[41] Blevins, op. cit., p. 10.

Krauss and her band won the Best New Bluegrass Band of 1986 category at the Kentucky Fried Chicken Bluegrass Music Festival. Part of the reward was a Nashville recording contract which was produced by Sam Bush. On August 11, 1986, *People* magazine gave her full coverage.

While Krauss was still with **Classified Grass**, Ken Irwin of Rounder Records received a demo of this band with Krauss on fiddle and vocals. It was pleasant, but not enough to really stimulate him beyond wondering what she would sound like when she became older. When she was fifteen, Dave Samuelson of Puritan Records saw her at a gospel sing and told Irwin about her. Irwin found that "she was extremely professional" and became very excited about her music. She soon signed to do an LP for Rounder and to play at the prestigious Newport Folk Festival. Irwin remembered, "We had never even heard her in person before we signed her. That's *extremely* unusual. In fact, it just about flies in the face of all rationality!"[42]

Late in 1986, Krauss (15) signed with Rounder and recorded the album "Too Late to Cry,"[43] produced by Ken Irwin. Released in 1987 soon after she was seventeen, the album did well but not exceptionally so. Soon she began working with Jeff White (guitar). Alison took part in the Masters of the Folk Violin tour sponsored by the National Council for the Traditional Arts.

The blucgrass world was still slow to appreciate women vocalists—especially one so young and with no bluegrass pedigree yet. There were still many holdouts who insisted that women couldn't sing bluegrass. But about that time, IBMA began to be an influential factor in bluegrass and began giving significant exposure to women in bluegrass. By the time that her second LP ("Two Highways") won a Grammy nomination, some

Alison Krauss and Union Station, 1990. L to R: Adam Steffey, Barry Bales, Alison Krauss, Alison Brown, Tim Stafford.

real momentum was building. The 1991 Grammy award ("I've Got That Old Feeling") pushed her importance in the bluegrass community still further. And because the band was able to cross over to other music charts, Krauss is often given credit for doing the most in recent years to raise bluegrass music to the forefront of the outside world.

By this time, she had established her style and become very good at it. But she wanted "to learn why things work" so she enrolled into the University of Illinois School of Music. By 1988, she was a fully-developed and skilled fiddler. She no longer made an effort to "listen to [other fiddle players] and learn licks anymore. I used to do that. I'll try to take something that someone else does and apply it. But I don't try and sound like someone else because then they will say that she's trying to sound like so-and-so."[44]

In October 1988, members of **Alison Krauss and Union Station** were Krauss (fiddle), Mike Harman (banjo, emcee), Jeff White (guitar) and John Pennell[45] (electric guitar). For their "Two Highways" album they added Jerry Douglas on resonator guitar and Brent Truitt, mandolin. The album received a Grammy nomination.

Members of **Alison Krauss and Union Station** in 1990 included Krauss (fiddle), Alison Brown[46] (banjo) and three former members of **Dusty Miller**: Adam Steffey (mandolin), Tim Stafford (guitar) and Barry Bales (bass).

Krauss was featured in *Rolling Stone* magazine in October 1990, probably because of her new video, "I've Got That Old Feeling." According to *USA Today*, "'I've Got That Old Feeling' is as 'cutting edge' as anything around. Krauss' incredibly nimble, clear voice—recalling a young Dolly Parton—and soulful fiddle convey a passion and vitality that will surprise anybody who

---

[42]Jack Tottle, "Alison Krauss and Union Station," *Bluegrass Unlimited*, May, 1991, p. 23. Ken Irwin had actually seen her earlier at a SPBGMA contest but didn't realize her potential at that time so he didn't pay any attention to her at that time.

[43] "Too Late to Cry" included musicians Sam Bush, Russ Barenberg, Roy Huskey Jr., Jerry Douglas, Tony Trischka, John Schmaltz and Lonnie Meeker.

[44]Rick Kubetz, "Union Station," *Bluegrass Unlimited*, October, 1988, p. 58.

[45] As of 1996, Pennell lived in Franklin, TN, and played in a band led by Chris Jones. He also taught guitar and bass on a part-time basis. He writes songs so that people can recognize who wrote them. He says that is the mark of a good songwriter—song writer identification. Mike Harman won the Colorado State Championship in 1985 and soon got a job with the Harman Family Band and the Sally Mountain Show. Jeff White was twice the Indiana State Flatpicking Champion and has his own solo CD.

[46] Alison Brown was from the San Francisco Bay Area where she played with Heartland in a duo with her husband, and earlier with Stuart Duncan, John Hickman and Larry Bulaich in Gold Rush. While in college in Massachusetts, she played banjo with Northern Lights. She went on to record several solo banjo projects.

expects bluegrass to drone. This is one of the few albums bound to please anyone."[47] The project received a Grammy award. The video went to #1 nationally. It was voted Album of the Year at IBMA in 1991 as was her "Every Time You Say Good-bye" in 1993.

Author Jack Tottle wrote of Krauss that "Alison's voice has a wonderful clarity and precision which appeals to a broad range of listeners. Her instrumental work is not only technically excellent, it is also beautifully creative and exciting even to someone who has listened to decades of the great bluegrass fiddlers."[48] She received IBMA's award for Female Vocalist of the Year in 1990, 1991, 1993 and 1995 and SPBGMA's Female Vocalist of the Year.

In late 1991, Ron Block joined on banjo and guitar when Alison Brown left. Members were now Krauss (fiddle), Tim Stafford (guitar), Block (banjo, guitar) and Barry Bales (bass). Stafford quit his job at East Tennessee State University in 1992 to tour full-time. He was replaced by Dan Tyminski, formerly of the **Lonesome River Band**. By 1995, Stafford led **Blue Highway**.

The promotion of Alison Krauss is steered by Alison said Rounder's Ken Irwin. She has the potential, and has had the offers, to go pop country but chooses to be at the top of the bluegrass field instead of being an "also ran" in country music. Besides that, she would have to adapt her music to electric basses, lap steels and the other instruments which characterizes country music. She would have to change her music all around to try and fit into the mold. She chooses not to do so. If one recalls the switch from bluegrass to pop country by Ricky Skaggs, Skaggs seems to have gotten lost in the fold. According to Ken Irwin, "Alison has brought more attention to bluegrass than Ricky Skaggs ever has in ten years. And Alison has done it in much less time than that."[49] Her group won IBMA Entertainer of the Year in 1991 and 1995. At the 1995 Country Music Awards ceremony she won Female Vocalist of the Year, the Horizon Award, Single of the Year ("When You Say Nothing at All") and Recorded Event of the Year ("Somewhere in the Vicinity of the Heart" with **Shenandoah**). She was the first from an independent label to win a CMA award in 27 years, according to *USA Today*. Her 1994 Rounder CD 0325 "Now That I've Found You—A Collection" sold over one million copies (platinum) within a year and became the first bluegrass album to do so. It crossed-over to the country music field and brought unprecedented independent label sales as a result. *Time* picked the recording as the #2 album of 1995 (#1 was by **Smashing Pumpkins**; #3 was by Bruce Springsteen).

[47]Tottle, op. cit., p. 20.
[48]Ibid., p. 20.
[49]From a July 27, 1994, telephone conversation with Mr. Irwin.

Regional Bluegrass - Table of Contents

Regional Bluegrass

While bluegrass music in its raw and original form may be said to have originated in the deep South, it didn't stay there. Bluegrass enthusiasts all over the nation listened to records, learned to play it, and came up with their own "slant" on bluegrass. While in certain parts of the country there is a jazz influence, in others there is a concentration on keeping it traditional. In still others there seems to be an emphasis on instrumental technique or vocal harmonies. In any case, the music takes on the influences of the local people playing it.

John Hartford on the origins of bluegrass

In a 1992 telephone interview, John Hartford spoke about his opinions of the origins of bluegrass music. He indicated that if he were to speak on the subject it might conflict with the personal relationship he has with all of the pioneers of this music. But he added, "I'll tell you this: it all comes out of old-time fiddling—a lot of it—and old-time music is older than classical music. It goes way back to bagpipe melodies. We're talking about a music that predates Bach and Mozart and those people. All this music comes from Scotch-Irish."

John Hartford

Hartford also feels that 1922 (when Eck Robertson recorded what is generally accepted as the first country music record: a fiddle tune) was not necessarily the first year that fiddle tunes were put on wax. "There were fiddle tunes being cut on records back in the teens. I think they started recording in 1890, but they wouldn't necessarily be called 'country' music. You have to remember that there's a time in any kind of music when it's not called what it is ... because there is a time when bluegrass music was not called 'bluegrass.'

"And the same goes for country music. And a lot of the music that bluegrass comes from was played in the cities. Chicago had a tremendous Irish fiddling convention. And New York still does this. Irish players are getting off the boat every day and live in Brooklyn. Brooklyn, New York, has one of the largest enclaves of Irish/old-time fiddling in the entire country and they are all isolated up there in the hills and hollows of Brooklyn just like they were in the Appalachians. In other words, the path of the fiddle coming from Ireland and Scotland to this country, and then coming down the Ohio Valley, isn't something that happened in the early days; it's still going on. That river of music has never stopped.

"We were touring New York State last year and we started looking on the map and all these Irish names of all these towns and everything like that, and Irish restaurants along the highway, and we'd pull in there. Here there were signs in Gaelic and records on the jukebox of fiddle tunes played by Irish bands. You just lop off a couple of the ornaments and turn a few of them around and you've got, basically, what *we* play. They have a tendency to use a few more accordions and things than we do, and you won't hear any five-string banjo picking, but you *will* hear the music. And the timing and phrasing is there, too. You take Irish fiddling, lop off some of the ornaments of it, and you can get closer to the old-time phrasing than you can about any way else. Basically, an Irish lilt is a swing. A lot of Irish lilt is five-string banjo picking—what gives it that drive."[1]

The geographical center of bluegrass origins

The tri-cities area of Bristol, Johnson City, and Kingsport, Tennessee, may not be *the* place bluegrass originated, but certainly it was nurtured there. Within about one hundred miles of the three cities were born

"Brooklyn, New York, has one of the largest enclaves of Irish/old-time fiddling in the entire country and they are all isolated up there in the hills and hollows of Brooklyn just like they were in the Appalachians." —John Hartford

[1] Telephone interview, March 18, 1992.

such bluegrass and traditional country performers such as Ralph and Stanley Carter, Earl Scruggs, Red Rector, Jim and Jesse McReynolds, Bob and Sonny Osborne, Don Reno, Snuffy Jenkins, Red Smiley, the Carter family, Jim Eanes, Jimmy Martin, Wiley and Zeke Morris, Bill and Earl Bolick, Carl Story, Melvin and Ray Goins, Doyle Lawson, Kenny Baker, Ricky Skaggs, Paul Mullins, Roy Acuff, Dolly Parton, Chet Atkins, Carl and J.P. Sauceman, Raymond Fairchild, Ernest and Hattie Stoneman, Billy Baker, Tater Tate, Benny Sims, Ralph

Eric Weissberg and Bill Clifton, c. 1964

Mayo, Porter Church, Jethro Burns, Ernie Ford, George Shuffler, Bill Napier, Jack Cooke, Mark Pruett, Bobby and Dallas Smith and Tommy Jarrell. They all came from places such as Flint Hill, Pike County, Clinch Mountain, Roane County and Cumberland Gap.

This region was filled with back porch picking on Saturday nights; it seems that the main form of family entertainment in the area was playing music with friends. Nearly everyone played an instrument. They played the music they grew up with and loved. It was pure, simple and wholesome. WCYB's Farm and Fun Time (Bristol) was powerful and came in clear to their homes, helping to perpetuate their music even further when touring bands made the radio station their home. WNOX, a couple hundred miles away with its Mid-Day Merry-Go-Round, was also strong enough to reach these folks and played this music as well.

The music was good and was predominant in the area, even through the Elvis era. Even today the music's roots are strong there. Ralph Stanley's recent recording project of Grayson and Whitter songs shows just one person's love of the music he grew up with.

There one can visit the Music Department and its Center for Appalachian Studies and Services. Jack Tottle, mandolinist/historian/educator, has directed ETSU's Bluegrass and Country Music Program since 1982. Guitarist Tim Stafford, also from the area and with **Blue Highway** as of 1997, also taught music classes there. Courses include instruction on all bluegrass music instruments, and bluegrass and country music history.

Don Owens, XERF, and bluegrass in the nation's Capitol

According to author H. Conway Gandy, Don Owens "is probably *the* person most responsible for the popularity of bluegrass in the Washington, D.C., area where bluegrass sprouted, took root, and grew into what it is today."[2]

Owens was a deejay on various radio stations in the area including "Radio Rodeo" (pronounced Row-day-oh) on Connie B. Gay's WGAY about 1950. He played the country music of the day including Doc Williams, Jimmie Rodgers, Hank Snow and Ernest Tubb. He was an accomplished musician, having played bass in the **Blue Mountain Boys**[3]. He also made several recordings during his music career. He was manager for several bands including Jim Eanes, and the **Blue Grass Champs**. He booked Patsy Cline in the Washington area.

In the mid-'50s, Owens moved to XERF, Del Rio, Texas, to spin records on that station where his music reached the entire southern part of the nation. The station was operated just across the border in Mexico to avoid the FCC licensing restrictions of the United States which limited AM radio stations to 50,000 watts. Some of these X-stations may have used up to half a million watts of power and reached into Canada at night and even further occasionally. The **Carter Family**

Don Owens. Photo courtesy Jim Clark.

2 H. Conway Gandy, "Don Owens," *Bluegrass Unlimited*, November, 1987, p. 68.

3 With Curly Smith (fiddle), Charlie Fetzer (Dobro) and Perry Westland (guitar).

gained considerable exposure there (1938 to 1942). The station paid its bills by operating a mail-order business for various products. Record spinner Wolfman Jack (Robert Smith) made as much as $30,000 a month plying his trade and selling his advertisers' products. He gained even more popularity after he appeared in "American Graffiti," a George Lucas film.

A change in the late-night format at the station led to Owens move back to Washington to work on WARL, Arlington, Virginia. There he learned salesmanship. He could "sell ice boxes to Eskimos" over the radio. WARL was the station where Connie B. Gay gained fame as announcer and deejay. WARL was probably the first station to program one hundred percent country music. After Owens became well-known on the radio, he began producing live concerts with bluegrass and country acts. Shows included a summer moonlight cruise down the Potomac River on a cruise line.

During the late '50s, Owens became one of the first people to begin the term "bluegrass" to define a certain type of music that he programmed on his radio shows. He hosted the "Don Owens Jamboree" on WTTG-TV from 1957 to 1960 in Raleigh, North Carolina.

Owens died April 21, 1963, after an auto accident at age thirty-two.

Washington, D.C.— a hotbed of bluegrass activity

Another one of the reasons that the nation's Capitol was a center for bluegrass music is because of the bars which served as venues for it: the Shamrock in Georgetown was home to the **Country Gentlemen**; in the late '60s, the Red Fox Inn in Bethesda was the home for **Cliff Waldron and the New Shades of Grass**; and in the '70s, the Red Fox Inn was home to the **Seldom Scene** until they moved to the Birchmere.

Buzz Busby and the Bayou Boys. L to R: Buzz Busby, John Hall, Pete Pike, Don Stover, Donnie Bryant. Seated: Connie B. Gay.

And *Bluegrass Unlimited* magazine was close by; its mere existence in the late sixties proved that bluegrass was expanding in the area.

When Eddie Adcock joined the **Country Gentlemen** in 1958, there were a few bands in the Washington, D.C., area: the **Country Gentlemen**, **Buzz Busby and the Bayou Boys**, **Benny and Vallie Cain and the Country Clan**, the **Stonemans**. These bands were significant factors in making the capitol city the hotbed for bluegrass that it is today. As of 1975, there were thirty bluegrass groups in the area. According to Adcock, "The bluegrass music that people are listening to today did not come from Kentucky—it came from the rolling hills of Washington, D.C.. Here's Bill Monroe sounding a certain way in 1957, and now listen to one of his releases today. Bill Monroe and Ralph Stanley stayed the farthest away from the **Gentlemen** sound of anybody, and damned if they don't sound a little bit like them. Listen to them—you can tell."

While John Duffey was a member of the **Seldom Scene** about 1980, he was asked if he ever considered joining the Grand Ole Opry. He smiled and gloated, "I remember several years ago some of the officials of the Opry came to where we were playing in Bethesda. They said, 'We certainly would like to have you on the Opry.' And it just tickled me to death to say, 'We don't need it.' There was a time when we would have shined their shoes for them to be a part of that sort of thing. But then, with the success we were having with the **Scene**, who needs to move to Nashville? There's more work in Washington."[4]

Duffey, who was born and raised in the area, spoke about the growth of the substantial bluegrass audience in the Washington area, "The music's been on the radio around here since about 1946. It was the Appalachian influx that first brought it here since so many people migrated here during and after the Second World War. Everybody was looking for a job."

By the mid-'80s, one listener-supported FM station which played many hours of bluegrass daily was WAMU in the Washington area. A survey of their listeners found that while fifteen percent of the programming was bluegrass music, forty-three percent of the money pledged to the station was for bluegrass music. Dick Spottswood had his Dick Spottswood Hour. He convinced the station to air forty hours of bluegrass a week. His history with the station goes back to 1966 where his program called Bluegrass Unlimited ran for seven years. Later on, other deejays on the station gained their own personal fame there, one of which was Eddie Stubbs who was the fiddler with the **Johnson Mountain Boys**. Stubbs, in the spring of 1995, took over a vacant announcer spot on the Grand Ole Opry. He continued his Eddie Stubbs Show from his new home in Nashville.

4 Dix Bruce, "John Duffey Interview," *Mandolin World News*, Vol VI, #II, Summer, 1981, p. 10.

Promoter Ray Davis

The promotion of bluegrass music is one of the key ingredients to the continuance of bluegrass music today. Without the promoters, the music would not be nearly as popular today as it is. Ray Davis is an important promoter who has spent more than twenty-five years bringing bluegrass to the Baltimore area, and continues doing so into the 1990s. His sponsor was usually Johnny's Auto Sales.

Davis began his career in 1948 when, at fifteen, he sang bluegrass on WDOV, Dover, Delaware; he also emceed on the pop radio station. In 1950, he emceed at Baltimore's Old Hippodrome. In 1954, Davis joined XERF for a year in Del Rio, Texas/Villa Acuna, Mexico, and frequently transmitted at 150,000 watts—strong enough to interfere with a local cable television station which complained to the Federal Communications Commission. The FCC investigated, but the over-powering signal continued.

Back in Washington, Davis featured many of the same records played by other radio stations. In 1962, Davis began producing his own records under the Wango label. His first record featured Clyde Moody on the twelve-string guitar. He later produced the **Stanley Brothers**, Don Reno, Red Smiley, Bill Harrell and Charlie Moore. In 1975, Davis promoted concerts for artists including Larry Sparks, Del McCoury, Ted Lundy, Jimmy Martin and Reno and Harrell's band. Said Davis, "We've promoted a lot of shows and the only ones that never lost money were bluegrass. Maybe I'm an outlaw and do it because everyone says you can't make a living doing it but I've done it. I've been working close, but I've lived."[5]

The tri-cities area of Bristol, Johnson City, and Kingsport, Tennessee, may not the place bluegrass originated, but certainly it was nurtured there.

Benny and Vallie Cain and the Country Clan of the Washington area

This husband and wife team began their first band in 1949. This band was not bluegrass initially, but soon after they heard the bluegrass sound of Toby Stroud's **Blue Mountain Boys** which was playing on WWVA, they changed their music toward bluegrass.

Benny and Vallie Cain. Photo courtesy Jim Clark.

In 1950, Benny and Vallie Cain moved to the Washington, D.C., area where they formed a bluegrass band.[6] The new band played at WINC and was sponsored by a chain of jewelry stores.[7]

The Cains changed the band name from **Country Cousins** to **Country Clan** in 1953. They played on WGAY, Silver Spring, Maryland, and sent a weekly tape back to WINC. Donnie Bryant joined on banjo. When Bryant left, Pete (Roberts) Kuykendall took his place in 1956 for a couple of years. Scott Stoneman was on fiddle with the band. At various times, other band members included bassist Tom Gray, fiddler Art Wooten, and banjoists Don Stover, Bill Emerson, Billy Wheeler and Johnnie Whisnant. They were a very active band in the Washington area and helped establish its reputation as a center for bluegrass music. The bluegrass style of the **Country Clan** used the songs of the **Blue Sky Boys**, **Delmore Brothers**, and the **Monroe Brothers**. They used their own distinctive harmony.

The **Country Clan** performed for Congress on Capitol Hill in June of 1967. They were the first band to play for this traditional affair which precedes the annual baseball game between the Democrats and the Republicans.

[5] Quotation from a June issue of *Bluegrass Unlimited* magazine, year unknown.

[6] With Richard Peters (banjo) and Larry Leahy (bass, Leahy would later be in the car crash which led to the formation of the Country Gentlemen in 1957). Occasionally, Patsy Cline, trying to get a start in her style of commercial music, sang with the Cains on the station, but not on the bluegrass numbers with the band. The Cains insisted she join Sammy Moss and the Blue Mountain Boys in Berkeley Springs.

[7] This chain, the Jewel Box, was also sponsoring Dinah Shore down South.

America's Music | Bluegrass

Benny Cain became an authority on stringed instruments—especially vintage Gibson mandolins. He has a complete list of model, serial numbers, date, condition and owner. The list is sometimes consulted during insurance claims.

The importance of New York City on bluegrass

Bob Applebaum, a master mandolinist now in the Los Angeles area, grew up in the New York area during the 1950s and '60s which was an era of infancy for the New York City bluegrass scene. This was the period when Frank Wakefield, John Herald, David Grisman, Andy Statman, Eric Weissberg, Peter Wernick, Roger Sprung, Tony Trischka and others[8] were all active.

He remembered what it was like to play bluegrass in "The Big Apple." In a 1992 interview he explained that the importance of New York City in the history of bluegrass cannot be overestimated. "In the early '60s there was a bluegrass scene," he said. "There were already players in the area like Eric Weissberg, and he had come out of quasi-bluegrass folk bands like the **Tarriers** which included Marshall Brickman. Weissberg was playing banjo in the area at the time. Roger Sprung was in the area and I remember a whole bunch of us going out and buying his first album because there was this guitar player, Doc Watson, who *really* played bluegrass guitar and played leads. And I think that first Roger Sprung album had a profound effect on a lot of players in terms of increasing interest in the area.

"If you look, today, at the music and you look at figures who are very prominent in the bluegrass world in 1992, names that have made major impacts like Bela Fleck, Tony Trischka, or Pete Wernick or David Grisman or players like Jody Stecher who was here today[9], Barry Mitterhoff, Mark Schatz. We're talking about New Yorkers. Those people have made prominent—not controlling, prominent—contributions to the popularization and to the direction of the music. Certainly one has to appreciate that when the head of the IBMA is a Columbia University doctorate who played music and learned in and around Washington Square and Greenwich Village. The place of New York City in bluegrass music has to be considered, I think.

"In the early sixties—and the tradition is pretty much unchanged today—on Sunday, mostly in the spring and summer, musicians and interested people would gather around the fountain in Washington Square in Greenwich Village and they would play. And I would take the bus from Newark, which is as close to New York City as any of the boroughs—it's forty-five minutes—and there you would see Bill Keith and David Grisman and Jody Stecher and Eric Weissberg and they

were playing this music and generating an excitement. And it was part of a very vibrant New York bluegrass scene. Besides people like Eric Weissberg, there were two principal bluegrass players in those years: Winnie Winston who went on to be known as a pedal steel player, and Steve Arkin, who played with Monroe for a while.

Roger Sprung

"There was an enormous amount of experimentation in the sixties influenced by the American contemporary jazz scene in New York. One of the most exciting bands in the area at the time was **Breakfast Special**. Andy Statman, undoubtedly one of the most creative and brilliant mandolin players—eccentric at times, but quite capable of playing extraordinarily accurate and exciting Monroe style. And he knows the music. Stacy Phillips (who wrote a book on bluegrass resonator guitar playing) innovated on the resonator guitar which pre-staged what Jerry Douglas would do later. Tony Trischka was on banjo. Kenny Kosek, who played very 'outside' fiddle—here was a band that was taking traditional bluegrass, and they were quite capable of sounding like the hottest bluegrass band twenty years ahead of its time, and then going off into harmonic and rhythmic directions. They worked with a drummer named Richard Crooks. It would be dynamic, exciting and challenging in 1990—and they were doing it in late 1960s and early 1970s! You can hear some of the concepts of this if you

How to play the 5-string Banjo by Pete Seeger

Third Edition Revised · 1962

[8] Including Gene Lowinger, Steve Arkin, Kenny Kosek and Jody Stecher.
[9] IBMA's World of Bluegrass, September, 1992, Owensboro, Kentucky.

listen to Tony Trischka's 'Heartland' album. You can get some sense of the intensely dynamic experimental range that these guys went into. It's out of that context that Bela Fleck learns, being influenced inevitably by Tony Trischka, Pete Wernick, Marty Cutler—who I feel is the earliest banjo player to really look into fusion jazz and adapt the banjo to that.

"Now the **Greenbriar Boys**, who recorded on Vanguard Records in those years, had Eric Weissberg in the band originally and was replaced by Bob Yellin—if my history is correct—there was Ralph Rinzler who went on to the Smithsonian. And his work at the Smithsonian was very instrumental—pardon the pun—in building the reputation of Bill Monroe in the artistic world...in the professional world. The **Greenbriar Boys** functioned similar to the way that the **Dillards** helped popularize bluegrass on the West Coast. It became the focus of the urban scene. The **Greenbriar Boys** were one of the centers of the music in the New York City area. When Ralph Rinzler left the **Greenbriar Boys**, he was replaced by Frank Wakefield.

"My earliest recollection of Frank Wakefield is his coming to New York with the **Greenbriar Boys**. Now, Frank is from Tennessee and he came from his associations with Red Allen [and the **Kentuckians**] in the Ohio area. In that same time period, David Grisman and a group of players who come from Jewish ethnic backgrounds—Andy Statman, Grisman, Mitterhoff, and myself and I'm sure many others—well, here's David Grisman becoming associated with Red Allen; Frank Wakefield coming from New York and being associated with the **Greenbriar Boys**. And so you're starting to get very clear open lines of communications between these different cultures: urban, rural, educated, and it pre-stages what we are seeing here today [at this meeting of IBMA]. It's a wonderful thing. We're seeing people from all these different walks of life and different regions and different ethnic heritages beginning to exchange this music very regularly. And I can remember, with my AM radio if the cloud cover was good, I could get WWVA in New Jersey. And the thrill of hearing Red Allen live, and hearing David Grisman playing with Red Allen. This was a very exciting period.

"Those dynamics, I really believe, have had a significant contribution to the shape of bluegrass music in general and even organizations like this. It's not accidental that someone who is a very hard-working academic who knows about organization, who knows how to write, knows how to communicate, and has a profound love and respect for the people and the traditions of the music would come to become the President of the organization. A city kid!"

Bela Fleck—
"There's not a lot of demand for banjo players in New York City."

In an interview on the "USA Today" television show in May 1989, Bela Fleck was asked about his banjo playing in New York City. "There is not a lot of demand for banjo players in New York City," he replied. "That's why I had to leave. But at least it was different than what everyone else was doing. I think I made a lot of friends over a long period of time with it but, at first, I got a little bit of flack from guys from New York—it seemed stupid to them. But I was real serious about it. They were going to take my lunch money and knock me in the gutter...so none of them broke my banjo anyway."

Eric Weissberg

Photo courtesy Eric Weissberg.

Eric Weissberg—
"Dueling Banjos" and more. The early New York bluegrass scene.

Eric Weissberg was born in the lower east side of New York City August 16, 1939. There he grew up and went to the Little Red Schoolhouse in Greenwich Village where he met Pete Seeger and started following Seeger's banjo technique about 1947. His father bought him his first guitar and banjo.

At that time, Seeger was living on McDougal Street. On Saturday mornings he used to have little shindigs for kids which he called "Wing Dings." Weissberg's mother would drop him off there about nine and pick him up at noon. Lead Belly was there. Woody (Guthrie) would come, Cisco Houston, too. Weissberg explained in a 1993 telephone interview, "When Pete (Seeger) was writing his first banjo instruction manual, he realized that he had never actually taught anybody how to play, so he developed the notion of having six or eight

America's Music — Bluegrass

people come once a week and have a group lesson. There he could impart what he knew so he could see how it would work teaching. I was lucky enough to be one of those people. I was somewhere around eight or nine then. I used to go to camp in the Catskills near Woodstock where I live now. He used to come there also. So I would see him all the time."

Weissberg began playing three-finger bluegrass banjo after he heard Earl Scruggs on a record in 1951. After that, he became a regular at New York City's Sunday meeting place for bluegrassers: Washington Square. Roger Sprung was there on banjo. And so was Willie Dykeman. Dykeman, from Summit, New Jersey, came every Sunday in addition to accompanying some square dancers on 35th Street. "He had lights inside," said Weissberg. "This was pre-plastic head era. So to keep the tension on the head—keep the head dried out—he put Christmas lights inside. The red and green lights made it dry out in damp weather. But he was a pretty good player! Willie Dykeman was the first guy, I think, that I actually saw do the pegs thing. He didn't have Scruggs tuners; he just tuned the strings. And I hadn't even heard Earl do it yet. He was doin' it in the Square. The first I ever saw play it—close up—was Mike Steig, son of William Steig, the cartoonist—and we were playing together in an assembly or something in junior high school. He played it right in my ear. I was playing the fiddle. I was about eleven or twelve. The banjo was like, level with my ear. And he was doin' this picking in my ear. And I had only heard—up until that time—Pete Seeger's style, which was strumming, basically. So, I was freaking out through the whole thing. Well, he never did actually show me anything. I had to get his girlfriend to show me what he was doing. She told me what the basics of it were. So I never did actually see him do it because he was behind me. But Willie Dykeman was a good banjo player. He is important because he was one of *the* bluegrass guys—and there was only three of us then in about 1951: Willie, Roger Sprung and me." By 1954, Weissberg played the Scruggs style well enough to audition on banjo and to be accepted to the New York High School of Music and Art as a bass major. He did some recording during this period and graduated in 1957.

"And then later in the '50s, Marshall (Brickman) was already at the University of Wisconsin (1957)—he had skipped a year. I was graduating high school and I wanted to go there so I went up there and we roomed together there with another banjo player. It was there that John Herald came up to me and introduced himself because he remembered me from Washington Square. I

"We're seeing people from all these different walks of life and different regions and different ethnic heritages beginning to exchange this music very regularly." —Bob Applebaum

didn't remember him. He wasn't playing any instrument then. We both (Weissberg and Herald) left Wisconsin after one year and we both came back to New York and formed the **Greenbriar Boys** with Bob Yellin in 1958."

By 1959, Weissberg was playing publicly on a regular basis. Among the people to hear this style for the first time—close up—was Bill Keith who had been playing tenor and classical banjo styles until this point.[10] From this point, Keith switched to a bluegrass banjo.

"Then at Wisconsin I was a music/bass major," continued Weissman. "I came back and figured out that I was going to become a symphonic bass player so I wanted to go to Juilliard and study with my teacher— which I did. Then in December of '59, Pete [Seeger] left the **Weavers**. The **Tarriers** were playing at the Village Gate on a bill with Leon Bibb. Eric Darling replaced Pete in the **Weavers**, and he had to leave the **Tarriers** right in the middle of a three-week gig. So Leon, with whom I'd played bass that summer at the Newport Folk Festival, suggested to Bob and Clarence that I fill out their trio as bass player. A few days went by and they discovered that I also played both the banjo and the guitar. This was Bob Carey and Clarence Cooper at the time. By the end of that three-week gig they asked me to join the group. I finished out that semester and joined them and we started touring everywhere."

In 1961, Weissberg and Marshall Brickman[11] heard Bill Keith at Charlie Rothchild's apartment play his melodic style which he had highly developed in the ensuing years. Weissberg and Brickman then went out and developed this style also, and soon recorded "Folk Banjo Styles" which came out on Elektra. On this LP they performed "Devil's Dream" in the melodic style.

Weissberg recalled that his playing included up to eight scale notes in a row in the melodic style before he first heard Bill Keith do his melodic picking. But this was for embellishment and was not of the same caliber that Keith soon developed. When Keith began performing his melodic picking, it was used in whole songs and very much more complex than Weissberg had done up to that point. So, by early 1963, Elektra released Weissberg and Brickman's "New Dimensions in Blue-

---

[10] This date according to Eric Weissberg in a January 1993 interview. This is different than the 1957 date which Bill Keith remembers, which was about when Keith bought Pete Seeger's banjo book and began learning the three-finger banjo style. According to Weissberg though, he recalled that Bill Keith told him that it was on a beach that he first heard the style. Weissberg remembered that he first met Bill Keith at the 1959 Newport Folk Festival. He recalled that Bill Keith, up to that point, was studying and playing the styles of classical banjoists such as Billy Faier, Paul Cadwell, Fred Van Eps and those who played intricate, classical tunes using the three-finger style which incorporated a note-for-note type of playing.

[11] In the summer of 1962, Marshall Brickman joined the Tarriers. He had graduated from the U. of Wisconsin as a music major and was planning to return to New York City and go to Juilliard. He later became a comedy writer for television and a movie director.

grass" LP with musicians Weissberg (banjo, mandolin, guitar), Brickman (banjo, guitar), Gordon Terry (fiddle) and Clarence White (guitar).

"When the folk craze started petering out around '65 or around there," continued Weissberg, "we did a tour in Russia with Judy Collins and it just sort of trickled down.[12] We disbanded and I went on the road with Judy as her accompanist for a year and a half and then I said that I'd done enough touring and that I wanted to stay in New York and be a studio guy. So I just did. I started doing studio work exclusively in about '67. And basically that's what I've been doing since then. Since then I guess I've done between eight and ten thousand sessions plus all the other stuff I've played with the Metropolitan Opera and all different kinds of things."

Weissberg became famous for the soundtrack of the movie "Deliverance." He played banjo and Steve Mandell played guitar. He spoke of how he got that job, "Oddly enough, the 'Dueling Banjo' thing was also interconnected with Bill Keith. He actually got the first call for it but he was in Europe at the time on a concert tour and he couldn't come back because it was only supposed to be for that one scene—the first scene at the gas station. So he suggested that I be called. So I got called for it and, of course, it turned into what it turned into. He's actually a little uptight about it although we do it in our show. He's not really mad at me about it, just at how unlucky the timing was for him. Bill and I are good friends and it's really nothing personal between us. We have re-formed the **Blue Velvet Band** and call it the **New Blue Velvet Band**."

"I'm still doing studio work and, since 1992, I have been playing guitar for Art Garfunkel when he tours, and with Tom Paxton, and as a solo, singing and picking."

The Nashville scene[13]

Charmaine Lanham, a resident of the Nashville bluegrass scene since the early 1970s, spoke of the regional and geographic characteristics of Nashville. She told this writer in a 1993 interview, "Bluegrass is a geographical music in a lot of ways. We could say that it came from the mountains, but it's more than just mountain music. It's mountain music and Bill Monroe and black blues and black dancing and old-timey fiddle tunes and that sort of thing.

"I think until the last ten years, the geographic differences in the music were real important. And now, of course, they have associations all over the country which are working together to make a big umbrella of bluegrass which would mean that different groups of

people will be coming together and learning from each other. The rhythm will probably will be shared and the tunes will be shared and it will probably tend to have vast regional differences. But up until maybe the middle '80s, all the regions of the country were real distinct in their groups.

"There's a real powerful group in Washington, D.C., that later became the IBMA group that's in Kentucky now. On the West Coast there was the northern California scene and the southern California scene and the New York scene. These were all different—real different. And then there was the South where the music is just part of the culture—it really is. It's not a scene as much as it is a way of life. It's a language understood in the South. That makes the South unique.

"We've got two scenes here in Nashville: We've got the bluegrass Opry stars and the bluegrass community. And [the Opry stars are] part of the community, but they're also part of their own community of Opry people that really overlaps very little.

"The tie-in that I know about is the West Coast in northern California and how the bluegrass clubs in Nashville got started. So that's my particular reference.

"I guess Bob and Ingrid Fowler (**Styx River Ferry**) were the instigators of the bluegrass music scene in San Francisco.[14] They talked Paul Lampert, of Paul's Saloon, into doing bluegrass there. And by the time it ended up, it had a two-decade run as a bluegrass club which, under one format, is a lot for any kind of night club. Bob and Ingrid played there and started bluegrass there and my husband (Marty Lanham) played banjo with them from 1970 to 1972 when they left San Francisco and we all came back here (to Nashville) and we continued playing music—not as the **Styx River Ferry**. But what happened was we—from the West Coast, which was myself, Marty, Bob and Ingrid and Roland White—we got together with Red and Birdy Smith and Jim Bornstein and we started the Station Inn here.

"Roland (White) wasn't one of the original owners. The actual ownership of the club was Bob Fowler, Marty Lanham, Red Smith and Jim Bornstein. Me and Birdy and Roland were the unofficial break-our-back helpers with whatever-was-happening type of guys. Roland was one of the energy people—he did as much work as anybody and he gathered the musicians and he did everything

12 I think Mr. Weissberg meant "lost its energy."

13 From an interview with Charmaine Lanham in Nashville April 17, 1993. The interview has been truncated for brevity and applicability to the subject of bluegrass as a regional music.

14 Actually, the origins of bluegrass music in this area goes back even earlier. But her statement serves as frame of reference for the rest of the story.

America's Music — Bluegrass

from mop the floor to run the jams. He and Marty and Bob Fowler instigated the jam sessions. Bob was a genius for getting musicians together.

"Well, this diverse crowd got together from the old Dusty Roads Tavern which was a place where they played country music—you go in there and jam—and it was near the Salvation Army so you'd have all the Salvation Army...we called them the 'Sally Anne's'...they were the ones drying out from the alcohol. They come in there and get a quart of Sterling Beer and listen to the music. And the music was any-body who happened to stumble in. They had these old guitars with linoleum tops and bad, old strings. And Bobby and Evelyn Green would let the country pickers come in there and they picked those old guitars. There was just a bunch of really bad music one night and then the next night you might see everybody from the Grand Ole Opry. You might see Paul Warren and Roland White. A bunch of them would come in there and park in the back so Lester Flatt wouldn't go by and see that they were at a nightclub and playing music 'cause he didn't allow that. And that was their bluegrass night. And another night there would be some real country stars come in there, but we never mixed bluegrass and country nights. You never played bluegrass on a country music night. Of course, you had everybody, from those who would come in there and bang on those old, dead linoleum guitars that were never guitars, to people like Benny Martin and Kenny Baker and Bob Fowler and Marty and all of them on Martin guitars and the best instruments in the world. And you'd go from seeing the best music to...it was pot luck, anything could happen there... One night I saw Benny Martin, Kenny Baker and Paul Warren triple-fiddling. I would have liked to have preserved that in stone but nobody had a tape recorder and nobody had a camera. I'm a photographer, and in those days we had just come to town and we were both working for Gruhn Guitars and I didn't have the money to be a photographer and get the film. We were just really scraping...

"So this was before the Station Inn, before the Bluegrass Inn, and this was the only place in town we had to play. So this group from California, Ingrid and Bob and Kim Young and Steve Young—the man who wrote 'Seven Bridges Road'—and Ed Dye and Bruce Nemerov, Pat Enright, Alan O'Bryant and Billy and Terry Smith (the Smith brothers), Mike Hartgrove of the **Bluegrass Cardinals**, who was at that time with Billy and Terry Smith. They were all kids. We had all this scene and no place to play. So when the Station Inn started, all these people rolled in from all over the country would come here to record and do things like that and want to go out and have fun and would come to the Station Inn. Bob always knew how to get people up on the stage and off and we'd have these great jam

sessions like when Vassar Clements and John McEuen would come in and jam or Kenny Baker or Bill Monroe.

"The Station Inn started in April 1974. This was two years after the Lanhams had come to town. Roland had been there probably a decade before that. This Dusty Roads [thing] had been going on for years and was the only place to go. And when the Opry was downtown it was just *the* place to be after hours. But then the Opry moved to Briley Parkway. It was the only place that you could just jam. We had the best jamming in the world in Nashville; we still have. There's not another city in the world that has jamming like we have.

"At the same time, Earl Snead started the Bluegrass Inn and he had a real successful place. His format was like having Jimmy Martin and the **Whites** and different bands. The longest band that worked for them was Hubert Davis (and the **Season Travelers**) and then Hubert and them took it over, but that was much later. When Hubert and Ruby took it over it was only Hubert and Ruby playing there for years and years. It was by Vanderbilt University and that's what kept them going.

"We've got two scenes here in Nashville: We've got the bluegrass Opry stars and the bluegrass community." —Charmaine Lanham

---

And after they moved they were never that successful. And by that time, Hubert was in ill health. But they really needed that collegiate crowd. So we had the two bluegrass clubs. The Station Inn's format was to have a house band, lots of guests and guest bands. It was successful—it's still successful.

"The old Station Inn that we started was in another location than it is now. But what has endured with the Station Inn is that the format is never changed. And that format is that it is a community center for the bluegrass people whoever comes through town, but also for whoever lives here. It's the place that we've all gathered.

"But Nashville is separate from Owensboro. It's separate from Washington, D.C.. It's no longer a part of the West Coast. In '83, when J.T. (Gray, owner) started having problems in the winter, we got to thinking if he can't keep it open what are we going to do to keep our community center? So we started the Nashville Bluegrass Music Association. And the purpose of it was that if we run out of a place to play music, we have a newsletter and a way to keep up with each other and we could go to the full moon parties which Ed Walker had until last year (1992).

"The Opry and the Musician's Union have conspired together to make it real rough for our community to do anything. For example, Vic Willis, of the Union, called me on the carpet when we started our association in 1983. We started it in this little dive called The Springwater. The guests were a *Who's Who* of Nashville bluegrass: Bela, Jerry, Marty Lanham, Roland White...all these wonderful people. Alan Munde was in town and was a guest and we had his name in the paper and Vic Willis called me up and he said, 'You can't do this! There's no contract!' I said this is a family thing. Nobody was making any money. 'Oh, well that's against union rules.' And I said that it's just a place families can get together, we can pick together. The children growing up can pick with the older ones and so forth. He kept telling us we can't do that. They fought us all the way. We've had to leave our functions out of the paper to keep them from buggin' us."

"I think the geographical differences are a great thing," continued Lanham. "At the same time, I think they can lead to a pulling apart. So it's all the way people want to do it.

"Roland White grew up in southern California playing bluegrass music from records and from old-time records and from Bill Monroe records, and it was after he was an adult that he came back to play with Bill Monroe. So you know that Roland's rhythm was a California influence coming back to play with, and soak up, that Bill Monroe influence. And I know Roland got a lot from Bill Monroe. But he *had* a lot when he got with Bill Monroe.

"At the very end of Clarence's life, he and Roland were going to get together. Roland was going to come from the Bill Monroe and **Flatt and Scruggs** influence. Clarence was going to come from the **Byrds** and recording with [Linda] Ronstadt and being in that studio scene with Herb Pedersen and all those people in L.A.. And they were gettin' together once again and bringin' all that bluegrass back and becoming a bluegrass band again as the **New Kentucky Colonels** and doin' what they started to do before Roland got drafted and he and Clarence went different ways.

"I think that Roland getting drafted was probably a tragedy for their music and family. It was probably just one of many events which were against them. I think that Herb Pedersen and Chris Hillman and that whole Berkeley scene had a huge influence as well. ...I think that without the California influence, the Station Inn

never would have started. And I think it's kept going by people from all over the country.

"We have a very close-knit community here in Nashville. And a lot of people come here and try to capture that and take it home to their town and have a community just like ours. I think that's what the international bluegrass community is trying to do and be. But it's only Nashville that does this and the only way that it can spread and go back out to the country is for it to be an open exchange of communities. It mustn't limit people like 'I'm from the Washington crowd and the only bands we recognize are the **Seldom Scene**, the **Country Gentlemen**, the **Bluegrass Cardinals**' and so on. It's a big family with lots of branches, and within the branches people love each other and step all over each others' toes and get mad at each other and all the branches might be doing the same thing collectively to each other.

Laurie Lewis and Kathy Kallick

"Nobody in this music is going to get terribly rich or famous. When I see the Joe Stuarts of this world—who was one of the finest bluegrass musicians who ever lived, and I'm not even sure how long anyone will even know his name—then I think that there's more to this than just stars and awards and everything else."

West Coast bluegrass styles versus East Coast styles

East Coast acceptance of a West Coast band comes slowly. In order to break into the eastern bluegrass scene, a touring West Coast band needs to make as much money as the East Coast headliners in order to make expenses. But in order to get to that point of acceptance, they'd need to "prostitute" themselves in many East Coast tours before it would begin to pay off.

One such band which accepted this challenge is Kathy Kallick's **Good Ol' Persons**[15] of the San Francisco Bay Area. Kallick and bassist Bethany Raine commented that "Back east I've actually been scolded for playing a song in the 'wrong' way. There's a rift between the coasts. Laurie Lewis has had to work really hard and spend a lot of time working the East Coast. She's a pioneer but it's still not easy. We have a much easier time playing in Europe than on the East Coast. The European audiences don't care that we were

[15] The band was founded by Kathy Kallick and Laurie Lewis back in 1975 when they added Sue Shelasky, Dorothy Baxter and Barbara Mendelsohn. The name was a takeoff from Frank Wakefield's Good Ol' Boys which played in the area at the time. The time was right for such a name because of the public's attention to words such as "chairperson" and "mail carrier." A few years later, the band evolved to Kallick (guitar), Paul Shelasky (fiddle), John Reischman (mandolin), Sally Van Meter (Dobro, banjo) and Bethany Raine (bass). When Shelasky left in the late '80s for a good-paying, steady job at Disneyland, Kevin Wimmer took his place.

from the West Coast. As far as they're concerned, we're from the United States and we're playing traditional American music."[16]

The West Coast seems to have produced a different kind of bluegrass than the East Coast. While the eastern bands are very much traditionally-oriented, mandolinist John Reischman commented that in the West Coast area, "There is no conscious vision of what the band should sound like. We just ended up being a band together, bringing our different influences and the music we like. Everybody is open to trying new things." Kallick added, "It's harder for us as a group to work out a song that *isn't* an original. I want to have a vision of a song as something that hasn't been done. If we have an original song, we don't have somebody else's version to confuse us."[17]

San Francisco Bay Area bluegrass. An early history—briefly.

The path to bluegrass music in the Bay Area began about 1953 when Neil V. Rosenberg met Mayne Smith. By 1955, Smith, Rosenberg and Scott Hambly were going to folk jams and in 1957 switched from nylon strings to steel (which had more of a bluegrass sound) to their guitars—which they liked. With their new bluegrass strings they began playing their version of folk music at the KPFA studios.

Author Sandy Rothman was on the scene at the time and described West Coast bluegrass, "Playing bluegrass in Berkeley at that time wasn't the easiest thing in the world to do. For one thing the folk song atmosphere, created largely by the work of Barry Olivier with its emphasis on quiet ballads, understated delivery and solo and duet singers, wasn't entirely

"California musicians tend to lay back..."

This Californian (though born in Denver, Colorado) spoke about the difference between East Coast and West Coast bluegrass bands, "California musicians tend to lay back on the beat whereas East Coast players tend to push the beat—at least at the present time [1985]."[19] — Steve Pottier

compatible with the powerful bluegrass sound, even in trio form. And too, this was the West Coast. Most people had never heard this kind of music before. Bluegrass came to the area through the folk music revival, not a country music context; the audiences were folk audiences."

There was a large movement toward folk singing during those years, and before long the "American Banjo—Scruggs Style" LP was released and became a learning tool for everyone trying to learn the banjo—including Rosenberg and Smith.

In 1958, Rosenberg and Smith, both freshmen at Oberlin College in Oberlin, Ohio, spent their spring break in New York City where they heard bluegrass live for the first time, performed at a party by Eric Weissberg and Marshall Brickman. Rosenberg remembered that "Some of the East Coast musicians had a kind of chip-on-the-shoulder attitude but they were ahead of us musically. Alice Gerrard, Mike Seeger and others were very helpful to us...I felt like we were following them. They also introduced us to the mystique of instruments and music."[18]

That summer, Rosenberg, Smith and Hambly made thirty-six hand-duplicated copies of a twelve-inch acetate recording and given or sold to friends. The songs were "Little Maggie" and "Jesse James." There at college, Rosenberg and some Oberlin classmates formed the **Lorain County String Band** (early 1959). His summer of 1959 was spent in Berkeley, California, and there Scott Hambly, Mayne Smith, Pete Berg and Rosenberg formed the **Redwood County Ramblers**. They played wherever they could. He returned to Oberlin that September after the group made a second demo tape. He re-joined his Oberlin classmates again to form the **Plum Creek Boys** (January 1960). Mayne Smith did not return to Oberlin but decided to stay in Berkeley until the next year.

Scott Hambly, according to Rosenberg in a 1995 note to this writer, was very important in the California bluegrass scene during those early years. He wrote, "Not only was he the key person in the **Redwood County Ramblers**—the only one who was in the band all the time between 1959 and 1964—but he was generally regarded as one of the leading mandolin players in the region, not just in the Bay Area but also in L.A.. In 1961, while Roland White was in the Army, Scott regularly sat in on mandolin in the **Country Boys**, flying down several times a month for gigs at The Ash Grove and elsewhere. He also backed up Mac Wiseman in a show, and auditioned for mandolinist with **Flatt and Scruggs** during this time period. In 1962, Chris Hillman flew up regularly to take mandolin

[16] J.D. Kleinke, "Omnigrass Anyone? The Good Ol' Persons and the Can't-Label-Us Blues," *Bluegrass Unlimited*, March, 1991, p. 24. For efficiency, the comments of both Kallick and Raine are combined in this quote.

[17] Ibid, p. 19.

[18] Sandy Rothman, "Rambling in Redwood Canyon: The Routes of Bay Area Bluegrass, Part Two," *Bluegrass Unlimited*, June, 1991, p. 60.

[19] Sandy Rothman, "Butch Waller's High Country—Conclusion, *Bluegrass Unlimited*, October, 1985, p. 20.

lessons from Scott in Berkeley. Scott's record and tape collection was, during this period, unsurpassed in the region so he was widely known amongst the small number of people who were into bluegrass as an expert about bands, styles, and songs. He was in the USAF from 1964 to 1967 and then lived in L.A. from '68 to, I believe, '71. When John Hickman first came to L.A., he played in a band with Scott awhile and Scott gigged a lot in the L.A. area during that period."

"I remember fantasizing," said Mayne Smith, "that someday the word 'bluegrass' would become common knowledge. It was awkward—it was hard to figure out how to describe what it was we were doing. It did have a cultural status—people were applying a label to it—but we had to educate people about the music in order to get them to come and see us."[20] The bluegrass singing style was relatively alien to the area so the group spent most of their repertoire on instrumentals. The audiences had to get used to the power of the banjo and the drive of the music these men played—it was so very different than folk music with which everybody was familiar.

The **Plum Creek Boys** opened the show at Antioch College in March 5th of 1960 when the **Osborne Brothers** gave their first college concert. "Everyone was starting to know a lot more about bluegrass," said Rosenberg. "I learned a lot by watching. I remember Benny Birchfield showed me the second break to 'Earl's Breakdown' at the Antioch show."

Rosenberg told an anecdote of the appearance of a band they saw at WWVA's World's Original Jamboree radio show when the **Plum Creek Boys** were in the audience. "They announced the last act—a name we were not too familiar with, being new to bluegrass—and out came what we thought was the funniest combina-

The Vern Williams Band, 1980. L to R: Ed Neff, Keith Little, Vern Williams, Delbert Williams

tion of physical types we'd ever seen. The guitarist and mandolinist were quite chubby, the fiddler tall and broad-shouldered, and the banjo picker was so skinny that it appeared his Mastertone might pull him down at any moment. We didn't have time to laugh, for the moment they reached the mike, the guitar hit an E chord and the banjo player started playing the wildest single-note stuff we had ever heard! Surprised? We were stunned—we'd never heard of Jimmy Martin or

High Country, 1971. L to R: Bruce Nemerov, Ed Neff, Rich Wilbur, Lonny Feiner, Butch Waller

J.D. Crowe or Paul Williams or Johnny Dacus and we'd never heard 'Hold Whatcha Got.'"[21]

Their new formation of the **Redwood Canyon Ramblers** in 1960 was similar in format to hot bluegrass bands on the East Coast, complete with a comedian. Rosenberg and Smith recruited former jazz bassist Tom Glass who became the "Toby" or comedian in the band. Rosenberg noted that "This was before the Equal Rights Amendment for bass players. Earlier, the banjo player was a comedian,[22] but Earl Scruggs changed that. Reno and Smiley solved the problem by everyone costuming, thereby singling no one out. The **Kentucky Colonels** did the same."[23]

The **Redwood Canyon Ramblers** established a tradition of regular bluegrass at Berkeley's folk clubs all through the '60s and '70s. The band had offers to continue as a full-time band and probably would have done quite well but members considered music too risky an occupation and decided instead to go back to college. Rosenberg received a Ph.D. in 1970.

In approximately 1960, Butch Waller began taking mandolin lessons from Scott Hambly. Sandy Rothman got a banjo lesson from Neil Rosenberg, as did Rick Shubb. Rothman and Waller, along with Waller's friends Herb Pedersen and Rick Shubb, were devoted followers of the **Redwood Canyon Ramblers.** Waller formed the **Pine Valley Boys**[24] in 1963, a band which lasted until banjoist Herb Pedersen left to join **Vern and Ray** in

[20] Sandy Rothman, "Rambling in Redwood Canyon: The Routes of Bay Area Bluegrass, Part I," *Bluegrass Unlimited*, May, 1991, p. 56.

[21] Ibid, p. 61.

[22] Rosenberg was probably referring to Snuffy Jenkins or Stringbean. In many early bands, however, the comedian was most often on bass.

[23] Rothman, Part Two, op. cit., p. 62.

[24] The second of the bluegrass bands in the S.F. Bay Area was probably the Pine Ridge Ramblers. Members were Jerry Garcia, Sandy Rothman (banjo), Bert Johnson (guitar) and Bill Wood (bass).

Nashville in late 1964. In 1968, Waller formed **High Country**, a band which featured the Bay Area's finest musicians through the years.

Mayne Smith's 1964 master thesis, "Bluegrass Music and Musicians: An Introductory Study of a Musical Style in Its Cultural Context" (MA, Folklore, Indiana University, 1964) was probably the first serious study of bluegrass music. Then, in 1965, Smith wrote "An Introduction to Bluegrass." Published in the *Journal of American Folklore*, it was the first article on bluegrass in a scholarly journal. It was reprinted in *Bluegrass Unlimited* in their first year of publishing. Smith left academia in 1965 as a potential career change and became involved in the Los Angeles music scene—performing, record producing, songwriting, instrument repair, and running the sound system at The Ash Grove folk club (where the **Kentucky Colonels** played regularly). He played the resonator guitar, steel, guitar and banjo as a session man in L.A. studios—mostly in the new genre of acoustic/country/folk/rock.

In 1969, Paul Lampert bought the Paragon Bar in San Francisco and renamed it Paul's Saloon. Not a bluegrass fan at the time, he actually had no intention of having music there at his location on Scott Street but bluegrass and related music arrived there when Bob and Ingrid Fowler (**Styx River Ferry**) asked to play there. Attendance was usually less than fifteen people during those early days. By 1984, audiences of over 300 were known to frequent the bar on a Saturday night.

Pat Enright founded **Phantoms of the Opry** in 1969. He was soon joined by notables Laurie Lewis and Paul Shelasky in the early '70s. They won the band contest at Bill Monroe's 7th Annual Bean Blossom Festival.[25]

"Cousin Al's Bluegrass Show" was a popular radio program in Northern California. Al Knoth later went on to host the West Coast-famous KFAT bluegrass shows in Gilroy, California. In 1987, he started a syndicated radio show on commercial radio on KTOM and KPIG in the Monterey and Watsonville areas. The next year, he gave up his perennial position with listener-supported KCSM (College of San Mateo) to pursue these ventures more vigorously and for pay. Most of the region's bluegrass shows were on listener-supported FM radio stations where the deejays were volunteers.

About 1973, Mike Seeger hosted a show which led to the creation of the California Bluegrass Association. At the show was the **Homestead Act** with Elmo and Patsy Shropshire and John Hedgecoth. The show was

fully sponsored and very popular. Carol and Ron Masters worked with Seeger on the event. When Seeger left, the show ceased.

About that time, The People's Republic of China sent a delegation to the Bay Area. Carl Pagter arranged for a bluegrass band play for them and the Chinese audience loved them.[26] The gig was sponsored by Kaiser Engineers, who later called on Pagter to book many such events. This gave Pagter the contacts necessary to begin the California Bluegrass Association in late 1974. He was the founder and its first president.

Hard Times Bluegrass Band, c. 1976. L to R: Randy Hupp, Stuart Duncan, Geoff Stelling, Larry Bulaich. Photo courtesy Larry Bulaich.

Also about that time, A **Touch of Grass**[27] was formed by Bob Lawrence. **Over Easy** featured Jerry and Gregg Canote, Bill Iberti, Dave Holcomb and bassist Todd Phillips, who later went to perform with David Grisman's early quintet. The **Great American Music Band** as formed to play in San Francisco's Great American Music Hall. While a member of this band, Grisman taught mandolin in Sausalito, California.

Southern California bluegrass

Larry Bulaich[28] is an Oregonian educator who spent his formative bluegrass years in the Los Angeles area. He recalled that "I first saw the **Dillards** at UCLA. That really rattled my cage because they had the show, the original tunes, they had the ethnic/hillbilly characters they played. Their instrumentals were just phenomenal to me. And I still think that Doug Dillard is one of the cleanest banjo players I've ever heard. That blew me away. I was also a product of influences of the **Kingston Trio**, **Peter, Paul and Mary** and many others.

---

[25] Other bluegrass bands began to appear on the scene. There was David Grisman's first Bay Area band, Smoky Grass Boys, where he played in San Francisco's Cedar Alley bar with members Jerry Garcia (banjo, guitar), Herb Pedersen (guitar), Bert Johnson (guitar), Rick Shubb (banjo), Sandy Rothman (multi-instrumentalist) and others through the years. Joe Kimbro formed his Bear Creek Valley Boys in 1970. Appearing for a year already was Styx River Ferry with Bob and Ingrid Fowler, and others including Ed Neff, and Marty Lanham. Queen of the Rodeo was a band based in Santa Cruz. Homestead Act featured Elmo Shropshire (banjo), John Hedgecoth (banjo, fiddle) John Pierson (guitar) and was soon joined by Pat Trigg (guitar). Elmo and Pat married and became Elmo and Patsy which became famous for its "Grandma Got Run Over By a Reindeer." Rick Shubb and the Hired Hands began in 1972, followed by his Shubb, Wilson and Shubb.

[26] Band members were Aric Leavitt, Jay Quisenberry and John Murphy.

[27] Bert Johnson, Paul Siese and Mike Sanders.

[28] This text from an interview with Larry Bulaich in 1993.

"The **Kentucky Colonels** were playing: Clarence White, Roland White, Leroy Mack, Eric White, Roger Bush, Billy Ray Lathum. Great, great group!" Bulaich recalled that the **Golden State Boys**[29] were in the area at the time as well.

During the '70s, a group called **Wild Hickory Nuts** played in the area. The significance of this band on the bluegrass music of the area is that so many of the members went on to other groups popular even today. Craig Smith was on banjo, Darryl Boom was on guitar, Dennis Fetchet played mandolin and fiddle, Bill Bryson played bass and guitar. These last three men were stalwarts of the Los Angeles bluegrass scene for many years to come.

Back about 1975, Bulaich began playing music with Stuart Duncan, Alison Brown, Geoff Stelling and John Hickman. Bulaich recalled that Dick Tyner was one of his biggest influences in the music because, at one of Tyner's Golden West Bluegrass Festivals, Tyner put together a contest band which included Bulaich (guitar), Stuart Duncan (fiddle), Tyner (banjo) and Randy Huff (bass). This led to the formation of **Pain in the Grass** and gave him connections which would further his bluegrass career.

When Tyner quit the band in 1977, Bulaich, Alison Brown, Stuart Duncan, Barry Silver and John Hickman formed **Gold Rush**. "John Hickman joined us and that, right there with my friendship with John, was the beginning of my education in bluegrass," said Bulaich. "I mean, he taught me so much just by example or by just talking about it: its history, where it comes from, how it's survived, and so forth. I've never believed that John Hickman has been as much appreciated as he should be. I thought he knew more about bluegrass in one little finger than the rest of us in our whole body. He is an amazing, amazing person—his playing, his knowledge. He just seems to be on top of everything. John played with us and Alison Brown played resonator guitar and occasionally would play a banjo duet with John. Stuart played fiddle and mandolin and myself, guitar, and Barry Silver played the upright bass. And Barry could sing quite a bit—sing most of the parts. And the band was getting the job done there at Magic Mountain. Pretty soon John had to quit. He was doin' some full-time stuff with Byron (Berline) and Alison moved from resonator guitar to banjo but she occasionally played resonator guitar on the cowboy stuff. And we were doing swing tunes and I was starting to learn

Butch Waller's High Country, c. 1980. L to R: Jim Moss, Butch Waller, Larry Hughes, Larry Cohea, Steve Swan

cowboy music a little bit. And it was about this time that I realized that I was never cut out to be a full-time bluegrass singer; I just don't sing high enough.

"We were still called **Gold Rush** after John quit. Some people in California did not like us doin' cowboy songs and Bob Wills tunes. Barry left us and we got Ron Greenberg who did a good job on the bass. **Gold Rush** played up until June of '78 and our last great job at Grass Valley. A lot of groups play swing music today and nobody particularly jumps on their cases about it. As **Gold Rush**, we started playing different places than **Pain in the Grass** did. We played, for example, at a west Hollywood night spot called The Troubadour and tried to do different stuff with our bluegrass roots.

"Stuart and Alison were working together and creating a solo album[30] and had a lot of things worked out. I'd had a wonderful time playing with them because they are really nice kids and their parents are really fine people. Working with Stuart and Alison was amazing! I always felt as though the two had a special talent—I don't know if you call it genius or gifted—or whatever it is. They both are able to soak up an idea instantly and reproduce it; whether it's singing, memorizing, playing, harmony playing—long, convoluted lines of playing harmony—instantly they'd have this up. To sit there and watch it as their guitar player was really amazing. It sure would be a kick to do a concert with them now.

"Today (1993), I look at the careers that Stuart, John Hickman, Alison Brown and John Moore have, and it really pleases me. To have been touched by these virtuosos and super people is really treasured and satisfying." As of 1996, Bulaich performed in **Foxfire** in Oregon.

Bill Bryson—
Southern California's
stalwart bassist

In a March 25, 1995, interview, Bill Bryson told of his experience in Southern California bluegrass country. "I heard my first bluegrass band, the **Country Boys**, in 1959 or '60. I was interested in folk music then and that was the live, hard-core bluegrass I had heard. It was during the folk music boom."

29 With (Hal) Poindexter, Herb Rice and Don Parmley.

30 This album was "Pre-Sequel" (Ridge Runner Records, 1981) with Brown (banjo, Dobro), Duncan (fiddle, mandolin, guitar), Steve Libbea (guitar, mandolin) and Gene Libbea (bass).

"Roger Bush was with them when they were still the **Country Boys**. As a matter of fact, I was listening to some tapes on the way up (to this festival in Palo Alto, California) when, in 1962, when Roland White had gone into the service. The band was Roger, Billy Ray Lathum, Scott Hambly playing mandolin, and Leroy Mack (McNees). Oddly enough, Leroy was doing all the emcee work. Roger was known as the emcee for the **Kentucky Colonels**, but at that time Leroy was doing all of it.

"The **Dillards** came over in '62. Actually, there was quite a lot going on then. I remember when the **Dillards** came out I was at The Ash Grove the night the **Colonels** and the **Greenbriar Boys** were on the bill. I think it was '63 or '64. There was an active bluegrass scene, but you had to look a little bit harder for it. The **Colonels** and the **Country Boys** were playing in places far removed from folk music that was available in the college and high school scene at the time. They were playing in places like Lakewood and El Monte and an area of Los Angeles where the parents were working in the [World War II] effort. That's where the big defense plants were. And that's where that music kind of stayed—it was 'hillbilly' music. In Pasadena you could hear the **Kingston Trio**. If you went down to Lakewood or El Monte you could hear the **Country Boys** or country-western music. We didn't have country-western music in the upper-middle class white neighborhood; there was no place you could hear it. You went down across the tracks to the freeway and that's the place you could hear it.

"So they were part of that scene. They didn't really become part of the concert scene. People forget that. Bluegrass wasn't a big part of folk music—at least in Southern California; it was country-western music. It was a big, different thing. It wasn't under the old microscope, you know.

"There was change going on, and even back then it wasn't too tough to see the Hootenanny syndrome was a singer-songwriter kind of thing and the bluegrass thing was just a much stronger music—a much rawer music. And by the time **Flatt and Scruggs** started doing college concerts and things like that, I think it was one of the greatest things that ever happened to them; I'm sure they did, too. First of all because it extended their audience, and second of all being able to play nicer places, more money, less travel time. And it was flattering having people all of a sudden examining the music and listening to what you did. And all of a sudden you were a part of academia, as opposed to just doing the gigs.

"And Clarence and Roland (White) were doing it for a living. Like most of the people out West, they got their first exposure to bluegrass from records. The music of the West Coast is just a mirror of what Los Angeles was doing at the time. During the War, the population expanded tremendously. A lot of the people from the Southeast and Southwest brought their music with them (to the defense plants). By the same token, it's the most eclectic blend of things in the nation—there was very little regional separation in southern California. You had everybody jammed in there together; there was no place farther to go west. It was inevitable that the music would change because of the surroundings.

"Los Angeles was becoming the recording capitol of the world, as opposed to New York, for popular music. L.A. had some 'hellacious' guitar players and a lot of studio players, and that is *still* there! L.A. is a very competitive scene now. It's a great place for musicians to live; you can't get bored and you can't get complacent.

"You had a great jazz scene in L.A. all during the '40s. Remember, too, that the radio and the War service was extremely important in the rise of country music in the United States. People in all parts of the country were being exposed to country music for the first time [as a result of World War Two]. And people became much more mobile after the War and all the influences came as a result. When I went into the service, I'd never really been outside of southern California. All of a sudden I was in a squad full of guys from South Carolina.

Bill Bryson

"But I think that what happened with bluegrass in L.A. was a very natural progression. [For example], people like Chris Hillman starting out with Don Parmley and Vern and Rex Gosdin. From there, they got involved with the **Byrds** and Crosby and those guys was a very natural progression. In 1986, when Herb (Pedersen) and Chris formed **Desert Rose**, I had known Herb from bluegrass and known Chris from rock and country-rock efforts. We were all bluegrass players; that's where we started."

As of 1995, Mr. Bryson was in Southern California's **Laurel Canyon Ramblers** with Herb Pedersen (banjo), Billy Ray Lathum (guitar) and Kenny Blackwell (mandolin). They recorded "Rambler's Blues" album for Sugar Hill with guests Byron Berline (fiddle) and Leroy "Mack" McNees (resonator guitar).

Alan Munde—
"I refused to change the way I thought or played."

Munde said that, in general, the people in the East "have strong opinions about things and it's hard for them to see any variance. Bluegrass banjo players often get channeled into a very narrow view of the music. In Oklahoma I was viewed as just another musician who happened to play the banjo."[31]

"Bluegrass music has always been oriented toward, if not totally dominated by, the eastern portion of the country. Being from Oklahoma worked against me, but I refused to change the way I thought or played just to fit in with the eastern style...you don't have to live in the East to play this music."

Jack Tottle

Jack Tottle— educator, musician and enthusiast— "This is northern bluegrass."

In 1978, Rounder released "Tasty Licks" by Jack Tottle, Robin Kincaid, Bela Fleck, Stacy Phillips, Paul Kahn and guest Bobby Hicks. The liner notes by Dick Spottswood tried to describe the music of **Tasty Licks** at that time:

This is Northern Bluegrass. Maybe it hasn't been around long enough to establish traditions, but it's a force that's arrived and produced its own hierarchy of good musicians and bands. Adventurous people like Roger Sprung, Bill Keith and David Grisman began years ago to fuse southern vocal and instrumental styles with modern eclectic concepts of harmony and rhythm. Others took courage and began creating their own brand of traditionally-based banjo while simultaneously expanding its possibilities according to their individual tastes and ideas.

*Appropriately, **Tasty Licks** shows a restlessness of style. Much of their excitement is created by novel vocal harmonies combined with lightning chord changes and* abrupt rhythmic transitions. Their music is chock full of these surprises, and full appreciation requires constant attention and alertness on the part of the listener. Yet **Tasty Licks** surely does not use this arsenal of devices for their own sake, nor are they used in order for each soloist to show off his own particular bag of tricks. What enhances their music more than anything else is the unity of vocal and instrumental work, and that the demanding load of their adventurous music is shared skillfully by all. If its individual soloists are impressive, more so is the degree to which each has pooled his talents for the sake of a unified expression. It is a rare achievement in modern bluegrass.*

Tottle was already well known as the author of *Bluegrass Mandolin* (Oak) and *How to Play Mandolin* (Acorn). *Bluegrass Mandolin* was translated into Japanese, sold over 50,000 copies, and remains the most popular book ever written about bluegrass mandolin playing. Due to the success of the book, Rounder released Tottle's solo LP "Back Road Mandolin." His writing became more prominent when Rounder hired him to write liner notes for many of their albums. Resonator guitarist Stacy Phillips (also on the aforementioned album) was known for his album on Revonah, "All Old Friends," and for his two books published by Oak: *Bluegrass Fiddle Styles* (with Ken Kosek) and *The Dobro Book*.

While Tottle's 1978 LP may have been representative of his eight years in Boston, his other projects better reflected his upbringing in Virginia and in South Carolina in the military. Projects which show these southern roots of bluegrass include "Raise a Ruckus" (**Lonesome River Boys**), his two years with **Don Stover and the White Oak Mountain Boys** just prior to founding **Tasty Licks**, "Anchored to the Shore" (**Tasty Licks**, whose members then included Pat Enright, Bela Fleck and Mark Schatz), and his years as director of the ETSU Bluegrass Band. Frank Godbey on the liner notes of "Anchored": "Welcome to the second album by **Tasty Licks**. For the past few years this band has been successfully establishing a reputation as one of the better progressive groups in the Northeast, so it may come as a surprise to many of their listeners who know them only from their first Rounder album or from earlier New England appearances, that this same **Tasty Licks**, with a few personnel changes, has returned to the roots to produce an album of solid traditional-styled bluegrass."

One of the reasons Tottle left his **Tasty Licks** (1979) was the long, harsh winters of the Northeast. "I suddenly realized the more you stayed with it, the more you had to be prepared to travel more and more. To me, there were times when it seemed like the world of professional music was driving hundreds of miles to pick up a check and playing a few songs while you were there even though you were really too tired to play. So much work went into the planning and business ends that music was actually a very small part of the whole thing."[32]

[31] George A. Ghetia, "Friday Morning with Alan Munde," *Bluegrass Unlimited*, July, 1987, p. 24.

[32] Tim Stafford, "Jack Tottle: Artist, Author, Bluegrass Ambassador" (Part One), *Bluegrass Unlimited*, August, 1989, p. 29.

America's Music | Bluegrass

Tottle took up residence on a farm in Scott County in southern Virginia. There he joined the **Payroll Boys** and they recorded "Fields Where We Once Played" for June Appal. During that period, he began giving guitar lessons for Clinch Valley College. He then approached East Tennessee State University about his idea of a more structured, formal, collegiate curriculum on bluegrass. One of the first courses he began teaching after he initiated the Bluegrass and Country Music Program at ETSU was a course on the history of bluegrass. He is now on the faculty of the Center for Appalachian Studies and Services and is leader of the ETSU bluegrass band.

In a 1989 interview with fellow educator Tim Stafford, Tottle said he likes the new bands in bluegrass. "One thing that's nice about a lot of the newer bands is that they're combining traditional material with their own material. To me, the bands that will try different things appeals to me even though I like the traditional sound a great deal. It's like any other kind of music—it has to develop and change. You have to decide for yourself if you like the way it's changing or not. You can't say, 'How long can we keep it the same?' because no music has ever stayed the same except maybe classical music, which is all written down and the composers are legends."[33] He likes classical music but feels that the spontaneity of bluegrass is much more interesting.

Tottle likes to teach music with a simple method: he tries to keep students from over-playing. "I guess a lot of us have a tendency to want to play beyond what our technical limitations are. I know that when I first started playing I wanted to play the hardest breaks—I didn't even want to worry about learning the easy ones. I wish there had been someone there to sit me down and say, 'Hold on! We'll get to that. But first, let's get this one *really* solid.' I guess that's the role I perform a lot of times with students."[34]

Tottle has some interesting insights on society, culture, and the music of young people, "I don't listen to enough rock music to really understand it these days (1989), but it seems to me there's a lot of anger in it—especially in heavy metal music; [it] sounds angry to me. Obviously, you can understand why a music that incorporated that would have appeal for people going through adolescence. There is a time when you're going through that transition from child to adult and you're frustrated. There are all sorts of things you want but can't have yet

and there's a lot of confusion and rebellion. So there's anger and sexuality expressed in the music. There's also a lot of sexuality in country music, but it's not a theme in bluegrass all that much. If you think about what type of movies are popular with young people, you see the same thing: "Rambo," "Dirty Dancing," etc.. There's either a lot of sexuality or a lot of violence and a very fast pace. These aren't the only things young people respond to, but they're certainly visible and very available in our society. Maybe we could do some market research about our audience. My feeling is that violence, anger, and sexuality are not the most satisfying things to build your life around—and there are lots of kids who feel that way, too—it could be interesting."[35]

"One of the things that is appealing about bluegrass is that it is non-mechanical. As all these synthesizers get more sophisticated and they sound more and more like acoustic instruments, there are always going to be people who like the sound of strings vibrating against wood and you can't duplicate it—especially the feel of it. Pressing a key will never replace the feel of drawing a bow across the strings—the roughness of the strings, the vibrating instrument, all the physical sensations can't be replaced, even though the sound can be simulated to some extent. There will always be people who respond to that rather than the razzle-dazzle of electronic music or the highly-produced popular music."[36]

In 1991, Tottle was awarded the Outstanding Achievement Award of Tennessee on behalf of the members of the ETSU Bluegrass Band for their participation in the Soviet Union's International Folk Arts Festival. The next year, he was appointed to the IBMA Board of Directors, representing Print Media and Education. In 1993, during his tour of the Czech Republic and Slovakia, he became the first U.S. bluegrass performer to perform with a band comprised entirely of Czech and Slovak musicians. He is an assistant professor at ETSU whose alumni include Tim Stafford (leader of **Blue Highway**, 1996), Barry Bales, Adam Steffey (who are members of **Alison Krauss and Union Station** as of 1996), Marcus Smith and Beth Stevens, and he continues to record regularly.

33 Tim Stafford, "An Interview with Jack Tottle," September, 1989, p. 34. This the conclusion to "Bluegrass Ambassador," *BU*, Aug. '89.

34 Ibid., p. 34.

35 Ibid., p. 37

36 Tim Stafford, "An Interview with Jack Tottle," September, 1989, pp. 37,38. This the conclusion to "Bluegrass Ambassador" *BU*, Aug. '89.

Chapter 17

The Studio Musicians and their Music - Table of Contents

The Studio Musicians and Their Music

Bluegrass in the recording studio—by Dick Weissman

There are two sorts of recording sessions that feature bluegrass musicians. In "pure" bluegrass recording sessions, a band or a singer hires bluegrass musicians of their choice to augment their sound or to add some new ingredient to it. There is another sort of session which can be for an album, a movie or television soundtrack, or a radio or television commercial. In this sort of undertaking, one or more musicians are added to give a sort of glimpse of a bluegrass sound, rather than reproducing the actual sound of bluegrass. For the purpose of this section of *America's Music: Bluegrass*, I will refer to these sorts of sessions as "semi-bluegrass" sessions.

To my knowledge, no musician has ever been able to make a living simply by playing on other people's "pure" bluegrass records. A handful of players in Nashville, New York and Los Angeles have developed reputations as folk/country/bluegrass specialists. The difference between the two sorts of studio calls is that in the first sort of session, the record is going out to bluegrass fans who are quite familiar with the music and have a specific idea of how it should sound. In the case of the semi-bluegrass sessions, the musician is usually obligated to please the producer and/or the recording artist. To the general audience, it is probably enough for a fiddle or banjo player to play very fast to identify the music to them.

Over the years, a number of bluegrass players have played on the semi-bluegrass sessions. In New York, Eric Weissberg has probably played more different instruments on more recording sessions than anyone else. Other studio bluegrass players over the years have included Marshall Brickman, Matt Glaser, Marc Horowitz, Barry Kornfield, Bill Keith, Steve Mandell, Larry Packer, Paul Prestopino, Dick Rosmini, Tony Trischka and me. Note that many of these players are not "pure" bluegrass pickers, but are familiar enough with the style to add a bluegrass "flavor" to recording sessions.

Bobby Thompson was, for many years, the "king" of the semi-bluegrass sessions in Nashville. Mike Auldridge, Kenny Baker, Sam Bush, Vassar Clements, Jerry Douglas, Bobby Hicks, Vic Jordan, John McEuen, Curtis McPeake, Mark O'Connor, Ricky Skaggs, Buddy Spicher and several dozen guitar pickers did the work in Music City. There were also many sessions at Bias and Bigmo studios in the Washington, D.C., area.

Doug Dillard was one of the first active studio pickers in Los Angeles, and others included Byron Berline, Glenn Campbell, Dan Crary, Johnny Gimble, John Hickman, Bill Knopf, Joe Maphis, John McEuen and Merle Travis. Such players as David Grisman, Bela Fleck, Alan Munde and Tony Rice were apt to show up on sessions recorded in any of these music centers, or even on recordings made in such cities as Austin or San Francisco.

There are several rather odd things about semi-bluegrass sessions. For example, I would never describe myself as a bluegrass player yet I played bluegrass on quite a few sessions. (My playing is eclectic and uses a combination of folk techniques with a jazz influence.) This is because what constitutes a bluegrass sound on a commercial with a thirty-piece orchestra (not an unusual situation in New York) can be ten seconds of a Scruggs roll. Another aspect of bluegrass as a studio style is that there are many sessions in Nashville that might include a tune where a producer wants a banjo, but one or two others that need to be recorded on the same session where the musician must be able to play rhythm guitar. In an interview with Bobby Thompson that I did several years ago for an article in *Frets* magazine, he described to me how he had to learn to play rhythm guitar in order to make a living in the Nashville studios. Developing this expertise enabled him to play in the staff band for "Hee Haw," on the "Ralph Emery Show," and so on. He said that this would not have been possible if he had restricted himself to banjo.

Another continuing theme in studio work is the issue of reading music and playing with musicians not found in bluegrass bands, such as trumpet or saxophone players, drummers and percussionists. In the New York and Los Angeles sessions, an arranger may very well have written out a banjo or fiddle part, note-for-note. Usually the session producer will allow a musician to use that part as a road map, and to make up his or her own variation on it. But once in awhile, the producer is absolutely insistent on the musician playing the part "as written." This can result in an occasional nasty situation because most of the studio set don't really understand, for example, the function of the fifth string on the banjo. In commercials, it is quite common to have two or three key changes in the course of a thirty-second piece of music. Thanks to over-dubbing and the use of separate tracks for different instruments, it is usually possible to give the producer what he wants.

Why do musicians do studio work? First of all, there's the money. In the major recording centers, most of the work is done with union contracts. For an album, a session is divided into three-hour increments and the wage is slightly over $250 for the three hours. Even if a musician does an eight-bar harmonica over-dub, they are supposed to receive the union minimum. Other sessions, such as film work, television or commercials, pay in the same, general hourly range, although the minimum calls are different. Commercials require a one-hour minimum call. In addition to these wage minimums, players receive bonuses in the form of re-payment for re-used commercials and a sort of bonus pool system for those playing on records and for film score. Musicians who do regular work also become eligible for sizable pension payments, something that rarely happens through live performances. The very top players demand double or triple the union minimum, so they can earn a fair amount of money during the period that they are in high demand.

Another advantage of studio work is that the scene and personnel constantly change. A studio musician may have to play in seven or eight different musical styles in a single film scoring session, or with different musical artists on, say, five different records recorded in the same week. When a player is involved in a boring or tedious session, she can look forward to the notion that tomorrow's session will probably involve a different artist and musical arranger. In other words, no matter how bad a session is, it will soon go away. A performing musician stuck with a bad band leader can only escape by quitting, and then he will be out of work.

Another aspect of studio work is that because the recording process has become so highly developed, it is possible to do things that are musically subtle and enjoyable for the players. In a live performance situation, particularly in an outdoor stadium, something that works beautifully on a record may be inaudible.

Playing with top rhythm sections in the major recording centers is also a challenge that affords a creative musician the opportunity to learn and grow as a player. Different drummers and bass players may play

Don Reno

just in front of or behind the beat. The average bluegrass player may not be aware of these subtleties, and may even have trouble hearing them. This creates a higher level of musical awareness. An example of this sort of thing happened to me once when I was in a club with my friend Eric Weissberg, the performer on the "Deliverance" record. We realized that the performer was keeping time from one musical bar to another, but that within the bars themselves he was actually playing out of meter. This created an overall feeling that something was wrong with the rhythm. The average person might have found themselves disconcerted by this fairly complex problem and would probably not have understood what was wrong. I doubt that either Eric or I would have been able to pinpoint this problem if we hadn't each done a considerable amount of recording work.

The bad news for studio musicians is that they are rapidly being replaced by machines and electronic samples. Furthermore, the hottest player of the day may be an unknown two years from now as different styles and players come into vogue. In fact, many studio musicians phase themselves out of the studio after a certain amount of time because they suffer burnout from continual demands from producers or arrangers. Others stop freelancing because they prefer to concentrate on their music instead of other people's music.

Don Reno—
"The best stuff I ever did cut was haphazard."

This veteran of hundreds of recordings said, "I think some of the best stuff I ever did was cut, you know, haphazard. I think you're actually more yourself when you cut that way because you're not under the pressure of trying to please the man in the front office—you're cutting what you want to cut and what you feel like cutting."[1]

Jerry Douglas, Stuart Duncan and Barry Poss on selecting a producer

In addition to being one of the busiest studio musicians in Nashville in the early 1990s, a large portion of resonator guitarist Jerry Douglas' work these days is the production of recordings of artists such as Alison

[1] Bill Vernon, "The Don Reno Story, Part 1: Early Years," *Muleskinner News*, p. 10.

Americas Music | Bluegrass

L to R: Tony and Wyatt Rice, and Jerry Douglas with the Tony Rice Unit.

Krauss, the **Nashville Bluegrass Band**, Maura O'Connell, and others. He told this writer how an artist selects a producer, "The record label usually suggests somebody. It's up to the artist then to figure out whether out they can relate to the way the producer works. Number one factor is trust their judgment on the way they think about the song and how they would go about creating the sound for the record."

Fiddler Duncan also understands the importance of a good session producer. A producer, such as Bela Fleck who produces most of the **Nashville Bluegrass Band** recordings, has the last say as to the quality of each band member's playing. "The producer has to push someone to the maximum without making the musician mad so it will sound worse."[2]

Barry Poss, the head of Sugar Hill Records, spoke of the responsibilities of a record producer. "I think it's important for a producer to make some decisions about what it is you're trying to get and why you are there. In recording a traditional performer, you've already re-moved him from his natural setting of playing for and with friends. So get rid of all this excess baggage that says this music is recorded 'naturally.' My feeling is that a producer is entrusted with presenting a performer to an audience, most of whom will never see that person... My job was to try to get more of a theme, a concept, to tie the album together."[3]

Stuart Duncan on his move to the Nashville area and on studio microphone placement

Fiddler Duncan broke into the fiercely competitive Nashville scene by hard, repetitive work. He explained how he did it, "I see musicians all the time in lounges who really impress me. Usually I exchange cards with them and I can think of at least one occasion when that card got to a producer who called me for a session. I'm not much of a self-promoting person; it's just foreign to me. How do you tell people you're good? It's just a matter of opinion anyway."[4] His first session jobs were with Randy Travis. Four months later he did his next one, that time with Vince Gill.

Stuart Duncan left the Los Angeles area in 1980 when he began attending South Plains College as a bluegrass music major for a year. There he learned about ensembles, sound technology, and music theory. "I also gained a lot of studio expertise there; it has been very helpful in Nashville. One of the engineers there would experiment a lot with microphone placement for my fiddle. I learned a lot about mic placement and setting up a room. I seem to get a lot better sound of any session I go to now because I know where to put the mic on my mandolin or where to put it in relation to my fiddle. There are certain ways to get the sound you want. Directly in front of the f-hole is not where you want to be with a Neumann U-87 because the cardioid pattern on it goes in a weird, circular manner, so you catch it where the pattern is moving. You've got to turn it at an angle so it hits where the vibrations of the fiddle are coming out."[5] He changes the relative position between the microphone and the instrument, depending on the type of microphone. The college course gave him the opportunity to learn this. If he were in a studio session, time and cost of the studio would not have allowed this experimentation.[6]

Stuart Duncan

2 Barry Brower, "Stuart Duncan—Keeping the Bass Player Awake," *Bluegrass Unlimited,* May, 1989, p. 45.

3 Wayne Erbsen, "Barry Poss and Sugar Hill Records," *Bluegrass Unlimited,* October, 1982, p. 29.

4 Barry Brower, "Stuart Duncan—Keeping the Bass Player Awake," *Bluegrass Unlimited,* May, 1989, p. 44.

5 Ibid., p. 42.

6 In a 1993 telephone interview, he added that "there are different patterns on different mics." Then, referring again to the U-87, "I wouldn't want to face the 87 at parallel to the body of the instrument if I was close-mic-ing. Now if you were putting the mic far away—to get a different sound— sometimes that wouldn't matter as much because the pattern is wider." Other microphones have different characteristics and used for different purposes. He especially likes the C-24 for a warm, authentic sound for analog tape (as opposed to a less warm digital tape).

Vic Jordan—
"I like to concentrate on one song at a time and get it right."

In February 1974, banjoist Vic Jordan quit the road to pursue a better family life and more session work. Jordan became known for his Nashville studio recording sessions. In a 1992 telephone interview with Mr. Jordan, he compared studio work with bluegrass festival work, "You get away from straight bluegrass in the studios. There's a lot more emphasis on rhythm instruments, like bass and drums, and keeping the time consistent. When Bobby Thompson and I did some of those festival workshops, we'd each be trying to get the other one to take the lead. It takes awhile before you could get that looseness and attack that a true bluegrass player uses in person. The studio feeling is different—much tighter."

Vic Jordan

"My mentor was Bobby Thompson and it's really been great. Session work is really wonderful—you never know what you're going to do when the producer calls—there's always a variety. They call you and you show up with your instruments." Jordan has recorded with Dolly Parton, the **Oak Ridge Boys**, Charlie Pride, Loretta Lynn, Ray Charles, Porter Wagoner and others. He played in the movies "Concrete Cowboy" with guitarist Jerry Reed and actor Burt Reynolds, "Coal Miner's Daughter" and "Smoky and the Bandit II."

He likes some of the aspects of studio recording. "I like to concentrate on one song at a time and get it right. It's very controlled in the studio and what you don't play is just as important as what you do. They

usually give us some chord charts and it's good to hear it come together quickly. The pressure can help you, and the engineers hear things very well. It's challenging because there's different stuff all the time. They don't want you to just re-cycle your old ideas."

What he doesn't like: "It's normal to take four to six weeks to get paid for a date." And, "Very few producers really understand the banjo. They don't really know what to tell you about what they want you to play. There are some who understand, though. It's hard to cope with some of the different keys. Once I had a date that had a bunch of key changes. I actually had to have another fellow stand next to me and move the fifth string capo around each time we modulated."

About 1973, Vic Jordan got together with Bobby Thompson in the studio under the band name **Neaphonic String Band**. They did tunes such as "Roanoke," "Cheyenne" and "Flint Hill Special.[7] Recorded for Direct Disc Records, the session was recorded directly to the disc—omitting the tape. There was no stopping for a whole side of the album; any mistakes were not corrected except to record the entire side. Under these conditions, creativity and spontaneity seemed to be at their peak. The musicians go all out and can really get into the "groove". When tape is used, it gives the ability to do considerable re-recording but musicians can lose the feeling of a complete and soulful musical performance.

When asked if country recording sessions differ from bluegrass Jordan responded, "Country musicians spread out and use earphones to separate the sound and hear themselves. Bluegrass groups don't like to be spread out; they want to hear each other."[8] He feels that union scale for studio work was too high, driving some musicians away because studios were doing less and less recording because of the cost. Scale was, with pension and health payments, $282 in 1994 for a three-hour session. Many studio musicians moved to where it was cheaper to live and recorded locally. As a result, recording studios popped up everywhere in addition to a high concentration at Music Row in Nashville.

Curtis McPeake—
"I like drums but, don't think they always sound good in a bluegrass setting."

Banjoist Curtis McPeake did session work during the 1960s. He found it financially rewarding but frustrating to have to work through a producer's preconceived ideas of how a banjo player should take part in the "Nashville sound". "Session work is more serious

7 Other musicians were Buddy Spicher and Pete Dawson (fiddle), Paul Gordon and Jody Drumright (mandolin), Harold Bradley (rhythm guitar), Jim Glaser and Roy Huskey Jr. (bass) and others.

8 David Robinson, "Vic Jordan," *Pickin'*, August, 1974, p. 9. In a 1996 interview he said that country musicians nowadays gather around one mic more often but that in 1974, the time of this quotation, the quote held true.

work," he said. "Occasionally, I'd get into a session where everything was loose and we'd all get to cooking. But you might end up working for some producer that had no concept of the Tennessee styles, and if you put in a good banjo lick you might hear the mic click, 'Sorry, we don't want it to sound like bluegrass. We love what you're doing but we don't want it on this record.' They wanted banjo on it but just didn't want anybody to hear it. If you tinkled along with just a little bit of a roll, they'd accept that. Once when Jim Reeves was recording, I went in and recorded one-half of one chorus, two lines in a song! Why would a producer even hire a banjo player if he didn't want him more than that?"[9]

He found that he likes bluegrass with a heavier rhythm section "but I don't push it because a lot of people frown on it. I like drums but don't think they always sound good in a bluegrass setting, especially if you want to keep the music a little more pure. If I'm cutting instrumentals in a studio, I like drums. You just get better rhythm that way. I've also used piano. Electric bass is fine but I'd rather hear doghouse [bass] in a typical setting."[10]

The Lester Flatt Show. L to R: Jake Tullock, Roland White, Vic Jordan, Lester Flatt, Paul Warren, Josh Graves.

Blaine Sprouse— "When you're working on your own record, it makes you nervous."

By 1981, fiddler Sprouse had recorded two of his own albums: "Blaine Sprouse" and "Summertime." He spoke of his experience of being in a studio, "A recording studio is completely different for me than playing in front of a live audience; it's hard for me to really let go and play relaxed in the studio. It's something you just have to learn... It was a lot more comfortable doing my second album. When you're working on your own record, it makes you nervous. When you're doing a session for someone else you don't feel quite so responsible for everything that's going on. But, of course, it's always important to give your best effort no matter what the situation."[11]

Bobby Thompson— a bluegrass musician's indoctrination into Nashville's music numbering system

"Once I played a [orchestra leader] Fred Waring session. He walked in with the charts, every note was written, and there were no chord symbols at all. He raised his baton, and no one played a note. Finally, a piano player (Beegie Cruser Adair) went around and wrote the chords out for us and explained to Fred what the problem was. He was amazed that we couldn't read music. And then he was amazed at what we played just from the chord symbols. Then next day, he came in with everything written out in the Nashville number system."[12]

During this period of studio work, Thompson and fiddler Buddy Spicher worked together a lot. Spicher got his start as a studio musician by fiddling with different groups on the Opry and being invited to their recording sessions. The two men recorded "Area Code 615." Heavily influenced by the "Nashville sound", it opened the doors to their popularity. Other top studio musicians on the LP were Norbert Putnam, David Briggs, Wayne Moss, Kenny Buttrey, Mack Gayden, Weldon Myrick and Charlie McCoy. This group of musicians, known as the "Area Code 615" musicians, played only one concert to popularize the LP. Their foremost responsibility was to session work and not to be on tour. They actually did two albums. The group was also called to back up Linda Ronstadt and Ray Charles on "Hee Haw." After the second LP, the "Area Code 615" musicians broke up. Six months to a year later some of the same musicians and some additional musicians started **Barefoot Jerry**. Thompson was in and out of that group through their four or five albums.

About Bobby Thompson's success as a studio musician, Buddy Spicher said, "Well, actually there's probably a lot of fiddle players and a lot of banjo players that are a lot better. Quite a few, anyway, that would be able to play what me and Bob does on a session, but that's just in one field. What makes Bob so great on the banjo is that he knows every kind of tune imaginable.

9 Joe Ross, "An Interview with Curtis McPeak," *Bluegrass Unlimited*, July, 1992, p. 44.

10 Joe Ross, "An Interview with Curtis McPeake," *Bluegrass Unlimited*, July, 1992, p. 43.

11 Stephanie Ledgin, "Blaine Sprouse - Pick of the Bluegrass Fiddle Crop," *Bluegrass Unlimited*, November, 1982, p. 20.

12 Dick Weissman, "The Nine Lives of a Nashville Cat, Bobby Thompson," *Frets*, February, 1989, p. 32.

He knows music inside and out, whereas the typical bluegrass fiddle player or banjo player doesn't. The only bad thing about that particular music, [is] so many of the musicians get awfully hung up on it (just like classical music) and therefore they get locked in to just that. You have to keep an open mind and accept all kinds of music, I think. Then you become a better player—a better bluegrass player, a better pop player—whatever, because of it."[13]

Earl Scruggs's recording of "Earl's Breakdown"

An interview by Doug Hutchens on his radio show brought Earl's comments about a favorite tune. Though he doesn't have a favorite song, "I will say that the one, I guess, that really launched the banjo further, as far as a

Earl Scruggs

tune that I had written, was 'Foggy Mountain Breakdown.'[14] Of course, I have a pretty good feeling for, like 'Earl's Breakdown' or 'Flint Hill Special,' because of the tuners. Of course, that's been used so much that some of those tunes like that I like pretty well." He invented D-tuners about 1948.

Mr. Scruggs went on to describe the recording of "Earl's Breakdown," "I recorded that thing without a tuner at all, and my banjo at the time had bone buttons on it. We went into the studio and were using Howard Forrester as a fiddle player and Howard is a tremendous fiddle player but he never plays a tune twice the same way. So we went into that tune—I had written a tune and about half-way knew it myself and I knew the tuning part had to go in there—we took that thing and I did real good and I used the standard pegs as opposed to the tuners that had stops on it. The tune went great up until the very end of the thing—and I goofed it. And Howdy Forrester, he just outdid himself, I thought, with the fiddle break. And Don Law was the A & R man. Back in those days we didn't have twelve or twenty-four tracks, we only had monaural. I said, 'Hold that and let me put a shave and a haircut on it or let me try it again.' And I messed around and met Don Law and he said, 'Well Earl, it won't take but three minutes to do it over.' I said, 'You cain't do things over like that!' He said, 'Oh you can do it again.' I said save that one and let's do it again and let's see which one turns out the best. And I didn't know it, but he ran the tape back to the very start and we did it again and erased over the first cut. And that's always been a sore spot, every time I think about that, because neither Howard Forrester and I, either one, did it like we did that one take."

Blake Williams recording with Bill Monroe

"Recording with Bill has been an experience because he hears *everything* that's happening in the entire studio—from the harmony that the fiddlers are playing to each note of the backup."[15]

[13] Doug Green, "Nashville Cats: Blue Grass Style. Bobby Thompson and Buddy Spicher," *Bluegrass Unlimited*, February, 1974, p. 25.

[14] As of 1994, the song had been played over a million times on the radio.

[15] Michelle Putnam, "Blake Williams—The Sparta Flash," *Bluegrass Unlimited*, January, 1990, p. 55.

Chapter 18

Carlton Haney— The Man Responsible for the Bluegrass Festival? [1]

Sonny Osborne described Carlton Haney to the audience at the 1994 International Bluegrass Music Association Awards Ceremony, "If it weren't for that little man (and he pointed to Mr. Haney in the audience), we probably wouldn't be here today."

Carlton Haney was deeply entwined with Bill Monroe—the music *and* the man beginning in 1954 when Monroe hired him to be the manager for the **Blue Grass Boys**. He studied every aspect of the music that Monroe produced. Haney shares his thoughts in these pages. His words give us the idea that this music was created by just one man. Was it? Read on. The six-hour, March 15, 1992, conversation with Mr. Haney has been condensed and edited for a reading continuity.

Born September 19, 1928, in Reidsville, North Carolina (where he lives as of 1997), Carlton Haney received a Award of Merit at the 1990 IBMA Awards Ceremony. This was well-deserved because of Haney's many accomplishments in bluegrass music; he was one of the most influential promoters of country and blue-grass music during the 1960s and '70s and he intro-duced a different type of outdoor bluegrass show which was held on an autumn weekend for three straight days. Although many promoters had done weekend concerts before, Haney's was different (and significant) because this show at Cantrell's Horse Farm in Fincastle, Vir-ginia, on September 3, 4, and 5, 1965, also included workshops and three solid days of bluegrass music. The event marked a new beginning for bluegrass music.

During the course of a 1992 telephone interview, the subject came around to Bill Clifton's "festival" in 1961, and the bluegrass world's recognition that Carlton Haney was the originator of bluegrass festivals. We pick up the conversation on this topic.

Barry Willis: Bill Clifton did a thing at Luray— a one-day festival, I believe.

Carlton Haney: It wasn't a festival. It was just a one-day...you can call it that if you want to. It was a one-day, all-day bluegrass... Bill Malone said that Clifton ran the first bluegrass festival... Everybody just assumes that's the truth because Bill Malone said it. But that's not true. Bill Clifton knows he didn't.

Let me tell you what I think. I come to Richmond, Virginia, and was managing and bookin' Reno and Smiley and Bill Monroe. I moved to Richmond and there was this guy who owned a place called Watermelon Park in Berryville, Virginia—John U. Miller. I had Reno and Smiley up there and they had Sunday shows up there on the river. I booked them up there and then he wanted Bill Monroe and I booked Bill Monroe up there and then I booked Mac Wiseman up there and several of their Sunday shows. And that went on for a year or two.

There was a disc jockey in Washington, D.C., named Don Owens. Don Owens and him was gonna put on a thing. John Miller had called Don Owens and said, "I want to hire five bands—all bluegrass bands."

And Don Owens called me and said, "Can you get Bill Monroe? And I want Reno and Smiley and Mac Wiseman and Jimmy Martin." (Mr. Haney recalled it was called "Bluegrass Day" and was August 14, 1960.)

I said, "What are y'all gonna do?"

He said, "John's gone crazy. He wants the **Stanley Brothers**."

I was bookin' them. And I said, "Hell, I can get 'em if you want 'em. You want 'em all one day?"

He said, "Yeah."

So I started callin' 'em. Stanley? Yeah. Reno and Smiley? Yeah. Mac Wiseman? Yeah. Jimmy Martin? Yeah. Got a-hold of Monroe. "I can't do it."

"Why?"

"I'm in Birmingham, Alabama, on Saturday."

Oh God! I called [Owens] back. He says, "Well, is he open on Sunday?"

"Yeah"

---

[1] Dear Reader, Carlton is a great storyteller and extremely accurate in recalling his memories to this writer. But bear in mind that his quotes of other individuals are often embellished with colorful adjectives and language. When he describes a conversation with Ricky Skaggs, for instance, many of the swear words are his, not Ricky's.

"Well then, fly him to Washington."

This place is about forty miles outside of Washington. Fly him to Washington? I said, "You can't fly the whole band..."

"Just him! Somebody else can play for him." I called him back and told him that they would all be there.

"I can't play without my band."

I said, "Well, Bill, this is a special thing."

"Well, I'll have to buy Joe Stuart a ticket." Now Joe can play guitar, fiddle, banjo. So he knew he wouldn't be up there without a man who could play *time*. We wasn't talkin' *time* but I know what Bill was thinkin'—you know, somebody that Bill could depend on. Anyway, they agreed to fly 'em so they did. And John Miller put on the first all-bluegrass day ever put on...before Bill Clifton ever did. And the phone is listed in Berryville, Virginia...John U. Miller.[2]

So I booked shows there for him. When I got into country, I booked George Jones and Porter Wagoner and Dolly Parton and everything. So I put on Fincastle in '65 and '66 and the guys wanted $2000 to rent the place in '67. I said, "Hell, man. I don't take in but three."

Well, that was it so I got in my car and went to Berryville and told John Miller I had a bluegrass festival I'd run two years in a row now on Labor Day and did he want to run it with me. "No. That's too cold Labor Day."

Well, I said, "That's when I got it started."

He said, "Well, you can use the park and I'll run the concessions." So I put on '67 and '68. And the people started comin' in there. That was the festival at the place of Berryville at Watermelon Park. That's where I moved the festival.

But John Miller put on the first all-bluegrass day ever put on. It was his idea to get all of them there in one day.

Now I'm gonna tell you somethin' that's in my book [which I am writing]. The first bluegrass festival was not in Fincastle in 1965. The first bluegrass festival was in the National Guard Armory in Roanoke, Virginia, in 1963. Bill Monroe, the **Stanley Brothers**, Mac Wiseman, Reno and Smiley, Clyde Moody, Jim Eanes...and I put it on in there on New Year's Day. And I was gonna put it on the next year in Richmond, Virginia, and rented the Mosque Auditorium and advertised it for '64 in Richmond because the Old Dominion Barn Dance[3] we had run was a good place. It snowed eigh-

teen inches New Years of '64. We had to cancel it. I said, "Well, I ain't gonna run no more on New Years. I'm gonna change it to another holiday: Labor Day—go outdoors. So then I went out there and rented a horse farm in '65 and put it on in Fincastle—Cantrell's Horse Farm. But the first one... There's a man in Roxboro, North Carolina, got a ticket that he bought to that first one [at the Roanoke Armory]. And I've offered him $500 for it, he won't sell it.

Willis: Right now, the people seem to relate the actual beginnings of the festivals with what goes on now, which is three- and four-day things, and the first one was there in Fincastle. Wasn't it three and four days with workshops associated with it?

Haney: Yeah. You see the thing in the armory was a one-day thing but I call it... You see, when I moved to Fincastle, even when I moved to Berryville in '67, I still called it the Roanoke Bluegrass Festival. The first three-day thing was at Fincastle. Okay. But the first thing that I put on was there in that armory and I called it the Roanoke Bluegrass Festival.

But John Miller run the first bluegrass day and that's where Bill Clifton got the idea. Him and Don Owens run it in '59 or '60. And they had a crowd of cars backed up two miles back from this river... (*unintelligible*). Tremendous crowd.

To the Berryville, VA, festival at Watermelon Park, 1995.

[2] John U. Miller died August 30, 1994. Just before he died, Mr. Miller told his son, John Miller Jr., to get in touch with Carlton Haney and have him put on one more festival—for old times' sake—at the old Berryville, VA, site. Young Miller did that and Haney was quick to follow through. Haney, Miller and associates put $50,000 into Berryville's Watermelon Park in the form of roads, fences, and conveniences for the July 4-9, 1995, festival. The improvements were long-term; Haney and Miller intended that the festival would continue annually and, under their guidance, would grow to be one of the biggest and best, said Haney.

[3] Actually, the Old Dominion Barn Dance had ceased to exist in 1957 and was now called the New Dominion Barn Dance when Carlton Haney took over as the show's manager. The previous manager was "Sunshine" Sue Workman. Both shows were broadcast on 50,000-watt WRVA of Richmond, Virginia. The original show began about 1947 with artists such as Chet Atkins, Grandpa Jones, the CARTER FAMILY, Merle Travis and Joe and Rose Maphis.

In April of 1955, Haney re-formed RENO AND SMILEY and, as their manager, got them an audition with Sue for the Old Dominion Barn Dance. She gave them a regular spot at $150 per week. They stayed at the Barn Dance until Sue decided to close it in 1957. WRVA sold the Barn Dance to Haney for $1 who then took over its management. In the 1960s, the Virginia Life Insurance sold the old, decrepit building, closed it down, and the dangerous building was torn down. Haney moved the New Dominion Barn Dance to the smaller Belleview Theater (a movie theater). After the festivals got going, Haney needed the time to devote to the festivals, so he closed it down.

Carlton Haney (L) and John U. Miller Jr. at Watermelon Park, 1995

Carlton Haney on Bill Monroe and the origins of bluegrass

The conversation with Mr. Haney included many topics which could well appear in other parts of this book, but to assure some sort of continuity, the greatly-condensed interview is recounted only in this chapter. Carlton Haney was Bill Monroe's first manager, beginning in 1954. We now pick up the interview at a discussion Bill Monroe when he was in the **Monroe Brothers** with Charlie. Their duet was one in which two headstrong individuals sang country music together.

Willis: You think that Charlie was holding Bill Monroe back.

Haney: No. He wasn't holding him back. How much older was Charlie than Bill? Charlie was born in 1903. Bill was born in 1911. So when Charlie was eighteen, Bill was ten. So when Charlie was twenty-eight, Bill was twenty. So Bill was just a younger brother followin' along with him. Charlie had to look after him and everything. So he was tellin' him what to play and everything. So when he would sing a song, Bill would tickle...you know, he would play on the mandolin. And Charlie told me that...well, he sung "White House Blues" like Bill sung it 'cause Charlie Poole had it out on record. So they was just brothers. They played together. They didn't know they was never goin' to be nothin'. Or great. Or create nothin'. Monroe just played the mandolin with his older brother and they sung.

And then they had a quarrel or something and they split up and Bill goes to Arkansas somewhere with a bunch and he comes back to Atlanta, Georgia, and he's playin' around and he gets [Clyde] Moody. And he takes

an old Jimmie Rodgers song, puts it up in a high key and sings it different. And Clyde Moody does "Six White Horses" and Tommy Magness does "Katy Hill" and Bill sung the "Dog House Blues" or some blues and Bill done an instrumental and they done six numbers—October 7th, 1940.

Then in 1941, Clyde had left, Tommy Magness had left, Art Wooten was the fiddle player and they recorded. The bass player, Cousin Wilbur, sung on "In the Pines." He sung on "In the Pines" and then Art Wooten fiddled "Back Up and Push" and Monroe sung. "Orange Blossom Special," now that's a scarce Monroe record. That one will bring a couple of hundred dollars. And on the other side, this bass player, "Cousin Wilbur," used to sing a "Coupon Song." That was on the back of "Orange Blossom Special." It didn't sell, so there wasn't many of them made so that's why that record is scarce. I don't know where there's but three of them. And that was in the second session and all. So Monroe was just feelin' around.

And then Clyde come back to work with him, stayed 'til '44. They never made no records in there because the War was goin' on and you couldn't get lacquer—World War II. So then Clyde left in '44 and he tried to make it again with "Six White Horses" but it was under Bill Monroe's name. Then he (Bill) got Chubby Wise, Stringbean, Sally Forrester. Now Howdy Forrester was a fiddle player who worked with Acuff. So they made some records in '45. "Footprints in the Snow" and others and again, Bill just got a band together and played. And he had to have someone who could sing—I forgot who was playin' guitar then unless it was that Pete Pyle. So they made them records.

Okay. In '46, he's got **Flatt and Scruggs** and he does songs that he wrote: "Blue Moon of Kentucky" and all them. And that's what started it all on its way because they played the melody of the things that he wrote—made up. 'Cause you didn't have anything 'til then except old songs he was doin' a new way. So then he did his own thing there, his own music. He wrote it! And Flatt and Scruggs played it. So he kept writin'. And he kept writin'. They kept playin'. And Wiseman, the two he done with Wiseman changed the sound. When Wiseman left, Jimmy Martin and Rudy Lyle and Vassar Clements changed the sound.

Willis: They changed the Monroe sound?

Haney: Sure. They changed from the **Flatt and Scruggs** sound or the Mac Wiseman sound. It was a different thing. Lyle played the banjo in the three-finger roll but it was different from Scruggs and different from Reno. Reno played rolls with Monroe. He didn't play that [Monroe] stuff.

Charlie and Bill Monroe

When he left Bill, he said, "I can't play like the rest of them so I'll learn something else." So when he recorded in '52 he kicked off "I'm Using My Bible for a Roadmap" different. See, he worked for a guy named Arthur Smith[4] in Charlotte, North Carolina. He was a good guitar man.

Willis: And the tenor banjo, too.

Haney: Well, he could play any instrument. But he had a million-seller record called "Guitar Boogie." But Reno would play with him and play banjo like the guitar. He'd just keep his little finger two frets ahead and made the first string, E. On the banjo it's D. But if you note two half-tones ahead of D, it's E. So he kept his little finger two frets ahead and played the rest of them like Smith played the guitar. Then he found out he could play harmony that way because the string up above you is the third tone above the string below you... So there's the harmony right there. See, all you got to do is know how to note which two strings—it's structured that way, the instrument is.

So he got to playin' harmony with hisself. And he liked that. It fit Red and then he wrote all their songs from "I'm Using My Bible for a Roadmap," "Talk of the Town," "I Know You're Married But I Love You Still,"

all of them. So he had something to sing and play. The Stanleys wrote theirs. See, what hurt Martin is he never could write. He had a few hits. What hurt Wiseman—he had to get old English ballads, Irish. They got away with that but then Jim and Jesse never could write. Then when you get on up, the **Country Gentlemen** never could write. So what would Richard Petty be without the race car?[5] So you see, unless you write...they couldn't write—the **Country Gentlemen** had a couple good songs there that could be some good material.[6]

Willis: They went to the library (of Congress) for a lot of that stuff, too.

Haney: Yeah. Yeah. And then Kuykendall and then Gary Henderson up there in Virginia. And Larry Sparks never could write. Del McCoury never could write. So they never had nothin' to sing but somebody else's material. If Loretta or Dolly couldn't have wrote there never would have been no Loretta and Dolly. I mean what happened to Billy Jo Spears? [And] the one that had "Satin Sheets," Jeanie Pruitt, never could write. Buck Owens could write.

Willis: Well, Elvis made it without writing, didn't he?

Haney: But he had sex. He put sex in front of the public.

Now back to this "Blue Moon of Kentucky." Presley did it in 4/4 time. He sung on every beat. Monroe wrote it as a waltz. It's a waltz—that's 3/4 time. You sing it on one and you hold it over two rhythm beats. But Presley put it in 4/4 time. I was with Monroe the first time he heard it.

"What's that?" He woke up ridin' in the back of an Oldsmobile.

I said, "I don't know, Bill. I know 'Blue Moon of Kentucky' and I ain't never heard that." We got to a phone and called that radio station. They said it's a song recorded by a guy named Elvis Presley. Bill was madder than hell that he done that song like that. Two or three weeks [later] and we were in a hotel room and this guy calls me from Memphis and said, "Y'all playin' a live-stock auction in Tupelo, Mississippi?"

---

4 Arthur "Guitar Boogie" Smith, of "Dueling Banjos" fame, played tenor banjo opposite Don Reno's 5-string on "Feuding Banjos."

5 Haney, in July 1995, elaborated on this. His example was that if Richard Petty were to present himself to a racing team and tell them that he was the best driver in the world and that they should sponsor him, he probably wouldn't have gotten very far. But if he said the same thing while pointing to his race car which was on the trailer in the parking lot, the sponsor now had an opportunity to have him back up his words. And, of course, after he ran a couple of laps in his car, that would serve as proof that his product—his talent *and* his car—was worthy of their support.

6 In other sections of this book, it is described that the festivals were having a hard time existing due to the "non-family" orientation and that they almost died because of the unruliness which drove away fans. But there is more to this. We must now address the topic of songwriting, according to Carlton Haney; here's why:

Before Bill Monroe, there were no bluegrass songs—those songs written specifically for bluegrass. When Bill Monroe started writing extensively, the repertoire for bluegrass started getting larger. And other writers—Lester Flatt, Earl Scruggs, Curly Seckler, etc.—increased the quantity of bluegrass songs as well. But into the early 1970s, it seemed like the same thirty songs were being played and sung over and over by all the groups. The audiences were getting bored and attendance was dropping. Enter the progressive groups and the newgrass groups with their new songs and new styles. Audiences got larger as the songwriting increased. And into the 1980s, the songwriting increased in all styles of bluegrass and even more so into the 1990s.

As of 1995, we find that the future of bluegrass is safe. For as long as people continue to buy banjos and mandolins, they will play bluegrass. As the sales of these instruments continue, so will bluegrass.

I said, "Yeah, we're there on Tuesday, the ninth."
You see, they had these auction things where they'd
auction cattle off. Had a dirt floor in it and they got
seats on each side as grandstands and they run the
cattle through there and sell 'em. And we'd play 'em.
We'd put a truck bed in there and we'd play in them
things. We was gonna play the one in Tupelo, Mississippi, and this guy said, "Well, there's a boy who done
recorded Bill Monroe's song down here and he wants to
sing on that show."

I said, "Who is it?"

He said, "Elvis Presley."

I said, "Bill, that boy that's done your song lives out
in Tupelo and he wants to sing on the stage Tuesday
night."

"Well, you tell him to come up there."

So I told him to come up there.

The guy said, "How much you payin'?"

I said, "I don't know. You gotta pay him?"

He says, "Well, he wants to get something." I said,
"How much you pay him, Bill?"

"Tell him I'll give him $15."

"He'll take it." [And we gave him $15 per night for
three nights]. Presley was there. Monroe backed him up
and he sung "Blue Moon of Kentucky." Then Bill went
back to Nashville and recorded it. It started it out as a
waltz and then the fiddles changed it to the time
Presley had it in. And now you've heard the "rest of the
story."

Now picking up on a different part of the conversation...

Willis: You mentioned the importance of the musician's
location on the stage earlier: the fiddler next to the
guitar or whatever. That it makes a big difference in not

Lester Flatt and Earl Scruggs

only how the musicians react to each other but also how
it comes out in the total sound.

Haney: ...There's another thing. Musicians move their
instruments around. Well, you can't move 'em—there's
sound comin' out of them. Any time you move one, you
move those sound waves and mess up your harmonics.

Willis: Well, if your harmonics are wrong, and every
once in awhile you get it right, it must be awfully
inconsistent at that point, wouldn't it?

Haney: Well, you see, Monroe, once he puts a mandolin
up to the mike he never moves it while he's playin' it.

Willis: He doesn't work the mike like a lot of people
like to do, huh?

Haney: He puts the mandolin where it's supposed to be
and stays there until he gets done playin' the note
because if he moves it, he's gonna move the tones and
the vibrations, you see. It's like shootin' water out of a
hose pipe and you want to shoot it into that tub over
there. If you move the nozzle around, you ain't gonna
hit the tub, are you? Well, the sound comin' out of the
hole in that instrument—every time you move it, it
goes in a little different direction. It's *that* delicate. I
mean it's like me talkin' to you and turnin' around
sideways. You see what I'm sayin'? So it's all...and with
Monroe, you just learn to do it. It's like a young'un that
you raise. He just learns to be like Daddy or Mommy.
So with Monroe, you do it. The music starts to gettin'
better. He controls it. You just play with him. And he
gets it right.

Willis: It is said that the most significant thing in
Monroe's career was when he was booked into the
colleges, out of the South and into the northern colleges, by Ralph Rinzler. When he took over, it all of a
sudden started giving Monroe recognition that he never
had before.

Haney: That's not true.

Willis: What was the change, then? How do you see it?

Haney: He never played ten colleges. He might have
played one or two. He may have took him up there
some place, but at that time we couldn't make enough
money to eat on. The biggest change in Monroe's life
and his music was the festivals. And every one of us,
without the festivals every one of us would have done
starved. It gave 'em a place to play.

Now I was runnin' coliseum shows and I put the
Osbornes with country acts—Conway Twitty, Loretta

Lynn, Porter Wagoner, Dolly Parton. In fact, in '65 and '66, I run Fincastle. When I moved the thing to Berryville in '67, I called Porter Wagoner and asked him...he had called me and told me he wanted to hear one of these. He said... "I remember I used to come and see Bill Monroe in Missouri. I remember one night Jackie Phelps and Don Reno was playin' with him and they started to tune and Don's banjo was out of tune and Bill just stopped and said, 'Don, you got to tune that banjo.'

"And Phelps said, 'Yeah, Bill. Tell him to get it tuned.'

"And Bill turned to Phelps, 'It wouldn't hurt you to touch up that guitar a little bit.'"

Porter never forgot it. So I run two festivals and he told me he wanted to come and see one of them. 'Cause I was workin' him 80 days a year, you know. I told [Porter] I had to move it up to Berryville, Virginia, and he [wanted to bring his band down there and play and agreed to be advertised for the 1967 festival].[7]

The first bluegrass festival I was givin' Monroe $450/day. He called me on Wednesday and didn't have a banjo player. I had a list [of banjo players] and I said, "Let me read you these."

And I come to Lamar Grier. He said, "Who is that?"

"That boy up in Washington [that] we saw in Richmond."

"Oh, yeah. I liked him."

I said, "All right. I'll call him." I called Lamar Grier and told him would he come to Berryville, right outside of Roanoke, and play with Bill Monroe that weekend—he might get a job. You see, Bill Monroe came with a band that didn't have a banjo player to the first festival for $450 a day. I found the receipts to the motel where they stayed—a room cost $3.50 a night and didn't no more than two stay in it. [That was in] '65.

He said, "Yeah." So then Bill called me back in two or three hours and said I had to send him $400—he didn't have enough money to come so I wired him $400. And he come to the first festival. And Lamar Grier said that was the first time he had ever seen him.

But the thing is that the festivals—'68 Berryville was the second one up there—began to click; '69 they were clickin'. There was twelve by '70. By 1975, there was 300. So the festivals saved the music. If it hadn't been the festivals it would have died! Because Jim and Jesse was tryin' to record somethin' else. Mac Wiseman was recordin' "One Mint Julep" with pianos and all. **Reno and Smiley** was makin' a livin' because we was on TV. Flatt and Scruggs was makin' a livin' because Martha White was feedin' 'em and Jim and Jesse. Jimmy

Martin—I don't know where he was and there weren't nobody else. Mac Wiseman didn't have a band. Mac's always made a livin'. He could work country-type things. So the festivals saved the music. It would have been dead long ago. There would have been no new bands—never been no more. Never would have been no **Country Gentlemen** 'cause nobody had ever heard of them out of Washington. Or the **Seldom Scene**. Duffey left the Country Gentlemen, formed a band, called me in '72 or '71, said he was comin' to Camp Springs with a new group. I said, "What's their name?"

"Seldom Scene."

I said, "Well, nobody will know who they are. I'll just advertise you as a special guest." And I did. So without the festivals you wouldn't have any bluegrass music today. Even Monroe, he would have made a livin' 'cause he's played the Opry. But when I had the first festival there wasn't nigh a one of them would draw 50 people but Flatt and Scruggs and Reno and Smiley.

Willis: Yeah. I guess Jim Eanes, I think he told me that he didn't get paid that first year but you promised to pay him the second year and, by golly, you made expenses and paid 'em for two years that second time.

Haney: Yeah. That's right. And at the first one, I couldn't pay the Stanleys but $150 of their $300. That's all they was gettin' a day. So the next year... Carter died December the second and was unable to come to the second one. And I paid Ralph at the third one—the first one up at Berryville—the $150 for the first one.

Willis: How did you make a living out of all this? That sounds like a tough way to go.

Haney: I had **Reno and Smiley**. We had a television show every morning at Roanoke and I got $75 a week from the television station. Each one of us got $75—five of us. We started that in '56. I was livin' on the...I had a Cadillac. I would book 'em, they played shows and they drew. They were the best show on the East Coast. I could get $300 for a Sunday in parks and all. And we played schoolhouse off that television and [we'd] have 5, 6, 700 people at a schoolhouse. They seen us on television and we'd make $230, 60, 70 with a PTA sponsor or something. We'd get the date at the schoolhouse and we'd give them thirty percent, we got seventy. We'd make $2-250 on a Friday and then on Saturday we'd make $500. We'd split it $100 apiece and we'd give 75 to the television station. So we was makin' $175 apiece.

---

[7] Haney continued in an interesting anecdote about Dolly Parton: "About three weeks before that, he called me and told me Norma Jean had quit and he was gonna bring another girl singer if he could find one and did I know where there was any girl singers. I said, 'Yeah, there's one...' He said, 'I'll tell you what you do. You just get me five and have 'em down here next week and you be down here with 'em.' I said, 'All right.' So I got a girl named Shirley Hunter, one named Mary Click, one named Dolly Parton and two more and I met him down there and he listened to 'em and they all left and the next day he told me he was goin' to take the one from Roanoke named Shirley Hunter. I called her and she'd got back home with her husband. She had two kids and she decided she wasn't gonna go. So then Porter said, 'Okay. Let's take that girl from Sevierville.' I called and she said, 'Yeah.' So she come with Porter Wagoner to the third bluegrass festival and sung two songs—'cause that's all the band had a chance to rehearse with her—that was Dolly Parton."

America's Music | Bluegrass

Willis: Don didn't hold on to his money very well, did he?

Haney: He opened a car lot up and got into the car business and lost it.

We pick up another part of the conversation...

Haney: You see, they put Bill Monroc and Earl Scruggs and Lester Flatt on the Hall of Honor [at the Bluegrass Museum]. What happened to Chubby Wise? He's the only man besides Monroe that worked every Columbia recording. He worked on the first session in '45 with Stringbean and the accordion player, Sally Forrester, then in '46, '47 with Flatt and Scruggs. '49 was the Wiseman and Rudy Lyle festivals *(unintelligible)*. [They recorded] "Sweetheart of Mine, Don't You Hear Me Calling"/"Traveling Down That Lonesome Road" and there was two instrumentals in there that Mac played the guitar on and Rudy played banjo. A lot of people say Mac Wiseman made two records with Bill Monroe—he made four! But two of them was instrumentals and he just played guitar.

Monroe gave [their music] *time*. Old-time music you flog *(unintelligible)* the banjos and all

Don Reno (L) and Red Smiley

and sing on the melody note. It's like 4-4 time. 1936, 7 and 8, J.E. Mainer and **Mainer's Mountaineers** and so and so and so and so who played string music—there wasn't a lot of them, but the ones that were around—Zeke and Wiley Morris—wrote songs. All that was old-time music because it had no rhythm beat in it to separate the melody notes.

And my opinion, when Monroe formed his band in 1939, after him and Charlie broke up in the last of '38, they went to Little Rock, Arkansas, because he had never been there, he wasn't known there and the name of the band was the **Kentuckians**. All right. He came back to Atlanta three months later. In April, he found out that Charlie had named his band the **Kentucky Pardners**. So his being the **Kentuckians**, he was afraid that people would get them confused so he changed the name to the **Blue Grass Boys.**

Now, after [Cleo] Davis left he hired a guitar and singer from [Cherokee] North Carolina who played the guitar like no man has ever played it in country or bluegrass music: Clyde Moody. Moody used a finger pick and a thumb and he had a slap lick—rhythm lick—like a black blues guitar. And he played that with Monroe. And in my opinion, that's where Monroe got that

rhythm lick. Moody sings on the note and he hits the strings, or comes up with his finger, and played a rhythm lick between every melody note. And I can mail you tapes that I recorded of him live. He lived here, and in Danville, Virginia. Me and him was friends—I wouldn't have been in the business without Clyde Moody. That's where I met Melissa (Monroe)—at his house. That's where I met Monroe the second time for him to know who I was. I met him [earlier] at another show and spoke to him but that was just a show. But in my opinion he got the rhythm lick...because if you will listen with your earphones plugged into the amplifier, Moody is playing the mandolin on the 'Mule Skinner Blues.' Who was playing guitar? Monroe. Do you know why?

Willis: [I'm told] because Monroe didn't feel comfortable enough on the mandolin yet.

Haney: No. [This was because] they couldn't play that time. If you'll listen to the time on the "Mule Skinner Blues" it's like a three-lick time. It's got a lick on it like he used on the mandolin. It's like a dog runnin' with three legs. And he played guitar on another record on the next session. I don't know which one it was—one of those fast ones that I can't remember right now. If you'll listen, it's the same guitar lick. It's got to be Monroe playing guitar on that one song in the second session.

Now on the first session, Moody was working with him—the first recorded session October 7, 1940. The next year, when he recorded in '41, Moody had left. Now if you'll listen with your earphones you'll hear Moody—right at the end of "Mule Skinner Blues" you'll hear four or five licks on the mandolin just exactly like Monroe plays rhythm—in between the melody notes. You'll hear it. And that's Moody! Clyde Moody told me he was playing the mandolin. He said, "I didn't know but three chords on the mandolin and I wanted to get paid on the session. So I'm just chunkin' the neck of it." Of course, they just used one mike in those days to record on. But you can hear it if you get earphones and plug into the amplifier and listen to what's inside the amplifier. You will hear Moody, in several places, do that. You will hear it—right at the end of the song is where you can hear it the best. There's three or four licks of it.

Now in my opinion, that lick...Monroe had never heard it before because with Charlie he played the mandolin all the time while he was singing. He never played on one record that they made where he played rhythm. He always just played the mandolin—notes, notes. So in '45 you don't hear any rhythm licks on the songs they recorded: "True Life Blues," "Footprints in the Snow" where Stringbean was somewhere in there on the banjo. You won't find no rhythm licks from Monroe then. And then with Flatt and Scruggs and the song "I'm Goin' Back to Old Kentucky," that's the first time you can hear Monroe doin' those licks. That's the first one. You've got to hunt it down. There's just two or three little places you can hear it.

Willis: You know, it's often said—along that same topic—that one of the problems that Monroe had through the years is rarely finding people that could keep up with him on stage. By that I mean they aren't nearly as good as he is.

Haney: He's a genius! He played just good enough to be the best one. In other words, if you were a bad player he didn't show you up. He just played just good enough to be better than you are. If you was a good player, he played just good enough to play better than you are. If you was great, like Scruggs or Flatt or Reno, he still beat your pants off.

Did you ever hear the "stories" I did on stage from '65 to '70? I did eight "stories"[8] on Sundays at those festivals. I would go on stage, me and Monroe, at one o'clock. Nobody spoke. Nobody knew what musicians he was to play with or what song he was to play until five seconds before I told him. And every musician at the festival—sixty of 'em—had to come on stage and play with Monroe. And they were five or six hours long.

And no man spoke or picked a song and no man knew who he was going to play with or what song he was going to do until I told them over the microphone.

This was for the '65, '66, '67, '68 festivals. Then in '69 and '70 I did two each year, one in Berryville and I opened my place here in North Carolina and did one. That made eight stories. And at the eighth, I announced that I wouldn't do another one. And that was all Monroe. He stayed on the stage the whole five hours—never left the stage. And every musician—I put bands together.

At the first festival I told them I was going to do a "story" on Sunday on Bill Monroe's life, so I planned this thing and I got on stage at one o'clock and I called him up there and I said, "Well, Clyde Moody was the first guitar player. Where's Clyde?"

And he come up and I said, "Let's do 'In the Pines.'" And they sung "In the Pines" first time in fifteen years. And some more songs and then I said, let's see now, the second band—we don't have Flatt and Scruggs here, so his next band was Mac Wiseman, Don Reno and Benny Martin—and they were all here at the festival. Well, they come up and Mac and him did "Sweetheart of Mine, Can't You Hear Me Calling?" They hadn't sung together in eighteen years. And Reno played the banjo and Martin played the fiddle, just like they recorded it. "Mollie and Tenbrooks," "Orange Blossom Special" just like they did it on shows. And I'd put the next band together. The next year I did it again, and by '68, every musician who'd worked with him come just to get to sing with him again.

And '69 and '70 was out of this world because everybody was there—except Flatt and Scruggs—they wouldn't come. Tex Logan, Benny Martin, Chubby Wise, Clyde Moody. In '69, Chubby came from Dallas, Texas, and I put Chubby and Clyde Moody and Benny Martin and Bill Monroe together. I taped all of that. Not only that, I taped every concert, every band, every note of music for twelve years played at my festivals.

The reason I put on these festivals is to show the world this music. The "Beverly Hillbillies" in '65 was on television. People had heard it. Bill Keith told me, "I thought Flatt and Scruggs was the creator." I mean, they had never heard of Bill Monroe! He [Bill Keith] came to my house in Roanoke with his banjo and wanted to meet Earl Scruggs and didn't know how. I said, "You want to meet Bill Monroe."

Carlton Haney (L) and Neil Rosenberg at the International Bluegrass Music Museum story-telling session during the World of Bluegrass, 1994.

---

8 These "stories" that Haney told must have been fascinating. He's a very emotional man who loves this music, lives it daily, and can relate events which occurred down through the years—accurately. He described his story on Bill Monroe's life at the June 1970 festival (probably at Camp Springs, MD) in the paragraph and we can get the idea that the stories were a sort of "This Is Your Life" chronology of the featured artist. He stopped his stories in 1970, but scheduled his next one to be at his July 1995 festival—which he promised to be the biggest story of all. The festival at Berryville, Virginia, which Carlton spoke of, was full of all the wonderful characteristics of his older festivals, but was poorly attended. It may have been his last.

Tater Tate, in a 1993 interview, recalled what this "story" that Haney told is: "The best I know is that it was just mostly...he was so involved in bluegrass music, he just loved it so well, that he just wanted to [tell] the history from when it first started. He made it more or less a life's dream to get all that stuff together and organize it. Sometimes he would tell the story of RENO AND SMILEY, and the next time he might be on a story of Mac Wiseman. It would be a biography [of the groups]. He told how bluegrass had progressed—like gettin' into the colleges and that sort of thing. Haney, hisself, was just so wrapped up in bluegrass music...he just loved all phases of it."

Chubby Wise (R) telling a "story" to Carlton Haney at Haney's 1995 festival.

And I told him about Bill Monroe and he said, "Yeah. I want to work with the man. And I took him to Nashville. Well, I told him to go on. It was on Wednesday; I'll be there on Friday at the Clarkston Hotel. So I met him Friday and took him to Bill Monroe and he hired him that day—Brad Keith. I got most of Monroe's musicians for him...Bobby Hicks lives right down the road from me now. Works for Ricky Skaggs. Got him a job with Monroe in '54. You can talk to Monroe [that] he's the best fiddler in the world—he is. Best harmony. He plays the harmony exactly like Monroe—note-for-note.

Willis: Yes. I think it was Charlie Cline who told me that you just have to teach Bobby Hicks something one time and he'd immediately be able to do it on stage in harmony.

Haney: He's as good, note-for-note, as Monroe. The only thing is, he can't write songs and Monroe can. Monroe wrote instrumentals; Hicks never made up one. I stood up many times to see Monroe play it one time for him and he played it note-for-note. In fact, he was twenty years old standing in my living room—he lived on the end of the street I lived on, we had a little ol' band. I had a new record, "Get Up John," a 78 I just bought of Monroe's and I hollered at Bobby to come on down.

I said, "Bobby, bring your fiddle." I said, "Listen to this new Monroe record." And I played it. And Monroe's got a strange tunin' on that. It's sort of like "Black Mountain Rag." But what he's done is: the first string on your mandolin is E. The second string is A. And he's tuned one of the E strings up to A. And he tunes one of

the top strings down to F# and the other one up to D. And Bobby's standing there listening to it and got his fiddle, and by the time the record finished he had tuned that fiddle exactly like Monroe's mandolin. And when I moved the needle back and started it again he played with the record. And ever since then, you just have to play it for him one time. And he knows every harmony part. See, he can play two parts at the same time. And then he goes back—[like on] Skaggs' records he likes to go back and dub in the third part cause he knows exactly every note that he has played.

But the thing of it is that this music was created from one man's brain.

Haney and I then had a short conversation which led to a discussion of Clyde Moody.

Haney: There wasn't nobody there but Monroe, Flatt, Scruggs, Rainwater and Chubby Wise. He was there. He showed Flatt the guitar runs. And let me tell you this. When you listen to "Blue Moon of Kentucky" in those first sessions they did, all of them come out of the lines making Flatt's guitar run and all Scruggs could play—and you could hear him play on the banjo—was Flatt's guitar runs over and over and over.

Willis: Cleo Davis says he invented the G-run.

Charlie Smith telling a "story" at Carlton Haney's 1995 festvial

Haney: He may have. I don't think he invented it because there was black musicians playin' it and it was just a run [that goes with the music].

Willis: Wade Mainer says that Riley Puckett was probably using that G-run before this time. And Lester says that he didn't invent the run [even though he is given credit for it].

Haney: Clyde Moody didn't use that. Then Flatt come in there and 'cause Flatt had seen Moody with Monroe and all, he had picked up that finger pick. That's where he told me he got it from. There never was another one with a pick on their index finger—just Moody and Flatt. Flatt told me he saw Bill's show a time or two when Clyde was working with him and that's where he got it from. But Clyde never really used the run. He used an entirely different kind of guitar. Then when Flatt come in there and started playing the guitar, Chubby wound up playing the guitar in order to fit the music. If you don't believe it, listen to the hymns which everybody thinks is Flatt. That's Chubby Wise! *[Author's note: a conversation with Chubby Wise verifies this. See the Chubby Wise biography in the Fiddle chapter of this book.]*

The conversation with Mr. Haney then went back to Bill Monroe...

Haney: Monroe knows what chord he's in. That's all he knows. If you ask him, "How did that go, Bill?" He'll just play it for you again. You say, "Wait a minute," and he plays it for you again. When he plays it enough, you'll find you'll know where the notes are. I mean, he just plays it again 'til you get it. 'Cause if you stay with him you'll know every note on the neck of that instrument. You stay a year and a half you're going to know. You've got to stay there a year and a half, or two years. Then you're going to play just like him. And every man got it from him!

Scruggs didn't have no more to do with bluegrass—in creatin' it—except his part. His 184th part. There has been 184 or maybe 187 now, musicians work with Monroe. And each one is 187th of bluegrass. Monroe created it, played it, formed it, made it.

Willis: He had Stringbean doin' some drop-thumb frailing.

Haney: He was frailing. He was a comedian. He wasn't no banjo picker. He was hired as a comedian. He was working for Charlie [Monroe] and Charlie's show was hot in the Carolinas. And Bill hired Stringbean away from Charlie's show to get him like Charlie.

Stringbean

Willis: I heard that he was hired because he was a good baseball player—he could hit anything that people pitched.

Haney: That's a good point. That's what I was hired for. When I went to work for Monroe, I was the catcher. This was '54.

Willis: You were just on the road with the tent shows, huh?

Haney: I never played a note of music in my life.[9] Or sung a song. But I can tell you what he does, and every note of it. I didn't want to play; I wanted to be a manager...I wanted to be in the business end. Now I don't know how to tell you other than just tell you, see.

...Bobby Hicks, if you talk about musicians and all...1970, two singers came into Reidsville and I let 'em in 'cause they didn't have enough money—the festival ticket was $20 for three days. If they'd bought two tickets they couldn't have gotten back to Kentucky. They said they sung and played so I said, "You can sing and play for your tickets. What do you play?" "Stanley Brothers." I said, "Come on. Ralph's here. I'll have him have you on his show." One of them was named Ricky Skaggs and the other one...

Willis: Keith Whitley.

Haney: And the other one was Keith Whitley. Three years later they came to me and said, "They tell me you can tell us how to sing."

I said, "I cain't tell you how to sing." See, at that time I didn't know all this...I knew it, but I didn't know how to tell you what Monroe did. Five years ago, I quit everything I was doing and was packin' up all my records and tapes and all—it had been twenty-eight years—and I'd give up on finding out what Monroe did to all them men, and the twenty-eight years I had wasted in trying to prove that he created bluegrass music. So Jimmy Arnold—he's a banjo player. Have you ever heard of him?

Willis: Yeah. He's also a great guitar player, too. *(now deceased)*

Haney: He's a great damn musician, man. And a fiddle player like you can't believe! Him and Hicks set an' play

---

9 Actually, this is not completely true. Just after Carlton joined Monroe's band as his band manager, Monroe put him on the acoustic bass and taught him how to play the instrument with the band. Haney related that it was not very fulfilling and, many times, he said to himself, "Is this all I'm going to do for the rest of my life—pull this stupid string?" So that period of Mr. Haney's life was over, and he could concentrate on managing the band.

all the time. They live right here together. So Arnold come to my house and I said, "Jimmy, did you know I had all these tapes in here?" There's a room full—800 of 'em. Reel to reel that I recorded at the festivals. I said, "Let me play you something of Monroe here. I want you to play with him." I put it on and he started playin' with him with the guitar and would get out of time. And I said, "What's wrong, Jimmy?"

"Hell, you cain't play with Monroe!"

"Why?"

"Because he don't play time like nobody else."

"Why?"

"Hell, I don't know why. What do you mean why?"

I said, "Well, why can't you stay with him?"

"You'll have to work with him a year or two."

I said, "Well, what does he do, Jim?"

He says, "I don't know what he does. He just has perfect time."

I said, "What do you mean perfect time?"

"He plays perfect time and that's the reason we can't stay with him." He wouldn't even touch the banjo...

Vassar Clements would call me in Roanoke crying on the phone, "Man, get me a job with someone who can keep time like Monroe."

"There ain't nobody, Vassar."

He went crazy. He went crazy...his wife would call me and say, "What are we going to do with him?"

I said, "You can't do nothin' with him." And that's the reason he ain't playin' [unintelligible] on that Nitty Gritty album and got a little fame. He can't play with nobody.[10] Benny Martin can't play with nobody. It's a different time—it's perfect! And Benny Martin has a right hand nearest to Monroe of any man...him and Hicks. Benny Martin is a powerful fiddle player, man.

Benny Martin was with him in '48 and '49. Chubby quit in '47 or '8 for a while. Benny went to work and worked a year and a half. And he quit an' Chubby went back to work with Monroe in '49 because he recorded

on the Mac Wiseman songs and then quit again in '50 and went to work for Hank Snow.

And there was the time in 1977 when Skaggs was with **Boone Creek** at my festival. And he was trying to play "Big Mon" on the fiddle. We walked up there and he quit and he said, "I wish I knowed that."

I said, "Here's the guy that can show it to you."

Skaggs says, "Yeah, everybody can show you."

I said, "This is Bobby Hicks. Bobby, this is a guy named Ricky Skaggs."

Skaggs said, "You mean *the* Bobby Hicks?" 'Cause he had never been to a festival and nobody had ever seen him 'til '77.

And Hicks said, "I don't know that I can remember [the song]."

Skaggs said, "Show me how that goes."

Hicks said he didn't have his fiddle. I said, "I brought your fiddle, Bobby."

"Did you?" He done told me not to bring it and put him off on the other guys, you know. See, 'cause he knows how musicians are and if he went down there with his fiddle they would all think he was going to show them how to play.

And Skaggs said, "Show me." Hicks hesitated.

"Don't you want to show me?" [asked Skaggs.] 'Cause he (Hicks) had never been to a festival and he didn't know that's what they done was swap licks and swap tunes and learn how.

He said, "Do you want me to show you?"

He said, "Yeah. Give me my fiddle." So he showed him. He took his fingers and put 'em two or three places.

Skaggs said, "I'll be damned![11] Why couldn't I have figured that out?"

They got done and I said, "Sing one Ricky." And I've been after Ricky for five years to sing on the other beat. I didn't know how to tell him. I kept tellin' him he was singin' back'ards. That's what I was tellin' him then. You're singin' back'ards. See, 'cause I don't play and

---

[10] This writer asked Vassar about this. He couldn't remember one way or the other.

[11] Dear Reader, this is sort of a touchy subject. Allow me to elaborate.

Bobby Hicks read this conversation, as told verbatim by Carlton Haney; he had some rather interesting reactions. Hicks said that Skaggs would never use this kind of language—words such as "damned" or "son of a bitch" and words of this ilk. So what we have here is a story told by Carlton in his own words and color. Hicks actually laughed when he found how the words portrayed on these pages actually captured the personality of Carlton Haney. That's the way he talks, he told this writer.

The bottom line here, Reader, is that Mr. Haney sometimes embellishes his stories with his own language. Most people do, I suppose. But if you can get past the swear words that he uses and consider that his language is not meant to reflect adversely on anyone and is only meant to tell a story, please allow Mr. Haney to get his point across to you. His "point," in this case, is that Bill Monroe had a certain way of affecting those individuals who played with his band. So, please, enjoy the talents of one of bluegrass music's best story-tellers.

Mr. Hicks also said that this conversation between him and Skaggs "may have been true but I don't remember any of it." But he didn't deny that it occurred, either. Hicks recalls vividly, however, that the first time that he and Skaggs met, Skaggs was most impressed with Bobby's five-string fiddle.

And the part about calling Bill Monroe a "son of a bitch" (according to this story) would *never* have been true because Hicks would never have called his boss such a name—and he still wouldn't. Remember that this is *still* a story told by Carlton Haney.

Hicks does agree that the gist of the story which Haney told was true. He *was* affected by Bill Monroe. "I was playing bluegrass; that's all I ever played. And when I went to work with Monroe, it felt like a different timing. And I discovered then that there was a right way and a wrong way. Monroe taught me how to play bluegrass. I was playing Monroe's bluegrass before I joined him but it just didn't *feel* the same until I was in the band with Monroe. There's just something about that chop on that mandolin that puts a whole different feel in the music. I'm not saying that what I was playing earlier was different than when I joined him. I'm just saying that we didn't have a Bill Monroe in the band I was playing with. There was a *whole* different feel when he was back there chopping that mandolin. It's not that the music is different; Bill Monroe makes it feel different."—Bobby Hicks, September, 1995, interview at IBMA.

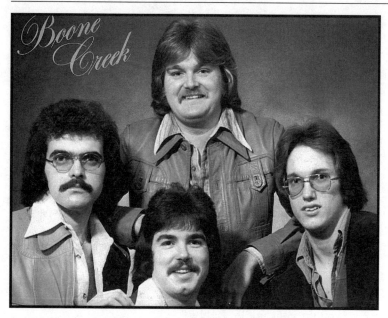

Ricky Skaggs and Boone Creek, Rounder Records #0081.

sing. I just knew he was over there on the other beat and didn't know there was two beats in all this stuff.

So he started singin' and Hicks looked at me. I looked at him and just shook my head and Skaggs stopped and said, "What is it?"

I said, "[Like I said before], you're singin' back'ards."

[Skaggs] said, "Hot damn, Bobby. Would you show me what he's talkin' about? He's been after me for five years on this."

And Hicks said, "You want me to?"

He said, "Yeah."

"Well, I'm gonna start playin'. You sing with my fiddle, but when I start doin' something else don't you come over there, 'cause I'm gonna play some *time* for you."

Bobby started playing time on the fiddle just like Monroe's mandolin. He could make it sound exactly like Monroe's mandolin. Right in between. Pushin'.

Skaggs' eyes got big as two eggs. "Let's sing another one." He sung another one and he got through that and he stopped and looked at Hicks and said, "I will be damned. You mean to tell me I've been doin' it wrong all my life?"

Hicks said, "If you been doin' it that way you have."

I said, "I've been tryin' to tell you for four years, Ricky."

He said, "Let's do another one." Bobby really showed him some fiddle, you know. He had never heard nothing like that 'cause he had not been to Nashville. So somebody hollered "Boone Creek's on!" They went up the stairs to the stage and me and Bobby go out the back of my stage and Hicks takes hold of the back of my arm and stops me. Now I'm at my festival with the **Country Gentlemen**, the **Seldom Scene**, everybody.

He said, "Let me ask you something."

I said, "What is it, Bobby?"

"Don't everybody here know they are playin' wrong?"

"No."

"Well, can't they hear it?"

I said, "No, and neither did you when I took you to Nashville in 1954 and got you a job with Monroe."[12]

"Hell, man, I ain't never played like that now." He got mad now. "I know damn well I ain't never played like 'at."

I said, "You did, Bobby. One man changed you."

He thought for ten seconds and said, "I will be damned! Is that what he done to me?"

Willis: He didn't even realize it?

Haney: He didn't realize it. He said, "I will be damned. Is that what that son of a bitch done to me."

I said, "That's what he done to every man that worked with him. Now you tell me what you done to Skaggs."

"Hell, I don't know!"

"Bobby, I've done wasted twenty-some years and I can't tell you. You tell me what you done to Skaggs."

"I don't know! He was wrong!"

"What do you mean he was wrong?"

"He was just wrong! Everybody here is wrong! The time is wrong!"

"Well, tell me how to..."

"I can't tell you—I can show you. You get a guitar."

I said, "I don't play! You know I don't play."

"I'll be damned. You mean they don't know they are wrong?"

"That's right. Neither did you when I took you down yonder."

"Well, you are right. He taught me everything I know, didn't he?"

I said, "That's right—every note you know."

We now pick up a different part of the conversation.

Haney: But you see, this thing of... All these musicians developed their own styles because Monroe never did let you play like another man. Now listen to this. In the fifties—I told you that I hired all the musicians for about ten years. He'd just tell me when one would quit and see if I could find another banjo player. And fiddle players. I found this fiddle player. No, it was a banjo player. We [were] in the back of the Opry and the guy in the back was showin' off the other musicians tryin' out. And they do a song and he does a little Scruggs—you know, down on the neck and everything—that poppin' thing Scruggs does.

A m e r i c a s M u s i c | B l u e g r a s s

12 Bobby Hicks, in a 1995 conversation elaborated: "He didn't take me to Nashville. He lives in Reidsville, I live in Greensboro which is like 20-25 miles apart. He came to my house in Greensboro one night and asked me if I would play bass with Bill Monroe's band for two weeks that he had booked in the area. Monroe didn't have a bass player so he wanted me to go and play bass for him in two weeks in 1954, which I did. By the time those two weeks were over with, Monroe asked me to come to Nashville with him and he would let me play a fiddle tune on every show and let somebody else play bass for one song. So when he asked me to come with him I said yes. Being on the Grand Ole Opry is every musician's dream when they are first starting to play. So, sure, I came with him to Nashville. And that's how I got to Nashville."

Monroe says, "I wouldn't play like that." That's all that he said. He just said he didn't want that in the song so they done another one and they got in it and he done a little thumb—Don Reno, you know. He looked at the other musicians and grinned a little bit, you know. And Monroe said, "I wouldn't play that way either."

I slipped around behind him and said, "Son, don't play like nobody else. You play like yourself."

He said, "What?"

"Play like yourself." I didn't want to scare him. I thought of whispering to him.

He said, "What! How do you do that?"

Monroe's tunin' the mandolin a little bit. Turns and looks at him and said, "You learn what everybody else knows—and then never play it." That's what he taught every man. You learn what Scruggs and Reno and Rudy Lyle did, and don't you play it.

Willis: Oh! I see what you mean. Develop your own style... But, there is a certain element of folks out there that say if you want to play a certain song with Bill Monroe you've got to sound exactly like the fiddle that played it on the original recording, the banjo player that played it on the original...

Haney: Not true. If he hires a musician to go to work for him, if he's gonna do "Uncle Pen," there's no way you can play it on the fiddle unless you play it like Red Taylor played it because that's the melody. You don't have to get the tone necessarily, but you got to get the same notes because Taylor played the melody.[13]

The conversation evolved to the timing of different bluegrass groups. Jimmy Martin's timing— it came from Bill Monroe!

Haney: Every one of them is a little different in a way, but Martin's probably the closest to Monroe of any man. When he gets a new musician, he has the same problem Monroe does: they can't keep time with him. I've seen Jimmy have to stop, they'd be so far off. You see, unless you was up there as a musician, you wouldn't understand it. It's like a trottin' horse; if he breaks stride he has to stop all over. It's that way with Monroe's music.

When he's playin' up there and he's playin' rhythm and you see him ticklin' the mandolin, that's because whoever he's playin' with just got out of time and the only way he can get hisself back in time is to tickle the mandolin and pick the beat back up. Every time he does that ticklin'— you know, doing the rhythm or backup—it means that whoever is singin' had done sung off beat. Not off key now—but off the beat—and Monroe has to do that to get back in time.

Willis: You've noticed that happening, huh?

Haney: I've been with him. I know every move. I know everything he thinks. I know everything. And I know exactly how he does it and why he does it. And you get right back in time when you do that 'cause, see, what you are doin' is doubled the lick. He's doubled it and then he picked the beat back up. And then he gets back with the singer. If you work with Monroe a lot, you will get those two beats completely separated. The rhythm beat will come out of the left side of the brain, and the melody beat will come out of the right side. Then when that gets to happenin' they are like a half a minute between 'em. It's the most amazin' thing.

Mr. Haney's efforts the past several years have been dedicated to teaching the" Monroe sound" in his Bluegrass Learning Center near his home in Reidsville, North Carolina. He explained his obsession with the subject.

Haney: I started unpackin' the tapes and listenin' to 'em. They had never been rewound or played. All these reels. And I started listenin' to 'em. And I could find in there all this stuff, and I started practicing—just my hands and feet—'til I can play Monroe's time, show you and talk at the same time. I've been practicin' five years. I'm buildin' a learnin' center out here where I'm gonna put my tapes and I'm writin' all this down. And a hundred years from now a kid can come in here and hear sixty hours of Monroe, **Country Gentlemen**, **Seldom Scene**, Ralph Stanley, **Osborne Brothers**, every big one that's ever played.

...Eighty percent of all country musicians have no idea what triads are and how they are built and how these tones are done or nothin' about it. Jim Eanes come down here the other day and saw me workin' on it. "What are you doin'?"

I said, "Jim, make me a G chord on that guitar." I said, "What notes are you makin'?"

"Hell, I don't know."

I said, "You don't know what notes you are makin'?"

"No. What do you mean?"

"Well now, you are hittin' all six strings there. Why are you hittin' 'em there?"

"Well, because that's a G chord. That's the way they showed me how to make a G chord."

"Do you know what notes is in G chord?"

"Hell, no!"

"Do you know what notes is in C chord?"

"No. I just know where to put my fingers."

I said, "How do you know what you are singin'?"

"I sing what tone the guitar makes."

See? They have no idea.

On the subject of the "high, lonesome sound," Mr. Haney had lots to say.

---

[13] The essence of this statement is that a person should stick to the melody—the melody *is* the song, and that's what Monroe did. What Haney means here is that Monroe always plays the melody, so it follows that Monroe does a song the way it should be done.

Willis: Charlie Cline said that when he was with Monroe they invented the *high, lonesome sound* right there. Do you agree with that?

Haney: Chubby Wise invented it. They did "Voice from on High," the gospel song... You see, "Footprints in the Snow" has that *high, lonesome sound* in it. The lonesome sound came from the fiddle... Nobody had put it in singin' and played the melody. Acuff had Tommy Magness who had worked with Monroe and who worked on the "Muleskinner Blues" record. He was Acuff's fiddle player and he played on the "Muleskinner Blues." Magness just fakes the song—he don't play the melody. He's just playin' the chords. He don't know it note-for-note. It had never been done until Chubby Wise done it on "Footprints in the Snow." And that, to me, in the instruments, is the *high, lonesome sound.*[14]

Willis: While we're talking about other folks—Kenny [Baker] and Josh [Graves] told me that Bill and Charlie had the worst duo they had ever heard. I said that I had never heard that before because they seemed to have been the standard of the brother-industry, well one of them, at that time.

Haney: Charlie liked to sing in high C. Nobody else had sung in C. Mainers, the **Morris Brothers**, the **Callahan Brothers**, Riley Puckett and Gid Tanner...nobody done it in C. And they could do it in C. B natural is Bill's key now. He didn't like C that much. Charlie just strained him. But Charlie liked C. The **Blue Sky Boys** couldn't. **Mainer's Mountaineers** couldn't. **Callahan Brothers**, Pappy Sherrill and Snuffy Jenkins and all them— nobody could sing it in C.

Bill Monroe never fired a musician, Mr. Haney declared. This seemed a bit astounding to this writer so I've since spoken to many people who might know—they confirmed what Mr. Haney said. Haney elaborated:

Haney: This goes for any man that worked with him. If he finds you, you got a job 'til you quit. You know he can make it rough on you, and if you ain't carrying your end of the road he'll make it rough on you. He'll do that by tellin' you, "You ain't playin' right. Now you get in here!"

"What do you want me to do?"

"You get that time right! Now you get in here!"

Martin's got Monroe's time. If you can't play it, he can't play with you. And if you can't play Monroe's time, Monroe can't play with you. You'll mess him up. Monroe don't lie to you that he's gonna give you time to learn it. He knows you gonna develop it; every man has. And he knows that it takes that. But if you ain't carryin' your end, if you ain't wantin' to play that guitar two or three hours a day, if you ain't wantin' to do it...if you're wantin' to lollygag around and run around with a bunch of gals at night or mess around, he ain't gonna put up with that. He'll just make it so rough on you that you say, "Hell, I'm gonna quit." You quit then.

Kenny (Baker) was with him for years. I don't know why he quit, but Monroe ain't never mistreated no musicians other than back when I was with him we couldn't make enough to pay. We couldn't make it! When we didn't have it, we didn't have it. He was broke and he didn't have it. He tried. You could leave any time you wanted to. That's the way it was. And a lot of 'em left. But there ain't nigh a one of 'em that don't love that man, worship him, respect him. and nigh a one of 'em will say a word against him. And he's never told a lie to no man in his life. You'll never find one man tell you or me that Monroe's ever told a lie. And he's never took a drink of alcohol... He don't like it. He never took a drink or smoked a cigarette. That's the reason he's eighty years old and he can still sing. But the music come from him. It's *his* music!

You know Scruggs and Reno—I lived with Reno ten years. He's the greatest all-around musician I've ever seen. He could play a banjo, a fiddle, a guitar, a bass, a mandolin. His banjo playin' was so complicated that it was not copied so it was never popular like Scruggs' was.

It was just Reno and he recorded a song called "Follow the Leader." And I saw a banjo player come into my stage underneath—Jimmy Arnold was up there—and this smart aleck guy had his banjo and walked up.

"I hear you are Jimmy Arnold."

"Well, yeah. I am."

"I hear you play a pretty good banjo. Let's pick one."

Arnold said, "Well, what do you want to pick?"

"Anything. You pick it."

J.E. Mainer and his Mountaineers

[14] Mr. Haney later elaborated that the entire *high, lonesome sound* originated from the voice of Bill Monroe. He explained that when Monroe sang tenor to a lead singer, he left the octave in which the song is sung and Monroe would tenor it in the next highest octave. Musically speaking, Haney explained that's twenty half-steps above the melody. This is especially apparent in "Sweetheart of Mine" and "Mighty Dark to Travel." Haney said that the person who comes closest today to what Monroe did is John Duffey, but explained that Duffey has to go into falsetto in order to reach it.

But back to a fuller explanation of what Monroe had Wise play with the BLUE GRASS BOYS. Haney explained that Monroe taught Wise to play the songs he wrote note-for-note, and in the same key and hand position on the fiddle, what the melody was—and Monroe had him do it in the "long bow." technique of fiddling. The first song Chubby did this way was Monroe's "True Life Blues" followed by "Footprints in the Snow." Haney: "It's Monroe's voice on the fiddle—that's your *high, lonesome sound.*"

And I could tell, boy. Arnold was really gettin' pissed off. Arnold said, "Well, no. You pick one. If you want to pick, I'll let you pick it."

"No. You go ahead and pick one."

Arnold said, "All right, let's play 'Follow the Leader' by Reno."

"Oh, wait a minute! Hell, I ain't too much on Reno."

He said, "Well, hell, you ain't no banjo picker." And the guy left because nobody can play that but Arnold and Reno. Reno taught it to him. And that's the ultimate. You mention that to a banjo player you'll see him put his banjo in the case. Reno did a lot of things. I liked his style. A lot of people liked Scruggs' tone. Scruggs gets a tone no man will ever get. Reno knew the neck of one, and no one will ever know the neck of one like he did. He played two-part and three-part harmonies.

On the topic of the serious injury to Bill Monroe's mandolin, Haney recalled:

Haney: The repairs on Monroe's mandolin (by Charlie Derrington) were close to the original sound—it'll never be like it was before it was busted up. Never. It's a shame. But he's got it pretty close. Closer than I thought he would. I can remember when I was doin' those stories on stage with him, he could hit a 4th string after he got it into perfect tune...you see, if he was one vibration off he'd work with that thing and then it would shake that whole stage. I got some notes on these tapes. You would not believe it's just a note off the mandolin when he was tunin' it. It's the prettiest thing you ever heard. It's the greatest instrument in the world. It's a shame.

I can remember when he first got it back from Gibson when I first went to work with him and he had set it...he had a box of strings in the case and he had put the mandolin in there—he had the original case, you know one of them old ones in the shape of the mandolin? He had a box of strings in it and he had a mandolin in it and he shut the lid down, fastened it, and when he went to get it out the next time, he broke the neck a little. So he sent it back to Gibson to have it fixed. And because he had scratched up the front of it a little bit with the picks and all—playin' it all them years—they refinished it. Well, when it come back, I thought he was gonna die, man. And I had no idea what was goin' on. And he got it out and I said, "That's pretty, man."

He said (abruptly), "Don't you talk to me!"

See, I didn't know. He went on upstairs and I went up 'ere and went up to his room and he was settin' there on the bed with a pocket knife scratchin' the paint off of it. Every bit of it...down on the floor. I said, "Bill, what are you doin'?"

"It's my mandolin, ain't it?

I said, "Yes, sir."

"Well, by God I'll do what I want to with it!"

And he scraped every bit of the paint off of it. He played it for ten years with that varnish gone. And then he took a knife and he cut somethin' in the top of it. He took a piece of two-inch adhesive tape and put over it and told me never to tell what was under there. And I've never told. I will in my book but I ain't gonna tell until then.

Carlton Haney promoted concerts to a very large extent until about 1987 and began devoting most of his time to the study of Bill Monroe and, as he put it, "What did Monroe do to 'em. I had to give up trying to figure it out. I had to get this other (Blue Grass Music Learning Center) done. I just done give up and figured I wasn't ever goin' to ever find out. And it's so plain once you find it. You learn to pat your left and right foot and then pat along with country or anything and then listen to how many of them will sing—especially beginnin' the 2nd and 3rd lines of the verse—they'll sing on that rhythm beat every time. And that puts them one off. And they're never with you no more. Because that's a rhythm lick. You sing when you make a note 'cause it's got a tone to it. And that's what Monroe does; just straightens you out and makes you play so you can get overtones on the sound. And then you can't believe how easy it is to play when the rhythm is correct. Like Mac Magaha told me, 'I looked down to see if that was me playin'.' You can't miss. You can't get out of time yourself and it just fits."

Wrapping up, the rest of this interview with Carlton Haney included much that had already been said before. But, in addition, he said that the future of bluegrass music was one of impending doom for bluegrass because Bill Monroe, when he passes on, will take with him all that made bluegrass what it is.

One last point. Mr. Haney has kept track of the popularity of bluegrass music through the years and he noted that it is more popular today than it ever has been. And he feels certain that as long as people keep on buying and playing banjos and Martin guitars, bluegrass will continue to thrive. And the recent sales of the instruments prove that it will continue in its climb in popularity.

Chapter 19

Americas Music | Bluegrass

The Festivals - Table of Contents

The Festivals

The event of the bluegrass festival in America is one of the reasons that bluegrass music is as popular as it is. From the traveling medicine shows and its accompanying entertainment to sell their product, to the gatherings at old-time fiddle contests and the traveling tent shows, the modern bluegrass festival has become a truly American phenomenon as a result of these events. One might even go so far to say that the industry of bluegrass music promotion, some of the independent record labels, and most of the acoustic instrument industry exist because of the festival. Bluegrass music has not only existed because of these events, it has thrived. And entire industries were created to support it. Here is the story of the bluegrass festivals.

Bascom Lamar Lunsford— the "Minstrel Man of Appalachia"

In 1928, at Asheville, North Carolina, Bascom Lamar Lunsford held his first big folk festival. It was significant enough to change history: the festival brought Appalachian music to the general population.

Lunsford hated the hillbilly stereotype and fought to eliminate it by bringing this music to the forefront. At that time, Asheville prided itself as being modern and cosmopolitan. Lunsford had the opportunity to show the local people their history and music when the promoters of the Rhododendron Festival asked him to put on a folk show. The festival was supposed to attract real estate investors to the city and Lunsford's part was to be on the side as "entertainment" for the people. The festival preparations were scoffed at by others who promoted music; they didn't see any way people of any quantity would arrive to view the music. They were wrong. They came out in droves and proved to the folks in the "big city" that this music was important. 5000 people showed up and the sideshow turned out to be the main attraction. The annual event became The Mountain Dance and Folk Festival. This was the first of

many festivals to spring up throughout the country. And from his dance contests came precision clogging. Purists argued that taps and costumes bastardized the art form, but there is no doubt that Lunsford had pushed Appalachian dance and music into the cultural mainstream of America.

Lunsford was born in 1882 on South Turkey Creek in Mars Hill near Leicester, South Carolina. He grew up playing mountain music but made a career of collecting it. He was a performer, songwriter and a collector with a passion for the music of the mountains. In 1963, at age 81, he was still active in this pursuit. He toured the world as a performer, became a renowned folklorist, was featured on a CBS television documentary, and performed for President and Mrs. Roosevelt.

During his search for mountain music and dance, he might stay with a person one evening, or he might stay for two weeks; it depended upon what he could learn from the person. Lunsford searched for traditional Appalachian music uninfluenced by outside popular music. Where most people saw these musicians sitting

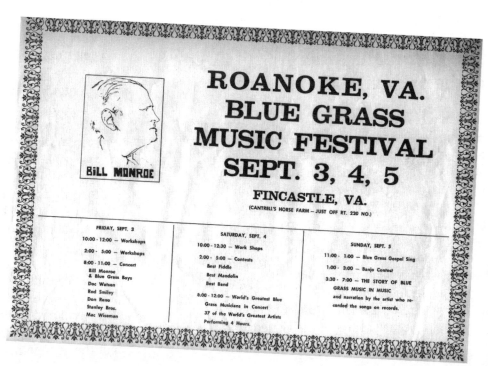

A restaurant placemat advertising Carlton Haney's first bluegrass festival. Donated by Tom Gray.

around on the porch playing music, Lunsford saw talent; even the least capable musician was of interest to him. What he was after could only be found in peoples' homes, not on records.

He was enthusiastic about buck dancing. He took what people did as a social activity and identified it as an indigenous art form. His favorite buck dancer and player was Bill McElreath. Lunsford held regular competitions in North Carolina for dancers and musicians alike. This rekindled the spirit and skill of mountain dancing.

Lunsford could remember hundreds of songs. At Columbia University in New York in 1935, he recited 315 songs from memory over a period of two weeks. "It was a tiring two weeks for him, as he performed for long periods each day before two microphones used to record his songs on aluminum discs. As Lunsford points out from time to time in the recording, he sometimes forgot stanzas and lines to songs in trying to recall at one time all the songs he knew."[1] He recorded his entire repertoire for the Library of Congress in 1949 which became forty-five double-faced 16-inch originals. Songs included "To the Pines, To the Pines," "Darling Cora," "Sally Ann," "Reuben," "Little Willie," "The Roving Gambler," "Cripple Creek," Old Mountain Dew," "Old Joe Clark," and many other tunes which later became bluegrass standards. His 1935 recording session included many of the above-mentioned songs, though not quite as many.

Lunsford wrote "Mountain Dew." He traded all rights to the song for a train ticket home[2]. He died in September 4, 1973. The Mountain Dance and Folk Festival continues.

Patsy Montana's idea of the origins of the festivals

An interview in 1991 with Patsy Montana showed some insight on the beginnings of bluegrass festivals. She told this writer, "I think that one reason for the success of the present day bluegrass festivals is just a leftover from my day. We used to call it 'all day singing and dinner on the ground.' It was a chance for people to get together and sing together and communicate. Of course, in my day it was religious songs, you know. It's the same love then as the festivals now." This was usually a social affair in church houses, she said. They would dress up in their best clothes and it was a chance to get together in a social situation. These summer events still occur in parts of the United States."

Bill Monroe purchases the future site of the Bean Blossom, Indiana, festival

In 1951, Bill Monroe bought the Brown County Jamboree, a country music park at Bean Blossom, Indiana. The Jamboree was established in the mid-1930s. Instead of the tent, which had been used for years, a barn was built as a concert hall in 1941. Monroe's music personnel connections and skills enabled the Jamboree to grow much faster than before he purchased it. He established an annual bluegrass festival there in 1967 after several years of using the park every Sunday for summer concerts.

Harley Bray on the 1958 Bean Blossom "festival" in Indiana

Harley, a banjoist who is still active in the Seattle area, described the early Bean Blossom one-day shows, "One time we went down to Bean Blossom and Monroe didn't have a band together. The banjo player he had was mad at Bill. He was there with his banjo and he didn't want to play but he was making himself available in case Bill would apologize and ask him to play.[3] Bill didn't ask him. The banjo I owned had the original calf skin head on it but it was completely worn out and actually split on the ring that morning. I tried to borrow this guy's banjo but he was holdin' out. He thought he was gonna get to play.

"There was this big platform at Bean Blossom, I guess they square danced on it. It wasn't there after 1960, but that day cars were parked all around it and Bill was there with a fiddle player from Nashville, and Red, Francis and I played with him. It was sprinkling off and on and so Bill told everyone to stay in their car and instead of applauding, honk their horn! That was the strangest feeling! I was really nervous and Bill asked me what instrumental I wanted to play and the only thing I could think of was 'Bluegrass Breakdown,' so I started it out and boy, I played it fast!"[4]

As a result of this exposure, Harley was asked by Monroe to join his band. But he wanted to stay with **Red Cravens and the Bray Brothers**[5]; Harley, Nate, Francis and Red felt that they were just beginning to put things together and didn't want to split up. How-

[1] "The Personal Folksong Collection of Bascom Lamar Lunsford," a thesis by Anne Winsmore Beard, Miami University, 1959.

[2] It is also reported that Scott Wiseman, of Lulu Belle and Scotty, bought the rights to the song for $25 but generously shared half the royalties with Lunsford.

[3] Harley told this writer that this banjo player was a friend and didn't want to give his name. Harley said that this man was holding out to be paid for past performances and was trying to force Mr. Monroe into paying him. But, as many ex-Blue Grass Boys have learned, no one forces Bill Monroe to do anything. The fact that this banjo player had not been paid is not an unusual circumstance with Monroe's band. That was a less-than-prosperous time in the history of the band and Monroe was having to cut corners where he could. Sidemen in the business at that time made pitifully-low wages on which to try to live. This is one of the main reasons the turnover in bluegrass bands was/is so high.

[4] Barry Brower, "Harley Bray, Bluegrass Gentleman," *Bluegrass Unlimited*, July, 1984, p. 65.

[5] In 1961, Harley and the band got a similar offer from Jimmy Martin when J.D. Crowe left.

American Music — Bluegrass

ever, the band did play a summer as Monroe's host band at Bean Blossom.

During their frequent appearances at the Bean Blossom events, Harley recalled that "This afforded Nate a number of musical opportunities to swap with Monroe. Late at night, long after the audience and the rest of the musicians had departed, the two mandolinists would sit on a bench showing each other their versions of fiddle tunes and breakdowns, scarcely stopping to talk about them. Typically, Bill would play a line or two and Nate would echo back, perhaps adding some variations of his own. No doubt Monroe was pleased to hear a younger man making such good sense out of the music he had created."[6]

Bill Clifton and the 1961 bluegrass "festival"

In 1961, Clifton organized what some people recognize as the first bluegrass festival, a one-day event at Luray, Virginia, on July 4th. This "Bluegrass Day" (as it was advertised) featured Bill Monroe and a reunion of many of his early musicians.[7] Monroe invited ex-Blue Grass Boys Mac Wiseman, Carter Stanley and Jack Cooke to the stage to re-create some of their old performances together. Tickets were $6. The eight hours of bluegrass at Luray also featured the **Country Gentlemen**, Bill Clifton, **Jim and Jesse**, Mac Wiseman and the **Stanley Brothers**.

Clifton's Bluegrass Day, at Oak Leaf Park, was held in conjunction with the Shenandoah Valley radio stations owned by Richard F. Lewis. The park had shows every Sunday from May 28th until September 17th, and featured various acts through the summer. This led Mr. Clifton to a job as one of the organizers of the 1963 Newport Folk Festival where many bluegrass and folk acts played on the same stage.

Also in attendance were Carlton Haney and Don Reno, whom Haney managed. In a March 1989 interview, Pete Kuykendall told of Clifton's 1961 event. Evidently, Clifton couldn't hire **Reno and Smiley** for that festival because Haney would not compromise on the price.[8]

This poster is in the Station Inn, Nashville.

Mr. Clifton's event doesn't get the ultimate credit for being the *first* because it was a one-day event—not a three-day event such as the one Carlton Haney promoted in 1965 which fits the pattern of the festivals we know it today. It served as a forerunner to Haney's 1965 shindig. Haney's festival was also different because it was in an empty field—previous bluegrass events were usually in a country music park of some kind.

Neil Rosenberg on Bean Blossom in the early sixties

"The first time I saw Bill Monroe at Bean Blossom (after Rosenberg moved to Indiana in 1961) there weren't probably more than twenty in the audience. And it was no big deal. People weren't coming out to Bean Blossom because, very frequently, Bill would be advertised and he wouldn't show up. Something else would have happened and he wouldn't be around. And you never knew who would be in the band.

"That all changed dramatically when Ralph Rinzler became his manager in 1963. I remember the first show of the season. It was really an exciting thing. Not only was it good music, but also here's this guy, Bill Keith, who I'd been hearing about from people in the folk revival network in Boston, Berkeley etc., and here's one of the local boys in Monroe's Band.

"In addition, there were people around that I'd met at Bean Blossom—people from Indiana and people who had moved up from the South: North Carolina, Tennessee, and Kentucky and these people felt Bill Monroe deserved to be better known. All of us had a kind of common cause in sort of promoting and trying to get Bill to promote Bean Blossom—to make it more than just another country music jamboree.

"We did all kinds of things during that year that I managed it. For example, we made it into Bill Monroe's Brown County Jamboree. We had the folk people come out and paint the signs and change it from Brown County Jamboree to Bill Monroe's Brown County Jamboree. And it's funny, Bill didn't really know if he

[6] Paul Birch, "Nate Bray," *Mandolin World News*, Vol IV, no. 1., p. 14.

[7] Monroe's band at the time was Tony Ellis (banjo), Billy Baker (fiddle) and Bessie Lee Mauldin (bass). Carlton Haney and John V. Miller held a similar "Bluegrass Day" on Aug. 14, 1960.

[8] Haney held his own one-day "Roanoke Bluegrass Festival", as Mr. Haney called it, on New Years Day of 1963 in Roanoke at the National Guard Armory.

like that. He really didn't really see the point, it seems to me at that time, about using his name to promote either bluegrass in general or the Jamboree. And it took a lot of convincing to get him to bring in bluegrass acts."[9] The Jamboree was bought in 1951 and except for the years that Rosenberg was hired to manage it, Birch Monroe ran it.

The first bluegrass festival—1965

Carlton Haney initiated what is now known as the "first bluegrass festival".[10] It was at Fincastle, Virginia, near Roanoke. It was first bluegrass event of its kind because it was three days long (September 3, 4 and 5) and featured many of the same events as today's festivals such as instruction workshops and crafts sales.

The site of the festival was at Cantrell's Horse Farm. John Palmer, Pam Magaha (wife of fiddler Mac Magaha) and others built benches and swept leaves to prepare for the fans. No one had any idea how popular the festival concept was to become. The bands especially enjoyed the function because they were scheduled to play at the same location for three days instead of their normal routine of jumping into their car after a concert and driving 700 to 1000 miles to their next job. They also enjoyed having an opportunity to meet their fans. One reason for the Roanoke site was because of the broadcasting of the very powerful WDBJ which covered areas of North Carolina, Virginia, West Virginia, and Tennessee.

Featured bands at the festival included: on Friday, Doc Watson, **Blue Grass Boys**, **Tennessee Cut-Ups**, **Stanley Brothers**, the **Bluegrass Cut-Ups**, Mac Wiseman; on Saturday, various workshops, fiddle, mandolin and band contests, and the performances of the above groups; and on Sunday, Blue Grass Gospel Sing, banjo contest and Carlton Haney's own "The Story of Bluegrass Music in Music and Narration by the Artist Who Recorded the Songs on Records."[11]

The camper and water facilities were woefully inadequate for the many visitors (around 1000 for the weekend by some estimates). Haney wasn't able to pay all the musicians that year but asked, and received, their cooperation that he would make good on what he owed them when he could, which he did at the next year's festival.

Tater Tate at the first festival

Tater Tate was with Red Smiley's **Bluegrass Cut-Ups** band with John Palmer, Billy Edwards and Gene

Clarence "Tater" Tate at Grass Valley, CA festival, 1987.

Burrows at Carlton Haney's festival in 1965. He spoke of that event, "The first one wasn't a tremendous success. They was several people just out there on the farm—you know, Cantrell's farm up there in Fincastle. At that time, you know, there wasn't a lot of small groups and stuff around, so actually, as far as I know, they had everyone at the festival. There was the Stanleys, and Monroe, and Red Smiley, Jimmy Martin, Mac Wiseman. They were limited back then; there wasn't many bluegrass groups then."

While many of the other groups had to travel to Fincastle for this festival, Tate and his group were based in Roanoke, Virginia, and close to home. "We were at home in our back door, more or less. We lived four or five miles from the place." They worked the festival for the next several years until "there got to be so many of them you couldn't make 'em all."

Allen Mills on the legendary Carlton Haney

A founding member of **Lost and Found**, Allen Mills, remembered Carlton Haney who, in the early 1960s, was perhaps the largest promoter of country shows in the world. At the King Records studio in Cincinnati about that time, "Carlton had us and the **Easter Brothers** there one night, along with some other groups. And, like, the stage was there, and there were the wings, and he had boards—like a bench—and all the artists who did that show came out and set on the stage while Bill Monroe come on. But I loved his music so good..."

[9] Jack Tottle, "Neil Rosenberg at East Tennessee University," *Bluegrass Unlimited*, October, 1987, p. 64.

[10] Technically, the first bluegrass festival may have been held in 1958. Art Menius discovered that a "Blue Grass Festival" was held December 19th and 20th when the University of Louisville basketball team hosted such an event at Freedom Hall in Louisville, Kentucky. The event was a basketball game which they called a "Blue Grass Festival", probably because it was held in the bluegrass state of Kentucky and a "festival" because there were several college teams in attendance. The event ended with the University of North Carolina defeating Notre Dame (81-77) and Northwestern (78-64).

[11] At that festival, David Freeman of New York City was there selling records. Active since the 1950s in collecting and the sales of this music, he founded County Records in 1963. He continues today as its manager. The mail-order outlet, County Sales, was started in 1965.

He reminisced, "By 1946, I was big enough that Momma and Daddy would let me play the radio by myself at night, and I would listen to Monroe. And I loved his music so much that, when I went and set down, when he first started playin' 'Mule Skinner Blues,' tears rolled out of my eyes. And I'm a fifty-one year-old and I'm not ashamed to admit that because I loved it and I'm not ashamed of the feelin' and how I felt about the music. You see, if you love the music, it just gets in you and you can't get it out and the only way you can supply it is to continue to be around it. It's more addictive than any dope or anything. It's just the joy of being around the people of this music that you can't find a replacement in it.

"I saw Clyde Moody and Bill Monroe together on that stage and that was unheard of. To me, the first festival I ever saw was New Year's Day, 1963, in Roanoke, Virginia, at the National Guard Armory. I saw Bill Monroe, the **Stanley Brothers** and **Reno and Smiley** do an afternoon show on one day and all the people would set down and watch. That was the first festival I ever saw."

The Roanoke event was Haney's first bluegrass concert of this type. He later became famous for his three-day festival in 1965, but this was his first "festival". Mills continued, "The music had not separated in those days; it was all the same. **Reno and Smiley** was pretty hot. They were headlining shows of country artists. You can see that on some of the posters of the day. **Reno and Smiley** was almost God in Ohio.

"What Carlton was doin' was—and I saw this at the American Theater in Roanoke, Virginia—I saw Jim Reeves, Margie Bowes, the **Wilburn Brothers** I believe, Grandpa Jones, **Flatt and Scruggs** and **Reno and Smiley** all on the same show at one theater one night. Carlton was great! He was the first man to take country music and fill up a 13,000 seat auditorium in Greensboro, North Carolina. Nobody else was ever doin' it. He was buyin' Porter Wagoner for $1500. In '59 or so, Carlton had a '57 Cadillac El Dorado. He was goin' out, settin' those shows and workin' the door for **Reno and Smiley**. He would rent the theater and sold the tickets. He would do this all over. He would come back and I would ask him where he had been. He said he'd been up to Columbus, Ohio. I was just burnin'. And I would go home and get me a map and see where Columbus was...wantin' to do it bad!

"There was a time when Carlton was a pleasure to talk to. 'Cause if he talked with you much, he would tell you something. Man, he was in the thick of things. He was makin' history and when he turned around, people took notice. He was dynamite! He was big! You can check on the impact of Haney and find a lot of nega-

tives, but he was the biggest thing in country music for what he was makin' happen.

"He made me so mad in 1975 when we was just learnin' to pick. I told him that I wanted to work [his festival at] Camp Springs. He was doin' that down there. He said, 'Look, can you sell tickets?' I said, 'Well, I ain't never done it, but I'll try to go over to the gate and do it.' He said, 'No! I ain't talkin' about.. I mean *can you sell tickets*? I got to have twelve bands that can sell tickets. If you can sell tickets I can use you. Create a demand and I can use you.' That made me so mad I wanted to bust him in the mouth. Later I found out what he was talkin' about. But it was his way of tellin' me that 'If you ain't gonna do nothin' for me I can't use you.' So I was determined I was goin' to sell tickets somewhere. That made me more determined. I wanted to get into this business and do somethin' with it. But he had a funny way of tellin' you stuff like that. But I respected it. At that time, he still was a powerful man."[12]

The Blue Sky Boys and bluegrass music

While the **Blue Sky Boys**, Earl and Bill Bolick, have insisted that they are not bluegrass, they have definitely influenced the music. The close-harmony style of music of the **Blue Sky Boys** and the **Delmore Brothers** has been carried on through the years by groups such as **Jim and Jesse**, the **Louvin Brothers**, Ray and Ina Patterson[13], the **Whitstein Brothers**, the **Tashians** and the **Nashville Bluegrass Band**. A main venue for groups such as these has been bluegrass festivals.

Bill Monroe. Photo courtesy Jan Willis.

[12] From a 1992 interview at IBMA.

[13] As of 1996, Ray (mandolin) and Ina (guitar) Patterson were still active in the music near their home in Colorado Springs, Colorado. This duo played nationally for many years until Ina's hearing aid was disturbed by sound systems to the extent that they had to quit public performances.

"Jumbo" of Japan's Lost City Mad Dogs meets Bill Monroe at a 1983 festival. Photo courtesy Jan Willis.

In a 1991 telephone interview, Bill Bolick spoke about the bluegrass circuit which he and his brother Earl experienced in the early 1970s, "The reason I don't play at bluegrass festivals is because what I saw is that they are too rough. Mainly what I saw was drunks and people on dope. You can take a small group and they'll get together for one band, they'll get encores and this and that. A group that's been out of existence as long as we have—I don't like to compete with people like that. It isn't fair. It puts us at a disadvantage because Earl and I couldn't get together. I don't see how we done it (got together again and practiced for the aforementioned 1974 festival). I don't have that much nerve anymore. I just don't think it's fair because people will say, 'Aw, they will understand.' Well, they *don't* understand! If you get up there and entertain, they expect you to be just as good as you were years ago—and that's the way they judge you. I read some of their reviews and stuff and I just am not going to subject myself to stuff like that because Earl and I have a very distinctive style of singing. We can't do it playing once every ten or fifteen years...and especially quitting in-between times. I feel they more or less invite you as a freak thing. They want to see what you look like after all these years. For that reason I haven't wanted to play any of them. And Earl is even more like that than me."

In a further communication with Mr. Bolick he added, "We played five festivals in 1974. The festivals we played at Camp Springs, North Carolina, were pretty much under control, as was the festival we played at Terrell, North Carolina. However, the festivals near Berryville, Virginia, and Gettysburg, Pennsylvania, were pretty bad. In fact, Mr. Miller, who owned the park near Berryville, stated he would close his park down

entirely before he would allow it to be taken over by hippies, drunks and people on dope. I think he did close it down not long after we were there. I have a newspaper article in my files now, taken from the Greensboro, North Carolina, paper to verify this. This was in 1974 and I have no idea as to how most of the festivals are today... The Union Grove Fiddler's Convention, which was of great renown, was forced to close because of the crime and dope it brought with it. Union Grove is only thirty to forty miles from [our hometown of] Hickory." He added that there were also personal reasons for not wanting to play at the festivals.

The festival scene in the seventies

Tom Gray, who was active with the **Seldom Scene** for nearly two decades, told this writer that "The festivals had become very big in the seventies. There were a lot of young people and a lot of them caused trouble at the festivals. There were problems at festivals with drugs with those who we referred to as 'boogie freaks' who would just act crazy. They were all young people and rather rowdy. And then the motorcycle gangs came in and there was violence. There had been murders in the late seventies. So the festival promoters who wanted it to survive had to restructure them to make them family festivals. They would restrict how or if alcohol could be consumed. There would be no public display of alcohol. There would be uniformed security. Of course, there would be no illegal drugs permitted. Or dogs, or motorcycles on the festival grounds. If you arrived on a motorcycle you had to park it at the gate and walk in. There were all [kinds of] innovative ways of managing the festival to keep them under control.

"And so eventually they did get under control and they are much more pleasant to go to now, but the crowds aren't as big. So the musicians who were used to having all the work they could handle at these monster festivals were faced with a smaller audience— and now an aging audience, because the boogie freaks didn't come back."[14]

In *Bluegrass Unlimited* we read, "It has come to our attention that many localities are still passing ordinances to prohibit outdoor local gatherings or to make having one so difficult so as to limit them without a ban. Unfortunately, although bluegrass festivals are severely hampered by these rules, they are usually not the cause for their being enacted.

"So what we are asking is that the members of our bluegrass audience watch for these things in your community and get out and speak in behalf of the bluegrass festival. If you don't, you may find yourself driving long distances again just to see your favorite once a year."[15]

[14] Quotation during an 1989 interview at the home of Tom Gray in Kensington, Maryland.
[15] *Bluegrass Unlimited*, November, 1976, p. 12.

A pioneer act appears at a modern festival for the first time

In 1971, Ken Swerliss was an enthusiast of folk music who sought out the old stars of the music to play at the San Luis Obisbo (California) Folk Festival. Swerliss, who worked for Warner Brothers Pictures, lured pioneer resonator guitarist Cliff Carlisle and his partner, Wilbur Ball, out of retirement.

On April 30th, Carlisle and Ball were present there at Cal Poly. They were dressed smartly in suits and ties—a contrast to the dress of the typical folk festival attendee who may not have worn even a shirt. The duo was very nervous; they had never been to a college concert before and half-expected a riot to occur. It became an enlightening experience to them because many of the students had researched the duo and studied their music. They were asked questions about who was on what recording, and it turned out that the students knew more about their music than the pair could remember. During the concert, the duo would hear the students yelling out requests for songs they popularized many years earlier such as "Waiting for a Train." The two veterans were now able to understand the importance of their music and its historical significance. And, seeing that people were still appreciating it brought tears to Carlisles's eyes. Carlisle died in 1983. Ball continued performing.

Lester Flatt

In his last interview, Flatt spoke about festivals, "The good ones will [stay around]," he said. "A few you can count on to stay around. But there's going to be a lot of them that are going to go. You're going to have to keep a good festival and something that the people can take their families to, or they are not going to be there too many times."[16]

"Letters" on festival character of the 1970s

Kathy Kaplan, of New York City, in 1973 sent a letter to *Bluegrass Unlimited* about festival audiences, "While we are all eager to see bluegrass flourish, in our zeal we must not act oblivious to the exploitive [sic] measures that are being taken by certain promoters. The new crowds are, among other things, rapidly changing the character of festivals. Perhaps the fact that people are beginning to feel that festivals are no longer a good place to bring the family is not a great issue with many, but what about the utter lack of respect that's been shown to many of our greatest musicians at these events?

Tex Logan (L) and Carlton Haney at Haney's 1995 festival in Berryville, VA.

"The fact that the Woodstock generation *is* seemingly becoming the majority at some of these events is giving grounds to the fears expressed by the locals. And somehow the news always gets national exposure. I believe that anyone who cares about the future of traditional music should boycott these festivals."

In another letter in *BU* several years later (September 1980), Bob Dickerson of Valdosta, Georgia, suggested that promoters rate their festivals in a manner which lets attendees know what type of rules the festival has:

G - The family festival. Absolutely no dogs, drinking or drugs in the concert area.
PG - For families also. Drinking allowed, but not to excess. Strictly enforced.
R - Get as drunk as you want, but if you bother your neighbors, you will be expelled.
X - Anything goes. Definitely not recommended for those who would like to enjoy the music.

Art Stamper

Fiddler Stamper spoke about festivals, "Lots of times at these festivals, in order to profit more, they'll hire some groups that don't have it together and that gives some people who don't know anything about bluegrass the wrong impression of bluegrass music. If they're not well known, I think they should be auditioned by qualified judges. This is just one man's opinion, but it would keep the true image of bluegrass music."[17]

---

16 Marty Stuart, "Lester Flatt Memories," an interview with Curly Seckler, *Bluegrass Unlimited*, May, 1986, p. 85.

17 Marty Godbey, "The Lost Fiddler—Art Stamper," *Bluegrass Unlimited*, November, 1982, p. 27.

The New Grass Revival in June 1973. L to R: Courtney Johnson, Sam Bush, Curtis Burch, Ebo Walker.

Rual Yarbrough speaks on festivals and country music

A 1992 telephone interview with banjoist/store owner Rual Yarbrough added to the topic of festivals, "At one time, I think a few people thought bluegrass might get to be as big as country ever was. It was headed in that direction at one time [because of the festivals]. It was just goin' so big. A lot of the country artists even tried to get on the bandwagon. They started carrying a banjo and they wanted to get booked on the bluegrass festivals. They were seeing something that they liked. I don't really know what happened to that. The radio stations, for one thing, won't play bluegrass music and that keeps it choked out some. A lot of people have a tendency to class bluegrass music a little bit lower than we do. We face that now in church. We just sing in church. When they see you walkin' in with a fiddle or a banjo they kind of look at you like you're some hillbilly or something."

Back to the subject of festivals, Yarbrough said, "I think they did a lot for bluegrass. Definitely! 'Cause I don't think it would ever be like it is [if it] wasn't for the festivals."

The business of festivals

As of 1989, promotion of bluegrass festivals was big business in the South. Colonel Tom Riggs, well known emcee, pizza franchise owner, and entrepreneur, and Bill Barrett were members of the American Bluegrass Network which launched twelve festivals throughout the area using the same well-known bands. They got a good bargain with the bands by dealing in quantity (hopefully assuring a profit) thereby assuring more festivals in the future.

The festivals are, indeed, well-respected methods of bringing money into a community. "One single, two-day bluegrass festival in Louisville [in 1987] contributed

more than $900,000 to the state's economy and generated more than $63,000 in tax revenue—the equivalent of twenty-eight full-time jobs. Further, the development office has found than more than seventy percent of travelers polled in a recent survey indicated that festivals and similar events influenced their decision to visit Kentucky."[18]

Don Parmley

Band leader Don Parmley spoke of his areas of concern. "A lot of times, getting one band off stage and another one on is the worst handled part of a festival. When an emcee is forced to stand out there and tell corny jokes and ask if everybody's having a good time [it] aggravates a lot of people.

"And these poor sound people run themselves to death to try and change the microphones in one minute so the next band can come runnin' out there and the first three songs be wasted because the sound's not right. If a minimum of ten minutes were set aside on the schedule for each band to change, the sound man could play recorded music while a band member from the next band did a quick setup and sound check and it wouldn't bother people. It's just another area in which bluegrass needs more professionalism." Parmley also wants stage lighting to reach the same standards used by a big country show.

He continued, "Some things that artists can do to help promoters is to announce your upcoming shows and encourage people to come to them. Showing up at the park early so the promoter doesn't have to worry about whether you'll make it helps. And your agent should let a promoter know well in advance if you have a scheduling problem, like having an unusually long way to go to your next date. This way, the promoter can make out his schedule and take this into consideration. I'm a firm believer that if the festival management has a

The Hillmen. L to R: Chris Hillman, Don Parmley, Rex Gosdin, Vern Gosdin.

[18] This quote by Kentucky's Secretary of the Department of Tourism, *International Bluegrass*, 1991 September/October highlighted the importance of bluegrass music.

typed or printed schedule, then no artist should try to get that schedule changed on the day of the festival. Sometimes a fan has a schedule and gets there by a certain time in order to see a favorite artist only to find the artist went on early by changing show times at the last minute and has already left the park; that's not good."[19]

Jam busting—an issue at festivals

Now that the festivals have brought together huge numbers of fans at one place, a problem has been created just because people are people. The problem of getting along became much easier when the whole atmosphere of the festivals moved toward a "family event" rather than an event which would invite drugs and troublemakers.

But a new problem seems to be present which concerns many festival attendees—that of jamming at a campsite and the courtesy which must be shown to fellow jammers. One letter sent to *Bluegrass Unlimited*[20] addressed the matter. Some folks complain about it, some write about it, some merely put up with it. Richard Arnold of Earlville, New York, told that there's room for everyone in most jams but there are limits. He wrote, "Beginners can also be insensitive in certain situations. I was at a festival last summer and was in a really good progressive bluegrass and new acoustic jam when this woman steps into the center of the circle and starts clawhammering 'Old Joe Clark' on a banjo that was cheap and out of tune. That really puts a damper on a hot jam. It's no fun trying to play a hot, progressive instrumental if nobody knows the chords or can follow. Even though I do progressive music, I still love to kick off old bluegrass standards with good friends. I feel sorry for anybody who hasn't had this experience and can't enjoy the fellowship that bluegrass music has to offer."

This is the flyer which helped bring in 17,000 people to the 1972 Culpeper Bluegrass Folk Festival. It was promoted and originated by Jim Clark.

[19] Brett F. Devan, "The Bluegrass Cardinals, Synonym for Vocal Harmony," *Bluegrass Unlimited*, May, 1986, p. 9.

[20] "Letters," *Bluegrass Unlimited*, January, 1991, p. 9.

The Business of Bluegrass - Table of Contents

The Business of Bluegrass

Earning a living in the bluegrass music business has several peculiarities which all boil down to the fact that there's less money in it than most other forms of music and it is less lucrative for business people and musicians alike. These pages will identify many of the problems—and rewards—of those who actively participated in this very difficult business which could end up being an ordeal were it not for the love of the music by the people in it.

From stories about individuals included in this chapter, you can get an idea of what the artist had to go through in order to play his music as his/her occupation. Occasionally, you'll find that the musician had to have a day job to be able to afford to play his music. You'll probably notice that most of the people who were trying to stay in the music had to be dedicated—motivated by a love of the music—to remain in it. You might contrast this with other jobs—even other forms of music— where a person stays in that field simply because it pays well.

Bluegrass and the music business— by Dick Weissman[1]

Bluegrass is a very small segment of the international music business in terms of record sales. This is an important point to bluegrass artists, managers, and promoters because what it means is that the major record companies have little interest in recording or promoting bluegrass music.

Generally, artists rely on recordings in order to get playing jobs. There are two sorts of recording contracts that are commonly used. Some small companies use what is referred to as a "one off" deal. In this sort of deal, the company agrees to record an album and there is no further commitment on either side to continue the relationship between the artist and the record company. The large record companies generally want an artist to make a five-year commitment, or to record a specific number of albums for them. There are options in the contract, but they are almost always on the record company side. In other words, a company like MCA gets the artist to make a specific time or product commitment, but the record company can back off after each year of the contract. It is important for the reader to understand the following points:

- Some eighty-five percent of the record business in the entire world is controlled by six multi-national record companies: WEA (Warner Brothers, Elektra, Atlantic) is the only American-owned company in the bunch. The other five are BMG (RCA), Capitol (EMI), MCA, Polygram and Sony. All of these companies are involved to a greater or lesser extent in various media enterprises such as film and television, recording studio operation, concert promotion, book and magazine publishing, music publishing, and the selling of such merchandise as T-shirts and tour jackets. They also distribute and press their own recordings as well as some recordings on smaller labels.

- Recording contracts include small or large advances and payments for recording. Most artists make comparatively little money from recording because royalties are not paid until the costs of making the recordings are paid back to the company. Large company rock or country albums may be budgeted at $250,000 and up. Many bluegrass recordings are budgeted at $5000-$10,000. It is difficult to compete with the more extravagant productions on recording of people like Garth Brooks or Michael Jackson on pygmy-sized budgets. Another record company cost that is quite common is for one of the large companies to give away over five thousand copies of a record to radio stations and music critics. There are quit a few excellent bluegrass albums that will never even *sell* that many albums.

- A typical, fair, starting royalty for beginning artists is ten percent of the retail selling price of the recording.

- Many aspects of recording contracts are highly negotiable, especially the question of who owns the publishing rights if the artist is also a songwriter. The record company generally tries to option these rights, but sometimes the artist is able to keep all or half of these rights. Publishing becomes a particularly important source of potential revenue if other artists record the song in future years, or if the song receives continual and extensive airplay, print rights, and any other uses of a song.

Artists generally get recording contracts through contacts utilized by personal managers and music business attorneys. Other sources include music publishers, personal contacts that the artist may have, music business organizations like ASCAP or BMI and,

---

[1] This brief section is by Dick Weissman, who teaches in a Music Business Degree Program at the University of Colorado at Denver. He is the author of six books about music and the music business including *The Music Business: Career Opportunities, and Self Defense*, Crown Publishing and *Making a Living in Your Local Music Market*, Hal Leonard Publishing.

to a lesser extent, radio station personnel or booking agents. Occasionally, a record company signs an artist who sent in an unsolicited tape, but this is definitely a long shot.

Booking agents obtain work for artists. These agents solicit clubs, festivals, colleges or other venues. They usually take fifteen to twenty percent of the artist's gross for these services. Personal managers monitor the overall career of the artist and make sure that booking agents, record companies and others are giving the artist the best possible deal. Managers are paid anywhere from ten percent to the fifty percent that Colonel Tom Parker took from Elvis' earnings. The usual amount is fifteen to twenty-five.

Because bluegrass makes few people wealthy, there is a shortage of high-powered business people who want to manage, book or promote bluegrass acts. Until and unless bluegrass produces its own Garth Brooks or Madonna, record companies, promoters and managers are liable to have relatively little interest in the music. The few bluegrass songs that have "crossed over" into general popularity, like "Foggy Mountain Breakdown," "Dueling Banjos" and the recent Alison Krauss album, are the exception to the rule.

Asher and Little Jimmie Sizemore— a popular father and son act

Many of the first-generation country radio stars in the 1930s were young, but none as young as the nation's premier child star in country music: Little Jimmy Sizemore. Dressed in a satin cowboy outfit, with his father Asher Sizemore, the kid was really cute. He was a fully-developed harmony singer to his father by age five. He could sing more than two hundred songs from memory.

Asher and Little Jimmie Sizemore

According to author Charles Wolfe, "Much of Little Jimmy's success came from the fertile brain of his father (1906-1973), a pleasant if undistinguished singer who was one of the great innovators in country music promotion. He was quick to follow Bradley Kincaid's lead in pioneering the use of paperback songbooks to sell over the air (in his long career he produced about as many as Kincaid), and through complex system of 'leasing wires' and cutting entire fifteen-minute programs onto large sixteen-inch transcription discs, Asher was able to syndicate his programs throughout the South and Midwest. He also watched his copyrights on songs very carefully and worked to place songs he owned or published with other acts such as Frankie Moore's **Log Cabin Boys**."[2]

Henry Ford— a promoter of fiddle music and square dances

Automobile magnate Henry Ford was very active in the promotion of old-time fiddle contests at his dealerships in hundreds of communities across the land. Art Menius wrote, "Held on Saturday nights, local contest winners advanced to state competitions in larger cities and eventually to a national championship in Detroit. 'Ford's Fiddlin' Five,' who averaged seventy years of age, popularized square dancing and old-time music on Ford-sponsored tours. At the Ford winter home in Ft. Myers, Florida, he used to roll up the rug, hire a band and a caller, and hold a square dance.

"His promotion of fiddling and square dancing did leave lasting results," continued Menius. "It helped spread country music across the nation at the very time when record companies were beginning to promote the old-time sound, which Ford enjoyed for the very same sentimental reasons that millions of rural Americans did. Fiddlers' contests became an established part of life in the rural South. The famed Union Grove, North Carolina, event, for example, began in 1925. The fiddling craze helped George D. Hay to convince the management of Nashville radio station WSM to permit him to go ahead with the barn dance show that became the Grand Ole Opry."[3]

By 1926, in spite of Ford's activities which were effectively spreading old-time fiddling, only the South seemed to embrace the musical art form; it seemed to die outside of the South except for "pockets" of old-time string band music in upstate New York, Upper New England and the Ozarks. Ford then turned his energies toward his museum and toward experimental schools in the Greenfield Village complex in Detroit.

2 Charles Wolfe, album cover notes on the Old Homestead recording "Songs of the Soil."
3 Art Menius, "Our Ford: Old-Time Fiddling and Dancing," *Bluegrass Unlimited*, February, 1992, p. 39.

The early days of the Lonesome Pine Fiddlers—"Bring your outlaws, your in-laws, grandmas, bring anybody, and come as you are."

This band was formed in 1937. By 1939, the Cline brothers, Curly Ray (fiddle) and Ned (tenor banjo), with their brother-in-law Ezra (also known as "Cousin Ezra," whose use of the bass fiddle was one of the few in use at the time) were hired by Gordon Jennings' group which was sponsored by Bi-tone, supposedly a medicinal water additive. Back in those days, hillbilly bands had to get a sponsor if they were to be able to make a living in music. Curly Ray recalled, "If you didn't get a sponsor, you didn't get paid. We played for Syrup of Black Draught for a dollar fifty each while, of course, Porter Wagoner or somebody like that would be raking it in at the Grand Ole Opry for the same sponsor. But you could buy a steak for forty cents back then and a hot dog cost a nickel."[4]

Jennings played guitar and sang with the group on WHIS, Bluefield, West Virginia. Often they had to perform other manual labor-type jobs before they could afford the gas to get to their gigs—Bi-tone didn't pay much. If the group wanted to eat, they brought food from home, borrowing electricity to cook. This is another one of many cases in the early history of this music where the protagonists wanted to play music for a living but had to supplement their music income with a day job so that they could afford to do what their heart desired—which was to play music full-time.

Ezra sold candy during the concert to help pay the bills. The performances became known as "candy shows". Charlie Cline described the event. "What we did, we played those because you didn't have to book nothing—only get a market. And the market would let us use their electricity 'cause they wanted the business—we had five or six hundred people out there in the parking lot. We made up a trailer with a stage on it. We could book one today and then go out and play it because we had a PA set up on the car [to advertise the show] and we'd go all throughout all the communities and valleys. We'd announce that the **Lonesome Pine Fiddlers** were playing—bring your outlaws, in-laws, grandmas, bring anybody, come as you are. Don't even change your clothes, barefooted, with overalls; any way

you want to come. And they would. And they would come out there and stand—no seats now."

Ezra paid $8 per night plus room and board (in 1951) "and all the chickens we could get from the sponsor. Every Saturday morning, my sister, Margaret, would cook chicken and dumplin's from Freeman's market, our sponsor," added Charlie.

Charlie Cline played on and off with Bill Monroe from 1951 to 1956. He and Jimmy Martin recalled the hard times when, "We traveled 100,000 miles with Bill Monroe, sleeping on shoulders. And maybe get a bath when we could find a sink and a rag. We played seven days a week, five shows a day. A lot of the time we wouldn't get to the motel until it was all over. We'd have to stop at a fillin' station and shave. We were always runnin' a little late. There were no freeways then. The only one which I can remember, when I was with Bill, was the Pennsylvania Turnpike. We had all them crooked single-lane roads. We hit deers and stuff."[5] Cline also played fiddle on "Roanoke" and the tom-tom (actually it was just pounding on a guitar) on "Cheyenne." He played baseball with Monroe's team for a short while. When he was knocked on his rear with a line drive and almost killed, he quit baseball.

Mr. Cline, in 1989 at Kissimmee, Florida, spoke about the difficulty of being on the road in order to make a living in this music. "I'll tell ya, if young people knew what pioneers of bluegrass went through...it's not just all glory like it is now. People have it a lot easier now than they did back then. You notice the roads now. We didn't have four lanes back then. We went on pig trails and one lanes and I remember there were one or two turnpikes like the Pennsylvania Turnpike. We would really rejoice when we knew we were going to be on that toll road. The cost wasn't important. We'd travel 100,000 to 150,000 miles a year, seven days a week with Bill. It was hard, but just like I tell young people today, you gotta like it... If you don't learn it this way and you have it easy, when a little hard times come, you'll quit."

Life in a typical touring band in the old days—Snuffy Jenkins, Pappy Sherrill and their WIS Hillbillies

"Throughout the decade of 1937-1947, the **WIS Hillbillies** traveled more than 250,000 miles to entertain more than 600,000 people in personal appearances

Snuffy Jenkins (L) and Pappy Sherrill, 1969. Photo courtesy Pappy Sherrill.

[4] Quotation by Charlie and Curly Ray Cline from the article by Janice Brown McDonald, *Bluegrass Unlimited*, September, 1988, p. 25.

[5] From a live interview at the 1992 IBMA convention, Owensboro, Kentucky.

throughout South Carolina, North Carolina, Georgia, Virginia and Tennessee."[6] They traveled an average of 2,000 miles per month or more.

In 1939, Dewitt "Snuffy" Jenkins was with **Byron Parker and the WIS Hillbillies**. He remembered, "We didn't even have a PA system. We'd play a lot of these little old rabbit school houses down there. Wouldn't hold over a couple hundred, you know. Fifteen and twenty-five cents [admission] and five of us made a living like that. No electricity."[7]

"To ride along with the **Hillbillies** en route to a personal appearance was an education in itself. The entire group would laugh, talk, and continuously make little jokes about each other. And, it was on these trips that they worked out most of their material. All five members of the organization would usually try out their version of various tunes and accept suggestions from the others on how to improve... Upon arrival at the school, or wherever their personal appearance was to take place, they would split up into teams. Snuffy usually took care of selling the tickets. Someone else would get the amplifier equipment and the instruments set up on stage (they first used loud speakers in 1939)... And no one had more fun than did the **Hillbillies** themselves! Some of their most popular routines included 'Snuffy Cures a Snakebite,' 'Smoke, Smoke, Smoke,' Snuffy as the undertaker in 'Dead or Alive,' and 'Hookeyville School.' Although the play-let was written out, they would seldom follow the script exactly. When it was all over, the long trip home to Columbia frequently ended as late as three in the morning."[8]

Their concerts at Columbia's Township Auditorium were often followed by a square dance. The hall seated 3,500 and was usually filled to capacity. After these late nights, they were up again to play an 8:30 a.m. and a live noon show six days a week. They were booked six months solid. But this employment *did* have the advantage of being at home every night. Bands which joined the Grand Ole Opry didn't have that benefit; those folks were on the road constantly.

Snuffy recalled, "Back then, we had the show dates but couldn't get the gas to travel. The government was rationing gasoline and we barely got enough to get to the radio station. Farmers, however, could purchase gas without coupons. Our largest audience was farmers and we could always go up to a farmer's house late at night, and once they knew who we were, they would always provide gas for us to return to Columbia."[9]

When Byron Parker died in 1948, Snuffy and Pappy took over the band and it became **Snuffy Jenkins and Pappy Sherrill and the Hired Hands**. The **Hired Hands** played primarily for school houses in a circuit now known as the "kerosene circuit". "When electricity had reached some of the remote areas, we started carrying a PA system and would set up the microphones up on stage even if they didn't have electricity. It made things look good," laughed Snuffy.[10]

They used to "pack the house everywhere we went" when they played at schoolhouses, said Pappy Sherrill. Radio and live concerts were the only entertainment available for rural people. In 1953, when television came into the picture, bands no longer had the radio stations at which to play. The audiences no longer had to come to their live performances; instead, they could see them on television. And it certainly didn't help that more and more groups were being formed and taking a portion of the dollars available. Pappy Sherrill told this writer that recently, in 1990, there were probably 10,000 musicians in Nashville trying to make a living. That certainly makes it difficult for anyone, no matter how good they are. But if a group got a break with a good record company which promoted them correctly, they could make a significant sum of money. It seems that in modern times, connections in the business are essential—more so than in the early days.

Sherrill made his living in the car business (Chevrolet) in later years when traveling with the band became too hard. Another event that also made touring difficult was when schools consolidated—they closed a lot of them down and no longer provided the same type of venue they were used to. But at twenty-five cents admission, and the sponsor taking thirty-five percent of that, times were very hard.

Snuffy's years at WIS eventually had to end about 1970 because "I quit on account of my health. I was starving to death."[11] He got a day job at a Chevrolet dealer in Columbia, continuing to play as long as his health held out.

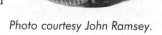

Photo courtesy John Ramsey.

[6] Steve Libby, "South Carolinians in the Entertainment World," *The South Carolina Magazine*, vol. 12, no. 1, January, 1949. pp. 21, 26.

[7] Tony Trischka, "Snuffy Jenkins," *Bluegrass Unlimited*, October, 1977, pp. 20, 21.

[8] WIS-DOM, February, 1948, vol. 3, no. 5, p. 3.

[9] Ray Thigpen, "A Legend in His Own Time," *Bluegrass Unlimited*, June, 1987, p. 9.

[10] Ibid., p. 9

[11] Trischka, op. cit., p. 21.

Jim Shumate speaks of Monroe's tent shows and the baseball team

Fiddler Jim Shumate spoke about the summer tent shows of the forties while he was working with the **Blue Grass Boys**. Beginning in the summer of 1943, Bill Monroe set up a system of shows which toured with tents, a caravan of trucks to carry them, and the crew to set them up. This was probably a copy of what the Opry began in the early 1930s. Shumate vividly remembered, "There was a tent crew that went along ahead of us. When we got there, everything was ready to go. We had a big tent that held about three or four thousand people, plus bleachers and chairs. They'd put the chairs down out front. They were reserved, and the bleachers were different prices. It was like a carnival, so to speak, except it was under one big roof—one tent. They had a popcorn machine and all that stuff. Lester Flatt's wife operated the popcorn machine. She was one of the Stacy sisters that used to be with Charlie Monroe years ago.

"We had quite a [baseball] team back then. We'd get to town early, usually around three or four o'clock. I'd go to the pool hall or somewhere where I could find some young guys and ask them if they had a baseball team there in town. Most of them did, and I'd tell 'em who we was and that we had a bluegrass team and we'd like to challenge 'em. Oh, Man! They'd get busy and get their gang together and meet us at the field. Sometimes they'd meet us in an hour. We did that all over the country. Sometimes we had good crowds just for a ball game. We had a lot of fun. We had uniforms and everything. I played shortstop and was a pretty good hitter, too. I could lay the timber to that ball! String pitched. He was a good pitcher. I believe Lester played third base. We had two or three of the tent crew boys that were good ball players. Bill played pitcher, but he was a better hitter than anything else. I've seen him just bust bats and break 'em wide open. They'd just splinter when he'd hit 'em."[12]

Mac Wiseman—
"The worst thing that can happen to a musical form is for it to become static and keep repeating itself."

In a 1987 interview, Mac Wiseman spoke of the music Nashville was putting out at the time. He said, "A lot of 'slick' music is being recorded in Nashville. They're geared to hit-making like Tin Pan Alley and New York studios were years ago... Bluegrass is looking for new markets and directions to grow in. This is a sure sign of good health in the music business. The worst thing that can happen to a musical form is for it to become static and keep repeating itself. That's what's happening in Top 40 country music."[13]

Wiseman spoke of the hard times of the '40s and '50s, especially during the winter. "Well, we just kept plugging along when things wasn't as good. It was touch and go but we survived. You just had to cinch up your belt a little bit. We played dances and things like that—things that people could do in the winter time when they couldn't get out and attend open-air shows, of course. Usually that was our main thing to pay our grocery bills and rent, so to speak. In the winter time, folks—rural folks—would go out on Saturday nights, kick up their heels a little bit, have a little toddy... After you've had snow on the ground for a couple of weeks everybody gets cabin fever and wants to get out.

"A lot of it was call-in and write-in, you see, where they'd listen to you on the radio. You had daily shows, early morning shows and sometimes noontime shows and you'd be limited as to how much you could travel—the distance you could make—maybe a hundred, a hundred and fifty miles. But that was usually the coverage of your radio station anyhow. People were listening to us because back then we didn't usually have records. We worked on a percentage basis—very few guarantees back then. We just worked for our percentage in the PTAs and the VFWs and the local organizations that would sponsor you. They were fundraising ventures that they depended on [for their income]. You worked for seventy or eighty percent of the door and you did your advertising on your radio show and supplied them with some window cards and fliers and such as that to promote locally with.

"And theaters. You used to play a lot of theaters. You go in and play thirty or forty minutes and they run the movie and the news and the cartoon and then you come back and do another one. You'd play three or four shows a day. Back then, instead of booking the theaters individually, I'd go to Washington or Baltimore or places where [the local theaters] booked their films, then just go to the theater houses and sit down with the date book and you'd book for thirty, sixty days at a time. They route you right with the movie, see. So that simplified the booking thing. One thing that put the damper on that before they started going to clusters—the concept they have today in the malls and such as that—they put those wide screens in and that did away with your stage space. So that was the beginning of the end for the theater business. Quite often they'd even have to take the first few rows of seats out to make room for [the wide screens]...

"And drive-ins came along; that was a big, big thing. In the early '50s when TV became so competitive, in the summertime we'd play an awful lot of drive-in theaters. We'd play from the top of the concession

---

[12] Wayne Erbsen, "Jim Shumate—Bluegrass Fiddler Supreme," *Bluegrass Unlimited*, April, 1979, pp. 19, 20.

[13] J. Wesley Clark and J. Michael Hosford, "Mac Wiseman: Once More with Feeling," *Bluegrass Unlimited*, August, 1987, p. 18.

stand. Or some of 'em had stages built at the bottom of the screen but your sound system was hooked right into your speakers to the cars. And instead of gettin' applause you'd get horns tooted.

"We traveled in cars then and...before the days of television...you'd go and do the theaters and schools and stuff like that by yourself and after TV came in, well, they had to resort to the package shows to get people out of the house. The package show concept was when I started [working as a single without a traveling band] because in the early '50s, right at my peak of record success, promoters in California and overseas and places like that would contact me and put me on package shows and they didn't want the band because of the additional transportation costs they'd have to pay. They always had a staff band to back three or four people that were there on the package. A typical example would be myself and Lefty Frizell and the **Maddox Brothers and Rose** and Ernest Tubb on a package. They'd have a staff band that would back Lefty and myself—we both worked as singles. That's why I disbanded [the **Country Boys**]. It helped me to cut down my touring schedule because I didn't have to maintain a backup band. If you wanted to keep a good band, you couldn't turn 'em loose in the wintertime and expect 'em to be there when you needed 'em in the spring."[14]

Walter V. Saunders spoke about a popular Wiseman song, "The song 'Love Letters in the Sand' was first recorded by Mac Wiseman in 1953 for Dot. It was so successful that Dot Records had their crooner Pat Boone record it in 1957. This version had one less verse because Boone sang it slower. It was also successful—so much so that Dot re-recorded Wiseman's original version which did very well the second time around also."[15]

When asked to give advice to aspiring professional bluegrass pickers who desire to make a living from bluegrass music, Wiseman replied, "I think it would be extremely difficult, really, because they have to play a lot of small jobs and things like that just to maintain a living for four or five people in a group. I really don't see how some of them do survive during the winter months, to be honest with you, 'cause...you don't have those small venues that we used to play just to make, more or less, living expenses."[16]

The "lean years"

"By the late forties, it was no longer economically feasible to keep...large ensembles [such as the ten- to fifteen-piece band of **Bob Wills and the Texas Playboys**] on the road, and smaller groups like those of Ernest Tubb (rhythm section, lead guitar, and steel) and Hank Williams (steel, fiddle, rhythm section, and sometimes lead guitar) became the rule."[17]

The 1950s were very lean years in the country music business. Some people put the blame on the commercialization of music which was occurring in Nashville. The **Blue Sky Boys** dropped from the music completely. Bill Bolick was so frustrated that he put his mandolin under his bed—not to touch it again for another five years. Hank Williams was doing okay. Some months he earned $100,000; he was the exception. Well known country bands, in order to draw a decent crowd, had to tour together. One such tour included Roy Acuff, Little Jimmy Dickens, **Johnny and Jack**, Kitty Wells and dancer Robert Lunn.

When Elvis came along in 1954 and made such a tremendous impact on music of the day, musicians really had to give him credit: "Anyone capable of making a living in this climate has got to be good," they said.

"For a while there," said Mr. Bolick, "in the so-called country music line, we [**Blue Sky Boys**] were second only to Eddy Arnold with Victor. Of course, maybe we sold 100,000, he sold a million. But I felt that even back then, had we even one-tenth the publicity that Victor was giving to him, that we could have done much better than what we did. I always felt that there was plenty of room for our type of music, and I think even today there is quite a demand for it, could people get it. But it is almost an impossibility to find one of our records, even though they are available, in any of the modern music stores today. They simply will not handle them. They're after the fast buck, and although we weren't overnight sellers, in a period of time we were good, steady sellers."[18]

Half the fan mail to WNAO[19] (Raleigh, North Carolina) was addressed to the **Blue Sky Boys** but their income didn't seem to reflect their popularity. Television was just getting its start but was not affecting their income. What *did* influence their finances was the effect of so many new radio stations coming into being and in competition with each other. In order to make a good living in the country music business, performers found it necessary to be on one of the large 50,000 watt stations. About that time, radio station policy began to require that songs be dedicated to listeners to increase the radio audience.

In February of 1951, the Bolick brothers abruptly retired from music. In retrospect, this was a good move considering the increasing difficulty in trying to earn a

14 Roland Kausen, "Fall Bluegrass Blues?" *Bluegrass Unlimited*, October, 1991, pp. 31, 32.

15 "Notes and Queries," *Bluegrass Unlimited*, October 1986, p. 9.

16 Kausen, op. cit., p. 33.

17 Larry Sandberg and Dick Weissman, *The Folk Music Sourcebook*, (New York: Alfred A. Knopf, 1976), p. 98.

18 1991 telephone interview.

19 Now WKIX-AM 850.

living in music. Many musicians endured the hard times that the fifties had in store for them, hoping that things would get better—which finally occurred in the mid-sixties. Bill Bolick joined the U.S. Postal Service as his day job. Earl retired from music to Tucker, Georgia. They never thought they would play again. If they had known they would record again in twelve years, they would have kept up with their music. Instead, they laid their instruments down.

Red Allen on the hard, winter months, or, "It's according to how much you love the stuff."

Red Allen spoke of how the bluegrass music business decreased during the winter, "Oh yea, yes. It's always been this way. It was rough when I picked it 'til the sixties. Sixties, it was all right. But the '50s were the roughest years. Flatt and Scruggs, they're about the only ones who could carry a full band because Martha White...had a deal with them. Bill Monroe couldn't afford a full band and that's why he had so many people workin' with him. When we used to work, we'd be without a bass player. We couldn't afford a bass player—just the guitar, the mandolin and the banjo."

Red Allen (far right) and the Osborne brothers.

"Me and Frank Wakefield and Noah Crase and people like that worked the clubs here in Dayton. But I worked the year 'round. I was working six nights a week in clubs here in Dayton in the early '50s...at least four nights a week. Back in the '50s, when me 'n' the Osbornes was workin' together when they first came back to town, Sonny went to work in a box factory or somethin' like that and Bobby went to work drivin' a bread truck. Then me and Bob went to work at NCR, National Cash Register. But I worked at General Motors, I worked at Frigidaire. I went to GM in '48 and I worked until about 1951, playin' music in clubs. It'll make an old man out of you. You could never make a living through the '50s playing bluegrass. There weren't that many places to play. It was hard. It was hard

years."[20] Soon after 1984, Red Allen retired from full-time music. The last twenty years of his musical career were the most financially rewarding.

He spoke of Jimmy Martin, "You got to know Jimmy... He's a good entertainer, a good singer but he's let this g...damn music drive him crazy. He lives [it]. Some people let it get to them. You see, this music was never that important to me. I done it to keep from having to work in a hard, manual labor job because I had no education, you know. And it was better than gettin' out there and diggin' a damn ditch. But if I knew then what I know now, if I seen a banjo picker or a mandolin player comin' toward the house I would have shot him."[21]

Red Allen feels strongly about many matters; the materialism of today's bluegrass musicians is one of them. "What I got in this music business—there are so many people who [just] want to impress people they've got something. And I always look at bluegrass pickers. Back in the fifties, you couldn't make a living at this [music], you know, until the festivals started. Bill Monroe couldn't keep a band—he couldn't pay 'em. And Flatt and Scruggs, they could keep a band 'cause Martha White was sponsoring 'em. And the rest of them were just playing around. Hell, you could get Bill Monroe for $250 in a beer joint here in Dayton, Ohio. Me and the Osbornes had a #10 record out in the nation—'Once More' was #10—and we was working for a beer joint down here in Dayton for $15 apiece a night and playin' in Wheeling for $11 apiece on Saturday night. I would have gone into some other sort of f... music if I knowed that bluegrass was goin' to be like that. I would have got into something I could have made some f... money at, you know. I guess people's doin' all right now with the festival thing but they ain't everybody doin' all right. There'll always be three or four bluegrass bands can make a livin' at it and the rest of them is carryin' it and help bringin' the crowd in and makin' no money.

"It seems like to me that these fellas, for prestige, got to get themselves a bus or something like that. I never believed in that. I just wanted to pick my music and go ahead and just travel and do my thing. I never believed in putting on a big front, you know, or trying to be somebody you're not. I never [cared] what the next man has got. I got what I wanted or [what] I could afford. If Bill Monroe comes out here and jumps off a cliff, half these bluegrass mandolin players'll do the same thing. I never looked up to people like that myself."

When asked to give advice to aspiring professional bluegrass pickers, Red Allen said, "Not to take it serious and not ever try to make a livin' at it. It's accordin' to how you love the stuff. You might make a good livin', but you have to be on the Opry; somethin' like that to do that. That's the way it is. Reno and

20 Kausen, op. cit., pp. 30, 32. 33.

21 From a 1992 telephone interview with Mr. Allen.

Smiley worked themselves to death just tryin' to make a livin'. People say you can't quit!"[22]

Lester Flatt with Bill Monroe and the Blue Grass Boys—"Monroe was making all the money, yet he was doing less work than the sidemen."

Jake Lambert's biography of Lester Flatt described the money Lester Flatt and Earl Scruggs were making when they were members of Bill Monroe's band. "Flatt and Scruggs, as well as the rest of the boys, were making about sixty dollars a week; and that wasn't bad money, with the exception of the long hours. Lester Flatt did the emcee work on all the shows while Earl took care of the money. Earl was the only one in the group that had a high school education. Earl told me that on many Saturdays (after a week of touring), when the **Blue Grass Boys** rolled into Nashville, he would be carrying from five to seven thousand dollars. So both Flatt and Scruggs could see where the money was. They knew it would never be made as 'side men' but as the 'star' or leader. Monroe was making all the money, yet he was doing less work than the side men."[23]

By June of 1948, the band of **Flatt and Scruggs** had, of course, formed, moved a few times, added several personnel to the band, and played on several radio stations. Now at WCYB in Bristol, Tennessee, "They put out their souvenir songbooks. The songbook served several purposes: it could make the band a little money, but more importantly it could gauge audience size in those pre-Neilson rating days. In less than two weeks, they had sold 10,000 copies of their first songbook."[24]

Flatt and Scruggs and the rock and roll era—"If you can't be seen or heard, you just as well stay at the house."

Until the mid-1950s, venues for bluegrass bands were mostly schoolhouses, theaters and parks. The rock and roll era then struck with a vengeance. Earl Scruggs described it this way, "The next thing that happened that almost sunk a lot of country acts—both—was the rock and roll days. They came in about '55 and '56. Well, we had come here in 1953 for Martha White. When I say here [I mean] at Nashville, Tennessee. In 1955, I guess it was, they put us on a chain of television stations. Well, we had our own built-in audience that watched us. The format of the radio stations went rock and roll. They just completely dropped country music and with the virgin days—if I can call it that—of television..., I'll say this whether it's right or wrong, the Grand Ole Opry just wasn't bein' listened to like it was back in '48 and '47 along in there. We were on six live television shows a week for Martha White [and we was doin' all right while others were not fortunate enough to have a sponsor like we did]."[25]

Louise Scruggs took over the business end of Earl's career with **Flatt and Scruggs** in 1956. "When she first started booking **Flatt and Scruggs** in 1956," wrote Tony Trischka, "the country music industry was reeling from the influence of Elvis Presley, leaving very few country stars (not to mention bluegrass band leaders!) even able to carry a band full-time. By keeping **Flatt and Scruggs** working throughout this difficult period, Louise made it possible for Earl to stay in music and continue his development as a banjo player. The connections she made to get **Flatt and Scruggs** (and later the **Earl Scruggs Revue**) on national television, movie soundtracks and many other diverse venues were a critical link in the widespread exposure of Earl and his banjo—this exposure being the largest single factor to date in the growth of nationwide and worldwide interest in the five-string banjo. Through all the years of Earl's stellar work on center stage, Louise's unsung, behind-the-scenes efforts have had a major role in keeping him there."[26] Louise, matriarch of the Scruggs family, worked hard, twelve to fourteen hours a day with the telephone and typewriter. She managed the group and rarely had an opportunity to travel with the band. "She enjoys her office work and if she stays gone long she gets pretty snowed in with paperwork," said Earl.

There seemed to be something about the Scruggs' business acumen which helped keep their band busy all the time and in ventures which would benefit the band financially. While the management of other bands in bluegrass was competent, it appears that the management of **Flatt and Scruggs**, and later the **Earl Scruggs Revue**, made them quite well-to-do. Between the decisions of Earl and Louise, they appeared to have an insight which was uncanny and kept them on the "cutting edge" of the music business. Such decisions included their Hollywood television excursions including "Beverly Hillbillies" and "Green Acres," being asked to provide background music for movies such as "Bonnie and Clyde," the decision for Earl to be on John and Bill McEuen's "Will the Circle Be Unbroken" LP,

---

22 Kausen, op. cit., p. 33.

23 Jake Lambert with Curly Sechler, *The Good Things Out Weigh the Bad, A Biography of Lester Flatt*, (Hendersonville: A Jay-Lyn Publication, 1982), p. 7.

24 From the liner notes of the CMH LP "A Living Legend—Lester Flatt and the Nashville Grass."

25 This was the end of the tape given to me by Doug Hutchens. The rest of that conversation was missing so I'll just try to end it as if Mr. Scruggs might have done.

26 Tony Trischka and Peter Wernick, *Masters of the 5-String Banjo*, p. 22.

and numerous real estate purchases which have paid off well.

According to Steve Cooley (banjoist with the **Dillards**) in a 1991 interview, "At the time when folklorists (such as Ralph Rinzler) were 'discovering' bluegrass [in the late '50s or early '60s], **Flatt and Scruggs** continued to carry on as a country style act in performance and recording. When bluegrass had no place to go in country or pop, they were slick and polished enough to be entertaining and musical in concerts at colleges and folk or pop venues. Other acts, Monroe, **Reno and Smiley**, etc., were more focused at a rural or specialized audience in a regional setting. **Flatt and Scruggs** consistently made well-crafted studio projects that were radio-ready. Other bluegrass acts weren't always radio ready."

"It seems like to me that these fellas, for prestige, got to get themselves a bus or something like that. I never believed in that. I just wanted to pick my music and go ahead and just travel and do my thing." —Red Allen

By 1978, Earl Scruggs was thoroughly involved with his sons in their **Earl Scruggs Revue**. *Pickin'* magazine (August 1978) was able to obtain a rare, in-depth interview with Mr. Scruggs along with sons Steve, Randy, and Gary Scruggs, and Taylor Rhodes. "Actually," said Scruggs, "when I write to a promoter, I forbid him to advertise that [our music] is a bluegrass show because when you do that, you mislead the public, I believe. We're not really into bluegrass; we do traditional tunes as well as modern tunes." Earl described their new music as "Just music, I guess. There's no way to label it and I'd like people to get away from labelin' music anyway... So we just play the instruments and I imagine that we go in 'most any direction." The group recorded on **Flatt and Scruggs'** old label, Columbia.

Scruggs continued, "Another thing that's been a great asset, they're goin' strong into good sound equipment. I've always believed that if you couldn't be seen or heard, you just as well stay at the house. Now, they're using much better lights and much better sound than in the old days. I remember the days when you used to work to one mike. And when the power went off

you worked with no mike at all. You could get by with it then, but you can't do it now with all the electric instruments and the big auditoriums." The days of the 300-seat schoolhouse were gone for the **Revue**. "The overhead expense eliminated that," he said.

Curly Seckler and touring with Flatt and Scruggs—"Back then I didn't mind the cold weather."

In a 1992 telephone interview, Mr. Seckler spoke of what the life of a full-time bluegrass musician was like. "I went to work in the music in 1935...we were workin' radio. Of course, back then all you had was radio. We was doin' live shows...and we'd go into a place and work it as far as the station would reach. Most of the stations was around a thousand [watts] or something like that and some of 'em less and we'd play that out for a year or so and then we'd move on to another station. That kept us pretty busy. Back then I didn't mind the cold weather.

"Rock and roll changed it for a lot of people but it never did harm us in any way. When I say 'us,' of course, I was workin' with Lester and them at the time. It would have took a stick o' dynamite loaded at both ends to harm that group. Now, we didn't have no hard times, period! It just wasn't such a thing.

"You worked seven days a week; there wasn't no letups. At one time, we was doin' live TV shows all across the country. We had 'em just week-in and week-out—just one to the other. There wasn't no letups. I was over at 'Nashville Now'...tellin' some things that actually did happen in my early years and they thought it was a tale, but is actually is not. Times was so hard, at certain times of the year when the corn [was in the] fields in the country and the roastin' ears were just right, gosh, we thought the first three rows in any corn field belonged to entertainers. So I've seen some rough days in this business. I've seen some bad days. I mean real bad. But you just had that urge to stay in there and stay with it."[27]

The beginning of the phenomenon called "Elvis Presley"

In the early '50s, Elvis Presley appeared at several country/bluegrass events as a country artist, complete with the cowboy hat and scarf.[28] Critics believed he had

[27] Kausen, op. cit., pp. 30, 31.

[28] Elvis sang Red Foley's "Old Shep" at age ten and won a talent contest. At age nineteen, he appeared on the Grand Ole Opry. His early country music days were often spent touring with Wanda Jackson, Mother Maybelle and the Carter Sisters, the Louvin Brothers and Janie Frickie. He was an "instinctive performer who could make a traditional blues or gospel or hillbilly song sound as if it belonged to him alone." He was an exceedingly charismatic singer who had an unshakable hold on his audience just by doing what he did naturally. He was a balladeer and he was a showman. He is one of country music's top ten important figures." Quotation from *Life's* 1994 special issue on country music. The magazine rated various country artists in the following order, beginning with number one: Hank Williams, the Carter Family, Jimmie Rodgers, Patsy Cline, Bill Monroe, Chet Atkins, Bob Wills, Ernest Tubb, Gene Autry and Elvis. Flatt and Scruggs came in at spot #25 and were the only other bluegrass group in the top 100. Interestingly, *Life's* all-time country band included bluegrassers Vassar Clements, Jerry Douglas, Bill Monroe, Earl Scruggs, Doc Watson and Emmylou Harris—six bluegrass artists.

a future but were unable to categorize his music into either country or rock and roll.

Presley first appeared on the Opry September 25, 1954, to a subdued audience of country music lovers. They were expecting something quite wonderful and groundbreaking; his reputation for being a great performer and the sexiest man in show business was well deserved even at this early date. They went away with the general opinion like: "Is that all he does—shake his leg? Where's the country music?"

He moved on to the Louisiana Hayride where he became a member. His first appearance was October 16, 1954. The Hayride was more liberal and open-minded. It was here that Hank Williams began his career and returned to when he was "kicked off" the Opry for drinking. The Hayride introduced such artists as Johnny Horton, Faron Young and Webb Pierce. Many of these would become stars and move on to the Opry. One possible reason many of these stars left the Hayride was to avoid the competition

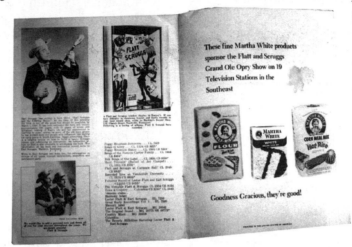

of Elvis Presley. His affect on girls and, in turn, record sales was awesome. According to Opry historian Chet Hagan, "From 1953—when rock and roll began—to 1960, the Grand Ole Opry ticket buyers had fallen off by forty-four percent."[29] Many boys who saw the reaction of their girlfriends to Elvis decided not to fight it but to join it. Buddy Holly and Buddy Knox soon had their own rock and roll tunes on the radio.

Presley signed with RCA in August 1955, playing rockabilly. His band was the **Blue Moon Boys,** named after Monroe's "Blue Moon of Kentucky." Though some record companies considered rock and roll a fad, most left traditional music and pushed the pop-oriented product on deejays—whether or not they liked it! Country music and bluegrass was changed forever.

The recording industry in 1954

"Those of you under thirty can hardly appreciate the state of the art of bluegrass music in the late '50s," wrote Frank U. Childrey. "Country music was reeling under the impact of rock 'n' roll. Bands—good bands at that—were disbanding wholesale; those that stayed together were traveling long hours over bad roads in worn out automobiles to play in gritty little country music parks and the proverbial smoke-filled beer joints

just to stay alive. That country music in general and bluegrass survived at all is an amazing phenomenon. While many people cite the bluegrass festival movement, begun by Bill Clifton in Luray, Virginia, in 1961, and later Carlton Haney at the now-historic 1965 and 1966 Fincastle, Virginia, and the Bill Monroe-produced festivals as major turning points in bluegrass music's history, other facts were also influential. For one thing, knowledgeable and musically sophisticated aficionados were writing about the music: Pete Kuykendall in *Disc Collector*, Ralph Rinzler in *Sing Out!*, Mike Seeger, Richard Spottswood, Mayne Smith and Neil V. Rosenberg, among others. Of course, Alan Lomax's [article] 'Folk Music with Overdrive'—Flatt and Scruggs' article in *Esquire*—was also important. Second, when Monroe showed [up] at the second Fincastle festival, he brought with him a band that was playing quite literally as if its life depended on it. Within a year, this publication (*Bluegrass Unlimited*) was founded and the rest, as they say, is history."[30]

Author Childrey then explained that, as of 1988, bluegrass had become a profitable industry—a viable style of music which could not be denied. "But despite bluegrass music's much-deserved, long-overdue and amazingly substantial successes, there are plenty of veteran bluegrass musicians who helped write the book in the '50s only to be late for the current '80s gravy train. Reasons for this are as complex as they are numerous. In some cases, these musicians just plain gave up. Others, unwilling to compromise their styles, found that what was acceptable to some in the '50s was considered archaic and unwelcome in the '80s. 'Hard' bluegrass, like 'hard' country, unless performed by neo-traditionalists perceived and marketed as hip, just doesn't sell. Still others have come out of retirement and are being heralded as authentic innovators and are working, apparently, for more money and under better working conditions than they have ever experienced." The author referred to Bill Napier, veteran 1950s flatpicker, the subject of his record review.

Lance LeRoy— a bluegrass fan first, then a promoter

Lance LeRoy (born May 26, 1930) grew up in northeastern Georgia, in Tignall. Every day, during the school lunch break, he hurried home to listen to the

29 Chet Hagan, *Grand Ole Opry: The Complete Story of a Great American Institution and Its Stars* (New York: Henry Holt, 1989), ppp. 181, 182.

30 Quotation from a record review of "Bill Napier—Larry Taylor, Country Boy's Life," by Frank U. Childrey in the September, 1988, issue of *Bluegrass Unlimited*.

Crossroads Follies on WSB, Atlanta, and to **Pap and the WIS Hillbillies** on WIS at Columbia, South Carolina. The LeRoy home was a center of activity every Saturday night when they put a radio speaker in the window of their home so the 25 to 75 people in their yard could listen to the Opry. They loved Uncle Dave Macon, Roy Acuff, Bill Monroe, Minnie Pearl, Curly Fox, Fiddlin' Arthur Smith, Bradley Kincaid and others.

LeRoy took up the fiddle in the eighth grade and was a fiddler in a band 1946-'47. Every Saturday night, each of the band members tried to memorize the words to songs Lester and Earl did on the Opry that night with the **Blue Grass Boys**. They immediately went home and tried to re-create that song on their own.

LeRoy remembered that there used to be a feeling of excitement in the old days when the curtain was raised on the artist for whom you had traveled so far to see perform. The audience consisted of small-town folks from the same area, and they all knew each other. They would mingle before show time until the moment would arrive. The excitement was heavy as they raised the curtain. LeRoy reminisced, "I can't describe how exciting and thrilling it was! We don't get a thrill like than when bands come on today. One of the reasons is because there was an aura of mystery about it then. With no television to see what the band members looked like, sometimes we didn't know who was who until they got their instruments out."[31]

Earl Scruggs spoke of LeRoy, "Lance used to live in Georgia and when we were working through there he would drive for miles to see the shows. He'd always be there and we always looked forward to Lance coming around to the shows. He's been a fan of bluegrass for many years before getting into the business end of it."[32] LeRoy's obsession is his record collection which contains over 9,000 45s and 78s and over 8,500 LPs.

By 1952, LeRoy had become good friends with Lester and Earl and, by 1966, with Paul Warren. His day job was an internal auditor for a finance company. This led to doing the accounting and income tax work for Flatt after **Flatt and Scruggs** broke up. According to LeRoy, Flatt was a good entertainer but a poor businessman. When it came to money matters and promotional activities when Flatt was with Scruggs, he'd just as soon not do it. So the burden then fell on Louise Scruggs who then took on the responsibility with a competence and zeal that made them the best-paid band in the business for many, many years.

When Lester and Earl split up in 1969, Lester asked Lance to be his Manager/Booking Agent. He accepted, then began touring with **Lester Flatt and the Nash-** ville Grass. Though he didn't drive the bus, he had the 4 a.m. shift to ride "shotgun" to keep the driver awake—a practice on which Lester insisted.

In 1977, LeRoy and Flatt formed a booking agency: The Lancer Agency. The name came from combining their two first names. When the bookings for Lester's band became less frequent and reliable due to Lester's health, LeRoy began booking the **Bluegrass Cardinals** in April 1978 and this assured the continuance of the Agency. LeRoy said, "Without them there's no question that I would never have survived in the agency... When it comes to pure class, they're the closest thing I've seen to **Flatt and Scruggs**."[33]

Fiddler Glen Duncan knows of LeRoy's expertise in the field: "Whenever I've had a question about who wrote a certain song, or if somebody would call me as a reference wanting to know who had written a certain song, I'd always call Lance and 99 times out of 100 he could give it to you right off the top of his head!."[34] "I think [Lance] deserves to be [in the Bluegrass Hall of Fame] because bluegrass music wouldn't be anywhere near where it is today had it not been for Lance LeRoy."[35]

Eddie Adcock— "I like being on the 'cuttin' edge.'"

Mr. Adcock has been in the music business from the early 1950s until the present. He's a great example of those who are able to adapt their music—their job—to what the public demands. Those who were *not* able to adapt had a tougher time in this business. But Adcock had the talent and the motivation to stay in music as his main source of income for all his adult life.

Eddie Adcock left home at age fifteen, continuing to help support his family back in Scottsville, Virginia. "I think the thing that made me want to attack [music] professionally, almost before I was big enough to leave home, was I had a choice between that and farming...the decision wasn't really that hard." But like many musicians of the early 1950s, it was necessary to work at a day job. So the next year, he began a seven-year period where he boxed semi-professionally. During the late '60s, he won thirty-four straight drag races in his car "Mr. Banjo."

In 1954, Adcock toured with **Smoky Graves and the Blue Star Boys** and its tent shows. The years between 1949 to 1955 were those in which a person could make a decent living in music, but a slump after this period made it very difficult for the next decade.[36]

---

[31] Traci Todd, "Lance LeRoy, Part 1 of 2," *Bluegrass Unlimited*, February, 1993, p. 45.

[32] Ibid., p. 44.

[33] Ibid., p. 48.

[34] Ibid., p. 47.

[35] From a 1994 telephone conversation with this writer.

[36] According to Adcock, this slump in country music was caused by Elvis Presley and rock 'n' roll.

In order to pull out of this recession, a market had to be created for bluegrass; the **Country Gentlemen** was a part of this resurgence. When bluegrass was introduced by the **Gentlemen** into colleges, they became an important contributor to its revival; the first college they played at was Oberlin (Ohio) in May of 1961. By 1963, **Flatt and Scruggs** had followed the **Gents'** lead and were playing the college circuit.

When Adcock joined Mac Wiseman's **Country Boys** in 1956, they were regulars on WRVA's Old Dominion Barn Dance.[37] Wiseman paid Adcock $90 per week—a lot of money for that time. "There was weeks that I made $300—selling songbooks in Canada to 3400 to 3500 people. That's what Mac drew in those days. There has never been a star as big as Mac in bluegrass music—a lot of people don't know that—I sure as hell hope there will be some day. And something else, Mac never missed having a hit record in a ten-year period yet. No [other] bluegrasser can say that. His last one was about ten years ago, 'Johnny's Cash and Charlie's Pride.' He's got more hits than anybody. I was in that last band as his banjo player [Adcock was the last full-time banjo player Wiseman ever had]. Mac moved to California and worked as an A & R man for Dot (1956). He made his fortune playing on the road. He still probably makes more today than any of us." Wiseman soon dissolved his **Country Boys** and began working as a solo act with pick-up bands wherever he performed.

About the time that the Elvis Presley phenomenon hit the world Adcock was working with Mac's **Country Boys** and doing okay. But "When Elvis hit, he hit every music industry so hard that they had to revamp and figure out what to do. The only person selling records at this point in time was Elvis Presley and no one else. Country music said, 'Let's add horns and symphonies or whatever the hell we can find to add to try to get a different light ahead of us.' Bluegrass people said, 'I wouldn't add no horn in my music if it was the last damn thing I ever did in my life. So the bluegrass people separated from the country. Up until Elvis, bluegrass and country were one and the same music... The public knew nothing about bluegrass music until that separation and it got to where, in about 1958, it had a totally different identity. So bluegrass waited it out; and although it's been slow, it's working. We have our own identity now."[38]

Along those lines, Adcock added, "The interests of the Country Music Association could care less about bluegrass music; they don't care about us. IBMA [the International Bluegrass Music Association] will. And perhaps the CMA will take some of the credit. That's okay. That's where our roots are."[39]

"Nashville can only control *their* country music; it can't control any other kind of music. Bluegrass is one of those *other* kinds of music which Nashville can't control. I really think that it's just not enough in demand. I think that if the stations played it, immediately there would be a success in this business. It's primed and it's ready to go. But without support, it can't or won't. But I don't think there's any conspiracy against it. I think they've always disliked it, and they still do."[40]

In 1956, Adcock joined Bill Harrell's **Rocky Mountain Boys** in Washington, D.C., replacing Donnie Bryant who joined the military.[41] Adcock's tenure with Harrell's band was fairly short; this band broke up when Harrell entered the military that year. They played music in the bluegrass style, strongly influenced by rock and roll music which was becoming popular.[42] They made about $12.50 each for each of their three or four nights per week performances. He also worked with the **Stoneman Family** and **Buzz Busby and the Bayou Boys** during the same period. In late 1958, he joined the **Country Gentlemen**, replacing Porter Church on banjo.

Adcock left the **Country Gentlemen** in 1970 after twelve years, went to California and began a jazz, jazz-rock, and country-rock band, performing under the name "Clinton Kodack." He explained he's always had trouble doing anything but bluegrass under his real name. He did well financially with this venture which lasted until he returned to the East Coast and formed the **II Generation** in 1971. "I have tried to play what I feel I want to play...no matter what's popular. I left a good position with the **Country Gentlemen**—just gave it up. Freely donated it to whoever wanted it, just to get back on the cuttin' edge again. I like being on the cuttin' edge. You don't make as much money, but it's fun."[43]

The Adcocks, Eddie and Martha Hearon, disbanded their bluegrass/rock group, the **II Generation**, in 1984, and went to work with David Allan Coe, with Eddie as Coe's band leader. They made excellent money. Eddie and Martha were the core of his band until leaving in the spring of 1985. Adcock said, "Coe loved the bluegrass feel in his music. We enjoyed the freedom that we

---

[37] Adcock still didn't often use a roll in his banjo playing .

[38] From a 1990 interview with Adcock at Owensboro, Kentucky.

[39] This is a condensed, though accurate, paraphrase. The "credit" Mr. Adcock spoke of was an optimistic observation that he saw as the success of the bluegrass music business due to the IBMA. He predicted that mainstream country music would see bluegrass getting more popular and assume responsibility for its new-found popularity (if it ever happens).

[40] Tom Henderson, "On the Cuttin' Edge...with Eddie Adcock," *Pickin'*, October, 1975.

[41] Band members were Harrell (guitar), Carl Nelson (fiddle), Smiley Hobbs (mandolin), Adcock (banjo) and Roy Self (bass).

[42] Scott Stoneman labeled Adcock a "rock and roll banjo picker"—a label which fit.

[43] Tom Henderson, "On the Cuttin' Edge...with Eddie Adcock," *Pickin'*, October, 1975.

had with the variety of stuff that we played."[44] Eddie played gitbo, acoustic guitar, fiddle and mandolin. Adcock once told an audience, "They tell me I'm old and I play weird. But what can you expect from a bluegrass performer who counts Van Halen as a major musical influence?"

Adcock gave some advice to the person planning to be a full-time musician, "It seems to me that a lot of musicians complain that the music just won't support them and I ask, 'Well, how much time do you put into it?' And most of them do put a lot of time into practicing their picking, but almost no time into the business! And that's where I think they are wrong. Martha and I spend our days calling this man or that man, looking and finding work [also doing promotion]. You know, it takes commitment and sometimes you starve a little. Hell, I've gone out and starved with the best of 'em."[45]

Wilma Lee Cooper on her husband, Stoney Cooper— "Stoney had great foresight."

Wilma Lee spoke of her late partner and husband, "Stoney had a great foresight; it's what they call ESP now. He could foresee things ahead down the road before they happened. He could see where the industry was going—how it was pointed. I remember back in the Wheeling days around 1950, we were working high school auditoriums and the parks. One day he said to me, 'I think we ought to try to work a drive-in theater. I see drive-in theaters being a big business for shows.' So he booked one, and my goodness! We had every speaker filled up and no place to put the rest of the folks who wanted to get in. After that, we started working the drive-in theaters in the summer. Then, other acts picked up on the idea."[46]

Jim Eanes— "We did it for the love of the music."

During the early '50s, when Eanes formed his **Shenandoah Valley Boys**, Eanes and his band played tent shows or, as he described it, "cow pastures and anything else. It was a lot of fun then—just starting out. We didn't do it for the monetary gains 'cause we didn't expect that much out of it. We did it for the love of the music. Today (1990) I'm still doing it for the love of the music. That's what it's all about...meeting people, picking up new fans, and meeting old fans."[47]

"Bluegrass is a specialty music. It's been distorted by the people who are tryin' to promote it and they don't know what they're promotin'. It's just like the country back in the early '50s when they were called 'hillbillies'. They got into Nashville, made a little money and bought 'em a cowboy suit, and they didn't want to be called 'hillbillies'. So they all changed that when they started the DJ convention. I was one of the charter members on that thing so Ernest Tubb walked up and said, 'We're all from the country, let's call it "country"'. So they started country, see. Western swing was already there so they called it 'country and western'. But that's my type of country music—in the early '50s and '60s. But as I say, everything has got to change. Today it's country rock—it's a damn shame!

"Nobody's gonna get rich in bluegrass. Bluegrass came along in '65, actually, when the festivals started. Everybody looked down their nose at Carlton Haney and said, 'You are crazy, man. You can't get people in a cow pasture!' But he proved 'em wrong. So actually, although it was **Bill Monroe and the Blue Grass Boys** in the early days, it wasn't bluegrass. Actually, the music was *not* bluegrass. It was a type of bluegrass that most of 'em are playin' today but it was not called 'bluegrass.' It was called 'hillbilly' or whatever."[48]

The business of Jim and Jesse— "If you're going to play bluegrass music, do it because you love it."

In 1951, Jim and Jesse McReynolds moved to WPFB, Middletown, Ohio, where they worked for Smoky Ward as a featured duet on Ward's television and radio variety show using the name, **McReynolds Brothers**. Jim and Jesse also performed on the show as the **Virginia Trio** with Larry Roll (lead vocals, rhythm guitar. Roll also wrote "A Memory of You," later recorded by Smoky Ward) and Dave Woolum (bass). They sang mostly gospel tunes. It was with this band that they made their first recordings for Gateway Records and featured Jesse's cross-picking. With Gateway, they recorded eight songs, issued ten years later as "Sacred Songs of the Virginia Trio" by Ultra-Sonic. Author Scott Hambly wrote, "In retrospect, this was the first instance of a recurring sense of proprietary disenfranchisement. Jesse feels that he and Jim would have fared better from the fruits of their artistic efforts if they had been able to gain possession, and hence control, of the masters from the Gateway session. Jesse reports that these masters have been sold several times to owners who re-pressed and sold them without their permission

44 Logan Neill, "The Eddie Adcock Band—Accentuating the Unconventional," Quotation by Eddie Adcock, *Southern News*, November/December, 1989, p. 9.

45 Ibid., p. 9.

46 Wayne W. Daniel, "Wilma Lee Cooper—America's Most Authentic Mountain Singer," *Bluegrass Unlimited*, p. 17.

47 Quotation from an interview at Owensboro, Kentucky, 1991.

48 1991 interview.

> *"A country artist can make more money in three or four years with some hits than a bluegrass picker can make in a lifetime, but it's a livin'. "* —Jesse McReynolds

and without paying them any royalties. Jesse suspects that this material is presently available in LP form on budget labels."[49]

Jim and Jesse and the Virginia Boys acquired a job playing in Pensacola, Florida, on WEAR-TV and on WTVY, Dothan, Alabama, about 1957. These jobs were sponsored by John Dodson's Marina and Crestview Mobile Homes Companies in Florida. Jesse recalled, "That was a big thing then because we went down there and got into things like that and we worked for Ford Tractor and then they co-sponsored with a local construction company. We worked three TV shows for Ford Tractor Company (WSAV, WALB, and WCTV in 1956)." They put on a huge number of miles on their cars. They would work Savannah on Tuesday; on Thursday they were in Pensacola, and then back to Dothan.

Scott Hambly wrote, "Recording contracts were difficult to come by in the late 1950s. Rockabilly and rock and roll had the debilitating effect of drawing away large segments of the country audience and causing most record companies to shun bluegrass bands. **Jim and Jesse**, purveyors of a conservative, traditional form of American music were, of course, numbered among those who were victims of the lean years in country music. Three years had elapsed since their last sessions for Capitol. With years of intervening experience, polish and a fine band, **Jim and Jesse** needed records for airplay in the national market."[50] That's where Don Pierce, of Starday Records, came in. **Jim and Jesse** signed a recording contract with Starday. Songs included "Border Ride" and "Let Me Whisper."[51] The brothers had an arrangement where Starday would only distribute the records; they would have to be recorded, mixed, and produced elsewhere. It was a commercial success but this arrangement with Starday was similar to several years ago with Ultra-Sonic and Gateway: beyond their control and without royalties.

In January of 1959, **Jim and Jesse** left Live Oak, Florida, and moved to Valdosta, Georgia. The **Stanley Brothers** replaced them in Live Oak. Martha White

Flour Mills began a sponsorship of **Jim and Jesse** on their tours, some television shows, and occasional guest spots on the Opry. The sponsorship by Martha White helped their popularity immensely and helped get them on the Opry as permanent members in 1964.

On the strength of their Columbia recordings, they made their first guest appearance on the Grand Ole Opry on January 28, 1961. Jim said, "There's a lot of exposure and, of course, prestige there with the Opry. It got us a lot of bookings and some package shows that we never would have accomplished any other way." Jesse added, "It meant a lot more airplay on our records. I'd noticed that before we got on."[52]

The membership in the Opry also opened the door to a support network. Jim remembered, "They had a news release thing that they were always sending out to all the deejays. Back then, on Friday nights, WSM had a 'Mister DJ USA' thing that Grant Turner was in charge of. Grant would take the DJ and the artist out to dinner after everything. We went on several of those and we got to know those guys. It's just personal contact that meant a lot. No other way [other than being members of the Opry] could you get involved in stuff like that."[53]

Their music changed with the times and often alienated their old fans. Jim said, "I think that a lot of the narrow-mindedness that has been attributed to bluegrass fans is really more from die hards and some of the promoters. When we were doing the 'Diesel on My Tail' thing, for instance, the fans accepted it. They must have accepted it; the criticism we would get was mainly from the other entertainers. There's just something about the music business where if it's successful, there's always somebody ready to knock it."[54]

"We are working more now (1991) than we did, say, ten years ago," said Jesse. "It's holding up pretty steady as far as makin' a livin'. But that's as far as bluegrass artists are concerned. A country artist can make more money in three or four years with some hits than a bluegrass picker can make in a lifetime, but it's a livin'. It's a volume-type thing; we have to work a lot." He also explained that although his band was doing well, smaller bands who were trying to make a living in the music have it pretty rough; there are so many of them and there isn't that much money. "People ask me for my advice on what to do with a new band. I tell them, 'If you're going to play bluegrass music, do it because you love it; because you're not going to get rich from it.' Flatt and Scruggs came as close as anyone to getting rich. But they were pioneers and got in on the college circuit [where the money is]."

[49] Scott Hambly, "Jim and Jesse—Reprising Their 'Epic' Best," *Bluegrass Unlimited*, August, 1986, p. 10.

[50] Scott Hambly, from the album cover of "The Jim and Jesse Story," April, 1980.

[51] "Whisper" was written by their guitar player, Don McHan, who specialized in gospel tunes.

[52] Art Menius, "Jim and Jesse Celebrate Opry Anniversary with All-Star Recording," *Bluegrass Unlimited*, May, 1991, p. 35.

[53] Ibid., p. 36.

[54] Robert K. Oermann, "Jim and Jesse: Testing the Boundaries of Bluegrass Music—With a Little Help from Charlie Louvin," *Bluegrass Unlimited*, September, 1982, p. 19.

Bobby Atkins—
"It was so cold you couldn't hardly stand it."

In 1954, banjoist Bobby Atkins joined the **Blue Grass Boys** the first of three times. This time it was for only three days. "I got so homesick that I came back home, for I had not been away from home before.[55]

"At that time, it was Bill, Bobby Hicks, Charlie Cline, Jackie Phelps (bass) and myself. I was okay until the sun went down. When the sun went down, I was some kind of lonesome person! They had a old hotel down there in Luverne, Alabama, that didn't have heat in it, see. Some of the window lights were broke out. They had some kindling laying around so you could build a fire 'cause it was so cold you couldn't hardly stand it. But I was so homesick that I just went to bed and cried. I didn't have no money so Carlton Haney bought my clothes and everything that I had when I first went with Bill. I won't never forget him for that."[56]

He spoke of the hard times with Bill Monroe during the subsequent times he was with the **Blue Grass Boys**. "We got to where we wasn't getting paid. I don't hold nothin' against nobody. Vassar don't. None of us does. But we got to where we played eight months, and in the fall of the year when we didn't have too many shows, we got to where we didn't get paid, see, like we should. So we quit. I quit. And when I quit, Bobby Smith and Vassar Clements both quit at the same time. It was three weeks later that he (Monroe) went and played Carnegie Hall. Benny Jarrell, Frank Wakefield, Red Allen and a bass player out of Roxboro, North Carolina, played the shows that Bill had around Virginia and North Carolina because Bill didn't have a band." Atkins would have loved to play Carnegie Hall but he didn't know about it. In hindsight, to Atkins this was the "clunker" to have just worked with Bill Monroe and not be called for the job.

Atkins spoke about a curse which has afflicted many a musician—alcohol—a condition which sometimes cannot be controlled. "For years, I didn't drink nothin'. But I got to drinkin' a lot. Joe (Stone) got to drinkin' a lot. The whole band got to drinkin' a lot. We'd go somewhere and be late. In fact, we were doing more harm to ourselves than we were good. So I just called Joe (Stone) and I told him that I was going to start my own group and you can start yours. 'Cause like we're doing, we're just not doin' no good at all."

Norman Blake on playing the music he likes versus making a living— "I feel that show business defeats a lot of creativity."

Mr. Blake spoke of his music, "You can obviously tell I'm not into the commercial aspects of show business because I feel that show business defeats a lot of creativity. Any time you've got to sell it, you've got to compromise it a little bit. I haven't sat up a thousand nights burning the midnight oil to figure out a bunch of super peachy-keen arrangements. I just play the music I feel like playing when I'm on stage. I usually play what's in my head. That's what comes out—good or bad—whether people like it or not. It's no heavy intellectual number.

"When the rock and roll thing came along, I was all but wiped out. You couldn't sell country music. You couldn't sell bluegrass."[57] This demise of bluegrass affected Blake in a personal way. But he bolstered himself up and started writing songs about his life experiences.[58] "I think a lot of musicians have gone through that," Blake explained. "They've been put down, and it takes a lot to bolster your confidence enough to go out and get your trip on and say, 'All right, I'm going to do it whether you like it or not. It's a little different from what you're used to hearing, and don't put me down for it. Here it comes, I hope you're ready for it.'"[59]

"The musicians in bluegrass—all of them— have really hurt the music. There is so much jealousy and unprofessionalism in bluegrass it just makes me sick..." —J. D. Crowe

---

[55] Atkins took Hubert Davis' place on banjo. He took the place of Buck Trent the second time with Monroe.

[56] From a 1992 telephone interview. In an interview with Carlton Haney in 1991, Mr. Haney recalled: "So he (Atkins) worked awhile. The first week we went to Florida, he wouldn't turn the light out in the bedroom in the hotel room and the other boys couldn't sleep and they come and got me and I went down there and said, 'What's the matter?' He said, 'I can't sleep with the light out.' I said, 'It's night. You all got to play tomorrow. You got to turn that light out.' 'I can't sleep with the light out.' And after three days Bill told me to take him home 'cause he couldn't get a hotel room for him and the boys couldn't sleep with the light on. So I took him home after three days. He was awful [home]sick and he couldn't sleep with that light out. It wasn't long and I run out of banjo players and I called him up again. This was maybe a year or a year and a half later. I said, 'Bobby, I need a banjo player. Bill needs a banjo player and I ain't got a soul.' 'I'll come. I'll be alright this time. I can sleep with the light out. I've been doin' it at home.'"

[57] Mary Jane Bolle, "Norman Blake," *Bluegrass Unlimited*, October, 1973, p. 9.

[58] One of the characters of his past was Sullivan, a gatherer of the ginseng root in northern Georgia. Blake wrote and recorded "Ginseng Sullivan."

[59] Bolle, op. cit., p. 9.

J.D. Crowe—
"You may not succeed anyway, but you sure won't if you don't act professionally."

In a 1981 interview with Marty Godbey, J.D. Crowe talked about professionalism, "I study more than just picking; I study the whole realm of the business, like when I was with Jimmy [Martin] around Nashville. I guess I was raised up around professional musicians. This [business] is what puts meat on my table and when you look at it that way, you want to succeed. You many not succeed anyway," he laughed, "but you sure won't if you don't act professionally!"

He added, "The musicians in bluegrass—all of them—have really hurt the music. There is so much jealousy and unprofessionalism in bluegrass it just makes me sick...they just try to keep it within their certain circle. And when it starts getting outside that circle they want to start putting their feet down."[60]

Crowe commented on the frequent personnel changes. "Every time you get a new picture made, it was three months and somebody would leave. It never fails. Then you're stuck with 500 pictures. The good musicians get tired and want to try something new even, though [that] may not last long. That's fine! If a person stays in a band about four years, you've got the best out of them. At the time, we enjoyed it, burnt hell out of a lot of songs, and put it down like it should have been done. Everybody had a good time and we've still got good relationships.

"Every time you change people, I could no way keep the sound. Especially after Tony and Ricky left. There was no way to bring in somebody else and sound that way. I'd have to start over and get the sound that we could make together and I knew that. That's where a lot of people make a mistake. There's no way that anybody could beat what we did so there was no use tryin' and I know that, so that's why I did what I did."[61]

While many musicians feel that it is easier now to make a living in bluegrass music than it used to be, Crowe explained, "Well, it's according to what you call 'a livin'.' Music is like a lot of things: it's not consistent. And, too, you only get out of it what you put in it. But there's a few little discrepancies in *that* thing, too. A lot of it is luck and being at the right place at the right time. A lot of it's who you know. There's a lot of good pickers that aren't even known and probably never will be. And you have to understand that it's a different time than it was back then, too. We could talk about this for six hours. When you talk about this, you have to cover the whole spectrum of the music business from the '40s on 'til now—the *time* it was, the *why* it happened. It's just totally different now."

In a 1992 interview with this writer, Crowe discussed how he ran his band. After considering that some band leaders are autocratic and some are partnerships where each musician is free to play his own feelings, he replied, "Well, you've got a set pattern; you've got to know the material you want to do and the way you want to do it. So that's just the way it has to be. You can't have everybody going in different directions." He tries to preserve a certain "J.D. Crowe sound" up to a point, "But I'm not beyond doing other things if it sounds good." When playing a song which has already been played or recorded, each member of Crowe's band is free to play what has been played and recorded earlier in that person's own style but with the restriction that it must *fit*. He said, "Everybody plays different but you got to play with the band...you don't play by yourself. You go with what fits the flow of the music and the groove. That's the way it has to be."

Jimmy Martin—
Trying to find players with a professional attitude

Jimmy Martin spoke of the qualities of a professional musician, "I try to find players with a professional attitude: those people who hate to make a mistake. If J.D. or Bill Emerson made a mistake, down in the dressing room you'd hear them nearly break their banjo putting it in the case. You never have to get on a pro musician about messing up your song because he'll stand there and feel guilty himself. They were pros from start to finish..."[62]

Hubert Davis—
"One day, bluegrass music is gonna be on top."

"It's always gonna be there," said banjoist/band leader Hubert Davis. "Just like I say about bluegrass music...people's put it down, put it down. I used to talk to the guys when I worked in the mill and say, 'One day bluegrass music is gonna be on top.' [They would reply] 'Ah no, that'll never happen.' But I've always had that in my mind. That's one reason why I never did quit. And I know guys that's quit that's good banjo players—good bluegrass pickers—and told me, '...can't make no money at this bluegrass music. I've done quit. Get me an electric guitar.' Or, 'I've got my religion; I don't play

60 Leon Smith, "Talking with the Stars: Two Interviews from a 'Bluegrass Hornbook,'" *Bluegrass Unlimited*, July, 1981, p. 17. (Note: "Bluegrass Hornbook" was a summer radio program on National Public Radio.)

61 Ross, "The Talented J.D. Crowe," *Bluegrass Unlimited*, November, 1990, p. 21.

62 Ibid., pp. 22, 23.

it no more.' And just as quick as bluegrass has grown and got to where they can make some money I see where they've dropped their religion and started playing the banjo again. I've heard country stars say, 'Get that mess off the stage so the show can go on.' And then in later years they come up with a banjo on their records."[63] About these country artists who made these comments, he insists that those people are driven by the dollar—which really has nothing to do with the essence or experience of making music.

Dean Webb—
"Purists get mad at you if you change anything."

Webb recalled that just as the **Dillards** was getting its start in this music in the early '60s in Southern California, "Folk music *looked* like it was still going pretty well. Actually, it was winding down in popularity; it was really fading out. Of course, we didn't know it at the time. [We thought] it could be a gold mine! Go to California and play bluegrass—just like we'd always wanted to do—and get paid for it! So we created what was an identifiable music and kept it pretty image-conscious [including] the way we'd dress—almost like Daniel Boone with fringe shirts and moccasins. The songs all fit into the image: 'Old Man at the Mill' and 'Polly Vaughn.' The songs created the image and all worked for us. Then, after you do a thing for a while, you get tired of it. It becomes confining—whether it's bluegrass or anything. Everybody had his own concept of what it is. That's why all the purists get mad at you if you change anything."[64] Even though the **Dillards** went through three albums with that image, they knew all along that their band did not play traditional bluegrass.

John Duffey—
"I don't want to save up to go on tour."

On March 4, 1969, John Duffey left the **Country Gentlemen**, needing a break from music and touring and the music business in general. He also suffered much frustration with no monetary reward only the promise of royalties and from the various recording companies used by the **Country Gentlemen**. "It was like savin' up to go on tour. The other guys, Eddie and Charlie, wanted to go anywhere for five bucks and I told them than we'd never get a decent price if you keep on doing that! I don't want to save up to go on tour. I should get paid to go on tour. In addition to that, there were the hassles of the business and I was getting pretty successful with my instrument-repair business. Hell, I could stay home and not put up with all that shit and get by."[65]

"No matter what I personally do, I still don't forget what I really like. Unfortunately, what I really like will not make you a living. You've got to diversify a little bit. For instance, we can't go out and do all of Bill Monroe's songs and be—shall we say—a band ourselves or a separate entity. We just become clones. And who wants to see that? The original is still around. I love just straight-ahead, hard-driving bluegrass music."

"There's a revival in folk music right now (1987) that's getting hot, and I think it will have an effect on bluegrass music. I might be mistaken, but bluegrass seems to be in a recession right now. I think this folk music revival is going to do what it did in the '60s. There's a hell of an audience that's going to come into bluegrass from the folk side."[66]

Mike Auldridge then commented about the use of drums on their last three albums, "There's enough talent in the band that, if we worked at it, we could compete with anybody. But it's real hard to walk out on stage at some of the (mixed) country and bluegrass festivals. Acoustic music just sounds weak by comparison; there's no bottom end. And the same thing happens on the radio. You've got to be able to have a little stronger bottom end, rhythm wise. You could do that in a way that a song like 'Old Train' wouldn't really change." But this viewpoint was not shared by everyone. Bassist Tom Gray disagreed with this view so strongly that he eventually had to quit the **Seldom Scene**.

Posed the question, "If you had to do your musical career differently would you do things differently?" Duffey responded, "Yea, I would have taken up my uncle's offer in Florida to send me to law school and come down and take over his practice in Miami. I would never advise anybody to get into this business. I mean, after a long period of time, I finally managed to succeed at it. But, it's like my wife and I say, things will work out right. Now that we can afford to do it, we're not physically able." This new "afford-ability" factor came into his life when the **Seldom Scene** began to gain significant audiences in the mid-70s."[67]

[63] Bruce Nemerov, "Hubert Davis—Down Home Banjo Picker," *Bluegrass Unlimited*, January, 1977, pp. 20, 21.

[64] Interview by Bob Alekno. "Dean Webb Interview," *Mandolin World News*, Winter 1980-1981, Vol V, #IV, p. 15.

[65] Live interview, 1993. He didn't own a shop. He was given space in the basement for a shop at Arlington Music. He was the first person to do Martin Guitar warranty work outside the Martin factory.

[66] Art Menius, "The New Seldom Scene Article," *Bluegrass Unlimited*, July, 1987, p. 16.

[67] Live interview, 1993.

Tony Ellis on working with Bill Monroe in the early 1960s

Bill Monroe paid Ellis and most of his other hired hands union scale (the minimum wage established by the Musician's Union). This means he was paid only when they worked. There are other pay arrangements a musician can possibly work out, but union scale probably applied to most of the musicians who worked for Monroe. This pay arrangement was adequate during the summer but during the winter it was best to be a single person without a lot of financial obligations to be able to survive. $800 was a good month. In a band which was structured as a "band-leader and sidemen" situation, the band owners made all the money and the members made out the best they could.[68]

Adding to this difficulty was Monroe's method of booking concerts. He didn't have an agent at that particular time to go out and promote the band (this was to change in early 1963 when Ralph Rinzler took over that responsibility). Monroe did have the opportunity to get large jobs by paying Artist's Service Bureau in Nashville, but he felt that the fifteen to twenty percent they charged was too much. Instead, Monroe took smaller jobs, and paid a ten percent fee to the booking agent or whoever booked the band into a venue.

After Rinzler joined as Monroe's manager, the **Blue Grass Boys** had some terrific musicians, such as Bill Keith and Kenny Baker, who helped keep the band, musically, at the performance peak of any of the bands he'd had through the years. Audiences were fascinated by their skill and began to appreciate the band as a pioneer in American folk music. Monroe highlighted each individual's skills on stage and, together with the additional bookings that the band got through the work of Rinzler, they gained a momentum as a band that thrust the band name toward the top in the public's recognition of bluegrass bands. Up until that point, only the touring bands or the local bands were generally known by the public. And Monroe was suddenly gaining recognition as the "Father of Bluegrass Music" according to the label given him by Rinzler.

But as well as they were doing in the recognition department and as tight as their band was, promoter/manager Carlton Haney still had to wire Monroe money so that Monroe could hire a band to appear at the Fincastle, Virginia, festival in 1965. The "Father of Bluegrass Music" momentum spread rapidly, however, and, together with the advent of the festivals, Monroe became better able to keep a band together from that time on.

Bill Clifton

William Marburg, later known as Bill Clifton, became an educated man with a Masters Degree in Business Administration. This sets him apart from most of his bluegrass contemporaries, many of whom never even completed high school. He was a stock broker before he found that he could make a living as a full-time American folk musician in Britain. Clifton cautiously weighed the possibility of dropping his day job to pursue music full-time. The jump from the security of having a well-paying day job would be a big one—an important one. He followed his heart, left the broker business, and for the next ten years was in Britain making folk and bluegrass music.

Raymond Fairchild— "The people who've made bluegrass music what it is today have lived it."

"If you're out there playing a show, you've got to play from the heart. You've got to feel it; you've got to live it. A lot of people sing, but they have their mind on something else while they're singing. You can tell by the sound of it where it's coming from. The people who've made bluegrass music what it is today, Buddy, they've lived it. Back when bluegrass first started, you know they couldn't have been making much money doin' it. But they wouldn't change; they wouldn't quit.

"Just the other night I done a show with Don Reno in Blue Ridge, Georgia. Man, he was so sick. Most of these young musicians who claim to like bluegrass would have been at home in bed with somebody rubbing their chests with Vicks salve. But Don Reno was up there doing his show. Any minute it looked like it was going to be his last breath. Now, I ain't kidding. He told me he had something like bronchitis and felt like he was smothering. He'd talk awhile and then take a deep breath. That's love. That's what's helped bluegrass music out—people like that.

"Bill Monroe's traveled the roads many, many times and didn't always make money. So did Ralph and Carter Stanley. Ralph has told me many times they'd have to play a show before they could eat. I've seen Ralph and Carter come into Spruce Pine, North Carolina, back in the fifties and play for eight or ten people. They were playing on a percentage basis and people were paying thirty or forty cents to get in, so you can figure out how much they made. It was the love of it that kept 'em going.

"I love it. There's some great young musicians, but they don't understand what the hard life is. If it boiled down to the hard times again, they'd be quittin'. They

68 Monroe once told Ellis that during a seven-year period which included the times Lester and Earl were with him, he made two and a half million dollars.

wouldn't have the backbone to stand up. They don't love it well enough where they'd hang with it and play for nothing. Them fellers played for years and years and never made nothing: Bill Monroe, Reno and Smiley, Mac Wiseman, Ralph and Carter, the Goins Brothers. That's who we can thank now. They're the ones who handed it down on a silver platter. It was fellers back then that held it together."[69]

He spoke of the importance of having experience in the entertainment business, "You can't stay in this business thirty-five years and not know what you're doing. I can get up before any audience in the United States and before the third number, I know what to do. That's important when being a band leader."

The formation of the Country Music Association

About 1957, Don Pierce and Owen Bradley met in Nashville to discuss creation of a new trade organization to be named the Country Music Association (CMA), soon to be formed to counteract the tremendous influence that rock and roll music was having on the youth of America (and, of course, the music business). It was meant to instill a sense of identity to the music—hopefully to increase the number of radio stations playing the music. Among the many artists who were once considered a part of country music who then became established in rock and roll were Elvis Presley, Carl Perkins, Buddy Holly, Sonny James, Jerry Lee Lewis and the Everly brothers.

Tom Gray on bluegrass and the Country Music Association, Elvis, and the Seldom Scene

In a 1989 interview with Gray in his home, he spoke about bluegrass and the Country Music Association and how the CMA intentionally tried to eliminate bluegrass music. "In the early '60s, there was a deliberate attempt by the CMA to eliminate bluegrass from country music programming. It was the intent to make country look more urban. They thought that anything which was traditional, folky—anything not slick—should be avoided. The Chet Atkins/Nashville sound was to be promoted. Music that could be looked upon as old-fashioned...something [like] the average mountaineer sitting on his front porch might play on his banjo was to be avoided. And bluegrass had that image. So they advised country music radio stations to base their format around the Nashville sound and they should avoid bluegrass. They should not play Kitty Wells because she sings through her nose. A lot of the country music radio stations at that time followed that lead

and they stopped playing bluegrass. There were a few of them that still did, but bluegrass was sort of driven off into a corner... I blame a lot of the demise of the bluegrass radio audience on the leadership of CMA, which I think was Chet Atkins at that time.

"The big market that bluegrass had in the forties when Bill Monroe was new and fresh...had gradually faded. And when Elvis hit, he just destroyed what was left of any market at all for bluegrass. He dominated what had been the country market. Then many of the radio stations would cross over and you couldn't really tell the rockabilly from country or some of the rock and roll that was being played then. Elvis was sort of in-between then. He was the new, exciting thing and a lot of other music was left behind without a market once Elvis came along. And bluegrass was hurt a lot by that. But when folk music began to get popular again in the sixties, then this music being traditional and acoustic folk music found a new audience—you could perform in college campuses and for the first time bluegrass was moved out of the southeastern states.

"In the early '60s there was a deliberate attempt by the CMA to eliminate bluegrass from country music programming." —Tom Gray

Gray spoke of the final days he was in the **Scene**, which he was in from 1972 until 1987. The **Seldom Scene** sought a larger audience, he explained. "We were at a plateau. Our income had reached a high point in 1985. It stayed about the same. It was gradually becoming harder to keep our calendar full. During the first ten years of the **Seldom Scene** we never had an agent—we didn't need one. John Duffey would just answer the phone. Sometimes he would say 'yes' and sometimes he would say 'no.' He'd never have to solicit work. He would ration us by price and this made us the best paid bluegrass band in the business for several years." Being equal partners in the band made this situation quite lucrative for band members.

"Friend, no one has taken bluegrass anywhere. Either you play bluegrass or you don't."

According to J.R. Hornyak of Sherrill, New York, the Country Music Association was created, according to its own guidelines, to "preserve" and "save" country

69 Wayne Erbsen, "Raymond Fairchild—Making His Own Way," *Bluegrass Unlimited*, March, 1982, p. 16.

music. But what it ended up doing is breaking any ties with what had slowly evolved to be known as country music, [and it] was no longer in vogue. It was replaced by all the gadgets and rhythm instruments which the "Nashville sound" found pertinent. *This* sound was what was to be played on the radio—nothing else! *This* sound was what was to be shoved down the public's throat and was to be accepted. After all, the CMA and the Nashville producers knew what's best for the public. Right? The old, country music which was its history was put in a corner and labeled as "hillbilly" and not up the standards of the industry's new sound. As author Hornyak explained, "Gone was the simplistic and historic primarily acoustic instrumentation, replaced by mass electrification, amplification, percussion and other instrumentation to alter the sound. Its true sound was no longer considered the 'trend'. Gone also were the country ballads of family, home, strife, railroads or heartfelt love, replaced largely by bedroom ballads, cheatin' songs, and other topics not remotely resembling country music's true character and roots. These old messages weren't in vogue."[70] Reflecting on how radio stations seldom play the old songs which are country music's history, he wrote, "How are young performers to know where bluegrass is headed when they don't know where it's been?"

"Even comedy," he continued, "long an integral part of country music, was discouraged—and discontinued was the country music award for it... Today, Nashville performers envision themselves as strutting sex symbols as they clutch a microphone and slink along, often crooning some lustful ditty."

He also analyzed another aspect of the future of bluegrass. "Most amusing, yet annoying, are those who parrot [that] bluegrass is 'stifled' and it must 'grow' or it will 'stagnate.' These are favorite expressions by those who seek (intentionally or unintentionally) to destroy it from within. The suggestion is that bluegrass needs an overhaul, but generally the speaker stops short of any explicits. "Beware these wolves in sheep's clothing who say, 'I love bluegrass BUT...' No 'Buts!' Why would anyone seek to compromise that which he truly loves? If one doesn't *love* bluegrass, perhaps he should do something else. Ricky Skaggs, for one, abdicated to pop country. Fine." [Author's note: Ricky returned to Bluegrass in 1997.]

Moving to still another topic, the writer was annoyed by "those insiders who seek to corrupt our music by suggesting they're 'taking bluegrass in new directions!' Friend, no one has *ever* taken bluegrass anywhere! Either you play bluegrass or you don't."

He closed optimistically, "Yes, bluegrass can grow—achieve new direction within the confines of un-amplified acoustic instrumentation without selling-out instrumentally or lyrically. No forced evolution—

abandoning its rural roots or suggesting the festival stage be property of established, full-time bands, or those recognized by any one self-appointed group of spokesmen for this music—should ever be tolerated if bluegrass is to remain the grassroots country music of the people."

David Grisman— touring with Red Allen and paying your bluegrass dues

As a member of **Red Allen and the Kentuckian**s in 1965, they all drove to Wheeling, West Virginia, to perform on the WWVA Jamboree. While touring with his foursome, Grisman remembered that Allen only bought "one [motel] room for everybody. We'd take the beds apart. We'd have two beds and he'd take the mattresses off the top and sort of make four beds out of it. I tell people, 'Hey man! You haven't paid your bluegrass dues until you've slept in between Red Allen and Bobby Diamond' (he laughed). I remember once they lost the key. We were staying in some motel in Pennsylvania and they lowered me in through the bathroom window. They lowered me by my feet and I landed on the toilet on my hands."[71]

Doyle Lawson— keeping a band's sound consistent

Doyle Lawson is a band leader who hires musicians to fulfill the sound which he has established—a system similar to that of Jimmy Martin and Bill Monroe. When band members move on to other bands, such as when three members of one of his band configurations left to form **IIIrd Tyme Out**, they must be replaced with individuals who can do the same task at least as well.

It's more difficult to own your own band, Lawson told this writer. It's much easier to just work for someone else, get a paycheck, and simply play as the band leader requires. That's easy. What Lawson has to avoid, in order to keep his own **Quicksilver** sound, is allow the banjo player to play and sing in any style he wants. Or allow the bass player or the guitarist to do the same. It is not only important for him to keep the certain sound that the band has, it is equally important that it not change significantly as new members come and go.

It took a long time for Lawson to find his own sound which people can recognize. By keeping it the same from year to year, it somewhat assures product reliability and being able to be hired by promoters who expect his band to perform just like they did when they hired **Doyle Lawson and Quicksilver** some years before.

70 J.R. Hornyak, "Letters," *Bluegrass Unlimited*, May, 1991, p. 8.
71 Interview, 1993.

Jimmy Martin—
"Bluegrass is not something to get on stage or out in the parking lot and do it every which way."

Jimmy Martin spoke about how hard the work was in the old days, especially in the slow season of winter. "When I was with Bill Monroe we played in the wintertime seven days a week. But we played most of the shows for percentage...just for the door... Bill started me off at $60 a week. Then I got to $90 a week and had to pay my hotel bills and things and eat out of that, and travel seven days and nights a week—any time he could get a show date. Maybe [we'd] get off three or four days for Christmas, then right back on the Grand Ole Opry and right back in the snow and sleet and rain and playin' show dates seven nights a week. I went as high as a week and not even get into bed or lay down on the couch or anything. One thing, it was hard work and it made me know what livin' was. But you see, I was raised on a farm and had to saw wood and dig ditches and work on the farm and I thought that was a lot easier than being on the farm. I liked it better, but I got more sleep on the farm."[72]

Martin's **Sunny Mountain Boys** in 1957 were Martin, J.D. Crowe (banjo), Johnny Dacus (fiddle) and Paul Williams (mandolin[73]). This was Martin's favorite group and brought the most success—especially significant because the band was competing with Elvis' popularity. But while other bluegrass bands were having significant problems finding venues for their music, Elvis didn't affect the success of Martin's band at all. While others told him that he would have to get an electric guitar to compete, "I think we was on the Louisiana Hayride as guests two times and I think we took two and three encores with the banjo, mandolin and guitar—and they hired me a bass player. And it's been doing that ever since. Elvis didn't hurt me whatsoever. I would have liked to open up his show for him and showed him how bluegrass could win over at his show."[74]

Martin has had many different musicians since his band of the early sixties. "It's hard to keep entertainers

Jimmy Martin

today—harder than ever," he said. "They get a little bit mad at you because you're trying to get your music down, and they don't want to work hard at getting your songs sounding good... I love bluegrass music better than anyone who ever wore a pair of shoes. But today, my outfit changes very often. Lots of people say to me, 'Jimmy, if you paid the boys more they would stay with you.' But that's not the reason, because every Sunny Mountain Boy ever worked for me—every year—I give them raises, and the good pickers who can sing real good get good salaries. Some of them can't travel that much or can't live in Nashville. It would be better to live in Nashville where they can ride the bus with me and rehearse and get the songs down professionally. You see, bluegrass is not just something to just get on stage or out in the parking lot and do it just every which way. Bluegrass is played by harmony singing. But lots of musicians don't know how to tone in their voices with someone else's. You just don't get that overnight. You learn it and study it. They don't *study* it today, and get out in the parking lots and jam. To make good grades in school you've got to study the books. Like Ricky Skaggs, let's give him a big hand. He studied it with the Stanleys and he worked hard. And when he made his break, he already knew what he was going to do. And I've never heard him do a bad thing yet, even though he's put electric steels, and guitars. And what he's making a hit on is still bluegrass because he studied it first, and he ain't never going to forget bluegrass.

"And the band has got to be powerful and come on strong—just as good as the trio voices. A lot of times today you hear good harmony singing, but the band is not even together.

"Today, bluegrass bands like to get out and jam better than working at getting the songs down that they have to make a living at. If they don't get to do exactly what they want to do, then they quit you."[75] "You've got to be professional. You've got to get your music in harmony; you've got to get your singing in harmony; you've got to have plenty of power in it. You can't sound weak. Bluegrass music has to sound strong to get the records played on the radio."[76]

Martin refuses to go on today's television shows until he feels the sound of his band is right—up to his

---

72 Roland Kausen, "Fall Bluegrass Blues?" *Bluegrass Unlimited*, October, 1991, p. 30.

73 Bill Gill was their mandolinist in June.

74 1992 interview, Grass Valley, CA.

75 Strickland, op. cit., p. 21.

76 Ibid., p. 22.

standards. He has received offers to appear on the "Fire on the Mountain" and "Nashville Now" television shows and the Opry. But "Unless I got a real tight band sounding good, I'm better off to just go coon hunting and stay out of it. Because I have seen bluegrass on television and shows that absolutely—and pardon me, I don't want to hurt any body's feeling—not getting it. And other people who've heard it say it sounds terrible. Well, you're not doing anything for bluegrass then, you're just letting it go down. We've lost the sound. We've lost the rhythm and timing of bluegrass."[77] Even a drummer doesn't hold it together. "Each musician has got to hold it up there on his own, bring out a good tone, and tone it together."

Sonny Osborne— "Everything in your life is commercialized."

Sonny Osborne is always busy with his business of music. "I relax when there is something to relax about. But if you're going to be in the business, you've got to be in the business. You can't just be into it a little bit and out of it a little bit—in my mind anyway. You work as hard as you possibly can, as hard as you did when you were fifteen, sixteen, seventeen years old. If you don't do it that way, then you're cheating yourself and everybody else. While you *can* make it, it's best to make it because it won't always be there. That's the reason for that."[78]

"The business side of it, to me, is a lot like the music side. You work as hard as you can to perfect a certain kind of break or note or something like that, and in the business side of it you work hard to perfect that, too. You work as many dates and get as much money out of it as you can. Everybody says you're not supposed to look at the commercial part of the entertainment business of music; just play for the music itself. I think that's bull. Everything in your life is commercialized. We all think that way, too. It might look good, or sound good, but you still can't make a living by not being commercial—just for the music itself. So there's more—a lot more—that goes into the business side of music. You work as hard on that as you do the other."[79]

Sonny has spent a lot of time thinking about the tradeoffs between the career move into music, its lack of security, its tremendous time and energy commitments, and the costs of taking that road. The costs were "My life. It's a pretty fair trade. That's about all any of us have to give: our time and what we are—what we

know mentally. We trade that for security. And I kept some for myself."

If he were to do it again, "Number one, I would have gotten a good education—which I don't have—which has cost me a great deal: not in money, but in time. With an education you are able to think your way through and not have to go trial and error,. And that's the way we had to do it because we weren't knowledgeable enough to do it the other way. That's the first thing I would do.

"I would stay completely away from alcohol and speed, which I didn't do, and I had to learn the hard way. They took a little bit of my mind away. Of course, they gave me some things in return, I guess—I don't know what yet. Let me see, they probably shortened my life by ten or fifteen years. I won't know until the time comes. Maybe in some other life. Speed kind of helped me in a way, though, because with speed you're able to out-think yourself. Alcohol is really bad. I think that is what I would stay away from most of all—alcohol and all kinds of drugs."[80] He quit alcohol in 1968, and the rest about 1977.

"As far as the business side of it, I think we did what we could do in the early days with the knowledge we had. There wasn't anybody to ask, either, in those days, because we were among the first bluegrass bands in existence. Besides us, there was Lester and Earl, Monroe, the Stanley Brothers and Jim and Jesse. We started in 1953, so we were right in the beginning. There was nobody there to ask what was right or wrong. I really wouldn't change the music all that much."[81]

Paul Adkins, 1991.

[77] Strickland, op. cit., p. 24.

[78] Glenna H. Fisher, "The Osborne Brothers," *Bluegrass Unlimited*, July, 1984, p. 10.

[79] Ibid., p.11.

[80] Ibid., pp. 15, 16.

[81] Ibid., p. 16.

Paul Adkins—
"I think that the most important thing is to satisfy your customers."

After many years as a sideman in the bands of Larry Sparks, Glen Duncan, J.D. Crowe and Bill Harrell, Paul Adkins broke out on his own with the **Borderline Band** in January 1988.[82] The name "Borderline" came from Paul's belief that the band's music was on the borderline of bluegrass and other styles.

His new band brought realization that surviving in this bluegrass world as a band leader is tough. "You just don't know how hard it is to promote yourself until you have to really go out and do it. Just trying to get promoters—who don't know you—sold on the idea that you *can* attract an audience to their show is something that's tough to do."

Adkins recognizes that finding one's own sound, as a band unit, is important to the formula for making a living in bluegrass. "I suppose most groups really want to have a sound all their own," he said. "We built ours around original material and arrangements and that pretty much guarantees that we're different. It's been interesting from my standpoint to watch how this band's music has evolved. I had a desire at first to get really hot pickers and singers. But what I really wanted was a band that had their hearts in the music that I wanted to make."[83]

"This is my business. It's just the same as any other business. Long before we even set foot on a stage I had set some realistic musical and financial goals for this group. I think that the most important thing is to satisfy your customers. If you strive to do that you will make yourself successful a whole lot sooner."[84]

Don and David Parmley—
"If you don't want to travel, you ain't got no business in the business."

David Parmley's solo album for Sugar Hill in 1989 was "I Know a Good Thing." This was his announcement to the world that he had other talents other than bluegrass. He spoke of the business, "The whole thing in this business is to try to get your name recognized. That's the name of the game: to get more jobs. You can't make a name for the **Bluegrass Cardinals** by goin'

out and recordin' a bunch of old classics. Not that I've got anything against 'em—I love 'em. But it seems to me that every band that's ever been successful had to come up with some new material—something that the people will recognize and associate with that band. But even if we get most of our material from other sources, we still try to do it in the traditional style."

David Parmley then spoke of bluegrass videos, "It may be a small part now, but down the road in, say, ten years, I think it will be a major part of every project that comes out. At this point, the only stations I'm familiar with that play a video is The Nashville Network (TNN) and Country Music Television (CMT). Alison (Krauss) has opened some doors there. Of course, if too many bluegrass people start trying to put a video out just so they've got a video and it's not good quality, then that's just going to set bluegrass back another twenty years. Anybody can put out a poor quality video just like anybody can have a record printed.

"I think bluegrass music needs to be more business oriented than it has in the past. It's probably the only form of music where there are acts out there working and promoters can walk up to the artist and book dates. You know, you can't call George Strait at his house and book him and the reason is—not because he doesn't want to talk to promoters—but because he can't handle all that business and work the road and play music and travel and record and do the interviews and all the other things he has to do.[85]

In the same article, Randy Graham spoke of the International Bluegrass Music Association, "I think IBMA has done a great deal, especially in terms of creating more media awareness and hopefully broadening the audience. There are some initial aims and goals that were spoken of early on that I wish they'd kinda get back to and that's some group insurance for musicians. I don't know where that stands right now but I'd like to see it come about now. But I'd like to see it come about so that people who devote their lives to the industry could receive some benefits from it."

At an interview at Ken Seaman's 1993 MidWinter Bluegrass Festival, Don Parmley mentioned that his job is not easy. "What you do while you're up there on the stage is the easiest part of the business. When you get done here, you got to get in that bus and go six or eight hundred miles or a thousand to do a show the next day. A lot of people don't think about that part of it. That's part of the business, and if you don't want to travel you

---

82 Paul Adkins and the Borderline Band recorded its "Lay It on the Line" LP for Old Homestead and the band started touring in January 1988 just as soon as the LP was ready for sale. The band was formed on January 16th with Adkins (guitar), Ron Pennington (mandolin), Ned Luberecki (banjo) and Tom Gray (bass).

Recruiting Gray into another band was not easy because "Tom had just left the Scene and I was pretty sure that he wouldn't be interested. So I didn't really come out and ask him if he wanted the job." But the job intrigued Gray so he joined within a week. When the band evolved into a full-time touring band, Gray had to drop out due to the time commitments of his day job. Robin Smith joined on bass. The Borderline Band signed with Rebel Records in 1989 and recorded the all-gospel "Wings of Gold." Robin Smith and Fred Travers (resonator guitar) joined the band just before this recording.

83 Logan B. Neill, "Paul Adkins and the Borderline Band Are on the Right Track," *Bluegrass Southern News*, September/October, 1989, p. 20.

84 Ibid., p. 20.

85 Brett F. Devan, "The Bluegrass Cardinals. The Traditional Sound of the Creative Original Vocal Trio," *Bluegrass Unlimited*, November, 1991, p. 20.

ain't got no business in the business. You got to travel if you're going to make a living at it."

The spreading popularity of bluegrass music

In the early 1980s, the popularity of bluegrass music seemed to be spreading. According to a letter by Dave Freeman, founder of County Records, his record company was producing one-third more, to possibly double, the number of strictly bluegrass albums when compared to as little as four or five years earlier.[86]

Butch Robins— "You've always got to look at it like a job."

About making a living in music, Robins said, "When you get right down to it, you've always got to look at it like a job. It can't be any other way. You've always got to be physically and mentally in shape to pull it off. I've been more conscious here lately about developing a professional attitude about my playing than I've ever been. I'm conscious of the thing that I show up on time or ahead of time to do my job, not be temperamental, make do with what is at hand, and keep on getting by like any other wandering minstrel does. I'm trying to carry an image about me that I can take pride in and letting people know I'm a friendly sort of fellow instead of someone who'll just run and hide from them—which I have been known to do before."[87]

Bill Harrell on "comin' through" on tours and on local associations

Harrell spoke of booking his band and the process of being hired at a less-than-festival-rate-of-pay when the band is "coming through" the area en route to another gig. His stature in the business, and having been in it for forty years, built up some feelings about which some promoters may not want to hear. He told this writer, "'Comin' through' is one of those things which I wish had never happened. And the reason I wish it had never happened is—and I blame a lot of the bluegrass bands for it—is 'comin' through' and they want to get you for next to nothing. When you are 'comin' through,' frankly, I don't want $500 for 'comin' through.' It's not fair for the people who pay me my price: And if they've got time to advertise, they should be able to put on a show and pay my price. Of course, a weekday is a little cheaper. I just won't play these 'comin' through' things. Some of these bands play for $400 or $500 just to get it. I'm not that hungry. I'm not tryin' to be stuck-up about

it at all either, but I figure that if I'm not worth at least $1000 passin' through, then they don't want me anyhow.

"I understand the instances where, perhaps the geographic area would not support that much money. Or the band does it to get the exposure to the people who don't see them and, of course, you do sell a lot of recording product, and so forth. I use my good friend, Mac Wiseman, as a good example. He hardly plays any 'comin' through' prices—he's got a price and that's what you pay. And he's worth it!

"These [local bluegrass] organizations ought to get out and hawk these advanced tickets and get behind the thing if they want somebody with a name to come through and put a show on. I know; I've done it my own self: rented buildings out the last couple years and just

Butch Robins

filled them to the rafters and told them I didn't want nothin' but the gate." Mr. Harrell related that he recently rented a 300-seat hall for $300. He hired a radio personality as emcee to help plug the concert on the airwaves, and hawked tickets. Before the concert, he had 150 tickets sold. He put on a show and put 311 people in there for $10 a head. The hall owners came to him later and thought Harrell should give them some more money. But Bill felt that their food sales, booze sales and rental fee was quite sufficient, thank you. After all, that was the original deal. "I can't do that in Colorado 'cause I'm not there to hawk those tickets and go around to different organizations... I could tell any of these bluegrass organizations how to put a show on and how to do it to get the community behind it. [I'd tell them] to sell ads in a book where I'd tell them that this is gonna be a show and we're expectin' a large crowd. Would you like to buy some tickets for your special customers and would you like to buy space in this pamphlet which we give out at the festival. If these bluegrass organizations have a common interest, it

86 "Letters to the Editor," July 1980 issue of *Bluegrass Unlimited* magazine
87 Barry Silver, "Butch Robins," *Bluegrass Unlimited*, May, 1979, p. 55.

seems to me to be a very simple matter for each person who belongs to the organization to get out and hawk eight or ten tickets apiece and put a good price on it. I know, I did it!"[88]

Blaine Sprouse—
"As a featured artist, you have to entertain people."

While Sprouse was the fiddler with **James Monroe and the Midnight Ramblers**, the group occasionally worked double bills with the **Blue Grass Boys**. Here he learned, "In this business you meet a lot of people and you have a lot of acquaintances. That's the nature of the business, I guess."[89]

In 1982, he was co-owner in the **Bluegrass Band**. He spoke of owning his own band, "In this band, it's not just musical knowledge you have develop, it's also business knowledge. When you're in business for yourself and not working as a sideman, you have a lot to learn. As a featured artist, you have to entertain people. I've found that I need to learn more about that and concentrate more on developing my technical abilities and my stage presence."[90]

Pat Enright—
"I think people are a little burned out on popular music."

Enright spoke about his decision to play music full-time, "My upbringing was to get an education, have a career. In choosing music, you have to forget all that and go ahead with [music] because you feel that's absolutely what you should do. You have to decide once and for all that you're going to do whatever it takes to make a living at music until, maybe, it becomes obvious that you have no business doing it."[91]

In 1985, the **Nashville Bluegrass Band** added Stuart Duncan and recorded Rounder's "My Native Home" (they used Blaine Sprouse on fiddle before Duncan). When Duncan joined, he was twenty-four. Since he had been playing music since he was seven years old, he probably had more musical experience than any of the other band members. It was hard, financially, to split the income five ways but they realized it was a good move.

In a 1987 interview, Enright talked about the rise in the popularity of bluegrass music. "I see it on the road and playing some of the festivals. I think people are a little burned out on popular music. People are ready for a change. A lot of the musicians who are suddenly attracting notice have been around for several years now. There are a lot of fine musicians around and a lot of them are here in Nashville—which is another good reason to be here. But it has only been only the last five or six years that Nashville music people have looked around and realized that there is a huge audience that likes bluegrass and related music. I think a lot of people in the music are becoming wise to the fact that there is a huge audience out there for different kinds of music and that they ought to tap into it. You can't ignore Jerry Douglas, Mark O'Connor or Bela Fleck—they're just too good. Jerry, Mark, the **New Grass Revival**, all have major label contracts now with complete control of what they do. That's a good sign. Bluegrass isn't just regional music and hasn't been for a long time."[92]

"Bluegrass has been the 'unwanted child of country music' since the invention of the multi-track recorder and the advent of the 'Nashville sound.' Until recently, any mention of 'bluegrass,' or 'traditional,' or 'banjo,' would have had a producer at a country recording session reaching for the Maalox. But now, more than ever, artists and producers are looking to the music's roots for new songs and different sounds. And it must be working, because the current country charts are filled with songs, either from the traditional sources or written in a straight-ahead, traditional style. Everything comes 'round again."[93]

Larry Cohea
on the fans of this music

Larry Cohea, banjoist for **High Country**, spoke about bluegrass fans, "One thing I've never understood is how people won't spend any money on [bluegrass music]. I don't know what it is, but you can play rock and roll or punk music or something, and the kids by the thousands will take the last five bucks they've got and go down and buy a ticket to see some run-of-the-mill rock band. Yet bluegrass fans—some of them making a good living—but they won't spend five bucks. They won't get out of the house and drive across town if they have to park. I never understood that."[94]

[88] From a 1993 telephone interview.

[89] Wayne W. Daniel, "Blaine Sprouse—Fiddler Turned Scholar," *Bluegrass Unlimited*, November, 1988. The nature he referred to was probably the mobile aspect of the job—the effect of which tends to inhibit roots.

[90] Stephanie Ledgin, "Blaine Sprouse—Pick of the Bluegrass Fiddle Crop," *Bluegrass Unlimited*, November, 1982.

[91] Alana J. White, "Pat Enright," *Bluegrass Unlimited*, December, 1987, p. 59.

[92] White, op. cit., p. 61.

[93] From the liner notes of High Country's first Turquoise Records LP, "Blue Highway."

[94] Sandy Rothman, "Butch Waller's High Country - Part 1," *Bluegrass Unlimited*, September, 1985.

Jerry Douglas—
"I didn't have to struggle through like Red Allen and Jimmy Martin and those guys."

In a person's career development, timing is very important. This certainly hold true in the case of Jerry Douglas. He began his musical career at the peak of the bluegrass festivals phenomenon. His first professional job was at the top of the bluegrass field as session resonator guitarist with the **Country Gentlemen** in the summer of 1973. Ten years earlier would have made a significant difference in him and his musical exposure. Douglas recalled, "I didn't have to struggle through like Red Allen and Jimmy Martin and those guys. They had the hardest road for a bluegrass musician. They were playing in some pretty rough clubs behind chicken wire and the like. The big part of it was transportation; the roads in the whole country were different. There weren't these huge interstates which have direct lines from one part of the country to another. And the vehicles they rode in were not as plush and comfortable. They didn't use airplanes because they didn't make enough money to afford the tickets. I never did have to do that and I'm glad I didn't have to do that. But I don't think that would have changed my tenacity. I think I would have stayed with it no matter what."[95]

In 1985, after seven years with the **Whites**, Douglas quit to get away from the 200-250 days per year of touring and being tired all the time. When they first began touring together they used vans. As time went on they became able to afford a bus, adding a new dimension to the concept of touring. "It makes your playing a lot better," he said. "You stay in tune a lot better, your ears aren't worn out from listening to the road, you can sleep, you can walk; it's just a lot easier on you and allows you to play a lot better."[96]

He spoke about being on the road and how it makes a person into a different person, "I'd feel it coming over me when I'd get off the bus and go out to talk with somebody. They always knew me but I never knew them. So I'd immediately shift into Jerry Douglas, **Whites'** band member or Jerry Douglas on the road. It's strange to have so many good friends all across the country with their names and faces running together. You start getting superficial. I could see it coming and I just didn't want to be that way. I wanted to see what it's like to live a normal life, to have a personal life, to spend time at home with my wife, Jill. You know I have a son, Grant, from my previous marriage and Jill has a son, Patrick. We're hoping to expand our family one of these days. The road musicians' schedule just doesn't allow a family man to be home enough."[97]

Professionalism in bluegrass—
"It doesn't happen overnight or in a parking lot."

Writer/performer Steve Stephenson of Virginia Beach, Virginia, wrote an essay about how bluegrass performers must increase their professionalism.[98] "But what is professionalism?, he asked. "Mr. Webster defines it as 'The conduct, aims and qualities that characterize a profession or professional person.' Lofty words but true nonetheless. Let's look a little closer and examine the words. Conduct. What do you suppose the bluegrass fan thinks when he sees his favorite artist or group drunk, smoked up, dressed like bums, or acting like fools when on or off stage? How many would-be bluegrass fans, probably attending their first festival, will attend another? How many other bluegrass groups will be hurt by the loss of these people and their purchasing dollar?

"Look at the second word in the definition: aims. The aim of every bluegrass group should be the entertainment of the audience and the furtherance of bluegrass music. But people are not entertained nor music furthered by sloppy-looking musicians putting on a sloppy performance and looking like they are bored by the whole business. It's hard to soar with eagles when you are surrounded by turkeys.

"Look at the last and maybe the most important word of all: qualities... Anyone who pays the prices necessarily charged today to attend a first class festival is entitled to quality entertainment from quality groups and performers. Frankly, some promoters would do well to look at the quality of some of the performers they book as fill-bands. I don't mean that a band should be given a chance unless they have umpteen albums out and super credentials, but I do think that promoters have an obligation to the audience to see that the bands they book can, at least, carry their portion of the show in a manner that does credit to bluegrass in general. Most top names in bluegrass today will tell you that one of the things that hurts bluegrass most is the appearance on stage of people representing themselves as a bluegrass band who can neither play their instruments, nor sing, nor entertain in a quality manner. One of the most charming things about bluegrass music is that people who can learn three or four chords on a guitar, banjo or mandolin can get together for an evening of fun and music and who knows? Most of the great names in

---

[95] From a telephone 1993 telephone interview.

[96] Ibid.

[97] Bobby Wolfe, "The Jerry Douglas Story," *Bluegrass Unlimited*, August, 1991, p. 24.

[98] In "Letters" to the editor in *Bluegrass Unlimited*'s December 1980 issue,

bluegrass started in just such a fashion. But you wouldn't learn three or four chords on a piano and then try to pass for a concert pianist. Why, then, do these people try to pass as a professional bluegrass band until they are ready? To change a group of musicians into a well-disciplined band requires weeks and months of practice and hard work, learning together the fine points of the music and each other's capabilities along the way. I doesn't happen overnight or in a festival parking lot.

"However, I know of no greater feeling on this earth than the pleasure I feel at the conclusion of a good performance, or the release of a good album. To those bands just starting out, or to those a little further along the way, I assure you the work and tears it takes are worth it.

"I hope that all performers and groups reading these thoughts will take a moment for some soul searching. Happily, most of the top names in the business recognized long ago the ideas spelled out above; that's why they are tops today. People want performers they can look up to, and then after the show, mingle with them, have pictures taken with them, and ask questions. Bluegrass music will continue to grow as it has, and even faster so long as its growth is solid and built on the foundation of the great bands and artists of the past who recognized that professional music is a business and, as such, must be run like any other business that in order to survive, must create and market quality merchandise.

· "If bluegrass music is to grow, its performers must grow first.
· "If bluegrass music is to be elevated above the cow pasture, its performers will have to be elevated above the cow pasture first.
· "If bluegrass music is to be appreciated throughout the world as an art form, its performers are going to have to become professional artists first."

Country Music Pioneer Association

The Country Music Pioneer Association was formed in Nashville in 1986 to perpetuate country music. Ex-Blue Grass Boy Clyde Moody was the first president.

Guest editorial in
Bluegrass Unlimited

Joe Ross, frequent contributor to *Bluegrass Unlimited*[99] and leader of his own bands through the years, feels that there is a need to professionalize bluegrass

music. He was clear to point out that "professionalize" is not the same as "commercialize". Ross asked bands to ask themselves several specific questions:

1) How do we look?
2) How do we dress?
3) What image are we trying to convey?
4) How's our emcee work?
5) Is our show choreographed?
6) Is our performance paced like a jet heading for the sky?
7) Do we capitalize on our personalities and musical skills—instrumental as well as vocal talents?
8) Can we give interesting interviews?
9) Does our image convey success, enthusiasm, energy, dedication and perseverance?

Ross insists that "Keeping these thoughts in mind will result in a higher grade of bluegrass without compromising the music's integrity."

Neil Rosenberg on
the problem of alcohol and drugs

In an interview with Jack Tottle, Rosenberg was asked about the problem of alcohol and drugs for the professional musician. "First of all," he said, "I think the situation of being a professional musician is one that, in this circumstance, just leads to health problems in a general way. If you are traveling all the time, you can't eat the way you should, you are constantly under stress, you are always trying to make ends meet. You have to deal with promoters who are under a lot of stress themselves and often solve problems in ways that don't help the musician.[100]

"To me, the problem of alcoholism and drug abuse is a problem that really has socio-economic causes. How people deal with that often has to do with how they deal with their career. I think drinking and drugs often serves as an escape for facing the difficult problems of how one handles one's career.

"Bill Monroe is very interesting in that regard. I always noticed that Bill didn't drink and that he spent time exercising. Also, he would always meditate before he went on stage."[101] This meditation, according to Rosenberg and Peter Rowan, was the reason he would never sweat on stage; Monroe would simply will himself not to sweat. Rosenberg continued, "There is sort of an inner strength that Monroe has always had, for whatever reason, because of his personality. I think the other successful musicians have all had ways of dealing with these things through their own sort of mental health."[102]

---

99 The guest editorial in the February 1987 issue of *Bluegrass Unlimited*.

100 This is an apparent reference to the fact that at time promoters may fail to pay performers as agreed, sometimes citing low attendance at a show.

101 Jack Tottle, "Neil Rosenberg at East Tennessee University," *Bluegrass Unlimited*, October, 1987, p. 69.

102 Ibid., p. 69.

The breakup of the Johnson Mountain Boys— "Music is an 'extra.' It can be a way of life, but not a livelihood."

After 1987's formal declaration of the **Johnson Mountain Boys** breakup, it was official as of February 20th, 1988. But, unofficially, it dragged on a little while the band reaped the benefits of a full-house wherever they would go in concerts listed as their final performance. The story of this group's final days is interesting because it sheds a bright light on what it takes to be a professional bluegrass musician and on the public's reaction at the demise of one of its most popular recent groups.

Dudley Connell had been full-time in bluegrass since 1980. The pressures of "accounting, bookkeeping, payroll, numerous tax and bank deposits, correspondence, and business management had replaced my former dream of becoming a professional musician," he wrote.[103] Leaving his family for trips became more and more painful, and during the slow season of winter he saw his "nest egg" dwindle. Connell said, "I couldn't enjoy the slow season with my family as I once did." His bottom line was, "Don't misunderstand; I love bluegrass. But I feel you have to justify in your own mind whether or not the hard work brings an adequate reward." He looked forward to bluegrass on a part-time basis.

Two months later, *Bluegrass Unlimited* published many responses to Connell's announcement in its "Letters" section including:

> If bluegrass is going to continue as a viable form it must have an infusion of younger talent who know what the music is all about, and this young talent must be able to at least earn a decent living from the music. There are other good, young bluegrass bands out there but few have generated the unanimous acclaim given to the *Johnson Mountain Boys*. It's ironic that *J-M-B* is forced to break up because it finds low monetary gain doesn't justify the pressures and frustrations. Exactly what are we, as bluegrass fans, willing to support?[104]

and,

> It doesn't surprise me that the music industry doesn't have a job for someone like that because driving endless miles, doing repetitious songs until your eyes glaze over, working eighty hours a week with no fringe benefits or paid holidays, and then going home to bookkeeping, inventories, maintenance and repair—all for little money— does not constitute the stuff that attracts genius. Dudley is not leaving the field because the work is too hard and/or because the money is too little. His reason, like his music, is more 'traditional.' He is leaving so he can be with and support his family. He has discovered...what musicians have long known: music is an 'extra.' It can be a way of life but not a livelihood."[105]

The demise of bluegrass, continued.

On March 6th, 1987, *The Washington Post* newspaper featured an article by columnist Richard Harrington which spoke of the demise of bluegrass music. The article used the announced breakup of J-M-B as the tip of the iceberg and professed that the whole genre of bluegrass was doomed to failure.

While a sensationalist columnist for a newspaper wrote these words of impending doom, IBMA President Peter Wernick was quick to discredit the journalist's presumptions. While Wernick agreed that the traditional-style bluegrass bands have trouble earning a living, he insisted that those bands are quantitatively in the minority when all bands earning a living in the music are considered. Wernick used his own **Hot Rize** as an example of a band which was doing quite well at the time by mixing traditional bluegrass with more contemporary stylings (and comedy) which seem to appeal to a larger audience.

Though the loss of **J-M-B** was sad, Dave Freeman of Record Depot Distributors, Roanoke, Virginia, said it was not significant enough to indicate the death-knell of all bluegrass. He wrote, "I am sure there are dozens—if not hundreds—of bluegrass bands throughout this country that would be happy indeed to command the personal appearance fees that the **Johnson Mountain Boys** did, play the number of show dates per year they played, and sold the number of records, tapes and T-shirts off the table that they sold at shows."[106]

There was an inference in the *Post* article that there were no young people interested in this music—that its audience and participants were old and finite. Ricky Skaggs, Keith Whitley, Sam Bush and many others who started in this music before they were ten would take issue here. Skaggs would probably be among the first to admit that it is difficult for a youngster who is interested in this music to be different than his/her classmates when rock music is so dominant in their social structure. Skaggs did it; he broke away from the mold. Occasionally, teenagers write to Skaggs for support in

[103] Dudley Connell, "Guest Editorial," *Bluegrass Unlimited*, February, 1988, p. 16.

[104] Jerry Barney, Fergus Falls, MN.

[105] "Letters," *Bluegrass Unlimited*, May, 1988. The second letter was contributed by Ron Thomason, Dry Branch Fire Squad.

[106] "Letters," *Bluegrass Unlimited*, May, 1988.

their problem of being laughed at and ridiculed by fellow classmates. He, himself, has been there and offers them encouragement in this fight against significant odds. Skaggs was once assigned a school project to write about somebody famous. He wrote about the Stanley Brothers whom he idolized. The teacher didn't recognize the Stanleys at all and gave him an incomplete/failing grade with which he was unable to graduate from high school. The irony of this story is, now that he is famous and can hold large fund raisers for his hometown of Louisa, Kentucky, they want him back and they treat him with the utmost respect and affection. Funny how money can influence a person's outlook. I wonder how that teacher feels now.

Dudley Connell several years after the breakup of the Johnson Mountain Boys

In 1992, a few years after their breakup in 1988, the **Johnson Mountain Boys** won awards from IBMA and re-formed to tour again. Connell reflected on the event of their breakup, "I probably don't feel the same way I felt back in 1988. At that particular time, I had a child that was three years old, we were on the road some two hundred days a year. I don't remember what I was making—I can't remember now—maybe ten or fifteen thousand dollars a year, something like that. And my wife was working full-time and we were in one of the more expensive counties in the U.S., just outside of Washington, D.C.. The thing that we had, and have, is there is a lot of opportunities for employment there. So I guess there is quite a pull to not be away so much and to spend time with your family and make more money. But you know something I found after leaving the business—you know I left the business for a year and a half to two years—I really realized how important the music was, let alone any financial reward. Just to get out and play and perform means more to me than perhaps I realized in 1988.

"I don't think anyone can dispute my affection for bluegrass music; I've always loved the music. It's just a matter of how I chose to make my living. I don't think you have to make your living at it to love it. People can feel any way they want about why we disbanded. The reason we broke up was for a career change and didn't reflect on how much we love the music. We just wanted to try something else for a while. We were young men with a little education and just wanted to try something else. And I found, in some ways, that bluegrass has more to offer than the material or the sane world" (he laughed).[107]

Support your recording artist with cash

A man from West Virginia wrote to "Letters" in *Bluegrass Unlimited* that he was concerned about the practice of copying a friend's recordings instead of buying a new recording. He insisted that if everyone would spend a few extra dollars which would go directly to the band, "They would have a direct, active role in keeping him singing, which would keep him recording in someone's studio, which would keep the publishers supplying him with new songs, which would keep the songwriters writing." He went on to warn us. "Saying that you don't do it that often or that you only record certain groups doesn't excuse you. That one tape every couple of months *does* matter. Bluegrass music needs the financial support a lot more than the blank tape manufacturers."[108]

Worldwide Bluegrass Music Month

New York City resident Bob Wolff was the person responsible for the effort to get Congress to acknowledge the month of May as "Worldwide Bluegrass Music Month." He started to push for the Month in 1987 to order to draw attention to bluegrass music and to expose the music to more people. About promoting bluegrass during Bluegrass Month, he said, "There are no regulations except that whatever you do should put the music in contact with people in your area on their 'turf' and continue the tradition of attending bluegrass as a family experience."

Allen Mills— "You do without things to get to play the music."

In a 1992 interview with **Lost and Found** founding member Allen Mills, he explained that he recognized how difficult it is to keep a band together. He founded the band in 1973 with Dempsey Young, Roger Hardy and Gene Parker. Soon, Bubba Chandler and Steve Thomas were with the band. "It makes you appreciate the perseverance of Bill Monroe. We've got the same problem today because there's not enough venues to play to do it on a professional basis. You have to subsidize your income and it makes you a harder, better musician really if you can do it. You got to love the music. But you do without things to get to play the music... There are a lot of unsung heroes in this music that need to be talked about: like Jim and Jesse and the

107 From an interview at the 1992 IBMA convention, Owensboro, Kentucky.
108 Letter in *Bluegrass Unlimited*, May, 1989, p. 6. Mike Blackburn, of Tornado, West Virginia.

Osbornes. They've had personnel changes come and go and they've got a successful group."[109]

There are a lot of groups today, Mills went on to explain, which are successful in this music but only use it to have fun. If they had to give up their day jobs for the music they wouldn't do it because of the loss of their income. The music isn't important enough to them to rely on it one hundred percent. "But me, I don't want to do nothin' else. But I don't hold it against them; that's just the way they are. I just can't be that way, but they can. They've probably got a lot more fans than I have bein' the other way."

The creation of IBMA

In 1985, a bluegrass trade association was created to help bring recognition of bluegrass music to the media and the rest of the nation. Later named the International Bluegrass Music Association (IBMA), it planned to solicit all types of bluegrass organizations to find out what they wanted IBMA to do. The first meeting was held at the sumptuous board room in Nashville's BMI (Broadcast Music Inc.) headquarters.

Dr. Banjo was the first bluegrass act at the newly opened Riverpark Center in Owensboro. It is next to the IBM Museum (1991).

Art Menius (then working for the Linear Group, producers of "Fire on the Mountain" on TNN) had been developing plans for an industry organization. Meanwhile, Lance LeRoy stepped forward and initiated a meeting to establish the organization. There at the June meeting were LeRoy, Menius, Sonny Osborne, Pete Kuykendall, Milton Harkey, Bill and James Monroe (Bill bought lunch for everyone there at Shoney's), Jim and Jesse McReynolds, Mac Wiseman, Larry Jones, Ray Hicks, John Hartin, Joe Carr, Len Holsclaw, Doyle Lawson, Randall Hylton and a few others. They seemed to all agree that bluegrass music was on its last legs; no

bluegrass group had been signed to a major country label since the 1970s, the number of festivals had declined since 1977, and the only recent superstars were Doyle Lawson's **Quicksilver**, **Hot Rize** and **Johnson Mountain Boys**.

They met again in August with many of the same individuals as the June meeting. They named the organization and elected a Board of Directors who were Kuykendall, Lawson, Allen Mills, Sonny Osborne and Barry Poss. Norman Adams and John Hartin became alternate Board members, Hylton was voted treasurer and Menius became the secretary and soon became Acting Executive Director. Peter Wernick was later selected as President, a position he holds into the mid-1990s as "the only president the IBMA has ever needed." They were on the way to becoming a successful organization. By the end of 1985, they had fifty-five individual members, eleven organizational members and fourteen patrons (now called Grass Roots Club).

In August of 1985, "Bluegrass with Class" was a festival event sponsored by the Owensboro-Daviess County Tourist Commission. It featured the **Osborne Brothers** with the Owensboro Symphony, the **Whites**, the **Bluegrass Cardinals**, **Jim and Jesse** and the **Johnson Mountain Boys**. Overlooking the Ohio River from English Park, it was free. The next year, IBMA moved their activities from Nashville to Owensboro, Kentucky. Owensboro continued to exhibit its interest in bluegrass by holding other "Bluegrass with Class" events.

Doyle Lawson was one of the people involved in the inception of IBMA. He spoke about the International Bluegrass Music Association, "It was formed as a trade association for the good of the music and not for one person or group of people. It was formed to better the music—to structure it to where it could be a legitimate business and turning it into a working, growing, thriving thing as opposed to just sort of everybody splashing around in the waters. But we're not looking to change the music. Everything evolves with time. No matter how much you try to keep it one way, it'll change some."[110]

The IBMA may have been formed to keep bluegrass from dying. "Of course, we're worried about it," said Lawson. "I'll worry about it when it reaches a certain plateau and never seems to get any smaller but never seems to get much bigger. I'll worry then, because you have to attract some new fans at some point in time, since the old ones get old with you... People will lose their enthusiasm if there aren't any new people coming along getting excited, saying, 'Oh, I've just discovered bluegrass!'"[111]

A 1986 guest editorial in the March issue of *Bluegrass Unlimited* by Art Menius gave some insights for

[109] From a 1992 interview at IBMA.

[110] Tim Stafford, "A View from Home—A Discussion with Doyle Lawson," *Bluegrass Unlimited*, October, 1987, p. 45.

[111] Ibid., p. 46.

Pete Wernick talks with Mary Tyler Daub at the IBMA, 1994

the reason for the Association's creation, "The Country Music Association (CMA) came about in order to make country a popular music. As a side effect, it created crossover stars such as Parton and Rogers. In so doing, country music lost its very 'countryness.' IBMA has no intention of doing the same to, or for, bluegrass. Bluegrass was commercial in the context of 1946; it is not in the context of 1986 tastes... IBMA is not here to change the music or the people who support it. What we want to change is: great musicians starving for their art, shoddy business practices, poor or no promotion, negative public images, second rate productions, and shoe-string budgets."

The IBMA held its first trade show (called the "World of Bluegrass"), Fan Fest, and showcase in August 1986. Bluegrass Week in late September now consists of a convention attended by more than 1500 musicians, business people and fans. The International Bluegrass Music Awards began in 1990 and aired internationally on radio. The outreach program places the best of bluegrass in schools.

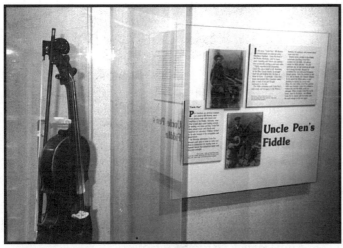

Uncle Pen's fiddle hanging in the IBM Museum.

As soon as Art Menius was appointed Acting Executive Director of IBMA, he announced the formation of the Bluegrass News Service. It was created to be the publicity arm of IBMA and to answer any questions about bluegrass and provide any information someone would need about the music.

Menius was later hired full-time as Editor of the association's newsletter, *International Bluegrass*. Menius, in 1990, spoke of the impact of IBMA, "Probably the most significant thing, as simple as it sounds, is just getting the people in bluegrass to think of ourselves as an industry and as a community: to realize that whether we're in Queensland, Australia, or Bangor, Maine, or Eureka, California, that we have common interests and common strengths." By that time, there were 1000 members of IBMA. In attendance at the IBMA meeting were John Hartford, Doyle Lawson, Sonny Osborne, Roland White and others.

In the March 1986 issue of *Bluegrass Unlimited*, Joe Ross wrote about the IBMA, "I found it very interesting that the goals for the IBMA are very similar to those that led to the creation of the Country Music Disc Jockey's Association in 1957. The CMA's creation was undertaken to revitalize country music by representing the interests of performers, producers and retailers to the business world. The CMA felt that increasing the number of radio stations playing country would lead to increased listeners, and thus make the music more widely marketable and expand country music's urban appeal. To achieve such a goal, the 'Nashville sound' was created that emphasized electric guitars, drums, piano, pedal steel, horns and echo chambers. Some recordings that also included choruses and string sections could be more appropriately labeled 'pop' music. This movement toward a 'Nashville sound' gained its impetus from the direct competition by rock and roll music, and the trend was successful. The record companies, and most performers too, were happy as record sales increased and the appeal of country music was broadened. The result, of course, was that country music changed its identity and, in the process, lost touch with its origins, its roots."

Ross went on to describe that bluegrass didn't fit into this mold that CMA had forged. Presumably, the banjo, fiddle, and mandolin were too "folky". Bluegrass instrumental breaks and fills were probably thought by some 'Nashville sound' proponent to clutter or confuse the music which should focus on the vocals. And finally, a stigma was associated with bluegrass music primarily due to its origins as a music of the poor, rural whites of Appalachia. Country music record company producers wanted nothing to do with our musical style with current negative connotations.

"Despite the widespread exclusion of bluegrass in Nashville over the years, certain events were monumental for bluegrass and showed that Nashville at least recognized its existence as a part of America's country music heritage. From the first bluegrass festival in Roanoke in 1965, the events grew and were hard to ignore. In 1970, Bill Monroe was elected to the Country Music Hall of Fame. In 1971, the annual CMA Awards recognized the **Osborne Brothers** as Best Vocal Group of that year. Also in 1971, William Ivey and Doug Green brought a good background and understanding of bluegrass to the Country Music Foundation, Nashville's foremost country music research organization. In 1970, Nashville booking agencies were started that dealt solely with bluegrass talent. Unfortunately, few bluegrass groups have become regular members of the Grand Ole Opry over the last two decades. However, I can't think of any since Jim and Jesse [McReynolds] and the Osborne brothers joined in 1964."

An article by Ray Hicks in the December 1985 issue of *Bluegrass Unlimited* reported on the formation of IBMA and indicated that the trade association would "neither be a preservationist organization nor will seek to change the music to make it more popular." Ross commented on the statement affirmatively, "This is essential if the identity of bluegrass is to survive."

Ross then spoke of the increased radio programming of progressive bluegrass in the late '60s and early '70s which led to the progressive trend within the music which is happening today as well. "Perhaps this is what is needed to revitalize bluegrass. However, if the newly-created IBMA is not careful, we could find direct rebellion by fans against the compromising of the music solely to achieve commercial success."

Following Art Menius' tenure, Dan Hays became IBMA Executive Director in August 1990. IBMA now boasts a world-wide membership and increasingly reflects the international nature of bluegrass in the 1990s. The fears that prompted its founding have been replaced by an industry enjoying unprecedented success.

On November 30, 1990, groundbreaking occurred for the River Park Center in Owensboro, Kentucky, which was to house the IBMA offices as well as the International Bluegrass Music Museum and a performing arts center to be used by the City and during IBMA events. The Museum opened in Owensboro on a limited basis in 1993 (officially in 1995), boasted some strong collections, and presented some outstanding programs and exhibits during Bluegrass Week. The Museum suffered from staff turnover. During the winter of 1996/1997, some serious questions arose concerning its staffing, funding and governance, including the City of Owensboro's commanding presence on the Board of Directors of the Museum.

IBMA awards

The annual inductees into the IBMA Hall of Honor were:
1991— Bill Monroe, Earl Scruggs, Lester Flatt
1992— Carter and Ralph Stanley, Don Reno, Red Smiley
1993— Jim and Jesse McReynolds, Mac Wiseman
1994— Sonny and Bobby Osborne
1995— Jimmy Martin
1996— Peter V. Kuykendall, the classic Country Gentlemen
1997— Josh Graves

Earl Eugene Scruggs' Hall of Honor plaque.

Awards of Merit went to:
1986— Alfred Brumley, Ray Davis, Bill Monroe, Ruby Baker Moody, Cuzin' Isaac Page, Dr. Neil V. Rosenberg
1987— Dewitt "Snuffy" Jenkins, Bill Jones, Don Owens, Ralph Rinzler, Charlie Waller
1988— John Duffey, Tom Henderson, Peter V. Kuykendall, Ola Belle Reed, Earl Scruggs, Bill Vernon
1989— Lester Flatt, David Freeman, Kathy Kaplan, Robert Larkin, Dr. Bill C. Malone
1990— Carlton Haney, Wade Mainer, Joe Stuart, Dr. Charles Wolfe
1991— Don Stover, Ralph Epperson, Bill Bolick, Earl Bolick (**Blue Sky Boys**)

1992— Bill Clifton, Josh Graves, Lloyd Loar, Charlie and Ira Louvin

1993— Curly Ray Cline, Hazel Dickens, Jim Eanes, Dick Freeland

1994— Johnny and Jack with Kitty Wells, Wilma Lee Cooper, Lance LeRoy, Ken Irwin

1995— Joe Val, Rose Maddox, Mike Seeger, Saburo and Toshio Watanabe

1996— G.B. Grayson, George Shuffler, Curly Seckler, Martha White Flour Company

1997— Mary Tyler Doub, Vern Williams and Ray Park, Kenny Baker, Benny Martin

Print Media Personality awards went to:
1990— Art Menius
1991— Peter V. Kuykendall
1992— Hub Nitchie
1993— Edward Morris
1994— John Wright
1995— Frank Godbey
1996— Wayne Bledsoe
1997— Murphy Henry

Broadcast Personality awards went to:
1990— Orin Friesen
1991— Lee Michael Dempsey
1992— Dell Davis
1993— Col. Tom Riggs
1994— Frank Javorsek
1995— Wayne Rice
1996— Eddie Stubbs
1997— Bill Knowlton

The bluegrass portion of the music market

According to *Music Business International*,[112] 64% of all music records are sold in record stores, 11% are sold via record clubs, 21% are sold in "other stores" (such as Wal-Mart, etc.), 3.8% are sold by mail order. Rock sold 36% of all music, followed by Urban Contemporary (18%), Country (12.5%), Pop (11.7%), Jazz (4.3%), Classical (3.9%), Christian/Gospel (3.5%), all others (8%). Bluegrass music fits into the "all others" and "country" categories. In 1993, 330 million CDs were sold, along with 360 million cassettes. The retail music sales figure that year was 8.3 billion dollars and expected to go higher in successive years. Warner Brothers was the easy leader in the worldwide record-sales market in 1992 with 30.7% followed by BMG (19.4%) and the rest.

The Bluegrass Consumer

According to the 1995 Simmons Market Research on the bluegrass record buyer, when compared to the average U.S. consumer, the bluegrass consumer showed the following characteristics:
- #1 leisure activity is listening to music
- consumed 45 million colas/diet colas per week (two more than general population)
- twice as likely to earn more than $75,000/year
- more likely to paint, draw or sculpt
- more likely to buy Martha White flour
- more likely to water ski
- more likely to play a musical instrument
- almost three times as likely to own a full-size motor home

And according to "Bluegrass Market Research Report" by Pete Wernick in 1994, "Since 1985, the number of people who like bluegrass music has grown by 15 million—the largest rise in numbers and in sharpness of increase of all kinds of music studied in both 1985 and 1992." This date, notes Wernick, is when IBMA came into being. And he also noted that bluegrass came in a lowly 17th (0.7%) as the "most-liked" music of all types and that country was the dominant leader in these rankings at 21.3% followed by rock (12.9%), gospel (9.7%) and easy listening (9.3%).

Bill Monroe's Hall of Honor plaque.

Record Companies - Table of Contents

Record Companies

The effect of a strike and World War II

In 1942, the American Federation of Musicians struck against the record companies, demanding royalties for their songs when they were played on the radio and the juke box. This took almost two years to settle.

As a result of the strike against Decca, Columbia and Victor, a few small, independent record companies were formed to provide a place for musicians to continue to record. Capitol was formed in Hollywood with enough money to ensure longevity. King Records was formed in 1943 in Cincinnati and concentrated almost exclusively in the fields of country music and rhythm and blues. In 1946, Rich-R-Tone Records came into existence. The chronological order of these companies is as follows:

- King (1943, founded by Syd Nathan, now owned by Gusto)
- Mercury (1945, now owned by Polygram)
- 4 Star (1945, founded by Bill McCall, now based in Nashville)
- Bullet (1945, last release was in the early 1950s)
- Vogue (1946, short-lived)
- Sterling (1946, until 1948)
- Rich-R-Tone (September 1946, founded by Jim Stanton, revived in Nashville by Stanton in the 1970s)
- Imperial (1948)
- Dot (1950, founded by record store owner Randy Wood, eventually moved to the West Coast and merged with ABC-Paramount which was absorbed by MCA)
- Sun (1952, by Sam Phillips)
- Starday (ca. 1953, founded in Texas by Jack Starnes and H.W. "Pappy" Daily, merged with Mercury for a short time, then with King in 1960s. Now owned by Gusto Records)
- Hickory (1954, by Roy Acuff, Fred Rose and Wesley Rose. Now owned by Gaylord Publishing Company)
- Monument (1958, bankrupt by mid-1980s)
- County (1963, by Dave Freeman)
- Rebel (mid-1960s, by Dick Freeland)
- Rounder (1970)
- Flying Fish (1974)
- Sugar Hill (c. 1978)

Another interesting factor of importance to the record industry during the WW II years was that the shellac compound used in the production of records became non-existent when the Japanese dominated the control of Pacific shipping routes. The only way new records could be made in America was to take an old record and melt it down so that the wax could be used to record the newer artists. Old record collectors may still remember this period with a shudder as they try to imagine how many now-priceless treasures were destroyed in order to turn out new Frank Sinatra hits. This accounts for the lack of recordings during this period by important artists in country and bluegrass music.

The story of Rich-R-Tone Records

In the fall of 1946, Rich-R-Tone was founded with minimum financing by Johnson City, Tennessee, businessman Jim Hobart "Hobe" Stanton. Groups who began their recording career there were the **Stanley Brothers**, the **Bailey Brothers**, the **Church Brothers** and **Wilma Lee and Stoney Cooper**. Rich-R-Tone "was probably the first independent country label devoted to traditional music forms and originating in the same area as the music."[1] A real fan of country music, Stanton's new recording company seemed to be just what was needed because the larger production companies (Columbia, RCA Victor, Decca) were ignoring the music, seeking the more commercial types of music and holding out for artists of that ilk who promised large financial gains.

Stanton's music career began in the juke box business where he replaced records in the machines. He worked at this for several years but, as he said, he "became a critic. Instead of doing the job I should have done, like put the records on and collect nickels, I found something wrong with every record I put on the machine." This led to a strong drive to get into the record business himself, which he did when he founded Rich-R-Tone.

Stanton's first artist to record was Jim Hall who recorded "Waiting in Old Caroline"/"Rainbow at Midnight" in the studios of WOPI in Bristol. It sold well with the limited distribution which Stanton provided. Stanton remembered, "I was so new at it and knew absolutely nothing. I didn't know how to distribute records so I loaded them and hit the record shops. [The response was] real good. And I really sold records, but I only had one distribution point and that was the trunk of my car. So we'd press a thousand of them and I'd go peddle them and then call the plant in St. Louis and

[1] Charles K. Wolfe, *Tennessee Strings*, (Knoxville: The University of Knoxville Press, 1977), p. 92.

they'd press another thousand and I'd go peddle them. And word really spread from one town to another up through Kentucky, West Virginia, and then it got into Pennsylvania, and then I was, from then on, just deluged with artists and entertainers wanting to get on record. It was just a novelty to people then. It started spreading on its own. The distributors...which I was unaware of earlier...from Charlotte, Nashville, Atlanta would actually hunt me and call me on the telephone and give me orders—wholesale distributors that handled the majors. You know, I could feel the door opening up... King Records was doing the same thing and you could hear word about King all around these places. You know, I look back on it now and I think what a fine life it was. Nowadays, a record label is, ho hum, you know. There's record labels like Exxon stations."[2]

Up until that point, it was virtually unheard of that an artist would carry his own records to sell; they usually just told the audience to go to a record store to buy them. It wasn't long before Stanton began to realize that some of his artists and distributors would sell records and some would not. He was very fortunate that his first few recordings were hits; it gave him a sense that no matter what he would record, he could sell. Stanton continued, "I suppose I really loaded the label down with too many different things and that's one of the mistakes I made that I later realized. I hadn't really caught on to the fact that certain magnetism has to be with that talent to make it click and sell records. Others, in my opinion that were just as good, they just didn't. And even until yet I just don't understand the full meaning of that." He signed the **Caudill Family** of Whitesburg, Kentucky, **Wilma Lee and Stoney Cooper,** the **Stanley Brothers,** Curley Lambert and Curley Parker with their **Pine Ridge Ramblers, Glen Neaves and the Grayson County Boys,** the **Bailey Brothers,** and the **Sauceman Brothers** with their **Hillbilly Ramblers Quartet.**

Stanton was respectful in all his dealings with the artists and the distributors as well. If he ordered a pressing a thousand copies, he bought the entire quantity and tried to sell them all. It wasn't like the larger labels such as Columbia, Decca, RCA, which would return what they couldn't sell. "We could sell like 5000 **Stanley Brothers** in Kentucky, and absolutely could not give one away in Georgia... I've gone into department stores, like in Atlanta, Georgia, and to a salesgirl I knew well and if I put a bluegrass sound on her turntable it would embarrass her to the point that she would look around to see who was listening and in turn it would reflect back on me. I would be embarrassed for doing it. I think that the social non-acceptance of certain music hurt us then socially. I think that people's social habits was a bad situation in those days. People tied a banjo and fiddle with Kentucky, with coal mining, with rural hillbillies and, socially—people that were more educated, maybe more socially prominent—they turned their nose down at it. Pretty soon the campuses got the folk thing rolling. That introduced the banjo and now, thank goodness, all music is music... It's finally broken through. I used to book Lester and Earl into tiny little schoolhouses propped up on sticks in the coal fields and really it was the best bookings I could get them. And then years later, after we lost track of each other, I'm sitting home watching TV and they're on UCLA campus; 30,000 people raving, and I can't believe it."[3]

During the mid-'50s, Kate Peters came to Stanton's desk and asked him how much she would have to pay him to record her record. What a neat concept this was! Somebody actually paying him to do a job! He had always presumed the expenses himself. He took the arbitrary amount of $92.50, formed Folk Star Records for this purpose, and produced her record. This was the beginning of custom bluegrass records.

Though he tried to be as professional as possible, he never held the signed artists to their contracts. "I could have incorporated, I am sure, and I could have gotten some good, strong people into the organization and it would have been a big, famous company today, probably. But as time went on, I kept operating a little country way and many, many labels just kept cropping up and smothering it into the crowd... I guess the thing that really scared me was losing my own personal contact with the artists myself. I didn't want a board of people sitting around making decisions on talent. I sort of wanted to be that myself so maybe it was a mistake; maybe it wasn't. Maybe it was ego. I don't know what it was but, and then again, maybe it was because that was what I love and I didn't really want to swap a chunk of my love for somebody's money... All I can say is that, right or wrong, that's the way I did it. But I lost talent

> "You know, I look back on it now and I think what a fine life it was. Nowadays, a record label is, ho hum, you know. There's record labels like Exxon stations." —Jim Stanton

2 Interview of Jim Stanton for "The Rich-R-Tone Story, The Early Days of Bluegrass, Volume 5," a booklet of background material for Rounder's record of the same name. P. 2.
3 Ibid., p. 4.

America's Music — Bluegrass

that was good because of big companies that was more attractive. That happened with the **Stanley Brothers**, it happened with Stoney and Wilma Lee Cooper. And I remember Stoney calling me on the telephone. He'd had an audition with Grand Ole Opry and Columbia Records and he sort of hinted and indicated he'd like to be out from under the contract so I said, 'Do you want out?' And he said yes, so I said okay." Stanton was thoroughly understanding and not at all regretful about allowing these big artists out of their contracts. The big record companies had the artists contact Rich-R-Tone directly to cancel the contract instead of calling him themselves. This way, Stanton would be much more inclined to let them go.

There were hundreds of labels which disbanded due to the "Elvis Presley era". Stanton had to close down the operation because of lack of distribution and finances for promotion. Stanton's custom gospel label, Skyland, released between 400 to 500 albums. Stanton later became Chief Engineer at United Music World Recording Studios, West Columbia, South Carolina.

After the 1960s, many small record companies sprang up with minimum financing. Many were owned by artists who found it profitable to produce their own records (Jim and Jesse McReynolds created their own Old Dominion Records, for instance). County, Rebel, Rounder, Flying Fish and Ridge Runner were among those companies which were formed for profit, but which had a basic premise of a love of the music. Beginning in 1965, bluegrass festivals were a major source of retail sales for these labels—a distribution source which Jim Stanton didn't have when he was active.

Record producer Don Pierce, Starday and Mercury Records

Don Pierce was a businessman who revolutionized the country music industry by being able to acquire locally-popular artists for Starday such as George Jones and Porter Wagoner, and by being able to promote their records in a business-like manner.

Neil Rosenberg, bluegrass historian, once heard a tape of an interview with Don Pierce by Doug Green (of the Country Music Foundation). It chronicled the rather confusing mergers and splits with Starday Records and Mercury Records. According to Rosenberg's recollection of the tape in a 1992 interview at IBMA, "Don Pierce started in the music business in Los Angeles in the late '40s after World War II with 4 Star Records. He built 4 Star Records up and was responsible for their country catalog. Around 1952, he became involved with Starday with its founders Jack Starnes and Pappy Dailey

in Texas. He worked in partnership for a few years and he and Dailey bought out Starnes and moved to Nashville (1955). Then they got a deal with Mercury Records to do all of their production work (1956) in country music in Nashville. This lasted eighteen months and that's why you see a lot of Mercury masters in the Starday catalog to this day. Then they split up; Mercury and Starday again became separate entities. Dailey left the operation (to found D Records in Texas), and Pierce became the sole head [of Starday].

After Starday was founded, Pierce signed **Jim and Jesse and the Virginia Boys**, the **Stanley Brothers**, **Buzz Busby and the Bayou Boys**, **Bill Harrell and the Virginians**, the **Country Gentlemen** and several others. As rock and roll began to dominate the tastes of America, the larger labels were soon to take advantage of this new boom and ignore those types of music who were not of that ilk. They hired big-selling talent away from the smaller labels and forced bluegrass artists to record on the smaller labels. Only Bill Monroe (Decca) and **Flatt and Scruggs** (Columbia) remained on major labels. And **Flatt and Scruggs** was only allowed to stay with Columbia if they would modify their sound toward current popular music trends.

As of 1958, Don Pierce was the new manager of Starday which was no longer connected with Mercury. Now that the Starday-Mercury arrangement was ended, Mercury now had a reduced involvement in country music except for a few major artists like George Jones. Starday was planning activities on a national scale. Under the direction of Pierce, Starday soon released albums by Jim Eanes and the **Stanley Brothers**.

Don Pierce left Starday Records in 1970 and the company became bankrupt in 1971. In 1972, Starday was bought and became more successful by recording artists such as Larry Sparks, Charlie Monroe, Don Reno and Bill Harrell and J.D. Crowe. In 1975, Starday Records and King Records were purchased by Gusto Records of Nashville.

"The main thing I got from the [Doug Green] interview," continued Rosenberg, "was the importance of publishing rights. He didn't care that much about the artists or even about promoting the records. The thing that came first was securing as many publishing rights and hanging onto them, because that was what made money in the record business. He was very astute as far as promotion goes. He recognized this whole thing about labeling bluegrass music and selling it as such on LPs before anyone else...in the fifties." Pierce knew, about 1959, that any record with the word "banjo" would sell. One of the first Starday bluegrass sampler LPs, "Banjo in the Hills," came out in 1959 followed by many others with a banjo on the cover.

Norman Blake on the big labels— "If it doesn't sell, they'll drop you immediately."

In 1976, now in a career partnership with his wife Nancy, Norman and Nancy Blake signed a three-album contract with Takoma records. Blake spoke about the smaller labels, "One advantage of recording for an independent label is I was able to get a big, multiple-album contract. On the big labels, they'll put their money out for you on one record, but if it doesn't sell they'll drop you immediately... On an independent label, they'll give you full, artistic control. I like the idea of not having to answer to anyone."[4]

Ralph Stanley on Rebel Records— "I figure after thirty-nine years I know about how I want me to sound."

Ralph recorded with Rebel for many years beginning in 1971. The label allowed him to play anything he wanted on a record. He was fortunate in this way, for many groups who record music are often forced to use studio musicians or play the kind of music the record company wants it to play. Ralph said, "That's why I'm with Rebel. I can pick my own material and do it up the way I want to and send it to them. They don't show up at the studio. When I get ready to make an album I tell them I want to make an album, I record it, send it in to them, no questions asked. I figure after thirty-nine years I know about how I want me to sound."[5]

Vassar Clements on the power of record companies

When asked of a main factor which [as of 1984] influences the music and artists in it, Clements told of the tremendous power of the record companies, "They will let you do what you want to do, but only within a certain category; it has to be consistent with something they know. What they feel comfortable with is what they put out on the airwaves—and that's what gets sold. Variety is very lacking.

"If I were to want to go in and do one jazz tune and one country tune and one bluegrass tune, they can't go for that because I found out later that in order for a record to do anything you've got to have a category to put it in. If they can't put that in a category they'd have to throw it over into miscellaneous. And then it's not country, it's not rock, it's not anything. So there has to be a continuity to it, you know."[6]

Dave Freeman, Barry Poss, County Records and Sugar Hill

County Records was founded in 1963 by Dave Freeman. Its first release, "Old-Time Fiddle Classics" (County 501), was a re-release of the 1920s music by twelve different old-time artists—an anthology—which featured fiddle music and laid the foundations of hillbilly music. The next three albums were also anthologies. "Mountain Songs" (County 504) was still in print in 1990.

Those first albums were sparsely labeled. Charles Wolfe wrote, "Part of this lack of liner notes was due to the fact that historical research in early country music was almost non-existent, and there was very little information about many of the early bands or singers. Some reviewers at the time complained at this, but Freeman later noted that, in those days, it would have cost him thousands of dollars in the [research if the albums were annotated] as well as most historical albums are today."[7]

Freeman began his County Sales catalog of recordings for sale in 1965. The *Newsletter*, later called *County Sales Newsletter*, originally contained miscellaneous information. According to Freeman's editorial in the March-April 1972 *Newsletter*, "In the past few years, the picture has changed considerably with regard to the production of bluegrass and old-time records. The great majority of such records are now issued by the smaller, little-known companies, or by the artists themselves."[8]

To be closer to his rural customers, Freeman moved his operations from New York City to Floyd, Virginia, in the Blue Ridge Mountains in 1974. Then he set up Record Depot, a mail-order distributor in Roanoke, which specialized in thirty-five different labels of bluegrass and old-time music. In 1991, Freeman reported that he handled about 150 labels.

Freeman remarked, "Nowadays, I don't think the major companies would be interested in anything that sold less than 25,000 copies. I heard that when Decca-MCA cleaned house awhile back, they used 40,000 as a bottom-line figure. I really expected them to even cut [Bill] Monroe. Unlike other companies, County does not really care all that much whether an artist sells a lot of the records himself, or tours a lot. There have

---

4 Ken Moffitt, "Norman Blake, *Bluegrass Unlimited*, November, 1982, p. 11.

5 From a 1985 interview in Portland, Oregon.

6 From a 1992 telephone interview.

7 Charles Wolfe, "Dave Freeman and County Records," *Bluegrass Unlimited*, December, 1980, p. 52.

8 Ibid., p. 53.

been artists on our 700 series [old-time banjo and fiddle] who have never sold a single record themselves. In the past, if I believed in a record enough to put it out, it never bothered me one iota if the group broke up the next day or never sold one record on tour. That's one of the reasons we started Sugar Hill. [It] was to produce more active groups, groups that do get out and appear a lot, where we can afford to sink more into production and promotion."[9]

In 1975, Barry Poss answered Dave Freeman's ad for an opening for a graphic artist at County Records. For the next three years, he was in record production. "As I recall, Barry and I came up with the idea of a new label together, though the idea for the name 'Sugar Hill' was Barry's. Specifically, we were looking for a subsidiary label on which to put out more contemporary material which I did not want to issue on County. Basically, the first six to eight releases on Sugar Hill were done while I still owned Sugar Hill. Barry did most of the production work. What led to the splitting up of County and Sugar Hill was my acquisition of the Rebel label (from Dick Freeland) in October 1979. This was a large enough label that when I bought it, it took considerable time, space and money to operate the label (Rebel) so I sold my share of Sugar Hill to Barry in order to devote more time to Rebel and County."[10]

One of the early artists to be recorded by Freeman and Poss was **Buck White and the Down Home Folks.** Buck White's new music (it has evolved considerably through the years) was not bluegrass and Freeman could not comfortably produce their music on the County label. With Sugar Hill, Poss and Freeman could feature electric instruments, drums and studio production sound. Before long, Sugar Hill Records featured Ricky Skaggs, the **Country Gentlemen,** and the **Seldom Scene.** Many other popular groups were quick to recognize that their records would be distributed better than some other labels with which they had been associated.

In a 1989 interview, Barry Poss noted that Sugar Hill then seemed to be on the verge of a breakthrough in bluegrass record sales. "There was a review a couple of years ago that compared us a little to Sun Records of the 1950s. And you can look and see that there is a contem-

"Nowadays, I don't think the major companies would be interested in anything that sold less than 25,000 copies. I heard that when Decca-MCA cleaned house awhile back, they used 40,000 as a bottom-line figure." —Dave Freeman

porary feel to the music we are putting out—contemporary, with a nod towards traditional roots. We consciously release only about fifteen records a year so it's easy for a person who is 'buying the label' to take a chance on someone he's never heard."[11]

While the sales of records by the small, independent labels has always been tough, Poss pointed out in a 1996 conversation that "the same thing is true with the majors. Everybody thinks that the majors have an easy time getting all their product out there. That's not true either. Their retailers will 'cherry-pick' the major label offerings. In a lot of ways, we may actually be *better* represented. [In any case], in this particular retail environment, because we're not dealing with independents and we're not dealing with small chains, we're dealing with national chains (Wal-Mart, Tower, etc.) who pretty much buy based on turnover—the vast number of copies sold over a short product of time. And, clearly, bluegrass product is not of that sort. But that's no different than it was twenty years ago."

Poss said, "We get a fair number of letters from groups wanting to record for Sugar Hill; that's probably the toughest part of this job. I'm still a music fan, and when I go to a show and tell the performers that I like what they did, I don't necessarily mean that I want to do a record...we're pretty restricted (for marketing reasons) to groups that are either touring full-time or known on a national basis."[12]

Poss has some advice for bands: "I think it is very important for groups to learn to do things simply. There's a real lesson to be learned by subtlety and understatement. It's especially important for bands just starting out to resist getting complicated too soon. You've really got to master the complex job of getting at the elegance of simple arrangements."[13]

Hazel Dickens on Rounder Records

About 1980, Rounder released Hazel Dickens' first Rounder album, "Hard Hitting Songs for Hard Hit People." Dickens likes recording for Rounder Records; it seems to appreciate her style of music and has an excellent distribution system.

[9] Charles Wolfe, "Dave Freeman and County Records," *Bluegrass Unlimited*, December, 1980, p. 54

[10] Dave Freeman's letter to me, February 12, 1993.

[11] "Barry Poss: On Record with Sugar Hill," *Southern Bluegrass News*, September/October 1989, p. 16.

[12] Wayne Erbsen, "Barry Poss and Sugar Hill Records," *Bluegrass Unlimited*, October, 1982, p. 33.

[13] Ibid., p. 33.

Rounder Records

Rounder Records, of Massachusetts, the company was founded in 1970 by college students Ken Irwin, Marian Leighton, and Bill Nowlin to "make a few recordings." Sometimes they came out with unusual recordings. At that time, the trio preferred hard-core bluegrass artists to the homogenized bluegrass sound of Washington, D.C.. They later experimented with progressive music. Their first recording projects were George Pegram (two-finger style banjo), the rather progressive **Spark Gap Wonder Boys** of nearby Cambridge, followed by the more traditional **Joe Val and the New England Bluegrass Boys**. They later featured artists such as Buzz Busby and Leon Morris, **J.D. Crowe and the New South**, Norman Blake, Vassar Clements, Pete "Oswald" Kirby, Ricky Skaggs, David Grisman and Tony Rice. By 1985, Rounder Records was a powerful force in bluegrass music.

In 1975, one of their most significant recordings was "J.D. Crowe and the New South" with Crowe, Skaggs, Rice, Slone and Douglas. "The aim here," explained Ken, "was not for an isolated commercial success but for a broader, less provincial approach to bluegrass—what Marian calls 'taking it from just being a parochial music to see it be understood and appreciated for where it fits in the overall context of music.'"[14]

By that time, bluegrass had its own identity. It was not a form of folk music; neither was it a part of country music. When bluegrass festivals became popular, bluegrass had come into its own. Liner notes on LPs were often very complete and became a source of historical data for those in a quest for more knowledge of this music. Rounder's founders, each from an academic background, were helpful in this practice. Author Dave Haney wrote, "In fact, education provides the key to understanding how and why this company has grown and changed over the last fifteen years, especially in terms of its relationship with bluegrass music... [The Rounder people] point to the several generations of banjo players, for example, that evolved from Bill Keith's innovations in the '60s, to Tony Trischka's experiments in the '70s, to the current (1986) prominence of Bela Fleck and Tony Furtado.

Another place that Rounder feels that it is different from other labels is its pre-recording discussions with its artist with career progression in mind. They were trying to get away from the idea that a record company was merely a place for a group to get a record made. Rounder wanted to work with groups which had plans to stay together for some time after the record release. Where some record companies treat the bottom line as their god, Rounder followed the traditions of other small labels like Rich-R-Tone which focused on the artists' music, placing Company income behind the purity of the music.

In the mid-eighties, the development of New Acoustic Music came from acoustic musicians with incredible skill from backgrounds of bluegrass, jazz, classical, and other styles. The result was super musicians creating sophisticated compositions in a new style. The musicians on the forefront of this activity included Rounder artists Tony Rice, David Grisman, Tony Trischka, Andy Statman, Mike Marshall and Darol Anger. According to Ken Irwin in 1994, the name actually came from Anger. Rounder publicized and promoted the New Acoustic Music name to the point where it reached larger audiences.

Rounder's interest in the early days of bluegrass led them to travel south and interview and collect photographs of many of the lesser-known artists who recorded during the early years of the music as part of a grant from the National Endowment for the Humanities. The materials resulted in a series of reissues called "The Early Days of Bluegrass" which helped create a demand for the music of obscure, early bluegrass and pre-bluegrass recordings. The series featured entire albums by **Connie and Babe**, the **Sauceman Brothers**, the **Church Brothers**, and Bill Clifton as well as a number of compilations which included early recording by Red Allen, Frank Wakefield, the **Lilly Brothers** and many others whose later recordings were to gain national recognition.

In 1985, Rounder released "Rose of My Heart" by the **Whitstein Brothers**. This traditional, brothers-duet music was archaic by today's more popular progressive bluegrass but showed the audience's renewed appreciation of the music in the style of the **Louvin Brothers**, the **Delmore Brothers**, and the **Blue Sky Boys**—the close-harmony style.

The practice of a record company bringing together popular artists in bluegrass who did not normally tour or play together was also becoming popular. One such project was that of **Dreadful Snakes**. Spearheaded by Jerry Douglas and Bela Fleck, other musicians were Pat Enright, Blaine Sprouse, Roland White, Jerry Douglas and Mark Hembree. Their album was "Snakes Alive" (1984). 1981 marked the creation of the **Bluegrass Album Band** with Tony Rice, J.D. Crowe, Doyle Lawson and Bobby Hicks. This project, originally intended to be a Tony Rice record, eventually expanded into five LPs (and later compact discs) and the group was occasionally booked at bluegrass festivals in this form. (As a side note, the mere existence of such a traditional-sounding bluegrass band in that era of "progressive evolution" gave notice to the world that traditional, straight-ahead bluegrass would never die. People would love it and play it in spite of its "archaic" sound and its age; it would continue to thrive for many years into the foreseeable future.

On June 14, 1923, Fiddlin' John Carson recorded the record acknowledged to be one of the first (if not *the* first) in country music. Rounder released the recordings in 1976 with the title "The Old Hen Cackled and the Rooster's Going to Crow." The album is considered by many as a "must" in record collecting.

By 1995, Rounder recording artist Alison Krauss had sold over 1,000,000 copies of her recording "Now That I've Found You"—a Collection." Also on Rounder's roster were the **Johnson Mountain Boys**, the **Del McCoury Band**, **IIIrd Tyme Out**, Laurie Lewis, the **Dry Branch Fire Squad** and James King.

Old Homestead Records

In 1971, Old Homestead Records was founded by deejay John Morris, frequent contributor to *Bluegrass Unlimited*, in the basement of his home in Brighton, Michigan. He operated the record company in his spare time from his full-time job as a pharmacist at Brighton's University Hospital. Early records were mainly from his personal collection of (as of 1980) 15,000 78s, 5000 45s, and 3000 LPs. One of his big success stories early in this career was when his label recorded Larry Sparks' "Bluegrass, Old and New" and **Mainer's Mountaineers**.

CMH Records

CMH Records began operations in Los Angeles in 1976. It founder was Martin Haerle, a former employee of Starday, United Artists and Arthur "Guitar Boogie" Smith. They featured the music of Mac Wiseman, Benny Martin, Don Reno, Eddie Adcock, Lester Flatt, the **Stonemans** and the **Osborne Brothers**.

Flying Fish Records

Flying Fish Records was founded in Chicago in 1974 by Bruce Kaplan. At one time, it was one of the premier bluegrass labels. It featured Lester Flatt, Mike Auldridge, **New Grass Revival**, **Country Gazette** and John Hartford in addition to a large selection of folk artists. Kaplan died in 1994. In 1995, Rounder Records purchased Flying Fish and consolidated its operations in Cambridge.

Ridge Runner Records

This Texas label began from Mike "Slim" Richey's invitation to Alan Munde, who was recording with United Artists at the time, to record a banjo LP. Munde accepted and "Banjo Sandwich" came out in 1975. Richey was now in the record business. Subsequent albums were a re-release of "Poor Richard's Almanac" (which American Heritage had released earlier)[15], followed by a fiddle album by Dave Ferguson, a resonator guitar LP by Dan Huckabee, an album by Roland White, and one by Buck White and the **Down Home Folks** (which guested Jerry Douglas and Ricky Skaggs) in late 1978.

Richey's earlier involvement in music was as a distributor and sales outlet at his Warehouse Music Sales of Fort Worth, Texas, and for Martin guitars. This evolved to sales at bluegrass festivals and at his store up to 1968. Richey is still active in music in Austin.

Fiddler Benny Thomason, Ridge Runner Records owner Slim Richey and fiddler Robert Bowlin in Dallas, TX, early 1980's. Photo courtesy Jan Willis.

WEBCO Records of Virginia

WEBCO Records started business February 1, 1980. Wayne E. Busbice, brother to musician Bernarr Graham "Buzz Busby" Busbice, founded WEBCO Records as a philanthropic endeavor to help his brother and other musician friends record cheaply. WEBCO stood for <u>W</u>ayne <u>E</u>. <u>B</u>usbice <u>CO</u>mpany; the Busbice brothers were active in the Washington, D.C., area. Their facilities handled recordings, a sound studio, and Old Home Place Publishing. The first recording was "Buzz Busby—Pioneer of Bluegrass Music" with

[15] According to Slim Richey in a 1996 telephone conversation, the recording was made in a room in Sam Bush's grandmother's house; the sound was deadened by hanging quilts around the room. American Heritage had released the recording without permission of the artists who were very disappointed at receiving no proceeds for their efforts.

musicians Eddie Stubbs (still in high school), Dudley Connell and Lamar Grier. Subsequent recordings were of Larry Stephenson, Carl Nelson, Darrell Sanders, Jim Eanes, Paul Adkins, Chris Warner, Karen Spence, James King, Jimmy Gaudreau and the duo of Wayne and Buzz which they called the **Busby Brothers.**

The company was taken over (not sold) in 1989 by Bill Emerson (the famous banjo player) and his son, John Emerson, and the name became WEBCO Records of Virginia. And to differentiate, Busbice's old company became WEBCO Records of Maryland, which is where the label began. Busbice kept many of the assets of the old company and the rights to re-release the recordings later. He taught John the business and dropped quietly from the recording industry for awhile until he released some earlier projects on compact disc. Bill (who was for a time Wayne's A & R man) became involved with the business when a recording by himself and Pete Goble, "The Tennessee Nights of 1949," came into being.

The label soon signed the **Larry Stephenson Band** and gained considerable credibility. The next year, they won an award for recognition that its artists re-

ceived the most radio programming, the most releases that year, and the size of their catalog. There were two categories: Category One included the large labels such as Sugar Hill and Rounder; Category Two included everyone else. The award was given every year by Colonel Tom Riggs on his syndicated radio show "Corn Bread Jamboree" which, in 1995, became the first syndicated show (180 radio stations) to be produced on compact disc.

In 1993, WEBCO was bought by Pinecastle Records (owned by Tom Riggs) and the label became Pinecastle/WEBCO Records. John Emerson stayed on as consultant and producer for a year. As of 1995, WEBCO was a wholly-owned subsidiary of Pinecastle. The **Larry Stephenson Band** (and possibly the **Reno Brothers**) successfully transitioned from WEBCO to the WEBCO/Pinecastle label.

Pinecastle Records

Pinecastle Records was founded in the summer of 1990; its goal was to promote new talent to prominence. The first artist recorded was Mitch Harrell, followed by the **Gary Ferguson Band**, Fred Travers, the **Bass Mountain Boys**, the **Beaver Creek Band**, **Petticoat Junction**, David Crowe, **Redwing** and Terry Eldridge. When they signed the **Osborne Brothers** in late 1993, it helped the other artists feel respectful of their label because they had a "big" name on it, for it was intended to give the label increased credibility. The label's biggest success, second to signing the Osbornes, was **Rarely Herd**, according to owner Tom Riggs.

The Pizza Hut® Bluegrass Showdown is a significant source of new artists, for its annual winner is offered a recording contract with Pinecastle. Most bands accept the offer. Some of these artists are **New Vintage Bluegrass Band** (1994 champions), **Special Delivery** (1993 champs), **Foxfire** (1993 runner-up) and **Appalachian Trail** (1995).

Kenny Baker (L) and Slim Richey. Photo courtesy Jan Willis.

Instrument Companies and Makers - Table of Contents

Instrument Companies and Makers

One of the most noticeable things about musicians of all types is their pride in their instruments—whether it is a Selmer brand trumpet, a Stradivarius violin or a Gretsch guitar. Along with this intense interest in his or her "ax" often comes a curiosity about the company which made it. Here's a brief sketch about several of those companies involved in bluegrass music.

A theory on the origin of an instrument's sound

The tone of an acoustic instrument such as the guitar or mandolin comes from the wood of the entire instrument. While it is true that the vibrating top is the most important part—the part that drives it—the back and sides also have a significant effect on the sound of the instrument. According to George Gruhn in a 1996 conversation, "If it has good tone, good volume, good response, it will have a good top. But instruments, for example guitars, sound notably different with back and sides of mahogany, maple or rosewood. And you can pretty well tell the rosewood guitar with your eyes closed. They each have a distinctly different tone."

"Many guitarists have learned that the use of the capo often improves the tone, but do not know why," wrote North Carolina instrument builder Roger Sturgill.[1] "The reason why is the effect produced by the change in pitch." He explained that when an instrument is built, the top is supposed to vibrate in 'sync' with its strings. Some tops vibrate with the frequency of the shorter strings created by the capo. One can now understand why it is so difficult why an instrument which in 'sync' with all its strings is so very hard to build.

C.F. Martin & Co., Est. 1833

The story of the acoustic guitar in America could well begin with Christian Friedrich "C.F." Martin (born January 31, 1796), who founded his own guitar company in America in 1833.

C.F. "Chris" Martin IV recently related that his great-great-great-great-great grandfather, Johann Georg Martin, the father of C.F. Martin, was a cabinet maker and guitar maker since about 1800 in the town of Markneukirchen in the German area of Saxony (a part

of East Germany from 1945 to 1990). The town, not accessible to westerners until recently, was home to many violin and guitar makers—but especially violin makers, for the guitar was regarded as a lower class of instrument than the violin and its makers were not given much respect. Young C.F. learned guitar making from his father then found the noted violin and guitar maker, Johann Stauffer of Vienna, with whom to apprentice. He soon became Stauffer's shop foreman.

C.F. quit Stauffer's shop after receiving some well-deserved recognition for building quality guitars, and by 1825 was employed by Karl Kuhle in Vienna, was married, and had a son, Christian Frederick Martin Jr.. After all of this, he moved back to his homeland to build guitars. But he received such antagonism from the violin community in Markneukirchen that he left Germany in 1833 to the United States to be where he was free to set up shop and a full-service music store in New York City (at the site of the entrance of the Holland tunnel). Martin moved to Nazareth, Pennsylvania, in 1839, an area which closely resembled his home in Germany, and began building guitars full-time, shipping them to his marketing contacts in NYC.

[1] David A. Sturgill, "Notes on Stringed Instruments," *Bluegrass Unlimited*, January, 1972, p. 5.

By 1850, C.F. was not only building them, he was making significant changes in guitar design to the extent that they no longer resembled guitars he made in "the big apple". He broadened the lower bout to give his guitars a deeper tone as well as a sleeker, more graceful, body shape than their European antecedents. They became less ornamented and less fancy for the tastes of his new country. And he became famous for perfecting (but he did not invent) X-bracing circa 1850 within many of his guitars. An 1850 factory expansion gave notice to the world that he was beginning to mass-produce guitars in several sizes and shapes.

The company was known as C.F. Martin and Company in 1867 when C.F. (age 91) shared the company with partners C.F. Martin Jr. (born in Vienna October 2, 1825) and nephew C.F. Hartman who had both already worked with the company for the past twenty-five years. The founder died in 1873. C.F. Jr. took over the company in the 1880s. By that time, the Martin guitar name was quite well known.

By the 1870s, the Martin Company was building a louder guitar to compete with the volume of the popular five-string banjo; they introduced the Size 00 in 1877. The demand for an even louder guitar brought the even larger Size 000 in 1902. However, the line only sold 104 in the first twenty years of production. The sizes of Martin's guitars began with the smallest being size 5 and increased with the numbers 4, 3, 2, 1,0, 00 and 000. The even larger dreadnought series followed with the "D" designation.

C.F. Jr.'s son, Frank Henry Martin (22) took over the company when Jr. (63) died in 1888. Fortunately for the company, Frank Henry, like his father and grandfather, had grown up working in the guitar business.

By that time, the mandolin was on its way to supplanting the banjo as the most popular fretted instrument, so Frank Henry began building bowlback or "taterbug" mandolins in 1895. The mandolin sales were quite brisk for the company and they made more mandolins than guitars through 1913. About that time, Gibson's mandolin came out with an easier-to-use carved back, and the bowlback became obsolete. Martin then abandoned the bowlback and responded with a more guitar-like mandolin which had a flat back and sold well for them.

The banjo, by the 1910s in its four-string versions, was becoming popular as evidenced by photos of the Mummers Parade in Philadelphia. Martin got into the banjo business in 1923, but right back out three years later.

Turn of the century A.T. Juhlin guitar. Its 22 inches across the bout helps give it the volume to compete with the louder instruments. Photo courtesy John Ramsey.

It was the Hawaiian music fad which significantly helped Martin financially when it began to make guitars for strictly this kind of music. These Hawaiian models accounted for greater than fifteen percent of Martin's total production in 1927. The Hawaiian guitar, which first appeared in their 1922 catalog, had louder, steel strings. This was the model 2-17. Until this time, while some Martin guitars could be ordered with either gut or steel strings, this was the first one catalogued *only* as a steel-stringed guitar and was not available with gut strings. It used mahogany for its top, back, sides and neck. As Chris Martin (born 1955) explained, the reason for the need to build steel-stringed guitars was because "Banjo and mandolin orchestras were forming and guitar players were jealous. They didn't want to just sit at home and play parlor music, they wanted to go out and gig. So they'd show up at the gig with their gut-stringed guitar, and it'd be like, 'Go sit in the back.' So there was a demand from the market to put the type of string from the banjo and mandolin on the guitar. Initially in our catalogs, I believe in the 1920s, it said 'gut-string standard, steel-string optional.' And then by the 1930s, the gut-stringed guitar and the Martin company started to become two different animals."[2] Construction changed to include a steel bar by 1934, and bridges were given larger surface area to adhere to the top, among other changes.

The Hawaiian music era also spawned the ukulele popularity, to which Martin was quick to respond. In 1916, Martin began building ukuleles—high quality instruments, not novelty or cheap. The sales of the ukes helped Martin's survival through the tenor banjo era of the 1920s.

Beginning about 1929, four-string banjoists began switching to the more versatile guitar. And making the transition easy was Martin's tenor guitar—which had a tenor banjo neck on a guitar body—introduced two years earlier. Helping the company though the Depression were the pictures of the very popular Jimmie Rodgers with his steel-stringed Martin—great advertisement.

1931 was a big year for Martin when they introduced both the archtop guitars and the first big-body dreadnoughts. The archtop was invented by Orville Gibson and perfected during the days of Lloyd Loar. It became a favorite of jazz band players in the 1930s. Epiphone, of New York, had a line of f-hole guitars this year as well. The archtops made by Martin were not as strong acoustically as those of Gibson, Epiphone or Gretsch, so production didn't last long. Martin's answer to more volume became a larger body with

2 Walter Carter, *The Martin Book* (London, England: GPI Books, 1995), p. 30.

the 'dreadnought' designation after the famous British battleship HMS Dreadnought.

The importance of the D- line of guitars cannot be overstated. Walter Carter wrote, "In country and bluegrass, and later folk music and any other musical setting where the guitarist required power and sustain, Martin dreadnoughts were considered to be without equal." Gene Autry, a Martin user "since I could walk," bought a D-18 and then a D-45 (1933)—actually, he bought the *first* D-45 made by Martin. Autry gave Martin great exposure. Martin became *the* guitar in bluegrass. "Lester Flatt was one of the many guitarists in the **Blue Grass Boys** who played a dreadnought.[3] Although he was never known as a lead player, his influence on guitar buyers was still enormous by virtue of his position as the front man for **Flatt and Scruggs**. In the early 1950s, Flatt played a D-18 but his more familiar guitar was his next one: a D-28. He bought it used, and then had it customized in 1956 by Mike Longworth, then a Chattanooga, Tennessee, high school kid, later head of Martin's customer relations. Longworth inlaid oversized diamonds and squares on the fingerboard, plus a 'Lester' block. He also added an oversized pick guard of leather, which he says was 'One of the dumbest ideas I ever had.'[4] Soon after, Nashville guitar maker J.W. Gower replaced the leather guard with one of tortoiseshell plastic. By the end of the 1950s, for bluegrass players, there was only one guitar: a Martin D-28."

According to Mike Longworth, the dreadnought was originally designed by Frank Henry Martin for the Oliver Ditson Company and came out in a twelve-fret version in 1916. When the Ditson store went out of business in the 1920s, the model fell into disuse until 1931 when Martin decided to try and find some more business. The fourteen-fret version, which is popular today, came out in 1934. The electric guitar was becoming an important trend in musical instruments in the late '40s but Martin did not follow except for a few electric instruments on a small scale. They kept building fine acoustic instruments and capitalized on the popularity of bluegrass and folk music.

When the folk boom came with the **Kingston Trio** singing and playing "Tom Dooley," Bob Shane, Nick Reynolds and Dave Guard all played Martins. As a result, thousands of folk guitarists chose Martin and the company began to have problems meeting demand which now exceeded 6,000 per year. They built a new factory with 65,000 square feet and production jumped to over 10,000 in 1965 and an all-time record in 1971 of 22,637.

Frank Henry Martin retired in 1945 and died in 1948. He passed the reins of the company to son C.F. Martin III, called "Fritz" or "Fred" by friends. He was the only head of the company who could be called an accomplished musician and often performed in public. Chris Martin became Martin's leader in 1986 when Fred died.

Orville Gibson, the Gibson Company and Lloyd Loar

Orville Gibson[5] first gained notoriety through his use of old, seasoned wood for his instruments—he made a violin from the wood of the old Town Hall of Boston. Gibson was an experimenter and an innovator, and by the turn of the century he was producing uncommonly large, carved mandolins which had fret scale length—nut to bridge—two inches longer than most other manufacturers; his archtop guitars were at least three inches wider across the lower bout, and as wide as eighteen inches.

---

[3] Flatt was not the only one who used a Martin. Charlie Monroe used a D-45. There was also Jim McReynolds, Mac Wiseman and Red Smiley and many of Monroe's guitarists; they seemed to all play Martin dreadnoughts. This helped establish the sound of bluegrass as we know it.

[4] Carter, op. cit., p. 43.

In a 1996 conversation, Mike Longworth explained how he came to work on Lester's guitar. "Back in the fifties, I was a high school kid and I would hang out posters for Flatt and Scruggs. So they would send me a batch of posters a week or two in advance. So what happened is that Lester and Earl played a six-day circuit of TV shows and they worked Chattanooga on Wednesday. So a week or so before, I would receive a stack of posters or whatever and I'd go and hang 'em up on trees and barbershops and wherever I could put 'em up. And I was also doin' pearl inlay work. I did a banjo for myself, and although it wasn't marked, it was number one of my professional inlay jobs. And number two was for an inexpensive guitar for a girl in my high school hillbilly band. Number three was a Dobro that I inlayed for Buck Graves. I don't know any name for it (like 'Cliff' or 'Julie') but I think the pattern had a bunch of diamonds in it. So he promptly sold it to Kelly McCormick of the McCormick Brothers. I think it had L-3 on it for 'my professional inlay job number three.' Number four was Curly Seckler's mandolin. He had an F-2. By current standards it looked somewhat crude, but I did it. I put an F-4 flowerpot on it. And the L-4 is on there but it's under the truss-rod cover. Now L-5 was Lester's guitar. What you will see is a pearl block there, done like a Mastertone block, but it said, 'Lester.' It's just above where I inlayed the L-5. I got the idea from the Gibson Mastertone block. Marty Stuart has the guitar. Remember that I was still in high school at the time and I didn't know Gibson had made an L-5 guitar. The L-5 was Longworth number five and it had nothing to do with the Gibson guitar. I did that for Lester about 1956.

"As far as I know, I was one of the first Martin inlay artists and I didn't have anyone to learn from—I had to teach myself—so the early work, by current standards, is a little crude in comparison to people that might have had a bigger jump-start than I did 'cause I didn't have anybody to look at.

"And I put on that leather pick guard on Lester's guitar, too. Most stupid things a man ever did! But Lester, with that long stroke he had, was wearing down below the pickguard—I think between the pickguard and the bridge but right below the saddle of the bridge—and he was starting to wear through the wood there. And he asked me to make him a pick guard that would cover that area. The only thing that I had at home was a leather suitcase so I cut that suitcase up and stuck that on there. So I guess I originated the 'Lester Flatt pickguard.' But you and I both know now that leather doesn't have much tone quality to it so in short order Lester had that taken off and had a man by the name of J.W. Gower make a similar guard out of plastic. The leather was on there only about two months or so. Gower was actually the father of the Grammer guitar. But back in the fifties he had a little shop in his garage out in the Woodbine section of Nashville. And I did some of the inlay work for Gower. Anyhow, after the leather was replaced with plastic, the guitar was fine. I saw the guitar sometime later with a pickguard that looked like a bat wing or something. I don't know who did that one."

[5] 1856-1918. Gibson was born in Chateaugay, NY. For more on Gibson, see the Bluegrass Mandolin chapter in this book.

Orville's only patent was No. 598,245, issued February 1, 1898, for his ideas on the construction of a mandolin—a carved top and back, and with sides that were cut from a solid piece of wood rather than being bent from thin strips. Roger Siminoff wrote, "Orville felt that the bent, multi-pieced back of the then-popular bowlback mandolins did not possess that degree of sensitive resonance and vibratory action necessary to produce the power and quality of tone and melody found in his instruments."[6]

In 1902, Orville and a group of Kalamazoo, Michigan, investors formed the Gibson Mandolin-Guitar Mfg. Co., Ltd., soon to be simply the Gibson Mandolin-Guitar Co..[7] Orville worked initially as a consultant. In 1909, Gibson sent him home to New York and they paid him not to come to the factory. In 1915, his contract was re-written to allow him to receive royalties from his work. The consensus of Orville's work through the years is that his instruments were difficult to play and had an inferior sound to that of the instruments that the Gibson Company was making by 1908. As a result, many of Orville's ideas on guitar design were abandoned in favor of the size and dimensions which other manufacturers used.

As for the mandolins, the company did not abandon Orville's designs but kept the ideas and continued to improve upon them. Orville lived long enough to see his company rise to prominence and success in the production of mandolins and guitars. He died in 1918 in a New York sanatorium of chronic endocarditis.

The time between 1918 and 1924 is significant because of the employment of people such as Lloyd Loar, and Gibson's introduction of the style-5 Master series. These included Master Model Mandolins (F-5s), Master Model Guitars (L-5s) and the Master Model TB-5 Banjos (the tenor banjo from which the Mastertone name was derived).

The all-new Gibson banjo introduced in February 1925 had a spring-loaded tone chamber and a full, wooden resonator. Variations which grew from this seed were to become the standard of excellence for banjos around the world. The pre-War four- and five-string Mastertone models were style -3, -4, Granada, -5, Bella Voce, Florentine and All-American in order of price.

Also just prior to the War were the -6, TB-75 and the top-tension models -7, -12 and -18.

Mylar plastic heads came along in the early 1950s. By that time, the technical advancements and quality control through the years put the Gibson banjos in a position of building top-quality products, and its banjo production department was ready for the onslaught of orders which would come as a result of bluegrass music.

Very few banjos were produced during the early '50s. Companies like Bacon had dropped from the scene. Virtually the only banjo manufacturers were Gibson, Vega and Gretsch. And Gibson's quality during this time was not nearly as good as their pre-War production.

About 1966, when Stan Rendel became president after Ted McCarty left, Gibson made a lot of changes to make the instruments easier to build. And, contrary to the beliefs of many Gibson advocates, they were generally not more durable. The re-tooling was simply for labor-saving purposes. George Gruhn told this writer, "Their flattop guitars were not more durable. If anything, they fell apart!" This became known as the "Norlin era" because the company was owned by Norlin Industries, Inc.. Their new strategy put more emphasis on profit than design or quality control. "The thin-rimmed Mastertone banjos and the mandolins of the 1960s were like soundless stage props next to older models."[8] These changes affected the company so drastically that by 1984 they had to close their plant in Kalamazoo, Michigan.[9]

The realization that they had to get back to building better instruments to gain better profits forced them into a re-think and a re-introduction of models which did so well for them in establishing the Gibson reputation for building fine instruments. Their guitar models included the Hummingbird, the Dove, the round-shouldered J-45s, and the 1950s J-200. They dropped the ineffective "double-X" bracing system (in use since 1971) and re-instituted small, tapered braces in a "single-X" arrangement.

During an interview at the 1990 Telluride Festival, Rick Turner, of Gibson USA, told that the new models of Gibson's guitars were now built of the same materials

[6] Roger Siminoff, "The Golden Banjos 20 Golden Years, 1918 to 1938," *Frets*, January, 1981, p. 24.

[7] The Gibson Guitar Corporation is the company's official name today. Gibson USA is a logo, not a corporate name.

[8] Carter, op. cit. *Gibson Guitars*, p. 227. Statement by George Gruhn.

[9] Also contributing to this plant's closure was, according to Gruhn, "because it was a union plant and they wanted to have a non-union plant and Tennessee was a right-to-work state and labor was much cheaper here. I think that had a great deal to do with it. They may say otherwise, but that's really why they did it."—1996 telephone interview.

and design as the pre-War instruments with which people can now sell to finance a home. Gibson's new instruments were better sounding than the Norlin era units. A similar change in construction techniques occurred in their production of their banjos and mandolins. The new banjos had the approximate sound as was popular in the pre-War units that made the Mastertone series famous. And the mandolins followed, more closely, the work of Lloyd Loar and they soon became the standard of the bluegrass industry.

In 1984, Gibson began building the Earl Scruggs Model banjo which Scruggs endorsed (he had a Vega-endorsing arrangement in the 1960s). He spoke about this event, "It started with the idea to do a Scruggs Model banjo and that's what they did, and it was very good. But a year or so after that, Greg Rich and some other people came in and, Buddy, he's a perfectionist. And, not throwin' off on the first banjos that they made because the sound was there, but Greg has put it back to the old pre-War style. I mean you can't tell it—or I can't tell it—from the pre-War banjos. Now they had a lot of pre-War banjos over the years and I believe that taking the Scruggs banjos they are buildin' now—just lay down a dozen of them—I believe that just about every one of them will come up to the best old pre-War banjo would come up to. I've never seen anything like it. They just don't miss a trick. And I think a whole lot of it is the perfection that goes into it and how well they put it together. They've got the very best of metal that goes in it. They use the very best wood. And I just don't know what they could do to improve it."[10]

The DOBRO®, the National guitar and the Dopyera brothers

George Beauchamp was the true catalyst for the invention of the resonator guitar. He was an excellent, professional steel guitar player on the vaudeville circuit during the 1920s. During that period, he began a determined search for a louder, improved guitar. By that time, there were at least two plausible means of amplifying a guitar's sound: mechanical and electrical. Electrical amplification wouldn't reach reality until the next decade when advances in electronics, such as the vacuum tube which was invented in 1906 but not ready for installation into amplifiers until the mid-'20s, would permit the sound to be satisfactory to those desiring more volume.

Mechanical amplification had been around since 1860 when it was tried in England, but it was not thoroughly developed until Beauchamp found inventor John Dopyera.[11] When Beauchamp asked John to build an amplified instrument, "He was on the verge of shaking up the whole guitar industry."[12] John was a true inventor who had earlier success with an improved shipping crate, a machine used in making picture frames, and numerous amplified acoustic instruments. John went to work on Beauchamp's project and came up with a tri-cone design which was a significant breakthrough in the development of mechanical amplification. "John described the moment he and Rudy first strung up the prototype, apparently Beauchamp was not present, 'The tone of my tri-plate flowed like a river. I went home and told my wife, "Jesus, we got a hell of a something here!"'" This patent was applied for in 1926 and granted in 1930.

Once the brothers had developed the patent to their satisfaction, they began building them, using the name "Nationals," the same name they used on their banjos. The original National instrument line included the tri-cones in Spanish and Hawaiian guitars, four-string tenor guitars, a mandolin and a ukulele. By 1928, business at National was great. Their instruments were expensive and ornate, but played by nearly every major steel guitar recording artist and performer. The company did well during the first few years.

The volume of their all-metal National guitars, their durability, and their modern appearance (they fit right in with the new Art Deco style begun in France a couple of years before) made them an instant success, especially with blues artists who played their Nationals in the non-lap (Spanish) style. The increased amplification was an especially important reason for its popularity; it gave the instrument the capability to compete with louder instruments of a band. "The DOBRO® was originally built with a Spanish neck, but since it developed concurrently with Hawaiian music, the Dopyeras were soon building square neck guitars for this style of playing."[13]

All of the first Nationals from 1927 to 1929 were made from German silver. The very first ones were handmade by John and Rudy Dopyera. While most of National's instruments were metal, wood body Nationals were also made in some of the earliest tri-cone prototypes. By the late 1930s, National was putting their hardware onto and into the wooden guitar bodies made by Harmony, Kay and even Gibson, whose woodworking was much better than what National could do. National bought the bodies for $5 to $10, installed $5 worth of hardware, and sold them for $29 to $55.

In 1929, John and Rudy formed the Dobro Manufacturing Company, later called the Dobro Corporation, LTD., to make the new single-cone Dobro instruments

[10] Doug Hutchens interview for his radio show. Date unknown.

[11] John was born in Austro-Hungary, on July 6, 1893. He was brought to the U.S. by his immigrating parents in 1908. They settled in southern California. By the mid-'20s, John and his brother Rudy had designed improved banjos that they built in their shop, and they had several applicable patents.

[12] Bob Brozman, *The History and Artistry of National Resonator Instruments* (Fullerton: Centerstream Publishing, 1993), p. 21.

[13] James L. McCoy, "The 'Hound Dog' Dobro Guitar," *Bluegrass Unlimited*, March 1971, pp. 12, 15.

(Dobro is short for the Dopyera Brothers. Also, "dobro" means "good" in their native Slavic language). National soon followed suit with their own single-cone design. The National-style cone is a simple, dome shape with the bridge mounted on the peak of the dome. The DOBRO®-style cone is shaped differently, uses a different bridge, and produces a softer, less metallic sound with more sustain. "From the very beginning of production, Hawaiian and blues musicians were attracted to the National, whereas the Dobro was favored by Cajun, bluegrass and white country guitarists."[14] Soon the DOBRO® became a registered brand name which is used generically to define most resonator-type guitars.

The National and Dobro companies merged in 1934 to become National-Dobro. The company established a "branch" in Chicago in 1936 but John and Rudy stayed in California with the company.

By 1933, Dobro had an electric instrument on the market. Though it made little or no historical impact, the research that Dobro was doing would pay off in a couple of years. "Producing electric guitars changed the whole character of the National-Dobro's enterprise. For one thing, electric steel guitars required less craftsmanship. The bodies and pickups were simple to make. The trick was making it all sound good through an amplifier."[15]

Production of the DOBRO® was stopped in 1941 to help the War effort (they needed metal for airplanes and so forth) until 1946. In the late 1950s, the DOBRO® was being manufactured by Emil Dopyera's Original Musical Instrument Company (O.M.I.) in Long Beach and later in Huntington Beach, California. During the 1960s, The Mosrite Company owned the Dobro name while Rudy and Emil "Ed" Dopyera (John was no longer involved in the manufacture of the DOBRO®) continued to build their instrument. It was manufactured by, or the design licensed to, several different companies. Through the years, various guitar makers such as Gretsch, Regal, and Kay bought Dobro's resonators to install in their own instruments. O.M.I. still made both DOBRO® and National cones, spun or stamped.

In the mid-'60s, Ed and Rudy Dopyera began manufacturing DOBRO®s after a twenty-plus year break. Author James McCoy explained, "Its comeback was marked with frustrations and disappointment. Various problems arose from modifications imposed upon it by promoters and after several years of being kicked around, the name DOBRO® no longer stood for the original fine instrument."[16] In 1967, Ed and Rudy decided to manufacture the guitar in its original form under a new name, the "Hound Dog". This was the nickname given to the style of playing with a steel bar.

"Julie" and "Cliff," owned and used by Josh Graves.

In September 1972, advertising appear in *Bluegrass Unlimited* for a resonator mandolin. It was created by Rudy Dopyera.

Guitar luthier J.W. Gallagher

On June 21, 1979, John William (J.W.) Gallagher, the luthier from Harris, North Carolina, died of a heart attack. His guitars were used by famous owners such as Doc and Merle Watson, Steve and Randy Scruggs, Chris Jones and Grandpa Jones.

Gallagher worked with wood all his life, building a fiddle at ten years old. He opened up the Gallagher Cabinet Shop where he built furniture in 1939. After a period of working with the Shelby Guitar Shop of Shelbyville, Tennessee, in 1965 he started his own guitar shop with his son, Don, in Wartrace, Tennessee, as J.W. Gallagher and Son.

In a 1995 telephone interview with Don Gallagher, he explained how his company had become associated with Doc Watson and how the Doc Watson Model evolved, "My father and I started making guitars in 1965. In 1965, we went to the Union Grove Fiddlers Convention in North Carolina. That's where we met Doc and Merle. We had two guitars with us there, a G-70 and a G-50, which we had taken to show. On Saturday night, Doc and Merle happened by at the festival and they were just playing under a tree there. Dad went up and introduced himself to Merle, and Merle invited us to come by their house in Deep Gap on the way home from Union Grove. So, Sunday afternoon, we

[14] Brozman, *National Resonator Instruments*, op. cit., p. 197. This portion of the book was written by Gary Atkinson.
[15] Ibid., p. 41.
[16] McCoy, op. cit..

stopped there and Doc played on the two guitars that we had. And the one that he really liked was the mahogany (G-50). My father told him that he was welcome to use the guitar if he wanted but, if in some point in time he decided he didn't want to play it any more, we would appreciate him giving it back to us.

Gallagher continued, "In 1974, Doc sent Merle down to the shop here with a Les Paul Gibson (an electric guitar) for us to take a look at the neck because he wanted us to make him a new guitar and what he wanted was the neck size shaped more like a Les Paul Gibson—the main feature being that it was a sixteenth-inch wider than the standard guitar. So we made that new guitar with a 1 3/4-inch neck and it was a little more rounded in the back than traditional guitars had been up 'til that point in time. We embellished it—it was mahogany[17]. Doc liked the sound of mahogany which had traditionally been the stepchild of the guitar; rosewood was what usually received the more elaborate ornamentation. We used the ebony fingerboard and bridge and trimmed it in herringbone and 'voiced' the top bracing[18]—we made an upscale mahogany guitar, basically. That was the first Doc Watson Model (1968), per se, and we gradually made a first guitar for Merle then." The Gallaghers made their first cut-away guitar for Merle in 1974, enabling Merle to do more slide-guitar playing.

"At the point at which we started making guitars in the early '60s, the guitar was really just beginning to come into its own as a musical instrument. Prior to that time, it had basically been used as a rhythm instrument which meant that what you wanted was a big, booming bass. When we first started making the guitar, people like Doc Watson were taking the guitar, transposing fiddle tunes, and flatpicking. So we designed a guitar that had a good balance across the range, with a good,

Don Gallagher with Dick Pierle (L) and author (center) at the 1996 IBMA trade show.

strong projection that was a very playable guitar on up the fingerboard (the G-50 and G-70 which they took to Union Grove were among the first ever designed for this purpose). And I think that's why Doc liked it. It was an acoustic guitar which was really designed to play the lead on. The mahogany he preferred had good note definition."

The J.W. Gallagher and Son company continues to thrive in 1996. Doc plays a Gallagher cut-away.

Bluegrass instruments and the Asians

In the mid-1950s, Japan began importing low-quality guitars into American stores. The guitars were often made of cheaper materials, such as plywood instead of the higher quality and the more expensive types of wood. The guitars had little effect on American high-quality instruments but ruined the market for the companies which had been supplying the low end of the market—especially Kay and Harmony. Kay was gone by 1970. By 1974, Harmony was gone. Some of the names of the defunct companies later came back as imports.

George Gruhn told this writer that the Japanese "were able to produce a guitar for a third the price the Americans could do it. American labor cost was at least four times as much as Japanese labor back then. Not now. Look at any old music catalog of the period and you'll see there were student-made guitars—student-grade instruments—and they were all American. When the Japanese came in, they out-competed the Americans on that and simply drove the Americans out of the market. When things were sold on price only in a low student-model bracket, price was everything. They out-competed companies like Harmony, Kay and Regal. Those companies were simply driven out of business. And companies like Martin and Gibson retreated into *only* the high-end stuff and dropped a lot of their low-end stuff. So Martin quit making things like mahogany-top cheap guitars. They got out of the market when the Japanese came in because they couldn't compete effectively.

"The Japanese had a different market niche. What they took over was the low end of the market, and as time went on they started taking over some of the mid-market. They never, really, took over the top-end market. They never really took away sales from Martin or Gibson to anything like the extent they did from Harmony, Kay and Regal. Later, what's happened is that the Koreans have come in and the Japanese are now out-competed by the Koreans. And you find *very* few Japanese guitars sold in the U.S. today because the low-end market now is Korea, India, Indonesia and even Mexico; Japan is too expensive now. But I certainly

[17] This refers to the body of the guitar. The top of most guitars—the part that resonates—is usually spruce.

[18] Voicing, Mr. Gallagher explained, was a technique of "scalloping" the top braces.

[believe] that the Japanese bluegrass instruments are certainly not as good as the Americans. It didn't affect my business or Martin or Gibson; what it killed was the low-end stuff.

"In the old days", continued Gruhn, "there wasn't much in between—you went from a cheap instrument straight up to a Martin or a Gibson. Now, and later when the Japanese came in, they could buy a real cheap one and then they could go up to a medium-grade Japanese one and they sometimes never moved any further. At that time, it kind of *did* hurt Martin and Gibson because there was a sort of a mid-market for amateur players who did not want to spend the Martin or Gibson price. They knew they weren't getting a Martin or a Gibson, and it did take a certain segment of the market like the more expensive Alvarez guitars, those things. The Japanese did get a pretty firm foothold on the mid-market.

"The banjo production by Japan and Korea was *way* down by 1994. But not guitar production. The Koreans are making as many guitars as ever and the Japanese are making far less. And when you start getting into Indonesia, you get into this *huge* production coming on-line now in Indonesia, in India, still lots of production in Korea. Banjo production is *way* down in the overseas market but guitar market is still very strong and, if anything, is increasing."[19]

Walter Carter wrote, "By the 1970s, with a large part of the American market sewn up, Japanese companies such as Yamaha and Ibanez shifted their focus from producing copies of American guitars to designing their own. Part of the reason was confidence in their own abilities to produce better instruments. But a larger part was that Taiwan and Korea, with much lower labor costs than Japanese companies, were undercutting Japan in the low-end market. No matter. After their advances in the American marketplace, these Asian exporters were now a force to be reckoned with."[20]

Ironically, the influx of the less expensive instruments probably helped the American instrument industry in the long run. It had enabled people to buy guitars (for instance) at an affordable price, develop an interest in playing, and they would often "move up" to a better quality guitar later. Guitar makers such as J.W. Gallagher and Son were not adversely affected by the quantity of cheaper guitars on the market. Indeed, it probably assured their longevity as a profitable business[21] because players came to appreciate the better quality of the high-end American units.

By 1994, the market for American-built instruments had jumped by leaps and bounds—especially in the market for the older, pre-War instruments made by Gibson and Martin. The American manufacturers became more plentiful and profitable. Many small shops had began on shoe-string budgets (Ome, Stelling, Deering, Mossman, Gallagher, etc.) and became successful by concentrating on building quality instruments. The Asians countered this market by producing some fine-quality instruments which compete very favorably with the American luthiers.

Randy Wood, luthier

One prominent instrument luthier is Randy Wood. His early experience in instrument building and repair includes major work at Rual Yarbrough's music shop in Muscle Shoals, Alabama, and then with Tut Taylor and George Gruhn to form GTR, Inc. in January 1970 (which became Gruhn Guitars in 1976). When he left GTR in September 1972, he and Tut Taylor and Grant Boatwright founded the Old-Time Picking Parlor, a music store which was featured in the movie "Nashville Coyote" (a Disney film). The band in the movie was, in fact, the Parlor's house band.

Author Janice Brown McDonald described an incident which has become legend. She wrote, "Randy was entrusted with the repair of Bill Monroe's mandolin which needed a new fingerboard.[22] 'That meant I had to keep it three or four days so I could work on it and when I told Bill that, he asked me if I wouldn't mind taking it home with me every night and not leave it at the Parlor after hours. Well, actually, he asked me if I

Author (L) with Randy Wood at the 1997 IBMA conference in Louisville, KY.

[19] 1996 interview.

[20] Walter Carter and others, *Gibson Guitars, 100 Years of an American Icon* (Los Angeles: General Publishing Group, 1994), p. 251. Section by Tom Mulhern.

[21] The situation, however, was not without its problems; there were several Japanese copies of the Gallagher guitar. This didn't bother the Gallaghers very much. But when some copies were being sold as Gallagher guitars. One of the most blatant incidents was in about 1974 when one company even used the Gallagher trademark. And when another Japanese company made copies/fakes using the Gallagher name, it became a matter of international importance and forced the Gallaghers to act accordingly with the American Embassy in Japan.

[22] According to luthier/author Tony Williamson of Mandolin Central (a distributor of Randy Wood mandolins), Bill's mandolin also had a hole in it due to the pick wearing through the top. Randy was the first person to work on Bill's mandolin since the Gibson re-finishing fiasco of the mid-'50s. Wood built several exact duplicates of Bill's famous F-5 in a period well before most other luthiers began building them.

wouldn't mind taking it home with me and sleeping with it every night so I'd be sure and not let anything happen to it.'"[23] A 1996 conversation with Randy Wood in 1996 brought light to this topic. Monroe had said those words to Wood mostly in jest. "He didn't particularly want me to leave the mandolin at the store. He didn't expect me to take it home and put it under my bed." Wood explained that he traveled with Monroe during the late 1960s when Rual Yarbrough was with the **Blue Grass Boys** and that he dressed the frets of Monroe's mandolin during that period. The legendary fingerboard replacement happened in 1972 or 1973. "I actually did replace the fingerboard at that time. He was pleased with the job. He thought that the old nut sounded better than the new one I put on. The old one was terribly worn—we had to shim the nut up in order to even make it work 'cause it had a new fingerboard and new frets on it. It was almost impossible to make it work right. The spacing was terrible on it. The neck on Monroe's mandolin is unusually narrow anyway. But that was Bill; that was what he wanted.

Bill was pleased with the work, he just thought it didn't sound like it was supposed to sound and he thought that the old nut would make it sound like it was supposed to sound. Norman Blake played the mandolin and thought it sounded fine. But people get those things in their head— not only Bill, but a lot of pickers—and they remember a particular sound [they want]. And with guys like Bill, you just go along with it. So after I put the old nut back on, he was happy with

The original Ode Banjo Company. L to R: Chuck Ogsbury, Justin Pierce, Darius Darwin, Dave Walden, c. 1961. Photo courtesy Chuck Ogsbury.

it. The action wasn't nearly as good then; it was playable, but just barely. Eventually, we did put a new nut on there. It became an absolute necessity.

"But Bill, for years, when he would wear the frets out on his mandolin, he wouldn't have the frets replaced. He would send it back to Gibson and have the whole fingerboard replaced because he didn't think you could replace the frets and make it play right. And that was the reason I replaced the board. Later on, he consented just to have the frets replaced. But for years, he didn't think that you could make the mandolin play right if you replaced the frets.

"When I was traveling some with him and everyone else would be asleep, Bill liked to set up a lot late at night and we'd set there and talk for hours." And, remembering the time in the 1950s when Monroe scraped the varnish off the mandolin, "Bill has told me he scraped it both with a piece of glass *and* a pocketknife."

Wood sold the Old-Time Pickin' Parlor in 1978 and moved to Savannah, Georgia, where he now owns Randy Wood Guitars. His F-5 copies are highly sought after by bluegrass musicians, especially in the Southeast.

Vintage instruments

George Gruhn, a well-known author/store owner and contributor to *Bluegrass Unlimited*[24], spoke of a topic he knows well: vintage bluegrass instruments. "There are some real differences between bluegrass and country. For one thing, in spite of the broad appeal and considerable popularity of bluegrass, no bluegrass performer has had the degree of commercial success or record sales of such country performers as Randy Travis or Hank Williams Jr.. Put simply, there are no platinum-selling bluegrass albums.

"On the other hand," continued Gruhn, "bluegrass music has had a profound impact on sales of musical instruments because a very high percentage of bluegrass fans are not simply listeners who buy records, tapes and CDs, but they are also players who strive to achieve some of the same sounds that they hear on-stage or on record from their idols. Therefore, a performer such as Bill Monroe has probably done more to promote sales of mandolins than someone like Ricky Skaggs whose latest album will undoubtedly sell more in both numbers and dollar volume than any album Bill ever put out. Certainly **Flatt and Scruggs** had considerable success, but if we gauge it in terms of numbers of instruments sold as a result of people listening to their music, Earl has had far more impact on banjo sales than many performers with multi-platinum sales have had on the market for their

[23] Janice Brown McDonald, "Randy Wood—Woodworking Wizard," *Bluegrass Unlimited*, May, 1989, p. 36.

[24] Gruhn in 1996: "I'm a contributor not only to *Bluegrass Unlimited* but numerous other magazines. *BU* is a very limited part of my writing. I'm a monthly columnist for *Vintage Guitar* magazine. I've done numerous columns for *Acoustic Guitar* magazine. Some for *Guitar World*. I've been a columnist for *Guitar Player* for many years. And while I've done a fair number of articles for *Bluegrass Unlimited* and don't wish to downplay that, it's certainly not my main thing.

"I've been in the vintage instrument business since the early '60s as far as wheeling and dealing. But I've had a shop since January of '70. I was one of the first who had a mail-order catalog and did a fair amount of export of vintage instruments and wrote four books on vintage guitars, banjos and mandolins. So I think those are important contributions I have done over the years."

particular instrument."[25] Gruhn also added that the country music market for instruments is much more stable than it is in rock and roll, which may have fads which last only a year.

About the F-5 mandolin and Bill Monroe, Gruhn felt that "it can be said that this particular relationship of Bill with his F-5 is an especially strong bond since a lot of Bill's current sound has been almost a partnership between Bill and that style mandolin. If one listens to his early recordings before he had the F-5, he didn't have that driving chop sound. He played a more traditional old-time style. Had he not gotten the F-5, he might have continued playing in the old style and altered the entire tradition of bluegrass."[26]

Chuck Ogsbury and Ode/Ome Banjos

The production of Ode banjos was begun in 1960 by Chuck Ogsbury in Boulder, Colorado. Ode, according to Ogsbury, means "path, way, or music and song". Ogsbury first sold the "Peoples' Banjo," which consisted of a one-piece tone ring and rim, for $70 . This original design be-came the basis for most of the earlier mass-produced Japanese, Korean and Stewart McDonald banjos. Soon Kix Stewart, a graduate from Industrial Arts of Athens, Ohio, started working for Ogsbury. Stewart redesigned the wood-rimmed banjos. The Stewart McDonald Banjo Company grew out of this working arrangement.

In 1963-64, Ode totally redesigned its banjo in the form of the A through F line which had a wood rim with

a bell-brass tone rim and one-piece, cast, brass resonator flange.

Stewart moved to Ohio in 1965. Ogsbury sold Ode to the Baldwin Piano and Organ Company.[27] Ogsbury worked for Baldwin for six months, then disappeared into the wilderness for the next five years.

Baldwin moved Ode to Fayetteville, Arkansas, in 1967 and manufactured Odes under the name Baldwin, and then back to Ode until 1982. He says that the collectible Odes are now the ones made prior to the Baldwin takeover.

In the late '60s, Kix Stewart started a music store where he met Bill McDonald and began making banjos in a chicken coop in the hills of Athens, Ohio. After a year of questionable success, Ogsbury suggested that they make kits. This Stewart-McDonald mail-order business turned out to be very profitable. About 1985, Stewart bought McDonald out. McDonald then moved to Bozeman, Montana.

Ogsbury and three other partners started Ome in 1970, a company whose name means "the universal sound". One of Ome's mandolin builders during the mid-'70s was Mike Kemnitzer, who later went to Michigan and began making Nugget mandolins.

The Baldwin conglomerate became bankrupt in 1982. At the time, they owned Gretsch guitars, Sho-Bud Pedal Steel Guitars and Burns Guitars. They also owned savings and loan companies. At bankruptcy, a Nashville mogul bought all the fretted instrument division. It then sold Gretsch and Ode to Fred Gretsch Jr.. Gretsch still owns the names Ode and Gretsch and still builds guitars.

As of 1997, Chuck Ogsbury's The Ome Company built four and five-string banjos in Boulder for bluegrass, jazz and frailing.

Chuck Erikson and Erika Banjos[28]

There are many little-known luthiers in the bluegrass business. Charles W. Erikson is a luthier whose experience goes back to the early 1960s in Denver, Colorado, where he became involved as an owner in a banjo shop. In 1965, he moved to the Los Angeles, California, area and began his own Erika Banjos in Van Nuys.

In the early 1960s, the folk boom was just coming to an end in California. But Erickson didn't know this when he got into building banjos. His original objective was to build a banjo which he could wholesale out, not have a lot of money in, be reasonably priced, and which would have good hardware and sound good. He bought tooling and materials for this purpose, but just before he

[25] George Gruhn, "The Musical Instrument Market—The Bluegrass Instrument Market," *Bluegrass Unlimited*, May, 1990, p. 88.

[26] George Gruhn, "The Musical Instrument Market—The Bluegrass Instrument Market," *Bluegrass Unlimited*, May, 1990, p. 89.

[27] C.C. "Clyde" Richelieu had plans to buy Ode from Ogsbury but he ended up being instrumental in the sale of the Ode Banjo Company to Baldwin for Ogsbury. Richelieu now makes his own Richelieu Banjos.

[28] Interview in Chico, California, at the Acoustic Music and Media Conference, March 8, 1992.

got production into high gear, the folk boom died and people were having trouble selling what instruments they had on hand. His instruments sounded good, but because of their metal pot construction, he found there was an aversion from banjoists buying a banjo without wood in its pot construction. He got away from the idea of building multiple instruments and was forced to build custom instruments one at a time. While he put many instruments together, only two dozen were made where all the parts and work was his.

At The Ash Grove during the 1960s, he made friends with the **Kentucky Colonels** and the **Dillards**. He ended up doing a lot of repair work for Billy Ray Latham and Clarence White. He knew Roland White and was in the band's circle of friends; they all lived within a couple miles of his shop. Byron Berline lived close. When John Hickman came into town (before he joined his first band), Erikson sold him a banjo and made him a neck so he could play his music at his lumber yard day job. There in Van Nuys he did repair work for Doug Dillard, Clarence White, David Lindley, John Hickman, John Hartford, Larry McNeeley, Billy Ray Latham, Jefferson Airplane, Alan Munde, Bob Cox, Pat Cloud, Shuggy Otis, Don Parmley, Bill Keith, Herb Pedersen, Bernie Leadon and others.

Now that Fender is no longer making banjos, "There's a funny story about John Hartford that probably can be told," related Erikson. "At the time, he was real big from the 'Glen Campbell Goodtime Hour.' He wrote 'Gentle on My Mind' and this really got him going. We kind of got to be buddies; we went out and did stuff together. The thing about big artists, at least then, was I never built a lot for them because they were being given free instruments from the big factories. They'd pay them to take the instrument out and use them in public. If the artist would pay, like, three grand for a custom instrument, they'd never get to use it on stage anyway because they always had these contracts with Gibson and Fender and everybody.

"Well, John was approached by Fender. They wanted to give him a top-of-the-line Fender banjo. He went to the factory and they told him to pick one out. He said, 'Well, I'll tell you what. How 'bout if I pick out several of them, take them home and try them for a night, and I'll bring them back and take one of them.' They said that was okay. So they gave him six banjos and he didn't take them home at all. He came right over to my shop. We tore every one of those banjos down to its component parts; we had piles of parts. Put them all in one big pile—all the tension hoops, all the pots, all the tone rings. We weighed all the parts and labeled 'em with weights and then we hung 'em on strings and gonged them and recorded what note they registered at. And then we also tried all the different parts for fit—like the tone rings onto the pot, and the necks to the pot, and et

cetera. We found the stuff that fit the best that had the optimum weight, and had the best ring to it, and we took all the best parts from six instruments and put them into one. We were up all night long until daybreak the next day doing this. And these were all serial-numbered banjos.

"We ran into such things as one instrument had a tone ring on it where it was such a sloppy fit that they wrapped masking tape around the pot just so the tone ring wouldn't shift around on it. And there were others that fit really well. But we took all the best parts and put them on one instrument. And the thing was really a cannon; it was really a good instrument. And then, for the heck of it, we took all the absolute worst parts and put them in another banjo to see how bad a banjo would come out of Fender. It wasn't all that bad! It still sounded pretty decent. And we were a little surprised. At the time, there was no way he could tell the factory what he did because they would hit the roof—about tearing these things down and switching serial numbers around—so he never told the factory what he did. But it wouldn't matter now.[29] But it was really interesting and very rare to get six instruments like that to be able to experiment around like that."

Erickson left the music business in 1981 but returned to it and by the 1990s was recognized as "The Duke of Pearl," one of the foremost suppliers of mother-of-pearl inlay materials.

Greg Deering and the Deering Banjo Company

One of the largest banjo companies in the world is the Deering Banjo Company located in Lemon Grove, California.

In 1969, Greg Deering built his first banjo. Soon he became an instrument repairman in a corner of The American Dream music store (co-operative) in Lemon Grove. Luthiers at this stage of skill development don't make much money, but the experience serves as an essential period to hone the expertise which would be necessary later. Deering then went to work for Bob Taylor (who would later be known for his Taylor Guitars) as an instrument repair person and banjo builder. Deering stayed there until Geoff Stelling offered him a partnership in his new Stelling Banjo Works in 1975 (Stelling had opened his company in Spring Valley, California, near San Diego, in 1974). Deering did all of the neck work, binding finish work, and most of the work on the resonators. In June, Stelling became uncomfortable having a partner so he split the company. Newlyweds Greg and Janet Deering formed the Deering Banjo Company which was then subcontracted by Stelling to help build his Stelling banjos.

The Deering/Stelling association ended in 1977 and the Deerings started all over again. The Deerings built mountain dulcimers until they could get geared up for banjo building. Janet became the business manager for the company. Greg Deering recalled that "There were times when Janet would take some dulcimers and drive them to San Francisco in order to get money in the bank in time to pay the rent."[30] They sold their dulcimers for $90 each.

Their dream was to build a quality banjo which sounded good and was priced less than the better-known banjos. They started out with a line of Deering Basic and Deering Intermediate models. Their steel rim sounded superior to most imported aluminum rim banjos. The success of these models formed the basis for prosperity of their company.

In a 1990 interview, Deering demonstrated that a popular Japanese banjo looked good next to expensive banjos, but when the tone ring was out and struck with a pen, it didn't ring at all. Deering explained that the Japanese, during the time they were flooding the market with banjos (when the movie "Deliverance" was popular), were cutting down in the areas which really counted. The quality of a banjo comes from attention to detail, explained Deering. It is important to notice how the fingerboard feels, how the corners of the frets feel, how well the truss rod works to adjust the neck, and the feel of the back of the neck. All the subtle details add up to the sum total. The Deering tone rings are made in a sand mold which can handle the higher temperatures required by the better alloys. He used to turn the rings on a lathe himself but found a computerized lathe which did the job with more reliability. Most of his time in banjo building is spent turning the rims, doing the neck work and the fancy inlay work. His crew of employees builds the entire banjo under one roof.

Geoff Stelling and the Stelling Banjo Works—getting a patent on his own banjo design

In the '70s, Stelling played banjo with the **San Diego Grass and Eclectic Company**, **Pacific...ly Bluegrass**, and in **Hard Times** with Stuart Duncan (fiddle, mandolin, age 11), Larry Bulaich (guitar) and Randy Hupp (bass).

From his years of playing banjos, Stelling developed an "ear" for how he thought a banjo should sound and, "as a player and mechanic, I tore banjos apart to see what made them work." He came up with some innovative ideas which were to soon be implemented in the manufacture of his banjos.

Stelling began his Stelling Banjo Works in 1974. Alan Munde played one of Stelling's first eight prototypes and liked it so well that he asked Stelling to make him one. Stelling immediately went out and applied for a patent on the tone ring. "But getting the patent wasn't easy. The patent office twice rejected the application because the words 'beveled edges' in Geoff's design description also appeared in a patent granted to a man named Lang in the 1920s. Stelling was planning a trip to the East so his lawyer suggested a visit to the patent office in person. Stelling explained, "So I took my old Mastertone and my Stelling to the patent examiner and explained all the theories of why banjos sound good. And I told him how I got my idea from propeller shafts [in the Navy], I hadn't even seen the Lang patent. I

30 From a 1990 interview in Winfield, Kansas.

America's Music | Bluegrass

said, 'Look, the Lang patent has so many parts no one would want to build one that way, let alone infringe on the patent.' So I played the Gibson, I played 'Pike County Breakdown,' and everybody on the second floor of the patent office heard it and came in to hear. Then I played my banjo and the examiner said, 'Yes your banjo does have the sound you say it does. I'm going to give you a patent.'"[31]

Getting down to the business of building banjos, Stelling contracted Greg Deering to exclusively build Stelling banjo necks in 1975 for a while. In the 1980s decade, Stelling moved his company to the East Coast, to Afton, Virginia, near the Shenandoah Mountains, to be closer to where the bulk of the bluegrass business is. As of 1995, he and his company had built 4,300 instruments.

The building of a Gibson F-5 replica from plans

Unicorn Musical Instruments was founded in 1971 by Rolfe Gerhardt. He built his first instrument in 1964, a tater bug mandolin with a five-string neck, while in a seminary at a parsonage basement in Maine. The Unicorn design was inspired by the book, "The Last Unicorn," by Peter Beagle.

In 1973, he built his first replica of Gibson's F-5 mandolin. He spoke of the so-called Lloyd Loar F-5 plans that he used, "Those plans are really deadly because they are not correct.[32] I don't know of a correct set anywhere. But I didn't find out how far they are off until I had a chance to sit down with a genuine Loar F-5 and really study it. I have a degree in engineering as well as the ministerial degree, but the mandolin research is really a seat-of-the-pants thing. When you study the ideas of master violin builders and remember when they did their work, you realize that all they had to work with was common sense. Precious little common sense had been applied to mandolin design since Loar made slight improvements on Gibson's basic model, and somehow Gibson got locked into that awful baroque look with points and scrolls. It was stylish back then, but as you can learn from the violin builders, a heavy instrument cannot project like a light one—the mass of it absorbs more of the vibration—so all that 'dead' wood, all that extra stuff, holds the sound back. The scroll also stiffens the top and back in one area and hampers its vibration.[33] Tom Morgan, noted instrument craftsman, commented about that in *Bluegrass Unlimited* some time ago. I really believe that the best sound,

consistently, will come from a well-built 'A' style body, but it has to be redesigned to give that sound, especially to give the bluegrass sound."[34]

Tom Nechville and the BANJO REVOLUTION!

Tom Nechville, from Bloomington, Minnesota, has a true love for banjo playing and building, as well as a background in manufacturing and sales. Although he had both the desire and qualifications for being a banjo manufacturer, he dismissed this career path as impractical until 1986 when he invented a new banjo design which he dubbed the "Heli-Mount." Nechville wrote that "The two-piece Heli-Mount is simply the most elegant and versatile banjo construction, providing unsurpassed professional musical tone. The added benefits of reliability, easy maintenance, capability of quick adjustment, interchangeable parts, and lighter weight make it an exceptional value in musical instruments."

Nechville spent the next five years learning the craft of making banjos. He patented his idea and displayed his banjos for sale at the 1991 IBMA trade show. In 1994, he was joined by his sister (and an editor of this book), Jamie L. Peterson, to help market the product line and publish the *Banjovia* newsletter.

By 1995, Nechville Musical Products had seven modern bluegrass instruments as well as interchangeable electric modules, six-string necks, and the NUVO neck with built-in "Capobility". In 1996, Nechville introduced a bridge which compensated for different gauges of banjo strings. His slogan "BANJO REVOLUTION!" is an attempt to bring attention to his ingenious new products and to unite banjo players who want the banjo to thrive into the future.

This is a recent German version of a National-Continental tri-cone guitar. It is made of bell brass and is nickle-plated. Photo courtesy John Ramsey.

[31] George Martin, "Stelling Banjo Works," *Bluegrass Unlimited*, March, 1976, pp. 26, 27.

[32] George Gruhn agreed: "Some of the plans are better than others. Most people agree: you can't build an F-5 that's right out of published plans. I haven't seen any correct plans published."

[33] Luthier Tony Williamson noted that if the scroll was made correctly, it would *not* hamper vibrations. He said that the scroll was designed by Orville Gibson to be an air column, like a woodwind. Same principle as the lyre-mandolin.

[34] Robert Gruene, "Unicorn Mandolins," *Bluegrass Unlimited*, March, 1977, p. 14.

Rich and Taylor banjos

Greg Rich became the Banjo Division Manager for the Gibson Guitar Company in 1987. The goal was to build banjos with the sound and quality which existed before W.W.II.. Rich said, "As Banjo Division manager, my goal was to bring a high quality back to Gibson with a group of people that I hand-picked and trained. I said, 'If we're gonna go back and do it right, then let's start with the tone rings— the meat of the matter— and let's get that ironed out. Then this is how we're gonna set our banjos up, this is how we're gonna color 'em, this is how we're gonna scrape 'em, this is how it's going to be done.' And when I finally showed the Gibson management what a Granada was supposed to be, it was kind a like they said, 'Whoa! That's a banjo!'"[35] He enjoyed the job but moved on in February 1993.

Rich and Taylor, Inc., was begun April 1, 1993, in Nashville and Mt. Juliet, Tennessee, by Mark Taylor, Greg Rich and Darrel Adkins (businessman, banjo player, concert and festival promoter). Rich and Taylor's line of instruments in 1995 consisted of five banjos and Tut Taylor's resonator guitars.

In the process of designing and creating a product, Taylor cautioned that "when you get to a certain point in life or get so big you say, 'I've got it; I don't need to do anymore,' that's when you're in trouble. There's always somebody out there experimenting to put one fine edge on it to make it better. And that's what we're in the process of doing now. We've found a way to translate the ideas Greg and I have had for a long time into a product that will be clearly superior to any tone ring that's on the market now. That's the American system: to do something better."[36]

[35] Brett F. Devan, "Rich and Taylor—Magnificent Artwork and the Elusive 'Prewar' Flathead Sound," *Bluegrass Unlimited*, March, 1995, p. 76.

[36] Ibid., p. 80. Rich and Taylor Banjos went out of business in 1995.

Chapter 23

The Invention of Bluegrass and Controversies - Table of Contents

The Invention of Bluegrass and Controversies

Who invented bluegrass music?

This chapter deals with this question as well as many others of a controversial nature, some of which came about from the earliest days of bluegrass. Within these pages is one opinion after another of who did what and when. While most books on a non-fiction subject present a premise and try to prove it within their pages, this project is a history book that doesn't try to prove a premise; it presents facts and opinions and allows the reader to weigh each and decide for himself.

Because people have such widely diverse and strong opinions about the actual beginnings of this music, we are probably not able to reconstruct its actual origins; it is doubtful that anyone can. We probably can't put an actual event or date that caused bluegrass to happen. But we can listen to the words of many of the people who were there at the origins of bluegrass. As you try to formulate the "truth" from the ideas expressed here, you may want to take note of the date of the statement if it is included. In many cases, the statement may be made so many years after the event that the person giving the viewpoint may be somewhat swayed by the years and the memory may be of a somewhat biased nature. Perhaps not. In any case, you will probably have enough information to form your own opinion about the subjects addressed here.

One may wonder if exposure of these sometimes sensitive matters about this music is healthy for its long-term vitality. It was suggested that bluegrass' dirty laundry should not be aired to the world. But perhaps, in this book, we can look at this music's heroes and these matters so close to them as items a reader needs to know in order to further explain what the music is and from whence it came.

Is all this controversy healthy? In a very real sense, yes. For if we didn't care about bluegrass we wouldn't talk about it, we wouldn't wonder about it, we wouldn't argue about it. If we didn't care, if we didn't wonder, if we didn't argue, it would probably cease to exist because no one would consider it important. And there are ways to discuss the topics rationally. Former Executive Director of the International Bluegrass Music Association, Art Menius, put it this way, "My suggestion [is] to encourage bluegrass fans to engage in productive activities that will keep our music strong, rather than encouraging activities as fractious and counterproductive as the intellectual masturbation of discussing the definition of bluegrass."[1]

Old-time music is now differentiated from modern music

In 1957, at the popular Old Time Fiddlers Convention, Union Grove, North Carolina, two categories of music were used: Modern—that music which included electric instruments; and Old-Time—acoustic music.

John Hartford on the beginnings of bluegrass

In a 1992 phone interview, Mr. Hartford spoke about the subject of who put the *drive* into banjo music. He agreed with many others that it was Earl Scruggs, but "Here's the way I feel about it. Everybody's all worried about who invented the style and it's obvious that three-finger banjo pickers have been around a long time—maybe since 1840. But my feeling about it is that if it wasn't for Earl Scruggs you wouldn't be worried about who invented it."

Herschel Sizemore on who invented bluegrass music

About the origins of bluegrass, the mandolinist from Sheffield, Alabama, said, "It will never be any smoother than the way the original group had: Lester Flatt, Bill

John Hartford

[1] Art Menius, "Letters," March, 1987, p. 15. This statement was made in the context of all the furor present in the many letters in *BU* in which people were trying to define bluegrass music by including and excluding certain artists who play bluegrass instruments and appear on the festival circuit. In this case it was about Tony Trischka.

Monroe, Chubby Wise and Earl Scruggs. To me, that's where bluegrass started."

But that was just the beginning. "A lot of things have advanced far beyond what they were then. Knowledge of instruments and of singing harmonies is so much greater [now]. Some of it is for the better, and some for the worse. For acoustical bluegrass, I think some of it has gone too far, but only if you want to define it as acoustical bluegrass. But everyone should be looking for their own sound. Just because you play the mandolin or banjo doesn't mean you have to play it like Bill Monroe or Earl Scruggs. I love what they did, respect them highly, but a person has got to create something else."[2]

Lance LeRoy and Len Holsclaw on the music of Scruggs and Monroe

A 1991 interview with booking agent Lance LeRoy told of his opinion of the picking of Earl Scruggs, "In my mind, *that* was the beginning of bluegrass music. When Earl came, that was my idea of the beginnings of bluegrass music. Again, in my opinion, and I'll tell you honestly and probably get some static on this, but I'll be glad to [back it up], the **Monroe Brothers** and then Bill [Monroe] in 1939; but Bill went on to an accordion and Andy Boyette played electric guitar with Bill in '43. I've heard Lester talk about that quite a lot in the years that I worked for Lester Flatt. The rhythm was not the same. It didn't have the three-finger style banjo. In my opinion, Earl made it complete. I don't say that Earl invented it—neither did Bill. Neither did Chubby Wise. Neither did Lester Flatt or the bass player Cedric Rainwater. None of the five invented it but it took all five of them to make it complete. And in my opinion, everything else was in place. It just took Earl to come in and make it complete. Stringbean had played two-finger clawhammer with him, you know. But, to me, Earl completed the process of making what we call 'bluegrass.' That was the original bluegrass band."

Adding to what Mr. LeRoy said, it seems that the rhythm of bluegrass *was* occasionally there with Monroe's band before Scruggs joined. It came from different sources including the rhythm guitar of Clyde Moody and Lester Flatt with a timing that was dictated by the rhythm of Monroe's powerful mandolin playing. As one listens to the songs in the years prior to Earl Scruggs, it becomes apparent that it was, indeed, "altogether different" than after he joined—as LeRoy said. The rhythm of Moody and Flatt and Monroe was there in his music occasionally, but it didn't seem important until Scruggs came along. Monroe actually changed his music a bit to fit that "fancy banjo" that was becoming so popular. The banjo playing of Scruggs

Herschel Sizemore

elevated Monroe's music to a different level. Scruggs' timing fit right into Monroe's style, and the banjo helped Monroe's band become even more popular than ever before. The audiences loved it and a new genre in music began to appear.

Len Holsclaw, manager for the **Country Gentlemen**, in an interview in 1989, told this writer that "Earl Scruggs and Lester Flatt's first band was probably the greatest bluegrass band that ever was. Without a doubt, that was one of the most talented—one of the most solid... When you go to bluegrass music [in the dictionary], you can put a picture of that band in there and you'd have [the ideal bluegrass band]. But, they never did go into a room with the design and purpose of forming the greatest bluegrass band in the world. Earl Scruggs was the greatest banjo player in the world and Flatt was what he was and you put all that together and it happened... If it hadn't been Lester Flatt playing the guitar, then Jimmy Martin might have been the greatest guitar player in the whole world. But the sound happened to be that sound. And that's the sound it was and nobody planned it that way at all. It was just, 'Hey I like the way you play. Let me hear something there.'" Holsclaw continued, "I think **Flatt and Scruggs** made Bill Monroe what he is today. I think they did him the biggest favor in the world. Pete Kuykendall and Ralph Rinzler and a bunch of pseudo-intellectuals labeled Monroe as the creator of bluegrass music. This is a complete myth. **Flatt and Scruggs** was a hillbilly band. Monroe's was a hillbilly band."

In an interview with Lester Flatt by Pete Kuykendall (*Bluegrass Unlimited*, January, 1971), Flatt said that the music he played was not bluegrass as named after Bill Monroe's group, the **Blue Grass Boys**, but **Flatt and Scruggs** music—a mere extension of country music. The name of the music was not impor-

2 Interview by David Grisman. "Herschel Sizemore Interview," *Mandolin World News*, Winter 1980-1981, Vol V, #IV, p. 10.

tant. It was only important that he could continue to play his music in the spirit of country people.

Pappy Sherrill, still active with his own band since 1935, speaks of bluegrass origins

In a 1991 telephone conversation, Sherrill spoke about the kind of music known as "country". "Back even before the early '30s, in the bands Riley Puckett and Gid Tanner and the **Skillet Lickers**, and Clayton McMichen and the **Georgia Wildcats**, that was when that music was known as 'country' music. Now, what they call 'country' is far from it. And I'll tell you, back then we used to be called the **WIS Hillbillies**. I don't believe you ever had any group on the Grand Ole Opry called 'hillbillies.' I don't know why they never did... But anyhow, Bill [Monroe] got that name 'blue grass' because he was from the bluegrass state. That's where it sprung from and since that time there were so many groups get together and they all got a bluegrass name to 'em. All of it arrived from regular old country music. And country, I mean like the old-timers played back there. Charlie and Bill, when they were together there wasn't nothin' known as 'bluegrass.' That all happened in 1940... You have to give credit to Bill for the invention of bluegrass music. He's the granddaddy of it; no doubt about that." Mr. Sherrill played shows with Monroe occasionally; some around Columbia, South Carolina.

Tater Tate

Carl Sauceman—
"But even before his time there was a lot of it out there...but they didn't know what they were doing."

In a 1989 telephone conversation, Carl Sauceman spoke of the origins of bluegrass music. "In my early years of show business, people didn't know what bluegrass music was. There wasn't no such word as 'bluegrass' music. You see, when Bill Monroe went to the Grand Ole Opry, the way that got started as bluegrass—he was from the bluegrass state of Kentucky. And I imagine somebody just said, 'Here's the bluegrass boy from the state of Kentucky.' And I guess it just stuck.

"You've got to give Bill credit because he has spread it, you understand. He had the means to do it—which was, of course, the Grand Ole Opry. Now Bill and Charlie were fabulous and they were some of the forerunners. They were before my time but I was big enough to know what they what they were doing. I knew their harmony and all like that—and appreciated it. Because of that, I won't try to take anything from him. But even before his time there was a lot of it out there...but they didn't know what they were doing. I did it in those days and didn't know what I was doing. I was just singin'. That's all I knew. I was raised up, not in the mountains but close to the mountains, and that's what they called 'mountain' music. But Bill, like myself, he didn't know to call it bluegrass music... If I had to say what started it, I give him credit for publicizing it. But we all knew it back then as plain ol' hillbilly music".

When this writer suggested that Monroe had changed the keys and tempo of hillbilly music and changed it into something else, Sauceman replied, "He didn't change anything, he just had the high voice; he just had to sing in the higher keys." Carl then spoke about a reference to picking up the speed of hillbilly music, "Wiley and Zeke [Morris] come that close to doing that [with their music]."

Tater Tate—
the name "bluegrass" didn't come until after the festivals started

In 1950, Clarence "Tater" Tate was a fourteen-year veteran of various bands. He reminisced about the time when he was in the Sauceman brothers' band at WCYB, "It wasn't called 'bluegrass' music then; it was just 'country' music. A lot of them called it 'mountain' music. It wasn't named 'bluegrass' at that time. That name didn't come into the picture until after the festivals started."[3] Before the 1965 'first' festival, Tate

The Invention of Bluegrass and Controversies

remembered folk festivals and other events where a few bands would be on the same program. But, he emphasized that the *first* festival was there at Cantrell's Horse Farm. He should know. He was there.

The first uses of the word "blue grass" as it pertaines to this music

Bill Monroe's booklet of his music, which came out about 1948, was called *Bill Monroe's Blue Grass Country Songs*. This was probably the first use, in print, of the name "blue grass" to describe his music.

According to Everett Lilly, the word "bluegrass" came about in the early fifties when audiences asked Flatt and Scruggs to do a tune they used to perform when they were with **Bill Monroe and the Blue Grass Boys.** The audience knew that Flatt and Scruggs disliked the term "Bill Monroe tune" so they began asking for a "bluegrass tune".

Prior to 1956, no one had written about the phenomenon called "bluegrass". It was still called "hillbilly" or "backwoods" music from the Appalachians (even though this new music's direct roots were not exclusive to the Appalachian Mountain area). Probably the first time the words "blue grass" appeared in media print to describe this music was in the September 15, 1956, issue of *Billboard* magazine (p. 66) which said that WCMS deejay Bob McLendon "has switched over to programming practically all bluegrass and true hillbilly material..."[4]

In October of 1959, an article on bluegrass music appeared in *Esquire* magazine. Written by folklorist Alan Lomax, famous for his substantial contributions of folk music to the Library of Congress in 1934, "Bluegrass Background: Folk Music with Overdrive" is credited with being the first widely-read appeal for Americans to recognize bluegrass music. Lomax co-founded the Newport Folk Foundation and served as an advisor to the Mountain Dance and Folk Festival in Asheville, North Carolina. He continued to be active in folk music through the '70s.

Lance LeRoy said, "I remember for a fact that by 1959 to 1960 a significant number of DJs were beginning to use [the term] 'bluegrass' in a generic sense. It seems pretty obvious that this surely must have been in deference to Monroe's band name, the **Blue Grass Boys.** We'll never know, but it just might be that someone in Decca Records' production department inadvertently played a hand in this when the label titled Monroe's first LP, released in 1958, 'Knee Deep in Blue Grass.' MGM really confirmed it when that label titled a 1962 **Osborne Brothers** LP simply 'Bluegrass Music.'"[5]

Neil Rosenberg credits Bill Knowlton with coining the term "traditional bluegrass" in 1961. Folkways released "Mountain Music: Bluegrass Style" in 1959.

Chubby Wise— "I'd say that the authentic bluegrass sound—I'd have to say that Lester Flatt put it on."

Wise was with the **Blue Grass Boys** as their fiddler when Earl Scruggs joined on banjo. He recalled that Scruggs' playing was just as good when he joined as when he left in 1948.

Asked if bluegrass music existed before Earl Scruggs and Lester Flatt arrived on the scene, Wise replied, "Yea. That was before Earl. When I went to work for Bill, the late Clyde Moody was playin' the flattop and singin' with him. And Stringbean was playin' the five-string with us, and a gentleman named 'Cousin Wilbur'—'cause Cousin Wilbur Wesbrooks was a comedian and played bass. And Howdy's wife, Billy—some people called her 'Sally Ann,' Wilene—she played accordion and sang with us. She was one of Bill's right-hand men. Of course, she sold tickets on the show. We was out under a tent when I worked for Bill.

"I'd say that the authentic bluegrass sound—I'd have to say that Lester Flatt put it on. As far as I'm concerned, I'm not throwing any bouquets at him because he's dead and gone, but he was a friend. But not only that, he was one of the best bluegrass lead singers for Bill Monroe that he ever had, or since, as far as I'm concerned.

[4] Neil V. Rosenberg, "Thirty Years Ago This Month," *Bluegrass Unlimited*, September, 1986.

[5] Traci Todd, "Lance LeRoy, Part 2 of 2," *Bluegrass Unlimited*, March, 1993, p. 44. Lance LeRoy is a veteran bluegrass fan, promoter and manager who is more fully discussed in the Pioneers chapter of this book.

"Before he really played bluegrass, he and his brother Charlie, as the **Monroe Brothers**, sang a duet but it wasn't strictly bluegrass; it was kind of a mountain flavor but you couldn't call it 'bluegrass'. He didn't start bluegrass until, I don't think, until he went onto the Grand Ole Opry, really."

Mr. Wise believes that the rhythm of bluegrass as we know it came about when Lester came on board—it was not there with Clyde Moody who was the guitarist just before Flatt.

Mac Wiseman—
"It was Bill's hard-driving style that created something."

Mac Wiseman spoke about the origin of bluegrass music, "I think it was the combination of Chubby Wise on fiddle, Lester Flatt on guitar and Earl Scruggs on banjo, being with Bill Monroe that was the start of bluegrass music from an identification viewpoint. It was Bill's hard-driving style that created something. Chubby's fiddling was learned from the fast licks of Monroe. Chubby had played predominantly blues and mountain style of fiddle before that.

"I don't think you can beat Earl Scruggs when it comes to rhythm and timing, but you can't shake Bill Monroe loose when it comes to rhythm and timing on his mandolin. Earl's style on the banjo added to the drive of Monroe on mandolin and vocals...

"As for the music today being called 'bluegrass', I have always contended that if Bill Monroe had been from Virginia and the Green Mountain [state rather] than being from the bluegrass state of Kentucky, his group would have been called the '**Green Mountain Boys**' and what is being played today would be called 'Green Mountain music'. Bill wasn't the first to start with the old-time music sound, but he started the kind of music [known] today as 'bluegrass' through his hard-driving and high-pitched style. You can't take that away from him."[6]

Jimmy Martin—
"If Bill Monroe started the style of bluegrass, he lost it in 1945 when Flatt and Scruggs went with him."

In a 1991 interview, Jimmy Martin spoke about Earl Scruggs and the beginnings of bluegrass as we know it. "What brought Earl Scruggs' banjer to life was Earl Scruggs. It wasn't no band (referring to the **Blue Grass Boys**). *He* made the band! If I must say so, Bill Monroe is the 'Father of Bluegrass'. He's my idol. But if Bill

Monroe started the style of bluegrass, he lost it in 1945 when Flatt and Scruggs went with him because they took a different style than Bill Monroe. His style absolutely changed from what Bill was a-playin'. It changed to Lester Flatt and Earl Scruggs style. They took a style to Bill Monroe that he'll never recover again. And they took it away from him again when they left. They took the same sound away from Monroe when they left. They took Cedric Rainwater, who was Bill's bass player. They took Earl Scruggs, Lester Flatt and Chubby Wise.

"I'm not going to toot my own horn but the whole world tells me this: 'When Lester and Earl left him, they took their sound. And Jimmy Martin took another sound with him when he left Bill Monroe.'"

Martin remembered that he once met Lester Flatt at Flatt's trailer park. After they sang and picked together, with Martin playing mandolin, Flatt promised that there would always be a place for Martin with him and Scruggs.

Curly Seckler—
Monroe's early music wasn't bluegrass

Mr. Seckler described Monroe's early band in this way, "Monroe had a accordion and a electric guitar when Lester went to work with him. And when Earl came in there, they turned his sound all the way around. [Monroe] had never played nothing like he calls 'bluegrass' music until Lester and Earl went to work with him. Now that's a true fact! And I never heard of bluegrass music, except what the **Morris Brothers** played, until Lester and Earl went to work with Bill. And Bill had never played no bluegrass music 'til then that I know of. Now, he's entitled to that name (Father of Bluegrass Music)—period! I'm glad he's got it because he deserves it. Because he was out there just a year or two before I went. But I would tell him today, if he was over here, that Charlie lacked two weeks of beatin' him to the Opry. Now we (**Charlie Monroe and the Kentucky Pardners**) was in Wheeling, West Virginia, when Charlie asked us if we would like to go to the Opry. I told him it was fine with me—wherever he goes; I was working for him. And he said we was scheduled to go in there for an audition in two weeks. Turned around and we [heard an announcement on WSM] one night and it said 'Bill Monroe and the Blue Grass Boys.' [Charlie] got up and left [the room]. So Bill beat him in there two or three weeks."[7]

Nashville Grass banjoist Larry Perkins agreed with Mr. Seckler, saying (separately) that if what Bill Monroe was playing before 1945 was called "bluegrass", then what his music evolved to after Earl Scruggs joined him was "something entirely different."

[6] Don Rhodes, *Bluegrass Unlimited*, July, 1975.

[7] Phone interview with Curly Seckler, June, 1992.

The history of bluegrass as defined by the banjo playing of Reno or Scruggs

In March of 1944, Don Reno became a U.S. Cavalry horseman in Merrill's Marauders which served in India, Burma and China. Reno did not regret his decision not to join Monroe as banjoist when the job was offered in 1943, for he was actually more interested in playing guitar at the time.

There have been extensive theoretical discussions about what the **Blue Grass Boys** would have been like if Reno had taken the place of Stringbean on the banjo instead of Earl Scruggs. According to Ronnie Reno in 1991, there wouldn't have been any difference—indicating that it was just the *time* for the banjo to make its mark in bluegrass. The importance of Earl Scruggs with the **Blue Grass Boys** seemed to be overrated, young Reno indicated. Earl certainly was good; his right hand technique was impeccable and his drive unmatched—by all but Don Reno. Ronnie Reno's father played the same way Earl did during that period; their skill and style were very much the same. A basic reason for this, he explained, is that they were both from the same part of the country and both were greatly influenced by Smith Hammett and Snuffy Jenkins, pioneers of the three-finger picking style. So by the time Reno was asked to join Monroe's band, they had styles which sounded very much the same.

But Reno chose to join the Army. Son Ronnie, looking back at history, feels that this was a mistake. As a result of choosing not to join Monroe, he feels his father never got the recognition he deserved. Earl made the right move when he joined one of the most dynamic groups the Opry had ever known. This new "fancy banjo" style of Earl Scruggs only helped to solidify the band's presence and influence on the WSM Saturday night show. Reno's banjo with the band would have had the same effect.

The reader may recall that Don Reno played banjo with the **Morris Brothers** band in the early '40s. His place on banjo with the band was then taken by young Earl Scruggs. During a 1993 interview with Zeke Morris on the subject of banjo players with the **Morris Brothers**, Zeke compared all of his banjo players up until that time: Joel Martin, Hoke Jenkins, Don Reno, then Earl Scruggs. Zeke noted that there was really no comparison between Reno and Scruggs. "That was a different style. But now Don was good! Don was a terrific player but it was entirely different style. Earl was so terrific with his style—you know with three-fingers—that nobody around, you know, was any better. Now, he and Joel Martin was the closest, I believe, I've ever heard and equal to each other, you know. Don was

more of scientific banjo picker 'cause Don could play in any key without changin' or tunin' up. He could play it in any key without that. And Don was a good guitar player, as well. He could tear a guitar up! He was just an all-around good musician.

"So Joel and Earl was playin' similar to each other but Joel was playin' a long time before Earl was. He wasn't as smooth as Earl, but as far as playin' the banjo he was just as good as Earl, but he wasn't as smooth. Old Earl, he would never miss a note whenever he was a-playin'; he'd hit every note. He was a nervous-type guy; his hands would shake but he'd never miss a note on the banjo. He was just a terrific banjo player and he would just fall right in anything that Wiley and me would sing, you see. He would take a break on it—it didn't make any difference what it was."

Earl Scruggs

During the course of the telephone interview, Zeke was given the following scenario: "There is a story that, in 1943, Bill Monroe offered Don Reno a job as the banjo player with the **Blue Grass Boys**. Do you remember that? (He answered no.) Well, Don said that he couldn't join because he was expecting to go into the military. So he went into the Army over in Burma into Merrill's Marauders and came out in 1948, after Earl had already been with Monroe for two years or so, you see. What do you suppose would have happened if Don Reno would have accepted that job with Bill Monroe on the Opry instead of Earl Scruggs?"

Zeke responded, "It wouldn't have lasted no time! Don wouldn't have put up with Bill's way of doin' things. Don had his own ideas about doin' things, you know. Don wasn't the type of banjo player that Bill would have liked. He just wouldn't have fit in. I don't

America's Music | Bluegrass

think Don would have played with him other than to get nationalized. He might have played with him awhile for that, but other than that I don't believe Don would have played with him."

The feud between Bill Monroe and Flatt and Scruggs according to Josh Graves

In 1955, Flatt and Scruggs became permanent members of the Opry. Until that time, they were only guests. Josh Graves spoke of Bill Monroe's attempts to keep Lester Flatt and Earl Scruggs off the Opry, "When they worked together [in the **Blue Grass Boys**] they were the best of friends and were a great band. As far as I'm concerned, that was bluegrass! When Lester and Earl went out on their own, there was some jealousy there and they didn't speak for twenty-two years; Bill was that way. I knew him before that and when I came in with **Flatt and Scruggs**, Bill wouldn't speak to me. But the boys in [Monroe's] band talked [to me]. They didn't want us to but we did. People like me and James Monroe and Joe Stuart talked a lot and that's how Flatt was booked at Bean Blossom. I'd go tell Lester good things Bill had said about him, and James [Monroe] would tell Bill the same things about Lester. So in '71 or '72, when Lester was asking about the June schedule, I told him we were going to Bean Blossom. He said, 'You've got to be kidding!' So when we got there, Bill came backstage, grabbed me and said, 'How's my boy?' Then [he] turned around and shook hands with Lester and welcomed him to Bean Blossom.

"Bill was on stage and said that folks wanted them to sing some songs together and Lester looked over at him and said, 'Can you still cut it?' I remember that. And when they hit the stage with those songs, I don't think there was a dry eye out there."[8]

Earl Scruggs and Bill Monroe also made up while Graves was with Flatt's band. Scruggs and his **Earl Scruggs Revue** performed at Bean Blossom to show off his new band which included Graves. Interestingly, Flatt wouldn't speak to Graves for the two years that Graves was with the **Revue**. Graves described the reason for leaving Flatt, "Well, we got to where we couldn't get along. And there was a lot of controversy in the group and I just got tired of hearing it."[9]

Curly Seckler on the Monroe/Flatt and Scruggs feud

There are many stories about the feud between Bill Monroe and Flatt and Scruggs. Mr. Seckler would not elaborate on this feud but did tell this writer that when **Flatt and Scruggs** was at its peak, Bill Monroe couldn't even keep a band together. Seckler described how popular the band of **Flatt and Scruggs and the Foggy Mountain Boys** was, "Lord, you couldn't carry the mail that they was gettin' home in that bus hardly. They were just stackin' 'em in!"

It has been said by some that when Monroe heard that **Flatt and Scruggs** was coming to Nashville, he said the only way they would look right in Nashville was on the street with a cup. It seems like "the upstarts," as they were called, had made it, too. Seckler added, "In my opinion, when he thinks that there ain't no room out here for the rest of us, I don't believe the good Lord would put a man here on earth if he didn't have something for him to do. There's room out there for everybody, I don't care who they are. Look at the thousands out there now makin' a livin' at it (bluegrass). He felt like that—that we weren't entitled to the Opry—but he'd better thank his good Lord every time he passes Sparta, Tennessee, get down on his knees and kiss Lester Flatt's grave—in my opinion! 'Cause if it hadn't been for us, I don't believe he would be where he is today. That's my honest opinion!"

Mr. Seckler emphasized that it was the group that Seckler was in at the time that got in the colleges and made the thing go. Monroe is well known for not being a businessman, but Lester and Earl viewed their music as a business—with a very tough manager, Louise Scruggs, to run it. According to Seckler, "We worked! We worked seven days a week, year in and year out. In my opinion, they're the ones who put it on the map."

When Carlton Haney first heard the word "bluegrass," and the origin of "the feud"[10]

"I met Melissa Monroe in Danville, Virginia, when Bill, her daddy, had the wreck in '53," Mr. Haney told this writer. "She was up there because there was a lady goin' up to see Bill at the hospital that Melissa didn't get along with, and that was Bessie Mauldin. And they got in a fight up there and Melissa beat her up pretty bad and Bessie would not hit her back because she was Bill's daughter. So they took her and sent her to Danville, Virginia, to stay with Clyde and Francis Moody until Bill got well at the hospital or didn't make it, one. They said he wasn't gonna live. So she stayed up there and I met her up there in '52 and started datin' her. And we were ridin' around two or three months later and her daddy did get well and went back and was on the Opry. And we was ridin' around on Saturday

8 Charles Wolfe, "Dave Freeman and County Records (Conclusion)," *Bluegrass Unlimited*, December, 1980, p. 55, pp. 29, 30.
9 Interview at Mr. Graves' home, November 1994.
10 From a July 1995 interview at his John U. Miller Memorial Festival at Watermelon Park, Berryville, Virginia.

night and listened to see if he got to playin' and one Saturday night there he was.

"She said, 'That's Daddy.'

"I said, 'Yea, I remember it.' And they sang 'The Little Girl and the Dreadful Snake' that night. And I said to her, 'You know, I don't understand that old-time music.'

"She said, 'That ain't old-time music.'

"I said, 'What is it?'

"'That's Daddy's. He don't play old-time music.'

"I said, 'What does he play, Melissa?'

"'Daddy don't play old-time music, he plays blue-grass music.'

"I said, 'Well, I don't understand it.'

"Now, I keep datin' her and finally I meet him in September and I book them in some schoolhouses and theaters in November. And he asked me what I did and I said I worked at a battery plant, makin' automobile batteries. He said, 'Well, if you ain't ever got nothin' to do, I want you to work for me.' So the more I lifted them batteries the heavier they got. So in December the first, I put in my notice—I had to work a thirty-day notice 'cause I was a production control man in the outer office. I put in my notice an' quit and went to work for him on the last week of December of '53 or the first week of January of '54 and went to Nashville. We did shows all through January, February, March, April, May.

"And he had a place in Indiana called Bean Blossom and he wanted to take me up there. We went up there and seen it and he played some dates up around in there. He sent me up there bookin' all through Indiana at schoolhouses—anything I could get. And then he wanted me to go and run Bean Blossom that summer. And I did. And I was out tryin' to book and all.

"And there was a Hedrick guy who ran a TV place and he had a little band and I went down there one time and they said Bill Monroe's manager was here. And I listened to them play and all, and said somethin' about bluegrass music—somethin' was said about it. And I just called it 'bluegrass' 'cause Melissa did. And I'd go out to theaters and tell them I wanted to bring them a bluegrass show—Bill Monroe music. So then years later, Neil Rosenberg interviewed this Hedrick guy and he says, 'Yea, he said it. He heard it somewhere.' Well, that was 1954, and that's where he heard it: from me. And I heard it from Melissa Monroe. And that's how it got called 'bluegrass' music.

"And when I was managin' **Reno and Smiley** in '55, John Palmer said that the first time he ever heard it was when he heard me call it that.

"And this 'feud' thing, do you know how that developed? They were down at the back of the Opry after they had left him and they were visitin'. And Bill asked them to come play a song on his show. Flatt said they

couldn't do it; 'We didn't bring our instruments.' Bill said okay. And when he left that night he happened to walk by their car and the banjo and guitar were in the back seat of the car. They had lied to Bill and he never spoke to them after that for eighteen years. And that's all the feud was. This was early '50s: '51 or '52. They were best friends in the world, they still are. There ain't never been no hatred between them. They thought the *world* of Monroe; both of them did as long as they lived.

"But when Monroe gets here Friday,[11] it'll be the first time me and him have spoke in twenty-five years. And we ain't never been mad at one another. He's just stubborn, and I'm stubborn, and I'm just as good a promoter as he is a picker. So I respect my end of the thing as much as his. But in 1970, I got to talkin' on stage and announced that I was going to build a hall of fame museum for this music. And he thought I was tryin' to take it over. He don't understand, see, things and how things are. Him and James have tried to promote and promote and promote and cain't do it. He admires me and Melvin Goins because we make it work. And we admire him 'cause he can play music and we can't. Now Melvin can, but [Bill] just doesn't have any business sense. All he knew was to play music—take that money and spend it and get out and play again. No investment, no nothin' until he bought Bean Blossom. And when I went to work for him in 1953, and left and went up there in '54, the payments got behind and was $500 a month. And I borrowed money from my daddy and made the payments for him to save it for him. He did not have enough work. He wasn't makin' enough money or keepin' it and we was about to lose it."

Lance LeRoy on Lester Flatt and Earl Scruggs

In 1992, Lance LeRoy spoke of Lester and Earl, "I realize it may create some controversy, but based on many years of hanging around Lester and Earl and working for and studying Lester's habits, I've often thought that if it hadn't been for Earl, there might never have been a Lester.

"Lester told me that a week and a half after Earl turned in his notice to Bill Monroe, Lester turned in his own notice. 'We'd been working seven days a week and almost never got a day off and I was worn out and tired. I decided to quit, too, and go back to the mill. Earl's gone and that takes a lot of the fun out of it for me. And no tellin' what kind of a banjo picker we'll get in here to take his place.'

"As far as I'm concerned, Earl and his recorded work still don't have any peers on the banjo or three-finger guitar. I'm sure that with just an average banjo player Lester would have done well, but I can't believe

11 Bill had a bout with pneumonia that week. His doctor made him promise to rest so he was unable to make the appearance.

his career would have ever reached the monumental proportions it did without Earl Scruggs as the other half of the act. They were a team, an entity, with a one-of-a-kind sort of charisma and class that I don't expect us to ever see again in bluegrass music.

"I don't know about Earl late on, but I know better than few people living that for Lester after they split up,[12] the magic was gone. The old-line fans realized it. I could read it in their eyes and in conversations, though nobody, including myself, would come right out and say it."[13]

Dan Crary on Earl Scruggs

Dr. Crary feels that the single most significant contribution to this music was the banjo playing of Earl Scruggs. He said Scruggs had a feel and drive for the music that no one else had at the time—including Don Reno. "When Scruggs was with Monroe, and later with **Flatt and Scruggs and the Foggy Mountain Boys**, the other musicians would get polite and somewhat subdued acceptance of their solo break. They were waiting for Scruggs to take another break. And when he did the crowd would absolutely go wild."[14]

Dr. Dan Crary

Roy Acuff

Author Don Rhodes wrote, "When I asked Acuff if he thought Earl Scruggs' banjo really defined bluegrass music, he replied, 'I don't know if the banjo had anything more to do with it than the mandolin or fiddle. Earl Scruggs had a special three-finger style and with him being with Bill Monroe, that started Scruggs being known as a bluegrass musician. His banjo style was nothing new to me. I had seen the three finger style

before Earl. I knew a woman in my hometown of Maynardville who had a three-finger roll.'"[15]

Charlie Cline on the origins of bluegrass music

Charlie, with the **Warrior River Boys** at the time of this interview in the late 1980s, was asked by this writer if Bill Monroe was, indeed, the "Father of Bluegrass Music". He replied, "No. He's really not. The popularity of bluegrass didn't start until the sixties. You see, the Stanley brothers actually promoted this term in Bristol and Norton and up in there, more than Monroe. They were giving credit to Monroe as having started the music [in order to promote their own music]. If you heard Bill Monroe on Columbia Records, you wouldn't think it was Bill Monroe. Earl Scruggs and Lester Flatt are the ones who started that sound. Bill had an accordion, an electric guitar on Columbia. Then he got Lester, who used to play mandolin with Charlie Monroe in 1942. And then Scruggs joined [in 1945]. [Note: all of Monroe's recordings with Lester and Earl were on Columbia.]

"After Scruggs left, Rudy Lyle was the banjo player. He was one of the best pickers around at that time. You'll find the late Rudy on 'The First Whippoorwill' and 'Rawhide' and 'White House Blues,' 'Sugar Coated Love' and 'Lonesome Truck Driver's Blues.' That's Rudy Lyle. He's underrated. Rudy Lyle and Jimmy Martin and me were all together in 'Y'all Come,' 'On and On' and 'White House Blues.' They wasn't many banjo pickers back then; you could count them on your hand... That's about all I can tell you about that. I don't want to be a-soundin' like Monroe was tellin' a story or nothin' like that. But somebody else gave him that name. He never did use that name... The reason that Monroe has become the 'Father of Bluegrass Music' is because he played in 1938."

Bill Monroe's first recorded tune— he used a guitar, not his mandolin

According to Wayne Erbsen's 1982 article in *Bluegrass Unlimited* which addressed the topic of why Bill Monroe recorded his first tune with a guitar and not his familiar mandolin, Erbsen wrote that much importance has been placed on the fact that Monroe, himself, played guitar on that first recording of "Mule Skinner Blues." Some writers have explained it by saying that Monroe played the guitar to give that special "bluegrass time" that only he could give. Erbsen concluded that it is

[12] On March 12, 1969, the announcement was made to the media. The split occurred a couple months earlier.

[13] Traci Todd, "Lance LeRoy, Part 2 of 2," *Bluegrass Unlimited*, February, 1993, p. 48.

[14] From a 1990 interview with this writer.

[15] Don Rhodes, "Roy Acuff, the Real Speckled Bird," *Bluegrass Unlimited*, May, 1979, p. 19.

more probable that Monroe simply felt more comfortable playing the guitar rather than the mandolin when he went to the microphone to sing solos.[16]

But Carlton Haney[17] said that Monroe knew what sound and rhythm he wanted on that tune—and the sound was that of the guitar. In order to get the rhythm and sound correct per Monroe's arrangement of the song, he had to play the rhythm guitar because Moody wasn't fully versed with this rhythm at the time. Moody had just replaced Cleo Davis on guitar. A careful listening to the recording can be heard Moody playing a subdued rhythm chop on Monroe's mandolin.

Chubby Wise followed Carl Story, not Howdy Forrester

Chubby Wise started with Bill Monroe in late 1943, after their regular fiddler, Carl Story, left to join the Navy. The way Mr. Wise recalled the story, however, is a little different. He remembered that he heard Bill Monroe announce on one of his radio shows that his regular fiddler was leaving for the Navy and the band needed a replacement. A 1994 discussion with Mr. Wise indicated that Monroe didn't mention the name of the departing fiddler. Because it is well known that Howdy Forrester left to join the Navy, it is commonly—and mistakenly—assumed that Chubby took his place. Even Mr. Wise often said it was Forrester he followed. But "Big Howdy" had left for the Navy in October of 1942. His place was taken by Carl Story for a year until Story joined the Navy in October of 1943. Carl Story recalled playing twin-fiddles with Forrester before Howdy left for the Navy. This sequence of events was constructed from a conversation with Mr. Story in 1994.

The formation of the Country Gentlemen and early D.C. bluegrass music

There are several versions of how the **Country Gentlemen** was formed and the events leading up to it. This section will set it straight.

In the Washington, D.C., area in June of 1957, Eddie Adcock played rhythm guitar with **Buzz Busby and the Bayou Boys.** He had just started with the band, replacing Charlie Waller. Bill Emerson was the banjoist. Vance Truell played bass. Buzz Busby played mandolin. Charlie Waller, according to interviews with Adcock and

Emerson and John Duffey, wasn't with the band at that time though he had done an occasional gig with them earlier.

Then the car accident occurred which resulted in the formation of the **Country Gentlemen**. Sonny Presley was driving and fell asleep at the wheel. The accident put him in the hospital for many weeks. Busby, Adcock and Truell were severely hurt also and spent time in a hospital. Bill Emerson was not in the car. It wrecked Adcock's 1927 Gibson Mastertone; it was a miracle that anyone was left alive in that car. To fulfill Busby's commitment to that regular gig at Bailey's Crossroads, Virginia, Busby asked Emerson to get a band together. So Emerson called John Duffey and Charlie Waller to replace Busby and Adcock. Bill Emerson started the band. Emerson did the calling. *He* started the **Country Gentlemen**.

When Adcock recovered from his injuries in August, he joined Bill Monroe's band for about six months then joined to the **Gents** in the winter of 1958.

Eddie Adcock on Don Reno's single-string banjo playing

There are many fans of bluegrass who are led to believe that, because Don Reno was so prominently known for his single-string banjo playing, he invented the style. Eddie Adcock, in a 1990 interview, wanted to set the record straight. He made it clear to this writer that "I believe that Don Reno was inspired by *my* single-string playing, and not vice-versa... You see, I began music playing flatpicked mandolin, guitar, and tenor banjo. Therefore I picked single-string style. Only later, when Scruggs with Monroe played Scottsville, Virginia's Victory Theater did I, at about age ten, even become aware of the use of thumb and finger-picks. But it would be years before I used them myself. What I did was simply to transfer my flatpick method to fingerpicks. It was single-string style therefore, and that's all I knew. I had no one to learn the roll from. My main exposure to banjo...I heard Scruggs on the Opry. I tried to duplicate his sounds with a flatpick on my brother Bill's old Gretsch tenor banjo."[18]

Additionally, during the '50s, Adcock's single-string playing was strongly influenced by Les Paul's very popular act. The act "made a big change in my single-string work during that time. I think I may have influenced much of Don Reno's single-string stuff from what I was doing. He didn't do too much single-string stuff

16 Wayne Erbsen, "Cleo Davis—The Original Blue Grass Boy," *Bluegrass Unlimited*, February, 1982, p. 63.

17 In a September 1994 conversation.

18 Quotation from a letter to *Frets* magazine March 1, 1988. This letter was sent to me by Mr. Adcock to help straighten the record on how *he* was the first to do single-string work, and not Don Reno.

Adcock continued in this thought: "I have always loved Don, God rest his soul, and his family. He was a sweet man and I am not telling this to try to shadow his greatness but merely to set the record a little straighter. Also that day, I showed Don my playing and he was extremely interested in my single-string style. He was playing mostly the moving chord style then. I didn't think I was very good but he liked what I did. And he shortly went and told Mac Wiseman, who was having hit record after hit record, and who had just lost Donnie Bryant, that he should take me on." There, with Wiseman's Country Boys, Adcock played both the roll and single-string styles.

The "ultimate" banjo of Earl Scruggs, and "the trade" according to Don Reno

In 1948, Don Reno acquired a 1934 Gibson RB-3 (with a -4 neck) Mastertone banjo in a trade of his own Mastertone Granada (flat-top tone-ring, which Reno got from Snuffy Jenkins for $90) with Earl Scruggs. Reno played this RB-3 (in addition to a Stelling) until his death in 1984. Reno traded the Granada banjo to Earl Scruggs, even after fiddle rosin (or some other substance) which was left in the case (and under the bed while he was in the Army) melted all over the banjo. Scruggs hadn't seen it since Reno went into the Army but was insistent, and simply *had* to have that banjo. Reno gave Scruggs a new Martin D-28 as part of the deal because "I don't want to cheat you. My banjo is not the best in the world, so I'll give you a Martin guitar and my banjo." Up until that time, Scruggs didn't have a banjo Reno felt was worth trading, wrote Reno in his autobiography.

"The trade" according to Earl Scruggs

"Actually, I first met Don (Reno) at a pickin' contest. It was in a little town in South Carolina. I can't even remember what year it was, but we were both young guys at the time. Later, when I first heard him on the radio, I remembered him from that contest.

"He was on WSPA in Spartanburg, South Carolina, a station I had played on, too. I'm not sure if he had a group of his own then, or was part of some other group. They were playing bluegrass but, of course, in those days it was called 'hillbilly' or 'country.' I remember he had a two-finger style at that time and was one of the best banjoists I'd ever heard.

"After I left Monroe, Bill heard him, and Don began playing with the **Blue Grass Boys**. I think he still had a two-finger style, or he was still mixing two-finger runs with this three-finger style.

"I got a banjo from Don. Lester and I were working with the **Foggy Mountain Boys** in Bristol, Tennessee. We were playing on a radio station there and Monroe came through town so we invited him and the band to go on our show. Don decided he wanted to trade banjos with me. I had a good Mastertone at the time, but I just heard something in his banjo that I liked. So even though mine was in better shape—I remember his was *really* messed up—we traded. He wanted mine bad

Eddie Adcock

when I first met him but it seemed that I would hear him do more after I had been doing it."[19]

"But the truth is, I think I *did* inspire him to play more single-string—but certainly not *my* single-string. You can ask his kid, Don Wayne Reno [who can play Reno-style exactly like Don Reno did]. He'll tell you that Eddie Adcock don't play a damn single note of Don Reno's single-string style. And at the same time, I can tell you that Don Reno didn't play a single note of my single-string style. We had a different approach—another way of doing things. We were both guitar players, which made our theories and ideas about playing a lot alike. But at the same time, they were different in the way they were delivered. He was big for barring things where I work out of a scale position. The way I always felt about that is that Don's sounds faster and mine *is* faster. He was reaching for it in a different way entirely. Because I came just a bit later on than he did, and I had a jazz guitarist show me the best method of playing that there ever was, he had to struggle to get some of the things I got with ease. By that time, Reno was too far along with his own style to change. And this wasn't because of talent. It was because he learned to do it the hard way. He did it wonderfully and got good results, but I did it easier because of what that jazz musician showed me."[20]

---

[19] Peter Kuykendall, "II Generation," *Bluegrass Unlimited*," March, 1975, p. 12.

Reno showed Adcock how to do the three-finger roll about 1954 or 1955. Up until that time, he was playing single-string banjo almost exclusively, with either fingerpicks or flatpick. The only roll he had taught himself was a rudimentary "backwards" one, a la "Doin' My Time." Adcock never frailed. Adcock's background was mandolin and tenor banjo so this significantly influenced his banjo style.

[20] From a live interview at the IBMA trade show in 1992.

enough that he offered me his banjo and a Martin guitar so it was a deal. I've continued using that banjo that I got from Don right up to the present day. But, I believe he stopped using the one I traded him that he wanted so bad; or he, at least, occasionally switched off to a Stelling banjo.

"It was hard to keep up with him after that. In those days, we worked all the time just to make a living. Often, you just didn't know how other people were doing, and where the other bands were working unless you heard them on the Grand Ole Opry. Other than myself, Don was the first three-finger-style banjo I heard on the Opry. Before us, there had been Uncle Dave Macon and Stringbean, and two-finger picking was their style.

"There were always a lot of young players talking to me in those days, trying to learn the style. I remember doing a couple of dates with the **Stanley Brothers** when Ralph was just learning it. He and Don might have been the first I heard doing it in public when it was catching on. But I never taught anything to Don. His original playing was strictly his own.

"It's hard to put a finger on Don's greatest contribution—he did so much. He was a band leader, a business manager, he sang, he did comedy, he wrote songs, as well as being a great banjo and guitar picker. He was a complete performer and musician."[21]

Scruggs, who bought the RB-3 Mastertone in the late '40s for $150, spoke of this banjo and others in an interview with Doug Hutchens for his "Bluegrass Today" syndicated radio show, "Well, first-off, back in 1948 Don Reno had the banjo that I have.[22] I had a good banjo, a RB-3 I believe it was, and he came through Bristol and he was wantin' my banjo. And his banjo, that I have now, was in bad shape. It was a Granada, gold-plated, but it looked like (tarnished) penny would look after it had been layin' out for ten years on the soil or somethin'. It looked terrible. Part of the metal part was broken on the thing but I could hear a tone in it that I liked. I didn't like the neck in it because it was a extra large neck, but anyway I traded with him. I give him my banjo for his banjo and a (D-) eighteen Martin guitar.

"Well, in a little while I contacted the Gibson people up in Kalamazoo—that's where they were at that time—and I asked them about cuttin' the neck down. They wrote me back and said they could do it but the neck would warp if they did it. Well, I was stubborn enough to believe that that old a-piece a wood might not warp and I just didn't want it the way it was so I sent it

back and they cut it down and they made it a nice-sized neck. But it did warp and I had to have another neck put in. But now it's all restored back the way it came from the factory back in 1932 or three, whenever it was made."

Scruggs didn't like gold on the banjo because it tarnished and lost its luster. Plus, repair work in gold during that period was difficult to obtain. He converted his Granada to chrome except for the tone ring and the outside part of the resonator. "I wouldn't touch that for nothin' in the world because that's where the sound is when you got a good neck mounted in there good. The tone is still there."

Jimmy Martin— "Well, I'm speaking to them if they would me."

In a 1991 interview with Jimmy Martin in California, Mr. Martin spoke about his present relationship with several bluegrass pioneers with whom he had worked who did not speak to him any longer. "Well, I'm speaking to them if they would me. But it seems like they turn their head, you know, and I ain't gonna reach and turn somebody's head and speak to 'em. Would you? When I go to visit the Grand Ole Opry, Bill Monroe and the Osborne brothers are the only ones who don't speak to me. Everybody else does; even the **Blue Grass Boys** and the **Osborne Brothers** band speak to me. But they [Monroe, Bob and Sonny Osborne] shun me in every way they can." Mr. Martin didn't seem to know why this was so. "I never have borrowed no money from them. I've never lied to 'em. I never tried to do nothing to hurt 'em. Put it this way: I'd like to buy them all a steak but I'm afraid they would choke [on it] when they were looking at me."

Lance LeRoy later explained why Jimmy Martin didn't seem to get along with many of the other artists. He explained, "Well, Jimmy's got a strong, outgoing personality—quite a showman. Jimmy's a good friend of mine. I think a lot of Jimmy and I'm very proud to call him my friend. He's a great guy. Part of it's probably jealousy. Jimmy's a great showman. You get Jimmy on the stage and he's pretty hard to compete with, Barry, and I think some of that is just jealousy on the part of other artists. Some of them cain't excite an audience like he does and they are jealous of it. I'll be honest

> *"Well, Jimmy's got a strong, outgoing personality—quite a showman. Jimmy's a good friend of mine. I think a lot of Jimmy and I'm very proud to call him my friend."* —Lance Leroy

21 Phil Hood, "Remembering Don Reno, Banjo's Eclectic Innovator," in *Frets*, April, 1985, p. 23.

22 Scruggs was referring to the Granada. Reno had bought the banjo from Snuffy Jenkins when Don first went to work for Arthur Smith. This was the same Gibson Mastertone that Snuffy bought from Fisher Hendley for $50.

with you. And some of them are good friends of mine, but I believe in calling a spade a spade.

"He's made some people mad, but it's all innocent. It's just Jimmy; it's just his nature, you know. When you get to talking to him in the daytime, he's a good business man. He manages his finances and his business well. He owns a nice home place in Nashville [area] in comfortable financial circumstances. I really think that it's mostly jealousy. He's offended some people, you know. Let's face it. But as for myself, Jimmy's a good friend of mine. I admire what he's done on record; some of those old Decca records were just tremendous. And the stuff he did with the Osborne brothers on RCA, it was just great. He's done a lot for bluegrass."

Jimmy Martin sets the record straight

Martin, in a 1991 interview with this writer, wanted to contradict some things that were false. "When I went to work with Bill, a lot of the magazines have said that Mac Wiseman was leaving Bill and Bill was looking for a replacement when he hired young Jimmy Martin. That was not so; Bill was not looking for a guitar player. I slipped in there and sung two songs with Bill[23] and Roy Acuff and the whole room was listening to me and Bill sing. And Roy Acuff looked at Bill and said, 'Bill, is that boy who's singin' with ya any kin to ya?' Bill said no. And Roy Acuff said, 'Boy he sure sounds good with ya. It sounds like you.' We sang two songs—I think it was 'Cabin Home on the Hill' and 'Mansions for Me.'[24] Bill took me off and talked to me and I told him I would go to work with him. He took me along the next week. And on all the shows I sung with him we encored three or four times.

"About a month after that, we done about twenty-one days [on tour] with the late, great Hank Williams, and **Lonzo and Oscar**, and Stringbeans and Little Jimmy Dickens. And me and Bill and Hank Williams would sing trios. You see, I know baritone, tenor, bass or lead in quartets. I sang baritone and Bill sang the tenor and Hank Williams would sing the lead. And when Bill got tired, I got Bill's mandolin and sang a few songs with Hank Williams. And I remember Hank looking at Bill and said, 'Bill, you better keep this boy. If you don't keep him I'm just going to get him in my group and get him a mandolin and let him play in my group and sing with me.' I sang tenor on 'I Saw the Light' with Hank,

you know." At Christmas time 1949, in Lake City, Florida, Wiseman gave his notice.

Paul Mullins and his nickname, "Moon"

In 1963, Briar Records released "The World Of Bluegrass" and featured the new song "(Come on Down the Mountain) Katy Daly." Paul Mullins wrote the music to this and a chorus to this song about a moonshiner. Russell Simms wrote the lyrics. The **Bluegrass Playboys**, the band with which he played at the time, recorded this tune in Cincinnati in October of 1962. They played to audiences as large as 30,000.

It has been rumored that his nickname "Moon" came from this song. But that is false. Paul took the name from the comic strip character because the two words, "Moon" and "Mullins," were recognizable together. It became his deejay "handle".

Allen Shelton's first professional banjo job

Banjoists Allen Shelton and Bobby Atkins were raised in the same area of North Carolina and learned to play banjo together. There is a story that Shelton only knew two songs when he hired on with Jim Eanes' **Shenandoah Valley Boys** in 1952. As the story goes, the song that Shelton auditioned with Eanes' group, "Cumberland Gap," was the only song he really knew. Bobby Atkins rebuked this rumor, "Allen could play *good* banjo before he went with Jim Eanes. He knew a lot of songs. Shelton played a dance every week. In fact, Allen started picking banjo before I did—and I'm older than he is."[25]

Kenny Baker on three special tunes held by Bill Monroe for "just the right fiddler"

In an interview with Kenny Baker in 1992, he elaborated on the legend of three songs which were supposedly held back by Bill Monroe for "just the right fiddler." Legend says that these songs were "Road to Columbus," "Jerusalem Ridge" and "Ashland Breakdown." Baker told this writer that Bill Monroe wrote "Road to Columbus," "Ashland Breakdown" and

---

[23] For this audition, Martin used Bill Monroe's D-28—the same one that Lester Flatt used. With this guitar Martin later recorded "Walking in Jerusalem Just Like John" and "I'll Meet You in Church Sunday Morning." When this guitar was cracked and went in for repairs "I used George Morgan's guitar. I didn't like it at all 'cause a little '35 Gibson will not come up with Monroe's mandolin." Here Mr. Martin verified the comments of many who speak reverently about Monroe's Lloyd Loar F-5 as being one of the most powerful and significant instruments in bluegrass music. In 1991, Martin was using a Martin Herringbone D-28, itself a magnificent-sounding instrument which can drown out most any other guitar in volume and tone.

[24] The reader has probably noticed that Mr. Martin contradicts himself when referring to the songs sung at the audition when compared to other quotations he made in his biography in the Pioneers chapter of this book. That's okay. Who can remember everything that happened to themselves when they were young—and very nervous?

[25] From a 1992 interview with Mr. Atkins at IBMA, Owensboro.

Kenny Baker

"Jerusalem Ridge"[26] on one weekend at a festival in Ashland, Kentucky. But the legend is incorrect.

Baker explained that when he was with Monroe at an early time with the band, Monroe had taught him several old tunes that Monroe's Uncle Pen had taught him. Monroe forgot about them for several years and it wasn't until the 1970s when Baker re-minded Monroe of the tunes. There were several of these tunes, eleven of them are on the 1972 MCA album "Uncle Pen." Examples are: "The Old Gray Mare Came Tearing Out of the Wilderness," "Kiss Me Waltz" and "Jenny Lynn." Baker had never heard these tunes before Monroe taught them to him the first time.

He continued to explain that Monroe had planned to do these songs on an album for many years but told Kenny he wouldn't record them until the right fiddle player came along. One day, after Baker brought the tunes back to Monroe's memory, he told Kenny he was going to record them. So, according to Baker, *he* must have been that certain fiddle player that Monroe was waiting for. That was an assumption Baker had to make, for Monroe normally isn't the type of person who would come out and say "Kenny, you're the best person in the world to record my Uncle Pen's songs." It's not very probable that Monroe would have said this for he was a quiet man and slow to give compliments of this nature.

A reason for quitting Monroe's band

On October 12, 1984, Kenny Baker left Bill Monroe's band after Monroe insisted that he play a tune ("Jerusalem Ridge") called up from the audience in Jemison, Alabama. According to Baker, "It was the last day we had here in this country and then we were to fly to Japan. I did the first show and started the second show and worked maybe twenty minutes in that. I did four fiddle numbers in a row and people kept on calling for that damn 'Jerusalem Ridge' you know. Bill said,

'Well, I'm sure Kenny wants to play it for you.' And when he says that, you can't do a damn thing about it. I just showed my fiddle to the audience and walked off. That's exactly what happened." Baker was so angered that he left the rest of the band to finish the show.

His departure didn't have anything to do with an old hand injury from a 1977 hunting knife as some authors have suggested. As in all things, of course, this was just the last of many incidents which put him over the edge. Yet, there is still no animosity toward his ex-boss. He was ready to pursue his solo career and had, at that time, written about 100 tunes and recorded twenty of his own albums. "When I left Monroe I really didn't have any idea of what I was planning to do, honestly. I left Bill on Friday and I did not make the first phone call [to book dates] and I had nineteen festivals booked by nine o'clock on Sunday evening." Baker and Monroe reconciled in 1995.

The controversy of J.D. Crowe's electrified music

In September 1973, *Bluegrass Unlimited* included a letter signed by "A Stone-deaf Ex-J.D. Crowe Fan" from Gary, Indiana. "While on vacation last week I stopped in Louisville, Kentucky, at the Rode Way Inn to enjoy the all new 'electrified' sound of **J.D. Crowe and the New South**. I can say that to anyone who remembers and appreciated the unmatched purity of J.D. Crowe's original sound with the **Kentucky Mountain Boys**, the overall effect of electrical pickups in the F-5, the Martin, the Mastertone, and Bobby Slone's fiddle, plus drums and electric bass is quite startling to say the least. The decibel range in which they play compares with any rock band around these days. Mr. Crowe suggested to me during one of their breaks that...following the example of the **Osborne Brothers** and the **Earl Scruggs Revue**, the electric-grass sound will probably be the trend more and more traditional bands will follow."

A 1992 interview with Crowe revealed his reaction to the letter, "All I can say to that guy—he's a purist and that's fine—but don't knock somebody else for doin' something they need to do. If he don't like it he can leave, is my opinion on this. I don't need them kind of people anyway. The music's gonna change anyway. They're not gonna stop it."[27]

By late 1973, you could find Crowe's records in both rock music stores as well as country music stores. Tony Rice said, "You just don't find bluegrass music stores! Bluegrass has either got to go country or get into rock because it doesn't seem like it's going anywhere on its

[26] In London, England, in 1975, Monroe spoke about his song, "Jerusalem Ridge," during a live concert: "It's wrote about part of my old home place, there in Kentucky. Back where we used to fox-hunt there was a ridge runnin' through the country there, where we fox-hunted, called Jerusalem Ridge. And I wrote this number—I want you to listen close to it..."

572

[27] Source of this quote was probably from Mr. Crowe in a 1994 conversation at IBMA.

own. It just doesn't seem to have enough push."[28] But he added, "A lot of people think we're trying to cut down bluegrass, but we're not. Everybody in the band loves bluegrass more than anything else in the world."[29] "As long as J.D. has played a five-string banjo and tried to do it for a living and nearly starved...it's much easier to take electrified instruments and get the general public and feed your mouth than it is to play straight bluegrass instruments and go hungry."[30]

John Duffey and "the Duck"

The "rumor mill" was working overtime when someone made a big deal about John Duffey and a mandolin called "the Duck". Here is his story:

When Duffey left the **Country Gentlemen** in 1969 he was replaced by Jimmy Gaudreau. Duffey semi-retired from music to his instrument repair store. It was during this time that he hand-built "the Duck", an odd-looking but good-sounding mandolin. Much has been rumored and written about this instrument but Duffey thinks that those who spend any time on the subject are wasting their time. To him, it was just a mandolin.

He used this mandolin between the time that his regular Gibson F-12 was stolen and recovered. "This friend of ours named Bobby Bryant, a banjo player, and I were always poking jokes at each other. I'd made some crack at him and he says something like, 'Well, it's no worse than that "Duck" *you're* playing.' You know, the thing looked like a duck or something (its points resembled wings). So out of this phase that popped out in the Red Fox Night Club (Bethesda) all of a sudden, all over the world, it's a 'Duck.'"[31] Later, Duffey told this

From The Bluegrass Album, Volume Four, Rounder Records. Top L to R: Jerry Douglas, Bobby Hicks, J.D. Crowe, Todd Phillips. Bottom L to R: Doyle Lawson, Tony Rice.

writer, "I didn't call it anything. It was just a mandolin—an odd-looking mandolin. It had points which had a purpose to them. I fooled around with the points being hollow. If I cared to I could actually change the tone of the instrument by filling up one of the points or the other depending... Jimmy Gaudreau helped me test the thing that way. I would use real fine sand just as a filler, just pour it in the thing, and he would play it and I could listen and see what had changed; it had a lot of possibilities. I played it for a long while. There was even a chance that the Martin Company might consider building it. But I actually had made the neck a little too narrow to suit me and didn't put an adjustable truss rod—I put in a solid truss rod because that's the Martin way—and it just needs another neck. And I'm the type of person who, if I've got something that works, that's no worse than anything else. The only reason I built it is because I didn't have a mandolin. In fact, the one I'm playing now has been stolen. I had two of them stolen. Both of them came back."[32]

Dave Freeman on northern versus southern bluegrass bands

About the bluegrass music produced by groups north of the Mason-Dixon Line, record producer Dave Freeman said, "I never had anything against revival bands as such. What I was objecting to, it was sort of a gut feeling that they (the bands of the north) hadn't put in their time. It was like the city bluegrass group, which I feel the same way about, ten to fifteen years ago in the North. They were interested, they had the enthusiasm, they'd heard a fair amount of the stuff, but they hadn't enough time as a group to put it together... I've heard a lot of young groups today play on stage songs they learned off County reissues—they did a great job, sometimes, but I'm not going to put that on record again."[33]

David Grisman on the cultural differences between northerners and southerners

The New Yorker, David Grisman, a veteran of the bluegrass band of Kentuckian Red Allen in 1965, spoke of how a city boy was different from southerners, "Well, I dug those cultural differences. It was grits and country ham. I was always a non-conformist, and this was about as different as you could get in the early sixties. Also, I

[28] Mary Jane Bolle, "Happy Medium—J.D. Crowe and the New South," *Bluegrass Unlimited*, February, 1974, p. 7.

[29] Ibid., p. 8.

[30] Leon Smith, "Talking with the Stars: Two Interviews from a 'Bluegrass Hornbook,' *Bluegrass Unlimited*, July, 1981, p. 19.

[31] Dix Bruce, "John Duffey Interview," *Mandolin World News*, Summer, 1981, p. 16.

[32] From an interview with Duffey in 1993.

[33] Charles Wolfe, "Dave Freeman and County Records," *Bluegrass Unlimited*, December, 1980, p. 55.

thought it was fantastic music. It seemed to come from a different place and time and it rang true. People didn't have that lick—that authentic sound. Getting to play with Red allowed me to sound more authentic. When you listen to a **Stanley Brothers** record, it's just got that sound...there's no way you can learn to do that."[34]

During the 1989 recording session for Grisman's "Home Is Where the Heart Is," "[Red] gave me lots of tips, mostly about part-singing and phrasing. It was like folk medicine. These guys don't technically say very much, but they'll say, 'Play the song.' Even on this session some of that happened. We were doing 'Love Come Home' which didn't end up on the album. I got this idea to start it with just the banjo solo on the melody. Then on that A chord, the seven chord in the key of B, the whole band would come in. On one take Porter [Church] would kick it off and all of a sudden he stopped and said (serious voice), 'I'm sorry, I didn't play the song.' In other words, these guys have a real strict idea of how they want to play the melody. That's very important to bluegrass musicians to play the melody and play it right."[35]

Robert Cantwell analyzes the Seldom Scene

In the April 1974 issue of *Bluegrass Unlimited*, Bob Cantwell[36] wrote "Is the 'Scene' Grass?" It asks about the word 'traditional' as applied to bluegrass music. He concluded that the **Seldom Scene** is progressive in a traditional sense but noted, "I would like very much to say that Bill Monroe is 'good, solid and traditional' but his genius, like all genius, is more erratic. It was his early penchant for experimentation that brought bluegrass into existence and his continued striving for excellence that has brought him both brilliant successes and occasional obscure mistakes.

"In any case he [Monroe] is certainly 'progressive' in some sense, especially when seen against the background of traditional music that nurtured him. And, what about **Flatt and Scruggs**, Jim and Jesse, Don Reno, Jimmy Martin, the **Country Gentlemen**? No one will argue that these musicians are good and solid; but are they traditional?" Cantwell later concluded that Monroe's music in 1945 was progressive for the time and that it is now considered traditional.

Mr. Cantwell's thoughts introduce another question: whether a person should classify the music and all its branches. While the **Scene** uses bluegrass instrumentation, the members don't consider themselves a bluegrass band in the tradition of Monroe, the **Stanley Brothers** *or* **Flatt and Scruggs**. They aim for a considerably different sound and feel to their music. They don't have any intention of being a clone of another band. So, is the **Scene** grass? Probably not. Should we have to classify them as one thing or another? Probably not. But the reality of the situation is that they don't care one way or the other what we do—they just want to play their music in a fashion which brings approval from their audiences and the monetary rewards which enable them to continue with their artistic endeavors.

Mr. Cantwell also raised the issue of whether to consider **Flatt and Scruggs** or the **Stanley Brothers** as belonging to a particular classification of the music—which might be considered "traditional". Again, however, our attempts to put these styles of music in a class are completely irrelevant to the issue of what their music means to them as artists. Lester Flatt would say he's just putting on a little country show. Ralph Stanley would undoubtedly say he plays a "mountain style" of music or "old-time" music which is an extension of the music which he and Carter used to play as kids. The brothers added the three-finger banjo style to their music only after Earl Scruggs had already made it popular. They then began their own version of bluegrass. Whatever they played in those early years, they probably could care less about how we, fifty some years later, categorize it. The early pioneers were simply playing the music they knew best in a style which they felt was commercial enough to support them financially.

The Seldom Scene, 1988. L to R: Ben Eldridge, John Duffey, Lou Reid.

[34] Dix Bruce, "David Grisman," *Bluegrass Unlimited*, February, 1989, p. 19.

[35] Ibid., p. 19.

[36] Cantwell wrote *Bluegrass Breakdown*, a scholarly analysis of Bill Monroe and his music. It is widely considered a path-breaking exercise in multi-disciplinary analysis, although a difficult read.

Back to the original issue, Mr. Cantwell, along with many others who like to label things, may tend to get carried away in over-analyzing the music to the point which might actually divide bluegrass lovers into factions—possibly even into dissenting and warring groups. In dissertations such as Cantwell's, authors may tend to try to intellectualize excessively and perhaps miss the enjoyment of the subject which the artists had in mind: music for the purpose of entertainment.[37]

The "Lester Flatt G run"

When Lester Flatt was with the **Blue Grass Boys**, he used what some refer to as the "Lester Flatt G-run". Flatt elaborated, "Well, a scissors G is what I call when you make a G chord with your thumb and your middle finger. But this little run that I make, I didn't think anything about it when I was using it. Actually, we were doing everything so fast that we needed to have a time-setter to come back in on. And that was actually what I was using it for, more than anything else. We started out like [the speed of] next week and there was a lot of live bands on stations about anywhere you wanted to tune them in and it seemed like you could hear them all doing it."[38] Even though Flatt said he didn't invent it[39], he felt that he was the first to do it on the Opry. His guitar style while he was Bill Monroe was different than anyone else had played. Flatt recalled, "I believe that's right. I had never heard it. I just lucked into it, I guess. I just played what I felt."[40]

Wade Mainer, a veteran of country music since the 1920s, knew about rhythms of not only country, but bluegrass as well. He recalled, in an interview with this writer, that "Clyde Moody was a very, very good rhythm guitar player. I wanted to use the two guitars, the banjo and the fiddle, see. But Clyde Moody... Zeke Morris was the one that really started the bluegrass guitar. I'm pretty sure. Before Clyde ever got into the music, why,

he was listening to the **Mainer Mountaineers** way before he got into the music. Zeke Morris had the bluegrass rhythm with his guitar! *He* made them runs. It was either Zeke or Clyde, one, was the one that made that 'Lester Flatt G-run!' That was established before Lester Flatt ever knew anything about the G-run on the guitar. Riley Puckett was the man that done that. You can go back to some of the old '20s recordings of the **Skillet Lickers** and you can hear it in there—the same way that they said that my banjo had the bluegrass lick on some of the records that we recorded in the '30s."

Josh Graves with Lester Flatt's new band in 1969

When Flatt and Scruggs split, Graves continued with the more traditional sound of **Lester Flatt and the Nashville Grass**. However, according to Graves the reason for him choosing one band over the other was not because of a musical preference (certainly the two men's groups were very different). Graves said, "Hell no! I just wanted to make a living." He loved both men and found it difficult to choose one over the other.[41]

Don Reno and the capo— according to Carlton Haney

There was an argument as to whether Don Reno used a capo. Carlton Haney responded, "I was with him from '55 'til he died and I never seen one on his banjo. But somebody wants to keep writin' that he was playin' at the 10th fret with his capo on. And I wrote that boy twice and told him that as far as I know Reno never owned one. And why he says that is he keeps listenin' to the record and he's *got* to be at the 10th fret with a capo... I told him and John Palmer told him. And he didn't own one. He didn't need one. I don't know where he's gettin' this from other than [as I described]."[42]

---

[37] Art Menius wrote in response to the above analysis: "I'll admit *Bluegrass Breakdown* proves a difficult read, but I feel this criticism of my friend Bob Cantwell is rather unfair. Bob picks banjo, guitar and mandolin and knows the joy of the music as well as anyone. *Bluegrass Breakdown* was not directly about that aspect. Cantwell attempted an intellectual high-wire act and thus produced a critically important work, whose significance lies largely outside the bluegrass world per se. *Bluegrass Breakdown* is a dense but path-breaking effort at multi-disciplinary analysis of the meaning of Bill Monroe's music in American culture. Like the Seldom Scene, I'd propose that he used bluegrass as a method, that *Bluegrass Breakdown* uses bluegrass as the means for an examination of folk culture and the creative genius of individual artists. Bluegrass proves the perfect choice since it combines older traditions and folk process with the creative genius of individual artists. As Henry Glassie has argued, everything is traditional since it draws on what has gone before it.

"His next book, *Ethnomimesis*, used the Festival of American Folklife to examine publicly supported folklife, the role of festivals and museums in folk culture, and the fascination of people with cultural artifacts of other cultures. I'd argue that the intended audience for *Bluegrass Breakdown* was no more bluegrass fans than Ethnomimesis aimed at people who like folk festivals and museums. While I certainly have my points of disagreement, I remain awestruck by his insights and his daring. Cantwell's latest effort takes on the folk revival of the 1960s."

[38] Marty Stuart, "Lester Flatt Memories, an interview with Curly Seckler," *Bluegrass Unlimited*, May, 1986, p. 81. This interview of Flatt was his last before his death. The band Flatt referred to here was the Blue Grass Boys.

[39] Cleo Davis, Monroe's first guitarist, claims to have invented it for the same reasons as Flatt describes here.

[40] Stuart, op. cit., p. 82. This could be another example of the same lick or technique being developed simultaneously and separately by different people. There are several instances of this in this music. After all, the music was relatively new, and creative musicians were developing what was necessary to do the job efficiently and effectively.

[41] And this love was reciprocated by all who knew him. He is, simply, one of those individuals who gives love wherever he goes.

[42] From a telephone interview.

Don Parmley and the Hillmen

Don Parmley is known for being in a band called the **Hillmen**. In truth, the **Hillmen** was a band which never actually played a show date. The band was really the **Blue Diamond Boys**, a good, working band which played from 1962 through 1964 in California.

Parmley explained that "The **Blue Diamond Boys** was myself, Vern Gosdin, (the late) Rex Gosdin and Chris Hillman. Vern and Rex and I were playing with the **Golden State Boys** (based in Los Angeles) and we were playing on a regular TV show called 'Country Music Time.' We had a difference of opinion with the manager of the **Golden State Boys** so Vern and Rex and I left them and got Chris [Hillman] to play mandolin and we formed a new group; Hal Poindexter and some other guys kept the **Golden State Boys**. Our new group got our own show on 'Country Music Time' and we ran a contest to see what we could name the band. From that, we picked a name that was sent in—the **Blue Diamond Boys**—so we used that name from then on until we disbanded. After we cut the album, the producer changed the [band's] name on it. When the album came out, it had the **Hillmen** on it. I reckon he was a big fan of Chris Hillman's. Of course, the thing was cut around '64 and didn't come out until about eight years later. I know when I went to the union hall to get my (recording session) check (when the album was finally released) the woman said, 'They must owe you about a million dollars in royalties!'

"It wasn't cut for Together Records to start with; it was cut for World-Pacific Records, based in New York. Glen Campbell did a twelve-string guitar instrumental album for the same label. Family problems developed with the management which is why our album got put on the shelf for all those years. It wasn't long after we recorded the album that the **Blue Diamond Boys** broke up. I don't remember exactly; it probably wasn't even a year. Chris Hillman got a job playin' electric bass with the **Byrds**."[43] The album was reissued by Sugar Hill Records in 1981, on compact disc in 1995. [See photo on page 500]

"Letters"—the old controversy of using an acoustic bass or an electric bass in bluegrass music

In the "Letters" section of the April 1972 issue of *Bluegrass Unlimited* magazine, Ronald Smith, of his **Sounds of Bluegrass** band in Winston-Salem, told of his concern about the future of the bass in bluegrass music. "I am deeply concerned about the controversy over the standard and electric bass. Even though the old doghouse sticks to all the traditions, it just doesn't deliver

the good, solid, hard-as-stone, backup that is needed in today's modern bluegrass. As much as I hate to say it, the good old doghouse doesn't stand out enough and is very easily mis-noted; both of these factors hurting the music greatly. Many bands, as mine, would like to change over to the electric bass, but as convention rules and judges feelings are now, it is really hard to win anything, if not harder to even get into the convention. As of now, my group still uses the standard bass. But in our search for the best of bluegrass, the electric bass would add an uncountable advantage. So please, let's strive to erase this feeling of distaste about the electric bass."

Two letters were sent in the next month in response the above. The first writer, Bill Mollman of the **Green Valley Ramblers**, took exception to the need for electric amplification of the bass and insisted that a good bassist seldom mis-notes, if ever. Mollman suggested that the bass volume could be enhanced by using a microphone. He closed the letter, "There is still no room for the electric bass in true bluegrass music, be it hard core traditional or progressive."

Another letter by a non-musician reads, "For those who enjoy playing and listening to electric instruments, there are many other fields where they would be welcomed with open arms and I say this is where they belong—good riddance."

More "Letters"

A "Letters" contribution from Steve Gilmore of Gering, Nebraska, to the November 1986 issue of *Bluegrass Unlimited* brought up an interesting point: "I want to voice a concern about the attitudes of some professional bluegrass bands toward their amateur counterparts.

"We live in western Nebraska, very close to Wyoming, and bluegrass here is as rare as hen's teeth. Our group has created a market for the music in these parts and we've been instrumental in educating the general public in bluegrass. To illustrate, prior to 1980 the only bluegrass band who had performed in our community was the **Dillards**. They had played almost fifteen years prior to that. Since that time, this area has seen the **Country Gazette** (twice), Doc Watson, the **Bluegrass Band**. Our group formed in 1979. And admittedly, we do a lot of copy material.

"Without groups like ours there might not be a market for the pros. We aren't interested in taking bookings from famous bands but we are interested in developing a market for bluegrass. Professional groups owe part of their success to bands like ours because:

    1) we promote bluegrass music.

    2) we expose a new audience to bluegrass.

America's Music | Bluegrass

43 Brett F. Devan, "The Bluegrass Cardinals. The Traditional Sound of the Creative Original Vocal Trio," *Bluegrass Unlimited*, November, 1991, pp. 17, 18.

3) we select some material that other bands do and thus expose audiences to the music of the pros.
4) we are able to offer an affordable price to non-profit organizations and small groups of business people for performances.
...and the list goes on.

"If bluegrass is to survive, it will take a combined effort of both pros and non-pros to promote the music. We love the music and the musicians who play it. Don't slight us because we don't make a living doing it."

The controversial music of Tony Trischka

Tony Trischka's "Sky-line Drive" was panned in the December 1986 issue of *Bluegrass Unlimited*. But it didn't bother Trischka because, as he explained in the next issue of the magazine's "Letters" section, "We have never claimed to be a blue-grass band...and we do not play Dawg or newgrass music. We play Skyline music."

Certainly Trischka has blue-grass roots; he learned them well from the influences of Jimmy Martin, the Stanleys and others. But the band was also influenced by Igor Stravinsky, too. "It's just frustrating, after all this time, to put up with the same 'traditional vs. progressive' arguments that were tedious fifteen years ago. There's traditional and there's progressive, and for some people the twain shall never meet. But there truly is room for both and that's healthy, and in fact necessary if the music is going to survive and grow. The last thing we need is polarization of the various acoustic camps. It's hard enough trying to earn a living playing this music without someone within the ranks fanning the flames of discord."[44]

That was Trischka's response. The reaction of other readers expressed other feelings to the topic and gives a good idea of this division of philosophies which seems to want to divide bluegrass enthusiasts. In subsequent articles of *Bluegrass Unlimited* we read, "I am inter-ested in what the musicians do on a record, not how they fail to meet the reviewer's arbitrary and obviously debatable standards. I consider **Tony Trischka and Skyline** an important part of bluegrass today."[45]

Tony Trischka

Other responses: "Bluegrass is Bill Monroe—a fact! Jazz, blues, whatever music is fine. If it ain't bluegrass, it ain't and that's a fact."[46] "It seems odd that on one hand you would feature an article on new acoustic music in your *bluegrass* magazine (which I felt was appropriate) but on the other hand employ reviewers who have not progressed, at least to the point of being open-minded!"[47] "It would be a shame if everyone sounded the same."[48]

Best Bluegrass Recording for 1990—a piano player!

The music awards show on television presented the Grammy for Best Bluegrass Recording to Bruce Hornsby and the **Nitty Gritty Dirt Band** for the track "The Valley Road" from the "Will the Circle Be Unbro-ken Vol. II" LP. This caused quite a stir in the bluegrass community because Hornsby played piano on the cut. A lot of bluegrass fans were incredu-lous at the award which bypassed many "legitimate" bluegrass artists.

In an editor's note in *Bluegrass Unlimited* (April 1990), it was explained that the award was for Best Bluegrass Recording, not Best Bluegrass Performance or Best Bluegrass Album as many outraged bluegrass fans thought. "The ques-tions that the experts had to resolve was 'does it have a bluegrass feel?' While 'Valley Road' may be a close call, I honestly think anyone who listens with a knowledge of blue-grass will agree—it does have a bluegrass sound."

The editorial went on to explain that the judges were not experts on bluegrass but were members of the National Academy of Recording Arts and Sciences, Inc. (NARAS). And only these members could vote. They voted on nineteen categories, only one of which was bluegrass. They voted on a *recording*, not an artist. With this understanding, perhaps we bluegrassers need not be offended and be able to enjoy the music.

A response to the topic by Orin Friesen gave his support for Hornsby's song as a valid recipient of the Grammy for Best Bluegrass Recording. While even Hornsby will be the first to admit that he is obviously not a bluegrass musician, the recording nevertheless "has the potential to bring many more fans to bluegrass music. I am pleased that an all-acoustic album not only

---

[44] "Letters," *Bluegrass Unlimited*, December, 1986, p. 9. A response by Tony Trischka.

[45] David Barnhart, *Bluegrass Unlimited*, March 1987, p. 10.

[46] George Stephens, Ibid., p. 10.

[47] Roger Williams, Ibid., p. 11.

[48] Eldred Hill, Ibid., p. 11.

won three Grammys, but was also voted Album of the Year by the Country Music Association. So what if 'The Valley Road' steps outside the boundaries of traditional bluegrass with its use of piano and drums? It isn't the first time and it won't be the last. Just listen to some of Lester Flatt's early solo albums on RCA with their pianos and drums and tell me that's not bluegrass. A lot of us are so busy drawing lines that we can't sit back and enjoy the music. I think we bluegrass fans owe a lot of thanks to Bruce Hornsby and the **Nitty Gritty Dirt Band** for all they've done to promote the music we love."[49]

Mr. Friesen may have had a good point, for the "Circle II" LP was the best-selling bluegrass recording in Charlottesville, Virginia, according to deejay David G. Blevins of WKAV radio. He said, "I believe in my head, and maybe in my heart, that 'Circle II' did more for bluegrass in 1989 than any of the other nominated albums combined. Don't get me wrong, I love all of them. But the other albums were mainly bought by bluegrass fans. Again, taking nothing away from these artists, they were probably 'preaching to the choir.'"[50]

Is it bluegrass or not?

In a guest editorial in *Bluegrass Unlimited*, Ron Thomason, founder of **Dry Branch Fire Squad**, discussed his recent refusal to be drawn into an argument as to whether a song is bluegrass or not. Thomason attacked a letter to *BU* which seemed to indicate that Alison Krauss doesn't sing bluegrass and shouldn't really be considered in the same category—bluegrass—as artists such as **Flatt and Scruggs** or Thomason's **Dry Branch Fire Squad**. Thomason wrote, "So whether you like 'I've Got That Old Feeling' or not, if you're in the bluegrass *business* you should be darned glad Alison Krauss won the Grammy. Ken Irwin and Rounder did good business in promoting her and we all benefited. Rounder only works with folks they like, and with Alison that's easy. She's nice, carries an excellent bluegrass band, does old songs with primitive intensity and she is young—basically a business's dream. If the bluegrass community does not embrace her, it will be to bluegrass's embarrassment and detriment, not Alison's. Let's just count our blessings that she was able to beat out the **Headhunters** and the pianists."

Krauss' video of "I've Got That Old Feeling" went to #1 on Country Music Television and got six plays per day during that period. The rating chart is strongly influenced by viewer response, especially in a case like this where the song is not getting commercial radio airplay.

Rounder Records had its best year, up to that point, in 1990. Probably a large part of this success is due to Krauss. Her Grammy for "I've Got That Old Feeling" also made Rounder the first independent label to win the Best Bluegrass Recording Grammy award.

Naming the *high, lonesome sound*

John Cohen feels confident that *he* invented the phrase "high, lonesome sound" when, in 1962, he made up the term to describe a name for the film he was making. He sought a term which "reflected my own feelings about the music." The music he was referring to, however, was not bluegrass but that of artists such as Roscoe Holcomb and Dillard Chandler. This music was entirely folk while only delving into portions of bluegrass when he admitted that "Bill Monroe made a guest appearance in the film, performing on the courthouse steps of Hazard (Kentucky) at a coal celebration on Labor Day. His voice had this same quality."[51] A distributor of educational films urged him to title it "Kentucky Mountain Music" so that it could be identified by region in his catalog, but "I insisted on this less clear, more unknown, more poetic title."

Not too long after Cohen's film came out, his friend Ralph Rinzler compiled and annotated an album of Bill Monroe's music for Decca, calling it "The High, Lonesome Sound of Bill Monroe." (Rinzler, Cohen relates, added the comma for proper grammar). Ralph "told me he got the idea for the title from my film and record (which was on Roscoe Holcomb's "The High Lonesome Sound" which came out just after the film). I was flattered to have my idea go traveling this way, to be seen by country people on a bluegrass record, and to describe their own music."

Cohen went on to describe a correspondence with historian Neil Rosenberg. "Among other questions, he asked if I had heard of the **Country Gentlemen**'s song 'High Lonesome,' and I said that I had seen the title listed although I had never heard the song. He conveyed this in print in this book, *Bluegrass: A History*, giving the impression that I had gotten the title from the **Country Gentlemen** (I hadn't). I had no idea that he was a big fan of theirs. I think he was shaping the history towards his own preferences. Historians always do this sort of thing."

Jimmy Martin defines the *high, lonesome sound*

When this writer (in 1991) asked Mr. Martin about to describe an important aspect of bluegrass music called the *high, lonesome sound,* he replied, "Well, I

49 Orin Friesen, "Letters," *Bluegrass Unlimited*, June, 1990, p. 9.
50 David G. Blevins, "Letters," June, 1990, p. 9.
51 John Cohen, "Naming the High Lonesome Sound," *Bluegrass Unlimited*, December, 1995, p. 42.

think Jimmy Martin set that in there for Bill Monroe because the keys that Lester sung the songs they recorded—me and Bill set 'em up about two or three more frets. That's where we got that *high, lonesome sound*.

"I remember one time we went to Sunset Park in West Grove, Pennsylvania. We started gathering around the car and someone asked, 'Which one is Bill and which one is Jimmy Martin? Man he's the best I've ever heard with you and I just want to meet him. We heard you last night and you all was really getting on up there and gittin' it.' And, I remember reading some magazine article that said Jimmy Martin set Monroe's music to a higher [plane]."

Jimmy Martin

Martin mentioned that he does a lot of his material with a blues influence, specifically the Hank Williams tune "I'm Blue and Lonesome, Too" and also "In the Pines." He said, "Bill always liked it when I put that lonesome break in my voice. He'd say, 'Do just a little bit more of that, Jimmy, and let me tenor it.'"

Strife at the Opry caused by Bill Monroe

Lance LeRoy, in a 1996 letter to this writer, told of a time when Bill Monroe tried to keep Flatt and Scruggs from the Opry." The fact is that in 1953 when Bill Monroe heard that Martha White Mills wanted Lester Flatt and Earl Scruggs to be members of the Grand Ole Opry and to host the regular Martha White time slot, Monroe, motivated only by pure jealousy and spite, apparently fought it bitterly with Opry management. He even circulated a petition backstage at the Opry for the other members to sign, stating that whoever signed it was opposed to Lester and Earl being made members of the cast. He succeeded in keeping them off for more than a year.

"Of course, any good journalist would ask at this juncture, 'Do you have proof?' I do, indeed, and the strongest kind of proof." LeRoy continued, "One night backstage at the Opry while it was still held in the Ryman Auditorium, Roy Acuff came in Lester's dressing room, one of the small rooms that were barely large enough to hold a five-piece band. It was in 1970 or 1971 and I think, possibly the latter. Roy began reminiscing with Lester and I stood there and heard Acuff relate an incident whereby Bill Monroe brought the petition to him. Acuff said he read it and it specified that Monroe's music belonged to him and that Lester and Earl should not be brought in to compete with him. Acuff said he signed it but very soon began to realize that the music belonged to Lester and Earl as much as to Monroe. He thereupon looked Monroe up, retrieved the petition, and made Monroe scratch his name off. He said he felt that Lester and Earl would be a credit to the Opry and had every right to be there. Acuff added that Ernest Tubb refused to sign it when it was presented to him by Monroe.

"I would like very much for you to quote me on this in your book and I stand behind every word of it. And proudly, The truth should be told. Hastily. late at night... Best Wishes." It was signed Lance LeRoy.

Around the World with an International Music - Table of Contents

Around the World with an International Music

Bluegrass is truly an international music today; you can find it on all five continents. Nations all over the globe have bluegrass bands and promoters of bluegrass who enable bluegrass bands to tour their country. The system of setting up an international tour often can be arranged through the band's international connections simply by a phone call or by e-mail.

Perhaps the earliest example of a foreign band to tour the United States is that of Japan's The **Bluegrass 45** onto the fruited plain in the early 1970s. Their tour, at the invitation of Dick Freeland (Rebel Records), included Bean Blossom (Indiana), Camp Springs Park (Reidsville, North Carolina) and Maryland. They recorded on Rebel (SLP-1502, 1507) and toured comfortably in a bus. Their bass player since they were formed in 1968, Toshio Watanabe, continues in bluegrass today by being the president of B.O.M. Service, Ltd., Hyogo, which helps spread bluegrass in Japan into the 1990s. They can be seen in the movie "Bluegrass Music, Country Soul" from the 1971 Camp Springs festival.

Bill Clifton— a bluegrass pioneer in England

As a bluegrass veteran in the United States, in 1963 Clifton moved to Britain. Clifton recalled, "When I arrived in England in September of '63, the Newport Folk Festival was fresh in everyone's mind. As one of the Founding Directors of that festival, I had been responsible for organizing the 'country-related' talent, and would-be festival organizers in England were looking for some help and guidance in organizing similarly styled festivals. The English Folk Song and Dance Society requested, and got, my help with the organization of their live-in festival at Keele University. And the organizers of the Cambridge Folk Festival sought not only my help in organization but also asked that I recommend and assist in booking artists from the U.S..

"If old-time and bluegrass music were to be given a proper respect by the media, it was of paramount importance to set up high-profile venues for quality musicians who were strong proponents for traditional American music. As a result of the interest shown by festival organizers and by the audiences I was encountering on a daily basis, I decided to undertake the booking of tours for a number of individuals and groups that included, but not limited to, Mike Seeger, the **New Lost City Ramblers** and **Bill Monroe and the Blue Grass Boys**. For these artists, it was their very first exposure to European audiences and, while monetary rewards were few, an awareness was established on the part of both the artists and the audiences which has led to wider acceptance and greater participation on the part of the international community."

After playing the local folk clubs there, he worked his way into radio and television. Clifton told how he became involved in bluegrass music in England, "That came about when Starday released records in England through English Decca, which were released on Decca's London label. This was about 1961 or 1962 when they started selling records over there. I had been over there

The Bluegrass 45 from their "Caravan" album, Rebel SLP-1507.

to England as a visitor, but not as a performer, so I had never really spent any time there. When Starday records were issued overseas, my records were among the first to become available and for some reason, they were accepted very well in England. (And the Mercury records came out on little EPs which were popular at the time.) There was a magazine, *Country Western Express*, which was promoting country music in England and taking polls as to what was the most popular record of the year. And all of a sudden, in early 1963, I found my songs voted in that Most Popular category. This

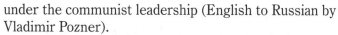

Bill Clifton at WINA. Photo courtesy of Ray and Ina Patterson.

was some sort of feedback which gave me a reason to look into going over there. I wrote to the editor of the magazine, George Haxell, and asked him if it made any sense to come over there." In spite of Haxell's warnings about visas, work permits and red tape at the British Embassy, Clifton went anyhow and was somehow let into the country in September 1963.

He immediately began recording on Decca. His single "Beatle Crazy" was based on Clifton's own amusement at the rock group which had garnered considerable national newspaper headlines but had only one single record to their credit at that time. Clifton's record came about when he asked Geoff Stevens, a songwriter for *Southern Music*, to write a "talking blues" song about the **Beatles**. Stevens said, "Sure. What's a talking blues?" Clifton showed him some talking blues from his songbook to give him an idea of how to do it. Stevens' first few attempts were without humor and therefore inappropriate for Clifton to sing. Clifton felt that the element of spontaneity would be lost if they didn't do something soon. In early November, they proceeded to record the song and it soon gained him considerable exposure. This success served as a springboard to many other jobs. By the time Clifton's record was released in December, the **Beatles** had two recordings on the charts. As a result of the newly-opened doors to Clifton, instead of staying in England six months, he stayed fifteen years.

Working full-time at music, he initially worked primarily in folk clubs as a soloist, did an occasional concert, and had his own Saturday night program on

BBC. By 1966, Clifton was playing six times a week in England. His BBC radio show was "Cellar Full of Folk," predecessor to the long-running (more than twenty years) "Country Meets Folk" program. Having a show on the BBC was quite an honor. He loved it and even managed to get the producer to let him do it live—rarely done by the BBC. And because this program aired all over Europe, he became much in demand in western Europe. And it probably influenced the folks at Radio Moscow to invite him to the Soviet Union in the summer of 1966 to do a one-hour program of traditional American music...the first ever under the communist leadership (English to Russian by Vladimir Pozner).

In England, Clifton played occasionally with a group of individuals who called themselves the **Echo Mountain Band**. The band was comprised solely of young students from a nearby school.[1] Interestingly, the only band of this type around in the early sixties was this one which was in Clifton's town of Sevenoaks, Kent. They frequently accompanied Clifton in England, Holland, Switzerland and Germany, on radio and television.

By 1967 Clifton felt he needed a break from traveling. He and his family joined the Peace Corps program in the Philippines where he served as regional director on the southernmost island of Mindanao.

In 1970, he returned to England, to work in the folk clubs and do radio, television, and concerts, and on the continent, as well. Clifton's pattern now was a commute between America and England so in 1975 he went back to the U.S. awhile for some recording and then back to England. It was during this period that Clifton partnered with Red Rector, one of bluegrass' best mandolinists. Clifton returned to the U.S. to stay in 1978 but still manages to do overseas tours in Europe, Japan, Australia and New Zealand—sometimes in the company of other musicians.

J.D. Crowe's tour of Japan

"Live in Japan" was recorded for Rounder in April of 1979 but not released in the U.S. until 1987. Musicians of **J.D. Crowe and the New South** included Crowe

[1] The Echo Mountain Band consisted of three "primary" musicians/singers: Richard (banjo) and Andrew (mandolin) Townend, and Mick Audsley (guitar/lead singer) who was the most active songwriter of the group. All three still maintain a high profile in Britain, performing together or in combination with other artists.

(banjo), Keith Whitley (guitar), Bobby Slone (fiddle), Jimmy Gaudreau (mandolin) and Steve Bryant (bass).

They did a parody of when **Flatt and Scruggs** were on the Martha White Radio Show. "We'd kick off with the 'Martha White Theme' then Keith would imitate Lester Flatt. Then we'd do a couple numbers. We did that a lot on shows and the people would love it, especially on the shows where the people would understand exactly what you were doing. In Japan, they knew exactly what we were doing. Even though a lot of them didn't speak English, they knew that sound."[2] Whitley soon embarked on his career as a country singer.

Flatt and Scruggs in Japan

Earl Scruggs told of the group's 1968 trip to Japan. It was a surprise to the band that their music was so popular there. They found that there were 500 bands there at the time, and very serious about this music.

"We went to Japan in '68. I don't know if any blue-grass-type groups had ever been there or not.[3] But we went over for I guess fifteen or seventeen days, something like that. And it was just unbelievable how they accepted us. It just blew my mind. I had no idea how popular the banjo was over there but I met one guy who was teachin' banjo and he had a little over two hundred students just himself. So it went real well and I've had a lot of personal contacts with Japanese people ever since.

"The first night we got there and we was playin' this auditorium and it was equivalent to Carnegie Hall. It was a real elite auditorium and apparently there had been a band there that didn't want to do any autographs so this manager asked if you would sign some autographs after the show. We said, 'Sure. We would be happy to.' Well, behind the stage they had a little corridor and one side of it was glass, as well as I remember, but they had a table set to where they couldn't get by us except on one side. They'd have to come by me first and I'd sign, and Lester'd sign [and] go on down to the end of the table. Well we signed until the time was runnin' low and the people knew that they wasn't gonna have enough time to get an autograph so they got to pushin' in so fast until they pushed this one glass panel down. Well, that wound it up with the promoters. They rushed us into a room, cut out all the lights, and it took a couple hours, I guess, before we ever got out. And they got us out with cigarette lighters, showin' us down the exits. I had fun with the guy for the rest of the tour. I'd say, 'Can we autograph tonight?' He'd say, 'No, no, no, no, no! No autographs! No autographs!' But it was really a wonderful experience."[4]

Charlie Waller's Country Gentlemen in Japan

Waller spoke of an early '70s tour of Japan, "It was amazing! I've never been treated so nice in my life. They wouldn't even let us carry our instruments. They had a bus with our name on it waiting for us when we got off the airplane. We played concerts all over Japan...and each show we did was sold out. We arrived at [a concert at a department store] and found a huge sign, 'Welcome Country Gentlemen.' We went up to the eighth floor, which had been cleared and roped off, and there was a large crowd waiting. What's funny was that this crowd was requesting songs that we've never recorded, songs that I thought they could have no way of knowing were in our repertoire."[5]

Bluegrass in Russia

In a 1989 tour into the Soviet Union, **Banjo Dan and the Mid-Nite Plowboys** remembered that the acceptance of bluegrass by the Russians was great. Author/banjoist Dan Lindner recalled, "The response was overwhelming. This was the first of seven formal concerts we were to do and the story repeated itself again and again. Tremendous enthusiasm, encores, autographs, gifts, questions in half a dozen languages, flowers. We were treated like heroes. Needless to say, we ate it up. If they had only allowed me to sell albums... But then, you can't take rubles out of the country."[6]

The tour also included Tbilisi. "Our farewell to Tbilisi was very emotional, as many of us had formed close friendships with our Georgian hosts, and our

Ex-Bluegrass 45 bass player Toshio Watanabe with author in 1992

[2] Joe Ross, "The Talented J.D. Crowe," *Bluegrass Unlimited*, November, 1990 p. 20.

[3] Flatt and Scruggs was the first.

[4] Doug Hutchens interview for his radio show, "Bluegrass Today."

[5] Nick Tosches, "Steering Clear of Electricity with Charlie Waller," *Bluegrass Unlimited*, September, 1974, p. 29.

[6] Dan Lindner, "Tour of a Lifetime—Banjo Dan and the Mid-nite Plowboys in the Soviet Union," *Bluegrass Unlimited*, July, 1989, p. 17.

teenagers had actually stayed overnight in homes—something unthinkable prior to Mr. Gorbachev's glasnost.

"We spent time with some wonderful people and had the opportunity of sharing songs in their parlors—around a piano or around the table. These are some of our fondest memories and are the kind that tourists staying in comfortable hotels, eating in tourist-oriented restaurants and spending their days sightseeing will never have."[7]

Bluegrass in Denmark

The manner in which many European musicians became interested in bluegrass music is very similar to the way many Americans did. Denmark's Flemming Buchardt of the **Grasshoppers** said, "I was interested in folk music in the early sixties. In the late sixties, I heard a tune on the radio. I think it was 'Darling Corey' by the **Brothers Four**. I really loved the sound of the banjo. When I heard the **Blue Ridge Mountain Boys** (with Herschel Sizemore), I realized that it was a style of music called 'bluegrass.' I saw some guys playing at a singing hall in Tivoli. I wanted to play the music..."[8]

Jens Therkildsen joined the group in 1974 on fiddle. "As a child in the fifties, there were Danish translations of folk songs and which featured tenor banjo, guitar and fiddle. I always liked the folk sound. In the late sixties, I heard 'Foggy Mountain Breakdown' on the Swedish Top Twenty. I didn't know it was bluegrass but my cousin had a lot of records. I taped a bluegrass sampler album and listened to those same ten songs for many years."[9]

Bluegrass in Italy

Italian Stefano Santangelo, banjo, mandolin and Autoharp player with the **Buffalo Ramblers**, explained how bluegrass and old-time music got started in Italy, "The music became popular some ten years ago (~1979) when a non-commercial music magazine called *Il Mucchio Selvaggio* started a column dealing with old-time and bluegrass music. This contributed to increasing the interest in this kind of the first bluegrass groups."

There are several groups today in Italy. Stefano continued, "Bluegrass music's appeal and popularity is linked with its freshness and with the opportunities the music provides to give one's personal interpretation and contribution through soloing. Old-time music has also become very popular due to its suitability for dance parties and its instrumental variety."[10]

Bluegrass in Switzerland

Swiss bluegrass probably began in the early 1960s when Ruedi "Hank" Dettwiler joined a local country band and began playing the five-string banjo with them; they then changed their name to **Country Pickers**. Dettwiler became influenced by the Pete Seeger banjo course and some written information by Bill Clifton, which came from England.

A 1966 concert in Basel (the second-largest city in Switzerland) which featured Cousin Emmy, the **Stanley Brothers**, the **New Lost City Ramblers**, and Roscoe Holcomb is still remembered as one of the momentous occasions that helped bluegrass get a foothold in Switzerland. European tours by American bands are stuff legends are made of and are fondly remembered by those in the audience. They recall the **Country Gentlemen**, the **Osborne Brothers**, Del McCoury, Joe Val, the **Bluegrass Cardinals** Dan Crary, **Hot Rize**, **Lost and Found**, **Cloud Valley** and **Whetstone Run**.

Bluegrass in Sweden

Swede Urban Haglund, bass player with Sweden's **Country Comfort**, became a bluegrass fan in 1962 (age fifteen) after hearing the **Osborne Brothers** on Swedish radio. He soon became a record collector, and he eventually had a bluegrass record and magazine collection which may be the best in Europe. The Swedish magazine *Kountry Korrall* includes a section on bluegrass.

About that same time, Tom Paley, of the **New Lost City Ramblers**, arrived in Stockholm and found that Sweden was experiencing a folk revival not unlike that which the U.S. was going through. Gottfrid Johansson's Music store sold stringed instruments and folk music records. Banjo devotees followed Pete Seeger's book but "The roll wasn't exactly right," said Haglund. "It was different than those commonly heard in bluegrass and didn't give the music any attack. So we had to live that for a few years until some of us flew over to the States and discovered the Scruggs style."[11]

Haglund and his brothers soon were in a family bluegrass band, followed by the **Bluegrass Swedes** in 1972, followed by **Country Comfort** which was founded in 1976 by Bobby Ahl.

In 1990, there were three bluegrass festivals in Sweden. One of them is organized by Leif Sunnerbrandt. He said, "I hold this festival because I love bluegrass. When I was eight years old, I heard something on the radio and loved it; it went right to my

[7] Dan Lindner, "Tour of a Lifetime—Banjo Dan and the Mid-nite Plowboys in the Soviet Union," *Bluegrass Unlimited*, July, 1989, p. 17.

[8] Joe Ross, "The Grasshoppers—Twenty Years of Danish Bluegrass," *Bluegrass Unlimited*, July, 1989, p. 31.

[9] Ibid., p. 32.

[10] Joe Ross, "The Buffalo Ramblers—Old-time and Bluegrass Music in Italy," *Bluegrass Unlimited*, July, 1989, p. 36.

[11] Joe Ross, "Bluegrass—How Swede It Is," *Bluegrass Unlimited*, July, 1989, p. 64.

heart. When I was eleven, I learned that this type of music is called 'bluegrass'. I am trying to teach the Swedish people to love it. I want people to listen. Give them five minutes and they love it!"

Swede Jan Johansson moved to North Carolina and fiddled with **New Vintage** as of 1995.

A perspective of bluegrass from The Netherlands

As much as we Americans would like to think that bluegrass is very popular in Europe, Mr. Carel van Melis, of Strictly Country Records, has a few illuminating things to tell us. Van Melis wrote to this writer in answer to some questions sent to him February 1996.

He wrote that "pop" music is by far the most popular music in Holland. "Bluegrass music has never been popular in our area—such as pop music. Bluegrass music is not popular. It is just good music for a certain number of people and, in my view, it will never be as popular as pop music, as I said. But...it will always be special music for special people. In that way, the bluegrass is not buried yet and shall never be. It's still alive."

His own background, from his childhood on, was influcnccd by American bluegrass and country music. He likes bluegrass because it "is uncomplicated, down to earth music. The difference with other music in Holland—as well in other countries—is that bluegrass music doesn't change so much in style like pop music. Bluegrass is recognizable, even after fifty years."

Mr. van Melis wrote this note of a matter which is of primary concern to him. He asked us to forgive any spelling or grammatical errors.

Dear Mr. Willis,

I hope I can help you a bit with this information. I can tell you about my own experience. Besides the SCR Agency, I'm running a country [music] club also (with five other members). I'm really proud to can tell that the "Stonevalley Foundation" is one of the most famous clubs in the world. I will not be arrogant, but I know where I'm talking about. (I've travelled a lot and visited country clubs all over the world).

Most of the time we have a full house. But generally it's difficult to get a full house but it has also a lot to do with the kind of publicity. In that way, I have a good advise for clubs.

Never be ashamed for what you are doing—in promoting the Bluegrass music. Don't call it "pop" or other stupid titles. If you do that—in hoping you get more people in—you get the wrong people. None of the "wrong people" would listen to the bluegrass

music, that means they start talking and producing a big noise. The real bluegrass fan will be disapointed and turn their back and never return. Call it "Bluegrass" and you get the right people who are coming just for the music. That's the way.

It's a hard time—special in the beginning—to make everything financial good but after awhile you will find out that this is the only right choice. You will see, after a few year, you get fans from all over the country and in my case even from out of foreign countries. Because the fans knowing "everybody in that hall has the same feeling" and creating a beautiful admosphere.

Again, don't be ashamed for what you are doing. Be clear, always.

Van Melis' comments came from a recent event in his country. He continued,

Alison Krauss did a gig in our country. And she is a great talent, there is no doubt about it. But...they go wrong because of the tour-management. They introduced Alison as a new pop-talent. There was a big promotion programme on radio but none of the announcers called her a "bluegrass artist." They call it pop or folk or even 'a pop singer who is influenced by Irish music.' (!?)

What is wrong with bluegrass?

On this moment...about two weeks later de radio has already forgotten Alison Krauss, also she's out of the pop-charts. The bad side of this experiment is that the real bluegrass lovers turn their back of now from Alison Krauss because of the pop-scene. In honesty...I am really angry because the organization didn't even inform the Dutch bluegrass scene about the Alison Krauss event. She has to be "POP," you know.

So this "bluegrass" event didn't help at all the bluegrass music. Nothing bad about Alison Krauss, she's still great.

According to Mr. Reink Janssen, "In the '50s and early '60s, bluegrass was quite unknown here. People who listened to country music came across the odd Flatt and Scruggs or Bill Monroe song, but that was about it. In the second half of the '60s, this started to change a little. The first Dutch bluegrass band founded itself (the Dutch Bluegrass Boys)—still active today!

"A big influence in those years was Bill Clifton's presence in Europe. He lived in England for about fifteen years (from 1963) and performed in many European counties, solo as well as with British bluegrass musicians (the Echo Mountain Boys). I saw them first in 1966 when they played in our country. Around that same time, I started ordering records from the USA, and the same Bill Clifton's "Mountain Bluegrass Songs" LP turned me really on to bluegrass music, leaving "country music" more or less behind me.

"The term "strictly country," as in my Strictly Country Records, came from a weekly national radio show, produced by Jo Eummelen, that started in the 1960s and lasted until the early '90s—it contained bluegrass and traditional country music. In the Netherlands, "strictly country" music is kind of the opposite of Top 40 country music, with bluegrass music as the main ingredient.

"Together with some friends, I founded Strictly Country magazine in 1971. Later on came the mail-order business for records and the Strictly Country Records. As of 1997, our record company has released over fifty albums. Pieter Groenveld has been the producer of the label since about 1980.

"During the 1970s, U.S. bluegrass artists would occasionally come to the Netherlands. They include Bill Monroe, Country Gazette, Jim and Jesse, Charlie Moore. Dutch bands began to play bluegrass. The earliest of these included the Country Ramblers, Smoketown Strut, the Bluegrass Clodhoppers.

"Around 1980, the bluegrass scene moved away some more from the country music scene. Small bluegrass festivals were organized, bluegrass concerts and tours emerged. The first tour I did myself was for Joe Val and the New England Bluegrass Boys in 1981, and since then many U.S. bands have toured this country and other parts of Europe.

"The interest in bluegrass music has grown gradually, but is still quite small in the Netherlands. Bluegrass festivals attract between 300 and 500 people and concerts are many times attended by less than a hundred people. In 1997, the Netherlands Bluegrass Music Associaion was formed and in 1998 they are organizing, for the first time, the European World of Bluegrass. The purpose is to bring together bluegrass people from all over Europe (plus the rest of the world) and, together, put this music more in the spotlight so more people in Europe will learn to know it."

Author Rick Lang described Janssen's tours, "During the tours, overnight accommodations are very expensive in Europe so quite often Rienk puts up the bands in his own home and while they are traveling,

The Sawtooth Mountain Boys in 1994. L to R: John Van Brocklin, Mike Eisler, Steve Waller, Hal Spence, Rollie Champe.

they stay with 'friends' along the way. In general, the tours are not money-making propositions and at best barely cover the costs involved. Sometimes the promoters lose money which they usually pay out of their own pockets. The European tours do, however, have some other important values which include: great exposure for the bands and performers; providing quality entertainment for the audiences; and above all, having many great experiences together. Everyone involved usually has a wonderful time and this more than outweighs the lack of monetary success."[12]

Steve Waller's European tours

Waller's **Sawtooth Mountain Boys** of Oregon was founded in 1964 with banjoist/fiddler Mike Eisler. Since then, the band has toured Europe several times.

After a tour of England in 1986, Waller observed that "Bluegrass fans are basically the same throughout the world; they are as different as they can be. They come from all walks of life but also share the same love for this captivating experience we call bluegrass... Fans in the West have progressed in their sophistication and understanding of the music and are close to being as knowledgeable about the music as those in the East due, in part, to the availability of records, festivals and concerts in the West."

Waller described the bluegrass fans of England, "They play well and are real avid fans. And the overwhelming thought we had is that they don't have any sort of concept of the hillbilly stigma attached to bluegrass as many people do in the U.S.. The English fans accept bluegrass for the fun music that it is. In one place we played, a bunch of punks came in with their hair in green-colored spikes; they were funny-looking, but real nice. They said they'd never met Americans before and really enjoyed the music."

In a 1994 interview with Waller, he said that many of the details for touring in Europe were handled by Reink Janssen of Strictly Country Records. All Americans have to do is get the time off from their day job to do the gigs. Strictly Country usually tours with the

12 Rick Lang, "Promoter Rienk Janssen—The Holland Connection," *Bluegrass Unlimited*, July, 1989, p. 78.

imported band and records them for later release as one of its "Live in Holland" albums.

The **Sawtooth Mountain Boys'** 1993 tour was arranged by Reink through the various "bluegrass clubs" as he called them. Though not strictly bluegrass, the clientele seem to like *any* of the music that America sends over of the country/bluegrass ilk. Waller said, "There's so much interest, it never ceases to amaze me. I was overwhelmed by the interest in England, let alone going to Holland Germany and Switzerland where they have bluegrass and country music clubs with all kinds of pickers and bands.

"Our 1993 tour was basically up and down the Rhine River Valley—on either side—into Holland, into Germany. We went into Switzerland up into the Alps and played at its capitol and in Baden-Baden which is sort of in the foothills. We played as far east as Ohm, Germany. Every place we played, it was either country music clubs or they have all kinds of country music, bluegrass,

Kenny Baker (L) and Josh Graves (R) with Warren Kennison, 1989 Rocky Mountain Bluegrass Festival.

folk music, and the people [really] come out for the show. They know that it's going to be a good show because they are presented regularly to them—like every few weeks or so.

"And what is demonstrated to us is that they like it all. They're not hung up on it being electric country or country rock or bluegrass or traditional bluegrass. They seem to like it all and they are very responsive. They give you very good receptions, they are very hospitable, they clap for breaks and they are knowledgeable. I mean, you can tell. And about half of the people speak English, so when you are giving your spiel, only half the people know what you're saying. The other half, well, they clap when they're supposed to clap. So that's kind of interesting. And there were a few places where only thirty percent understood English—but that's okay. Music is universal. They like the music. And even if they don't laugh at your jokes or clap, they have a very avid interest.

"The people there are very well organized. Reink Janssen, for instance, he loads up his little station wagon car with hundreds of CDs and tapes and drives to all the concerts with the band. He sets up a little store and he sells this stuff. The people come out and they expect it. It's a real neat added attraction to have all these CDs and stuff. He comes to America once a year and buy them directly from the manufacturers here and takes them back."

Waller finds that compact discs are much more popular in Europe than in America. He loaded up on cassettes before his tour, but found that he should have recorded his music on CDs.

Kenny Baker and Josh Graves on playing Europe

Baker and Josh Graves, partners beginning in 1984, enjoy the fans overseas. Baker said, "I believe the fans in Europe listen a little more intensely than they do here. If you make a change in any number, they'll let you know about it. And the older the songs you play for 'em, the better you'll be accepted."[13]

In October of 1986 Graves and Baker toured Europe. There they ate a lot of cheese. "Kenny lost ten pounds and had to borrow one of my belts," joked Josh. "It is so different—their music is about twenty years behind ours. They even liked my singing. I told Baker I might stage a comeback."[14] They were also popular in Japan. "They love our kind of music over there." said Josh.

Peter Rowan

Peter Rowan spoke about different audiences, "I think Texas audiences are the most overall-accepting. British audiences are quietly enthusiastic, but they keep coming back for more. Italian audiences, especially in the south of Italy, tend to go berserk when they hear the sound of bluegrass music and I like that a lot. The eastern seaboard changes all the time; Colorado is good. In Europe, the audiences are very, very sympathetic to an artist's attempt to communicate. And if they just know he's trying to do the best he can, they give something to him. And that helps you go beyond your boundaries."[15]

[13] Brett F. Devan, "Kenny Baker—One of the Masters," *Bluegrass Unlimited*, February, 1991, p. 24.

[14] Arlie Metheny, "Kenny Baker and Josh Graves—The Best Years of Their Lives," *Bluegrass Unlimited*, January, 1988, p. 28.

[15] Stephanie P. Ledgin, "A Candid Conversation with Peter Rowan," *Bluegrass Unlimited*, April, 1986, p. 15.

Chapter 25

The Future of Bluegrass - Table of Contents

The Future of Bluegrass

While no one can really know what the future holds, we can learn from the past, see the present, and give an opinion as to what the future may be.

When a person's bluegrass background and preference is the traditional bluegrass of the '40s and '50s, s/he may tend to treat future changes in the music with disdain and have little tolerance for how the music has changed through the years.

Another faction of bluegrass lovers may lean toward an appreciation of what people can do with their bluegrass roots and how they applied them to their own style. They may like the more progressive style of bluegrass which inevitably emerged simply because the world changes. These people understand that bluegrass today is not the same as bluegrass of the past for the same reasons as people are not the same as fifty years ago either.

Bluegrass music will continue to exist as long as people actively participate in its promotion, its controversy, and its performance as a musical form in front of the public. If it is ignored, it will certainly cease to exist! From the statements within this chapter from people who have lived the past of this music, we find many viewpoints about what the future of bluegrass may be.

Don Reno—
"I do like to see things progress."

"I think the push and drive that is behind bluegrass music will be here for many years. It's been here many years—I've seen the ups and downs in it, the cycles in it—it's in a good cycle now (December 1973). I think the cycle's going to continue, then there'll be a drop-off; there always has been. Then somebody will pull it out again. I think as long as we keep converting the young people, our music will always be here."

Reno also had some concerns about all the changes in the music. "That could be good. I do like to see things progress. They could run it a little too far-fetched and damage it. They'll be a hassle over it and they'll be some new stuff tried. It'll either go or it won't; but it won't hurt the good."[1]

Kenny Baker—
"God knows where it's going!"

"There'll be very few hard-core bluegrass pickers hardly left here in a few years probably...when [**Bill Monroe and the Blue Grass Boys**, **Jim and Jesse** and the **Osborne Brothers**] are gone, God knows where it's going. Progressive in bluegrass—I can't relate to that because they can't call it 'bluegrass'."[2]

Frank Buchanan—
former Blue Grass Boys guitarist

Buchanan feels that the "Monroe sound" will continue even if Mr. Monroe is not around to "teach" it. He said, "Bluegrass has gotten so popular, with the festivals and all, that I think it will continue." He metioned that the **Nashville Bluegrass Band** and **Traditional Grass** were two present-day bands (1992) which were properly carrying on the Monroe sound.[3]

Dan Crary—
"Bluegrass *is* going to change. There's no doubt about that."

When asked how bluegrass music might change in the future, Crary told this writer, "Bluegrass *is* going to change. There is no doubt about that. To me the issue is not whether it will change or not but whether it will change so much that it loses itself. The groups I like to listen to, both the old-time and the progressive groups, are the groups that have one foot solidly on traditional bluegrass. They have done their homework. They have listened carefully and studied **Flatt and Scruggs** and the **Stanley Brothers** and the founding fathers of bluegrass, and they have gotten that into their soul so that as they get up there and play newgrass music or whatever you want to call it—progressive bluegrass, new acoustic, whatever—you can still hear the soul of bluegrass coming through. And I'm not worried about the future of bluegrass if that's true.

"If people will start by listening to the people who invented the music and understand what they are doing and let that influence them, then I think what we want to do is for the young players to translate that into what feels right for them to play." Then "bluegrass music will

[1] Bill Vernon, "The Don Reno Story. Part Five—Don Reno Today," *Muleskinner News*, February, 1974, p. 20.

[2] Brett F. Devan, "Kenny Baker—One of the Masters," *Bluegrass Unlimited*, February, 1991, p. 24.

[3] 1992 interview at IBMA, Owensboro.

be around a long time and it will still sound like bluegrass but it won't be identical to that of the founding fathers."[4]

John Duffey—
The future of bluegrass depends on "whether they accept it or not."

Mr. Duffey commented on the future of bluegrass music, "I don't think anyone knows where any kind of music is going; it's basically relying on public appeal. I mean, [if] a lot of people decide they like it, times will get better. [If] a lot of people decide, 'I don't like it,' times are going to get worse. So I think it's really dictated by the public acceptance as to where it's going. You can't say, yourself, 'Hey, I'm going do this record and it's going to happen.' Bulls——! It's whether they accept it or not."[5]

Charles Sawtelle—
the future of bluegrass lies in its presentation

A 1985 interview of Charles Sawtelle, guitarist with **Hot Rize** at the time, revealed that he felt that the future of bluegrass music lies in its presentation. He said that good sound systems, lighting systems and the kind of things that people are used to seeing on television or from other sorts of musicians are the kinds of things with which bluegrass musicians must concern themselves. When that happens, bluegrass will gain better acceptance. He said that the days of stepping out of a car and onto the stage must change if bluegrass is to become more accepted.[6]

Tim O'Brien—
"Bluegrass is definitely here to stay."

In 1985, O'Brien spoke about his future career development. "The first thing I would say is that bluegrass is definitely here to stay—bluegrass and all the fringe music that goes with it: the swing, acoustic, Irish, and blues. Folk music fans, I guess, are really a loyal, hard-core following that's always going to be there. So I feel fortunate to be developing that phase at this point. There may come a time when I want to step out and do something a little different, but I can always

Tim O'Brien

come back and do a bluegrass thing, where I think the fans will always be."[7]

Three years after **Hot Rize** broke up and O'Brien was on his own with his various projects of recording, performing with his sister Mollie O'Brien and with his **Tim O'Brien and the O'Boys**, and other projects. O'Brien realized that giving up the security of a successful group such as **Hot Rize** was risky and full of second-guessing, but in view of his successive achievements in his career after **Hot Rize**, he realized "The only way you can measure your security as a performer is to look backwards. You can't look forwards because you don't know what's coming. But if you look back and say, 'Oh, I averaged this many gigs and sold this many records for the last three years,' then that means we'll probably be all right this year."[8]

Vic Jordan—
"There are so many good players..."

About the future of the banjo, Vic Jordan said in 1993, "I think that the banjo must progress as music moves forward. I think it will stay important in bluegrass but I think it will become more popular in other areas of music. We'll hear it in different kinds of music. It could fit into many of the rock styles. They're asking for more double-time sort of picking in the studios now. It's tough now because there are so many good players, yet less independent work for us to do."[9]

---

[4] Live interview, 1985, Peter Britt Festival, Jacksonville, Oregon.

[5] 1994 interview.

[6] 1985 interview, Eugene, Oregon.

[7] Don Stiernberg, "Interview—Tim O'Brien," *Mandolin World News*, June, 1984, p. 8.

[8] David McCarty, "Taking the Chance to Take a Chance." *Bluegrass Unlimited*, October, 1994, p. 19.

[9] From a 1993 telephone interview.

Carlton Haney—
"The only way you can reach greatness is to work with Bill Monroe."

On the topic of the future of bluegrass music and its preservation, it seemed that Haney was certainly hard at preserving bluegrass music with his Bluegrass Learning Center in Reidsville, North Carolina. But the way he described it, he seemed to indicate that bluegrass would soon whither away and die.

"They ain't never been but two hundred good bluegrass pickers. There ain't never been but seventy-five great ones. And there ain't never been but thirty that was really great. So if I can teach twenty per year, in five years that's a hundred. I don't have to teach but ten to keep it alive; twenty, or thirty come and learn.

"But they don't have Monroe to cap it off. So there will never be no more great ones because he was the only man that could make 'em. Larry Stephenson—never worked for Monroe. **Lonesome River Band**—good old band—you ever heard of them? They never worked with Monroe. They are just four or five musicians. They'll never be great. They're as good as they'll ever be right now. The only way you could reach that greatness is to work with him; [it's] the only way you could be Scruggs, or a Flatt, or a Wiseman, or a Martin, or a Benny Martin, or a Kenny Baker or whatever... 'Cause he's done quit makin' 'em now. You know, playin' those shows of his...they all stay with him now. There ain't no more. They can play. But the only way they can do it and be great is set down five years, two hours a day, with his records.

Carlton Haney

"Ricky Skaggs went. But he's left it because you can't make $500 a day doin' it. A whole band can't make $400 a day. I can hire all you want—good bands: Ricochet, Eric Ellis and them, Appalachian Trail. $500 a day. Five of them. They get $100 apiece. They can't live on that. If they work Friday, Saturday, Sunday, they can't live on $300 a week now."

Jimmy Martin—
"I'm makin' more money than I ever made in my life."

In a 1991 interview, Mr. Martin was asked what might happen to bluegrass music when he and the Osbornes and the Bill Monroes of the music are gone. "I'm proud you asked me that question. I think bluegrass music was way on the downfall and goin' out until Lester Flatt and Earl Scruggs got it more popular when they got on the 'Beverly Hillbillies.' And I think that me and the Osborne brothers and Lester Flatt and Earl Scruggs, in the last twenty-five years, has upped bluegrass music more than any individuals. The reason why I'm saying that is because we got it playin' on the radio where they about quit playin' it. And we got it played on the jukebox and was outselling everybody in records.

"Today it's hard to get on a major label 'cause they can't sell records. I've never tried to get on a major label since Decca fired me; they let the Osbornes, and Little Jimmy Dickens, and Kitty Wells, and Webb Pierce and Jimmy Davis go all at the same time. But they kept Bill Monroe. I don't know why. He wasn't selling close to the Osbornes or Jimmy Martin. At five percent royalties, I was getting $8000 to $9000 twice a year. They just wanted to go with groups like the **Oak Ridge Boys** who had holes in their tennis shoes and patches on their britches. It was just a guy there at Decca who didn't like bluegrass music. Period! I'm selling fifty times more records today than I ever did with Decca. I'm makin' more money and playing about thirty dates a year and more money than I ever made in my life."[10]

Curtis McPeake—
"You either progress or you stay backwards."

"Bluegrass has to grow. We need new blood, new innovations, new licks, new ideas. You either progress or you stay backwards. The music can't stay in the same spot forever."[11]

---

[10] 1991 interview, Grass Valley, California.

[11] Joe Ross, "An Interview with Curtis McPeake," *Bluegrass Unlimited*, July, 1992, p. 49.

Bobby Osborne—
"Bluegrass will never die."

Bobby Osborne talked about the old days and how the music has changed, "Of course, the music has changed a lot; you've got new people, new writers, new ideas for songs. Back in the days when we started, there were only three or four groups that played bluegrass: Bill Monroe, **Flatt and Scruggs**, **Reno and Smiley** and the **Stanley Brothers**. It was *all* traditional back then. Each group had its own style. When we came along we developed a style of our own. In the last few years, I've not heard anybody with a style that could be recognized so you could say, 'Well, that's so-and-so.' There should be someone like that.

Bobby Osborne

"I've thought a lot about the direction bluegrass is taking," continued Osborne. "A lot of people are trying to mix bluegrass with rock. Rock music is great but I don't think it can be played with bluegrass instruments with any effect. There will always be a certain number of people who stick to the traditional sound.

"That's another thing. Bluegrass is hard to do. It's a must for you to be a good picker and a good singer, too.

Not many people coming along nowadays can do both. So many people get just good enough to go on stage and then they don't try anymore. I'm a firm believer that no one is as good as he can be...

"As for the direction bluegrass is taking, I'm not sure. Some people say that if something happens to Bill Monroe bluegrass will die. But bluegrass will never die."[12]

About young pickers on the scene Mr. Osborne added, "I'm sure they listen to **Flatt and Scruggs**, Bill Monroe, our records and others, but they miss the basics like they way Earl Scruggs plays the banjo. If you don't play the banjo the way Earl plays, to me, you're playing something else. I just wish they'd listen to the songs on the records and learn them. When they learn the songs, hold exactly to the melody instead of changing them to where they're not original anymore. The way I figure it is if you are going to imitate somebody, get it as close as you can. If we do one of their songs [**Flatt and Scruggs**] we get the phrasing the way they did it. We did an album called 'Yesterday, Today, and the Osborne Brothers.' One side is exactly the way **Flatt and Scruggs** did it. The other side is our style of music. Sticking to tradition works."[13]

Little Jody Rainwater—
"The audience will be the judge."

Charles "Little Jody Rainwater" Johnson spoke about the music he was involved with for so many years, "I don't know where bluegrass is heading, but people are always going to like the music. People like good, old, plain, country music...nothing fancy. Just go out, be yourself, do right, and play good music. The audience will be the judge."[14]

Raymond Fairchild—
"Bluegrass is gonna go a long way."

Mr. Fairchild spoke about the future of bluegrass, "As long as people stick to their own style and learn something new and don't try and pick like somebody else, bluegrass is gonna go a long way. But if they don't get off this...copying Bill Monroe, trying to copy Jimmy Martin, trying to copy the Osborne brothers or any group that comes along, then bluegrass music's gonna be gone. It's gonna take sitting down and working. You got to work at anything you do. You can't sit back and wait for somebody else to make it and then copy it and go on stage and play it."[15]

---

[12] Glenna H. Fisher, "The Osborne Brothers," *Bluegrass Unlimited*, July, 1984, p. 12.

[13] Carol Sue Jeffrey, "Back to the Basics—Bobby Osborne," *Bluegrass Unlimited*, February, 1991, p. 38.

[14] John A. Hinton, "Jody Rainwater—Bluegrass Reflections," *Bluegrass Unlimited*, January, 1981, p. 40.

[15] Ibid.

Larry Sparks

Larry Sparks—
"Continue to spread the music or it may be lost."

When asked by this writer what he feels about the future of bluegrass music, Larry Sparks said that it is necessary for hard-core traditionalists to continue spreading the word or the music may be lost.

Buddy Spicher—
"Bluegrass is like old jazz; it's so great, it's *too* good."

As a veteran of the "Nashville sound" as well as of traditional bluegrass music, Buddy Spicher spoke about the commercial future of bluegrass music. "But I'm also afraid that bluegrass is like old jazz. It's so great, it's *too* good! It's over a lot of people's heads. They don't appreciate bluegrass because they don't know it. They don't understand it, so therefore it's not really commercial. So I don't know if there'll be a lot of success as far as money goes."[16]

Butch Waller—
"I don't think it will ever be real popular."

Long-time West Coast bluegrass musician Butch Waller gave his ideas about the future of bluegrass music. "There are several things that look good. It's

getting more and more acceptance. I don't think it will ever be real popular. In fact, I hope it won't be, because when things do get popular they just kind of get homogenized and lose what's unique about them. So I hope it'll just keep slowly building like it is and get the fan support that it needs. Bluegrass will always have a future. It seems like it will. In a way, it can be compared with jazz in the way that it's had this underground support going through the years. Jazz is not a really popular form of music but it keeps on going. People keep on playing and loving it."[17]

Rual Yarbrough—
"They're going to get some bad names like some of the rock festivals have."

About the future of bluegrass, in 1978 Mr. Yarbrough said, "Well, I wouldn't say bluegrass is dying out, but I think it's headed for some things they're going to have to keep a tight hold on to keep it from getting out of order. I see it happening at the festivals. They're going to get some bad names like some of the rock festivals have."[18]

Bill Emerson—
"People today have no idea how hard it was going through the fifties and sixties."

Bill Emerson recognizes that bluegrass has changed through the years and will continue to do so. And just like the old days, "bands today can make a living. I remember the volume of product we carried with the **Country Gentlemen**. Some people work at it and some don't. Jimmy Martin had us hawk the albums right on stage. When you got off the stage you'd take an armload of records through the crowd and come out with money stuffed in every pocket. There's money to be made but you have to go get it. Nobody's going to hand it to you."

Even if a band works hard at it, "It bothers me that they're playing a twenty-five year-old record (on the radio) from some band that's been out of the business for fifteen years. Why are they doing that when there's bands trying to make a living at it?"[19]

Emerson then referred to the past, "People today have no idea how hard it was going through the '50s and '60s. Bands ran the road in automobiles. If the pickings are slim today, you should have seen it then. There

16 Douglas B. Green, "Nashville Cats: Blue Grass Style—Bobby Thompson and Buddy Spicher," *Bluegrass Unlimited*, February, 1974, p. 25.

17 Sandy Rothman, "Butch Waller's High Country—Part 1", *Bluegrass Unlimited*, September, 1985.

18 Patricia Glenn, *Bluegrass Unlimited*, October, 1978.

19 Joe Ross, "Bill Emerson, Banjo Player Extraordinaire, *Bluegrass Unlimited*, March, 1992, p. 32.

weren't any festivals. Bands played school houses on percentage, roadhouses and little outdoor parks. Dedicated performers kept bluegrass going when it could have faded away. Carlton Haney just received recognition for his visionary contributions. I played the first bluegrass festival in Fincastle, Virginia, with Jimmy Martin in the '60s. After the festivals, Carlton got us all together and talked about the future of bluegrass. I can tell you, it all happened just as he said it would. I think the younger artists who have something good need all the support we can give them, but I won't forget the ones who paid big dues to make the music what it is."[20]

Bobby Atkins—
"Get some new material and play it *your* way!"

As a veteran of forty years in bluegrass music, Atkins reflected on the importance of keeping the old timers around to keep the music right, and of his appearance at IBMA with his own **Countrymen** and Vassar Clements. "It's going to take people like myself, like Scruggs and people that's played down through the years with [Bill Monroe] to *really* keep it going... And every band here today—and if you listen you know what I'm going to tell you is the truth—all young bands, unless they come up with someone like me or Reno or

Bobby Atkins

Scruggs, most of them bands sound just alike. When you hear one—this is what hurts what we are trying to do—everybody sounds alike. When you hear me, when you hear **Flatt and Scruggs**, when you hear Bill, Charlie, Jim Eanes, people like that, you know who they are by the time they hit their first four bars. Nowadays, if they don't tell you who they are, you don't know who they are."[21]

Another thing that he feels is hurting the music is lack of progress. While some bands insist that a song be played exactly like it was done on the record, Atkins feels this way, "I play 'Roanoke'; my band plays 'Roanoke.' But when Bill Monroe recorded that, the banjo only had a small part in it. Nowadays, I take the whole break in it on the banjo. Why do I have to do it like that was? I'm not going to do that way. This is what's hurtin' our kind of music. Lack of progress.

"And another thing that's hurtin' our music—every bluegrass festival you see are the same people on it. My mamma is ninety years old and she can't stand it when she hears Bill Monroe sing 'Blue Moon of Kentucky' because she has heard him sing it every time he has hit the stage. And the same thing applies to a re-release of an album I already have—but this one has a new cover. There's no point in me buying a new Bill Monroe album if it has the same songs on it that I already have. Somewhere along the line, somebody has got to make a little progress with it. I'm not sayin' just take it and ruin it with all kinds of doin's and play it like they are doin' a lot of country. In my book, that is more rock and roll than it is country. The way they're playing bluegrass these days is more jazz than bluegrass. I don't have anything against jazz, but I'd like to hear the tune more. But get you some new material and play it different! Play it your way!"

J.D. Crowe—
New bluegrass musicians "really don't feel it and they're not willing to do what it takes to learn it."

About the future of bluegrass music Crowe said, "The bluegrass industry needs somebody to book it the way country music does, otherwise it's never going anywhere. That would get rid of little dinky record companies and bad sound and amateur bands. That's the way I think it's going to have to be."[22]

---

[20] Ibid., p. 32.

[21] Continuing with his conversation that September 1991 evening in Owensboro, "It hurt my feelings. Look! We drove seven hundred miles up here and we got to looking at papers and magazines. Our name wasn't nothin'. More than makin' me mad, it hurt my feelings. I don't know if anybody can do anything about it, though. You see, if the younger people—the younger generation of bluegrass musicians—had to come up like I did... A lot of times, like when I was playing with bands like the Flint Hill Playboys, we'd have to divide a bag of popcorn or a bar of candy a day. And that's all we had to eat. So we loved it enough to stay with it. All right, you take nine out of ten of them today, if they had to do that it would make your head swim. They wouldn't stay in it long if they had to do that. That's what hurts me. I ain't mad at nobody. I just want people to settle down and see where it come from. Like me or Carlton Haney or all the pioneers of bluegrass music."

[22] Leon Smith, "Talking with the Stars: Two Interviews from a 'Bluegrass Hornbook'.", *Bluegrass Unlimited*, July, 1981, p. 19.

About new up-and-coming musicians, Crowe felt that "They're learning in a different fashion; they're learning what they hear but they really don't feel it and they're not willing to do what it takes to learn it. They want big money right at the beginning when they don't have the name and sometimes don't have the talent [to deserve it]. They think hot licks is where it is. It's impressive to musicians, but not many of them. They've either heard it already or done it on down through the years. Timing is the basis of music—the root of it—not hot licks! It's hard to explain timing. Most of it is really simple—just the touch, technique and feel of the timing."[23]

This is a highly structured music which is difficult to play, he said. Part of the blame is because of the frequent change in band members and the obligation of the leader to teach this new person. But another facet is that "Everybody has to want the same thing. That's what it boils down to. If they want to have a band and play in a band situation, the band sound is what they got to work on. That's what makes good bands. There are some real professional groups that created a kind of momentum, or controversy or excitement or whatever you want to call it, in a bluegrass band. I don't see or hear many bands doing that today. There's a lot of good pickers there but there aren't many with a band sound. Everybody sounds separate. And until you have that *one* sound—a *band* sound—you're not going to be successful. I'm not sure they realize how much it takes and what you have to sacrifice, the frustrations you go through. A lot of people won't do it, and in this day and time you can hardly afford to do it. But the groups that work for that 'band sound' will be the ones that are remembered."[24]

John Hartford and the IBMA

"I belong to the IBMA," said John Hartford. "I'm very fond of the IBMA and I'm fond of the people that are in the IBMA, but I'm not totally in agreement with the IBMA. I want to work for the good of the music, but I have definite feelings about the IBMA which I'll tell you. It may not be the popular view.

"I believe that, first of all, if somebody does not like bluegrass music, you will never get them to like blue-

"I believe that, first of all, if somebody does not like bluegrass music, you will never get them to like bluegrass music. If somebody does like bluegrass music, there's no way you can keep 'em from it." —John Hartford

grass music. If somebody does like bluegrass music, there's no way you can keep 'em from it.

"Bluegrass music right now is like a wonderful, small town that we all live in where we don't have to lock our doors at night. And if somebody gets into trouble, we all go and help 'em out with a benefit or whatever. But what the IBMA seeks to do, through whatever means, is to get the equivalent of General Electric or General Motors or somebody to come in on the outskirts of town and build a great big plant. And what that's gonna bring with it is all that kind of stuff that goes on in the outside world—crime, drugs, protesters, the ills of modern civilization—where we are gonna have to start locking our doors. When the music gets real popular we're gonna have to start locking our doors. When the music gets real popular we're gonna wind up having to share it with a whole lot of people we don't know, and right now, not only do we all know each other, but there's a good chance that a lot of us are related!

"I've watched the Country Music Association over the years and they've done a lot of good stuff for country music. But the old-timers that worked real hard to build the music are still the old-timers, and the people that are making all the money are people from New York and Los Angeles, people who didn't do any of that [hard work]. And, also, it's changed the music. It's changed the flavor of the music of the music and everything like that. Maybe one of the reasons that a lot of the old-timers don't support the IBMA is for that reason. They kind of have a feeling for that.

"I like the way it is now," Hartford went on to say, "and we have to be careful with it—not to try to get people to take it as a course in school and all that kind of stuff. I heard an interview with Isaac Stern, the great classical violinist, and he said that the great musicians don't take their music to the public. The great musicians stay where they are and play, and the public comes to them.

"Now, there's a lot of people in bluegrass that are not making a living from bluegrass but who want to be making a living in bluegrass, and they will violently disagree with me. And I don't really have an answer for that. I wish I did. But if they have to get in there and overcome those terrible odds [of becoming successful], then they'll come up with something new and different—something that's good and furthers everything."[25]

---

[23] Ibid., p. 19.

[24] Joe Ross, "Food for Thought from J.D. Crowe," *Bluegrass Unlimited*, November, 1990, p. 24.

[25] Julie Koehler, "The One and Only John Hartford, "*Bluegrass Now*, September/October, 1994, p. 7.

Keith Little—
"I don't see bluegrass as ever being real popular because you can't dance to it."

"Butch Waller and I have talked a lot about seeing bluegrass as being chamber music or something, where there are definite places to play and little societies or organizations that are interested in it and could promote tours. I don't see bluegrass as ever being real popular in the way it is for me, because you can't dance to it, it's not loud enough, and it doesn't lend itself to a club atmosphere that much. In and of itself I don't think it will ever be a super-popular music with the masses, but I do think it's going to last. It will probably be carried on from a performer's standpoint by groups and organizations that will support it in places where people can go and hear it, places like the Freight and Salvage (in Berkeley, California)."[26]

Burt Baumbach—
"There's a lack of professionalism."

Baumbach was 1980's Entertainer of the Year in Canadian bluegrass and he spoke of the Canadian bluegrass scene. Despite the fact that interest seems to have diminished in the past few years, "I think it's going to come around again, like anything else. I think what has happened with the bluegrass situation in Canada is that there's a lack of professionalism in some of the people putting on the festivals. And people who go for the first time to see a festival say, 'If that's what it's like then I'm not interested in it.' On the other hand, I think the musicians are starting to get more serious about what they should be doing and what they're expected to do. They should realize it whether they are full or part-time; they really shouldn't make the differentiation on stage."[27]

Allen Shelton—
"There must be something else to play besides 'Foggy Mountain Breakdown.'"

"Maybe my ideas were too different from other banjo pickers. I just wanted to play something a little different from what anyone else was playing. I thought there must be something else to play besides 'Foggy Mountain Breakdown.' I mean that's great, but... It was my opinion in those days they were trying to limit the banjo. In other words, you only wanted a banjo in a fast bluegrass tune and nothing else. I think it can be played in anything and folks these days have proved that, and I thought that all along. I guess that's just the way I think it ought to be. That's the way I hear it."[28] His opinion on the future of the banjo? "No limit" he told Peter Wernick in 1984.

Chris Thile at age ten. Photo taken minutes before he was runner-up in the mandolin contest at a Blythe, CA, festival. It is individuals like this who are the future of bluegrass.

26 Sandy Rothman, "Butch Waller's High Country, Part 2," *Bluegrass Unlimited*, September, 1985, p. 25.

27 Alynn Thomas, "The Dixie Flyers—A Canadian Bluegrass Tradition," *Bluegrass Unlimited*, May, 1986, pp. 60, 61.

28 Footnotes on "Shelton Special" (Rounder 0088) written by Tony Trischka.

Appendix A

Some of the publications devoted to bluegrass are listed here.

In July 1966, the first issue of *Bluegrass Unlimited* was printed. Its officers were: Chairman, Pete (Roberts) Kuykendall; Vice Chairman, David Freeman (owner of Rebel Records since 1963); Richard Spottswood, Treasurer; Gary Henderson; and Secretary, Dianne Sims. A full-year subscription was $3. The magazine wasn't intended to be much more than a newsletter with some record notices and a listing of who was playing where.

Muleskinner News was first published by Carlton Haney in 1970. Its editor was Fred Bartenstein who did most of the work. It was intended to compete directly with *BU*. As a result of the challenge, in the fall, *BU* changed its format to a more professional-looking journal and the staff went full-time.

Bossmen: Bill Monroe and Muddy Waters was published in 1971 by the Dial Press of New York (It was later reprinted in paperback by Da Capo Press, Inc.). It was written by Jim Rooney, a director of the Newport Folk Festival, and partner of Bill Keith.

The Hub Nitchie newsletter started in 1972. That first issue was supposed to be the last; it was called *The Banjo Information Clearing House* and was merely a bunch of classified ads for banjo-oriented suppliers around the country. (For two stamps extra you could also receive a free banjo song in tablature.) Printed by mimeograph machines and advertised for sale for $1, he said, "Well, that's it! I've nothing more to say. I don't know what I'm going to do if I ever put out another one of these things because I don't have anything more to say about the banjo."[1] By March of 1973, Nitchie had decided to do it again and called it *Banjo Tablature of the Month*. In November, his first issue of *The Monthly Newsletter That Covers the 5-String Banjo* was his first issue. The following February, the title was changed to *Banjo Newsletter*. While the earliest versions were written entirely by Nitchie, by 1979 he had so many contributors that he did very little contributing except editing and a few tabs.

In 1972, *The Bluegrass Songbook* was published by Collier Books; it was written by Dennis Cyporyn.

Bluegrass Songbook was published in 1976 by Oak Books, New York City. Written by Peter Wernick, the book focused on singing skills rather than instrument picking instruction. And Midtown Publishers, of Middletown, Ohio, published *Bluegrass Songbook with Over 500 Songs* in 1980, followed by Volume 2 in 1983. Wernick's *Bluegrass Banjo* came out in 1974 from Oak Publications and by 1995 had sold 200,000 copies.

In February 1974, *Pickin'* magazine was first published in New York by Douglas Tuchman. It ceased operations eight months after *Frets* magazine appeared in 1979.

Bob Artis' book, *Bluegrass*, was published in hard copy in 1975. The paperback came out the next year.

In 1981, *Wayne Erbsen's Backpocket Bluegrass Songbook* came out in a size where it would fit handily in a back pocket. Erbsen also wrote *A Manual on How to Play the 5-String Banjo for the Complete Ignoramus!*, *The Complete and Painless Guide to the Guitar for Young Beginners*, and *Starting Bluegrass Banjo from Scratch*, all published by Pembroke Music Company of New York.

Oak Publications published Tony Trischka's *Melodic Banjo* in 1976 and included a plastic record within its pages.

Oak published *Bluegrass Bass* by Ned Alterman and Richie Mintz in 1977 and had a plastic record within its pages. Roger Mason's *Teach Yourself Bluegrass Bass* (AMSCO Music Publishing Co, 1978) came out the following year.

Mandolin World News was published monthly. The magazine began in the basement of David Grisman in 1976. Its editor was Don Stiernberg.

In the fall of 1980, Ms Burney Garelick, of San Marcos, California, started her own magazine *Bluegrass Alternative and the National Fiddler*. It had a format similar to *Bluegrass Unlimited* but leaned toward fiddling activity throughout the United States. It started out as a 22-inch broadside but within a year it was a forty-page monthly magazine on coated stock. Garelick provided most of the work required to produce and distribute the product. The publication of the magazine ceased in 1983 when she found the workload for one person too much. She was also the editor for Dick Tyner's *Golden West Bluegrass* magazine; used for a time to promote Tyner's festivals in Norco, California.

In 1985, the University of Illinois Press published Neil V. Rosenberg's *Bluegrass: A History*. It became a bible for the music. As of 1994, he had sold 9,000 copies.

Bluegrass Now was first published in 1991. Based in Rolla, Missouri, the staff soon became its founder Wayne Bledsoe, Ray Hicks and Deb Ashby. Bledsoe began the periodical as a spin-off from his radio show, "Bluegrass for a Saturday Night," on the University of Missouri at Rolla station KUMR. Subscription rate for a year was $11.97.

In the early part of the 1990s decade, for retail sales of one million copies, *Earl Scruggs and the 5-String Banjo*, Scruggs received a gold book award from Peer-Southern.

5-String Quarterly, put together by Eddie Collins of Austin, Texas, was begun in early 1995 and ended its publication a year and a half later.

Cybergrass® The Internet Bluegrass Music Magazine is a venture which began in September 1992. It can only be accessed by the Internet system. Robert S. Cherry, of Colorado Springs, Colorado, is the creator, the editor and the publisher. Access to the magazine is achieved by the computer Internet address "http://www.banjo.com/" and was frequented by a truly international audience of half a million people each month as of 1997.

America's Music — Bluegrass

[1] Murphy Henry, "It's Been Nothing But Fun!—Hub Nitchie and *Banjo Newsletter*," *Bluegrass Unlimited*, August, 1989, p. 64.

Appendix B

The people of bluegrass
Personal data

First Name	Last Name	Nickname	Birthplace	Birthdate	Died
Roy Claxton	Acuff		nr Maynardville, TN	Sep 13, 1903	Nov 23, 1992
Raymond Thomas	Adams			Dec 4, 1979	
Raymond Thomas Jr.	Adams	Tom	Gettysburg, PA	Nov 17, 1958	
Eddie	Adcock		Scottsville, VA	Jun 21, 1938	
Martha	Adcock (Hearon)		SC	Oct 29, 1949	
Floyd Powhatan	Adkins	Chief Powhatan	Charles City County, VA	June 21, 1927	
Paul	Adkins			Sep 9, 1952	
David	Akeman	Stringbean	Annville, KY	Jun 14, 1914	Nov 10, 1973
Harley	Allen	Red	Hazard, KY	Feb 12, 1930	Apr 3, 1993
Neal	Allen			Feb 18, 1974	
Rick	Allred			May 8, 1960	
Irene	Amburgey (Carson)	Martha Carson	Neon, KY	May 19, 1921	
Bob	Amos		DE	Oct 24, 1957	
Jack	Anglin		Columbia, TN	May 13, 1916	Mar 7, 1963
Donald Lee	Anthony	Chubby	Lincolnton, NC	Dec 20, 1935	Feb 5, 1980
Eddie	Arnold		nr Henderson, TN	May 15, 1918	
Jimmy	Arnold		Galax, VA	Jun 11, 1952	Dec 26, 1992
Bob	Artis			Jul 26, 1946	
John	Ashby		Warrenton, VA	Oct 6, 1915	May 11, 1979
Clarence Tom	Ashley	T.C. or Tom	Mountain City, TN	Sep 20, 1895	Jun 2, 1967
Bobby	Atkins		Shoals, NC	May 22, 1933	
Chester Burton	Atkins	Chet	Luttrell, TN	Jun 20, 1924	
Mike	Auldridge		Washington, D.C.	Dec 30, 1938	
Tim	Austin			Jun 18, 1961	
Orvon Gene	Autry	Gene	Tioga, TX	Sep 29, 1907	
Homer	Bailes		Kanawha County, WV	May 8, 1922	
Johnnie	Bailes			Jun 24, 1918	Dec 21, 1989
Kyle	Bailes			May 7, 1915	March 3, 1996
Walter	Bailes			Jan 17, 1920	
Charlie	Bailey		Happy Valley, TN	Feb 9, 1916	
Danny	Bailey		Happy Valley, TN	Dec 1, 1919	
Deford	Bailey	Harmonica Wizard	Bellwood, TN	Dec 14, 1899	July 2, 1982
James	Bailey		Farmville, VA	Mar 22, 1957	
Billy	Baker		Pound, VA	July 4, 1936	
Kenny Clayton	Baker		Burdine, KY	Jun 26, 1926	
Jerome	Baldassari	Butch	Scranton, PA	Dec 11, 1952	
Barry	Bales		Kingsport, TN	Aug 23, 1969	
Brian	Barnes			Oct 28, 1959	
Kevin	Barnes		MN	May 14, 1957	
Wanda	Barnett			Oct 9, 1957	
Dr. Humphrey	Bate		Castallian Springs, TN	May 25, 1875	Jun 12, 1936
Terry	Baucom		Monroe, NC	Oct 6, 1952	
Mel	Bay		Bunker, MO	Feb 1915	May 14, 1997
Parlin Kenneth	Beaver	Pappy	nr Newport, TN	Mar 7, 1919	
Thom	Bentley		N. Hollywood, CA	Aug 1, 1956	
Byron	Berline		Caldwell, KS	Jul 6, 1944	
Barry	Berrier		Mt. Airy, NC	Oct 10, 1960	
Alan	Bibey		King, NC	Aug 24, 1964	
Elmer	Bird	The Banjo from Turkey Creek	Turkey Creek, WV	May 28, 1920	July 19, 1997
Bob	Black			Jun 14, 1949	
Cary	Black			Jul 17, 1950	
Nancy	Blake			June 11, 1952	
Norman	Blake		Chatanooga, TN	Mar 10, 1938	
Doug	Blevins		Iaeger, WV	Mar 27, 1953	
Lloyd	Blevins		Iaeger, WV	May 22, 1950	
Rubye	Blevins	Patsy Montana	Jessieville, AR	~Oct 30, 1914	May 3, 1996
Moran Lee	Boggs	Dock	Dooley, VA	Feb 7, 1898	Feb 7, 1971
Bill	Bolick		West Hickory, NC	Oct 29, 1917	
Earl	Bolick		West Hickory, NC	Nov 16, 1919	
Claude	Boone		Yancy County, NC	Feb 18, 1916	
Bill	Boutilier			Apr 16, 1926	
Larry	Boutilier			Oct 18, 1936	
Ken	Boutilier			July 10, 1946	
John R.	Bowman			Sep 15, 1970	
Rick	Bradstreet		Sioux City, IA	Sep 28, 1954	

First Name	Last Name	Nickname	Birthplace	Birthdate	Died
Kirk	Brandenberger		IA	Aug 16, 1955	
Rod	Brasfield		Smithville, MS	Aug 22, 1910	Sep 12, 1958
Francis Leon	Bray		Champaign, Il	Nov 3, 1931	
Harley Orville	Bray		nr Champaign, Il	Oct 7, 1934	
Jascha Nate	Bray	Nate	nr Champaign, Il	Mar 6, 1936	1970
Finley J.	Brewer	Jim		Mar 16, 1938	
Gary	Brewer	Stretch	KY	Apr 19, 1965	
Lee Kahle	Brewer				Aug 12, 1989
Gena	Britt		Star, NC	Apr 11, 1972	
Jim	Britton			Jun 7, 1972	
Jim	Brock		AL	Aug 5, 1934	
Alison	Brown			Aug 7, 1962	
Frank, Jr.	Brown	Hylo	River, KY	Apr 20, 1922	
Alfred E.	Brumley			Oct 29, 1905	Nov 15, 1977
Billy	Bryant			May 4, 1938	Mar 31, 1994
Boudleaux	Bryant		Shellman, GA	Feb 13, 1920	Jun 25, 1987
Matilda	Bryant	Felice	Milwaukee, WI	Aug 7, 1925	
Mike	Bub		Los Angeles, CA	Nov 13, 1964	
Frank	Buchanan		Spruce Pine, NC or Penland, NC	Mar 25, 1934	
James	Buchanan	Jim	NC	Jan 1, 1941	
Clay	Buckner		Cocoa Beach, FL	1954	
Daniel James	Buckner	Buck	Los Angeles, CA	Mar 26, 1941	
Keith	Bullard				Jan 25, 1982
Dan	Bump				Nov 22, 1992
Curtis	Burch		Montgomery, AL	Jan 24, 1945	
Elmer	Burchett				Sep 1977
Kenneth C	Burns	Jethro	Knoxville, TN	July 27, 1923 or Jan 10, 1920?	Feb 4, 1989
Gene	Burrows		Bedford County, VA	Sep 12, 1928	Sep 14, 1992
Bernarr Graham	Busbice	Buzz Busby	Eros, LA	Sep 6, 1933	
Wayne E.	Busbice		Chatham, LA	Mar 28, 1929	
Sam	Bush		Bowling Green, KY	Apr 13, 1952	
Carl	Butler		Knoxville, TN	Jun 2, 1927	Sep 4, 1992
Robert	Byrd	Honorable	NC	Nov 20, 1917	
Greg	Cahill		Chicago, Il	Dec 22, 1946	
James B.	Cain	Benny	New Haven, CT	May 21, 1921	
Vallie R.	Cain (Cave)		Kitzmiller, MD	July 19, 1927	Apr 15, 1993
Bill	Callahan		Madison County, NC	Mar 27, 1912	
Joe	Callahan		Madison County, NC	Jan 27, 1910	Sep 10, 1971
Alex	Campbell			1922	
Archie	Campbell		Bulls Gap, TN	Nov 17, 1914	Aug 29, 1957
Cecil	Campbell		Stokes County, NC	Mar 22, 1911	June 18, 1989
Sid	Campbell				Apr 21, 1987
Sarah Ophelia	Cannon (Colley)	Minnie Pearl	Centerville, TN	Oct 25, 1912	Mar 6, 1996
Bob	Carlin		New York City, NY	Mar 17, 1953	
Bill	Carlisle		Wakefield, KY	Dec 19, 1908	
Clifford Raymond	Carlisle	Cliff	Wakefield, KY	Mar 6, 1904	Apr 2, 1983
John	Carson	Fiddlin' John	Fannin County, GA	Mar 23, 1868	Dec 1949
Mike	Carson			Jun 27, 1937	
Alvin .Pleasant	Carter	A.P.	Maces Spring, VA	Dec 15, 1891	Nov 7, 1960
Ezra	Carter	Eck			
Janette	Carter		Maces Springs, VA	Jul 2, 1923	
Jason	Carter		Greenup County, KY	Feb 1, 1973	
Maybelle	Carter (Addington)	Mother Maybelle	Nicklesville, VA	May 10, 1909	Oct 22, 1978
Sara	Carter (Dougherty)		Wise Country, VA	July 21, 1898	Jan 8, 1979
Wilf	Carter	Montana Slim	Canada		Dec 5, 1996
Cynthia May	Carver	Cousin Emmy	nr Glasgow, KY (Lamb)	1903	Apr 11, 1980
Claude	Casey		Enoree, SC	Sep 13, 1912	
Roy Lee	Centers		Jackson, KY	Nov 8, 1944	May 2, 1974
Paul	Champion				Feb 16, 1986
Jean	Chapel				Aug 15, 1995
Robert Shannon	Cherry	Bob	Denver, CO	Dec 29, 1951	
Lew	Childre		Opp, AL	Nov 1, 1901	Dec 3, 1961

First Name	Last Name	Nickname	Birthplace	Birthdate	Died
Bill	Church		Wilkes County, NC	Sep 8, 1922	
Edwin	Church		Wilkes County, NC	July 29, 1925	
Porter	Church		Bristol, TN	Apr 17, 1934	Aug 18, 1995
Ralph	Church		Wilkes County, NC	Jun 28, 1928	
Manual D.	Clark	Speedy	Erwin, TN	Aug 6, 1906	
Millie	Clements		Florence, AL		
Vassar	Clements		Kinard, FL	Apr 25, 1928	
Zeke	Clements	Alabama Cowboy	Warrior, AL	Sep 11, 1911	Jun 4, 1994
Mike	Clevenger			Jan 28, 1959	
William August	Clifton (Marburg)	Bill	Riverwood, MD	Apr 5, 1931	
Charlie	Cline		Baisden, WV	Jun 6, 1931	
Ezra	Cline		Baisden, WV	1907	~1985
Ned	Cline		Baisden, WV	1920 or 1921	1944
Ray	Cline	Curly Ray	Baisden, WV	Jan 10, 1923	Aug 19, 1997
Doug	Cloud		Brewton, AL	Apr 26, 19xx?	
Pat	Cloud			Dec 23, 1950	
Larry	Cohea		Springfield, TN	Dec 18, 1946	
Paul	Cohen		Chicago, IL	Nov 10, 1908	Apr 1, 1970
Abner	Cole	Ab	Hope Hill, WV	1921	
T. Michael	Coleman			Jan 3, 1951	
William D.	Colleran	Mac Martin	Pittsburg, PA	Apr 4, 1925	
Bill	Colwell			Aug 14, 1962	
Mike	Compton		Meridian, MS		
Dudley	Connell		Shear, WV	Feb 18, 1956	
Jack	Cooke			Dec 6, 1936	
Dale Troy	Cooper	Stoney	Harman, WV	Oct 16, 1918	Mar 22, 1977
Wilma Lee	Cooper (Leary)		Valley Head, WV	Feb 7, 1921	
Lloyd	Copas	Cowboy	Muskogee, OK	July 15, 1913	Mar 5, 1963
Charles	Cordle	Chuck			Nov 10, 1967
Larry	Cordle			Nov 16, 1949	
Pete	Corum		NC	Nov 4, 1948	
Elizabeth	Cotten		Carrboro, NC	1893	Jun 29, 1987
Jason	County		Greenup County, KY		
Evelyn	Cox		LA	Jun 20, 1959	
Lynn	Cox		LA	Oct 11, 1960	
Sidney	Cox		LA	Jul 21, 1965	
Suzanne	Cox		LA	Jun 5, 1967	
Willard	Cox		LA	Jun 9, 1937	
Paul	Craft		Proctor, AR	1937	
Jerry	Crain			Jun 6, 1967	
Wayne	Crain			Sep 16, 1941	
Tommy	Crank		McKee, KY	Apr 13, 1926	
Dan	Crary		Kansas City, KS	Sep 29, 1939	
Robert	Cravens	Red	Champaign, Il	Jul 4, 1932	
Herman	Crook		Davidson County, TN	Dec 2, 1898	1988
Lewis	Crook		Troutsdale County, TN	1909	
James Dee	Crowe	J.D.	Lexington, KY	Aug 27, 1937	
Mack	Crowe	Banjo King of the Carolinas		Jan 5, 1897	Nov 8, 1966
Wayne	Crowe		Clayton, GA	Oct. 27, 1954	
William	Crowe	Josh	Clayton, GA	Oct 11, 1957	
John H.	Dacus	Johnny	Tennessee Mtn Fiddler		Apr 26, 1995
Pappy	Daily		Yoakum, TX	Feb 8, 1902	
Cleo	Davis		nr Cedartown, GA	Mar 9, 1919	
David	Davis		Cullman, PA	Feb 16,, 1961	
Hubert	Davis		Shelby, NC	1932	May 4, 1992
Jimmie H.	Davis		Beech Springs, LA	Sep 11, 1902	
Karl	Davis		Mt. Vernon, KY	1905	Jul 1979
Lynn	Davis			1914	
Ray	Davis		Wango, MD	May 2, 1933	
Buster	Deal	Buck	Gurley Bridge, WV	July 21, 1953	
Muriel	Deason	Kitty Wells	Nashville, TN	Aug 30, 1919	
Ray	Deaton		GA	Oct 6, 1952	
Greg	Deering		Boulder, CO	Jun 14, 1950	
Alton	Delmore		Elkmont, AL	Dec 25, 1908	Jun 8, 1964

First Name	Last Name	Nickname	Birthplace	Birthdate	Died
Rabon	Delmore		Elkmont, AL	Dec 3, 1916	Dec 4, 1952
Clark	Delozier			Dec 28, 1913	
Bob	Dick		Waterbury, CT	Apr 18, 1969	
Hazel	Dickens		Mercer County, WV	Jun 1, 1935	
Douglas	Dillard		E. St. Louis, IL	Mar 6, 1937	
Homer Earl	Dillard	Pop			Aug 29, 1990
Rodney	Dillard		E. St. Louis, IL	May 18, 1942	
Steve	Dilling		Raleigh, NC	Aug 5, 1965	
Dorsey	Dixon		Darlington, SC	Oct 14, 1897	Apr 17, 1968
Howard	Dixon		Darlington, SC	Jun 19, 1903	Mar 24, 1961
Henry	Dockery				Dec 21, 1990
John, Sr.	Dopyera				Jan 4, 1988
Jerry	Douglas	Flux	Warren, OH	May 28, 1956	
Mike	Drudge			Jul 1965	
Joseph Dudley	Drumright	Joe	Ft. Wayne, TX	Mar 29, 1929	Mar 29, 1996
John	Duffey		Washington, D.C.	Mar 4, 1934	Dec 10, 1996
Bill	Duncan		Charleston, WV	Feb 1, 1929	
Glen	Duncan		Columbus, OH	May 26, 1955	
Stuart	Duncan		Quantico, VA	Apr 14, 1964	
Pat	Dunford				Nov 10, 1976
Andy	Dye			Nov 2, 1959	
Homer Robert, Jr.	Eanes	Jim	Mountain Valley, VA	Dec 6, 1923	Nov 21, 1995
Ed	Easter		Mt. Airy, NC	Mar 28, 1934	
James	Easter		Mt. Airy, NC	Apr 24, 1932	
Jason	Easter		Mt. Airy, NC	Dec 4, 1975	
Jeff	Easter		Mt. Airy, NC	Mar 18, 1960	
Russell	Easter		Mt. Airy, NC	Apr 22, 1930	
Billy	Edwards		Tazewell County, VA	Sep 26, 1936	
Billy K.	Edwards				Jan 8, 1977
John	Edwards		Australia	1932	Dec 24, 1960
Ben	Eldridge		Richmond, VA	Aug 15, 1938	
Eric	Ellis		Wilkesboro, NC	Aug 12,1958	
Marvin	Ellis	Red	Arkadelphia, AR	Dec 21, 1929	
Paul Anthony	Ellis	Tony	Sylva, NC	Jul 29, 1939	
Charles	Elza	Kentucky Slim or the Little Darlin'	Harlan County, KY	Apr 4, 1912	Feb 23, 1996
John S.	Emerson			Jan 26, 1960	
William Hundley, Jr.	Emerson	Bill	Washington, D.C.	Jan 22, 1938	
Pat	Enright		Huntington, IN	Apr 22, 1945	
Boone	Estep				Mar 8, 1982
Dave	Evans		Portsmouth, OH	July 24, 1950	
Gerald	Evans			Jul 7, 1959	
Clay	Everhart		nr Lexington, NC	Jun 9, 1890	Dec 31, 1963
Leroy Robert	Eyler		Taneytown, MD	Oct 17, 1930	Jun 22, 1995
Tommy	Faile			Sep 15, 1928	
Raymond	Fairchild		Cherokee, NC	Mar 15, 1939	
Zane	Fairchild		Canton, NC	Jan 11, 1971	
Dewey	Farmer			Aug 6, 1942	
Shelton	Feazell			Jun 10, 1957	
Tom	Feller			Jul 11, 1973	
Ernest	Ferguson			July 16, 1918	
Ed	Ferris			Aug 12, 1934	Jun 24, 1993
Cathy	Fink		Baltimore, MD	Aug 9, 1953	
Lily	Fishman		Munich, Germany	1947	
Lester Raymond	Flatt		Sparta, TN	Jun 19, 1914	May 11, 1979
Bela	Fleck		New York City, NY	July 10, 1958	
Mike	Flemming			Sep 23, 1950	
Benjamin Francis	Ford	Whitey, Duke of Paducah	DeSoto, MO	May 12, 1901	Jun 20, 1986
Ernest Jennings	Ford	Tennessee Ernie	Bristol, TN	Feb 13, 1919	Oct 17, 1991
Howard	Forrester	Big Howdy	Hickman County, TN	Mar 31, 1922	Aug 1, 1987
Nick	Forster		Beirut, Lebanon	May 16, 1955	
Garley	Foster				Oct 5, 1968
William	Foster	Bill	Soddy-Daisy, TN	Jan 1, 1939	
Armin LeRoy	Fox	Curly	Graysville, TN	Nov 10, 1910	Nov 10, 1995

First Name	Last Name	Nickname	Birthplace	Birthdate	Died
Ruby	Fox (Owens)	Texas Ruby			Mar 29, 1963
Tom	Franks				Jun 11, 1977
Dick	Freeland			Jun 23, 19xx?	
Jess	Freiley				Jun 28, 1975
Tony	Furtado			Oct 18, 1967	
Harley	Gabbard		W. Harrison, IN	Dec 31, 1935	
John William	Gallagher	J.W.	Harris, NC	1915	Jun 21, 1979
Jerry	Garcia		Oakland, CA	1942	Aug 9, 1945
McRoy	Gardner		nr Conway, SC	Sep 3, 1944	
Robert A.	Gardner	Bob	Oliver Springs, TN	Dec 16, 1897	Sep 30, 1984
Steve	Garner			Feb 9, 1959	
Connie	Gately		TN		
James	Gaudreau	Jimmy	Wakefield, RI	Jul 3, 1946	
Connie B.	Gay		Lizard Lick, NC	Aug 22, 1914	Dec 3 or 4, 1989
Stoy	Geary		Rosine, KY		Jan 14, 1997
Lloyd	George	Lonzo	Haleyville, AL	June 24, 1924	1991
John	Gillis		GA	Dec 6, 1966	
Larry	Gillis		GA	Sep 24, 1962	
Lonnie	Glosson		Judsonia, AR	Feb 14, 1908	
Melvin	Goins		nr Bramwell, WV	Dec 30, 1933	
Ray	Goins		nr Bramwell, WV	Jan 3, 1936	
Wesley	Golding		Lambsburg, VA	1955	
Rex	Gosdin		Woodland, AL	193x	March 1978
Kenneth	Graham		Sherman, TX		July 1976
Bill	Grant		Hugo, OK	May 8, 19xx	
Juarez	Grant				Dec 31, 1992
Roy	Grant	Whitey	Shelby, NC	Apr 7, 1916	
Burkett	Graves	Buck or Josh	Tellico Plains, TN	Sep 27, 1927	
Tom	Gray		Chicago, Il	Feb 1, 1941	
George Banman	Grayson	G.B.	Ashe County, NC	Nov 11, 1887	Aug 13, 1930
Shannon	Grayson		Sunshine, NC	Sep 30, 1916	May 10, 1993
Bob	Green		Newark, NJ	1955	
Douglas	Green	Ranger Doug	MI	Mar 20, 1946	
John	Green	Buckwheat		Jun 20, 1953	
Richard	Greene		Los Angeles, CA	Nov 9, 1942	
Manuel A.	Greenhill	Manny			Apr 14, 1996
Jim	Greer		West Liberty, OH	Sep 3, 1942	
David	Grier		Washington, D.C.	Sep 23, 1961	
Lamar	Grier			Apr 15, 1938	
David	Grisman		Hackensack, NJ	Mar 23, 1945	
George	Gruhn		New York City, NY	Aug 21, 1945	
Martin	Haerle				Sep 4, 1990
Jimmy	Haley		NC	Jan 19, 1955	
Roy	Hall		Waynesville, NC	Jan 6, 1907	May 16, 1943
Smith	Hammett		Cleveland County, NC		Feb 1, 1930
Sonny	Hammond		Portland, OR	Oct 7, 1942	
Carlton	Haney		Reidsville, NC	Sep 19, 1928	
Leroy	Haney				Apr 14, 1981
Lillimae	Haney		nr Roundhead, OH	Mar 23, 1940	
Nick	Haney		Los Angeles, CA	Jan 16, 1957	
Esco	Hankins		Union County, TN	Jan 1, 1924	Nov 18, 1990
Tom	Hanway			Aug 20, 1961	
David	Hardy			Sep 11, 1955	
Milton	Harkey			Aug 20, 1948	
Sidney J.	Harkreader	Fiddlin' Sid			Mar 19, 1988
Jim	Harmon				Feb 1974
George William	Harrell	Bill	Attoway, VA	Sep 14, 1934	
Kelly	Harrell		Diapers Valley, VA	Sep 13, 1889	1942
Emmylou	Harris		Birmingham, AL	Apr 2, 1947	
John	Hartford		New York City	Dec 30, 1937	
Mike	Hartgrove		MO	Oct 27, 1955	
Dorsey Myree	Harvey		Irvin, KY	1935	Feb 20, 1988
Jan	Harvey			May 12, 1966	
Harold F.	Hawkins	Hawkshaw	Huntington, WV	Dec 22, 1921	Mar 5, 1963
Jim	Hawkins		Riverside, CA		Dec 17, 1976

First Name	Last Name	Nickname	Birthplace	Birthdate	Died
George D.	Hay	Solemn Old Judge	Attica, IN	Nov 9, 1895	May 8, 1968
Kerry	Hay			Feb 5, 1932	
Henry D.	Haynes	Homer	Knoxville, TN	July 27, 1918	1971
Dan	Hays		Ashland, KY	Feb 18, 1959	
Jim	Heffernan		Bronx, NY	1953	
Mark	Hembree			1954	
Gary	Henderson			Jul 17, 1944	
Tom	Henderson			Nov 23, 1937	
Allen	Hendricks		Madison, WI	Aug 19, 1946	
Bryan, Jr.	Henry	Red	Gainesville, FL	Nov 22, 1948	
Murphy	Henry			May 18, 1952	
Virginia	Hensley	Patsy Cline	Winchester, VA	Sep 8, 1932	Mar 5, 1963
Walter	Hensley			Mar 8, 1936	
John	Herald		New York City, NY	Sep 6, 1939	
Jack	Herrick		Teaneck, NJ	1949	
John	Hickman		Columbus, OH	Oct 7, 1942	
Bobby	Hicks		Newton, NC	Jul 21, 1933	
Jack	Hicks		Ashland, KY		
Nora Murphy	Hicks		Spartanburg, SC	May 18, 1952	
Eddie	Hill			Jun 4, 19xx	Jan 18, 1944
Ted	Hilliard		Newport News, VA	Nov 12, 1949	
Chris	Hillman		Los Angeles, CA	Dec 4, 1944	
John	Hisey			Jul 7, 1952	
Julian	Hobbs	Smiley			Jun 30, 1987
Robert Arnold	Hobbs		Roseboro, NC	June 14, 1931	Apr 6, 1996
Arval	Hogan		Robbinsville, NC	July 24, 1911	
Fairley	Holden		Gilmer County, GA	Oct 24, 1916	Oct 3, 1987
Milton	Holden	Jack	Pickens County, GA	Mar 13, 1915	
Len	Holsclaw			Nov 2, 1933	
Aubrey	Holt		Milan, IN	Aug 15, 1938	
Bill	Holt		Newport, TN	Aug 17, 1933	
David	Holt		Gatesville, TN	Oct 15, 1946	
Jerry	Holt		Cincinnati, OH	Aug 15, 1941	
Mark	Holt		Seattle, WA	Oct 23, 1963	
Tom	Holt			Jul 17, 1951	
Jim	Horn			Mar 25, 1932	
Randy	Howard				
Roger	Howard				Sep 15, 1985
Paul McCoy	Humphrey	Paul Williams			
Roy Milton	Huskey			Dec 17, 1956	Sep 6, 1997
Randall	Hylton		Willis, VA	Jan 8, 1945	
Kazuhiro	Inaba			Jun 12, 1960	
Kenny	Ingram			Aug 19, 1952	
Ken	Irwin			May 23, 1944	
Joe	Isaacs		Jackson County, KY	1947	
Carl	Jackson		Louisville, MS	Sep 18, 1953	
Harold Bradley	Jackson	Shot	Wilmington, NC	Sep 4, 1920	Jan 24, 1991
Milton	Jackson	Jack	Pickens County, GA	Mar 13, 1915	
Tommy	Jackson		Birmingham, AL	Mar 31, 1926	Dec 9, 1979
Ralph	James				Jan 5, 1976
Thomas Jefferson	Jarrell	Tommy	Round Peak, NC	Mar 1, 1901	Jan 28, 1985
Mitch	Jayne		Hammond, IN	July 5, 1930	
Sam Jr.	Jeffries			Jan 31, 1961	Jun 19, 1996
Dewitt	Jenkins	Snuffy	Harris, NC	Oct 27, 1908	Apr 30, 1990
Hoke	Jenkins		NC	Aug 4, 1917	1967
Verl	Jenkins	The Old Sheep Herder			
Sullivan	John Y.	Lonzo			June 5, 1967
Charles E.	Johnson	Little Jody Rainwater	Surrey County, NC	1921	
Courtney	Johnson		Barren County, KY	Dec 20, 1939	Jun 8 (or 7),1996
Enos	Johnson			Aug 17, 1928	
Albert Gene	Jones		White Top, VA	Feb 22, 1932	
Chris	Jones		Brooklyn, NY	Dec 7, 1959	
Clay	Jones			Oct 22, 1967	
Louis Marshall	Jones	Grandpa	Niagra, KY	Oct 20, 1913	

First Name	Last Name	Nickname	Birthplace	Birthdate	Died
Victor Howard	Jordan	Vic	Washington, D.C.	Oct 19, 1938	
Si	Kahn		Boston	Apr 23, 1944	
Bruce	Kaplan				Dec 15, 1992
Kathy	Kaplan		New York City, NY		Dec 11, 1983
Leslie C.	Keith		Pulaski County, VA	Mar 30, 1906	Dec 28, 1978 or Dec 28, 1977
William Bradford	Keith	Bill	Brockton, MA	Dec 20, 1939	
Clark	Kessinger		St. Albans, WV	July 27, 1896	Jun 4, 1975
Robin	Kessinger			Dec 14, 1955	
Dick	Kimmel			Feb 21, 1947	
Bradley	Kincaid		Gerrard County, KY	Jul 13, 1895	Sep 23, 1989 or Sep 23, 1990
	King	Curly			Dec 13, 1989
James	King		Martinsville, VA	Sep 9, 1958	
Fred	Kirby	Crazy Cavalier	Charlotte, NC	July 19, 1910	
Violet	Koehler				1974
Alison	Krauss		Decatur, Il	July 23, 1971	
George Edward	Krise	Speedy	Hinton, WV	May 7, 1922	
Kitsy	Kuykendall		MN	Jun 29, 1938	
Peter V.	Kuykendall	Pete Roberts	Northern VA	Jan 15, 1938	
John Lee	Lair		Livinston, KY	Jul 1, 1894	Nov 13, 1985
Darrell	Lambert	Pee Wee	Thacker WV	Aug 5, 1924	Jun 25, 1965
Richard Edward	Lambert	Curley	Broadnax, Va	Jun 13, 1930	Oct 22, 1982 or Oct 22, 1985
Jacob	Landers	Jake	Lawrence County, AL	Aug 14, 1938	
Bill	Lane				May 6, 1978
Daisy	Lange		Frankfort, IN		
Wayne	Lanham		Manassas, VA or Wash D.C??	Sep 14, 1959	
Mike	Lantz			Aug 12, 1957	
Billy Ray	Lathum		Cave City, AR	Jan 28, 19xx	
Nancy	Laur	Katie	Huntsville, AL		
Jack	Lawrence		Mooresville, NC	Oct 5, 1953	
Doyle	Lawson		Fordtown, TN	Apr 20, 1944	
Bert	Layne				Oct 29, 1982
Lily May	Ledford		Lexington, KY		Jul 14, 1985
Minnie Lena	Ledford	Black Eyed Susan			Jul 1987
Rosie	Ledford				Jul 24, 1976
Steve	Ledford		Bakersville, NC	Jun 2, 1906	Sep 19, 1980
Jack	Leiderman		Silver Spring, MD	Apr 19, 1955	
Lance	LeRoy		Tignall, GA	May 26, 1930	
Al	Lester		AL		May 14, 1991
Charles B.	Lewis		Lewis County, KY	Dec 11, 1950	
James Roy	Lewis	Pop	Lincolnton, GA	Sep 22, 1905	
Laurie	Lewis		Long Beach, CA	Sep 28, 1950	
Miggie	Lewis		Lincolnton, GA	May 22, 1926	
Mom	Lewis		Lincolnton, GA	Jun 20, 1996	
Polly	Lewis		Lincolnton, GA	Jan 23, 1937	
Roy	Lewis	Little Roy	Lincolnton, GA	Feb 24, 1942	
Travis	Lewis		Lincolnton, GA	Dec 26, 1958	
Wallace	Lewis		Lincolnton, GA	Jul 6, 1928	
Gene	Libbea		Huntington Beach, CA	Mar 22, 1953	
Gordon	Lightfoot		Orillia, Canada	Nov 17, 1938	
Charles Everett	Lilly	Everett	Clear Creek, WV	Jul 1, 1924	
Mike	Lilly			May 24, 1949	
Mitchell Burt	Lilly	"B"	Clear Creek WV	Dec 15, 1921	
Bill	Lineberry			Feb 27, 1935	
Keith	Little		Sonora, CA	Dec 14, 1955	
Babe	Lofton				Jul 16, 1993
Benjamin	Logan	Tex	Coahoma, TX	1927	
Alan	Lomax		Austin, TX	Jan 15, 1915	
John Avery	Lomax			1867	1948
Michael Keeton	Longworth	Mike	Chattanooga, TN	Nov 8,, 1938	
Charlie	Louvin (Loudermilk)		Rainsville, AL	July 7, 1927	
Ira	Louvin (Loudermilk)		Rainsville, AL	Apr 21, 1924	June 20, 1965

First Name	Last Name	Nickname	Birthplace	Birthdate	Died
Bill	Lowe		Hatfield, KY	May 8, 1930 or Apr 5, 1930?	
Gene	Lowinger		Newark, NH	Nov 10, 1942	
Bobby	Lundy				
Teddy Joe	Lundy	Ted	Galax, VA	Jun 26, 1937	Jun 23, 1980
Bascom Lamar	Lunsford		South Turkey Creek, SC	Mar 21, 1882	Sep 4, 1973
Jim	Lunsford				Sep 13, 1978
Lynwood	Lunsford		Roxboro, NC	Jan 31, 1962	
Rudy	Lyle			Mar 17, 1936	Feb 11, 1985
Ron	Lynam			Nov 5, 1954	
Claire	Lynch		AL	Feb 20, 1954	
Larry	Lynch			Mar 4, 1954	
David Harrison	Macon	Uncle Dave	Smart Station, TN	Oct 7, 1870	Mar 22, 1952
Cal	Maddox		Boaz, AL	Nov 3, 1915	1968
Cliff	Maddox		Boaz, AL	1912	1949
Henry	Maddox		Boaz, AL	Mar 19, 1928	1974
Roseea Arbana	Maddox (Brogdon)	Rose Maddox	Boaz, AL	Aug 15, 1925	
Mack	Magaha			Aug 1, 1929	
Joseph Emmett	Mainer	J.E.	Weaverville, NC	July 20, 1898	Jun 12, 1971
Wade	Mainer		Weaverville, NC	Apr 21, 1907	
Joe	Maphis		Suffolk, VA	May 12, 1921	
Rose Lee	Maphis		Baltimore, MD	Dec 29, 1922	
Ben	Marshall		Fort Gay, WV	Mar 20, 1956	
Dan Earl	Marshall		Crown City, OH	Jan 16, 1958	
Glen Chester	Marshall		Wayne, WV	Mar 20, 1926	
Judy	Marshall		Fort Gay, WV	Aug 1, 1951	
Asa	Martin		Winchester, KY	Jun 28, 1900	Aug 15, 1979
Benny	Martin		Sparta, TN	May 8, 1928	
C.F., III	Martin		Nazareth, PA	Sep 9, 1894	Jun 15, 1986
C.F., IV	Martin	Chris	Nazareth, PA	July 8, 1955	
Christian F., Jr	Martin		Vienna, Austria	Oct 2, 1825	Nov 15, 1888
Christian F., Sr.	Martin	C.F.	Markneukirchen, Germany	Jan 31, 1796	Feb 16, 1873
James H.	Martin	Jimmy	Sneedville, TN	Aug 10, 1927	
James P.	Martin	Slim	Murphy, NC	1920	Jun 29, 1975
Ray	Martin			1955	
William	Martin	Mac	Pittsburgh, PA	Apr 26, 1925	
Danny Lee	Masters				Jul 1, 1979
John Mace	Masters		Jacksonville, FL	May 26, 1913	
Lucille Ferndon	Masters		Homerville, GA	Sep 13, 1917	
Edd	Mayfield		Demmitt, TX	1926	July 1958
Ralph	Mayo				Sep 20, 1992
Maura	McCabe			Oct 17, 1957	
Jim	McCall		Chatham Hill, VA	Apr 30, 1930	
Haskell	McCormick			Jun 23, 1937	
Delano Floyd	McCoury	Del	Bakersville, NC	Feb 1, 1939	
Jerry	McCoury		PA	1948	
Robbie	McCoury		PA	Apr 30, 1971	
Ronnie	McCoury		PA	Mar 16, 1967	
Charlie	McCoy		Oak Hill, WV	Mar 28, 1941	
Willie	McDonald		Burlington, VT		
John	McEuen		Garden Grove, CA	Dec 19, 1945	
Lester	McFarland	Mac	nr Gray, KY	Feb 2, 1902	Jul 24, 1984
Clarence	McGarr	Mac			Jun 20, 1951
Kirk	McGee		Williamson County, TN	Nov 4, 1899	Oct 24, 1983
Sam	McGee	Flat-Top Pickin' Sam	nr Franklin, TN	May 1, 1894	Aug 21, 1975
Roy	McGinnis		Huntington, WV	May 12, 1926	
Alfred Don	McHan	Don			
Don	McHan		Bryson City, NC	July 11, 1933	
Vernon A.	McIntyre	Boatwhistle			Dec 20, 1980
Vernon Jr.	McIntyre		Cincinnati, OH		
Kate	McKenzie		Minneapolis, MN	Apr 25, 1952	
James	McKinney		Fort Payne, AL	Feb 26, 1957	
Raymond Kane	McLain			1930	
Raymond W.	McLain			Dec 18, 1953	

First Name	Last Name	Nickname	Birthplace	Birthdate	Died
David	McLaughlin		Washington, D.C.	Feb 13, 1958	
Peter	McLaughlin		Washington, D.C.	Nov 14, 1955	
Clayton	McMichen	Pappy	Allatoona, GA	Jan 26, 1900	Jan 3, 1970
Larry	McNeeley		Lafayette, IN	Jan 3, 1948	
Dewey	McPeak		Wytheville, VA	Aug 12, 1941	
Larry	McPeak		Wytheville, VA	Jul 13, 1947	
Mike	McPeak		Wytheville, VA	May 4, 1949	
Udell	McPeak		Wytheville, VA	June 12, 1953	
Curtis	McPeake			Oct 9, 1927	
James Monroe	McReynolds	Jim	Carfax. VA	Feb 13, 1927	
Jesse Lester	McReynolds		Carfax, VA	July 9, 1929	
Ralph	Meadows	Joe	Basin, WV	Dec 31, 1934	
Joseph Howell	Medford	Joe		Apr 2, 1932	Nov 16, 1993
Julian	Medlin	Greasy	Columbia, SC	Sep 18, 1910	Jul 15, 1982
Art	Menius		Raleigh, NC	Mar 4, 1955	
Ashley	Messenger		Massillon, OH	1956	
Landon	Messer		Kermit, WV	Apr 25, 1940	
Wilford	Messer				Aug 18, 1975
Walt	Michael		Bethesda, MD	Jun 20, 1946	
Tommy	Millard	Snowball	Canton, NC		
Arthur K.	Miller	Sonny			Nov 24, 1981
Roger	Miller		Fort Worth, TX	Jan 2, 1936	
Allen	Mills		nr Danville, VA	Nov 4, 1937	
Jim	Mills		Durham, NC	Dec 18, 1966	
Harold	Mitchell			Mar 22, 1938	
Barry	Mitterhoff		Newark, NJ	Sep 16, 1952	
Bertha	Monroe		Rosine, KY		Apr 1, 1997
Birch	Monroe		Rosine, KY	May 16, 1901	May 15, 1982
Charlie	Monroe		Rosine, KY	Jul 4, 1903	Sep 27, 1975
Harry	Monroe			Sep 8, 1890	Aug 20, 1954
James	Monroe		Nashville, TN	Mar 15, 1947	
James B.	Monroe	Buck		Oct 28, 1857	Jan 14, 1928
John	Monroe			May 17, 1896	Feb 1, 1962
Malissa A.	Monroe			Jul 12, 1870	Oct 31, 1921
Maude	Monroe			Nov 17, 1898	Dec 26, 1961
Melissa	Monroe		Nashville, TN		Dec 3, 1990
Speed	Monroe			Nov 30, 1884	Jan 14, 1967
William Smith	Monroe	Bill	Rosine, KY	Sep 13, 1911	Sep 9, 1996
Clyde Leonard	Moody	Carolina Woodchopper	Cherokee, NC	Sep 19, 1915	Apr 7, 1989
Charles Benjamin	Moore	Charlie	Piedmont, SC	Feb 13, 1935	Dec 24, 1979
Herbert R.	Moore	Buster	Bybee, TN	Oct 28, 1920	Nov 17, 1995
John W.	Moore	Bill			Apr 22, 1977
Lee	Moore	Coffee Drinking Nighthawk	Circleville, OH	Sep 24, 1914	Aug 17, 1997
Margaret	Moore (Bell)	Bonnie Lou		June 4, 1927	
Mary	Morgan			Oct 10, 1955	Aug 17, 1993
Russell	Moore		Pasadena, TX	Dec 21, 1963	
Tom	Morgan			Apr 19, 1932	
Claude	Morris	Zeke	Old Fort, NC	May 9, 1916	
George	Morris				
Lynn	Morris		San Antonio, TX	Oct 8, 1948	
Wiley	Morris		Old Fort, NC	Feb 1, 1919	Sep 22, 1990
Leon	Morris (Lamouroux)		Toronto, Canada	1935	
Harold	Morrison		Highlonesome, MO	Jan 30, 1931	Dec 21, 1993
Joe	Mullins			Oct 27, 1965	
Paul	Mullins	Moon Mullins	Frenchburg, KY	Sep 24, 1936	
Alan	Munde		Norman, OK	Nov 4, 1946	
J.W.	Murray	Jeff		Nov 12, 1969	
David	Nance		Oakridge, NC	1964	
William	Napier	Bill	Wise County, VA	Dec 17, 1935	
Howard	Nash	Panhandle Pete	NC		Oct 1972
Frank	Necessary		Boone's Camp, KY	Dec 20, 1935	
Ed	Neff		St. Louis, MO	Jan 16, 1946	
Ernie	Newton			Nov 7, 1909	
Mark	Newton			Feb 20, 1957	

First Name	Last Name	Nickname	Birthplace	Birthdate	Died
Hub	Nitchie				Oct 23, 1992
Charlie	Nixon				Jan 19, 1997
Tim	O'Brien		Wheeling, WV	Mar 16, 1954	
Alan	O'Bryant		Reidsville, NC	Dec 26, 1955	
Mark	O'Connor		Seattle, WA	Aug 4, (5?) 1961	
Jim	O'Neal	Uncle Jim			1982
Eli	Oberstein				Jun 12, 1960
Charles S.	Ogsbury	Chuck	Louisville, KY	Nov 9, 1938	
Andy	Olsen			Dec 4, 1944	
Robert	Osborne	Bobby	Hyden, KY	Dec 7, 1931	
Roland	Osborne	Sonny	Hyden, KY	Oct 29, 1937	
Wynn	Osborne		Nashville, TN	Aug 2, 1961	
Don	Owens			Aug 29, 1930	Apr 21, 1963
Ellis	Padgett				May 1969 or Jun 1973
Bob	Paisley		Ashe County, NC	Mar 14, 1931	
John	Palmer		Union, SC	May 28, 1927	Dec 26, 1993
Ray	Park		Treat, AR		
Byron	Parker	The Old Hired Hand	Hastings, IA	Sep 6, 1911	Oct 6, 1948
Charles	Parker	Rex	Maplewood, WV	Sep 30, 1921	
Curly	Parker				Sep 11, 1986
Eleanor	Parker (Neira)		Beard's Fork, WV	Feb 28, 1922	
David	Parmley		Los Angeles, CA	Feb 2, (1?) 1959	
Don	Parmley		nr Monticello, KY	Oct 19, 1933	
Gram	Parsons		Winter Haven, FL		Sep 19, 1973
Penny	Parsons			Feb 5, 1955	
Lester	Pate			Sep 12, 1944	
Ray	Patterson		Clayton, NM	Apr 17, 1926	
Ina	Patterson (Phelps)		Dexter, TX	Mar 13, 1929	
Herb	Pedersen		Berkeley, CA	Apr 27, 1944	
Ralph Sylvester	Peer		Kansas City, MO	May 22, 1892	Jan 19, 1960
Lonard	Peerce	Lonnie	Louisville, KY	July 27, 19xx or Jul 14, 1923?	May 31, 1996
Ron	Pennington		Springdale, AR		
Larry	Perkins		Grant County, IN	Jan 31, 1961	
Dale	Perry			Apr 2, 1962	
Evelyn Lang	Perry	Daisy			
Claude Jackson	Phelps	Jackie			Apr 22, 1990
Todd	Phillips		San Jose, CA	Apr 21, 1953	
Nick	Plaskias		Paris, France	1948	
Bill	Poffinberger			Jun 21, 1933	
Charlie	Poole		NC	Mar 22, 1892	May 21, 1931
Barry	Poss		Hamilton, Ontario	Sep 7, 1945	
Dale	Potter		Puxico, MO	Apr 28, 1929	Mar 14, 1996
Steve	Pottier		Denver, CO	Oct 18, 1948	
Billy	Powers				Sep 18, 1993
Elvis	Presley		East Tupelo, MS	Jan 8, 1935	Aug 1977
Tim	Prior		Fort Belvoir, VA	Jan 15, 1953	
Frank	Proffitt		Watauga County, NC	1913	1964
James R.	Prouty		Zanesville, OH	Dec 4, 1946	
Mark	Pruett		NC	Aug 19, 1951	
George Riley	Puckett		Alpharetta, GA	May 7, 1894	Jul 12, 1946
Pete	Pyle		Burnsville, MS	Apr 18, 1920	Mar 11, 1995
Louis	Pyrtle	Lou Reid	Winston-Salem, NC	Sep 13, 1954	
Mark	Rader			Apr 21, 1956	
Carmella	Ramsey			Sep 29, 1972	
Wayne	Raney		Wolf Bayou, AR	Aug 17, 1921	Jan 23, 1993
Bill	Rawlings			Apr 12, 19xx	
William Eugene	Rector	Red	Marshall, NC	Dec 15, 1929	May 31, 1990
Ola Belle	Reed (Campbell)		Lansing, NC		
Jim	Reeves		Panola County, TX	Aug 20, 1924	Jul 31, 1964
Gary B.	Reid			Oct 2, 1956	
Dale	Reno		Roanoke, VA	Feb 6, 1961	
Don	Reno		Spartanburg, SC	Feb 21, 1927	Oct 16, 1984
Don Wayne	Reno		Roanoke, VA	Feb 8, 1963	

First Name	Last Name	Nickname	Birthplace	Birthdate	Died
Ronnie	Reno		Buffalo, SC	Sep 28, 1947	
Verlon	Reno				Jun 1950
Dean	Reynolds		Houston, TX	Jan 27, 1932	
Anthony	Rice	Tony	Danville, VA	Jun 8, 1951	
Herbert Hoover	Rice				Nov 20, 1983
Larry	Rice			Apr 24, 1949	
Ronnie	Rice			Feb 22, 1955	
Wyatt	Rice			Jan 6, 1965	
Sharon Jean	Richardson	Deanie	Nashville, TN	Dec 18, 1971	
Mike	Richey	Slim	Atlanta, TX	Feb 11, 1938	
Johnny	Ridge		Gibsonville, NC	Nov 7, 1956	
Woodward Murice	Ritter	Tex	Panola, TX	Jan 12, 1907	Jan 2, 1974
Larry	Robbins		Montgomery County, MD	Apr 25, 1945	
Andrea	Roberts		Windfall, IN	July 12, 1966	
Doc	Roberts	Fiddlin' Doc		Apr 26, 1897	Aug 4, 1978
James William	Roberts (Carson)	James Carson	Richmond, KY	Feb 10, 1918	
Ben	Robertson		Athens, GA	Jan 12, 1946	
Alexander Campbell	Robertson	Eck	Delaney, AR	Aug 20, 1897 or Nov 20, 1887	Feb 17, 1975
Lonnie	Robertson				Feb 18, 1981
Clavin C.	Robins				May 21, 1980
Joseph	Robins	Butch			
Ralph	Robinson	Robbie			Nov 10, 1997
Jimmie	Rodgers		Meridian, MS	Sep 8, 1897	May 26, 1933
Danny	Rogers		Fort Collins, CO	Jan 3, 1946	
Robin	Roller		Dayton, OH	Nov 25, 1966	
Billy	Rose			Sep 22, 1963	
Bud	Rose				1975
Fred	Rose		Evansville, IN	Aug 24, 1897	Dec 1, 1954
Judy	Rose				Nov 25, 1990
Wesley H.	Rose		Chicago, IL	Feb 11, 1918	Apr 26, 1990
Neil V.	Rosenberg		Seattle, WA	Mar 21, 1939	
Phil	Rosenthal			Sep 30, 1948	
Ervin	Rouse				Jul 8, 1981
Peter	Rowan		Wayland, MA	Jul 3, 1942	
Gail	Rudisill			May 8, 1973	
Arnold W.	Ryan	Buck		May 2, 1925	Jan 7, 1982
Marty	Sachs		Bridgeport, CT	Jan 17, 1955	
Dean	Sapp			May 8, 1950	
Larry	Sargent		Norton, VA	Mar 15, 1953	
Arthur Edward	Satherley	Uncle Art	Bristol, England	Oct 19, 1889	Feb 10, 1986
Carl	Sauceman		Bright Hope Community, Greene CO, TN	Mar 6, 1922	
John Paul	Sauceman	J.P.	Greene County, TN	Mar 7, 1928	Oct 24, 1984
Owen	Saunders			May 10, 1973	
Charles	Sawtelle	Slade	Austin, TX	Sep 20, 1946	
Mark	Schatz		Philadelphia, PA	Apr 23, 1955	
Mike	Scott			May 14, 1962	
Tommy	Scott	Ramblin' Tommy Scott	Stephens County, GA	Jun 24, 1917	
Earl Eugene	Scruggs		near Shelby, NC	Jan 6, 1924	
Steven	Scruggs				Sep 23, 1992
Ken	Seaman			June 8, 1942	
John Ray	Sechler	Curly Seckler	nr China Grove, NC	Dec 25, 1919	
Mike	Seeger		New York, NY	Aug 15, 1933	
Everett	Sexton	Buster	Wytheville, VA	Dec 22, 1950	
Dusty	Shaver	Oscar August Quiddlemurp			May 1982
Sheehan		Shorty			Aug 13, 1983
Harry	Shelor	Ebo Walker		Oct 19, 1941	
Sammy	Shelor		Meadows of Dan, VA	Oct 10, 1962	
Raymond Allen	Shelton	Allen	nr Reidsville, NC	July 2, 1936	
Homer Lee	Sherrill	Pappy	Sherrill's Ford, NC	Mar 23, 1915	
Stephen H.	Sholes		Washington, DC	Feb 12, 1911	Apr 22, 1968
George Saunders	Shuffler		nr Valdese, NC	Apr 11, 1925	

First Name	Last Name	Nickname	Birthplace	Birthdate	Died
Jim	Shumate		Wilkes Co, NC	Oct 21, 1921	
Garland	Shuping			Feb 22, 1951	
Paul	Silvius		Cambridge, MA	July 15, 1954	
Vicki	Simmons			Jun 29, 1954	
Rickie	Simpkins		VA	Mar 10, 1955	
Ronnie	Simpkins		VA	Dec 31, 1950	
Benny	Sims		Sevierville, TN	1924	Dec 23, 1995
Charles	Sizemore	Charlie	Puncheon Creek, KY	Nov 23, 1960	
Herschel	Sizemore		Sheffield, AL	Aug 6, 1935	
Ricky	Skaggs		Cordell, KY	Jul 18, 1954	
Jimmie	Skinner		Blue Lick, KY	Apr 27, 1909	Oct 27, 1979
Anthony	Slater	Crazy Elmer			Mar 1980
Marion Try	Slaughter	Vernon Dalhart	Jefferson, Texas	April 6, 1883	Sep 15, (14?)1948
Shannon	Slaughter			Dec 13, 1965	
Bobby	Slone		Lexington, KY	June 13, 1936	
Leonard	Sly	Roy Rogers	Cincinnati, OH	Nov 5, 1911	
Andrew J.	Smick or Smik	Doc Williams	Tarrtown, PA	Jun 26, 1914	
Arthur Lee, Jr.	Smiley	Red	nr Asheville, NC	May 17, 1924 or 1925?	Jan 2, 1972
A.L.	Smith	Smitty	Oneida, TN	Aug 15, 1918	
Arthur	Smith	Fiddlin' Arthur	Bold Springs, TN	Apr 10, 1898	Feb 28, 1971
Arthur	Smith	Guitar Boogie	Kershaw, SC	Apr 1, 1921	
Bobby	Smith		Cookeville, TN	Jan 23, 1937	June 24, 1992
Carl	Smith		Maynardsville, TN	Mar 15, 1927	
Craig	Smith			June 6, 1956	
Dallas	Smith		nr Cookeville, TN	Jun 13, 1934	
Dick	Smith			Oct 4, 1943	
John O.	Smith	Tennessee	Oneida, TN	Mar 13, 1916	
Lloyd Mayne	Smith	Mayne	Boston, MA	Mar 15, 1939	
Marcus	Smith			Jan 16, 1971	
Ted	Smith		Oakland, CA	Dec 1, 1952	
Tim	Smith			May 29, 1955	
Jim	Smoak		Round O, SC		
Jill	Snider			Jan 11, 1972	
Mike	Snider			May 30, 1955	
John Kilby	Snow			May 28, 1906	Mar 20, 1980
Don	Sowards			Dec 4, 1930	
Larry	Sparks		Lebanon, OH	Sep 25, 1947	
Willis	Spears			Sep 13, 1940	
Blaine	Sprouse		Martinsburg, WV	Oct 11, 1956	
Roger	Sprung			Aug 29, 1930	
Tim	Stafford		Kingsport, TN	Sep 14, 1960	
Arthur	Stamper	Art	Knott County, KY	Nov 1, 1933	
Carter	Stanley		McClure, VA	Aug 27, 1925	Dec 1, 1966
Ralph Edmond	Stanley		Stratton, VA	Feb 25, 1927	
Ralph Edmond II	Stanley			Aug 20, 1978	
James Hobart	Stanton	Jim			July 15, 1989
Jack	Stapp			Dec 8, 1912	Dec 20, 1980
Orrin	Star			Mar 23, 1955	
Buddy	Starcher		nr Ripley, WV	Mar 16, 1906	
John	Starling		Lexington, VA	May 26, 1940	
Jody	Stecher		New York City	1946	
Adam	Steffey		Norfolk, VA	Nov 24, 1965	
Geoffrey	Stelling	Geoff		Jun 13, 1943	
Larry	Stephenson		Harrisonburg, VA	Oct 24, 1956	
Jim	Steptoe			Mar 19, 1951	
Ron	Stewart			Dec 11, 1965	
Billy	Stoneman				Apr 10, 1990
Calvin Scott	Stoneman	Scotty	Galax, VA	Aug 4, 1932	Mar 4, 1973
Dean	Stoneman		Galax, VA	Jun 12, 1930	Feb 28, 1989
Donna	Stoneman		Alexandria, VA	Feb 7, 1934	
Ernest V.	Stoneman	Pop	Monarat, VA	May 25, 1893	Jun 14, 1968
Jack	Stoneman				Apr 14, 1992
Jim	Stoneman	Jimmy	Washington, DC	Mar 8, 1937	

First Name	Last Name	Nickname	Birthplace	Birthdate	Died
Patsy	Stoneman		Galax, VA	May 27, 1925	
Van	Stoneman		Washington, DC	Dec 31, 1940	Jun 3, 1995
Veronica	Stoneman	Roni	Washington, DC	May 5, 1938	
Hattie	Stoneman (Frost)			1900	1976
Carl	Story		Lenoir, NC	May 29, 1916	Mar 31, 1995
Don	Stover		Ameagle, WV	Mar 6, 1928	Nov 11, 1996
Mike	Street		NC	Feb 9, 1960	
James Wilson	Stripling	Chick	GA		Nov 19, 1970
Charles Arnold	Stroud	Toby	Little Kate, OH	Aug 19, 1921	May 3, 1996
Joe	Stuart	Sparkplug		Feb 7, 1928	Sep 13, 1987
Marty	Stuart		Philadelphia, MS	Sep 30, 1958	
Eddie	Stubbs		Gaithersburg, MO	Nov 25, 1961	
Arthur	Sullivan				1957
Emmett	Sullivan		St. Stephens, AL	Jul 23, 1936	Apr 10, 1993
Enoch	Sullivan		St. Stephens, AL	Sep 18, 1933	
John	Sullivan	Lonzo	Edmonton, KY	July 7, 1917	June 5, 1967
Margie	Sullivan		Winnsboro, LA	Jan 22, 1933	
Rollin	Sullivan	Oscar	Edmonton, KY	Jan 19, 1919	
James Clell	Summey	Cousin Jody	nr Sieverville, TN	Dec 11, 1914	1976
Marion	Sumner			~1920	Aug 17, 1997
Ernie Jr.	Sykes		Long Island, NY	Nov 13, 1960	
Gid	Tanner	Laughing Gid	Dacula, GA	Jun 6, 1885	May 13, 1960
Gordon	Tanner				July 26, 1952
Johnny James	Tarleton	Jimmie	Chesterfield County, SC	May 8, 1892	1979
Clarence E.	Tate	Tater	Scott County, VA	Feb 4, 1931	
Dale	Taylor	Punch		Feb 5, 1965	
Earl	Taylor		Rose Hill, VA	Jun 17, 1929	Jan 28, 1984
Hartford	Taylor	Harty	Mt. Vernon, KY	1905	
Merle	Taylor	Red			May 3, 1987
Robert Arthur	Taylor	Tut	Baldwin County, GA	Nov 20, 1923	
Gordon	Terry		Decatur, AL	Oct 7, 1931	
Chris	Thile		Oceanside, CA	Feb 20, 1981	
Henry William	Thompson	Hank	Waco, TX	Sep 3, 1925	
Jesse Donald	Thompson	Uncle Jimmy	Baxter, TN	1948	Feb 17, 1931
Robert C.	Thompson	Bobby	Converse, NC	Jun 5, 1937	
Ozzie	Thorpe			Aug 28, 1964	
Bob	Tidwell				Jun 1977
Carl	Tipton				Sep 10, 1989
Glenn	Tolbert		Straight Mtn, AL	1949	
Jack	Tottle		Baltimore, MD	Nov 24, 1939	
Vance	Townsend			Sep 14, 1945	
Merle	Travis		Rosewood, KY	Nov 29, 1917	Oct 20, 1983
Anthony	Trischka	Tony	Syracuse, NY	Jan 16, 1949	
Herb	Trotman			Sep 14, 1944	
English P.	Tullock	Cousin Jake	TN	1922	June 18, 1988
Grant	Turner		Abilene, TX	May 17, 1912	Oct 19, 1991
Dan	Tyminski			Jun 20, 1967	
Richard	Underwood		Seabrook, MD	Jul 14, 1956	
Tommy	Vaden			Jun 15, 1925	
Joe	Valiante	Joe Val	Everett, MA	Jun 25, 1926	Jun 11, 1985
Dale	Vanderpool		OH	Dec 13, 1953	
Pendleton	Vandiver	Uncle Pen		1869	1932
Lowell	Varney		Crum, WV	Sep 21, 1936	
Bill	Vernon		CT or NY	Jul 4, 1937	Nov 20, 1996
Johnny	Vincent			1940	
Rhonda	Vincent		Kirksville, MO	July 13, 1962	
Franklin Delano	Wakefield	Frank	Emory Gap, TN	Jun 6, 1935	
Gary	Waldrep		Sand Mountain, AZ	Jul 18, 1963	
Cliff	Waldron		Jolo, WV	Apr 4, 1941	
Butch	Waller			Jan 19, 1944	
Charles Otis	Waller	Charlie	Jointerville, TX	Jan 19, 1935	
Dock	Walsh		Wilkes County, NC	Jul 23, 1901	May 28, 1967
Wade	Ward			1892	1971
Garnet	Warren	Fiddlin' Hank	Mt. Airy, NC	Apr 1, 1909	
Paul	Warren		Lyle, TN	May 17, 1918	Jan 12, 1978

First Name	Last Name	Nickname	Birthplace	Birthdate	Died
Toshio	Watanabe		Hyogo, Japan	Oct 1, 1946	
Arthel	Watson	Doc	Deep Gap, NC	Mar 3, 1923	
Dawn	Watson			Jan 19, 1962	
Eddie Merle	Watson	Merle	Deep Gap, NC	Feb 8, 1949	Oct 23, 1985
Jim	Watson		Durham, NC	1949	
Howard	Watts	Cedric Rainwater	Orlando, FL	1915	Jan 21, 1970
Dean	Webb		Independence, MO	Mar 28, 1937	
Eric	Weissberg		New York City, NY	Aug 16, 1939	
Peter	Wernick	Dr. Banjo	Bronx, NY	Feb 25, 1946	
Willie Egbert	Wesbrooks	Cousin Wilbur	Gibson County, TN		Aug 1984
Dottie	West		McMinnville, TN	Oct 11, 1932	Sep 5, 1991
Johnnie	Whisnant		Lenoir, NC	Dec 12, 1921	Feb 2, 1992
Buck	White		Wichita Falls, TX	Dec 13, 1930	
Cheryl	White		Abilene, TX	Jan 27, 1955	
Clarence	White		Lewiston, ME	Jun 7, 1944	Jul 15, 1973
Eric	White		Lewiston, ME	Jul 9, 1943	
Roland Joseph	White		Madawaska, ME	Apr 23, 1938	
Sharon	White		Abilene, TX	Dec 17, 1953	
Keith	Whitley		Sandy Hook, KY	Jul 1, 1954	May 9, 1989
Charles	Whitstein		Pineville, LA	Dec 11, 1948	
Robert	Whitstein	Bob	Pineville, LA	Mar 16, 1944	
Henry	Whitter		Fries, VA	Apr 6, 1892	1942?
Marshall	Wilborn		Austin, TX	Mar 12, 1952	
Rich	Wilbur				Jun 10, 1992
Benny	Williams		Bledsoe County, TN	Mar 28, 1931	
Blake	Williams	Sparta Flash	Sparta, TN	Oct 8, 1956	
Cohen T.	Williams				May 29, 1988
Delbert	Williams			1955	
Hiram	Williams	Hank	Mt. Olive, AL	Sep 17, 1923	Jan 1, 1953
James	Williams		Wythe County, VA	Feb 29, 1932	
Linda	Williams		Anniston, AL	July 7, 1949	
Robin	Williams		Winston-Salem, NC	Mar 16, 1949	
Rusty	Williams			Jan 18, 1954	
Vern	Williams		Newton County, AR	1932	
Cecil James	Williamson	Skeets			May 2, 1983
LaVerne	Williamson	Molly O'Day	McVeigh, KY	July 9, 1923	Dec 5, 1987
Barry Robert	Willis		Chicago, Il	Sep 20, 1945	
Janet Marie	Willis	Jan	Hammond, IN	Aug 13, 1953	
Marvin E.	Willis		Cleveland County, NC	Sep 8, 1916	
James Robert	Wills	Bob	Turkey, TX	Mar 6, 1905	May 13, 1975
Ed	Wilson		Brooklyn, NY	May 26, 1946	
Mike	Wilson		Burlington, NC	Sep 6, 1947	
Steve	Wilson			Mar 18, 1958	
Robert Russell	Wise (Dees)	Chubby	Lake City, Florida	Oct 2, 1915	Jan 6, 1996
Kent	Wiseman				Jun 6, 1964
Malcomb B.	Wiseman	Mac	Crimora, VA	May 23, 1925	
Scott	Wiseman	Skyland Scotty	nr Ingals, NC	Nov 8, 1909	Feb 1, 1981
Myrtle Eleanor	Wiseman (Cooper)	Lulu Belle	Boone, NC	Dec 24, 1913	
Terry	Woodward		Owensboro, KY	Jul 19, 1937	
Dave	Woolum				Mar 7, 1986
Art	Wooten		Mt. Airy, NC		Oct 6, 1986
Roger	Wooten			Feb 4, 1906	May 1975
Mary	Workman	Sunshine Sue			Jun 13, 1979
Johnny	Wright		Mt. Juliet, TN	May 13, 1914	
Art	Wydner				Jul 31, 1993
Rual Holt	Yarbrough		Lawrenceburg, TN	Jan 13, 1930	
Bill	Yates		Big Rock, VA	Apr 30, 1935	
Wayne	Yates		Manassa, VA	Apr 9, 1933	
Earl	Yeager			Nov 2, 1953	
Bob	Yellin		New York City, NY		
Rusty	York		Harlan County, KY	1935	
Dempsey	Young			Jul 1, 1954	
Glenn	Zankey		Pittsburgh, PA		

Index

Symbols

Mooney, Bob 160
Moore, Bob 205
Moore, Bonnie Lou and Buster 139
Moore, Charlie 201, 204, 365
Moore, Frankie 120
Moore, John 377, 460
Moore, Larry 114
Moore, Russell 319
Morgan, George 307
Morgan, Ray 162, 225
Morgan, Tom 209, 239, 285, 314
Morris brothers 40
Morris Brothers 17, 18, 63, 108, 135, 151, 152, 153, 159, 160, 173, 179, 223, 257, 375, 486, 563, 564
Morris, Dale 126
Morris, Edward 436, 531
Morris, George "Sambo" 13, 15, 27, 152, 256, 257
Morris, John 27, 539
Morris, Leon 287, 322
Morris, Lynn 440
Morris, Wiley 18, 63, 145, 152
Morris, Wiley and Zeke 145, 479, 561
Morris, Zeke 13, 18, 152, 160, 189, 564, 575
Morthland, John 120
Mosque Auditorium 474
Mosrite Company 548
Mountain Dance and Folk Festival 489, 562
Mueller, Eddie 135
Muleskinner 286, 355, 373, 403, 407
Muleskinner News 211, 220, 238, 240
Mullins, Joe 346
Mullins, Paul "Moon" 48, 69, 84, 96, 101, 107, 343, 378, 571
Munde, Alan 22, 42, 220, 288, 299, 357, 359, 373, 410, 413, 462, 539, 554
Murphy Brothers 212
Murphy, Alan and Aleta 349
Music Business International 531
Music City News 172, 230
Music Village USA 126
Musician's Union (AFM) 516
Mustard and Gravy 176
Myers, Ray 191

N

Nance, David 222
Napier, Bill 156, 344, 364, 508
Napier, Scott 379
"Nashville" (a film) 88
Nashville Bluegrass Band 361, 368, 371, 409, 465, 493, 523, 589
Nashville Bluegrass Music Association 455
Nashville Grass, Lester Flatt and the 125, 141, 144, 292, 338, 349, 373, 391, 509
"Nashville Now" (television show) 507
Nashville sound 69, 83, 593
Nashville's Reunion of Professional Enter-tainers 196
Natchez Express 261
Nathan, Bing 407
Nathan, Sydney 25, 68, 155, 156, 200, 204, 344, 364

National Academy of Recording Arts and Sciences (NARAS) 371, 577
National Association of Independent Record Dealers (NAIRD) 241, 439
National Banjo Picking Championship 440
National Barn Dance (WLS) 74, 75, 79, 83, 96, 114
National Bluegrass Banjo Championship 100
National Broadcasting System 79
National Council for the Traditional Arts 444
National Fiddle Championship 8
National Folk Festival 171, 175
National Guard Armory 474
National guitars 547
National Heritage Fellowship Award 17
National Life and Accident Insurance Company 75
National Observer 240
National Sick and Accident Association 75
Navy Band 270, 415
NBC Alka Seltzer National Barn Dance 431
Neaphonic String Band 468
Nechville Musical Products 555
Nechville, Tom 555
Nelson, Carl 211, 234, 268
Nelson, David 316
Nelson, Ken 205
New Coon Creek Girls 432, 441
New Dominion Barn Dance 87, 243
New England Bluegrass Boys 280, 538
New Grass Alliance 125
New Grass Revival 237, 300, 302, 320, 410, 413, 414, 416, 422, 443, 523
New Grass, Larry Stephenson and 322
New Group 270
New Lost City Ramblers 353, 406, 429, 581, 584
New Riders of the Purple Sage 403
New River Gang 388
New Shades of Grass, Emerson and Waldron and the 269, 387, 393, 449
New South 49, 273, 320, 395, 399, 400, 401, 412, 415, 416, 443, 538, 572, 582
New York City 73, 451
New York Folk Festival 124
New York Ramblers 352, 406
New York Times 187
Newgrass Music Festival 418, 577
Newport Folk Festival 5, 124, 167, 187, 207, 208, 233, 369, 373, 444, 453, 581
Newport Folk Foundation 562
Newton, Ernie 120
Nims, Debby 379
Nitty Gritty Dirt Band 307, 343, 359, 370, 375, 416, 417, 577
Nixon, Charlie 147
Noel Hotel 177
Noonday Jamboree 160
Norlin era 546
Norris, Fate 7
North Carolina Bluegrass Festival 28

North Carolina Cooper Boys 255
North Carolina Farm Hour 20, 257
North Carolina Ramblers, Charlie Poole and the 15, 254
Northeast Seaborn Band 340
Nowlin, Bill 538
Nugget mandolins 552

O

O'Boys, Tim O'Brien and the 299, 383
O'Brien, Mollie 590
O'Brien, Tim 53, 298, 423, 590
O'Bryant, Alan 323, 360
O'Connor, Mark 395, 418
O'Day, Molly 193, 194, 388, 433
O'Farrell, Michael 235
O'Roark, Michael 57
Oak Leaf Park 232, 491
Oberlin College 457, 510
Oberstein, Eli 81
Oermann, Robert K. 76
Ogsbury, Chuck 251, 552
Oklahoma Bluegrass Gentlemen 300, 358
Old and In the Way 403
Old Dad 95
Old Dominion Barn Dance 75, 87, 156, 172, 195, 234, 278, 474, 510
Old Farm Hour 193
Old Hickory 293
Old Home Place Publishing 539
Old Original Farm Hour 176
Old Time Fiddlers Convention 559
Old Time Pickin' Parlor 71, 389, 420, 550
Old-Time Country Music 125
old-time music 566
Old-Timers 388
Oliver Ditson Company 545
Ome Banjos 251, 552
Opryland USA 78, 84
Orange Mountain Boys 297
Original Musical Instrument Company (O.M.I.) 548
Osborne brothers 350, 570
Osborne Brothers 84, 125, 158, 171, 213, 216, 227, 228, 290, 318, 350, 361, 373, 384, 400, 421
Osborne Family, Lou Osborne and the 225
Osborne, Bob "Bobby" 46, 161, 215, 223, 592
Osborne, Bobby and Sonny 223, 530
Osborne, Robby 230
Osborne, Sonny 41, 121, 215, 217, 473, 520
Over Easy 459
Overcash, Chubby 15
Owens, Don 473, 530
Ozark Mountain Boys (Doug and Rodney Dillard) 275
Ozark Mountain Boys, Lucky Chatman and the 209, 239
Ozark Mountain Trio 281
Ozark Mountaineers 281
Ozark Opry 275